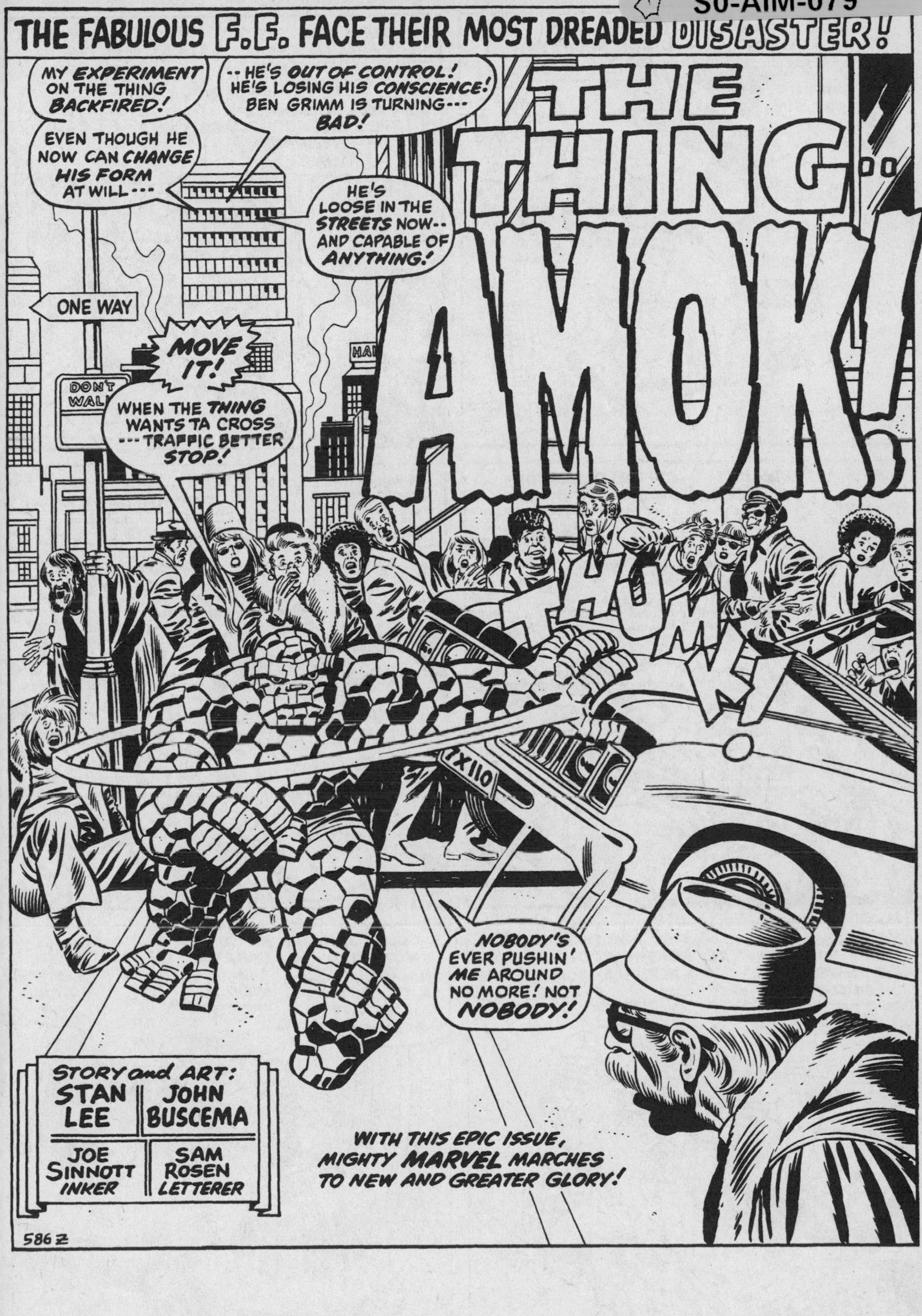
THE FABULOUS F.F. FACE THEIR MOST DREADED DISASTER!
THE THING.. AMOK!
MY EXPERIMENT ON THE THING BACKFIRED!
EVEN THOUGH HE NOW CAN CHANGE HIS FORM AT WILL---
-- HE'S OUT OF CONTROL! HE'S LOSING HIS CONSCIENCE! BEN GRIMM IS TURNING--- BAD!
HE'S LOOSE IN THE STREETS NOW-- AND CAPABLE OF ANYTHING!
ONE WAY
DON'T WALK
MOVE IT!
WHEN THE THING WANTS TA CROSS --- TRAFFIC BETTER STOP!
THUMK!
7X110
NOBODY'S EVER PUSHIN' ME AROUND NO MORE! NOT NOBODY!
STORY and ART: STAN LEE JOHN BUSCEMA
JOE SINNOTT INKER
SAM ROSEN LETTERER
WITH THIS EPIC ISSUE, MIGHTY MARVEL MARCHES TO NEW AND GREATER GLORY!
586 Z

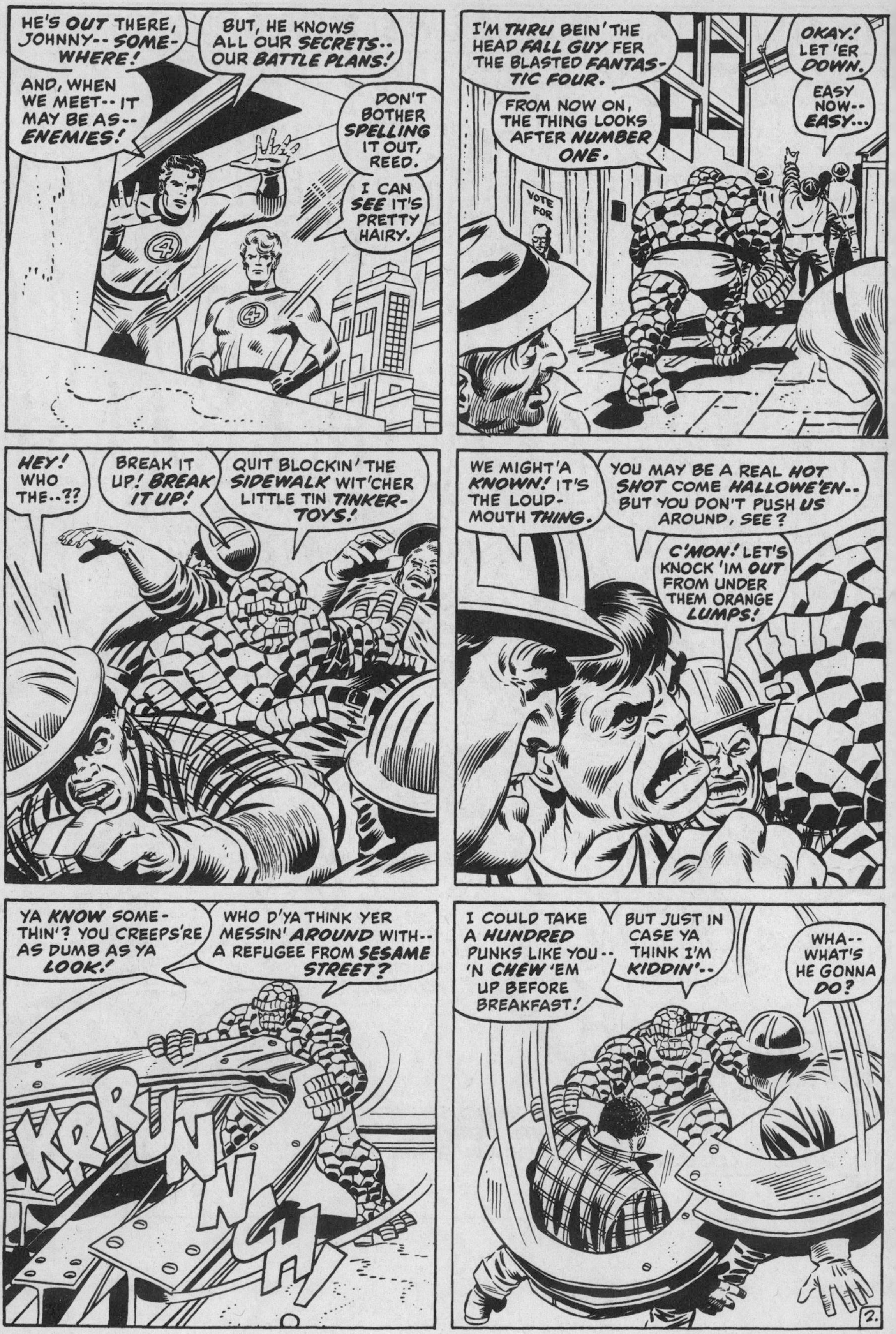

HE'S OUT THERE, JOHNNY-- SOME-WHERE!
AND, WHEN WE MEET-- IT MAY BE AS-- ENEMIES!
BUT, HE KNOWS ALL OUR SECRETS.. OUR BATTLE PLANS!
DON'T BOTHER SPELLING IT OUT, REED.
I CAN SEE IT'S PRETTY HAIRY.
I'M THRU BEIN' THE HEAD FALL GUY FER THE BLASTED FANTAS-TIC FOUR.
FROM NOW ON, THE THING LOOKS AFTER NUMBER ONE.
OKAY! LET 'ER DOWN.
EASY NOW-- EASY...
VOTE FOR
HEY! WHO THE--??
BREAK IT UP! BREAK IT UP!
QUIT BLOCKIN' THE SIDEWALK WIT'CHER LITTLE TIN TINKER-TOYS!
WE MIGHT'A KNOWN! IT'S THE LOUD-MOUTH THING.
YOU MAY BE A REAL HOT SHOT COME HALLOWE'EN-- BUT YOU DON'T PUSH US AROUND, SEE?
C'MON! LET'S KNOCK 'IM OUT FROM UNDER THEM ORANGE LUMPS!
YA KNOW SOME-THIN'? YOU CREEPS'RE AS DUMB AS YA LOOK!
WHO D'YA THINK YER MESSIN' AROUND WITH-- A REFUGEE FROM SESAME STREET?
KRRUNNCH
I COULD TAKE A HUNDRED PUNKS LIKE YOU-- 'N CHEW 'EM UP BEFORE BREAKFAST!
BUT JUST IN CASE YA THINK I'M KIDDIN'--
WHA-- WHAT'S HE GONNA DO?

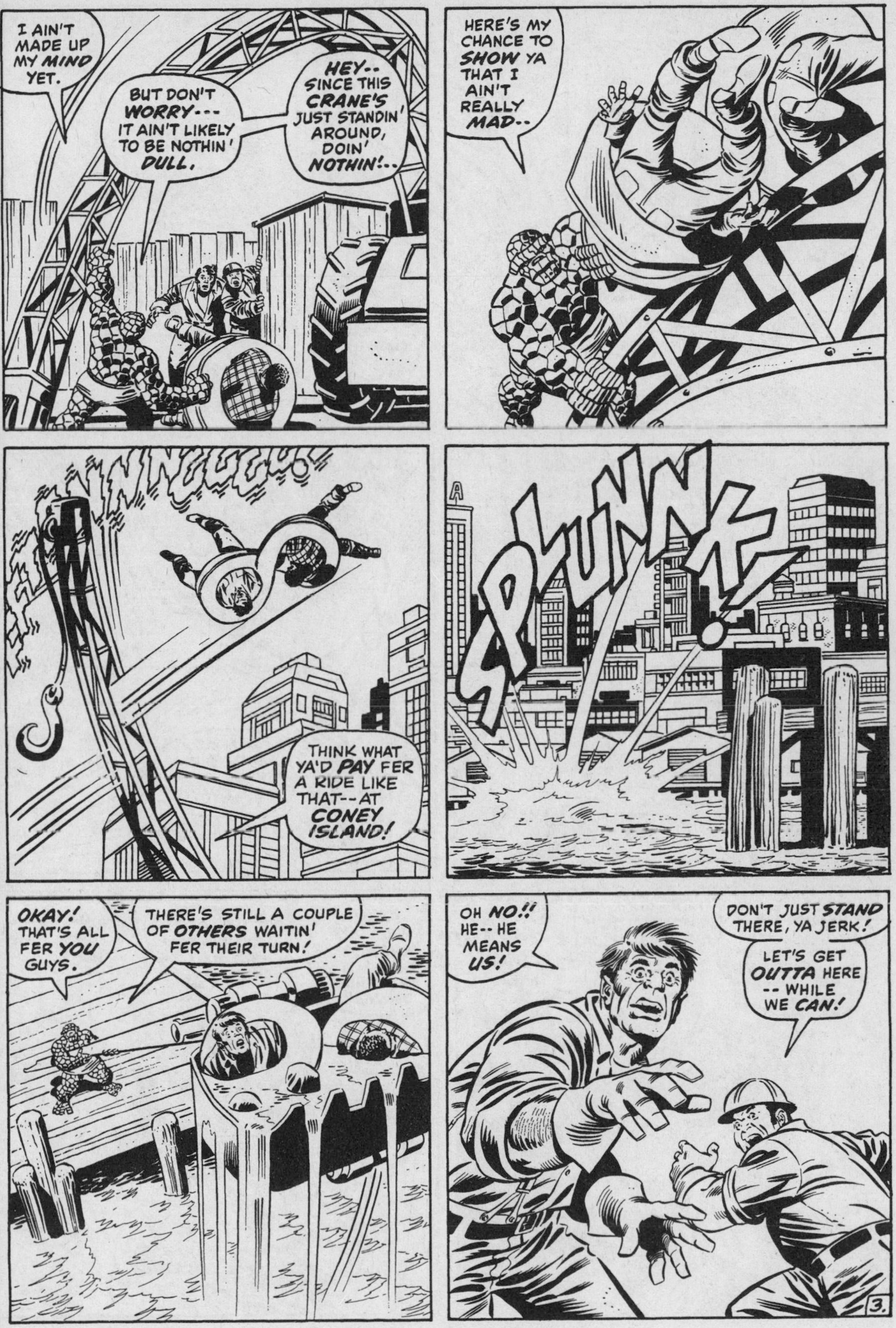
I AIN'T MADE UP MY MIND YET.
BUT DON'T WORRY--- IT AIN'T LIKELY TO BE NOTHIN' DULL.
HEY.. SINCE THIS CRANE'S JUST STANDIN' AROUND, DOIN' NOTHIN'..
HERE'S MY CHANCE TO SHOW YA THAT I AIN'T REALLY MAD..
THINK WHAT YA'D PAY FER A RIDE LIKE THAT--AT CONEY ISLAND!
SPLUNK
OKAY! THAT'S ALL FER YOU GUYS.
THERE'S STILL A COUPLE OF OTHERS WAITIN' FER THEIR TURN!
OH NO!! HE-- HE MEANS US!
DON'T JUST STAND THERE, YA JERK!
LET'S GET OUTTA HERE -- WHILE WE CAN!
3.

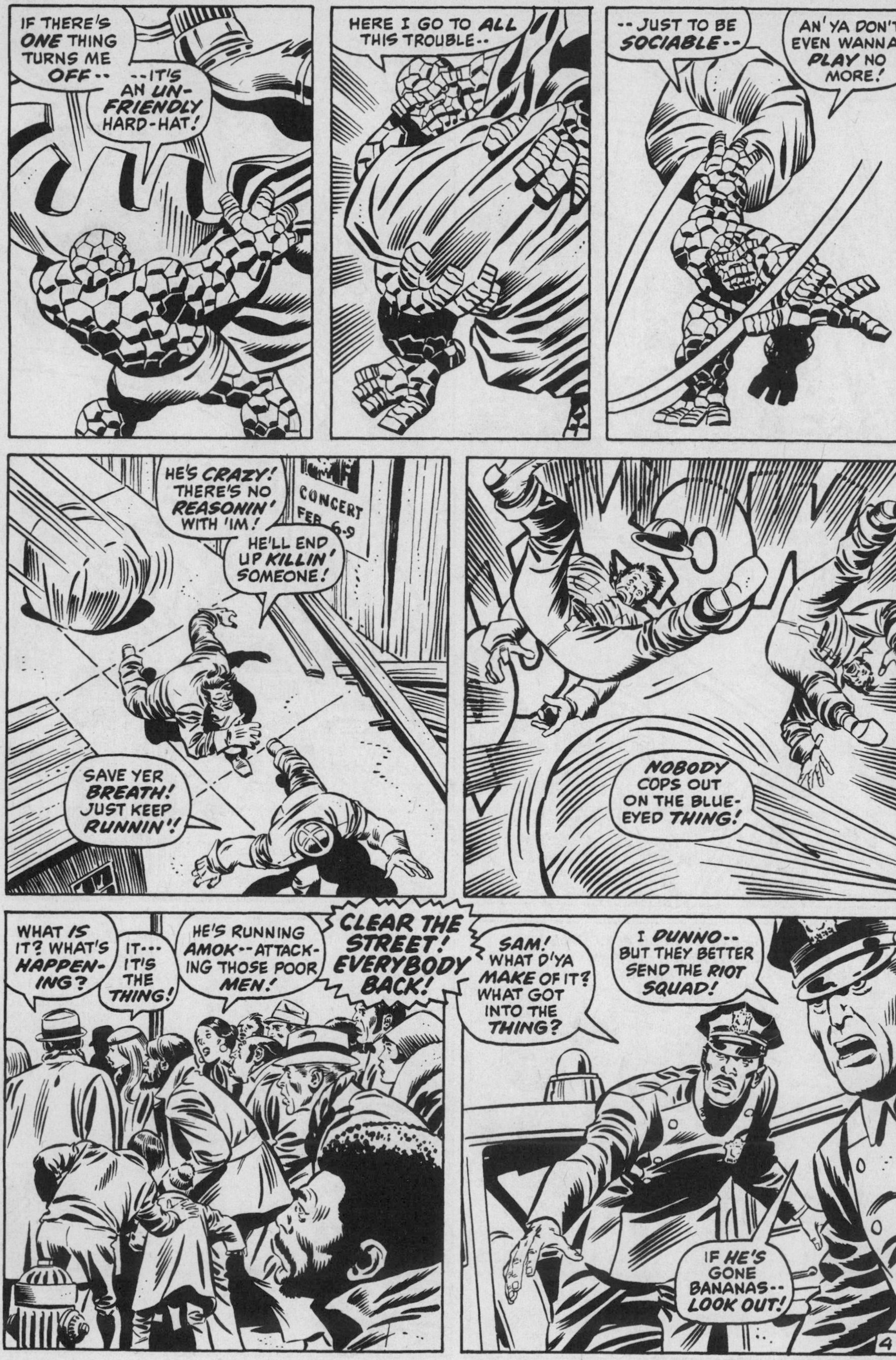
IF THERE'S ONE THING TURNS ME OFF--
--IT'S AN UN-FRIENDLY HARD-HAT!
HERE I GO TO ALL THIS TROUBLE--
--JUST TO BE SOCIABLE--
AN'YA DON'T EVEN WANNA PLAY NO MORE!
HE'S CRAZY! THERE'S NO REASONIN' WITH 'IM!
CONCERT FEB 6-9
HE'LL END UP KILLIN' SOMEONE!
SAVE YER BREATH! JUST KEEP RUNNIN'!
NOBODY COPS OUT ON THE BLUE-EYED THING!
WHAT IS IT? WHAT'S HAPPEN-ING?
IT--- IT'S THE THING!
HE'S RUNNING AMOK--ATTACK-ING THOSE POOR MEN!
CLEAR THE STREET! EVERYBODY BACK!
SAM! WHAT D'YA MAKE OF IT? WHAT GOT INTO THE THING?
I DUNNO-- BUT THEY BETTER SEND THE RIOT SQUAD!
IF HE'S GONE BANANAS-- LOOK OUT!
4

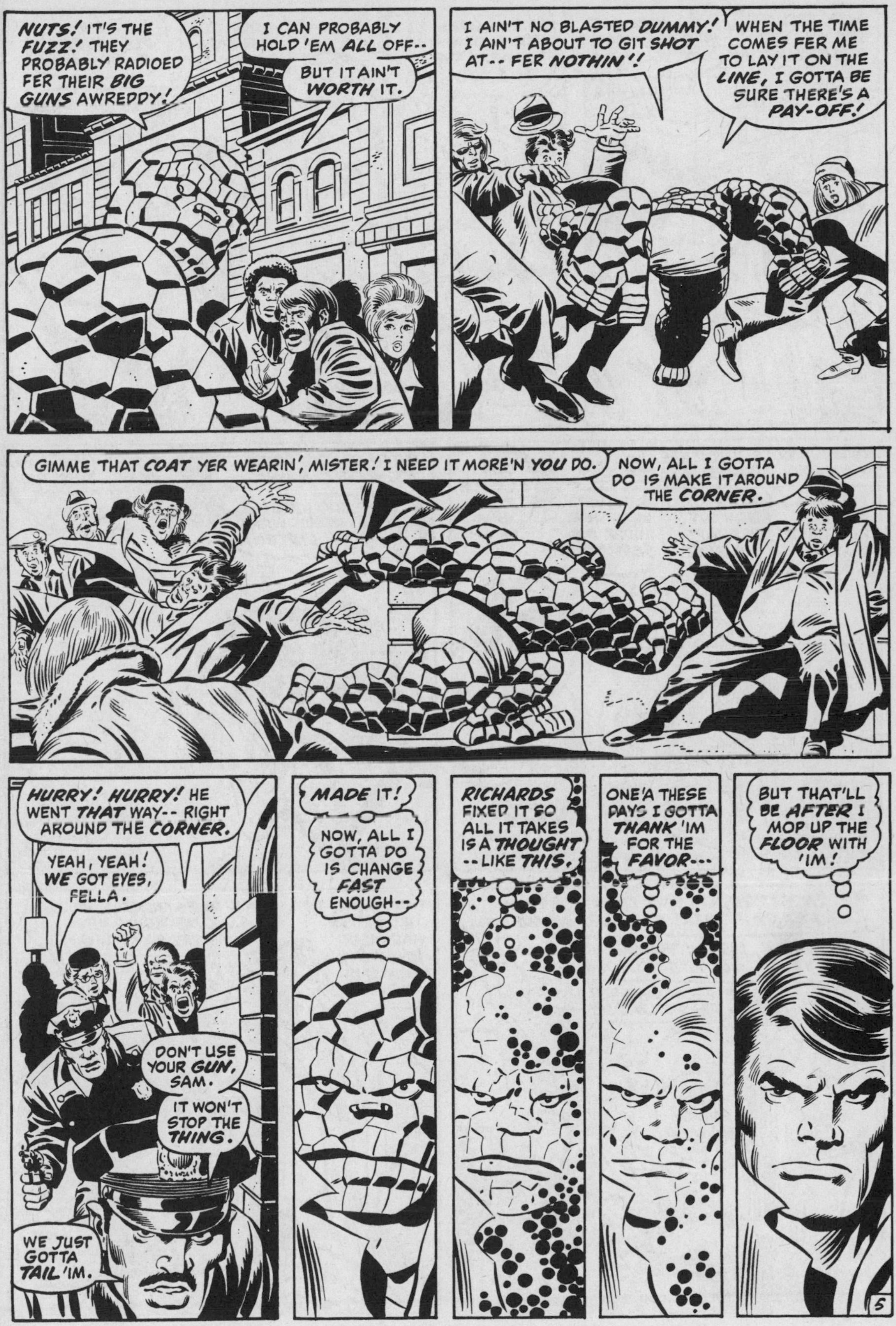

NUTS! IT'S THE FUZZ! THEY PROBABLY RADIOED FER THEIR BIG GUNS AWREDDY!
I CAN PROBABLY HOLD 'EM ALL OFF--
BUT IT AIN'T WORTH IT.
I AIN'T NO BLASTED DUMMY! I AIN'T ABOUT TO GIT SHOT AT-- FER NOTHIN'!
WHEN THE TIME COMES FER ME TO LAY IT ON THE LINE, I GOTTA BE SURE THERE'S A PAY-OFF!
GIMME THAT COAT YER WEARIN', MISTER! I NEED IT MORE'N YOU DO.
NOW, ALL I GOTTA DO IS MAKE IT AROUND THE CORNER.
HURRY! HURRY! HE WENT THAT WAY-- RIGHT AROUND THE CORNER.
YEAH, YEAH! WE GOT EYES, FELLA.
DON'T USE YOUR GUN, SAM.
IT WON'T STOP THE THING.
WE JUST GOTTA TAIL 'IM.
MADE IT!
NOW, ALL I GOTTA DO IS CHANGE FAST ENOUGH--
RICHARDS FIXED IT SO ALL IT TAKES IS A THOUGHT --LIKE THIS.
ONE'A THESE DAYS I GOTTA THANK 'IM FOR THE FAVOR---
BUT THAT'LL BE AFTER I MOP UP THE FLOOR WITH 'IM!
5

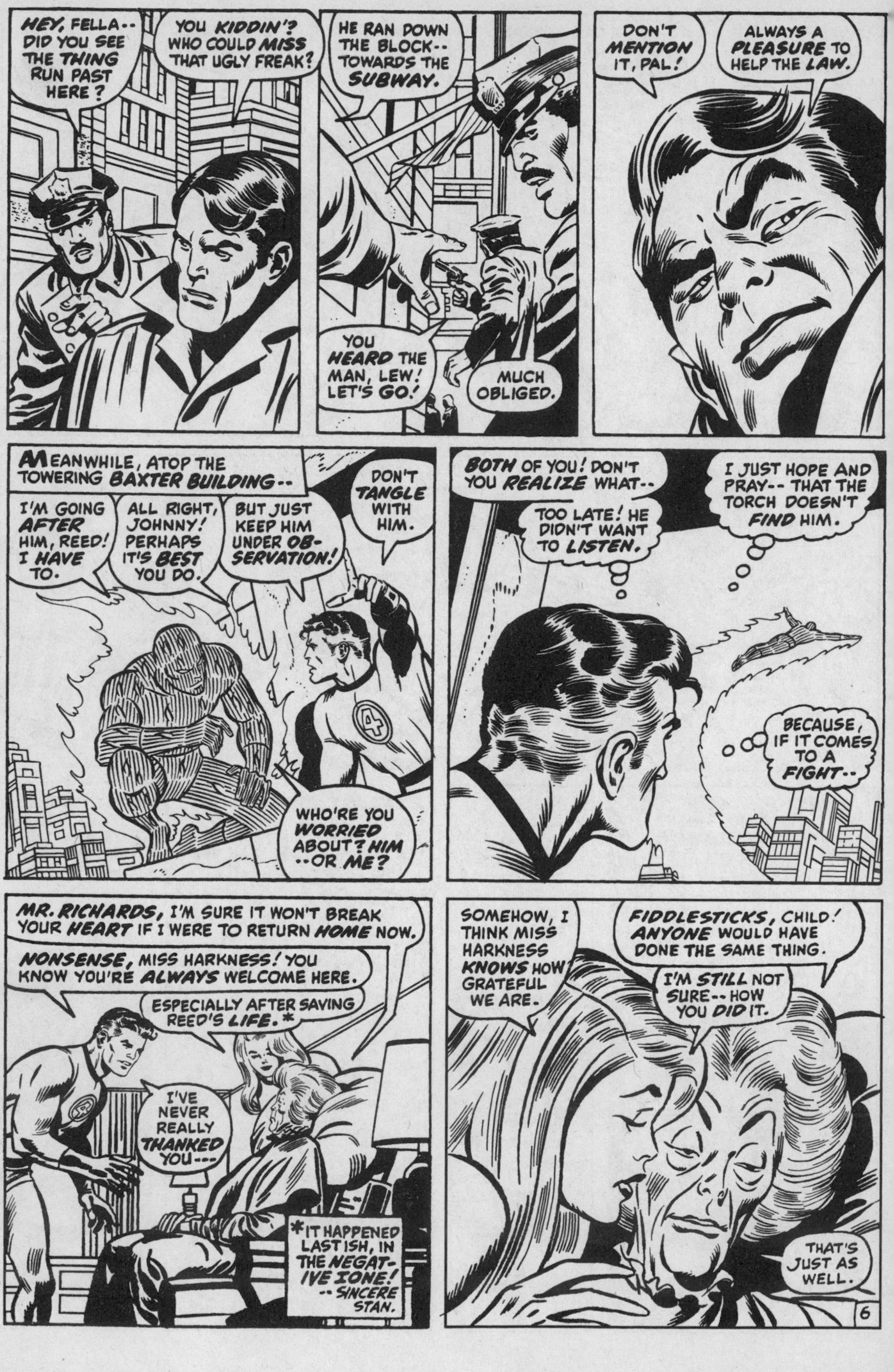
HEY, FELLA-- DID YOU SEE THE THING RUN PAST HERE?
YOU KIDDIN'? WHO COULD MISS THAT UGLY FREAK?
HE RAN DOWN THE BLOCK-- TOWARDS THE SUBWAY.
YOU HEARD THE MAN, LEW! LET'S GO!
MUCH OBLIGED.
DON'T MENTION IT, PAL!
ALWAYS A PLEASURE TO HELP THE LAW.
MEANWHILE, ATOP THE TOWERING BAXTER BUILDING--
I'M GOING AFTER HIM, REED! I HAVE TO.
ALL RIGHT, JOHNNY! PERHAPS IT'S BEST YOU DO.
BUT JUST KEEP HIM UNDER OB-SERVATION!
DON'T TANGLE WITH HIM.
WHO'RE YOU WORRIED ABOUT? HIM --OR ME?
BOTH OF YOU! DON'T YOU REALIZE WHAT--
TOO LATE! HE DIDN'T WANT TO LISTEN.
I JUST HOPE AND PRAY-- THAT THE TORCH DOESN'T FIND HIM.
BECAUSE, IF IT COMES TO A FIGHT--
MR. RICHARDS, I'M SURE IT WON'T BREAK YOUR HEART IF I WERE TO RETURN HOME NOW.
NONSENSE, MISS HARKNESS! YOU KNOW YOU'RE ALWAYS WELCOME HERE.
ESPECIALLY AFTER SAVING REED'S LIFE.*
I'VE NEVER REALLY THANKED YOU---
*IT HAPPENED LAST ISH, IN THE NEGATIVE ZONE! --SINCERE STAN.
SOMEHOW, I THINK MISS HARKNESS KNOWS HOW GRATEFUL WE ARE.
FIDDLESTICKS, CHILD! ANYONE WOULD HAVE DONE THE SAME THING.
I'M STILL NOT SURE-- HOW YOU DID IT.
THAT'S JUST AS WELL.
6

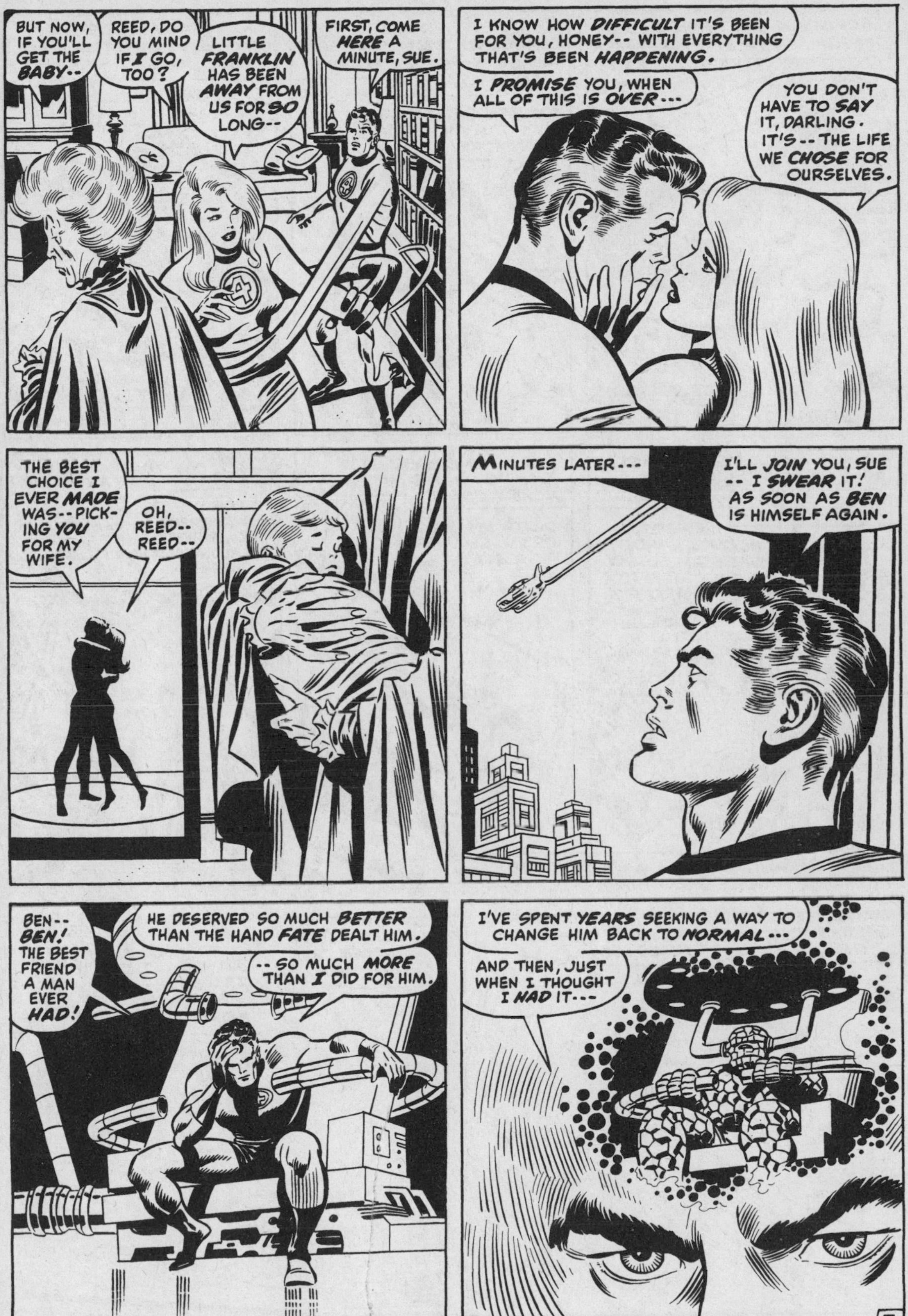

BUT NOW, IF YOU'LL GET THE BABY--
REED, DO YOU MIND IF I GO, TOO?
LITTLE FRANKLIN HAS BEEN AWAY FROM US FOR SO LONG--
FIRST, COME HERE A MINUTE, SUE.
I KNOW HOW DIFFICULT IT'S BEEN FOR YOU, HONEY-- WITH EVERYTHING THAT'S BEEN HAPPENING.
I PROMISE YOU, WHEN ALL OF THIS IS OVER---
YOU DON'T HAVE TO SAY IT, DARLING. IT'S -- THE LIFE WE CHOSE FOR OURSELVES.
THE BEST CHOICE I EVER MADE WAS--PICKING YOU FOR MY WIFE.
OH, REED-- REED--
MINUTES LATER---
I'LL JOIN YOU, SUE -- I SWEAR IT! AS SOON AS BEN IS HIMSELF AGAIN.
BEN-- BEN! THE BEST FRIEND A MAN EVER HAD!
HE DESERVED SO MUCH BETTER THAN THE HAND FATE DEALT HIM.
-- SO MUCH MORE THAN I DID FOR HIM.
I'VE SPENT YEARS SEEKING A WAY TO CHANGE HIM BACK TO NORMAL---
AND THEN, JUST WHEN I THOUGHT I HAD IT---
7.

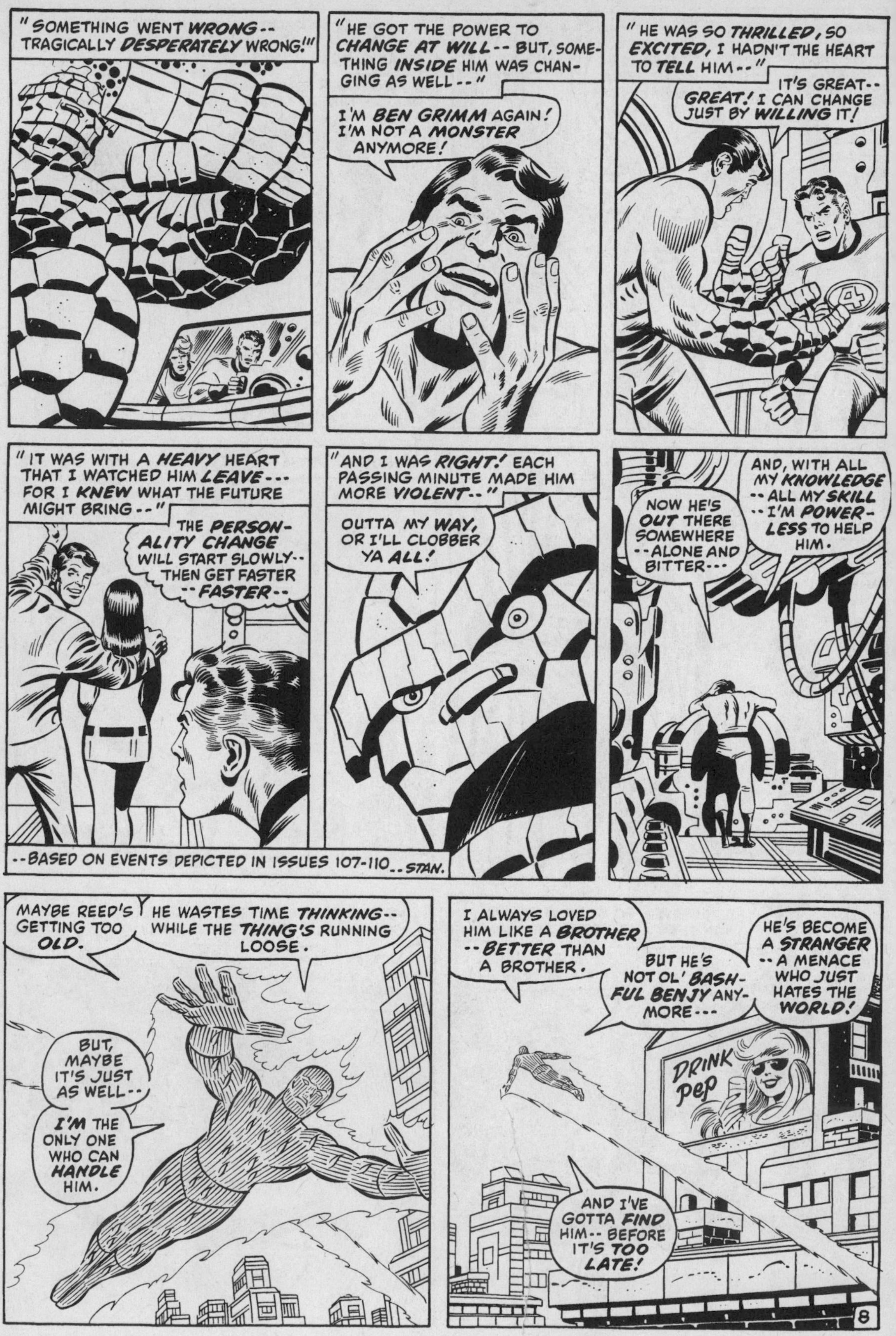

"SOMETHING WENT WRONG-- TRAGICALLY DESPERATELY WRONG!"
"HE GOT THE POWER TO CHANGE AT WILL-- BUT, SOMETHING INSIDE HIM WAS CHANGING AS WELL--"
I'M BEN GRIMM AGAIN! I'M NOT A MONSTER ANYMORE!
"HE WAS SO THRILLED, SO EXCITED, I HADN'T THE HEART TO TELL HIM--"
IT'S GREAT-- GREAT! I CAN CHANGE JUST BY WILLING IT!
"IT WAS WITH A HEAVY HEART THAT I WATCHED HIM LEAVE--- FOR I KNEW WHAT THE FUTURE MIGHT BRING--"
THE PERSONALITY CHANGE WILL START SLOWLY-- THEN GET FASTER --FASTER--
"AND I WAS RIGHT! EACH PASSING MINUTE MADE HIM MORE VIOLENT--"
OUTTA MY WAY, OR I'LL CLOBBER YA ALL!
--BASED ON EVENTS DEPICTED IN ISSUES 107-110..STAN.
NOW HE'S OUT THERE SOMEWHERE --ALONE AND BITTER---
AND, WITH ALL MY KNOWLEDGE --ALL MY SKILL --I'M POWERLESS TO HELP HIM.
MAYBE REED'S GETTING TOO OLD.
HE WASTES TIME THINKING-- WHILE THE THING'S RUNNING LOOSE.
BUT, MAYBE IT'S JUST AS WELL--
I'M THE ONLY ONE WHO CAN HANDLE HIM.
I ALWAYS LOVED HIM LIKE A BROTHER --BETTER THAN A BROTHER.
BUT HE'S NOT OL' BASHFUL BENJY ANYMORE---
HE'S BECOME A STRANGER --A MENACE WHO JUST HATES THE WORLD!
DRINK Pep
AND I'VE GOTTA FIND HIM-- BEFORE IT'S TOO LATE!

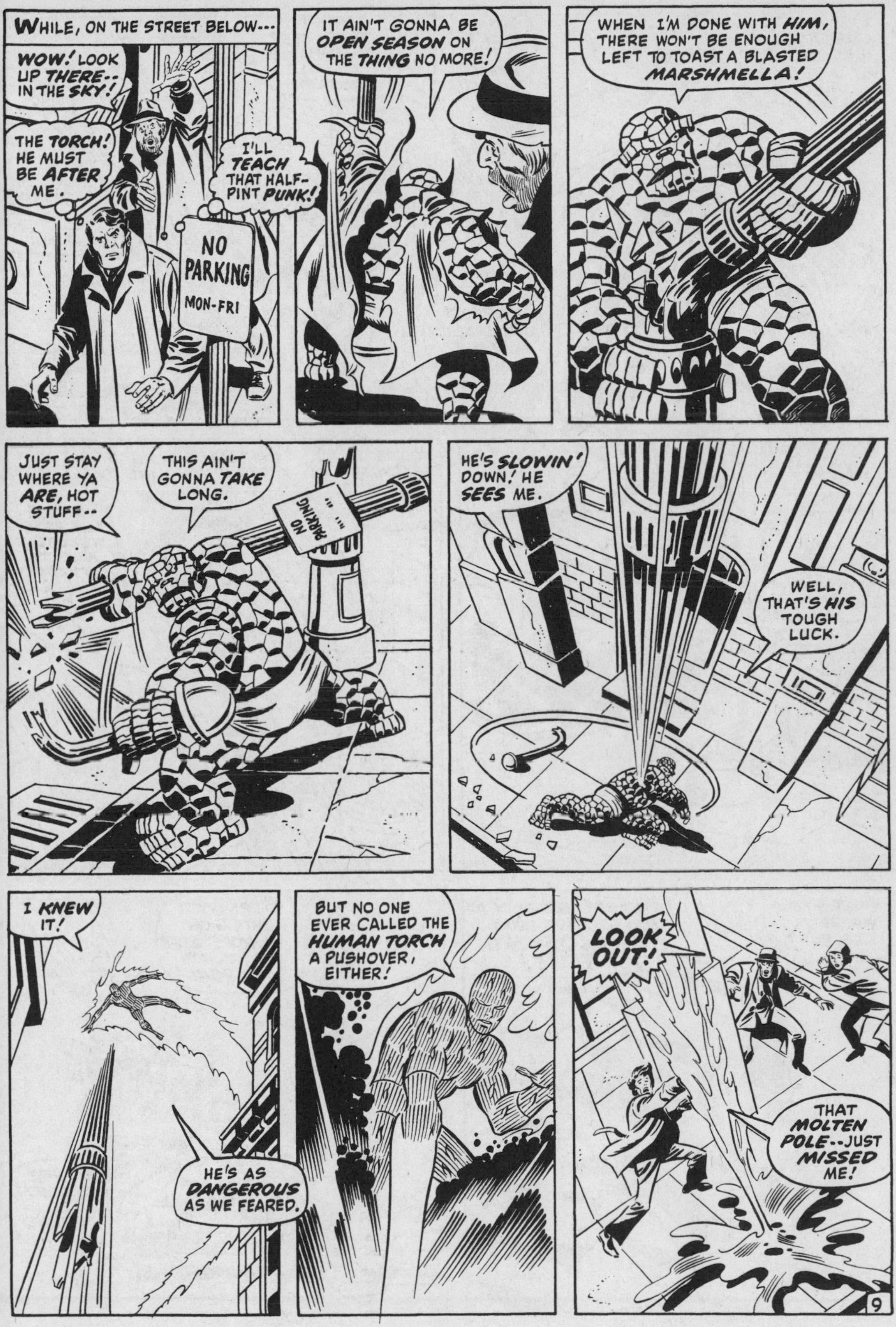
WHILE, ON THE STREET BELOW---
WOW! LOOK UP THERE-- IN THE SKY!
THE TORCH! HE MUST BE AFTER ME.
I'LL TEACH THAT HALF-PINT PUNK!
NO PARKING MON-FRI
IT AIN'T GONNA BE OPEN SEASON ON THE THING NO MORE!
WHEN I'M DONE WITH HIM, THERE WON'T BE ENOUGH LEFT TO TOAST A BLASTED MARSHMELLA!
JUST STAY WHERE YA ARE, HOT STUFF--
THIS AIN'T GONNA TAKE LONG.
NO PARKING
HE'S SLOWIN' DOWN! HE SEES ME.
WELL, THAT'S HIS TOUGH LUCK.
I KNEW IT!
HE'S AS DANGEROUS AS WE FEARED.
BUT NO ONE EVER CALLED THE HUMAN TORCH A PUSHOVER, EITHER!
LOOK OUT!
THAT MOLTEN POLE--JUST MISSED ME!

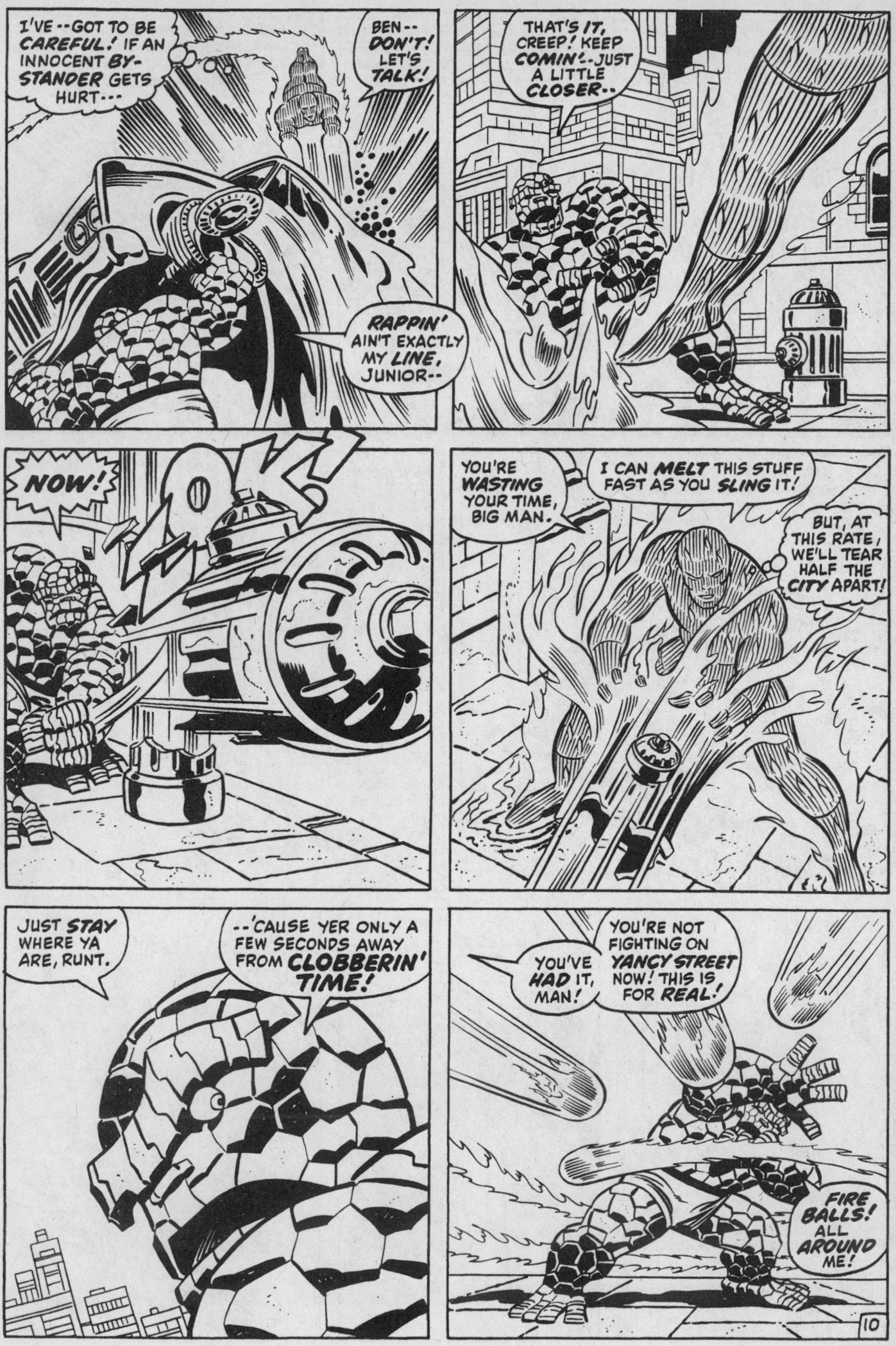
I'VE--GOT TO BE CAREFUL! IF AN INNOCENT BY-STANDER GETS HURT---
BEN--DON'T! LET'S TALK!
RAPPIN' AIN'T EXACTLY MY LINE, JUNIOR--
THAT'S IT, CREEP! KEEP COMIN'--JUST A LITTLE CLOSER..
NOW!
YOU'RE WASTING YOUR TIME, BIG MAN.
I CAN MELT THIS STUFF FAST AS YOU SLING IT!
BUT, AT THIS RATE, WE'LL TEAR HALF THE CITY APART!
JUST STAY WHERE YA ARE, RUNT.
--'CAUSE YER ONLY A FEW SECONDS AWAY FROM CLOBBERIN' TIME!
YOU'VE HAD IT, MAN!
YOU'RE NOT FIGHTING ON YANCY STREET NOW! THIS IS FOR REAL!
FIRE BALLS! ALL AROUND ME!

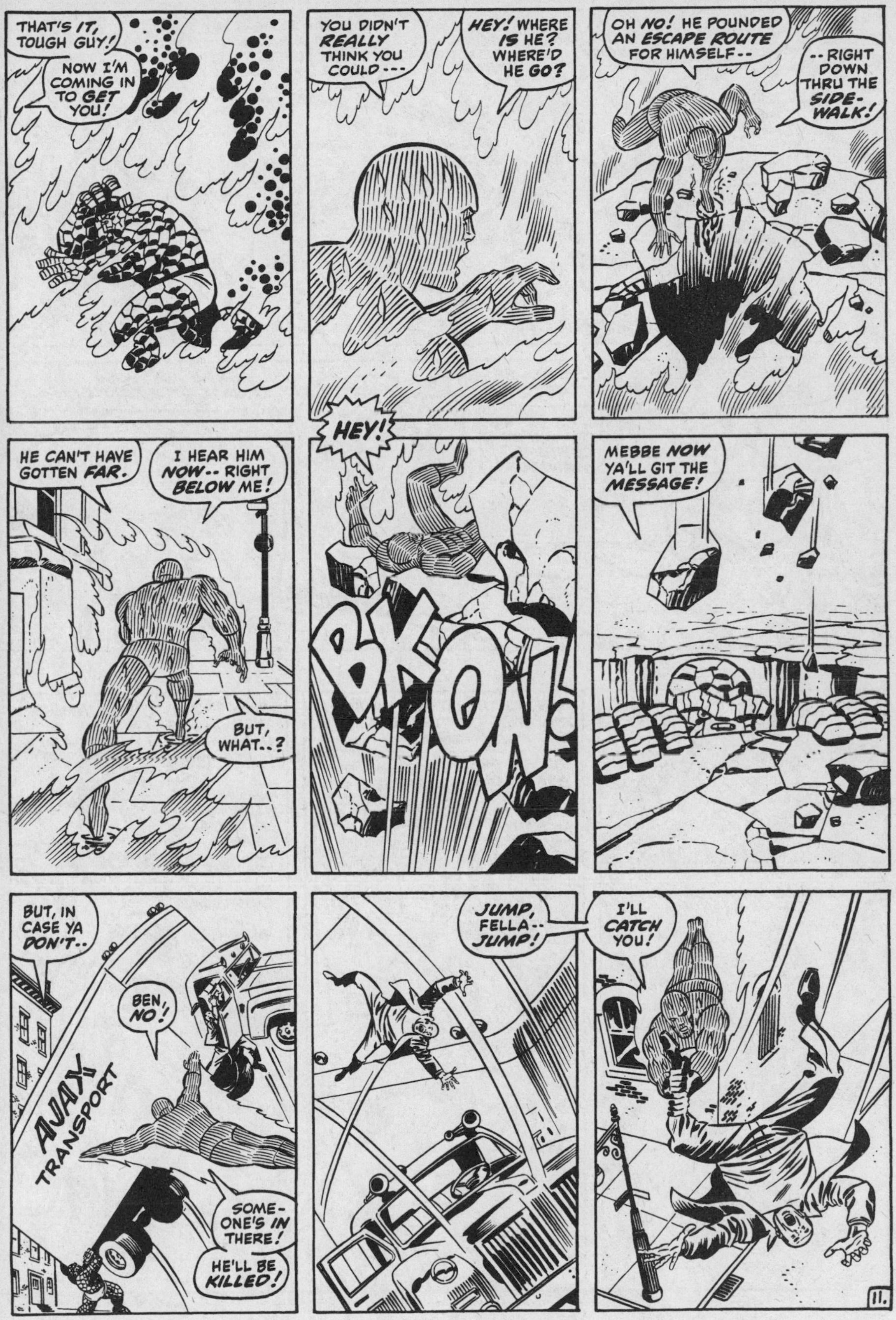
THAT'S IT, TOUGH GUY!
NOW I'M COMING IN TO GET YOU!
YOU DIDN'T REALLY THINK YOU COULD ---
HEY! WHERE IS HE? WHERE'D HE GO?
OH NO! HE POUNDED AN ESCAPE ROUTE FOR HIMSELF --
-- RIGHT DOWN THRU THE SIDE-WALK!
HE CAN'T HAVE GOTTEN FAR.
I HEAR HIM NOW -- RIGHT BELOW ME!
BUT, WHAT..?
HEY!
BKOW!
MEBBE NOW YA'LL GIT THE MESSAGE!
BUT, IN CASE YA DON'T..
BEN, NO!
AJAX TRANSPORT
SOME-ONE'S IN THERE!
HE'LL BE KILLED!
JUMP, FELLA -- JUMP!
I'LL CATCH YOU!
11.

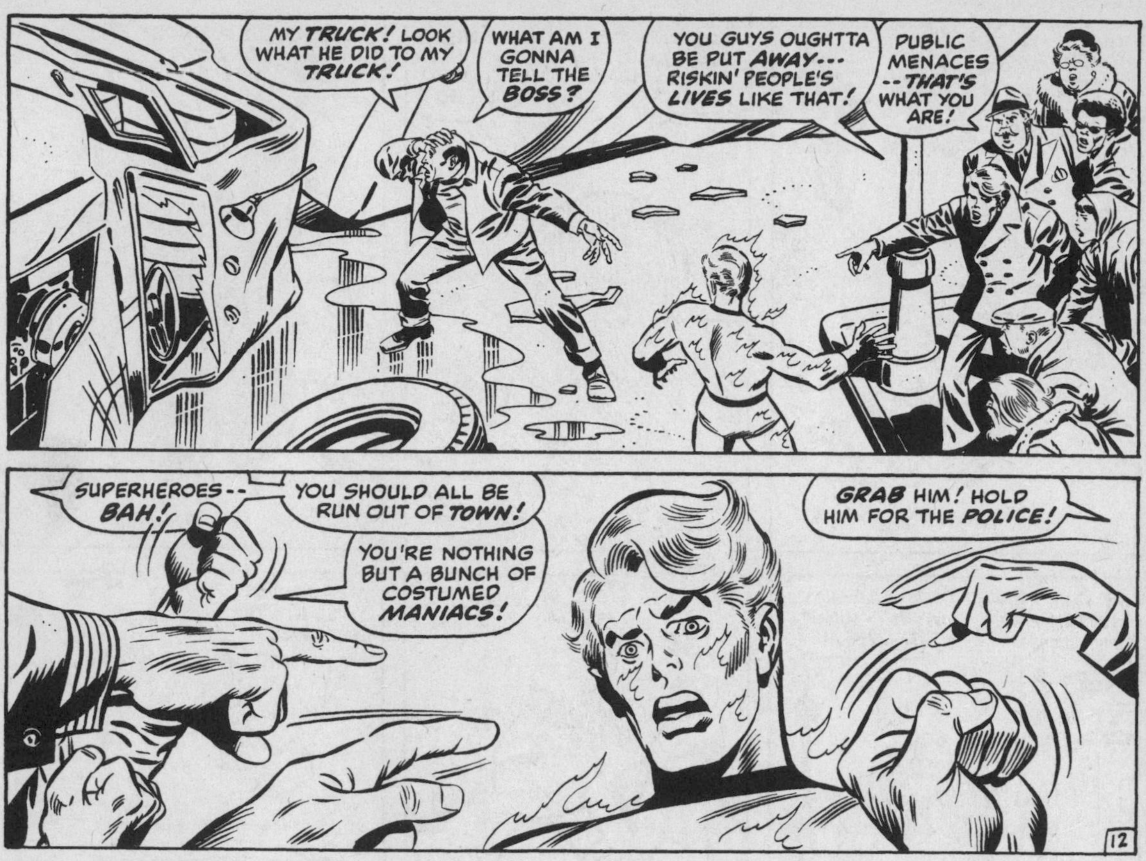
MY TRUCK! LOOK WHAT HE DID TO MY TRUCK!
WHAT AM I GONNA TELL THE BOSS?
YOU GUYS OUGHTTA BE PUT AWAY--- RISKIN' PEOPLE'S LIVES LIKE THAT!
PUBLIC MENACES --THAT'S WHAT YOU ARE!
SUPERHEROES-- BAH!
YOU SHOULD ALL BE RUN OUT OF TOWN!
YOU'RE NOTHING BUT A BUNCH OF COSTUMED MANIACS!
GRAB HIM! HOLD HIM FOR THE POLICE!
12

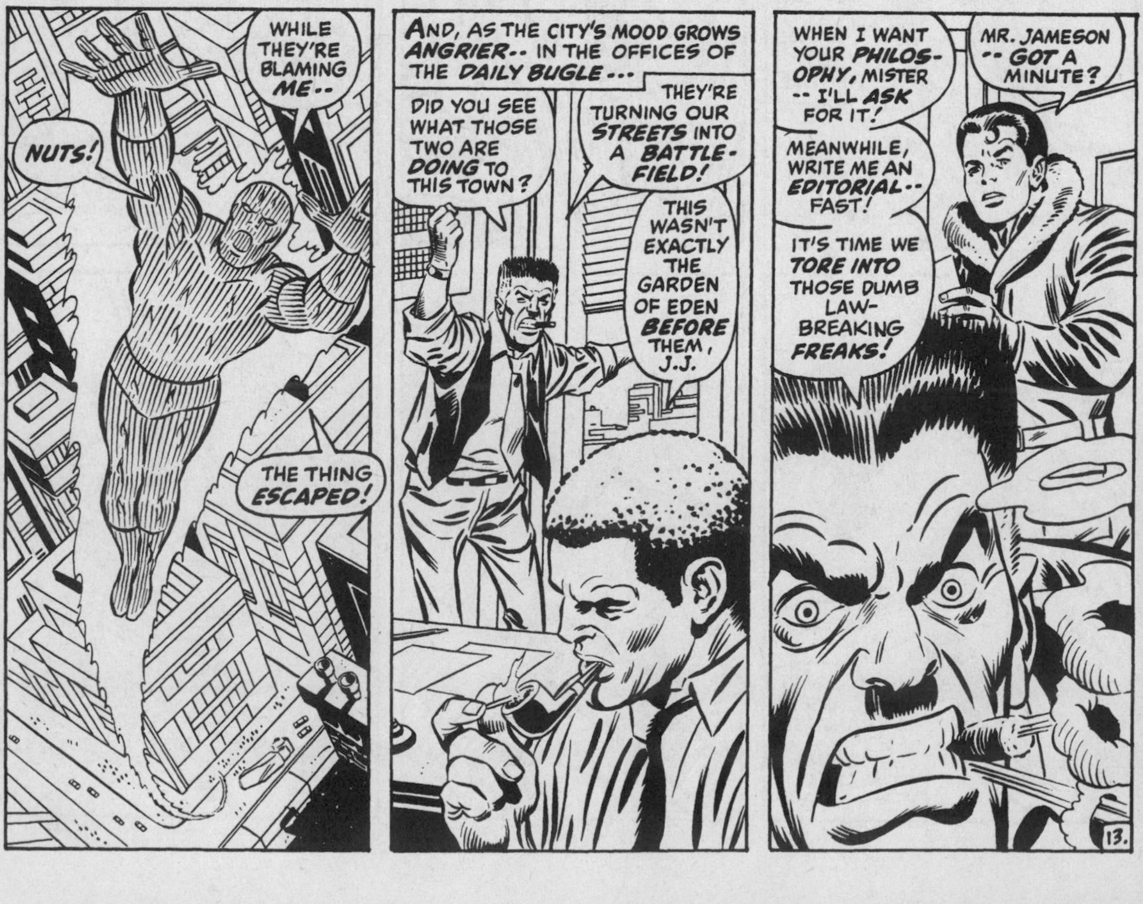
WHILE THEY'RE BLAMING ME--
NUTS!
THE THING ESCAPED!
AND, AS THE CITY'S MOOD GROWS ANGRIER-- IN THE OFFICES OF THE DAILY BUGLE...
DID YOU SEE WHAT THOSE TWO ARE DOING TO THIS TOWN?
THEY'RE TURNING OUR STREETS INTO A BATTLEFIELD!
THIS WASN'T EXACTLY THE GARDEN OF EDEN BEFORE THEM, J.J.
WHEN I WANT YOUR PHILOSOPHY, MISTER --I'LL ASK FOR IT!
MEANWHILE, WRITE ME AN EDITORIAL-- FAST!
IT'S TIME WE TORE INTO THOSE DUMB LAW-BREAKING FREAKS!
MR. JAMESON --GOT A MINUTE?
13.

I'VE-- GOT SOME *PHOTOS* FOR YOU.

SHADDUP, PARKER! CAN'T YOU SEE WE'RE *BUSY?*

WHAT'S *WITH* YOU, ROBBIE? YOU MY CITY EDITOR OR *NOT?*

I WANT THAT *EDITORIAL!*

I CAN'T *WRITE* IT IF I DON'T *FEEL* IT, J.J.!

THE *F.F.* HAVE DONE A *LOT* FOR THIS TOWN!

YEAH, THEY'VE DONE A *LOT*, ALL RIGHT!

AND IF WE DON'T *STOP* 'EM, THEY'LL *BURN* IT TO THE *GROUND!*

THEY'RE ALMOST AS *BAD* AS THAT WALL-CRAWLING WORM, *SPIDER-MAN!*

GIMME THAT *PORTABLE!*

I'LL WRITE THE COLUMN *MYSELF!*

AND THAT'S JUST THE *START* OF IT---

FOR, INSIDE THE *BAXTER BUILDING---*

RICHARDS! I WANT TO *SEE* YOU.

THIS TIME I MEAN *BUSINESS!*

THE F.F. HAS TWENTY-FOUR HOURS TO *MOVE OUT!*

PAY ATTENTION! I'M BREAKING YOUR *LEASE!*

RICHARDS-- I *MEAN* IT!

LOOK AT THE *CROWDS* DOWN THERE-- *DEMONSTRATING--* BECAUSE OF YOU.

WELL, IT'S A *FREE* COUNTRY.

NOT WHEN OUR OTHER *TENANTS* START COMPLAINING!

YOU'RE LOWERING THE *PROPERTY VALUES* IN THIS AREA!

SAVE OUR CITY

F.F. GO HOME!

BUT WE'VE A *JOB* TO DO. WE NEED A HEAD-QUARTERS... AND *THIS* IS *IT!*

FANTASTIC FOUR!

F.F. GO HOME!

YOU'VE *HAD* IT, RICHARDS! I'M TELLING YOU TO START *PACKING!*

THE FANTASTIC FOUR NO MORE!

WE D— NO MORE OF THE FANTASTIC FOUR!

GAINST THE WALL

14

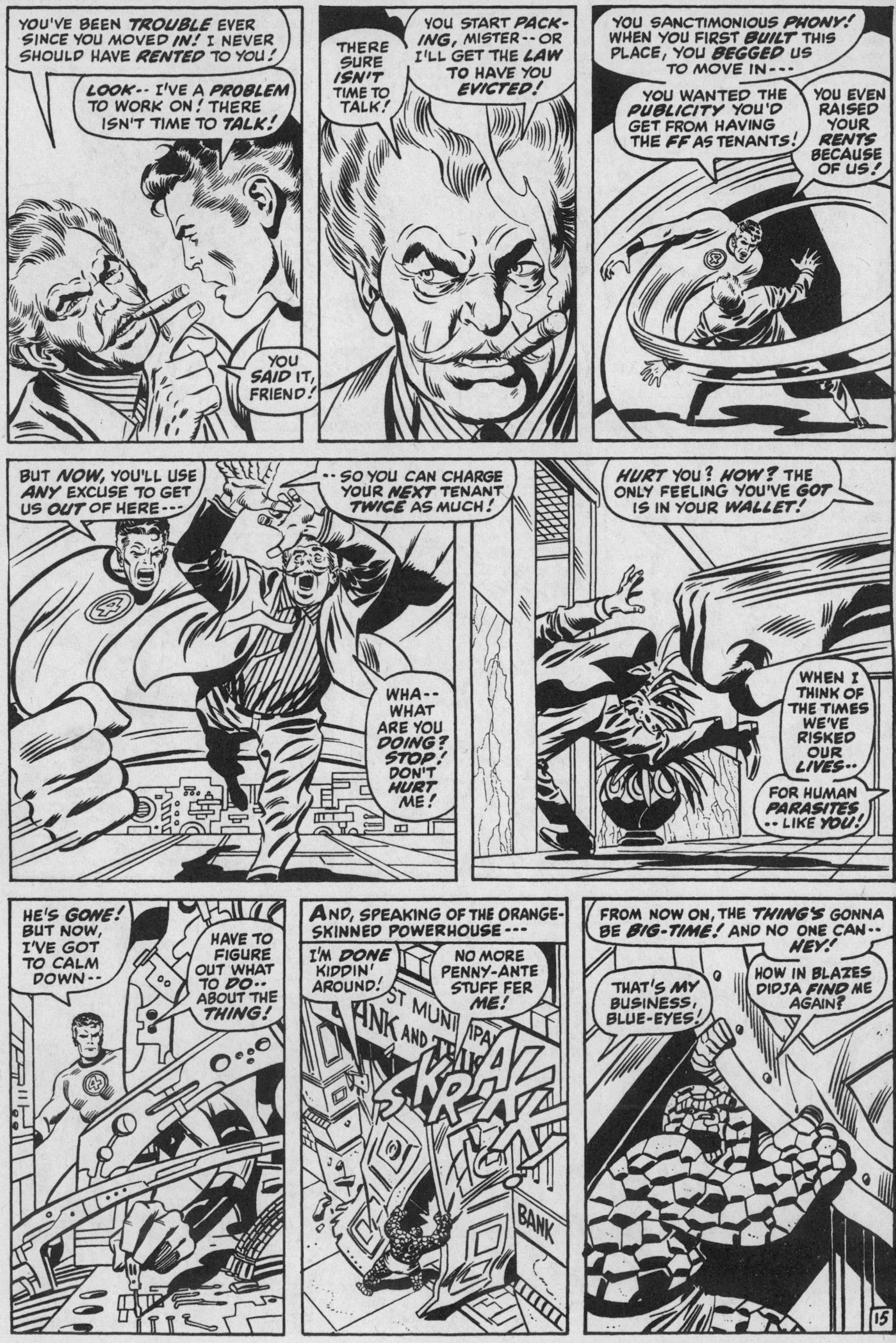
YOU'VE BEEN TROUBLE EVER SINCE YOU MOVED IN! I NEVER SHOULD HAVE RENTED TO YOU!
LOOK-- I'VE A PROBLEM TO WORK ON! THERE ISN'T TIME TO TALK!
YOU SAID IT, FRIEND!
THERE SURE ISN'T TIME TO TALK!
YOU START PACKING, MISTER--OR I'LL GET THE LAW TO HAVE YOU EVICTED!
YOU SANCTIMONIOUS PHONY! WHEN YOU FIRST BUILT THIS PLACE, YOU BEGGED US TO MOVE IN---
YOU WANTED THE PUBLICITY YOU'D GET FROM HAVING THE FF AS TENANTS!
YOU EVEN RAISED YOUR RENTS BECAUSE OF US!
BUT NOW, YOU'LL USE ANY EXCUSE TO GET US OUT OF HERE---
--SO YOU CAN CHARGE YOUR NEXT TENANT TWICE AS MUCH!
WHA--WHAT ARE YOU DOING? STOP! DON'T HURT ME!
HURT YOU? HOW? THE ONLY FEELING YOU'VE GOT IS IN YOUR WALLET!
WHEN I THINK OF THE TIMES WE'VE RISKED OUR LIVES..
FOR HUMAN PARASITES..LIKE YOU!
HE'S GONE! BUT NOW, I'VE GOT TO CALM DOWN--
HAVE TO FIGURE OUT WHAT TO DO..ABOUT THE THING!
AND, SPEAKING OF THE ORANGE-SKINNED POWERHOUSE---
I'M DONE KIDDIN' AROUND!
NO MORE PENNY-ANTE STUFF FER ME!
SKRAK
BANK
FROM NOW ON, THE THING'S GONNA BE BIG-TIME! AND NO ONE CAN-- HEY!
THAT'S MY BUSINESS, BLUE-EYES!
HOW IN BLAZES DIDJA FIND ME AGAIN?
15

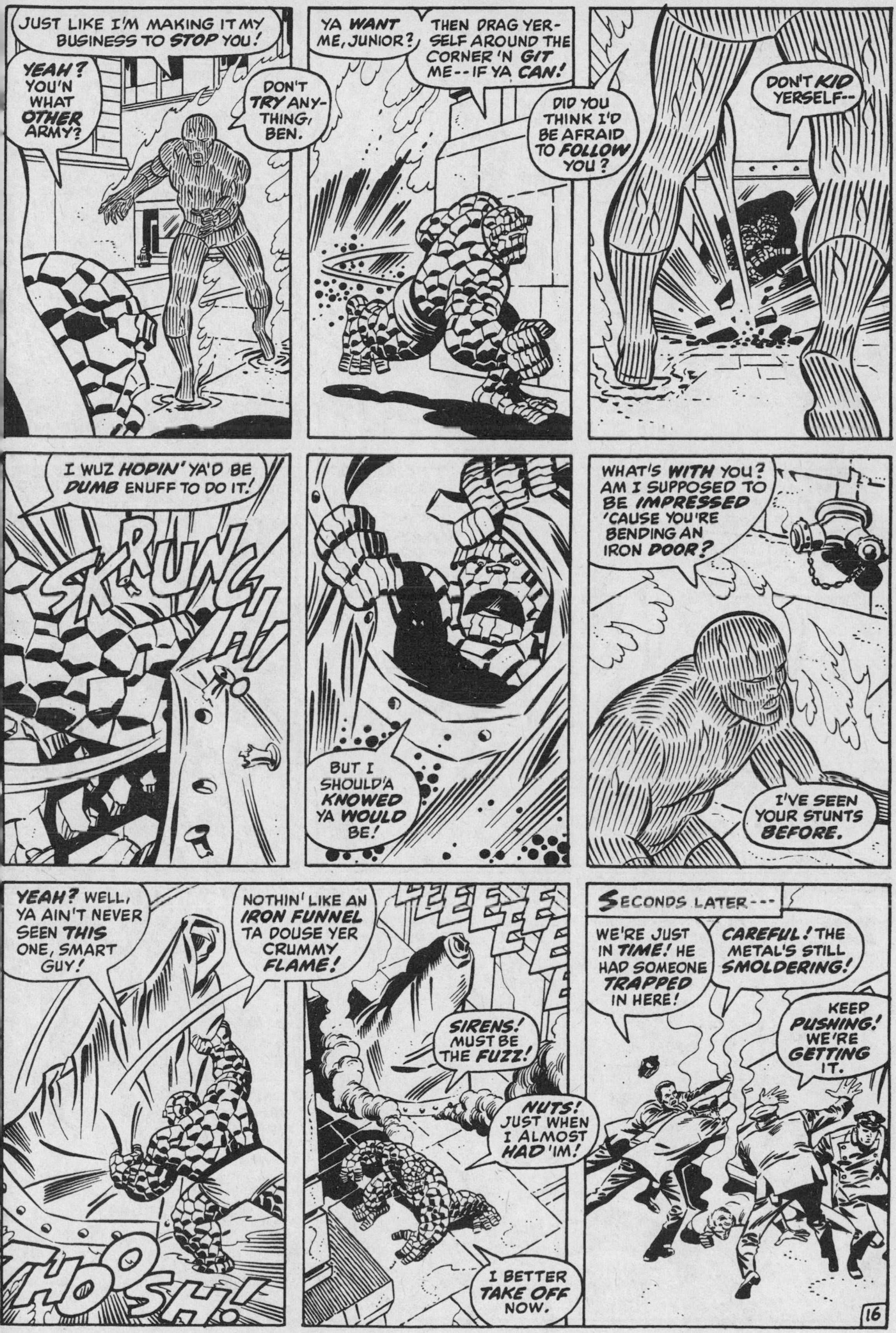
JUST LIKE I'M MAKING IT MY BUSINESS TO STOP YOU!
YEAH? YOU'N WHAT OTHER ARMY?
DON'T TRY ANYTHING, BEN.
YA WANT ME, JUNIOR?
THEN DRAG YERSELF AROUND THE CORNER 'N GIT ME--IF YA CAN!
DID YOU THINK I'D BE AFRAID TO FOLLOW YOU?
DON'T KID YERSELF--
I WUZ HOPIN' YA'D BE DUMB ENUFF TO DO IT!
SKRUNCH
BUT I SHOULD'A KNOWED YA WOULD BE!
WHAT'S WITH YOU? AM I SUPPOSED TO BE IMPRESSED 'CAUSE YOU'RE BENDING AN IRON DOOR?
I'VE SEEN YOUR STUNTS BEFORE.
YEAH? WELL, YA AIN'T NEVER SEEN THIS ONE, SMART GUY!
NOTHIN' LIKE AN IRON FUNNEL TA DOUSE YER CRUMMY FLAME!
THOOSH!
SIRENS! MUST BE THE FUZZ!
NUTS! JUST WHEN I ALMOST HAD 'IM!
I BETTER TAKE OFF NOW.
SECONDS LATER---
WE'RE JUST IN TIME! HE HAD SOMEONE TRAPPED IN HERE!
CAREFUL! THE METAL'S STILL SMOLDERING!
KEEP PUSHING! WE'RE GETTING IT.
16

Panel 1:
IT'S THE *TORCH!* IS HE *OKAY?*

NEVER MIND ABOUT *ME!* I'VE GOTTA FIND THE *THING.*

NOT *THIS* TIME, KID! THAT'S *OUR* JOB.

TAKE 'IM *IN!* HE'S GOT SOME *QUESTIONS* TO ANSWER.

Panel 2:
SURE, SURE-- WHATEVER YOU *SAY.*

--AFTER I FIND BEN GRIMM!

FLAME ON!

MEANWHILE, MANY MILES AWAY---

Panel 3:
--AND, IN *NEW YORK,* THE MAYOR IS URGING PEOPLE TO STAY OFF THE *STREETS,* UNTIL--

IT'S *BEN!* HE MUST BE STILL AT *LARGE!*

PERHAPS I SHOULD *RETURN*--

Panel 4:

I SUGGEST YOU REMAIN *HERE,* MY DEAR! THE *NEWS REPORT* HAS DISTURBED THE *BABY.*

BUT YOUR PRESENCE WILL *COMFORT* LITTLE FRANKLIN.

Panel 5:

HE *COULDN'T* HAVE HEARD THE TV, MRS. HARKNESS---

HE'S TWO ROOMS *AWAY*--- WITH THE DOOR *SHUT!*

I DIDN'T *SAY* HE HEARD IT, DEAR.

Panel 6:

PERHAPS I'D BETTER *CHECK* ON--*OH!*

I CAN HEAR HIM *CRYING* IN HIS ROOM.

Panel 7:

YOU WERE *RIGHT!*

HE KEPT MUMBLING *DA DA*--AS THOUGH HE'S WORRIED ABOUT HIS *FATHER!*

BUT, HOW COULD HE POSSIBLY--?

PERHAPS HE WAS HAVING A *CHILDISH DREAM.*

Panel 8:

AT ANY RATE, I *WILL* STAY A LITTLE *LONGER.*

IT'S BEEN SO *WONDERFUL*-- SPENDING ALL THIS *TIME* WITH HIM.

Panel 9:

IF ONLY --I WASN'T SO *WORRIED* --ABOUT THE *OTHERS.*

17.

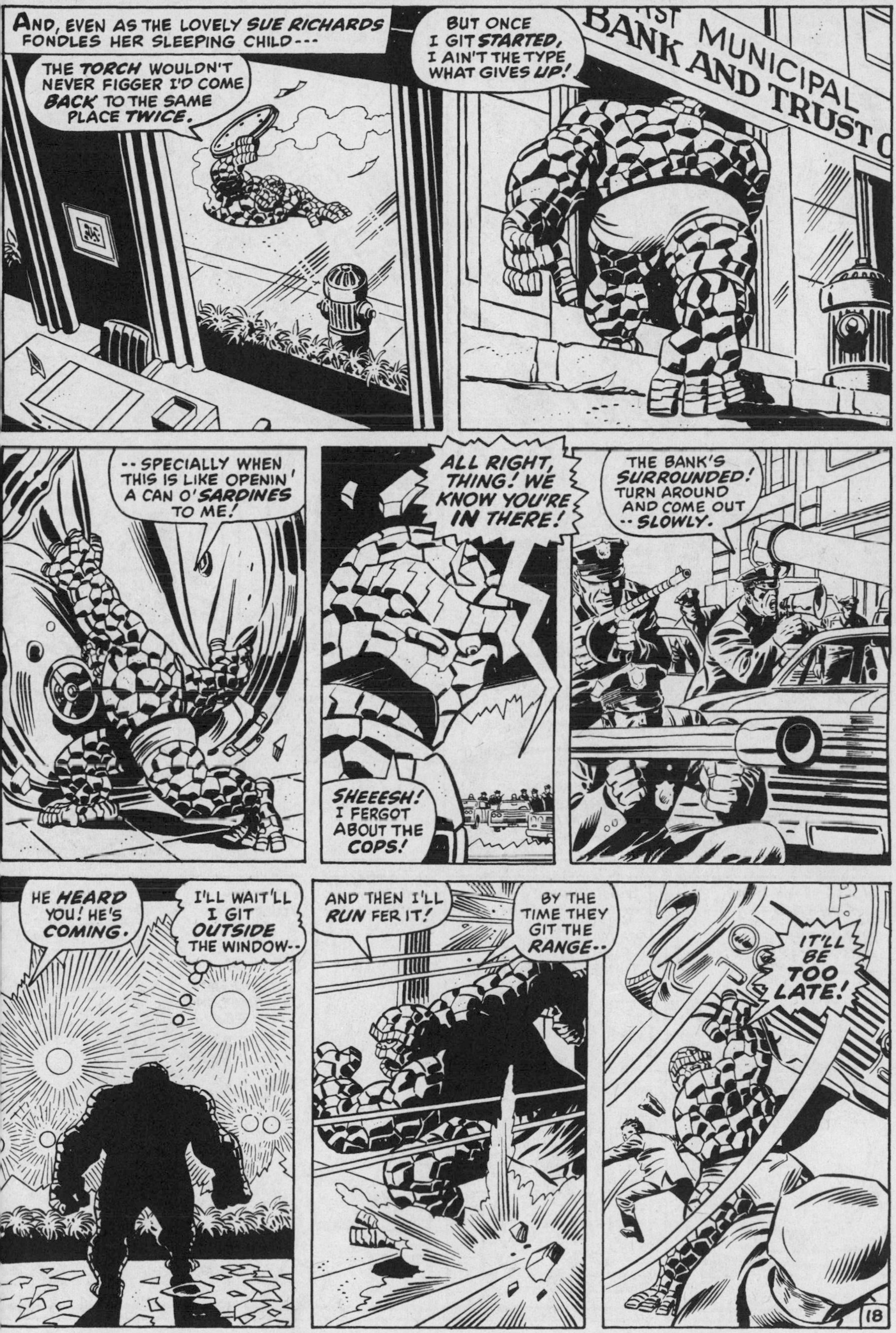

AND, EVEN AS THE LOVELY SUE RICHARDS FONDLES HER SLEEPING CHILD---
THE TORCH WOULDN'T NEVER FIGGER I'D COME BACK TO THE SAME PLACE TWICE.
BUT ONCE I GIT STARTED, I AIN'T THE TYPE WHAT GIVES UP!
FIRST MUNICIPAL BANK AND TRUST C
--SPECIALLY WHEN THIS IS LIKE OPENIN' A CAN O' SARDINES TO ME!
ALL RIGHT, THING! WE KNOW YOU'RE IN THERE!
SHEEESH! I FERGOT ABOUT THE COPS!
THE BANK'S SURROUNDED! TURN AROUND AND COME OUT --SLOWLY.
HE HEARD YOU! HE'S COMING.
I'LL WAIT'LL I GIT OUTSIDE THE WINDOW--
AND THEN I'LL RUN FER IT!
BY THE TIME THEY GIT THE RANGE--
IT'LL BE TOO LATE!
18

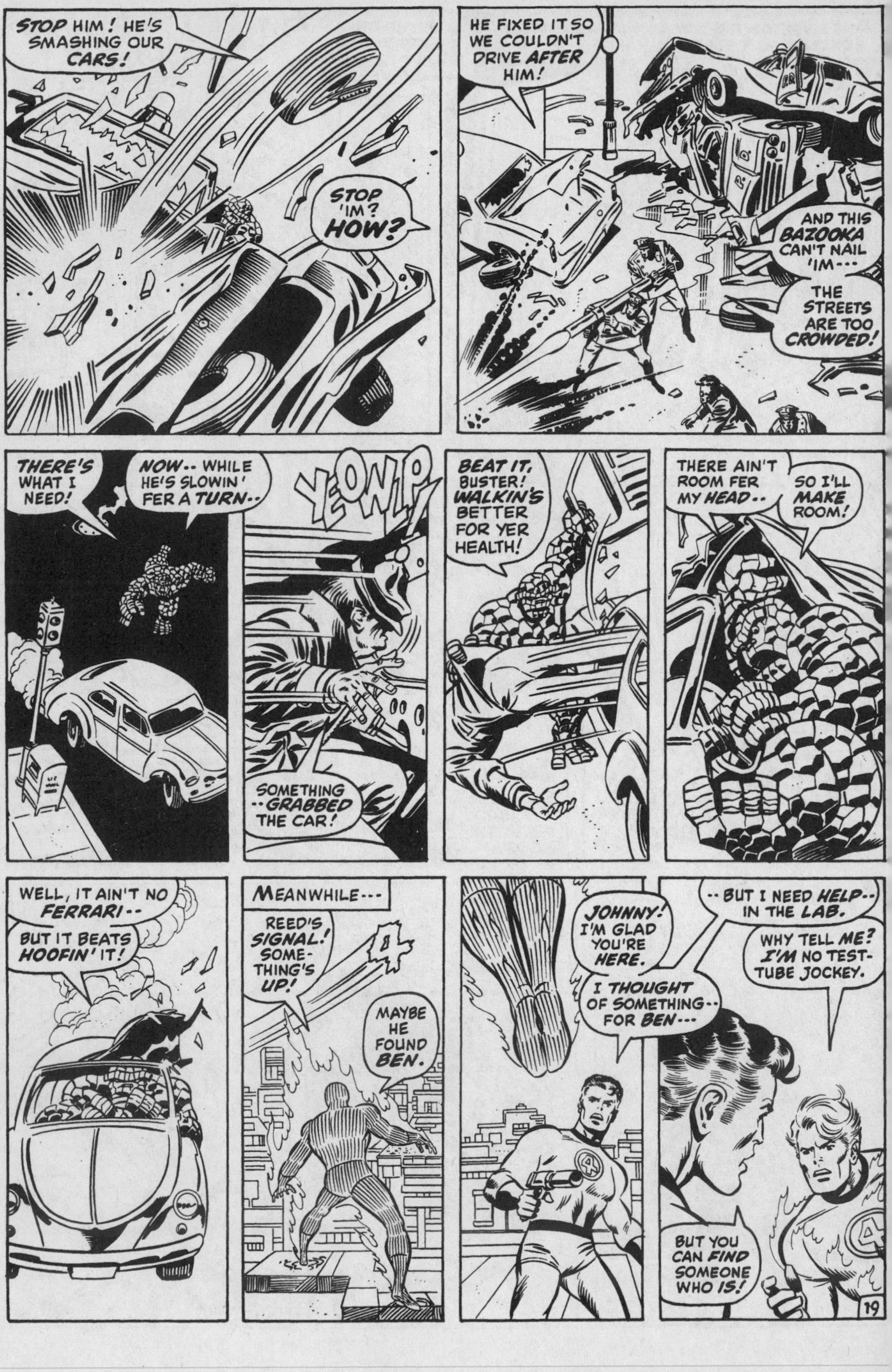
STOP HIM! HE'S SMASHING OUR CARS!
STOP 'IM? HOW?
HE FIXED IT SO WE COULDN'T DRIVE AFTER HIM!
AND THIS BAZOOKA CAN'T NAIL 'IM---
THE STREETS ARE TOO CROWDED!
THERE'S WHAT I NEED!
NOW-- WHILE HE'S SLOWIN' FER A TURN--
YEOWP
SOMETHING --GRABBED THE CAR!
BEAT IT, BUSTER! WALKIN'S BETTER FOR YER HEALTH!
THERE AIN'T ROOM FER MY HEAD--
SO I'LL MAKE ROOM!
WELL, IT AIN'T NO FERRARI--
BUT IT BEATS HOOFIN' IT!
MEANWHILE---
REED'S SIGNAL! SOME-THING'S UP!
MAYBE HE FOUND BEN.
JOHNNY! I'M GLAD YOU'RE HERE.
I THOUGHT OF SOMETHING-- FOR BEN---
-- BUT I NEED HELP-- IN THE LAB.
WHY TELL ME? I'M NO TEST-TUBE JOCKEY.
BUT YOU CAN FIND SOMEONE WHO IS!
19

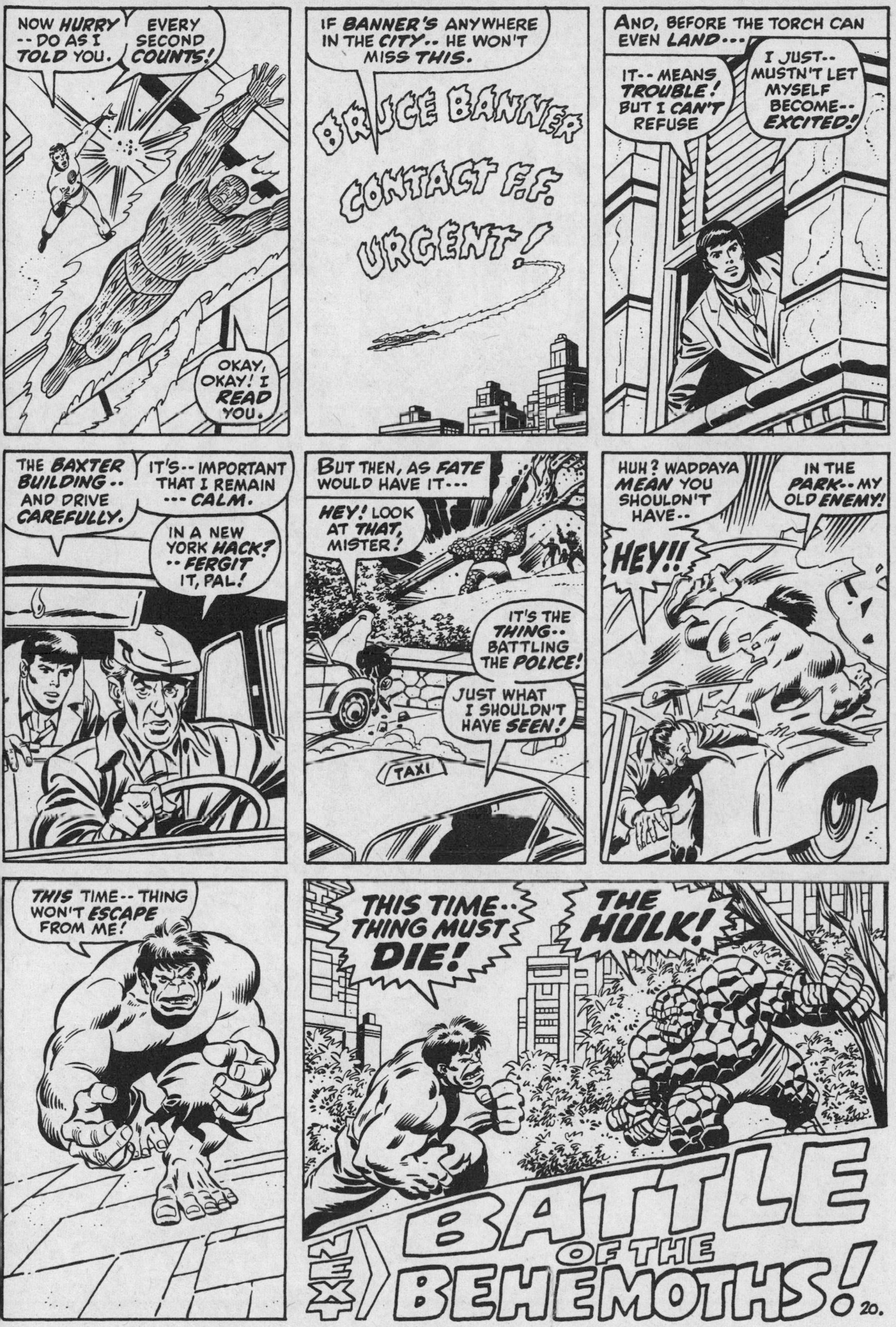
NOW HURRY -- DO AS I TOLD YOU.
EVERY SECOND COUNTS!
OKAY, OKAY! I READ YOU.
IF BANNER'S ANYWHERE IN THE CITY.. HE WON'T MISS THIS.
BRUCE BANNER
CONTACT F.F.
URGENT!
AND, BEFORE THE TORCH CAN EVEN LAND...
IT-- MEANS TROUBLE! BUT I CAN'T REFUSE
I JUST-- MUSTN'T LET MYSELF BECOME-- EXCITED!
THE BAXTER BUILDING -- AND DRIVE CAREFULLY.
IT'S-- IMPORTANT THAT I REMAIN --- CALM.
IN A NEW YORK HACK? -- FERGIT IT, PAL!
BUT THEN, AS FATE WOULD HAVE IT---
HEY! LOOK AT THAT, MISTER!
IT'S THE THING -- BATTLING THE POLICE!
JUST WHAT I SHOULDN'T HAVE SEEN!
TAXI
HUH? WADDAYA MEAN YOU SHOULDN'T HAVE--
IN THE PARK -- MY OLD ENEMY!
HEY!!
THIS TIME -- THING WON'T ESCAPE FROM ME!
THIS TIME -- THING MUST DIE!
THE HULK!
NEXT
BATTLE OF THE BEHEMOTHS!

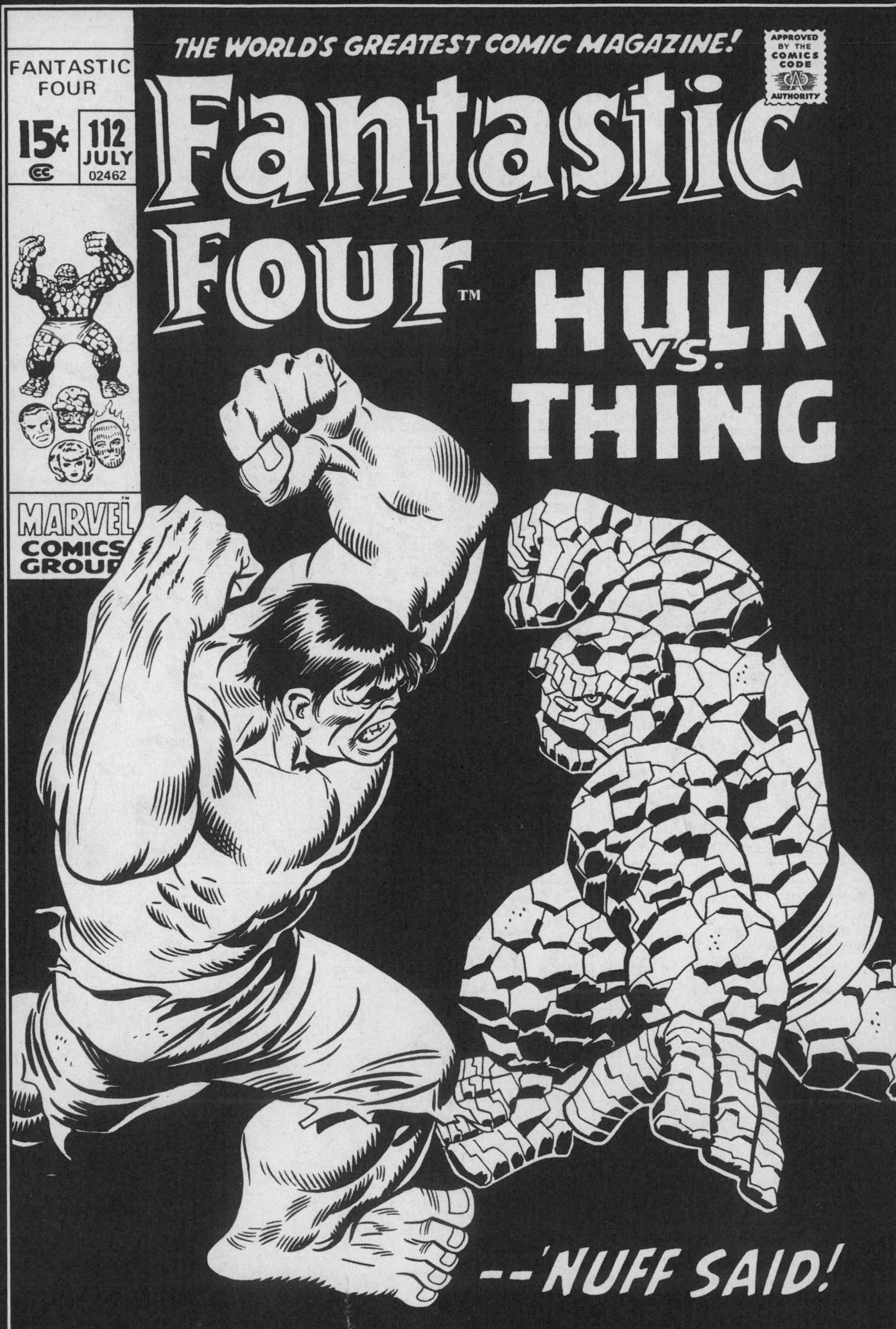
FANTASTIC FOUR
15¢
112
JULY
02462
CC
THE WORLD'S GREATEST COMIC MAGAZINE!
APPROVED BY THE COMICS CODE AUTHORITY
Fantastic Four™
HULK VS. THING
MARVEL COMICS GROUP
--'NUFF SAID!

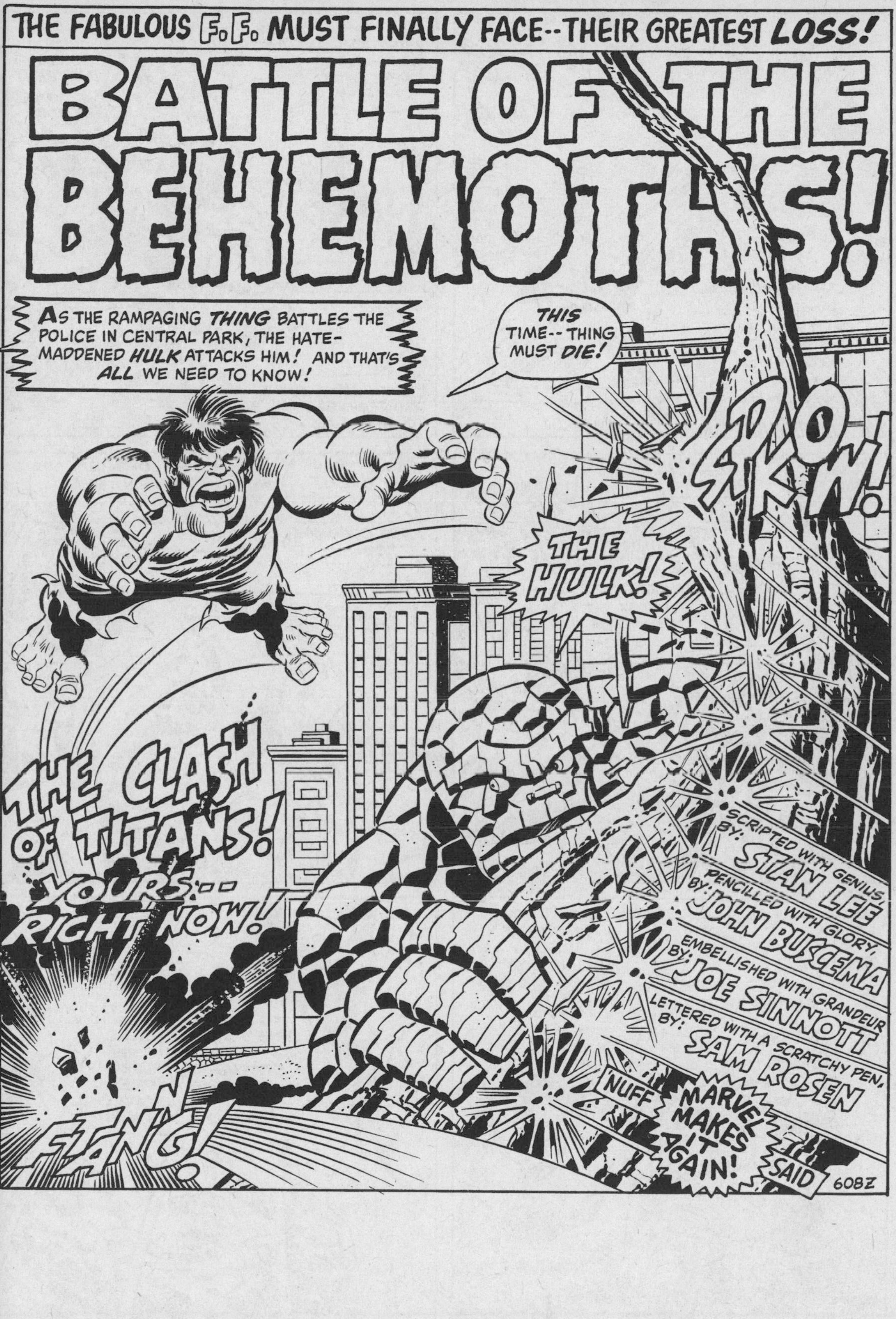

THE FABULOUS F.F. MUST FINALLY FACE--THEIR GREATEST LOSS!
BATTLE OF THE BEHEMOTHS!
AS THE RAMPAGING THING BATTLES THE POLICE IN CENTRAL PARK, THE HATE-MADDENED HULK ATTACKS HIM! AND THAT'S ALL WE NEED TO KNOW!
THIS TIME-- THING MUST DIE!
SPROW!
THE HULK!
THE CLASH OF TITANS! YOURS... RIGHT NOW!
SCRIPTED WITH GENIUS, BY: STAN LEE
PENCILLED WITH GLORY, BY: JOHN BUSCEMA
EMBELLISHED WITH GRANDEUR BY: JOE SINNOTT
LETTERED WITH A SCRATCHY PEN, BY: SAM ROSEN
NUFF SAID
MARVEL MAKES IT AGAIN!
FTANG!
608Z

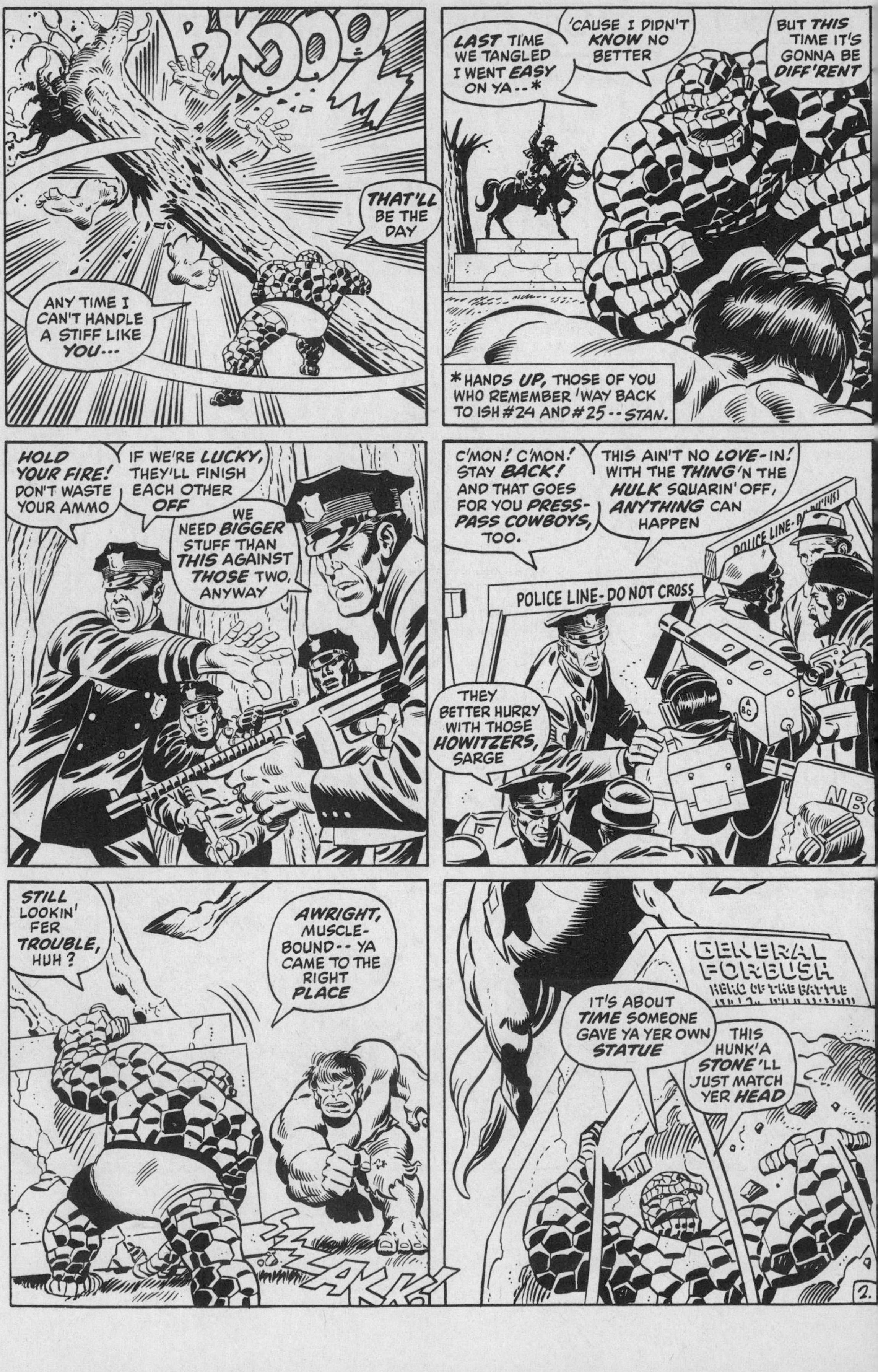

BKOOOM
ANY TIME I CAN'T HANDLE A STIFF LIKE YOU...
THAT'LL BE THE DAY
LAST TIME WE TANGLED I WENT EASY ON YA--*
'CAUSE I DIDN'T KNOW NO BETTER
BUT THIS TIME IT'S GONNA BE DIFF'RENT
*HANDS UP, THOSE OF YOU WHO REMEMBER 'WAY BACK TO ISH #24 AND #25--STAN.
HOLD YOUR FIRE! DON'T WASTE YOUR AMMO
IF WE'RE LUCKY, THEY'LL FINISH EACH OTHER OFF
WE NEED BIGGER STUFF THAN THIS AGAINST THOSE TWO, ANYWAY
C'MON! C'MON! STAY BACK! AND THAT GOES FOR YOU PRESS-PASS COWBOYS, TOO.
THIS AIN'T NO LOVE-IN! WITH THE THING 'N THE HULK SQUARIN' OFF, ANYTHING CAN HAPPEN
POLICE LINE-DO NOT CROSS
THEY BETTER HURRY WITH THOSE HOWITZERS, SARGE
STILL LOOKIN' FER TROUBLE, HUH?
AWRIGHT, MUSCLE-BOUND--YA CAME TO THE RIGHT PLACE
ZAKK!
GENERAL FORBUSH
HERO OF THE BATTLE
IT'S ABOUT TIME SOMEONE GAVE YA YER OWN STATUE
THIS HUNK'A STONE'LL JUST MATCH YER HEAD

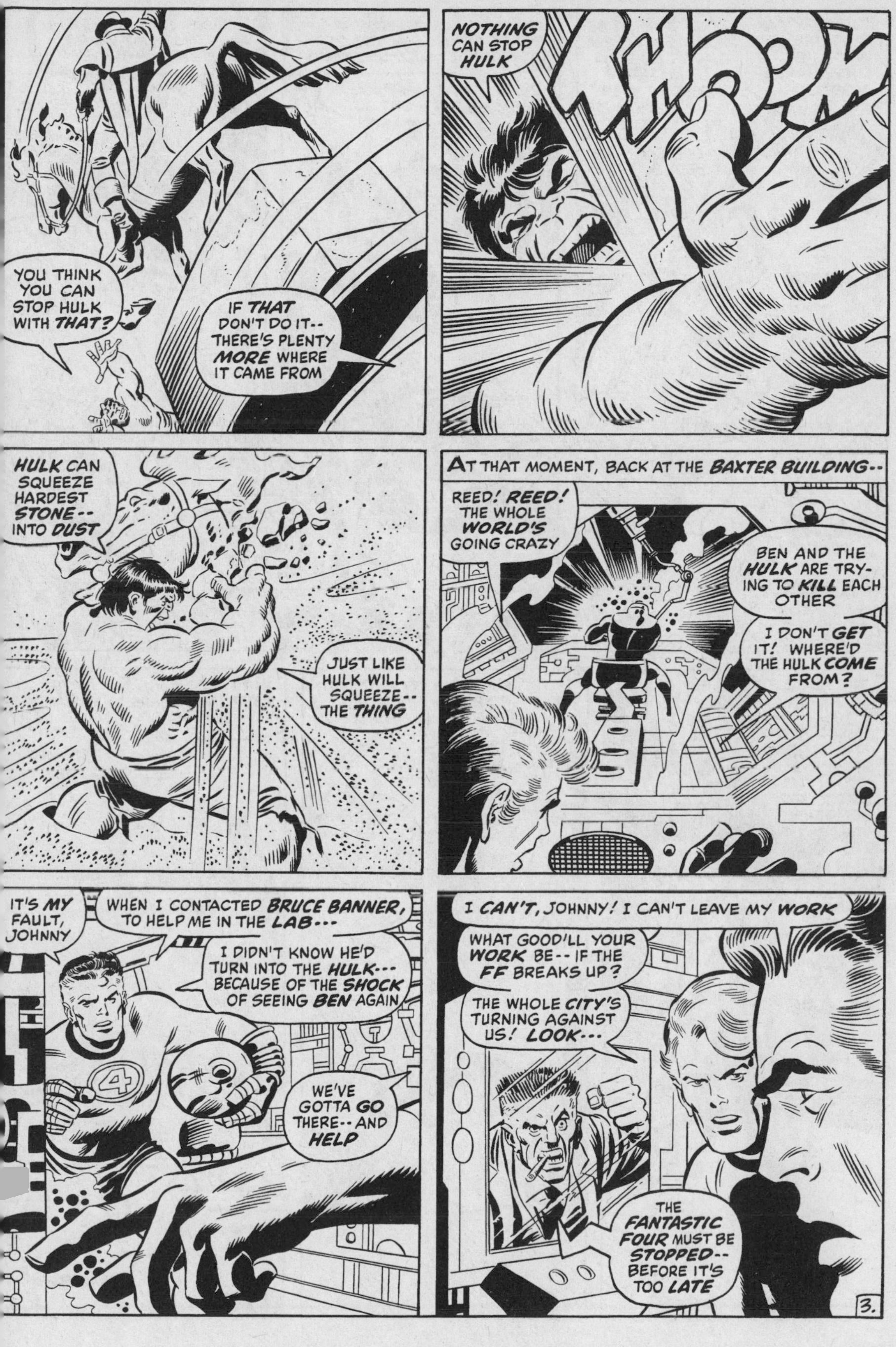

YOU THINK YOU CAN STOP HULK WITH THAT?
IF THAT DON'T DO IT-- THERE'S PLENTY MORE WHERE IT CAME FROM
NOTHING CAN STOP HULK
HULK CAN SQUEEZE HARDEST STONE-- INTO DUST
JUST LIKE HULK WILL SQUEEZE-- THE THING
AT THAT MOMENT, BACK AT THE BAXTER BUILDING--
REED! REED! THE WHOLE WORLD'S GOING CRAZY
BEN AND THE HULK ARE TRYING TO KILL EACH OTHER
I DON'T GET IT! WHERE'D THE HULK COME FROM?
IT'S MY FAULT, JOHNNY
WHEN I CONTACTED BRUCE BANNER, TO HELP ME IN THE LAB---
I DIDN'T KNOW HE'D TURN INTO THE HULK--- BECAUSE OF THE SHOCK OF SEEING BEN AGAIN
WE'VE GOTTA GO THERE-- AND HELP
I CAN'T, JOHNNY! I CAN'T LEAVE MY WORK
WHAT GOOD'LL YOUR WORK BE-- IF THE FF BREAKS UP?
THE WHOLE CITY'S TURNING AGAINST US! LOOK---
THE FANTASTIC FOUR MUST BE STOPPED-- BEFORE IT'S TOO LATE
3.

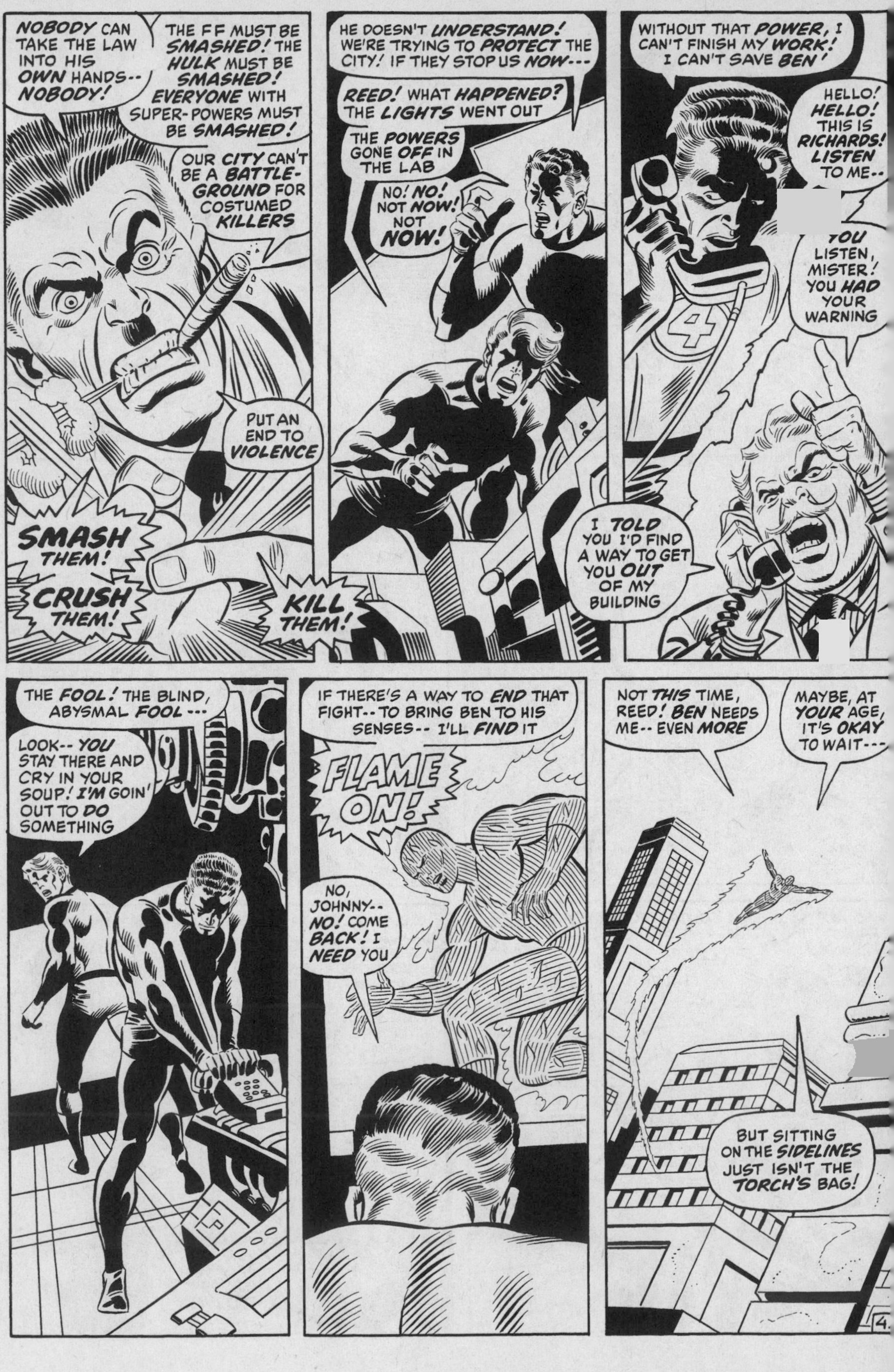
NOBODY CAN TAKE THE LAW INTO HIS OWN HANDS-- NOBODY!
THE FF MUST BE SMASHED! THE HULK MUST BE SMASHED! EVERYONE WITH SUPER-POWERS MUST BE SMASHED!
OUR CITY CAN'T BE A BATTLE-GROUND FOR COSTUMED KILLERS
PUT AN END TO VIOLENCE
SMASH THEM!
CRUSH THEM!
KILL THEM!
HE DOESN'T UNDERSTAND! WE'RE TRYING TO PROTECT THE CITY! IF THEY STOP US NOW---
REED! WHAT HAPPENED? THE LIGHTS WENT OUT
THE POWERS GONE OFF IN THE LAB
NO! NO! NOT NOW! NOT NOW!
WITHOUT THAT POWER, I CAN'T FINISH MY WORK! I CAN'T SAVE BEN!
HELLO! HELLO! THIS IS RICHARDS! LISTEN TO ME--
YOU LISTEN, MISTER! YOU HAD YOUR WARNING
I TOLD YOU I'D FIND A WAY TO GET YOU OUT OF MY BUILDING
THE FOOL! THE BLIND, ABYSMAL FOOL---
LOOK-- YOU STAY THERE AND CRY IN YOUR SOUP! I'M GOIN' OUT TO DO SOMETHING
IF THERE'S A WAY TO END THAT FIGHT-- TO BRING BEN TO HIS SENSES-- I'LL FIND IT
FLAME ON!
NO, JOHNNY-- NO! COME BACK! I NEED YOU
NOT THIS TIME, REED! BEN NEEDS ME-- EVEN MORE
MAYBE, AT YOUR AGE, IT'S OKAY TO WAIT---
BUT SITTING ON THE SIDELINES JUST ISN'T THE TORCH'S BAG!
4

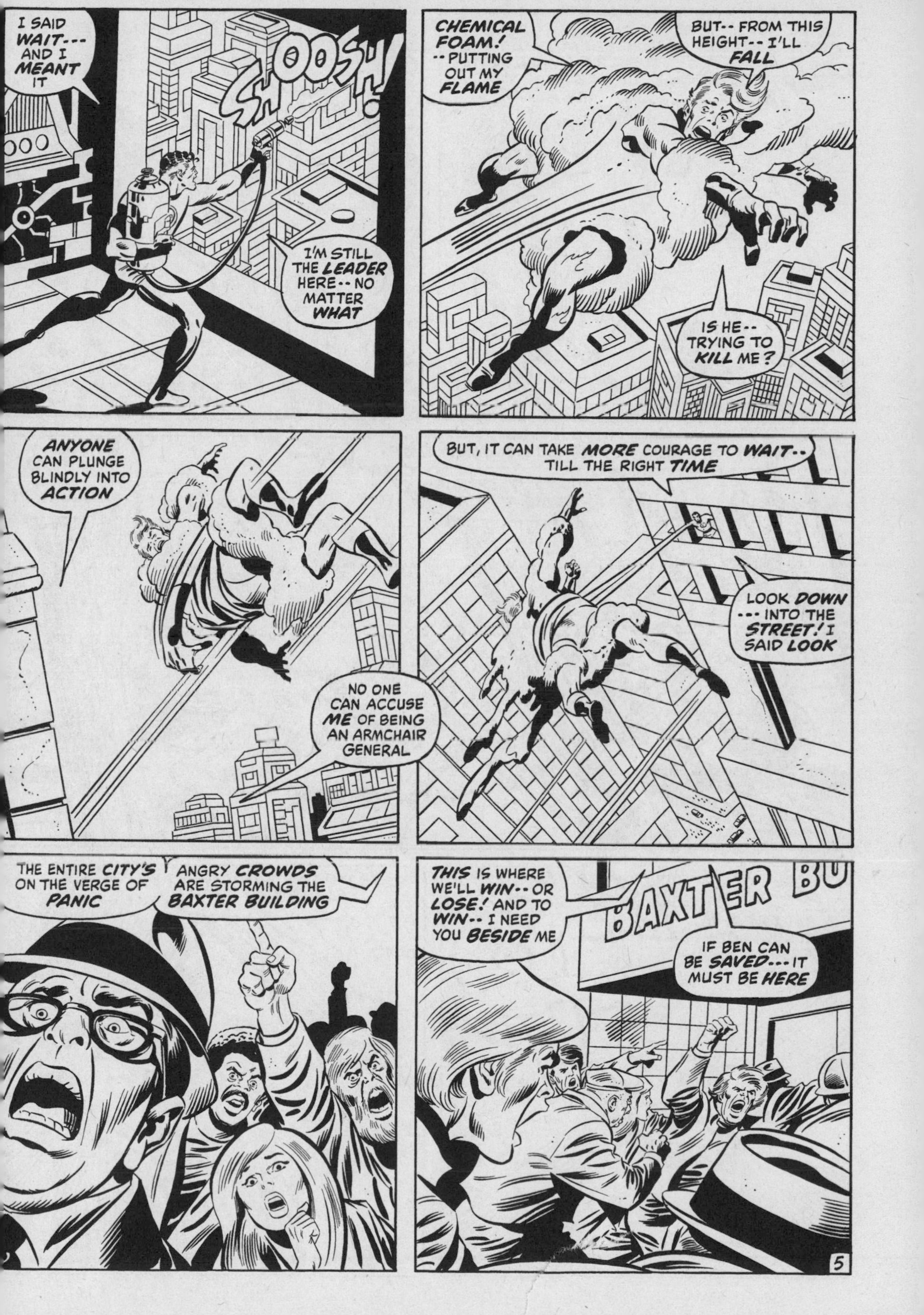
I SAID WAIT--- AND I MEANT IT
SHOOSH!
I'M STILL THE LEADER HERE-- NO MATTER WHAT
CHEMICAL FOAM! --PUTTING OUT MY FLAME
BUT-- FROM THIS HEIGHT-- I'LL FALL
IS HE-- TRYING TO KILL ME?
ANYONE CAN PLUNGE BLINDLY INTO ACTION
NO ONE CAN ACCUSE ME OF BEING AN ARMCHAIR GENERAL
BUT, IT CAN TAKE MORE COURAGE TO WAIT.. TILL THE RIGHT TIME
LOOK DOWN --- INTO THE STREET! I SAID LOOK
THE ENTIRE CITY'S ON THE VERGE OF PANIC
ANGRY CROWDS ARE STORMING THE BAXTER BUILDING
THIS IS WHERE WE'LL WIN-- OR LOSE! AND TO WIN-- I NEED YOU BESIDE ME
BAXTER BU
IF BEN CAN BE SAVED--- IT MUST BE HERE
5

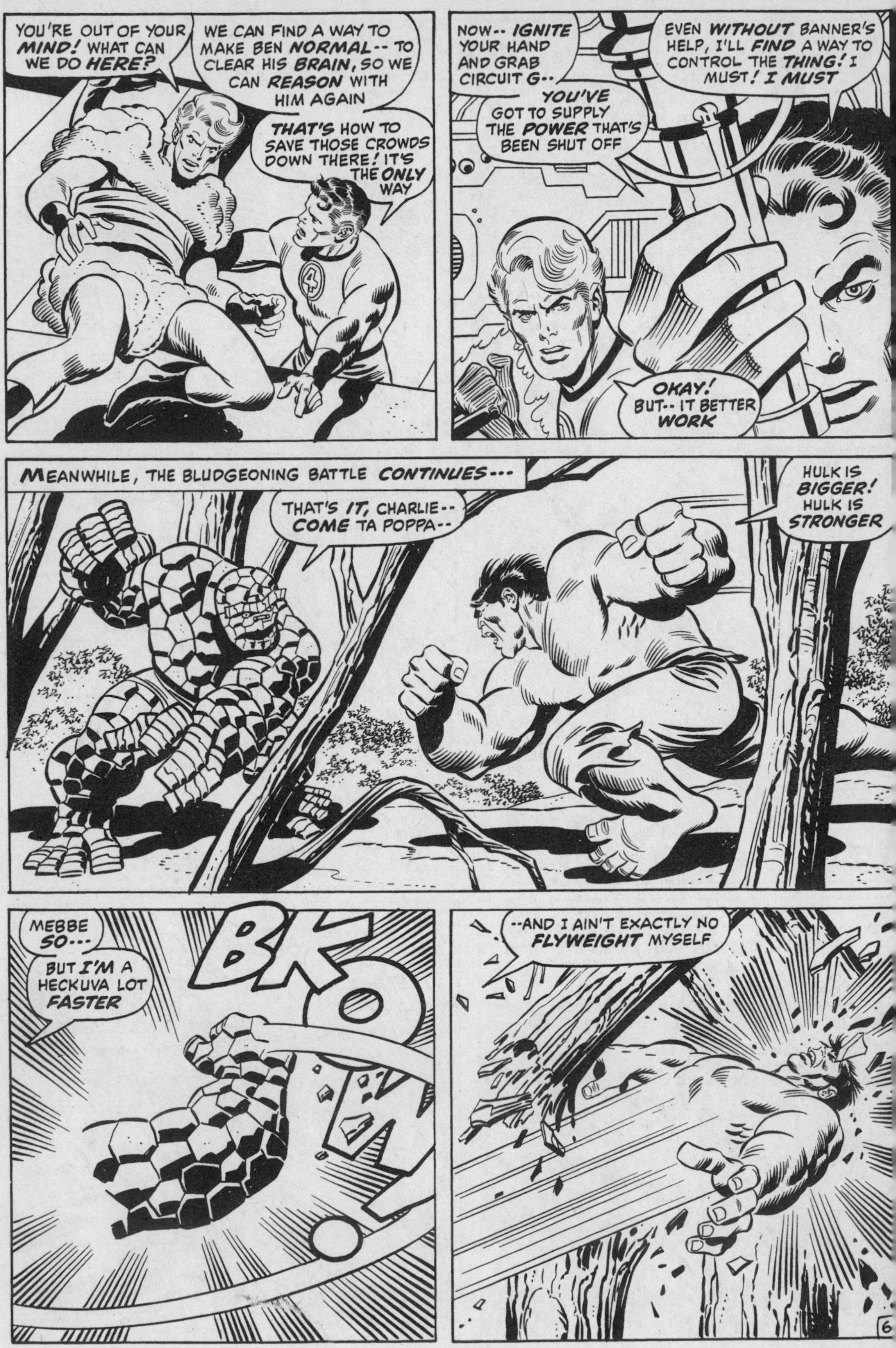

YOU'RE OUT OF YOUR MIND! WHAT CAN WE DO HERE?
WE CAN FIND A WAY TO MAKE BEN NORMAL-- TO CLEAR HIS BRAIN, SO WE CAN REASON WITH HIM AGAIN
THAT'S HOW TO SAVE THOSE CROWDS DOWN THERE! IT'S THE ONLY WAY
NOW-- IGNITE YOUR HAND AND GRAB CIRCUIT G--
YOU'VE GOT TO SUPPLY THE POWER THAT'S BEEN SHUT OFF
EVEN WITHOUT BANNER'S HELP, I'LL FIND A WAY TO CONTROL THE THING! I MUST! I MUST
OKAY! BUT-- IT BETTER WORK
MEANWHILE, THE BLUDGEONING BATTLE CONTINUES---
THAT'S IT, CHARLIE-- COME TA POPPA--
HULK IS BIGGER! HULK IS STRONGER
MEBBE SO---
BUT I'M A HECKUVA LOT FASTER
BKOOM
--AND I AIN'T EXACTLY NO FLYWEIGHT MYSELF

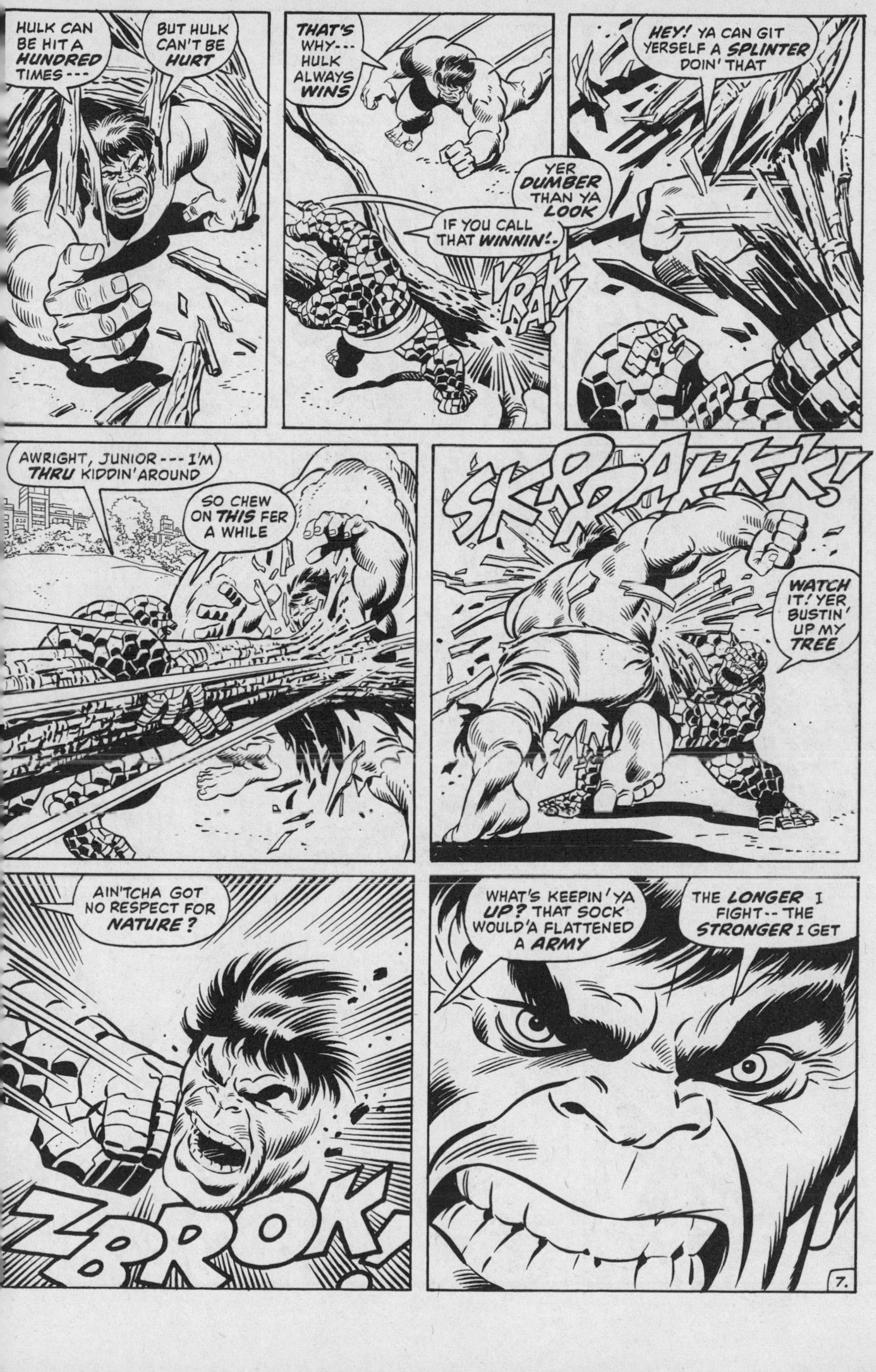
HULK CAN BE HIT A **HUNDRED** TIMES---
BUT HULK CAN'T BE **HURT**
THAT'S WHY--- HULK ALWAYS **WINS**
IF YOU CALL THAT **WINNIN'**..
YER **DUMBER** THAN YA **LOOK**
VRAK!
HEY! YA CAN GIT YERSELF A **SPLINTER** DOIN' THAT
AWRIGHT, JUNIOR --- I'M **THRU** KIDDIN' AROUND
SO CHEW ON **THIS** FER A WHILE
SKRAKK!
WATCH IT! YER BUSTIN' UP MY **TREE**
AIN'TCHA GOT NO RESPECT FOR **NATURE**?
ZBROK!
WHAT'S KEEPIN' YA **UP?** THAT SOCK WOULD'A FLATTENED A **ARMY**
THE **LONGER** I FIGHT -- THE **STRONGER** I GET
7.

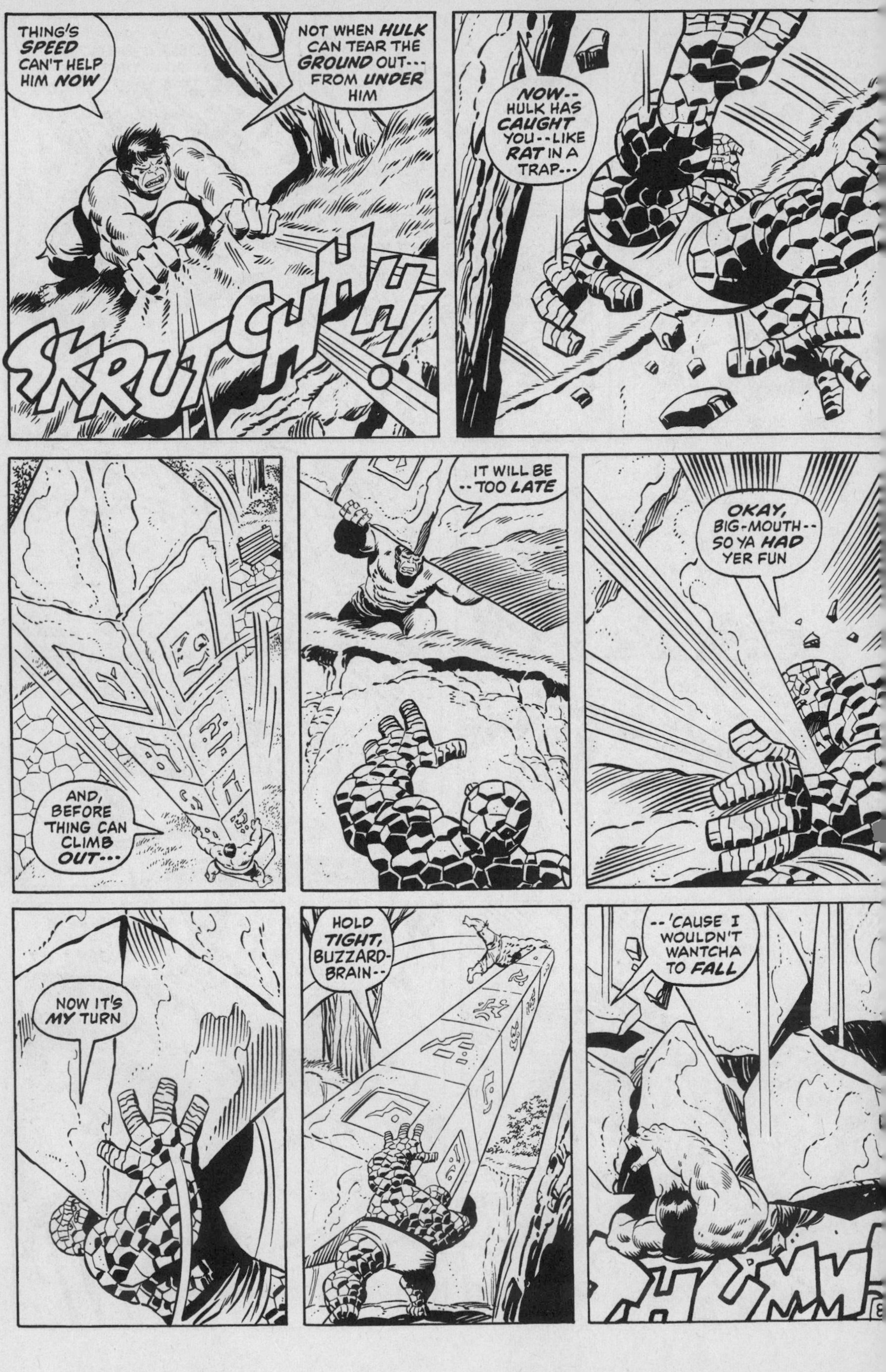
THING'S SPEED CAN'T HELP HIM NOW
NOT WHEN HULK CAN TEAR THE GROUND OUT--- FROM UNDER HIM
SKRUTCHHH!
NOW-- HULK HAS CAUGHT YOU--LIKE RAT IN A TRAP---
AND, BEFORE THING CAN CLIMB OUT---
IT WILL BE --TOO LATE
OKAY, BIG-MOUTH-- SO YA HAD YER FUN
NOW IT'S MY TURN
HOLD TIGHT, BUZZARD-BRAIN--
--'CAUSE I WOULDN'T WANTCHA TO FALL

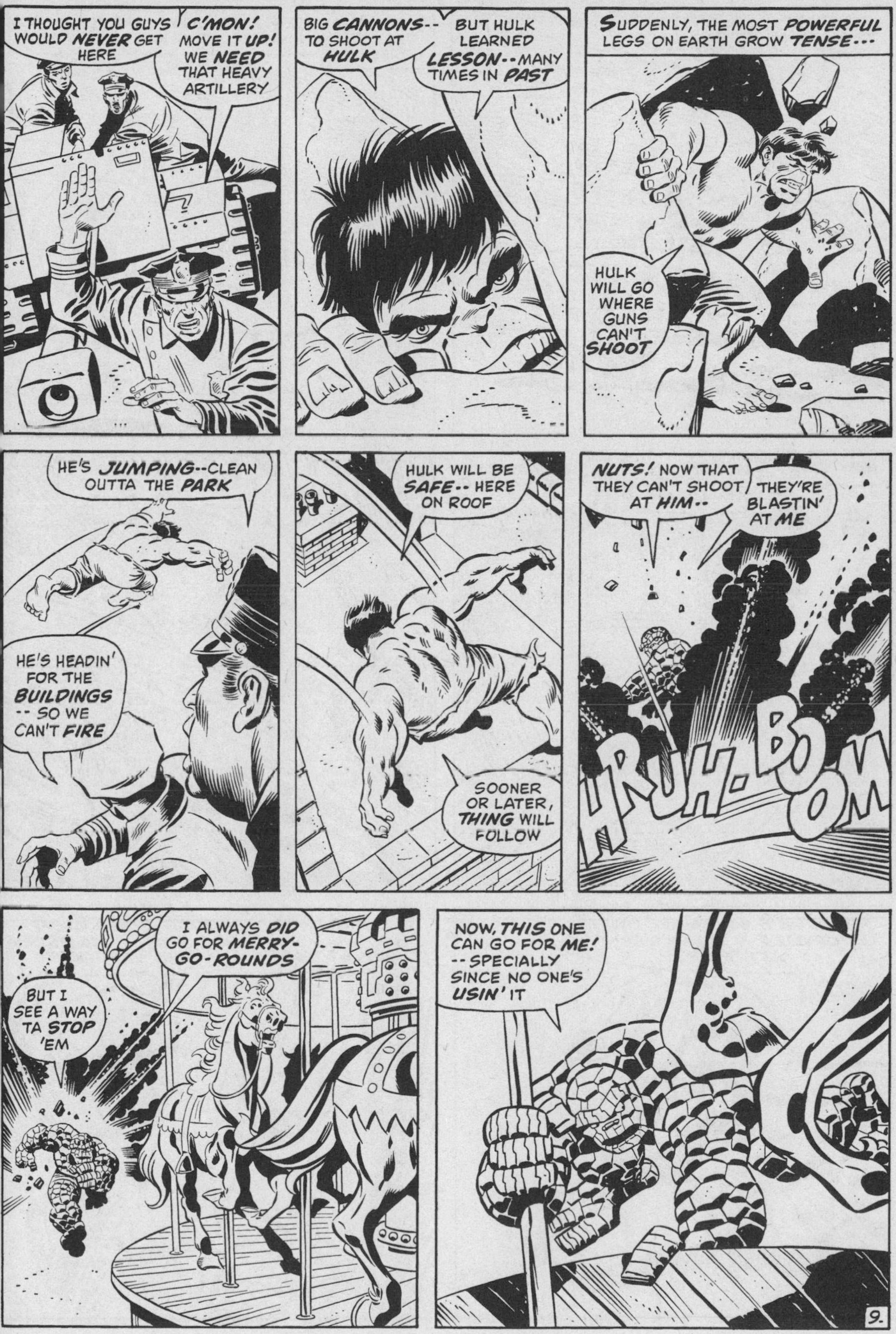
I THOUGHT YOU GUYS WOULD NEVER GET HERE
C'MON! MOVE IT UP! WE NEED THAT HEAVY ARTILLERY
BIG CANNONS-- TO SHOOT AT HULK
BUT HULK LEARNED LESSON--MANY TIMES IN PAST
SUDDENLY, THE MOST POWERFUL LEGS ON EARTH GROW TENSE---
HULK WILL GO WHERE GUNS CAN'T SHOOT
HE'S JUMPING--CLEAN OUTTA THE PARK
HE'S HEADIN' FOR THE BUILDINGS -- SO WE CAN'T FIRE
HULK WILL BE SAFE-- HERE ON ROOF
SOONER OR LATER, THING WILL FOLLOW
NUTS! NOW THAT THEY CAN'T SHOOT AT HIM--
THEY'RE BLASTIN' AT ME
HRUH-BOOM
I ALWAYS DID GO FOR MERRY-GO-ROUNDS
BUT I SEE A WAY TA STOP 'EM
NOW, THIS ONE CAN GO FOR ME! --SPECIALLY SINCE NO ONE'S USIN' IT
9.

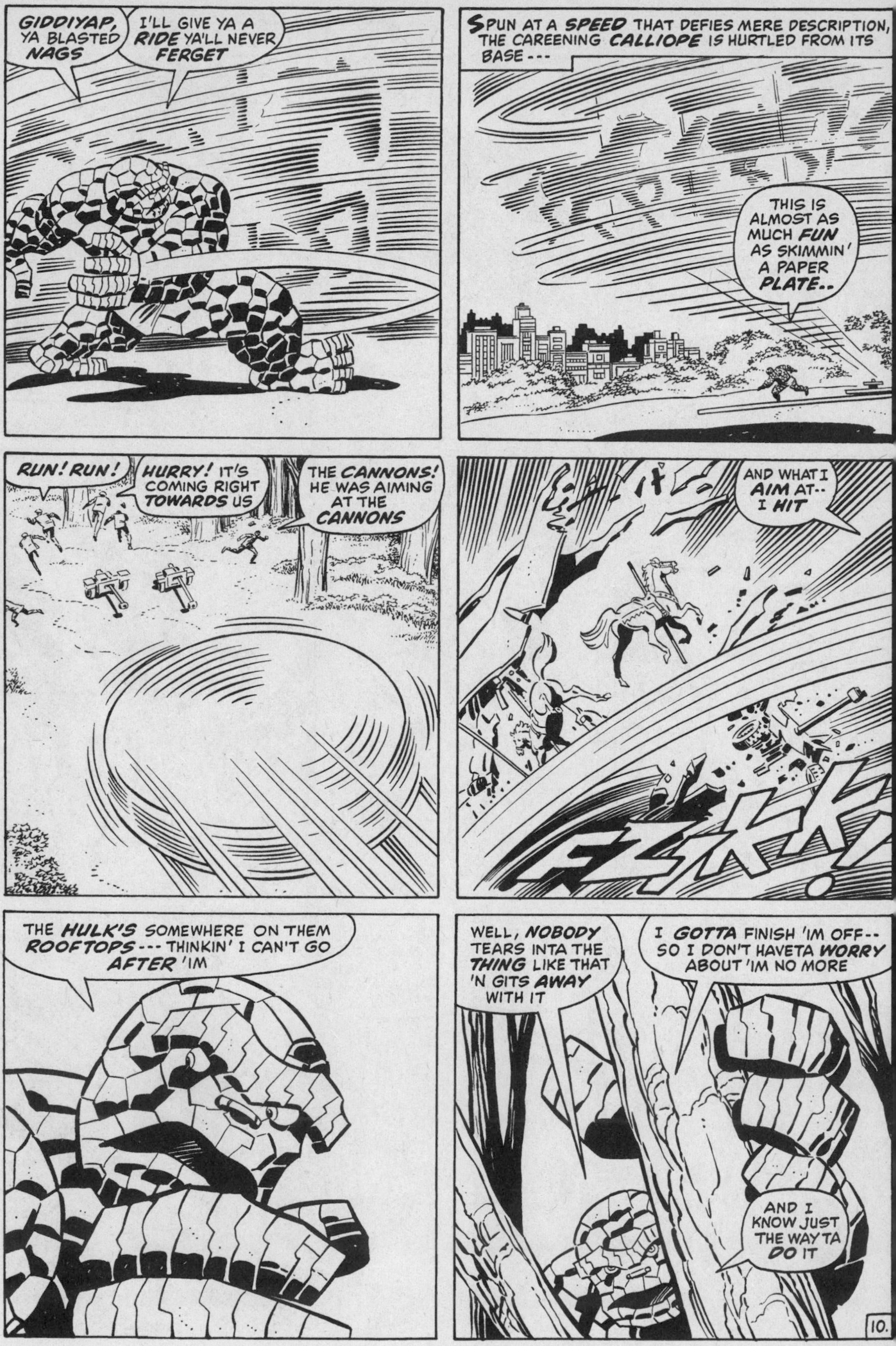
GIDDIYAP, YA BLASTED NAGS
I'LL GIVE YA A RIDE YA'LL NEVER FERGET
SPUN AT A SPEED THAT DEFIES MERE DESCRIPTION, THE CAREENING CALLIOPE IS HURTLED FROM ITS BASE---
THIS IS ALMOST AS MUCH FUN AS SKIMMIN' A PAPER PLATE..
RUN! RUN!
HURRY! IT'S COMING RIGHT TOWARDS US
THE CANNONS! HE WAS AIMING AT THE CANNONS
AND WHAT I AIM AT-- I HIT
THE HULK'S SOMEWHERE ON THEM ROOFTOPS--- THINKIN' I CAN'T GO AFTER 'IM
WELL, NOBODY TEARS INTA THE THING LIKE THAT 'N GITS AWAY WITH IT
I GOTTA FINISH 'IM OFF-- SO I DON'T HAVETA WORRY ABOUT 'IM NO MORE
AND I KNOW JUST THE WAY TA DO IT
10.

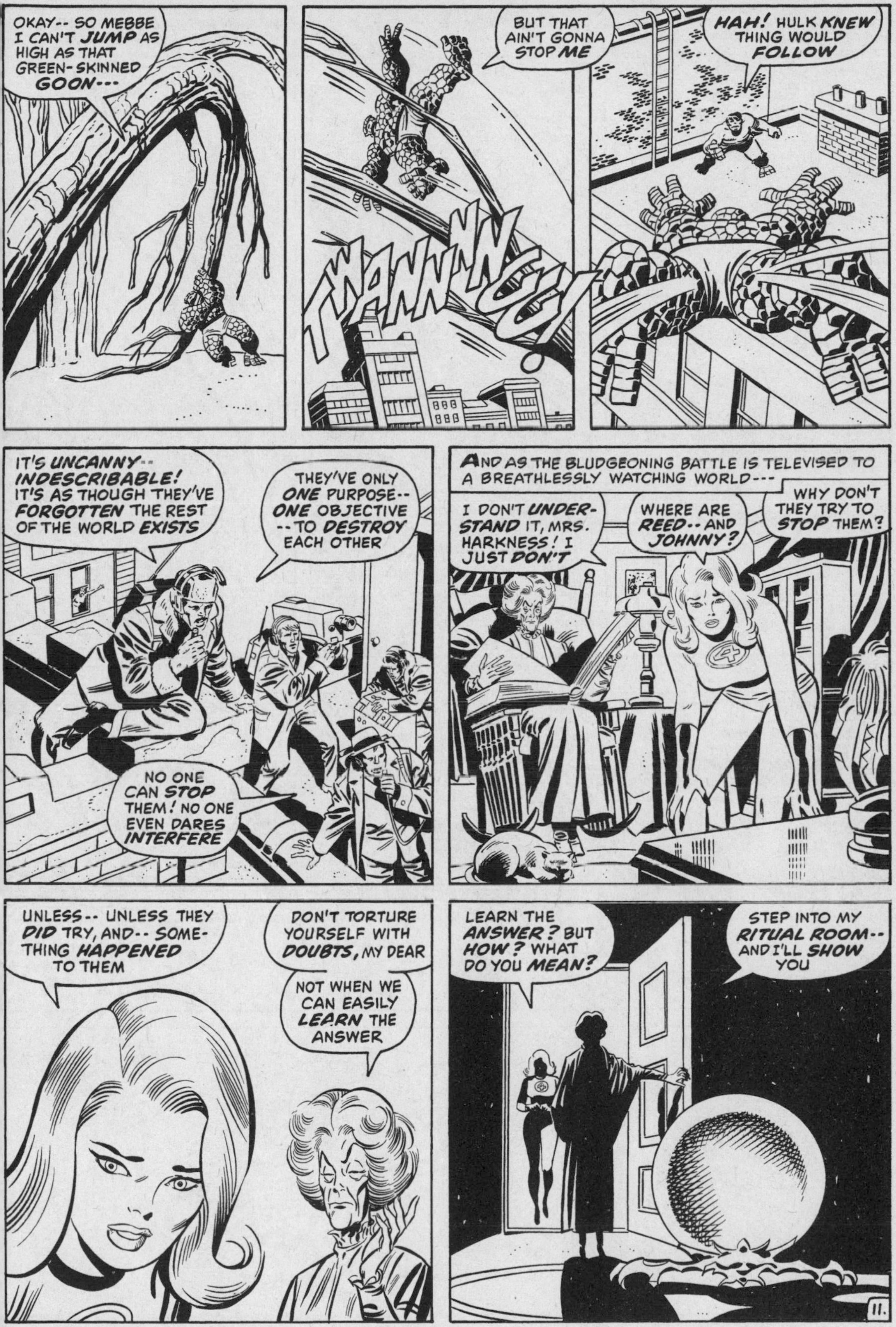
OKAY-- SO MEBBE I CAN'T JUMP AS HIGH AS THAT GREEN-SKINNED GOON---
BUT THAT AIN'T GONNA STOP ME
THANNNNGG!
HAH! HULK KNEW THING WOULD FOLLOW
IT'S UNCANNY-- INDESCRIBABLE! IT'S AS THOUGH THEY'VE FORGOTTEN THE REST OF THE WORLD EXISTS
THEY'VE ONLY ONE PURPOSE-- ONE OBJECTIVE --TO DESTROY EACH OTHER
NO ONE CAN STOP THEM! NO ONE EVEN DARES INTERFERE
AND AS THE BLUDGEONING BATTLE IS TELEVISED TO A BREATHLESSLY WATCHING WORLD---
I DON'T UNDERSTAND IT, MRS. HARKNESS! I JUST DON'T
WHERE ARE REED-- AND JOHNNY?
WHY DON'T THEY TRY TO STOP THEM?
UNLESS-- UNLESS THEY DID TRY, AND-- SOMETHING HAPPENED TO THEM
DON'T TORTURE YOURSELF WITH DOUBTS, MY DEAR
NOT WHEN WE CAN EASILY LEARN THE ANSWER
LEARN THE ANSWER? BUT HOW? WHAT DO YOU MEAN?
STEP INTO MY RITUAL ROOM-- AND I'LL SHOW YOU
11.

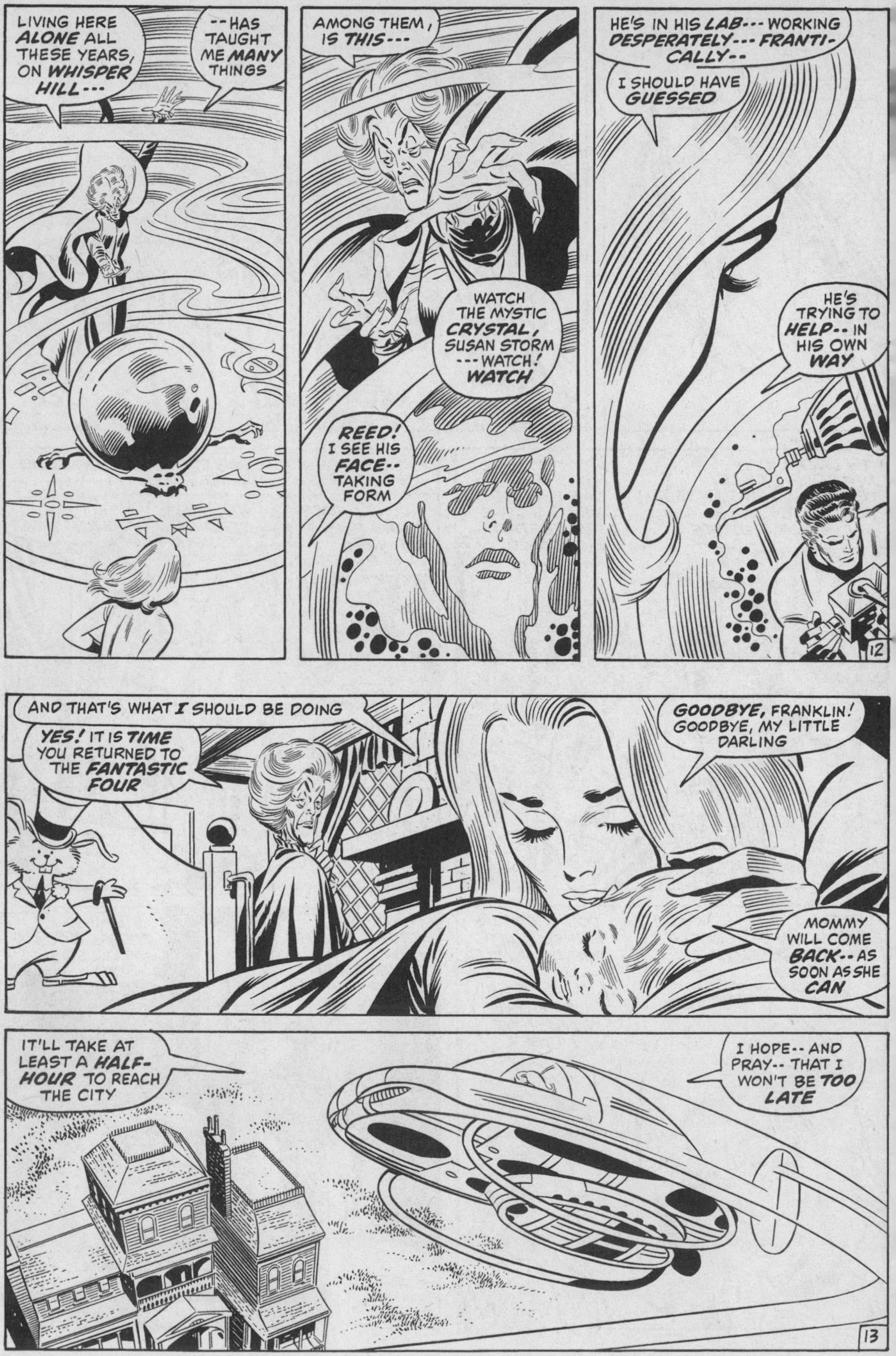
LIVING HERE ALONE ALL THESE YEARS, ON WHISPER HILL---
--HAS TAUGHT ME MANY THINGS
AMONG THEM, IS THIS---
WATCH THE MYSTIC CRYSTAL, SUSAN STORM ---WATCH! WATCH
REED! I SEE HIS FACE-- TAKING FORM
HE'S IN HIS LAB--- WORKING DESPERATELY--- FRANTI-CALLY--
I SHOULD HAVE GUESSED
HE'S TRYING TO HELP-- IN HIS OWN WAY
12
AND THAT'S WHAT I SHOULD BE DOING
YES! IT IS TIME YOU RETURNED TO THE FANTASTIC FOUR
GOODBYE, FRANKLIN! GOODBYE, MY LITTLE DARLING
MOMMY WILL COME BACK-- AS SOON AS SHE CAN
IT'LL TAKE AT LEAST A HALF-HOUR TO REACH THE CITY
I HOPE-- AND PRAY-- THAT I WON'T BE TOO LATE
13

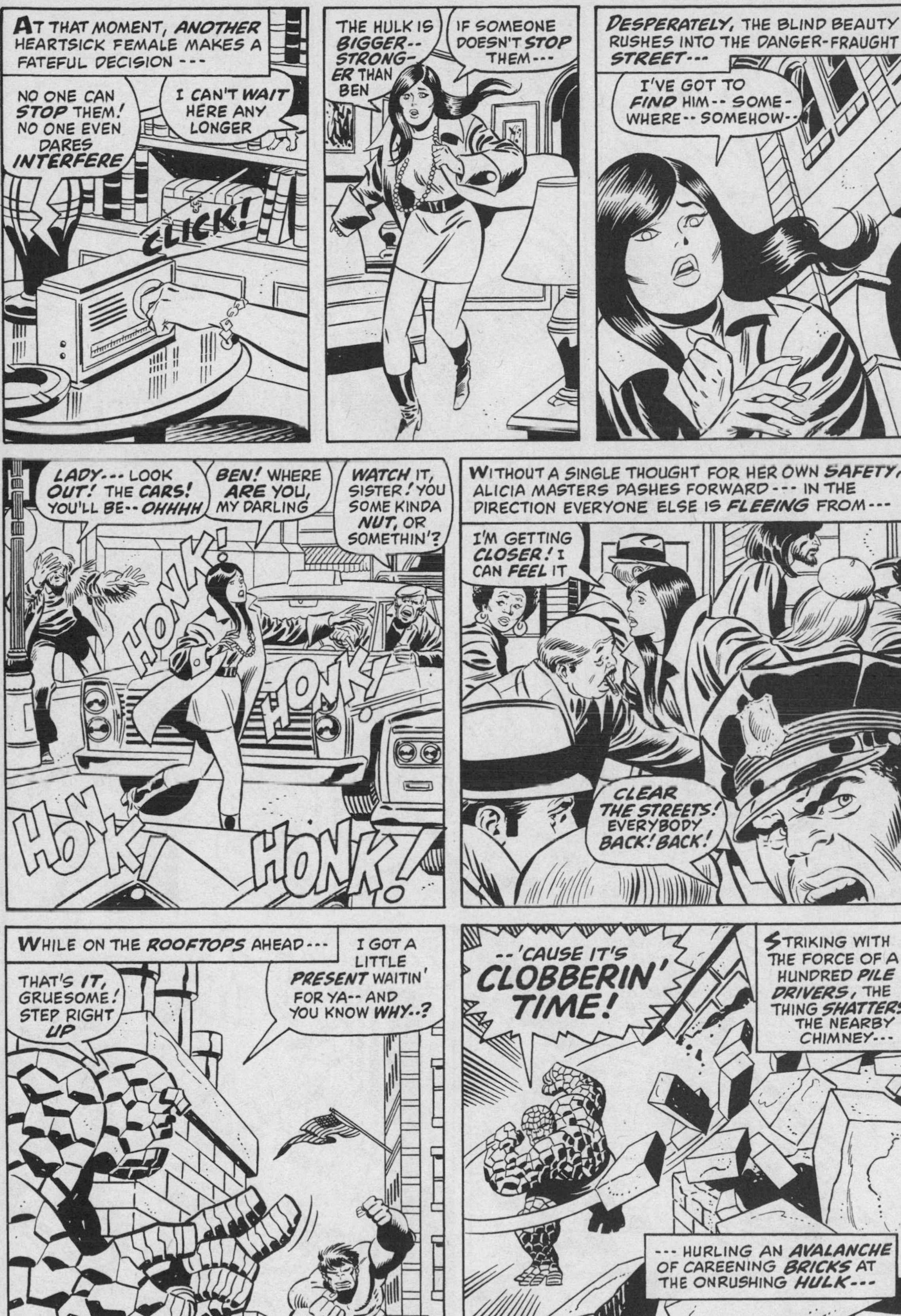

AT THAT MOMENT, ANOTHER HEARTSICK FEMALE MAKES A FATEFUL DECISION ---
NO ONE CAN STOP THEM! NO ONE EVEN DARES INTERFERE
I CAN'T WAIT HERE ANY LONGER
CLICK!
THE HULK IS BIGGER-- STRONGER THAN BEN
IF SOMEONE DOESN'T STOP THEM ---
DESPERATELY, THE BLIND BEAUTY RUSHES INTO THE DANGER-FRAUGHT STREET ---
I'VE GOT TO FIND HIM -- SOMEWHERE -- SOMEHOW --
LADY --- LOOK OUT! THE CARS! YOU'LL BE -- OHHHH
BEN! WHERE ARE YOU, MY DARLING
WATCH IT, SISTER! YOU SOME KINDA NUT, OR SOMETHIN'?
HONK!
HONK!
HONK!
HONK!
WITHOUT A SINGLE THOUGHT FOR HER OWN SAFETY, ALICIA MASTERS DASHES FORWARD --- IN THE DIRECTION EVERYONE ELSE IS FLEEING FROM ---
I'M GETTING CLOSER! I CAN FEEL IT
CLEAR THE STREETS! EVERYBODY BACK! BACK!
WHILE ON THE ROOFTOPS AHEAD ---
THAT'S IT, GRUESOME! STEP RIGHT UP
I GOT A LITTLE PRESENT WAITIN' FOR YA-- AND YOU KNOW WHY..?
--'CAUSE IT'S CLOBBERIN' TIME!
STRIKING WITH THE FORCE OF A HUNDRED PILE DRIVERS, THE THING SHATTERS THE NEARBY CHIMNEY ---
--- HURLING AN AVALANCHE OF CAREENING BRICKS AT THE ONRUSHING HULK ---
14

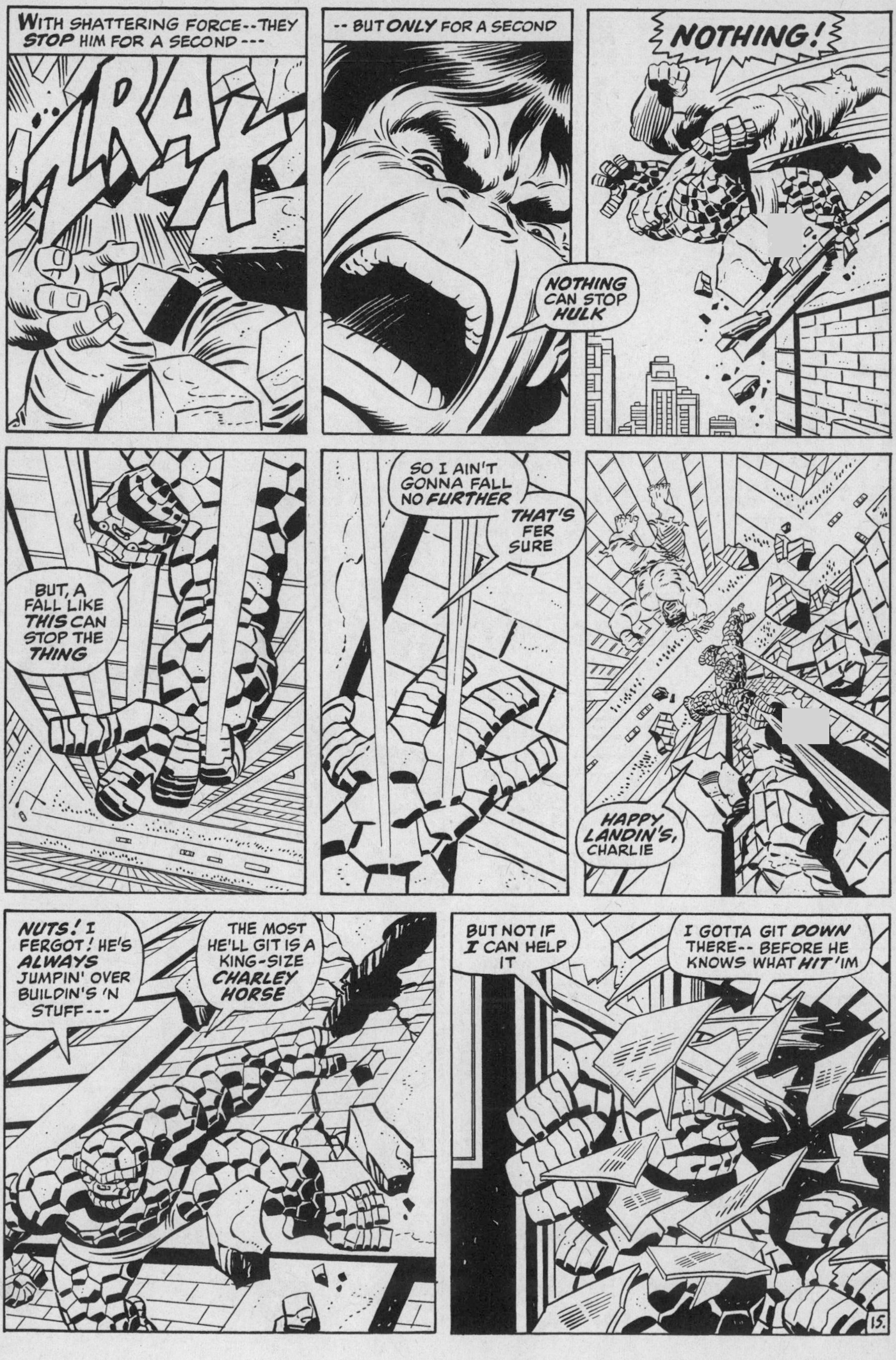
WITH SHATTERING FORCE--THEY STOP HIM FOR A SECOND---
KRAK
-- BUT ONLY FOR A SECOND
NOTHING CAN STOP HULK
NOTHING!
BUT, A FALL LIKE THIS CAN STOP THE THING
SO I AIN'T GONNA FALL NO FURTHER
THAT'S FER SURE
HAPPY LANDIN'S, CHARLIE
NUTS! I FERGOT! HE'S ALWAYS JUMPIN' OVER BUILDIN'S 'N STUFF---
THE MOST HE'LL GIT IS A KING-SIZE CHARLEY HORSE
BUT NOT IF I CAN HELP IT
I GOTTA GIT DOWN THERE-- BEFORE HE KNOWS WHAT HIT 'IM
15.

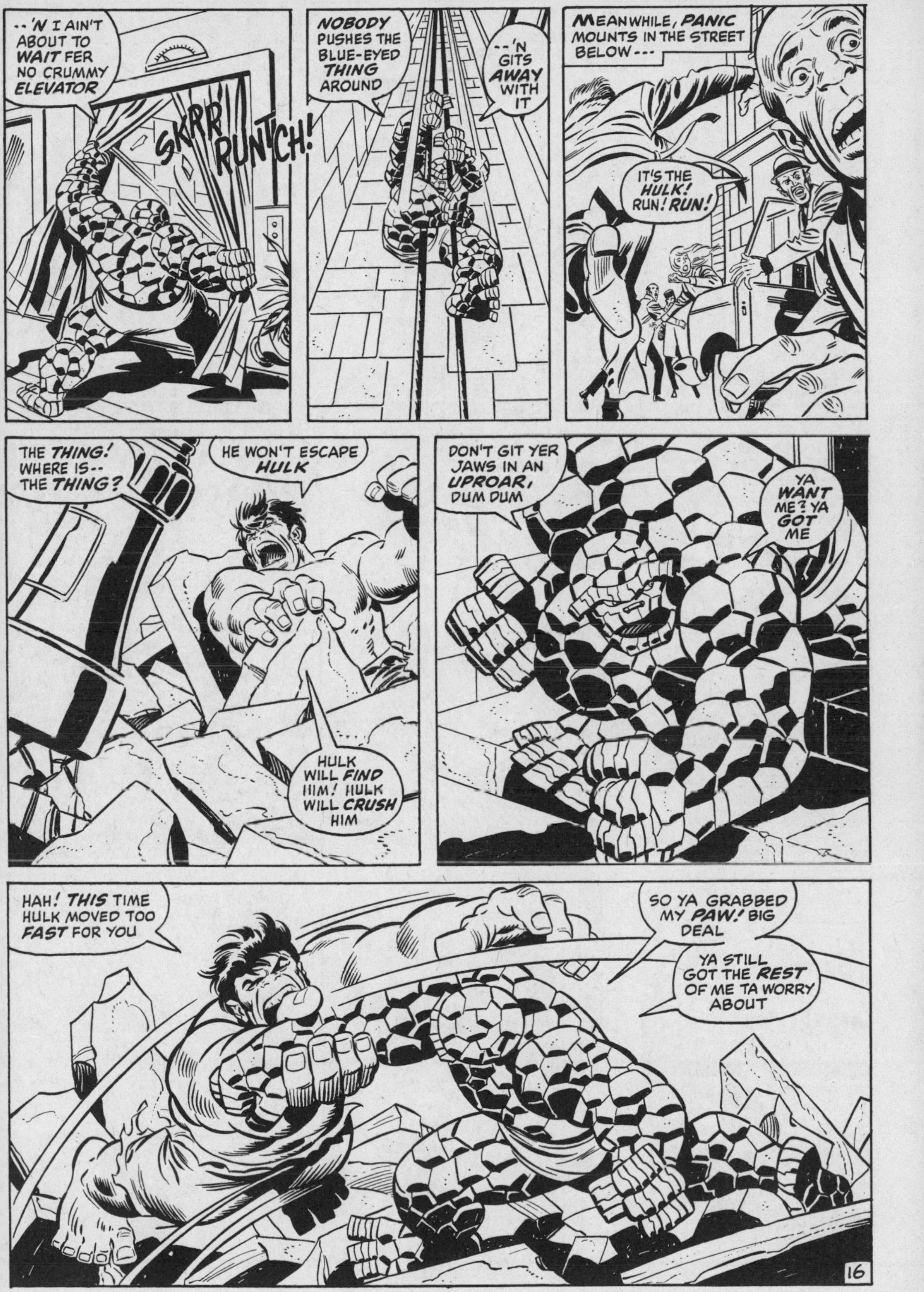
..'N I AIN'T ABOUT TO WAIT FER NO CRUMMY ELEVATOR
SKRR RUNTCH!
NOBODY PUSHES THE BLUE-EYED THING AROUND
--'N GITS AWAY WITH IT
MEANWHILE, PANIC MOUNTS IN THE STREET BELOW---
IT'S THE HULK! RUN! RUN!
THE THING! WHERE IS-- THE THING?
HE WON'T ESCAPE HULK
HULK WILL FIND HIM! HULK WILL CRUSH HIM
DON'T GIT YER JAWS IN AN UPROAR, DUM DUM
YA WANT ME? YA GOT ME
HAH! THIS TIME HULK MOVED TOO FAST FOR YOU
SO YA GRABBED MY PAW! BIG DEAL
YA STILL GOT THE REST OF ME TA WORRY ABOUT
16

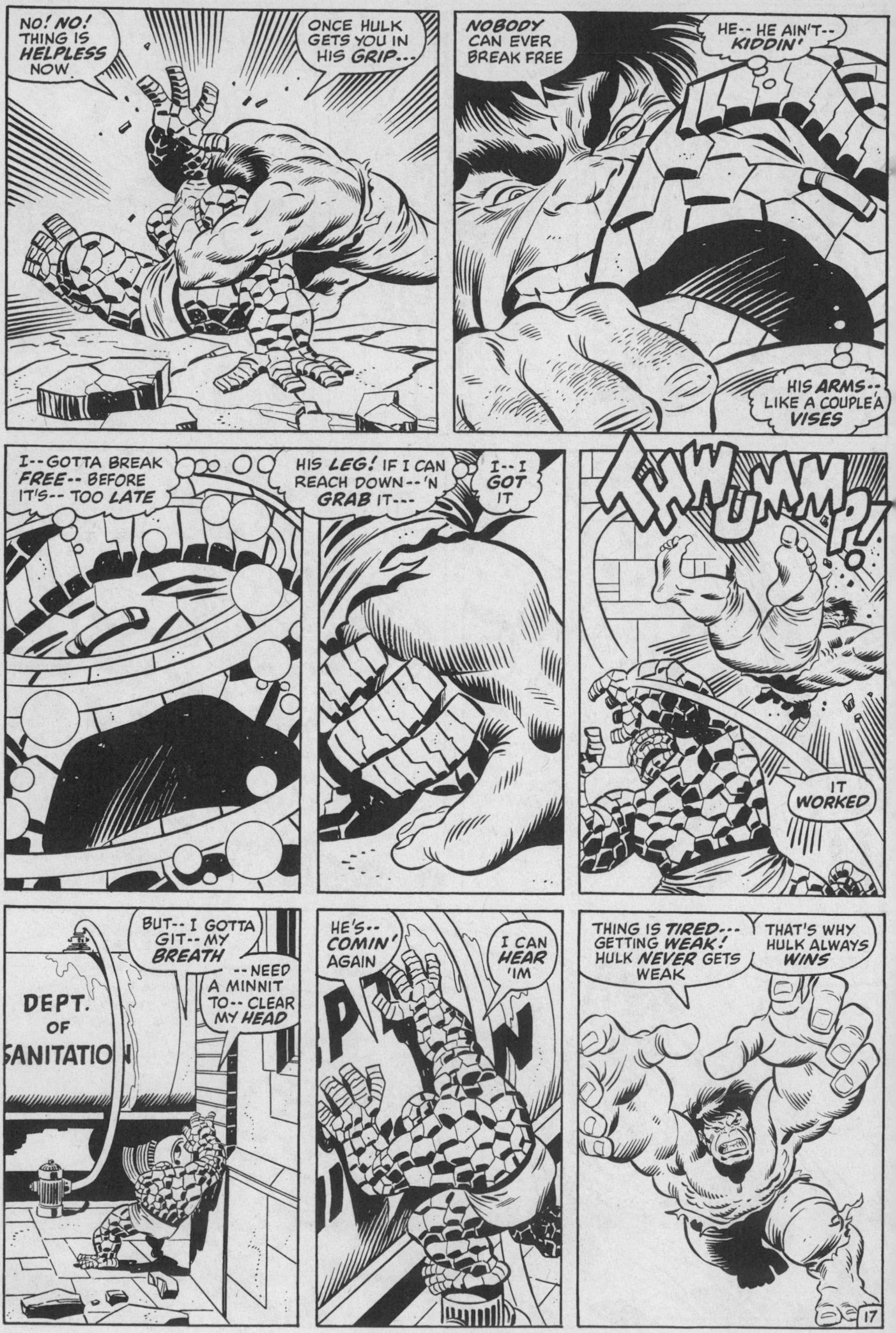
NO! NO! THING IS HELPLESS NOW.
ONCE HULK GETS YOU IN HIS GRIP...
NOBODY CAN EVER BREAK FREE
HE-- HE AIN'T-- KIDDIN'
HIS ARMS-- LIKE A COUPLE'A VISES
I-- GOTTA BREAK FREE-- BEFORE IT'S-- TOO LATE
HIS LEG! IF I CAN REACH DOWN--'N GRAB IT---
I-- I GOT IT
THWUMMP!
IT WORKED
BUT-- I GOTTA GIT-- MY BREATH
--NEED A MINNIT TO-- CLEAR MY HEAD
DEPT. OF SANITATIO
HE'S-- COMIN' AGAIN
I CAN HEAR 'IM
THING IS TIRED--- GETTING WEAK! HULK NEVER GETS WEAK
THAT'S WHY HULK ALWAYS WINS

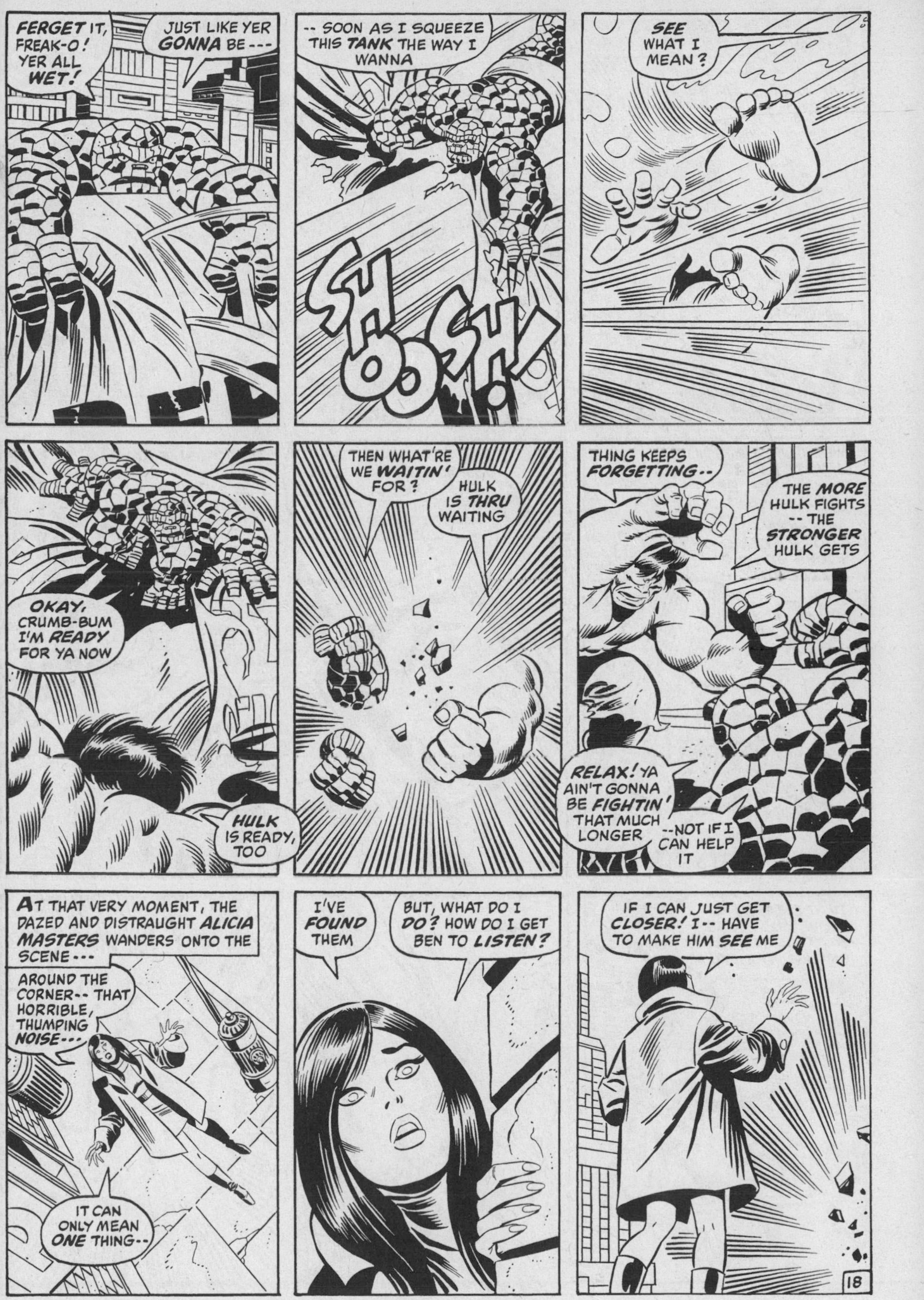
FERGET IT, FREAK-O! YER ALL WET!
JUST LIKE YER GONNA BE---
-- SOON AS I SQUEEZE THIS TANK THE WAY I WANNA
SHOOSH!
SEE WHAT I MEAN?
OKAY, CRUMB-BUM I'M READY FOR YA NOW
HULK IS READY, TOO
THEN WHAT'RE WE WAITIN' FOR?
HULK IS THRU WAITING
THING KEEPS FORGETTING--
THE MORE HULK FIGHTS -- THE STRONGER HULK GETS
RELAX! YA AIN'T GONNA BE FIGHTIN' THAT MUCH LONGER
--NOT IF I CAN HELP IT
AT THAT VERY MOMENT, THE DAZED AND DISTRAUGHT ALICIA MASTERS WANDERS ONTO THE SCENE---
AROUND THE CORNER-- THAT HORRIBLE, THUMPING NOISE---
IT CAN ONLY MEAN ONE THING--
I'VE FOUND THEM
BUT, WHAT DO I DO? HOW DO I GET BEN TO LISTEN?
IF I CAN JUST GET CLOSER! I-- HAVE TO MAKE HIM SEE ME
18

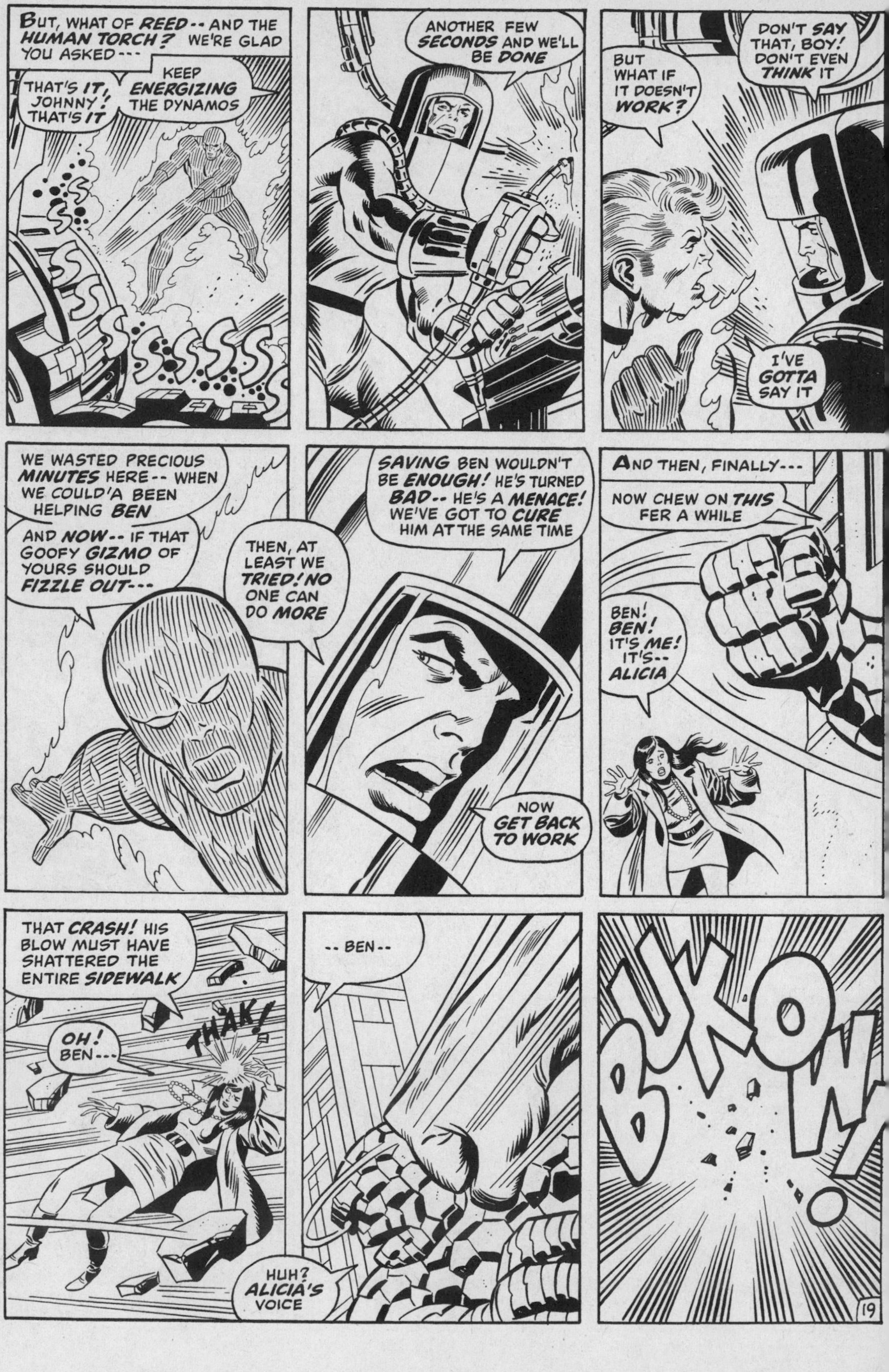

BUT, WHAT OF REED -- AND THE HUMAN TORCH? WE'RE GLAD YOU ASKED ---
THAT'S IT, JOHNNY! THAT'S IT
KEEP ENERGIZING THE DYNAMOS
SSSSSSSSS
ANOTHER FEW SECONDS AND WE'LL BE DONE
BUT WHAT IF IT DOESN'T WORK?
DON'T SAY THAT, BOY! DON'T EVEN THINK IT
I'VE GOTTA SAY IT
WE WASTED PRECIOUS MINUTES HERE -- WHEN WE COULD'A BEEN HELPING BEN
AND NOW -- IF THAT GOOFY GIZMO OF YOURS SHOULD FIZZLE OUT ---
THEN, AT LEAST WE TRIED! NO ONE CAN DO MORE
SAVING BEN WOULDN'T BE ENOUGH! HE'S TURNED BAD -- HE'S A MENACE! WE'VE GOT TO CURE HIM AT THE SAME TIME
NOW GET BACK TO WORK
AND THEN, FINALLY ---
NOW CHEW ON THIS FER A WHILE
BEN! BEN! IT'S ME! IT'S -- ALICIA
THAT CRASH! HIS BLOW MUST HAVE SHATTERED THE ENTIRE SIDEWALK
THAK!
OH! BEN ---
-- BEN --
HUH? ALICIA'S VOICE
BUKOOM!

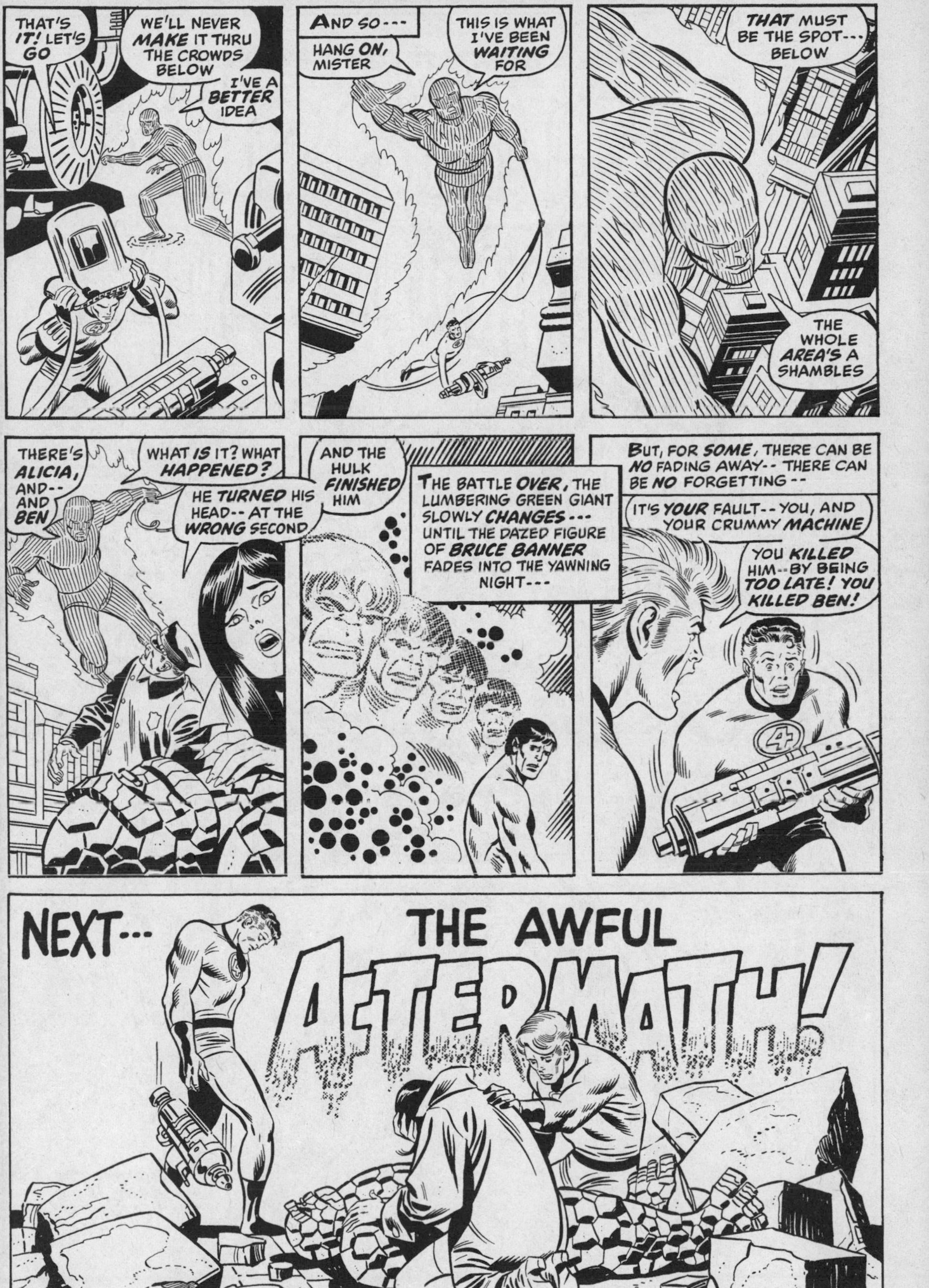

THAT'S IT! LET'S GO
WE'LL NEVER MAKE IT THRU THE CROWDS BELOW
I'VE A BETTER IDEA
AND SO---
HANG ON, MISTER
THIS IS WHAT I'VE BEEN WAITING FOR
THAT MUST BE THE SPOT--- BELOW
THE WHOLE AREA'S A SHAMBLES
THERE'S ALICIA, AND-- AND BEN
WHAT IS IT? WHAT HAPPENED?
HE TURNED HIS HEAD-- AT THE WRONG SECOND
AND THE HULK FINISHED HIM
THE BATTLE OVER, THE LUMBERING GREEN GIANT SLOWLY CHANGES--- UNTIL THE DAZED FIGURE OF BRUCE BANNER FADES INTO THE YAWNING NIGHT---
BUT, FOR SOME, THERE CAN BE NO FADING AWAY-- THERE CAN BE NO FORGETTING--
IT'S YOUR FAULT-- YOU, AND YOUR CRUMMY MACHINE
YOU KILLED HIM--BY BEING TOO LATE! YOU KILLED BEN!
NEXT---
THE AWFUL
AFTERMATH!

FANTASTIC FOUR
15¢
113
AUG
02462
THE WORLD'S GREATEST COMIC MAGAZINE!
APPROVED BY THE COMICS CODE AUTHORITY
Fantastic Four
THE COMING OF THE OVER-MIND!
MARVEL COMICS GROUP
THIS ONE HAS IT ALL!
THE FATE OF THE THING!
MISTER FANTASTIC FIGHTS BACK!
THE WATCHER SPEAKS!
THE TORCH IN ACTION!
...AND MUCH MUCH MORE!

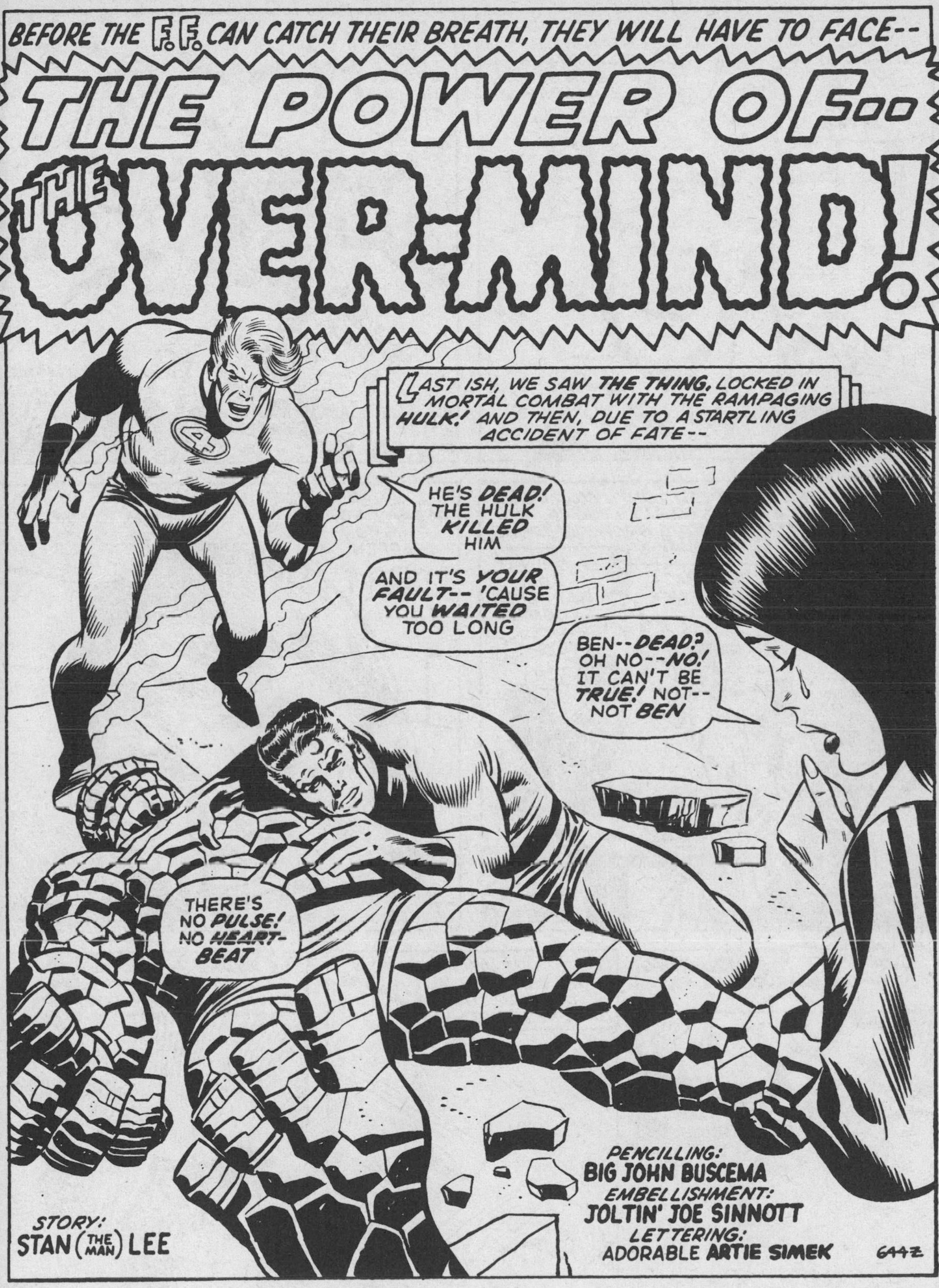
BEFORE THE F.F. CAN CATCH THEIR BREATH, THEY WILL HAVE TO FACE--
THE POWER OF... THE OVER-MIND!
LAST ISH, WE SAW THE THING, LOCKED IN MORTAL COMBAT WITH THE RAMPAGING HULK! AND THEN, DUE TO A STARTLING ACCIDENT OF FATE--
HE'S DEAD! THE HULK KILLED HIM
AND IT'S YOUR FAULT-- 'CAUSE YOU WAITED TOO LONG
BEN--DEAD? OH NO--NO! IT CAN'T BE TRUE! NOT--NOT BEN
THERE'S NO PULSE! NO HEART-BEAT
STORY: STAN (THE MAN) LEE
PENCILLING: BIG JOHN BUSCEMA
EMBELLISHMENT: JOLTIN' JOE SINNOTT
LETTERING: ADORABLE ARTIE SIMEK
6442

I **TOLD** you we should'a gotten here **SOONER!** but you wouldn't **LISTEN**

NO, NOT **YOU!** YOU HADDA STAY WITH YOUR **TEST TUBES** WHILE POOR BEN BATTLED **ALONE**

AND NOW-- IT'S **OVER!** THE HULK **KILLED** HIM

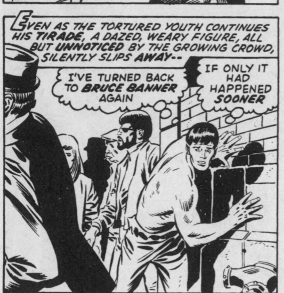

EVEN AS THE TORTURED YOUTH CONTINUES HIS **TIRADE**, A DAZED, WEARY FIGURE, ALL BUT **UNNOTICED** BY THE GROWING CROWD, SILENTLY SLIPS **AWAY**--

I'VE TURNED BACK TO **BRUCE BANNER** AGAIN

IF ONLY IT HAD HAPPENED **SOONER**

I NEVER **MEANT** FOR THIS TO HAPPEN

THE HULK DIDN'T WANT BEN GRIMM TO **DIE**

"WE WERE JUST **SQUARING** OFF--HE WAS **READY** FOR MY ATTACK--"

"BUT THEN, **UNEXPECTEDLY** --HE HEARD THE VOICE OF THE GIRL HE **LOVED**--"

BEN!

"HE TURNED--AND BEFORE I COULD **STOP** MY BLOW-- IT WAS ALL **OVER** FOR HIM"

2

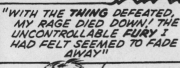

"WITH THE *THING* DEFEATED, MY RAGE DIED DOWN! THE UNCONTROLLABLE *FURY* I HAD FELT SEEMED TO FADE AWAY"

HE'S SO *STILL!* I--I CAN FEEL NO *HEARTBEAT*

AND NOW, I'M MY *NORMAL* SELF AGAIN

BUT, WHY COULDN'T *I* HAVE BEEN THE ONE--TO *DIE?*

*W*HILE, AROUND THE CORNER--

DO WE MOVE *IN* NOW, CAPTAIN?

RIGHT! OUR ORDERS ARE TO *ARREST* THE FANTASTIC FOUR

THERE'S ONLY *THREE* OF 'EM TO TACKLE!

THE THING'S *HAD* IT

STAND *BACK* THERE! LET US *THRU*

YOU AND THE KID ARE UNDER *ARREST*, RICHARDS

THEY'RE *MURDERERS!* THEY ALMOST *WRECKED* THE CITY

I'VE GOT MY ORDERS TO BRING YOU *IN*

YEAH! *UP* THE FF

YOU'RE *ARRESTING* US? FOR *WHAT?*

YOU *KIDDIN'?* LOOK AT THE *DAMAGE* YOU CAUSED

IT WAS POOR *BEN*-- FIGHTING FOR HIS *LIFE*

DON'T GIVE US ANY *TROUBLE,* MISTER! YOU CAN TELL IT TO THE *JUDGE*

KEEP BEN'S NAME *OUT* OF THIS, REED

LISTEN, JOHNNY-- THEY *MUSTN'T* TAKE US! I--JUST *THOUGHT* OF SOMETHING

IT'S TOO *LATE,* BIG BRAIN! BEN'S *FINISHED*-- AND SO ARE *YOU,* IN *MY* BOOK

3

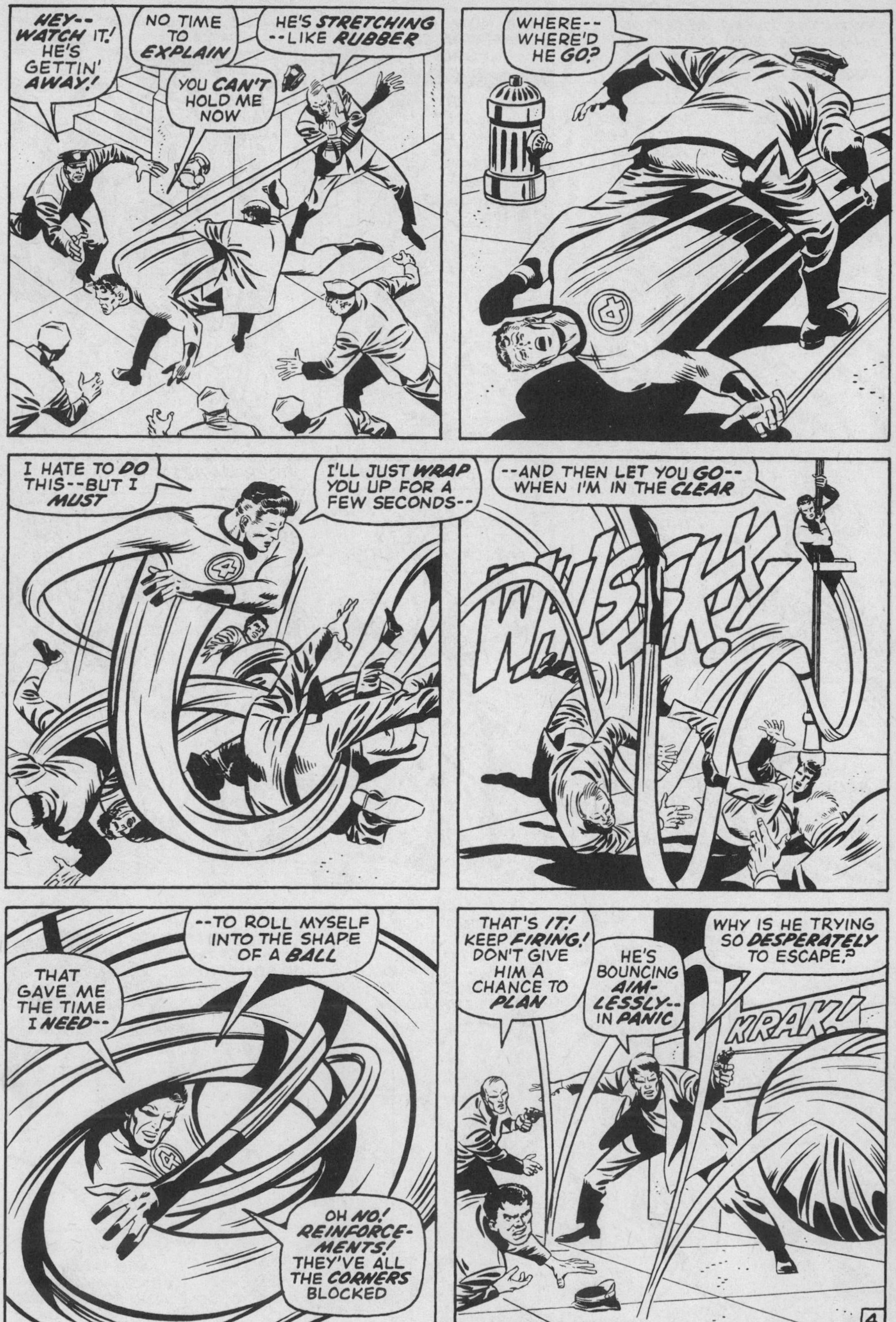
HEY-- WATCH IT! HE'S GETTIN' AWAY!
NO TIME TO EXPLAIN
HE'S STRETCHING --LIKE RUBBER
YOU CAN'T HOLD ME NOW
WHERE-- WHERE'D HE GO?
I HATE TO DO THIS--BUT I MUST
I'LL JUST WRAP YOU UP FOR A FEW SECONDS--
--AND THEN LET YOU GO-- WHEN I'M IN THE CLEAR
WHISSK-K!
THAT GAVE ME THE TIME I NEED--
--TO ROLL MYSELF INTO THE SHAPE OF A BALL
OH NO! REINFORCE-MENTS! THEY'VE ALL THE CORNERS BLOCKED
THAT'S IT! KEEP FIRING! DON'T GIVE HIM A CHANCE TO PLAN
HE'S BOUNCING AIM-LESSLY-- IN PANIC
WHY IS HE TRYING SO DESPERATELY TO ESCAPE?
KRAK!
4

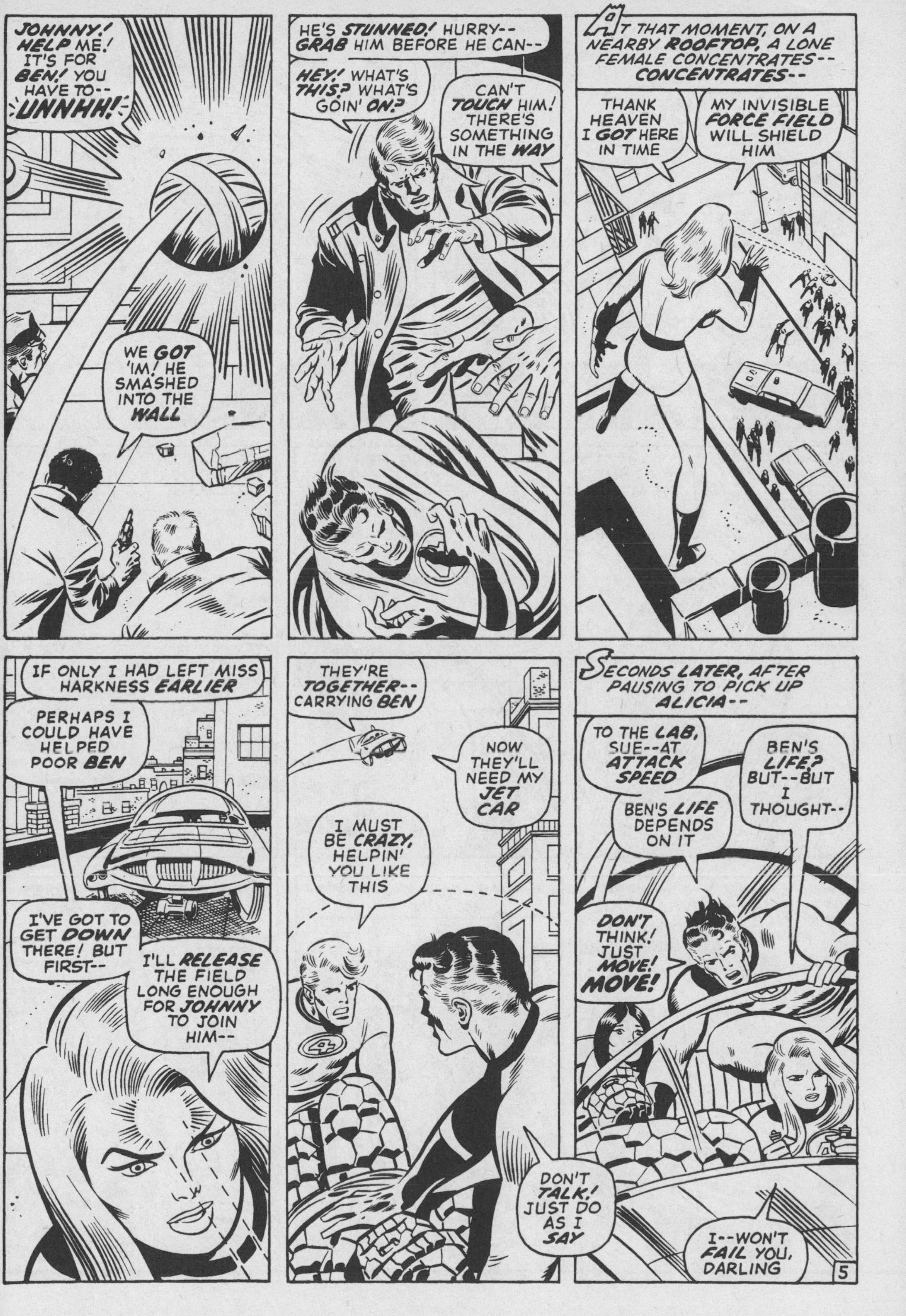
JOHNNY! HELP ME! IT'S FOR BEN! YOU HAVE TO-- UNNHH!
WE GOT 'IM! HE SMASHED INTO THE WALL
HE'S STUNNED! HURRY-- GRAB HIM BEFORE HE CAN--
HEY! WHAT'S THIS? WHAT'S GOIN' ON?
CAN'T TOUCH HIM! THERE'S SOMETHING IN THE WAY
AT THAT MOMENT, ON A NEARBY ROOFTOP, A LONE FEMALE CONCENTRATES-- CONCENTRATES--
THANK HEAVEN I GOT HERE IN TIME
MY INVISIBLE FORCE FIELD WILL SHIELD HIM
IF ONLY I HAD LEFT MISS HARKNESS EARLIER
PERHAPS I COULD HAVE HELPED POOR BEN
I'VE GOT TO GET DOWN THERE! BUT FIRST--
I'LL RELEASE THE FIELD LONG ENOUGH FOR JOHNNY TO JOIN HIM--
THEY'RE TOGETHER-- CARRYING BEN
NOW THEY'LL NEED MY JET CAR
I MUST BE CRAZY, HELPIN' YOU LIKE THIS
DON'T TALK! JUST DO AS I SAY
SECONDS LATER, AFTER PAUSING TO PICK UP ALICIA--
TO THE LAB, SUE--AT ATTACK SPEED
BEN'S LIFE DEPENDS ON IT
BEN'S LIFE? BUT--BUT I THOUGHT--
DON'T THINK! JUST MOVE! MOVE!
I--WON'T FAIL YOU, DARLING
5

JOHNNY! THERE'S NO ROOM IN THE CABIN

FLAME ON! FLY AFTER US

HURRY, KID! I'LL NEED YOU IN THE LAB

HE MUST HAVE FLIPPED! IF BEN'S DEAD, WHAT'S THE RUSH?

BUT, I MIGHT AS WELL SEE IT THRU

BRING HER IN FAST! EVERY SECOND COUNTS

HANG ON, REED

STAY IN THE SHIP! I'LL ACTIVATE THE AUTOMATIC LIFT

CLICK

THAT LIGHT IN THE SKY-- I NOTICED IT BEFORE

I WONDER WHAT IS?

NEVER MIND THAT! FLAME OFF!

WHILE, IN THE STREET BELOW--

THE F.F. MUST GO!

N.Y.-S! F.F. NO!

MAKE CITY SAFE!

UP THE F.F.

UP ALL SUPER HEROES

THEY LANDED ON THE ROOF

GET 'EM! BREAK DOWN THE DOOR

BAXTER

AND THEN, AS THE MOB'S EMOTION REACHES FEVER PITCH--

LOOK! IN THE SKY! WHAT IS IT?

IT'S HEADING FOR THE FF's PENTHOUSE

IT'S A TRICK! THEY'RE UP TO SOMETHING

6

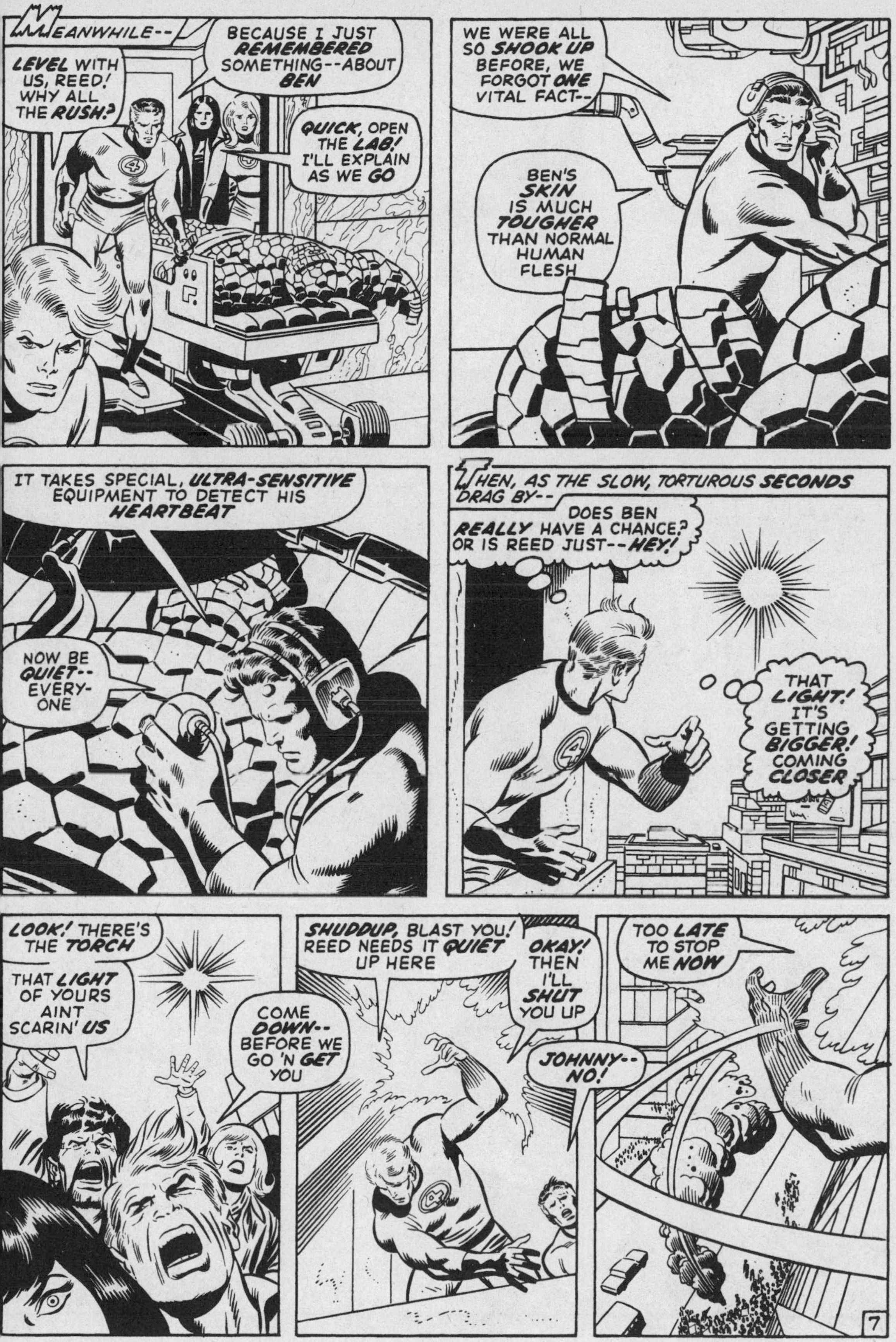
MEANWHILE--
LEVEL WITH US, REED! WHY ALL THE RUSH?
BECAUSE I JUST REMEMBERED SOMETHING--ABOUT BEN
QUICK, OPEN THE LAB! I'LL EXPLAIN AS WE GO
WE WERE ALL SO SHOOK UP BEFORE, WE FORGOT ONE VITAL FACT--
BEN'S SKIN IS MUCH TOUGHER THAN NORMAL HUMAN FLESH
IT TAKES SPECIAL, ULTRA-SENSITIVE EQUIPMENT TO DETECT HIS HEARTBEAT
NOW BE QUIET--EVERY-ONE
THEN, AS THE SLOW, TORTUROUS SECONDS DRAG BY--
DOES BEN REALLY HAVE A CHANCE? OR IS REED JUST--HEY!
THAT LIGHT! IT'S GETTING BIGGER! COMING CLOSER
LOOK! THERE'S THE TORCH
THAT LIGHT OF YOURS AINT SCARIN' US
COME DOWN--BEFORE WE GO 'N GET YOU
SHUDDUP, BLAST YOU! REED NEEDS IT QUIET UP HERE
OKAY! THEN I'LL SHUT YOU UP
JOHNNY--NO!
TOO LATE TO STOP ME NOW
7

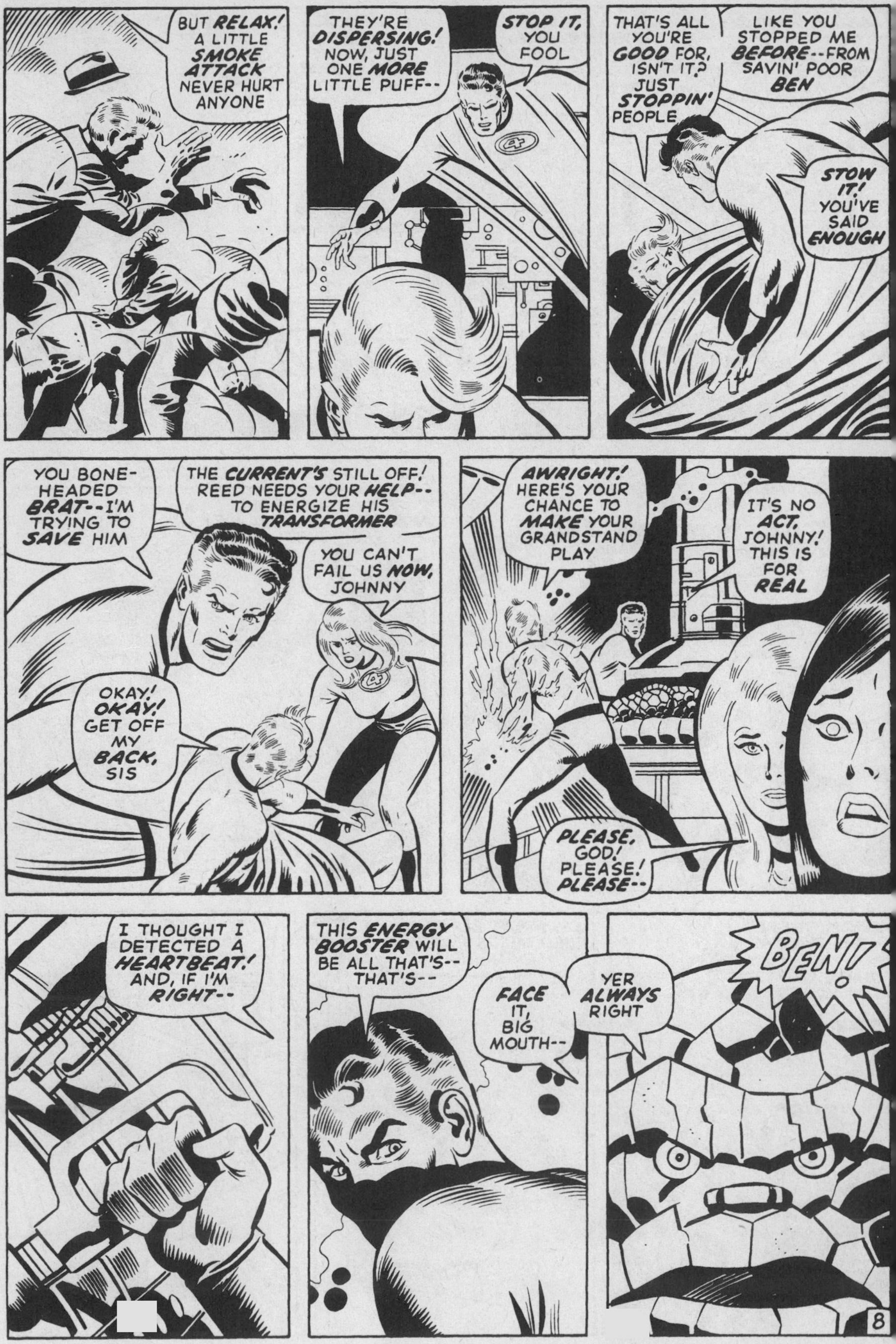
BUT RELAX! A LITTLE SMOKE ATTACK NEVER HURT ANYONE
THEY'RE DISPERSING! NOW, JUST ONE MORE LITTLE PUFF--
STOP IT, YOU FOOL
THAT'S ALL YOU'RE GOOD FOR, ISN'T IT? JUST STOPPIN' PEOPLE
LIKE YOU STOPPED ME BEFORE--FROM SAVIN' POOR BEN
STOW IT! YOU'VE SAID ENOUGH
YOU BONE-HEADED BRAT--I'M TRYING TO SAVE HIM
THE CURRENT'S STILL OFF! REED NEEDS YOUR HELP-- TO ENERGIZE HIS TRANSFORMER
YOU CAN'T FAIL US NOW, JOHNNY
OKAY! OKAY! GET OFF MY BACK, SIS
AWRIGHT! HERE'S YOUR CHANCE TO MAKE YOUR GRANDSTAND PLAY
IT'S NO ACT, JOHNNY! THIS IS FOR REAL
PLEASE, GOD! PLEASE! PLEASE--
I THOUGHT I DETECTED A HEARTBEAT! AND, IF I'M RIGHT--
THIS ENERGY BOOSTER WILL BE ALL THAT'S-- THAT'S--
FACE IT, BIG MOUTH--
YER ALWAYS RIGHT
BEN!
8

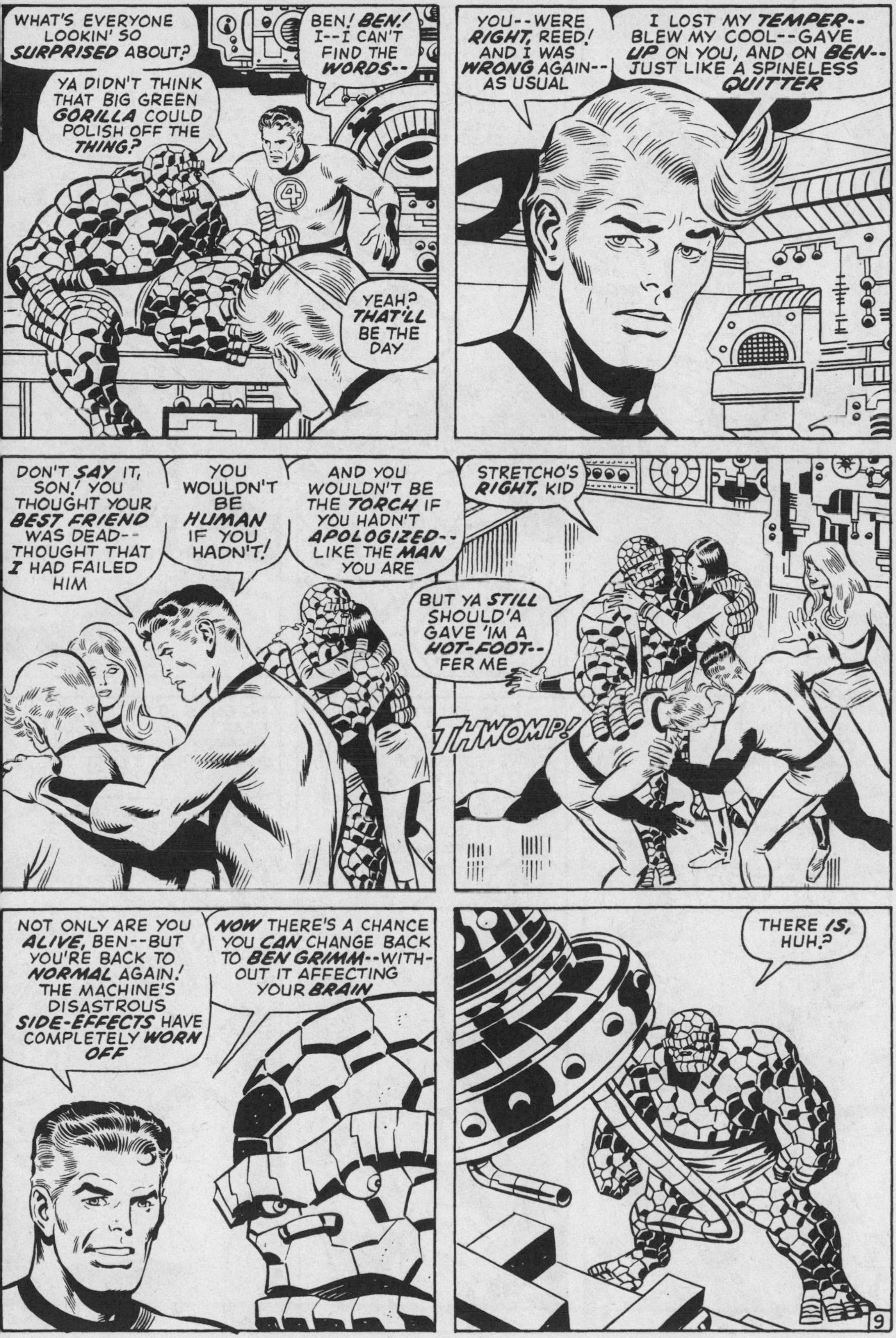
WHAT'S EVERYONE LOOKIN' SO SURPRISED ABOUT?
BEN! BEN! I--I CAN'T FIND THE WORDS--
YA DIDN'T THINK THAT BIG GREEN GORILLA COULD POLISH OFF THE THING?
YEAH? THAT'LL BE THE DAY
YOU--WERE RIGHT, REED! AND I WAS WRONG AGAIN--AS USUAL
I LOST MY TEMPER--BLEW MY COOL--GAVE UP ON YOU, AND ON BEN--JUST LIKE A SPINELESS QUITTER
DON'T SAY IT, SON! YOU THOUGHT YOUR BEST FRIEND WAS DEAD--THOUGHT THAT I HAD FAILED HIM
YOU WOULDN'T BE HUMAN IF YOU HADN'T!
AND YOU WOULDN'T BE THE TORCH IF YOU HADN'T APOLOGIZED--LIKE THE MAN YOU ARE
STRETCHO'S RIGHT, KID
BUT YA STILL SHOULD'A GAVE 'IM A HOT-FOOT--FER ME
THWOMP!
NOT ONLY ARE YOU ALIVE, BEN--BUT YOU'RE BACK TO NORMAL AGAIN! THE MACHINE'S DISASTROUS SIDE-EFFECTS HAVE COMPLETELY WORN OFF
NOW THERE'S A CHANCE YOU CAN CHANGE BACK TO BEN GRIMM--WITHOUT IT AFFECTING YOUR BRAIN
THERE IS, HUH?
9

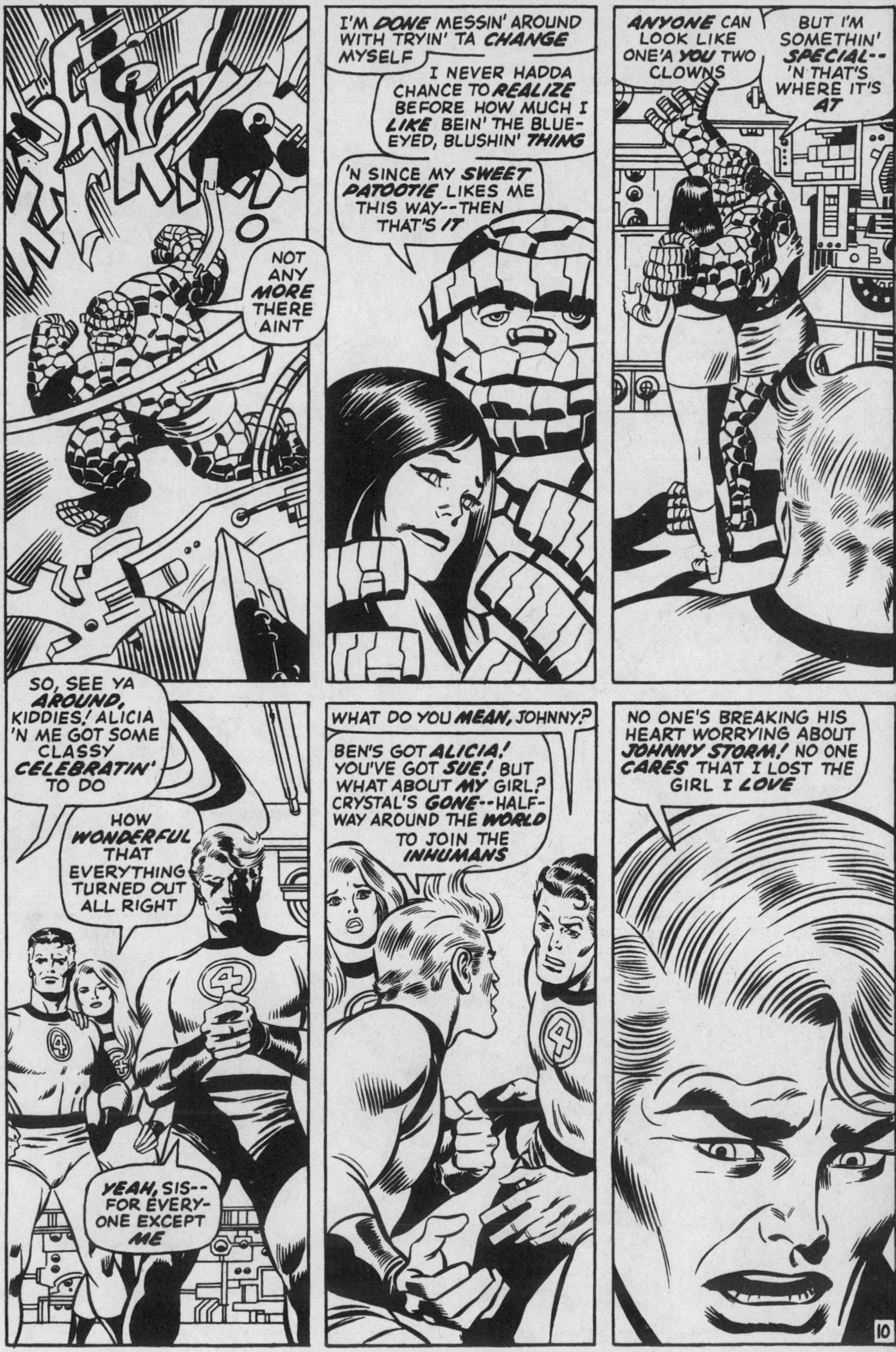
NOT ANY MORE THERE AINT
I'M DONE MESSIN' AROUND WITH TRYIN' TA CHANGE MYSELF
I NEVER HADDA CHANCE TO REALIZE BEFORE HOW MUCH I LIKE BEIN' THE BLUE-EYED, BLUSHIN' THING
'N SINCE MY SWEET PATOOTIE LIKES ME THIS WAY--THEN THAT'S IT
ANYONE CAN LOOK LIKE ONE'A YOU TWO CLOWNS
BUT I'M SOMETHIN' SPECIAL--'N THAT'S WHERE IT'S AT
SO, SEE YA AROUND, KIDDIES! ALICIA 'N ME GOT SOME CLASSY CELEBRATIN' TO DO
HOW WONDERFUL THAT EVERYTHING TURNED OUT ALL RIGHT
YEAH, SIS--FOR EVERY-ONE EXCEPT ME
WHAT DO YOU MEAN, JOHNNY?
BEN'S GOT ALICIA! YOU'VE GOT SUE! BUT WHAT ABOUT MY GIRL? CRYSTAL'S GONE--HALF-WAY AROUND THE WORLD TO JOIN THE INHUMANS
NO ONE'S BREAKING HIS HEART WORRYING ABOUT JOHNNY STORM! NO ONE CARES THAT I LOST THE GIRL I LOVE
10

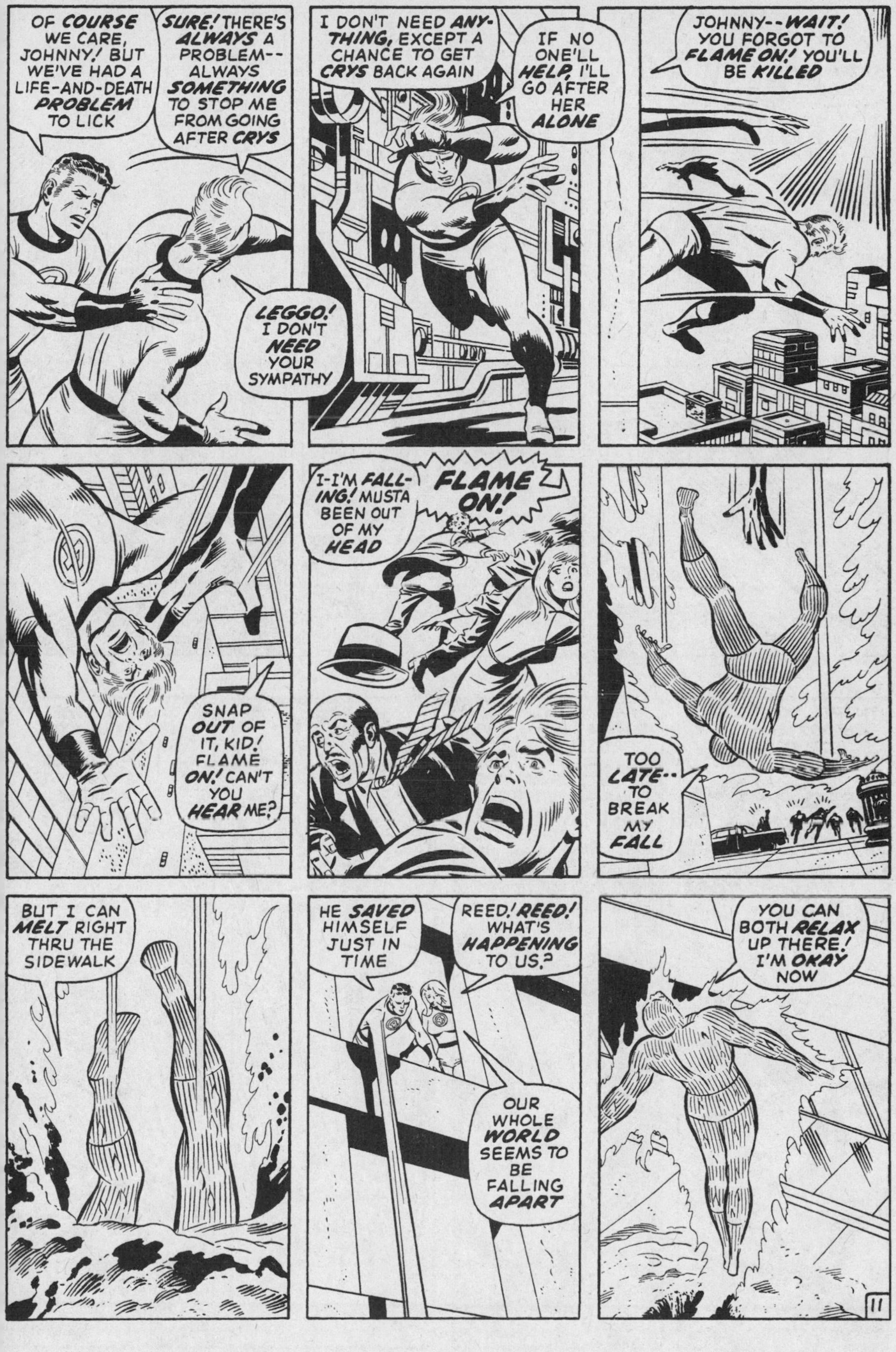
OF COURSE WE CARE, JOHNNY! BUT WE'VE HAD A LIFE-AND-DEATH PROBLEM TO LICK
SURE! THERE'S ALWAYS A PROBLEM-- ALWAYS SOMETHING TO STOP ME FROM GOING AFTER CRYS
LEGGO! I DON'T NEED YOUR SYMPATHY
I DON'T NEED ANYTHING, EXCEPT A CHANCE TO GET CRYS BACK AGAIN
IF NO ONE'LL HELP, I'LL GO AFTER HER ALONE
JOHNNY--WAIT! YOU FORGOT TO FLAME ON! YOU'LL BE KILLED
SNAP OUT OF IT, KID! FLAME ON! CAN'T YOU HEAR ME?
I-I'M FALLING! MUSTA BEEN OUT OF MY HEAD
FLAME ON!
TOO LATE-- TO BREAK MY FALL
BUT I CAN MELT RIGHT THRU THE SIDEWALK
HE SAVED HIMSELF JUST IN TIME
REED! REED! WHAT'S HAPPENING TO US?
OUR WHOLE WORLD SEEMS TO BE FALLING APART
YOU CAN BOTH RELAX UP THERE! I'M OKAY NOW
11

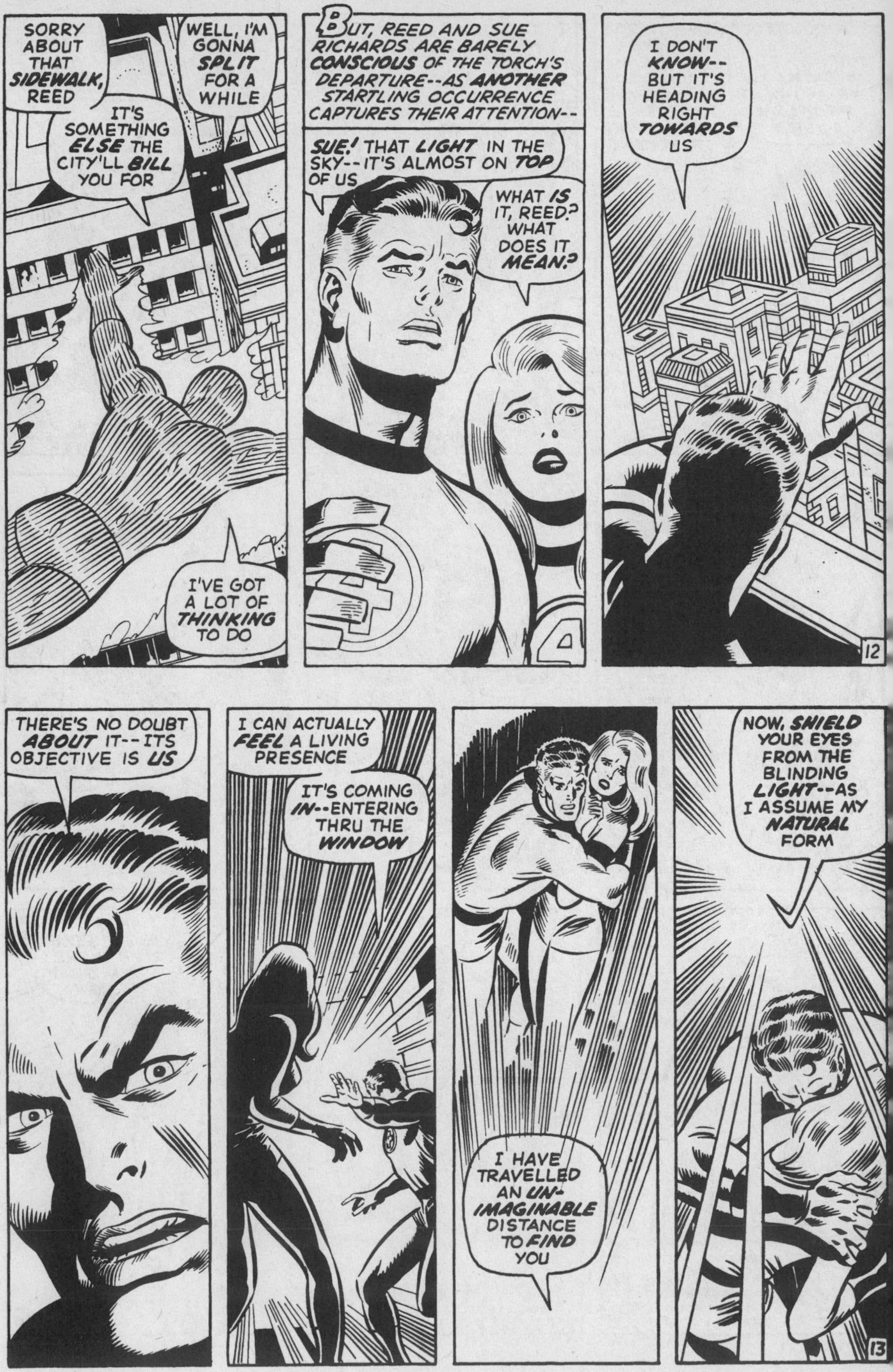
SORRY ABOUT THAT SIDEWALK, REED
IT'S SOMETHING ELSE THE CITY'LL BILL YOU FOR
WELL, I'M GONNA SPLIT FOR A WHILE
I'VE GOT A LOT OF THINKING TO DO
BUT, REED AND SUE RICHARDS ARE BARELY CONSCIOUS OF THE TORCH'S DEPARTURE--AS ANOTHER STARTLING OCCURRENCE CAPTURES THEIR ATTENTION--
SUE! THAT LIGHT IN THE SKY--IT'S ALMOST ON TOP OF US
WHAT IS IT, REED? WHAT DOES IT MEAN?
I DON'T KNOW--BUT IT'S HEADING RIGHT TOWARDS US
12
THERE'S NO DOUBT ABOUT IT--ITS OBJECTIVE IS US
I CAN ACTUALLY FEEL A LIVING PRESENCE
IT'S COMING IN--ENTERING THRU THE WINDOW
I HAVE TRAVELLED AN UN-IMAGINABLE DISTANCE TO FIND YOU
NOW, SHIELD YOUR EYES FROM THE BLINDING LIGHT--AS I ASSUME MY NATURAL FORM
13

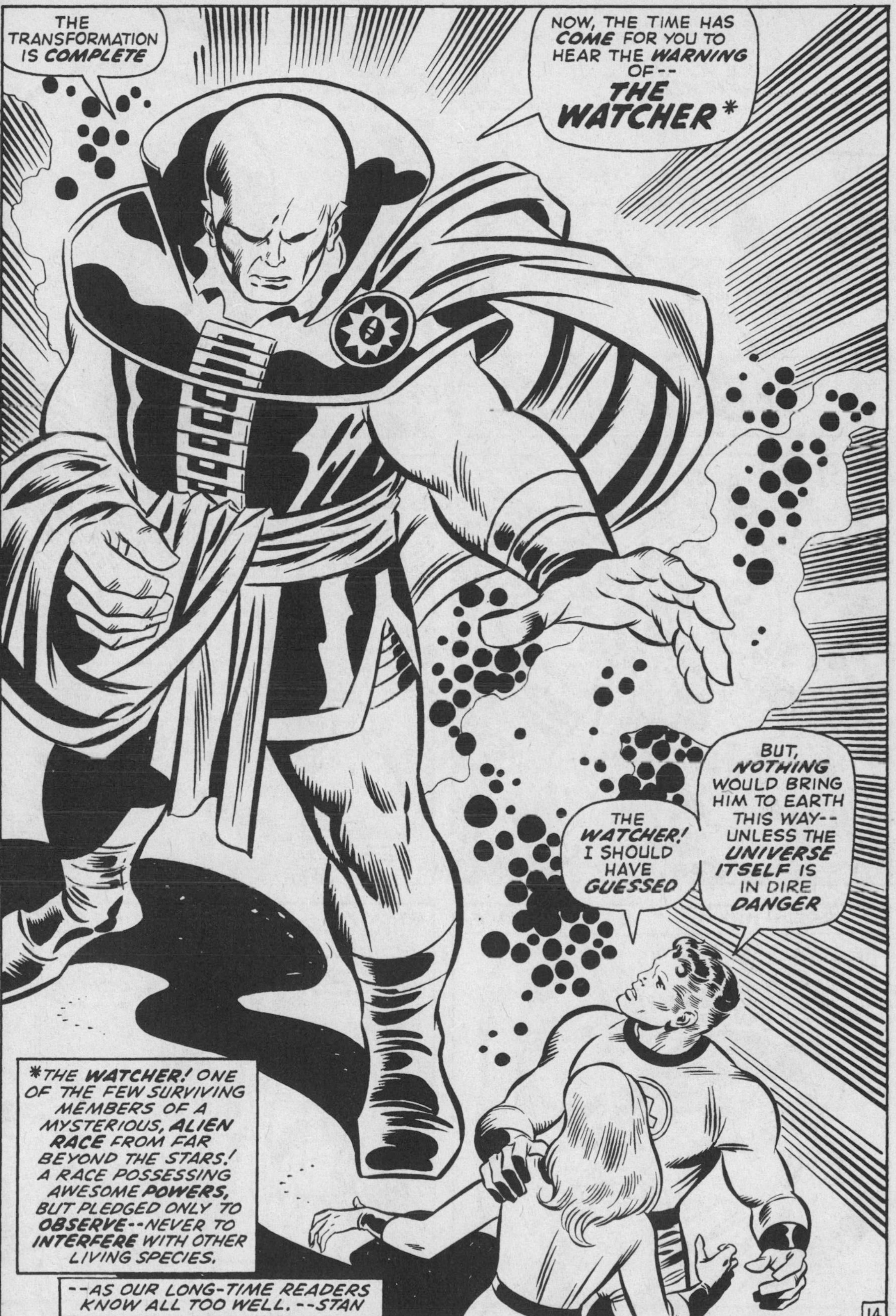
THE TRANSFORMATION IS COMPLETE
NOW, THE TIME HAS COME FOR YOU TO HEAR THE WARNING OF-- THE WATCHER*
THE WATCHER! I SHOULD HAVE GUESSED
BUT, NOTHING WOULD BRING HIM TO EARTH THIS WAY-- UNLESS THE UNIVERSE ITSELF IS IN DIRE DANGER
*THE WATCHER! ONE OF THE FEW SURVIVING MEMBERS OF A MYSTERIOUS, ALIEN RACE FROM FAR BEYOND THE STARS! A RACE POSSESSING AWESOME POWERS, BUT PLEDGED ONLY TO OBSERVE--NEVER TO INTERFERE WITH OTHER LIVING SPECIES.
--AS OUR LONG-TIME READERS KNOW ALL TOO WELL. --STAN
14

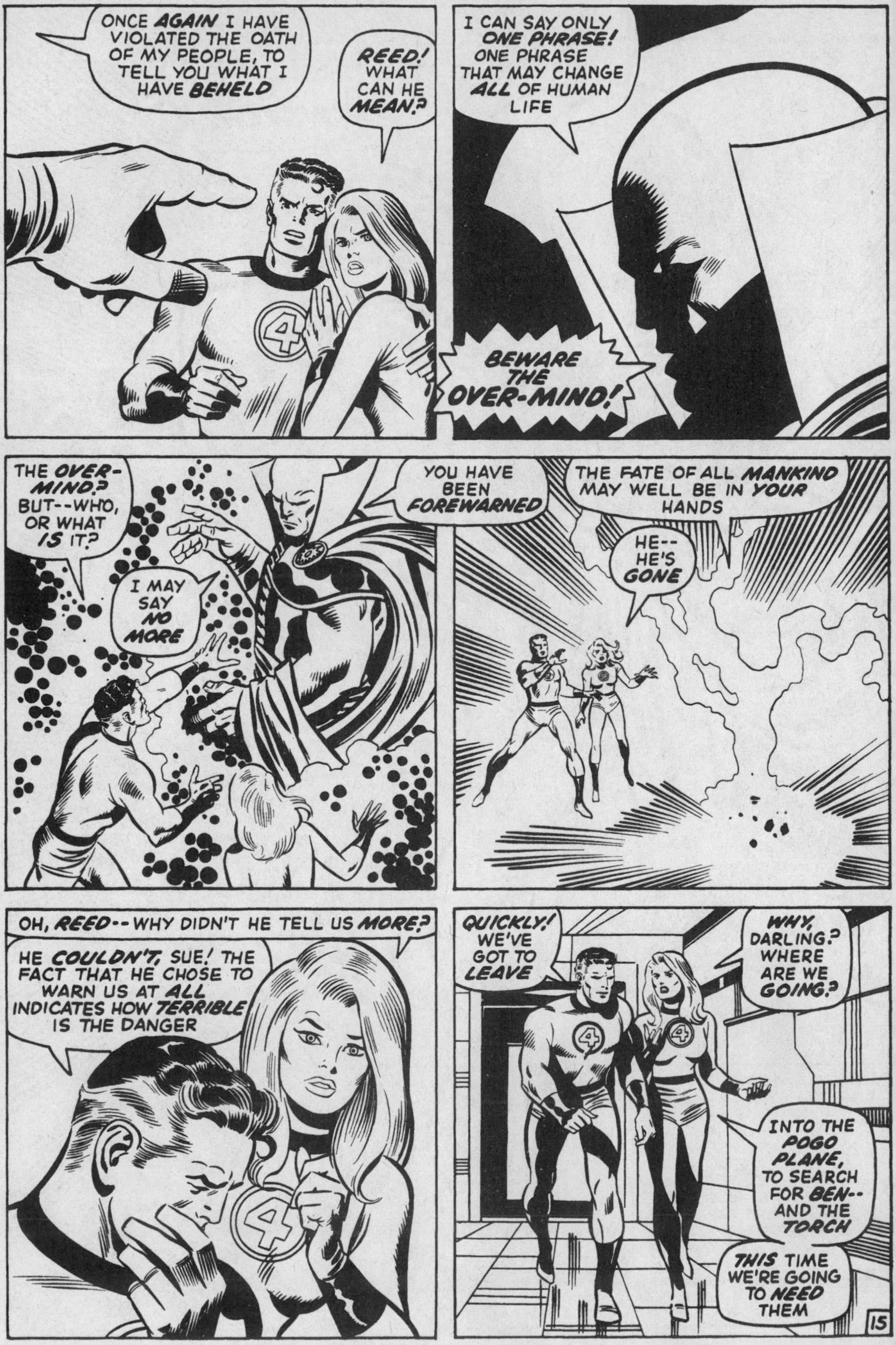
ONCE AGAIN I HAVE VIOLATED THE OATH OF MY PEOPLE, TO TELL YOU WHAT I HAVE BEHELD
REED! WHAT CAN HE MEAN?
I CAN SAY ONLY ONE PHRASE! ONE PHRASE THAT MAY CHANGE ALL OF HUMAN LIFE
BEWARE THE OVER-MIND!
THE OVER-MIND? BUT--WHO, OR WHAT IS IT?
I MAY SAY NO MORE
YOU HAVE BEEN FOREWARNED
THE FATE OF ALL MANKIND MAY WELL BE IN YOUR HANDS
HE--HE'S GONE
OH, REED--WHY DIDN'T HE TELL US MORE?
HE COULDN'T, SUE! THE FACT THAT HE CHOSE TO WARN US AT ALL INDICATES HOW TERRIBLE IS THE DANGER
QUICKLY! WE'VE GOT TO LEAVE
WHY, DARLING? WHERE ARE WE GOING?
INTO THE POGO PLANE, TO SEARCH FOR BEN--AND THE TORCH
THIS TIME WE'RE GOING TO NEED THEM

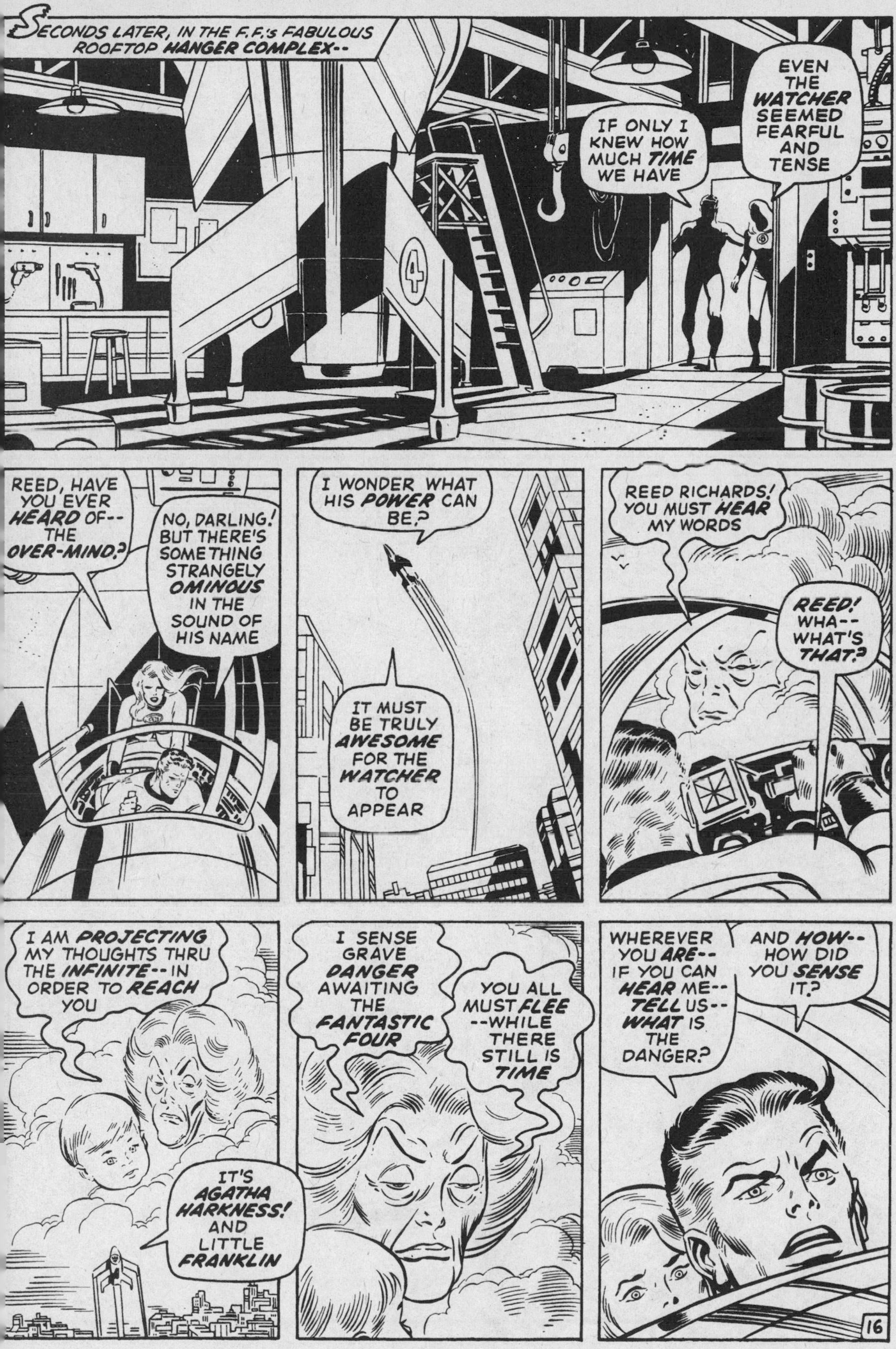

SECONDS LATER, IN THE F.F.'s FABULOUS ROOFTOP HANGER COMPLEX--
IF ONLY I KNEW HOW MUCH TIME WE HAVE
EVEN THE WATCHER SEEMED FEARFUL AND TENSE
REED, HAVE YOU EVER HEARD OF-- THE OVER-MIND?
NO, DARLING! BUT THERE'S SOMETHING STRANGELY OMINOUS IN THE SOUND OF HIS NAME
I WONDER WHAT HIS POWER CAN BE?
IT MUST BE TRULY AWESOME FOR THE WATCHER TO APPEAR
REED RICHARDS! YOU MUST HEAR MY WORDS
REED! WHA-- WHAT'S THAT?
I AM PROJECTING MY THOUGHTS THRU THE INFINITE-- IN ORDER TO REACH YOU
IT'S AGATHA HARKNESS! AND LITTLE FRANKLIN
I SENSE GRAVE DANGER AWAITING THE FANTASTIC FOUR
YOU ALL MUST FLEE --WHILE THERE STILL IS TIME
WHEREVER YOU ARE-- IF YOU CAN HEAR ME-- TELL US-- WHAT IS THE DANGER?
AND HOW-- HOW DID YOU SENSE IT?
16

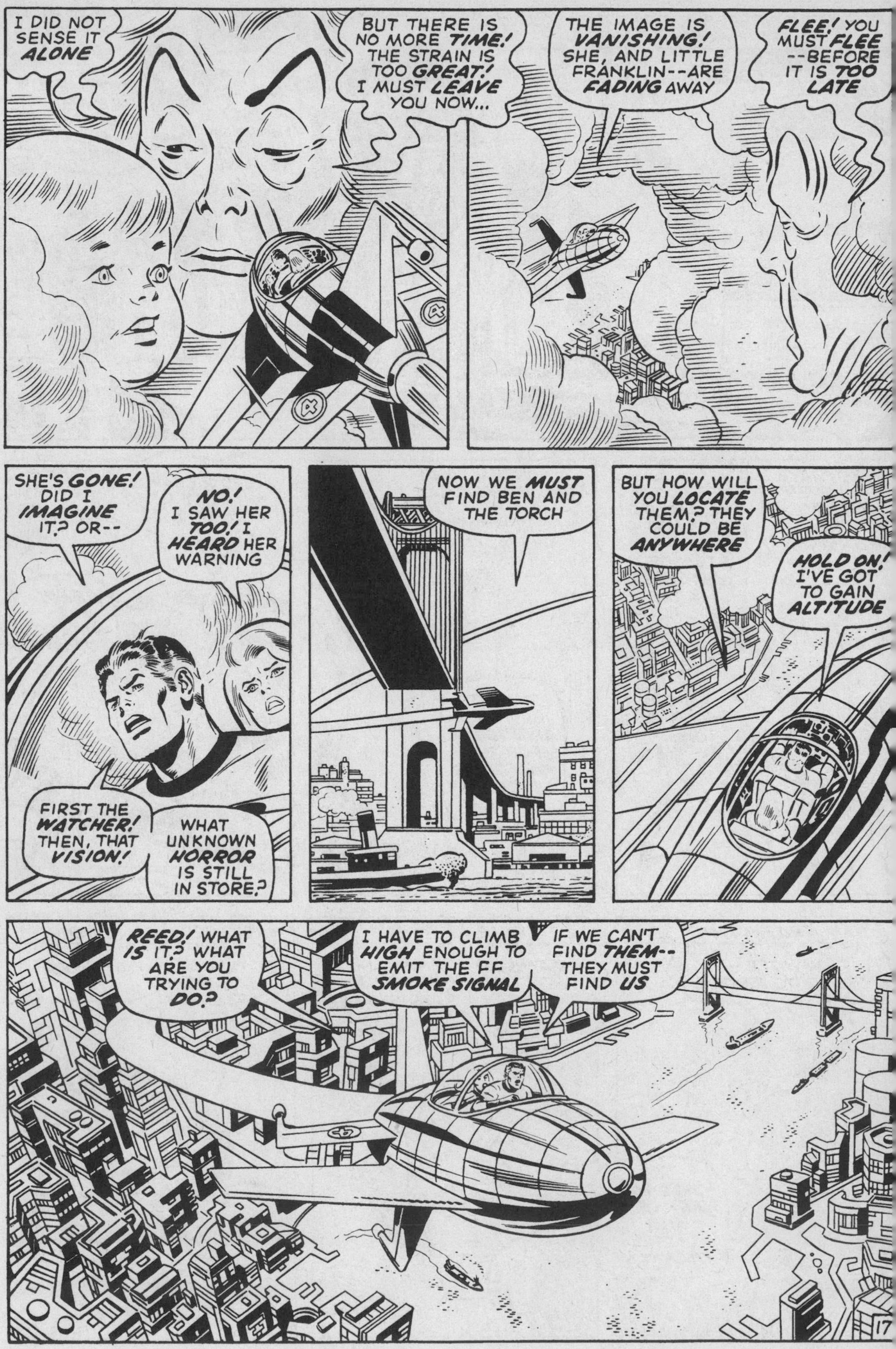
I DID NOT SENSE IT ALONE
BUT THERE IS NO MORE TIME! THE STRAIN IS TOO GREAT! I MUST LEAVE YOU NOW...
THE IMAGE IS VANISHING! SHE, AND LITTLE FRANKLIN--ARE FADING AWAY
FLEE! YOU MUST FLEE --BEFORE IT IS TOO LATE
SHE'S GONE! DID I IMAGINE IT? OR--
NO! I SAW HER TOO! I HEARD HER WARNING
FIRST THE WATCHER! THEN, THAT VISION!
WHAT UNKNOWN HORROR IS STILL IN STORE?
NOW WE MUST FIND BEN AND THE TORCH
BUT HOW WILL YOU LOCATE THEM? THEY COULD BE ANYWHERE
HOLD ON! I'VE GOT TO GAIN ALTITUDE
REED! WHAT IS IT? WHAT ARE YOU TRYING TO DO?
I HAVE TO CLIMB HIGH ENOUGH TO EMIT THE FF SMOKE SIGNAL
IF WE CAN'T FIND THEM--THEY MUST FIND US
17

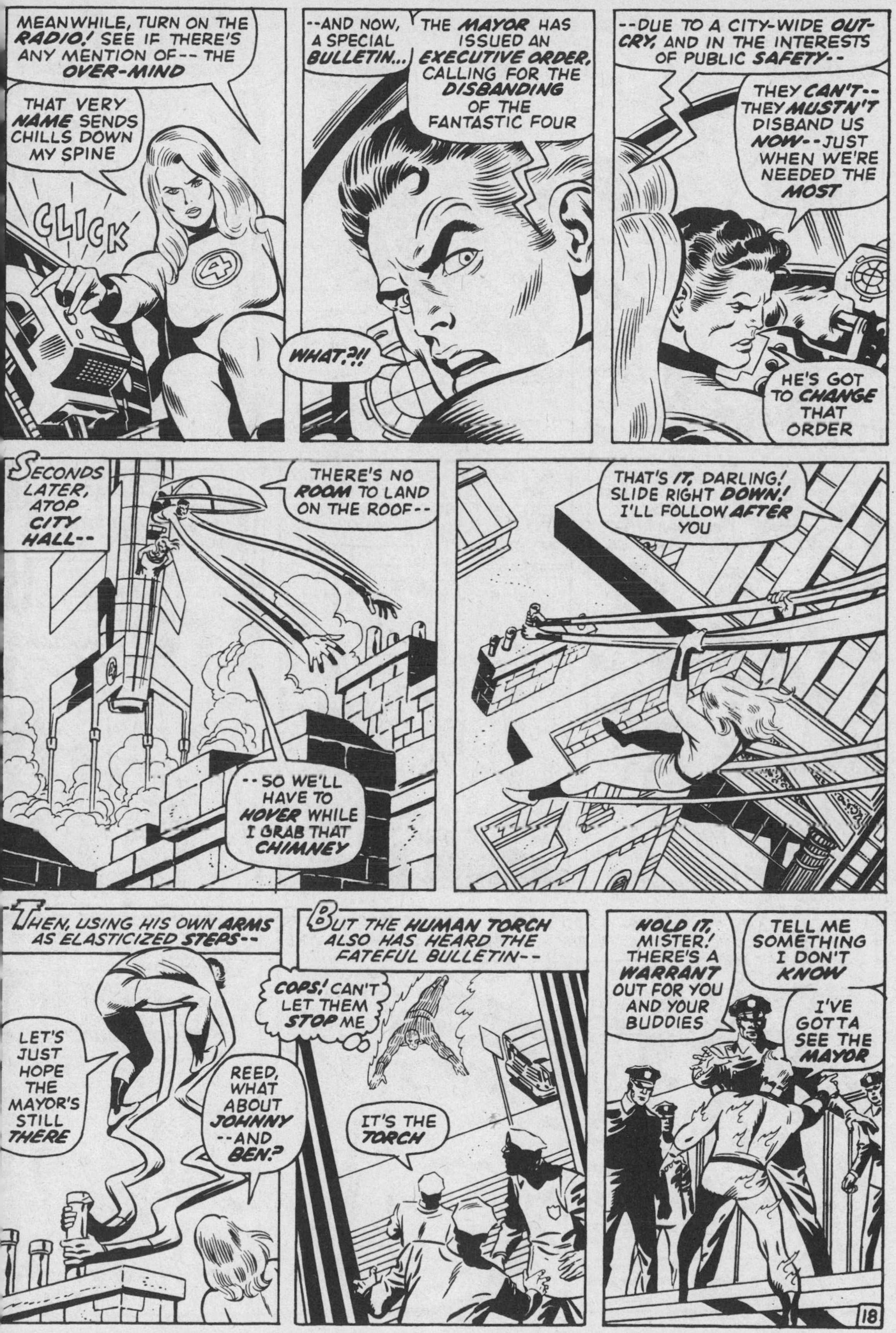
MEANWHILE, TURN ON THE RADIO! SEE IF THERE'S ANY MENTION OF-- THE OVER-MIND
THAT VERY NAME SENDS CHILLS DOWN MY SPINE
CLICK
--AND NOW, A SPECIAL BULLETIN...
THE MAYOR HAS ISSUED AN EXECUTIVE ORDER, CALLING FOR THE DISBANDING OF THE FANTASTIC FOUR
WHAT?!!
--DUE TO A CITY-WIDE OUT-CRY, AND IN THE INTERESTS OF PUBLIC SAFETY--
THEY CAN'T-- THEY MUSTN'T DISBAND US NOW--JUST WHEN WE'RE NEEDED THE MOST
HE'S GOT TO CHANGE THAT ORDER
SECONDS LATER, ATOP CITY HALL--
THERE'S NO ROOM TO LAND ON THE ROOF--
--SO WE'LL HAVE TO HOVER WHILE I GRAB THAT CHIMNEY
THAT'S IT, DARLING! SLIDE RIGHT DOWN! I'LL FOLLOW AFTER YOU
THEN, USING HIS OWN ARMS AS ELASTICIZED STEPS--
LET'S JUST HOPE THE MAYOR'S STILL THERE
REED, WHAT ABOUT JOHNNY --AND BEN?
BUT THE HUMAN TORCH ALSO HAS HEARD THE FATEFUL BULLETIN--
COPS! CAN'T LET THEM STOP ME
IT'S THE TORCH
HOLD IT, MISTER! THERE'S A WARRANT OUT FOR YOU AND YOUR BUDDIES
TELL ME SOMETHING I DON'T KNOW
I'VE GOTTA SEE THE MAYOR
18

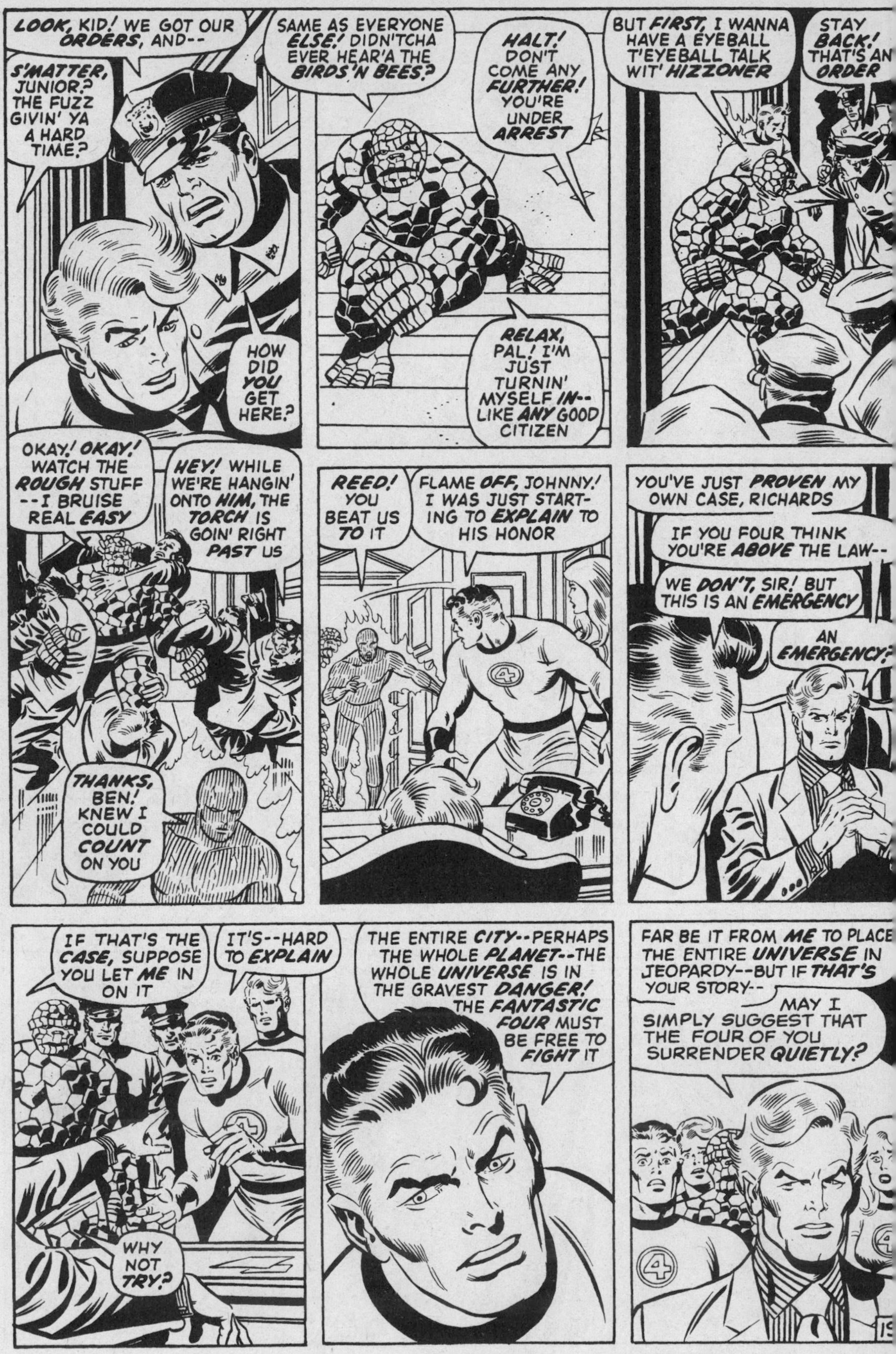

LOOK, KID! WE GOT OUR ORDERS, AND--
S'MATTER, JUNIOR? THE FUZZ GIVIN' YA A HARD TIME?
HOW DID YOU GET HERE?
SAME AS EVERYONE ELSE! DIDN'TCHA EVER HEAR'A THE BIRDS 'N BEES?
HALT! DON'T COME ANY FURTHER! YOU'RE UNDER ARREST
RELAX, PAL! I'M JUST TURNIN' MYSELF IN--LIKE ANY GOOD CITIZEN
BUT FIRST, I WANNA HAVE A EYEBALL T'EYEBALL TALK WIT' HIZZONER
STAY BACK! THAT'S AN ORDER
OKAY! OKAY! WATCH THE ROUGH STUFF --I BRUISE REAL EASY
HEY! WHILE WE'RE HANGIN' ONTO HIM, THE TORCH IS GOIN' RIGHT PAST US
THANKS, BEN! KNEW I COULD COUNT ON YOU
REED! YOU BEAT US TO IT
FLAME OFF, JOHNNY! I WAS JUST STARTING TO EXPLAIN TO HIS HONOR
YOU'VE JUST PROVEN MY OWN CASE, RICHARDS
IF YOU FOUR THINK YOU'RE ABOVE THE LAW--
WE DON'T, SIR! BUT THIS IS AN EMERGENCY
AN EMERGENCY?
IF THAT'S THE CASE, SUPPOSE YOU LET ME IN ON IT
IT'S--HARD TO EXPLAIN
WHY NOT TRY?
THE ENTIRE CITY--PERHAPS THE WHOLE PLANET--THE WHOLE UNIVERSE IS IN THE GRAVEST DANGER! THE FANTASTIC FOUR MUST BE FREE TO FIGHT IT
FAR BE IT FROM ME TO PLACE THE ENTIRE UNIVERSE IN JEOPARDY--BUT IF THAT'S YOUR STORY--
MAY I SIMPLY SUGGEST THAT THE FOUR OF YOU SURRENDER QUIETLY?
15

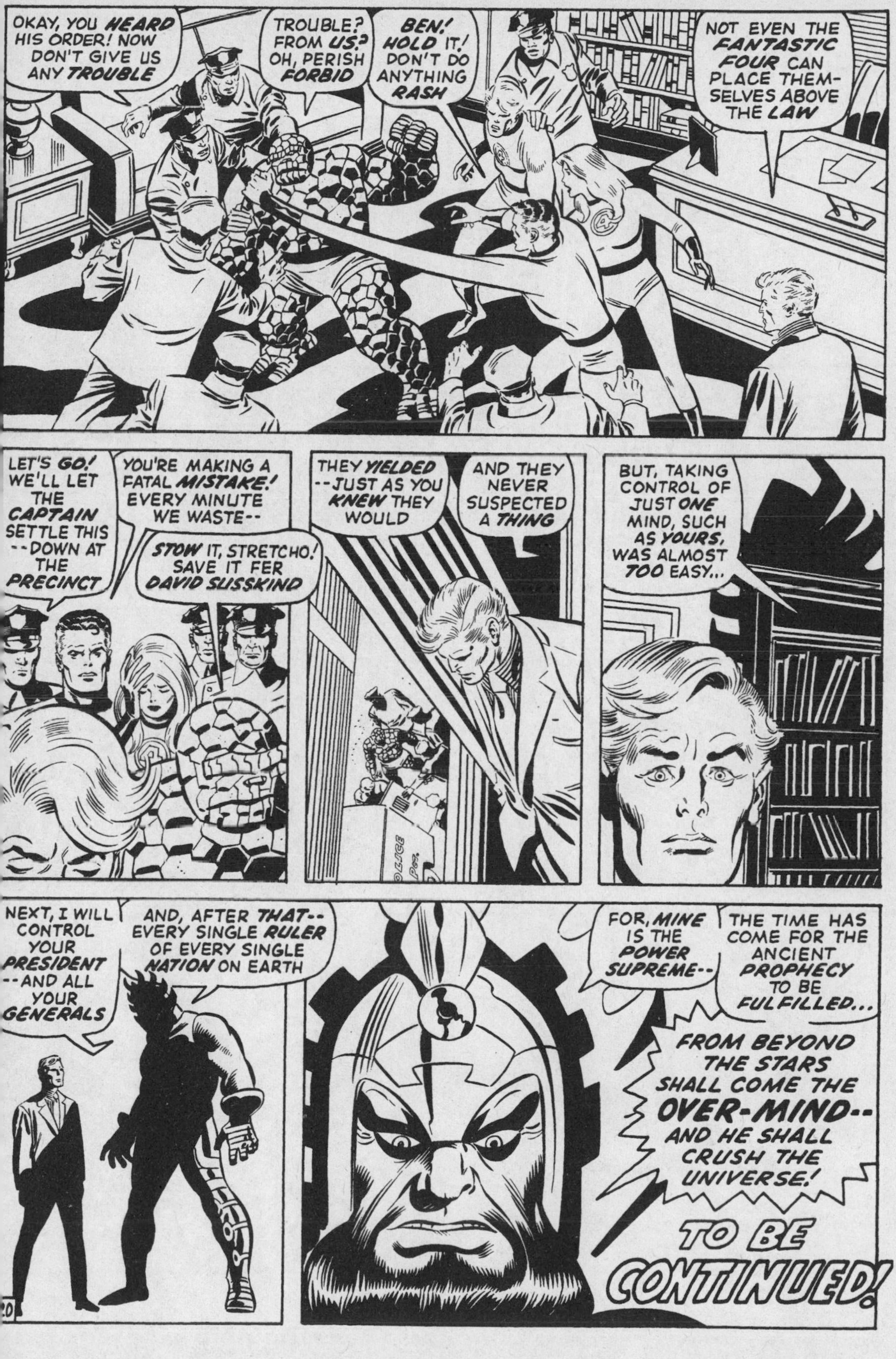
OKAY, YOU HEARD HIS ORDER! NOW DON'T GIVE US ANY TROUBLE
TROUBLE? FROM US? OH, PERISH FORBID
BEN! HOLD IT! DON'T DO ANYTHING RASH
NOT EVEN THE FANTASTIC FOUR CAN PLACE THEM-SELVES ABOVE THE LAW
LET'S GO! WE'LL LET THE CAPTAIN SETTLE THIS --DOWN AT THE PRECINCT
YOU'RE MAKING A FATAL MISTAKE! EVERY MINUTE WE WASTE--
STOW IT, STRETCHO! SAVE IT FER DAVID SUSSKIND
THEY YIELDED --JUST AS YOU KNEW THEY WOULD
AND THEY NEVER SUSPECTED A THING
POLICE
BUT, TAKING CONTROL OF JUST ONE MIND, SUCH AS YOURS, WAS ALMOST TOO EASY...
NEXT, I WILL CONTROL YOUR PRESIDENT --AND ALL YOUR GENERALS
AND, AFTER THAT-- EVERY SINGLE RULER OF EVERY SINGLE NATION ON EARTH
FOR, MINE IS THE POWER SUPREME--
THE TIME HAS COME FOR THE ANCIENT PROPHECY TO BE FULFILLED...
FROM BEYOND THE STARS SHALL COME THE OVER-MIND-- AND HE SHALL CRUSH THE UNIVERSE!
TO BE CONTINUED!

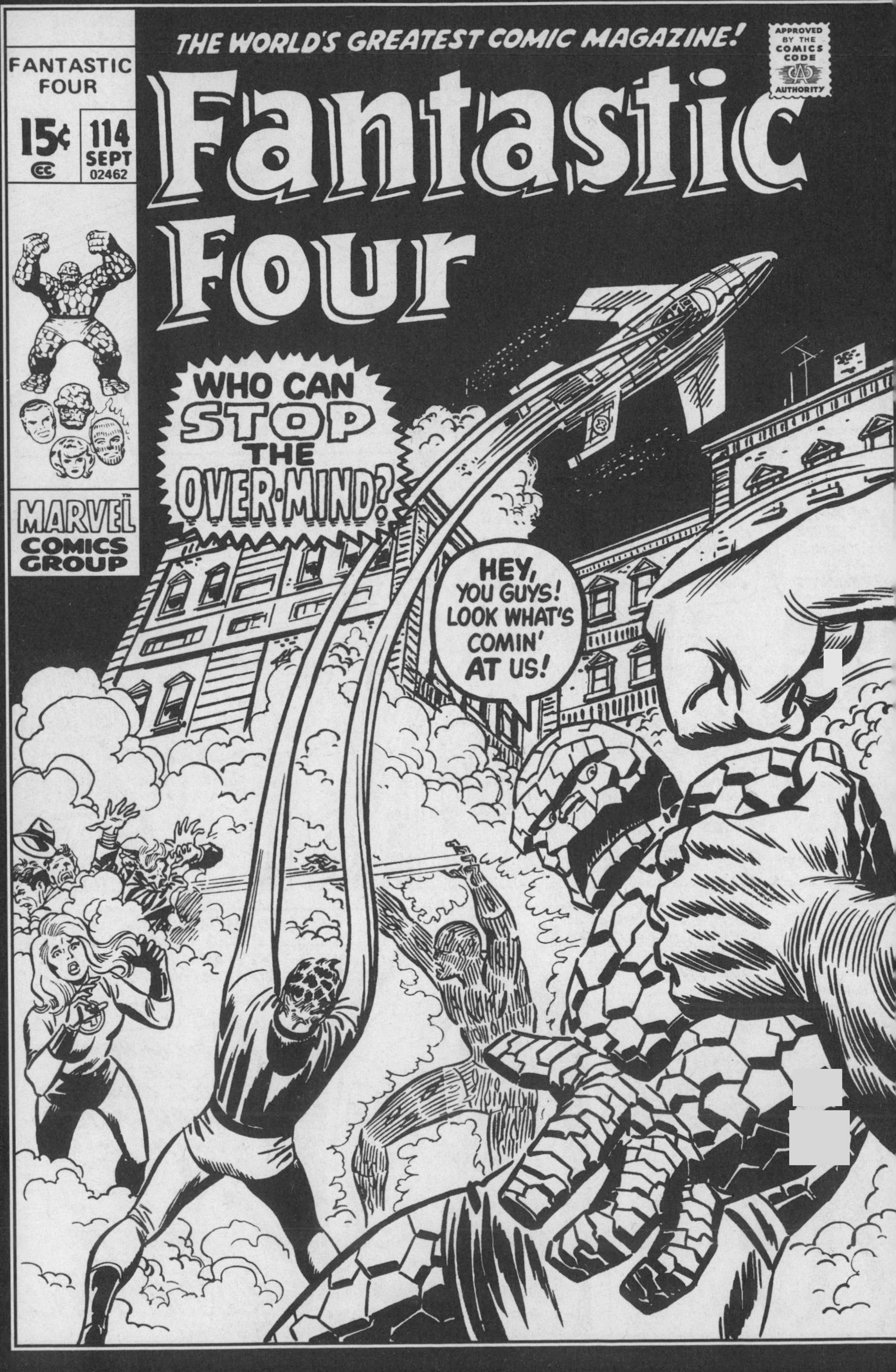
THE WORLD'S GREATEST COMIC MAGAZINE!
APPROVED BY THE COMICS CODE AUTHORITY
FANTASTIC FOUR
15¢
114 SEPT 02462
Fantastic Four
WHO CAN STOP THE OVER-MIND?
MARVEL COMICS GROUP
HEY, YOU GUYS! LOOK WHAT'S COMIN' AT US!

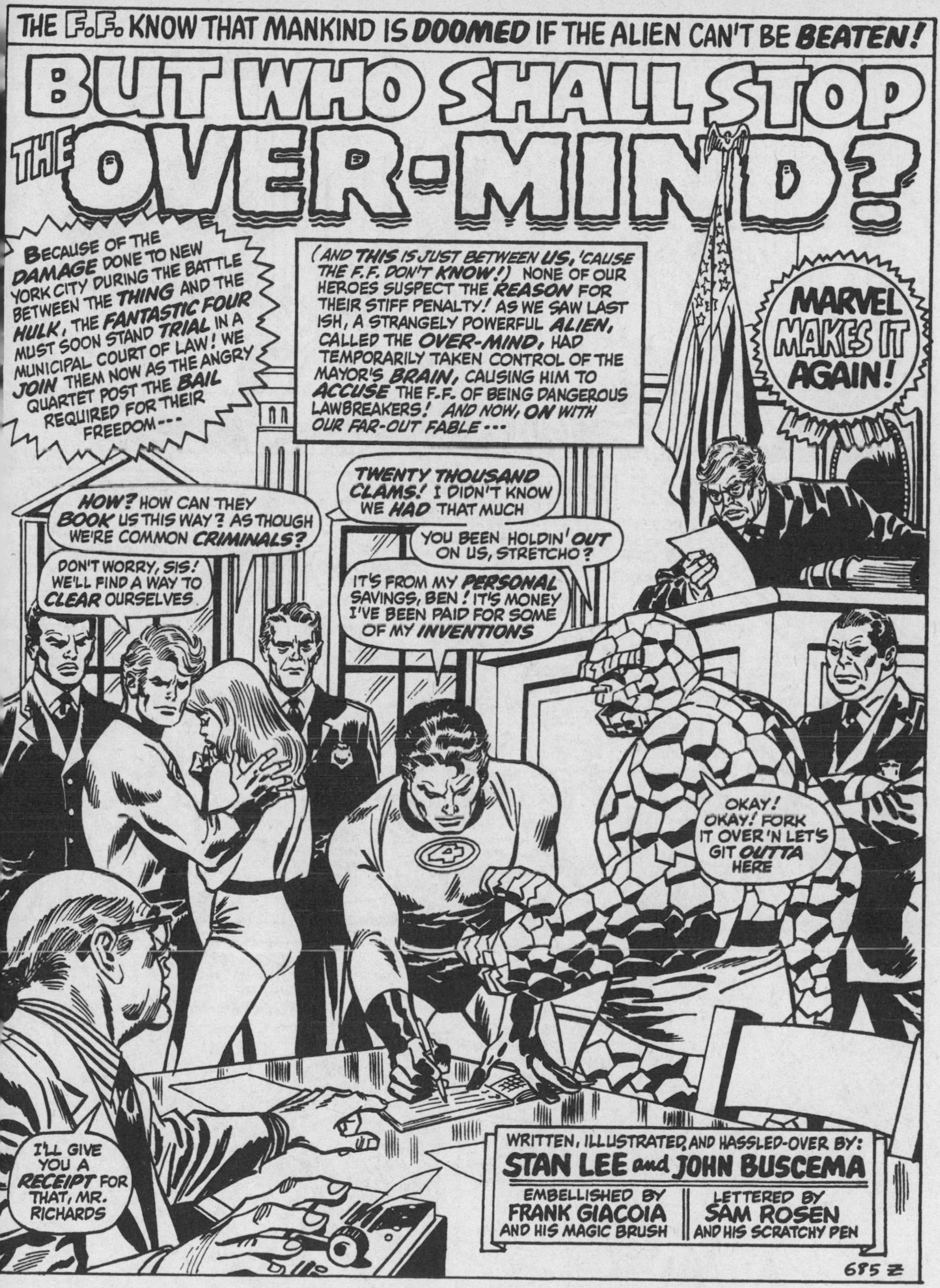
THE F.F. KNOW THAT MANKIND IS DOOMED IF THE ALIEN CAN'T BE BEATEN!
BUT WHO SHALL STOP THE OVER-MIND?
BECAUSE OF THE DAMAGE DONE TO NEW YORK CITY DURING THE BATTLE BETWEEN THE THING AND THE HULK, THE FANTASTIC FOUR MUST SOON STAND TRIAL IN A MUNICIPAL COURT OF LAW! WE JOIN THEM NOW AS THE ANGRY QUARTET POST THE BAIL REQUIRED FOR THEIR FREEDOM---
(AND THIS IS JUST BETWEEN US, 'CAUSE THE F.F. DON'T KNOW!) NONE OF OUR HEROES SUSPECT THE REASON FOR THEIR STIFF PENALTY! AS WE SAW LAST ISH, A STRANGELY POWERFUL ALIEN, CALLED THE OVER-MIND, HAD TEMPORARILY TAKEN CONTROL OF THE MAYOR'S BRAIN, CAUSING HIM TO ACCUSE THE F.F. OF BEING DANGEROUS LAWBREAKERS! AND NOW, ON WITH OUR FAR-OUT FABLE---
MARVEL MAKES IT AGAIN!
HOW? HOW CAN THEY BOOK US THIS WAY? AS THOUGH WE'RE COMMON CRIMINALS?
DON'T WORRY, SIS! WE'LL FIND A WAY TO CLEAR OURSELVES
TWENTY THOUSAND CLAMS! I DIDN'T KNOW WE HAD THAT MUCH
YOU BEEN HOLDIN' OUT ON US, STRETCHO?
IT'S FROM MY PERSONAL SAVINGS, BEN! IT'S MONEY I'VE BEEN PAID FOR SOME OF MY INVENTIONS
OKAY! OKAY! FORK IT OVER 'N LET'S GIT OUTTA HERE
I'LL GIVE YOU A RECEIPT FOR THAT, MR. RICHARDS
WRITTEN, ILLUSTRATED, AND HASSLED-OVER BY: STAN LEE and JOHN BUSCEMA
EMBELLISHED BY FRANK GIACOIA AND HIS MAGIC BRUSH
LETTERED BY SAM ROSEN AND HIS SCRATCHY PEN
685 Z

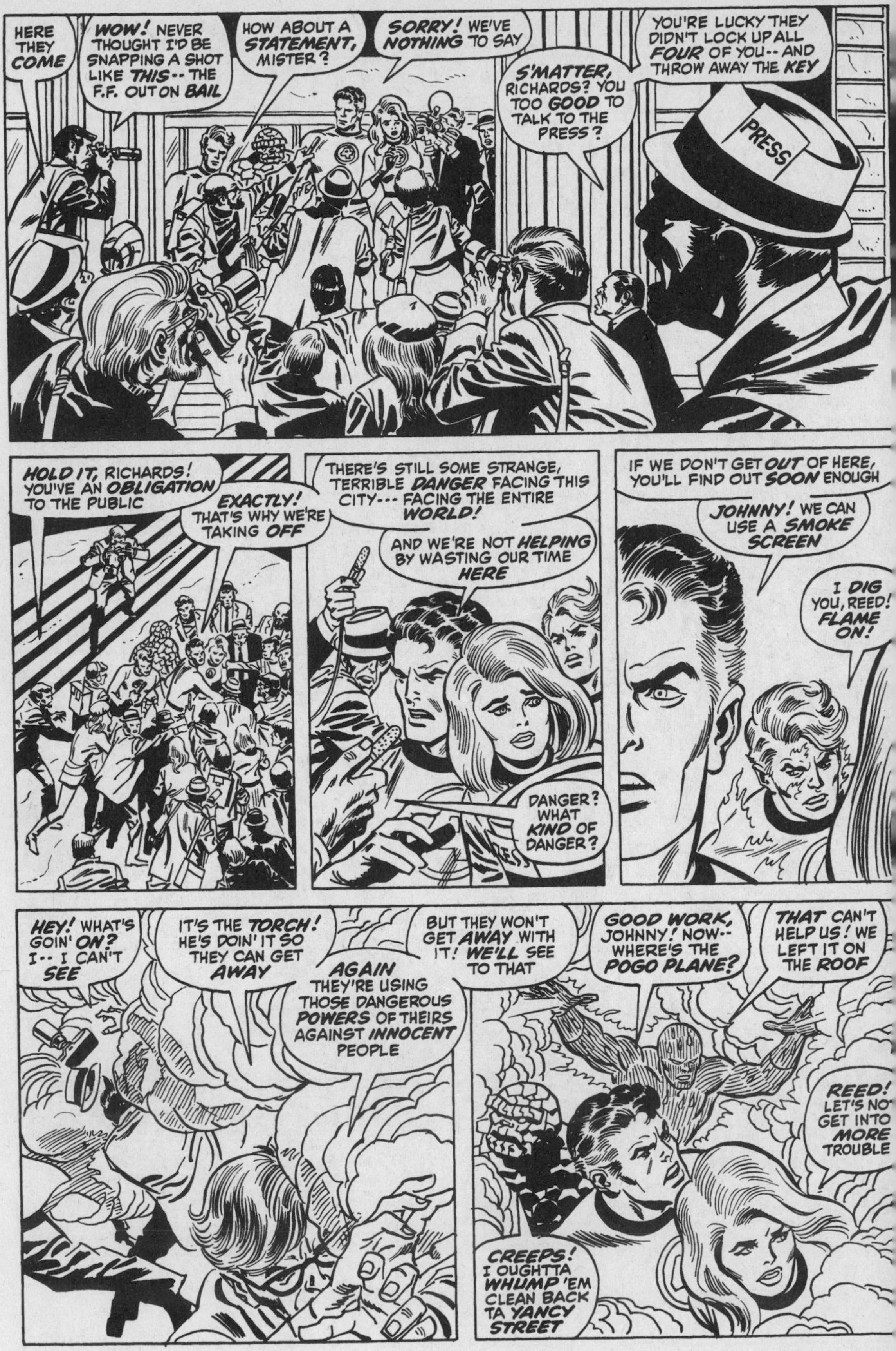
HERE THEY COME
WOW! NEVER THOUGHT I'D BE SNAPPING A SHOT LIKE THIS-- THE F.F. OUT ON BAIL
HOW ABOUT A STATEMENT, MISTER?
SORRY! WE'VE NOTHING TO SAY
S'MATTER, RICHARDS? YOU TOO GOOD TO TALK TO THE PRESS?
YOU'RE LUCKY THEY DIDN'T LOCK UP ALL FOUR OF YOU-- AND THROW AWAY THE KEY
PRESS
HOLD IT, RICHARDS! YOU'VE AN OBLIGATION TO THE PUBLIC
EXACTLY! THAT'S WHY WE'RE TAKING OFF
THERE'S STILL SOME STRANGE, TERRIBLE DANGER FACING THIS CITY--- FACING THE ENTIRE WORLD!
AND WE'RE NOT HELPING BY WASTING OUR TIME HERE
DANGER? WHAT KIND OF DANGER?
IF WE DON'T GET OUT OF HERE, YOU'LL FIND OUT SOON ENOUGH
JOHNNY! WE CAN USE A SMOKE SCREEN
I DIG YOU, REED! FLAME ON!
HEY! WHAT'S GOIN' ON? I-- I CAN'T SEE
IT'S THE TORCH! HE'S DOIN' IT SO THEY CAN GET AWAY
BUT THEY WON'T GET AWAY WITH IT! WE'LL SEE TO THAT
AGAIN THEY'RE USING THOSE DANGEROUS POWERS OF THEIRS AGAINST INNOCENT PEOPLE
GOOD WORK, JOHNNY! NOW-- WHERE'S THE POGO PLANE?
THAT CAN'T HELP US! WE LEFT IT ON THE ROOF
REED! LET'S NO GET INTO MORE TROUBLE
CREEPS! I OUGHTTA WHUMP 'EM CLEAN BACK TA YANCY STREET

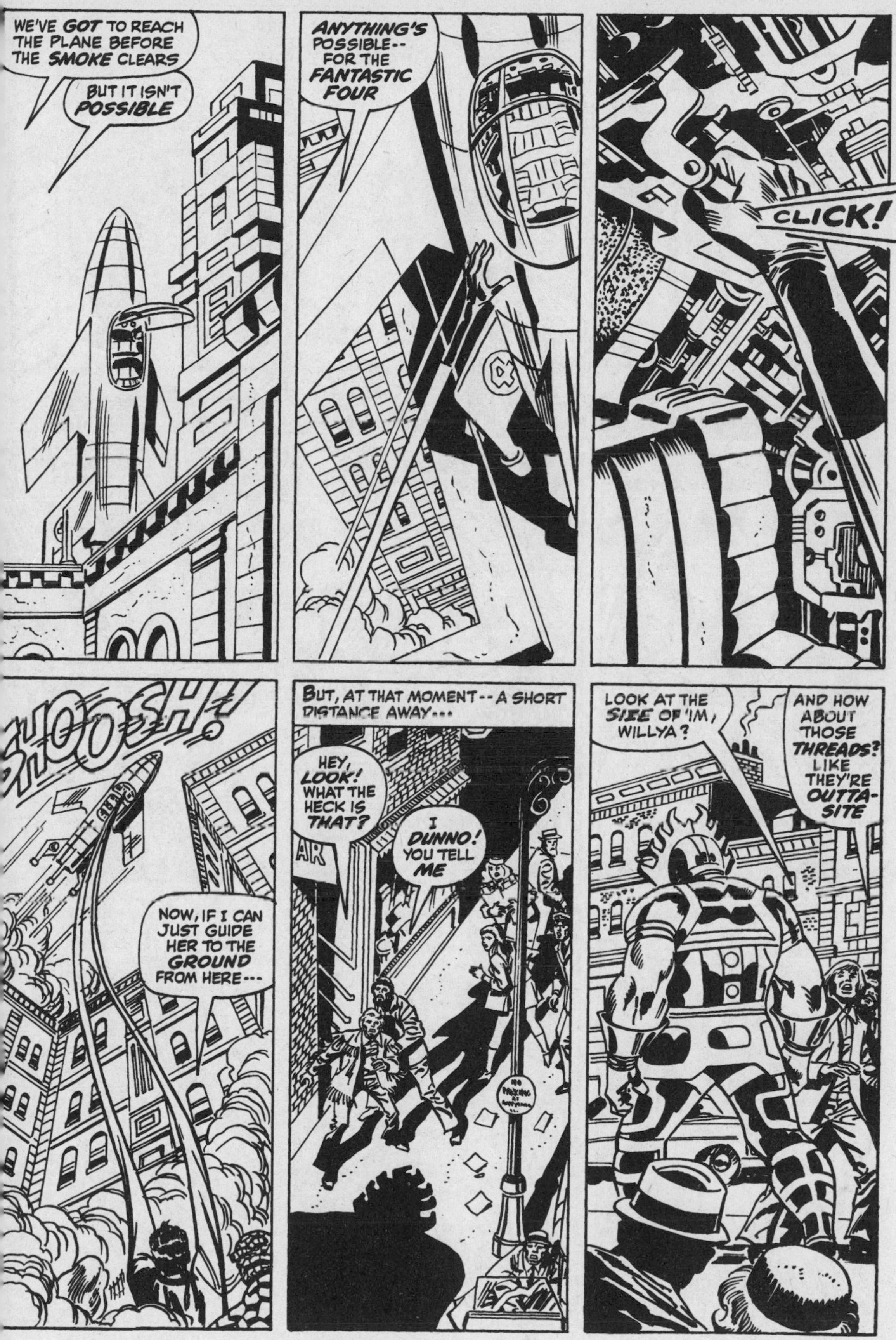

WE'VE GOT TO REACH THE PLANE BEFORE THE SMOKE CLEARS
BUT IT ISN'T POSSIBLE
ANYTHING'S POSSIBLE-- FOR THE FANTASTIC FOUR
CLICK!
SHOOSH!
NOW, IF I CAN JUST GUIDE HER TO THE GROUND FROM HERE---
BUT, AT THAT MOMENT-- A SHORT DISTANCE AWAY---
HEY, LOOK! WHAT THE HECK IS THAT?
I DUNNO! YOU TELL ME
LOOK AT THE SIZE OF 'IM, WILLYA?
AND HOW ABOUT THOSE THREADS? LIKE THEY'RE OUTTA-SITE

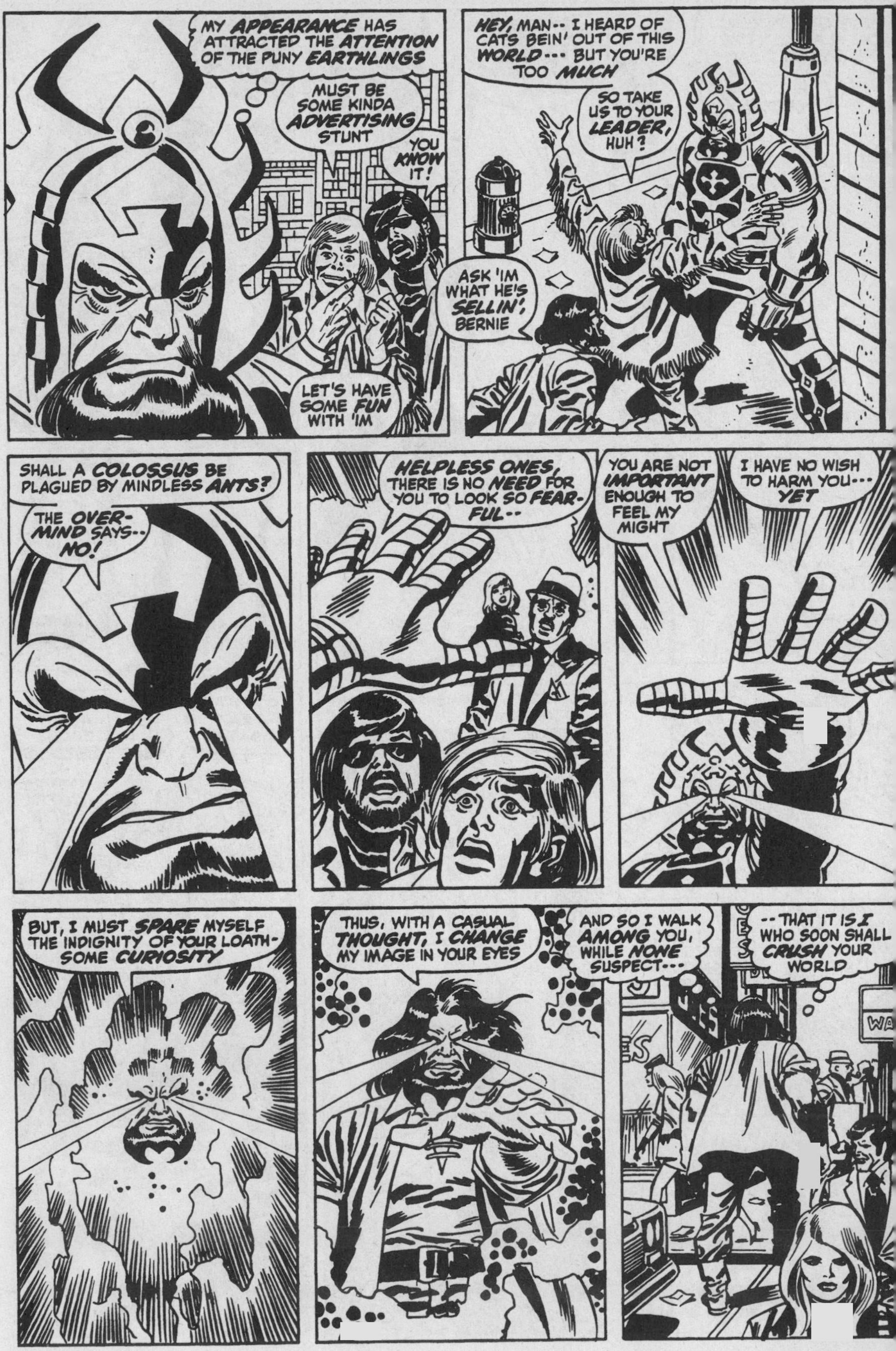
MY APPEARANCE HAS ATTRACTED THE ATTENTION OF THE PUNY EARTHLINGS
MUST BE SOME KINDA ADVERTISING STUNT
YOU KNOW IT!
LET'S HAVE SOME FUN WITH 'IM
HEY, MAN-- I HEARD OF CATS BEIN' OUT OF THIS WORLD--- BUT YOU'RE TOO MUCH
SO TAKE US TO YOUR LEADER, HUH?
ASK 'IM WHAT HE'S SELLIN', BERNIE
SHALL A COLOSSUS BE PLAGUED BY MINDLESS ANTS?
THE OVER-MIND SAYS-- NO!
HELPLESS ONES, THERE IS NO NEED FOR YOU TO LOOK SO FEAR-FUL--
YOU ARE NOT IMPORTANT ENOUGH TO FEEL MY MIGHT
I HAVE NO WISH TO HARM YOU--- YET
BUT, I MUST SPARE MYSELF THE INDIGNITY OF YOUR LOATH-SOME CURIOSITY
THUS, WITH A CASUAL THOUGHT, I CHANGE MY IMAGE IN YOUR EYES
AND SO I WALK AMONG YOU, WHILE NONE SUSPECT---
-- THAT IT IS I WHO SOON SHALL CRUSH YOUR WORLD

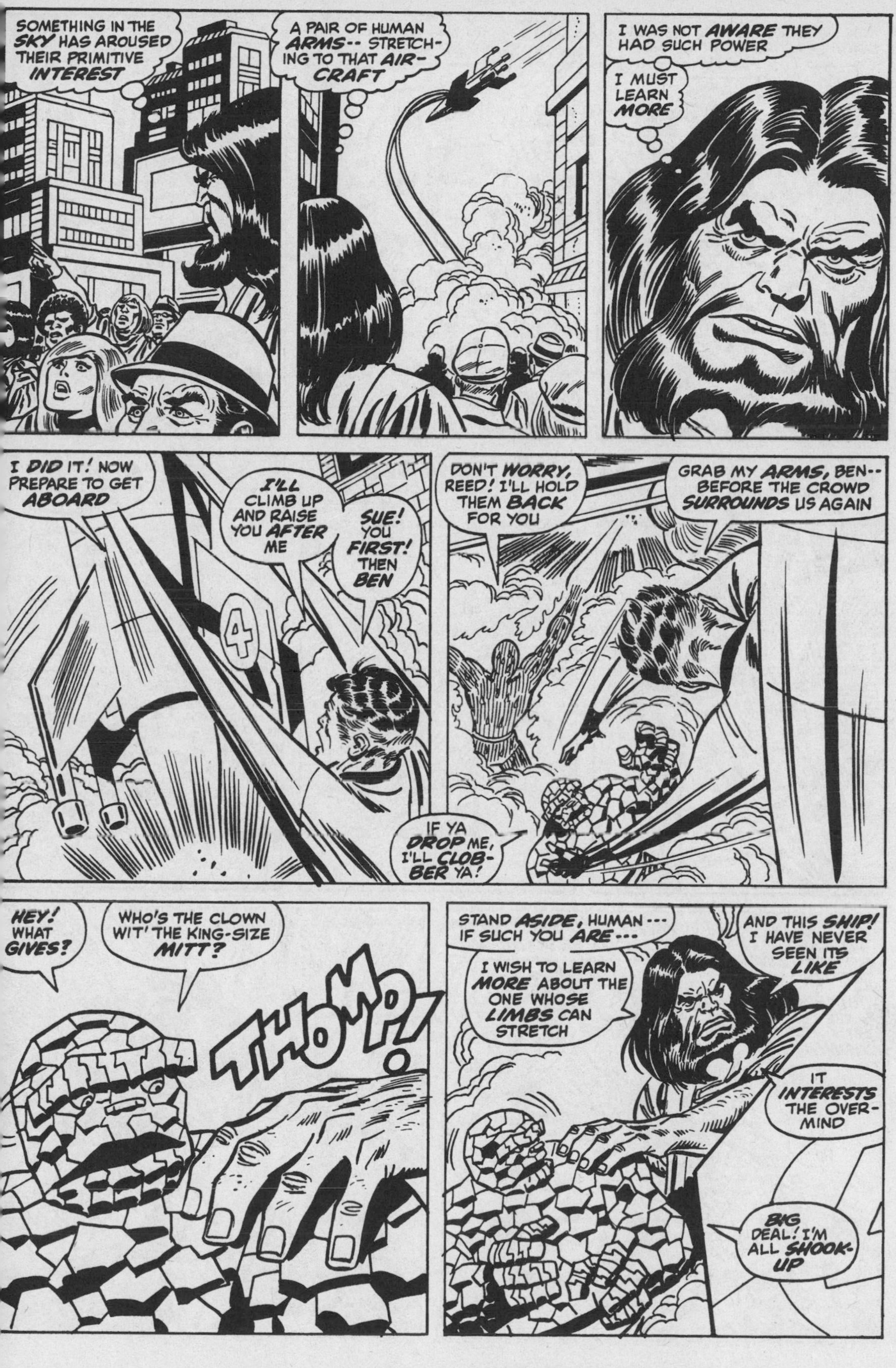
SOMETHING IN THE SKY HAS AROUSED THEIR PRIMITIVE INTEREST
A PAIR OF HUMAN ARMS-- STRETCHING TO THAT AIR-CRAFT
I WAS NOT AWARE THEY HAD SUCH POWER
I MUST LEARN MORE
I DID IT! NOW PREPARE TO GET ABOARD
I'LL CLIMB UP AND RAISE YOU AFTER ME
SUE! YOU FIRST! THEN BEN
DON'T WORRY, REED! I'LL HOLD THEM BACK FOR YOU
GRAB MY ARMS, BEN-- BEFORE THE CROWD SURROUNDS US AGAIN
IF YA DROP ME, I'LL CLOB-BER YA!
HEY! WHAT GIVES?
WHO'S THE CLOWN WIT' THE KING-SIZE MITT?
THOMP!
STAND ASIDE, HUMAN --- IF SUCH YOU ARE ---
I WISH TO LEARN MORE ABOUT THE ONE WHOSE LIMBS CAN STRETCH
AND THIS SHIP! I HAVE NEVER SEEN ITS LIKE
IT INTERESTS THE OVER-MIND
BIG DEAL! I'M ALL SHOOK-UP

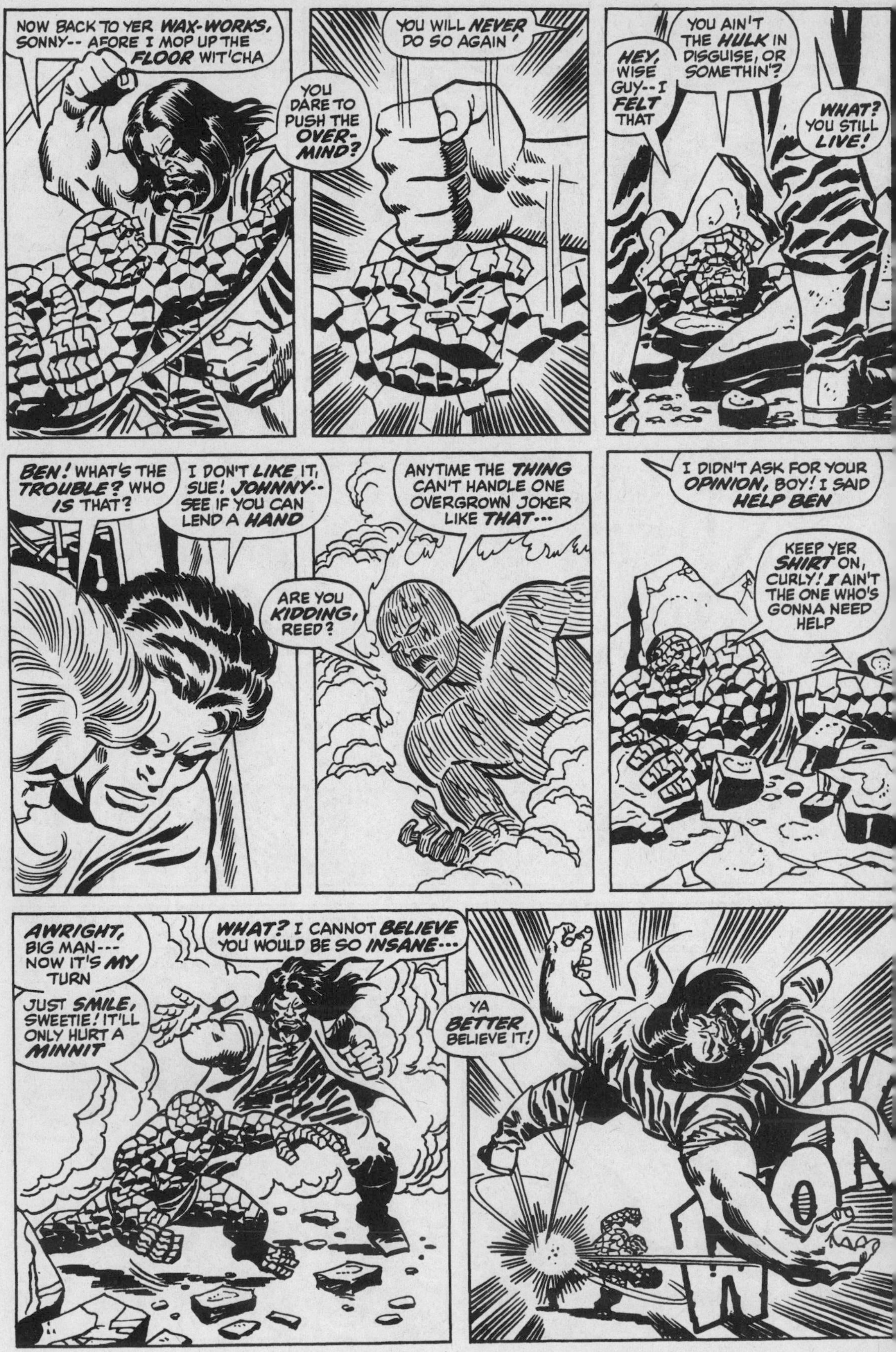
NOW BACK TO YER WAX-WORKS, SONNY-- AFORE I MOP UP THE FLOOR WIT'CHA
YOU DARE TO PUSH THE OVER-MIND?
YOU WILL NEVER DO SO AGAIN!
HEY, WISE GUY-- I FELT THAT
YOU AIN'T THE HULK IN DISGUISE, OR SOMETHIN'?
WHAT? YOU STILL LIVE!
BEN! WHAT'S THE TROUBLE? WHO IS THAT?
I DON'T LIKE IT, SUE! JOHNNY-- SEE IF YOU CAN LEND A HAND
ANYTIME THE THING CAN'T HANDLE ONE OVERGROWN JOKER LIKE THAT...
ARE YOU KIDDING, REED?
I DIDN'T ASK FOR YOUR OPINION, BOY! I SAID HELP BEN
KEEP YER SHIRT ON, CURLY! I AIN'T THE ONE WHO'S GONNA NEED HELP
AWRIGHT, BIG MAN--- NOW IT'S MY TURN
JUST SMILE, SWEETIE! IT'LL ONLY HURT A MINNIT
WHAT? I CANNOT BELIEVE YOU WOULD BE SO INSANE...
YA BETTER BELIEVE IT!

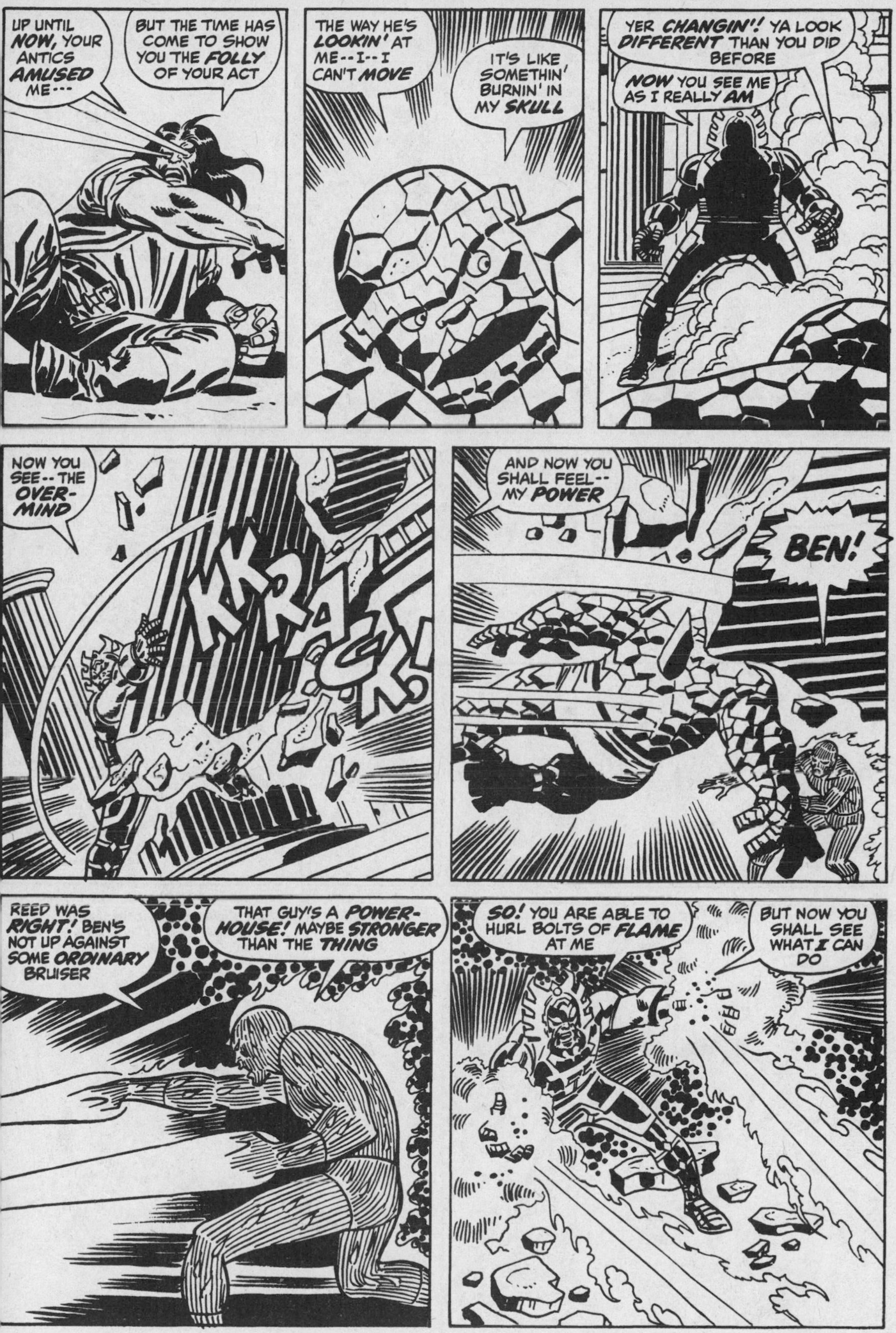

UP UNTIL NOW, YOUR ANTICS AMUSED ME---
BUT THE TIME HAS COME TO SHOW YOU THE FOLLY OF YOUR ACT
THE WAY HE'S LOOKIN' AT ME--I--I CAN'T MOVE
IT'S LIKE SOMETHIN' BURNIN' IN MY SKULL
YER CHANGIN'! YA LOOK DIFFERENT THAN YOU DID BEFORE
NOW YOU SEE ME AS I REALLY AM
NOW YOU SEE--THE OVER-MIND
KKRACK!
AND NOW YOU SHALL FEEL-- MY POWER
BEN!
REED WAS RIGHT! BEN'S NOT UP AGAINST SOME ORDINARY BRUISER
THAT GUY'S A POWER-HOUSE! MAYBE STRONGER THAN THE THING
SO! YOU ARE ABLE TO HURL BOLTS OF FLAME AT ME
BUT NOW YOU SHALL SEE WHAT I CAN DO

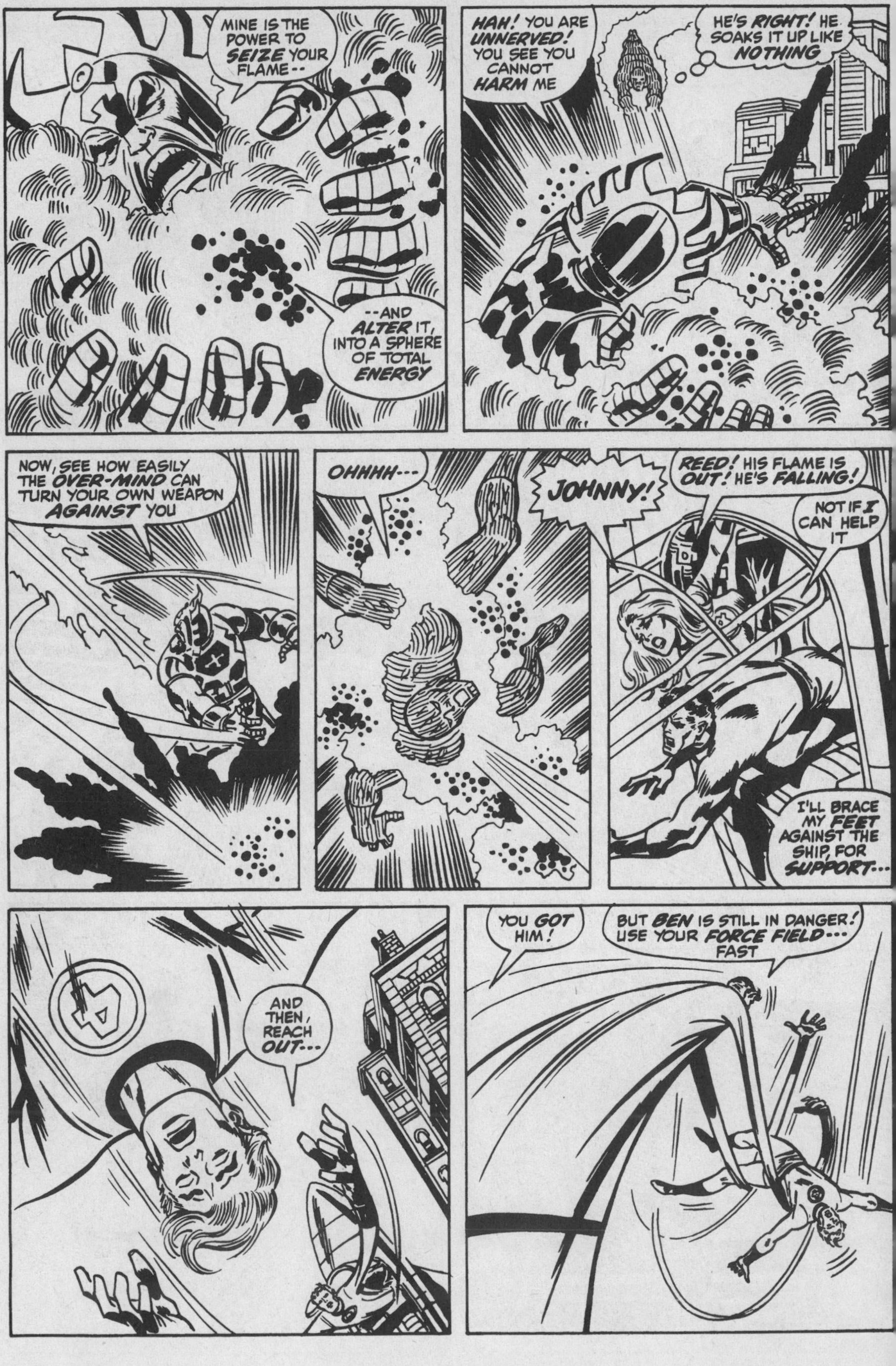
MINE IS THE POWER TO SEIZE YOUR FLAME--
--AND ALTER IT, INTO A SPHERE OF TOTAL ENERGY
HAH! YOU ARE UNNERVED! YOU SEE YOU CANNOT HARM ME
HE'S RIGHT! HE SOAKS IT UP LIKE NOTHING
NOW, SEE HOW EASILY THE OVER-MIND CAN TURN YOUR OWN WEAPON AGAINST YOU
OHHHH---
JOHNNY!
REED! HIS FLAME IS OUT! HE'S FALLING!
NOT IF I CAN HELP IT
I'LL BRACE MY FEET AGAINST THE SHIP, FOR SUPPORT...
AND THEN, REACH OUT...
YOU GOT HIM!
BUT BEN IS STILL IN DANGER! USE YOUR FORCE FIELD--- FAST

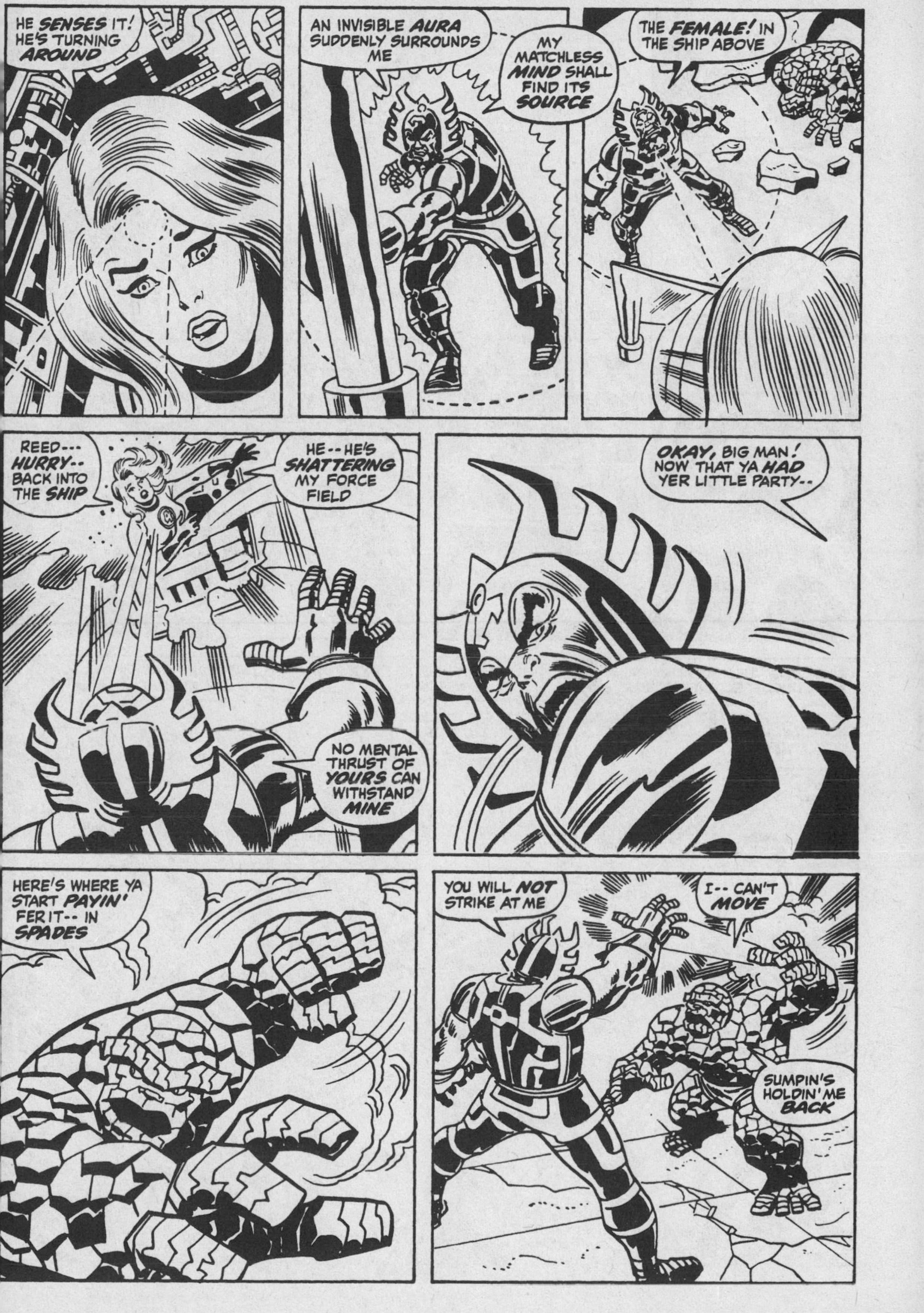
HE SENSES IT! HE'S TURNING AROUND
AN INVISIBLE AURA SUDDENLY SURROUNDS ME
MY MATCHLESS MIND SHALL FIND ITS SOURCE
THE FEMALE! IN THE SHIP ABOVE
REED--- HURRY-- BACK INTO THE SHIP
HE--HE'S SHATTERING MY FORCE FIELD
NO MENTAL THRUST OF YOURS CAN WITHSTAND MINE
OKAY, BIG MAN! NOW THAT YA HAD YER LITTLE PARTY--
HERE'S WHERE YA START PAYIN' FER IT-- IN SPADES
YOU WILL NOT STRIKE AT ME
I-- CAN'T MOVE
SUMPIN'S HOLDIN' ME BACK

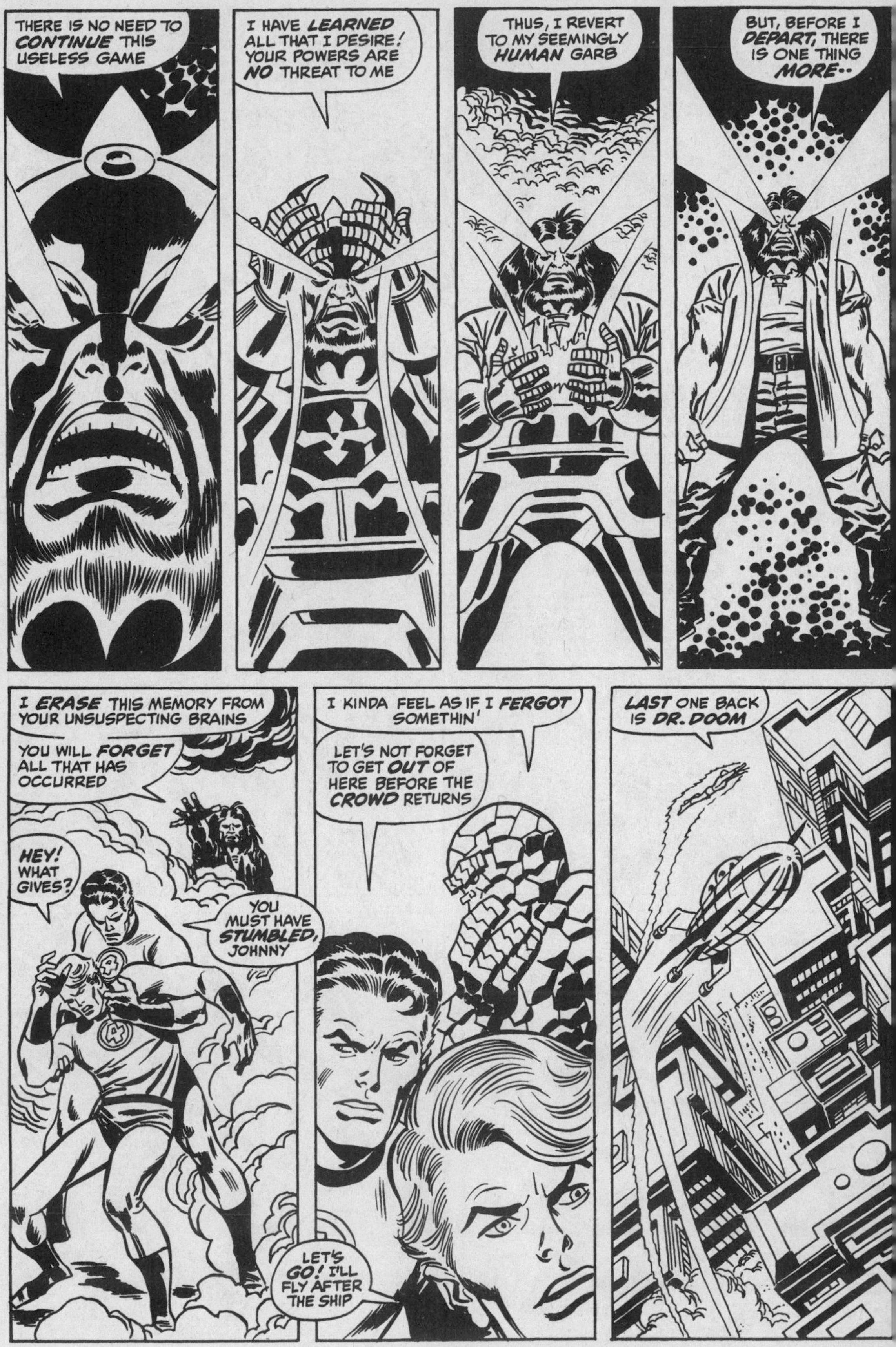

THERE IS NO NEED TO CONTINUE THIS USELESS GAME
I HAVE LEARNED ALL THAT I DESIRE! YOUR POWERS ARE NO THREAT TO ME
THUS, I REVERT TO MY SEEMINGLY HUMAN GARB
BUT, BEFORE I DEPART, THERE IS ONE THING MORE--
I ERASE THIS MEMORY FROM YOUR UNSUSPECTING BRAINS
YOU WILL FORGET ALL THAT HAS OCCURRED
HEY! WHAT GIVES?
YOU MUST HAVE STUMBLED, JOHNNY
I KINDA FEEL AS IF I FERGOT SOMETHIN'
LET'S NOT FORGET TO GET OUT OF HERE BEFORE THE CROWD RETURNS
LET'S GO! I'LL FLY AFTER THE SHIP
LAST ONE BACK IS DR. DOOM

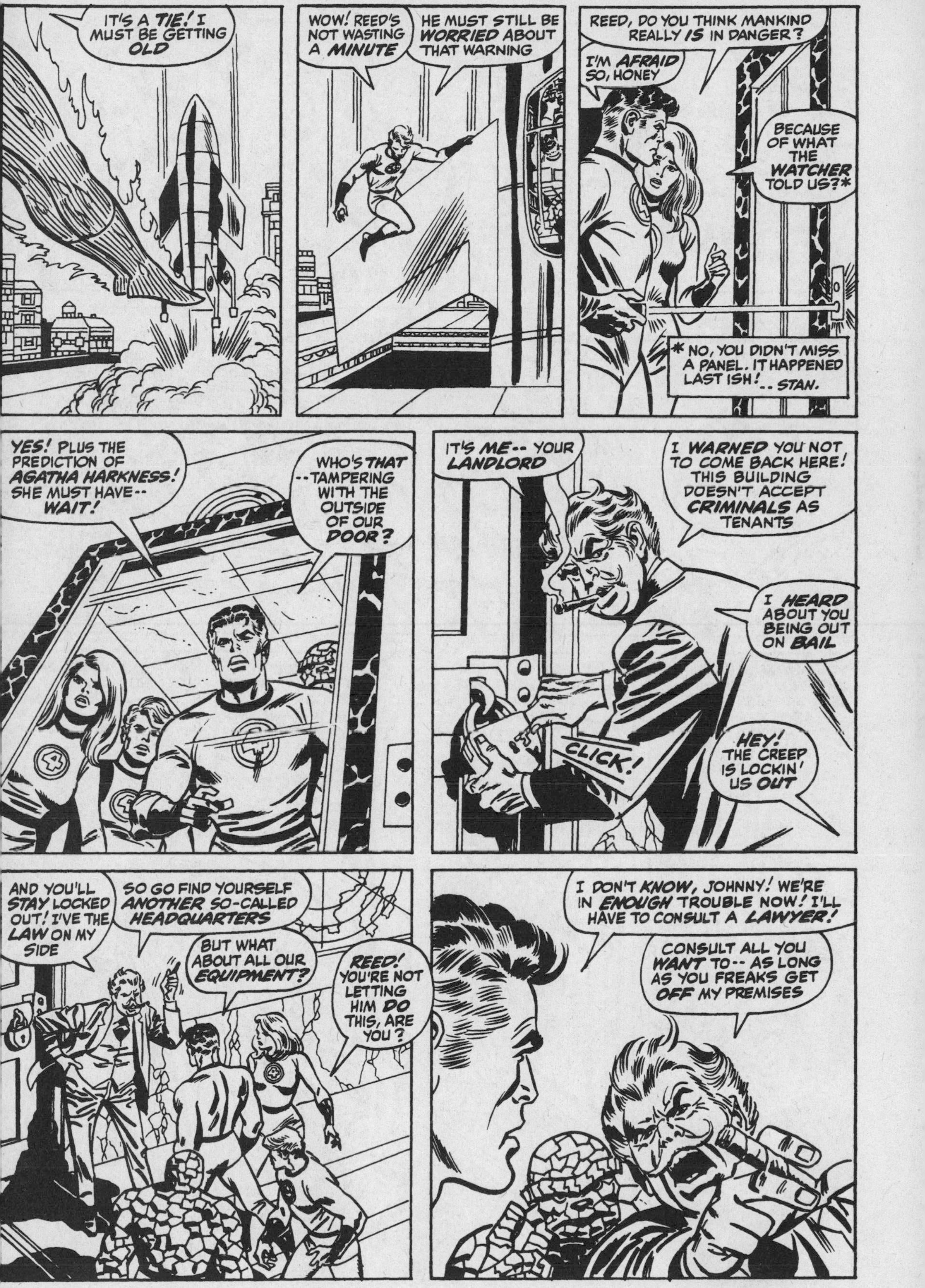
IT'S A TIE! I MUST BE GETTING OLD
WOW! REED'S NOT WASTING A MINUTE
HE MUST STILL BE WORRIED ABOUT THAT WARNING
REED, DO YOU THINK MANKIND REALLY IS IN DANGER?
I'M AFRAID SO, HONEY
BECAUSE OF WHAT THE WATCHER TOLD US?*
* NO, YOU DIDN'T MISS A PANEL. IT HAPPENED LAST ISH! -- STAN.
YES! PLUS THE PREDICTION OF AGATHA HARKNESS! SHE MUST HAVE-- WAIT!
WHO'S THAT --TAMPERING WITH THE OUTSIDE OF OUR DOOR?
IT'S ME-- YOUR LANDLORD
I WARNED YOU NOT TO COME BACK HERE! THIS BUILDING DOESN'T ACCEPT CRIMINALS AS TENANTS
I HEARD ABOUT YOU BEING OUT ON BAIL
CLICK!
HEY! THE CREEP IS LOCKIN' US OUT
AND YOU'LL STAY LOCKED OUT! I'VE THE LAW ON MY SIDE
SO GO FIND YOURSELF ANOTHER SO-CALLED HEADQUARTERS
BUT WHAT ABOUT ALL OUR EQUIPMENT?
REED! YOU'RE NOT LETTING HIM DO THIS, ARE YOU?
I DON'T KNOW, JOHNNY! WE'RE IN ENOUGH TROUBLE NOW! I'LL HAVE TO CONSULT A LAWYER!
CONSULT ALL YOU WANT TO-- AS LONG AS YOU FREAKS GET OFF MY PREMISES

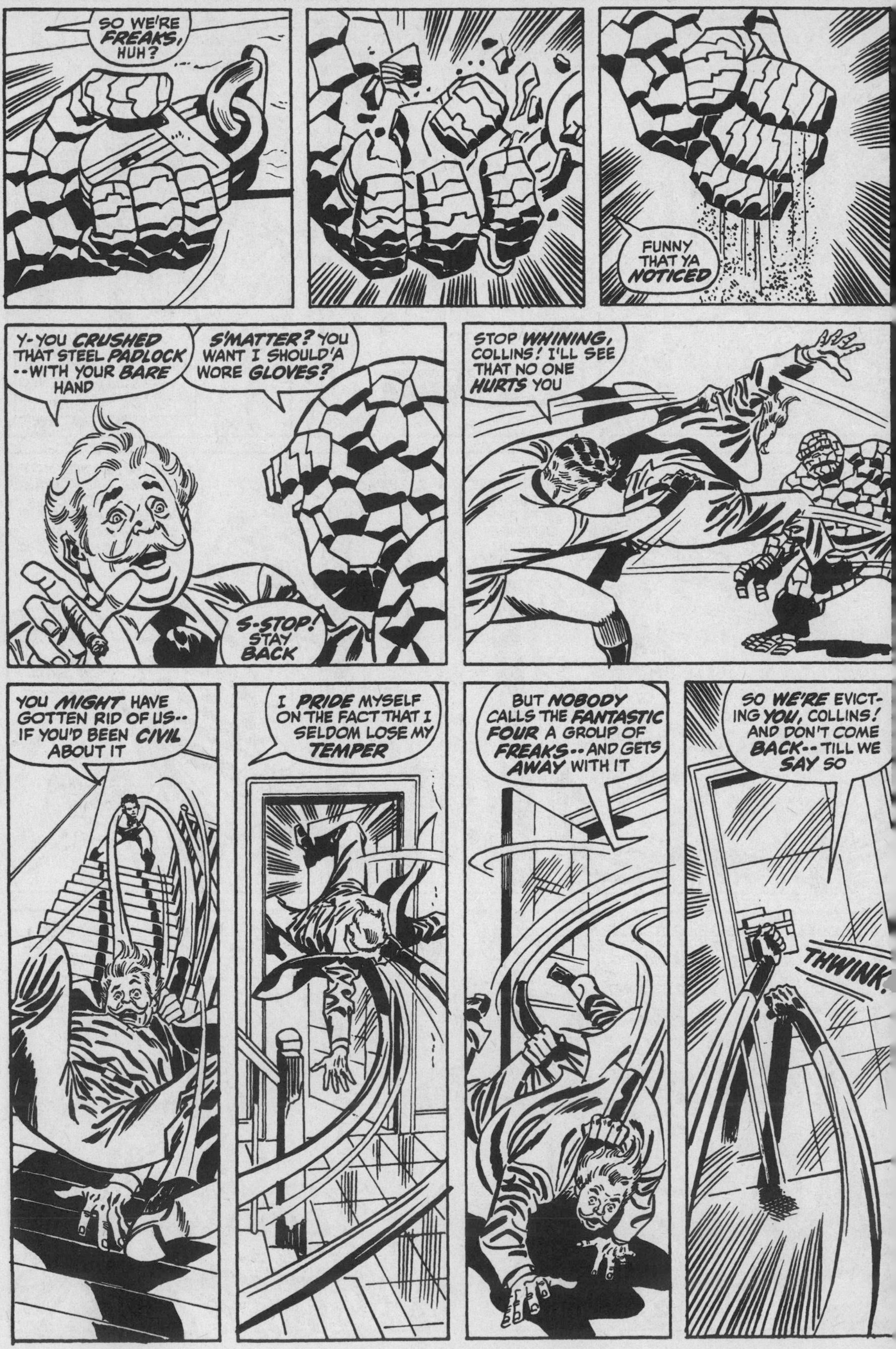
SO WE'RE FREAKS, HUH?
FUNNY THAT YA NOTICED
Y-YOU CRUSHED THAT STEEL PADLOCK --WITH YOUR BARE HAND
S'MATTER? YOU WANT I SHOULD'A WORE GLOVES?
S-STOP! STAY BACK
STOP WHINING, COLLINS! I'LL SEE THAT NO ONE HURTS YOU
YOU MIGHT HAVE GOTTEN RID OF US-- IF YOU'D BEEN CIVIL ABOUT IT
I PRIDE MYSELF ON THE FACT THAT I SELDOM LOSE MY TEMPER
BUT NOBODY CALLS THE FANTASTIC FOUR A GROUP OF FREAKS-- AND GETS AWAY WITH IT
SO WE'RE EVICTING YOU, COLLINS! AND DON'T COME BACK-- TILL WE SAY SO
THWINK!

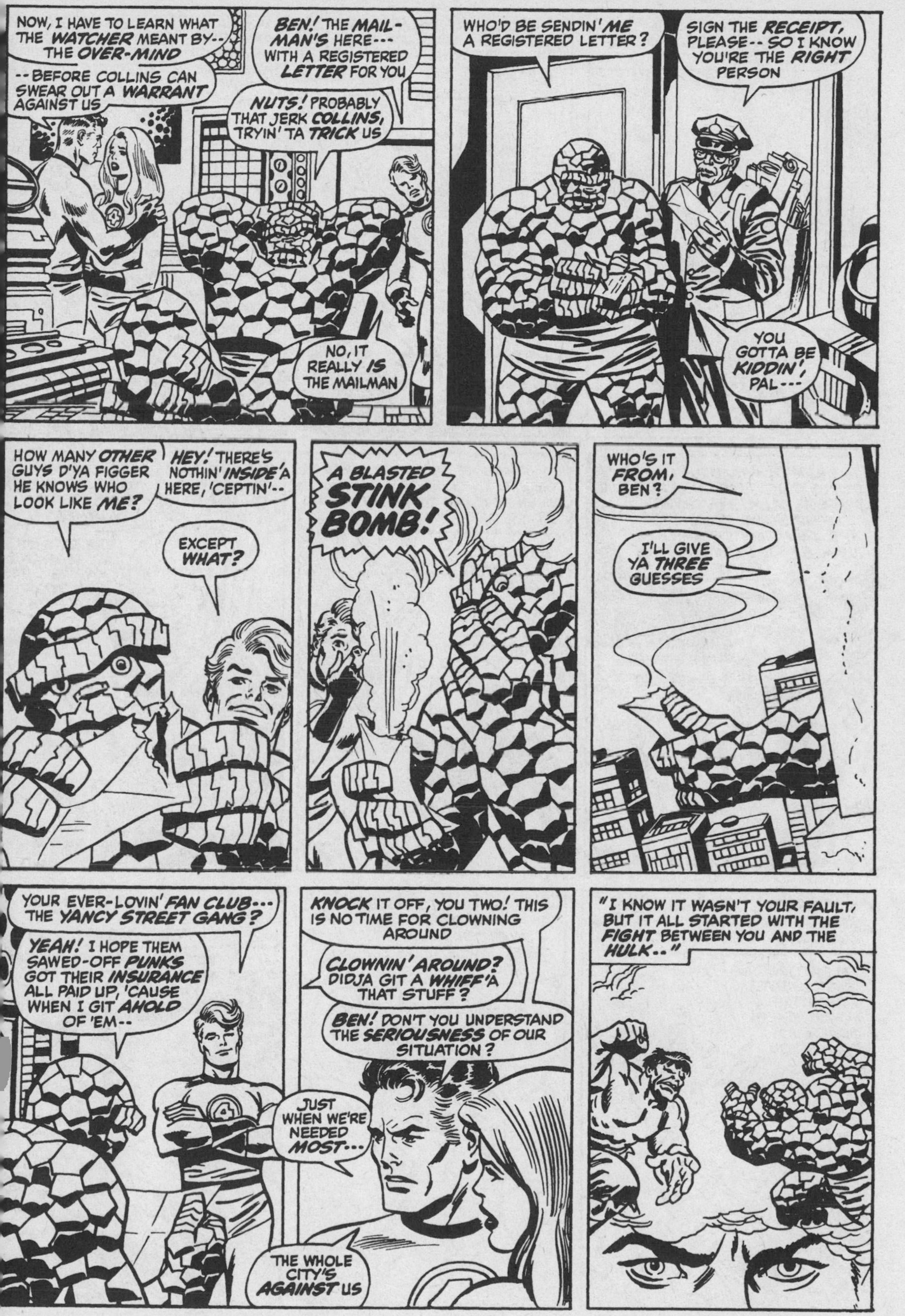
NOW, I HAVE TO LEARN WHAT THE WATCHER MEANT BY-- THE OVER-MIND
--BEFORE COLLINS CAN SWEAR OUT A WARRANT AGAINST US
BEN! THE MAIL-MAN'S HERE--- WITH A REGISTERED LETTER FOR YOU
NUTS! PROBABLY THAT JERK COLLINS, TRYIN' TA TRICK US
NO, IT REALLY IS THE MAILMAN
WHO'D BE SENDIN' ME A REGISTERED LETTER?
SIGN THE RECEIPT, PLEASE-- SO I KNOW YOU'RE THE RIGHT PERSON
YOU GOTTA BE KIDDIN', PAL---
HOW MANY OTHER GUYS D'YA FIGGER HE KNOWS WHO LOOK LIKE ME?
HEY! THERE'S NOTHIN' INSIDE 'A HERE, 'CEPTIN'--
EXCEPT WHAT?
A BLASTED STINK BOMB!
WHO'S IT FROM, BEN?
I'LL GIVE YA THREE GUESSES
YOUR EVER-LOVIN' FAN CLUB... THE YANCY STREET GANG?
YEAH! I HOPE THEM SAWED-OFF PUNKS GOT THEIR INSURANCE ALL PAID UP, 'CAUSE WHEN I GIT AHOLD OF 'EM--
KNOCK IT OFF, YOU TWO! THIS IS NO TIME FOR CLOWNING AROUND
CLOWNIN' AROUND? DIDJA GIT A WHIFF 'A THAT STUFF?
BEN! DON'T YOU UNDERSTAND THE SERIOUSNESS OF OUR SITUATION?
JUST WHEN WE'RE NEEDED MOST...
THE WHOLE CITY'S AGAINST US
"I KNOW IT WASN'T YOUR FAULT, BUT IT ALL STARTED WITH THE FIGHT BETWEEN YOU AND THE HULK.."

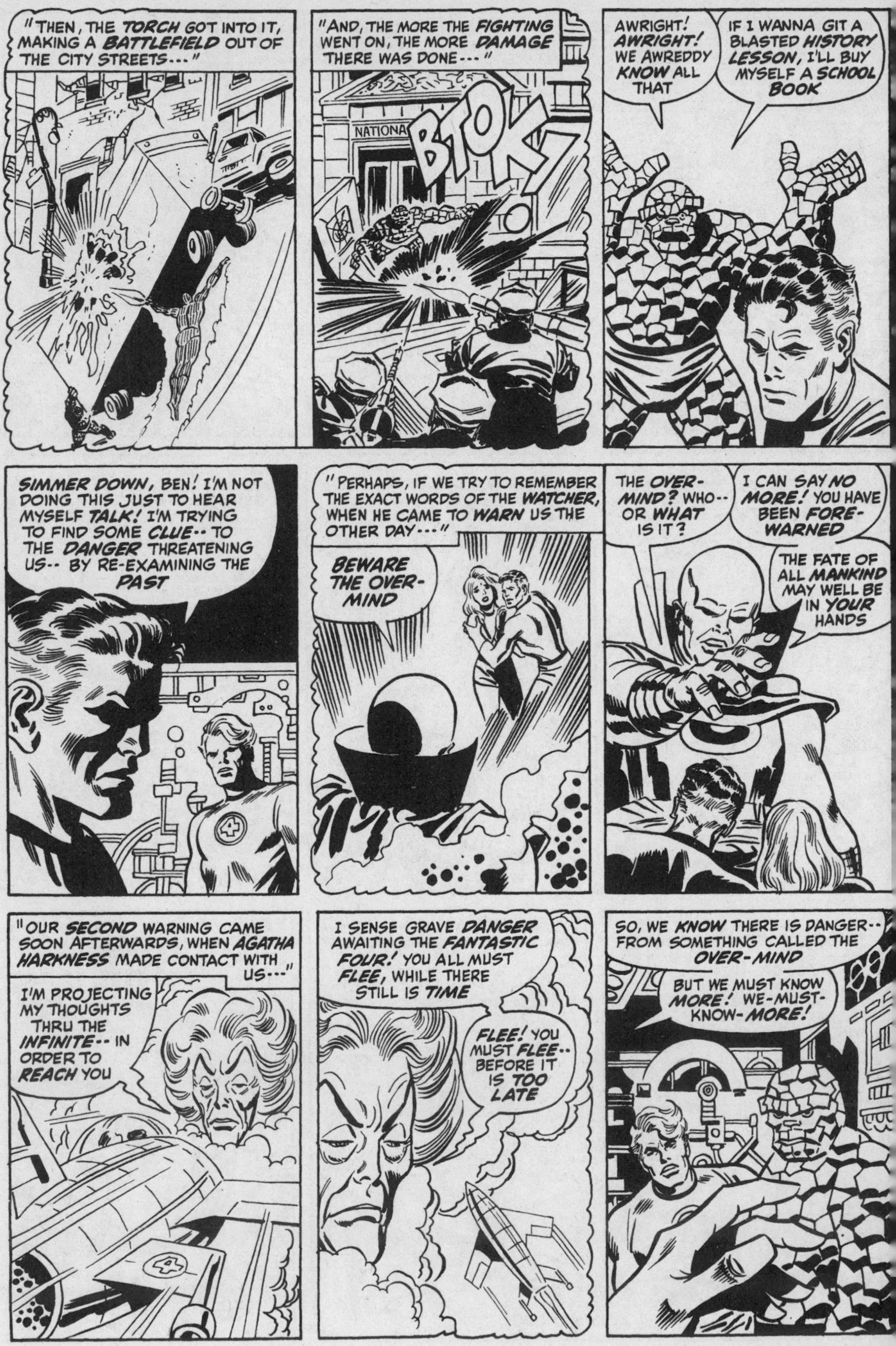
"THEN, THE TORCH GOT INTO IT, MAKING A BATTLEFIELD OUT OF THE CITY STREETS..."
"AND, THE MORE THE FIGHTING WENT ON, THE MORE DAMAGE THERE WAS DONE..."
NATIONA
BTOK
AWRIGHT! AWRIGHT! WE AWREDDY KNOW ALL THAT
IF I WANNA GIT A BLASTED HISTORY LESSON, I'LL BUY MYSELF A SCHOOL BOOK
SIMMER DOWN, BEN! I'M NOT DOING THIS JUST TO HEAR MYSELF TALK! I'M TRYING TO FIND SOME CLUE-- TO THE DANGER THREATENING US-- BY RE-EXAMINING THE PAST
"PERHAPS, IF WE TRY TO REMEMBER THE EXACT WORDS OF THE WATCHER, WHEN HE CAME TO WARN US THE OTHER DAY..."
BEWARE THE OVER-MIND
THE OVER-MIND? WHO-- OR WHAT IS IT?
I CAN SAY NO MORE! YOU HAVE BEEN FORE-WARNED
THE FATE OF ALL MANKIND MAY WELL BE IN YOUR HANDS
"OUR SECOND WARNING CAME SOON AFTERWARDS, WHEN AGATHA HARKNESS MADE CONTACT WITH US..."
I'M PROJECTING MY THOUGHTS THRU THE INFINITE-- IN ORDER TO REACH YOU
I SENSE GRAVE DANGER AWAITING THE FANTASTIC FOUR! YOU ALL MUST FLEE, WHILE THERE STILL IS TIME
FLEE! YOU MUST FLEE-- BEFORE IT IS TOO LATE
SO, WE KNOW THERE IS DANGER-- FROM SOMETHING CALLED THE OVER-MIND
BUT WE MUST KNOW MORE! WE-MUST-KNOW-MORE!

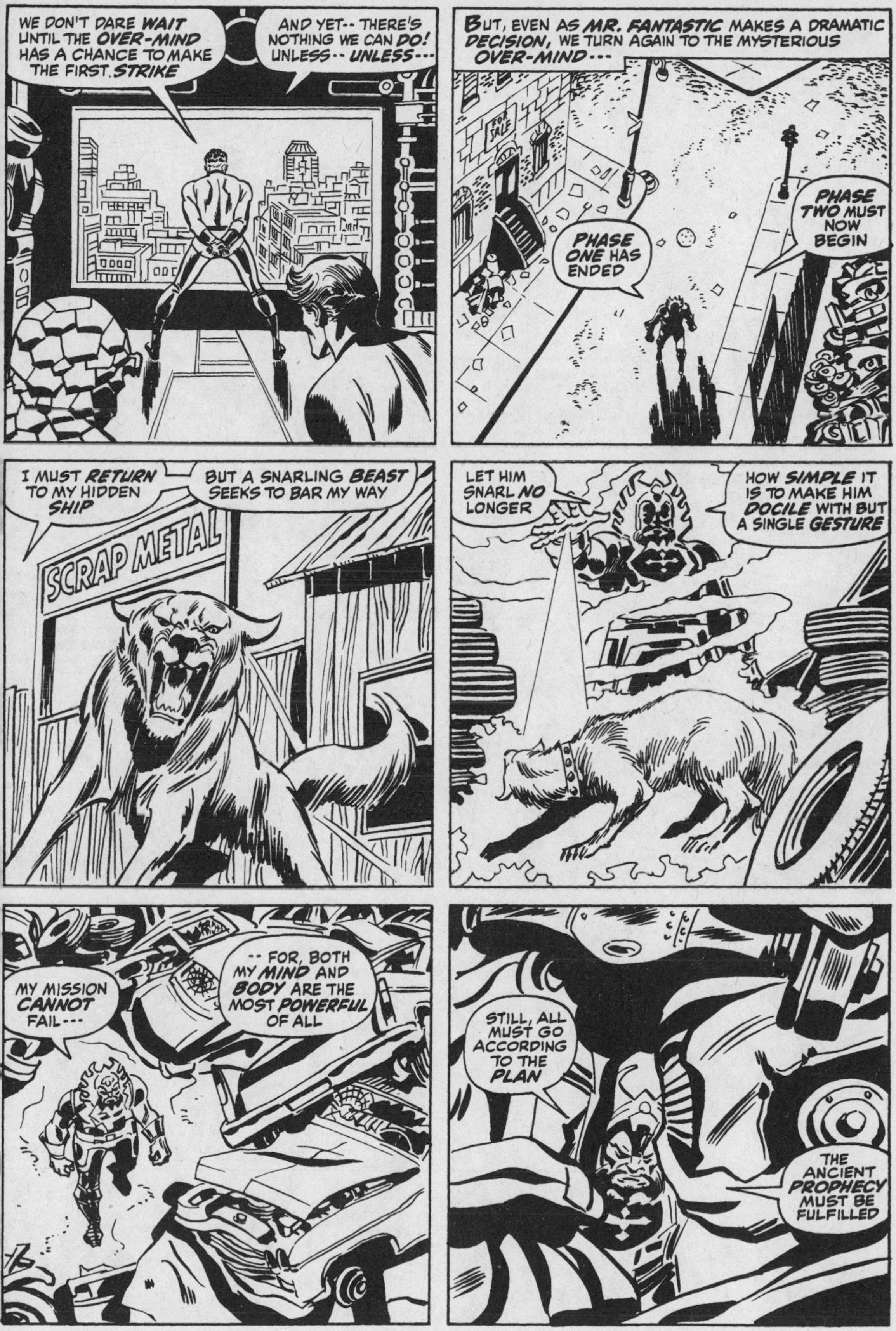
WE DON'T DARE WAIT UNTIL THE OVER-MIND HAS A CHANCE TO MAKE THE FIRST STRIKE
AND YET-- THERE'S NOTHING WE CAN DO! UNLESS-- UNLESS---
BUT, EVEN AS MR. FANTASTIC MAKES A DRAMATIC DECISION, WE TURN AGAIN TO THE MYSTERIOUS OVER-MIND---
FOR SALE
PHASE ONE HAS ENDED
PHASE TWO MUST NOW BEGIN
I MUST RETURN TO MY HIDDEN SHIP
BUT A SNARLING BEAST SEEKS TO BAR MY WAY
SCRAP METAL
LET HIM SNARL NO LONGER
HOW SIMPLE IT IS TO MAKE HIM DOCILE WITH BUT A SINGLE GESTURE
MY MISSION CANNOT FAIL---
-- FOR, BOTH MY MIND AND BODY ARE THE MOST POWERFUL OF ALL
STILL, ALL MUST GO ACCORDING TO THE PLAN
THE ANCIENT PROPHECY MUST BE FULFILLED

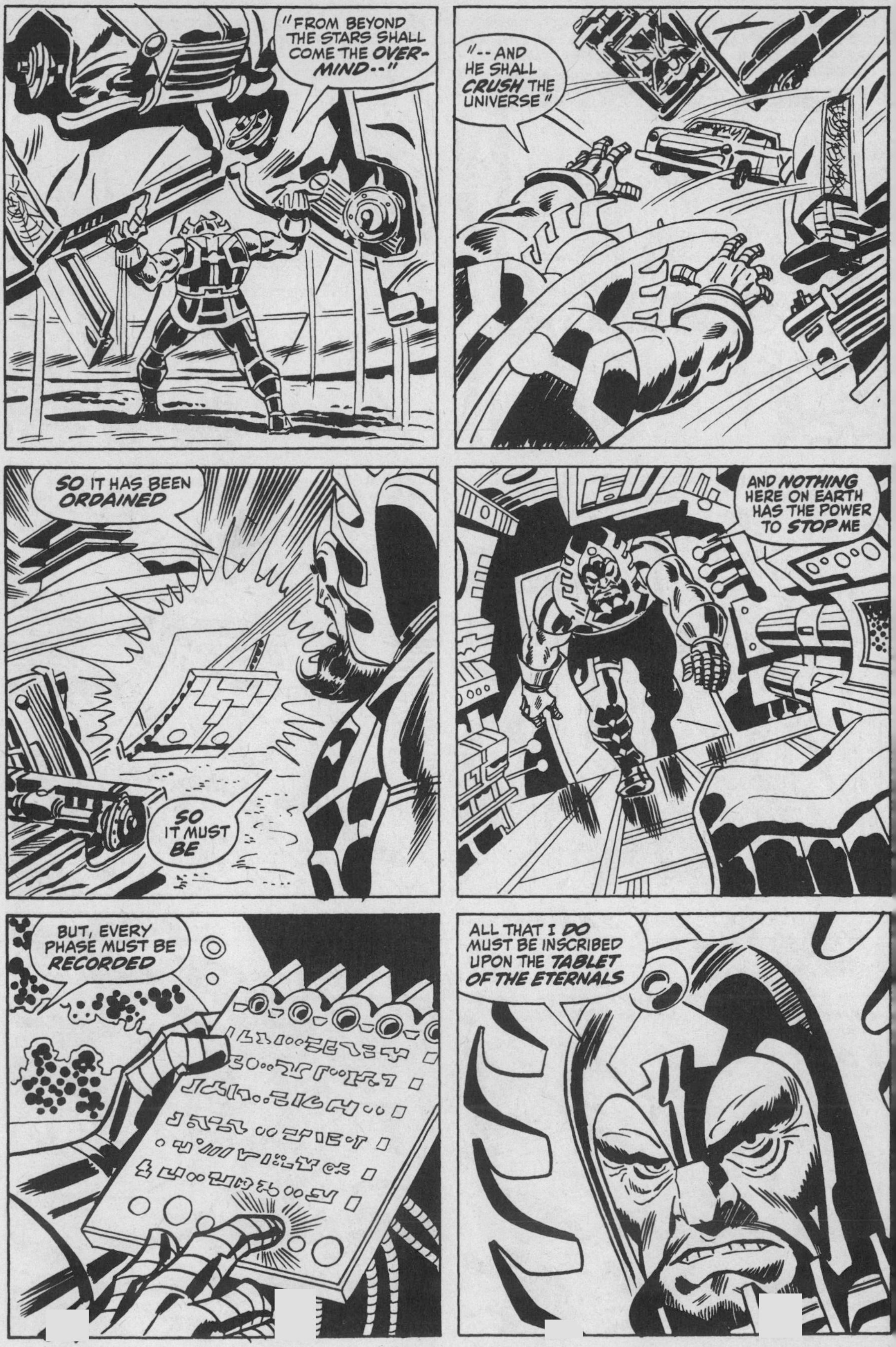
"FROM BEYOND THE STARS SHALL COME THE OVER-MIND--"
"--AND HE SHALL CRUSH THE UNIVERSE"
SO IT HAS BEEN ORDAINED
SO IT MUST BE
AND NOTHING HERE ON EARTH HAS THE POWER TO STOP ME
BUT, EVERY PHASE MUST BE RECORDED
ALL THAT I DO MUST BE INSCRIBED UPON THE TABLET OF THE ETERNALS

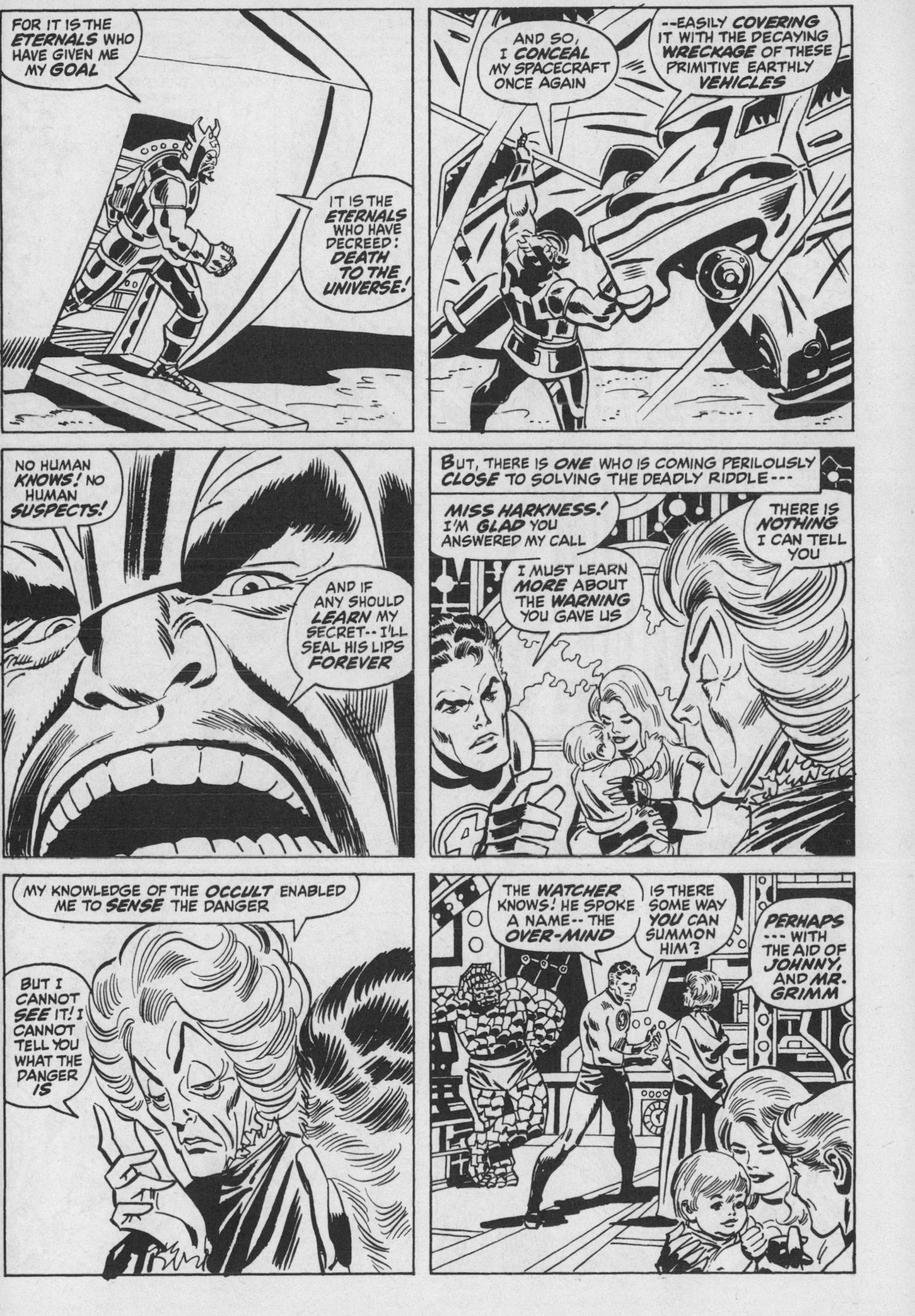
FOR IT IS THE ETERNALS WHO HAVE GIVEN ME MY GOAL
IT IS THE ETERNALS WHO HAVE DECREED: DEATH TO THE UNIVERSE!
AND SO, I CONCEAL MY SPACECRAFT ONCE AGAIN
--EASILY COVERING IT WITH THE DECAYING WRECKAGE OF THESE PRIMITIVE EARTHLY VEHICLES
NO HUMAN KNOWS! NO HUMAN SUSPECTS!
AND IF ANY SHOULD LEARN MY SECRET-- I'LL SEAL HIS LIPS FOREVER
BUT, THERE IS ONE WHO IS COMING PERILOUSLY CLOSE TO SOLVING THE DEADLY RIDDLE---
MISS HARKNESS! I'M GLAD YOU ANSWERED MY CALL
I MUST LEARN MORE ABOUT THE WARNING YOU GAVE US
THERE IS NOTHING I CAN TELL YOU
MY KNOWLEDGE OF THE OCCULT ENABLED ME TO SENSE THE DANGER
BUT I CANNOT SEE IT! I CANNOT TELL YOU WHAT THE DANGER IS
THE WATCHER KNOWS! HE SPOKE A NAME-- THE OVER-MIND
IS THERE SOME WAY YOU CAN SUMMON HIM?
PERHAPS --- WITH THE AID OF JOHNNY, AND MR. GRIMM

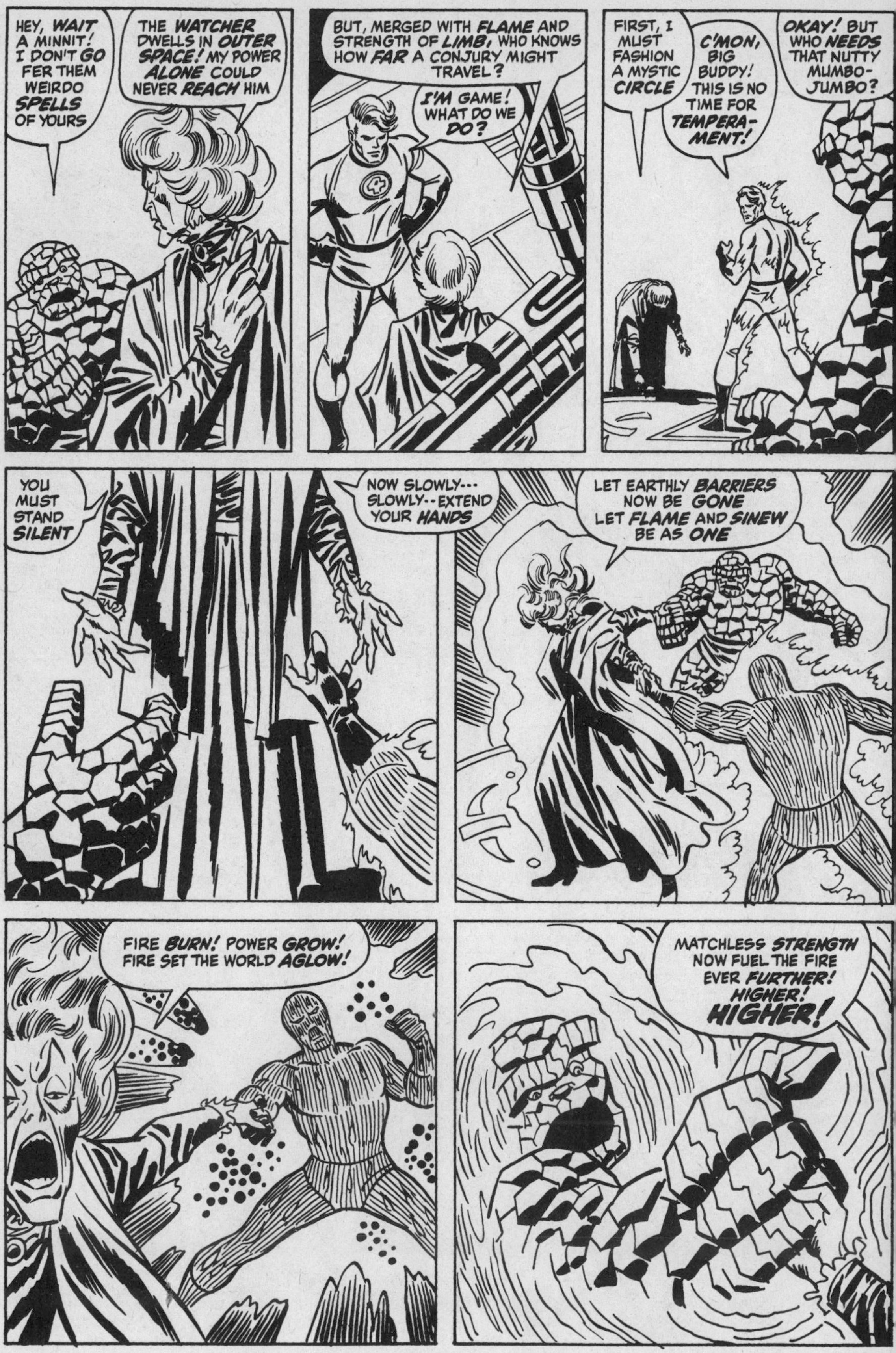
HEY, WAIT A MINNIT! I DON'T GO FER THEM WEIRDO SPELLS OF YOURS
THE WATCHER DWELLS IN OUTER SPACE! MY POWER ALONE COULD NEVER REACH HIM
BUT, MERGED WITH FLAME AND STRENGTH OF LIMB, WHO KNOWS HOW FAR A CONJURY MIGHT TRAVEL?
I'M GAME! WHAT DO WE DO?
FIRST, I MUST FASHION A MYSTIC CIRCLE
C'MON, BIG BUDDY! THIS IS NO TIME FOR TEMPERA-MENT!
OKAY! BUT WHO NEEDS THAT NUTTY MUMBO-JUMBO?
YOU MUST STAND SILENT
NOW SLOWLY--- SLOWLY--EXTEND YOUR HANDS
LET EARTHLY BARRIERS NOW BE GONE
LET FLAME AND SINEW BE AS ONE
FIRE BURN! POWER GROW! FIRE SET THE WORLD AGLOW!
MATCHLESS STRENGTH NOW FUEL THE FIRE EVER FURTHER! HIGHER! HIGHER!

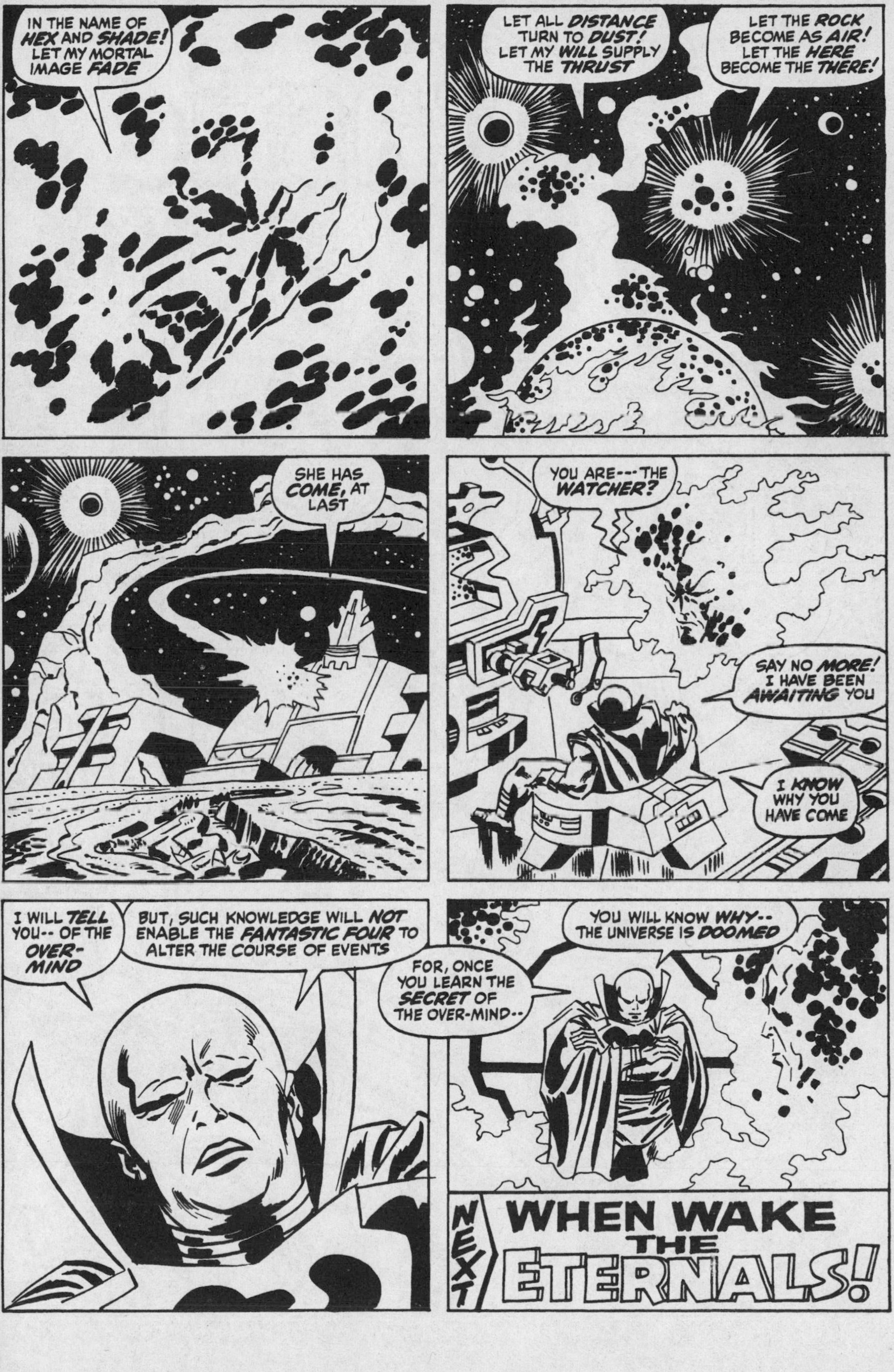

IN THE NAME OF HEX AND SHADE! LET MY MORTAL IMAGE FADE
LET ALL DISTANCE TURN TO DUST! LET MY WILL SUPPLY THE THRUST
LET THE ROCK BECOME AS AIR! LET THE HERE BECOME THE THERE!
SHE HAS COME, AT LAST
YOU ARE---THE WATCHER?
SAY NO MORE! I HAVE BEEN AWAITING YOU
I KNOW WHY YOU HAVE COME
I WILL TELL YOU-- OF THE OVER-MIND
BUT, SUCH KNOWLEDGE WILL NOT ENABLE THE FANTASTIC FOUR TO ALTER THE COURSE OF EVENTS
FOR, ONCE YOU LEARN THE SECRET OF THE OVER-MIND..
YOU WILL KNOW WHY-- THE UNIVERSE IS DOOMED
NEXT
WHEN WAKE THE ETERNALS!

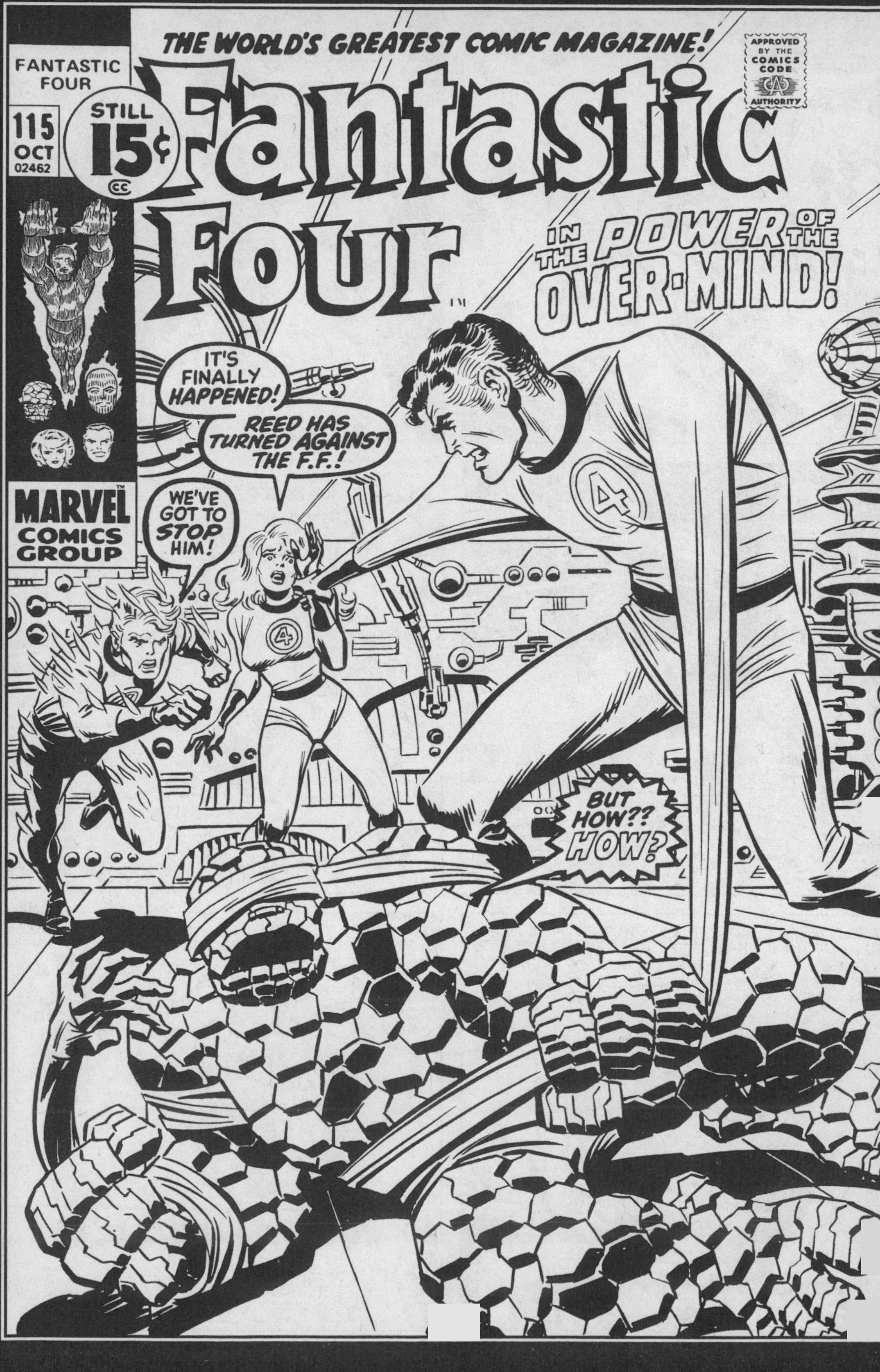
THE WORLD'S GREATEST COMIC MAGAZINE!
FANTASTIC FOUR
115
OCT
02462
STILL 15¢
APPROVED BY THE COMICS CODE AUTHORITY
Fantastic Four
IN THE POWER OF THE OVER-MIND!
MARVEL COMICS GROUP
IT'S FINALLY HAPPENED!
REED HAS TURNED AGAINST THE F.F.!
WE'VE GOT TO STOP HIM!
BUT HOW?? HOW?

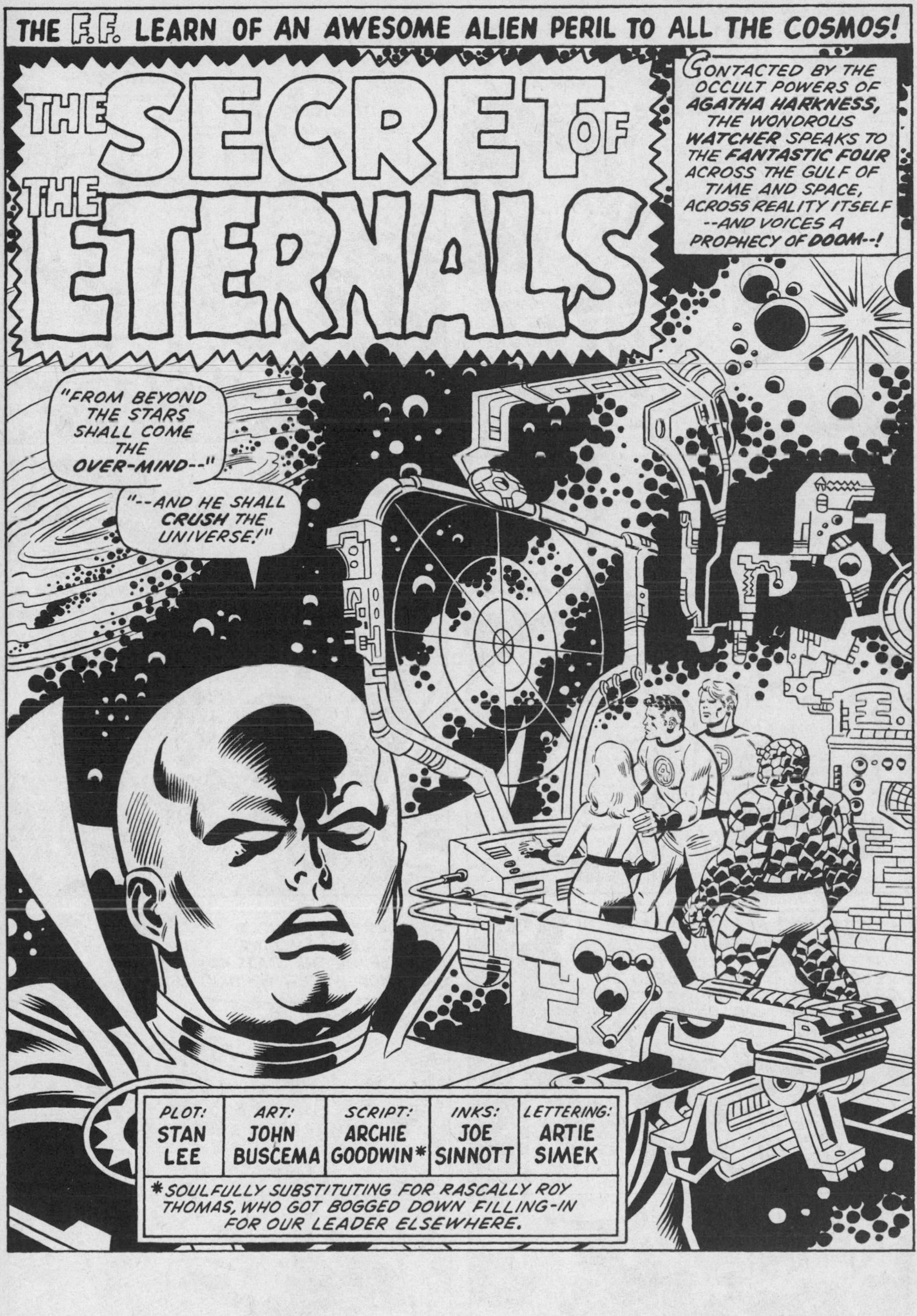
THE F.F. LEARN OF AN AWESOME ALIEN PERIL TO ALL THE COSMOS!
THE SECRET OF THE ETERNALS
CONTACTED BY THE OCCULT POWERS OF AGATHA HARKNESS, THE WONDROUS WATCHER SPEAKS TO THE FANTASTIC FOUR ACROSS THE GULF OF TIME AND SPACE, ACROSS REALITY ITSELF --AND VOICES A PROPHECY OF DOOM--!
"FROM BEYOND THE STARS SHALL COME THE OVER-MIND--"
"--AND HE SHALL CRUSH THE UNIVERSE!"
PLOT: STAN LEE
ART: JOHN BUSCEMA
SCRIPT: ARCHIE GOODWIN*
INKS: JOE SINNOTT
LETTERING: ARTIE SIMEK
*SOULFULLY SUBSTITUTING FOR RASCALLY ROY THOMAS, WHO GOT BOGGED DOWN FILLING-IN FOR OUR LEADER ELSEWHERE.

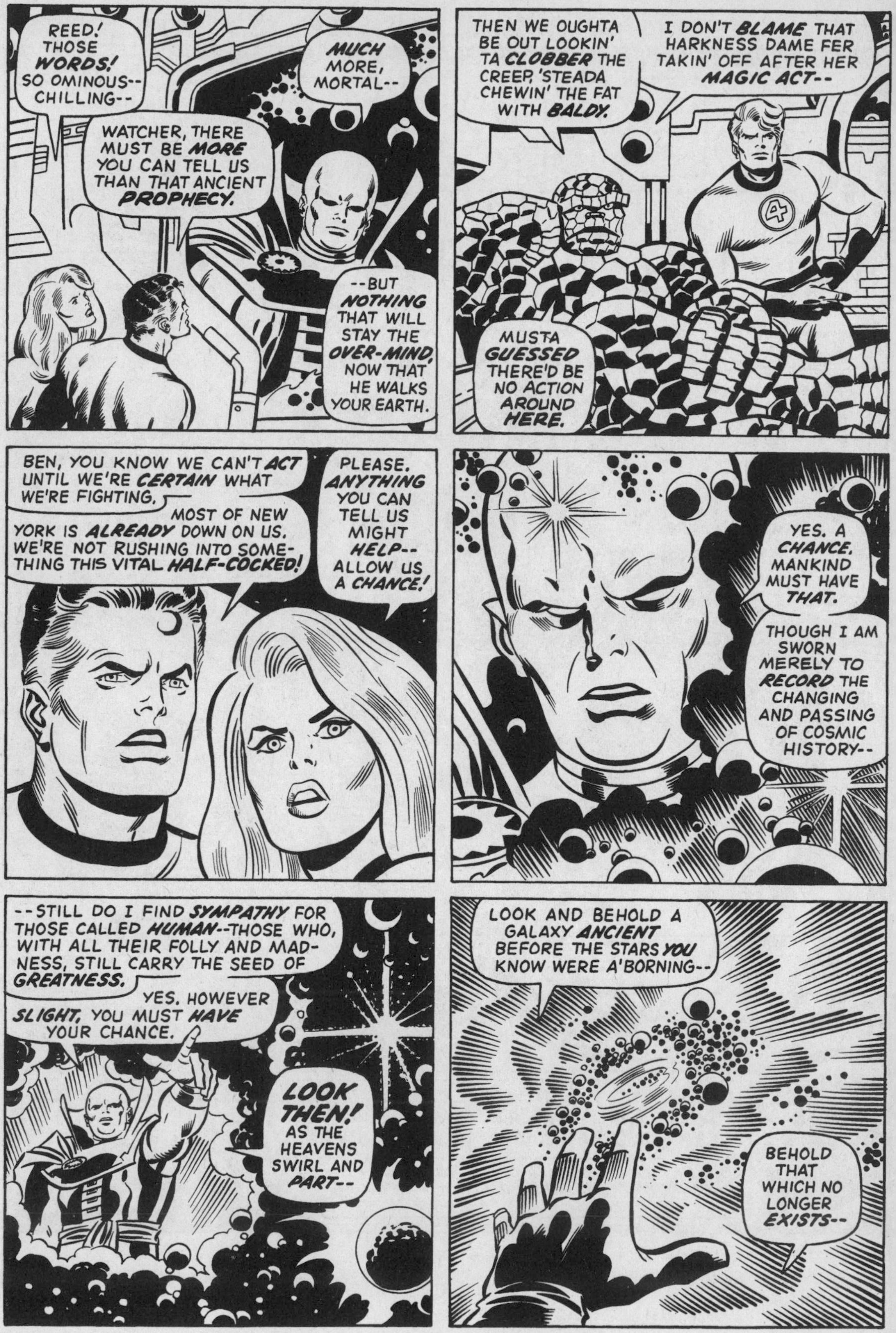
REED! THOSE WORDS! SO OMINOUS-- CHILLING--
WATCHER, THERE MUST BE MORE YOU CAN TELL US THAN THAT ANCIENT PROPHECY.
MUCH MORE, MORTAL--
--BUT NOTHING THAT WILL STAY THE OVER-MIND, NOW THAT HE WALKS YOUR EARTH.
I DON'T BLAME THAT HARKNESS DAME FER TAKIN' OFF AFTER HER MAGIC ACT--
THEN WE OUGHTA BE OUT LOOKIN' TA CLOBBER THE CREEP, 'STEADA CHEWIN' THE FAT WITH BALDY.
MUSTA GUESSED THERE'D BE NO ACTION AROUND HERE.
BEN, YOU KNOW WE CAN'T ACT UNTIL WE'RE CERTAIN WHAT WE'RE FIGHTING.
MOST OF NEW YORK IS ALREADY DOWN ON US. WE'RE NOT RUSHING INTO SOMETHING THIS VITAL HALF-COCKED!
PLEASE. ANYTHING YOU CAN TELL US MIGHT HELP-- ALLOW US A CHANCE!
YES. A CHANCE. MANKIND MUST HAVE THAT.
THOUGH I AM SWORN MERELY TO RECORD THE CHANGING AND PASSING OF COSMIC HISTORY--
--STILL DO I FIND SYMPATHY FOR THOSE CALLED HUMAN--THOSE WHO, WITH ALL THEIR FOLLY AND MADNESS, STILL CARRY THE SEED OF GREATNESS.
YES. HOWEVER SLIGHT, YOU MUST HAVE YOUR CHANCE.
LOOK THEN! AS THE HEAVENS SWIRL AND PART--
LOOK AND BEHOLD A GALAXY ANCIENT BEFORE THE STARS YOU KNOW WERE A'BORNING--
BEHOLD THAT WHICH NO LONGER EXISTS--

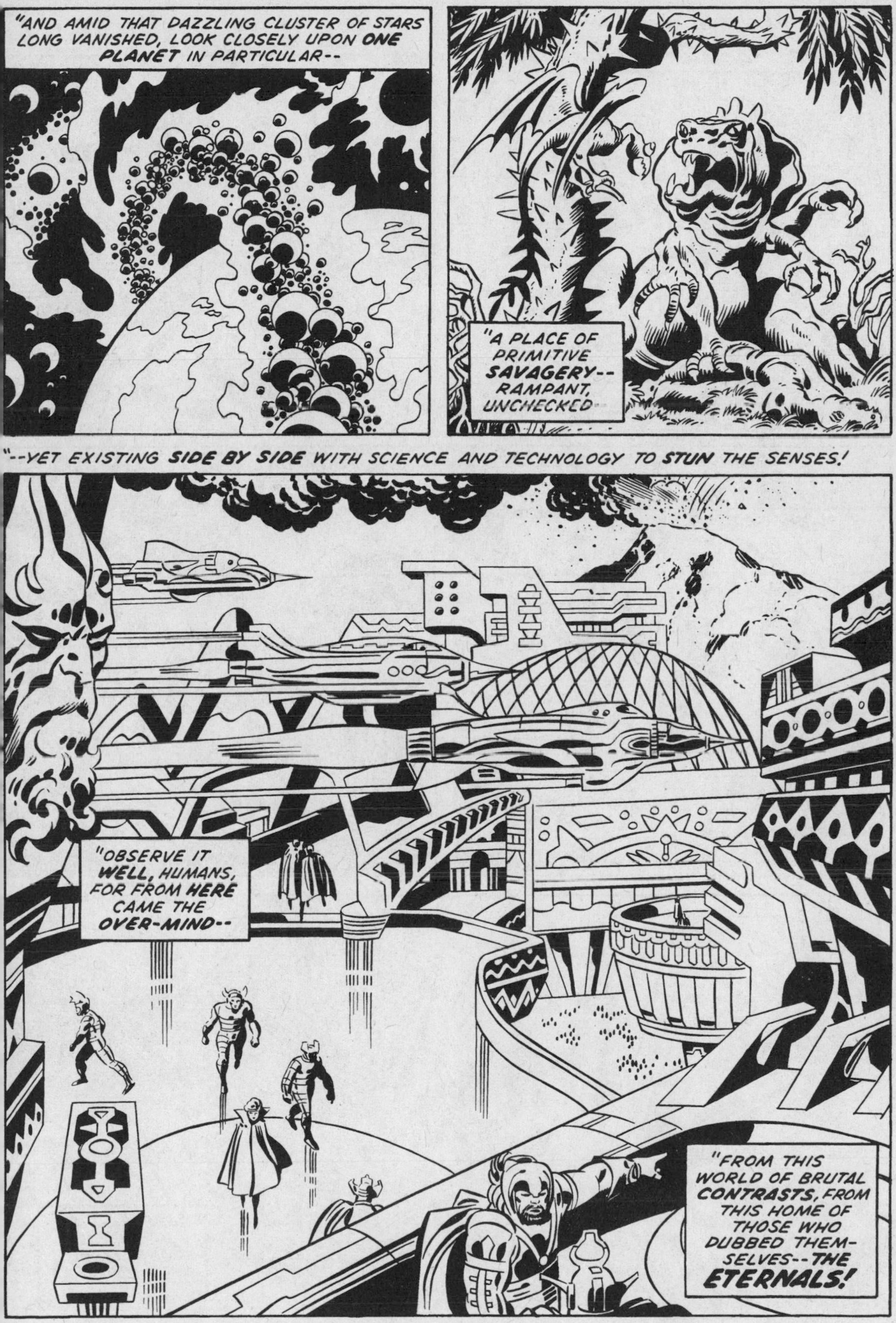
"AND AMID THAT DAZZLING CLUSTER OF STARS LONG VANISHED, LOOK CLOSELY UPON ONE PLANET IN PARTICULAR--
"A PLACE OF PRIMITIVE SAVAGERY--RAMPANT, UNCHECKED--
"--YET EXISTING SIDE BY SIDE WITH SCIENCE AND TECHNOLOGY TO STUN THE SENSES!
"OBSERVE IT WELL, HUMANS, FOR FROM HERE CAME THE OVER-MIND--
"FROM THIS WORLD OF BRUTAL CONTRASTS, FROM THIS HOME OF THOSE WHO DUBBED THEM-SELVES--THE ETERNALS!

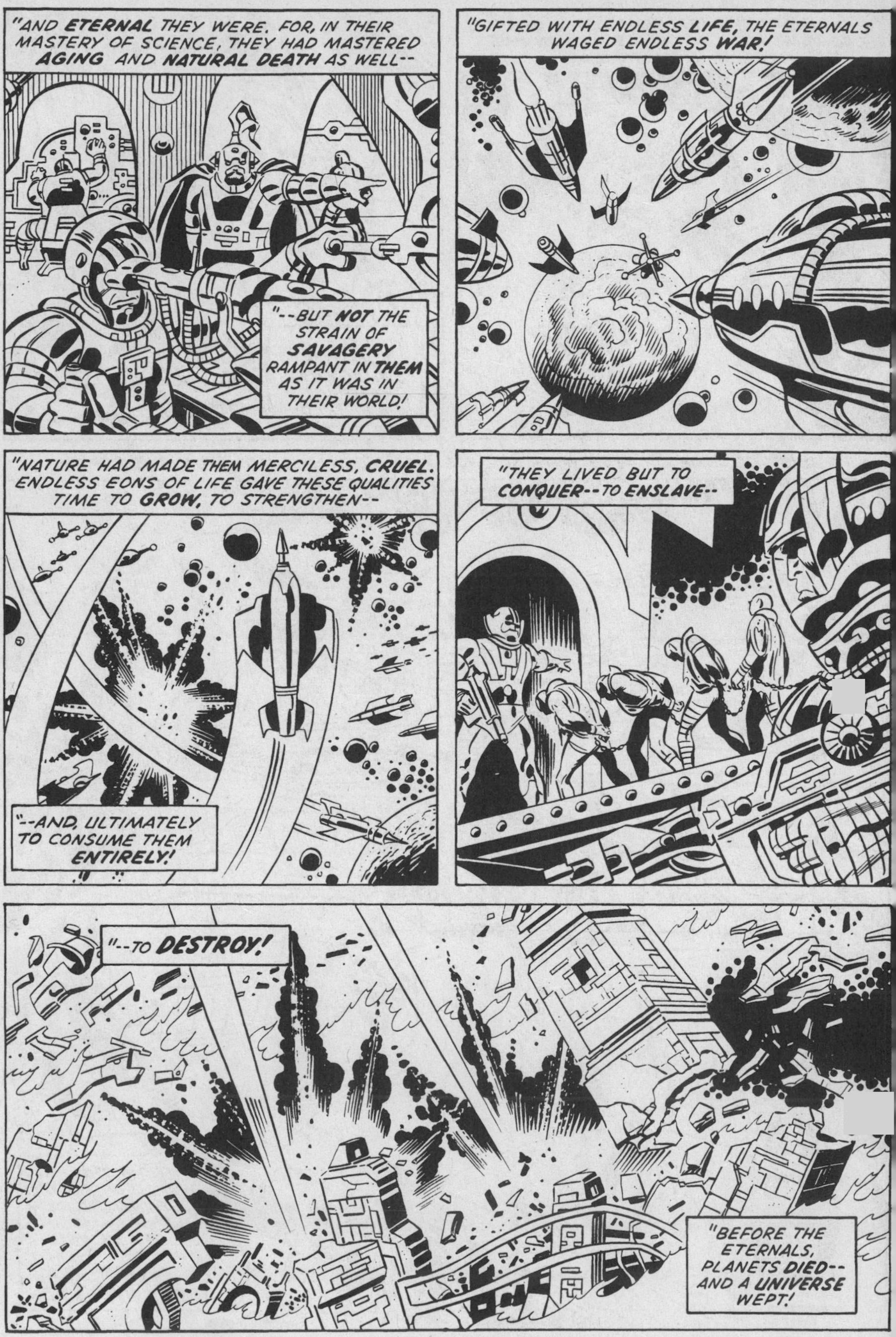
"AND ETERNAL THEY WERE. FOR, IN THEIR MASTERY OF SCIENCE, THEY HAD MASTERED AGING AND NATURAL DEATH AS WELL--
"--BUT NOT THE STRAIN OF SAVAGERY RAMPANT IN THEM AS IT WAS IN THEIR WORLD!
"GIFTED WITH ENDLESS LIFE, THE ETERNALS WAGED ENDLESS WAR!
"NATURE HAD MADE THEM MERCILESS, CRUEL. ENDLESS EONS OF LIFE GAVE THESE QUALITIES TIME TO GROW, TO STRENGTHEN--
"--AND, ULTIMATELY TO CONSUME THEM ENTIRELY!
"THEY LIVED BUT TO CONQUER--TO ENSLAVE--
"--TO DESTROY!
"BEFORE THE ETERNALS, PLANETS DIED--AND A UNIVERSE WEPT!

"THE ETERNALS WROTE THEIR NAME ACROSS THE STARS IN THE FLAMES OF DYING WORLDS-- NEVER KNOWING DEFEAT, ONLY VICTORY--AND ITS SPOILS.

THE SCOUTS HAVE NOT FOUND A WORTHY PLANET FOR CONQUEST IN AGES.

WHAT IF THERE ARE NO MORE, GROM? WHAT WILL MIGHTY WARRIORS SUCH AS YOU DO IF THERE IS PEACE?

PEACE?! PEACE IS LIKE DEATH, WOMAN-- FOR LESSER RACES-NOT FOR ETERNALS!

EVEN WHEN THERE ARE NO MORE WORLDS TO SMASH, THERE WILL ALWAYS BE--

--THE GAMES!

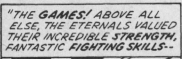

"THE GAMES! ABOVE ALL ELSE, THE ETERNALS VALUED THEIR INCREDIBLE STRENGTH, FANTASTIC FIGHTING SKILLS--

"--AND SO HELD BARBAROUS CONTESTS TO PROVE THEIR SUPERIORITY TO ALL CHALLENGERS--

"--MAN OR BEAST!

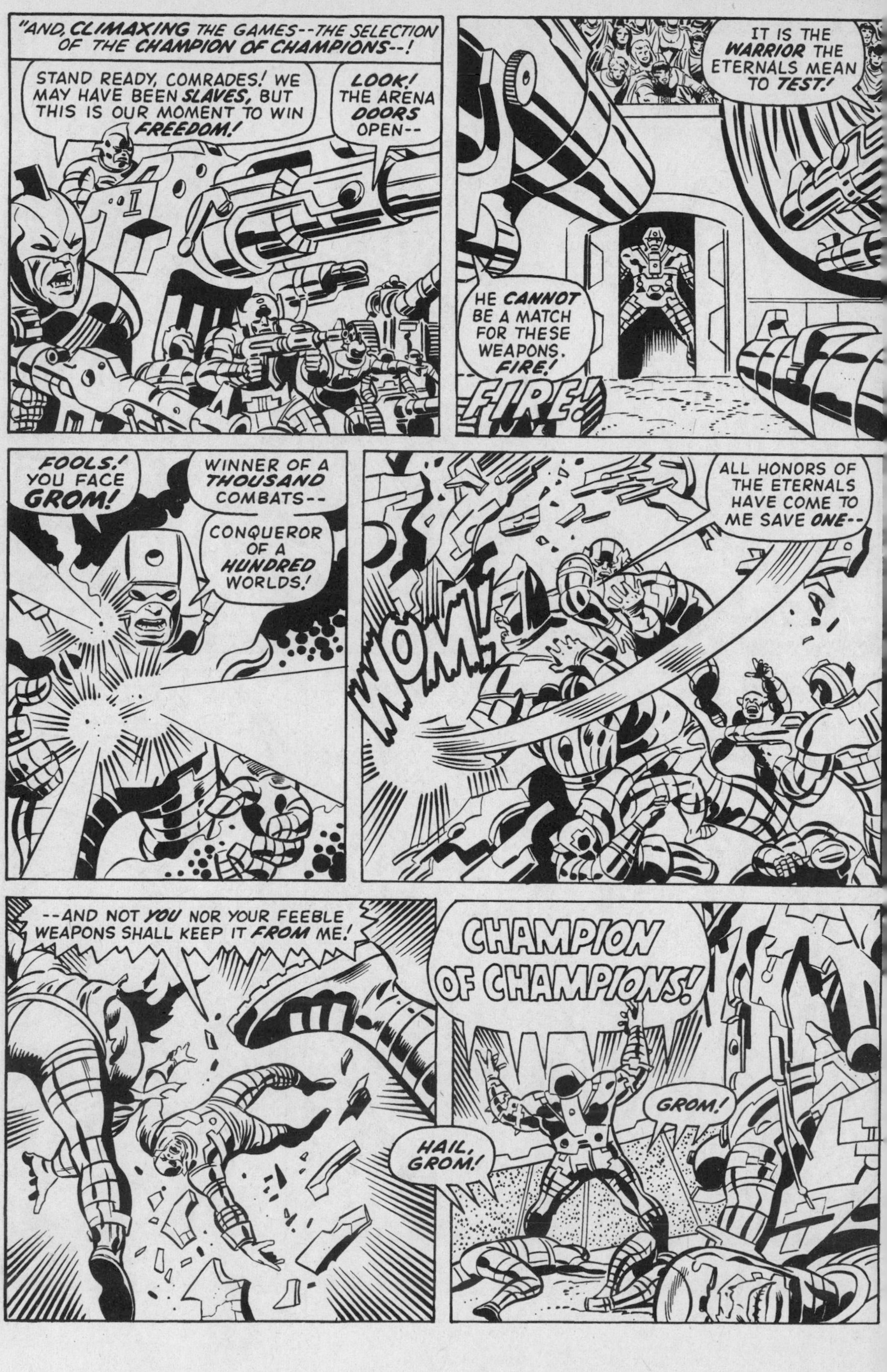
"AND, CLIMAXING THE GAMES--THE SELECTION OF THE CHAMPION OF CHAMPIONS--!
STAND READY, COMRADES! WE MAY HAVE BEEN SLAVES, BUT THIS IS OUR MOMENT TO WIN FREEDOM!
LOOK! THE ARENA DOORS OPEN--
IT IS THE WARRIOR THE ETERNALS MEAN TO TEST!
HE CANNOT BE A MATCH FOR THESE WEAPONS. FIRE!
FIRE!
FOOLS! YOU FACE GROM!
WINNER OF A THOUSAND COMBATS--
CONQUEROR OF A HUNDRED WORLDS!
ALL HONORS OF THE ETERNALS HAVE COME TO ME SAVE ONE--
WOM!
--AND NOT YOU NOR YOUR FEEBLE WEAPONS SHALL KEEP IT FROM ME!
CHAMPION OF CHAMPIONS!
GROM!
HAIL, GROM!

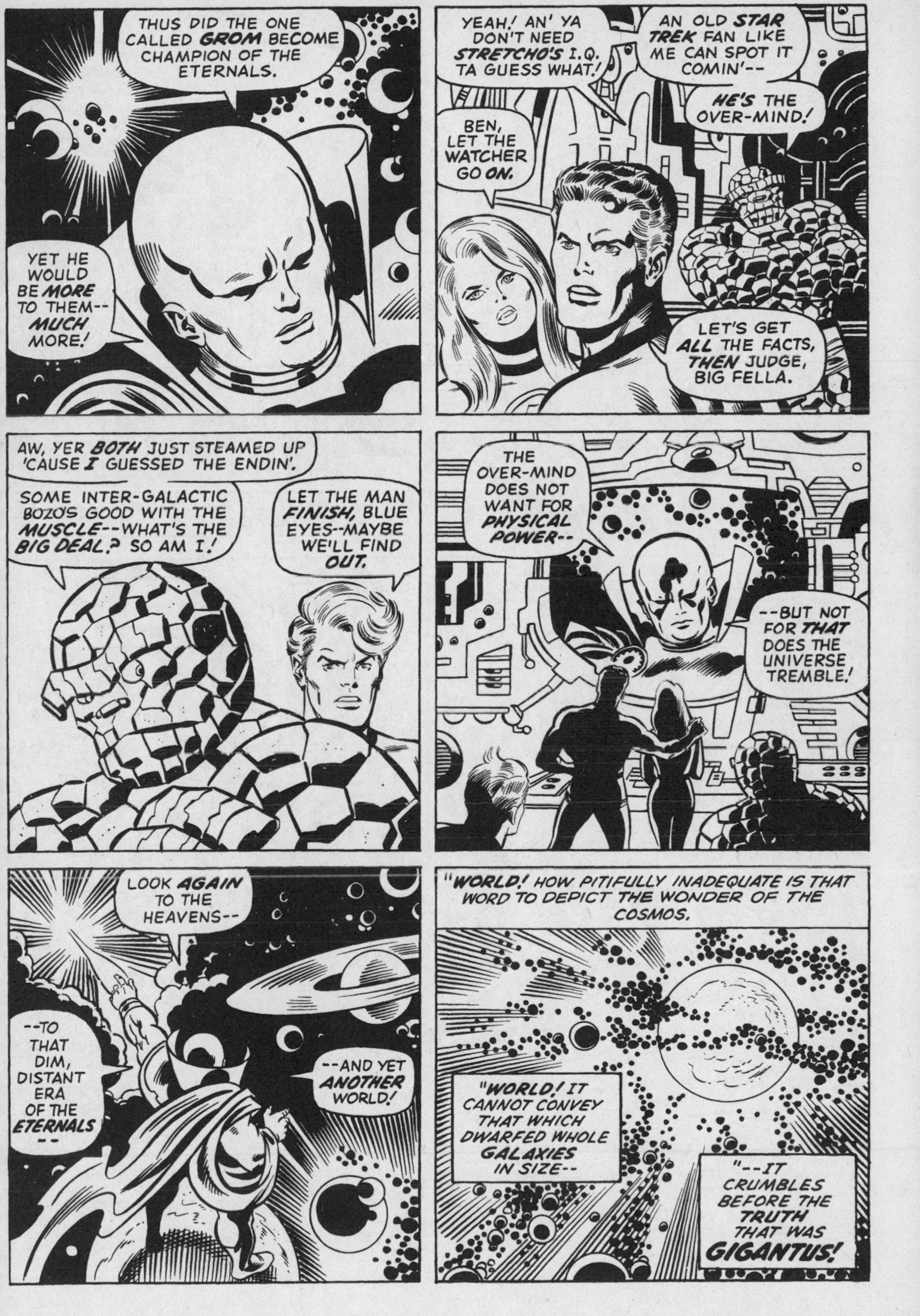
THUS DID THE ONE CALLED GROM BECOME CHAMPION OF THE ETERNALS.
YET HE WOULD BE MORE TO THEM-- MUCH MORE!
YEAH! AN' YA DON'T NEED STRETCHO'S I.Q. TA GUESS WHAT!
AN OLD STAR TREK FAN LIKE ME CAN SPOT IT COMIN'--
HE'S THE OVER-MIND!
BEN, LET THE WATCHER GO ON.
LET'S GET ALL THE FACTS, THEN JUDGE, BIG FELLA.
AW, YER BOTH JUST STEAMED UP 'CAUSE I GUESSED THE ENDIN'.
SOME INTER-GALACTIC BOZO'S GOOD WITH THE MUSCLE--WHAT'S THE BIG DEAL? SO AM I!
LET THE MAN FINISH, BLUE EYES--MAYBE WE'LL FIND OUT.
THE OVER-MIND DOES NOT WANT FOR PHYSICAL POWER--
--BUT NOT FOR THAT DOES THE UNIVERSE TREMBLE!
LOOK AGAIN TO THE HEAVENS--
--TO THAT DIM, DISTANT ERA OF THE ETERNALS --
--AND YET ANOTHER WORLD!
"WORLD! HOW PITIFULLY INADEQUATE IS THAT WORD TO DEPICT THE WONDER OF THE COSMOS.
"WORLD! IT CANNOT CONVEY THAT WHICH DWARFED WHOLE GALAXIES IN SIZE--
"--IT CRUMBLES BEFORE THE TRUTH THAT WAS GIGANTUS!

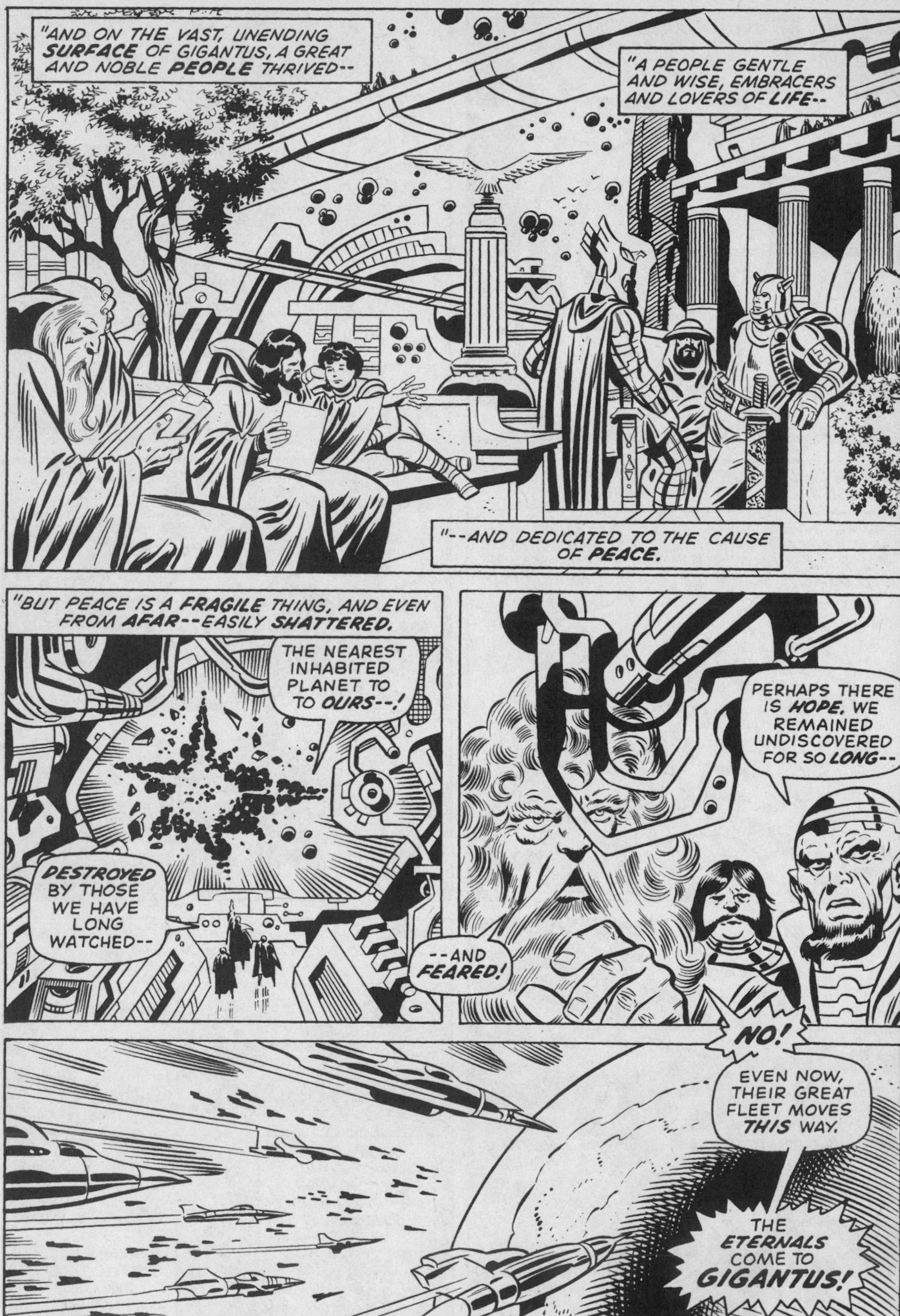
"AND ON THE VAST, UNENDING SURFACE OF GIGANTUS, A GREAT AND NOBLE PEOPLE THRIVED--
"A PEOPLE GENTLE AND WISE, EMBRACERS AND LOVERS OF LIFE--
"--AND DEDICATED TO THE CAUSE OF PEACE.
"BUT PEACE IS A FRAGILE THING, AND EVEN FROM AFAR--EASILY SHATTERED.
THE NEAREST INHABITED PLANET TO TO OURS--!
DESTROYED BY THOSE WE HAVE LONG WATCHED--
--AND FEARED!
PERHAPS THERE IS HOPE. WE REMAINED UNDISCOVERED FOR SO LONG--
NO!
EVEN NOW, THEIR GREAT FLEET MOVES THIS WAY.
THE ETERNALS COME TO GIGANTUS!

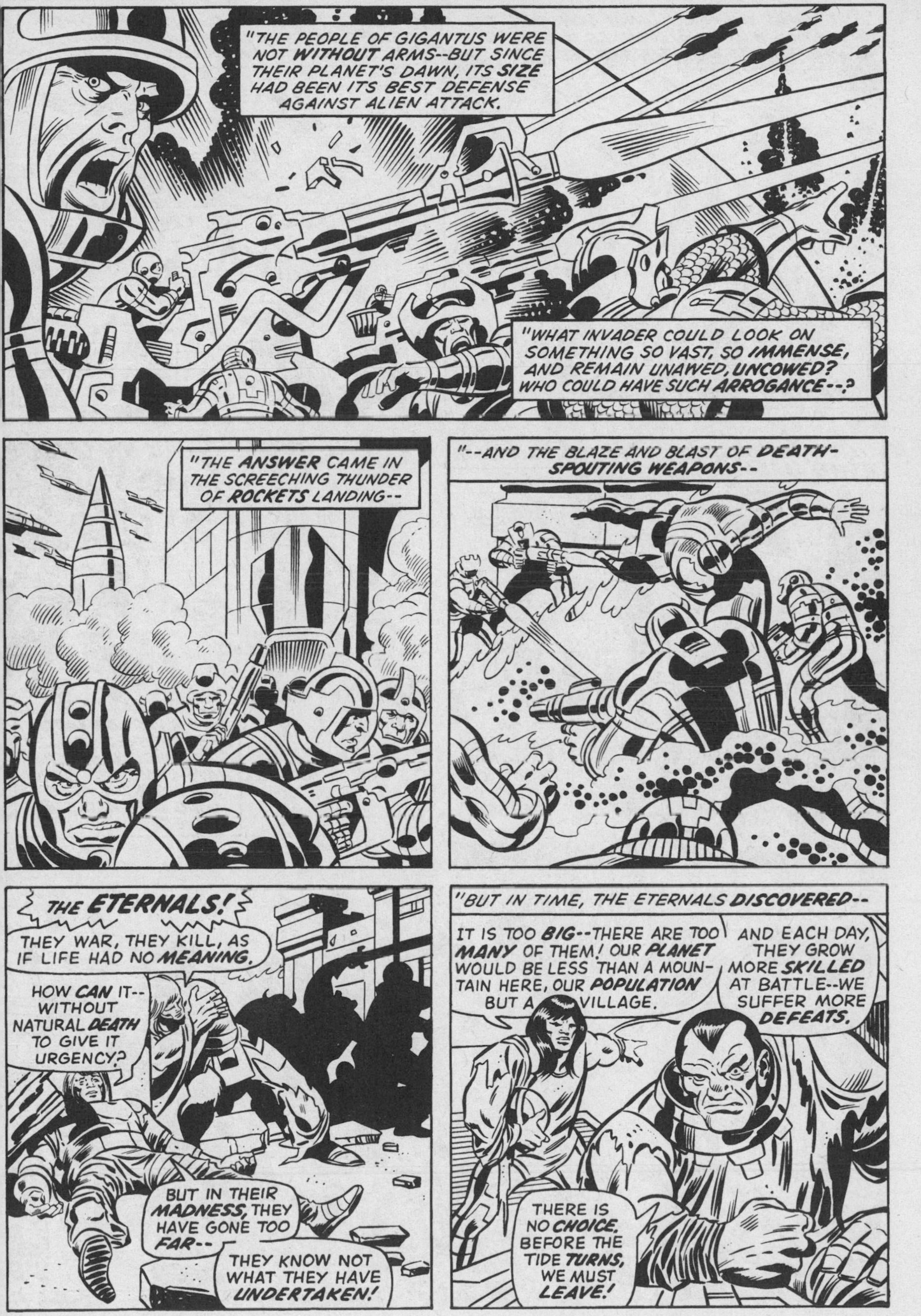
"THE PEOPLE OF GIGANTUS WERE NOT WITHOUT ARMS--BUT SINCE THEIR PLANET'S DAWN, ITS SIZE HAD BEEN ITS BEST DEFENSE AGAINST ALIEN ATTACK.
"WHAT INVADER COULD LOOK ON SOMETHING SO VAST, SO IMMENSE, AND REMAIN UNAWED, UNCOWED? WHO COULD HAVE SUCH ARROGANCE--?
"THE ANSWER CAME IN THE SCREECHING THUNDER OF ROCKETS LANDING--
"--AND THE BLAZE AND BLAST OF DEATH-SPOUTING WEAPONS--
THE ETERNALS!
THEY WAR, THEY KILL, AS IF LIFE HAD NO MEANING.
HOW CAN IT--WITHOUT NATURAL DEATH TO GIVE IT URGENCY?
BUT IN THEIR MADNESS, THEY HAVE GONE TOO FAR--
THEY KNOW NOT WHAT THEY HAVE UNDERTAKEN!
"BUT IN TIME, THE ETERNALS DISCOVERED--
IT IS TOO BIG--THERE ARE TOO MANY OF THEM! OUR PLANET WOULD BE LESS THAN A MOUNTAIN HERE, OUR POPULATION BUT A VILLAGE.
AND EACH DAY, THEY GROW MORE SKILLED AT BATTLE--WE SUFFER MORE DEFEATS.
THERE IS NO CHOICE. BEFORE THE TIDE TURNS, WE MUST LEAVE!

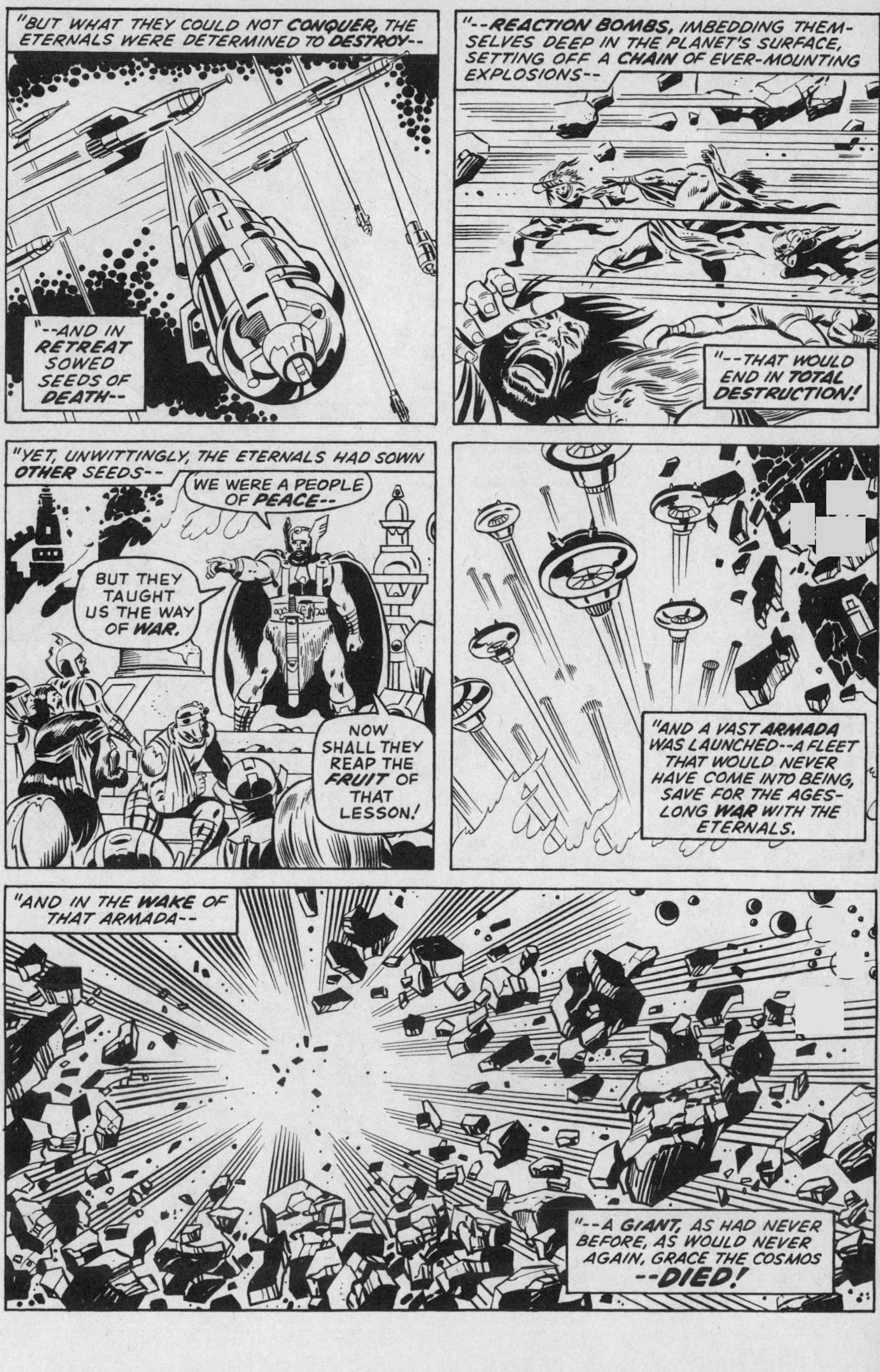
"BUT WHAT THEY COULD NOT CONQUER, THE ETERNALS WERE DETERMINED TO DESTROY--
"--AND IN RETREAT SOWED SEEDS OF DEATH--
"--REACTION BOMBS, IMBEDDING THEMSELVES DEEP IN THE PLANET'S SURFACE, SETTING OFF A CHAIN OF EVER-MOUNTING EXPLOSIONS--
"--THAT WOULD END IN TOTAL DESTRUCTION!
"YET, UNWITTINGLY, THE ETERNALS HAD SOWN OTHER SEEDS--
WE WERE A PEOPLE OF PEACE--
BUT THEY TAUGHT US THE WAY OF WAR.
NOW SHALL THEY REAP THE FRUIT OF THAT LESSON!
"AND A VAST ARMADA WAS LAUNCHED--A FLEET THAT WOULD NEVER HAVE COME INTO BEING, SAVE FOR THE AGES-LONG WAR WITH THE ETERNALS.
"AND IN THE WAKE OF THAT ARMADA--
"--A GIANT, AS HAD NEVER BEFORE, AS WOULD NEVER AGAIN, GRACE THE COSMOS --DIED!

"THE FRAGMENTS OF THAT GREATEST OF WORLDS WERE HURLED THROUGH THE UNIVERSE WITH CATACLYSMIC FURY--

"SOME TO VANISH IN GREAT MAELSTROMS OF SEARING, SWIRLING COSMIC ENERGY--

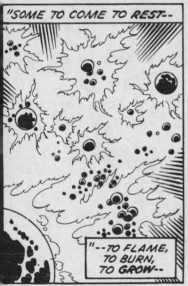

"SOME TO COME TO REST--

"--TO FLAME, TO BURN, TO GROW--

"TO LIVE AGAIN AS STARS, AS MOONS--

"--AS BLUE-GREEN PLANETS, FERTILE AND LUSH.

FOR SO IT HAS EVER BEEN IN THE UNIVERSE. EVERY ENDING BRINGS FORTH A NEW BEGINNING--

EACH BEGINNING MUST HAVE ITS END--

"--EVEN FOR ETERNALS!

IT IS IMPOSSIBLE-- IMPOSSIBLE!

WE HAVE NEVER BEEN UNDER ATTACK. NEVER! THEY COULD NOT DARE!

BUT, MY LORD-- SEE THE SCREEN! SHIPS IN NUMBERS TO DARKEN THE SKIES!

THEY SAY BUT A FRACTION OF GIGANTUS' POPULATION SURVIVED--

YET NEVER HAVE I BEHELD SUCH AN ARMADA.

WE ARE ETERNALS! NONE ARE OUR EQUALS --NO MATTER WHAT THEIR NUMBER.

OUR DEFENSES SHALL REPEL THEM-- DESTROY THEM!

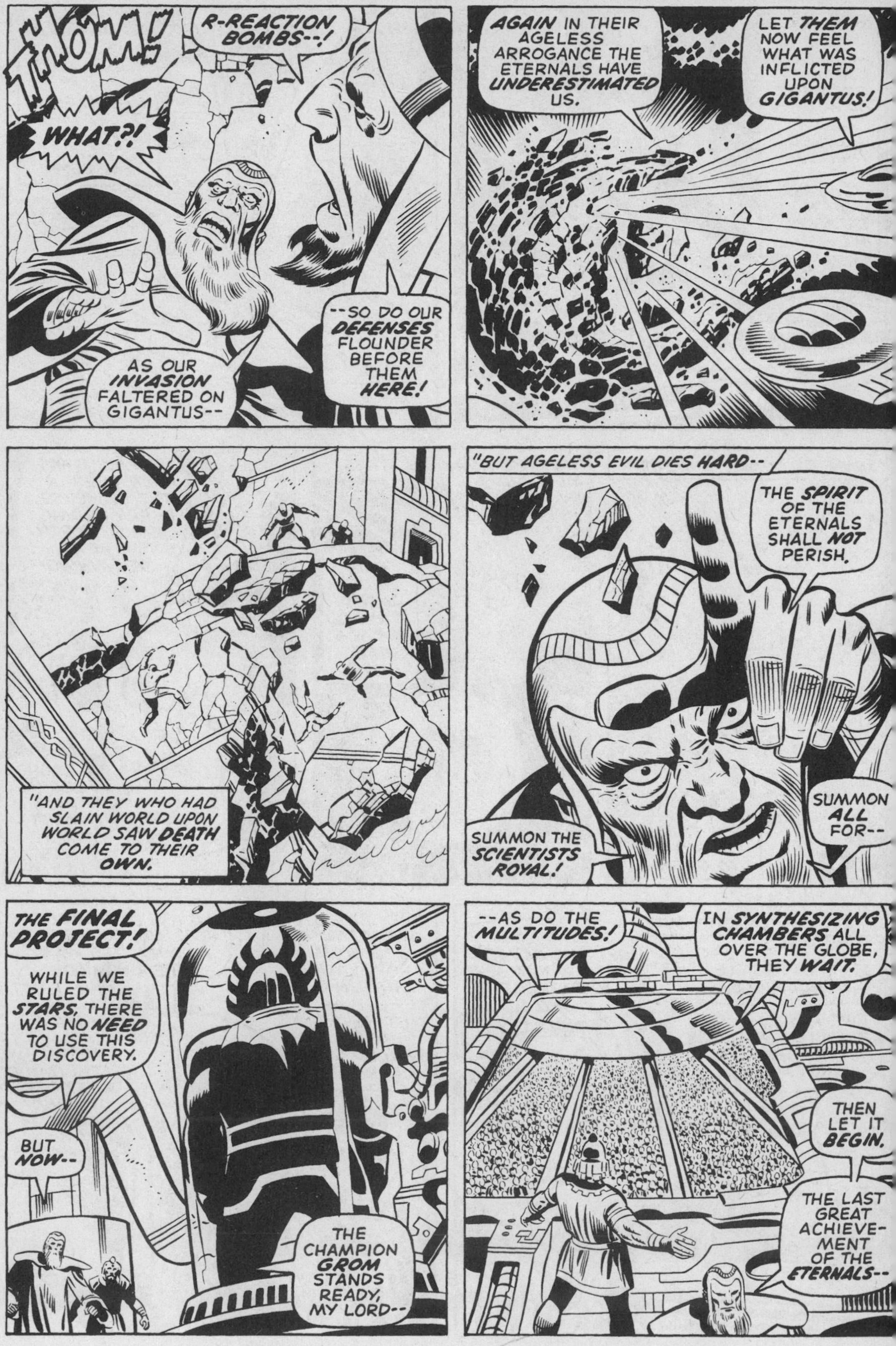
THOM!
R-REACTION BOMBS--!
WHAT?!
AS OUR INVASION FALTERED ON GIGANTUS--
--SO DO OUR DEFENSES FLOUNDER BEFORE THEM HERE!
AGAIN IN THEIR AGELESS ARROGANCE THE ETERNALS HAVE UNDERESTIMATED US.
LET THEM NOW FEEL WHAT WAS INFLICTED UPON GIGANTUS!
"AND THEY WHO HAD SLAIN WORLD UPON WORLD SAW DEATH COME TO THEIR OWN.
"BUT AGELESS EVIL DIES HARD--
THE SPIRIT OF THE ETERNALS SHALL NOT PERISH.
SUMMON THE SCIENTISTS ROYAL!
SUMMON ALL FOR--
THE FINAL PROJECT!
WHILE WE RULED THE STARS, THERE WAS NO NEED TO USE THIS DISCOVERY.
BUT NOW--
THE CHAMPION GROM STANDS READY, MY LORD--
--AS DO THE MULTITUDES!
IN SYNTHESIZING CHAMBERS ALL OVER THE GLOBE, THEY WAIT.
THEN LET IT BEGIN.
THE LAST GREAT ACHIEVEMENT OF THE ETERNALS--

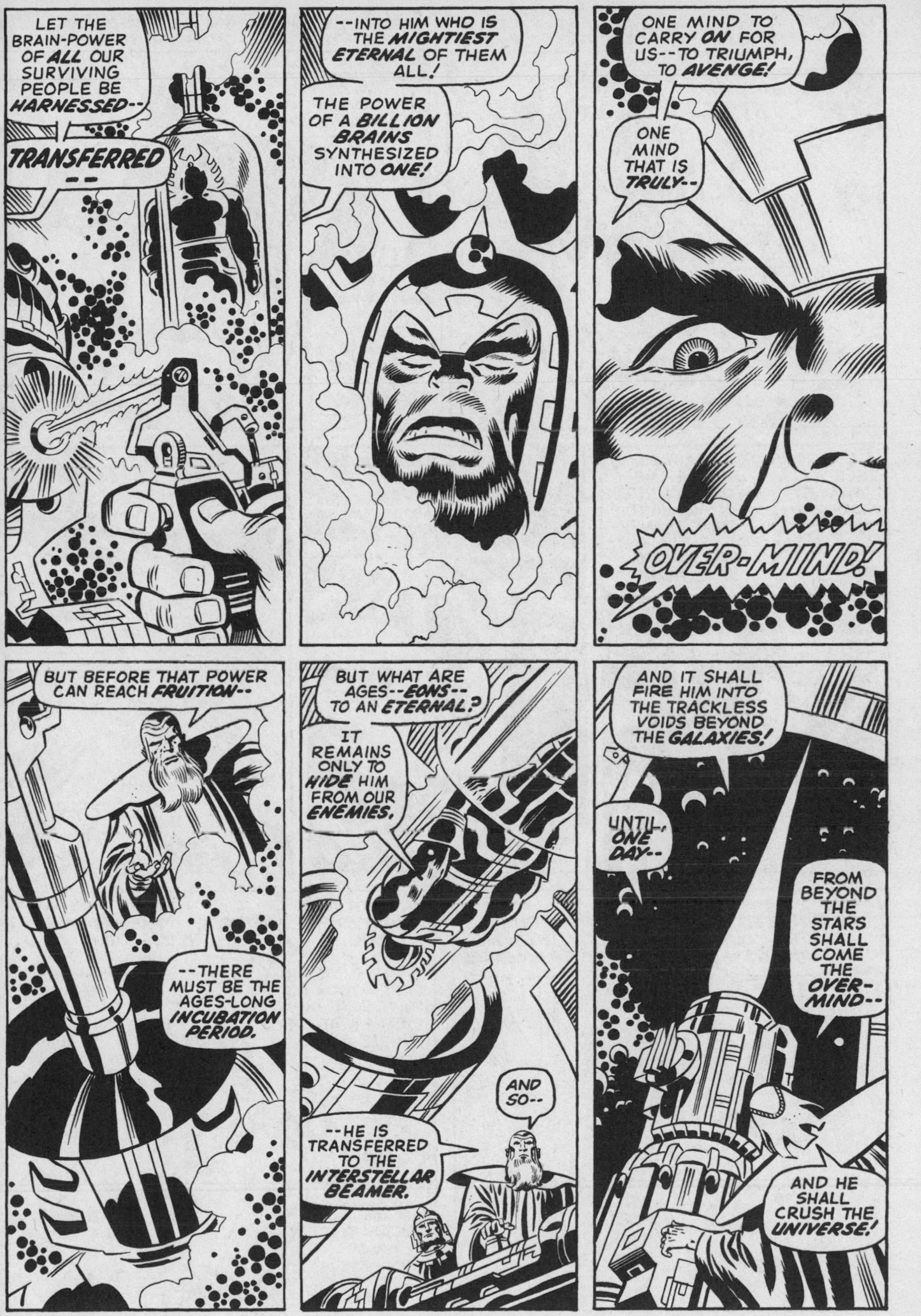
LET THE BRAIN-POWER OF ALL OUR SURVIVING PEOPLE BE HARNESSED--
TRANSFERRED --
--INTO HIM WHO IS THE MIGHTIEST ETERNAL OF THEM ALL!
THE POWER OF A BILLION BRAINS SYNTHESIZED INTO ONE!
ONE MIND TO CARRY ON FOR US--TO TRIUMPH, TO AVENGE!
ONE MIND THAT IS TRULY--
OVER-MIND!
BUT BEFORE THAT POWER CAN REACH FRUITION--
--THERE MUST BE THE AGES-LONG INCUBATION PERIOD.
BUT WHAT ARE AGES--EONS--TO AN ETERNAL?
IT REMAINS ONLY TO HIDE HIM FROM OUR ENEMIES.
AND SO--
--HE IS TRANSFERRED TO THE INTERSTELLAR BEAMER.
AND IT SHALL FIRE HIM INTO THE TRACKLESS VOIDS BEYOND THE GALAXIES!
UNTIL, ONE DAY--
FROM BEYOND THE STARS SHALL COME THE OVER-MIND--
AND HE SHALL CRUSH THE UNIVERSE!

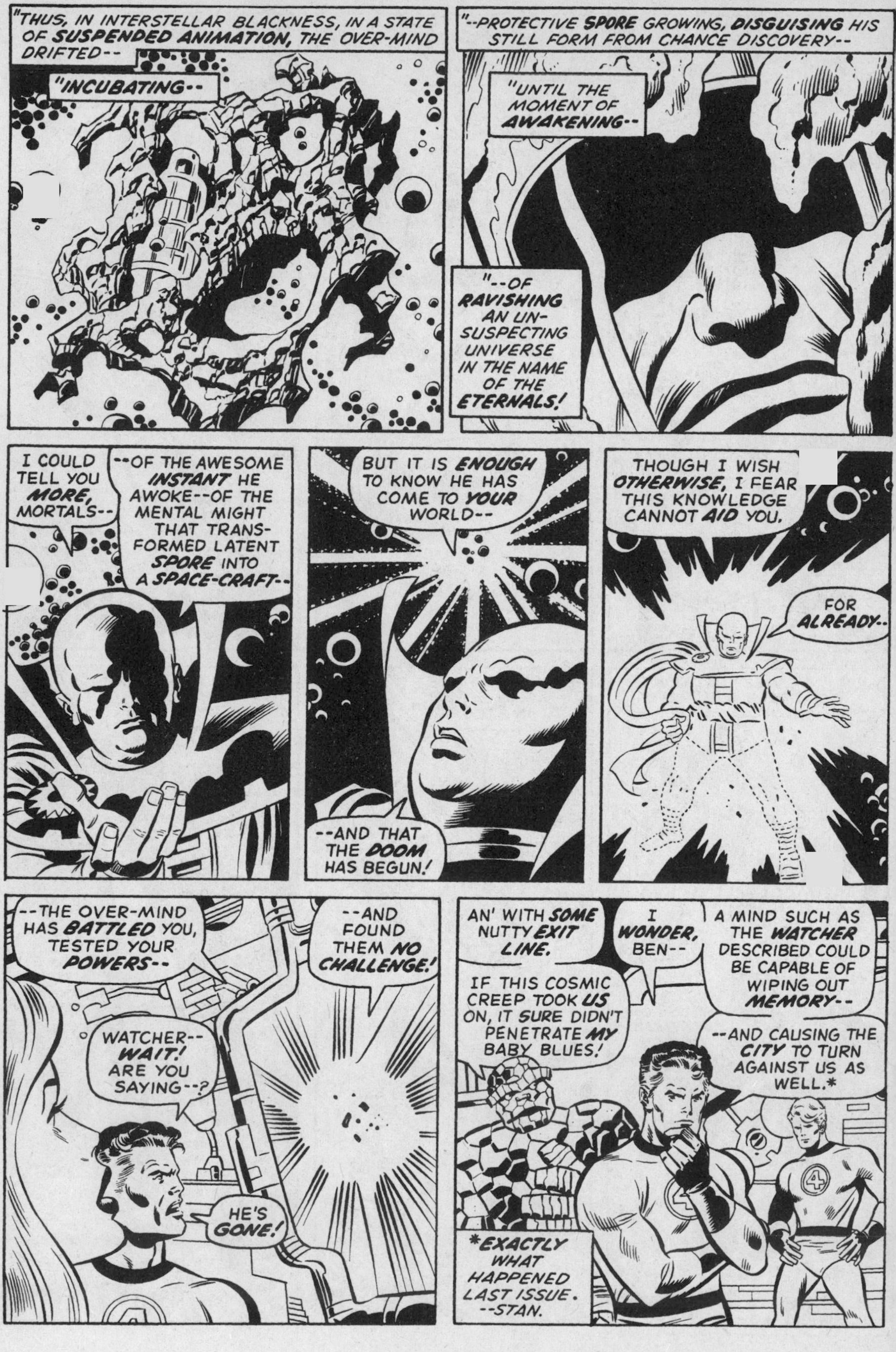
"THUS, IN INTERSTELLAR BLACKNESS, IN A STATE OF SUSPENDED ANIMATION, THE OVER-MIND DRIFTED--
"INCUBATING--
"--PROTECTIVE SPORE GROWING, DISGUISING HIS STILL FORM FROM CHANCE DISCOVERY--
"UNTIL THE MOMENT OF AWAKENING--
"--OF RAVISHING AN UN-SUSPECTING UNIVERSE IN THE NAME OF THE ETERNALS!
I COULD TELL YOU MORE, MORTALS--
--OF THE AWESOME INSTANT HE AWOKE--OF THE MENTAL MIGHT THAT TRANS-FORMED LATENT SPORE INTO A SPACE-CRAFT--
BUT IT IS ENOUGH TO KNOW HE HAS COME TO YOUR WORLD--
--AND THAT THE DOOM HAS BEGUN!
THOUGH I WISH OTHERWISE, I FEAR THIS KNOWLEDGE CANNOT AID YOU.
FOR ALREADY--
--THE OVER-MIND HAS BATTLED YOU, TESTED YOUR POWERS--
--AND FOUND THEM NO CHALLENGE!
WATCHER-- WAIT! ARE YOU SAYING--?
HE'S GONE!
AN' WITH SOME NUTTY EXIT LINE.
IF THIS COSMIC CREEP TOOK US ON, IT SURE DIDN'T PENETRATE MY BABY BLUES!
I WONDER, BEN--
A MIND SUCH AS THE WATCHER DESCRIBED COULD BE CAPABLE OF WIPING OUT MEMORY--
--AND CAUSING THE CITY TO TURN AGAINST US AS WELL.*
*EXACTLY WHAT HAPPENED LAST ISSUE. --STAN.

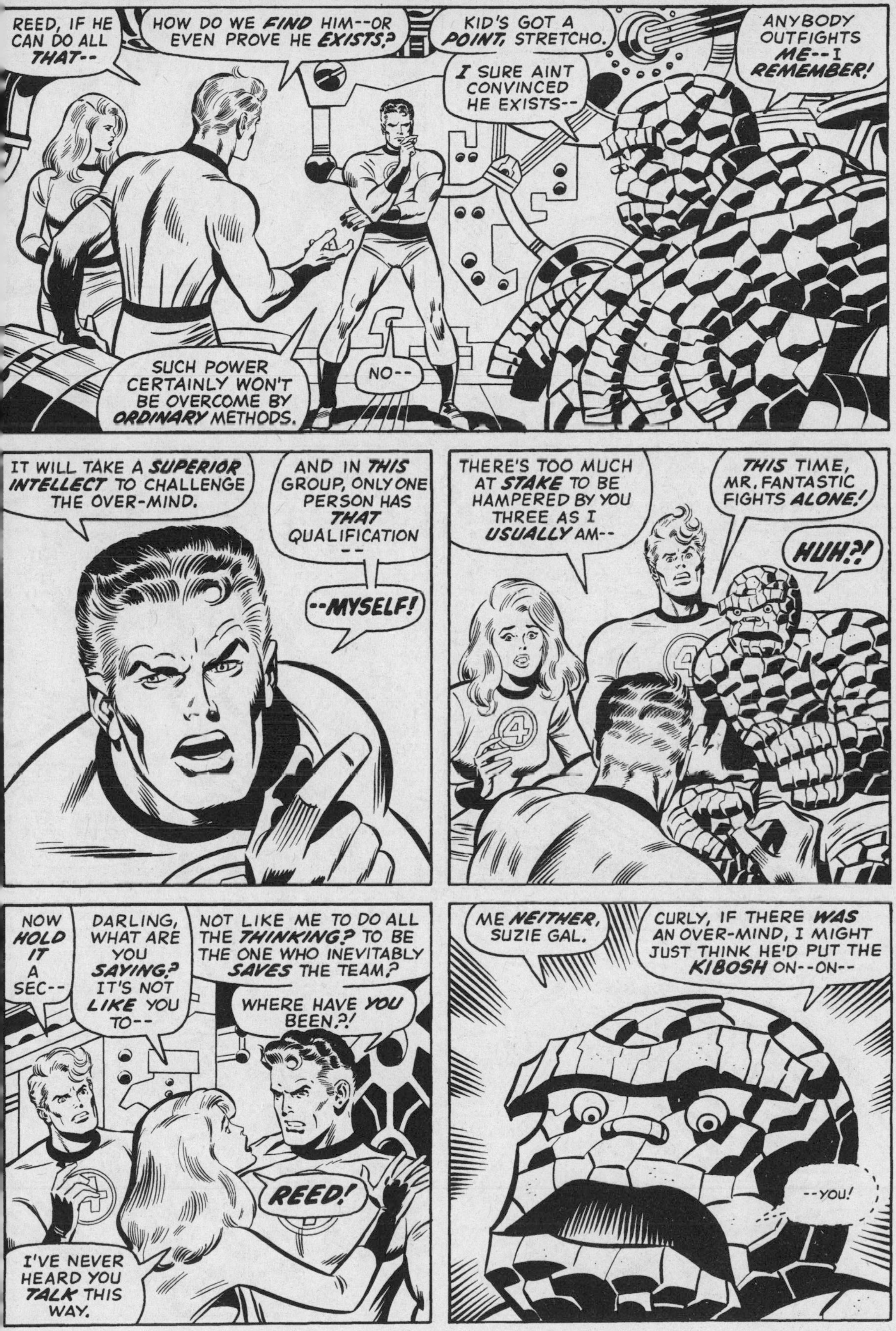
REED, IF HE CAN DO ALL THAT--
HOW DO WE FIND HIM--OR EVEN PROVE HE EXISTS?
SUCH POWER CERTAINLY WON'T BE OVERCOME BY ORDINARY METHODS.
NO--
KID'S GOT A POINT, STRETCHO.
I SURE AINT CONVINCED HE EXISTS--
ANYBODY OUTFIGHTS ME--I REMEMBER!
IT WILL TAKE A SUPERIOR INTELLECT TO CHALLENGE THE OVER-MIND.
AND IN THIS GROUP, ONLY ONE PERSON HAS THAT QUALIFICATION --
--MYSELF!
THERE'S TOO MUCH AT STAKE TO BE HAMPERED BY YOU THREE AS I USUALLY AM--
THIS TIME, MR. FANTASTIC FIGHTS ALONE!
HUH?!
NOW HOLD IT A SEC--
DARLING, WHAT ARE YOU SAYING? IT'S NOT LIKE YOU TO--
NOT LIKE ME TO DO ALL THE THINKING? TO BE THE ONE WHO INEVITABLY SAVES THE TEAM?
WHERE HAVE YOU BEEN?!
REED!
I'VE NEVER HEARD YOU TALK THIS WAY.
ME NEITHER, SUZIE GAL.
CURLY, IF THERE WAS AN OVER-MIND, I MIGHT JUST THINK HE'D PUT THE KIBOSH ON--ON--
--YOU!

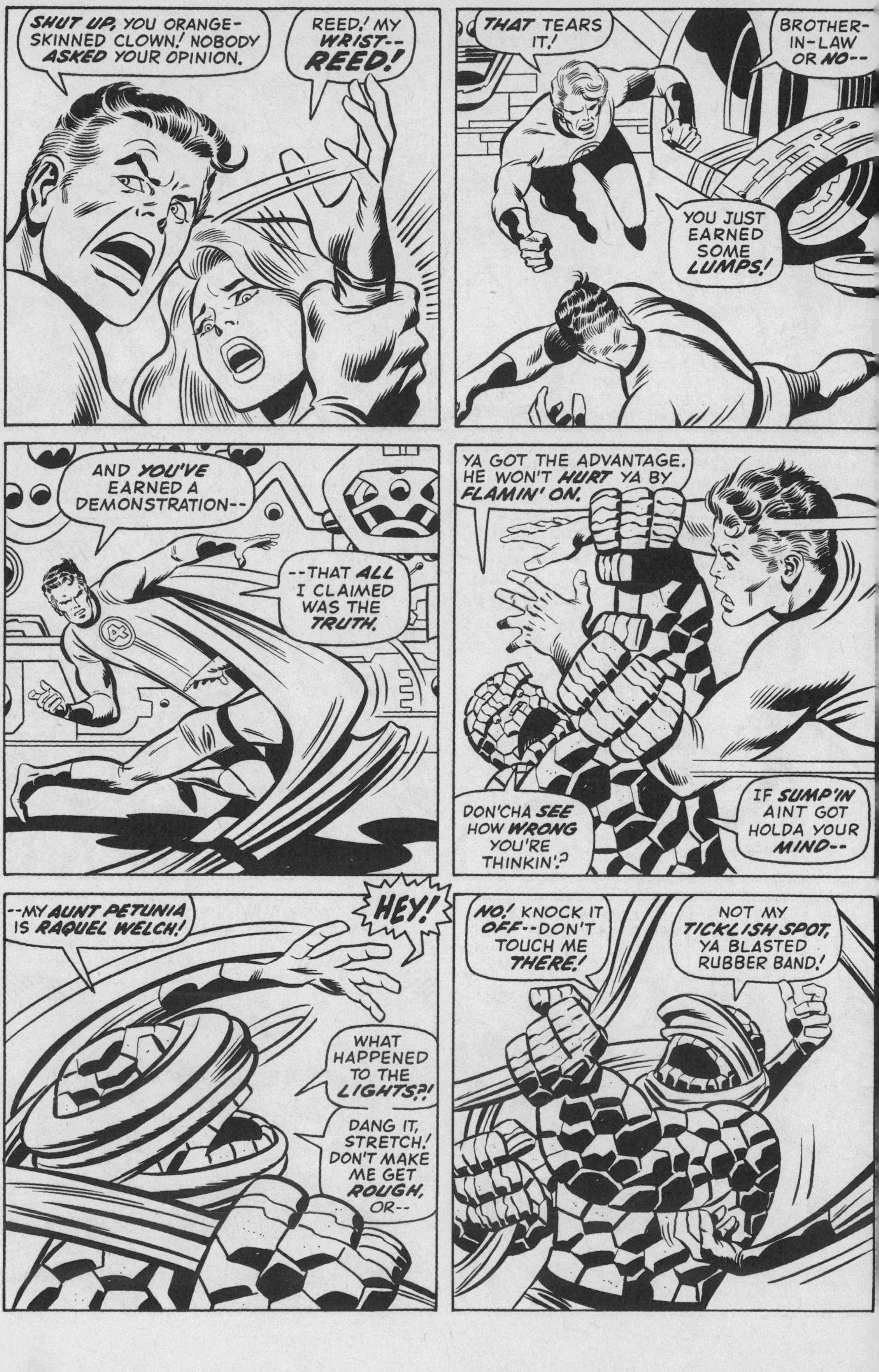
SHUT UP, YOU ORANGE-SKINNED CLOWN! NOBODY ASKED YOUR OPINION.
REED! MY WRIST-- REED!
THAT TEARS IT!
BROTHER-IN-LAW OR NO--
YOU JUST EARNED SOME LUMPS!
AND YOU'VE EARNED A DEMONSTRATION--
--THAT ALL I CLAIMED WAS THE TRUTH.
YA GOT THE ADVANTAGE. HE WON'T HURT YA BY FLAMIN' ON.
DON'CHA SEE HOW WRONG YOU'RE THINKIN'?
IF SUMP'IN AINT GOT HOLDA YOUR MIND--
--MY AUNT PETUNIA IS RAQUEL WELCH!
HEY!
WHAT HAPPENED TO THE LIGHTS?!
DANG IT, STRETCH! DON'T MAKE ME GET ROUGH, OR--
NO! KNOCK IT OFF--DON'T TOUCH ME THERE!
NOT MY TICKLISH SPOT, YA BLASTED RUBBER BAND!

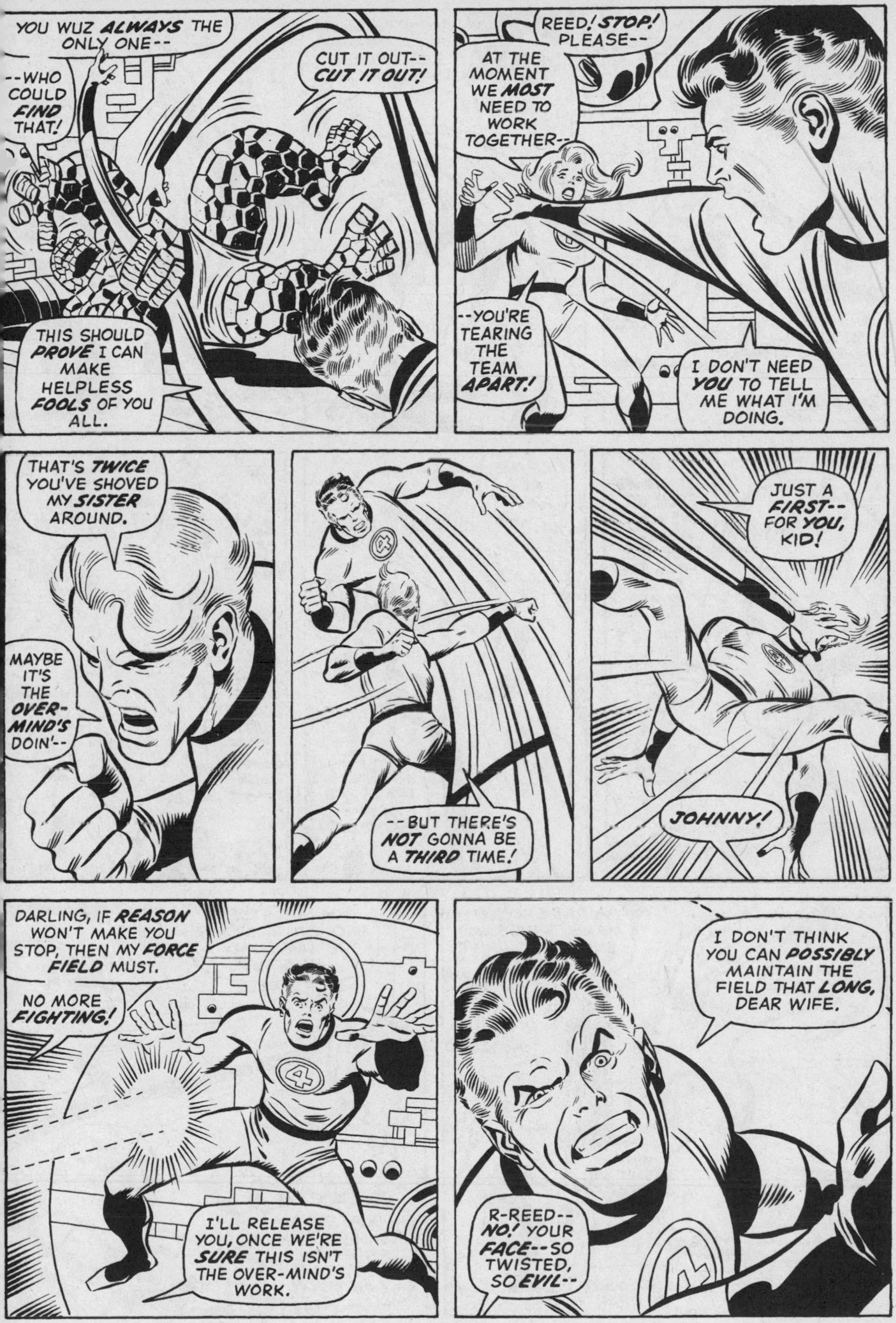
YOU WUZ ALWAYS THE ONLY ONE--
--WHO COULD FIND THAT!
CUT IT OUT-- CUT IT OUT!
THIS SHOULD PROVE I CAN MAKE HELPLESS FOOLS OF YOU ALL.
REED! STOP! PLEASE--
AT THE MOMENT WE MOST NEED TO WORK TOGETHER--
--YOU'RE TEARING THE TEAM APART!
I DON'T NEED YOU TO TELL ME WHAT I'M DOING.
THAT'S TWICE YOU'VE SHOVED MY SISTER AROUND.
MAYBE IT'S THE OVER-MIND'S DOIN'--
--BUT THERE'S NOT GONNA BE A THIRD TIME!
JUST A FIRST-- FOR YOU, KID!
JOHNNY!
DARLING, IF REASON WON'T MAKE YOU STOP, THEN MY FORCE FIELD MUST.
NO MORE FIGHTING!
I'LL RELEASE YOU, ONCE WE'RE SURE THIS ISN'T THE OVER-MIND'S WORK.
I DON'T THINK YOU CAN POSSIBLY MAINTAIN THE FIELD THAT LONG, DEAR WIFE.
R-REED-- NO! YOUR FACE--SO TWISTED, SO EVIL--

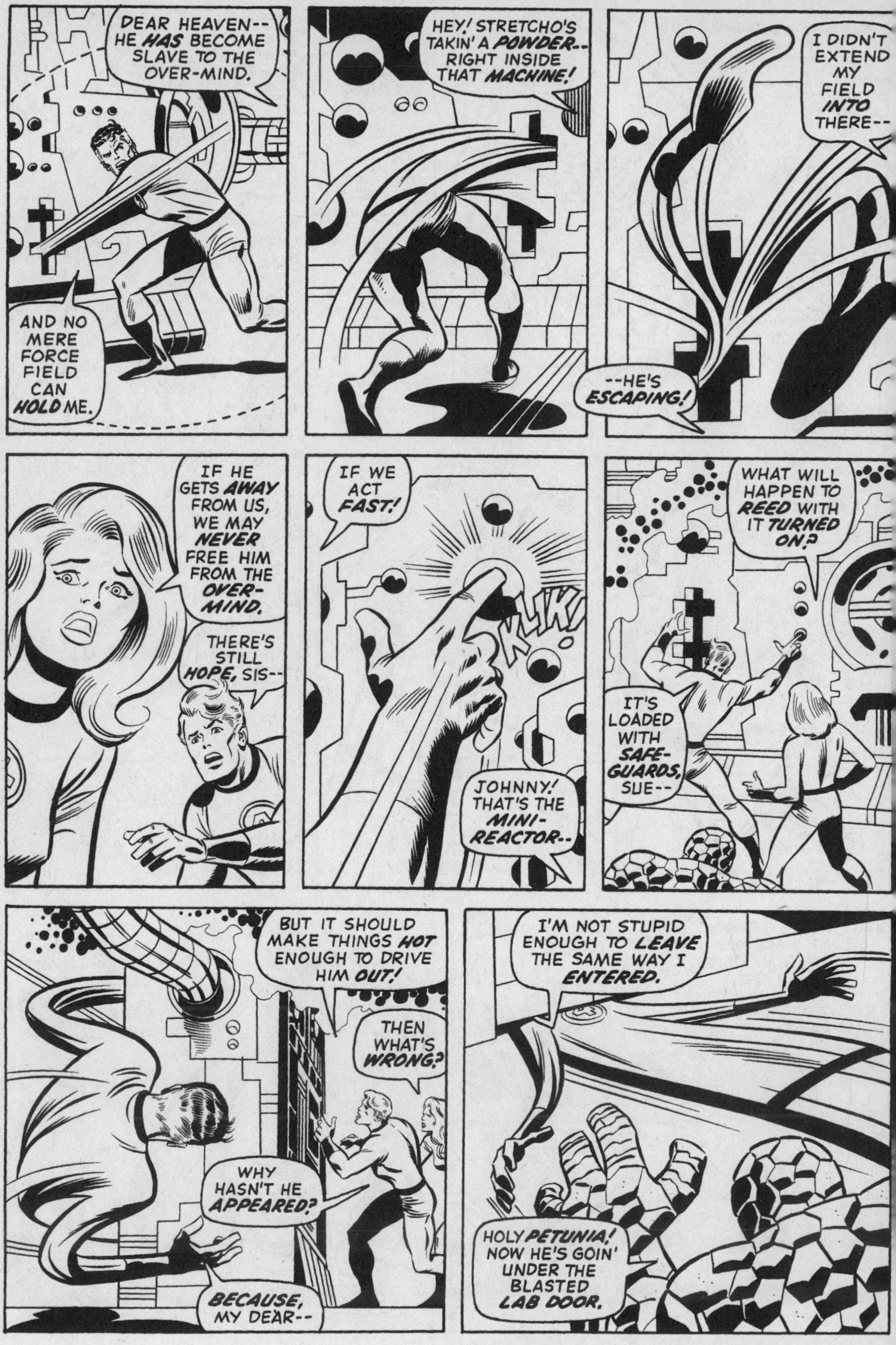
DEAR HEAVEN-- HE HAS BECOME SLAVE TO THE OVER-MIND.
AND NO MERE FORCE FIELD CAN HOLD ME.
HEY! STRETCHO'S TAKIN' A POWDER-- RIGHT INSIDE THAT MACHINE!
I DIDN'T EXTEND MY FIELD INTO THERE--
--HE'S ESCAPING!
IF HE GETS AWAY FROM US, WE MAY NEVER FREE HIM FROM THE OVER-MIND.
THERE'S STILL HOPE, SIS--
IF WE ACT FAST!
KLIK!
JOHNNY! THAT'S THE MINI-REACTOR--
WHAT WILL HAPPEN TO REED WITH IT TURNED ON?
IT'S LOADED WITH SAFE-GUARDS, SUE--
BUT IT SHOULD MAKE THINGS HOT ENOUGH TO DRIVE HIM OUT!
THEN WHAT'S WRONG?
WHY HASN'T HE APPEARED?
BECAUSE, MY DEAR--
I'M NOT STUPID ENOUGH TO LEAVE THE SAME WAY I ENTERED.
HOLY PETUNIA! NOW HE'S GOIN' UNDER THE BLASTED LAB DOOR.

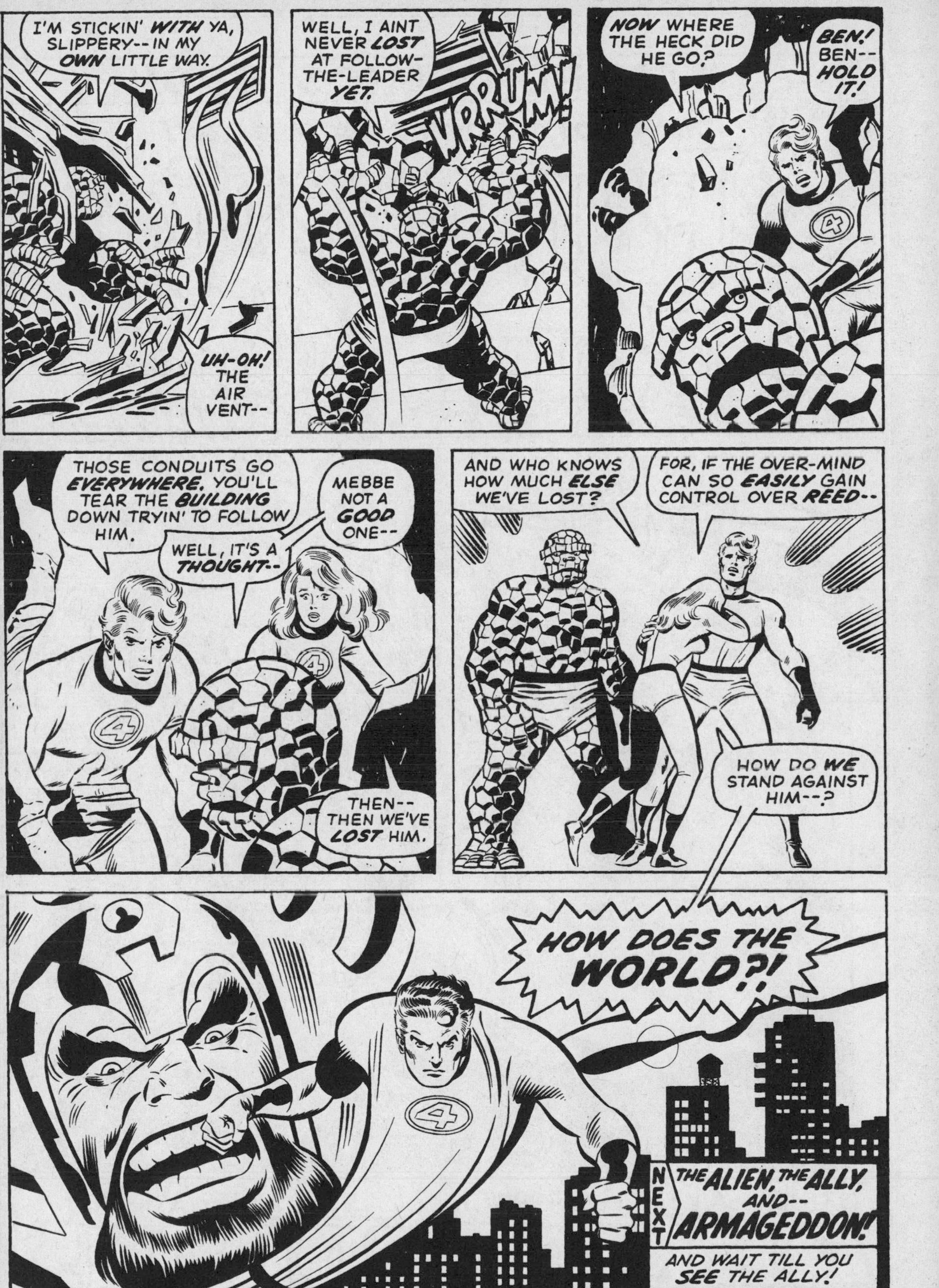
I'M STICKIN' WITH YA, SLIPPERY--IN MY OWN LITTLE WAY.
UH-OH! THE AIR VENT--
WELL, I AINT NEVER LOST AT FOLLOW-THE-LEADER YET.
VRRUM!
NOW WHERE THE HECK DID HE GO?
BEN! BEN--HOLD IT!
THOSE CONDUITS GO EVERYWHERE. YOU'LL TEAR THE BUILDING DOWN TRYIN' TO FOLLOW HIM.
WELL, IT'S A THOUGHT--
MEBBE NOT A GOOD ONE--
THEN--THEN WE'VE LOST HIM.
AND WHO KNOWS HOW MUCH ELSE WE'VE LOST?
FOR, IF THE OVER-MIND CAN SO EASILY GAIN CONTROL OVER REED--
HOW DO WE STAND AGAINST HIM--?
HOW DOES THE WORLD?!
NEXT
THE ALIEN, THE ALLY, AND--ARMAGEDDON!
AND WAIT TILL YOU SEE THE ALLY!

FANTASTIC FOUR
MARVEL COMICS GROUP™
25¢ CC
116 NOV 02462
THE WORLD'S GREATEST COMIC MAGAZINE!
APPROVED BY THE COMICS CODE AUTHORITY
Fantastic Four™
ALL-NEW THRILLS --AS REED RICHARDS IS REPLACED BY--- DOCTOR DOOM!
THE ALIEN... THE ALLY... AND
ARMAGEDDON!

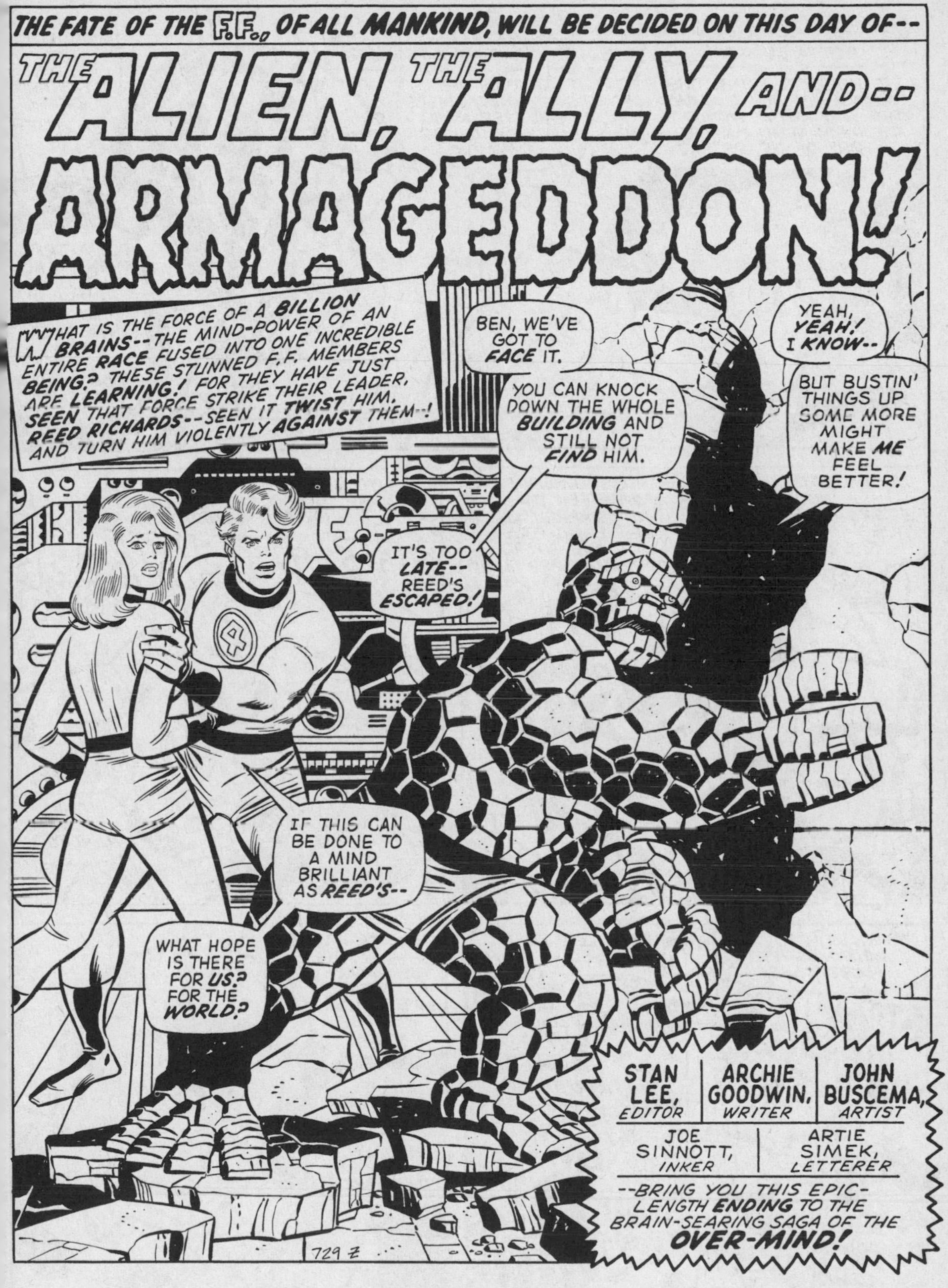

THE FATE OF THE F.F., OF ALL MANKIND, WILL BE DECIDED ON THIS DAY OF--
THE ALIEN, THE ALLY, AND-- ARMAGEDDON!
WHAT IS THE FORCE OF A BILLION BRAINS--THE MIND-POWER OF AN ENTIRE RACE FUSED INTO ONE INCREDIBLE BEING? THESE STUNNED F.F. MEMBERS ARE LEARNING! FOR THEY HAVE JUST SEEN THAT FORCE STRIKE THEIR LEADER, REED RICHARDS--SEEN IT TWIST HIM, AND TURN HIM VIOLENTLY AGAINST THEM--!
BEN, WE'VE GOT TO FACE IT.
YOU CAN KNOCK DOWN THE WHOLE BUILDING AND STILL NOT FIND HIM.
YEAH, YEAH! I KNOW--
BUT BUSTIN' THINGS UP SOME MORE MIGHT MAKE ME FEEL BETTER!
IT'S TOO LATE-- REED'S ESCAPED!
IF THIS CAN BE DONE TO A MIND BRILLIANT AS REED'S--
WHAT HOPE IS THERE FOR US? FOR THE WORLD?
STAN LEE, EDITOR
ARCHIE GOODWIN, WRITER
JOHN BUSCEMA, ARTIST
JOE SINNOTT, INKER
ARTIE SIMEK, LETTERER
--BRING YOU THIS EPIC-LENGTH ENDING TO THE BRAIN-SEARING SAGA OF THE OVER-MIND!
729 Z

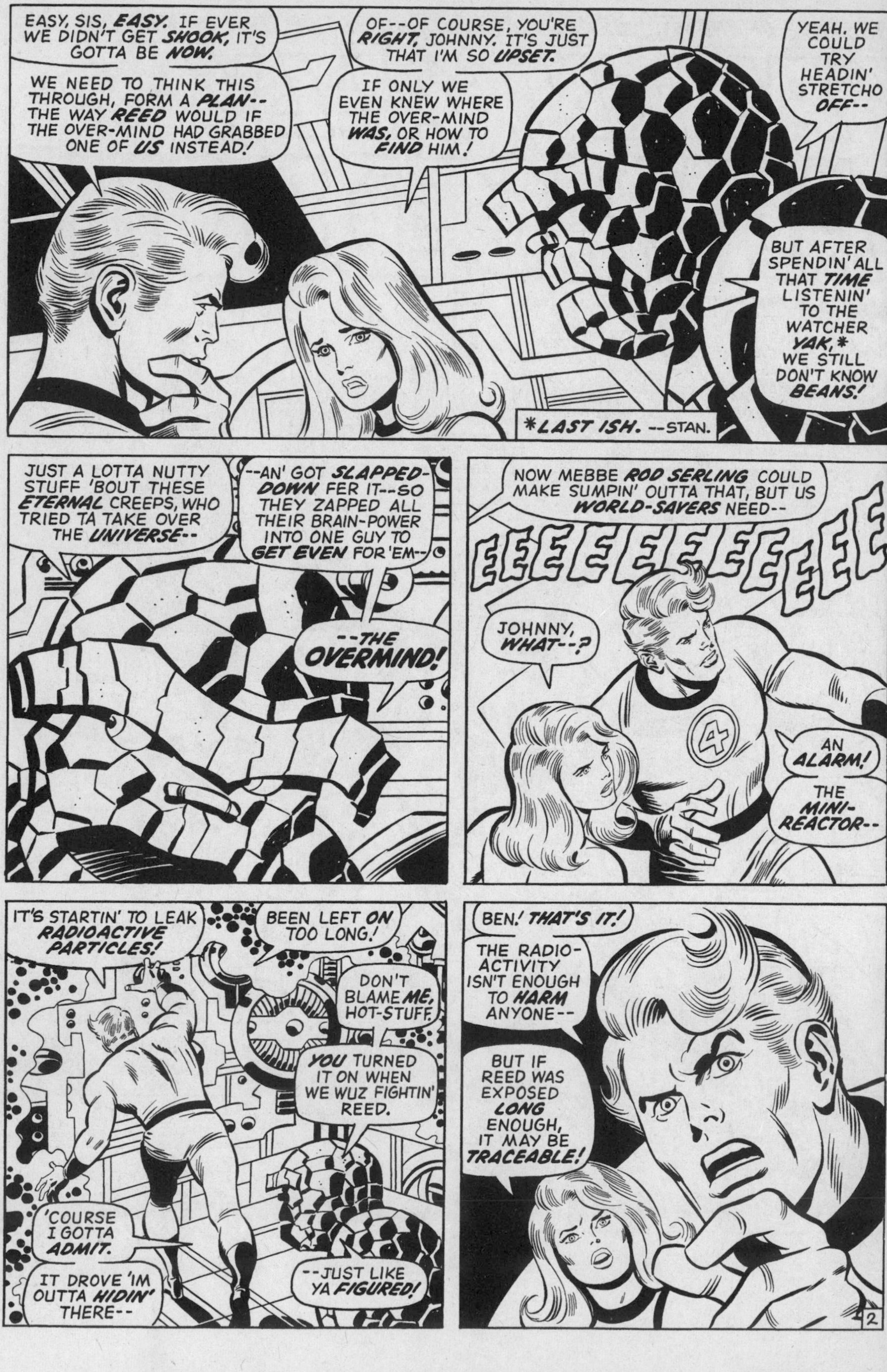
EASY, SIS, EASY. IF EVER WE DIDN'T GET SHOOK, IT'S GOTTA BE NOW.
WE NEED TO THINK THIS THROUGH, FORM A PLAN-- THE WAY REED WOULD IF THE OVER-MIND HAD GRABBED ONE OF US INSTEAD!
OF--OF COURSE, YOU'RE RIGHT, JOHNNY. IT'S JUST THAT I'M SO UPSET.
IF ONLY WE EVEN KNEW WHERE THE OVER-MIND WAS, OR HOW TO FIND HIM!
YEAH. WE COULD TRY HEADIN' STRETCHO OFF--
BUT AFTER SPENDIN' ALL THAT TIME LISTENIN' TO THE WATCHER YAK,* WE STILL DON'T KNOW BEANS!
*LAST ISH. --STAN.
JUST A LOTTA NUTTY STUFF 'BOUT THESE ETERNAL CREEPS, WHO TRIED TA TAKE OVER THE UNIVERSE--
--AN' GOT SLAPPED-DOWN FER IT--SO THEY ZAPPED ALL THEIR BRAIN-POWER INTO ONE GUY TO GET EVEN FOR 'EM--
--THE OVERMIND!
NOW MEBBE ROD SERLING COULD MAKE SUMPIN' OUTTA THAT, BUT US WORLD-SAVERS NEED--
EEEEEEEEEEEE
JOHNNY, WHAT--?
AN ALARM!
THE MINI-REACTOR--
IT'S STARTIN' TO LEAK RADIOACTIVE PARTICLES!
BEEN LEFT ON TOO LONG!
DON'T BLAME ME, HOT-STUFF.
YOU TURNED IT ON WHEN WE WUZ FIGHTIN' REED.
'COURSE I GOTTA ADMIT.
IT DROVE 'IM OUTTA HIDIN' THERE--
--JUST LIKE YA FIGURED!
BEN! THAT'S IT!
THE RADIO-ACTIVITY ISN'T ENOUGH TO HARM ANYONE--
BUT IF REED WAS EXPOSED LONG ENOUGH, IT MAY BE TRACEABLE!
2

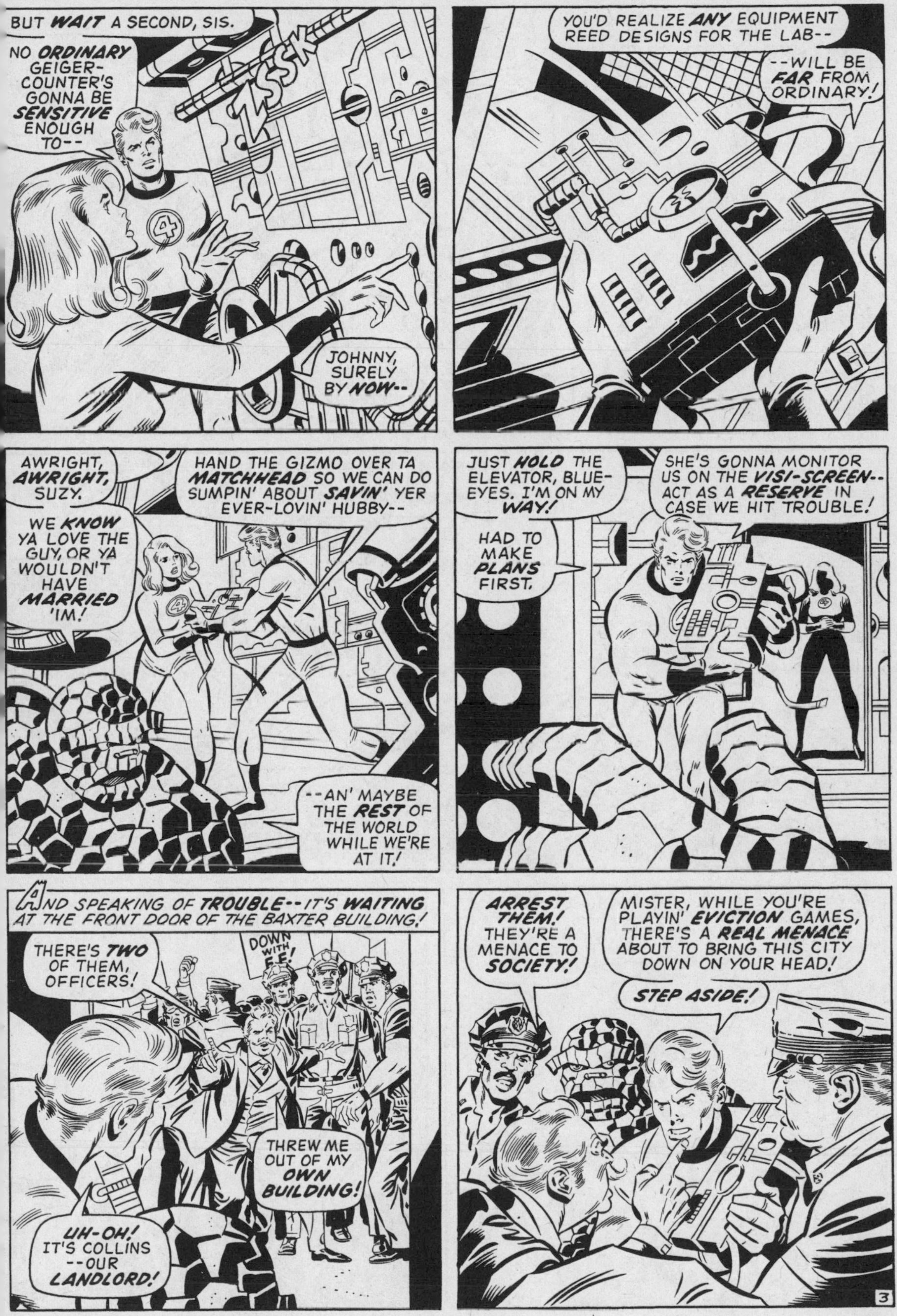

BUT WAIT A SECOND, SIS.
NO ORDINARY GEIGER-COUNTER'S GONNA BE SENSITIVE ENOUGH TO--
ZSSK
JOHNNY, SURELY BY NOW--
YOU'D REALIZE ANY EQUIPMENT REED DESIGNS FOR THE LAB--
--WILL BE FAR FROM ORDINARY!
AWRIGHT, AWRIGHT, SUZY.
WE KNOW YA LOVE THE GUY, OR YA WOULDN'T HAVE MARRIED 'IM!
HAND THE GIZMO OVER TA MATCHHEAD SO WE CAN DO SUMPIN' ABOUT SAVIN' YER EVER-LOVIN' HUBBY--
--AN' MAYBE THE REST OF THE WORLD WHILE WE'RE AT IT!
JUST HOLD THE ELEVATOR, BLUE-EYES. I'M ON MY WAY!
HAD TO MAKE PLANS FIRST.
SHE'S GONNA MONITOR US ON THE VISI-SCREEN-- ACT AS A RESERVE IN CASE WE HIT TROUBLE!
AND SPEAKING OF TROUBLE-- IT'S WAITING AT THE FRONT DOOR OF THE BAXTER BUILDING!
THERE'S TWO OF THEM, OFFICERS!
DOWN WITH F.F.!
THREW ME OUT OF MY OWN BUILDING!
UH-OH! IT'S COLLINS --OUR LANDLORD!
ARREST THEM! THEY'RE A MENACE TO SOCIETY!
MISTER, WHILE YOU'RE PLAYIN' EVICTION GAMES, THERE'S A REAL MENACE ABOUT TO BRING THIS CITY DOWN ON YOUR HEAD!
STEP ASIDE!
3

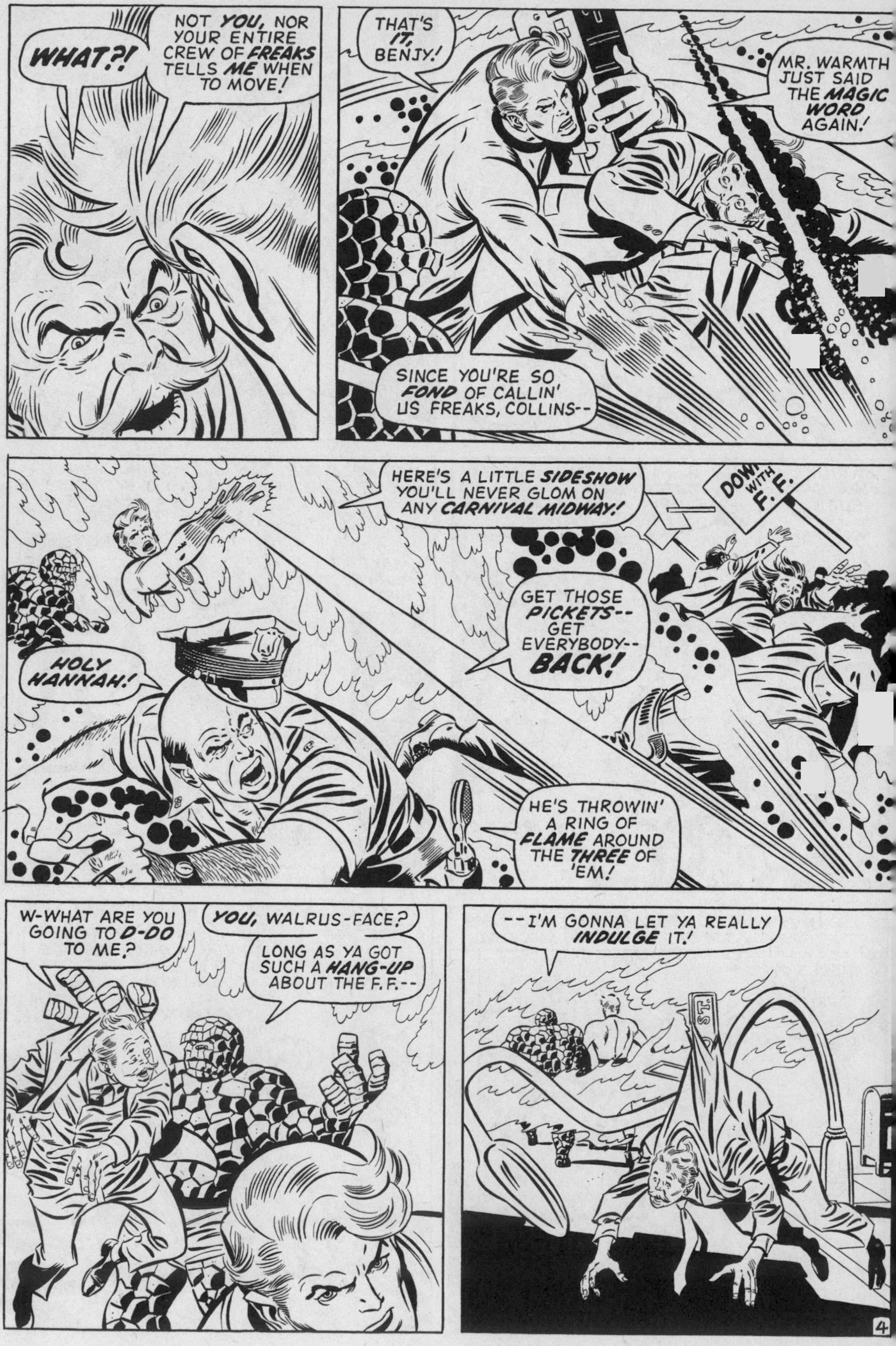

WHAT?!
NOT YOU, NOR YOUR ENTIRE CREW OF FREAKS TELLS ME WHEN TO MOVE!
THAT'S IT, BENJY!
MR. WARMTH JUST SAID THE MAGIC WORD AGAIN!
SINCE YOU'RE SO FOND OF CALLIN' US FREAKS, COLLINS--
HERE'S A LITTLE SIDESHOW YOU'LL NEVER GLOM ON ANY CARNIVAL MIDWAY!
WITH F.F.
HOLY HANNAH!
GET THOSE PICKETS-- GET EVERYBODY-- BACK!
HE'S THROWIN' A RING OF FLAME AROUND THE THREE OF 'EM!
W-WHAT ARE YOU GOING TO D-DO TO ME?
YOU, WALRUS-FACE?
LONG AS YA GOT SUCH A HANG-UP ABOUT THE F.F.--
--I'M GONNA LET YA REALLY INDULGE IT!
4

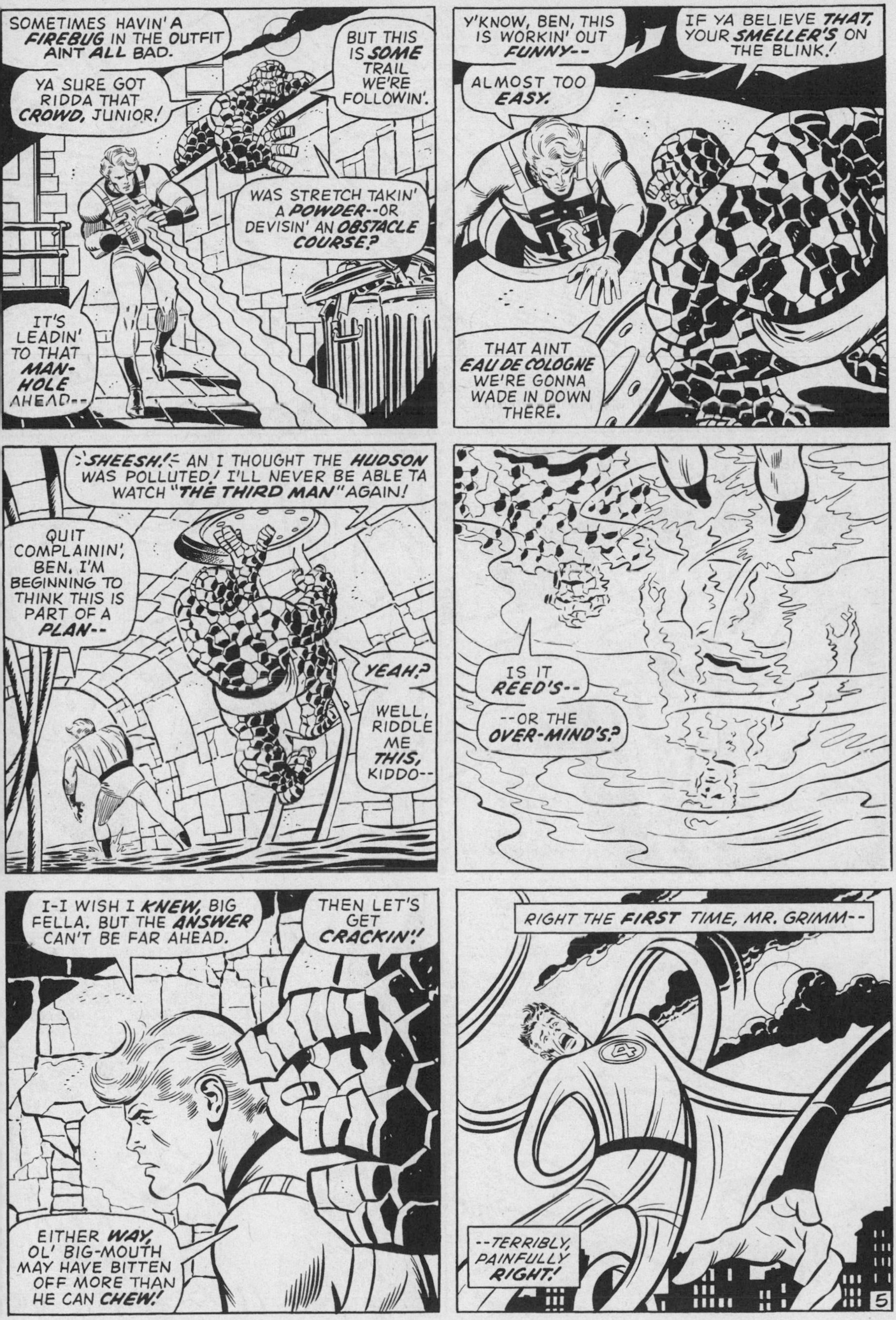
SOMETIMES HAVIN' A FIREBUG IN THE OUTFIT AINT ALL BAD.
YA SURE GOT RIDDA THAT CROWD, JUNIOR!
BUT THIS IS SOME TRAIL WE'RE FOLLOWIN'.
WAS STRETCH TAKIN' A POWDER--OR DEVISIN' AN OBSTACLE COURSE?
IT'S LEADIN' TO THAT MAN-HOLE AHEAD--
Y'KNOW, BEN, THIS IS WORKIN' OUT FUNNY--
ALMOST TOO EASY.
IF YA BELIEVE THAT, YOUR SMELLER'S ON THE BLINK!
THAT AINT EAU DE COLOGNE WE'RE GONNA WADE IN DOWN THERE.
SHEESH! AN I THOUGHT THE HUDSON WAS POLLUTED! I'LL NEVER BE ABLE TA WATCH "THE THIRD MAN" AGAIN!
QUIT COMPLAININ', BEN. I'M BEGINNING TO THINK THIS IS PART OF A PLAN--
YEAH?
WELL, RIDDLE ME THIS, KIDDO--
IS IT REED'S--
--OR THE OVER-MIND'S?
I-I WISH I KNEW, BIG FELLA. BUT THE ANSWER CAN'T BE FAR AHEAD.
THEN LET'S GET CRACKIN'!
EITHER WAY, OL' BIG-MOUTH MAY HAVE BITTEN OFF MORE THAN HE CAN CHEW!
RIGHT THE FIRST TIME, MR. GRIMM--
--TERRIBLY, PAINFULLY RIGHT!
5

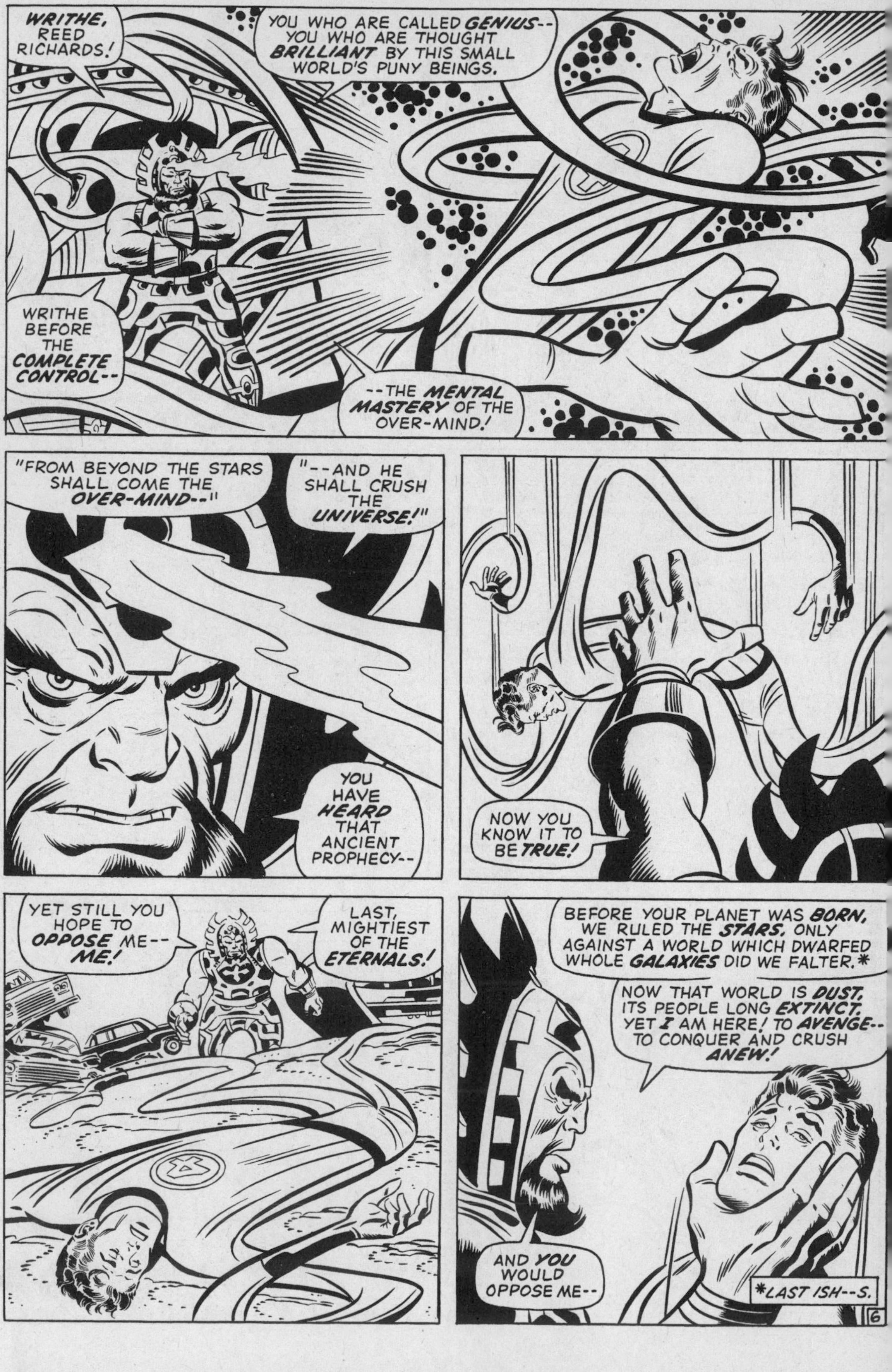
WRITHE, REED RICHARDS!
YOU WHO ARE CALLED GENIUS-- YOU WHO ARE THOUGHT BRILLIANT BY THIS SMALL WORLD'S PUNY BEINGS.
WRITHE BEFORE THE COMPLETE CONTROL--
--THE MENTAL MASTERY OF THE OVER-MIND!
"FROM BEYOND THE STARS SHALL COME THE OVER-MIND--"
"--AND HE SHALL CRUSH THE UNIVERSE!"
YOU HAVE HEARD THAT ANCIENT PROPHECY--
NOW YOU KNOW IT TO BE TRUE!
YET STILL YOU HOPE TO OPPOSE ME-- ME!
LAST, MIGHTIEST OF THE ETERNALS!
BEFORE YOUR PLANET WAS BORN, WE RULED THE STARS, ONLY AGAINST A WORLD WHICH DWARFED WHOLE GALAXIES DID WE FALTER.*
NOW THAT WORLD IS DUST, ITS PEOPLE LONG EXTINCT, YET I AM HERE! TO AVENGE-- TO CONQUER AND CRUSH ANEW!
AND YOU WOULD OPPOSE ME--
*LAST ISH--S.
6

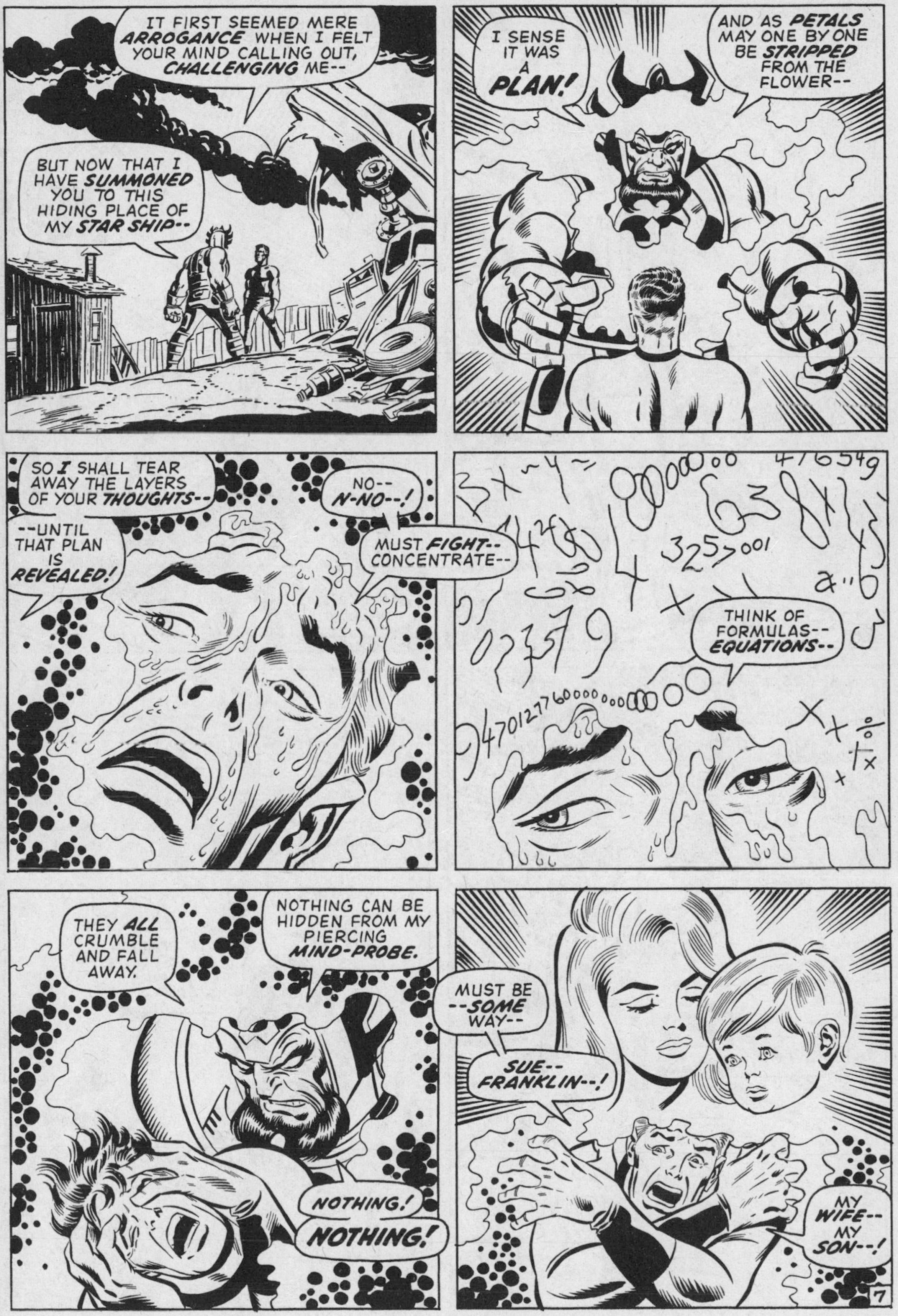
IT FIRST SEEMED MERE ARROGANCE WHEN I FELT YOUR MIND CALLING OUT, CHALLENGING ME--
BUT NOW THAT I HAVE SUMMONED YOU TO THIS HIDING PLACE OF MY STAR SHIP--
I SENSE IT WAS A PLAN!
AND AS PETALS MAY ONE BY ONE BE STRIPPED FROM THE FLOWER--
SO I SHALL TEAR AWAY THE LAYERS OF YOUR THOUGHTS--
--UNTIL THAT PLAN IS REVEALED!
NO-- N-NO--!
MUST FIGHT-- CONCENTRATE--
THINK OF FORMULAS-- EQUATIONS--
THEY ALL CRUMBLE AND FALL AWAY.
NOTHING CAN BE HIDDEN FROM MY PIERCING MIND-PROBE.
NOTHING!
NOTHING!
MUST BE --SOME WAY--
SUE-- FRANKLIN--!
MY WIFE-- MY SON--!

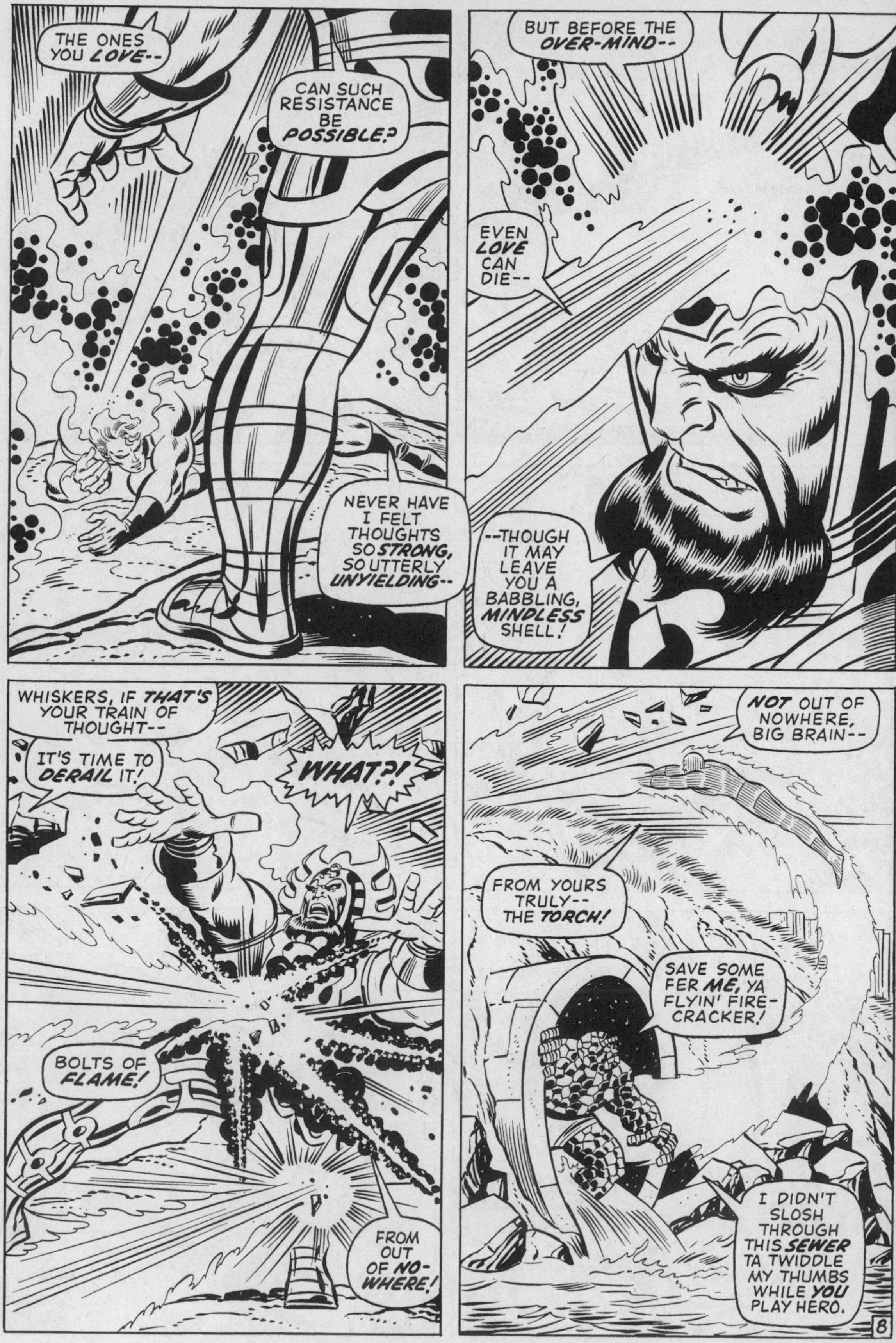
THE ONES YOU LOVE--
CAN SUCH RESISTANCE BE POSSIBLE?
NEVER HAVE I FELT THOUGHTS SO STRONG, SO UTTERLY UNYIELDING--
BUT BEFORE THE OVER-MIND--
EVEN LOVE CAN DIE--
--THOUGH IT MAY LEAVE YOU A BABBLING, MINDLESS SHELL!
WHISKERS, IF THAT'S YOUR TRAIN OF THOUGHT--
IT'S TIME TO DERAIL IT!
WHAT?!
BOLTS OF FLAME!
FROM OUT OF NO-WHERE!
NOT OUT OF NOWHERE, BIG BRAIN--
FROM YOURS TRULY-- THE TORCH!
SAVE SOME FER ME, YA FLYIN' FIRE-CRACKER!
I DIDN'T SLOSH THROUGH THIS SEWER TA TWIDDLE MY THUMBS WHILE YOU PLAY HERO.
8

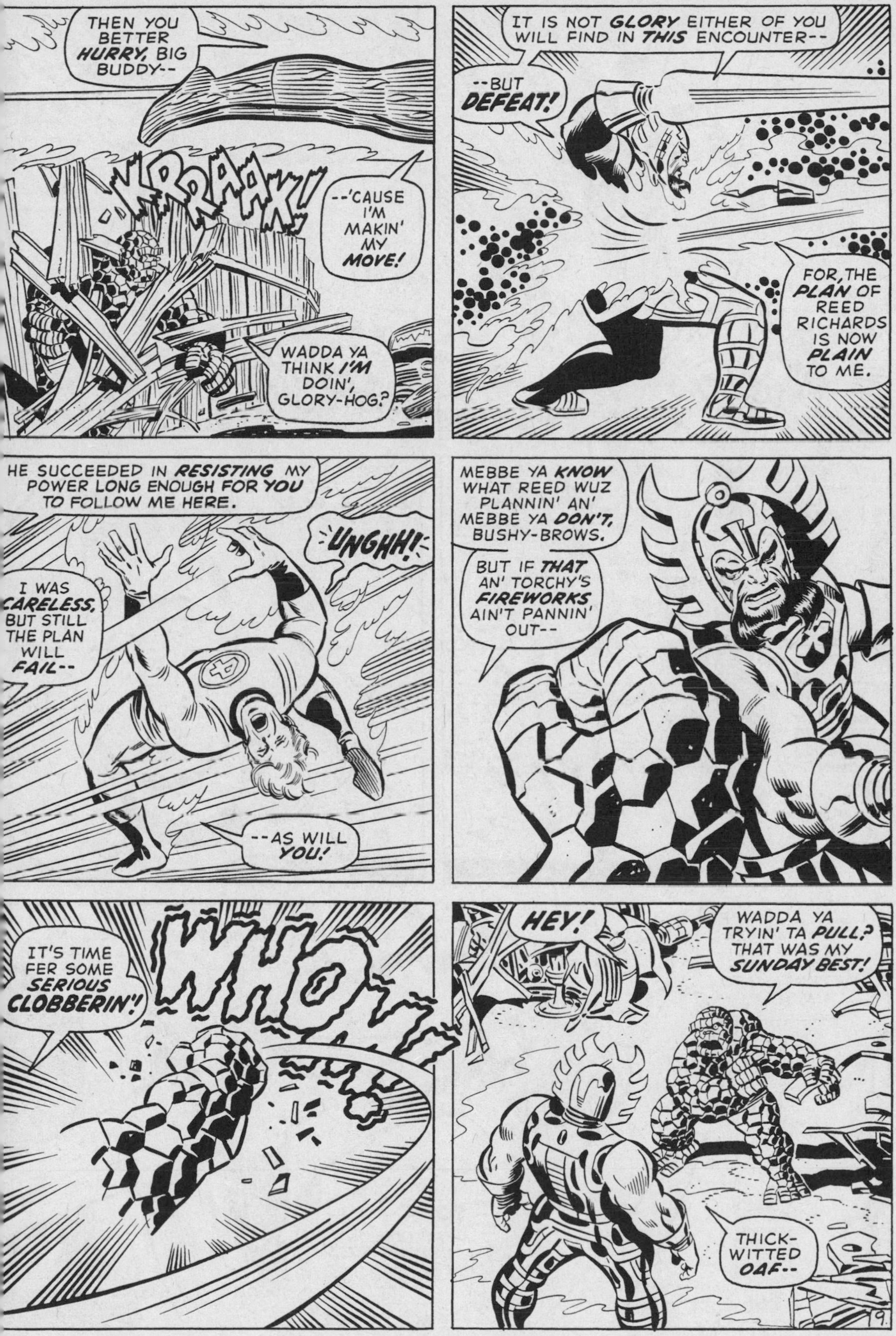

THEN YOU BETTER HURRY, BIG BUDDY--
KRRAAK!
--'CAUSE I'M MAKIN' MY MOVE!
WADDA YA THINK I'M DOIN', GLORY-HOG?
IT IS NOT GLORY EITHER OF YOU WILL FIND IN THIS ENCOUNTER--
--BUT DEFEAT!
FOR, THE PLAN OF REED RICHARDS IS NOW PLAIN TO ME.
HE SUCCEEDED IN RESISTING MY POWER LONG ENOUGH FOR YOU TO FOLLOW ME HERE.
UNGHH!
I WAS CARELESS, BUT STILL THE PLAN WILL FAIL--
--AS WILL YOU!
MEBBE YA KNOW WHAT REED WUZ PLANNIN' AN' MEBBE YA DON'T, BUSHY-BROWS.
BUT IF THAT AN' TORCHY'S FIREWORKS AIN'T PANNIN' OUT--
IT'S TIME FER SOME SERIOUS CLOBBERIN'!
WHOM
HEY!
WADDA YA TRYIN' TA PULL? THAT WAS MY SUNDAY BEST!
THICK-WITTED OAF--
19.

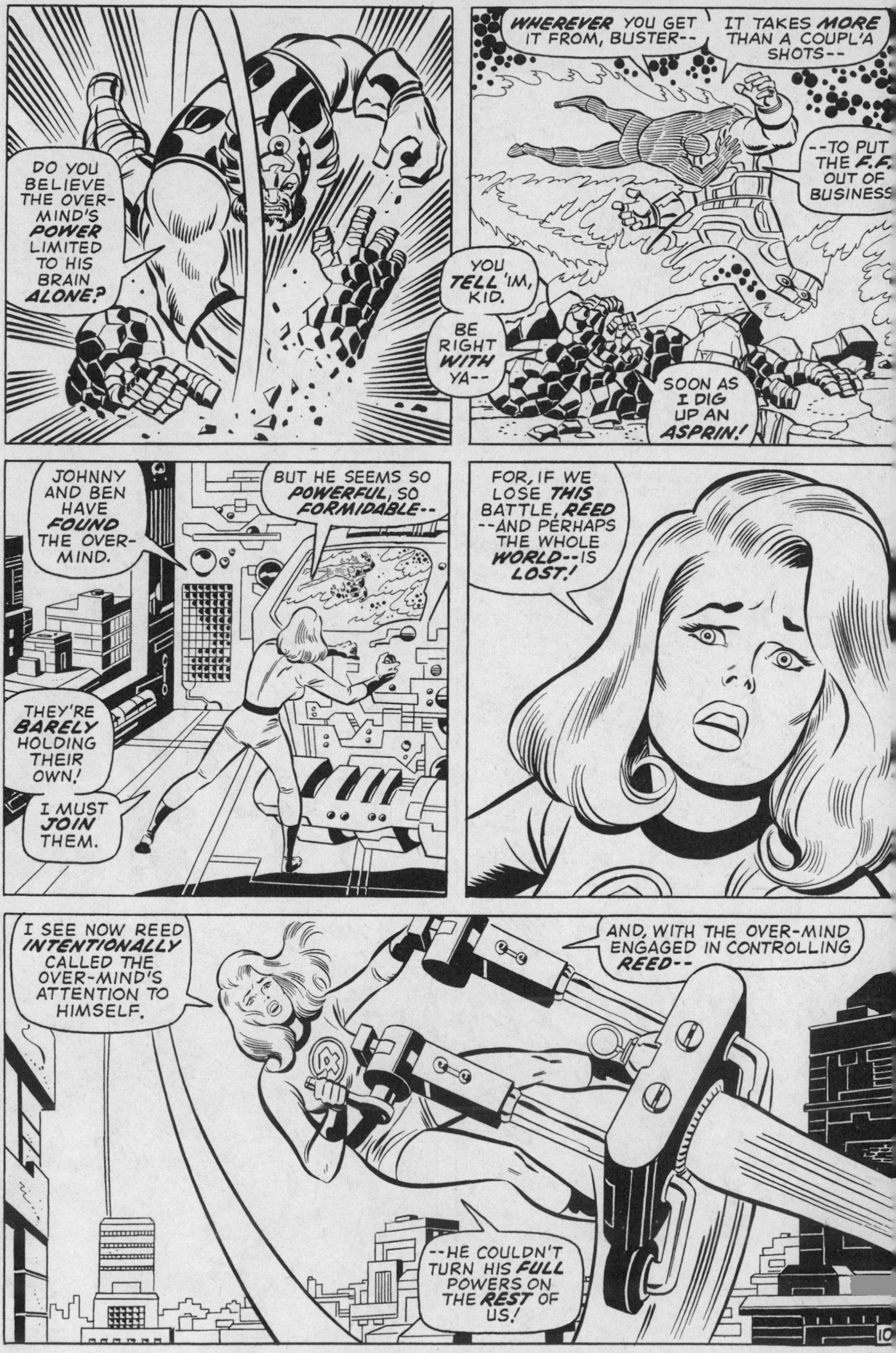
DO YOU BELIEVE THE OVER-MIND'S POWER LIMITED TO HIS BRAIN ALONE?
WHEREVER YOU GET IT FROM, BUSTER--
IT TAKES MORE THAN A COUPL'A SHOTS--
--TO PUT THE F.F. OUT OF BUSINESS
YOU TELL 'IM, KID.
BE RIGHT WITH YA--
SOON AS I DIG UP AN ASPRIN!
JOHNNY AND BEN HAVE FOUND THE OVER-MIND.
BUT HE SEEMS SO POWERFUL, SO FORMIDABLE--
THEY'RE BARELY HOLDING THEIR OWN!
I MUST JOIN THEM.
FOR, IF WE LOSE THIS BATTLE, REED --AND PERHAPS THE WHOLE WORLD--IS LOST!
I SEE NOW REED INTENTIONALLY CALLED THE OVER-MIND'S ATTENTION TO HIMSELF.
AND, WITH THE OVER-MIND ENGAGED IN CONTROLLING REED--
--HE COULDN'T TURN HIS FULL POWERS ON THE REST OF US!
10

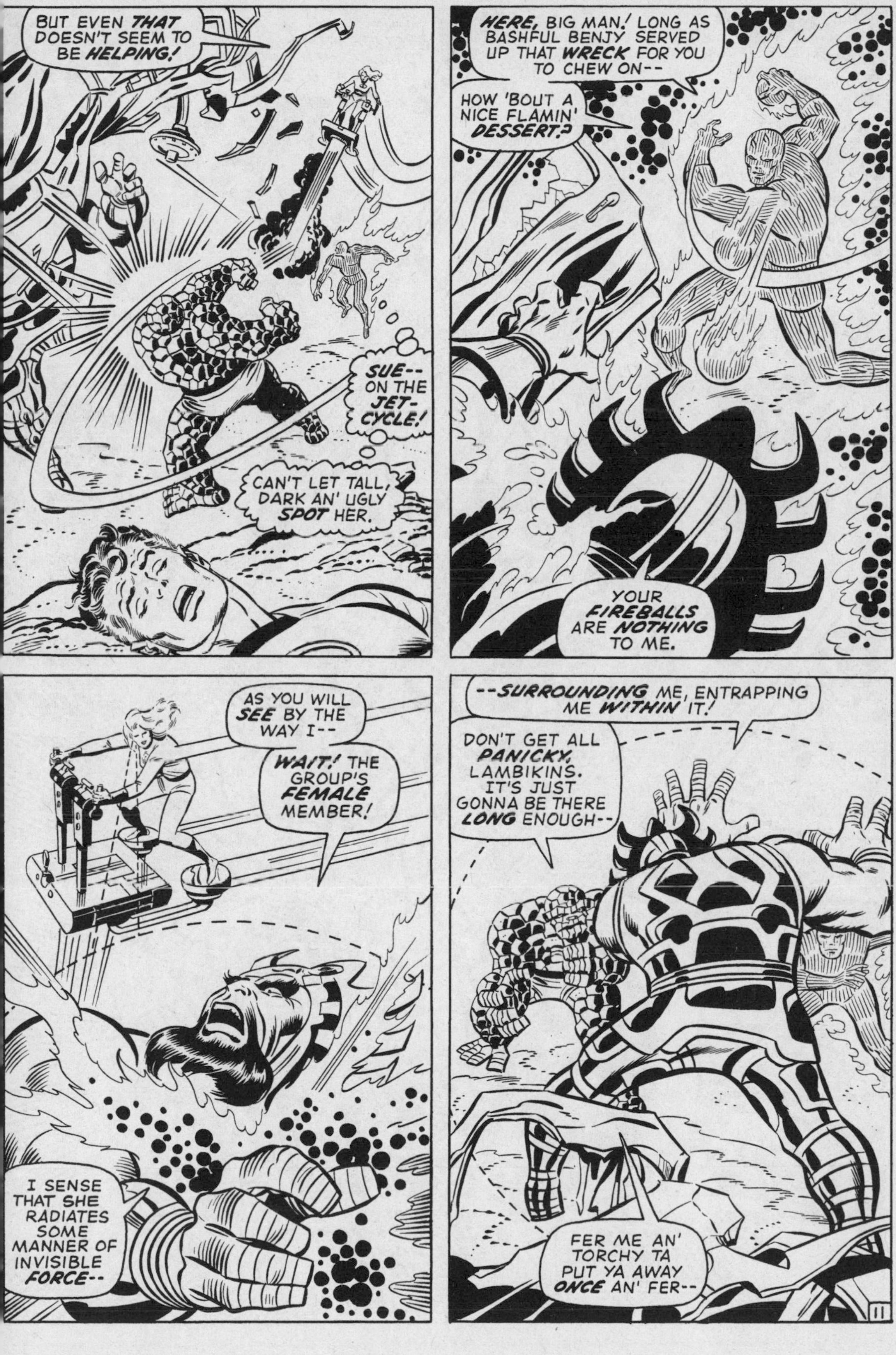
BUT EVEN THAT DOESN'T SEEM TO BE HELPING!
SUE-- ON THE JET-CYCLE!
CAN'T LET TALL, DARK AN' UGLY SPOT HER.
HERE, BIG MAN! LONG AS BASHFUL BENJY SERVED UP THAT WRECK FOR YOU TO CHEW ON--
HOW 'BOUT A NICE FLAMIN' DESSERT?
YOUR FIREBALLS ARE NOTHING TO ME.
AS YOU WILL SEE BY THE WAY I--
WAIT! THE GROUP'S FEMALE MEMBER!
I SENSE THAT SHE RADIATES SOME MANNER OF INVISIBLE FORCE--
--SURROUNDING ME, ENTRAPPING ME WITHIN IT!
DON'T GET ALL PANICKY, LAMBIKINS. IT'S JUST GONNA BE THERE LONG ENOUGH--
FER ME AN' TORCHY TA PUT YA AWAY ONCE AN' FER--
11

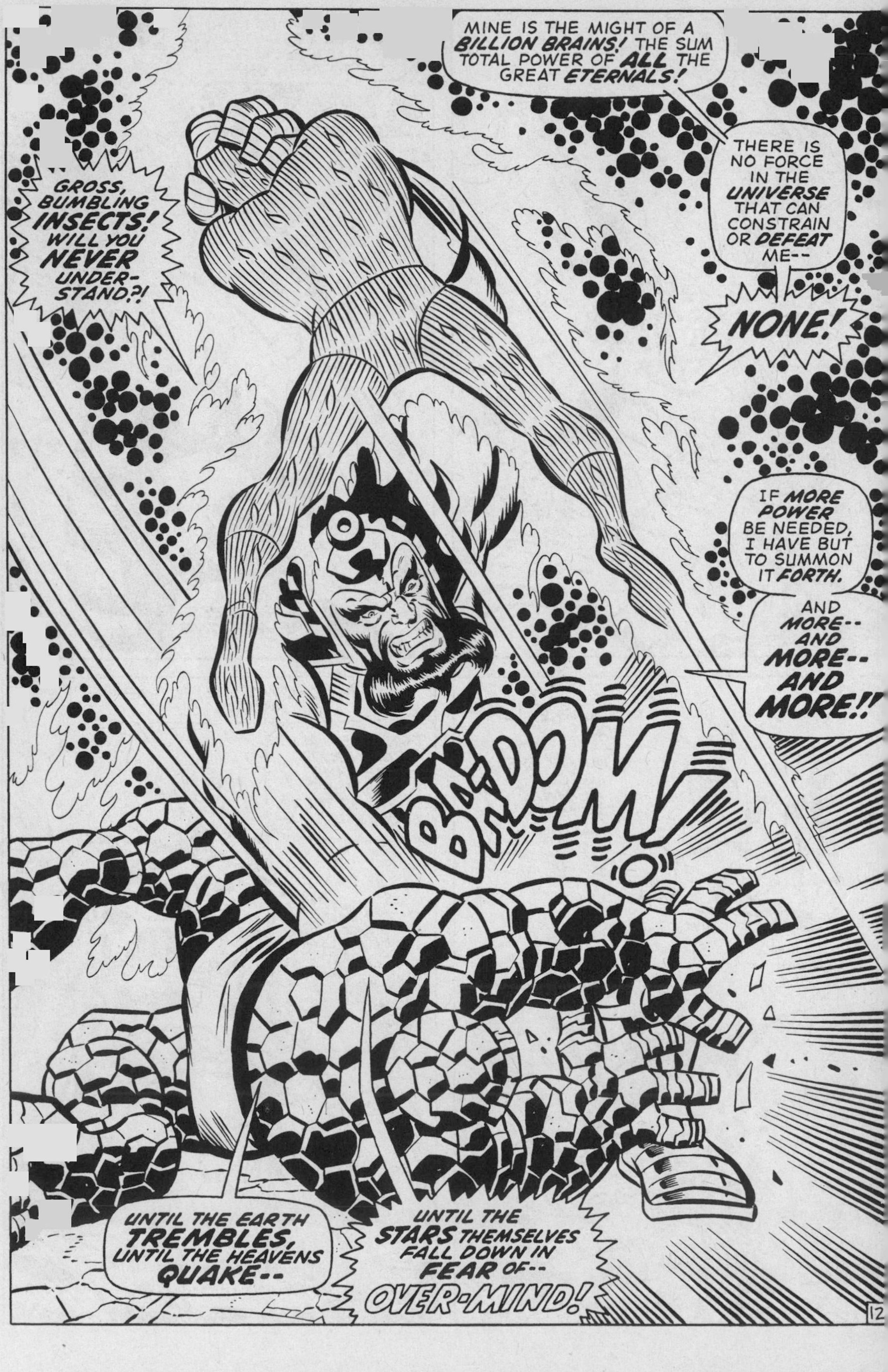
MINE IS THE MIGHT OF A BILLION BRAINS! THE SUM TOTAL POWER OF ALL THE GREAT ETERNALS!
GROSS, BUMBLING INSECTS! WILL YOU NEVER UNDER-STAND?!
THERE IS NO FORCE IN THE UNIVERSE THAT CAN CONSTRAIN OR DEFEAT ME--
NONE!
IF MORE POWER BE NEEDED, I HAVE BUT TO SUMMON IT FORTH.
AND MORE-- AND MORE-- AND MORE!!
BA-DOOM!
UNTIL THE EARTH TREMBLES, UNTIL THE HEAVENS QUAKE--
UNTIL THE STARS THEMSELVES FALL DOWN IN FEAR OF--
OVER-MIND!
12

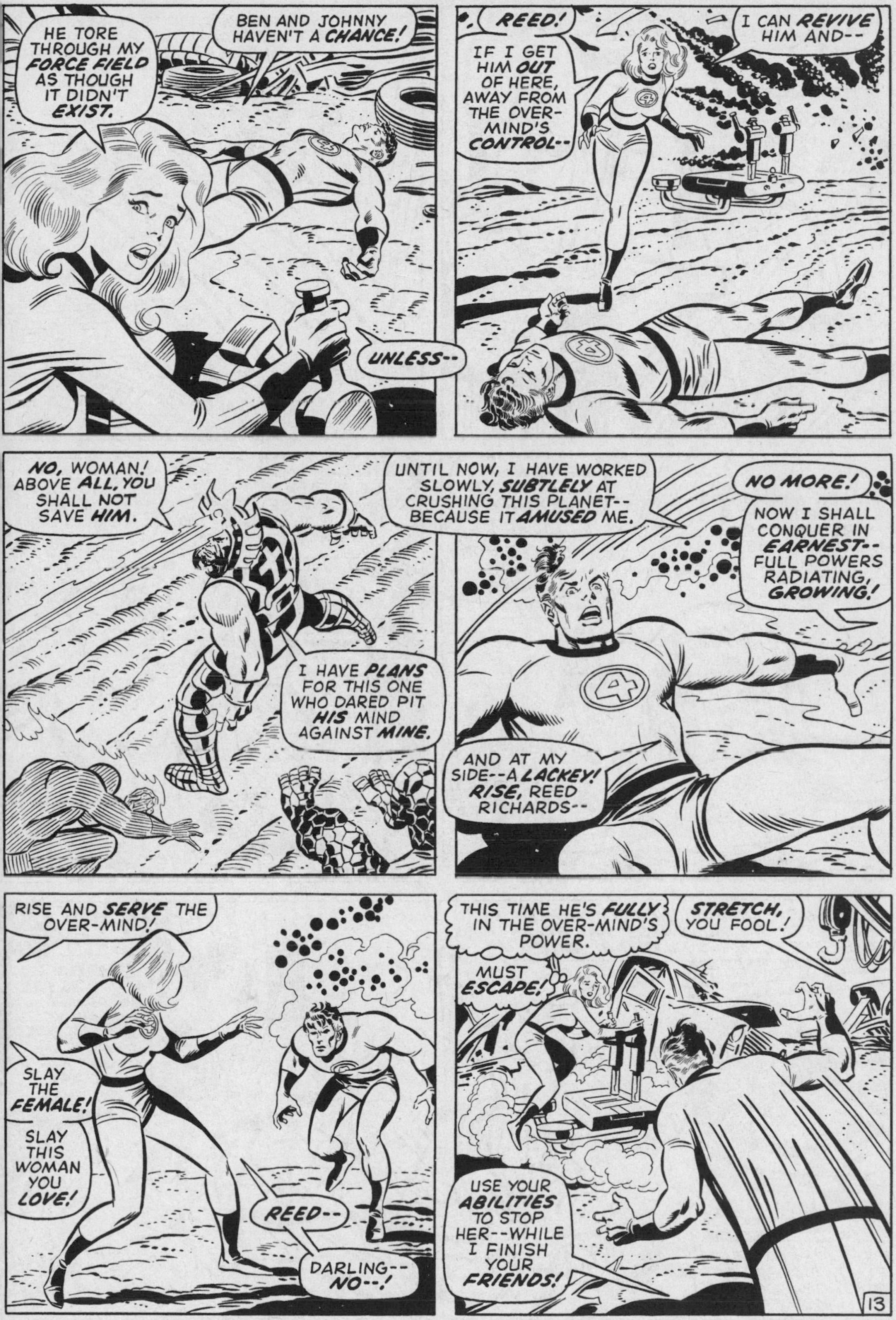
HE TORE THROUGH MY FORCE FIELD AS THOUGH IT DIDN'T EXIST.
BEN AND JOHNNY HAVEN'T A CHANCE!
UNLESS--
REED!
IF I GET HIM OUT OF HERE, AWAY FROM THE OVER-MIND'S CONTROL--
I CAN REVIVE HIM AND--
NO, WOMAN! ABOVE ALL, YOU SHALL NOT SAVE HIM.
I HAVE PLANS FOR THIS ONE WHO DARED PIT HIS MIND AGAINST MINE.
UNTIL NOW, I HAVE WORKED SLOWLY, SUBTLELY AT CRUSHING THIS PLANET-- BECAUSE IT AMUSED ME.
NO MORE!
NOW I SHALL CONQUER IN EARNEST-- FULL POWERS RADIATING, GROWING!
AND AT MY SIDE--A LACKEY! RISE, REED RICHARDS--
RISE AND SERVE THE OVER-MIND!
SLAY THE FEMALE!
SLAY THIS WOMAN YOU LOVE!
REED--
DARLING-- NO--!
THIS TIME HE'S FULLY IN THE OVER-MIND'S POWER.
MUST ESCAPE!
STRETCH, YOU FOOL!
USE YOUR ABILITIES TO STOP HER--WHILE I FINISH YOUR FRIENDS!
13

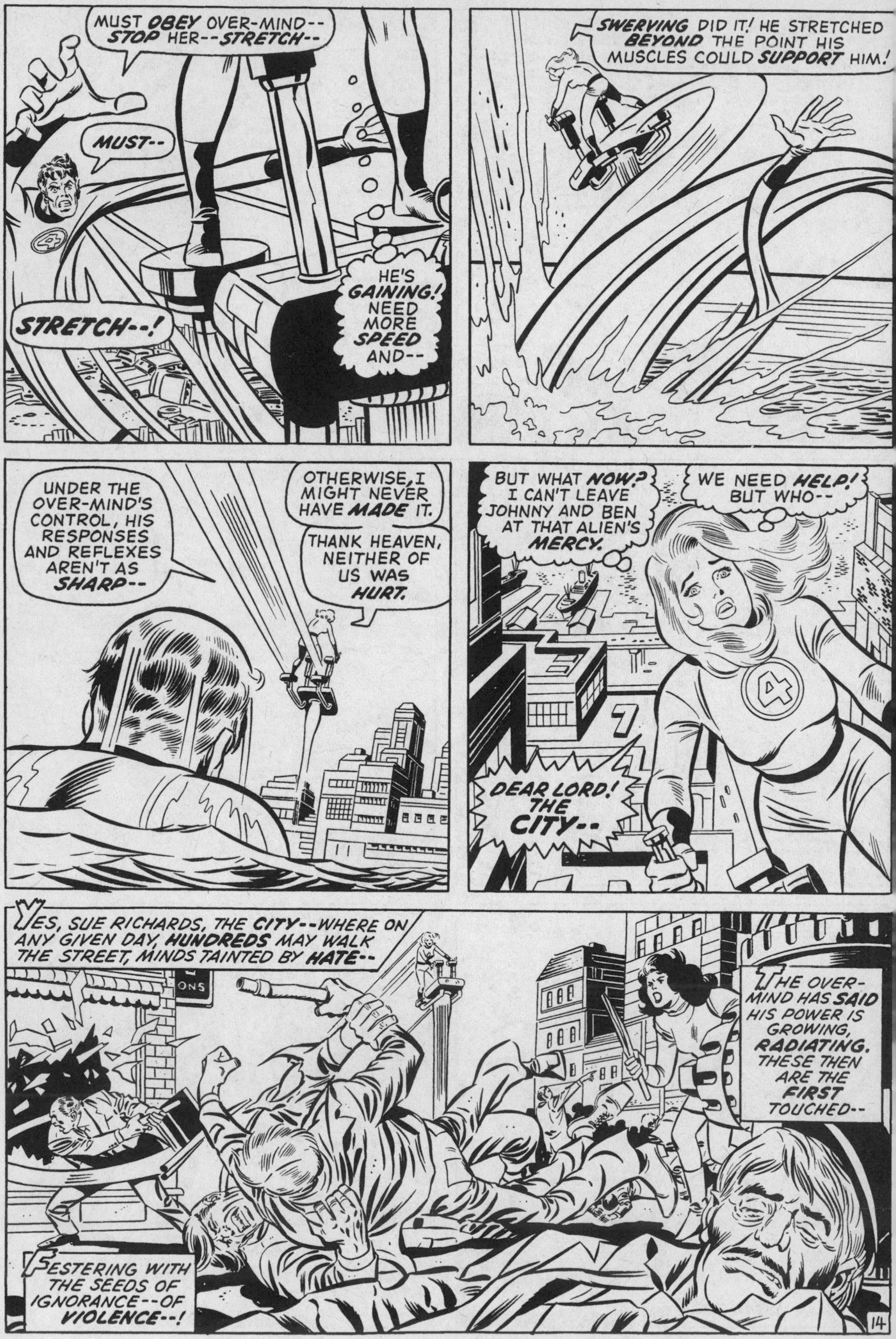
MUST OBEY OVER-MIND-- STOP HER--STRETCH--
MUST--
STRETCH--!
HE'S GAINING! NEED MORE SPEED AND--
SWERVING DID IT! HE STRETCHED BEYOND THE POINT HIS MUSCLES COULD SUPPORT HIM!
UNDER THE OVER-MIND'S CONTROL, HIS RESPONSES AND REFLEXES AREN'T AS SHARP--
OTHERWISE, I MIGHT NEVER HAVE MADE IT.
THANK HEAVEN, NEITHER OF US WAS HURT.
BUT WHAT NOW? I CAN'T LEAVE JOHNNY AND BEN AT THAT ALIEN'S MERCY.
WE NEED HELP! BUT WHO--
DEAR LORD! THE CITY--
YES, SUE RICHARDS, THE CITY--WHERE ON ANY GIVEN DAY, HUNDREDS MAY WALK THE STREET, MINDS TAINTED BY HATE--
THE OVER-MIND HAS SAID HIS POWER IS GROWING, RADIATING. THESE THEN ARE THE FIRST TOUCHED--
FESTERING WITH THE SEEDS OF IGNORANCE--OF VIOLENCE--!
14

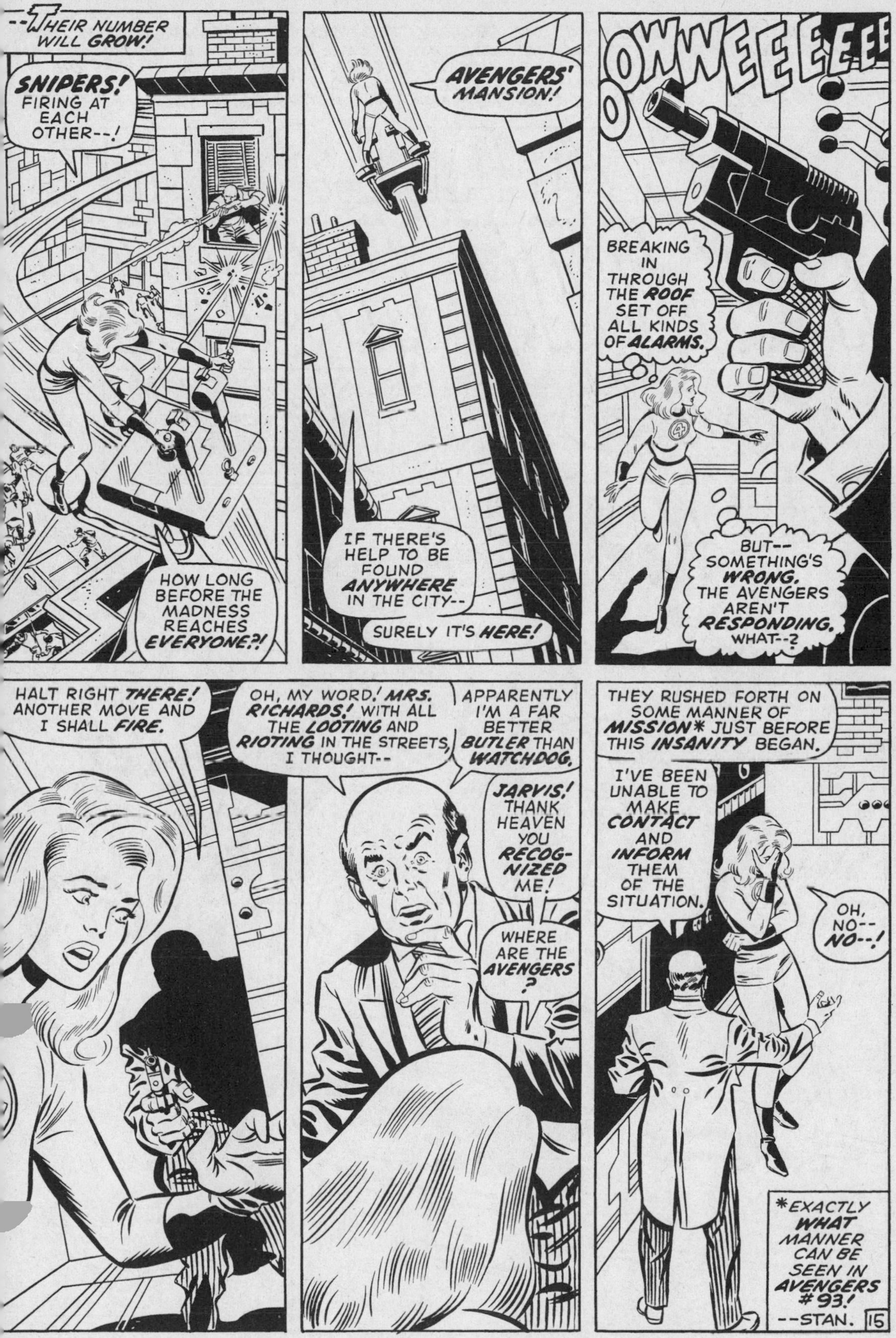
--THEIR NUMBER WILL GROW!
SNIPERS! FIRING AT EACH OTHER--!
HOW LONG BEFORE THE MADNESS REACHES EVERYONE?!
AVENGERS' MANSION!
IF THERE'S HELP TO BE FOUND ANYWHERE IN THE CITY--
SURELY IT'S HERE!
OWWEEEEEEE
BREAKING IN THROUGH THE ROOF SET OFF ALL KINDS OF ALARMS.
BUT-- SOMETHING'S WRONG. THE AVENGERS AREN'T RESPONDING. WHAT--?
HALT RIGHT THERE! ANOTHER MOVE AND I SHALL FIRE.
OH, MY WORD! MRS. RICHARDS! WITH ALL THE LOOTING AND RIOTING IN THE STREETS, I THOUGHT--
APPARENTLY I'M A FAR BETTER BUTLER THAN WATCHDOG.
JARVIS! THANK HEAVEN YOU RECOGNIZED ME!
WHERE ARE THE AVENGERS?
THEY RUSHED FORTH ON SOME MANNER OF MISSION* JUST BEFORE THIS INSANITY BEGAN.
I'VE BEEN UNABLE TO MAKE CONTACT AND INFORM THEM OF THE SITUATION.
OH, NO-- NO--!
*EXACTLY WHAT MANNER CAN BE SEEN IN AVENGERS #93! --STAN.
15

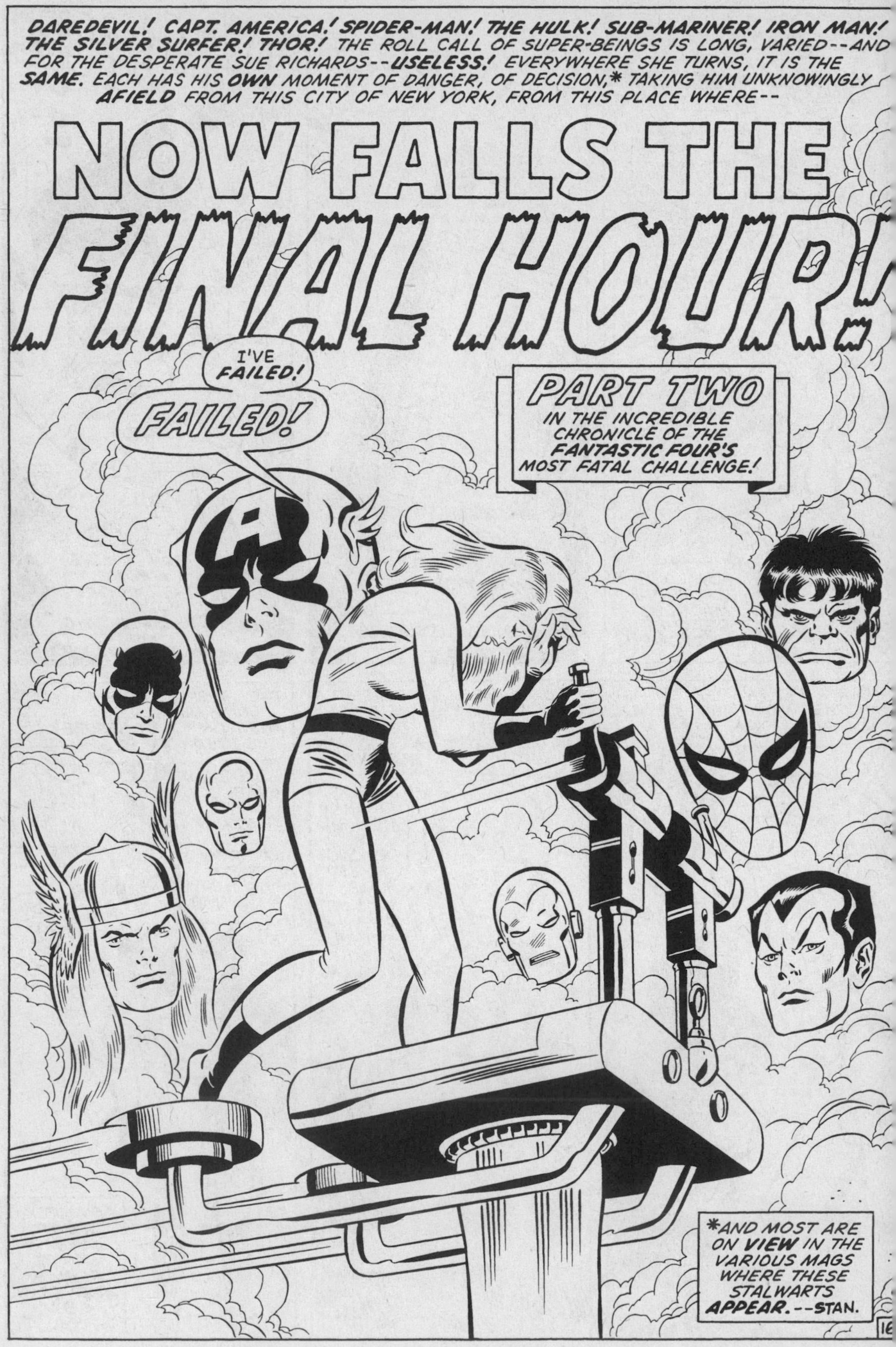
DAREDEVIL! CAPT. AMERICA! SPIDER-MAN! THE HULK! SUB-MARINER! IRON MAN! THE SILVER SURFER! THOR! THE ROLL CALL OF SUPER-BEINGS IS LONG, VARIED--AND FOR THE DESPERATE SUE RICHARDS--USELESS! EVERYWHERE SHE TURNS, IT IS THE SAME. EACH HAS HIS OWN MOMENT OF DANGER, OF DECISION,* TAKING HIM UNKNOWINGLY AFIELD FROM THIS CITY OF NEW YORK, FROM THIS PLACE WHERE--
NOW FALLS THE FINAL HOUR!
I'VE FAILED!
FAILED!
PART TWO IN THE INCREDIBLE CHRONICLE OF THE FANTASTIC FOUR'S MOST FATAL CHALLENGE!
*AND MOST ARE ON VIEW IN THE VARIOUS MAGS WHERE THESE STALWARTS APPEAR.--STAN.
16

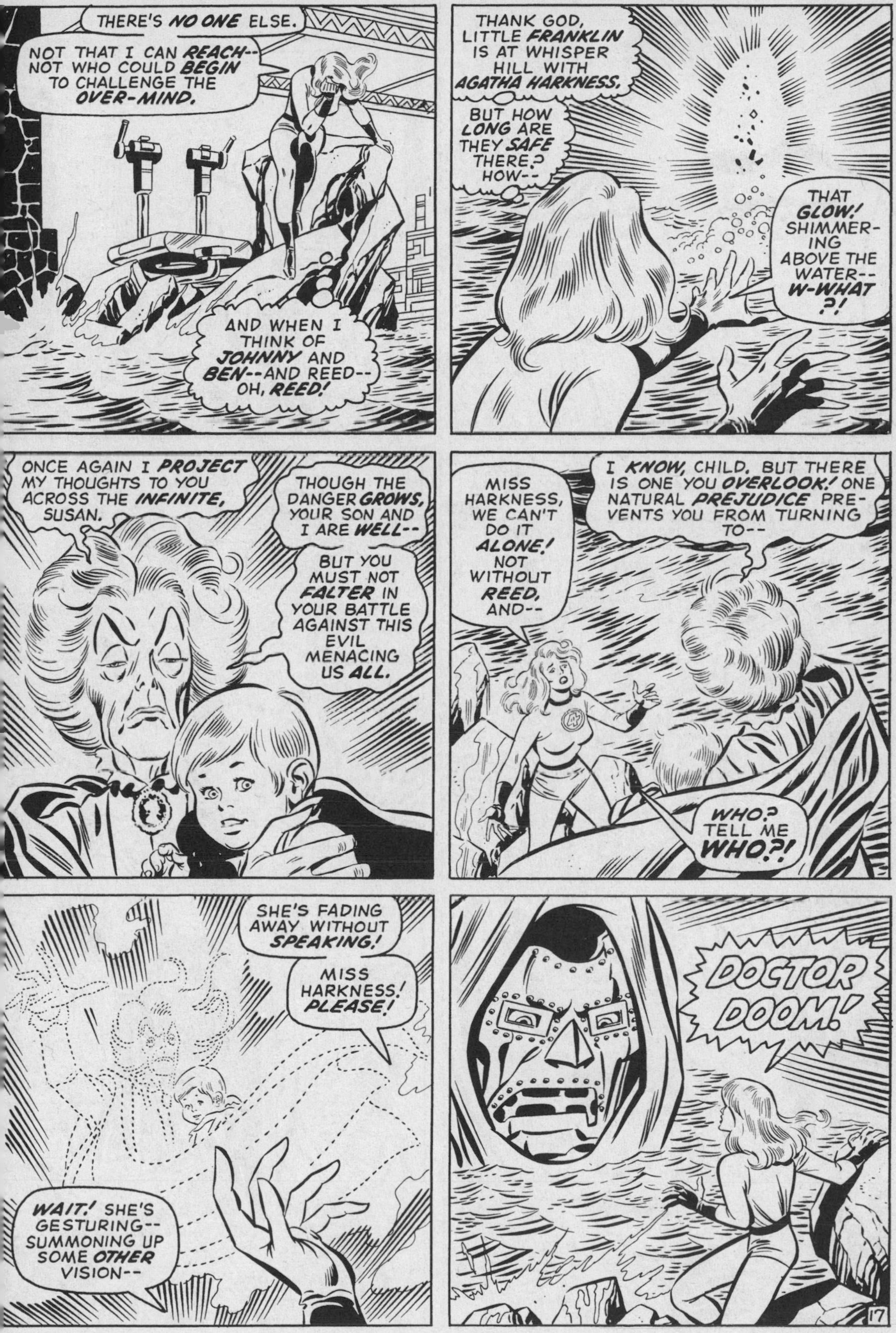
THERE'S NO ONE ELSE.
NOT THAT I CAN REACH-- NOT WHO COULD BEGIN TO CHALLENGE THE OVER-MIND.
AND WHEN I THINK OF JOHNNY AND BEN--AND REED-- OH, REED!
THANK GOD, LITTLE FRANKLIN IS AT WHISPER HILL WITH AGATHA HARKNESS.
BUT HOW LONG ARE THEY SAFE THERE? HOW--
THAT GLOW! SHIMMERING ABOVE THE WATER-- W-WHAT?!
ONCE AGAIN I PROJECT MY THOUGHTS TO YOU ACROSS THE INFINITE, SUSAN.
THOUGH THE DANGER GROWS, YOUR SON AND I ARE WELL--
BUT YOU MUST NOT FALTER IN YOUR BATTLE AGAINST THIS EVIL MENACING US ALL.
MISS HARKNESS, WE CAN'T DO IT ALONE! NOT WITHOUT REED, AND--
I KNOW, CHILD. BUT THERE IS ONE YOU OVERLOOK! ONE NATURAL PREJUDICE PREVENTS YOU FROM TURNING TO--
WHO? TELL ME WHO?!
SHE'S FADING AWAY WITHOUT SPEAKING!
MISS HARKNESS! PLEASE!
WAIT! SHE'S GESTURING-- SUMMONING UP SOME OTHER VISION--
DOCTOR DOOM!
17

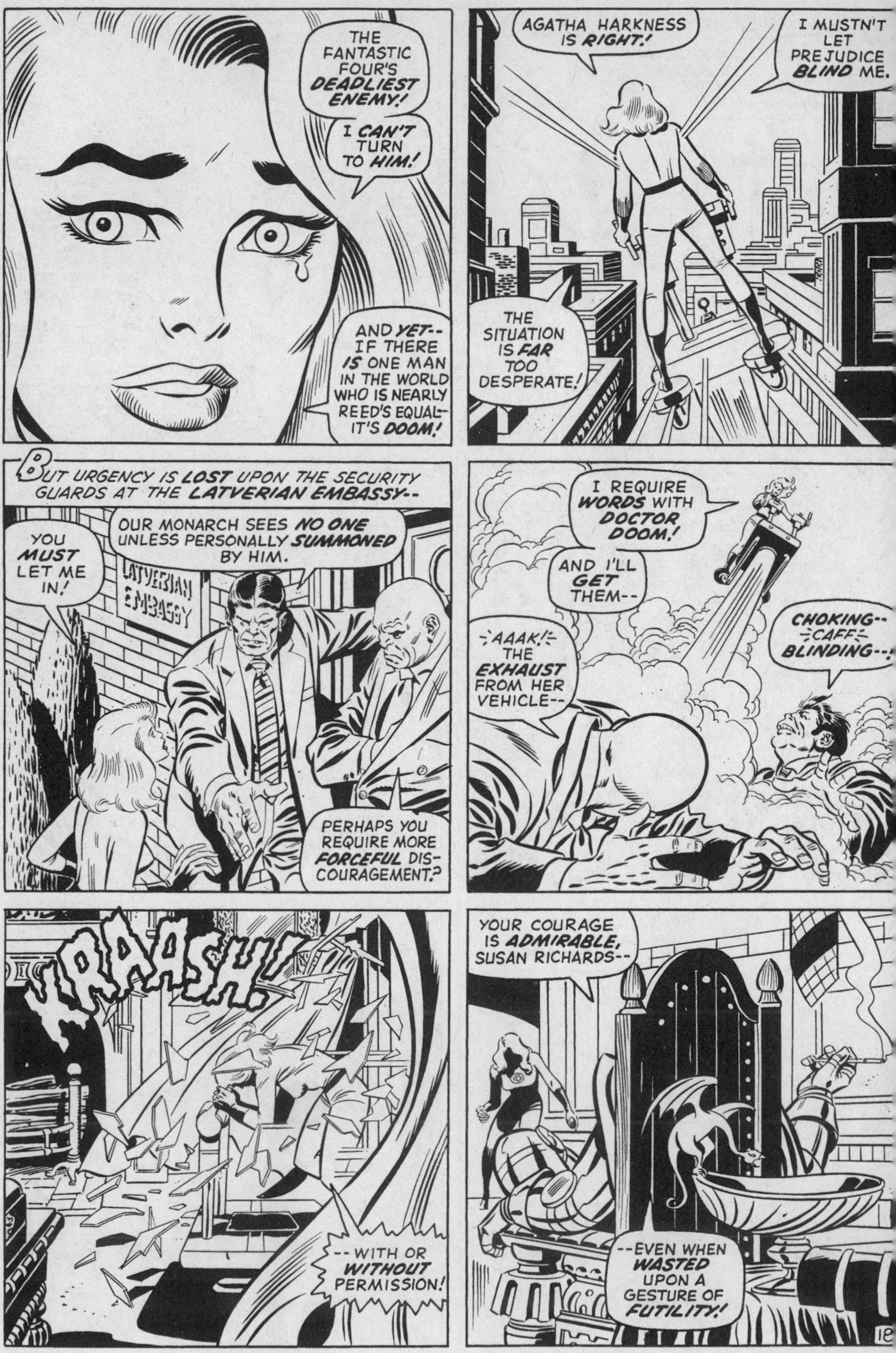
THE FANTASTIC FOUR'S DEADLIEST ENEMY!
I CAN'T TURN TO HIM!
AND YET-- IF THERE IS ONE MAN IN THE WORLD WHO IS NEARLY REED'S EQUAL-- IT'S DOOM!
AGATHA HARKNESS IS RIGHT!
I MUSTN'T LET PREJUDICE BLIND ME.
THE SITUATION IS FAR TOO DESPERATE!
BUT URGENCY IS LOST UPON THE SECURITY GUARDS AT THE LATVERIAN EMBASSY--
YOU MUST LET ME IN!
OUR MONARCH SEES NO ONE UNLESS PERSONALLY SUMMONED BY HIM.
LATVERIAN EMBASSY
PERHAPS YOU REQUIRE MORE FORCEFUL DISCOURAGEMENT?
I REQUIRE WORDS WITH DOCTOR DOOM!
AND I'LL GET THEM--
-AAAK!- THE EXHAUST FROM HER VEHICLE--
CHOKING-- -CAFF- BLINDING--
KRAASH!
--WITH OR WITHOUT PERMISSION!
YOUR COURAGE IS ADMIRABLE, SUSAN RICHARDS--
--EVEN WHEN WASTED UPON A GESTURE OF FUTILITY!
18

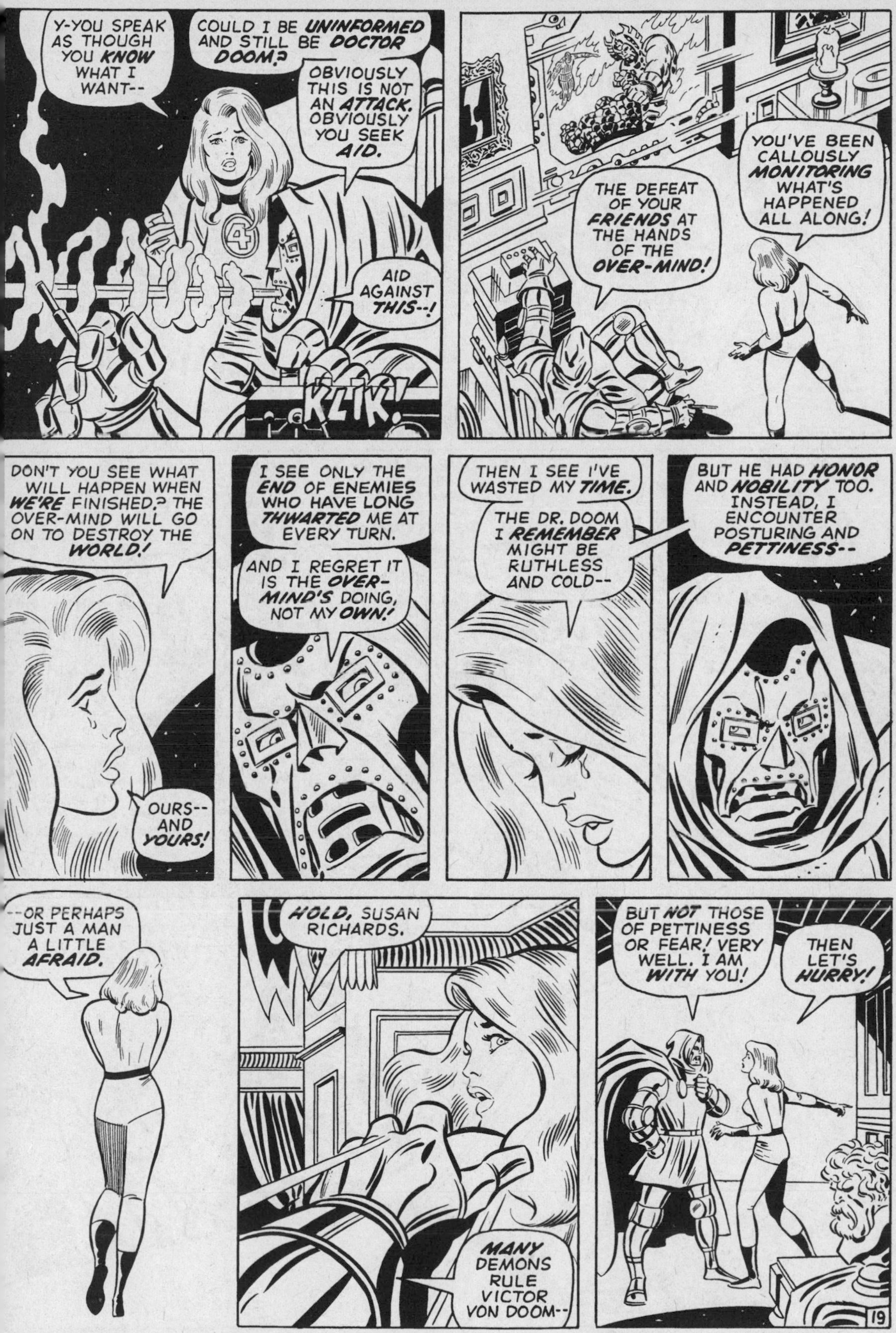
Y-YOU SPEAK AS THOUGH YOU KNOW WHAT I WANT--
COULD I BE UNINFORMED AND STILL BE DOCTOR DOOM?
OBVIOUSLY THIS IS NOT AN ATTACK. OBVIOUSLY YOU SEEK AID.
AID AGAINST THIS--!
KLIK!
YOU'VE BEEN CALLOUSLY MONITORING WHAT'S HAPPENED ALL ALONG!
THE DEFEAT OF YOUR FRIENDS AT THE HANDS OF THE OVER-MIND!
DON'T YOU SEE WHAT WILL HAPPEN WHEN WE'RE FINISHED? THE OVER-MIND WILL GO ON TO DESTROY THE WORLD!
OURS--AND YOURS!
I SEE ONLY THE END OF ENEMIES WHO HAVE LONG THWARTED ME AT EVERY TURN.
AND I REGRET IT IS THE OVER-MIND'S DOING, NOT MY OWN!
THEN I SEE I'VE WASTED MY TIME.
THE DR. DOOM I REMEMBER MIGHT BE RUTHLESS AND COLD--
BUT HE HAD HONOR AND NOBILITY TOO. INSTEAD, I ENCOUNTER POSTURING AND PETTINESS--
--OR PERHAPS JUST A MAN A LITTLE AFRAID.
HOLD, SUSAN RICHARDS.
MANY DEMONS RULE VICTOR VON DOOM--
BUT NOT THOSE OF PETTINESS OR FEAR! VERY WELL. I AM WITH YOU!
THEN LET'S HURRY!
19

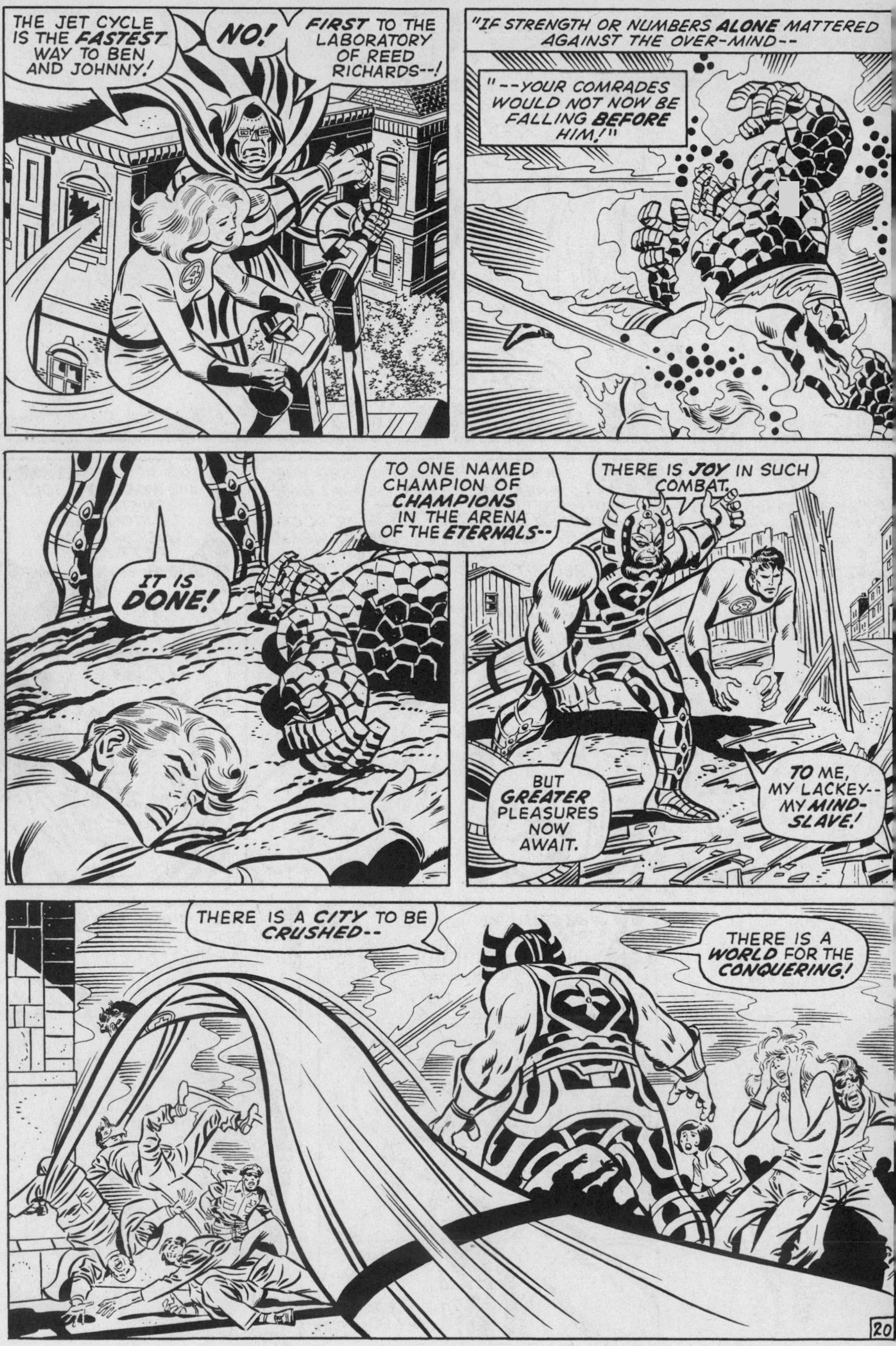
THE JET CYCLE IS THE FASTEST WAY TO BEN AND JOHNNY!
NO!
FIRST TO THE LABORATORY OF REED RICHARDS--!
"IF STRENGTH OR NUMBERS ALONE MATTERED AGAINST THE OVER-MIND--
"--YOUR COMRADES WOULD NOT NOW BE FALLING BEFORE HIM!"
IT IS DONE!
TO ONE NAMED CHAMPION OF CHAMPIONS IN THE ARENA OF THE ETERNALS--
THERE IS JOY IN SUCH COMBAT.
BUT GREATER PLEASURES NOW AWAIT.
TO ME, MY LACKEY-- MY MIND-SLAVE!
THERE IS A CITY TO BE CRUSHED--
THERE IS A WORLD FOR THE CONQUERING!

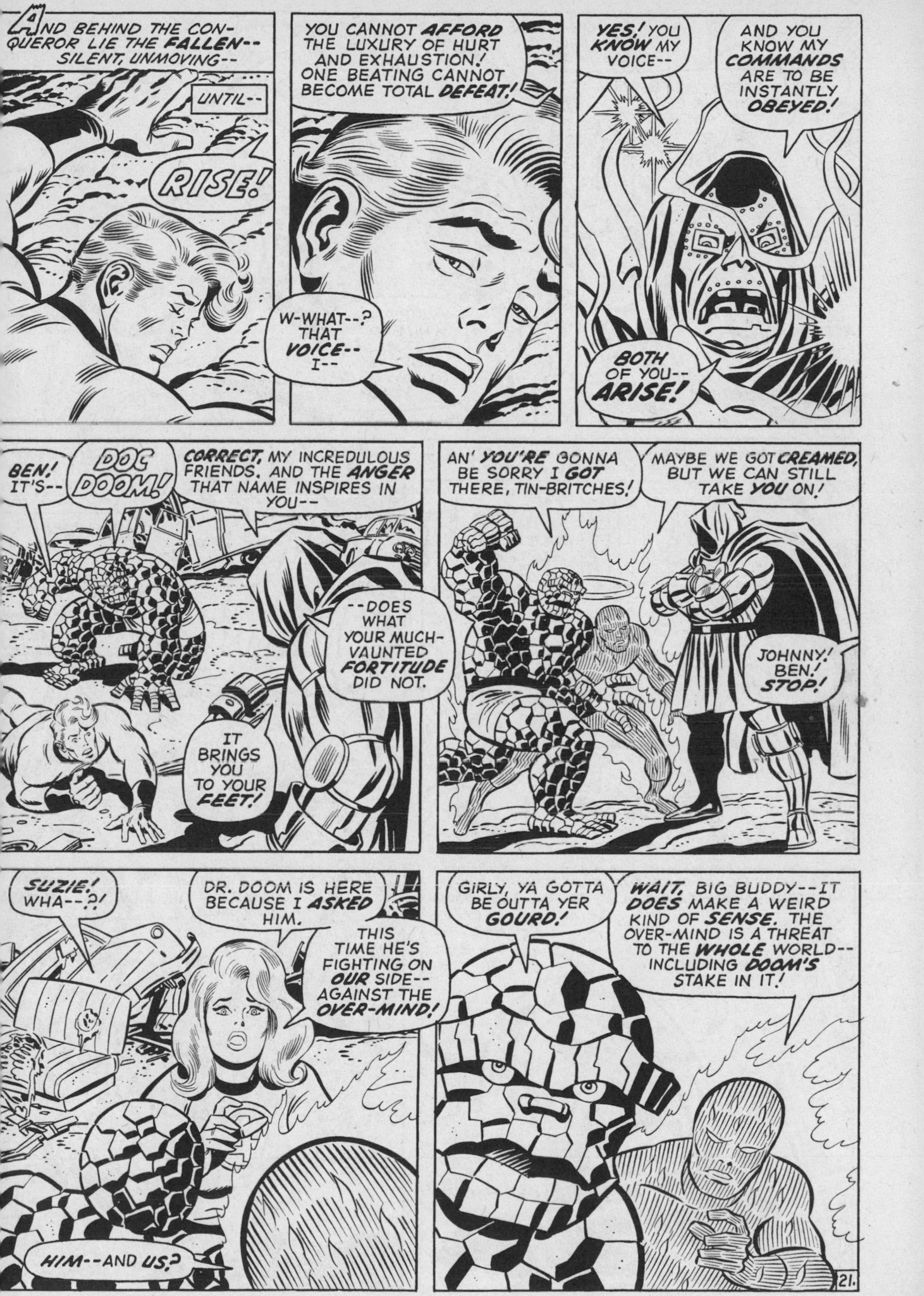
AND BEHIND THE CONQUEROR LIE THE FALLEN--SILENT, UNMOVING--
UNTIL--
RISE!
YOU CANNOT AFFORD THE LUXURY OF HURT AND EXHAUSTION! ONE BEATING CANNOT BECOME TOTAL DEFEAT!
W-WHAT--? THAT VOICE--I--
YES! YOU KNOW MY VOICE--
AND YOU KNOW MY COMMANDS ARE TO BE INSTANTLY OBEYED!
BOTH OF YOU--ARISE!
BEN! IT'S--
DOC DOOM!
CORRECT, MY INCREDULOUS FRIENDS. AND THE ANGER THAT NAME INSPIRES IN YOU--
--DOES WHAT YOUR MUCH-VAUNTED FORTITUDE DID NOT.
IT BRINGS YOU TO YOUR FEET!
AN' YOU'RE GONNA BE SORRY I GOT THERE, TIN-BRITCHES!
MAYBE WE GOT CREAMED, BUT WE CAN STILL TAKE YOU ON!
JOHNNY! BEN! STOP!
SUZIE! WHA--?!
DR. DOOM IS HERE BECAUSE I ASKED HIM.
THIS TIME HE'S FIGHTING ON OUR SIDE--AGAINST THE OVER-MIND!
HIM--AND US?
GIRLY, YA GOTTA BE OUTTA YER GOURD!
WAIT, BIG BUDDY--IT DOES MAKE A WEIRD KIND OF SENSE. THE OVER-MIND IS A THREAT TO THE WHOLE WORLD--INCLUDING DOOM'S STAKE IN IT!
21.

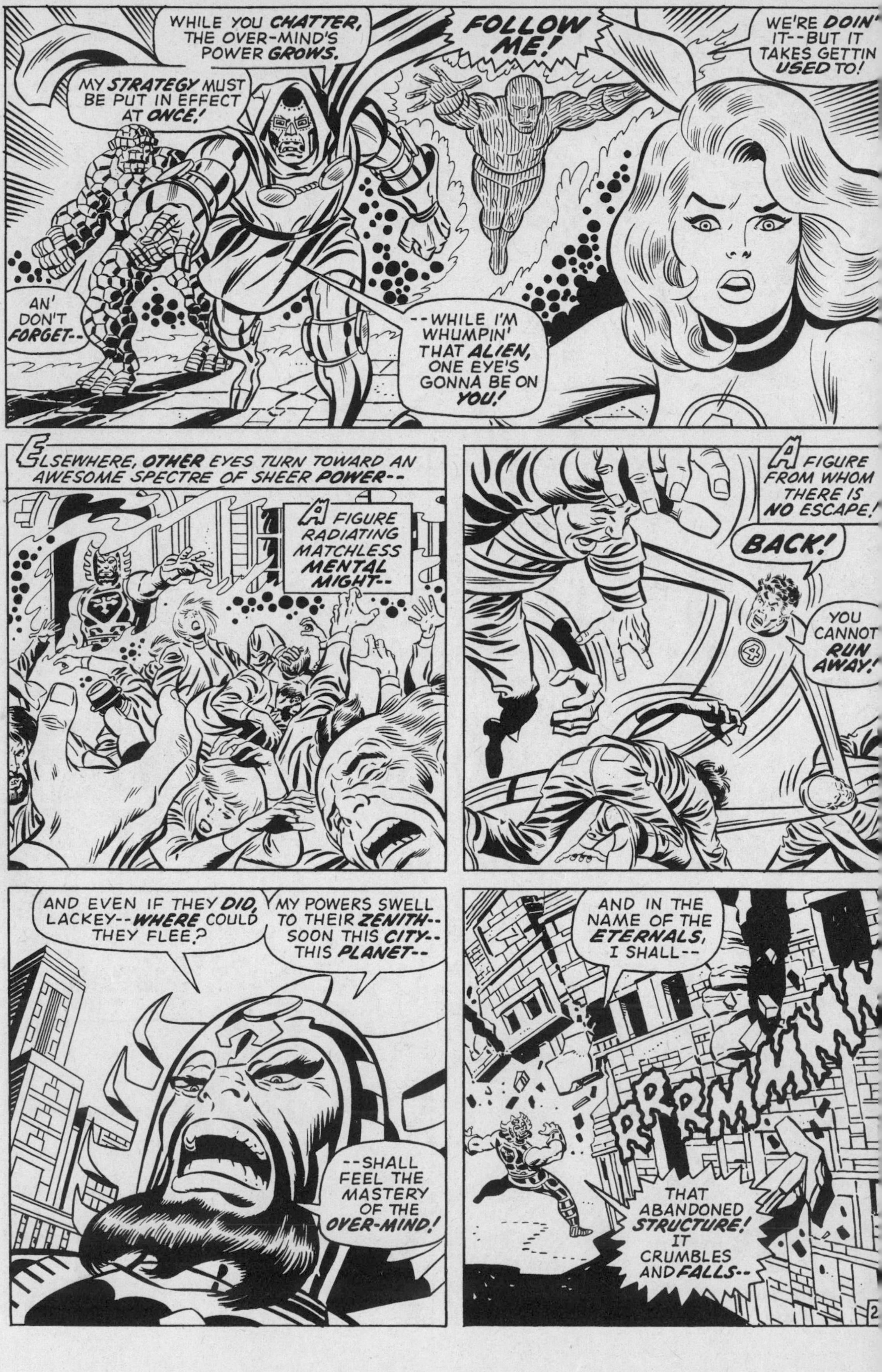
WHILE YOU CHATTER, THE OVER-MIND'S POWER GROWS.
MY STRATEGY MUST BE PUT IN EFFECT AT ONCE!
FOLLOW ME!
WE'RE DOIN' IT--BUT IT TAKES GETTIN USED TO!
AN' DON'T FORGET--
--WHILE I'M WHUMPIN' THAT ALIEN, ONE EYE'S GONNA BE ON YOU!
ELSEWHERE, OTHER EYES TURN TOWARD AN AWESOME SPECTRE OF SHEER POWER--
A FIGURE RADIATING MATCHLESS MENTAL MIGHT--
A FIGURE FROM WHOM THERE IS NO ESCAPE!
BACK!
YOU CANNOT RUN AWAY!
AND EVEN IF THEY DID, LACKEY--WHERE COULD THEY FLEE?
MY POWERS SWELL TO THEIR ZENITH--SOON THIS CITY--THIS PLANET--
--SHALL FEEL THE MASTERY OF THE OVER-MIND!
AND IN THE NAME OF THE ETERNALS, I SHALL--
RRRM
THAT ABANDONED STRUCTURE! IT CRUMBLES AND FALLS--
2

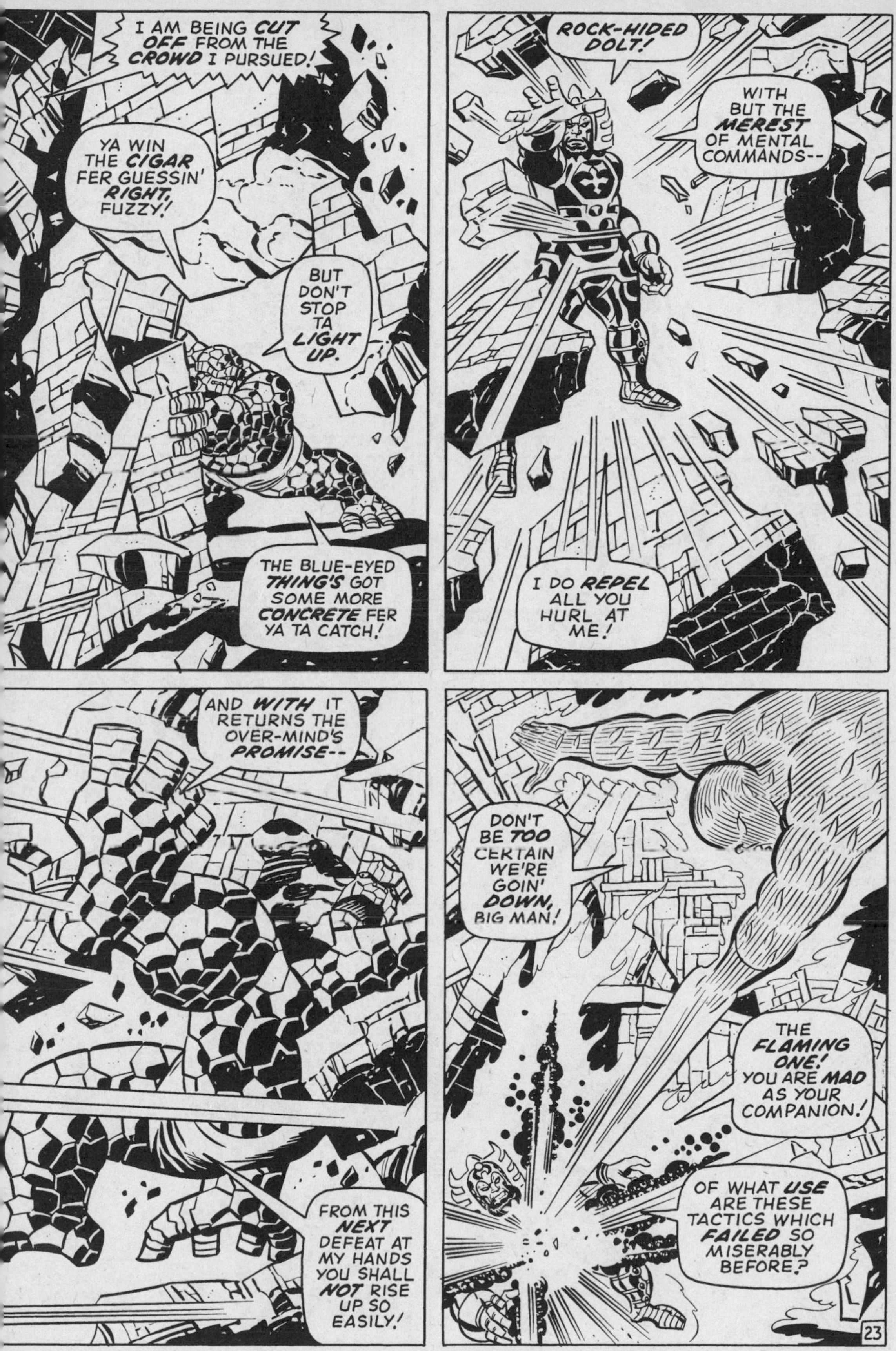
I AM BEING CUT OFF FROM THE CROWD I PURSUED!
YA WIN THE CIGAR FER GUESSIN' RIGHT, FUZZY!
BUT DON'T STOP TA LIGHT UP.
THE BLUE-EYED THING'S GOT SOME MORE CONCRETE FER YA TA CATCH!
ROCK-HIDED DOLT!
WITH BUT THE MEREST OF MENTAL COMMANDS--
I DO REPEL ALL YOU HURL AT ME!
AND WITH IT RETURNS THE OVER-MIND'S PROMISE--
FROM THIS NEXT DEFEAT AT MY HANDS YOU SHALL NOT RISE UP SO EASILY!
DON'T BE TOO CERTAIN WE'RE GOIN' DOWN, BIG MAN!
THE FLAMING ONE! YOU ARE MAD AS YOUR COMPANION!
OF WHAT USE ARE THESE TACTICS WHICH FAILED SO MISERABLY BEFORE?
23

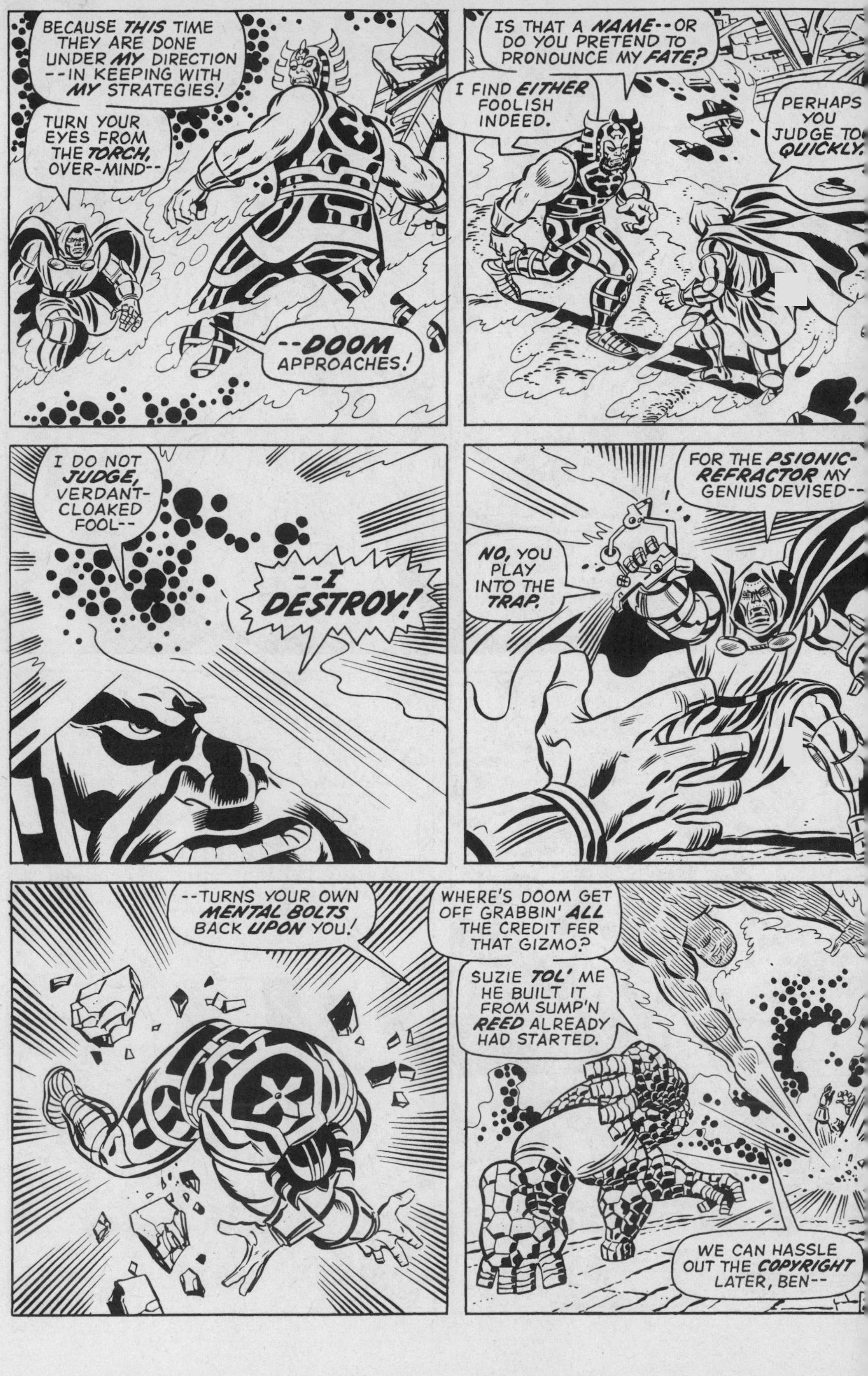
BECAUSE THIS TIME THEY ARE DONE UNDER MY DIRECTION --IN KEEPING WITH MY STRATEGIES!
TURN YOUR EYES FROM THE TORCH, OVER-MIND--
--DOOM APPROACHES!
IS THAT A NAME--OR DO YOU PRETEND TO PRONOUNCE MY FATE?
I FIND EITHER FOOLISH INDEED.
PERHAPS YOU JUDGE TOO QUICKLY!
I DO NOT JUDGE, VERDANT-CLOAKED FOOL--
--I DESTROY!
FOR THE PSIONIC-REFRACTOR MY GENIUS DEVISED--
NO, YOU PLAY INTO THE TRAP.
--TURNS YOUR OWN MENTAL BOLTS BACK UPON YOU!
WHERE'S DOOM GET OFF GRABBIN' ALL THE CREDIT FER THAT GIZMO?
SUZIE TOL' ME HE BUILT IT FROM SUMP'N REED ALREADY HAD STARTED.
WE CAN HASSLE OUT THE COPYRIGHT LATER, BEN--

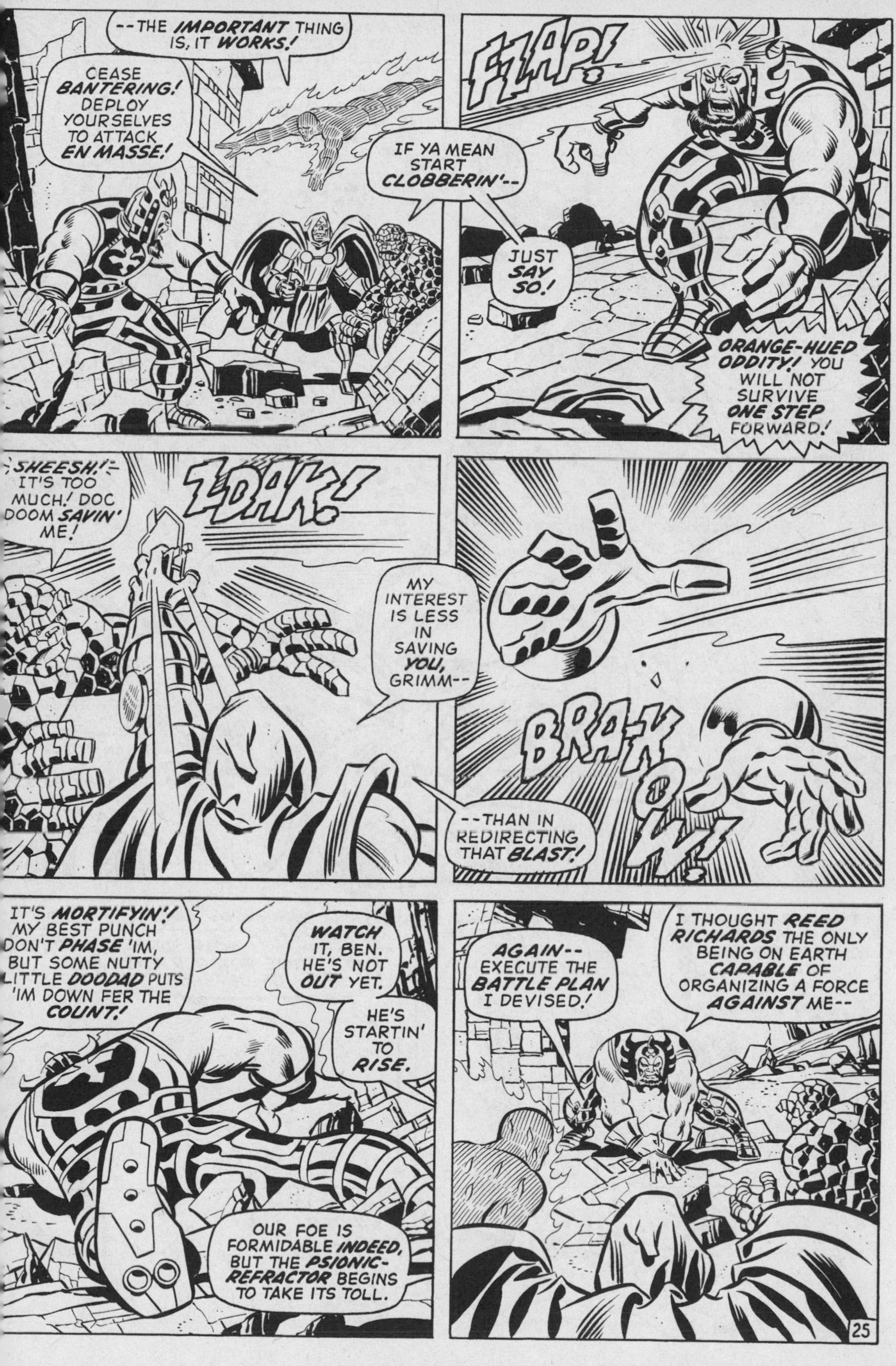
--THE IMPORTANT THING IS, IT WORKS!
CEASE BANTERING! DEPLOY YOURSELVES TO ATTACK EN MASSE!
IF YA MEAN START CLOBBERIN'--
JUST SAY SO!
FZAP!
ORANGE-HUED ODDITY! YOU WILL NOT SURVIVE ONE STEP FORWARD!
SHEESH! IT'S TOO MUCH! DOC DOOM SAVIN' ME!
ZDAK!
MY INTEREST IS LESS IN SAVING YOU, GRIMM--
--THAN IN REDIRECTING THAT BLAST!
BRAKOW!
IT'S MORTIFYIN'! MY BEST PUNCH DON'T PHASE 'IM, BUT SOME NUTTY LITTLE DOODAD PUTS 'IM DOWN FER THE COUNT!
WATCH IT, BEN. HE'S NOT OUT YET.
HE'S STARTIN' TO RISE.
OUR FOE IS FORMIDABLE INDEED, BUT THE PSIONIC-REFRACTOR BEGINS TO TAKE ITS TOLL.
AGAIN-- EXECUTE THE BATTLE PLAN I DEVISED!
I THOUGHT REED RICHARDS THE ONLY BEING ON EARTH CAPABLE OF ORGANIZING A FORCE AGAINST ME--
25

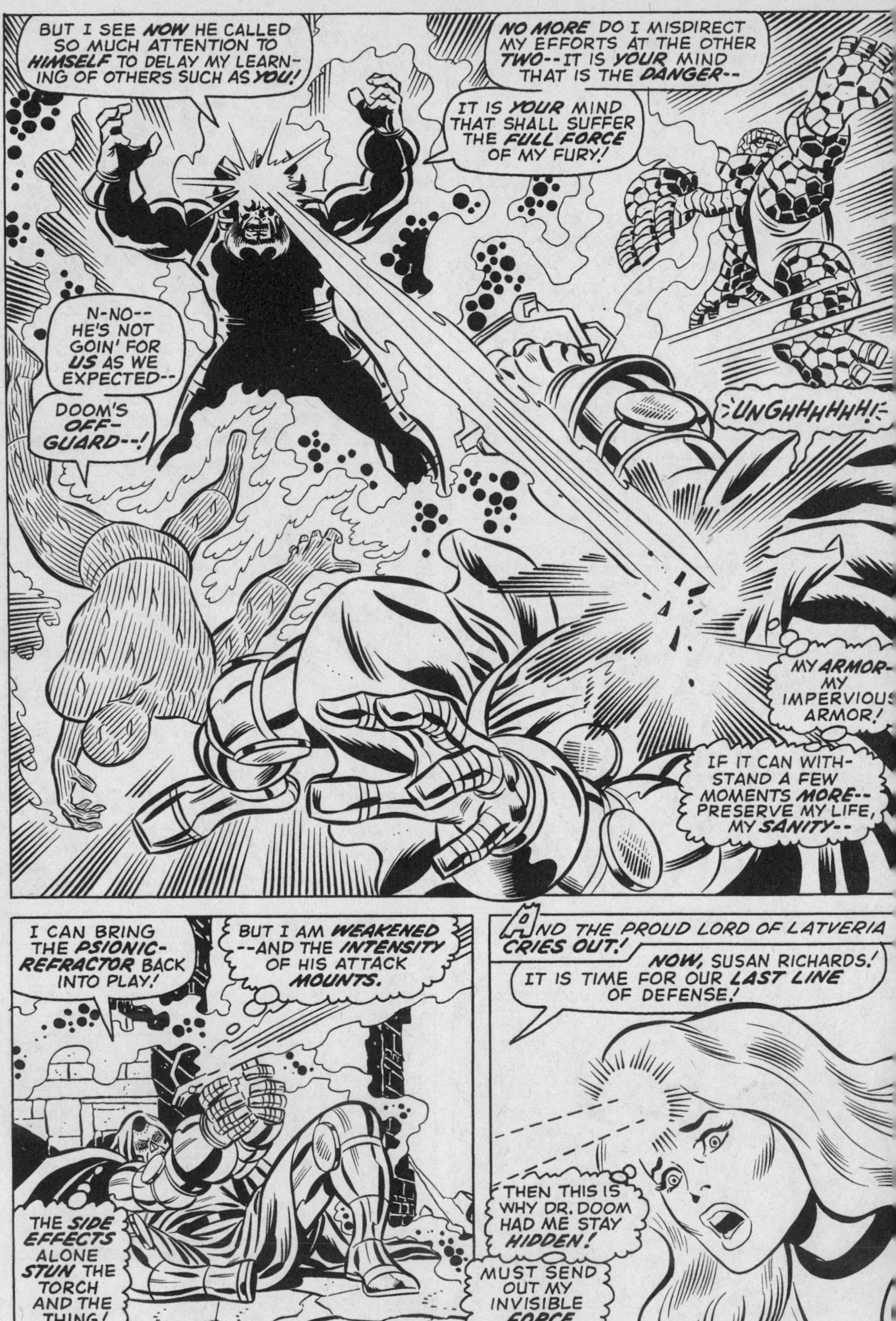
BUT I SEE NOW HE CALLED SO MUCH ATTENTION TO HIMSELF TO DELAY MY LEARNING OF OTHERS SUCH AS YOU!
NO MORE DO I MISDIRECT MY EFFORTS AT THE OTHER TWO--IT IS YOUR MIND THAT IS THE DANGER--
IT IS YOUR MIND THAT SHALL SUFFER THE FULL FORCE OF MY FURY!
N-NO-- HE'S NOT GOIN' FOR US AS WE EXPECTED--
DOOM'S OFF-GUARD--!
UNGHHHHHH!
MY ARMOR-- MY IMPERVIOUS ARMOR!
IF IT CAN WITHSTAND A FEW MOMENTS MORE-- PRESERVE MY LIFE, MY SANITY--
I CAN BRING THE PSIONIC-REFRACTOR BACK INTO PLAY!
BUT I AM WEAKENED --AND THE INTENSITY OF HIS ATTACK MOUNTS.
THE SIDE EFFECTS ALONE STUN THE TORCH AND THE THING!
AND THE PROUD LORD OF LATVERIA CRIES OUT!
NOW, SUSAN RICHARDS! IT IS TIME FOR OUR LAST LINE OF DEFENSE!
THEN THIS IS WHY DR. DOOM HAD ME STAY HIDDEN!
MUST SEND OUT MY INVISIBLE FORCE FIELD--

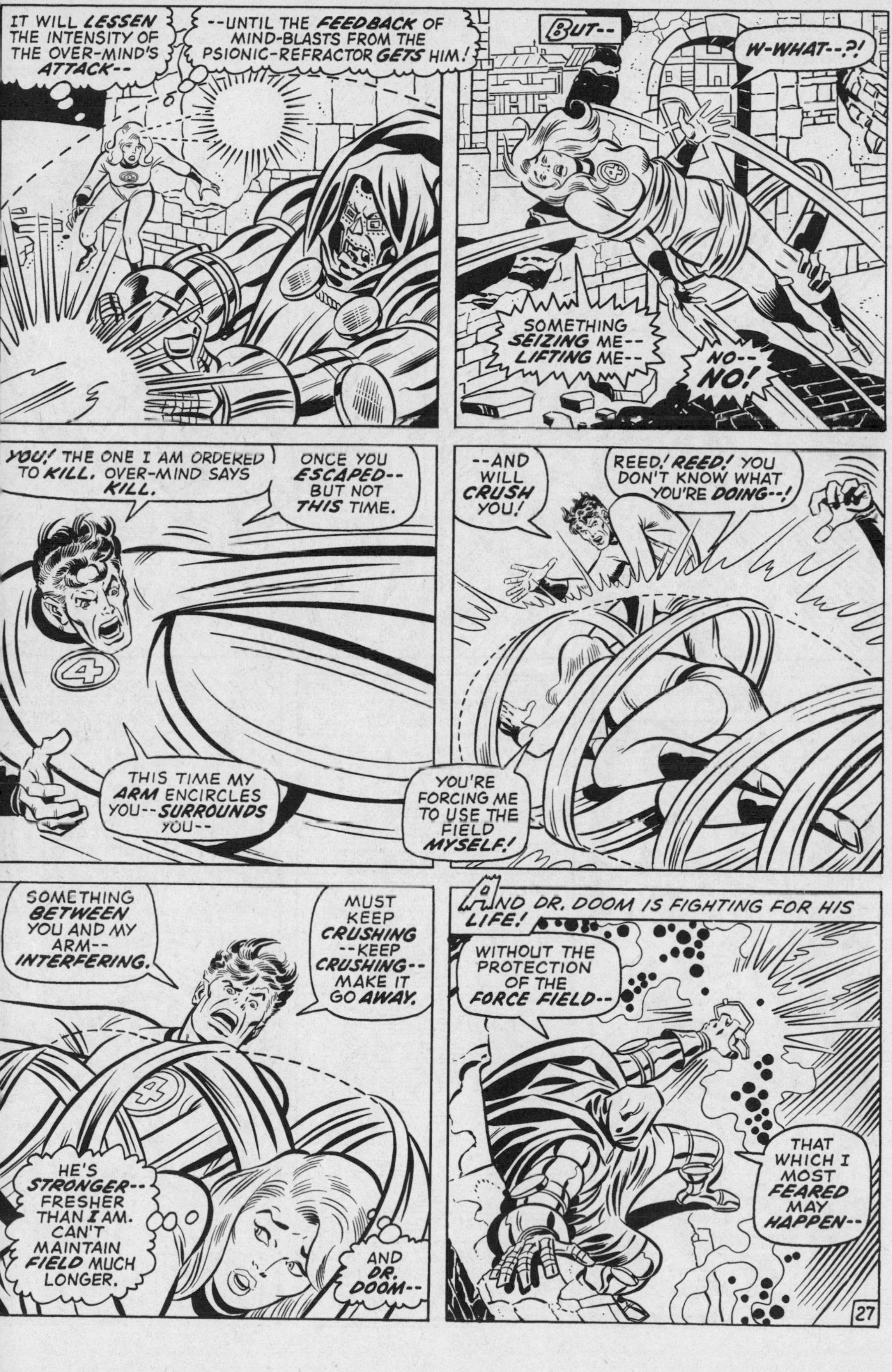
IT WILL LESSEN THE INTENSITY OF THE OVER-MIND'S ATTACK--
--UNTIL THE FEEDBACK OF MIND-BLASTS FROM THE PSIONIC-REFRACTOR GETS HIM!
BUT--
W-WHAT--?!
SOMETHING SEIZING ME--LIFTING ME--
NO--NO!
YOU! THE ONE I AM ORDERED TO KILL. OVER-MIND SAYS KILL.
ONCE YOU ESCAPED--BUT NOT THIS TIME.
THIS TIME MY ARM ENCIRCLES YOU--SURROUNDS YOU--
--AND WILL CRUSH YOU!
REED! REED! YOU DON'T KNOW WHAT YOU'RE DOING--!
YOU'RE FORCING ME TO USE THE FIELD MYSELF!
SOMETHING BETWEEN YOU AND MY ARM--INTERFERING.
MUST KEEP CRUSHING--KEEP CRUSHING--MAKE IT GO AWAY.
HE'S STRONGER--FRESHER THAN I AM. CAN'T MAINTAIN FIELD MUCH LONGER.
AND DR. DOOM--
AND DR. DOOM IS FIGHTING FOR HIS LIFE!
WITHOUT THE PROTECTION OF THE FORCE FIELD--
THAT WHICH I MOST FEARED MAY HAPPEN--
27

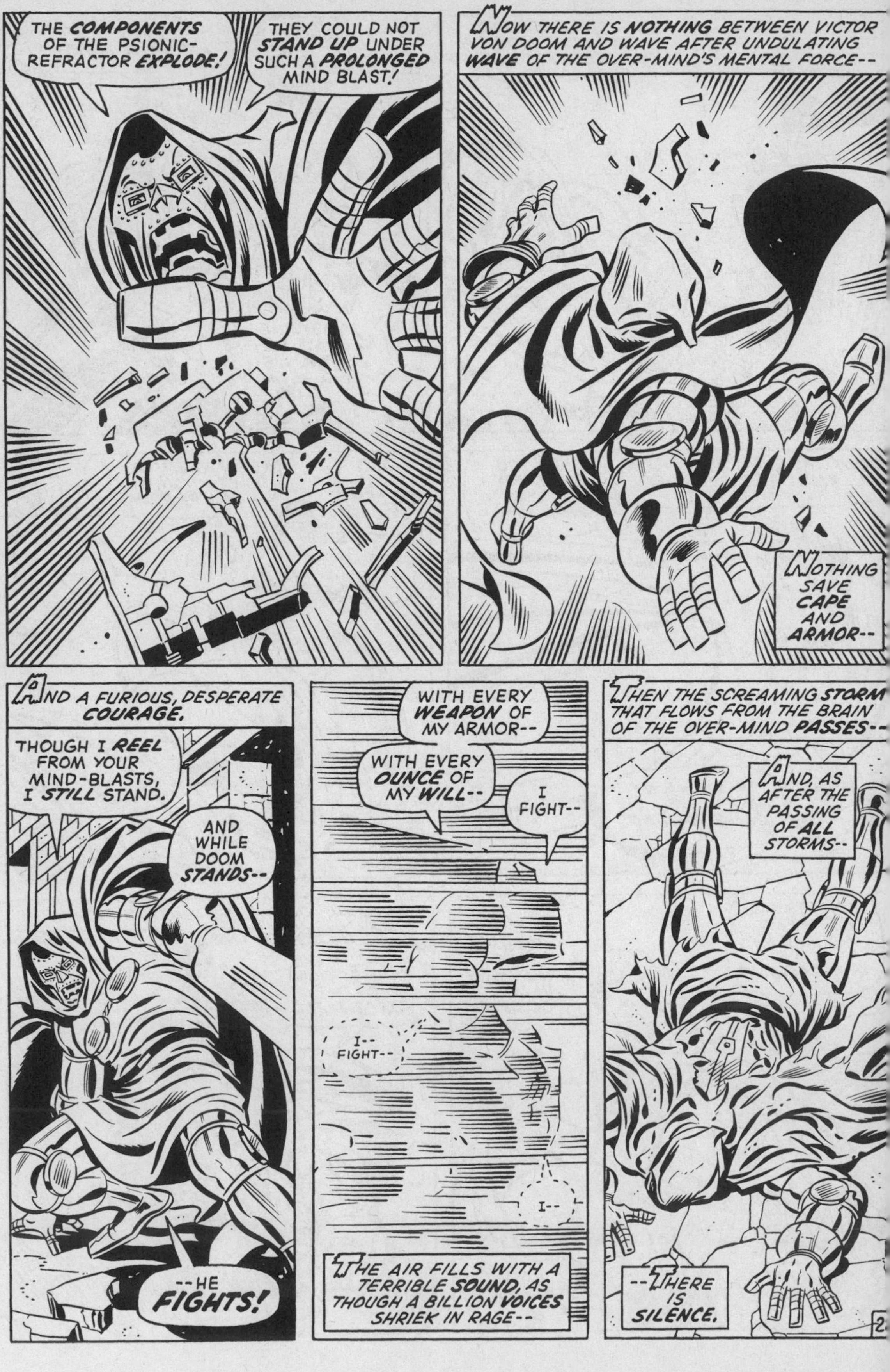
THE COMPONENTS OF THE PSIONIC-REFRACTOR EXPLODE!
THEY COULD NOT STAND UP UNDER SUCH A PROLONGED MIND BLAST!
NOW THERE IS NOTHING BETWEEN VICTOR VON DOOM AND WAVE AFTER UNDULATING WAVE OF THE OVER-MIND'S MENTAL FORCE--
NOTHING SAVE CAPE AND ARMOR--
AND A FURIOUS, DESPERATE COURAGE.
THOUGH I REEL FROM YOUR MIND-BLASTS, I STILL STAND.
AND WHILE DOOM STANDS--
--HE FIGHTS!
WITH EVERY WEAPON OF MY ARMOR--
WITH EVERY OUNCE OF MY WILL--
I FIGHT--
I-- FIGHT--
I--
THE AIR FILLS WITH A TERRIBLE SOUND, AS THOUGH A BILLION VOICES SHRIEK IN RAGE--
THEN THE SCREAMING STORM THAT FLOWS FROM THE BRAIN OF THE OVER-MIND PASSES--
AND, AS AFTER THE PASSING OF ALL STORMS--
--THERE IS SILENCE.
2

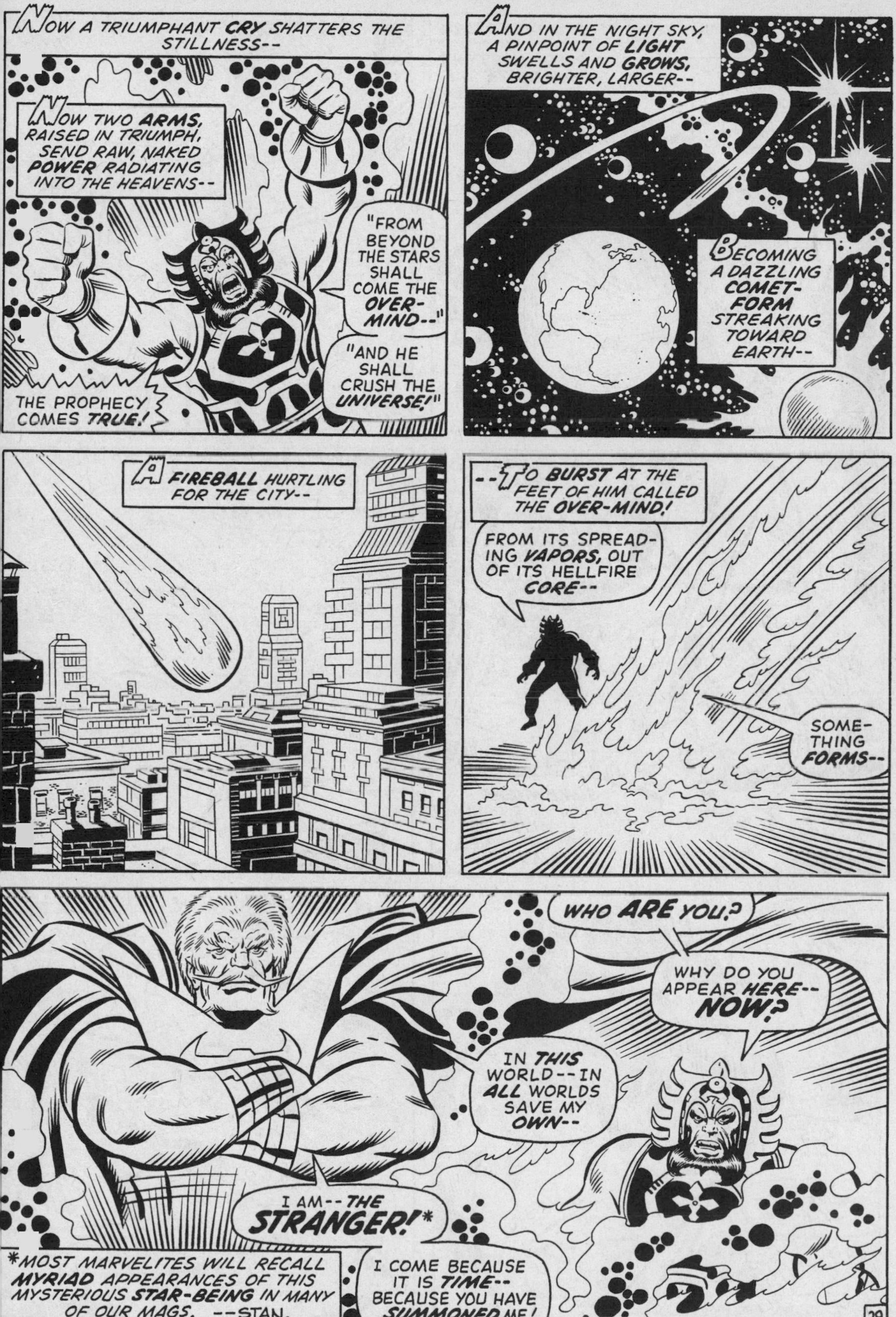
NOW A TRIUMPHANT CRY SHATTERS THE STILLNESS--
NOW TWO ARMS, RAISED IN TRIUMPH, SEND RAW, NAKED POWER RADIATING INTO THE HEAVENS--
"FROM BEYOND THE STARS SHALL COME THE OVER-MIND--"
"AND HE SHALL CRUSH THE UNIVERSE!"
THE PROPHECY COMES TRUE!
AND IN THE NIGHT SKY, A PINPOINT OF LIGHT SWELLS AND GROWS, BRIGHTER, LARGER--
BECOMING A DAZZLING COMET-FORM STREAKING TOWARD EARTH--
A FIREBALL HURTLING FOR THE CITY--
--TO BURST AT THE FEET OF HIM CALLED THE OVER-MIND!
FROM ITS SPREADING VAPORS, OUT OF ITS HELLFIRE CORE--
SOMETHING FORMS--
WHO ARE YOU?
WHY DO YOU APPEAR HERE-- NOW?
IN THIS WORLD--IN ALL WORLDS SAVE MY OWN--
I AM--THE STRANGER!*
*MOST MARVELITES WILL RECALL MYRIAD APPEARANCES OF THIS MYSTERIOUS STAR-BEING IN MANY OF OUR MAGS. --STAN.
I COME BECAUSE IT IS TIME-- BECAUSE YOU HAVE SUMMONED ME!
29

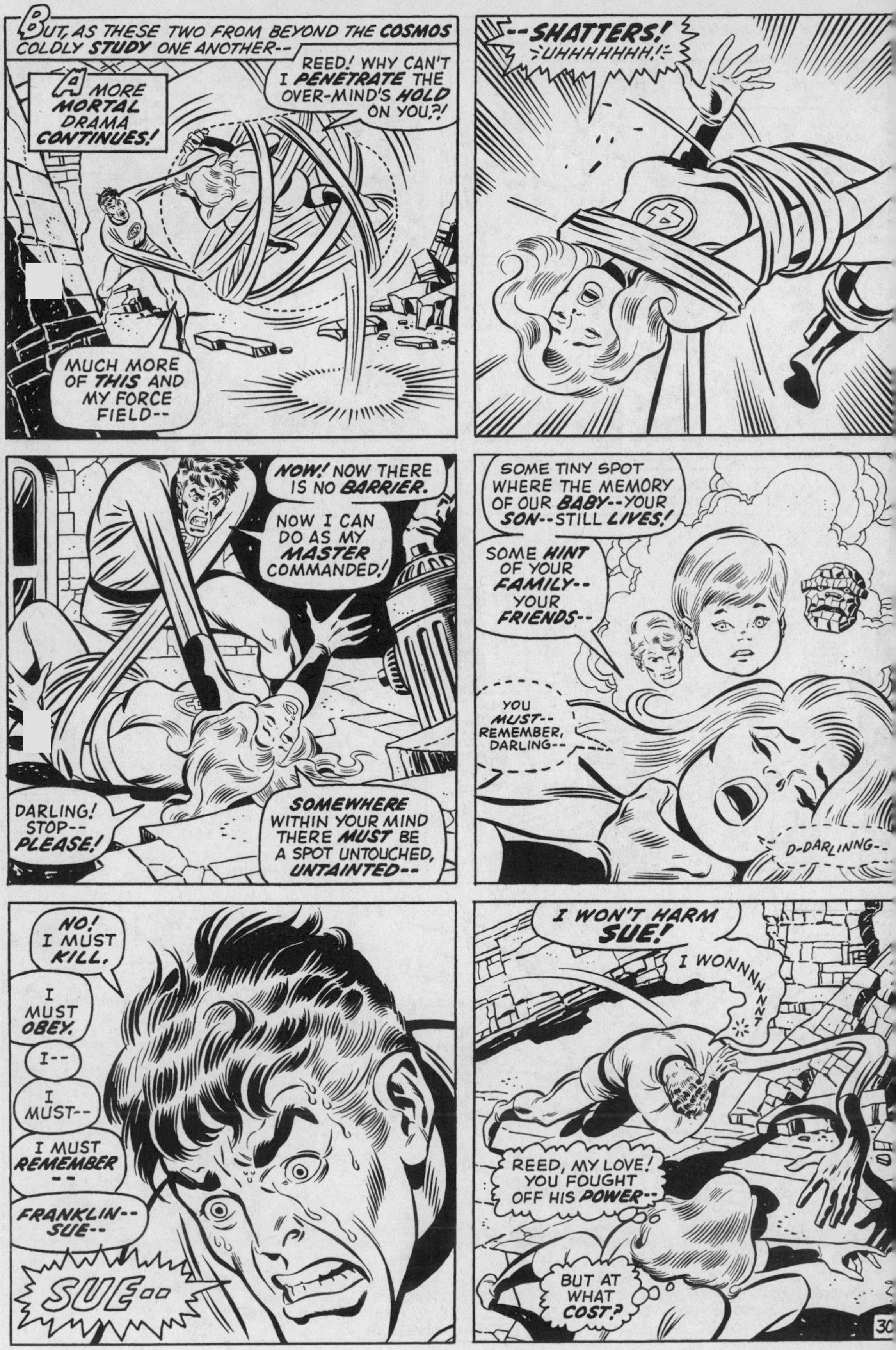

BUT, AS THESE TWO FROM BEYOND THE COSMOS COLDLY STUDY ONE ANOTHER--
A MORE MORTAL DRAMA CONTINUES!
REED! WHY CAN'T I PENETRATE THE OVER-MIND'S HOLD ON YOU?!
MUCH MORE OF THIS AND MY FORCE FIELD--
--SHATTERS!
UHHHHHHH!
NOW! NOW THERE IS NO BARRIER.
NOW I CAN DO AS MY MASTER COMMANDED!
DARLING! STOP-- PLEASE!
SOMEWHERE WITHIN YOUR MIND THERE MUST BE A SPOT UNTOUCHED, UNTAINTED--
SOME TINY SPOT WHERE THE MEMORY OF OUR BABY--YOUR SON--STILL LIVES!
SOME HINT OF YOUR FAMILY-- YOUR FRIENDS--
YOU MUST-- REMEMBER, DARLING--
D-DARLING--
NO! I MUST KILL.
I MUST OBEY.
I--
I MUST--
I MUST REMEMBER --
FRANKLIN-- SUE--
SUE--
I WON'T HARM SUE!
I WONNNNNNT
REED, MY LOVE! YOU FOUGHT OFF HIS POWER--
BUT AT WHAT COST?
30

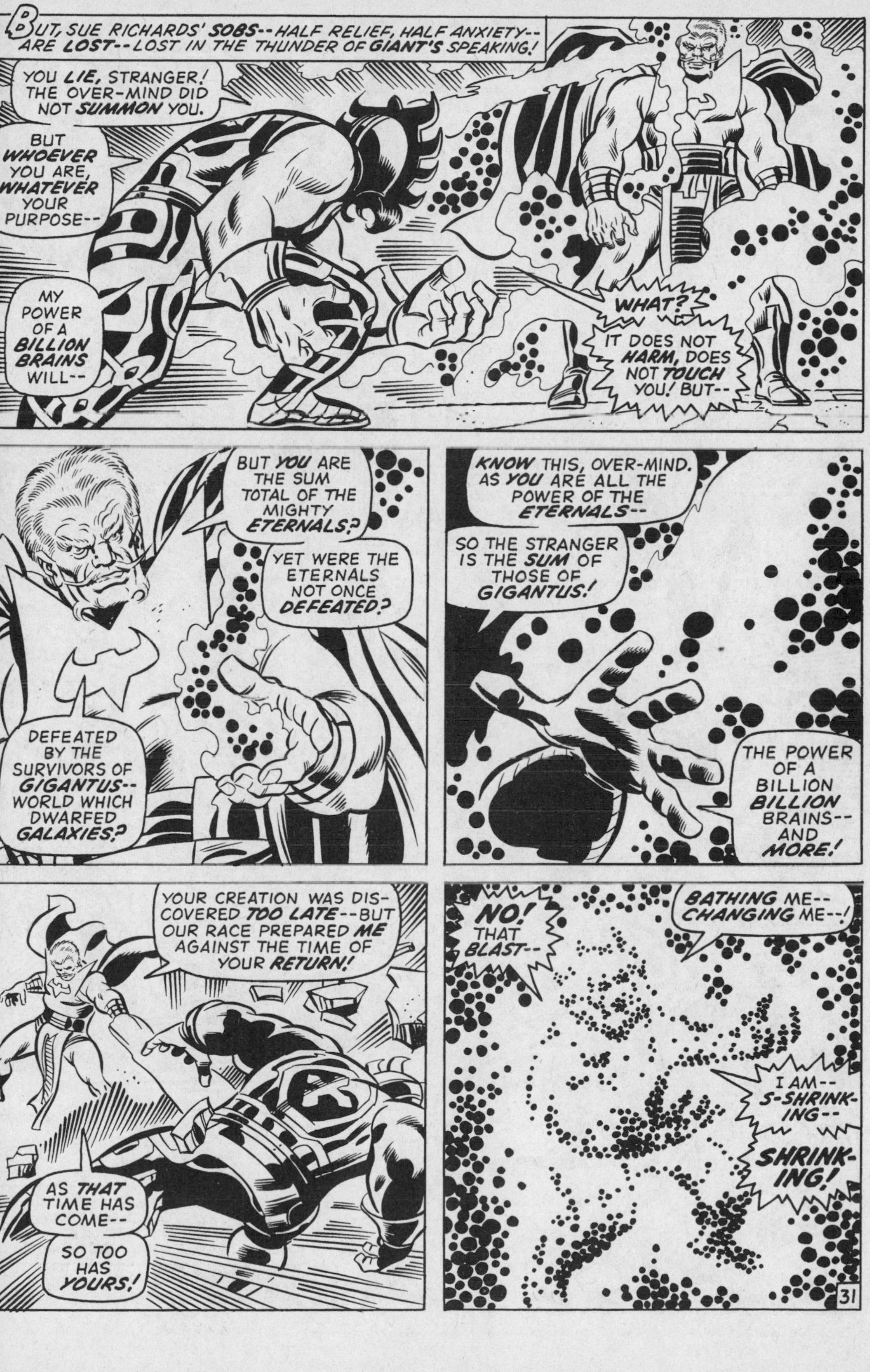
BUT, SUE RICHARDS' SOBS--HALF RELIEF, HALF ANXIETY--ARE LOST--LOST IN THE THUNDER OF GIANT'S SPEAKING!
YOU LIE, STRANGER! THE OVER-MIND DID NOT SUMMON YOU.
BUT WHOEVER YOU ARE, WHATEVER YOUR PURPOSE--
MY POWER OF A BILLION BRAINS WILL--
WHAT?
IT DOES NOT HARM, DOES NOT TOUCH YOU! BUT--
BUT YOU ARE THE SUM TOTAL OF THE MIGHTY ETERNALS?
YET WERE THE ETERNALS NOT ONCE DEFEATED?
DEFEATED BY THE SURVIVORS OF GIGANTUS--WORLD WHICH DWARFED GALAXIES?
KNOW THIS, OVER-MIND. AS YOU ARE ALL THE POWER OF THE ETERNALS--
SO THE STRANGER IS THE SUM OF THOSE OF GIGANTUS!
THE POWER OF A BILLION BILLION BRAINS--AND MORE!
YOUR CREATION WAS DISCOVERED TOO LATE--BUT OUR RACE PREPARED ME AGAINST THE TIME OF YOUR RETURN!
AS THAT TIME HAS COME--
SO TOO HAS YOURS!
NO! THAT BLAST--
BATHING ME--CHANGING ME--!
I AM--S-SHRINKING--
SHRINKING!
31

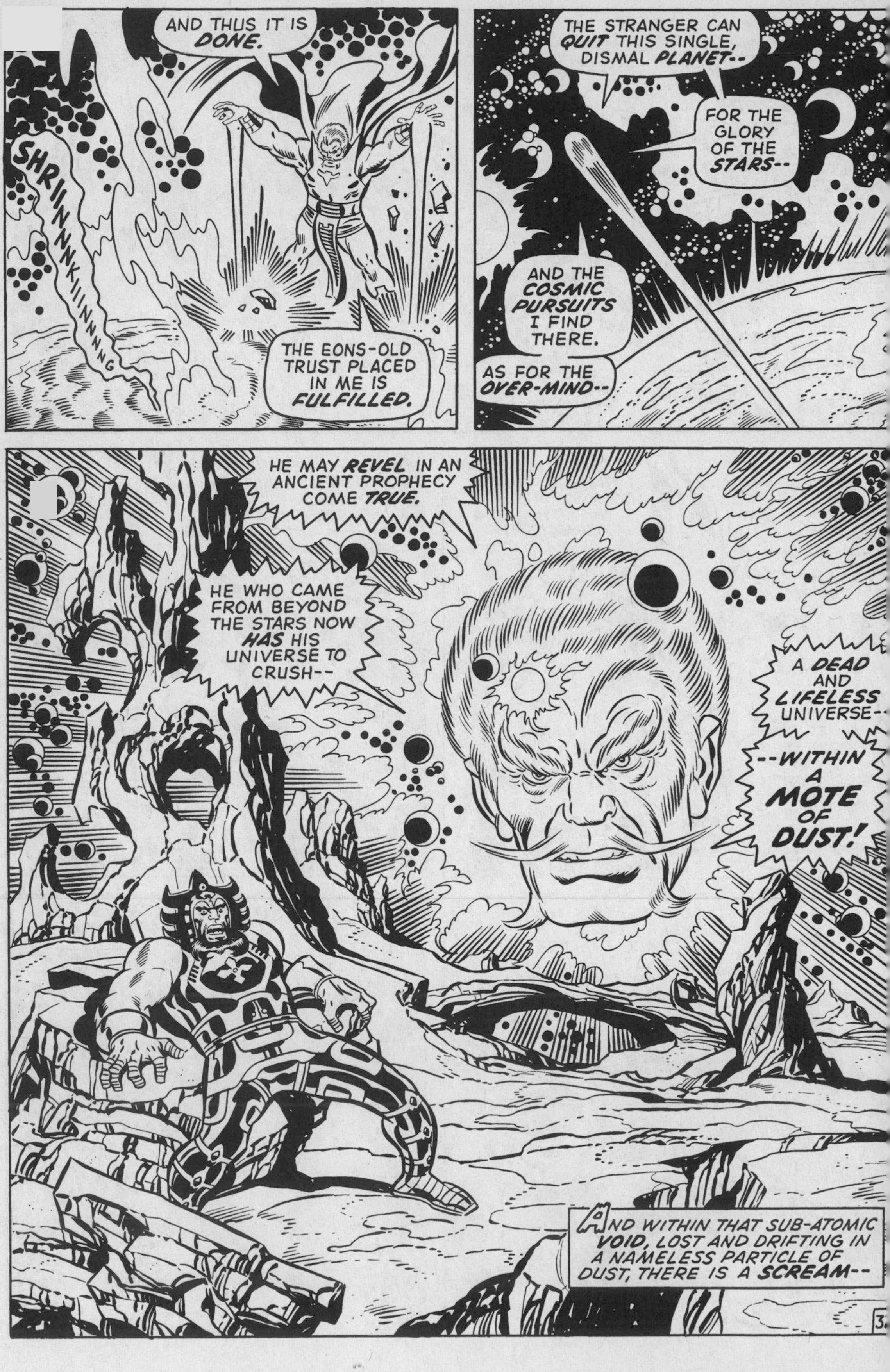
AND THUS IT IS DONE.
SHRIIINNNKIIINNNG
THE EONS-OLD TRUST PLACED IN ME IS FULFILLED.
THE STRANGER CAN QUIT THIS SINGLE, DISMAL PLANET--
FOR THE GLORY OF THE STARS--
AND THE COSMIC PURSUITS I FIND THERE.
AS FOR THE OVER-MIND--
HE MAY REVEL IN AN ANCIENT PROPHECY COME TRUE.
HE WHO CAME FROM BEYOND THE STARS NOW HAS HIS UNIVERSE TO CRUSH--
A DEAD AND LIFELESS UNIVERSE--
--WITHIN A MOTE OF DUST!
AND WITHIN THAT SUB-ATOMIC VOID, LOST AND DRIFTING IN A NAMELESS PARTICLE OF DUST, THERE IS A SCREAM--

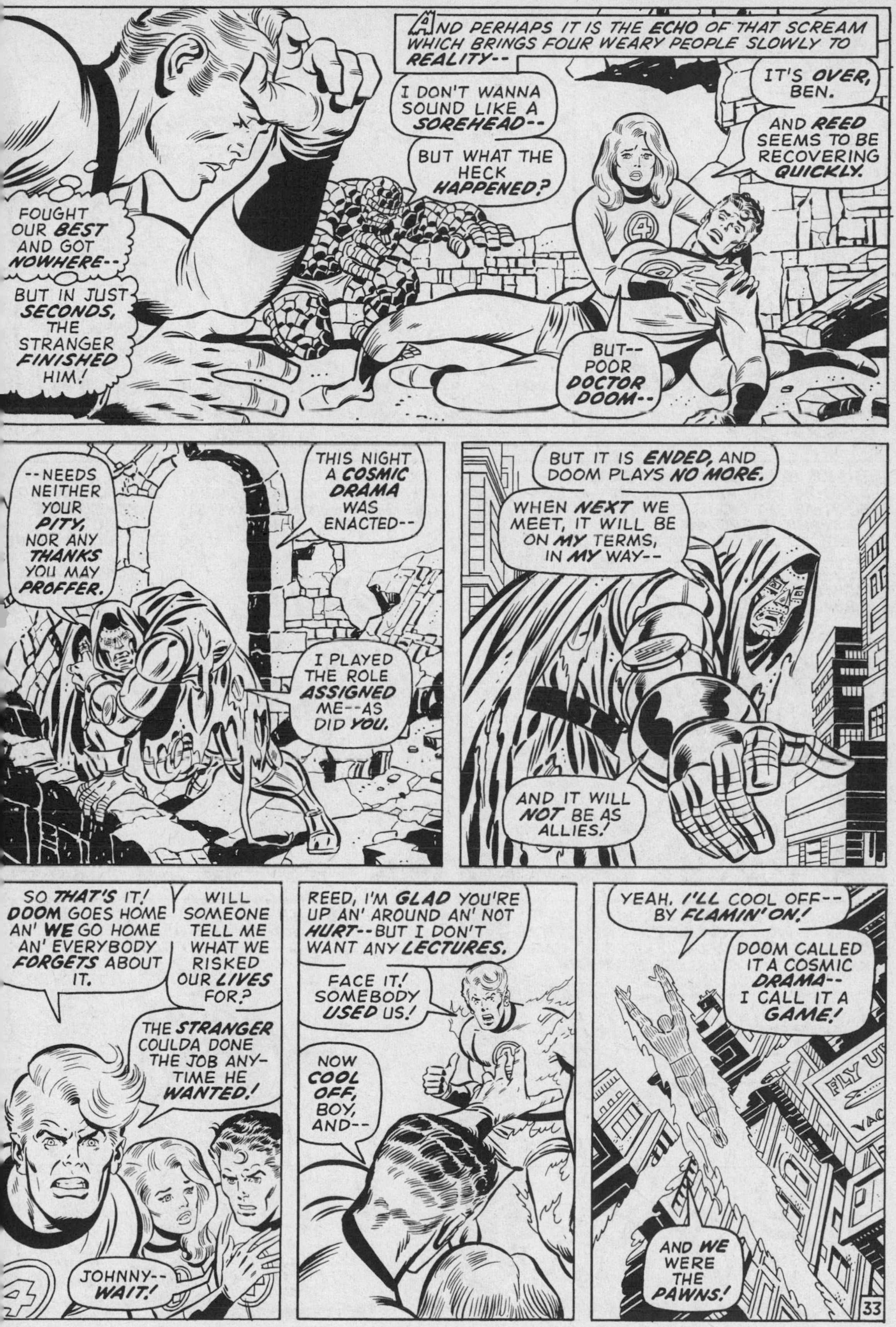
AND PERHAPS IT IS THE ECHO OF THAT SCREAM WHICH BRINGS FOUR WEARY PEOPLE SLOWLY TO REALITY--
FOUGHT OUR BEST AND GOT NOWHERE--
BUT IN JUST SECONDS, THE STRANGER FINISHED HIM!
I DON'T WANNA SOUND LIKE A SOREHEAD--
BUT WHAT THE HECK HAPPENED?
IT'S OVER, BEN.
AND REED SEEMS TO BE RECOVERING QUICKLY.
BUT-- POOR DOCTOR DOOM--
--NEEDS NEITHER YOUR PITY, NOR ANY THANKS YOU MAY PROFFER.
THIS NIGHT A COSMIC DRAMA WAS ENACTED--
I PLAYED THE ROLE ASSIGNED ME--AS DID YOU.
BUT IT IS ENDED, AND DOOM PLAYS NO MORE.
WHEN NEXT WE MEET, IT WILL BE ON MY TERMS, IN MY WAY--
AND IT WILL NOT BE AS ALLIES!
SO THAT'S IT! DOOM GOES HOME AN' WE GO HOME AN' EVERYBODY FORGETS ABOUT IT.
WILL SOMEONE TELL ME WHAT WE RISKED OUR LIVES FOR?
THE STRANGER COULDA DONE THE JOB ANY-TIME HE WANTED!
JOHNNY-- WAIT!
REED, I'M GLAD YOU'RE UP AN' AROUND AN' NOT HURT--BUT I DON'T WANT ANY LECTURES.
FACE IT! SOMEBODY USED US!
NOW COOL OFF, BOY, AND--
YEAH. I'LL COOL OFF-- BY FLAMIN' ON!
DOOM CALLED IT A COSMIC DRAMA-- I CALL IT A GAME!
AND WE WERE THE PAWNS!
FLY U
VAC
33

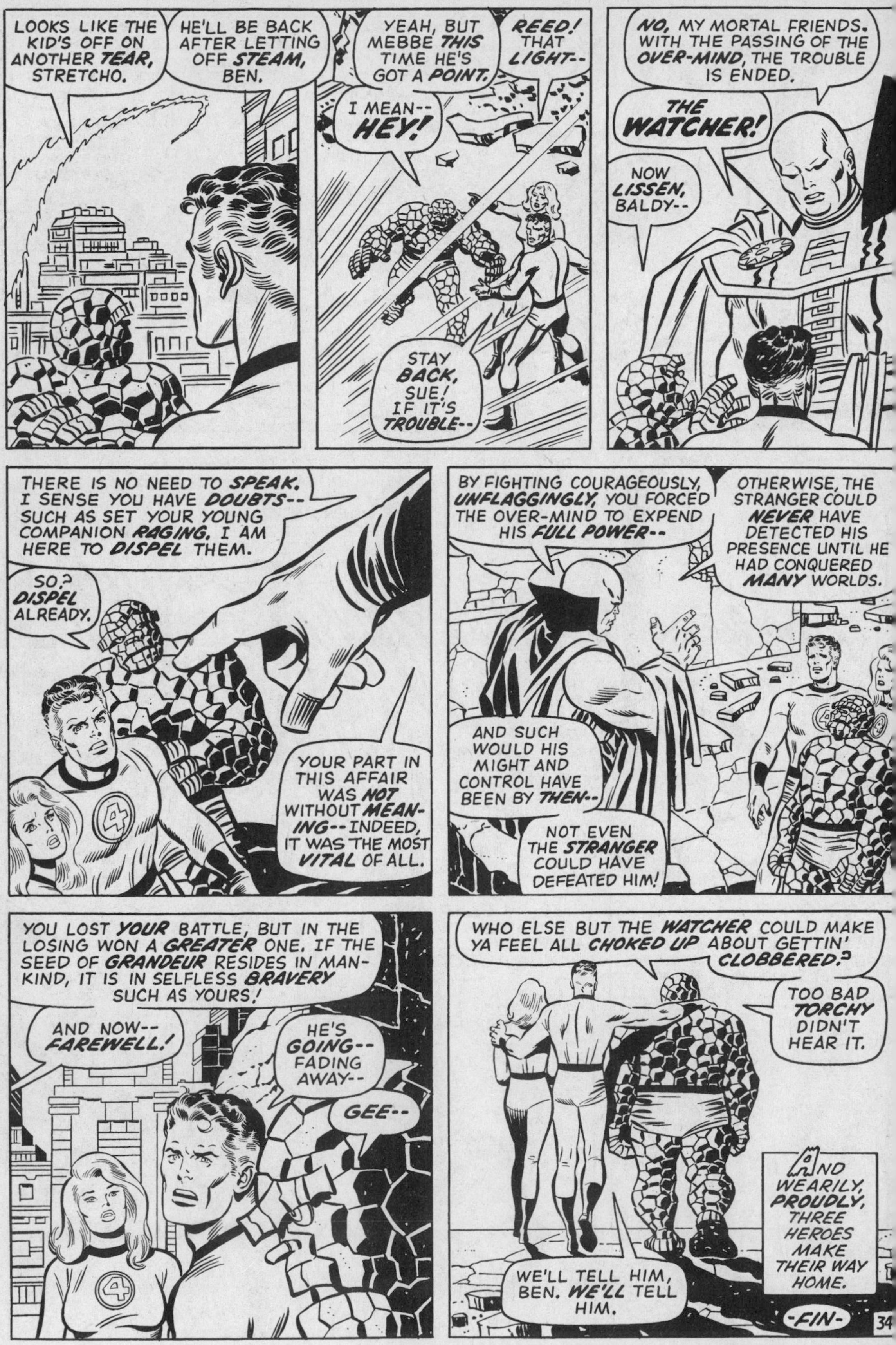
LOOKS LIKE THE KID'S OFF ON ANOTHER TEAR, STRETCHO.
HE'LL BE BACK AFTER LETTING OFF STEAM, BEN.
YEAH, BUT MEBBE THIS TIME HE'S GOT A POINT.
I MEAN-- HEY!
REED! THAT LIGHT--
STAY BACK, SUE! IF IT'S TROUBLE--
NO, MY MORTAL FRIENDS. WITH THE PASSING OF THE OVER-MIND, THE TROUBLE IS ENDED.
THE WATCHER!
NOW LISSEN, BALDY--
THERE IS NO NEED TO SPEAK. I SENSE YOU HAVE DOUBTS-- SUCH AS SET YOUR YOUNG COMPANION RAGING. I AM HERE TO DISPEL THEM.
SO? DISPEL ALREADY.
YOUR PART IN THIS AFFAIR WAS NOT WITHOUT MEANING-- INDEED, IT WAS THE MOST VITAL OF ALL.
BY FIGHTING COURAGEOUSLY, UNFLAGGINGLY, YOU FORCED THE OVER-MIND TO EXPEND HIS FULL POWER--
OTHERWISE, THE STRANGER COULD NEVER HAVE DETECTED HIS PRESENCE UNTIL HE HAD CONQUERED MANY WORLDS.
AND SUCH WOULD HIS MIGHT AND CONTROL HAVE BEEN BY THEN--
NOT EVEN THE STRANGER COULD HAVE DEFEATED HIM!
YOU LOST YOUR BATTLE, BUT IN THE LOSING WON A GREATER ONE. IF THE SEED OF GRANDEUR RESIDES IN MANKIND, IT IS IN SELFLESS BRAVERY SUCH AS YOURS!
AND NOW-- FAREWELL!
HE'S GOING-- FADING AWAY--
GEE--
WHO ELSE BUT THE WATCHER COULD MAKE YA FEEL ALL CHOKED UP ABOUT GETTIN' CLOBBERED?
TOO BAD TORCHY DIDN'T HEAR IT.
WE'LL TELL HIM, BEN. WE'LL TELL HIM.
AND WEARILY, PROUDLY, THREE HEROES MAKE THEIR WAY HOME.
-FIN-
34

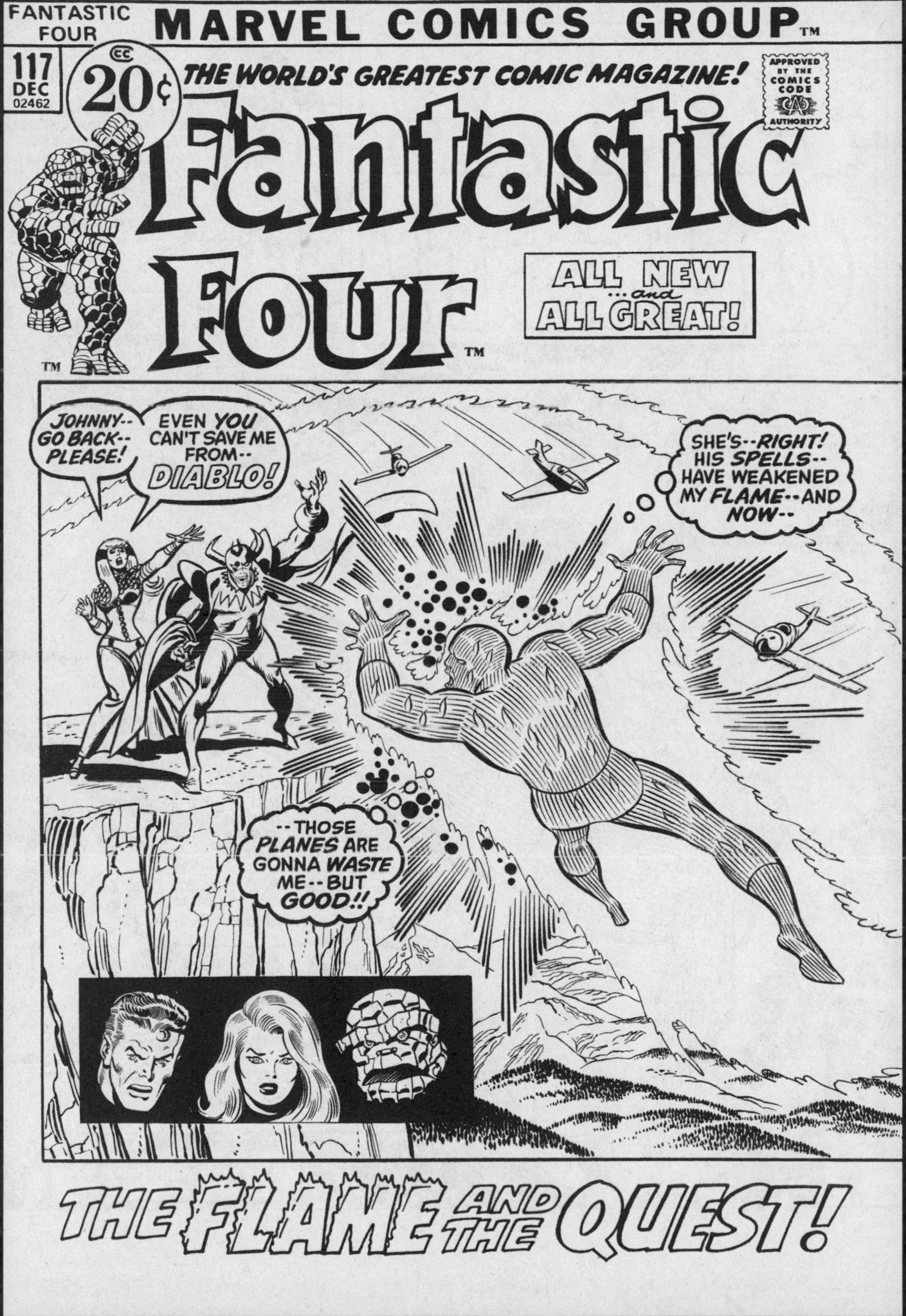

FANTASTIC FOUR
117 DEC 02462
MARVEL COMICS GROUP™
20¢
THE WORLD'S GREATEST COMIC MAGAZINE!
APPROVED BY THE COMICS CODE AUTHORITY
Fantastic Four™
ALL NEW ...and ALL GREAT!
JOHNNY-- GO BACK-- PLEASE!
EVEN YOU CAN'T SAVE ME FROM-- DIABLO!
SHE'S--RIGHT! HIS SPELLS-- HAVE WEAKENED MY FLAME--AND NOW--
--THOSE PLANES ARE GONNA WASTE ME--BUT GOOD!!
THE FLAME AND THE QUEST!

A RAMPAGING TORCH ABANDONS THE F.F. TO SEEK OUT THE GIRL HE LOVES.

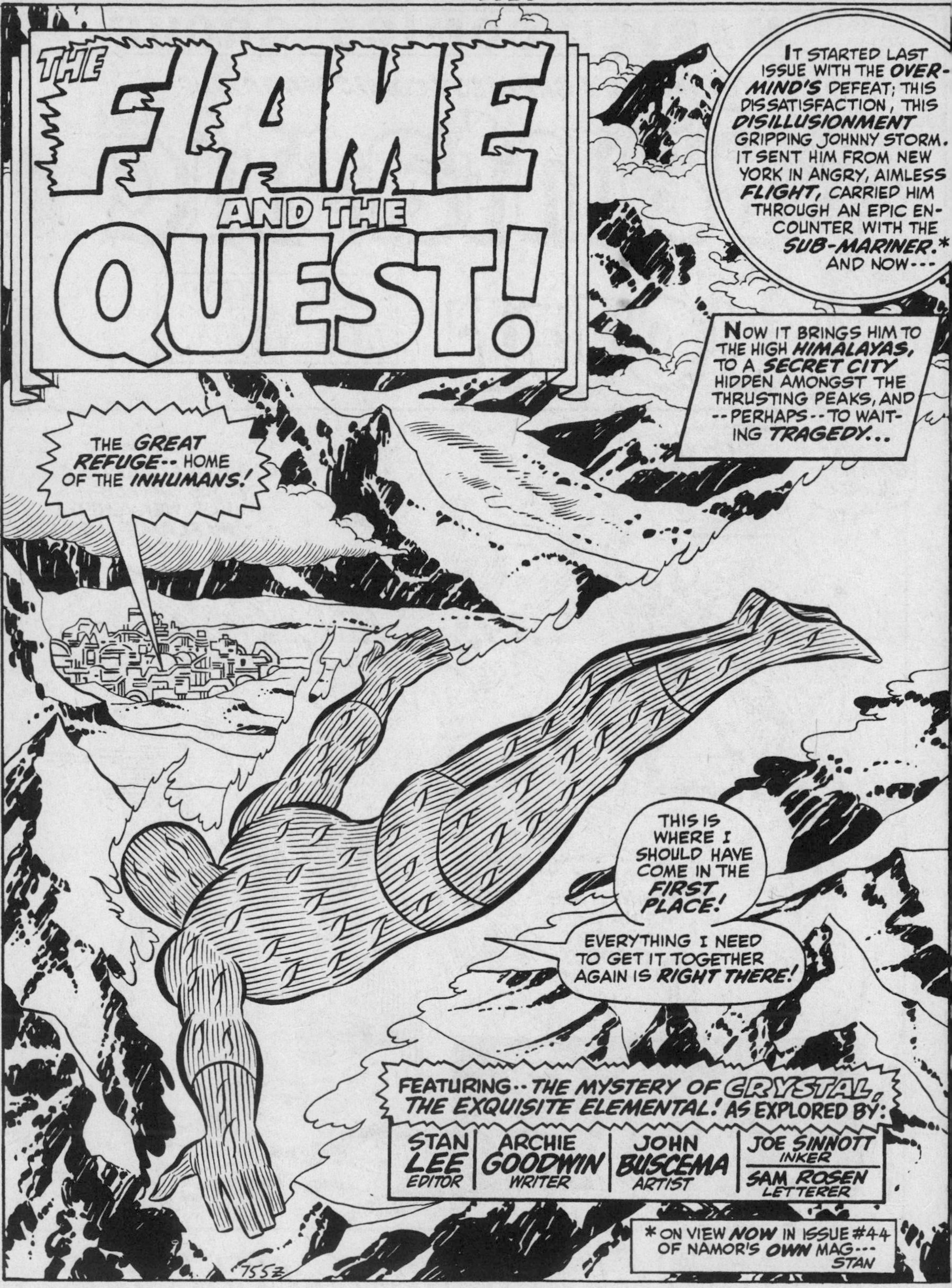
THE FLAME AND THE QUEST!
IT STARTED LAST ISSUE WITH THE OVER-MIND'S DEFEAT; THIS DISSATISFACTION, THIS DISILLUSIONMENT GRIPPING JOHNNY STORM. IT SENT HIM FROM NEW YORK IN ANGRY, AIMLESS FLIGHT, CARRIED HIM THROUGH AN EPIC ENCOUNTER WITH THE SUB-MARINER.* AND NOW---
NOW IT BRINGS HIM TO THE HIGH HIMALAYAS, TO A SECRET CITY HIDDEN AMONGST THE THRUSTING PEAKS, AND --PERHAPS-- TO WAITING TRAGEDY...
THE GREAT REFUGE-- HOME OF THE INHUMANS!
THIS IS WHERE I SHOULD HAVE COME IN THE FIRST PLACE!
EVERYTHING I NEED TO GET IT TOGETHER AGAIN IS RIGHT THERE!
FEATURING-- THE MYSTERY OF CRYSTAL, THE EXQUISITE ELEMENTAL! AS EXPLORED BY:
STAN LEE EDITOR
ARCHIE GOODWIN WRITER
JOHN BUSCEMA ARTIST
JOE SINNOTT INKER
SAM ROSEN LETTERER
* ON VIEW NOW IN ISSUE #44 OF NAMOR'S OWN MAG--- STAN
755Z

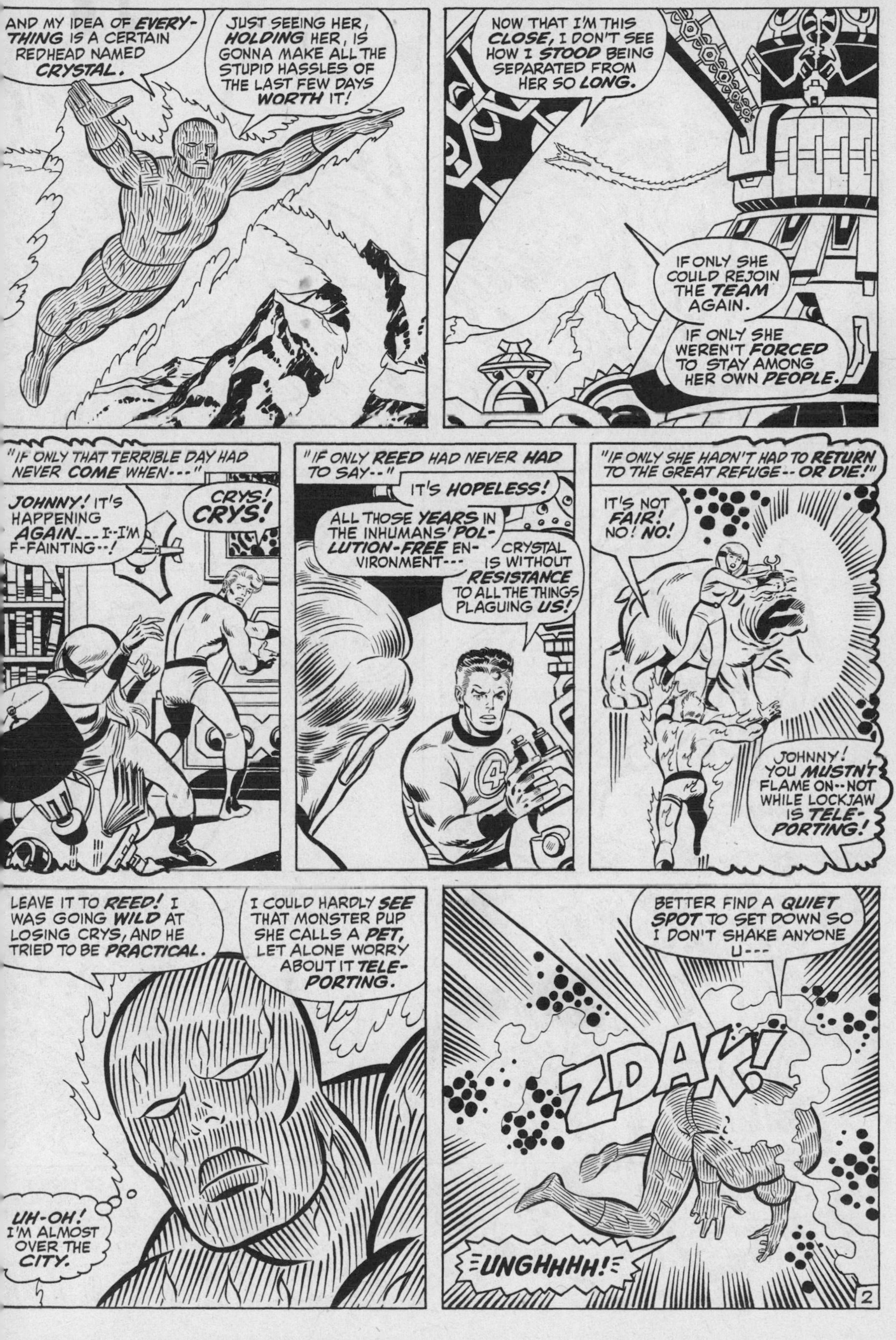
AND MY IDEA OF EVERYTHING IS A CERTAIN REDHEAD NAMED CRYSTAL.
JUST SEEING HER, HOLDING HER, IS GONNA MAKE ALL THE STUPID HASSLES OF THE LAST FEW DAYS WORTH IT!
NOW THAT I'M THIS CLOSE, I DON'T SEE HOW I STOOD BEING SEPARATED FROM HER SO LONG.
IF ONLY SHE COULD REJOIN THE TEAM AGAIN.
IF ONLY SHE WEREN'T FORCED TO STAY AMONG HER OWN PEOPLE.
"IF ONLY THAT TERRIBLE DAY HAD NEVER COME WHEN---"
JOHNNY! IT'S HAPPENING AGAIN--- I-I'M F-FAINTING--!
CRYS! CRYS!
"IF ONLY REED HAD NEVER HAD TO SAY--"
IT'S HOPELESS!
ALL THOSE YEARS IN THE INHUMANS' POLLUTION-FREE ENVIRONMENT---
CRYSTAL IS WITHOUT RESISTANCE TO ALL THE THINGS PLAGUING US!
"IF ONLY SHE HADN'T HAD TO RETURN TO THE GREAT REFUGE--OR DIE!"
IT'S NOT FAIR! NO! NO!
JOHNNY! YOU MUSTN'T FLAME ON--NOT WHILE LOCKJAW IS TELEPORTING!
LEAVE IT TO REED! I WAS GOING WILD AT LOSING CRYS, AND HE TRIED TO BE PRACTICAL.
I COULD HARDLY SEE THAT MONSTER PUP SHE CALLS A PET, LET ALONE WORRY ABOUT IT TELEPORTING.
UH-OH! I'M ALMOST OVER THE CITY.
BETTER FIND A QUIET SPOT TO SET DOWN SO I DON'T SHAKE ANYONE U---
ZDAK!
UNGHHHH!
2

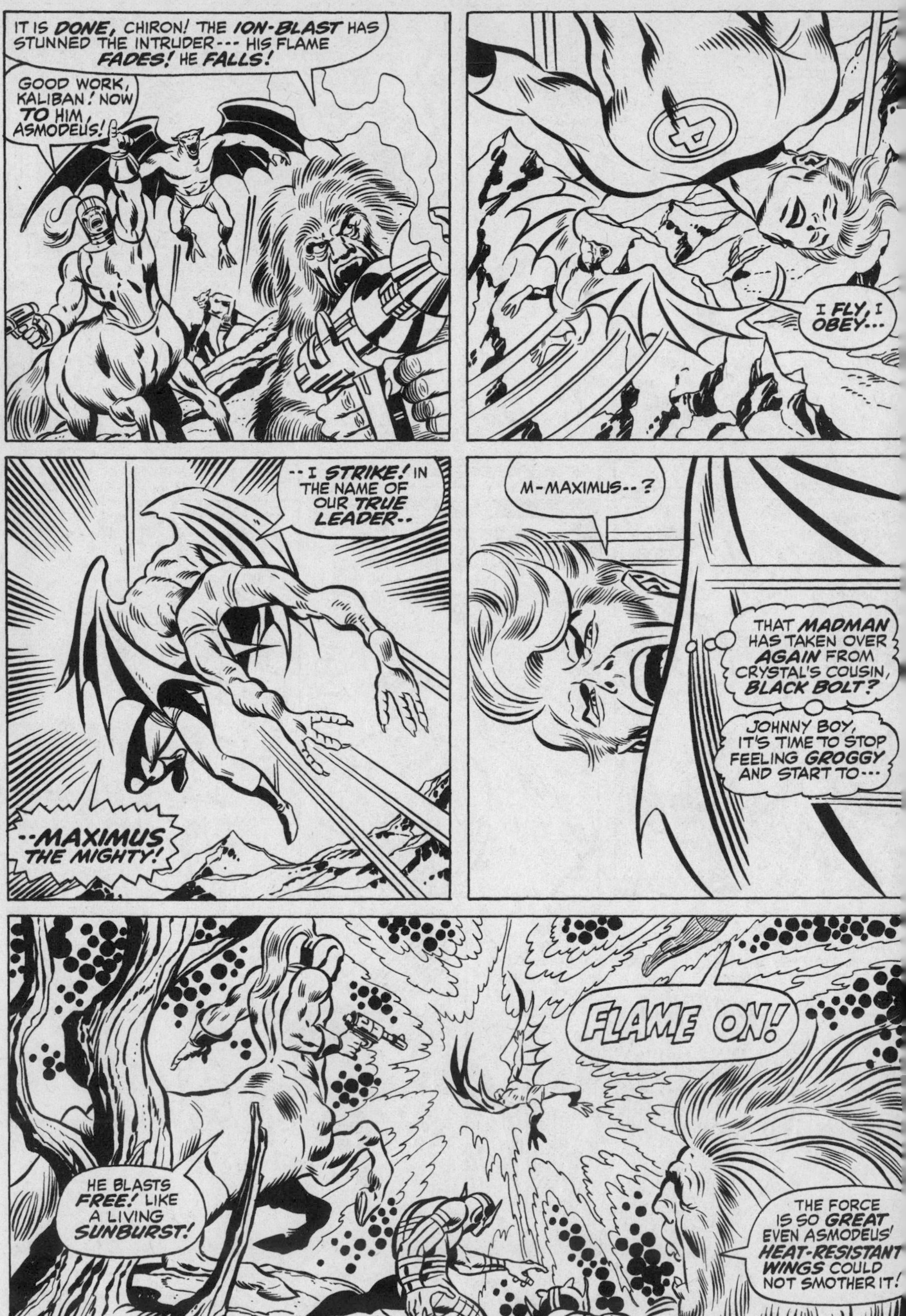
IT IS DONE, CHIRON! THE ION-BLAST HAS STUNNED THE INTRUDER--- HIS FLAME FADES! HE FALLS!
GOOD WORK, KALIBAN! NOW TO HIM, ASMODEUS!
I FLY, I OBEY---
--I STRIKE! IN THE NAME OF OUR TRUE LEADER--
--MAXIMUS THE MIGHTY!
M-MAXIMUS--?
THAT MADMAN HAS TAKEN OVER AGAIN FROM CRYSTAL'S COUSIN, BLACK BOLT?
JOHNNY BOY, IT'S TIME TO STOP FEELING GROGGY AND START TO---
FLAME ON!
HE BLASTS FREE! LIKE A LIVING SUNBURST!
THE FORCE IS SO GREAT EVEN ASMODEUS' HEAT-RESISTANT WINGS COULD NOT SMOTHER IT!
3

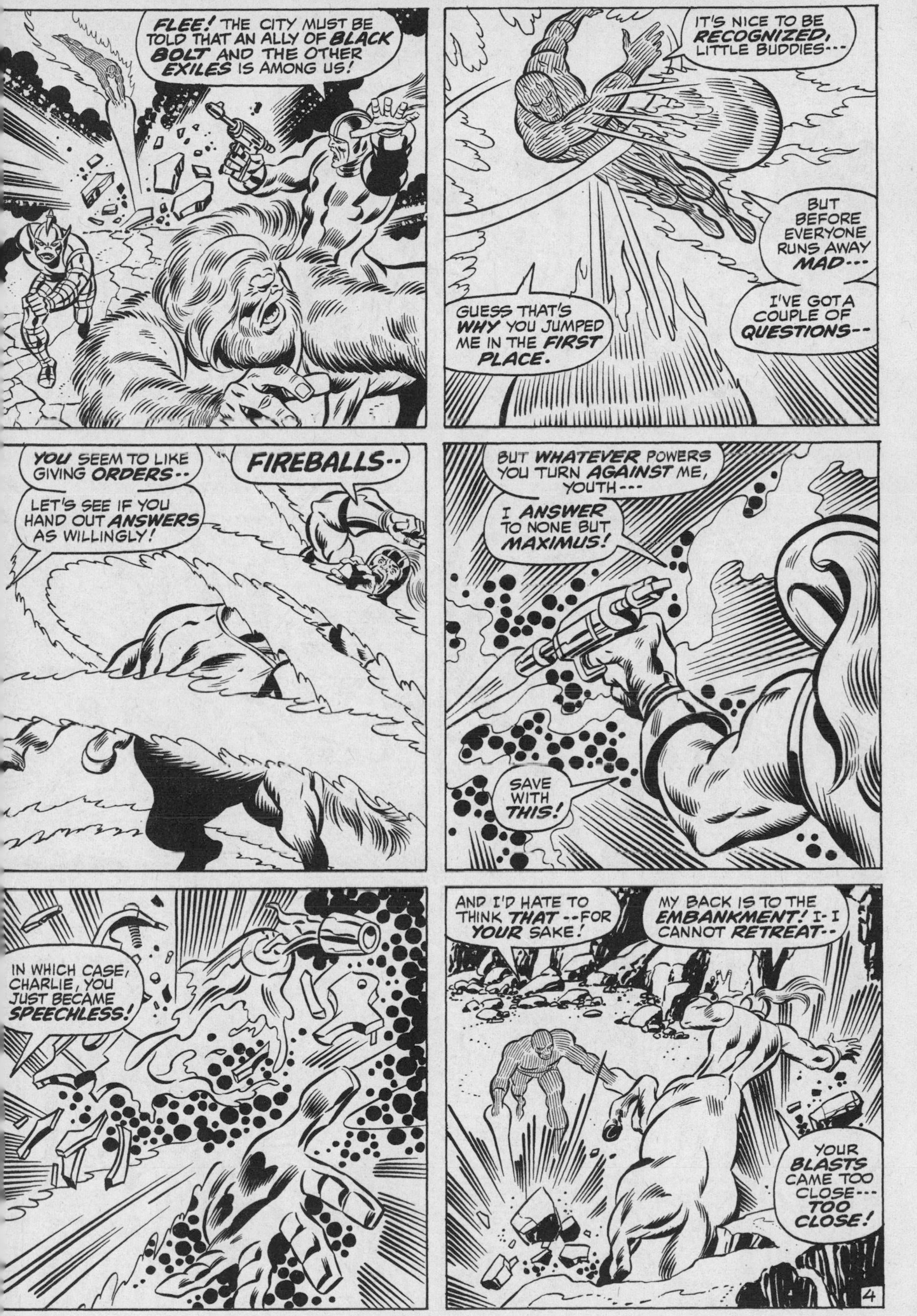
FLEE! THE CITY MUST BE TOLD THAT AN ALLY OF BLACK BOLT AND THE OTHER EXILES IS AMONG US!
IT'S NICE TO BE RECOGNIZED, LITTLE BUDDIES---
BUT BEFORE EVERYONE RUNS AWAY MAD---
GUESS THAT'S WHY YOU JUMPED ME IN THE FIRST PLACE.
I'VE GOT A COUPLE OF QUESTIONS--
YOU SEEM TO LIKE GIVING ORDERS--
LET'S SEE IF YOU HAND OUT ANSWERS AS WILLINGLY!
FIREBALLS--
BUT WHATEVER POWERS YOU TURN AGAINST ME, YOUTH---
I ANSWER TO NONE BUT MAXIMUS!
SAVE WITH THIS!
IN WHICH CASE, CHARLIE, YOU JUST BECAME SPEECHLESS!
AND I'D HATE TO THINK THAT --FOR YOUR SAKE!
MY BACK IS TO THE EMBANKMENT! I- I CANNOT RETREAT--
YOUR BLASTS CAME TOO CLOSE--- TOO CLOSE!

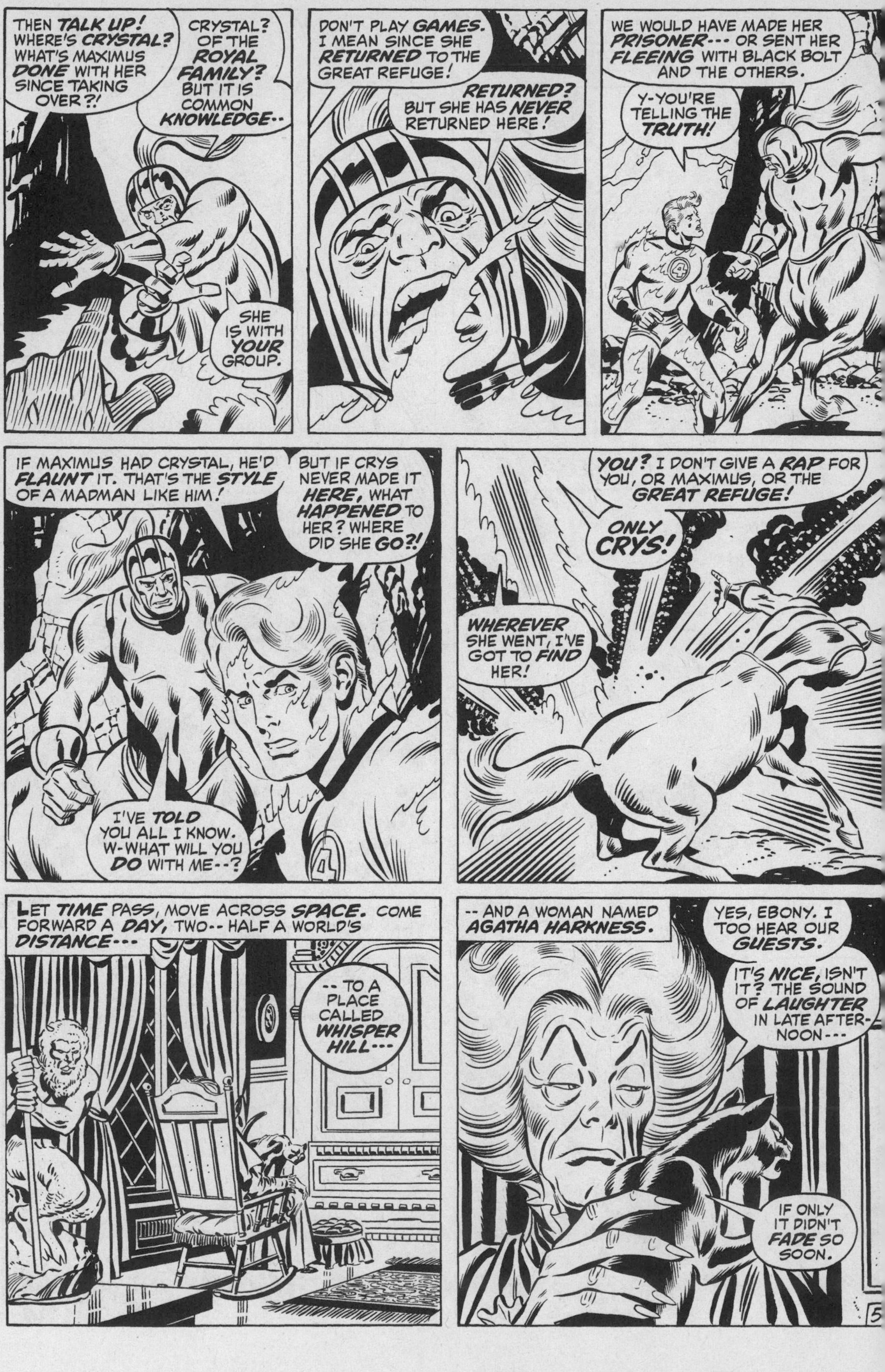
THEN TALK UP! WHERE'S CRYSTAL? WHAT'S MAXIMUS DONE WITH HER SINCE TAKING OVER?!
CRYSTAL? OF THE ROYAL FAMILY? BUT IT IS COMMON KNOWLEDGE..
SHE IS WITH YOUR GROUP.
DON'T PLAY GAMES. I MEAN SINCE SHE RETURNED TO THE GREAT REFUGE!
RETURNED? BUT SHE HAS NEVER RETURNED HERE!
WE WOULD HAVE MADE HER PRISONER--- OR SENT HER FLEEING WITH BLACK BOLT AND THE OTHERS.
Y-YOU'RE TELLING THE TRUTH!
IF MAXIMUS HAD CRYSTAL, HE'D FLAUNT IT. THAT'S THE STYLE OF A MADMAN LIKE HIM!
BUT IF CRYS NEVER MADE IT HERE, WHAT HAPPENED TO HER? WHERE DID SHE GO?!
I'VE TOLD YOU ALL I KNOW. W-WHAT WILL YOU DO WITH ME--?
YOU? I DON'T GIVE A RAP FOR YOU, OR MAXIMUS, OR THE GREAT REFUGE!
ONLY CRYS!
WHEREVER SHE WENT, I'VE GOT TO FIND HER!
LET TIME PASS, MOVE ACROSS SPACE. COME FORWARD A DAY, TWO-- HALF A WORLD'S DISTANCE---
-- TO A PLACE CALLED WHISPER HILL---
-- AND A WOMAN NAMED AGATHA HARKNESS.
YES, EBONY. I TOO HEAR OUR GUESTS.
IT'S NICE, ISN'T IT? THE SOUND OF LAUGHTER IN LATE AFTER-NOON---
IF ONLY IT DIDN'T FADE SO SOON.
5

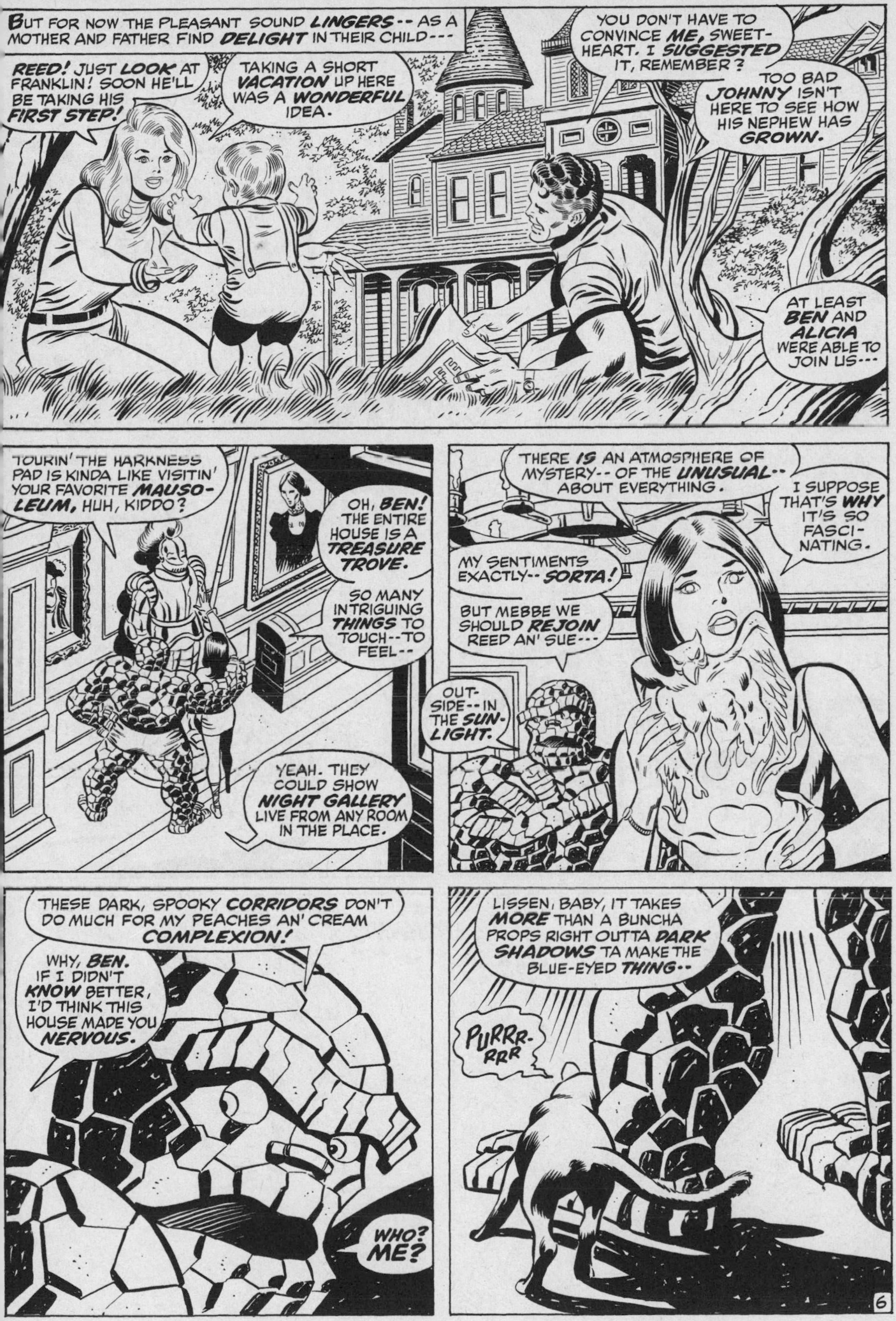

BUT FOR NOW THE PLEASANT SOUND LINGERS -- AS A MOTHER AND FATHER FIND DELIGHT IN THEIR CHILD---
REED! JUST LOOK AT FRANKLIN! SOON HE'LL BE TAKING HIS FIRST STEP!
TAKING A SHORT VACATION UP HERE WAS A WONDERFUL IDEA.
YOU DON'T HAVE TO CONVINCE ME, SWEET-HEART. I SUGGESTED IT, REMEMBER?
TOO BAD JOHNNY ISN'T HERE TO SEE HOW HIS NEPHEW HAS GROWN.
AT LEAST BEN AND ALICIA WERE ABLE TO JOIN US---
TOURIN' THE HARKNESS PAD IS KINDA LIKE VISITIN' YOUR FAVORITE MAUSO-LEUM, HUH, KIDDO?
OH, BEN! THE ENTIRE HOUSE IS A TREASURE TROVE.
SO MANY INTRIGUING THINGS TO TOUCH--TO FEEL--
YEAH. THEY COULD SHOW NIGHT GALLERY LIVE FROM ANY ROOM IN THE PLACE.
THERE IS AN ATMOSPHERE OF MYSTERY-- OF THE UNUSUAL-- ABOUT EVERYTHING.
I SUPPOSE THAT'S WHY IT'S SO FASCI-NATING.
MY SENTIMENTS EXACTLY-- SORTA!
BUT MEBBE WE SHOULD REJOIN REED AN' SUE---
OUT-SIDE--IN THE SUN-LIGHT.
THESE DARK, SPOOKY CORRIDORS DON'T DO MUCH FOR MY PEACHES AN' CREAM COMPLEXION!
WHY, BEN. IF I DIDN'T KNOW BETTER, I'D THINK THIS HOUSE MADE YOU NERVOUS.
WHO? ME?
LISSEN, BABY, IT TAKES MORE THAN A BUNCHA PROPS RIGHT OUTTA DARK SHADOWS TA MAKE THE BLUE-EYED THING--
PURRRR-RRR
6

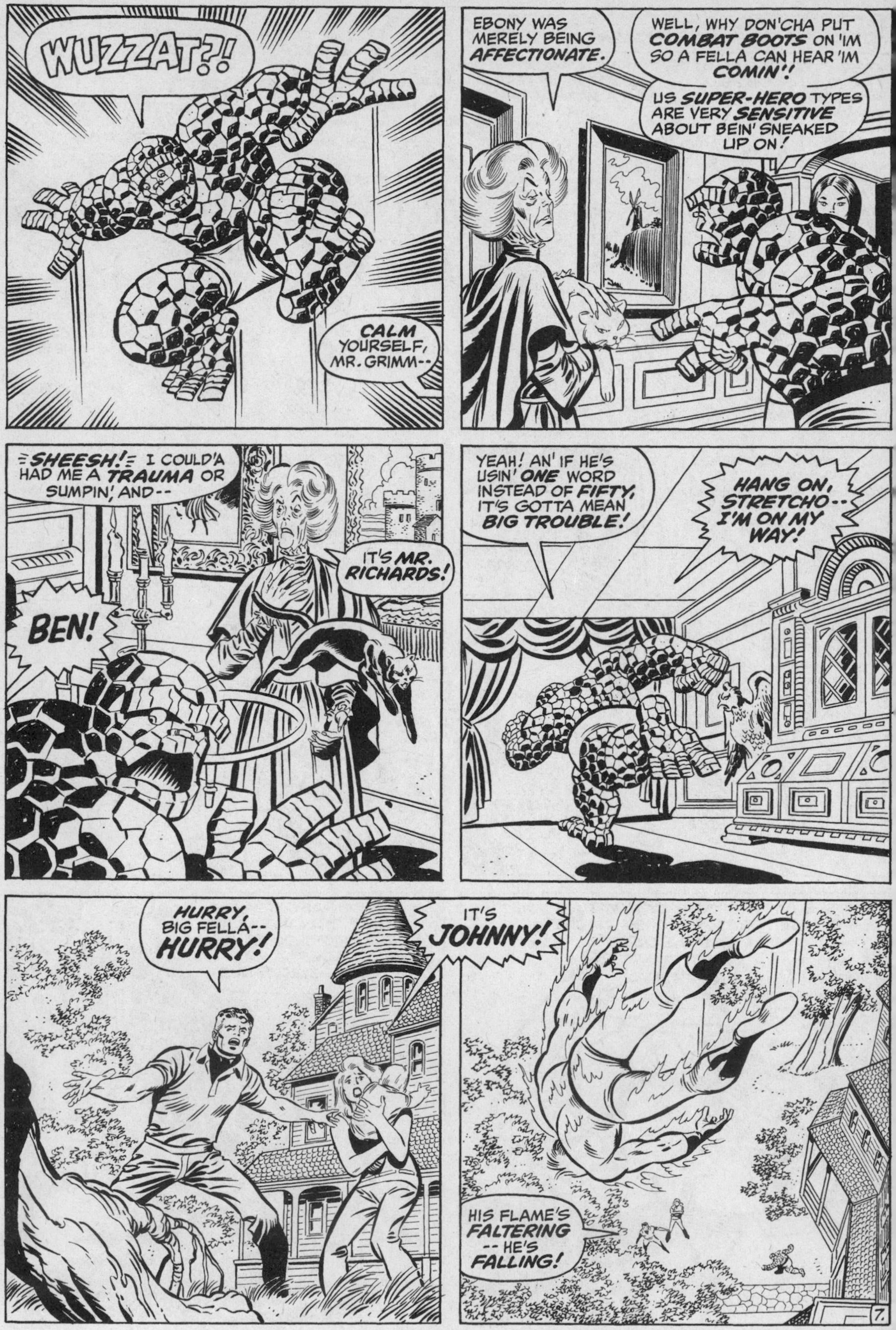
WUZZAT?!
CALM YOURSELF, MR. GRIMM--
EBONY WAS MERELY BEING AFFECTIONATE.
WELL, WHY DON'CHA PUT COMBAT BOOTS ON 'IM SO A FELLA CAN HEAR 'IM COMIN'!
US SUPER-HERO TYPES ARE VERY SENSITIVE ABOUT BEIN' SNEAKED UP ON!
SHEESH! I COULD'A HAD ME A TRAUMA OR SUMPIN', AND--
BEN!
IT'S MR. RICHARDS!
YEAH! AN' IF HE'S USIN' ONE WORD INSTEAD OF FIFTY, IT'S GOTTA MEAN BIG TROUBLE!
HANG ON, STRETCHO-- I'M ON MY WAY!
HURRY, BIG FELLA-- HURRY!
IT'S JOHNNY!
HIS FLAME'S FALTERING -- HE'S FALLING!
7.

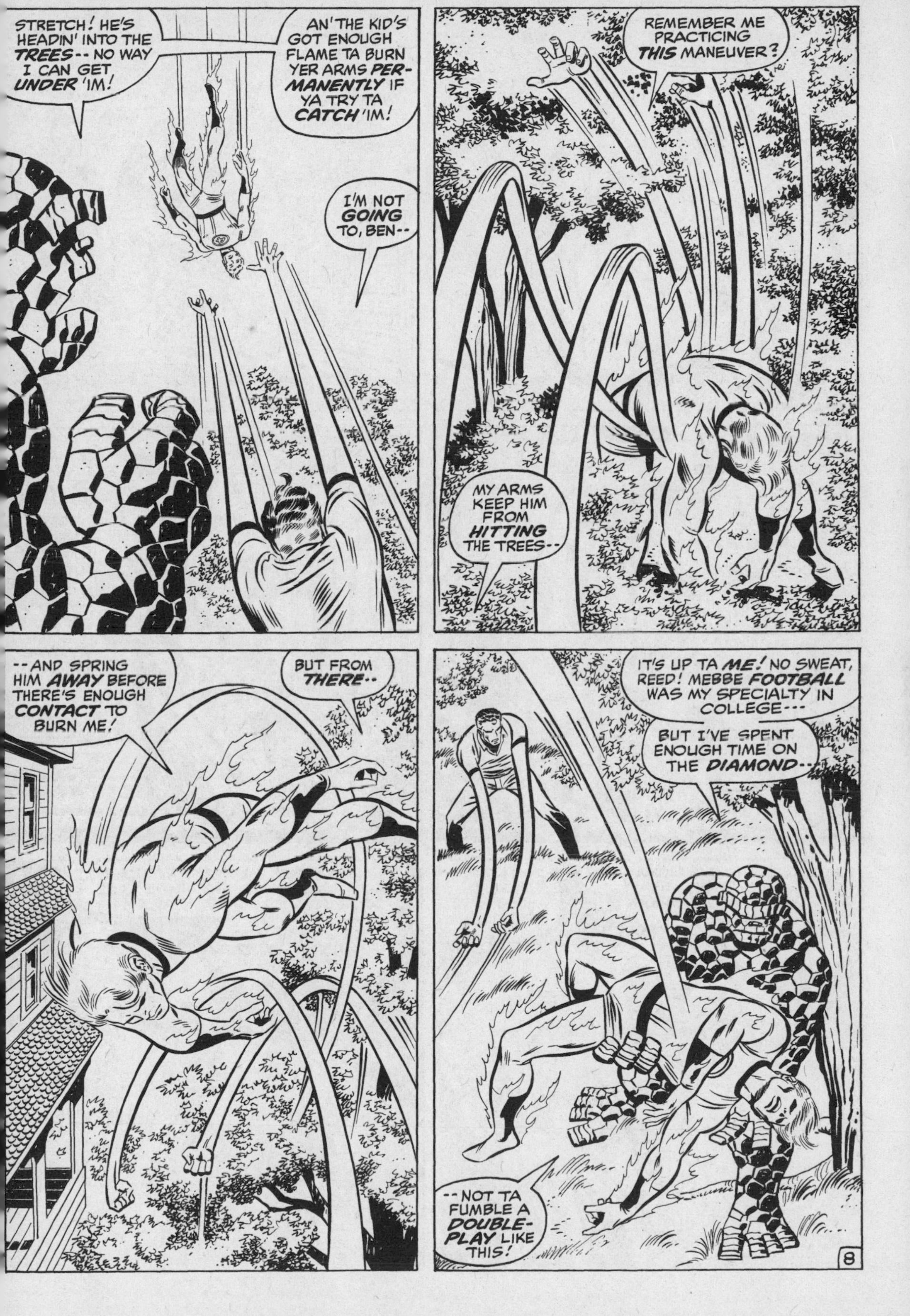
STRETCH! HE'S HEADIN' INTO THE TREES-- NO WAY I CAN GET UNDER 'IM!
AN' THE KID'S GOT ENOUGH FLAME TA BURN YER ARMS PER-MANENTLY IF YA TRY TA CATCH 'IM!
I'M NOT GOING TO, BEN--
REMEMBER ME PRACTICING THIS MANEUVER?
MY ARMS KEEP HIM FROM HITTING THE TREES--
--AND SPRING HIM AWAY BEFORE THERE'S ENOUGH CONTACT TO BURN ME!
BUT FROM THERE--
IT'S UP TA ME! NO SWEAT, REED! MEBBE FOOTBALL WAS MY SPECIALTY IN COLLEGE---
BUT I'VE SPENT ENOUGH TIME ON THE DIAMOND--
--NOT TA FUMBLE A DOUBLE-PLAY LIKE THIS!
8

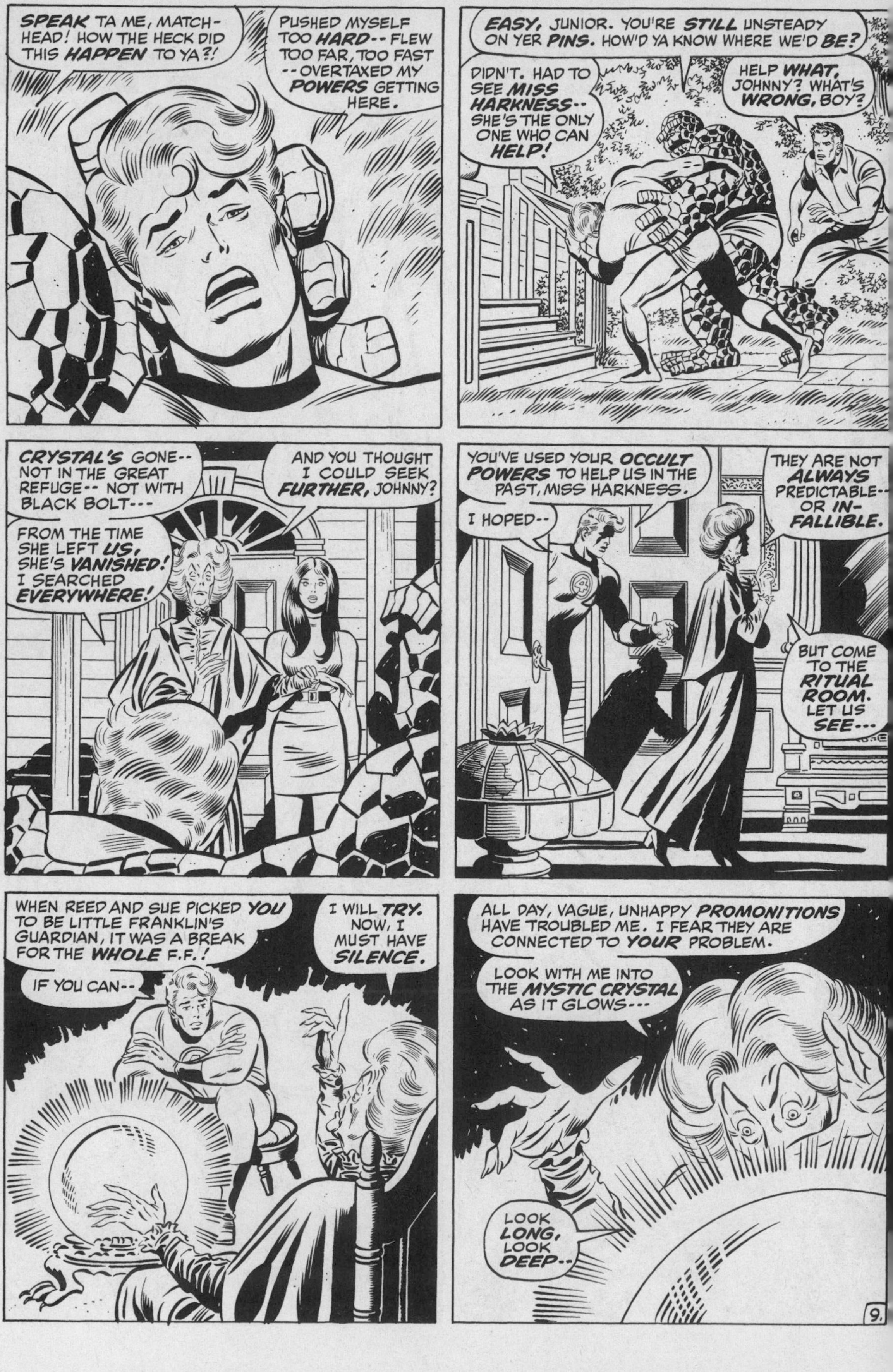
SPEAK TA ME, MATCH-HEAD! HOW THE HECK DID THIS HAPPEN TO YA?!
PUSHED MYSELF TOO HARD-- FLEW TOO FAR, TOO FAST --OVERTAXED MY POWERS GETTING HERE.
EASY, JUNIOR. YOU'RE STILL UNSTEADY ON YER PINS. HOW'D YA KNOW WHERE WE'D BE?
DIDN'T. HAD TO SEE MISS HARKNESS-- SHE'S THE ONLY ONE WHO CAN HELP!
HELP WHAT, JOHNNY? WHAT'S WRONG, BOY?
CRYSTAL'S GONE-- NOT IN THE GREAT REFUGE-- NOT WITH BLACK BOLT---
FROM THE TIME SHE LEFT US, SHE'S VANISHED! I SEARCHED EVERYWHERE!
AND YOU THOUGHT I COULD SEEK FURTHER, JOHNNY?
YOU'VE USED YOUR OCCULT POWERS TO HELP US IN THE PAST, MISS HARKNESS.
I HOPED--
THEY ARE NOT ALWAYS PREDICTABLE-- OR IN-FALLIBLE.
BUT COME TO THE RITUAL ROOM. LET US SEE---
WHEN REED AND SUE PICKED YOU TO BE LITTLE FRANKLIN'S GUARDIAN, IT WAS A BREAK FOR THE WHOLE F.F.!
IF YOU CAN--
I WILL TRY. NOW, I MUST HAVE SILENCE.
ALL DAY, VAGUE, UNHAPPY PROMONITIONS HAVE TROUBLED ME. I FEAR THEY ARE CONNECTED TO YOUR PROBLEM.
LOOK WITH ME INTO THE MYSTIC CRYSTAL AS IT GLOWS---
LOOK LONG, LOOK DEEP--
9.

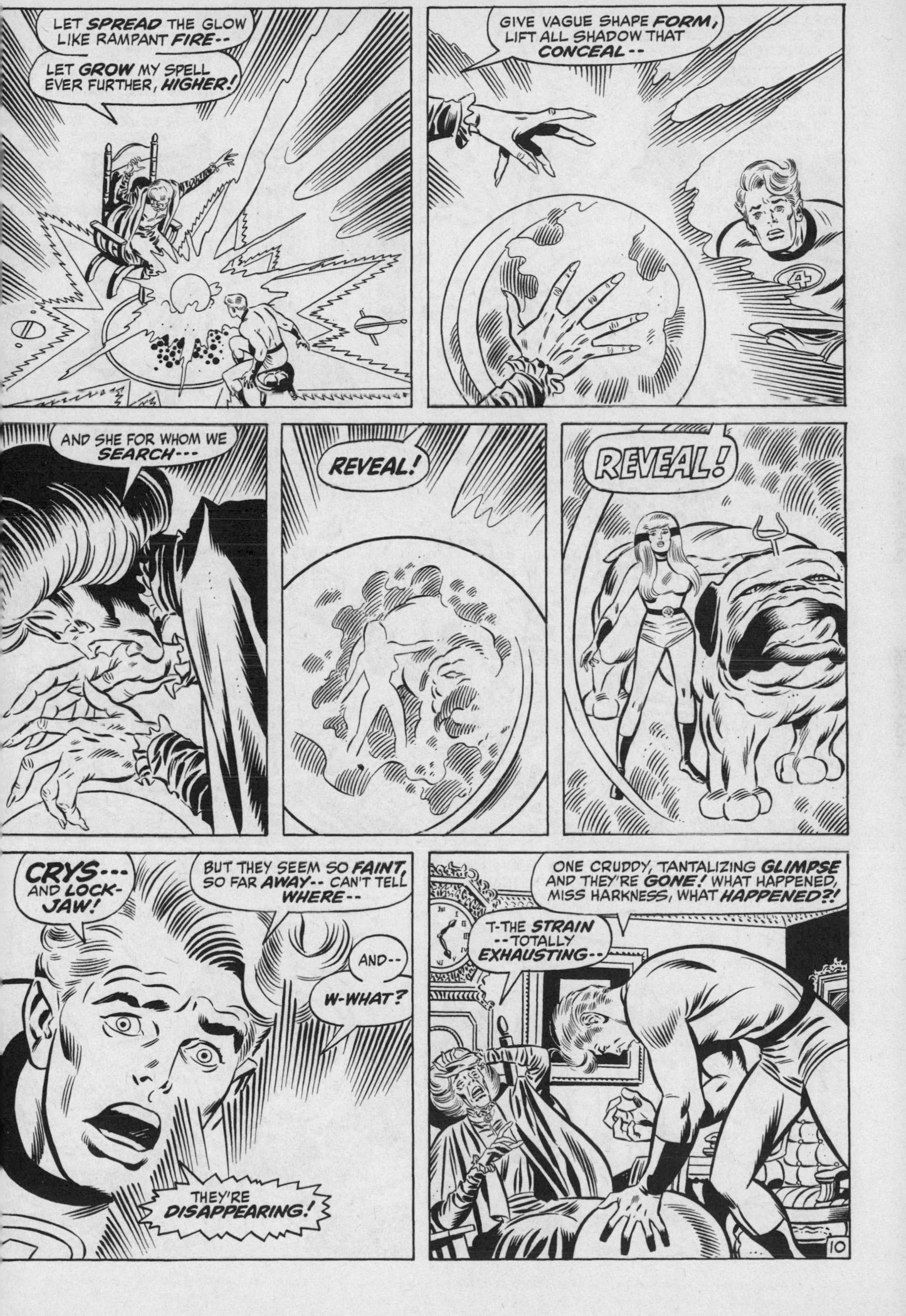
LET SPREAD THE GLOW LIKE RAMPANT FIRE--
LET GROW MY SPELL EVER FURTHER, HIGHER!
GIVE VAGUE SHAPE FORM, LIFT ALL SHADOW THAT CONCEAL--
AND SHE FOR WHOM WE SEARCH---
REVEAL!
REVEAL!
CRYS--- AND LOCK-JAW!
BUT THEY SEEM SO FAINT, SO FAR AWAY-- CAN'T TELL WHERE--
AND--
W-WHAT?
THEY'RE DISAPPEARING!
ONE CRUDDY, TANTALIZING GLIMPSE AND THEY'RE GONE! WHAT HAPPENED, MISS HARKNESS, WHAT HAPPENED?!
T-THE STRAIN --TOTALLY EXHAUSTING--
10

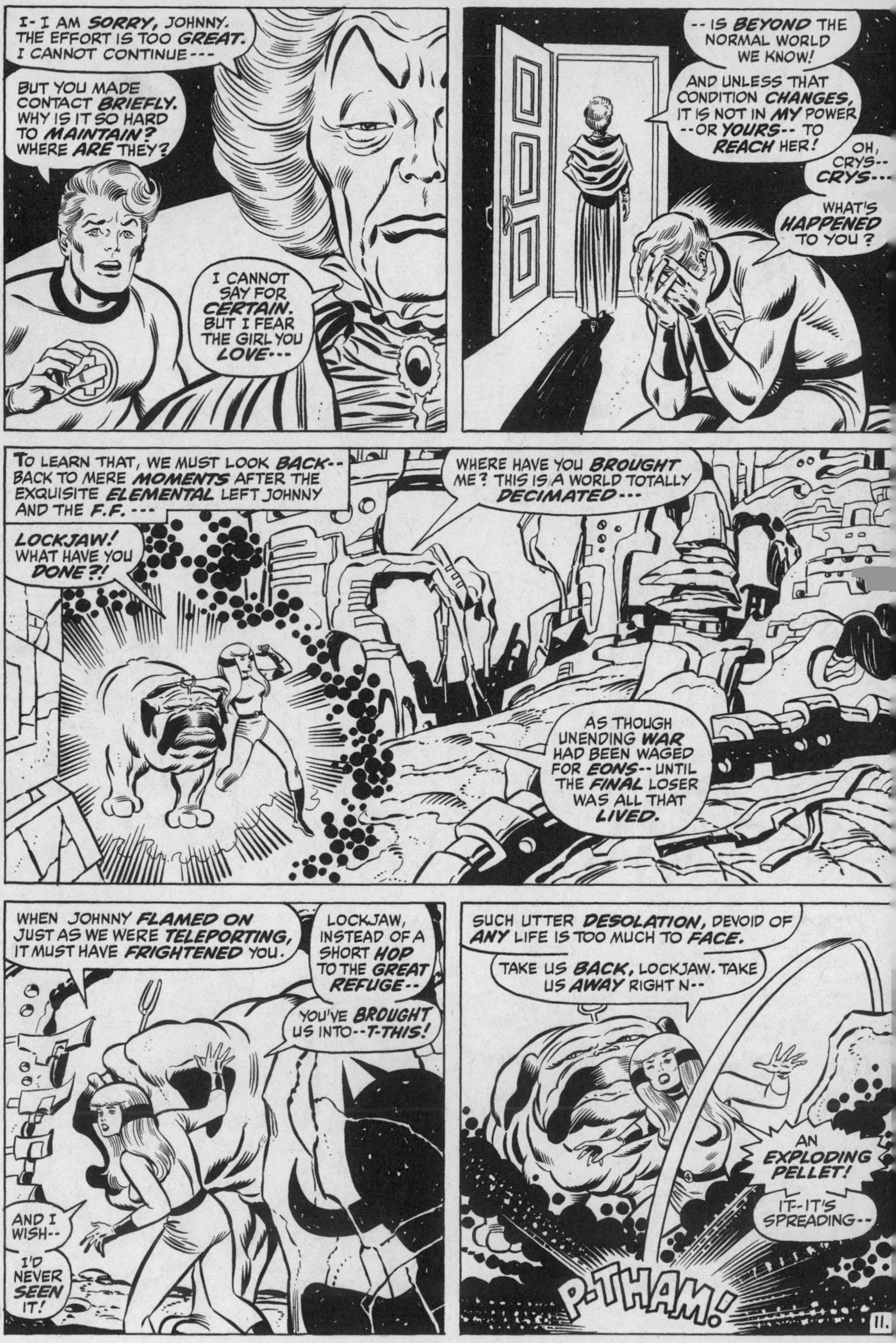
I- I AM SORRY, JOHNNY. THE EFFORT IS TOO GREAT. I CANNOT CONTINUE---
BUT YOU MADE CONTACT BRIEFLY. WHY IS IT SO HARD TO MAINTAIN? WHERE ARE THEY?
I CANNOT SAY FOR CERTAIN. BUT I FEAR THE GIRL YOU LOVE---
--IS BEYOND THE NORMAL WORLD WE KNOW!
AND UNLESS THAT CONDITION CHANGES, IT IS NOT IN MY POWER --OR YOURS-- TO REACH HER!
OH, CRYS-- CRYS---
WHAT'S HAPPENED TO YOU?
TO LEARN THAT, WE MUST LOOK BACK-- BACK TO MERE MOMENTS AFTER THE EXQUISITE ELEMENTAL LEFT JOHNNY AND THE F.F.---
LOCKJAW! WHAT HAVE YOU DONE?!
WHERE HAVE YOU BROUGHT ME? THIS IS A WORLD TOTALLY DECIMATED---
AS THOUGH UNENDING WAR HAD BEEN WAGED FOR EONS-- UNTIL THE FINAL LOSER WAS ALL THAT LIVED.
WHEN JOHNNY FLAMED ON JUST AS WE WERE TELEPORTING, IT MUST HAVE FRIGHTENED YOU.
LOCKJAW, INSTEAD OF A SHORT HOP TO THE GREAT REFUGE--
YOU'VE BROUGHT US INTO--T-THIS!
AND I WISH--
I'D NEVER SEEN IT!
SUCH UTTER DESOLATION, DEVOID OF ANY LIFE IS TOO MUCH TO FACE.
TAKE US BACK, LOCKJAW. TAKE US AWAY RIGHT N--
AN EXPLODING PELLET!
IT-IT'S SPREADING--
P-THAM!
11.

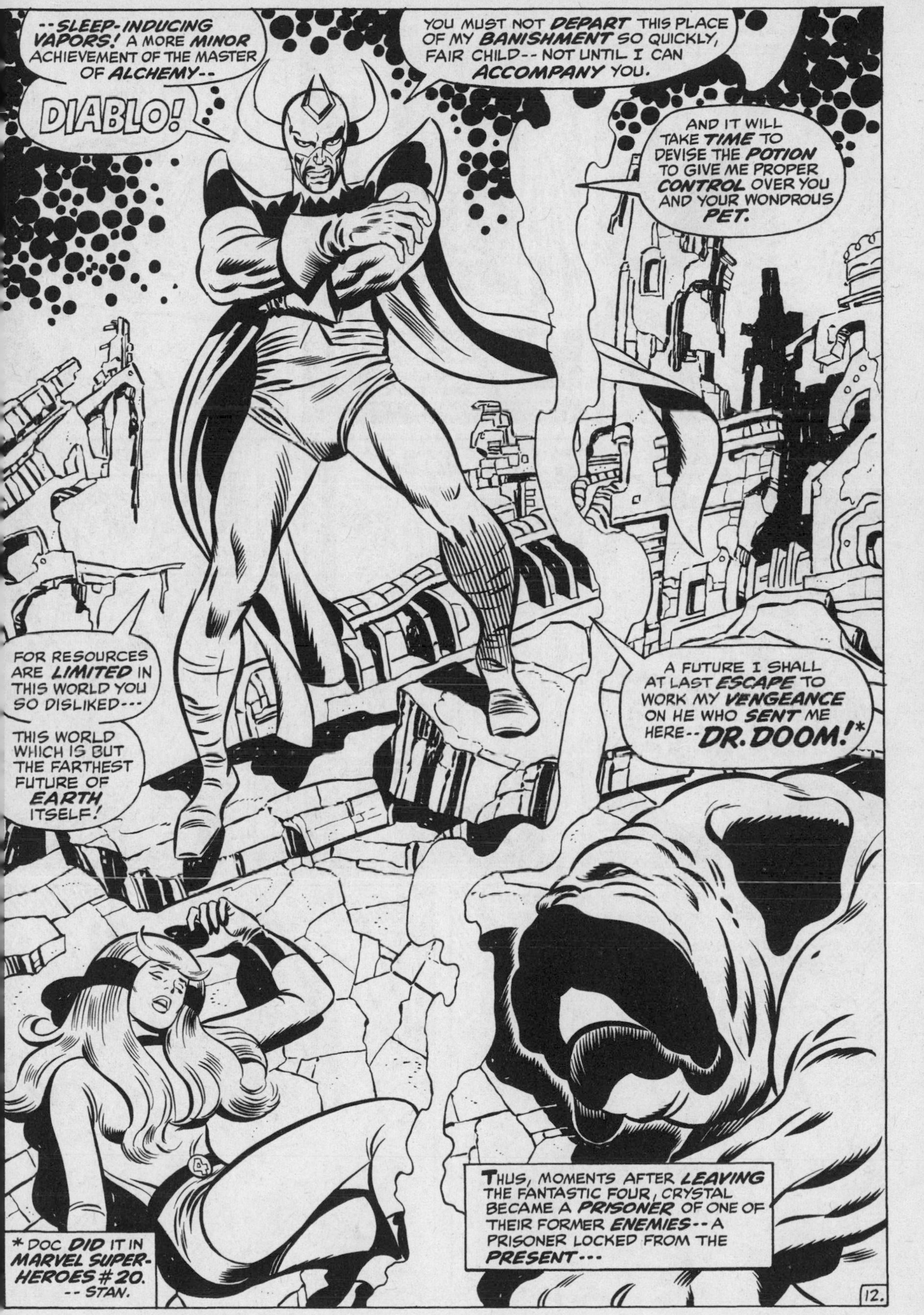
--SLEEP-INDUCING VAPORS! A MORE MINOR ACHIEVEMENT OF THE MASTER OF ALCHEMY--
DIABLO!
YOU MUST NOT DEPART THIS PLACE OF MY BANISHMENT SO QUICKLY, FAIR CHILD-- NOT UNTIL I CAN ACCOMPANY YOU.
AND IT WILL TAKE TIME TO DEVISE THE POTION TO GIVE ME PROPER CONTROL OVER YOU AND YOUR WONDROUS PET.
FOR RESOURCES ARE LIMITED IN THIS WORLD YOU SO DISLIKED---
THIS WORLD WHICH IS BUT THE FARTHEST FUTURE OF EARTH ITSELF!
A FUTURE I SHALL AT LAST ESCAPE TO WORK MY VENGEANCE ON HE WHO SENT ME HERE--DR. DOOM!*
THUS, MOMENTS AFTER LEAVING THE FANTASTIC FOUR, CRYSTAL BECAME A PRISONER OF ONE OF THEIR FORMER ENEMIES--A PRISONER LOCKED FROM THE PRESENT---
* DOC DID IT IN MARVEL SUPER-HEROES #20. -- STAN.
12.

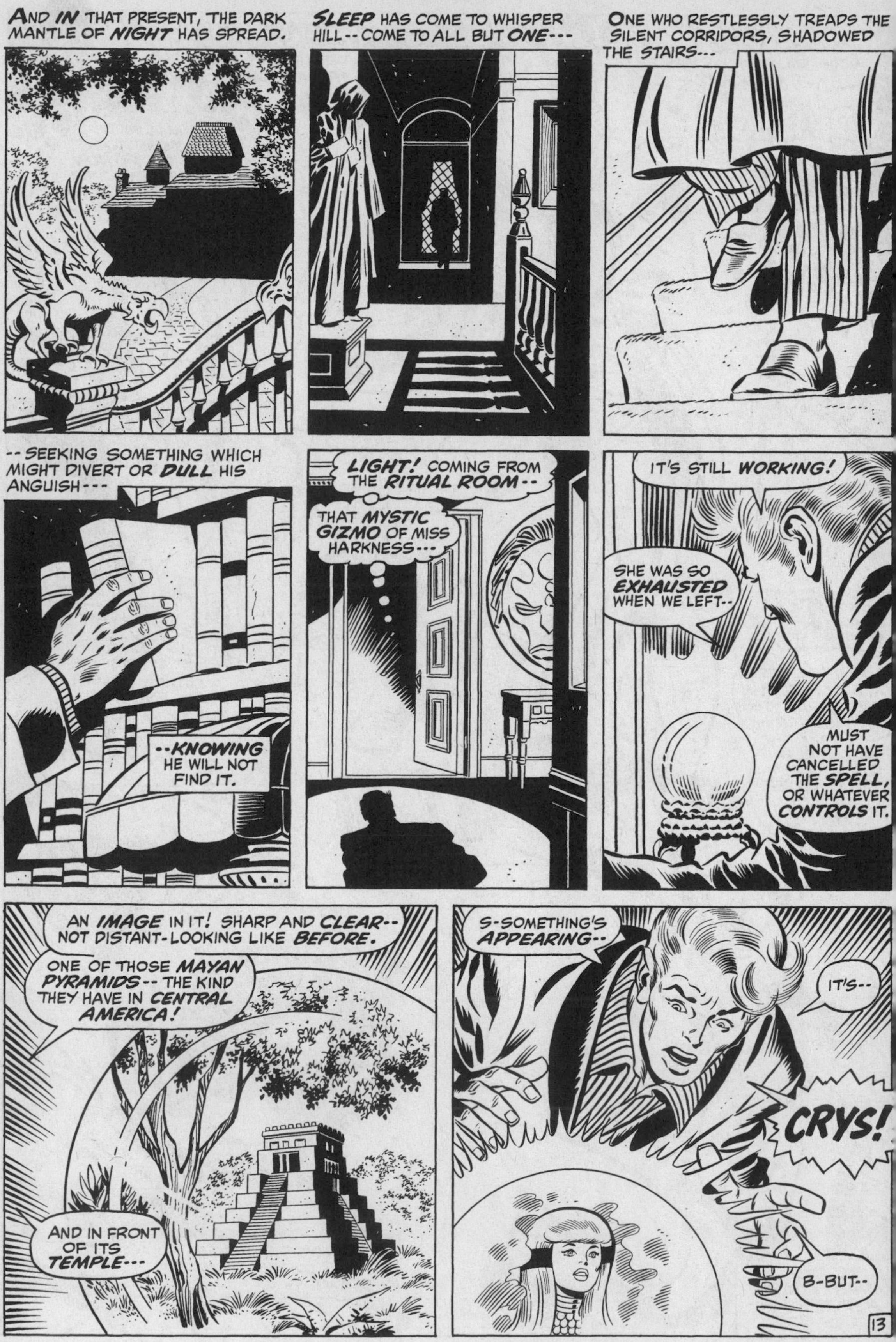
AND IN THAT PRESENT, THE DARK MANTLE OF NIGHT HAS SPREAD.
SLEEP HAS COME TO WHISPER HILL -- COME TO ALL BUT ONE---
ONE WHO RESTLESSLY TREADS THE SILENT CORRIDORS, SHADOWED THE STAIRS---
-- SEEKING SOMETHING WHICH MIGHT DIVERT OR DULL HIS ANGUISH---
--KNOWING HE WILL NOT FIND IT.
LIGHT! COMING FROM THE RITUAL ROOM--
THAT MYSTIC GIZMO OF MISS HARKNESS---
IT'S STILL WORKING!
SHE WAS SO EXHAUSTED WHEN WE LEFT--
MUST NOT HAVE CANCELLED THE SPELL, OR WHATEVER CONTROLS IT.
AN IMAGE IN IT! SHARP AND CLEAR-- NOT DISTANT-LOOKING LIKE BEFORE.
ONE OF THOSE MAYAN PYRAMIDS -- THE KIND THEY HAVE IN CENTRAL AMERICA!
AND IN FRONT OF ITS TEMPLE---
S-SOMETHING'S APPEARING--
IT'S--
CRYS!
B-BUT--
13

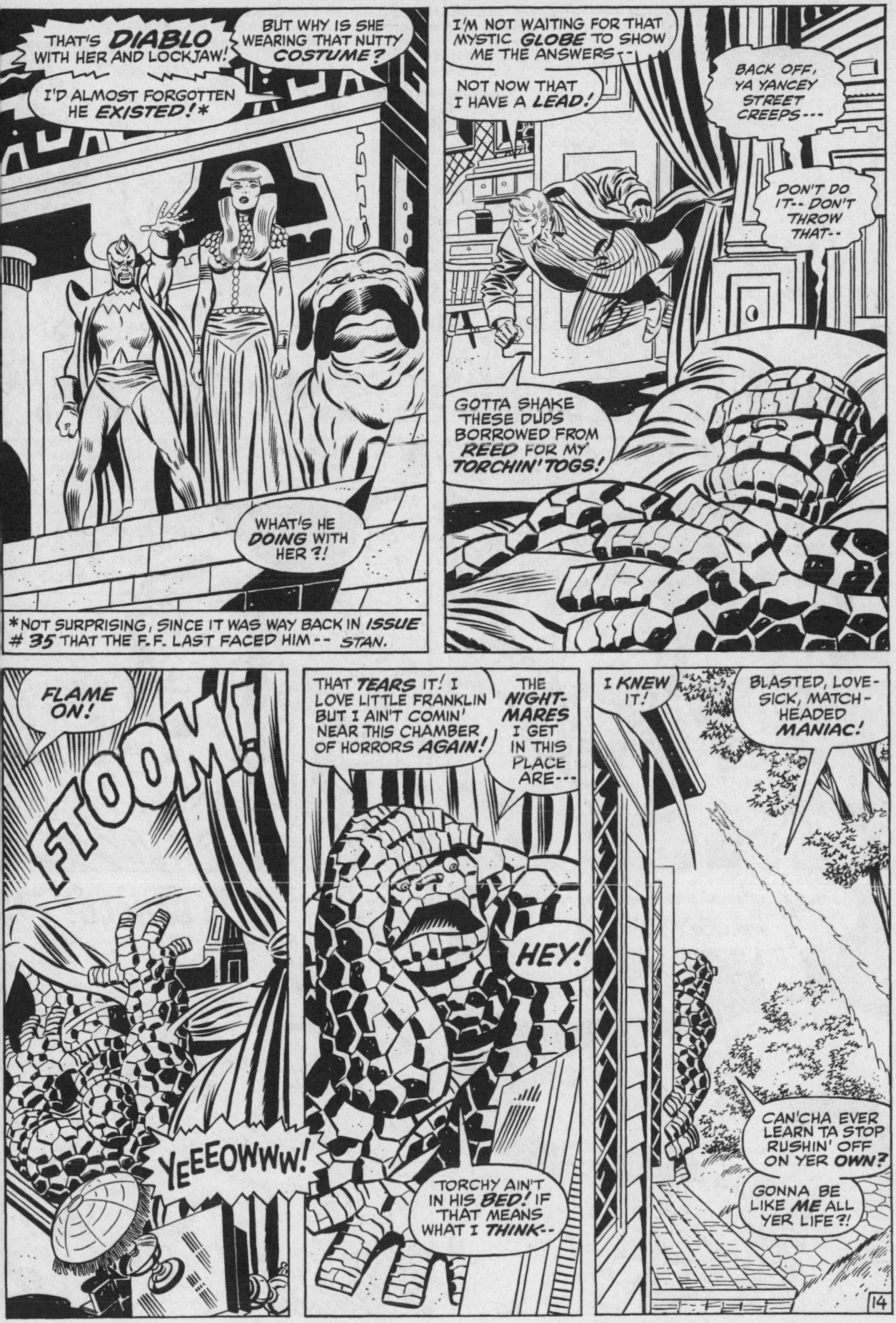
THAT'S DIABLO WITH HER AND LOCKJAW!
BUT WHY IS SHE WEARING THAT NUTTY COSTUME?
I'D ALMOST FORGOTTEN HE EXISTED!*
WHAT'S HE DOING WITH HER?!
*NOT SURPRISING, SINCE IT WAS WAY BACK IN ISSUE # 35 THAT THE F.F. LAST FACED HIM -- STAN.
I'M NOT WAITING FOR THAT MYSTIC GLOBE TO SHOW ME THE ANSWERS--
NOT NOW THAT I HAVE A LEAD!
BACK OFF, YA YANCEY STREET CREEPS---
DON'T DO IT-- DON'T THROW THAT--
GOTTA SHAKE THESE DUDS BORROWED FROM REED FOR MY TORCHIN' TOGS!
FLAME ON!
FTOOM!
YEEEOWWW!
THAT TEARS IT! I LOVE LITTLE FRANKLIN BUT I AIN'T COMIN' NEAR THIS CHAMBER OF HORRORS AGAIN!
THE NIGHT-MARES I GET IN THIS PLACE ARE---
HEY!
TORCHY AIN'T IN HIS BED! IF THAT MEANS WHAT I THINK-
I KNEW IT!
BLASTED, LOVE-SICK, MATCH-HEADED MANIAC!
CAN'CHA EVER LEARN TA STOP RUSHIN' OFF ON YER OWN?
GONNA BE LIKE ME ALL YER LIFE?!
14

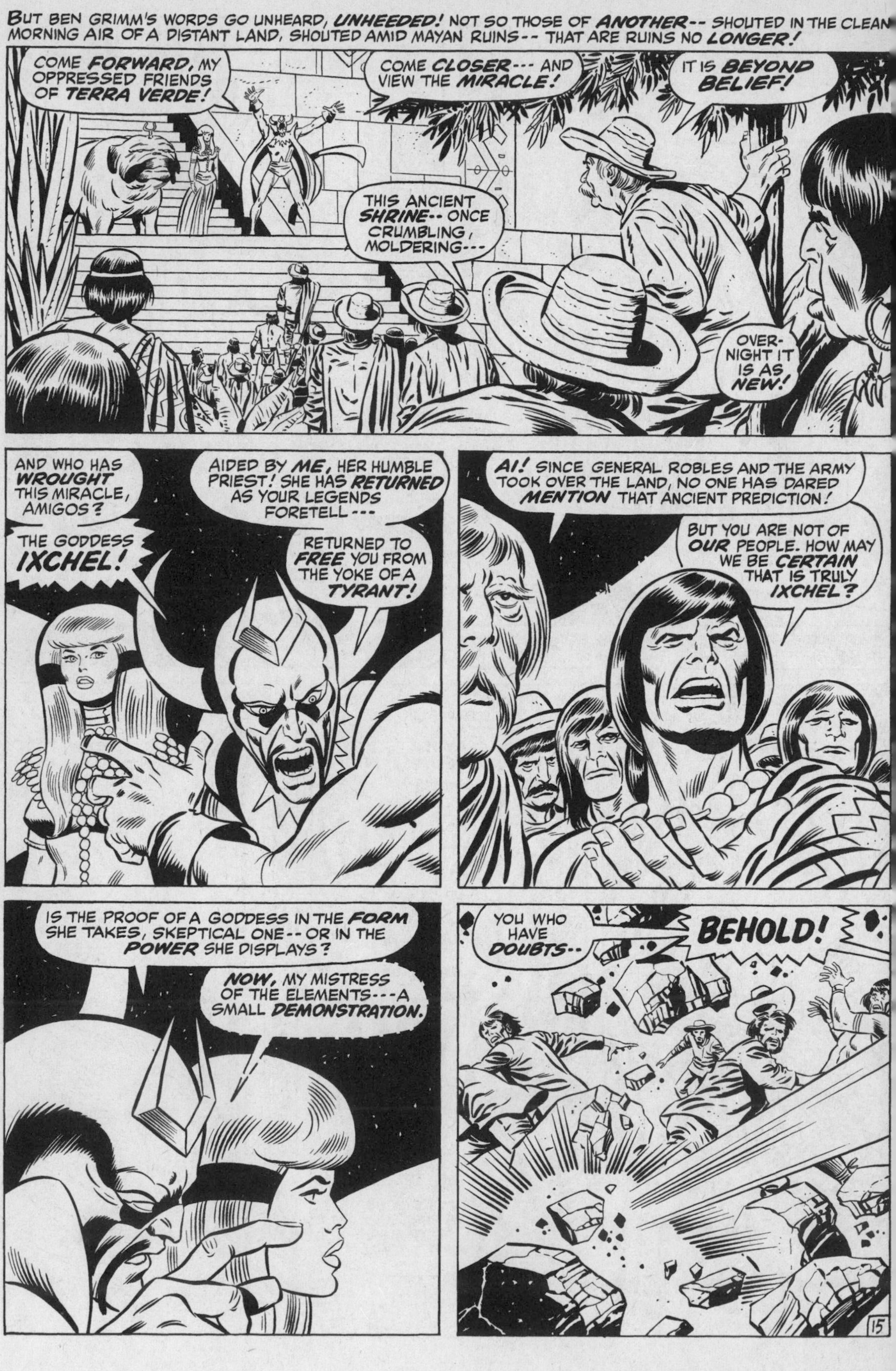

BUT BEN GRIMM'S WORDS GO UNHEARD, UNHEEDED! NOT SO THOSE OF ANOTHER-- SHOUTED IN THE CLEAN MORNING AIR OF A DISTANT LAND, SHOUTED AMID MAYAN RUINS-- THAT ARE RUINS NO LONGER!
COME FORWARD, MY OPPRESSED FRIENDS OF TERRA VERDE!
COME CLOSER--- AND VIEW THE MIRACLE!
IT IS BEYOND BELIEF!
THIS ANCIENT SHRINE-- ONCE CRUMBLING, MOLDERING---
OVER-NIGHT IT IS AS NEW!
AND WHO HAS WROUGHT THIS MIRACLE, AMIGOS?
AIDED BY ME, HER HUMBLE PRIEST! SHE HAS RETURNED AS YOUR LEGENDS FORETELL---
THE GODDESS IXCHEL!
RETURNED TO FREE YOU FROM THE YOKE OF A TYRANT!
AI! SINCE GENERAL ROBLES AND THE ARMY TOOK OVER THE LAND, NO ONE HAS DARED MENTION THAT ANCIENT PREDICTION!
BUT YOU ARE NOT OF OUR PEOPLE. HOW MAY WE BE CERTAIN THAT IS TRULY IXCHEL?
IS THE PROOF OF A GODDESS IN THE FORM SHE TAKES, SKEPTICAL ONE-- OR IN THE POWER SHE DISPLAYS?
NOW, MY MISTRESS OF THE ELEMENTS---A SMALL DEMONSTRATION.
YOU WHO HAVE DOUBTS--
BEHOLD!

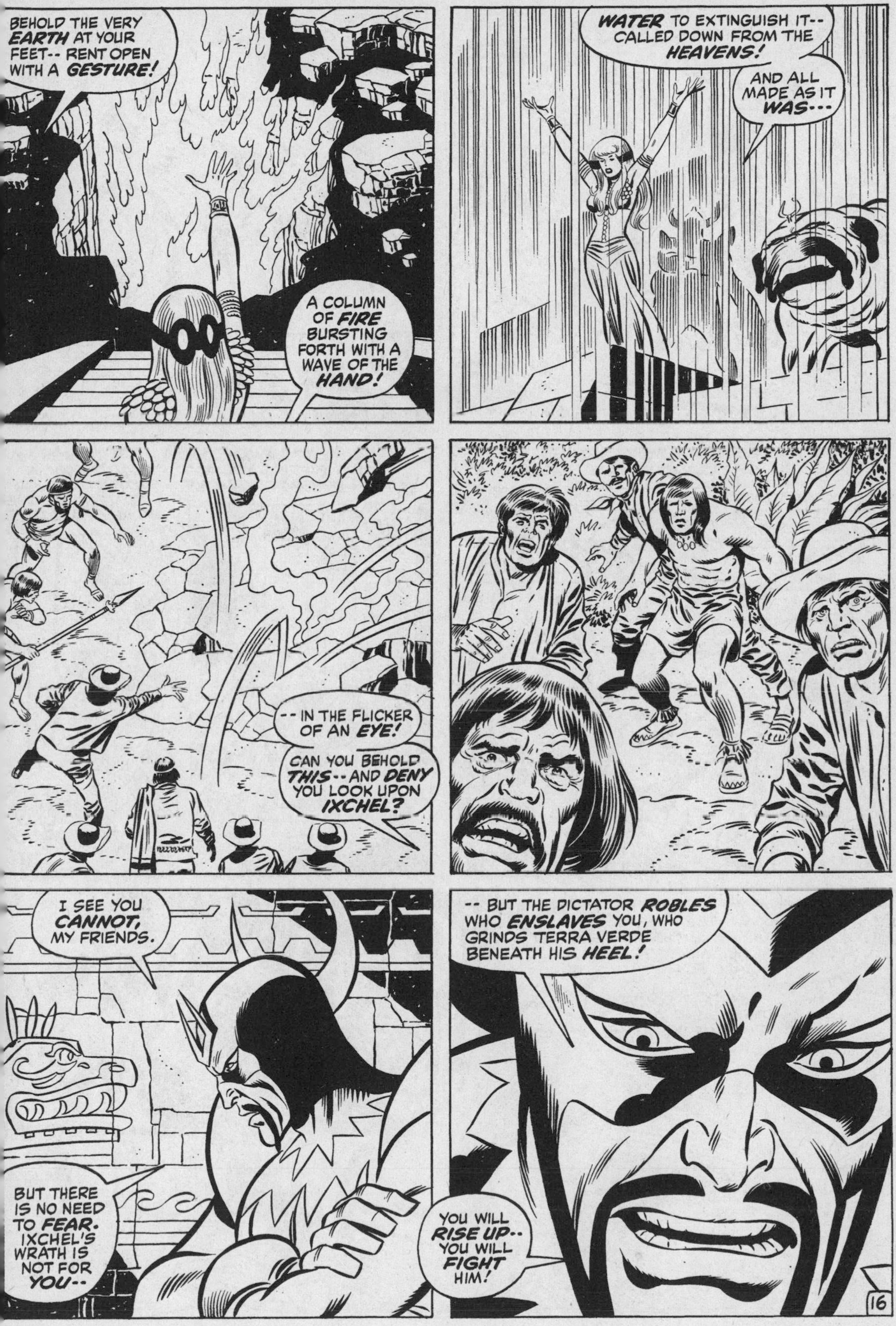
BEHOLD THE VERY EARTH AT YOUR FEET-- RENT OPEN WITH A GESTURE!
A COLUMN OF FIRE BURSTING FORTH WITH A WAVE OF THE HAND!
WATER TO EXTINGUISH IT-- CALLED DOWN FROM THE HEAVENS!
AND ALL MADE AS IT WAS---
--IN THE FLICKER OF AN EYE!
CAN YOU BEHOLD THIS--AND DENY YOU LOOK UPON IXCHEL?
I SEE YOU CANNOT, MY FRIENDS.
BUT THERE IS NO NEED TO FEAR. IXCHEL'S WRATH IS NOT FOR YOU--
--BUT THE DICTATOR ROBLES WHO ENSLAVES YOU, WHO GRINDS TERRA VERDE BENEATH HIS HEEL!
YOU WILL RISE UP-- YOU WILL FIGHT HIM!
16

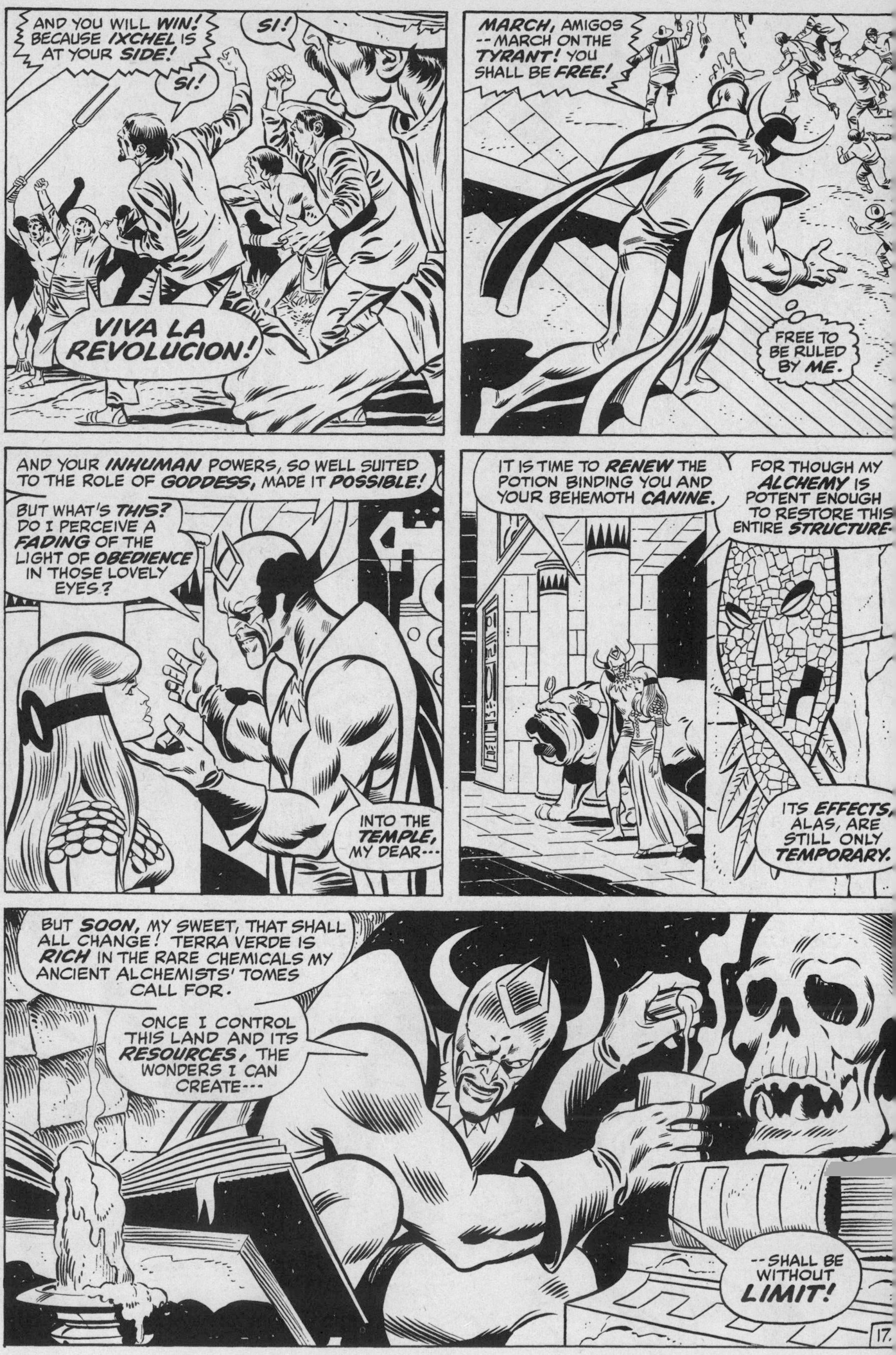
AND YOU WILL WIN! BECAUSE IXCHEL IS AT YOUR SIDE!
SI!
SI!
VIVA LA REVOLUCION!
MARCH, AMIGOS --MARCH ON THE TYRANT! YOU SHALL BE FREE!
FREE TO BE RULED BY ME.
AND YOUR INHUMAN POWERS, SO WELL SUITED TO THE ROLE OF GODDESS, MADE IT POSSIBLE!
BUT WHAT'S THIS? DO I PERCEIVE A FADING OF THE LIGHT OF OBEDIENCE IN THOSE LOVELY EYES?
INTO THE TEMPLE, MY DEAR---
IT IS TIME TO RENEW THE POTION BINDING YOU AND YOUR BEHEMOTH CANINE.
FOR THOUGH MY ALCHEMY IS POTENT ENOUGH TO RESTORE THIS ENTIRE STRUCTURE-
ITS EFFECTS, ALAS, ARE STILL ONLY TEMPORARY.
BUT SOON, MY SWEET, THAT SHALL ALL CHANGE! TERRA VERDE IS RICH IN THE RARE CHEMICALS MY ANCIENT ALCHEMISTS' TOMES CALL FOR.
ONCE I CONTROL THIS LAND AND ITS RESOURCES, THE WONDERS I CAN CREATE---
--SHALL BE WITHOUT LIMIT!
17

HOW *MANY* TIMES WHILE TRAPPED IN THAT BLEAK, DESOLATE *FUTURE*, I PLOTTED A MOVE SUCH AS THIS! BUT ONLY *YOUR* APPEARANCE MADE IT FEASIBLE.

HERE, MY *CHILD*--

YOU MAY DRINK TO OUR *SUCCESS!*

FOR WITH IT, I'LL HAVE MY OWN *COUNTRY,* UNIQUELY SUITED TO MY OWN *NEEDS*--

I'LL BE ON EQUAL FOOTING IN THE WORLD WITH *DOCTOR DOOM!*

AND THEN--*THEN*-- I SHALL WREAK *VENGEANCE* UPON HIM.

MEANWHILE, SOME MILES AWAY--AT THE *ROYAL PALACE* IN TERRA VERDE'S CAPITAL CITY---

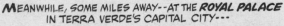

GENERAL ROBLES! THERE IS *TROUBLE* IN THE HILLS-- THE PEOPLE RISE IN *REVOLT!*

THEY BELIEVE THE GODDESS *IXCHEL* HAS RETURNED TO SET THEM *FREE,* IN FUL-FILLMENT OF THE OLD *LEGENDS!*

LUIS, YOU ARE A *FINE* HEAD OF SECRET POLICE--

IF ONLY YOU DIDN'T *SHOUT* SO.

A *BAD,* THING, SHOUTING--

SHOWS LACK OF *BREEDING,* LUIS. WITHOUT BREEDING, A MAN IS NO BETTER THAN A *PEASANT.*

AH, MY *POOR* PEASANTS-- SMALL WONDER THEY NEED THEIR *GENERAL* TO GUIDE THEM!

A *GODDESS,* YOU SAY, LUIS? THEY *BELIEVE* IN A GODDESS?

AH, MY POOR, FOOLISH *CHILDREN*--

18

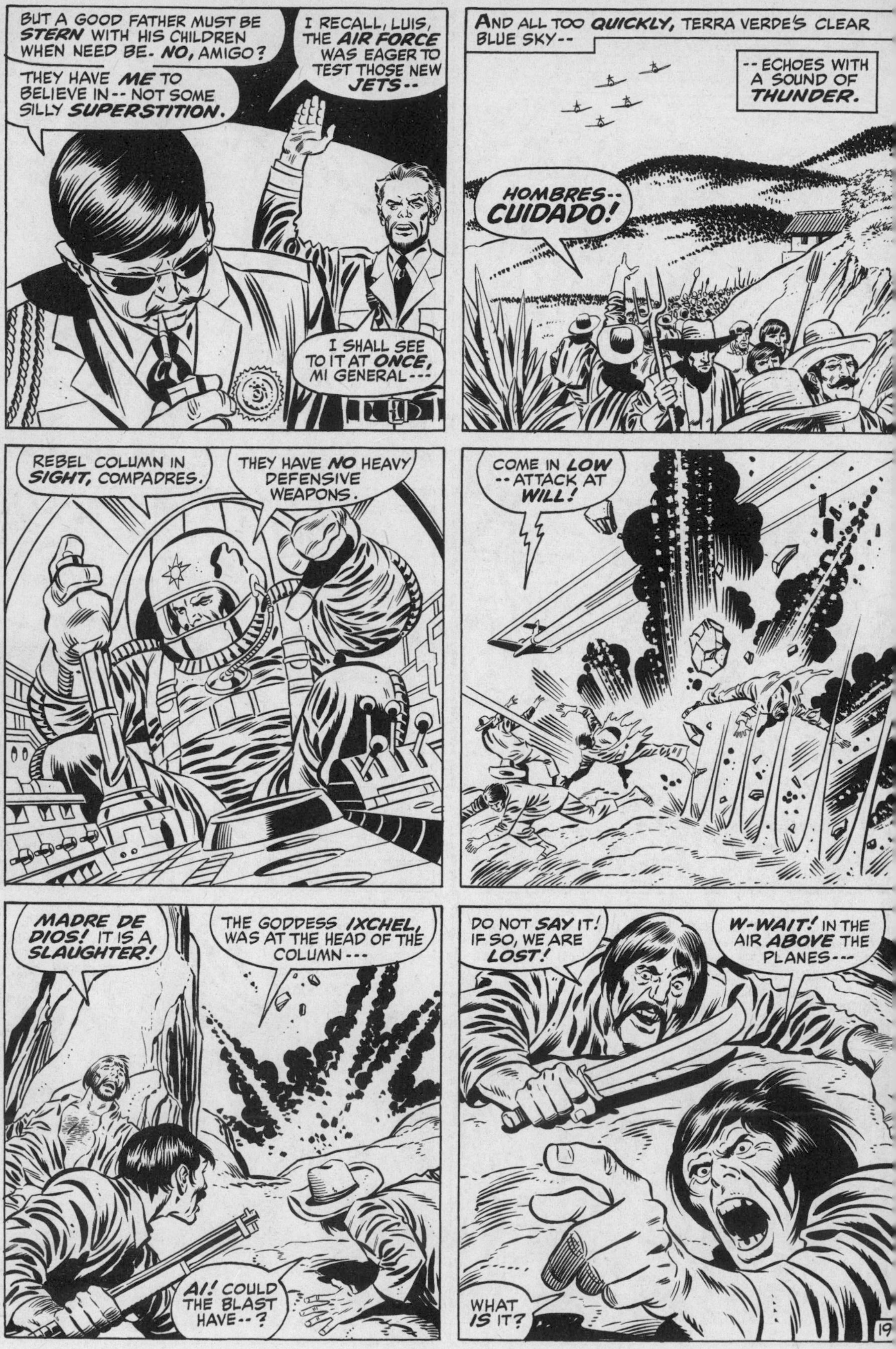
BUT A GOOD FATHER MUST BE STERN WITH HIS CHILDREN WHEN NEED BE. NO, AMIGO?
THEY HAVE ME TO BELIEVE IN-- NOT SOME SILLY SUPERSTITION.
I RECALL, LUIS, THE AIR FORCE WAS EAGER TO TEST THOSE NEW JETS--
I SHALL SEE TO IT AT ONCE, MI GENERAL---
AND ALL TOO QUICKLY, TERRA VERDE'S CLEAR BLUE SKY--
--ECHOES WITH A SOUND OF THUNDER.
HOMBRES.. CUIDADO!
REBEL COLUMN IN SIGHT, COMPADRES.
THEY HAVE NO HEAVY DEFENSIVE WEAPONS.
COME IN LOW --ATTACK AT WILL!
MADRE DE DIOS! IT IS A SLAUGHTER!
THE GODDESS IXCHEL, WAS AT THE HEAD OF THE COLUMN---
AI! COULD THE BLAST HAVE--?
DO NOT SAY IT! IF SO, WE ARE LOST!
W-WAIT! IN THE AIR ABOVE THE PLANES---
WHAT IS IT?

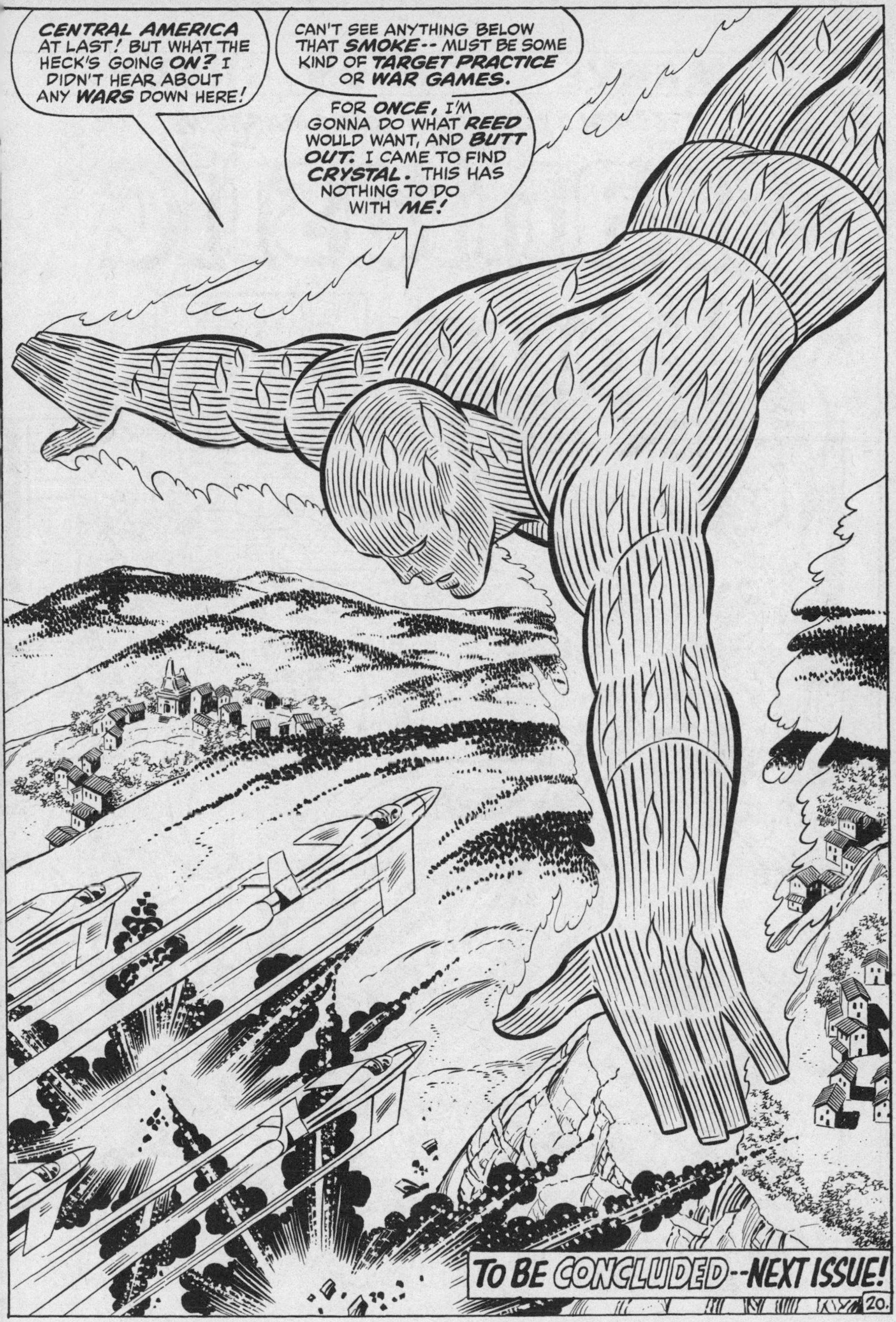
CENTRAL AMERICA AT LAST! BUT WHAT THE HECK'S GOING ON? I DIDN'T HEAR ABOUT ANY WARS DOWN HERE!
CAN'T SEE ANYTHING BELOW THAT SMOKE-- MUST BE SOME KIND OF TARGET PRACTICE OR WAR GAMES.
FOR ONCE, I'M GONNA DO WHAT REED WOULD WANT, AND BUTT OUT. I CAME TO FIND CRYSTAL. THIS HAS NOTHING TO DO WITH ME!
TO BE CONCLUDED--NEXT ISSUE!
20.

FANTASTIC FOUR
MARVEL COMICS GROUP
118 JAN 02462
20¢ CC
THE WORLD'S GREATEST COMIC MAGAZINE!
APPROVED BY THE COMICS CODE AUTHORITY
Fantastic Four
ALL NEW ...and ALL GREAT!
NO! YOU CAN'T HAVE TURNED AGAINST US!
NOT YOU!
WHY NOT-- WHEN CRYSTAL IS THE MOST POWERFUL INHUMAN OF ALL!!
THUNDER IN THE RUINS PLUS: THE THING FIGHTS ALONE!

AR FROM THE REST OF THE F.F., CAN THE TORCH ALONE DEFEAT THE DREAD DIABLO?

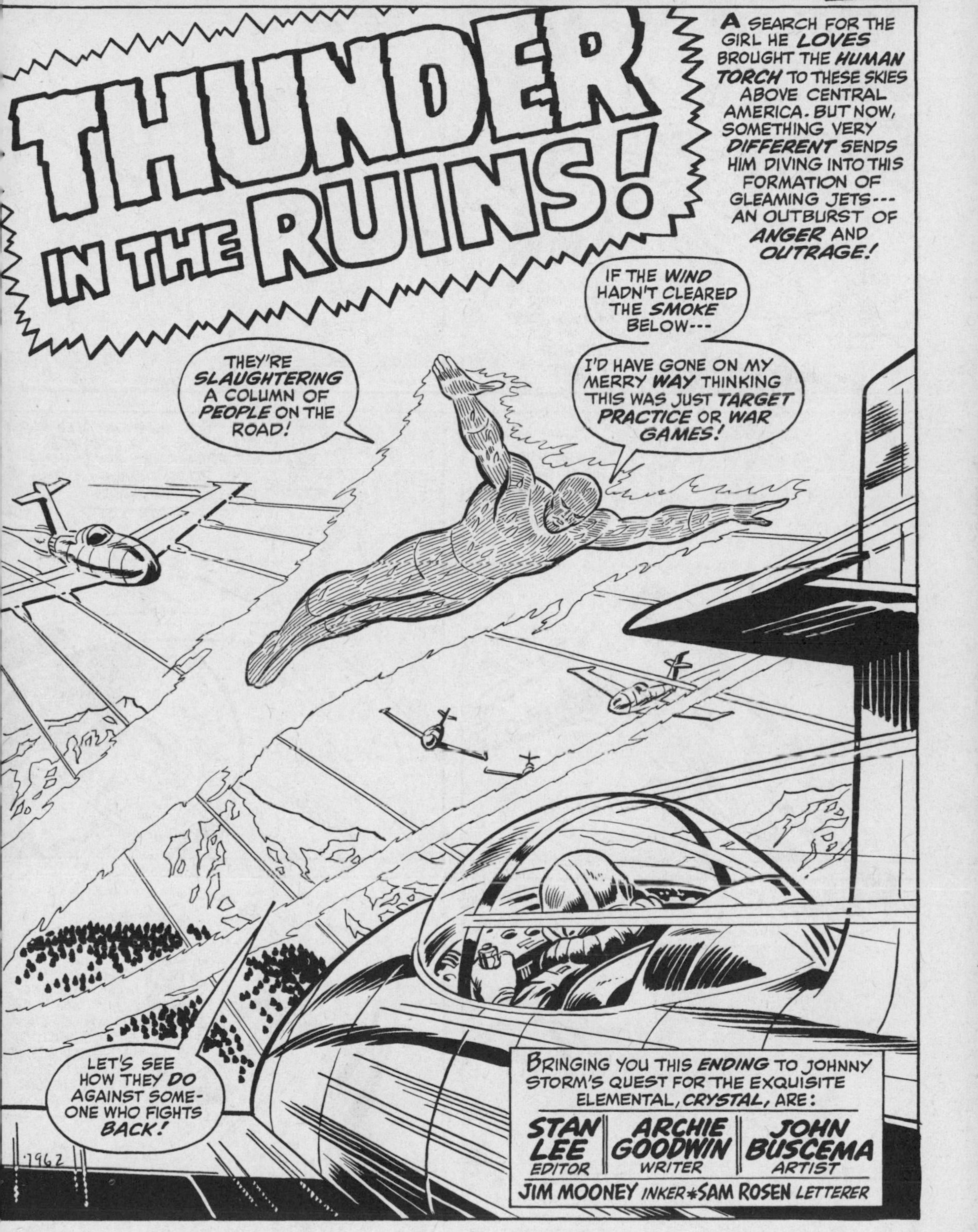
THUNDER IN THE RUINS!
A SEARCH FOR THE GIRL HE LOVES BROUGHT THE HUMAN TORCH TO THESE SKIES ABOVE CENTRAL AMERICA. BUT NOW, SOMETHING VERY DIFFERENT SENDS HIM DIVING INTO THIS FORMATION OF GLEAMING JETS--- AN OUTBURST OF ANGER AND OUTRAGE!
THEY'RE SLAUGHTERING A COLUMN OF PEOPLE ON THE ROAD!
IF THE WIND HADN'T CLEARED THE SMOKE BELOW---
I'D HAVE GONE ON MY MERRY WAY THINKING THIS WAS JUST TARGET PRACTICE OR WAR GAMES!
LET'S SEE HOW THEY DO AGAINST SOME-ONE WHO FIGHTS BACK!
BRINGING YOU THIS ENDING TO JOHNNY STORM'S QUEST FOR THE EXQUISITE ELEMENTAL, CRYSTAL, ARE:
STAN LEE EDITOR
ARCHIE GOODWIN WRITER
JOHN BUSCEMA ARTIST
JIM MOONEY INKER * SAM ROSEN LETTERER

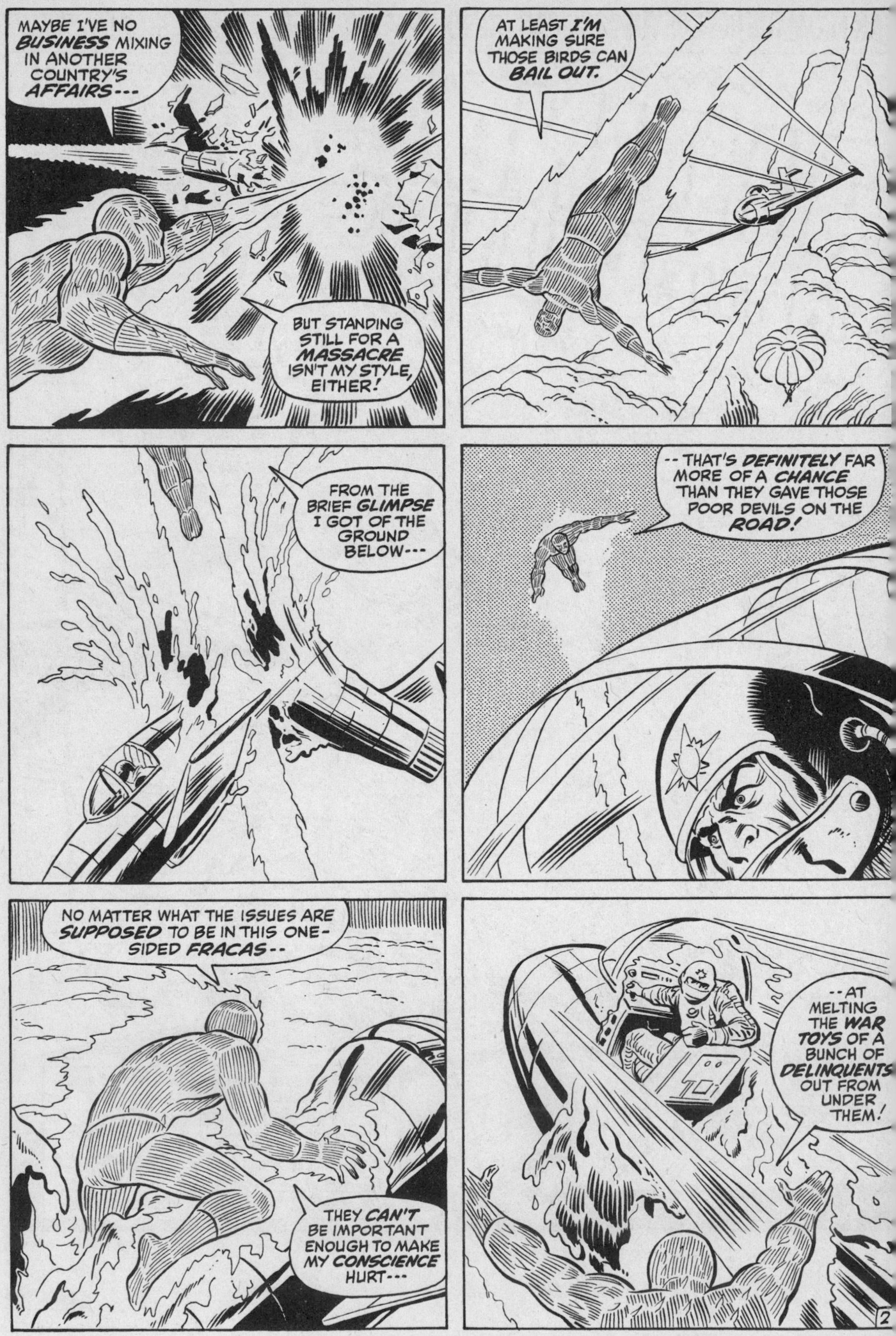
MAYBE I'VE NO BUSINESS MIXING IN ANOTHER COUNTRY'S AFFAIRS---
BUT STANDING STILL FOR A MASSACRE ISN'T MY STYLE, EITHER!
AT LEAST I'M MAKING SURE THOSE BIRDS CAN BAIL OUT.
FROM THE BRIEF GLIMPSE I GOT OF THE GROUND BELOW---
--THAT'S DEFINITELY FAR MORE OF A CHANCE THAN THEY GAVE THOSE POOR DEVILS ON THE ROAD!
NO MATTER WHAT THE ISSUES ARE SUPPOSED TO BE IN THIS ONE-SIDED FRACAS--
THEY CAN'T BE IMPORTANT ENOUGH TO MAKE MY CONSCIENCE HURT---
--AT MELTING THE WAR TOYS OF A BUNCH OF DELINQUENTS OUT FROM UNDER THEM!

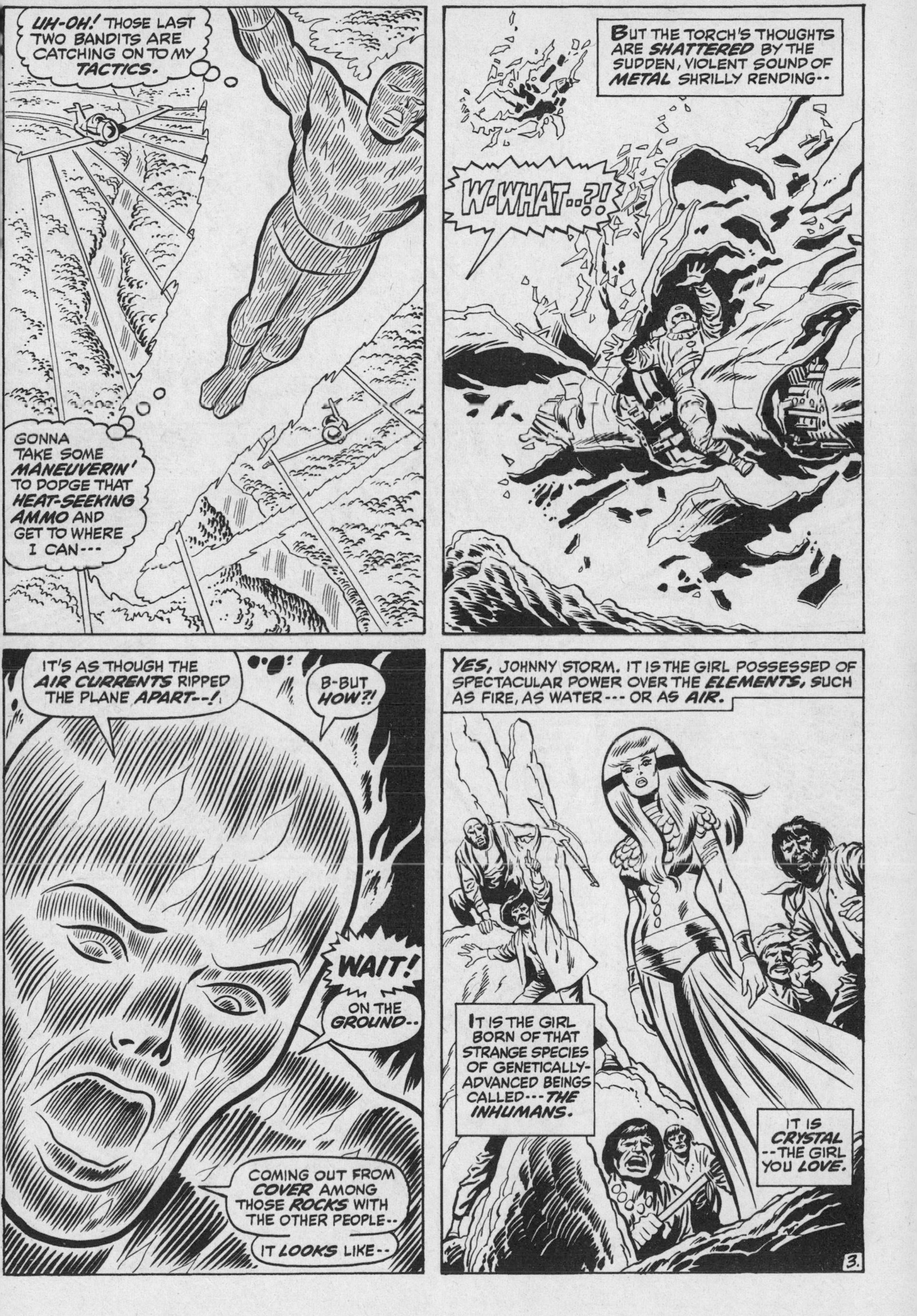
UH-OH! THOSE LAST TWO BANDITS ARE CATCHING ON TO MY TACTICS.
GONNA TAKE SOME MANEUVERIN' TO DODGE THAT HEAT-SEEKING AMMO AND GET TO WHERE I CAN---
BUT THE TORCH'S THOUGHTS ARE SHATTERED BY THE SUDDEN, VIOLENT SOUND OF METAL SHRILLY RENDING--
W-WHAT--?!
IT'S AS THOUGH THE AIR CURRENTS RIPPED THE PLANE APART--!
B-BUT HOW?!
WAIT!
ON THE GROUND--
COMING OUT FROM COVER AMONG THOSE ROCKS WITH THE OTHER PEOPLE--
IT LOOKS LIKE--
YES, JOHNNY STORM. IT IS THE GIRL POSSESSED OF SPECTACULAR POWER OVER THE ELEMENTS, SUCH AS FIRE, AS WATER--- OR AS AIR.
IT IS THE GIRL BORN OF THAT STRANGE SPECIES OF GENETICALLY-ADVANCED BEINGS CALLED---THE INHUMANS.
IT IS CRYSTAL --THE GIRL YOU LOVE.
3.

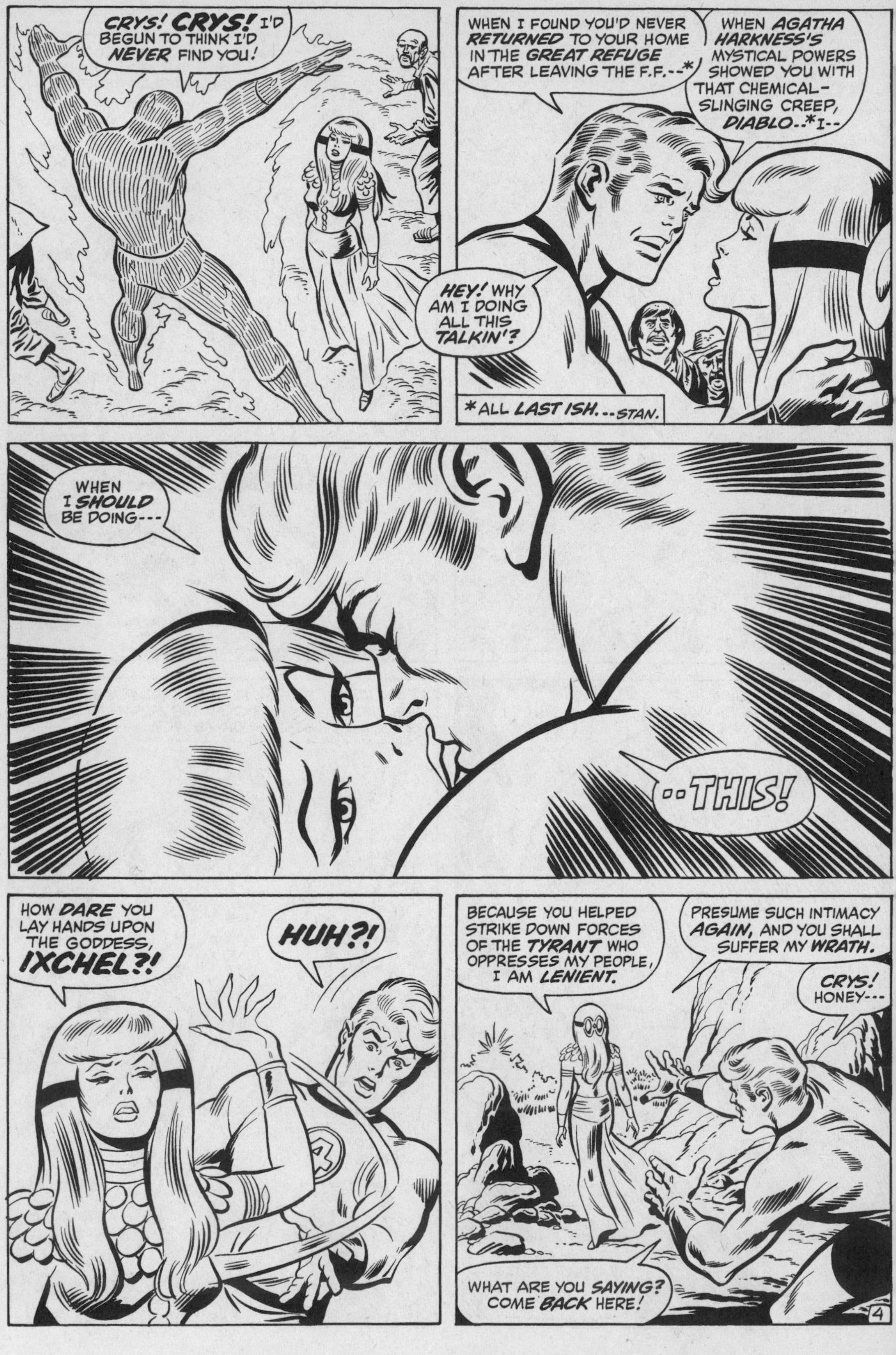
CRYS! CRYS! I'D BEGUN TO THINK I'D NEVER FIND YOU!
WHEN I FOUND YOU'D NEVER RETURNED TO YOUR HOME IN THE GREAT REFUGE AFTER LEAVING THE F.F.--*
WHEN AGATHA HARKNESS'S MYSTICAL POWERS SHOWED YOU WITH THAT CHEMICAL-SLINGING CREEP, DIABLO..*I--
HEY! WHY AM I DOING ALL THIS TALKIN'?
*ALL LAST ISH.--STAN.
WHEN I SHOULD BE DOING---
..THIS!
HOW DARE YOU LAY HANDS UPON THE GODDESS, IXCHEL?!
HUH?!
BECAUSE YOU HELPED STRIKE DOWN FORCES OF THE TYRANT WHO OPPRESSES MY PEOPLE, I AM LENIENT.
PRESUME SUCH INTIMACY AGAIN, AND YOU SHALL SUFFER MY WRATH.
CRYS! HONEY---
WHAT ARE YOU SAYING? COME BACK HERE!
4

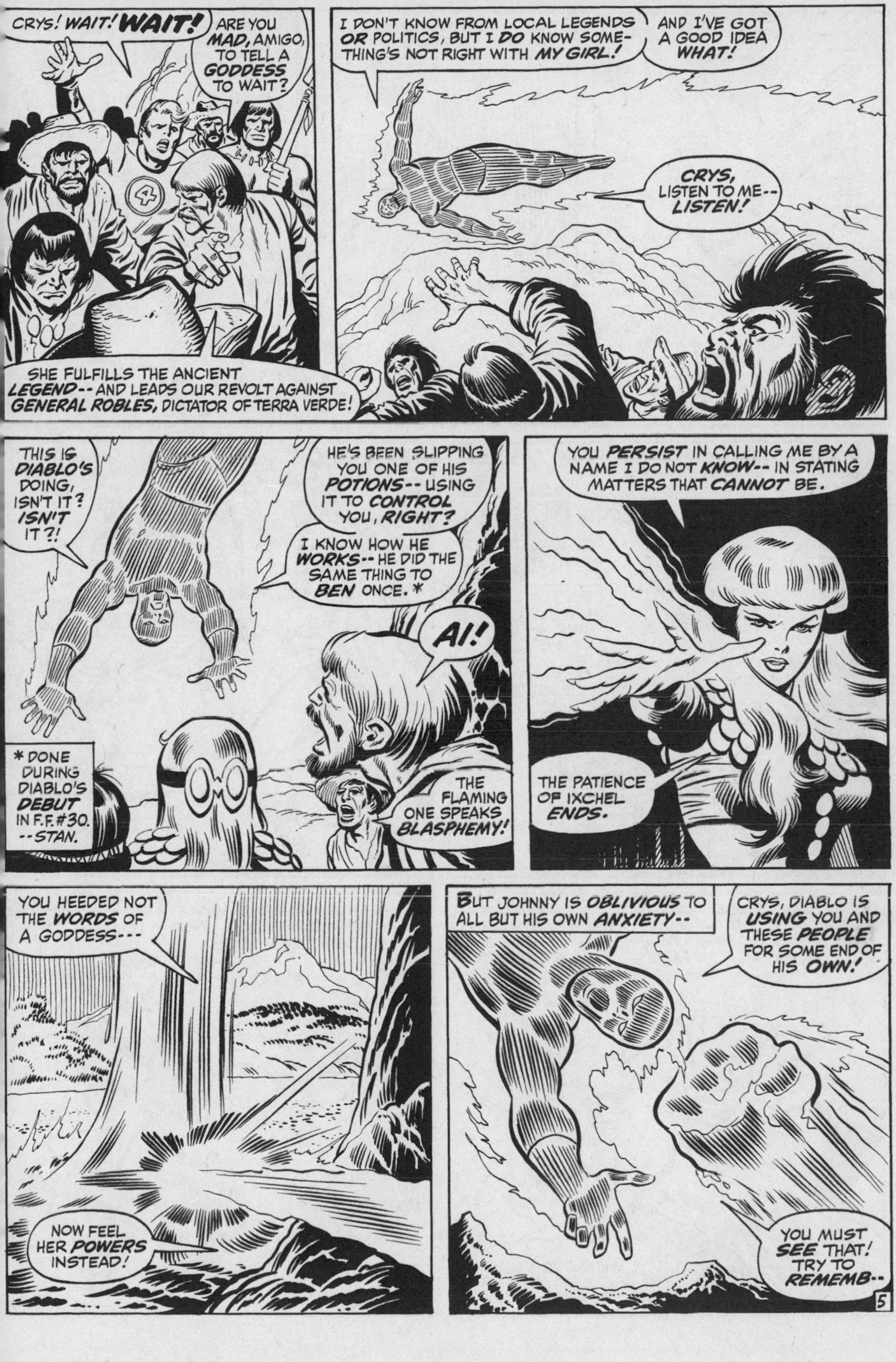
CRYS! WAIT! WAIT!
ARE YOU MAD, AMIGO, TO TELL A GODDESS TO WAIT?
SHE FULFILLS THE ANCIENT LEGEND-- AND LEADS OUR REVOLT AGAINST GENERAL ROBLES, DICTATOR OF TERRA VERDE!
I DON'T KNOW FROM LOCAL LEGENDS OR POLITICS, BUT I DO KNOW SOME-THING'S NOT RIGHT WITH MY GIRL!
AND I'VE GOT A GOOD IDEA WHAT!
CRYS, LISTEN TO ME-- LISTEN!
THIS IS DIABLO'S DOING, ISN'T IT? ISN'T IT?!
HE'S BEEN SLIPPING YOU ONE OF HIS POTIONS-- USING IT TO CONTROL YOU, RIGHT?
I KNOW HOW HE WORKS-- HE DID THE SAME THING TO BEN ONCE. *
AI!
THE FLAMING ONE SPEAKS BLASPHEMY!
* DONE DURING DIABLO'S DEBUT IN F.F. #30. --STAN.
YOU PERSIST IN CALLING ME BY A NAME I DO NOT KNOW-- IN STATING MATTERS THAT CANNOT BE.
THE PATIENCE OF IXCHEL ENDS.
YOU HEEDED NOT THE WORDS OF A GODDESS---
NOW FEEL HER POWERS INSTEAD!
BUT JOHNNY IS OBLIVIOUS TO ALL BUT HIS OWN ANXIETY--
CRYS, DIABLO IS USING YOU AND THESE PEOPLE FOR SOME END OF HIS OWN!
YOU MUST SEE THAT! TRY TO REMEMB--
5

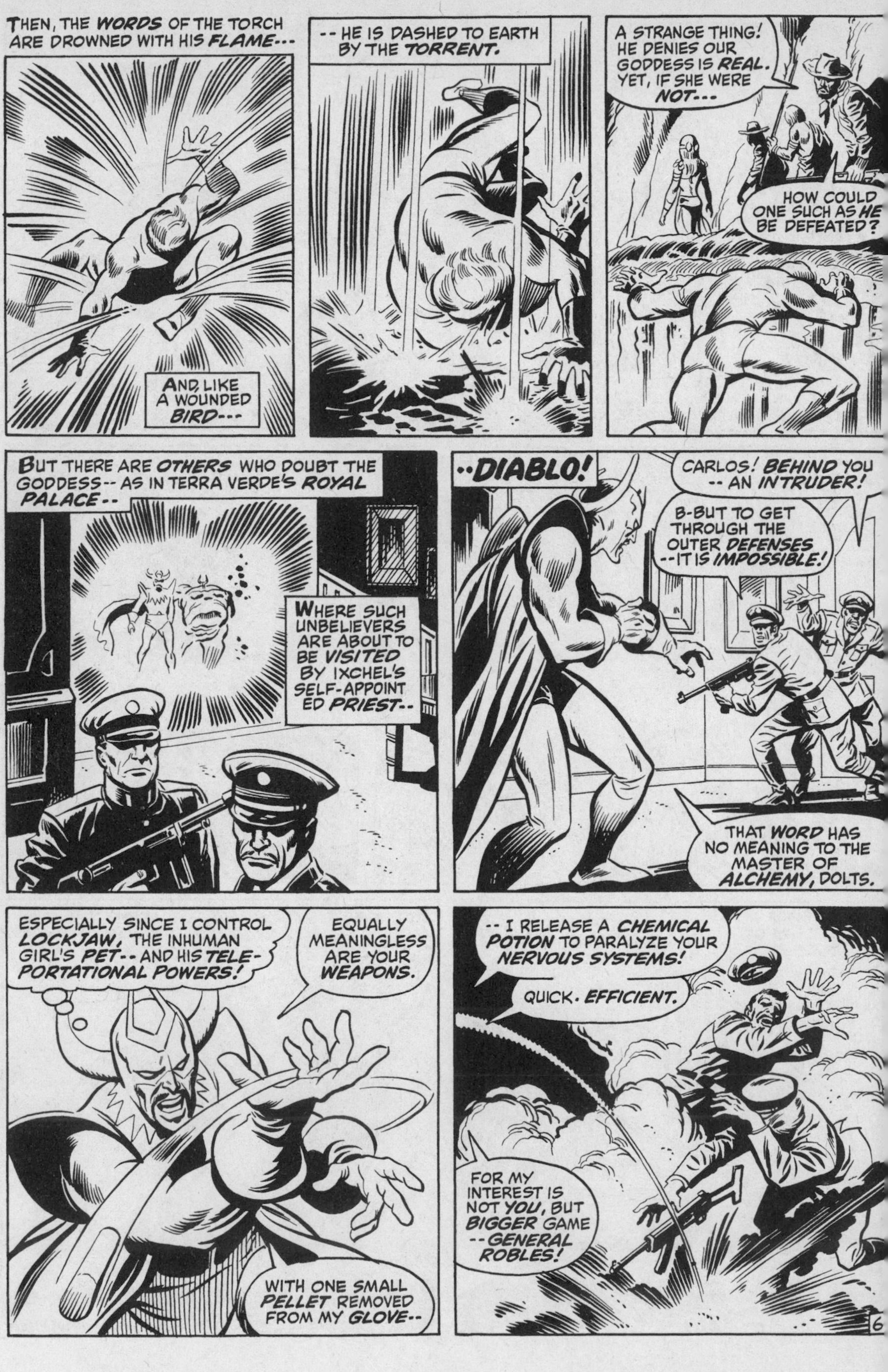
THEN, THE WORDS OF THE TORCH ARE DROWNED WITH HIS FLAME---
AND, LIKE A WOUNDED BIRD---
-- HE IS DASHED TO EARTH BY THE TORRENT.
A STRANGE THING! HE DENIES OUR GODDESS IS REAL. YET, IF SHE WERE NOT---
HOW COULD ONE SUCH AS HE BE DEFEATED?
BUT THERE ARE OTHERS WHO DOUBT THE GODDESS-- AS IN TERRA VERDE'S ROYAL PALACE--
WHERE SUCH UNBELIEVERS ARE ABOUT TO BE VISITED BY IXCHEL'S SELF-APPOINT ED PRIEST--
..DIABLO!
CARLOS! BEHIND YOU -- AN INTRUDER!
B-BUT TO GET THROUGH THE OUTER DEFENSES --IT IS IMPOSSIBLE!
THAT WORD HAS NO MEANING TO THE MASTER OF ALCHEMY, DOLTS.
ESPECIALLY SINCE I CONTROL LOCKJAW, THE INHUMAN GIRL'S PET-- AND HIS TELE-PORTATIONAL POWERS!
EQUALLY MEANINGLESS ARE YOUR WEAPONS.
WITH ONE SMALL PELLET REMOVED FROM MY GLOVE--
-- I RELEASE A CHEMICAL POTION TO PARALYZE YOUR NERVOUS SYSTEMS!
QUICK. EFFICIENT.
FOR MY INTEREST IS NOT YOU, BUT BIGGER GAME --GENERAL ROBLES!
6

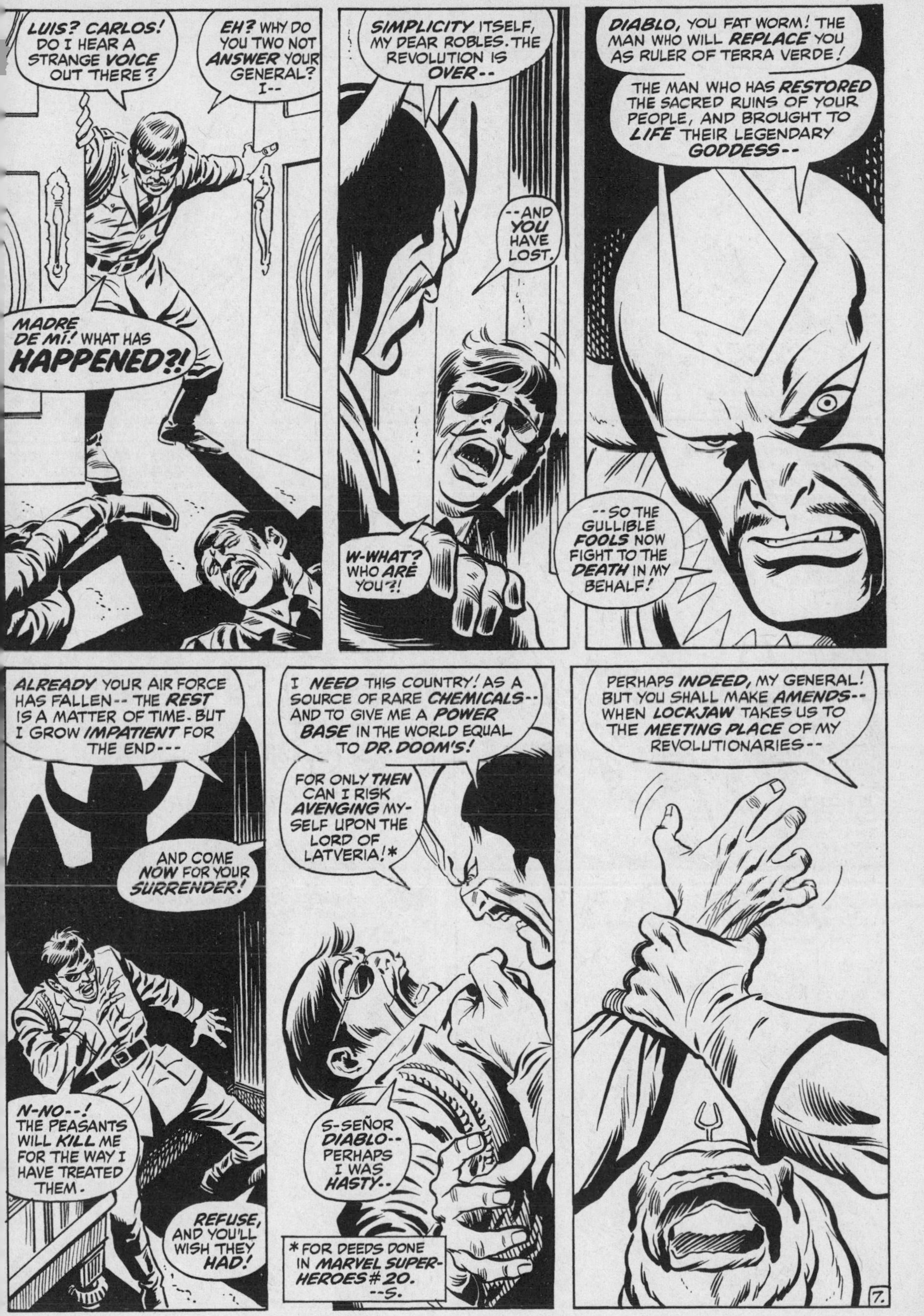
LUIS? CARLOS! DO I HEAR A STRANGE VOICE OUT THERE?
EH? WHY DO YOU TWO NOT ANSWER YOUR GENERAL? I--
MADRE DE MÍ! WHAT HAS HAPPENED?!
SIMPLICITY ITSELF, MY DEAR ROBLES. THE REVOLUTION IS OVER--
--AND YOU HAVE LOST.
W-WHAT? WHO ARE YOU?!
DIABLO, YOU FAT WORM! THE MAN WHO WILL REPLACE YOU AS RULER OF TERRA VERDE!
THE MAN WHO HAS RESTORED THE SACRED RUINS OF YOUR PEOPLE, AND BROUGHT TO LIFE THEIR LEGENDARY GODDESS--
--SO THE GULLIBLE FOOLS NOW FIGHT TO THE DEATH IN MY BEHALF!
ALREADY YOUR AIR FORCE HAS FALLEN-- THE REST IS A MATTER OF TIME. BUT I GROW IMPATIENT FOR THE END---
AND COME NOW FOR YOUR SURRENDER!
N-NO--! THE PEASANTS WILL KILL ME FOR THE WAY I HAVE TREATED THEM.
REFUSE, AND YOU'LL WISH THEY HAD!
I NEED THIS COUNTRY! AS A SOURCE OF RARE CHEMICALS-- AND TO GIVE ME A POWER BASE IN THE WORLD EQUAL TO DR. DOOM'S!
FOR ONLY THEN CAN I RISK AVENGING MYSELF UPON THE LORD OF LATVERIA!*
S-SEÑOR DIABLO-- PERHAPS I WAS HASTY..
*FOR DEEDS DONE IN MARVEL SUPER-HEROES #20. --S.
PERHAPS INDEED, MY GENERAL! BUT YOU SHALL MAKE AMENDS-- WHEN LOCKJAW TAKES US TO THE MEETING PLACE OF MY REVOLUTIONARIES--
7.

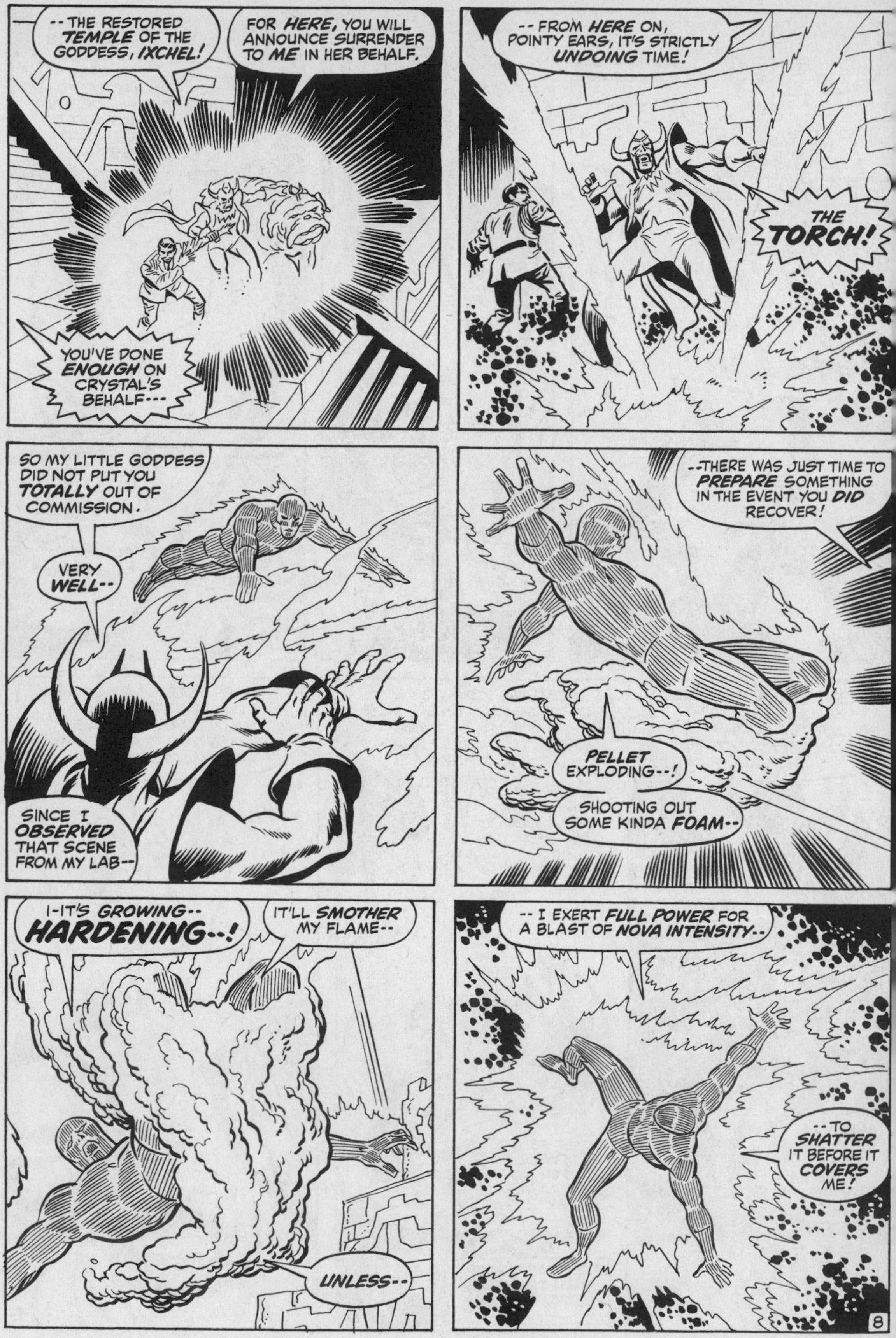
--THE RESTORED TEMPLE OF THE GODDESS, IXCHEL!
FOR HERE, YOU WILL ANNOUNCE SURRENDER TO ME IN HER BEHALF.
YOU'VE DONE ENOUGH ON CRYSTAL'S BEHALF---
--FROM HERE ON, POINTY EARS, IT'S STRICTLY UNDOING TIME!
THE TORCH!
SO MY LITTLE GODDESS DID NOT PUT YOU TOTALLY OUT OF COMMISSION.
VERY WELL--
SINCE I OBSERVED THAT SCENE FROM MY LAB--
--THERE WAS JUST TIME TO PREPARE SOMETHING IN THE EVENT YOU DID RECOVER!
PELLET EXPLODING--!
SHOOTING OUT SOME KINDA FOAM--
I-IT'S GROWING-- HARDENING--!
IT'LL SMOTHER MY FLAME--
UNLESS--
--I EXERT FULL POWER FOR A BLAST OF NOVA INTENSITY--
--TO SHATTER IT BEFORE IT COVERS ME!
8

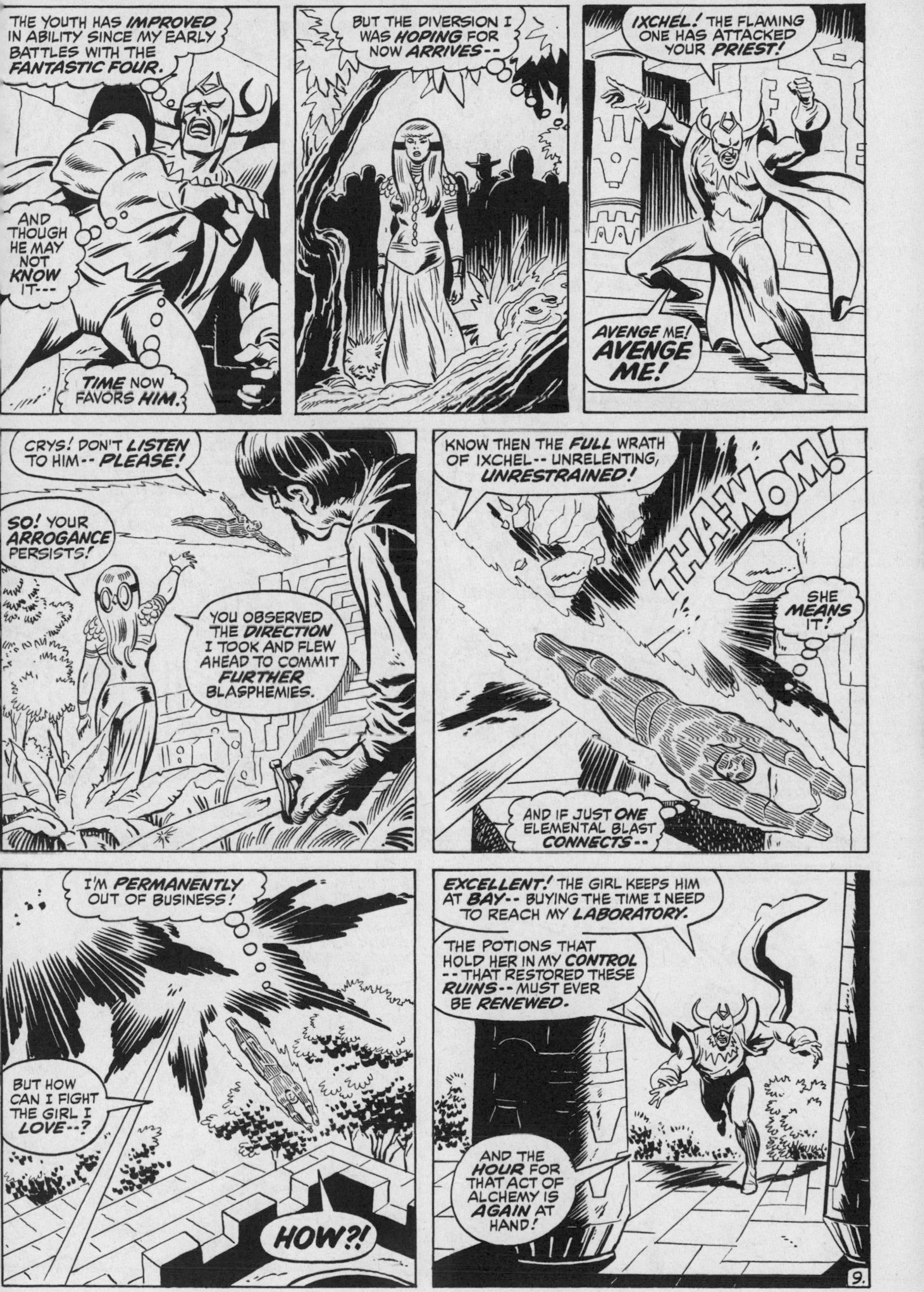
THE YOUTH HAS IMPROVED IN ABILITY SINCE MY EARLY BATTLES WITH THE FANTASTIC FOUR.
AND THOUGH HE MAY NOT KNOW IT---
TIME NOW FAVORS HIM.
BUT THE DIVERSION I WAS HOPING FOR NOW ARRIVES--
IXCHEL! THE FLAMING ONE HAS ATTACKED YOUR PRIEST!
AVENGE ME! AVENGE ME!
CRYS! DON'T LISTEN TO HIM-- PLEASE!
SO! YOUR ARROGANCE PERSISTS!
YOU OBSERVED THE DIRECTION I TOOK AND FLEW AHEAD TO COMMIT FURTHER BLASPHEMIES.
KNOW THEN THE FULL WRATH OF IXCHEL-- UNRELENTING, UNRESTRAINED!
THA-WOM!
SHE MEANS IT!
AND IF JUST ONE ELEMENTAL BLAST CONNECTS--
I'M PERMANENTLY OUT OF BUSINESS!
BUT HOW CAN I FIGHT THE GIRL I LOVE--?
HOW?!
EXCELLENT! THE GIRL KEEPS HIM AT BAY-- BUYING THE TIME I NEED TO REACH MY LABORATORY.
THE POTIONS THAT HOLD HER IN MY CONTROL -- THAT RESTORED THESE RUINS-- MUST EVER BE RENEWED.
AND THE HOUR FOR THAT ACT OF ALCHEMY IS AGAIN AT HAND!
9.

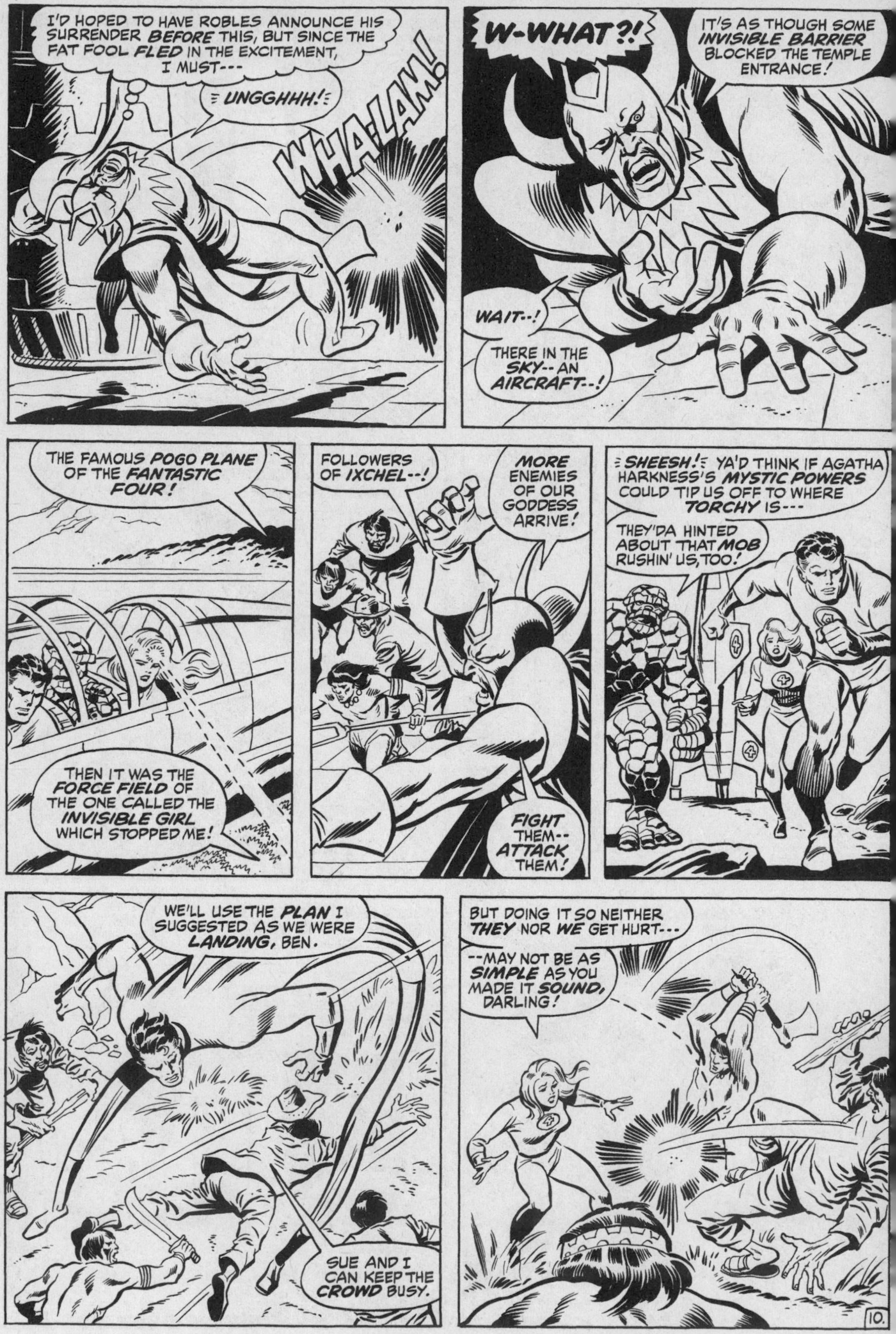
I'D HOPED TO HAVE ROBLES ANNOUNCE HIS SURRENDER BEFORE THIS, BUT SINCE THE FAT FOOL FLED IN THE EXCITEMENT, I MUST---
UNGGHHH!
WHA-LAM!
W-WHAT?!
IT'S AS THOUGH SOME INVISIBLE BARRIER BLOCKED THE TEMPLE ENTRANCE!
WAIT--!
THERE IN THE SKY-- AN AIRCRAFT--!
THE FAMOUS POGO PLANE OF THE FANTASTIC FOUR!
THEN IT WAS THE FORCE FIELD OF THE ONE CALLED THE INVISIBLE GIRL WHICH STOPPED ME!
FOLLOWERS OF IXCHEL--!
MORE ENEMIES OF OUR GODDESS ARRIVE!
FIGHT THEM-- ATTACK THEM!
SHEESH! YA'D THINK IF AGATHA HARKNESS'S MYSTIC POWERS COULD TIP US OFF TO WHERE TORCHY IS---
THEY'DA HINTED ABOUT THAT MOB RUSHIN' US, TOO!
WE'LL USE THE PLAN I SUGGESTED AS WE WERE LANDING, BEN.
SUE AND I CAN KEEP THE CROWD BUSY.
BUT DOING IT SO NEITHER THEY NOR WE GET HURT---
--MAY NOT BE AS SIMPLE AS YOU MADE IT SOUND, DARLING!
10.

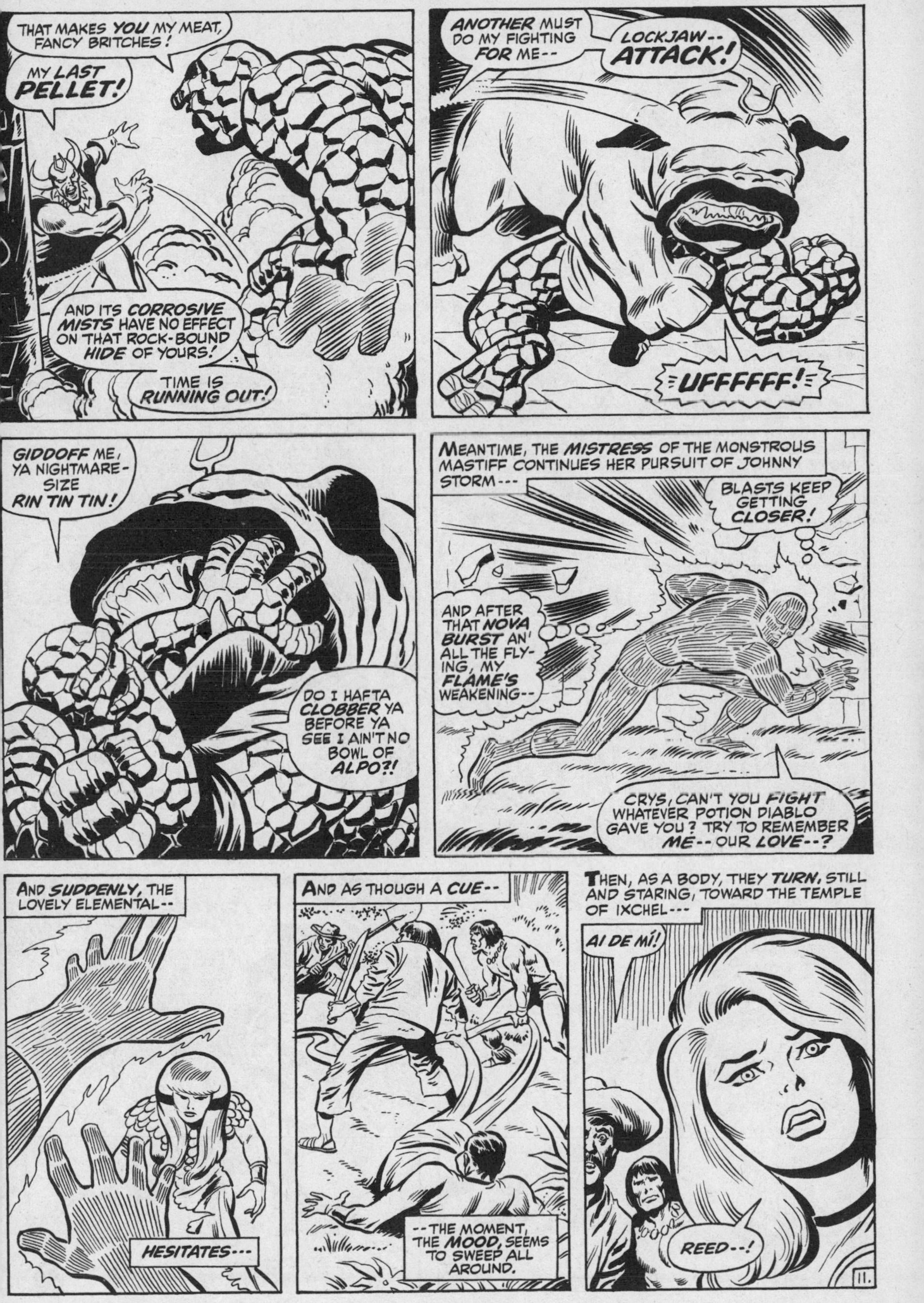
THAT MAKES YOU MY MEAT, FANCY BRITCHES!
MY LAST PELLET!
AND ITS CORROSIVE MISTS HAVE NO EFFECT ON THAT ROCK-BOUND HIDE OF YOURS!
TIME IS RUNNING OUT!
ANOTHER MUST DO MY FIGHTING FOR ME--
LOCKJAW-- ATTACK!
UFFFFFF!
GIDDOFF ME, YA NIGHTMARE-SIZE RIN TIN TIN!
DO I HAFTA CLOBBER YA BEFORE YA SEE I AIN'T NO BOWL OF ALPO?!
MEANTIME, THE MISTRESS OF THE MONSTROUS MASTIFF CONTINUES HER PURSUIT OF JOHNNY STORM---
BLASTS KEEP GETTING CLOSER!
AND AFTER THAT NOVA BURST AN' ALL THE FLYING, MY FLAME'S WEAKENING--
CRYS, CAN'T YOU FIGHT WHATEVER POTION DIABLO GAVE YOU? TRY TO REMEMBER ME-- OUR LOVE--?
AND SUDDENLY, THE LOVELY ELEMENTAL--
HESITATES---
AND AS THOUGH A CUE--
--THE MOMENT, THE MOOD, SEEMS TO SWEEP ALL AROUND.
THEN, AS A BODY, THEY TURN, STILL AND STARING, TOWARD THE TEMPLE OF IXCHEL---
AI DE MÍ!
REED--!
11.

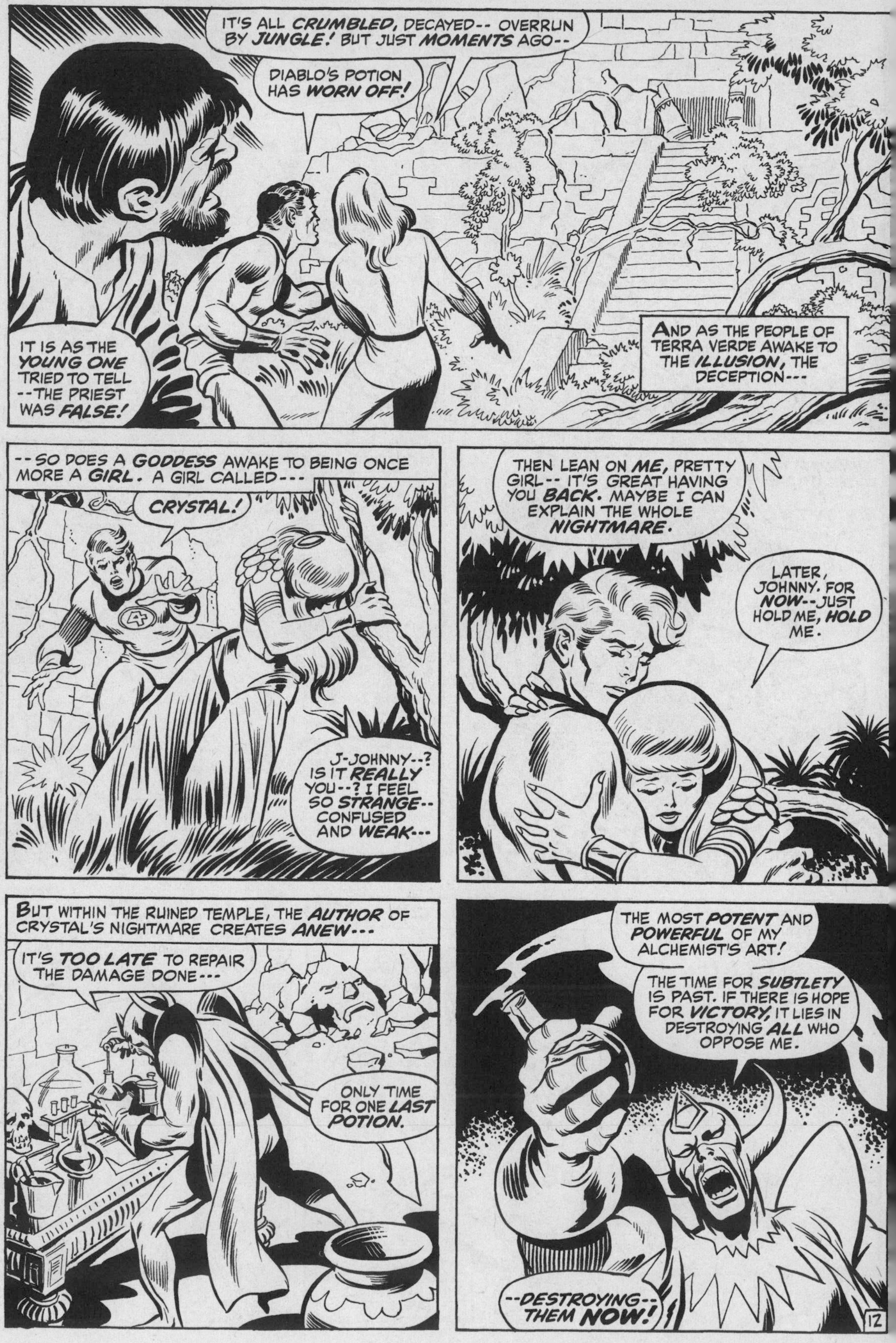
IT'S ALL CRUMBLED, DECAYED-- OVERRUN BY JUNGLE! BUT JUST MOMENTS AGO--
DIABLO'S POTION HAS WORN OFF!
IT IS AS THE YOUNG ONE TRIED TO TELL --THE PRIEST WAS FALSE!
AND AS THE PEOPLE OF TERRA VERDE AWAKE TO THE ILLUSION, THE DECEPTION---
--SO DOES A GODDESS AWAKE TO BEING ONCE MORE A GIRL. A GIRL CALLED---
CRYSTAL!
J-JOHNNY--? IS IT REALLY YOU--? I FEEL SO STRANGE-- CONFUSED AND WEAK---
THEN LEAN ON ME, PRETTY GIRL-- IT'S GREAT HAVING YOU BACK. MAYBE I CAN EXPLAIN THE WHOLE NIGHTMARE.
LATER, JOHNNY. FOR NOW--JUST HOLD ME, HOLD ME.
BUT WITHIN THE RUINED TEMPLE, THE AUTHOR OF CRYSTAL'S NIGHTMARE CREATES ANEW---
IT'S TOO LATE TO REPAIR THE DAMAGE DONE---
ONLY TIME FOR ONE LAST POTION.
THE MOST POTENT AND POWERFUL OF MY ALCHEMIST'S ART!
THE TIME FOR SUBTLETY IS PAST. IF THERE IS HOPE FOR VICTORY, IT LIES IN DESTROYING ALL WHO OPPOSE ME.
--DESTROYING-- THEM NOW!
12

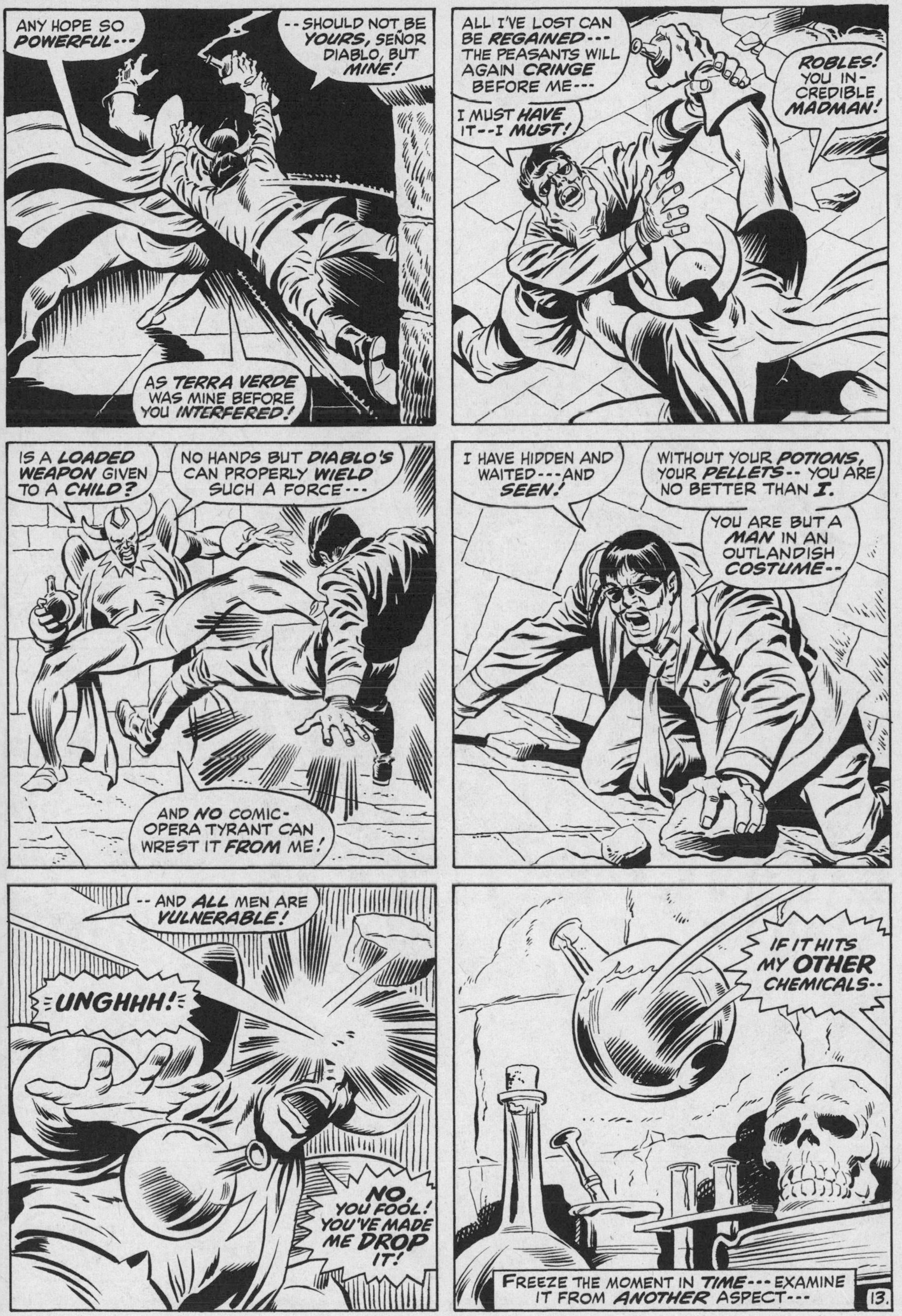
ANY HOPE SO POWERFUL---
--SHOULD NOT BE YOURS, SEÑOR DIABLO, BUT MINE!
AS TERRA VERDE WAS MINE BEFORE YOU INTERFERED!
ALL I'VE LOST CAN BE REGAINED--- THE PEASANTS WILL AGAIN CRINGE BEFORE ME---
I MUST HAVE IT--I MUST!
ROBLES! YOU IN-CREDIBLE MADMAN!
IS A LOADED WEAPON GIVEN TO A CHILD?
NO HANDS BUT DIABLO'S CAN PROPERLY WIELD SUCH A FORCE---
AND NO COMIC-OPERA TYRANT CAN WREST IT FROM ME!
I HAVE HIDDEN AND WAITED---AND SEEN!
WITHOUT YOUR POTIONS, YOUR PELLETS-- YOU ARE NO BETTER THAN I.
YOU ARE BUT A MAN IN AN OUTLANDISH COSTUME--
-- AND ALL MEN ARE VULNERABLE!
UNGHHH!
NO, YOU FOOL! YOU'VE MADE ME DROP IT!
IF IT HITS MY OTHER CHEMICALS--
FREEZE THE MOMENT IN TIME--- EXAMINE IT FROM ANOTHER ASPECT---
13.

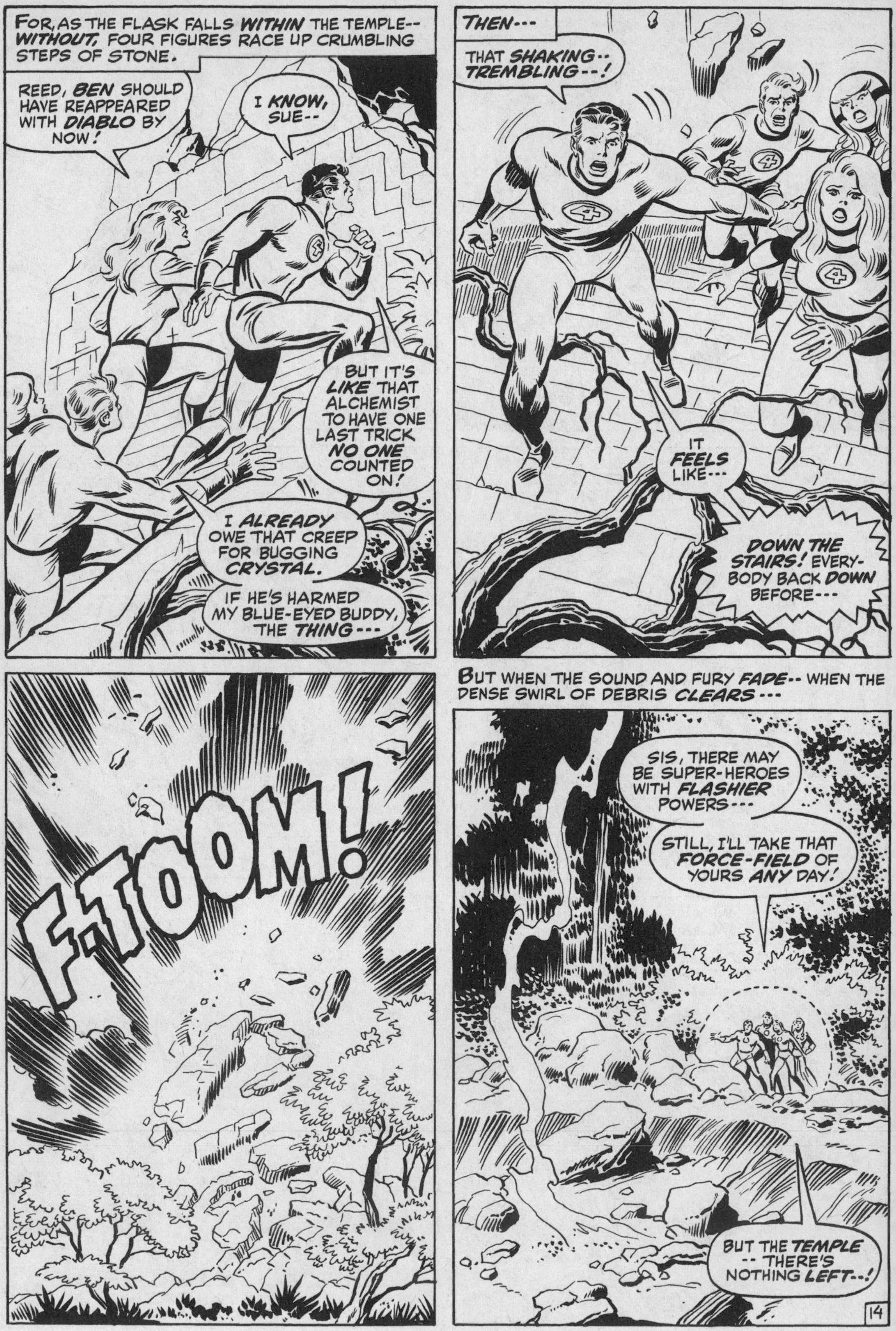
FOR, AS THE FLASK FALLS WITHIN THE TEMPLE-- WITHOUT, FOUR FIGURES RACE UP CRUMBLING STEPS OF STONE.
REED, BEN SHOULD HAVE REAPPEARED WITH DIABLO BY NOW!
I KNOW, SUE--
BUT IT'S LIKE THAT ALCHEMIST TO HAVE ONE LAST TRICK NO ONE COUNTED ON!
I ALREADY OWE THAT CREEP FOR BUGGING CRYSTAL.
IF HE'S HARMED MY BLUE-EYED BUDDY, THE THING---
THEN---
THAT SHAKING.. TREMBLING--!
IT FEELS LIKE---
DOWN THE STAIRS! EVERYBODY BACK DOWN BEFORE---
F-TOOM!
BUT WHEN THE SOUND AND FURY FADE-- WHEN THE DENSE SWIRL OF DEBRIS CLEARS---
SIS, THERE MAY BE SUPER-HEROES WITH FLASHIER POWERS---
STILL, I'LL TAKE THAT FORCE-FIELD OF YOURS ANY DAY!
BUT THE TEMPLE -- THERE'S NOTHING LEFT--!
14

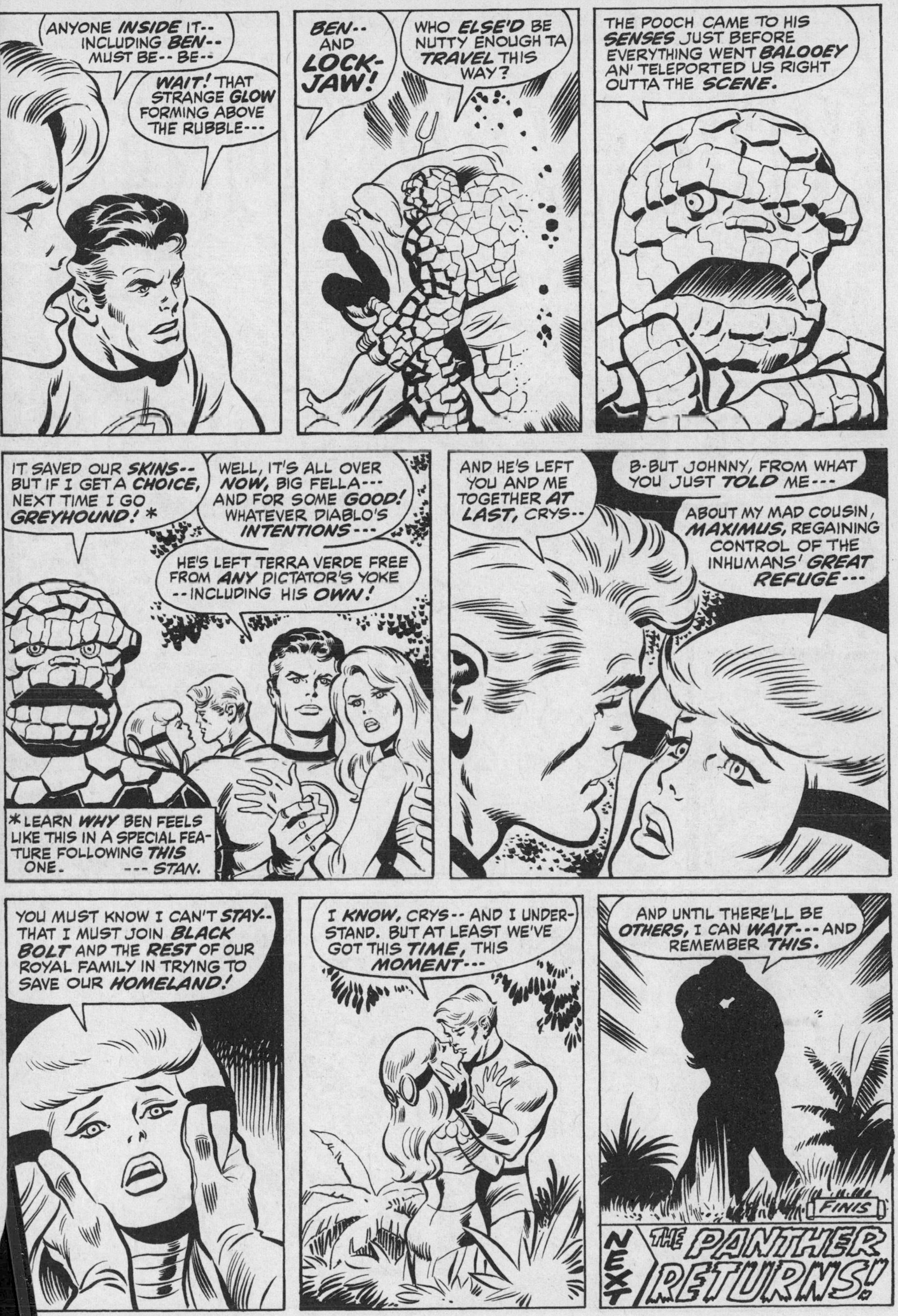
ANYONE INSIDE IT-- INCLUDING BEN-- MUST BE-- BE--
WAIT! THAT STRANGE GLOW FORMING ABOVE THE RUBBLE---
BEN-- AND LOCK-JAW!
WHO ELSE'D BE NUTTY ENOUGH TA TRAVEL THIS WAY?
THE POOCH CAME TO HIS SENSES JUST BEFORE EVERYTHING WENT BALOOEY AN' TELEPORTED US RIGHT OUTTA THE SCENE.
IT SAVED OUR SKINS-- BUT IF I GET A CHOICE, NEXT TIME I GO GREYHOUND! *
WELL, IT'S ALL OVER NOW, BIG FELLA--- AND FOR SOME GOOD! WHATEVER DIABLO'S INTENTIONS---
HE'S LEFT TERRA VERDE FREE FROM ANY DICTATOR'S YOKE --INCLUDING HIS OWN!
* LEARN WHY BEN FEELS LIKE THIS IN A SPECIAL FEATURE FOLLOWING THIS ONE. --- STAN.
AND HE'S LEFT YOU AND ME TOGETHER AT LAST, CRYS--
B-BUT JOHNNY, FROM WHAT YOU JUST TOLD ME---
ABOUT MY MAD COUSIN, MAXIMUS, REGAINING CONTROL OF THE INHUMANS' GREAT REFUGE---
YOU MUST KNOW I CAN'T STAY-- THAT I MUST JOIN BLACK BOLT AND THE REST OF OUR ROYAL FAMILY IN TRYING TO SAVE OUR HOMELAND!
I KNOW, CRYS-- AND I UNDERSTAND. BUT AT LEAST WE'VE GOT THIS TIME, THIS MOMENT---
AND UNTIL THERE'LL BE OTHERS, I CAN WAIT--- AND REMEMBER THIS.
FINIS
NEXT
THE PANTHER RETURNS!

STAN LEE, EDITOR • *ARCHIE GOODWIN*, WRITER • *JOHN BUSCEMA*, ARTIST • *JIM MOONEY*, INKER • *SAM ROSEN*, LETTERE
EXPLORE AN INSTANT IN ***TIME.*** AN INSTANT FROM THE PRECEDING ***STORY*** WHEN THE ***THING*** AND ***LOCKJAW*** TELEPORTED OUT OF AN ***EXPLOSION,*** AND FOR ITS ***DURATION*** ARE THRUST INTO---

WHAT MAD WORLD?

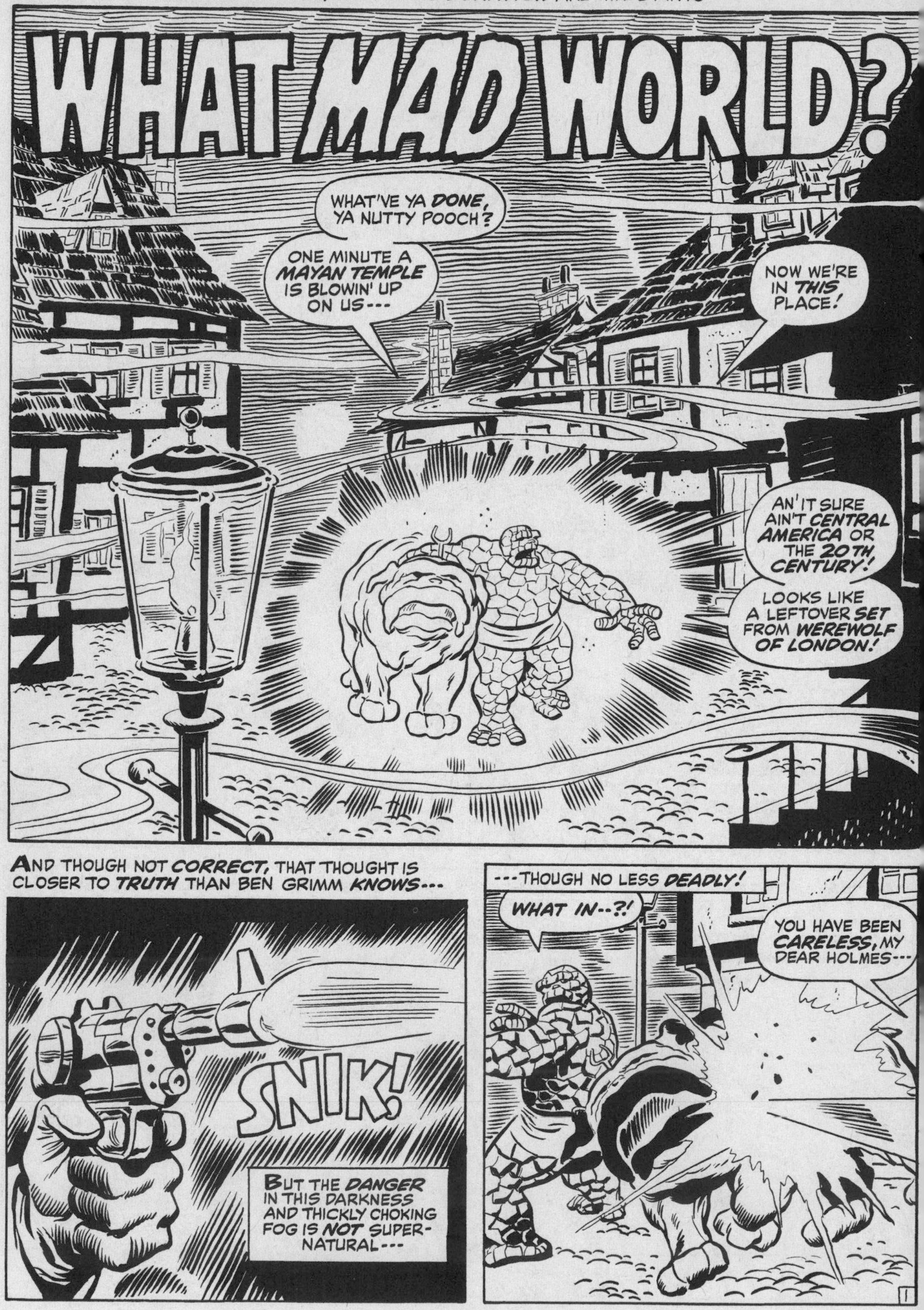

WHAT'VE YA DONE, YA NUTTY POOCH?
ONE MINUTE A MAYAN TEMPLE IS BLOWIN' UP ON US---
NOW WE'RE IN THIS PLACE!
AN' IT SURE AIN'T CENTRAL AMERICA OR THE 20TH CENTURY!
LOOKS LIKE A LEFTOVER SET FROM WEREWOLF OF LONDON!
AND THOUGH NOT CORRECT, THAT THOUGHT IS CLOSER TO TRUTH THAN BEN GRIMM KNOWS---
SNIK!
BUT THE DANGER IN THIS DARKNESS AND THICKLY CHOKING FOG IS NOT SUPER-NATURAL---
---THOUGH NO LESS DEADLY!
WHAT IN--?!
YOU HAVE BEEN CARELESS, MY DEAR HOLMES---
1

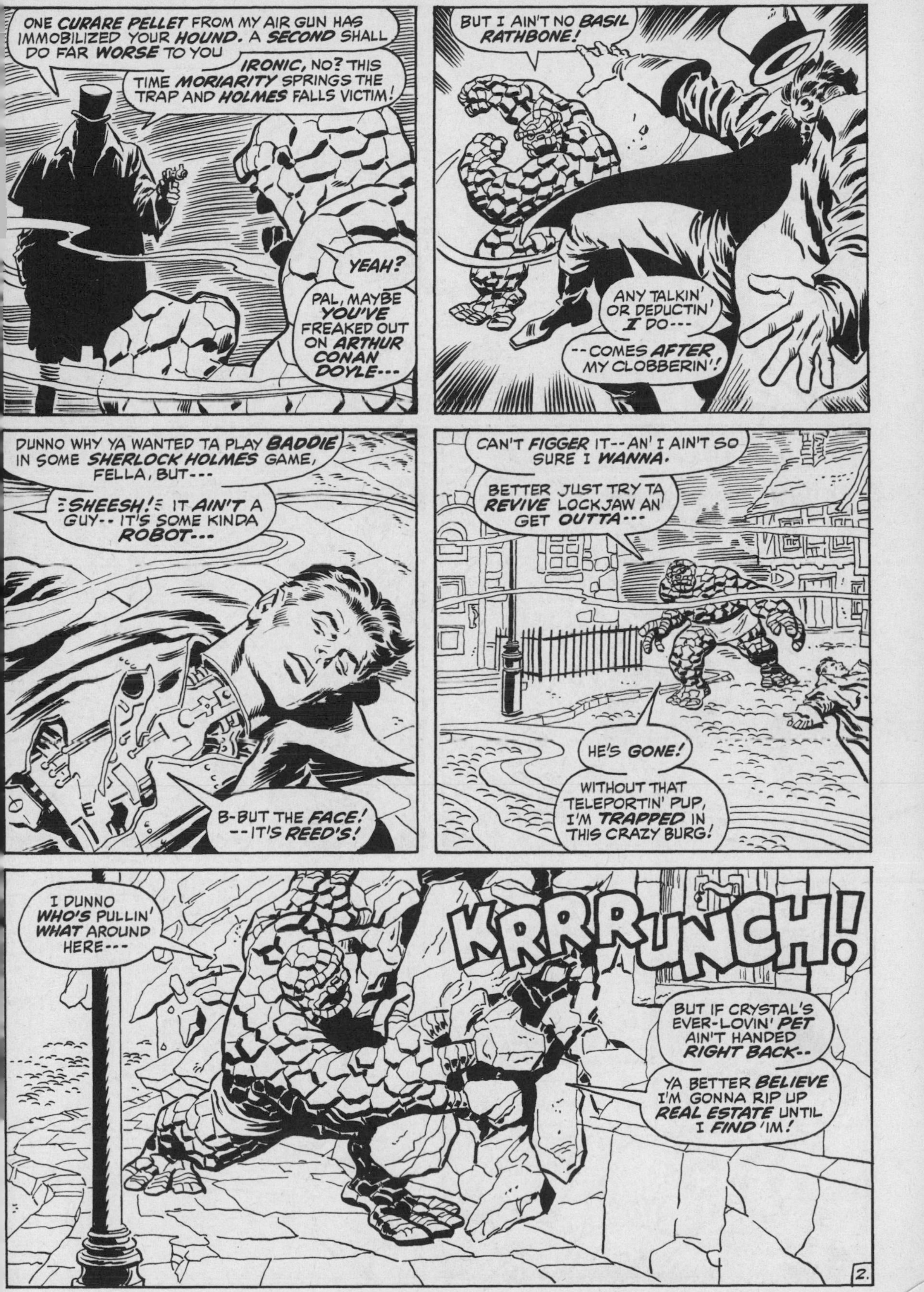
ONE CURARE PELLET FROM MY AIR GUN HAS IMMOBILIZED YOUR HOUND. A SECOND SHALL DO FAR WORSE TO YOU
IRONIC, NO? THIS TIME MORIARITY SPRINGS THE TRAP AND HOLMES FALLS VICTIM!
YEAH?
PAL, MAYBE YOU'VE FREAKED OUT ON ARTHUR CONAN DOYLE---
BUT I AIN'T NO BASIL RATHBONE!
ANY TALKIN' OR DEDUCTIN' I DO---
--COMES AFTER MY CLOBBERIN'!
DUNNO WHY YA WANTED TA PLAY BADDIE IN SOME SHERLOCK HOLMES GAME, FELLA, BUT---
SHEESH! IT AIN'T A GUY-- IT'S SOME KINDA ROBOT---
B-BUT THE FACE! --IT'S REED'S!
CAN'T FIGGER IT--AN' I AIN'T SO SURE I WANNA.
BETTER JUST TRY TA REVIVE LOCKJAW AN' GET OUTTA---
HE'S GONE!
WITHOUT THAT TELEPORTIN' PUP, I'M TRAPPED IN THIS CRAZY BURG!
I DUNNO WHO'S PULLIN' WHAT AROUND HERE---
KRRRUNCH!
BUT IF CRYSTAL'S EVER-LOVIN' PET AIN'T HANDED RIGHT BACK--
YA BETTER BELIEVE I'M GONNA RIP UP REAL ESTATE UNTIL I FIND 'IM!
2.

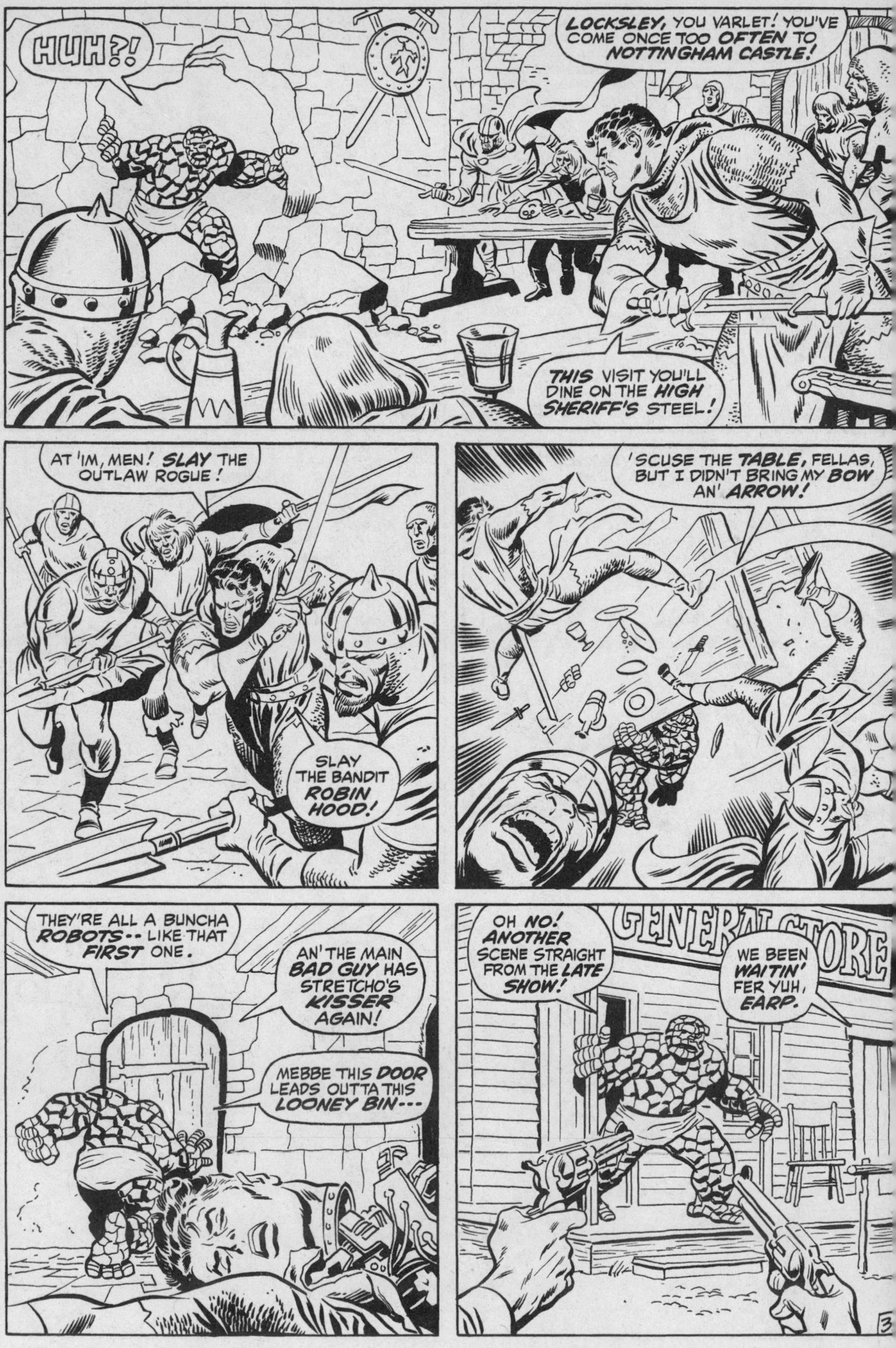
HUH?!
LOCKSLEY, YOU VARLET! YOU'VE COME ONCE TOO OFTEN TO NOTTINGHAM CASTLE!
THIS VISIT YOU'LL DINE ON THE HIGH SHERIFF'S STEEL!
AT 'IM, MEN! SLAY THE OUTLAW ROGUE!
SLAY THE BANDIT ROBIN HOOD!
'SCUSE THE TABLE, FELLAS, BUT I DIDN'T BRING MY BOW AN' ARROW!
THEY'RE ALL A BUNCHA ROBOTS -- LIKE THAT FIRST ONE.
AN' THE MAIN BAD GUY HAS STRETCHO'S KISSER AGAIN!
MEBBE THIS DOOR LEADS OUTTA THIS LOONEY BIN---
GENERAL STORE
OH NO! ANOTHER SCENE STRAIGHT FROM THE LATE SHOW!
WE BEEN WAITIN' FER YUH, EARP.
3

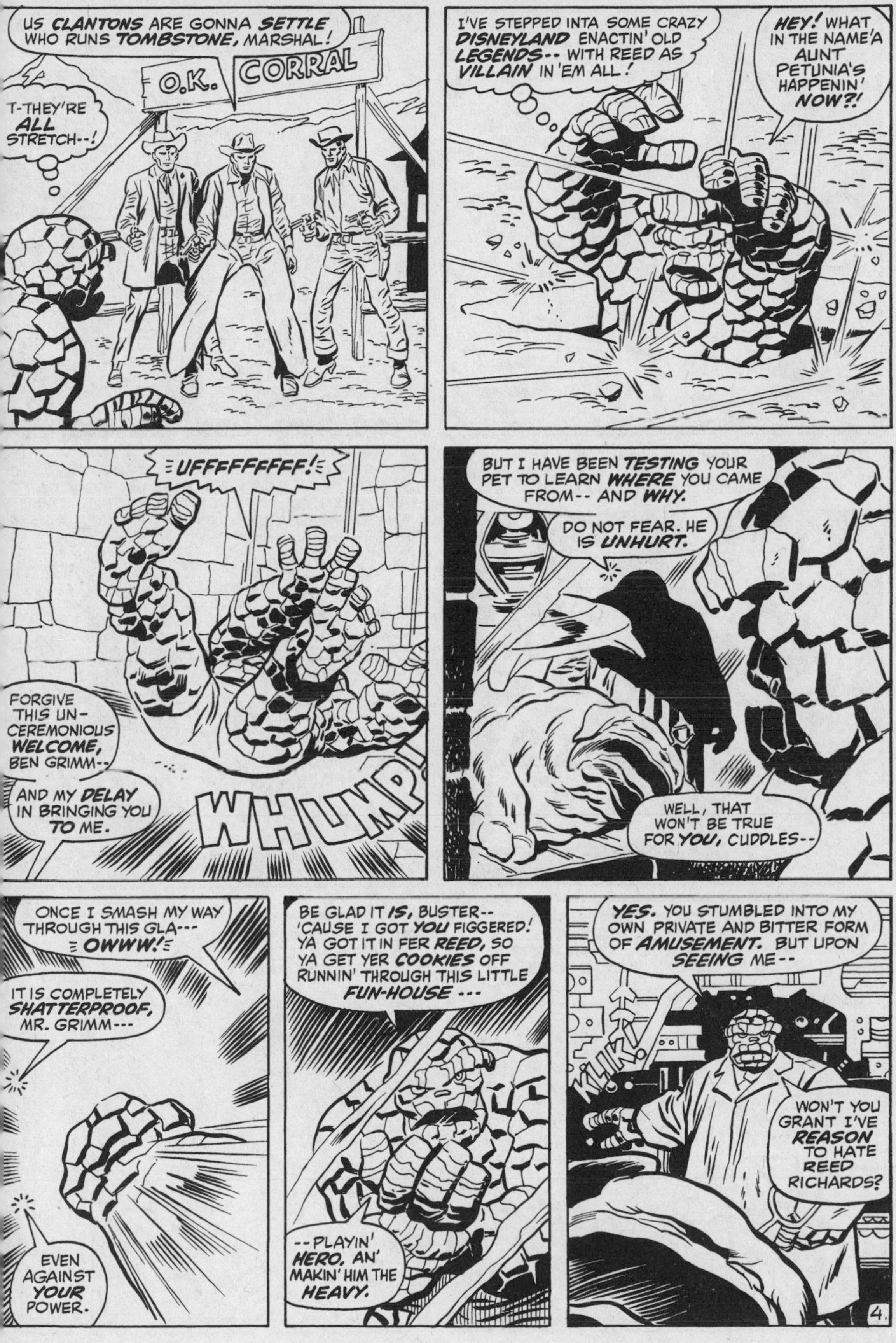
US CLANTONS ARE GONNA SETTLE WHO RUNS TOMBSTONE, MARSHAL!
O.K. CORRAL
T-THEY'RE ALL STRETCH--!
I'VE STEPPED INTA SOME CRAZY DISNEYLAND ENACTIN' OLD LEGENDS-- WITH REED AS VILLAIN IN 'EM ALL!
HEY! WHAT IN THE NAME'A AUNT PETUNIA'S HAPPENIN' NOW?!
UFFFFFFFFF!
FORGIVE THIS UN-CEREMONIOUS WELCOME, BEN GRIMM--
AND MY DELAY IN BRINGING YOU TO ME.
WHUMP!
BUT I HAVE BEEN TESTING YOUR PET TO LEARN WHERE YOU CAME FROM-- AND WHY.
DO NOT FEAR. HE IS UNHURT.
WELL, THAT WON'T BE TRUE FOR YOU, CUDDLES--
ONCE I SMASH MY WAY THROUGH THIS GLA--- OWWW!
IT IS COMPLETELY SHATTERPROOF, MR. GRIMM---
EVEN AGAINST YOUR POWER.
BE GLAD IT IS, BUSTER-- 'CAUSE I GOT YOU FIGGERED! YA GOT IT IN FER REED, SO YA GET YER COOKIES OFF RUNNIN' THROUGH THIS LITTLE FUN-HOUSE ---
--PLAYIN' HERO, AN' MAKIN' HIM THE HEAVY.
YES. YOU STUMBLED INTO MY OWN PRIVATE AND BITTER FORM OF AMUSEMENT. BUT UPON SEEING ME--
KLIK
WON'T YOU GRANT I'VE REASON TO HATE REED RICHARDS?
4.

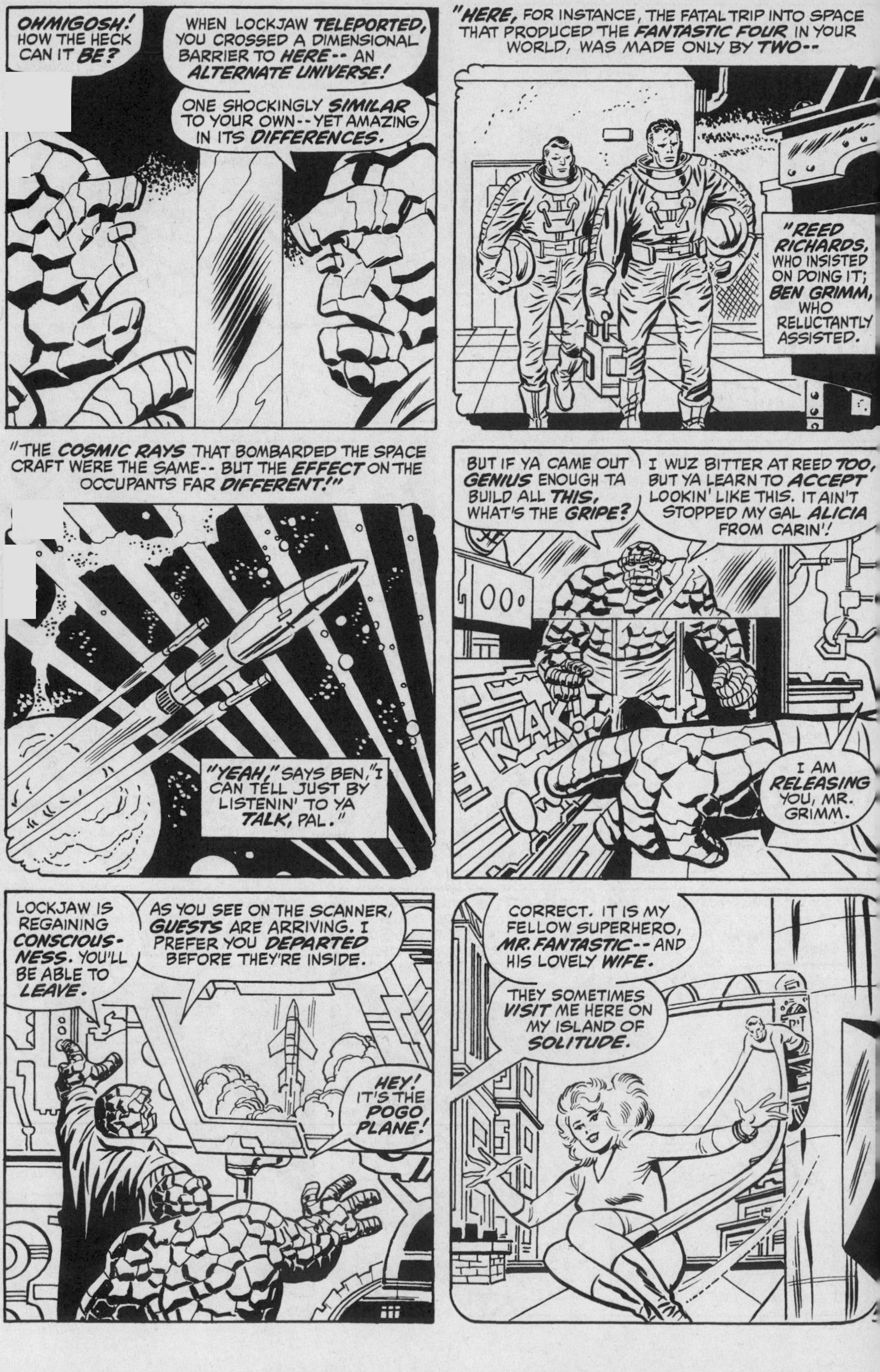
OHMIGOSH! HOW THE HECK CAN IT BE?
WHEN LOCKJAW TELEPORTED, YOU CROSSED A DIMENSIONAL BARRIER TO HERE-- AN ALTERNATE UNIVERSE!
ONE SHOCKINGLY SIMILAR TO YOUR OWN--YET AMAZING IN ITS DIFFERENCES.
"HERE, FOR INSTANCE, THE FATAL TRIP INTO SPACE THAT PRODUCED THE FANTASTIC FOUR IN YOUR WORLD, WAS MADE ONLY BY TWO--
"REED RICHARDS, WHO INSISTED ON DOING IT; BEN GRIMM, WHO RELUCTANTLY ASSISTED.
"THE COSMIC RAYS THAT BOMBARDED THE SPACE CRAFT WERE THE SAME-- BUT THE EFFECT ON THE OCCUPANTS FAR DIFFERENT!"
"YEAH," SAYS BEN, "I CAN TELL JUST BY LISTENIN' TO YA TALK, PAL."
BUT IF YA CAME OUT GENIUS ENOUGH TA BUILD ALL THIS, WHAT'S THE GRIPE?
I WUZ BITTER AT REED TOO, BUT YA LEARN TO ACCEPT LOOKIN' LIKE THIS. IT AIN'T STOPPED MY GAL ALICIA FROM CARIN'!
KLAK!
I AM RELEASING YOU, MR. GRIMM.
LOCKJAW IS REGAINING CONSCIOUS-NESS. YOU'LL BE ABLE TO LEAVE.
AS YOU SEE ON THE SCANNER, GUESTS ARE ARRIVING. I PREFER YOU DEPARTED BEFORE THEY'RE INSIDE.
HEY! IT'S THE POGO PLANE!
CORRECT. IT IS MY FELLOW SUPERHERO, MR. FANTASTIC-- AND HIS LOVELY WIFE.
THEY SOMETIMES VISIT ME HERE ON MY ISLAND OF SOLITUDE.

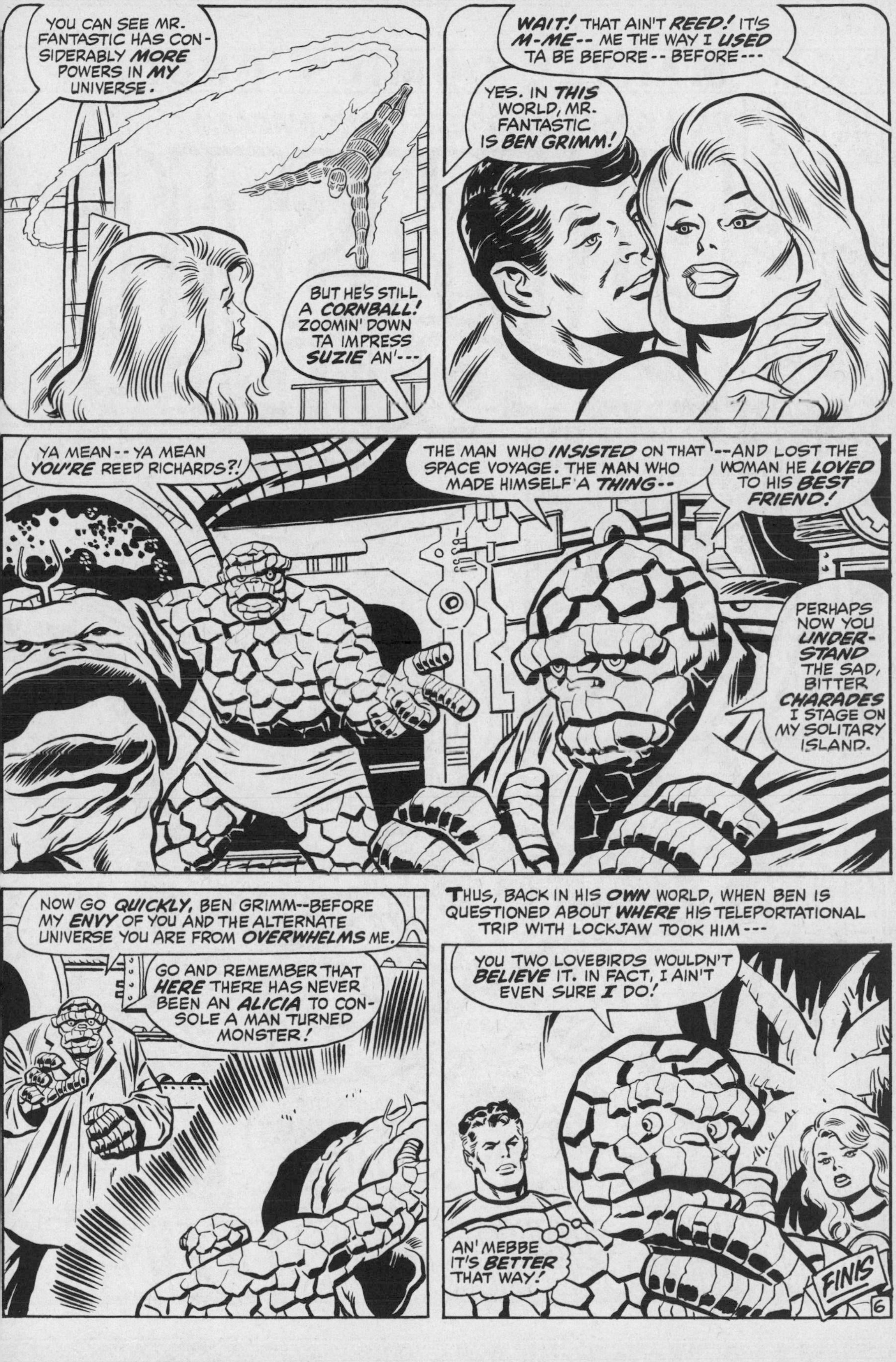
YOU CAN SEE MR. FANTASTIC HAS CONSIDERABLY MORE POWERS IN MY UNIVERSE.
BUT HE'S STILL A CORNBALL! ZOOMIN' DOWN TA IMPRESS SUZIE AN'---
WAIT! THAT AIN'T REED! IT'S M-ME-- ME THE WAY I USED TA BE BEFORE-- BEFORE---
YES. IN THIS WORLD, MR. FANTASTIC IS BEN GRIMM!
YA MEAN-- YA MEAN YOU'RE REED RICHARDS?!
THE MAN WHO INSISTED ON THAT SPACE VOYAGE. THE MAN WHO MADE HIMSELF A THING--
--AND LOST THE WOMAN HE LOVED TO HIS BEST FRIEND!
PERHAPS NOW YOU UNDERSTAND THE SAD, BITTER CHARADES I STAGE ON MY SOLITARY ISLAND.
NOW GO QUICKLY, BEN GRIMM--BEFORE MY ENVY OF YOU AND THE ALTERNATE UNIVERSE YOU ARE FROM OVERWHELMS ME.
GO AND REMEMBER THAT HERE THERE HAS NEVER BEEN AN ALICIA TO CONSOLE A MAN TURNED MONSTER!
THUS, BACK IN HIS OWN WORLD, WHEN BEN IS QUESTIONED ABOUT WHERE HIS TELEPORTATIONAL TRIP WITH LOCKJAW TOOK HIM---
YOU TWO LOVEBIRDS WOULDN'T BELIEVE IT. IN FACT, I AIN'T EVEN SURE I DO!
AN' MEBBE IT'S BETTER THAT WAY!
FINIS
6

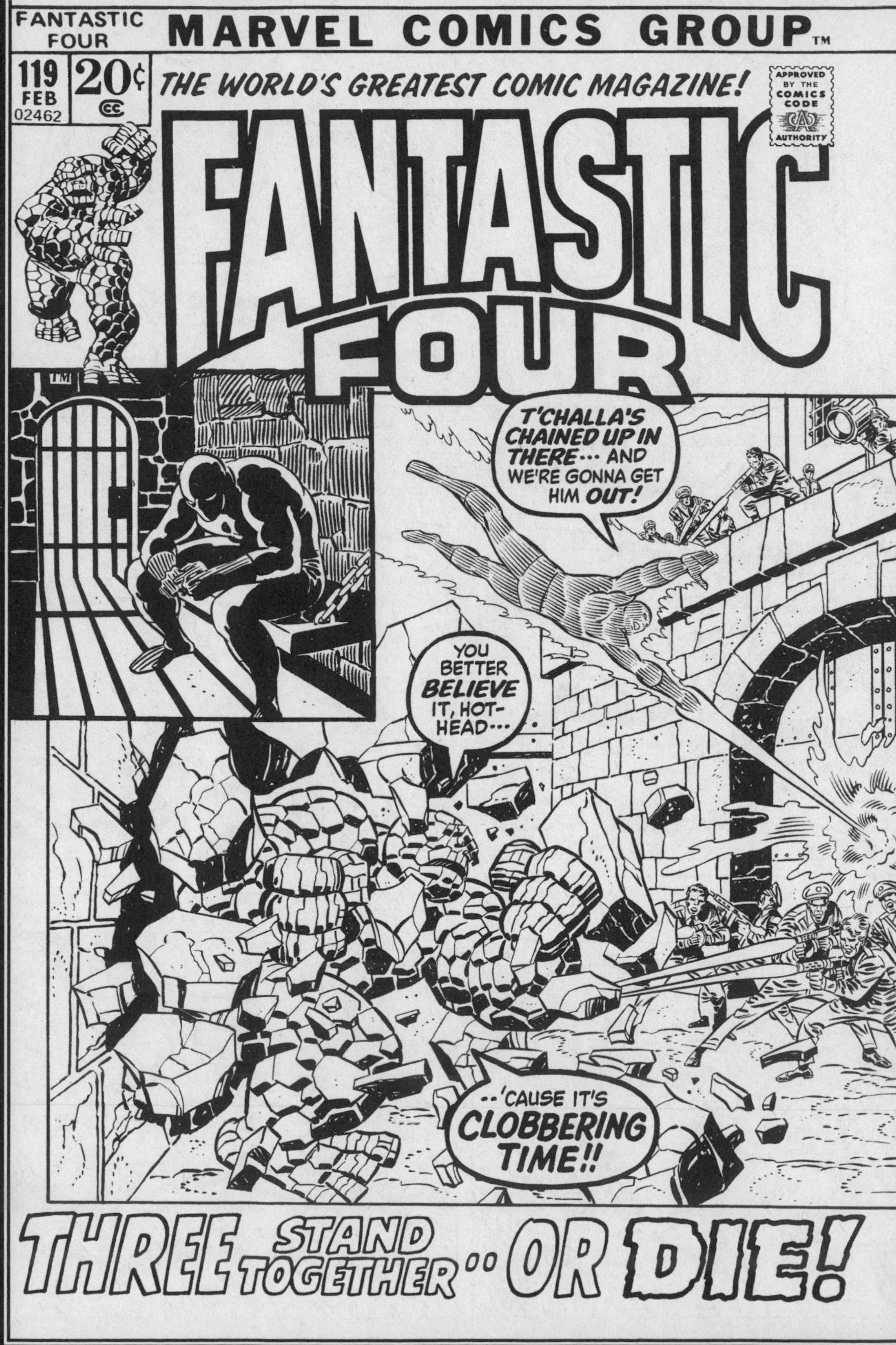
FANTASTIC FOUR
MARVEL COMICS GROUP™
119 FEB 02462
20¢
CC
THE WORLD'S GREATEST COMIC MAGAZINE!
APPROVED BY THE COMICS CODE AUTHORITY
FANTASTIC FOUR
TM
T'CHALLA'S CHAINED UP IN THERE... AND WE'RE GONNA GET HIM OUT!
YOU BETTER BELIEVE IT, HOT-HEAD...
...'CAUSE IT'S CLOBBERING TIME!!
THREE STAND TOGETHER.. OR DIE!

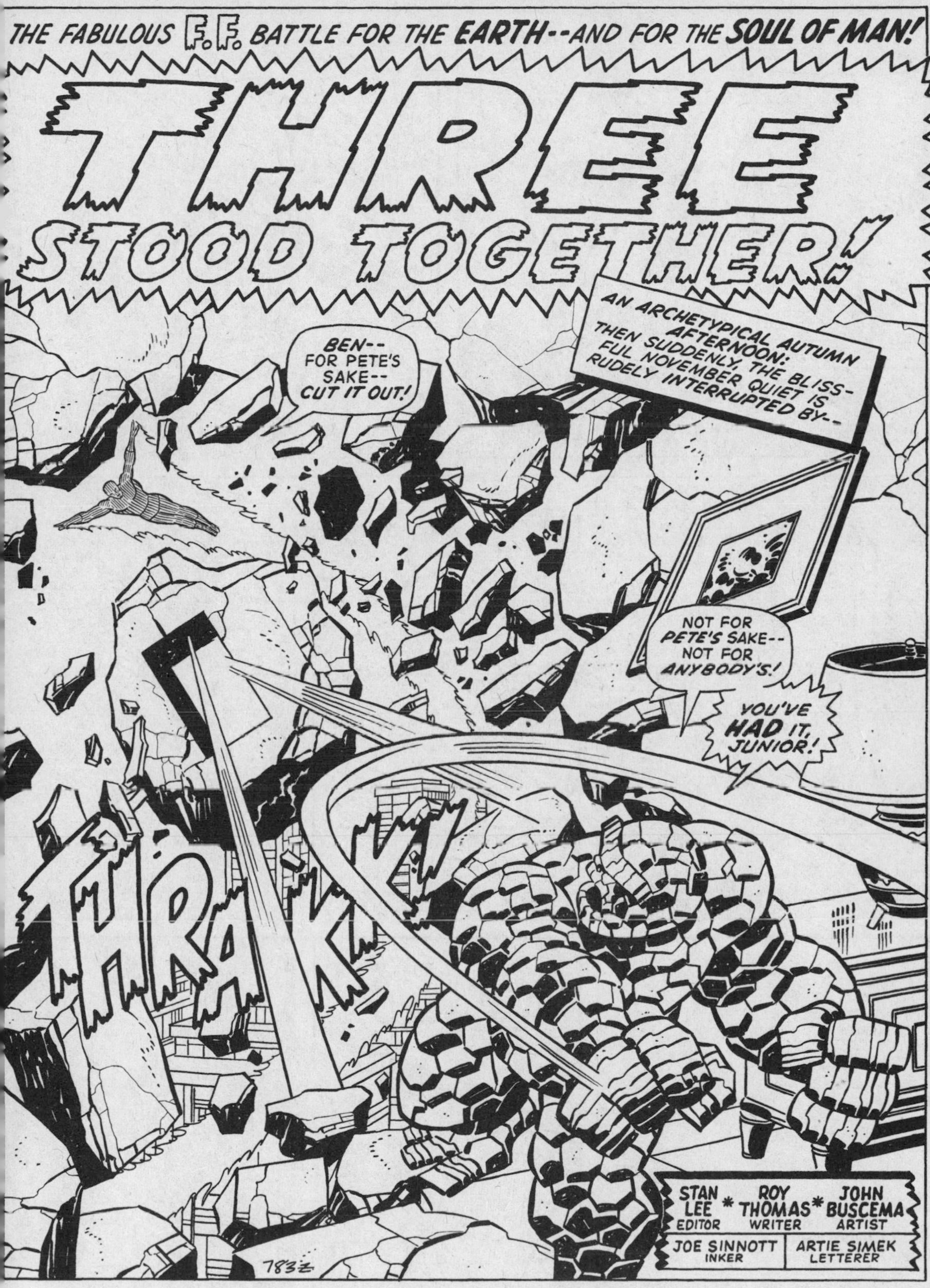
THE FABULOUS F.F. BATTLE FOR THE EARTH--AND FOR THE SOUL OF MAN!
THREE STOOD TOGETHER!
AN ARCHETYPICAL AUTUMN AFTERNOON: THEN SUDDENLY, THE BLISS-FUL NOVEMBER QUIET IS RUDELY INTERRUPTED BY--
BEN-- FOR PETE'S SAKE-- CUT IT OUT!
NOT FOR PETE'S SAKE-- NOT FOR ANYBODY'S!
YOU'VE HAD IT, JUNIOR!
THRAKK!
STAN LEE EDITOR * ROY THOMAS WRITER * JOHN BUSCEMA ARTIST
JOE SINNOTT INKER
ARTIE SIMEK LETTERER
783Z

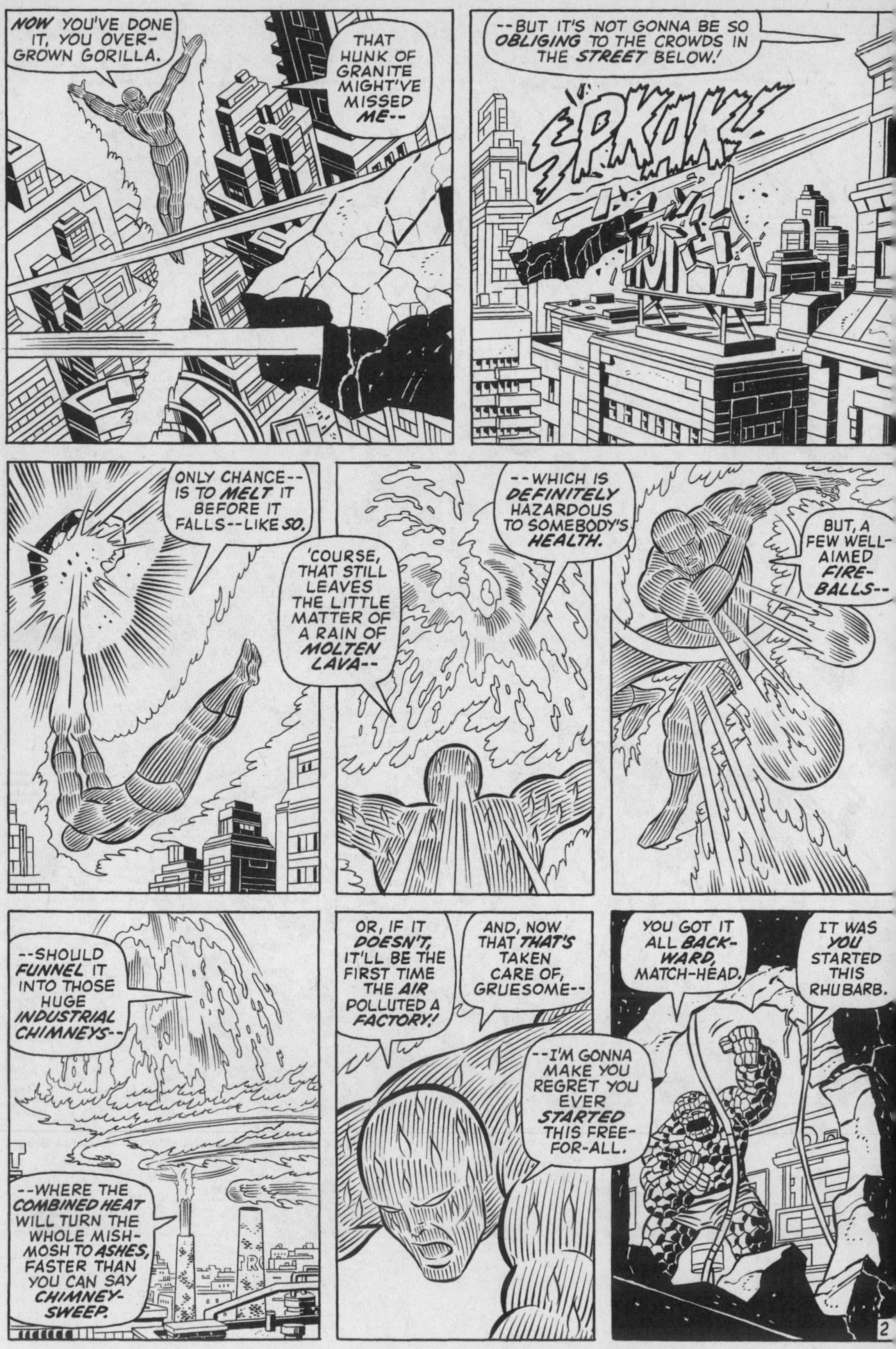
NOW YOU'VE DONE IT, YOU OVER-GROWN GORILLA.
THAT HUNK OF GRANITE MIGHT'VE MISSED ME--
--BUT IT'S NOT GONNA BE SO OBLIGING TO THE CROWDS IN THE STREET BELOW!
SPKAK!
ONLY CHANCE-- IS TO MELT IT BEFORE IT FALLS--LIKE SO.
'COURSE, THAT STILL LEAVES THE LITTLE MATTER OF A RAIN OF MOLTEN LAVA--
--WHICH IS DEFINITELY HAZARDOUS TO SOMEBODY'S HEALTH.
BUT, A FEW WELL-AIMED FIRE-BALLS--
--SHOULD FUNNEL IT INTO THOSE HUGE INDUSTRIAL CHIMNEYS--
--WHERE THE COMBINED HEAT WILL TURN THE WHOLE MISH-MOSH TO ASHES, FASTER THAN YOU CAN SAY CHIMNEY-SWEEP.
OR, IF IT DOESN'T, IT'LL BE THE FIRST TIME THE AIR POLLUTED A FACTORY!
AND, NOW THAT THAT'S TAKEN CARE OF, GRUESOME--
--I'M GONNA MAKE YOU REGRET YOU EVER STARTED THIS FREE-FOR-ALL.
YOU GOT IT ALL BACK-WARD, MATCH-HEAD.
IT WAS YOU STARTED THIS RHUBARB.

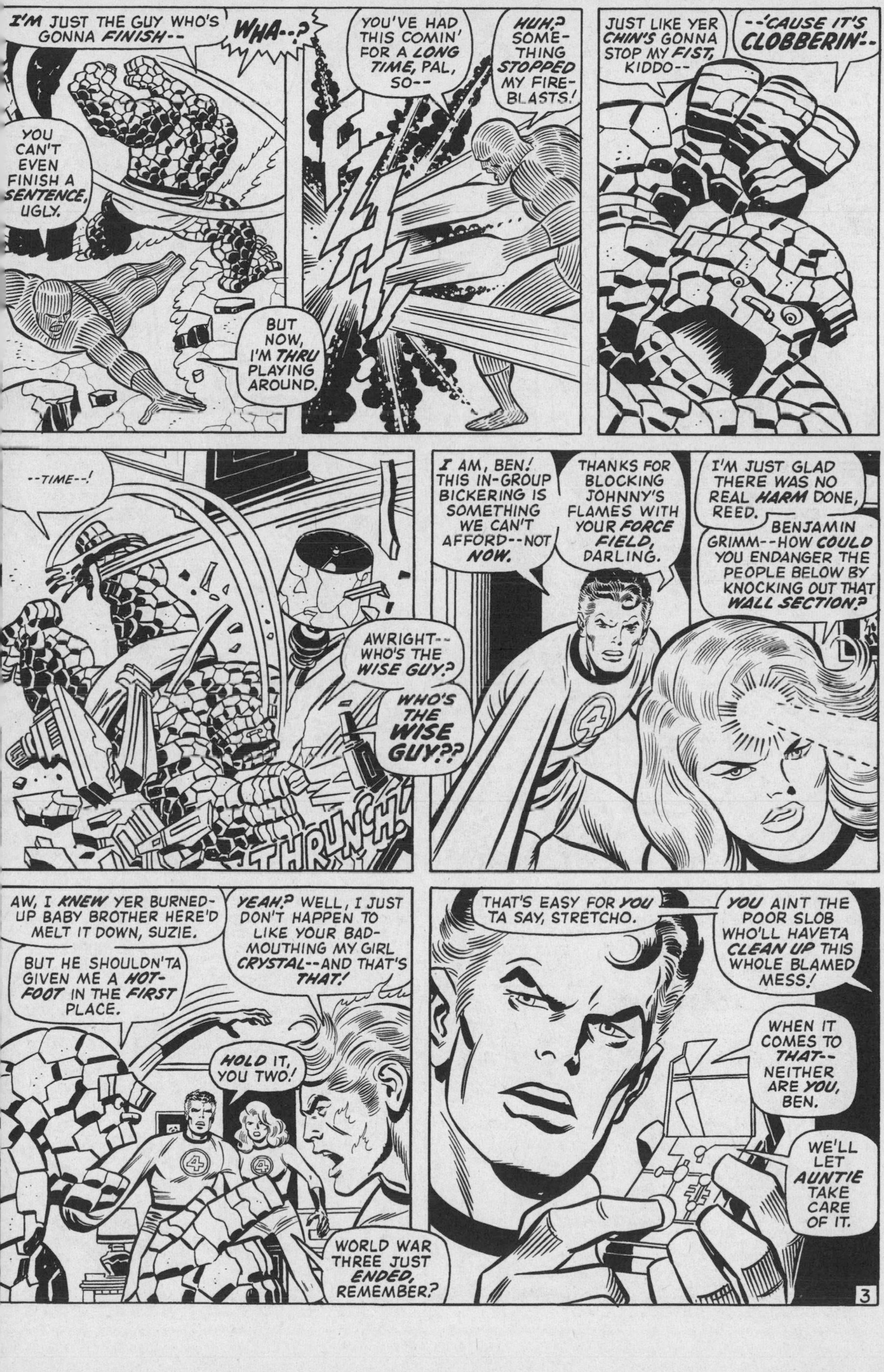

I'M JUST THE GUY WHO'S GONNA FINISH--
WHA--?
YOU CAN'T EVEN FINISH A SENTENCE, UGLY.
BUT NOW, I'M THRU PLAYING AROUND.
YOU'VE HAD THIS COMIN' FOR A LONG TIME, PAL, SO--
HUH? SOME-THING STOPPED MY FIRE-BLASTS!
JUST LIKE YER CHIN'S GONNA STOP MY FIST, KIDDO--
--'CAUSE IT'S CLOBBERIN'--
--TIME--!
AWRIGHT-- WHO'S THE WISE GUY?
WHO'S THE WISE GUY??
THRUNCH!
I AM, BEN! THIS IN-GROUP BICKERING IS SOMETHING WE CAN'T AFFORD--NOT NOW.
THANKS FOR BLOCKING JOHNNY'S FLAMES WITH YOUR FORCE FIELD, DARLING.
I'M JUST GLAD THERE WAS NO REAL HARM DONE, REED.
BENJAMIN GRIMM--HOW COULD YOU ENDANGER THE PEOPLE BELOW BY KNOCKING OUT THAT WALL SECTION?
AW, I KNEW YER BURNED-UP BABY BROTHER HERE'D MELT IT DOWN, SUZIE.
BUT HE SHOULDN'TA GIVEN ME A HOT-FOOT IN THE FIRST PLACE.
YEAH? WELL, I JUST DON'T HAPPEN TO LIKE YOUR BAD-MOUTHING MY GIRL CRYSTAL--AND THAT'S THAT!
HOLD IT, YOU TWO!
WORLD WAR THREE JUST ENDED, REMEMBER?
THAT'S EASY FOR YOU TA SAY, STRETCHO.
YOU AINT THE POOR SLOB WHO'LL HAVETA CLEAN UP THIS WHOLE BLAMED MESS!
WHEN IT COMES TO THAT-- NEITHER ARE YOU, BEN.
WE'LL LET AUNTIE TAKE CARE OF IT.
3

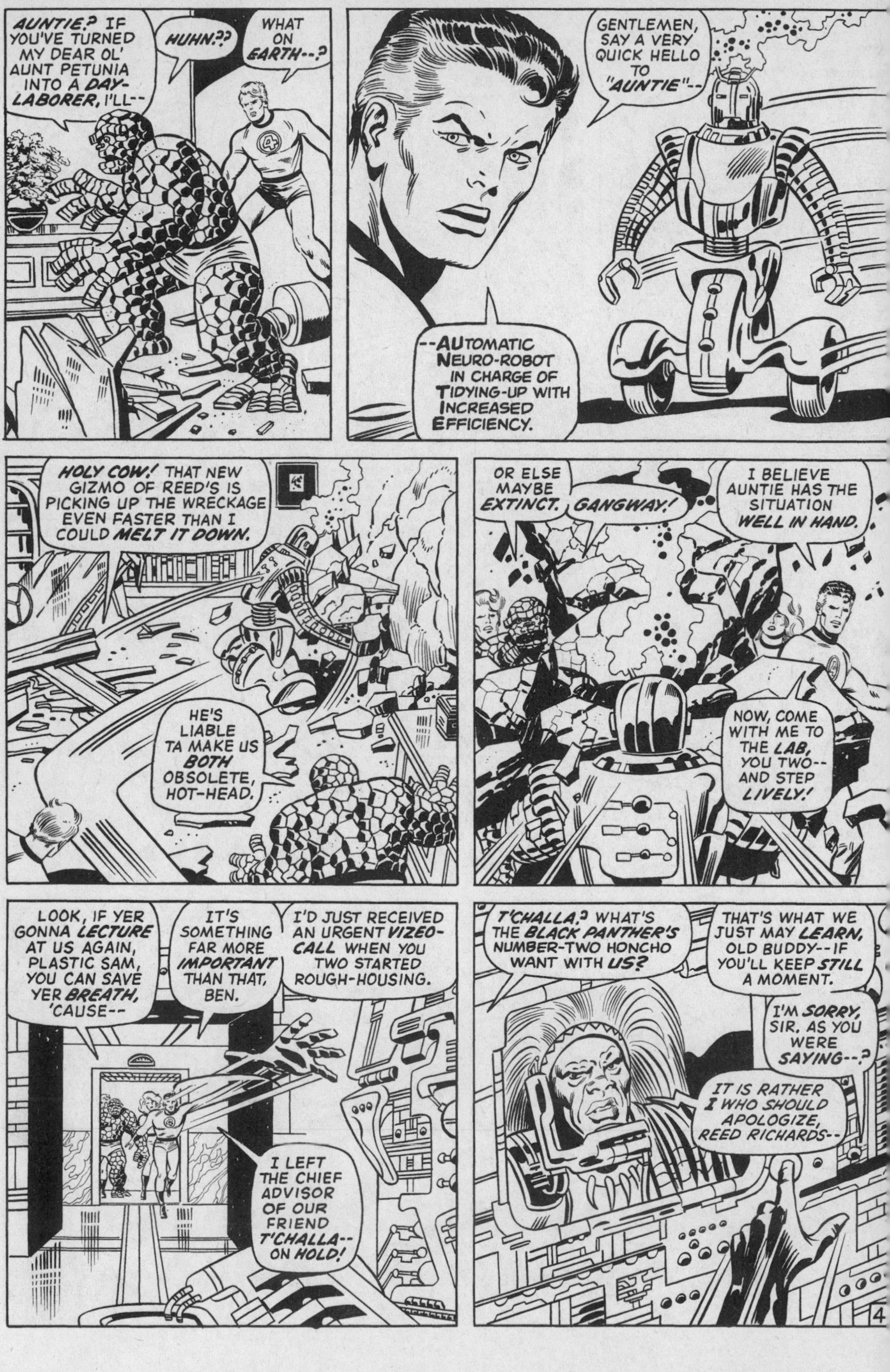
AUNTIE? IF YOU'VE TURNED MY DEAR OL' AUNT PETUNIA INTO A DAY-LABORER, I'LL--
HUHN??
WHAT ON EARTH--?
GENTLEMEN, SAY A VERY QUICK HELLO TO "AUNTIE"--
--AUTOMATIC NEURO-ROBOT IN CHARGE OF TIDYING-UP WITH INCREASED EFFICIENCY.
HOLY COW! THAT NEW GIZMO OF REED'S IS PICKING UP THE WRECKAGE EVEN FASTER THAN I COULD MELT IT DOWN.
HE'S LIABLE TA MAKE US BOTH OBSOLETE, HOT-HEAD.
OR ELSE MAYBE EXTINCT.
GANGWAY!
I BELIEVE AUNTIE HAS THE SITUATION WELL IN HAND.
NOW, COME WITH ME TO THE LAB, YOU TWO-- AND STEP LIVELY!
LOOK, IF YER GONNA LECTURE AT US AGAIN, PLASTIC SAM, YOU CAN SAVE YER BREATH, 'CAUSE--
IT'S SOMETHING FAR MORE IMPORTANT THAN THAT, BEN.
I'D JUST RECEIVED AN URGENT VIZEO-CALL WHEN YOU TWO STARTED ROUGH-HOUSING.
I LEFT THE CHIEF ADVISOR OF OUR FRIEND T'CHALLA-- ON HOLD!
T'CHALLA? WHAT'S THE BLACK PANTHER'S NUMBER-TWO HONCHO WANT WITH US?
THAT'S WHAT WE JUST MAY LEARN, OLD BUDDY-- IF YOU'LL KEEP STILL A MOMENT.
I'M SORRY, SIR, AS YOU WERE SAYING--?
IT IS RATHER I WHO SHOULD APOLOGIZE, REED RICHARDS--
4

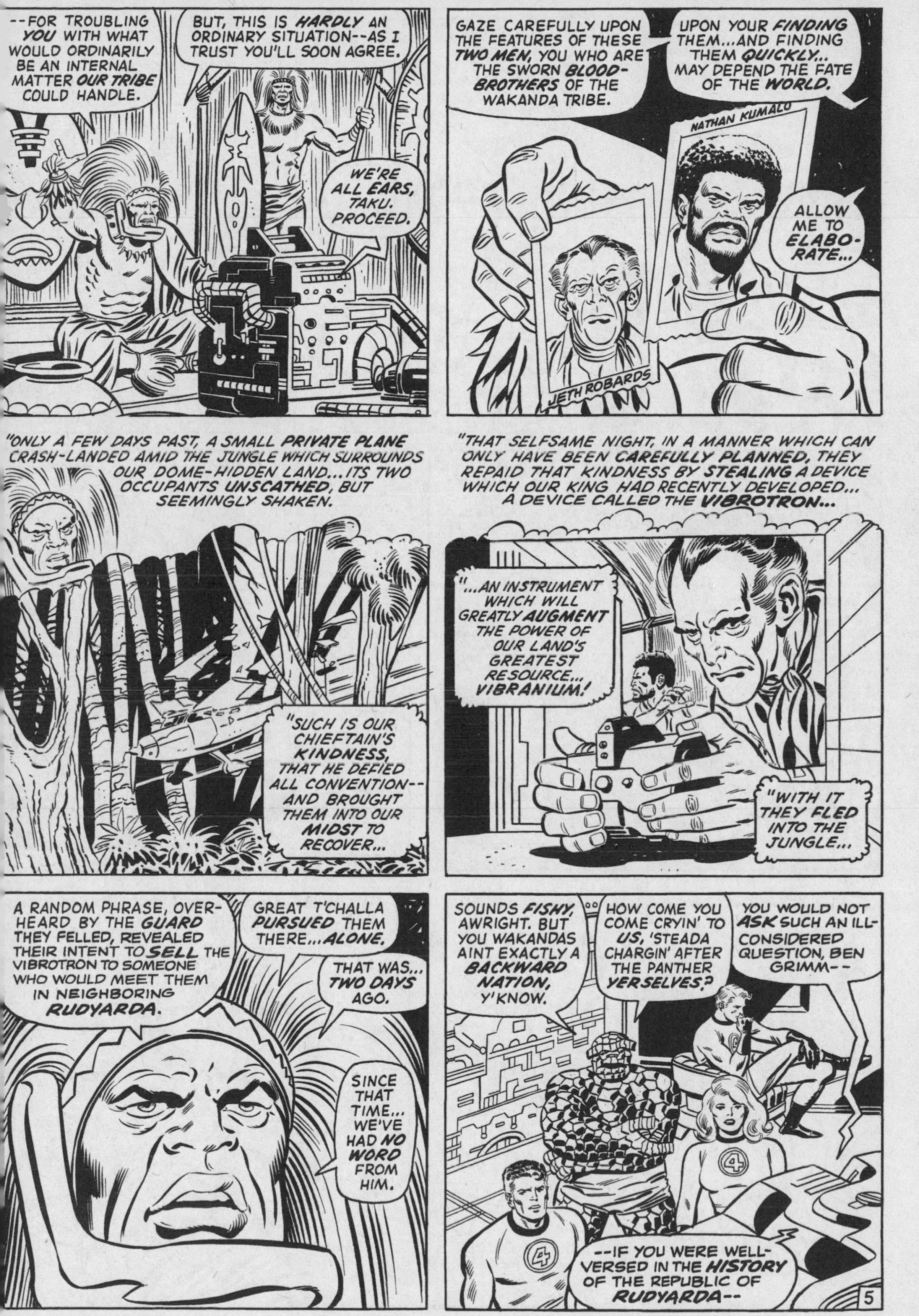
--FOR TROUBLING YOU WITH WHAT WOULD ORDINARILY BE AN INTERNAL MATTER OUR TRIBE COULD HANDLE.
BUT, THIS IS HARDLY AN ORDINARY SITUATION--AS I TRUST YOU'LL SOON AGREE.
WE'RE ALL EARS, TAKU. PROCEED.
GAZE CAREFULLY UPON THE FEATURES OF THESE TWO MEN, YOU WHO ARE THE SWORN BLOOD-BROTHERS OF THE WAKANDA TRIBE.
UPON YOUR FINDING THEM...AND FINDING THEM QUICKLY... MAY DEPEND THE FATE OF THE WORLD.
NATHAN KUMALO
JETH ROBARDS
ALLOW ME TO ELABO-RATE...
"ONLY A FEW DAYS PAST, A SMALL PRIVATE PLANE CRASH-LANDED AMID THE JUNGLE WHICH SURROUNDS OUR DOME-HIDDEN LAND... ITS TWO OCCUPANTS UNSCATHED, BUT SEEMINGLY SHAKEN.
"SUCH IS OUR CHIEFTAIN'S KINDNESS, THAT HE DEFIED ALL CONVENTION--AND BROUGHT THEM INTO OUR MIDST TO RECOVER...
"THAT SELFSAME NIGHT, IN A MANNER WHICH CAN ONLY HAVE BEEN CAREFULLY PLANNED, THEY REPAID THAT KINDNESS BY STEALING A DEVICE WHICH OUR KING HAD RECENTLY DEVELOPED... A DEVICE CALLED THE VIBROTRON...
"...AN INSTRUMENT WHICH WILL GREATLY AUGMENT THE POWER OF OUR LAND'S GREATEST RESOURCE... VIBRANIUM!
"WITH IT THEY FLED INTO THE JUNGLE...
A RANDOM PHRASE, OVER-HEARD BY THE GUARD THEY FELLED, REVEALED THEIR INTENT TO SELL THE VIBROTRON TO SOMEONE WHO WOULD MEET THEM IN NEIGHBORING RUDYARDA.
GREAT T'CHALLA PURSUED THEM THERE...ALONE.
THAT WAS... TWO DAYS AGO.
SINCE THAT TIME... WE'VE HAD NO WORD FROM HIM.
SOUNDS FISHY, AWRIGHT. BUT YOU WAKANDAS AINT EXACTLY A BACKWARD NATION, Y'KNOW.
HOW COME YOU COME CRYIN' TO US, 'STEADA CHARGIN' AFTER THE PANTHER YERSELVES?
YOU WOULD NOT ASK SUCH AN ILL-CONSIDERED QUESTION, BEN GRIMM--
--IF YOU WERE WELL-VERSED IN THE HISTORY OF THE REPUBLIC OF RUDYARDA--
5

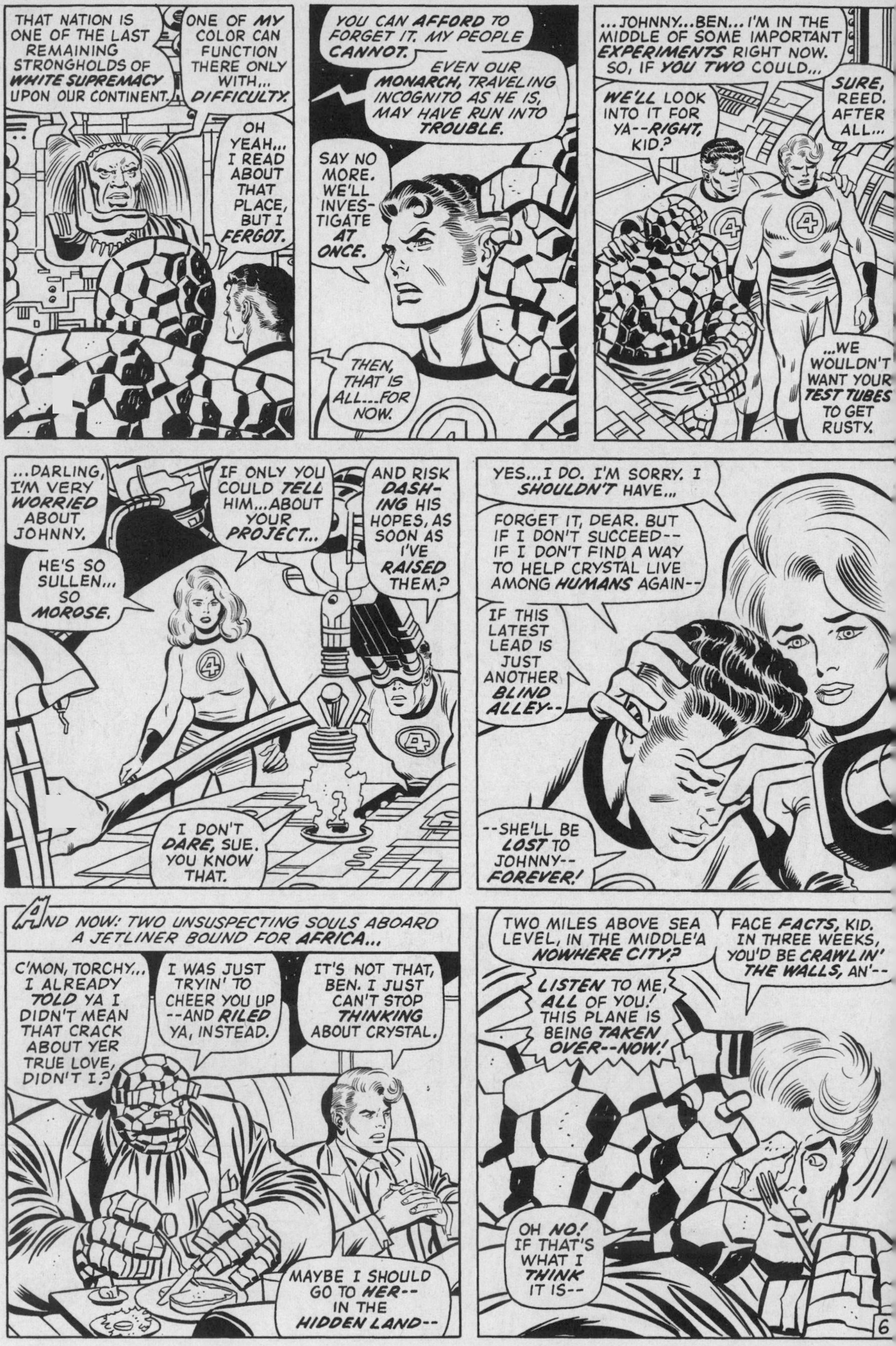
THAT NATION IS ONE OF THE LAST REMAINING STRONGHOLDS OF WHITE SUPREMACY UPON OUR CONTINENT.
ONE OF MY COLOR CAN FUNCTION THERE ONLY WITH... DIFFICULTY.
OH YEAH... I READ ABOUT THAT PLACE, BUT I FERGOT.
YOU CAN AFFORD TO FORGET IT. MY PEOPLE CANNOT.
EVEN OUR MONARCH, TRAVELING INCOGNITO AS HE IS, MAY HAVE RUN INTO TROUBLE.
SAY NO MORE. WE'LL INVESTIGATE AT ONCE.
THEN, THAT IS ALL...FOR NOW.
...JOHNNY...BEN... I'M IN THE MIDDLE OF SOME IMPORTANT EXPERIMENTS RIGHT NOW. SO, IF YOU TWO COULD...
WE'LL LOOK INTO IT FOR YA--RIGHT, KID?
SURE, REED. AFTER ALL...
...WE WOULDN'T WANT YOUR TEST TUBES TO GET RUSTY.
...DARLING, I'M VERY WORRIED ABOUT JOHNNY.
HE'S SO SULLEN... SO MOROSE.
IF ONLY YOU COULD TELL HIM...ABOUT YOUR PROJECT...
AND RISK DASHING HIS HOPES, AS SOON AS I'VE RAISED THEM?
I DON'T DARE, SUE. YOU KNOW THAT.
YES...I DO. I'M SORRY. I SHOULDN'T HAVE...
FORGET IT, DEAR. BUT IF I DON'T SUCCEED-- IF I DON'T FIND A WAY TO HELP CRYSTAL LIVE AMONG HUMANS AGAIN--
IF THIS LATEST LEAD IS JUST ANOTHER BLIND ALLEY--
--SHE'LL BE LOST TO JOHNNY-- FOREVER!
AND NOW: TWO UNSUSPECTING SOULS ABOARD A JETLINER BOUND FOR AFRICA...
C'MON, TORCHY... I ALREADY TOLD YA I DIDN'T MEAN THAT CRACK ABOUT YER TRUE LOVE, DIDN'T I?
I WAS JUST TRYIN' TO CHEER YOU UP --AND RILED YA, INSTEAD.
IT'S NOT THAT, BEN. I JUST CAN'T STOP THINKING ABOUT CRYSTAL.
MAYBE I SHOULD GO TO HER-- IN THE HIDDEN LAND--
TWO MILES ABOVE SEA LEVEL, IN THE MIDDLE'A NOWHERE CITY?
FACE FACTS, KID. IN THREE WEEKS, YOU'D BE CRAWLIN' THE WALLS, AN'--
LISTEN TO ME, ALL OF YOU! THIS PLANE IS BEING TAKEN OVER--NOW!
OH NO! IF THAT'S WHAT I THINK IT IS--
6

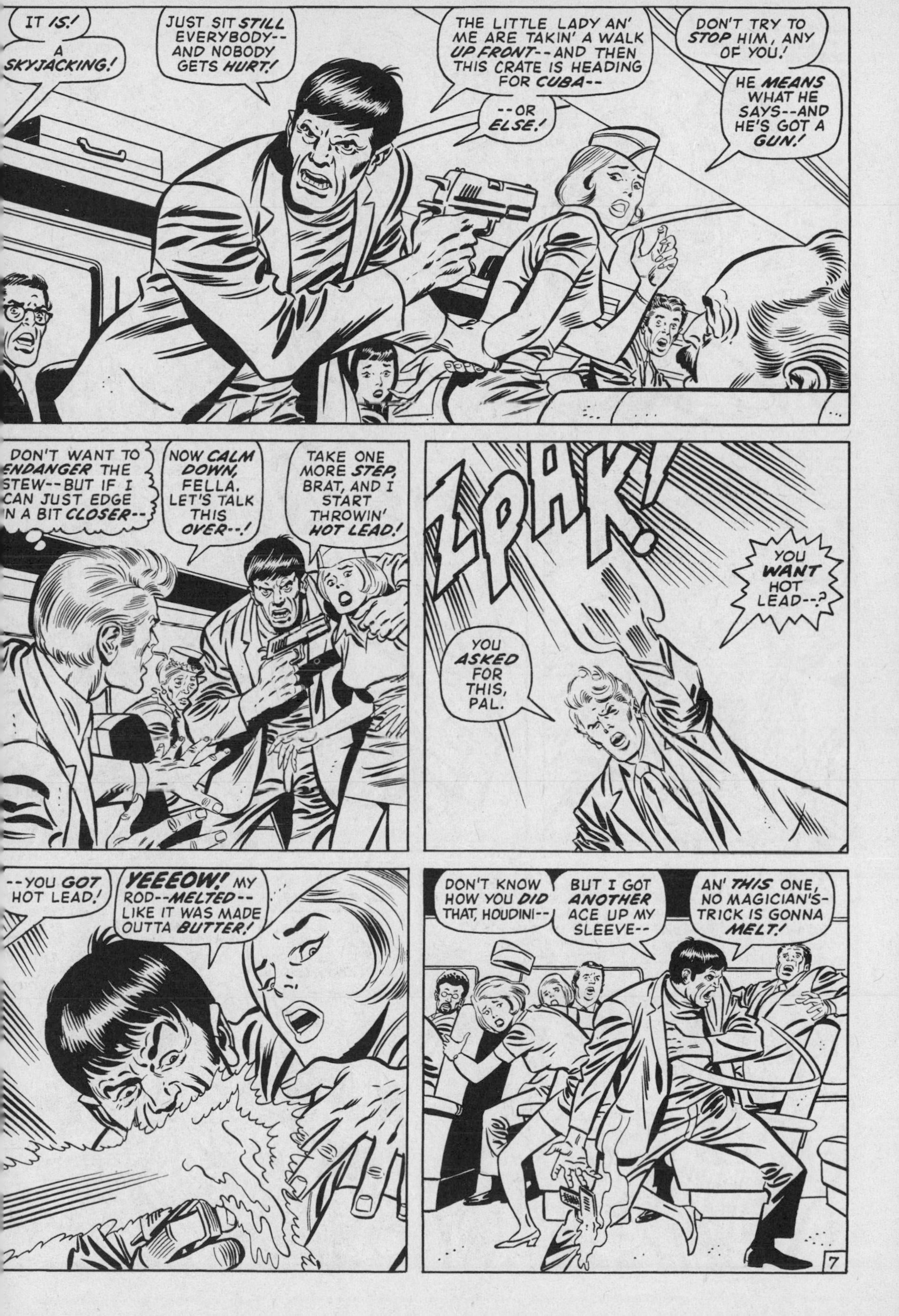
IT IS!
A SKYJACKING!
JUST SIT STILL EVERYBODY-- AND NOBODY GETS HURT!
THE LITTLE LADY AN' ME ARE TAKIN' A WALK UP FRONT--AND THEN THIS CRATE IS HEADING FOR CUBA--
--OR ELSE!
DON'T TRY TO STOP HIM, ANY OF YOU!
HE MEANS WHAT HE SAYS--AND HE'S GOT A GUN!
DON'T WANT TO ENDANGER THE STEW--BUT IF I CAN JUST EDGE IN A BIT CLOSER--
NOW CALM DOWN, FELLA. LET'S TALK THIS OVER--!
TAKE ONE MORE STEP, BRAT, AND I START THROWIN' HOT LEAD!
ZPAK!
YOU WANT HOT LEAD--?
YOU ASKED FOR THIS, PAL.
--YOU GOT HOT LEAD!
YEEEOW! MY ROD--MELTED-- LIKE IT WAS MADE OUTTA BUTTER!
DON'T KNOW HOW YOU DID THAT, HOUDINI--
BUT I GOT ANOTHER ACE UP MY SLEEVE--
AN' THIS ONE, NO MAGICIAN'S-TRICK IS GONNA MELT!
7

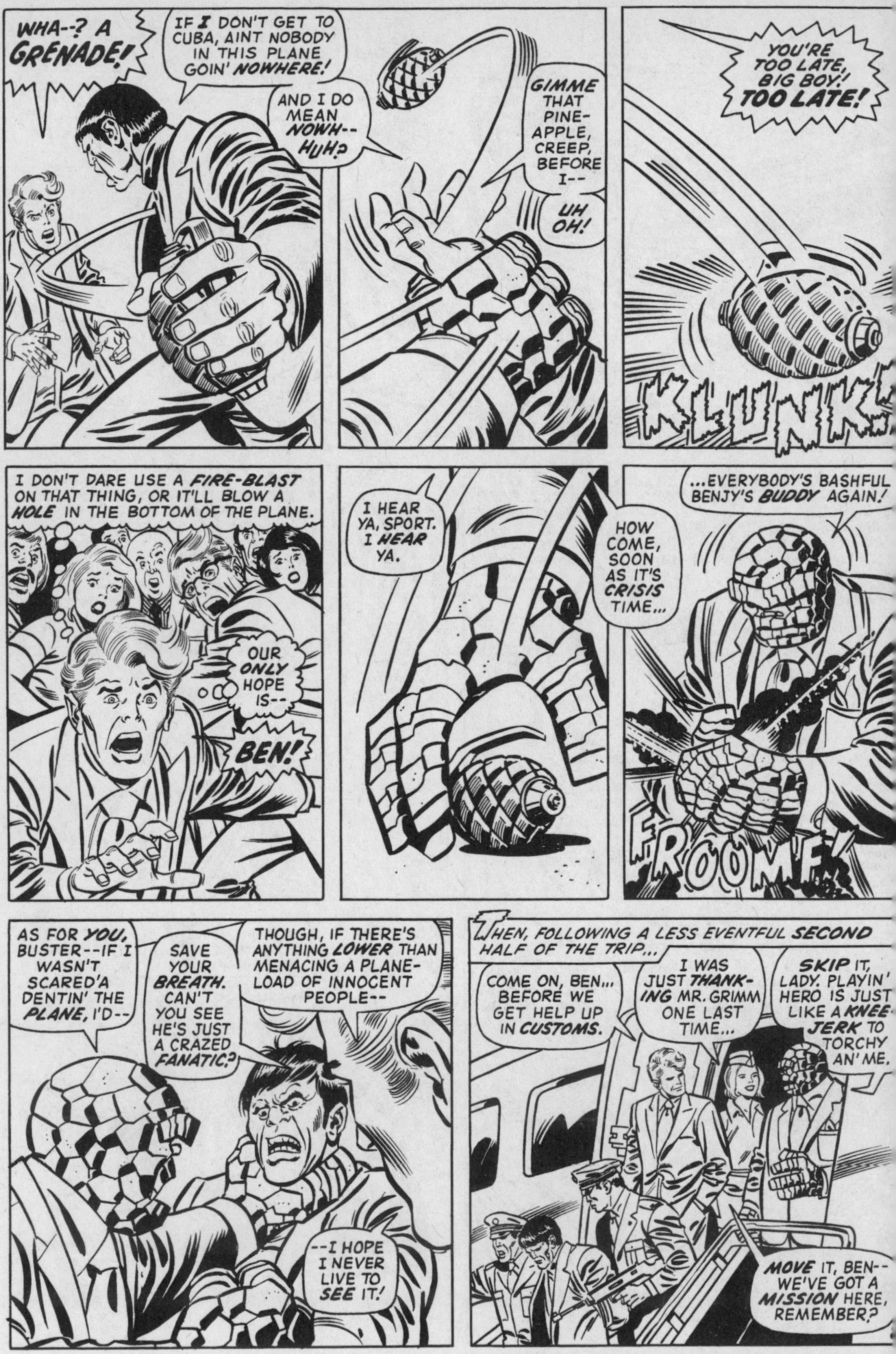
WHA--? A GRENADE!
IF I DON'T GET TO CUBA, AINT NOBODY IN THIS PLANE GOIN' NOWHERE!
AND I DO MEAN NOWH-- HUH?
GIMME THAT PINE-APPLE, CREEP, BEFORE I--
UH OH!
YOU'RE TOO LATE, BIG BOY! TOO LATE!
KLUNK!
I DON'T DARE USE A FIRE-BLAST ON THAT THING, OR IT'LL BLOW A HOLE IN THE BOTTOM OF THE PLANE.
OUR ONLY HOPE IS--
BEN!
I HEAR YA, SPORT. I HEAR YA.
HOW COME, SOON AS IT'S CRISIS TIME...
...EVERYBODY'S BASHFUL BENJY'S BUDDY AGAIN!
FROOMF!
AS FOR YOU, BUSTER--IF I WASN'T SCARED'A DENTIN' THE PLANE, I'D--
SAVE YOUR BREATH. CAN'T YOU SEE HE'S JUST A CRAZED FANATIC?
THOUGH, IF THERE'S ANYTHING LOWER THAN MENACING A PLANE-LOAD OF INNOCENT PEOPLE--
--I HOPE I NEVER LIVE TO SEE IT!
THEN, FOLLOWING A LESS EVENTFUL SECOND HALF OF THE TRIP...
COME ON, BEN... BEFORE WE GET HELP UP IN CUSTOMS.
I WAS JUST THANKING MR. GRIMM ONE LAST TIME...
SKIP IT, LADY. PLAYIN' HERO IS JUST LIKE A KNEE-JERK TO TORCHY AN' ME.
MOVE IT, BEN-- WE'VE GOT A MISSION HERE, REMEMBER?

Panel 1: YEAH, *I* REMEMBER, ALRIGHT. ONLY, I'M SURE GLAD WE'RE HERE TA SAVE THE WHOLE BLAMED *WORLD*... ...AN' NOT JUST SOME PLACE THAT DIVIDES ITS *OWN PEOPLE* INTO "EUROPEANS" AND "COLOREDS"...

EUROPEANS

COLOREDS

...OR I THINK I'D JUST *FERGIT* THE WHOLE THING!

Panel 2: AIR

NOW WHAT IN BLAZES--?

THAT'S THE *THIRD* EMPTY CAB'S PASSED ME BY LIKE I WUZ A *PLAGUE CASE*, OR ELSE MAYBE--

MAYBE A *BLACK MAN* TRYING TO GET TO *HARLEM,* MR. G.?

COLOREDS

EUROPEANS

YEAH... *SUMTHIN'* LIKE THAT.

VROOM

Panel 3: MAYBE I'LL JUST SLOW ONE OF 'EM *DOWN* A MITE... ...LET 'EM TAKE A *CLOSER* LOOK.

TAXI

LORD! WHAT THE--?

Panel 4: SAY, *I* KNOW YOU. YOU'RE THE *THING* --ONE OF THE AMERICAN *FANTASTIC FOUR.*

HOP *IN,* SIR. SORRY I DIDN'T *STOP* AT FIRST, BUT I TOOK YOU FOR-- I MEAN--

JUST TAKE US WHERE WE *TELL* YA, FELLA, AN' SHUT YER *YAP*...

...BEFORE I GET *SICK* ALL OVER YER BUGGY.

Panel 5:

NOW, KID, TELL ME SOMETHIN' *PLEASANT,* TO TAKE MY MIND OFF'A... THINGS.

T'CHALLA'S AIDE *CALLED BACK,* WHILE WE WERE PACKING...

LIKE *WHERE* WE'RE GOIN'!... AN' HOW WE KNOW TO *GO* THERE.

...SAID HE'D *FOUND* THIS ADDRESS FOR THE MAN *KUMALO.* 'COURSE, MAYBE KUMALO NEVER WENT BACK THERE...

...BUT WE STILL GOTTA *LOOK-SEE* HAVE A, HUH?

Panel 6:

ONE THING'S CERTAIN. IF HIM AN' ROBARDS *SOLD* THAT VIBRANIUM GIZMO ALREADY...

...THEY SURE AINT CASHED THE *CHECK.*

9

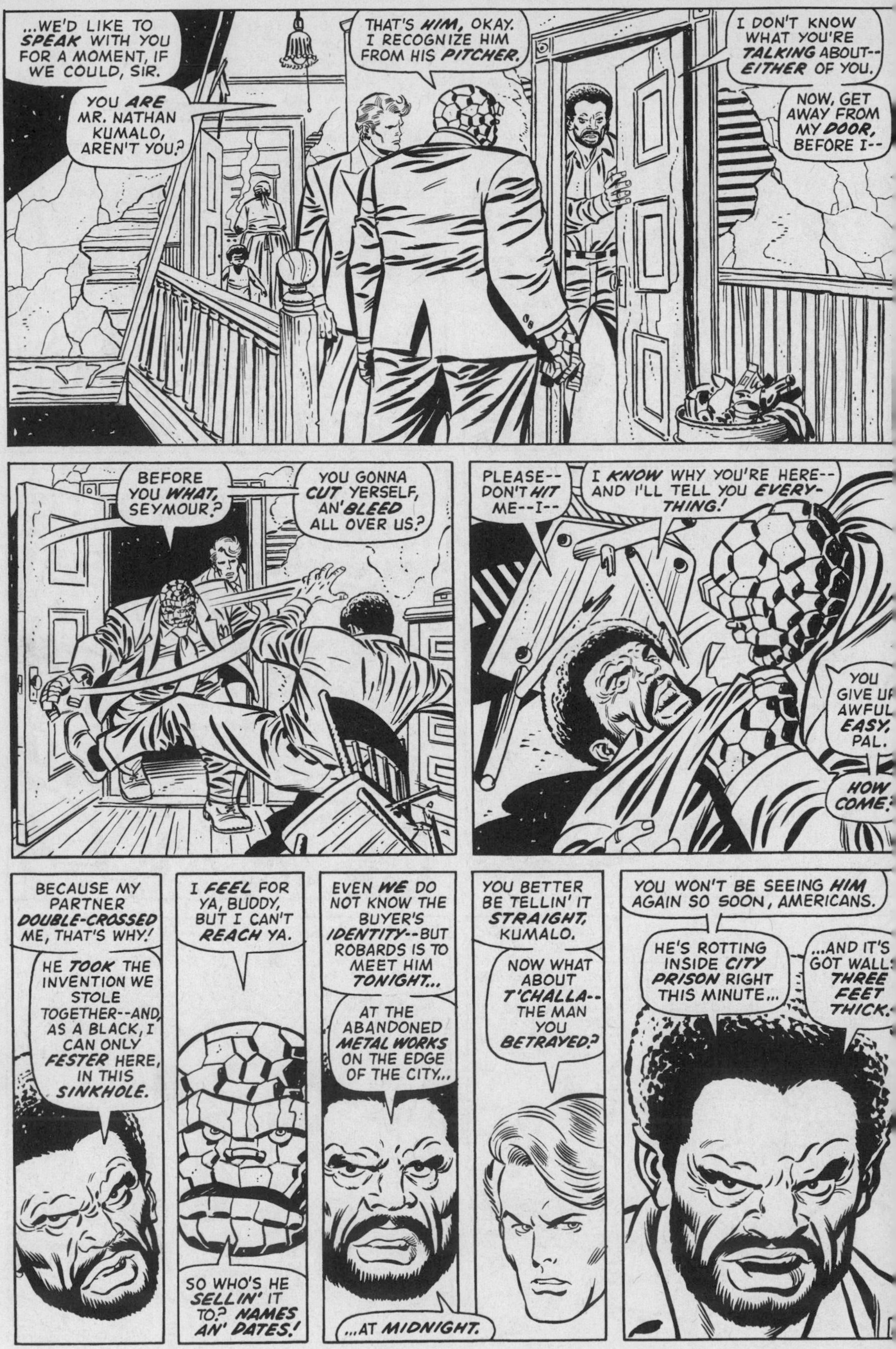
...WE'D LIKE TO SPEAK WITH YOU FOR A MOMENT, IF WE COULD, SIR.
YOU ARE MR. NATHAN KUMALO, AREN'T YOU?
THAT'S HIM, OKAY. I RECOGNIZE HIM FROM HIS PITCHER.
I DON'T KNOW WHAT YOU'RE TALKING ABOUT-- EITHER OF YOU.
NOW, GET AWAY FROM MY DOOR, BEFORE I--
BEFORE YOU WHAT, SEYMOUR?
YOU GONNA CUT YERSELF, AN' BLEED ALL OVER US?
PLEASE-- DON'T HIT ME--I--
I KNOW WHY YOU'RE HERE-- AND I'LL TELL YOU EVERY-THING!
YOU GIVE UP AWFUL EASY, PAL.
HOW COME?
BECAUSE MY PARTNER DOUBLE-CROSSED ME, THAT'S WHY!
HE TOOK THE INVENTION WE STOLE TOGETHER--AND, AS A BLACK, I CAN ONLY FESTER HERE, IN THIS SINKHOLE.
I FEEL FOR YA, BUDDY, BUT I CAN'T REACH YA.
SO WHO'S HE SELLIN' IT TO? NAMES AN' DATES!
EVEN WE DO NOT KNOW THE BUYER'S IDENTITY--BUT ROBARDS IS TO MEET HIM TONIGHT...
AT THE ABANDONED METAL WORKS ON THE EDGE OF THE CITY...
...AT MIDNIGHT.
YOU BETTER BE TELLIN' IT STRAIGHT, KUMALO.
NOW WHAT ABOUT T'CHALLA-- THE MAN YOU BETRAYED?
YOU WON'T BE SEEING HIM AGAIN SO SOON, AMERICANS.
HE'S ROTTING INSIDE CITY PRISON RIGHT THIS MINUTE...
...AND IT'S GOT WALLS THREE FEET THICK.

THEN, AS A STARTLED TWOSOME MULL OVER THAT LITTLE BOMBSHELL...

WELL, BEN? DO WE *BELIEVE* HIM, OR *DON'T* WE?

AW, HE'S TOO *CHICKEN* TO BE PUTTIN' US ON. I VOTE WE--

YOU'RE GOING TO DO *NOTHING*, EITHER OF YOU!

I'VE TAKEN *ENOUGH* OFF WHITE MEN TO LAST ME A *LIFETIME*.

AND THAT'S WHY YOU'RE BOTH GOING TO *DIE*--

--RIGHT *HERE*, RIGHT *NOW*-- IN THIS DINGY HOLE THAT *YOUR* KIND EXILED ME TO!

--EVER GONNA PUT THE *KIBOSH* ON AUNT PETUNIA'S FAVORITE *NEPHEW?*

--HERE, IN A PLACE AINT EVEN BEEN *CLEANED* IN A YEAR?

WHY, FACT IS, THIS WHOLE PLACE IS SO BLAMED *DUSTY*--THAT I'M PLUMB--ABOUT--TO--AAAAAA

CHOOOOO

BLAM

DON'T BOTHER TO GIT *UP*, PAL. *WE* KNOW THE WAY OUT.

BUT IF YOU TOL' US ANY *TALL TALES*-- YOU BETTER START *PACKIN'!*

Y-YOU'RE-- NOT GOING TO--PUT ME IN *PRISON*--?

YOU'RE ALREADY *IN* ONE, KUMALO --OR HADN'T YOU *NOTICED?*

C'MON, BEN--

11

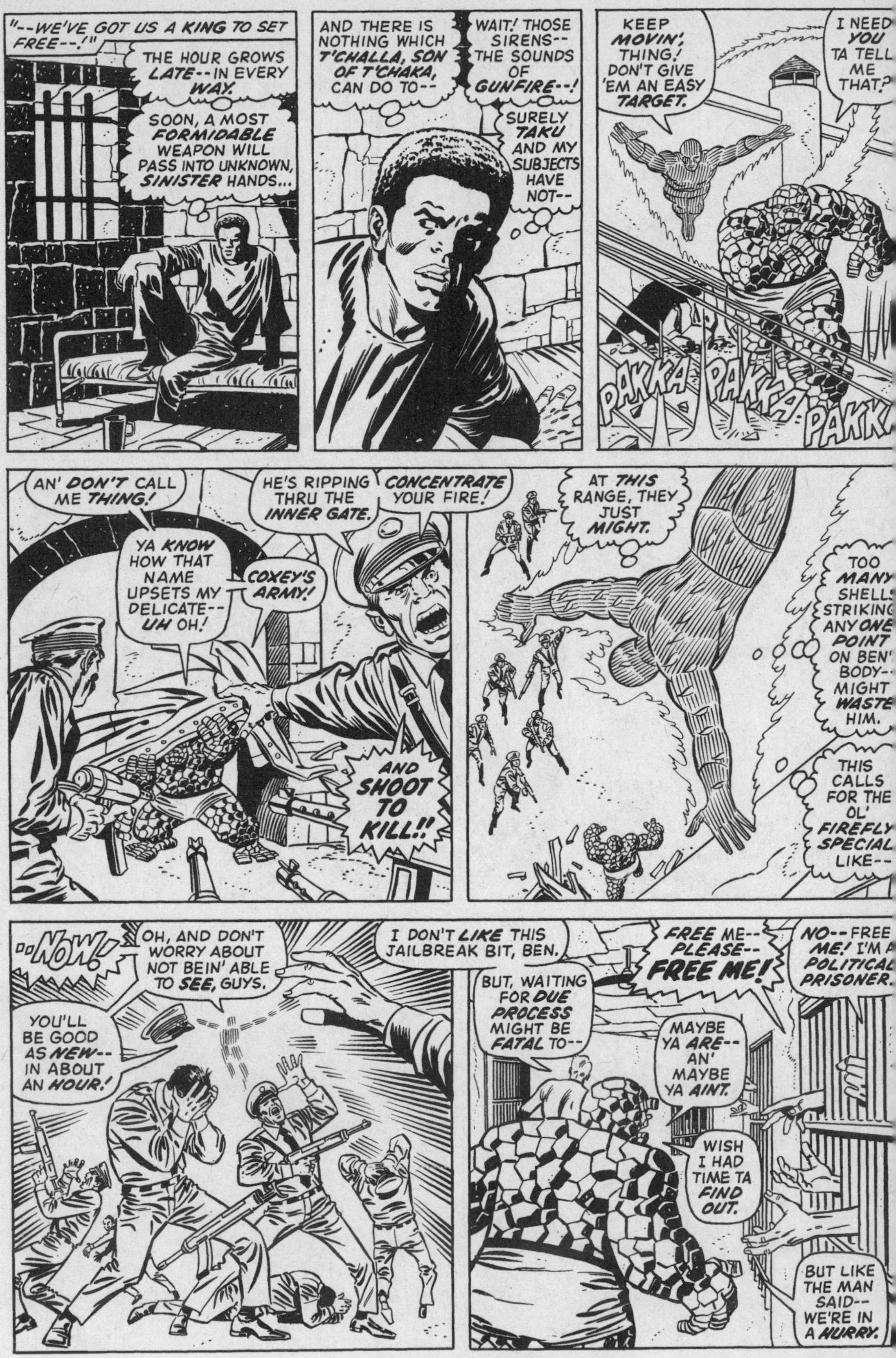
"--WE'VE GOT US A KING TO SET FREE--!"
THE HOUR GROWS LATE--IN EVERY WAY.
SOON, A MOST FORMIDABLE WEAPON WILL PASS INTO UNKNOWN, SINISTER HANDS...
AND THERE IS NOTHING WHICH T'CHALLA, SON OF T'CHAKA, CAN DO TO--
WAIT! THOSE SIRENS-- THE SOUNDS OF GUNFIRE--!
SURELY TAKU AND MY SUBJECTS HAVE NOT--
KEEP MOVIN', THING! DON'T GIVE 'EM AN EASY TARGET.
I NEED YOU TA TELL ME THAT?
PAKKA PAKKA PAKKA
AN' DON'T CALL ME THING!
YA KNOW HOW THAT NAME UPSETS MY DELICATE--UH OH!
HE'S RIPPING THRU THE INNER GATE.
COXEY'S ARMY!
CONCENTRATE YOUR FIRE!
AND SHOOT TO KILL!!
AT THIS RANGE, THEY JUST MIGHT.
TOO MANY SHELLS STRIKING ANY ONE POINT ON BEN' BODY-- MIGHT WASTE HIM.
THIS CALLS FOR THE OL' FIREFLY SPECIAL LIKE--
NOW!
OH, AND DON'T WORRY ABOUT NOT BEIN' ABLE TO SEE, GUYS.
YOU'LL BE GOOD AS NEW--IN ABOUT AN HOUR!
I DON'T LIKE THIS JAILBREAK BIT, BEN.
BUT, WAITING FOR DUE PROCESS MIGHT BE FATAL TO--
FREE ME--PLEASE--FREE ME!
NO--FREE ME! I'M A POLITICAL PRISONER.
MAYBE YA ARE--AN' MAYBE YA AINT.
WISH I HAD TIME TA FIND OUT.
BUT LIKE THE MAN SAID--WE'RE IN A HURRY.

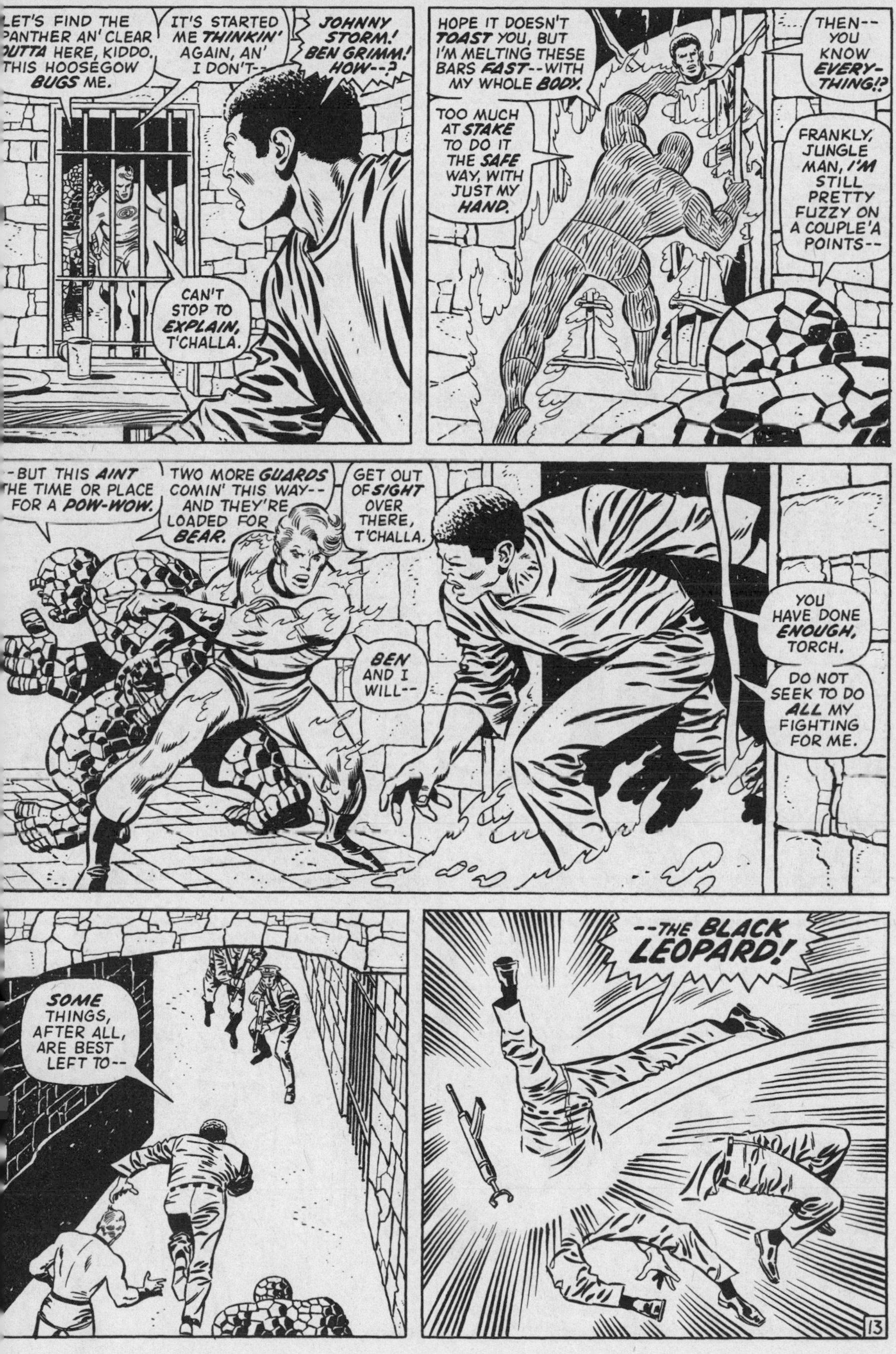

LET'S FIND THE PANTHER AN' CLEAR OUTTA HERE, KIDDO. THIS HOOSEGOW BUGS ME.
IT'S STARTED ME THINKIN' AGAIN, AN' I DON'T--
JOHNNY STORM! BEN GRIMM! HOW--?
CAN'T STOP TO EXPLAIN, T'CHALLA.
HOPE IT DOESN'T TOAST YOU, BUT I'M MELTING THESE BARS FAST--WITH MY WHOLE BODY.
TOO MUCH AT STAKE TO DO IT THE SAFE WAY, WITH JUST MY HAND.
THEN--YOU KNOW EVERYTHING!?
FRANKLY, JUNGLE MAN, I'M STILL PRETTY FUZZY ON A COUPLE'A POINTS--
--BUT THIS AINT THE TIME OR PLACE FOR A POW-WOW.
TWO MORE GUARDS COMIN' THIS WAY--AND THEY'RE LOADED FOR BEAR.
GET OUT OF SIGHT OVER THERE, T'CHALLA.
BEN AND I WILL--
YOU HAVE DONE ENOUGH, TORCH.
DO NOT SEEK TO DO ALL MY FIGHTING FOR ME.
SOME THINGS, AFTER ALL, ARE BEST LEFT TO--
--THE BLACK LEOPARD!
13

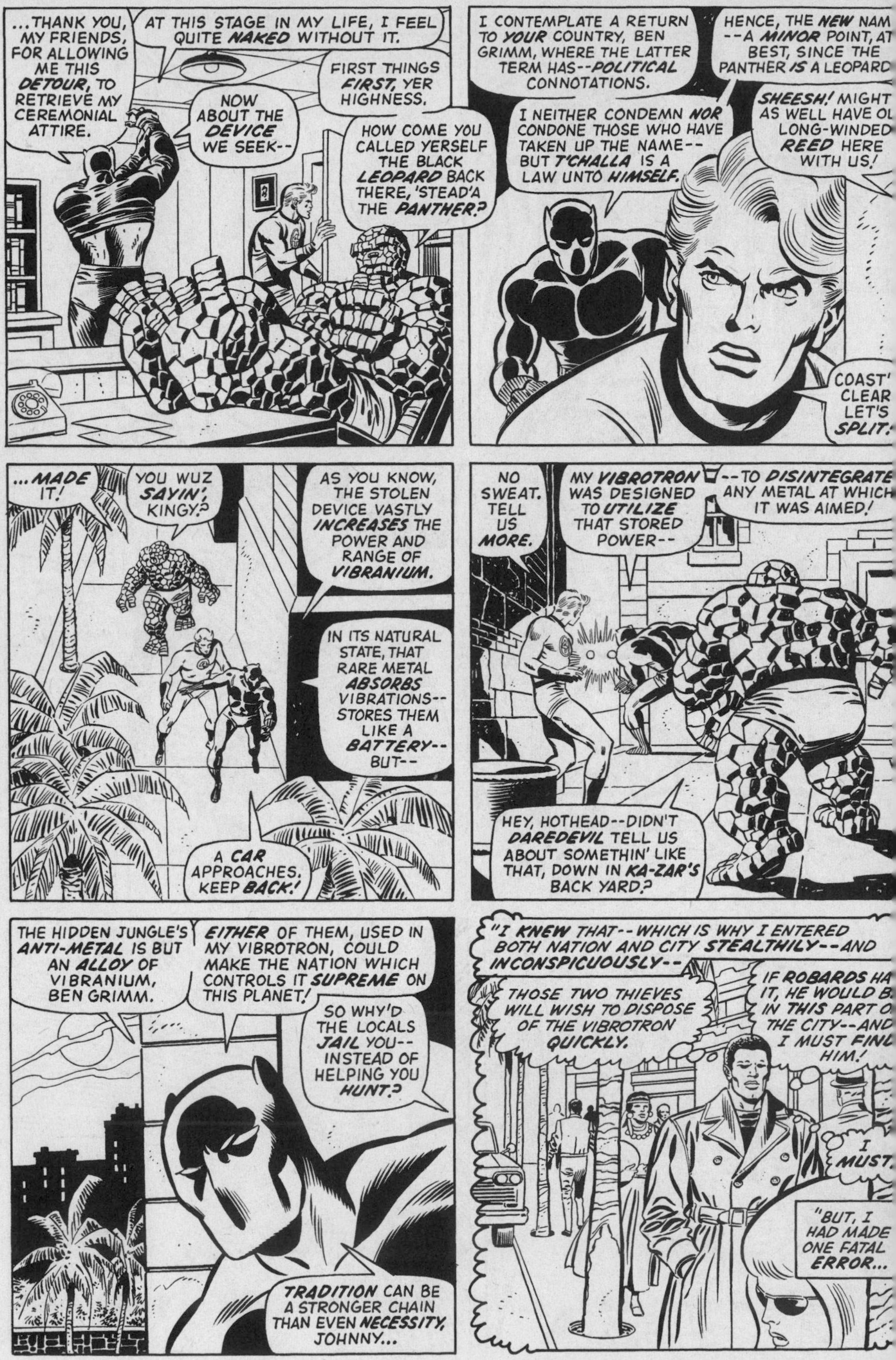
...THANK YOU, MY FRIENDS, FOR ALLOWING ME THIS DETOUR, TO RETRIEVE MY CEREMONIAL ATTIRE.
AT THIS STAGE IN MY LIFE, I FEEL QUITE NAKED WITHOUT IT.
FIRST THINGS FIRST, YER HIGHNESS.
NOW ABOUT THE DEVICE WE SEEK--
HOW COME YOU CALLED YERSELF THE BLACK LEOPARD BACK THERE, 'STEAD'A THE PANTHER?
I CONTEMPLATE A RETURN TO YOUR COUNTRY, BEN GRIMM, WHERE THE LATTER TERM HAS--POLITICAL CONNOTATIONS.
HENCE, THE NEW NAM --A MINOR POINT, AT BEST, SINCE THE PANTHER IS A LEOPARD
I NEITHER CONDEMN NOR CONDONE THOSE WHO HAVE TAKEN UP THE NAME--BUT T'CHALLA IS A LAW UNTO HIMSELF.
SHEESH! MIGHT AS WELL HAVE OL LONG-WINDED REED HERE WITH US!
COAST' CLEAR LET'S SPLIT!
...MADE IT!
YOU WUZ SAYIN', KINGY?
AS YOU KNOW, THE STOLEN DEVICE VASTLY INCREASES THE POWER AND RANGE OF VIBRANIUM.
IN ITS NATURAL STATE, THAT RARE METAL ABSORBS VIBRATIONS--STORES THEM LIKE A BATTERY--BUT--
A CAR APPROACHES. KEEP BACK!
NO SWEAT. TELL US MORE.
MY VIBROTRON WAS DESIGNED TO UTILIZE THAT STORED POWER--
--TO DISINTEGRATE ANY METAL AT WHICH IT WAS AIMED!
HEY, HOTHEAD--DIDN'T DAREDEVIL TELL US ABOUT SOMETHIN' LIKE THAT, DOWN IN KA-ZAR'S BACK YARD?
THE HIDDEN JUNGLE'S ANTI-METAL IS BUT AN ALLOY OF VIBRANIUM, BEN GRIMM.
EITHER OF THEM, USED IN MY VIBROTRON, COULD MAKE THE NATION WHICH CONTROLS IT SUPREME ON THIS PLANET!
SO WHY'D THE LOCALS JAIL YOU--INSTEAD OF HELPING YOU HUNT?
TRADITION CAN BE A STRONGER CHAIN THAN EVEN NECESSITY, JOHNNY...
"I KNEW THAT--WHICH IS WHY I ENTERED BOTH NATION AND CITY STEALTHILY--AND INCONSPICUOUSLY--
THOSE TWO THIEVES WILL WISH TO DISPOSE OF THE VIBROTRON QUICKLY.
IF ROBARDS HA IT, HE WOULD B IN THIS PART O THE CITY--AND I MUST FIN HIM!
I MUST.
"BUT, I HAD MADE ONE FATAL ERROR...

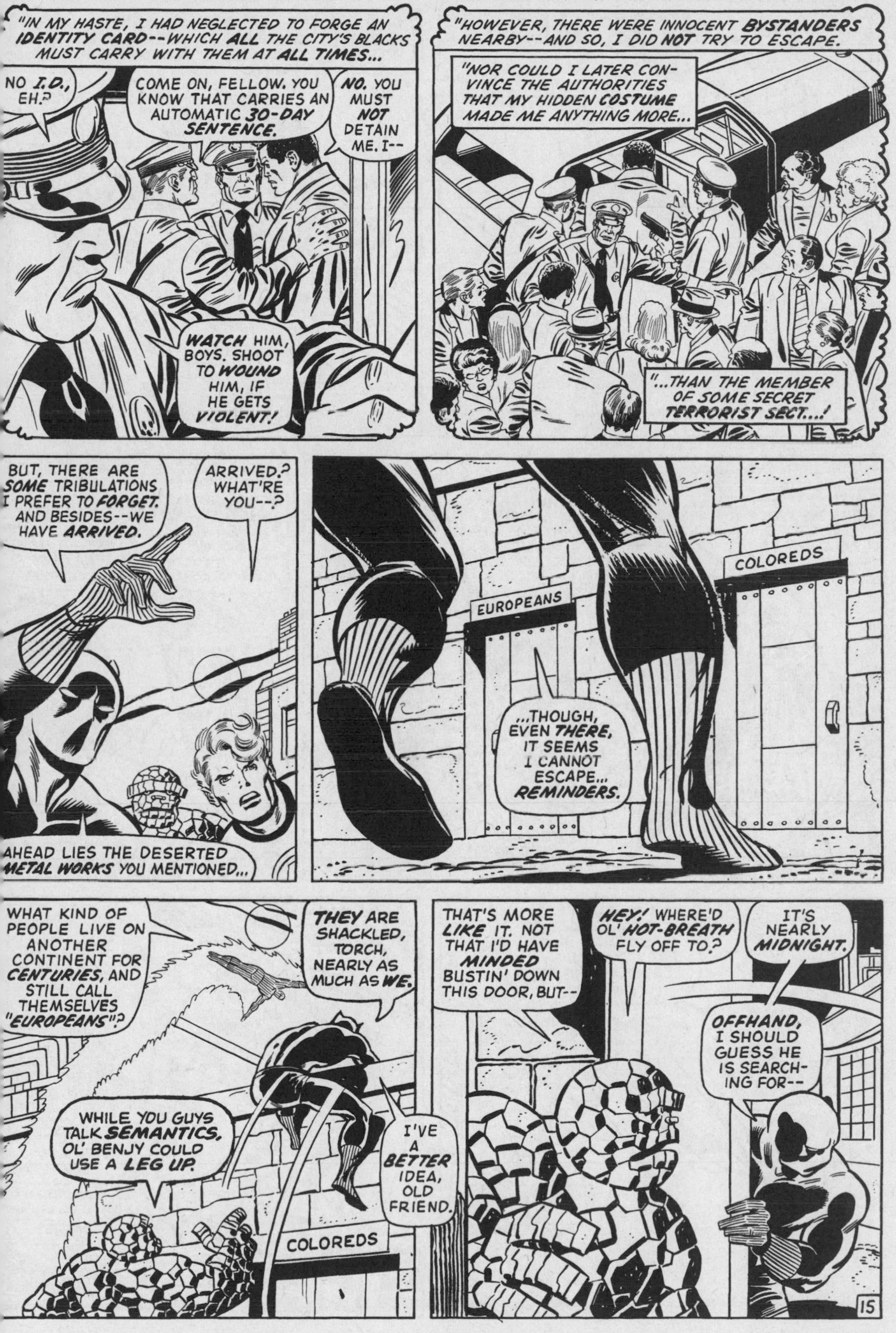
"IN MY HASTE, I HAD NEGLECTED TO FORGE AN IDENTITY CARD--WHICH ALL THE CITY'S BLACKS MUST CARRY WITH THEM AT ALL TIMES...
NO I.D., EH.?
COME ON, FELLOW. YOU KNOW THAT CARRIES AN AUTOMATIC 30-DAY SENTENCE.
NO. YOU MUST NOT DETAIN ME. I--
WATCH HIM, BOYS. SHOOT TO WOUND HIM, IF HE GETS VIOLENT!
"HOWEVER, THERE WERE INNOCENT BYSTANDERS NEARBY--AND SO, I DID NOT TRY TO ESCAPE.
"NOR COULD I LATER CONVINCE THE AUTHORITIES THAT MY HIDDEN COSTUME MADE ME ANYTHING MORE...
"...THAN THE MEMBER OF SOME SECRET TERRORIST SECT...!
BUT, THERE ARE SOME TRIBULATIONS I PREFER TO FORGET. AND BESIDES--WE HAVE ARRIVED.
ARRIVED.? WHAT'RE YOU--?
AHEAD LIES THE DESERTED METAL WORKS YOU MENTIONED...
EUROPEANS
COLOREDS
...THOUGH, EVEN THERE, IT SEEMS I CANNOT ESCAPE... REMINDERS.
WHAT KIND OF PEOPLE LIVE ON ANOTHER CONTINENT FOR CENTURIES, AND STILL CALL THEMSELVES "EUROPEANS"?
THEY ARE SHACKLED, TORCH, NEARLY AS MUCH AS WE.
WHILE YOU GUYS TALK SEMANTICS, OL' BENJY COULD USE A LEG UP.
I'VE A BETTER IDEA, OLD FRIEND.
COLOREDS
THAT'S MORE LIKE IT. NOT THAT I'D HAVE MINDED BUSTIN' DOWN THIS DOOR, BUT--
HEY! WHERE'D OL' HOT-BREATH FLY OFF TO?
IT'S NEARLY MIDNIGHT.
OFFHAND, I SHOULD GUESS HE IS SEARCHING FOR--
15

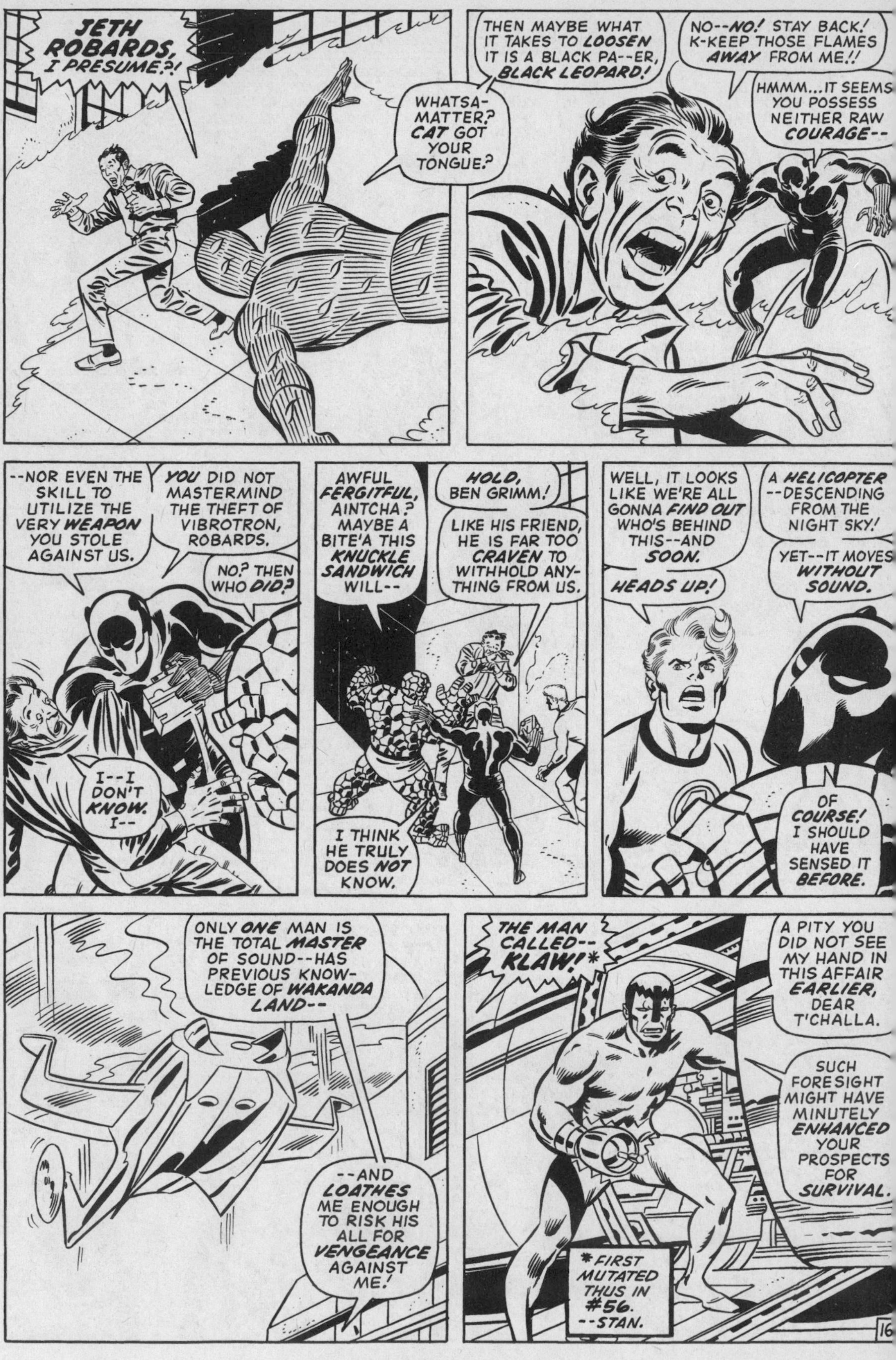
JETH ROBARDS, I PRESUME?!
WHATSA-MATTER? CAT GOT YOUR TONGUE?
THEN MAYBE WHAT IT TAKES TO LOOSEN IT IS A BLACK PA--ER, BLACK LEOPARD!
NO--NO! STAY BACK! K-KEEP THOSE FLAMES AWAY FROM ME!!
HMMM...IT SEEMS YOU POSSESS NEITHER RAW COURAGE--
--NOR EVEN THE SKILL TO UTILIZE THE VERY WEAPON YOU STOLE AGAINST US.
YOU DID NOT MASTERMIND THE THEFT OF VIBROTRON, ROBARDS.
NO? THEN WHO DID?
I--I DON'T KNOW. I--
AWFUL FERGITFUL, AINTCHA? MAYBE A BITE'A THIS KNUCKLE SANDWICH WILL--
HOLD, BEN GRIMM!
LIKE HIS FRIEND, HE IS FAR TOO CRAVEN TO WITHHOLD ANY-THING FROM US.
I THINK HE TRULY DOES NOT KNOW.
WELL, IT LOOKS LIKE WE'RE ALL GONNA FIND OUT WHO'S BEHIND THIS--AND SOON.
HEADS UP!
A HELICOPTER --DESCENDING FROM THE NIGHT SKY!
YET--IT MOVES WITHOUT SOUND.
OF COURSE! I SHOULD HAVE SENSED IT BEFORE.
ONLY ONE MAN IS THE TOTAL MASTER OF SOUND--HAS PREVIOUS KNOW-LEDGE OF WAKANDA LAND--
--AND LOATHES ME ENOUGH TO RISK HIS ALL FOR VENGEANCE AGAINST ME!
THE MAN CALLED--KLAW!*
A PITY YOU DID NOT SEE MY HAND IN THIS AFFAIR EARLIER, DEAR T'CHALLA.
SUCH FORESIGHT MIGHT HAVE MINUTELY ENHANCED YOUR PROSPECTS FOR SURVIVAL.
*FIRST MUTATED THUS IN #56. --STAN.
16

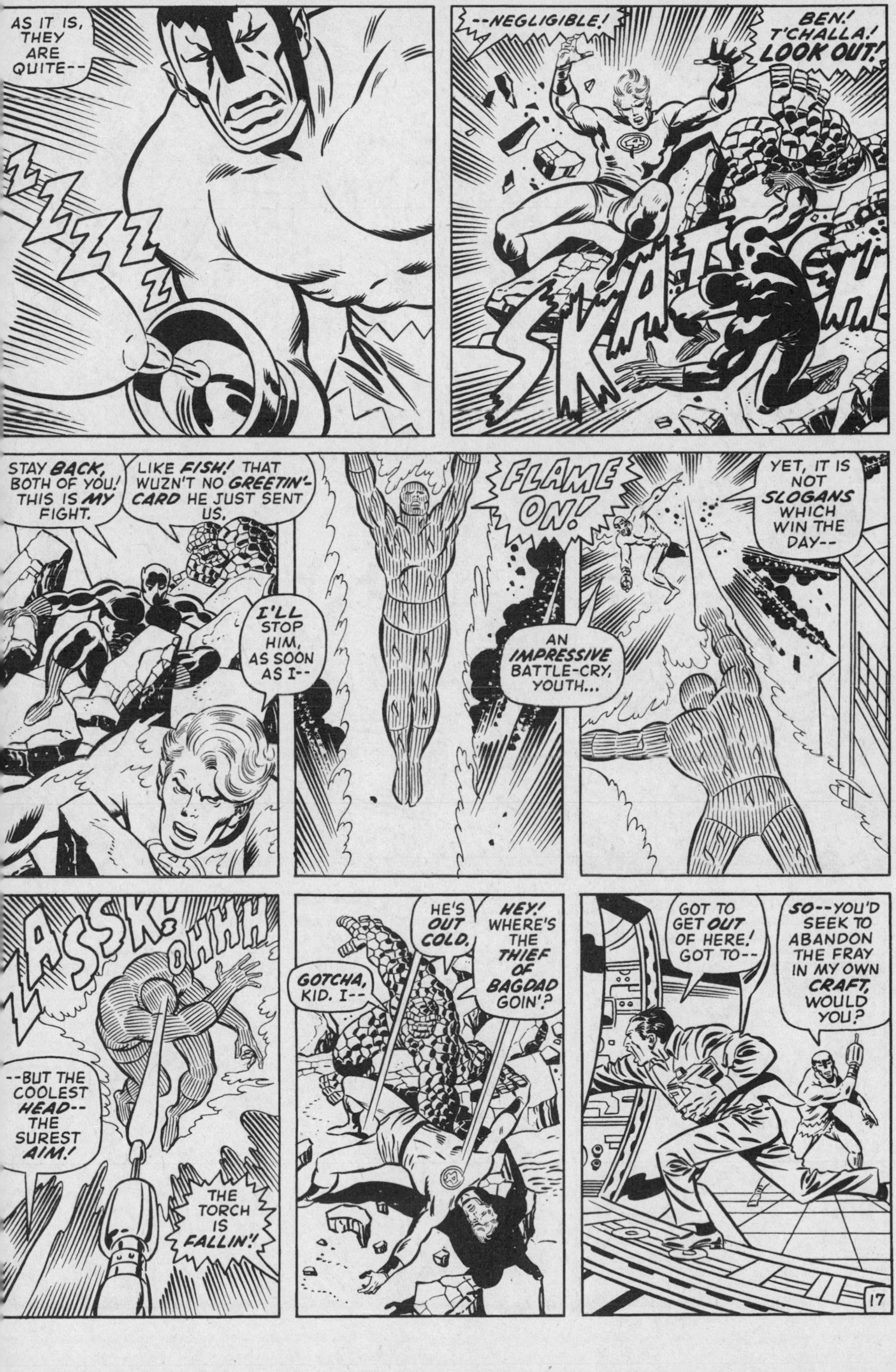

AS IT IS, THEY ARE QUITE--
ZZZZZZ
--NEGLIGIBLE!
BEN! T'CHALLA! LOOK OUT!
SKATCHH
STAY BACK, BOTH OF YOU! THIS IS MY FIGHT.
LIKE FISH! THAT WUZN'T NO GREETIN'-CARD HE JUST SENT US.
I'LL STOP HIM, AS SOON AS I--
FLAME ON!
AN IMPRESSIVE BATTLE-CRY, YOUTH...
YET, IT IS NOT SLOGANS WHICH WIN THE DAY--
ZASSK!
OHHH
--BUT THE COOLEST HEAD-- THE SUREST AIM!
THE TORCH IS FALLIN'!
HE'S OUT COLD.
HEY! WHERE'S THE THIEF OF BAGDAD GOIN'?
GOTCHA, KID. I--
GOT TO GET OUT OF HERE! GOT TO--
SO--YOU'D SEEK TO ABANDON THE FRAY IN MY OWN CRAFT, WOULD YOU?
17

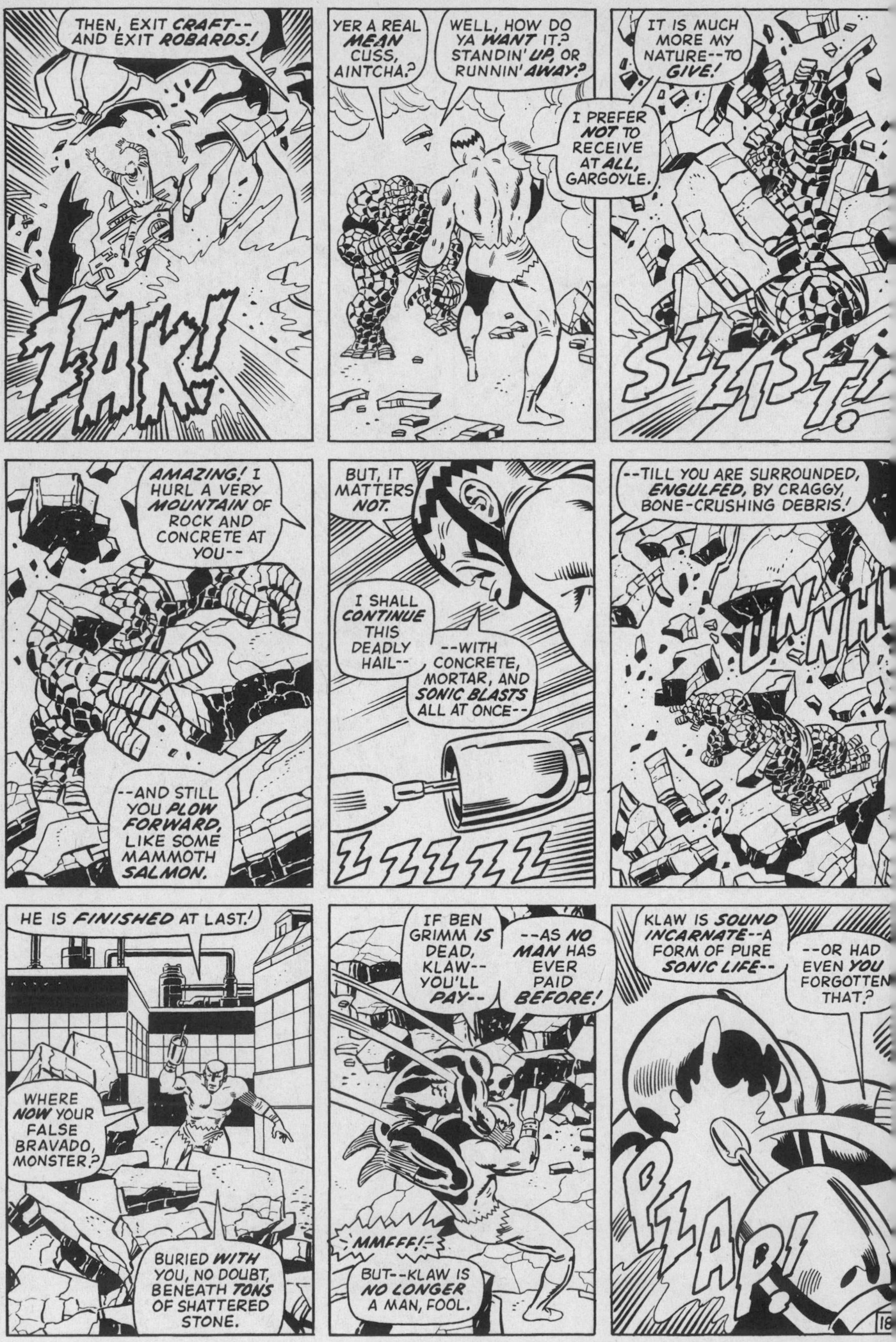
THEN, EXIT CRAFT-- AND EXIT ROBARDS!
ZAK!
YER A REAL MEAN CUSS, AINTCHA?
WELL, HOW DO YA WANT IT? STANDIN' UP, OR RUNNIN' AWAY?
I PREFER NOT TO RECEIVE AT ALL, GARGOYLE.
IT IS MUCH MORE MY NATURE--TO GIVE!
AMAZING! I HURL A VERY MOUNTAIN OF ROCK AND CONCRETE AT YOU--
--AND STILL YOU PLOW FORWARD, LIKE SOME MAMMOTH SALMON.
BUT, IT MATTERS NOT.
I SHALL CONTINUE THIS DEADLY HAIL--
--WITH CONCRETE, MORTAR, AND SONIC BLASTS ALL AT ONCE--
ZZZZZZ
--TILL YOU ARE SURROUNDED, ENGULFED, BY CRAGGY, BONE-CRUSHING DEBRIS.!
HE IS FINISHED AT LAST.!
WHERE NOW YOUR FALSE BRAVADO, MONSTER?
BURIED WITH YOU, NO DOUBT, BENEATH TONS OF SHATTERED STONE.
IF BEN GRIMM IS DEAD, KLAW-- YOU'LL PAY--
--AS NO MAN HAS EVER PAID BEFORE!
MMFFF!
BUT--KLAW IS NO LONGER A MAN, FOOL.
KLAW IS SOUND INCARNATE--A FORM OF PURE SONIC LIFE--
--OR HAD EVEN YOU FORGOTTEN THAT?
PZAP!
18

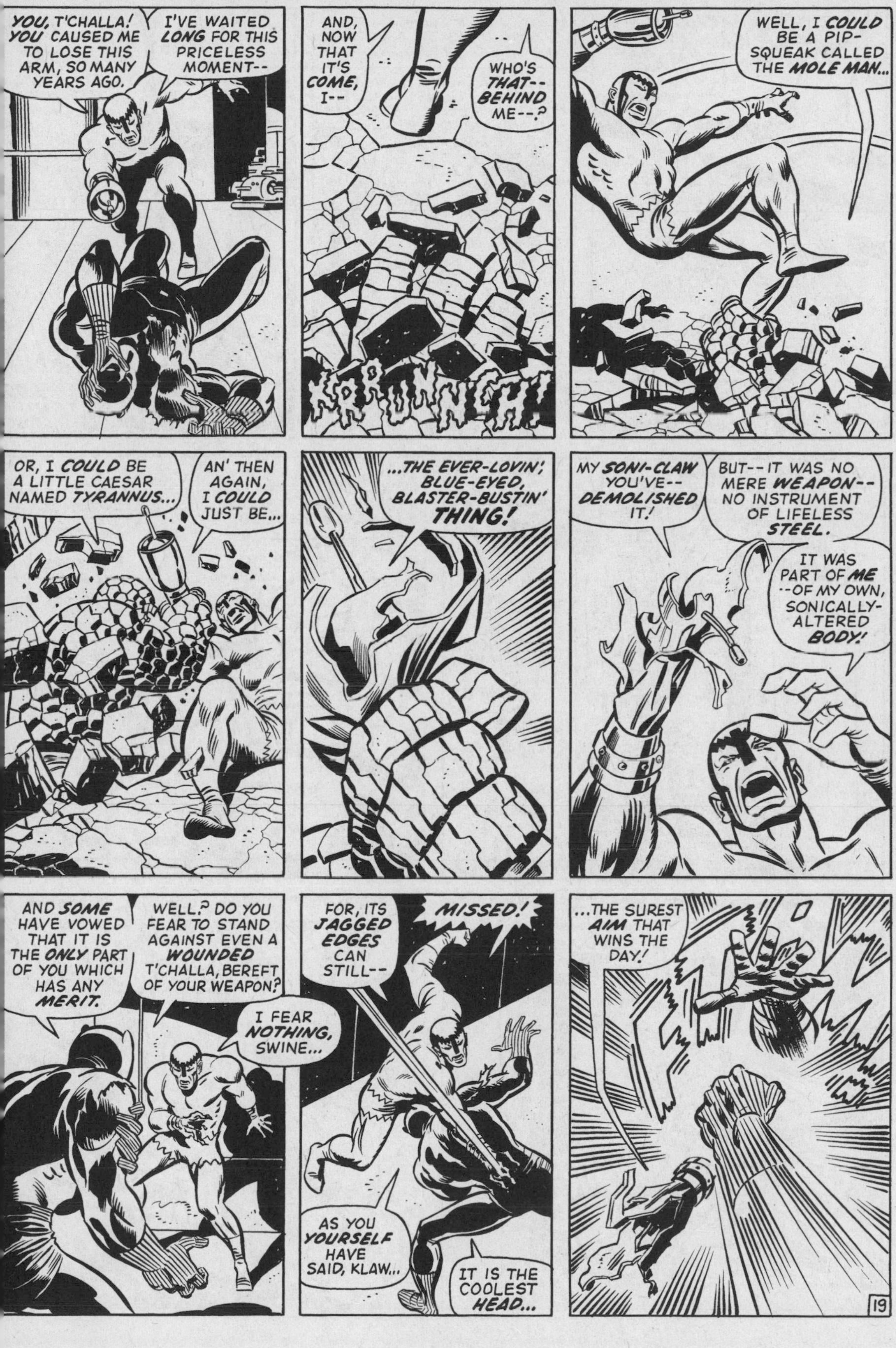
YOU, T'CHALLA! YOU CAUSED ME TO LOSE THIS ARM, SO MANY YEARS AGO.
I'VE WAITED LONG FOR THIS PRICELESS MOMENT--
AND, NOW THAT IT'S COME, I--
WHO'S THAT--BEHIND ME--?
KRRUNNCH!
WELL, I COULD BE A PIP-SQUEAK CALLED THE MOLE MAN...
OR, I COULD BE A LITTLE CAESAR NAMED TYRANNUS...
AN' THEN AGAIN, I COULD JUST BE...
...THE EVER-LOVIN', BLUE-EYED, BLASTER-BUSTIN' THING!
MY SONI-CLAW YOU'VE--DEMOLISHED IT!
BUT--IT WAS NO MERE WEAPON--NO INSTRUMENT OF LIFELESS STEEL.
IT WAS PART OF ME--OF MY OWN, SONICALLY-ALTERED BODY!
AND SOME HAVE VOWED THAT IT IS THE ONLY PART OF YOU WHICH HAS ANY MERIT.
WELL? DO YOU FEAR TO STAND AGAINST EVEN A WOUNDED T'CHALLA, BEREFT OF YOUR WEAPON?
I FEAR NOTHING, SWINE...
FOR, ITS JAGGED EDGES CAN STILL--
MISSED!
AS YOU YOURSELF HAVE SAID, KLAW...
IT IS THE COOLEST HEAD...
...THE SUREST AIM THAT WINS THE DAY!
19

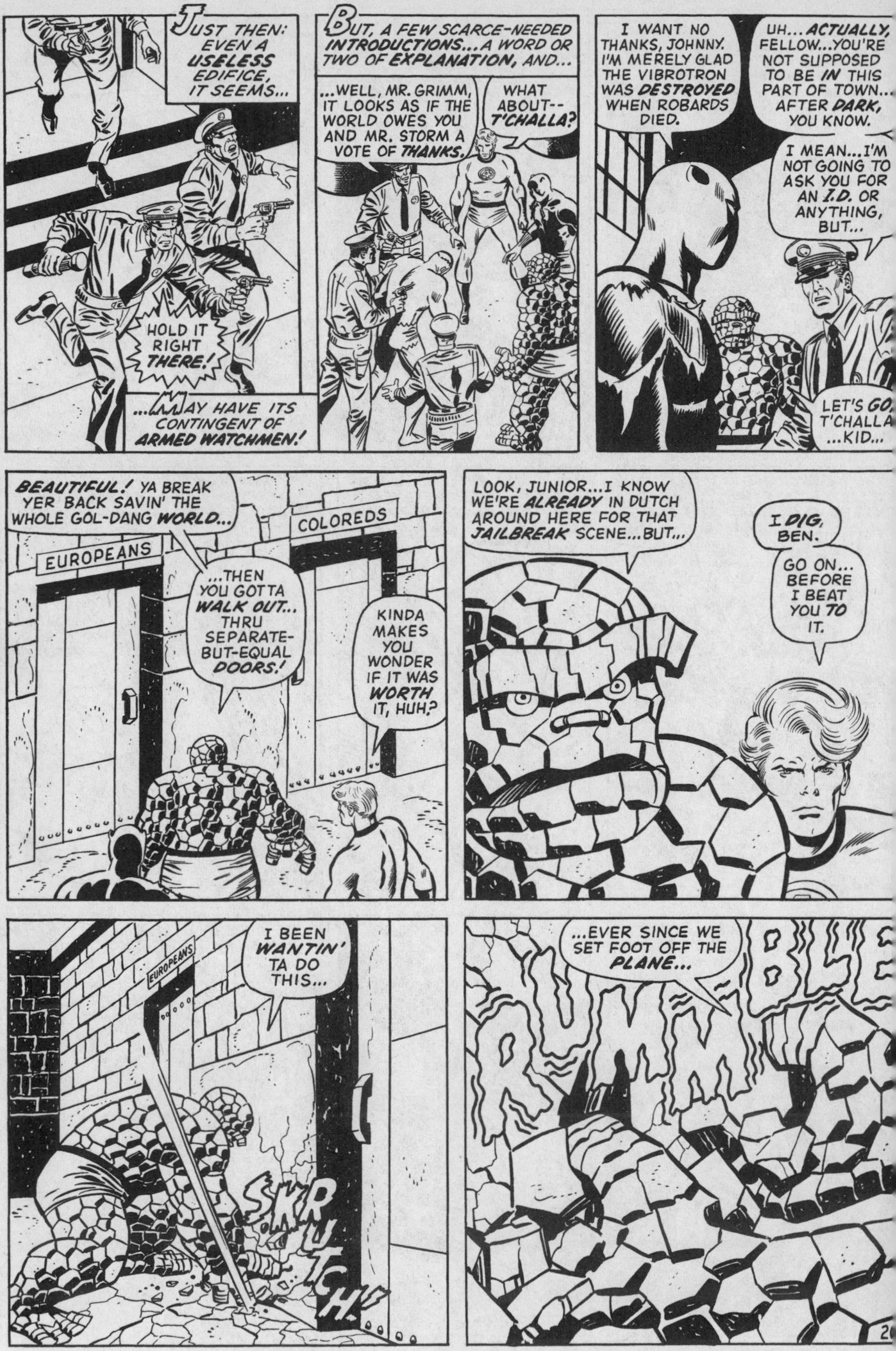

JUST THEN: EVEN A USELESS EDIFICE, IT SEEMS...
HOLD IT RIGHT THERE!
...MAY HAVE ITS CONTINGENT OF ARMED WATCHMEN!
BUT, A FEW SCARCE-NEEDED INTRODUCTIONS... A WORD OR TWO OF EXPLANATION, AND...
...WELL, MR. GRIMM, IT LOOKS AS IF THE WORLD OWES YOU AND MR. STORM A VOTE OF THANKS.
WHAT ABOUT-- T'CHALLA?
I WANT NO THANKS, JOHNNY. I'M MERELY GLAD THE VIBROTRON WAS DESTROYED WHEN ROBARDS DIED.
UH... ACTUALLY, FELLOW... YOU'RE NOT SUPPOSED TO BE IN THIS PART OF TOWN... AFTER DARK, YOU KNOW.
I MEAN... I'M NOT GOING TO ASK YOU FOR AN I.D. OR ANYTHING, BUT...
LET'S GO, T'CHALLA ...KID...
BEAUTIFUL! YA BREAK YER BACK SAVIN' THE WHOLE GOL-DANG WORLD...
EUROPEANS
COLOREDS
...THEN YOU GOTTA WALK OUT... THRU SEPARATE-BUT-EQUAL DOORS!
KINDA MAKES YOU WONDER IF IT WAS WORTH IT, HUH?
LOOK, JUNIOR... I KNOW WE'RE ALREADY IN DUTCH AROUND HERE FOR THAT JAILBREAK SCENE... BUT...
I DIG, BEN.
GO ON... BEFORE I BEAT YOU TO IT.
I BEEN WANTIN' TA DO THIS...
EUROPEANS
SKRUTCH!
...EVER SINCE WE SET FOOT OFF THE PLANE...

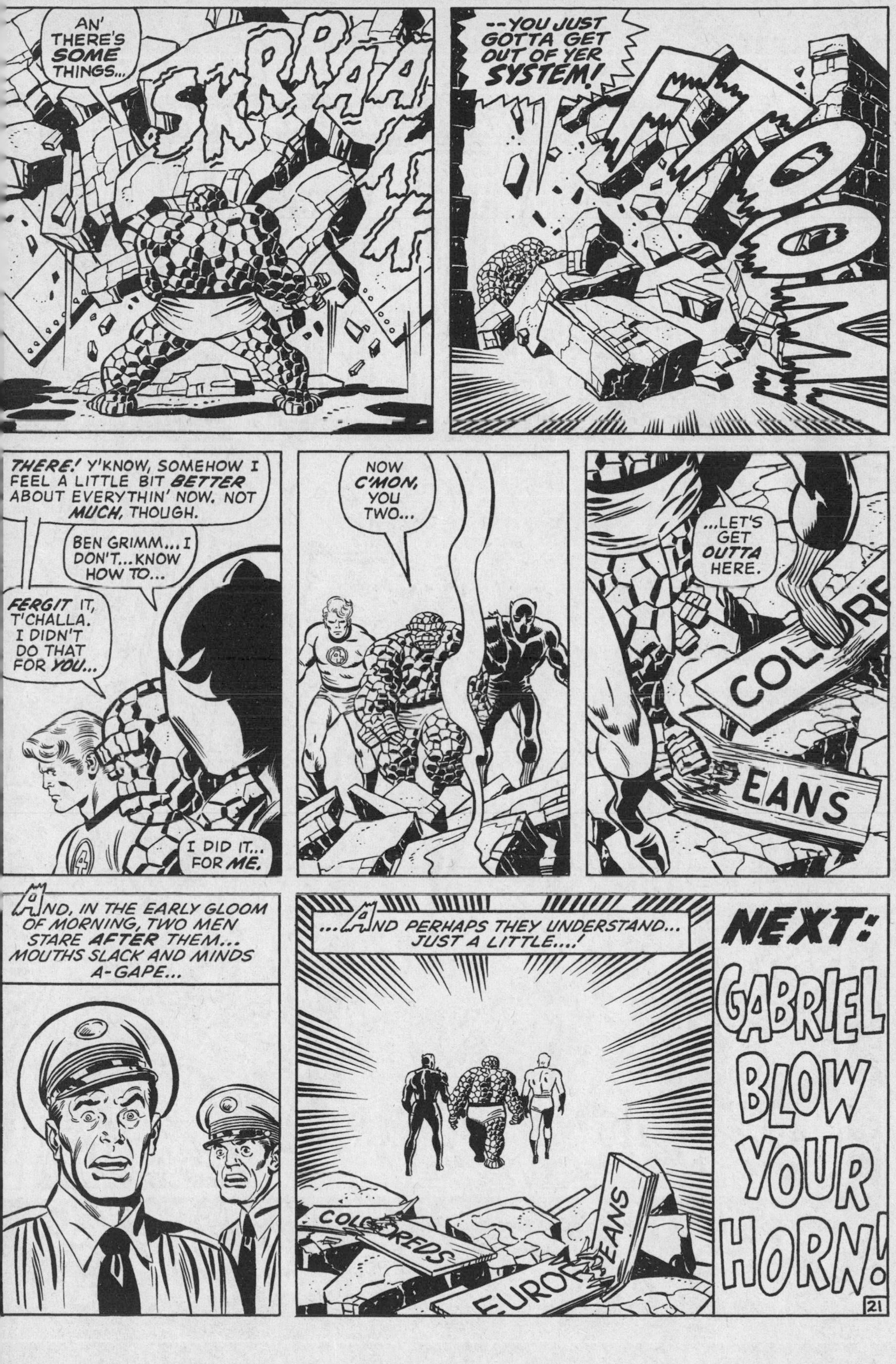
AN' THERE'S SOME THINGS...
SKRRAAAK
--YOU JUST GOTTA GET OUT OF YER SYSTEM!
FTOOOM
THERE! Y'KNOW, SOMEHOW I FEEL A LITTLE BIT BETTER ABOUT EVERYTHIN' NOW. NOT MUCH, THOUGH.
BEN GRIMM...I DON'T...KNOW HOW TO...
FERGIT IT, T'CHALLA. I DIDN'T DO THAT FOR YOU...
I DID IT... FOR ME.
NOW C'MON, YOU TWO...
...LET'S GET OUTTA HERE.
COLORE
EANS
AND, IN THE EARLY GLOOM OF MORNING, TWO MEN STARE AFTER THEM... MOUTHS SLACK AND MINDS A-GAPE...
...AND PERHAPS THEY UNDERSTAND... JUST A LITTLE....!
COLOREDS
EUROPEANS
NEXT:
GABRIEL BLOW YOUR HORN!
21

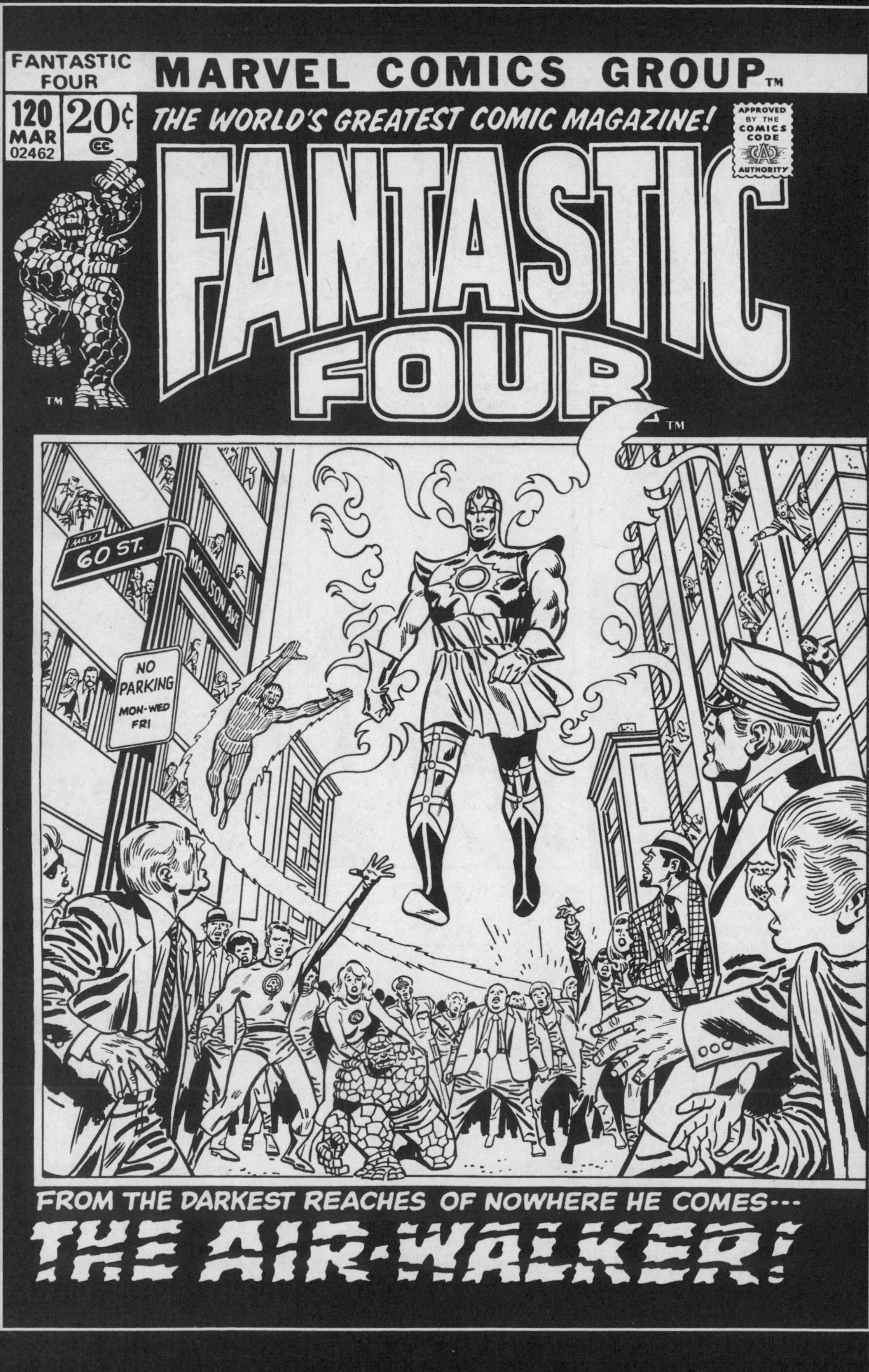

FANTASTIC FOUR
MARVEL COMICS GROUP™
120 MAR 02462
20¢
THE WORLD'S GREATEST COMIC MAGAZINE!
APPROVED BY THE COMICS CODE AUTHORITY
FANTASTIC FOUR™
60 ST.
MADISON AVE
NO PARKING MON-WED FRI
FROM THE DARKEST REACHES OF NOWHERE HE COMES---
THE AIR-WALKER!

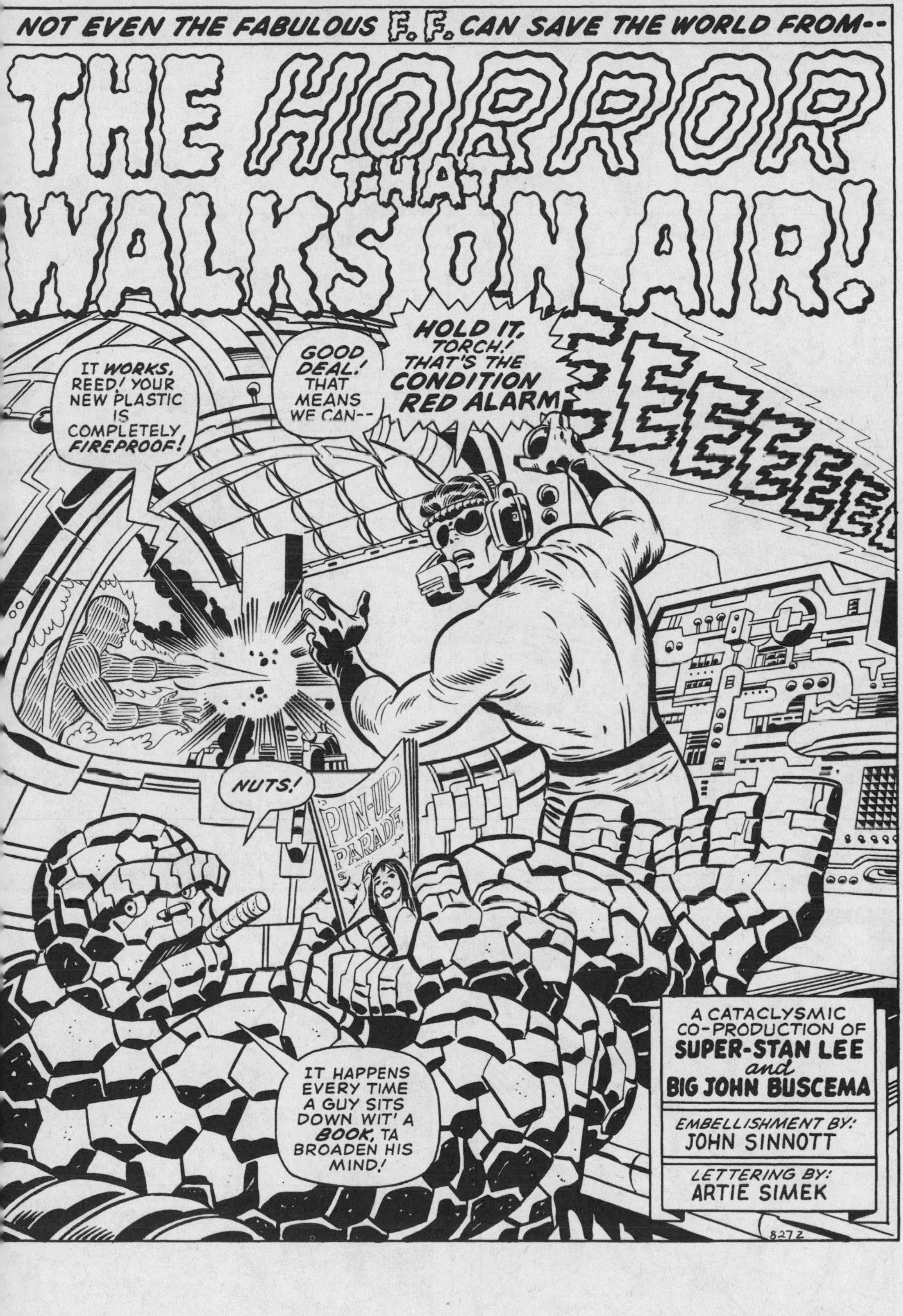
NOT EVEN THE FABULOUS F.F. CAN SAVE THE WORLD FROM--
THE HORROR THAT WALKS ON AIR!
IT WORKS, REED! YOUR NEW PLASTIC IS COMPLETELY FIREPROOF!
GOOD DEAL! THAT MEANS WE CAN--
HOLD IT, TORCH! THAT'S THE CONDITION RED ALARM!
EEEEEEE
NUTS!
PIN-UP PARADE
IT HAPPENS EVERY TIME A GUY SITS DOWN WIT' A BOOK, TA BROADEN HIS MIND!
A CATACLYSMIC CO-PRODUCTION OF SUPER-STAN LEE and BIG JOHN BUSCEMA
EMBELLISHMENT BY: JOHN SINNOTT
LETTERING BY: ARTIE SIMEK
8272

EEEE EEE EEEEEEE EEEE

COME ON! MOVE IT!

THAT ALARM MEANS DANGER!

WE'RE RIGHT WITH YOU, MISTER!

REED! WHAT IS IT? WHAT'S WRONG?

IS THAT THE CONDITION RED I HEAR?

YOU KNOW IT, SUE! IT MEANS THE BAXTER BUILDING'S UNDER ATTACK!

BUT--WHO WOULD DARE--WITH THE FANTASTIC FOUR UP HERE?

LOOK! OUT THE WINDOW! THAT MUST BE THE ANSWER!

STAY BACK! FIRST ONE TO MAKE A MOVE GETS IT!

SO THE F.F. HAS A PRIVATE ELEVATOR, HUH?

A FAT LOTTA GOOD THAT'S GONNA DO 'EM!

LET'S GO! IT'LL ALL BE OVER BEFORE THEY KNOW WHAT HIT 'EM!

CLICK

PH- O

29

28 O

26 O

HEY! THEY BLASTED THEIR WAY INTA THE ELEVATOR!

BRACE YOURSELVES! HERE THEY COME!

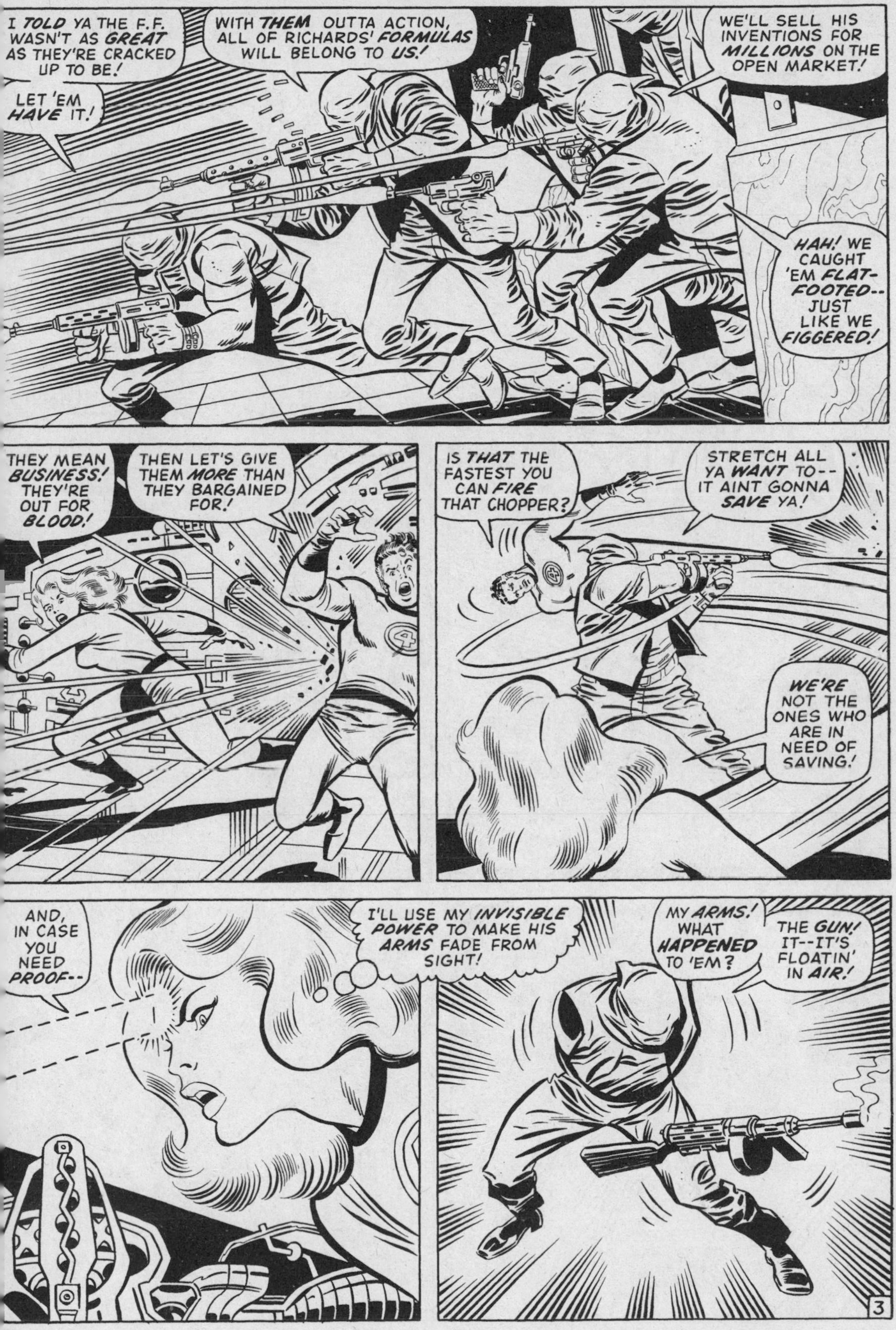

I TOLD YA THE F.F. WASN'T AS GREAT AS THEY'RE CRACKED UP TO BE!
LET 'EM HAVE IT!
WITH THEM OUTTA ACTION, ALL OF RICHARDS' FORMULAS WILL BELONG TO US!
WE'LL SELL HIS INVENTIONS FOR MILLIONS ON THE OPEN MARKET!
HAH! WE CAUGHT 'EM FLAT-FOOTED--JUST LIKE WE FIGGERED!
THEY MEAN BUSINESS! THEY'RE OUT FOR BLOOD!
THEN LET'S GIVE THEM MORE THAN THEY BARGAINED FOR!
IS THAT THE FASTEST YOU CAN FIRE THAT CHOPPER?
STRETCH ALL YA WANT TO--IT AINT GONNA SAVE YA!
WE'RE NOT THE ONES WHO ARE IN NEED OF SAVING!
AND, IN CASE YOU NEED PROOF--
I'LL USE MY INVISIBLE POWER TO MAKE HIS ARMS FADE FROM SIGHT!
MY ARMS! WHAT HAPPENED TO 'EM?
THE GUN! IT--IT'S FLOATIN' IN AIR!
3

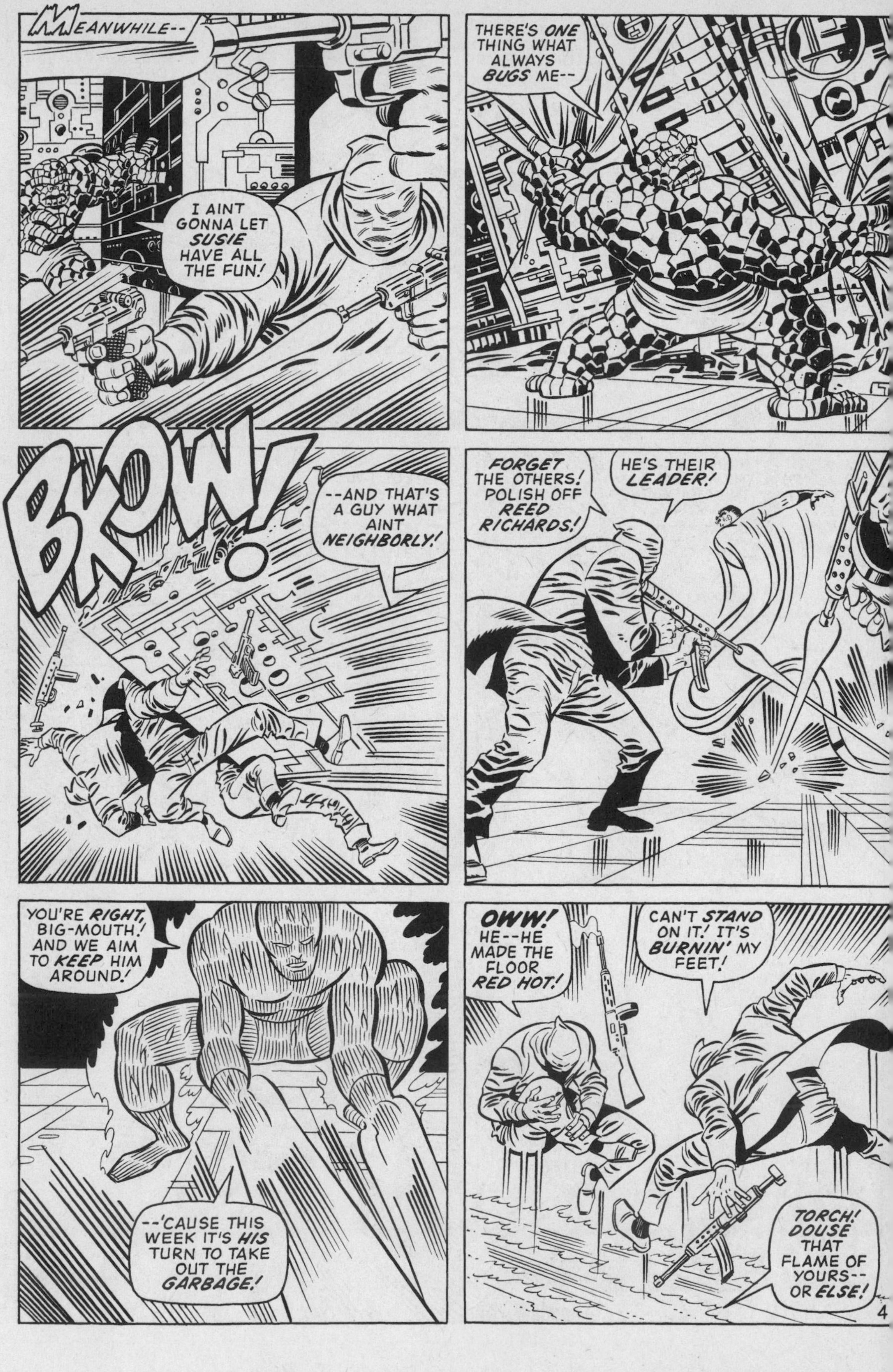
MEANWHILE--
I AINT GONNA LET SUSIE HAVE ALL THE FUN!
THERE'S ONE THING WHAT ALWAYS BUGS ME--
BKOW!
--AND THAT'S A GUY WHAT AINT NEIGHBORLY!
FORGET THE OTHERS! POLISH OFF REED RICHARDS!
HE'S THEIR LEADER!
YOU'RE RIGHT, BIG-MOUTH! AND WE AIM TO KEEP HIM AROUND!
--'CAUSE THIS WEEK IT'S HIS TURN TO TAKE OUT THE GARBAGE!
OWW! HE--HE MADE THE FLOOR RED HOT!
CAN'T STAND ON IT! IT'S BURNIN' MY FEET!
TORCH! DOUSE THAT FLAME OF YOURS-- OR ELSE!
4

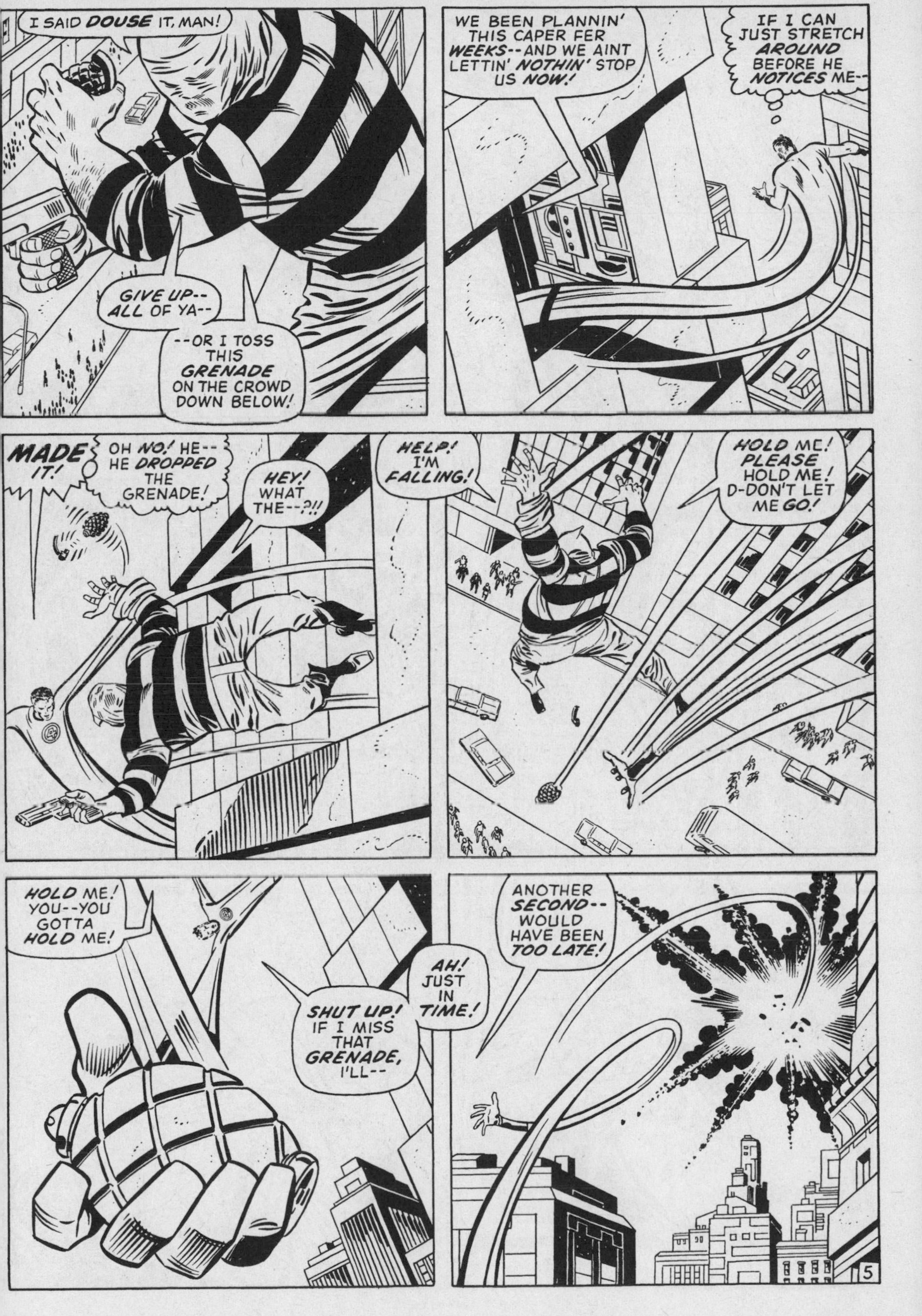
I SAID DOUSE IT, MAN!
GIVE UP-- ALL OF YA--
--OR I TOSS THIS GRENADE ON THE CROWD DOWN BELOW!
WE BEEN PLANNIN' THIS CAPER FER WEEKS--AND WE AINT LETTIN' NOTHIN' STOP US NOW!
IF I CAN JUST STRETCH AROUND BEFORE HE NOTICES ME--
MADE IT!
OH NO! HE-- HE DROPPED THE GRENADE!
HEY! WHAT THE--?!!
HELP! I'M FALLING!
HOLD ME! PLEASE HOLD ME! D-DON'T LET ME GO!
HOLD ME! YOU--YOU GOTTA HOLD ME!
SHUT UP! IF I MISS THAT GRENADE, I'LL--
AH! JUST IN TIME!
ANOTHER SECOND-- WOULD HAVE BEEN TOO LATE!
5

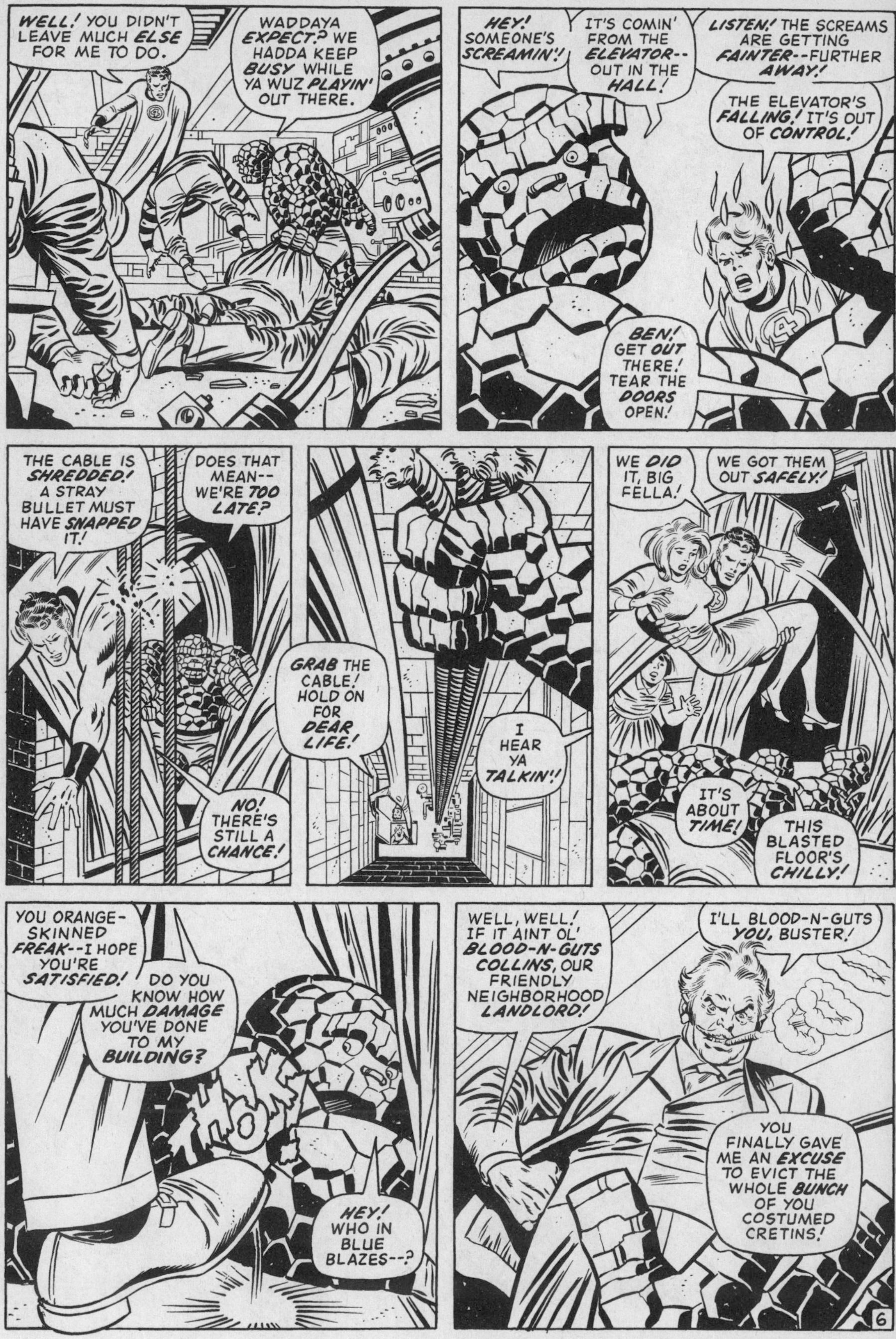
WELL! YOU DIDN'T LEAVE MUCH ELSE FOR ME TO DO.
WADDAYA EXPECT? WE HADDA KEEP BUSY WHILE YA WUZ PLAYIN' OUT THERE.
HEY! SOMEONE'S SCREAMIN'!
IT'S COMIN' FROM THE ELEVATOR-- OUT IN THE HALL!
LISTEN! THE SCREAMS ARE GETTING FAINTER--FURTHER AWAY!
THE ELEVATOR'S FALLING! IT'S OUT OF CONTROL!
BEN! GET OUT THERE! TEAR THE DOORS OPEN!
THE CABLE IS SHREDDED! A STRAY BULLET MUST HAVE SNAPPED IT!
DOES THAT MEAN-- WE'RE TOO LATE?
NO! THERE'S STILL A CHANCE!
GRAB THE CABLE! HOLD ON FOR DEAR LIFE!
I HEAR YA TALKIN'!
WE DID IT, BIG FELLA!
WE GOT THEM OUT SAFELY!
IT'S ABOUT TIME!
THIS BLASTED FLOOR'S CHILLY!
YOU ORANGE-SKINNED FREAK--I HOPE YOU'RE SATISFIED!
DO YOU KNOW HOW MUCH DAMAGE YOU'VE DONE TO MY BUILDING?
THOK
HEY! WHO IN BLUE BLAZES--?
WELL, WELL! IF IT AINT OL' BLOOD-N-GUTS COLLINS, OUR FRIENDLY NEIGHBORHOOD LANDLORD!
I'LL BLOOD-N-GUTS YOU, BUSTER!
YOU FINALLY GAVE ME AN EXCUSE TO EVICT THE WHOLE BUNCH OF YOU COSTUMED CRETINS!
6

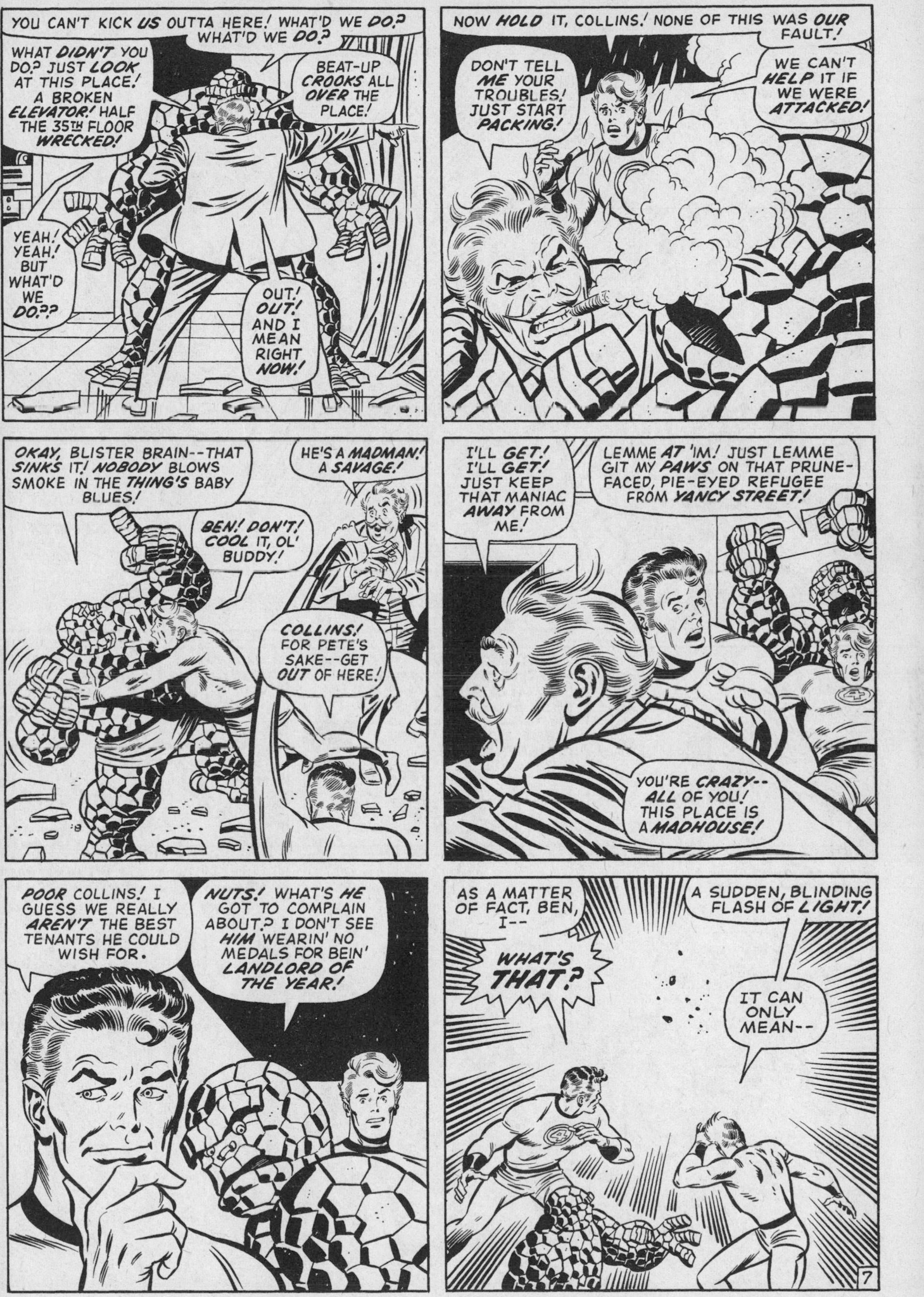

YOU CAN'T KICK **US** OUTTA HERE! WHAT'D WE **DO?** WHAT'D WE **DO?**
WHAT **DIDN'T** YOU DO? JUST **LOOK** AT THIS PLACE! A BROKEN **ELEVATOR!** HALF THE 35TH FLOOR **WRECKED!**
BEAT-UP **CROOKS** ALL **OVER** THE PLACE!
YEAH! YEAH! BUT WHAT'D WE **DO??**
OUT! **OUT!** AND I MEAN RIGHT **NOW!**
NOW **HOLD** IT, COLLINS! NONE OF THIS WAS **OUR** FAULT!
DON'T TELL **ME** YOUR TROUBLES! JUST START **PACKING!**
WE CAN'T **HELP** IT IF WE WERE **ATTACKED!**
OKAY, BLISTER BRAIN--THAT **SINKS** IT! **NOBODY** BLOWS SMOKE IN THE **THING'S** BABY BLUES!
HE'S A **MADMAN!** A **SAVAGE!**
BEN! DON'T! COOL IT, OL' BUDDY!
COLLINS! FOR PETE'S SAKE--GET **OUT** OF HERE!
I'LL **GET!** I'LL **GET!** JUST KEEP THAT MANIAC **AWAY** FROM ME!
LEMME **AT** 'IM! JUST LEMME GIT MY **PAWS** ON THAT PRUNE-FACED, PIE-EYED REFUGEE FROM **YANCY STREET!**
YOU'RE **CRAZY--** **ALL** OF YOU! THIS PLACE IS A **MADHOUSE!**
POOR COLLINS! I GUESS WE REALLY **AREN'T** THE BEST TENANTS HE COULD WISH FOR.
NUTS! WHAT'S **HE** GOT TO COMPLAIN ABOUT? I DON'T SEE **HIM** WEARIN' NO MEDALS FOR BEIN' **LANDLORD OF THE YEAR!**
AS A MATTER OF FACT, BEN, I--
WHAT'S THAT?
A SUDDEN, BLINDING FLASH OF **LIGHT!**
IT CAN ONLY MEAN--

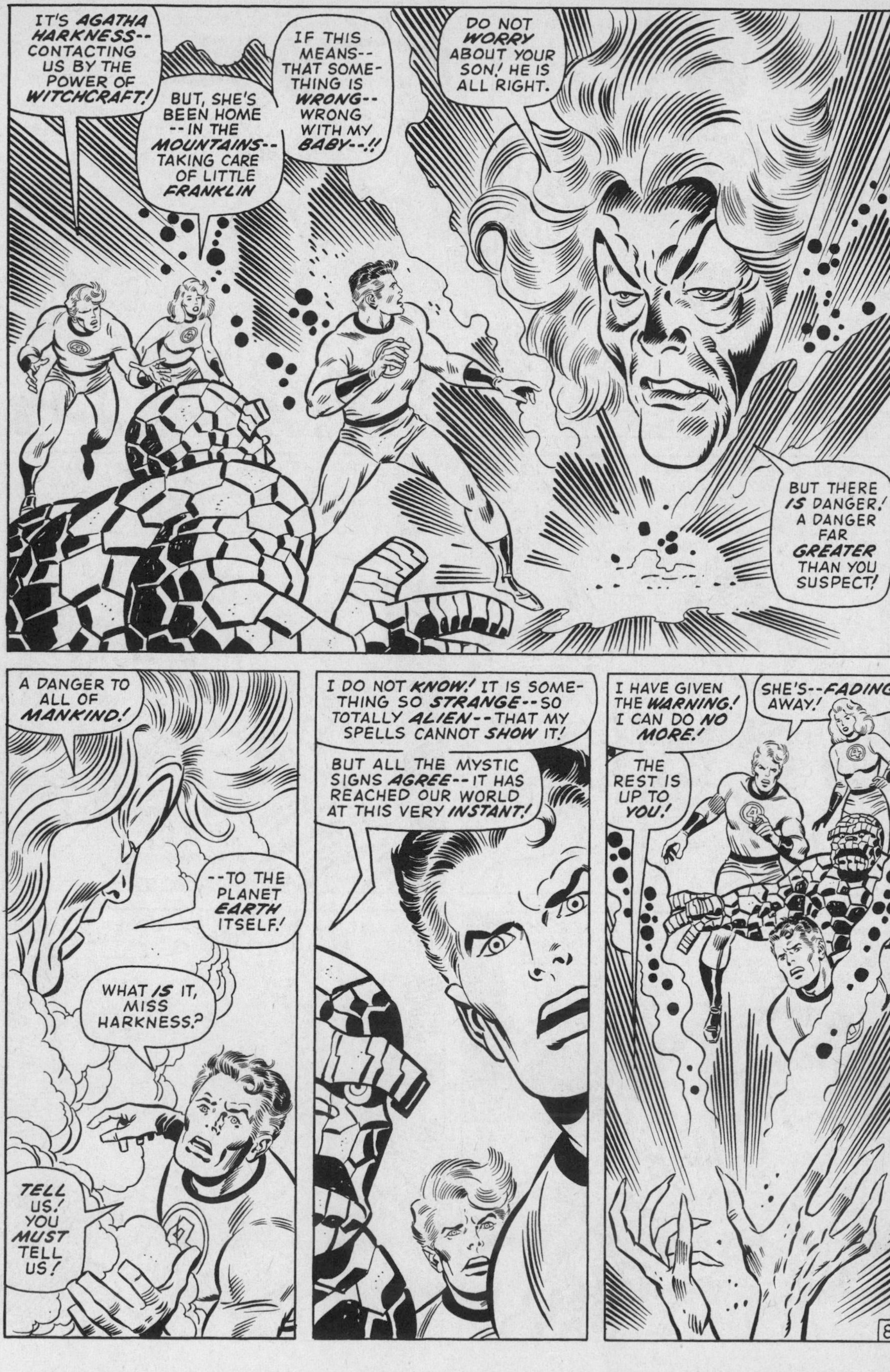
IT'S AGATHA HARKNESS--CONTACTING US BY THE POWER OF WITCHCRAFT!
BUT, SHE'S BEEN HOME --IN THE MOUNTAINS--TAKING CARE OF LITTLE FRANKLIN
IF THIS MEANS--THAT SOMETHING IS WRONG--WRONG WITH MY BABY--!!
DO NOT WORRY ABOUT YOUR SON! HE IS ALL RIGHT.
BUT THERE IS DANGER! A DANGER FAR GREATER THAN YOU SUSPECT!
A DANGER TO ALL OF MANKIND!
--TO THE PLANET EARTH ITSELF!
WHAT IS IT, MISS HARKNESS?
TELL US! YOU MUST TELL US!
I DO NOT KNOW! IT IS SOMETHING SO STRANGE--SO TOTALLY ALIEN--THAT MY SPELLS CANNOT SHOW IT!
BUT ALL THE MYSTIC SIGNS AGREE--IT HAS REACHED OUR WORLD AT THIS VERY INSTANT!
I HAVE GIVEN THE WARNING! I CAN DO NO MORE!
THE REST IS UP TO YOU!
SHE'S--FADING AWAY!
8

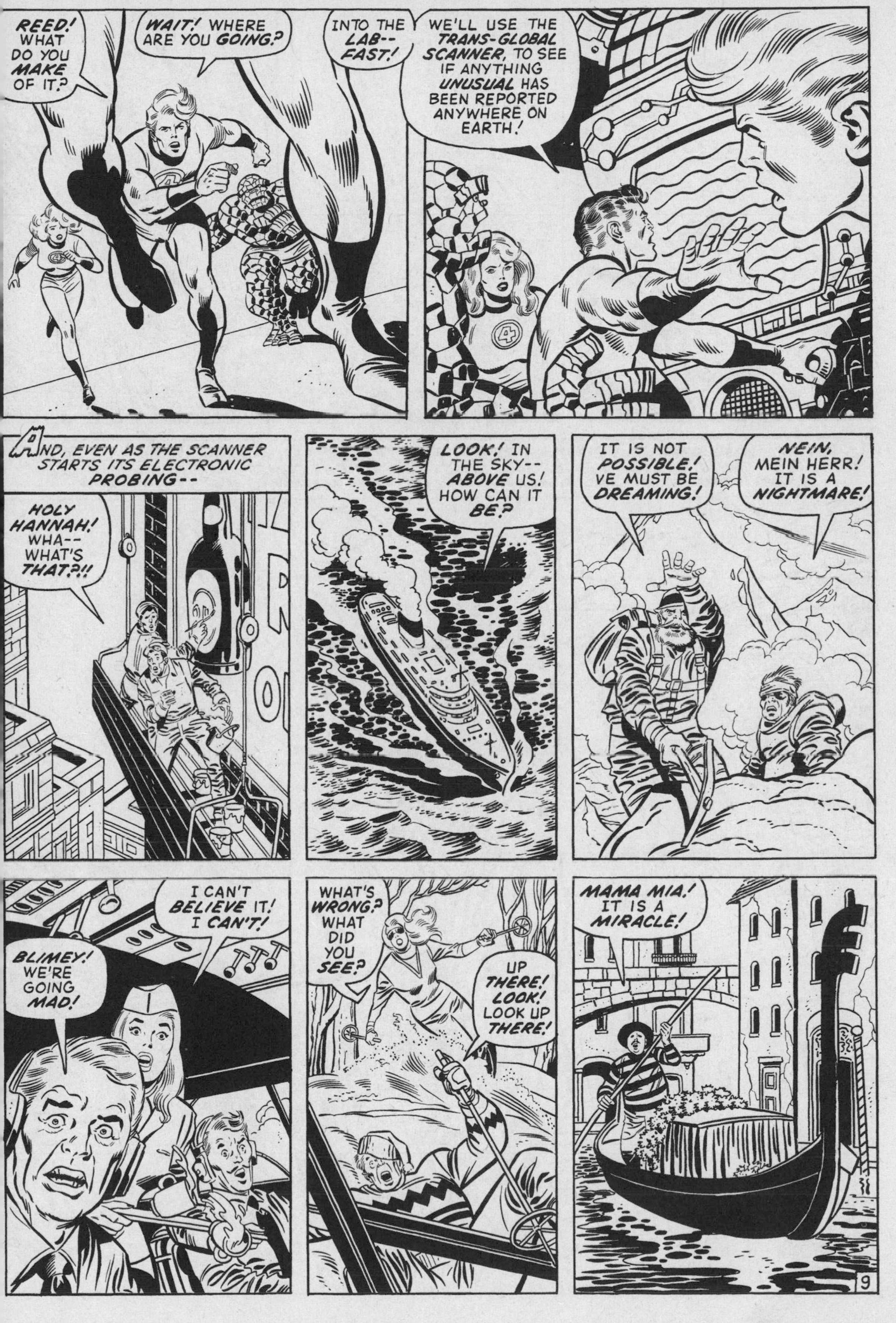
REED! WHAT DO YOU MAKE OF IT?
WAIT! WHERE ARE YOU GOING?
INTO THE LAB-- FAST!
WE'LL USE THE TRANS-GLOBAL SCANNER, TO SEE IF ANYTHING UNUSUAL HAS BEEN REPORTED ANYWHERE ON EARTH!
AND, EVEN AS THE SCANNER STARTS ITS ELECTRONIC PROBING--
HOLY HANNAH! WHA-- WHAT'S THAT?!!
LOOK! IN THE SKY-- ABOVE US! HOW CAN IT BE?
IT IS NOT POSSIBLE! VE MUST BE DREAMING!
NEIN, MEIN HERR! IT IS A NIGHTMARE!
I CAN'T BELIEVE IT! I CAN'T!
BLIMEY! WE'RE GOING MAD!
WHAT'S WRONG? WHAT DID YOU SEE?
UP THERE! LOOK! LOOK UP THERE!
MAMA MIA! IT IS A MIRACLE!
9

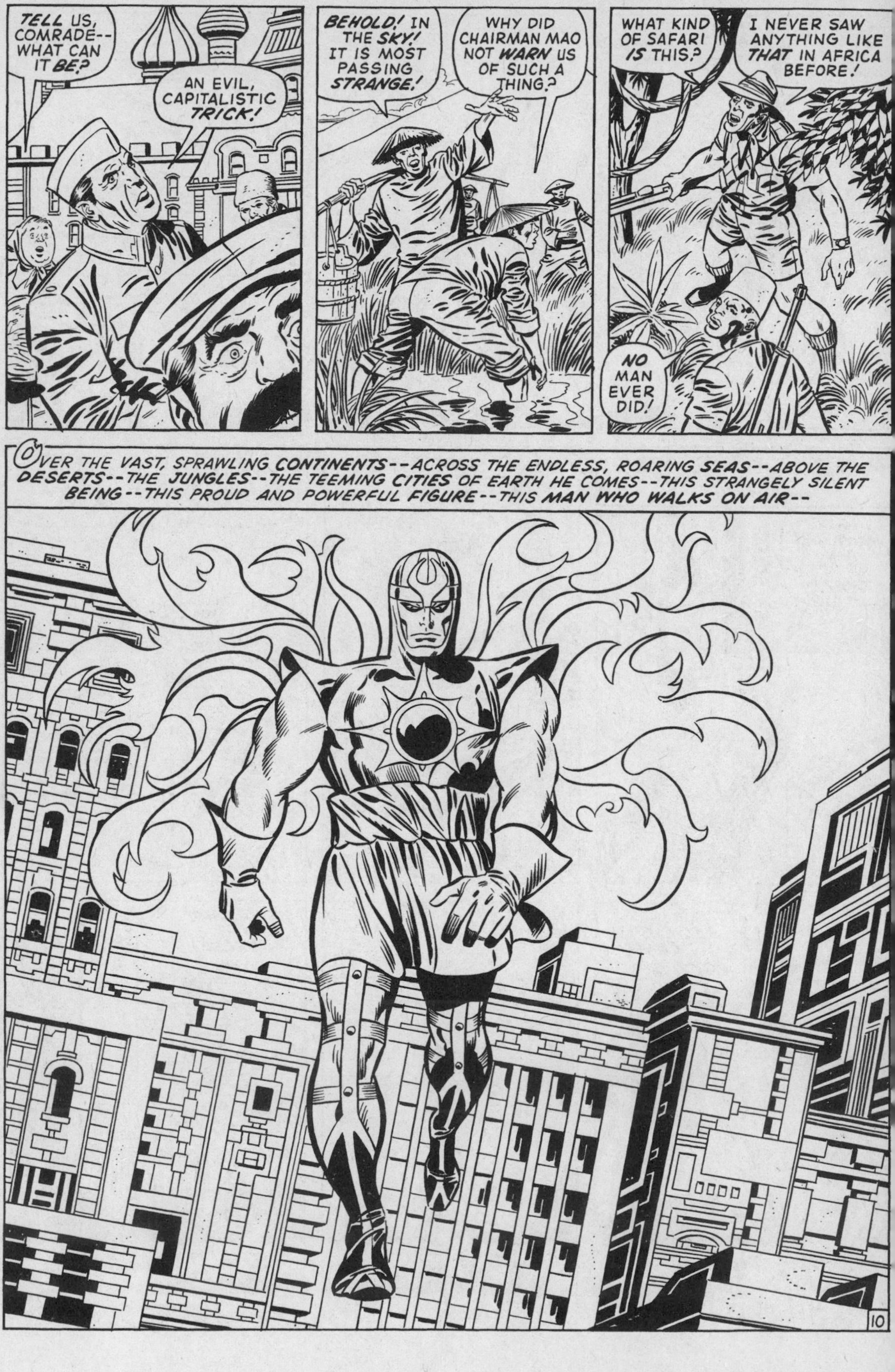
TELL US, COMRADE-- WHAT CAN IT BE?
AN EVIL, CAPITALISTIC TRICK!
BEHOLD! IN THE SKY! IT IS MOST PASSING STRANGE!
WHY DID CHAIRMAN MAO NOT WARN US OF SUCH A THING?
WHAT KIND OF SAFARI IS THIS?
I NEVER SAW ANYTHING LIKE THAT IN AFRICA BEFORE!
NO MAN EVER DID!
OVER THE VAST, SPRAWLING CONTINENTS--ACROSS THE ENDLESS, ROARING SEAS--ABOVE THE DESERTS--THE JUNGLES--THE TEEMING CITIES OF EARTH HE COMES--THIS STRANGELY SILENT BEING--THIS PROUD AND POWERFUL FIGURE--THIS MAN WHO WALKS ON AIR--
10

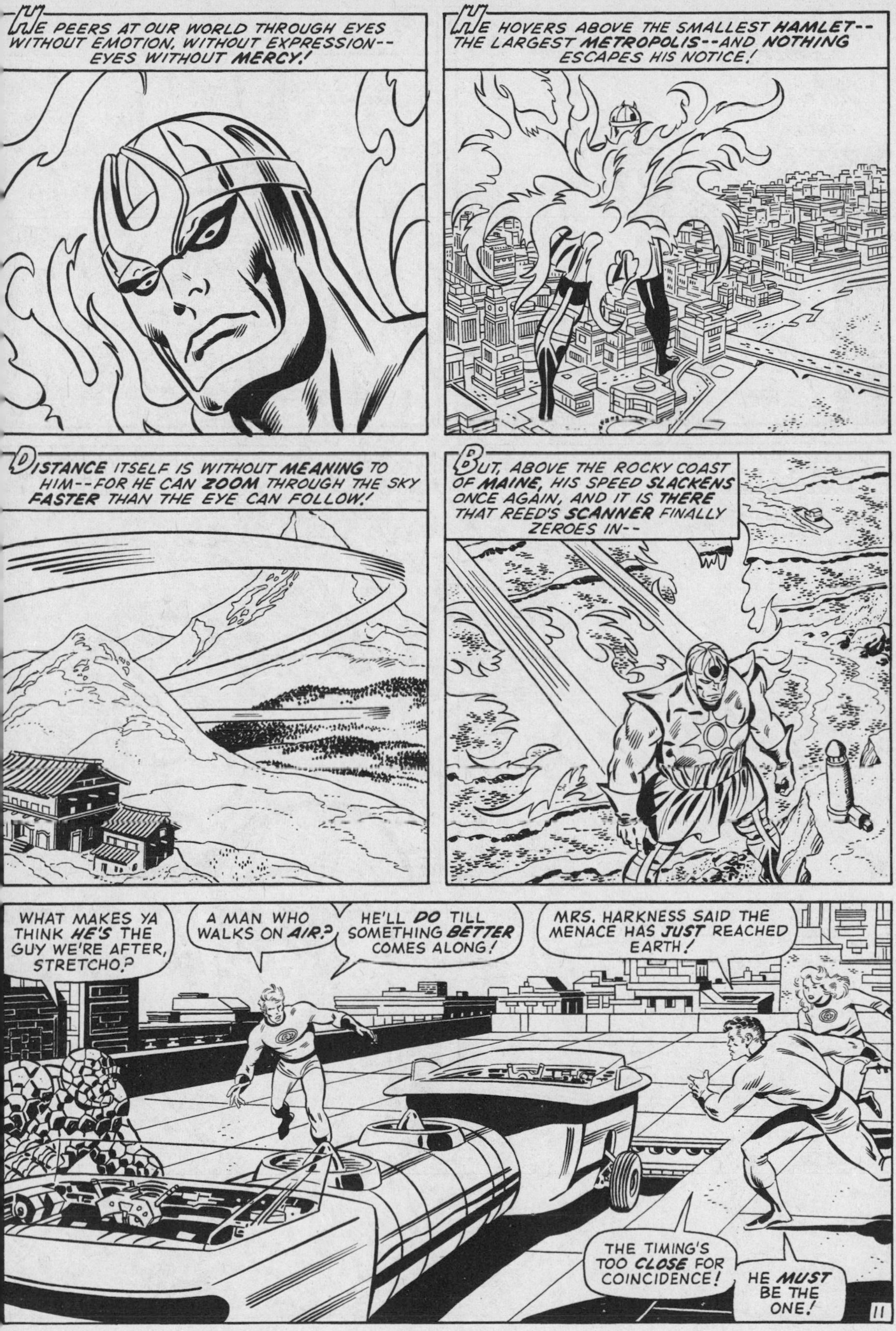
HE PEERS AT OUR WORLD THROUGH EYES WITHOUT EMOTION, WITHOUT EXPRESSION-- EYES WITHOUT MERCY!
HE HOVERS ABOVE THE SMALLEST HAMLET-- THE LARGEST METROPOLIS--AND NOTHING ESCAPES HIS NOTICE!
DISTANCE ITSELF IS WITHOUT MEANING TO HIM--FOR HE CAN ZOOM THROUGH THE SKY FASTER THAN THE EYE CAN FOLLOW!
BUT, ABOVE THE ROCKY COAST OF MAINE, HIS SPEED SLACKENS ONCE AGAIN, AND IT IS THERE THAT REED'S SCANNER FINALLY ZEROES IN--
WHAT MAKES YA THINK HE'S THE GUY WE'RE AFTER, STRETCHO?
A MAN WHO WALKS ON AIR?
HE'LL DO TILL SOMETHING BETTER COMES ALONG!
MRS. HARKNESS SAID THE MENACE HAS JUST REACHED EARTH!
THE TIMING'S TOO CLOSE FOR COINCIDENCE!
HE MUST BE THE ONE!
11

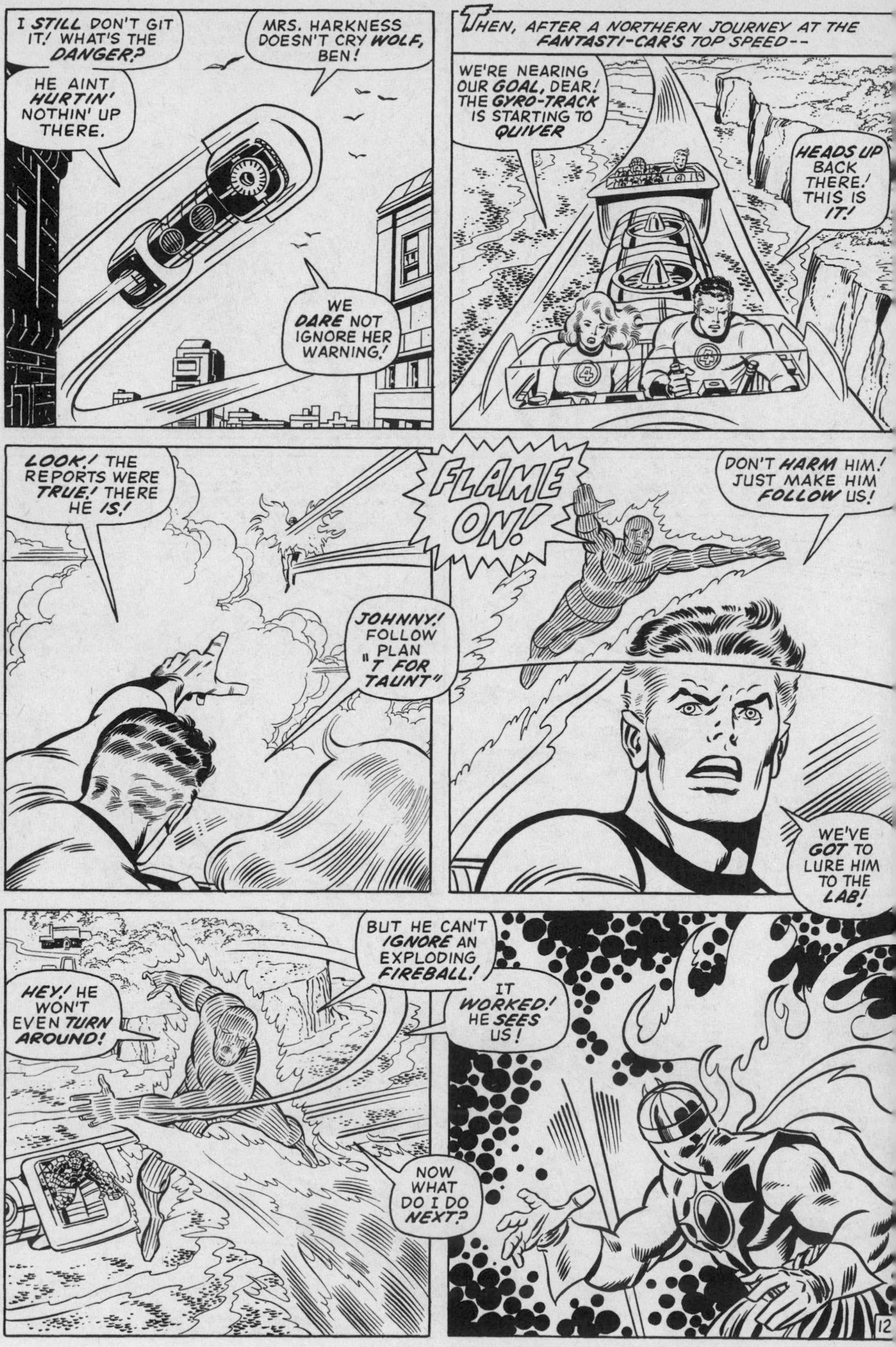

I STILL DON'T GIT IT! WHAT'S THE DANGER?
HE AINT HURTIN' NOTHIN' UP THERE.
MRS. HARKNESS DOESN'T CRY WOLF, BEN!
WE DARE NOT IGNORE HER WARNING!
THEN, AFTER A NORTHERN JOURNEY AT THE FANTASTI-CAR'S TOP SPEED--
WE'RE NEARING OUR GOAL, DEAR! THE GYRO-TRACK IS STARTING TO QUIVER
HEADS UP BACK THERE! THIS IS IT!
LOOK! THE REPORTS WERE TRUE! THERE HE IS!
JOHNNY! FOLLOW PLAN "T FOR TAUNT"
FLAME ON!
DON'T HARM HIM! JUST MAKE HIM FOLLOW US!
WE'VE GOT TO LURE HIM TO THE LAB!
HEY! HE WON'T EVEN TURN AROUND!
BUT HE CAN'T IGNORE AN EXPLODING FIREBALL!
NOW WHAT DO I DO NEXT?
IT WORKED! HE SEES US!
12

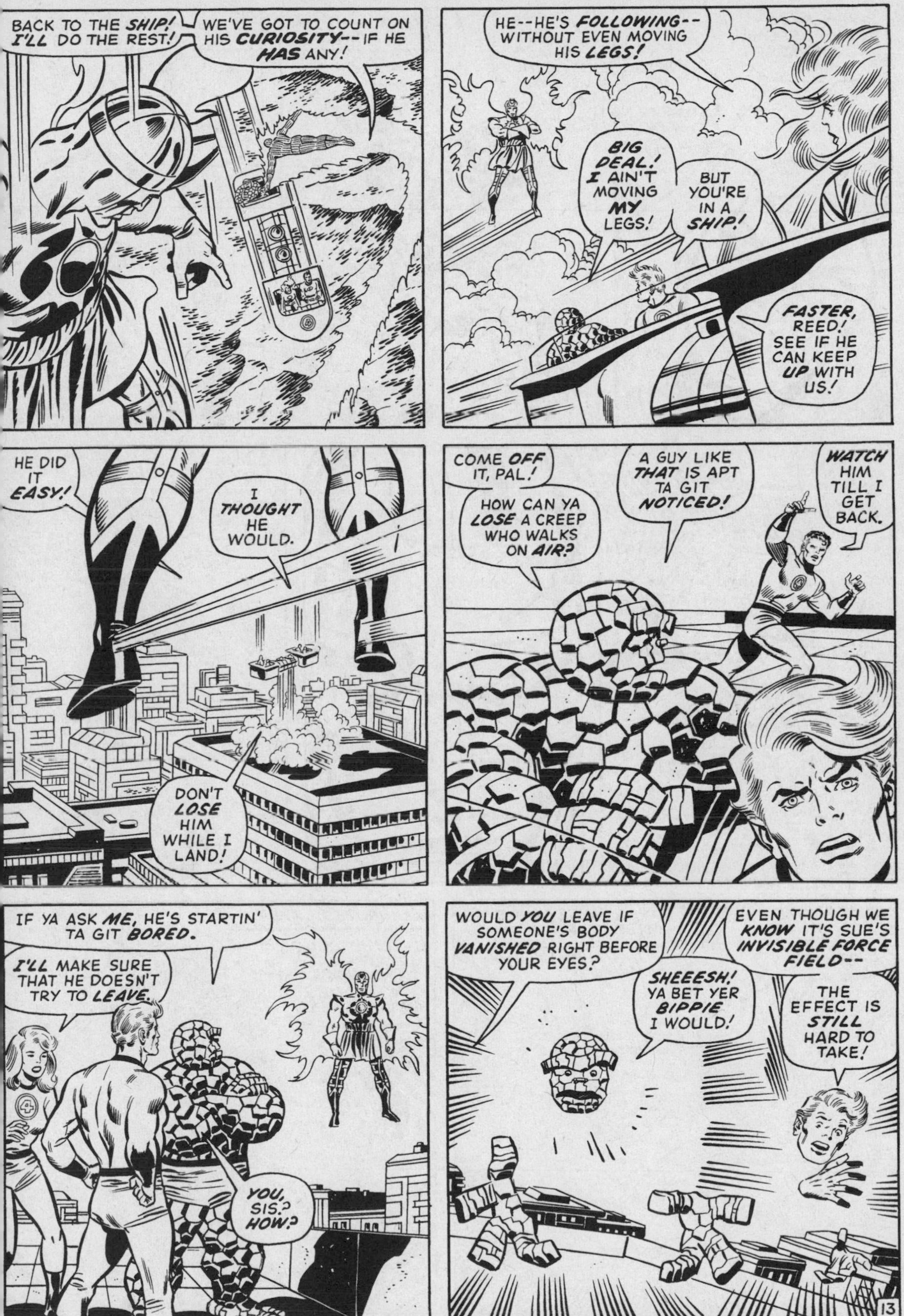
BACK TO THE SHIP! I'LL DO THE REST!
WE'VE GOT TO COUNT ON HIS CURIOSITY--IF HE HAS ANY!
HE--HE'S FOLLOWING--WITHOUT EVEN MOVING HIS LEGS!
BIG DEAL! I AIN'T MOVING MY LEGS!
BUT YOU'RE IN A SHIP!
FASTER, REED! SEE IF HE CAN KEEP UP WITH US!
HE DID IT EASY!
I THOUGHT HE WOULD.
DON'T LOSE HIM WHILE I LAND!
COME OFF IT, PAL!
HOW CAN YA LOSE A CREEP WHO WALKS ON AIR?
A GUY LIKE THAT IS APT TA GIT NOTICED!
WATCH HIM TILL I GET BACK.
IF YA ASK ME, HE'S STARTIN' TA GIT BORED.
I'LL MAKE SURE THAT HE DOESN'T TRY TO LEAVE.
YOU, SIS? HOW?
WOULD YOU LEAVE IF SOMEONE'S BODY VANISHED RIGHT BEFORE YOUR EYES?
SHEEESH! YA BET YER BIPPIE I WOULD!
EVEN THOUGH WE KNOW IT'S SUE'S INVISIBLE FORCE FIELD--
THE EFFECT IS STILL HARD TO TAKE!
13

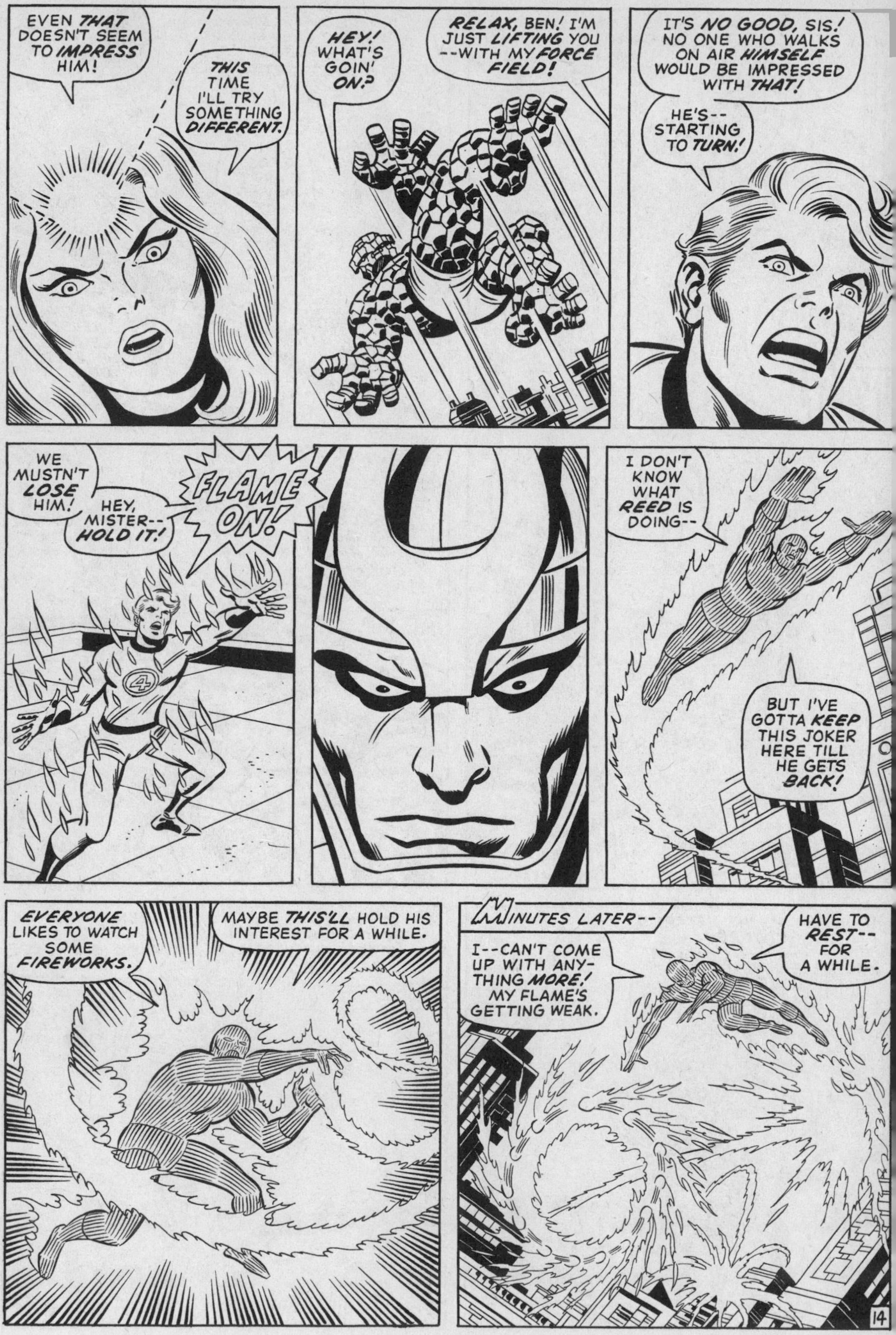
EVEN THAT DOESN'T SEEM TO IMPRESS HIM!
THIS TIME I'LL TRY SOMETHING DIFFERENT.
HEY! WHAT'S GOIN' ON?
RELAX, BEN! I'M JUST LIFTING YOU --WITH MY FORCE FIELD!
IT'S NO GOOD, SIS! NO ONE WHO WALKS ON AIR HIMSELF WOULD BE IMPRESSED WITH THAT!
HE'S-- STARTING TO TURN!
WE MUSTN'T LOSE HIM!
HEY, MISTER-- HOLD IT!
FLAME ON!
I DON'T KNOW WHAT REED IS DOING--
BUT I'VE GOTTA KEEP THIS JOKER HERE TILL HE GETS BACK!
EVERYONE LIKES TO WATCH SOME FIREWORKS.
MAYBE THIS'LL HOLD HIS INTEREST FOR A WHILE.
MINUTES LATER--
I--CAN'T COME UP WITH ANY-THING MORE! MY FLAME'S GETTING WEAK.
HAVE TO REST-- FOR A WHILE.
14

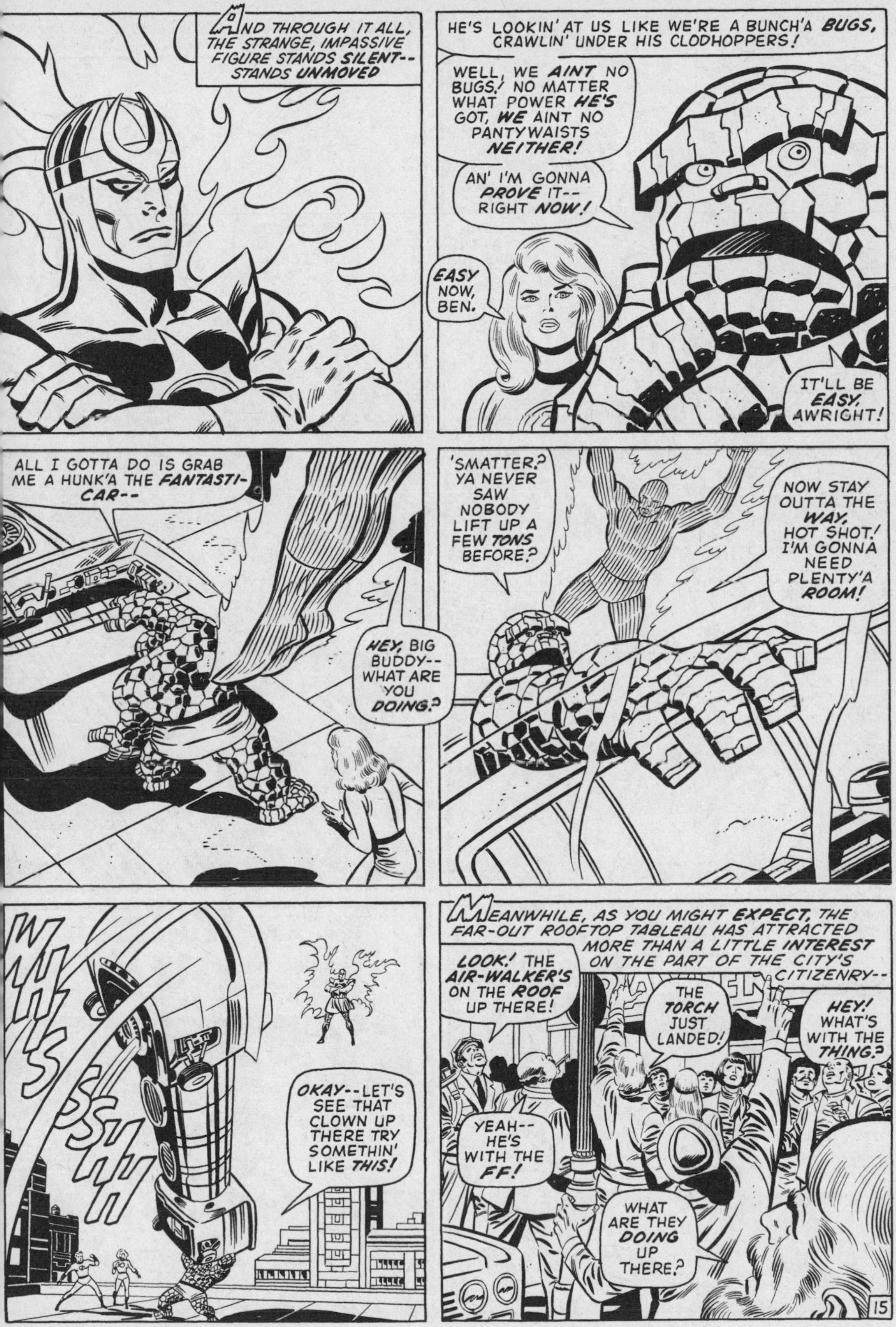
AND THROUGH IT ALL, THE STRANGE, IMPASSIVE FIGURE STANDS SILENT-- STANDS UNMOVED
HE'S LOOKIN' AT US LIKE WE'RE A BUNCH'A BUGS, CRAWLIN' UNDER HIS CLODHOPPERS!
WELL, WE AINT NO BUGS! NO MATTER WHAT POWER HE'S GOT, WE AINT NO PANTYWAISTS NEITHER!
AN' I'M GONNA PROVE IT-- RIGHT NOW!
EASY NOW, BEN.
IT'LL BE EASY, AWRIGHT!
ALL I GOTTA DO IS GRAB ME A HUNK'A THE FANTASTI-CAR--
HEY, BIG BUDDY-- WHAT ARE YOU DOING?
'SMATTER? YA NEVER SAW NOBODY LIFT UP A FEW TONS BEFORE?
NOW STAY OUTTA THE WAY, HOT SHOT! I'M GONNA NEED PLENTY'A ROOM!
WHSSHH
OKAY--LET'S SEE THAT CLOWN UP THERE TRY SOMETHIN' LIKE THIS!
MEANWHILE, AS YOU MIGHT EXPECT, THE FAR-OUT ROOFTOP TABLEAU HAS ATTRACTED MORE THAN A LITTLE INTEREST ON THE PART OF THE CITY'S CITIZENRY--
LOOK! THE AIR-WALKER'S ON THE ROOF UP THERE!
THE TORCH JUST LANDED!
HEY! WHAT'S WITH THE THING?
YEAH-- HE'S WITH THE FF!
WHAT ARE THEY DOING UP THERE?
15

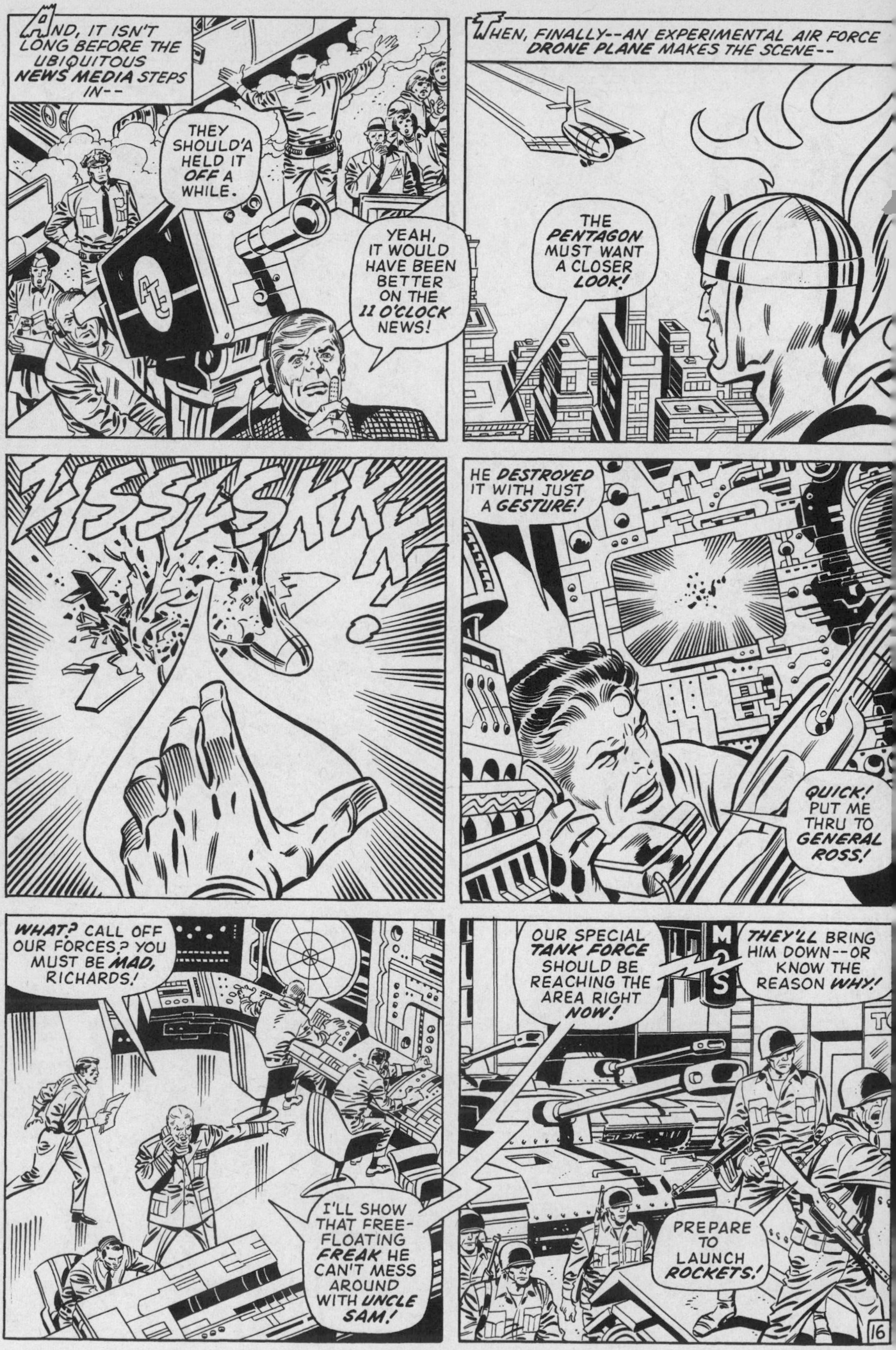
AND, IT ISN'T LONG BEFORE THE UBIQUITOUS NEWS MEDIA STEPS IN--
THEY SHOULD'A HELD IT OFF A WHILE.
YEAH, IT WOULD HAVE BEEN BETTER ON THE 11 O'CLOCK NEWS!
THEN, FINALLY--AN EXPERIMENTAL AIR FORCE DRONE PLANE MAKES THE SCENE--
THE PENTAGON MUST WANT A CLOSER LOOK!
ZSSSZSKK
HE DESTROYED IT WITH JUST A GESTURE!
QUICK! PUT ME THRU TO GENERAL ROSS!
WHAT? CALL OFF OUR FORCES? YOU MUST BE MAD, RICHARDS!
I'LL SHOW THAT FREE-FLOATING FREAK HE CAN'T MESS AROUND WITH UNCLE SAM!
OUR SPECIAL TANK FORCE SHOULD BE REACHING THE AREA RIGHT NOW!
THEY'LL BRING HIM DOWN--OR KNOW THE REASON WHY!
PREPARE TO LAUNCH ROCKETS!
16

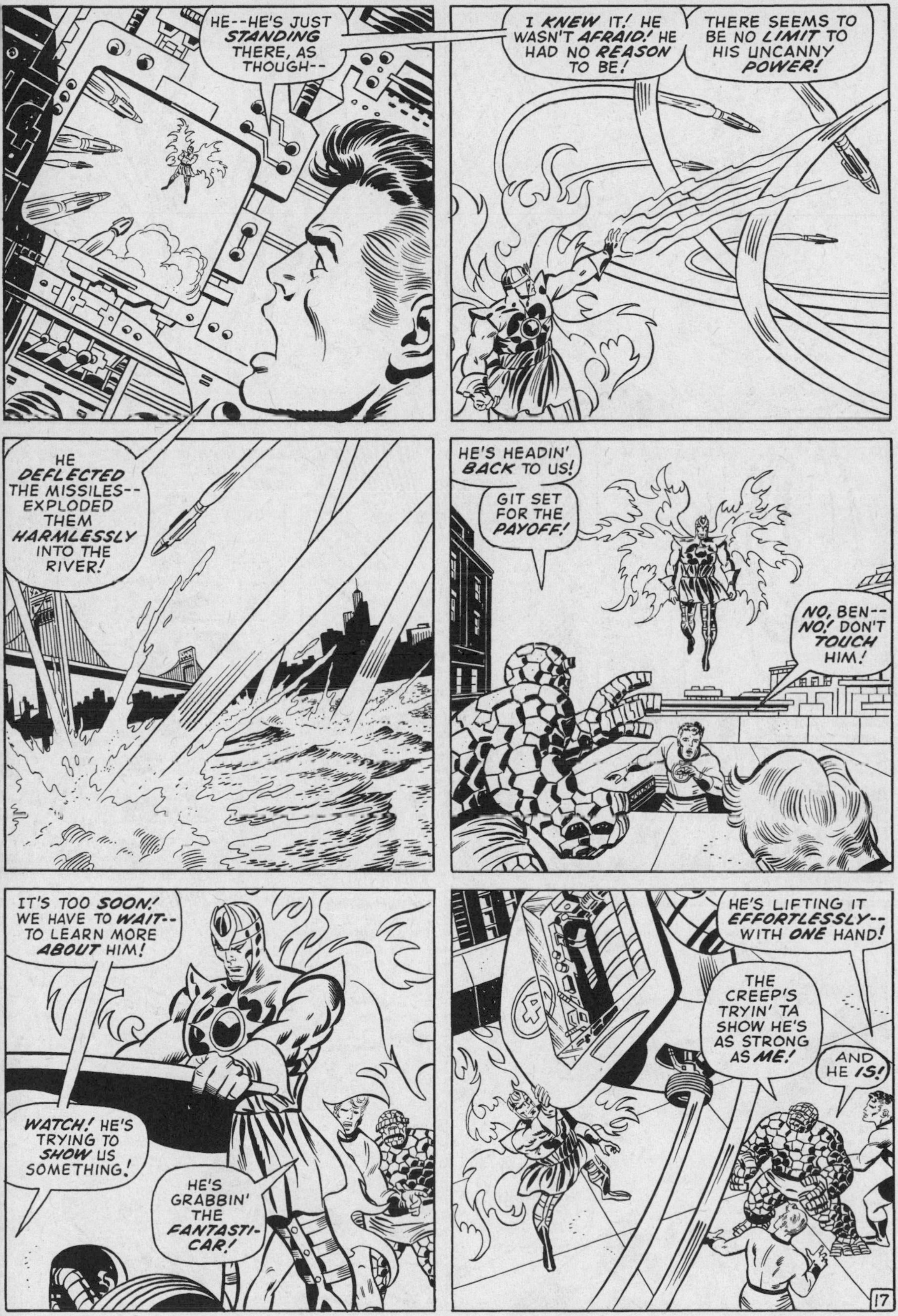
HE--HE'S JUST STANDING THERE, AS THOUGH--
I KNEW IT! HE WASN'T AFRAID! HE HAD NO REASON TO BE!
THERE SEEMS TO BE NO LIMIT TO HIS UNCANNY POWER!
HE DEFLECTED THE MISSILES--EXPLODED THEM HARMLESSLY INTO THE RIVER!
HE'S HEADIN' BACK TO US!
GIT SET FOR THE PAYOFF!
NO, BEN--NO! DON'T TOUCH HIM!
IT'S TOO SOON! WE HAVE TO WAIT--TO LEARN MORE ABOUT HIM!
WATCH! HE'S TRYING TO SHOW US SOMETHING!
HE'S GRABBIN' THE FANTASTI-CAR!
HE'S LIFTING IT EFFORTLESSLY--WITH ONE HAND!
THE CREEP'S TRYIN' TA SHOW HE'S AS STRONG AS ME!
AND HE IS!
17

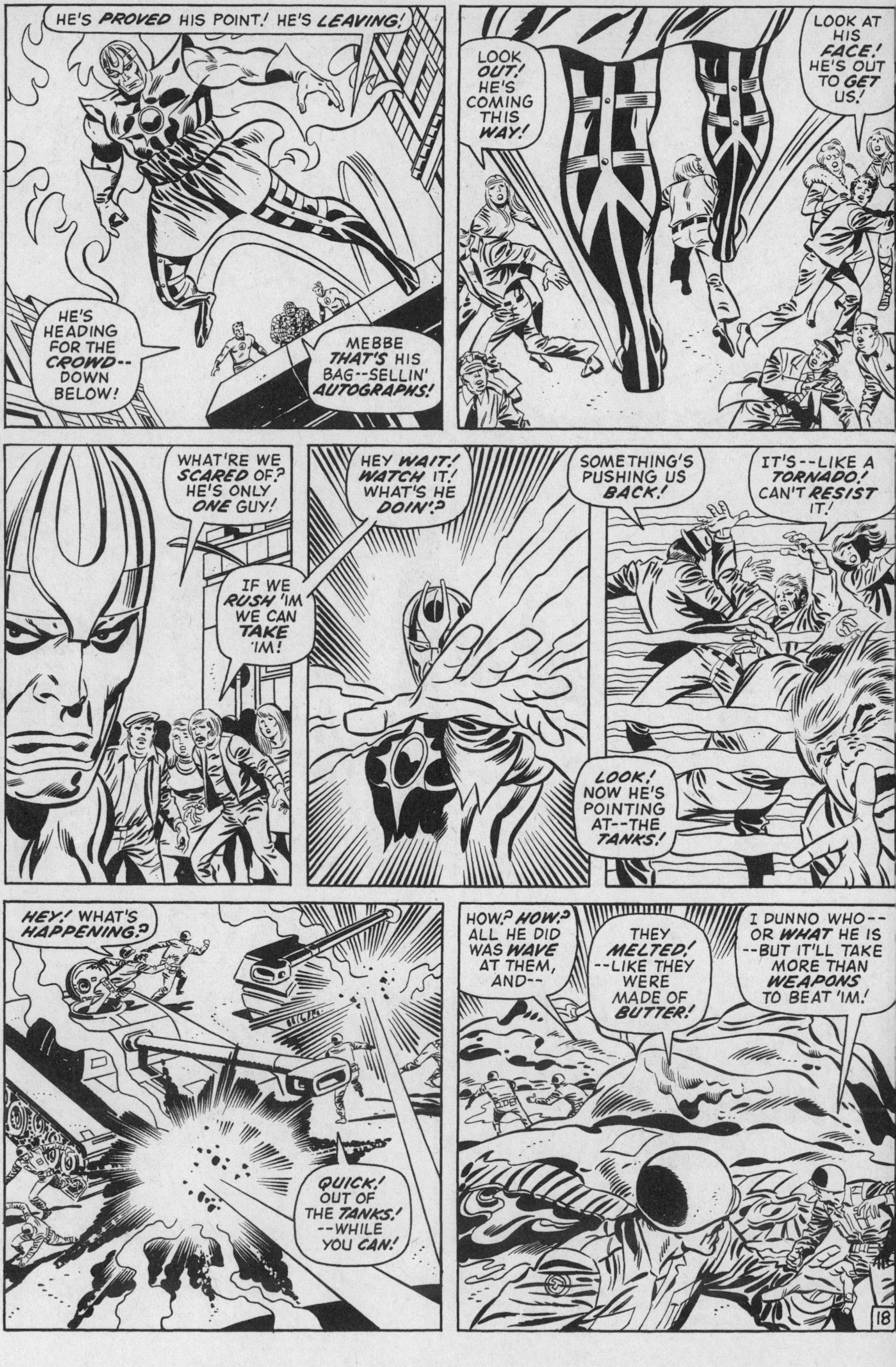
HE'S PROVED HIS POINT! HE'S LEAVING!
HE'S HEADING FOR THE CROWD-- DOWN BELOW!
MEBBE THAT'S HIS BAG--SELLIN' AUTOGRAPHS!
LOOK OUT! HE'S COMING THIS WAY!
LOOK AT HIS FACE! HE'S OUT TO GET US!
WHAT'RE WE SCARED OF? HE'S ONLY ONE GUY!
IF WE RUSH 'IM WE CAN TAKE 'IM!
HEY WAIT! WATCH IT! WHAT'S HE DOIN'?
SOMETHING'S PUSHING US BACK!
IT'S--LIKE A TORNADO! CAN'T RESIST IT!
LOOK! NOW HE'S POINTING AT--THE TANKS!
HEY! WHAT'S HAPPENING?
QUICK! OUT OF THE TANKS! --WHILE YOU CAN!
HOW? HOW? ALL HE DID WAS WAVE AT THEM, AND--
THEY MELTED! --LIKE THEY WERE MADE OF BUTTER!
I DUNNO WHO-- OR WHAT HE IS --BUT IT'LL TAKE MORE THAN WEAPONS TO BEAT 'IM!
18

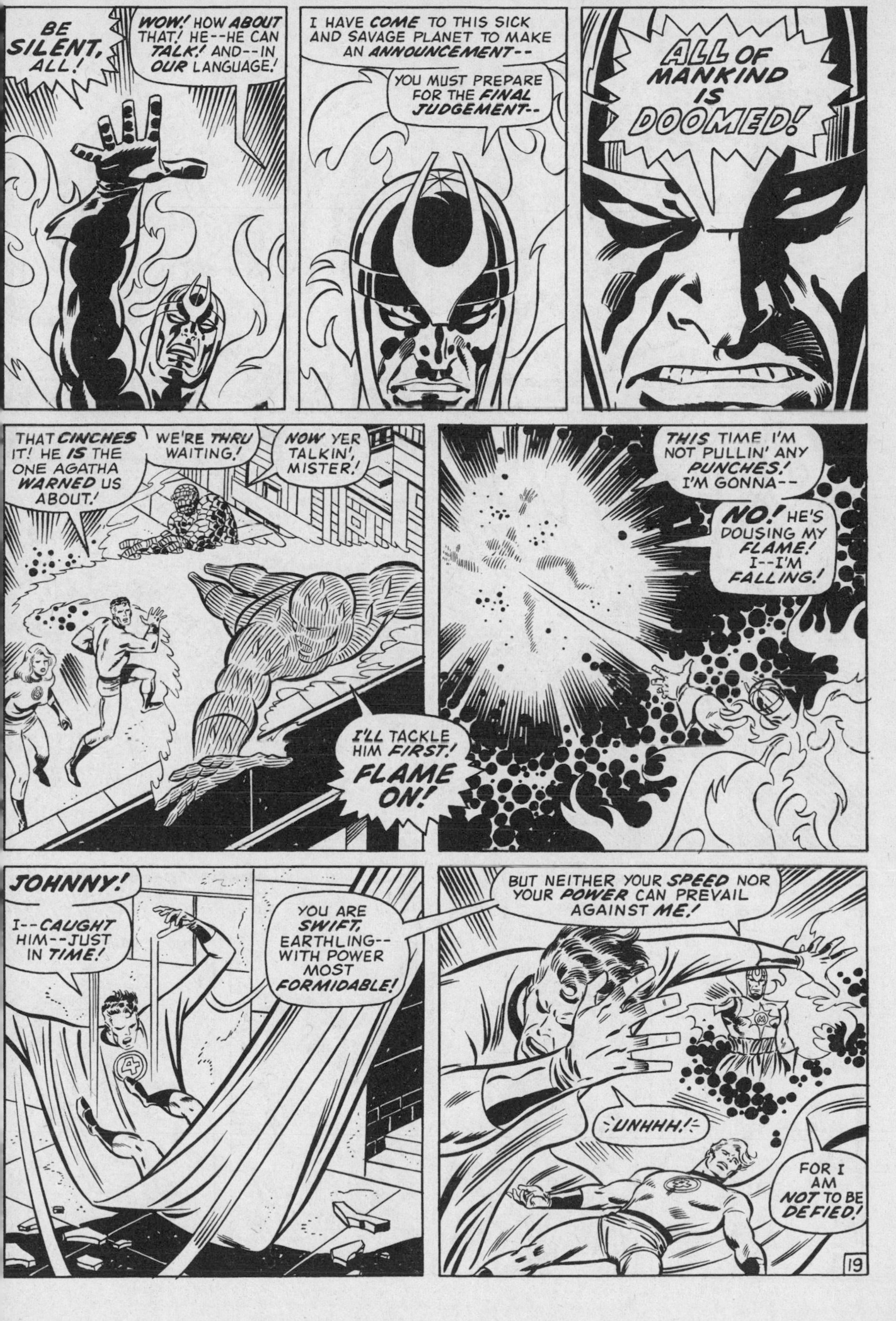

BE SILENT, ALL!
WOW! HOW ABOUT THAT! HE--HE CAN TALK! AND--IN OUR LANGUAGE!
I HAVE COME TO THIS SICK AND SAVAGE PLANET TO MAKE AN ANNOUNCEMENT--
YOU MUST PREPARE FOR THE FINAL JUDGEMENT--
ALL OF MANKIND IS DOOMED!
THAT CINCHES IT! HE IS THE ONE AGATHA WARNED US ABOUT!
WE'RE THRU WAITING!
NOW YER TALKIN', MISTER!
I'LL TACKLE HIM FIRST! FLAME ON!
THIS TIME I'M NOT PULLIN' ANY PUNCHES! I'M GONNA--
NO! HE'S DOUSING MY FLAME! I--I'M FALLING!
JOHNNY!
I--CAUGHT HIM--JUST IN TIME!
YOU ARE SWIFT, EARTHLING--WITH POWER MOST FORMIDABLE!
BUT NEITHER YOUR SPEED NOR YOUR POWER CAN PREVAIL AGAINST ME!
UNHHH!
FOR I AM NOT TO BE DEFIED!

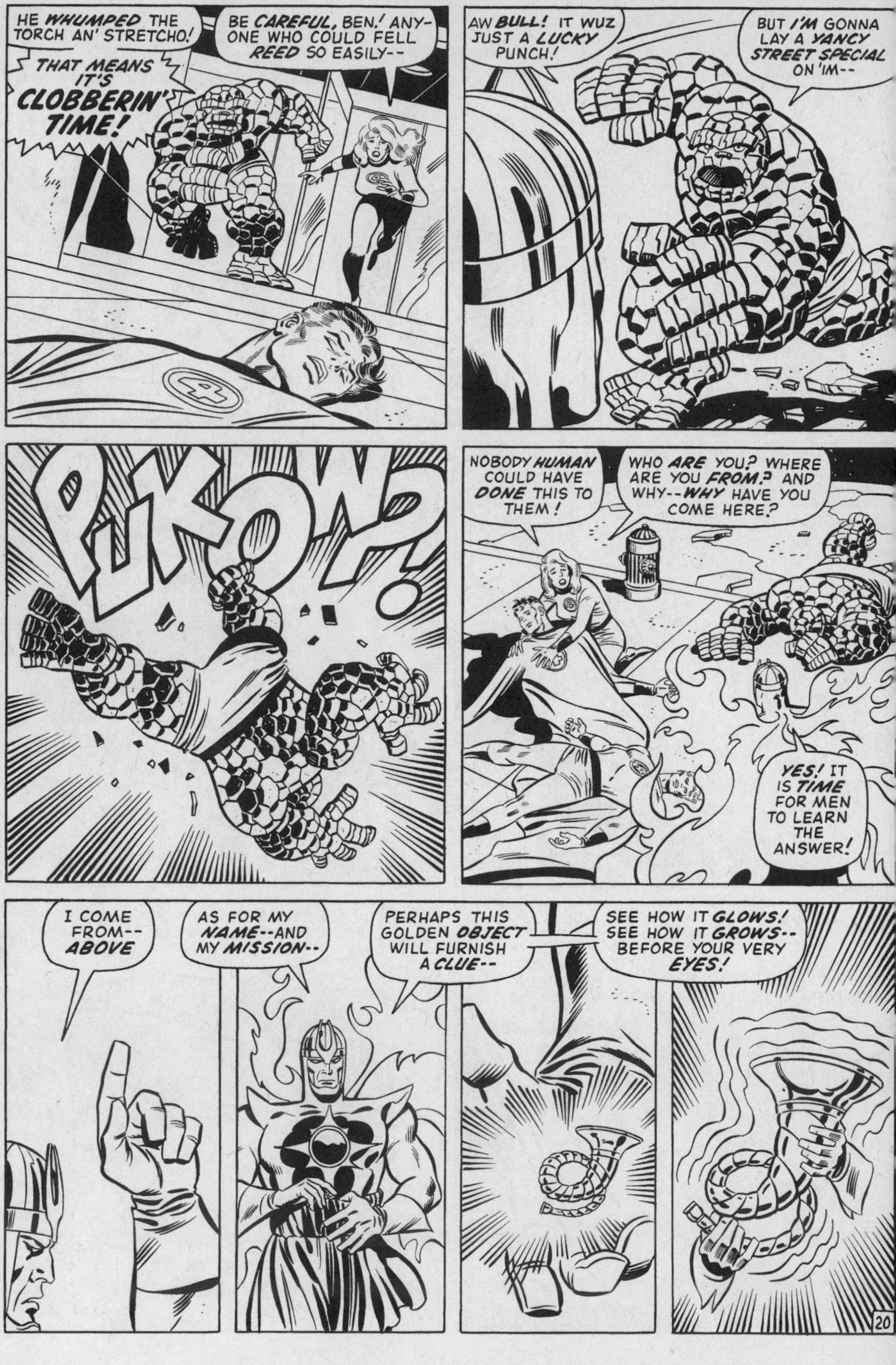
HE WHUMPED THE TORCH AN' STRETCHO!
THAT MEANS IT'S CLOBBERIN' TIME!
BE CAREFUL, BEN.! ANYONE WHO COULD FELL REED SO EASILY--
AW BULL! IT WUZ JUST A LUCKY PUNCH!
BUT I'M GONNA LAY A YANCY STREET SPECIAL ON 'IM--
PUKOWW!
NOBODY HUMAN COULD HAVE DONE THIS TO THEM!
WHO ARE YOU? WHERE ARE YOU FROM? AND WHY--WHY HAVE YOU COME HERE?
YES! IT IS TIME FOR MEN TO LEARN THE ANSWER!
I COME FROM-- ABOVE
AS FOR MY NAME--AND MY MISSION--
PERHAPS THIS GOLDEN OBJECT WILL FURNISH A CLUE--
SEE HOW IT GLOWS! SEE HOW IT GROWS-- BEFORE YOUR VERY EYES!
20

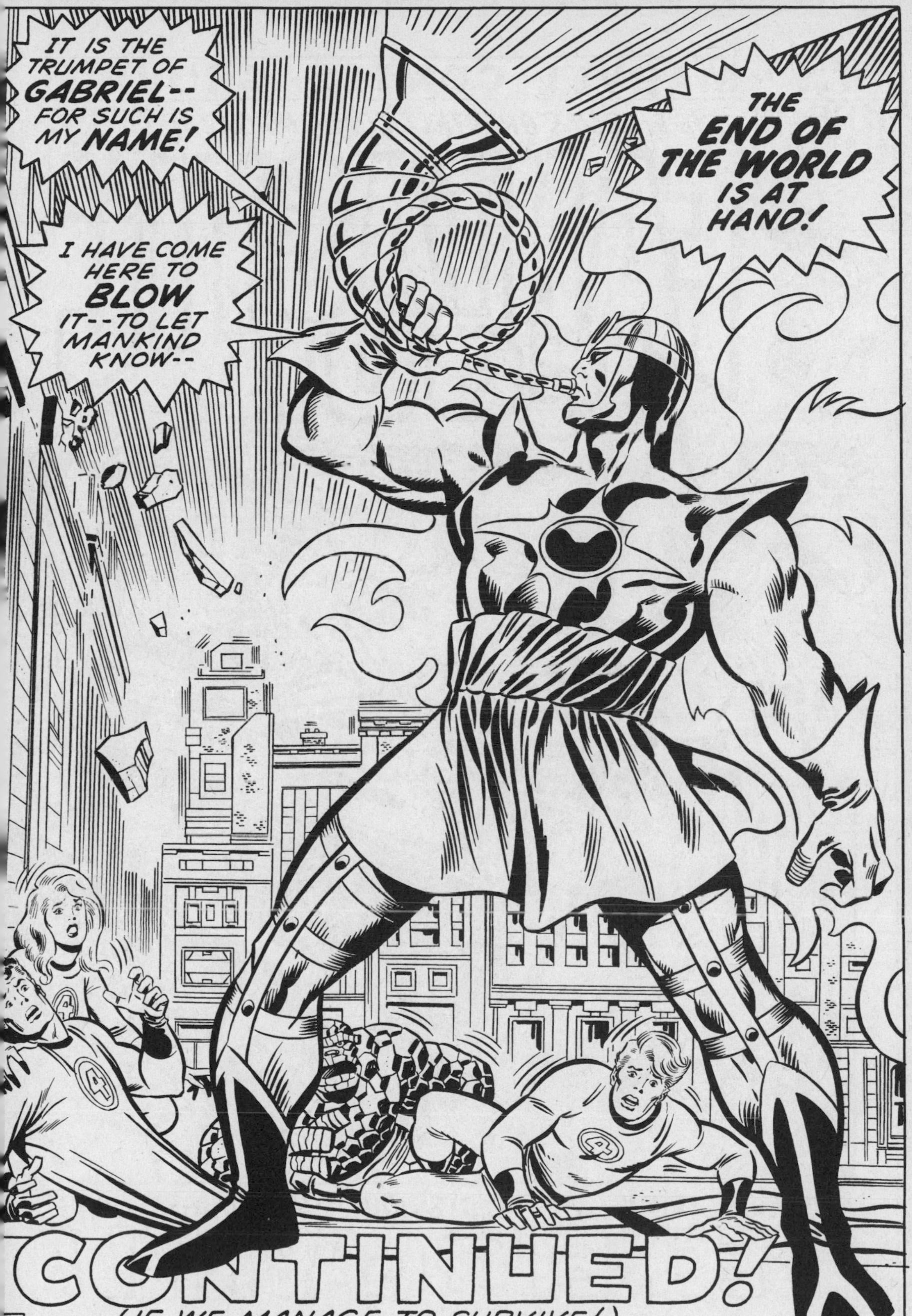
IT IS THE TRUMPET OF GABRIEL-- FOR SUCH IS MY NAME!
THE END OF THE WORLD IS AT HAND!
I HAVE COME HERE TO BLOW IT--TO LET MANKIND KNOW--
CONTINUED!
(IF WE MANAGE TO SURVIVE!)
21

FANTASTIC FOUR
MARVEL COMICS GROUP
121 APR 02462
20¢
THE WORLD'S GREATEST COMIC MAGAZINE!
APPROVED BY THE COMICS CODE AUTHORITY
FANTASTIC FOUR
FEATURING: THE SILVER SURFER!
IT'S MONSTROUS! IT'S MYSTERIOUS! IT'S MIND-BLOWING!
THE SECRET OF GABRIEL!

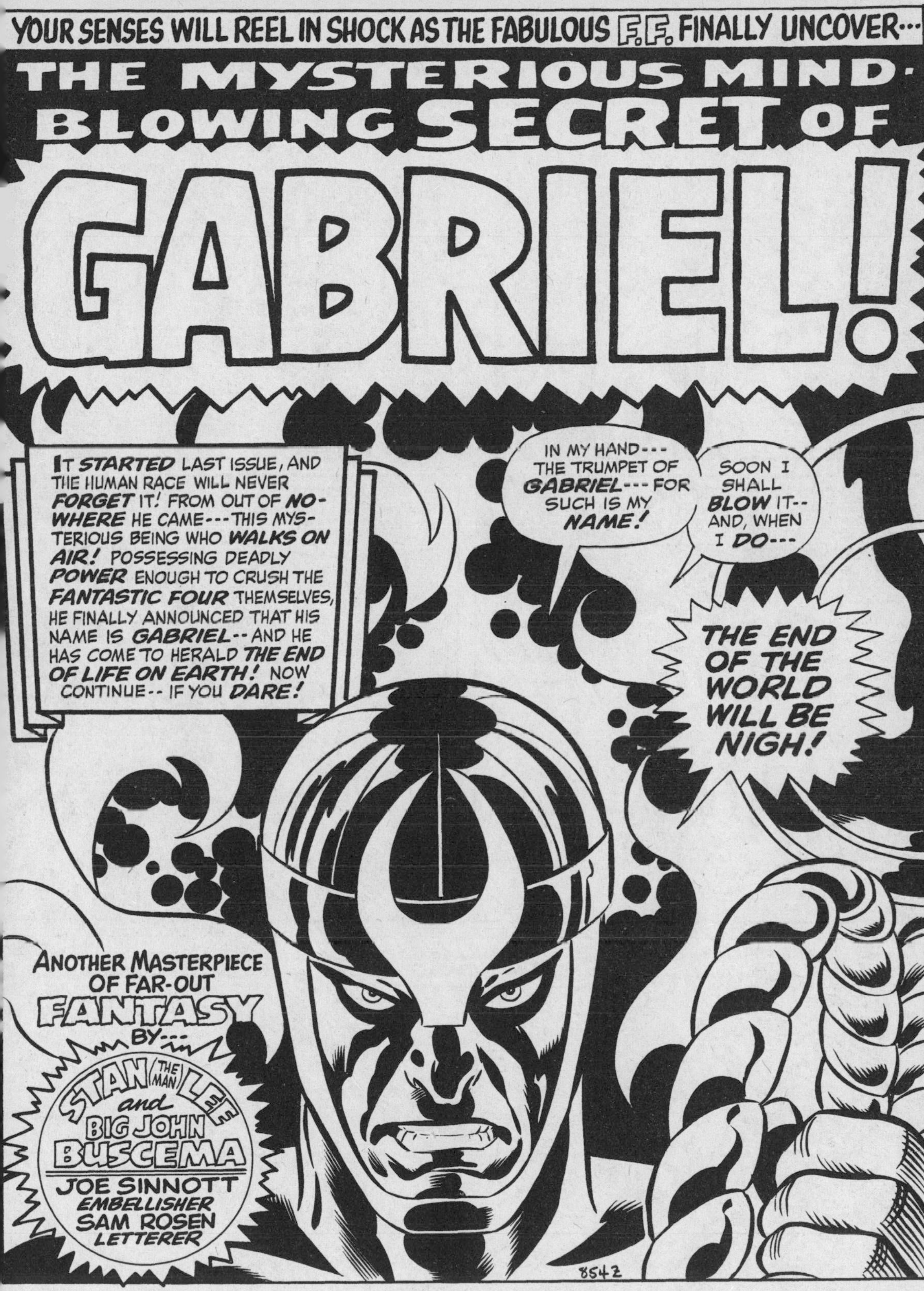
YOUR SENSES WILL REEL IN SHOCK AS THE FABULOUS F.F. FINALLY UNCOVER---
THE MYSTERIOUS MIND-BLOWING SECRET OF GABRIEL!
IT STARTED LAST ISSUE, AND THE HUMAN RACE WILL NEVER FORGET IT! FROM OUT OF NO-WHERE HE CAME---THIS MYSTERIOUS BEING WHO WALKS ON AIR! POSSESSING DEADLY POWER ENOUGH TO CRUSH THE FANTASTIC FOUR THEMSELVES, HE FINALLY ANNOUNCED THAT HIS NAME IS GABRIEL--AND HE HAS COME TO HERALD THE END OF LIFE ON EARTH! NOW CONTINUE--IF YOU DARE!
IN MY HAND--- THE TRUMPET OF GABRIEL---FOR SUCH IS MY NAME!
SOON I SHALL BLOW IT-- AND, WHEN I DO---
THE END OF THE WORLD WILL BE NIGH!
ANOTHER MASTERPIECE OF FAR-OUT FANTASY BY---
STAN (THE MAN) LEE and BIG JOHN BUSCEMA
JOE SINNOTT EMBELLISHER
SAM ROSEN LETTERER
8542

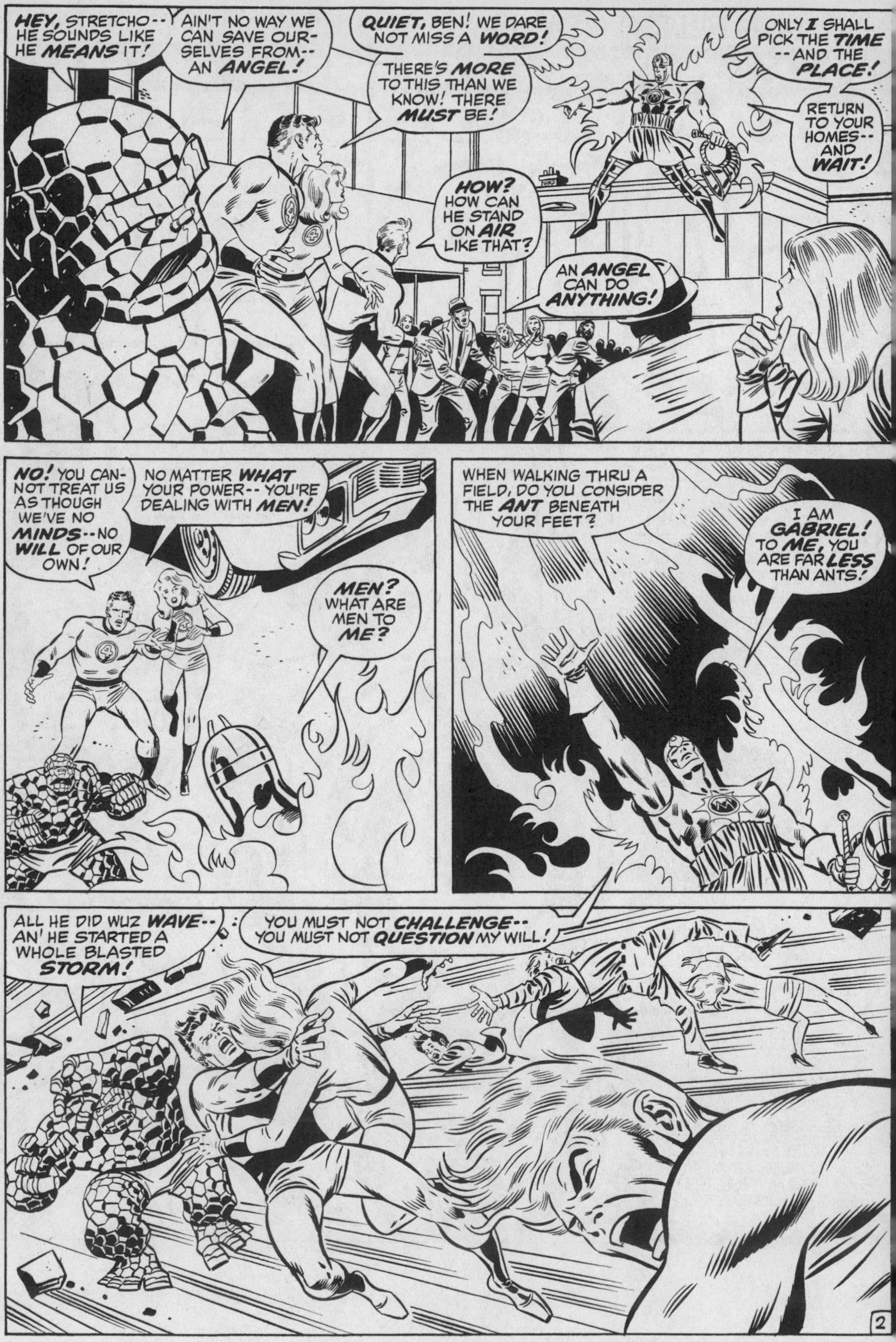
HEY, STRETCHO-- HE SOUNDS LIKE HE MEANS IT!
AIN'T NO WAY WE CAN SAVE OURSELVES FROM-- AN ANGEL!
QUIET, BEN! WE DARE NOT MISS A WORD!
THERE'S MORE TO THIS THAN WE KNOW! THERE MUST BE!
ONLY I SHALL PICK THE TIME --AND THE PLACE!
RETURN TO YOUR HOMES-- AND WAIT!
HOW? HOW CAN HE STAND ON AIR LIKE THAT?
AN ANGEL CAN DO ANYTHING!
NO! YOU CANNOT TREAT US AS THOUGH WE'VE NO MINDS--NO WILL OF OUR OWN!
NO MATTER WHAT YOUR POWER-- YOU'RE DEALING WITH MEN!
MEN? WHAT ARE MEN TO ME?
WHEN WALKING THRU A FIELD, DO YOU CONSIDER THE ANT BENEATH YOUR FEET?
I AM GABRIEL! TO ME, YOU ARE FAR LESS THAN ANTS!
ALL HE DID WUZ WAVE-- AN' HE STARTED A WHOLE BLASTED STORM!
YOU MUST NOT CHALLENGE-- YOU MUST NOT QUESTION MY WILL!
2

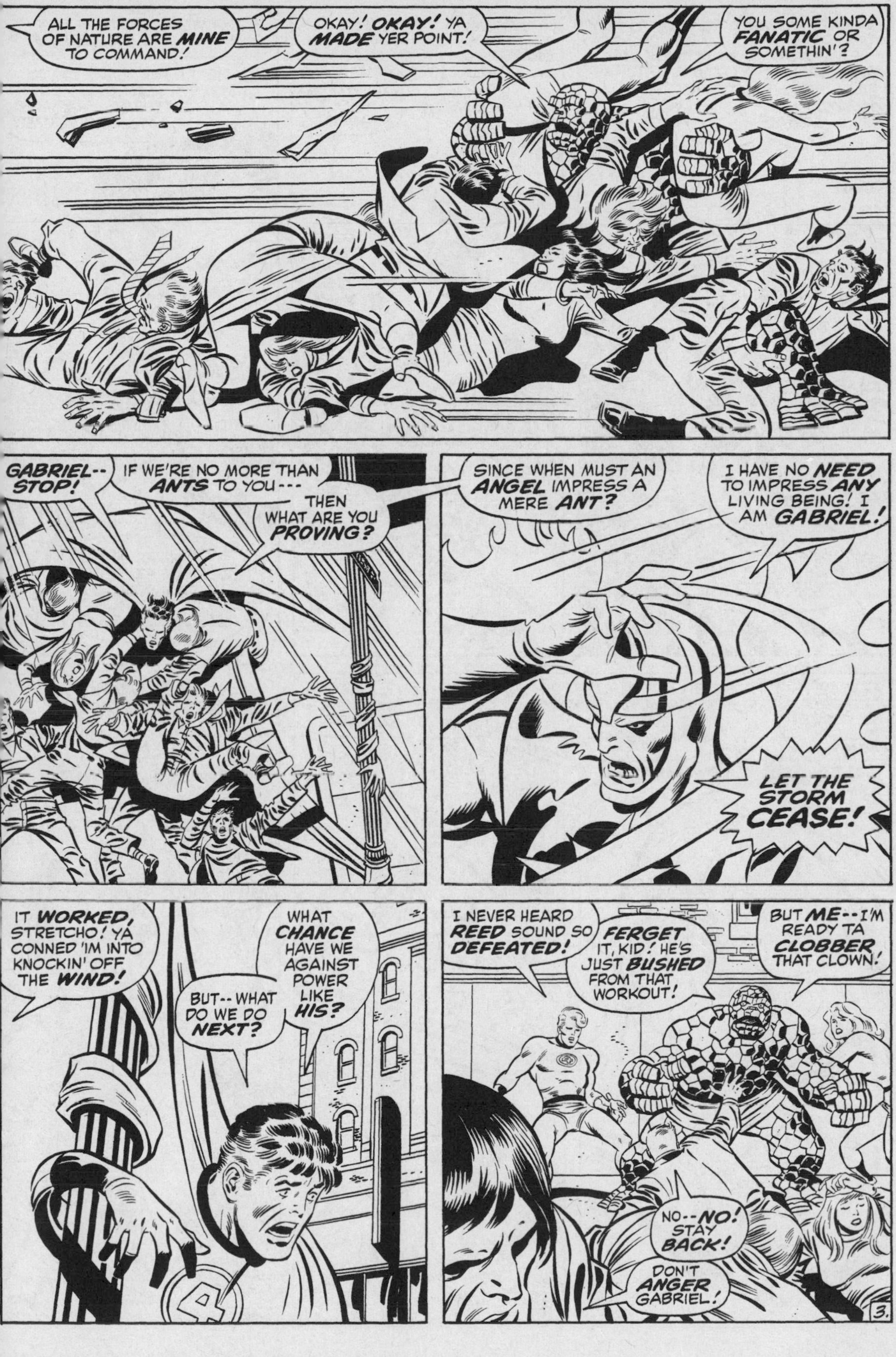
ALL THE FORCES OF NATURE ARE MINE TO COMMAND!
OKAY! OKAY! YA MADE YER POINT!
YOU SOME KINDA FANATIC OR SOMETHIN'?
GABRIEL-- STOP!
IF WE'RE NO MORE THAN ANTS TO YOU---
THEN WHAT ARE YOU PROVING?
SINCE WHEN MUST AN ANGEL IMPRESS A MERE ANT?
I HAVE NO NEED TO IMPRESS ANY LIVING BEING! I AM GABRIEL!
LET THE STORM CEASE!
IT WORKED, STRETCHO! YA CONNED 'IM INTO KNOCKIN' OFF THE WIND!
BUT-- WHAT DO WE DO NEXT?
WHAT CHANCE HAVE WE AGAINST POWER LIKE HIS?
I NEVER HEARD REED SOUND SO DEFEATED!
FERGET IT, KID! HE'S JUST BUSHED FROM THAT WORKOUT!
BUT ME-- I'M READY TA CLOBBER THAT CLOWN!
NO-- NO! STAY BACK!
DON'T ANGER GABRIEL!
3.

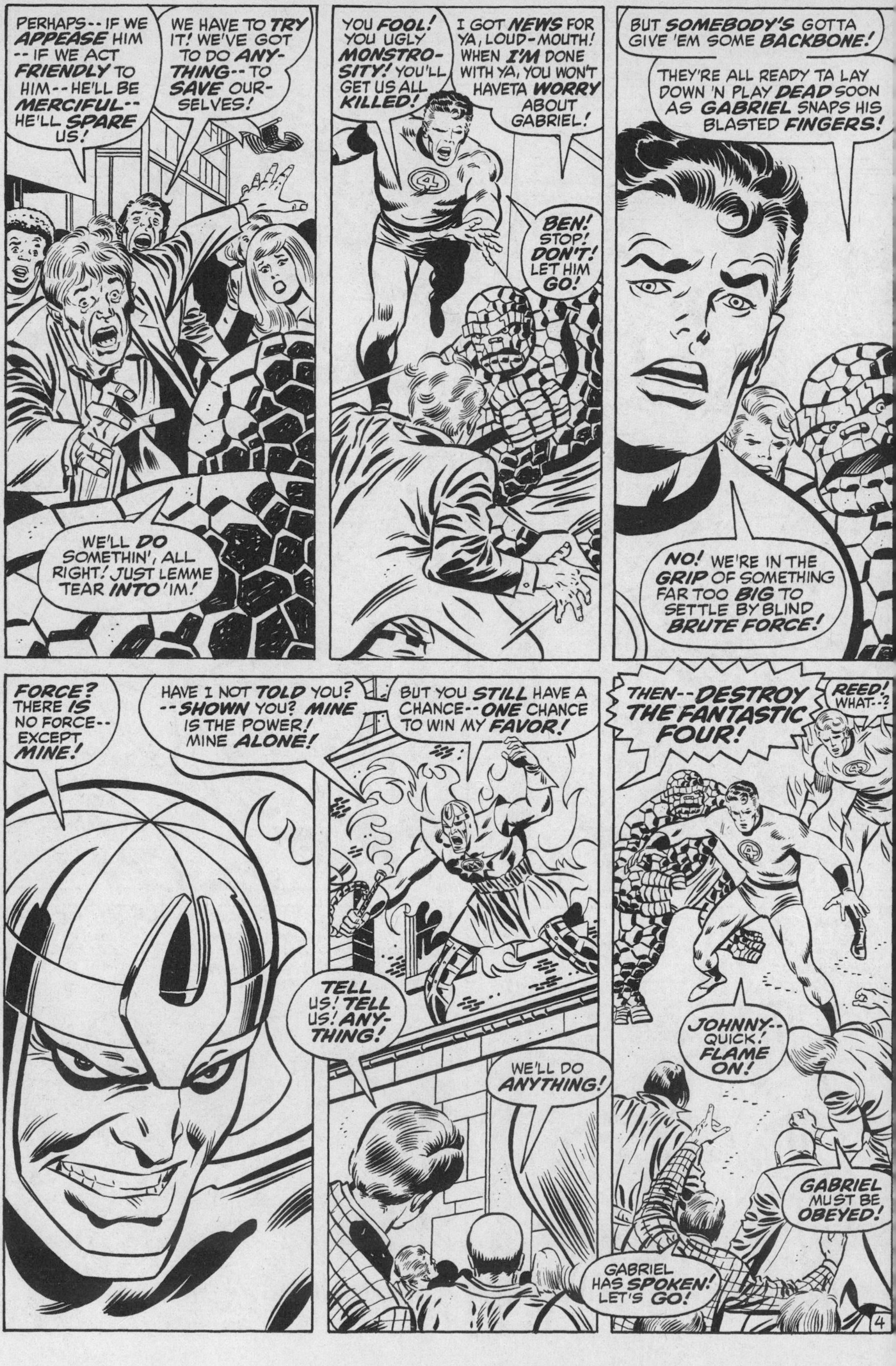
PERHAPS-- IF WE APPEASE HIM -- IF WE ACT FRIENDLY TO HIM-- HE'LL BE MERCIFUL-- HE'LL SPARE US!
WE HAVE TO TRY IT! WE'VE GOT TO DO ANY-THING-- TO SAVE OUR-SELVES!
WE'LL DO SOMETHIN', ALL RIGHT! JUST LEMME TEAR INTO 'IM!
YOU FOOL! YOU UGLY MONSTRO-SITY! YOU'LL GET US ALL KILLED!
I GOT NEWS FOR YA, LOUD-MOUTH! WHEN I'M DONE WITH YA, YOU WON'T HAVETA WORRY ABOUT GABRIEL!
BEN! STOP! DON'T! LET HIM GO!
BUT SOMEBODY'S GOTTA GIVE 'EM SOME BACKBONE!
THEY'RE ALL READY TA LAY DOWN 'N PLAY DEAD SOON AS GABRIEL SNAPS HIS BLASTED FINGERS!
NO! WE'RE IN THE GRIP OF SOMETHING FAR TOO BIG TO SETTLE BY BLIND BRUTE FORCE!
FORCE? THERE IS NO FORCE-- EXCEPT MINE!
HAVE I NOT TOLD YOU? --SHOWN YOU? MINE IS THE POWER! MINE ALONE!
BUT YOU STILL HAVE A CHANCE-- ONE CHANCE TO WIN MY FAVOR!
TELL US! TELL US! ANY-THING!
WE'LL DO ANYTHING!
THEN-- DESTROY THE FANTASTIC FOUR!
REED! WHAT--?
JOHNNY-- QUICK! FLAME ON!
GABRIEL MUST BE OBEYED!
GABRIEL HAS SPOKEN! LET'S GO!
4

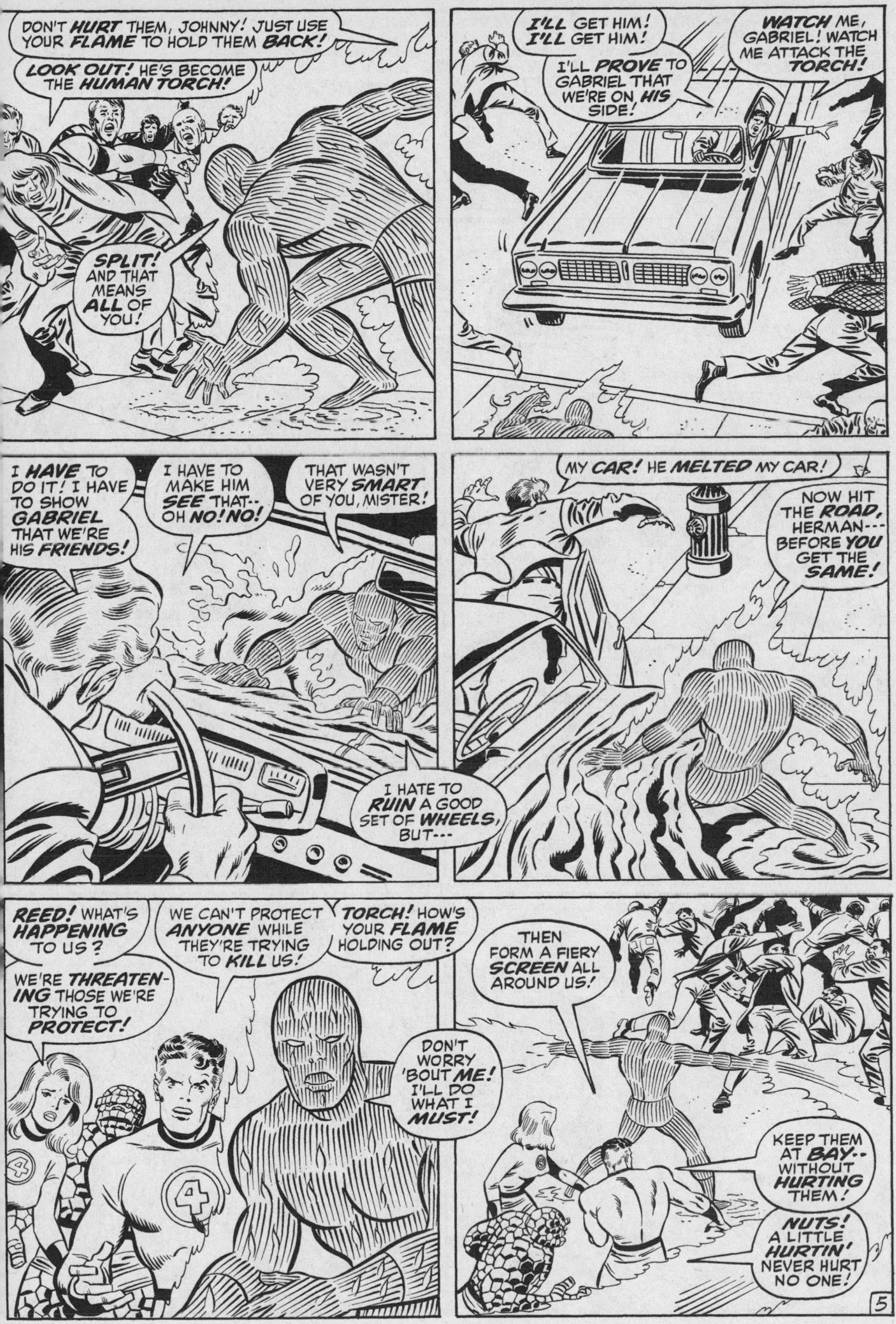
DON'T HURT THEM, JOHNNY! JUST USE YOUR FLAME TO HOLD THEM BACK!
LOOK OUT! HE'S BECOME THE HUMAN TORCH!
SPLIT! AND THAT MEANS ALL OF YOU!
I'LL GET HIM! I'LL GET HIM!
I'LL PROVE TO GABRIEL THAT WE'RE ON HIS SIDE!
WATCH ME, GABRIEL! WATCH ME ATTACK THE TORCH!
I HAVE TO DO IT! I HAVE TO SHOW GABRIEL THAT WE'RE HIS FRIENDS!
I HAVE TO MAKE HIM SEE THAT-- OH NO! NO!
THAT WASN'T VERY SMART OF YOU, MISTER!
I HATE TO RUIN A GOOD SET OF WHEELS, BUT---
MY CAR! HE MELTED MY CAR!
NOW HIT THE ROAD, HERMAN--- BEFORE YOU GET THE SAME!
REED! WHAT'S HAPPENING TO US?
WE'RE THREATENING THOSE WE'RE TRYING TO PROTECT!
WE CAN'T PROTECT ANYONE WHILE THEY'RE TRYING TO KILL US!
TORCH! HOW'S YOUR FLAME HOLDING OUT?
DON'T WORRY 'BOUT ME! I'LL DO WHAT I MUST!
THEN FORM A FIERY SCREEN ALL AROUND US!
KEEP THEM AT BAY-- WITHOUT HURTING THEM!
NUTS! A LITTLE HURTIN' NEVER HURT NO ONE!
5

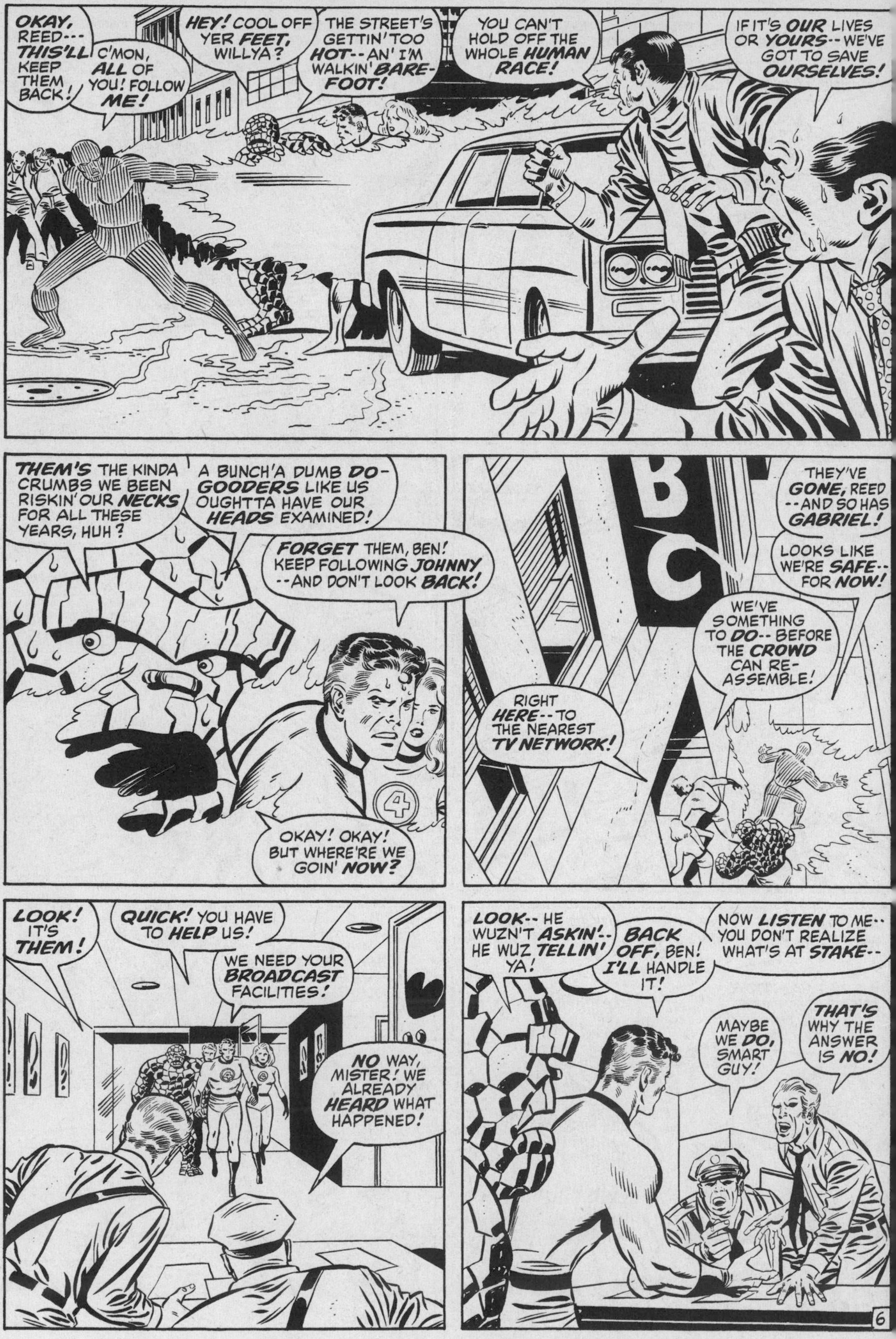
OKAY, REED--- THIS'LL KEEP THEM BACK!
C'MON, ALL OF YOU! FOLLOW ME!
HEY! COOL OFF YER FEET, WILLYA?
THE STREET'S GETTIN' TOO HOT--AN' I'M WALKIN' BARE-FOOT!
YOU CAN'T HOLD OFF THE WHOLE HUMAN RACE!
IF IT'S OUR LIVES OR YOURS--WE'VE GOT TO SAVE OURSELVES!
THEM'S THE KINDA CRUMBS WE BEEN RISKIN' OUR NECKS FOR ALL THESE YEARS, HUH?
A BUNCH'A DUMB DO-GOODERS LIKE US OUGHTTA HAVE OUR HEADS EXAMINED!
FORGET THEM, BEN! KEEP FOLLOWING JOHNNY --AND DON'T LOOK BACK!
OKAY! OKAY! BUT WHERE'RE WE GOIN' NOW?
B
C
THEY'VE GONE, REED --AND SO HAS GABRIEL!
LOOKS LIKE WE'RE SAFE-- FOR NOW!
WE'VE SOMETHING TO DO-- BEFORE THE CROWD CAN RE-ASSEMBLE!
RIGHT HERE--TO THE NEAREST TV NETWORK!
LOOK! IT'S THEM!
QUICK! YOU HAVE TO HELP US!
WE NEED YOUR BROADCAST FACILITIES!
NO WAY, MISTER! WE ALREADY HEARD WHAT HAPPENED!
LOOK-- HE WUZN'T ASKIN'-- HE WUZ TELLIN' YA!
BACK OFF, BEN! I'LL HANDLE IT!
NOW LISTEN TO ME-- YOU DON'T REALIZE WHAT'S AT STAKE--
MAYBE WE DO, SMART GUY!
THAT'S WHY THE ANSWER IS NO!
6

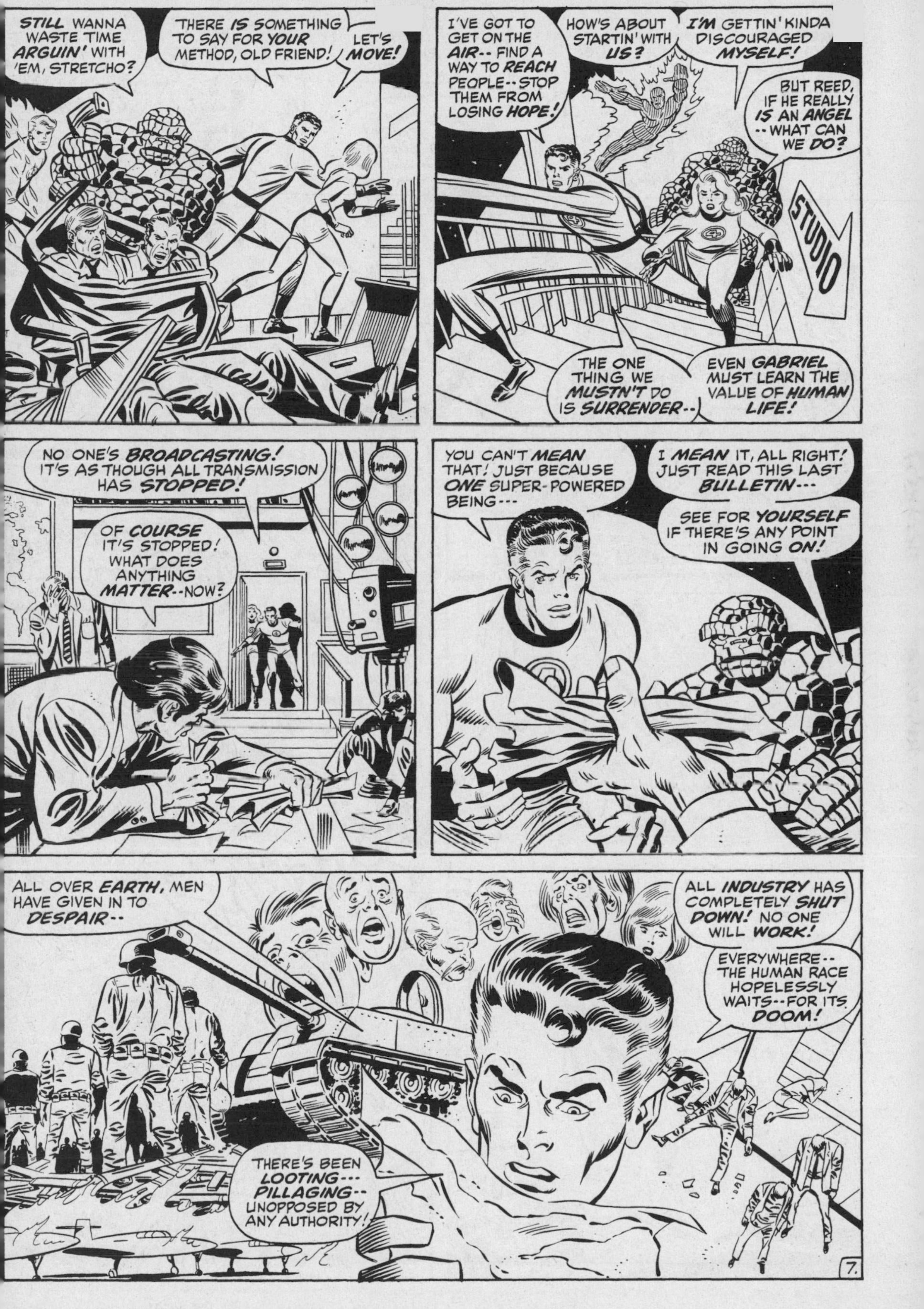

STILL WANNA WASTE TIME ARGUIN' WITH 'EM, STRETCHO?
THERE IS SOMETHING TO SAY FOR YOUR METHOD, OLD FRIEND!
LET'S MOVE!
I'VE GOT TO GET ON THE AIR-- FIND A WAY TO REACH PEOPLE-- STOP THEM FROM LOSING HOPE!
HOW'S ABOUT STARTIN' WITH US?
I'M GETTIN' KINDA DISCOURAGED MYSELF!
BUT REED, IF HE REALLY IS AN ANGEL -- WHAT CAN WE DO?
STUDIO
THE ONE THING WE MUSTN'T DO IS SURRENDER--
EVEN GABRIEL MUST LEARN THE VALUE OF HUMAN LIFE!
NO ONE'S BROADCASTING! IT'S AS THOUGH ALL TRANSMISSION HAS STOPPED!
OF COURSE IT'S STOPPED! WHAT DOES ANYTHING MATTER--NOW?
YOU CAN'T MEAN THAT! JUST BECAUSE ONE SUPER-POWERED BEING---
I MEAN IT, ALL RIGHT! JUST READ THIS LAST BULLETIN---
SEE FOR YOURSELF IF THERE'S ANY POINT IN GOING ON!
ALL OVER EARTH, MEN HAVE GIVEN IN TO DESPAIR--
ALL INDUSTRY HAS COMPLETELY SHUT DOWN! NO ONE WILL WORK!
EVERYWHERE-- THE HUMAN RACE HOPELESSLY WAITS--FOR ITS DOOM!
THERE'S BEEN LOOTING--- PILLAGING-- UNOPPOSED BY ANY AUTHORITY!

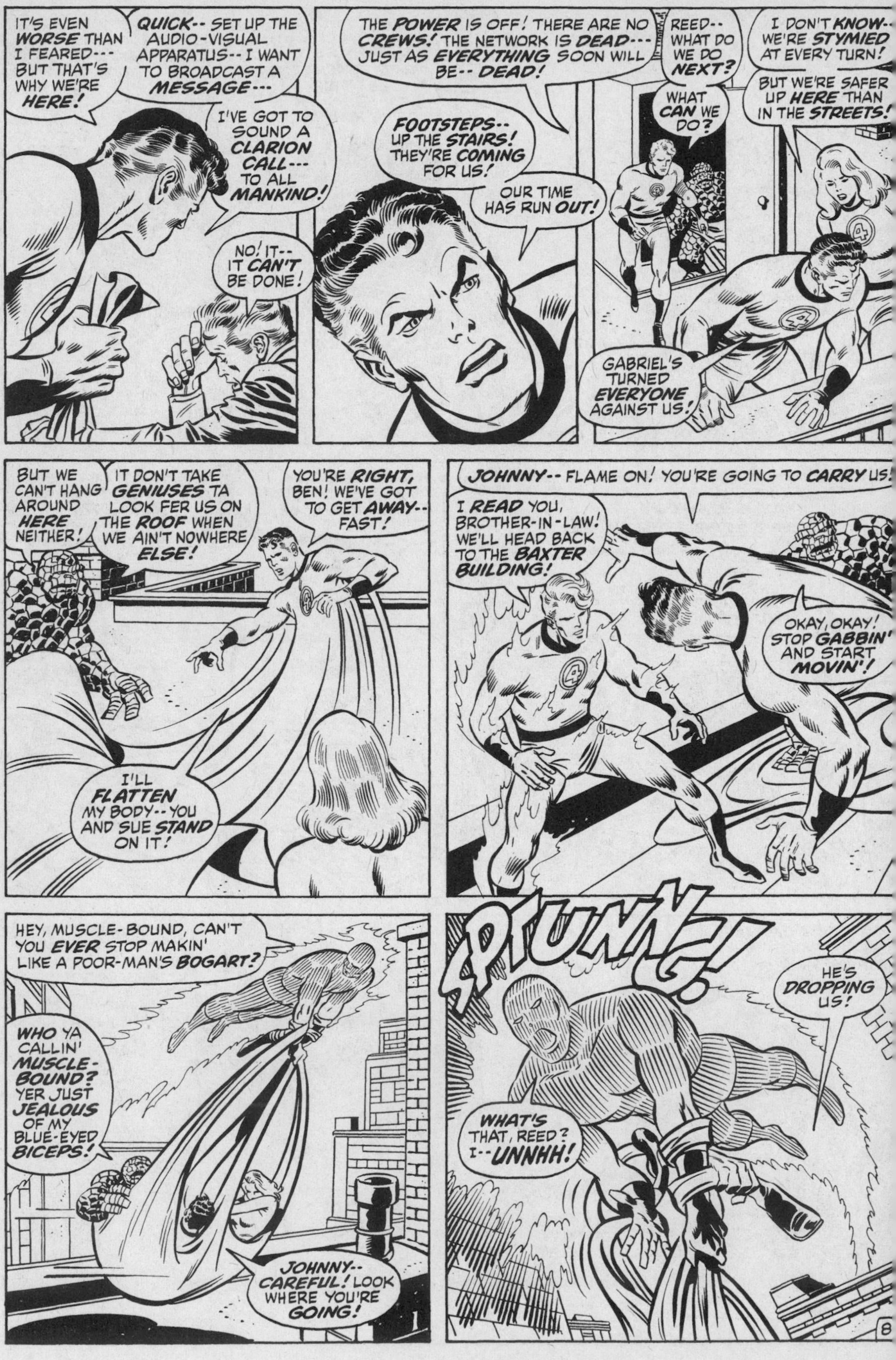
IT'S EVEN WORSE THAN I FEARED--- BUT THAT'S WHY WE'RE HERE!
QUICK-- SET UP THE AUDIO-VISUAL APPARATUS-- I WANT TO BROADCAST A MESSAGE---
I'VE GOT TO SOUND A CLARION CALL--- TO ALL MANKIND!
NO! IT-- IT CAN'T BE DONE!
THE POWER IS OFF! THERE ARE NO CREWS! THE NETWORK IS DEAD--- JUST AS EVERYTHING SOON WILL BE-- DEAD!
FOOTSTEPS-- UP THE STAIRS! THEY'RE COMING FOR US!
OUR TIME HAS RUN OUT!
REED-- WHAT DO WE DO NEXT?
WHAT CAN WE DO?
I DON'T KNOW-- WE'RE STYMIED AT EVERY TURN!
BUT WE'RE SAFER UP HERE THAN IN THE STREETS!
GABRIEL'S TURNED EVERYONE AGAINST US!
BUT WE CAN'T HANG AROUND HERE NEITHER!
IT DON'T TAKE GENIUSES TA LOOK FER US ON THE ROOF WHEN WE AIN'T NOWHERE ELSE!
YOU'RE RIGHT, BEN! WE'VE GOT TO GET AWAY-- FAST!
I'LL FLATTEN MY BODY-- YOU AND SUE STAND ON IT!
JOHNNY-- FLAME ON! YOU'RE GOING TO CARRY US!
I READ YOU, BROTHER-IN-LAW! WE'LL HEAD BACK TO THE BAXTER BUILDING!
OKAY, OKAY! STOP GABBIN' AND START MOVIN'!
HEY, MUSCLE-BOUND, CAN'T YOU EVER STOP MAKIN' LIKE A POOR-MAN'S BOGART?
WHO YA CALLIN' MUSCLE-BOUND? YER JUST JEALOUS OF MY BLUE-EYED BICEPS!
JOHNNY-- CAREFUL! LOOK WHERE YOU'RE GOING!
SPTUNNG!
HE'S DROPPING US!
WHAT'S THAT, REED? I-- UNNHH!
8

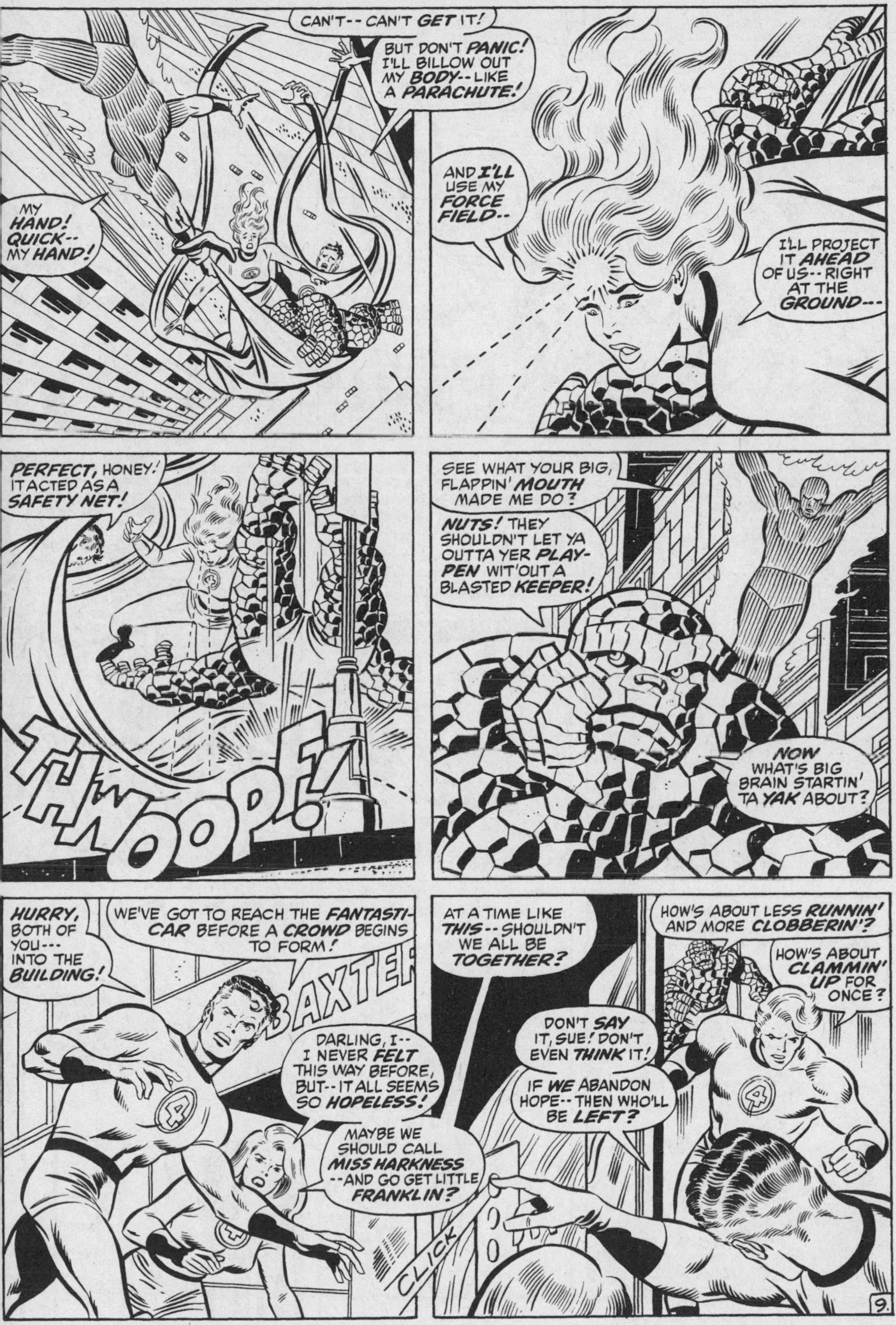
CAN'T-- CAN'T GET IT!
BUT DON'T PANIC! I'LL BILLOW OUT MY BODY--LIKE A PARACHUTE!
MY HAND! QUICK-- MY HAND!
AND I'LL USE MY FORCE FIELD--
I'LL PROJECT IT AHEAD OF US-- RIGHT AT THE GROUND---
PERFECT, HONEY! IT ACTED AS A SAFETY NET!
THWOOP.F.!
SEE WHAT YOUR BIG, FLAPPIN' MOUTH MADE ME DO?
NUTS! THEY SHOULDN'T LET YA OUTTA YER PLAY-PEN WIT'OUT A BLASTED KEEPER!
NOW WHAT'S BIG BRAIN STARTIN' TA YAK ABOUT?
HURRY, BOTH OF YOU--- INTO THE BUILDING!
WE'VE GOT TO REACH THE FANTASTI-CAR BEFORE A CROWD BEGINS TO FORM!
BAXTER
DARLING, I-- I NEVER FELT THIS WAY BEFORE, BUT--IT ALL SEEMS SO HOPELESS!
MAYBE WE SHOULD CALL MISS HARKNESS --AND GO GET LITTLE FRANKLIN?
AT A TIME LIKE THIS--SHOULDN'T WE ALL BE TOGETHER?
DON'T SAY IT, SUE! DON'T EVEN THINK IT!
IF WE ABANDON HOPE--THEN WHO'LL BE LEFT?
CLICK
HOW'S ABOUT LESS RUNNIN' AND MORE CLOBBERIN'?
HOW'S ABOUT CLAMMIN' UP FOR ONCE?
9.

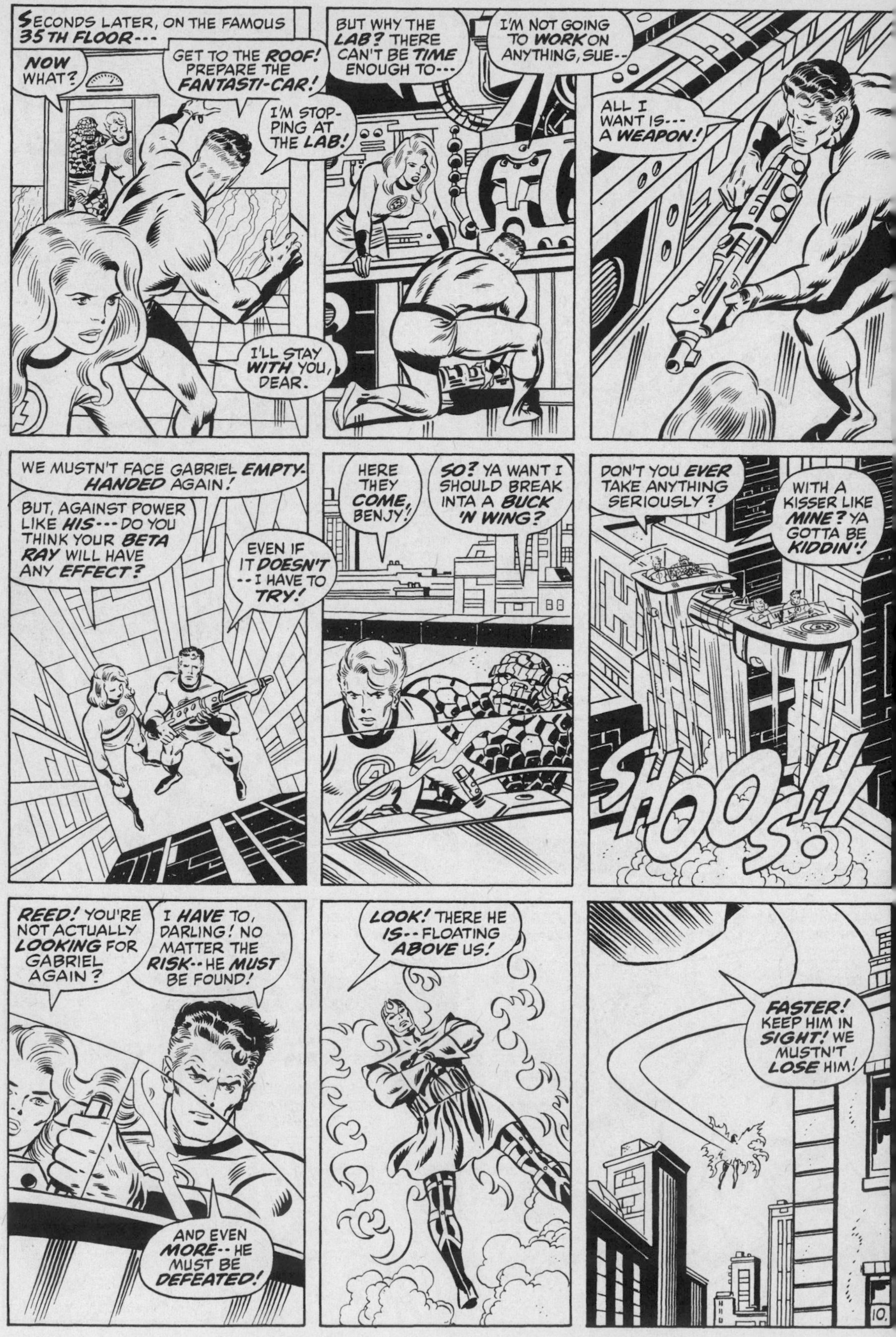
SECONDS LATER, ON THE FAMOUS 35TH FLOOR---
NOW WHAT?
GET TO THE ROOF! PREPARE THE FANTASTI-CAR!
I'M STOPPING AT THE LAB!
I'LL STAY WITH YOU, DEAR.
BUT WHY THE LAB? THERE CAN'T BE TIME ENOUGH TO---
I'M NOT GOING TO WORK ON ANYTHING, SUE--
ALL I WANT IS--- A WEAPON!
WE MUSTN'T FACE GABRIEL EMPTY-HANDED AGAIN!
BUT, AGAINST POWER LIKE HIS--- DO YOU THINK YOUR BETA RAY WILL HAVE ANY EFFECT?
EVEN IF IT DOESN'T --I HAVE TO TRY!
HERE THEY COME, BENJY!
SO? YA WANT I SHOULD BREAK INTA A BUCK 'N WING?
DON'T YOU EVER TAKE ANYTHING SERIOUSLY?
WITH A KISSER LIKE MINE? YA GOTTA BE KIDDIN'!
SHOOOSH!
REED! YOU'RE NOT ACTUALLY LOOKING FOR GABRIEL AGAIN?
I HAVE TO, DARLING! NO MATTER THE RISK--HE MUST BE FOUND!
AND EVEN MORE--HE MUST BE DEFEATED!
LOOK! THERE HE IS--FLOATING ABOVE US!
FASTER! KEEP HIM IN SIGHT! WE MUSTN'T LOSE HIM!
10

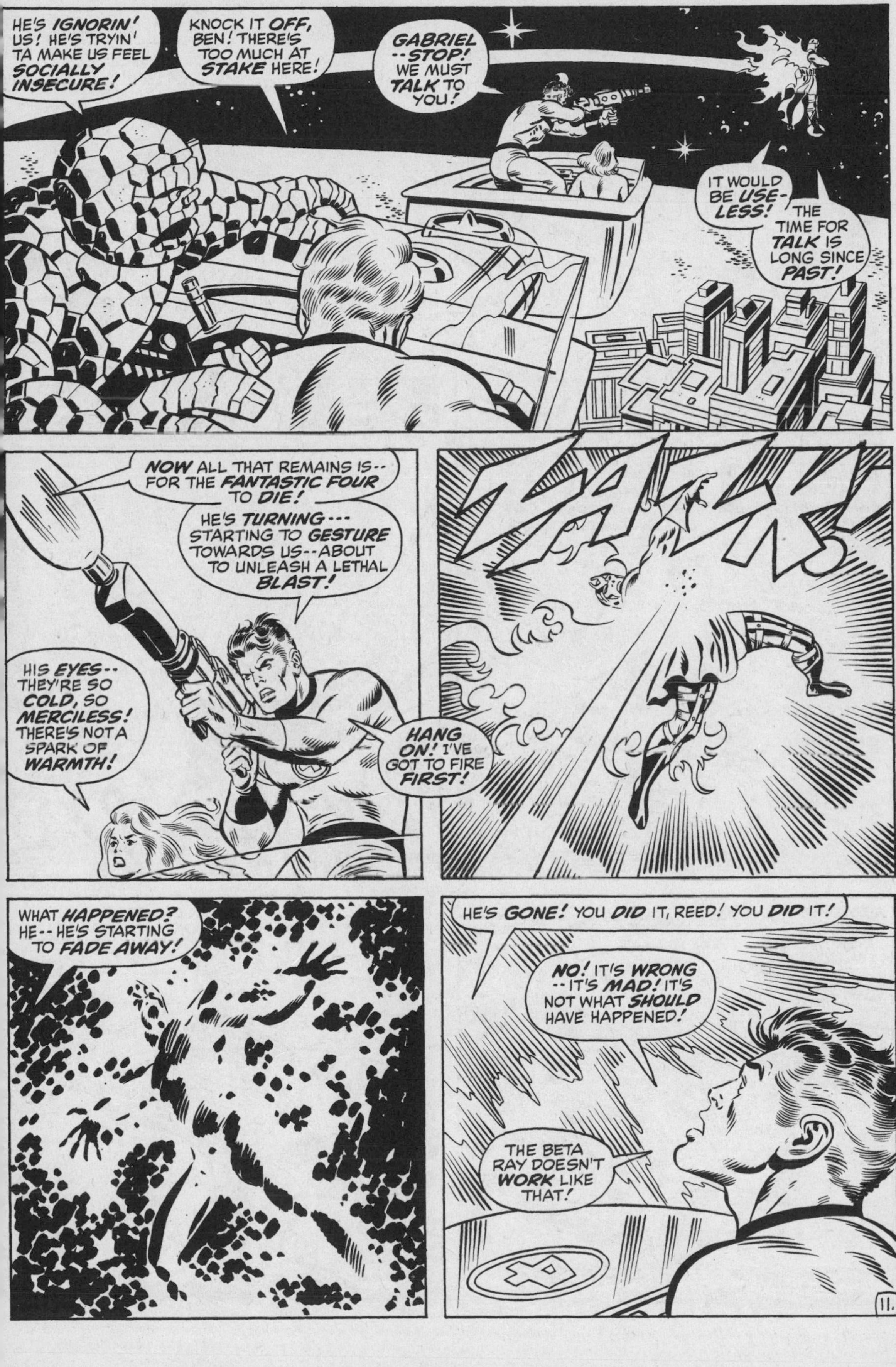
HE'S IGNORIN' US! HE'S TRYIN' TA MAKE US FEEL SOCIALLY INSECURE!
KNOCK IT OFF, BEN! THERE'S TOO MUCH AT STAKE HERE!
GABRIEL --STOP! WE MUST TALK TO YOU!
IT WOULD BE USE-LESS!
THE TIME FOR TALK IS LONG SINCE PAST!
NOW ALL THAT REMAINS IS-- FOR THE FANTASTIC FOUR TO DIE!
HE'S TURNING--- STARTING TO GESTURE TOWARDS US--ABOUT TO UNLEASH A LETHAL BLAST!
HIS EYES-- THEY'RE SO COLD, SO MERCILESS! THERE'S NOT A SPARK OF WARMTH!
HANG ON! I'VE GOT TO FIRE FIRST!
ZAZZK!
WHAT HAPPENED? HE-- HE'S STARTING TO FADE AWAY!
HE'S GONE! YOU DID IT, REED! YOU DID IT!
NO! IT'S WRONG --IT'S MAD! IT'S NOT WHAT SHOULD HAVE HAPPENED!
THE BETA RAY DOESN'T WORK LIKE THAT!
11.

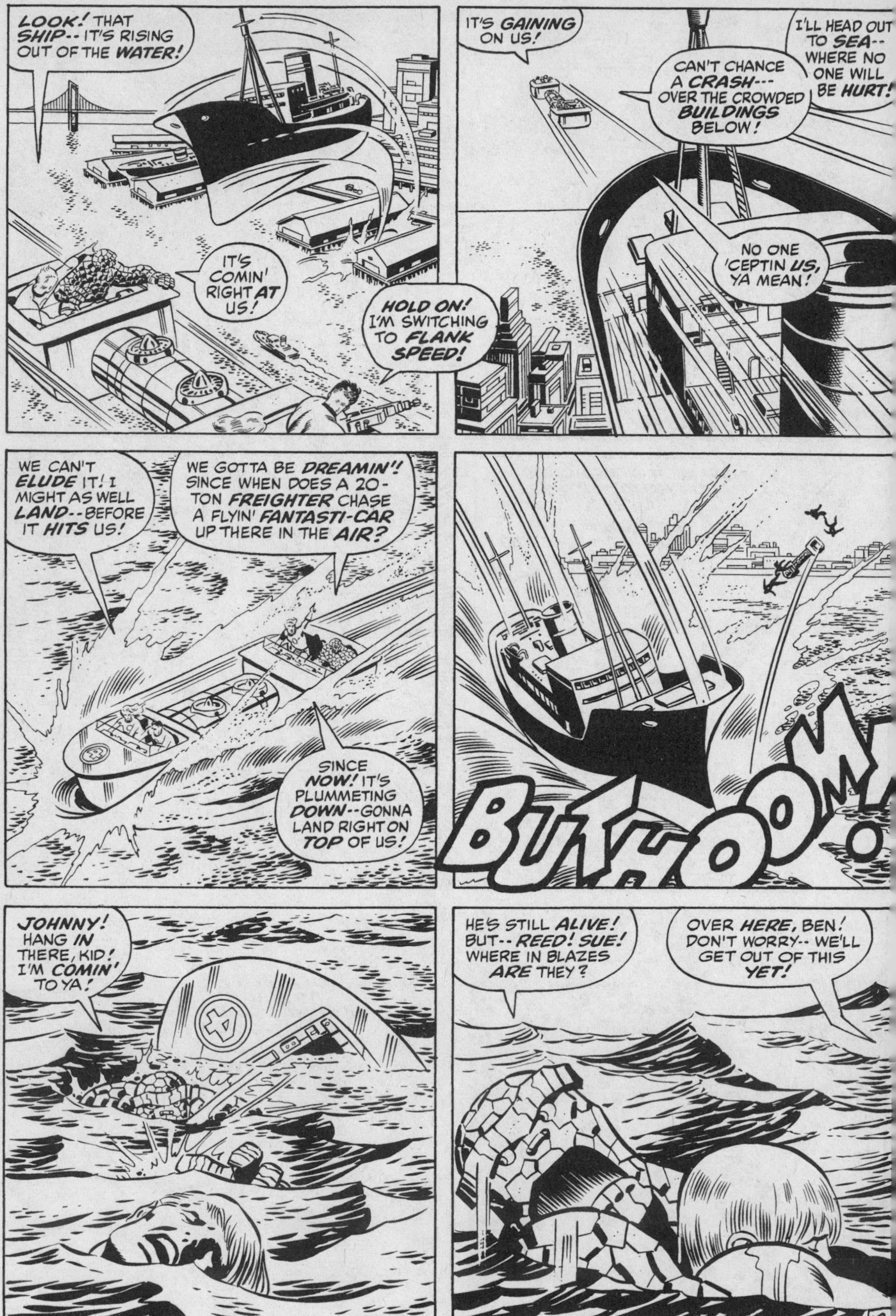

LOOK! THAT SHIP-- IT'S RISING OUT OF THE WATER!
IT'S COMIN' RIGHT AT US!
HOLD ON! I'M SWITCHING TO FLANK SPEED!
IT'S GAINING ON US!
CAN'T CHANCE A CRASH--- OVER THE CROWDED BUILDINGS BELOW!
I'LL HEAD OUT TO SEA-- WHERE NO ONE WILL BE HURT!
NO ONE 'CEPTIN US, YA MEAN!
WE CAN'T ELUDE IT! I MIGHT AS WELL LAND--BEFORE IT HITS US!
WE GOTTA BE DREAMIN'! SINCE WHEN DOES A 20-TON FREIGHTER CHASE A FLYIN' FANTASTI-CAR UP THERE IN THE AIR?
SINCE NOW! IT'S PLUMMETING DOWN--GONNA LAND RIGHT ON TOP OF US!
BUHOOOM!
JOHNNY! HANG IN THERE, KID! I'M COMIN' TO YA!
HE'S STILL ALIVE! BUT-- REED! SUE! WHERE IN BLAZES ARE THEY?
OVER HERE, BEN! DON'T WORRY-- WE'LL GET OUT OF THIS YET!
12

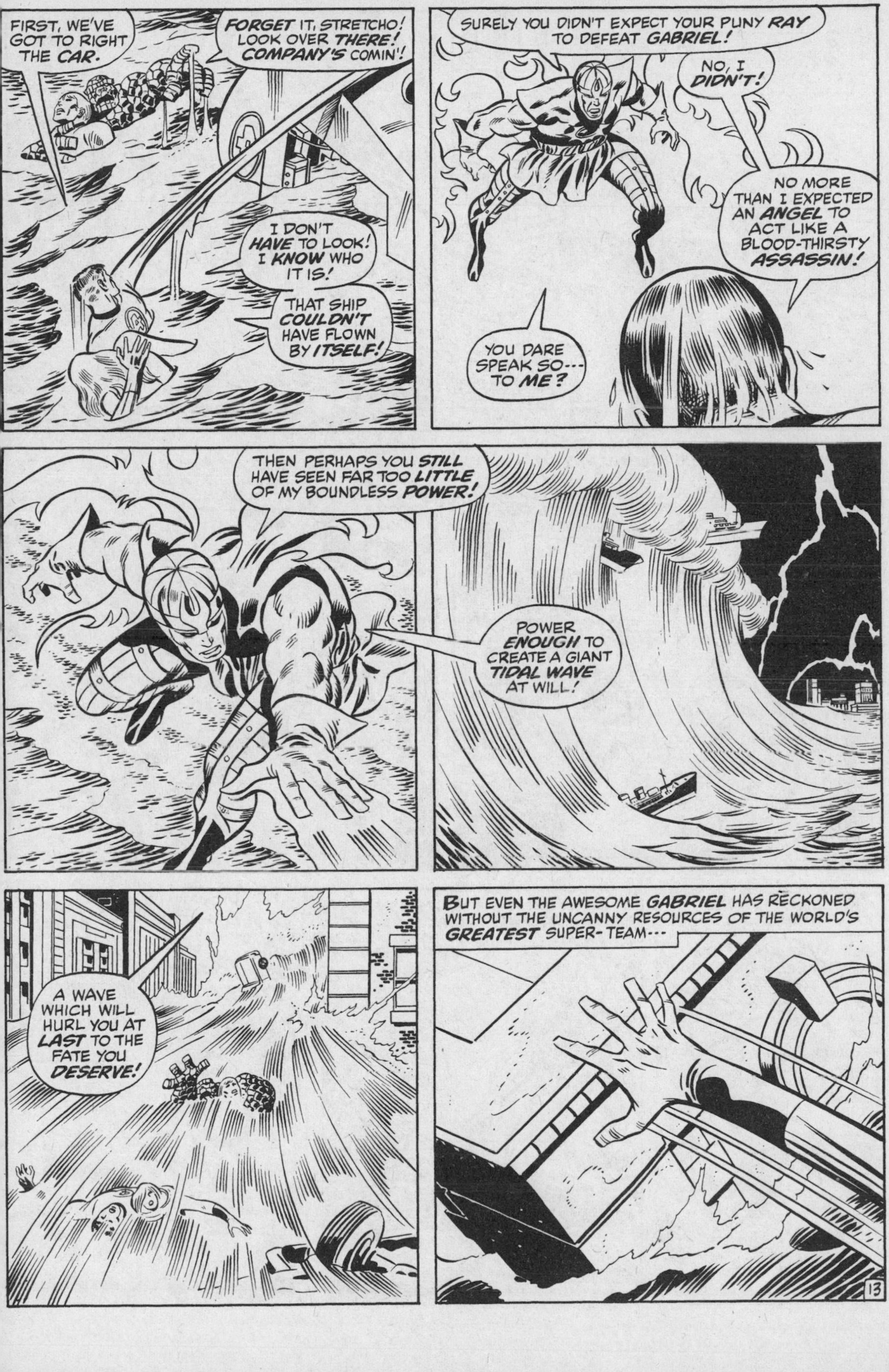

FIRST, WE'VE GOT TO RIGHT THE CAR.
FORGET IT, STRETCHO! LOOK OVER THERE! COMPANY'S COMIN'!
I DON'T HAVE TO LOOK! I KNOW WHO IT IS!
THAT SHIP COULDN'T HAVE FLOWN BY ITSELF!
SURELY YOU DIDN'T EXPECT YOUR PUNY RAY TO DEFEAT GABRIEL!
NO, I DIDN'T!
NO MORE THAN I EXPECTED AN ANGEL TO ACT LIKE A BLOOD-THIRSTY ASSASSIN!
YOU DARE SPEAK SO--- TO ME?
THEN PERHAPS YOU STILL HAVE SEEN FAR TOO LITTLE OF MY BOUNDLESS POWER!
POWER ENOUGH TO CREATE A GIANT TIDAL WAVE AT WILL!
A WAVE WHICH WILL HURL YOU AT LAST TO THE FATE YOU DESERVE!
BUT EVEN THE AWESOME GABRIEL HAS RECKONED WITHOUT THE UNCANNY RESOURCES OF THE WORLD'S GREATEST SUPER-TEAM---
13

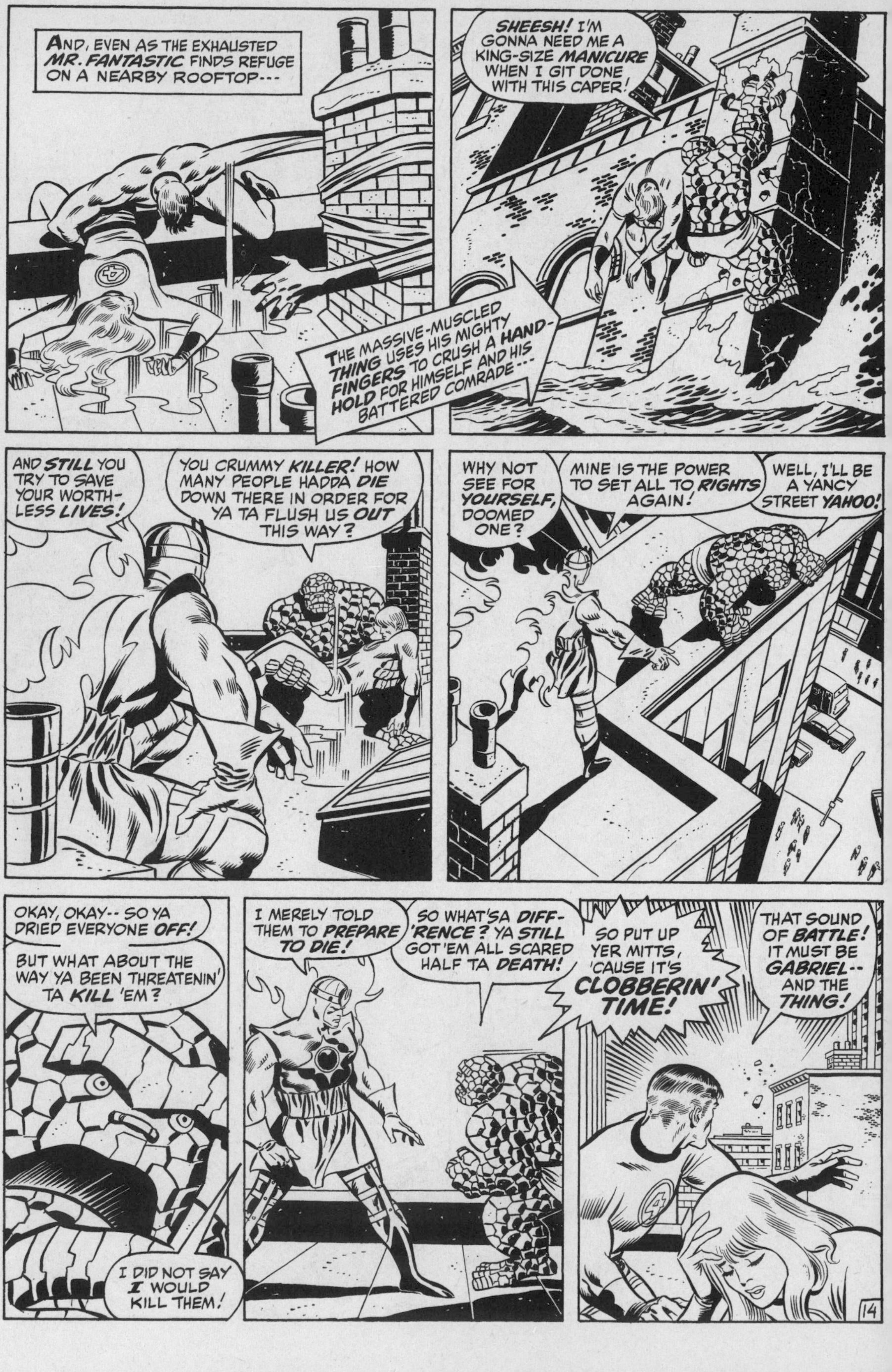
AND, EVEN AS THE EXHAUSTED MR. FANTASTIC FINDS REFUGE ON A NEARBY ROOFTOP---
THE MASSIVE-MUSCLED THING USES HIS MIGHTY FINGERS TO CRUSH A HAND-HOLD FOR HIMSELF AND HIS BATTERED COMRADE---
SHEESH! I'M GONNA NEED ME A KING-SIZE MANICURE WHEN I GIT DONE WITH THIS CAPER!
AND STILL YOU TRY TO SAVE YOUR WORTH-LESS LIVES!
YOU CRUMMY KILLER! HOW MANY PEOPLE HADDA DIE DOWN THERE IN ORDER FOR YA TA FLUSH US OUT THIS WAY?
WHY NOT SEE FOR YOURSELF, DOOMED ONE?
MINE IS THE POWER TO SET ALL TO RIGHTS AGAIN!
WELL, I'LL BE A YANCY STREET YAHOO!
OKAY, OKAY-- SO YA DRIED EVERYONE OFF!
BUT WHAT ABOUT THE WAY YA BEEN THREATENIN' TA KILL 'EM?
I DID NOT SAY I WOULD KILL THEM!
I MERELY TOLD THEM TO PREPARE TO DIE!
SO WHAT'SA DIFF-'RENCE? YA STILL GOT 'EM ALL SCARED HALF TA DEATH!
SO PUT UP YER MITTS, 'CAUSE IT'S CLOBBERIN' TIME!
THAT SOUND OF BATTLE! IT MUST BE GABRIEL-- AND THE THING!
14

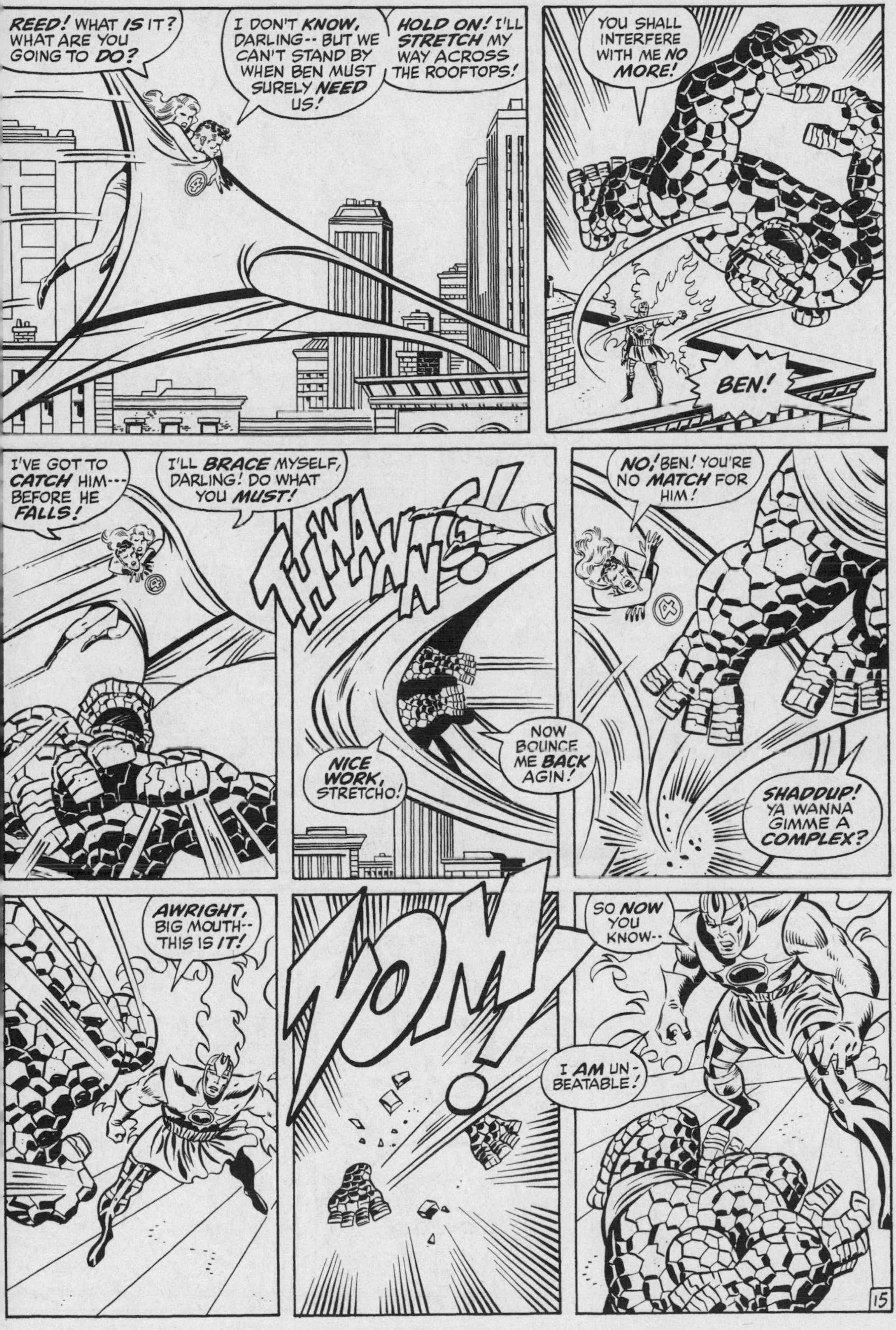
REED! WHAT IS IT? WHAT ARE YOU GOING TO DO?
I DON'T KNOW, DARLING-- BUT WE CAN'T STAND BY WHEN BEN MUST SURELY NEED US!
HOLD ON! I'LL STRETCH MY WAY ACROSS THE ROOFTOPS!
YOU SHALL INTERFERE WITH ME NO MORE!
BEN!
I'VE GOT TO CATCH HIM--- BEFORE HE FALLS!
I'LL BRACE MYSELF, DARLING! DO WHAT YOU MUST!
THWANNG!
NICE WORK, STRETCHO!
NOW BOUNCE ME BACK AGIN!
NO! BEN! YOU'RE NO MATCH FOR HIM!
SHADDUP! YA WANNA GIMME A COMPLEX?
AWRIGHT, BIG MOUTH-- THIS IS IT!
ZOOM
SO NOW YOU KNOW--
I AM UNBEATABLE!
15

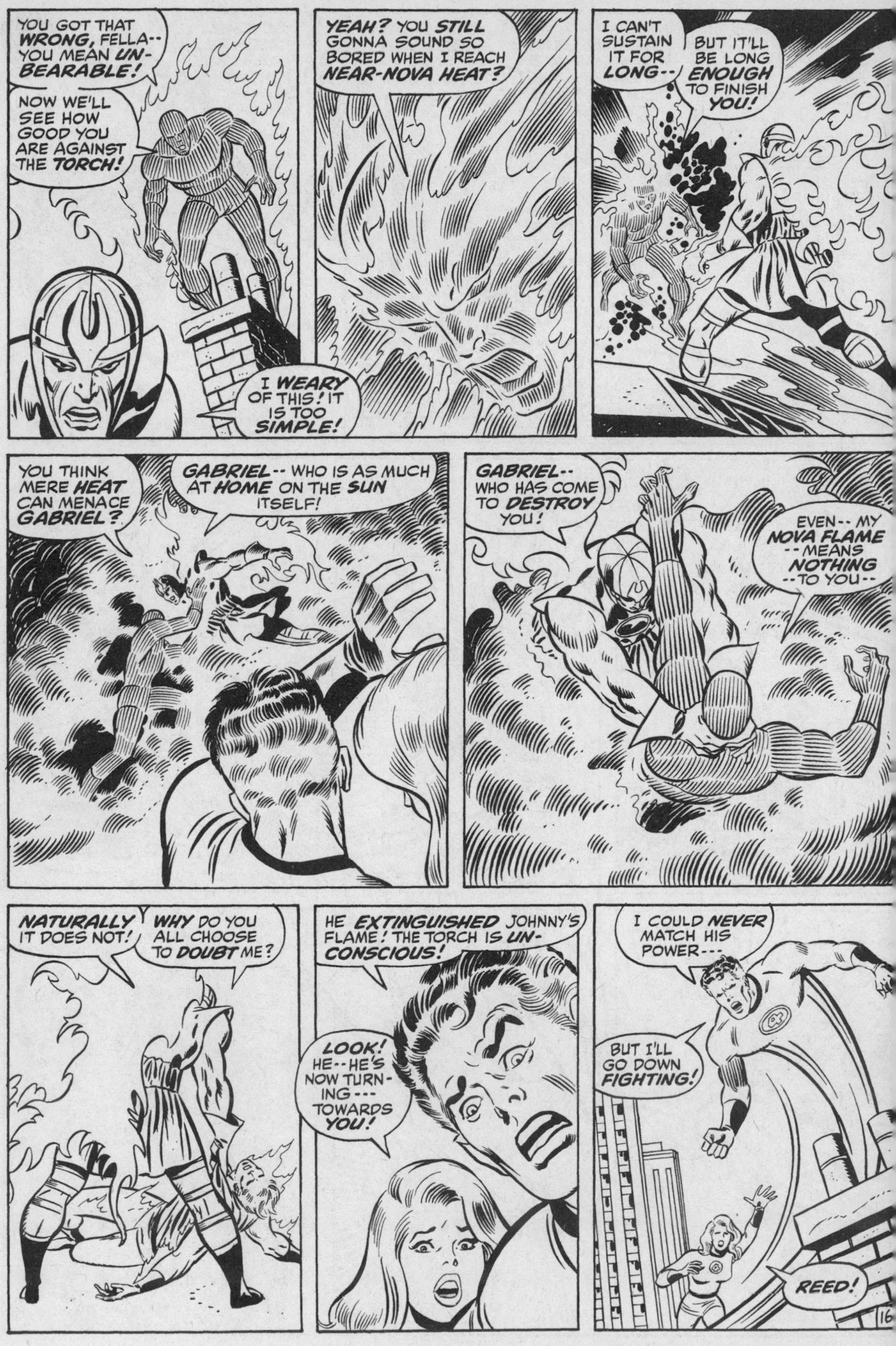
YOU GOT THAT WRONG, FELLA-- YOU MEAN UN-BEARABLE!
NOW WE'LL SEE HOW GOOD YOU ARE AGAINST THE TORCH!
YEAH? YOU STILL GONNA SOUND SO BORED WHEN I REACH NEAR-NOVA HEAT?
I WEARY OF THIS! IT IS TOO SIMPLE!
I CAN'T SUSTAIN IT FOR LONG--
BUT IT'LL BE LONG ENOUGH TO FINISH YOU!
YOU THINK MERE HEAT CAN MENACE GABRIEL?
GABRIEL-- WHO IS AS MUCH AT HOME ON THE SUN ITSELF!
GABRIEL-- WHO HAS COME TO DESTROY YOU!
EVEN-- MY NOVA FLAME --MEANS NOTHING --TO YOU--
NATURALLY IT DOES NOT!
WHY DO YOU ALL CHOOSE TO DOUBT ME?
HE EXTINGUISHED JOHNNY'S FLAME! THE TORCH IS UN-CONSCIOUS!
LOOK! HE--HE'S NOW TURN-ING--- TOWARDS YOU!
I COULD NEVER MATCH HIS POWER---
BUT I'LL GO DOWN FIGHTING!
REED!
16

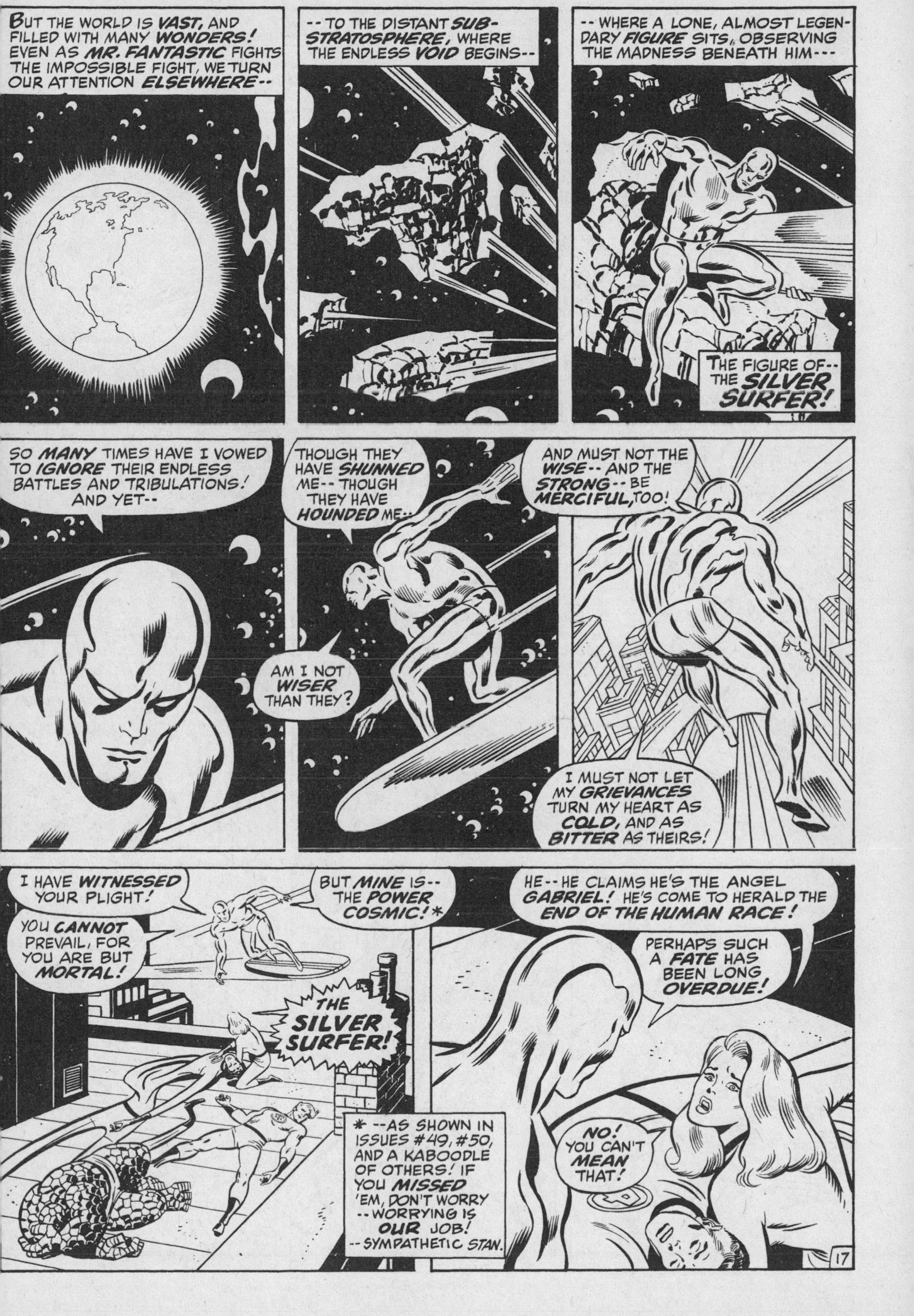

BUT THE WORLD IS VAST, AND FILLED WITH MANY WONDERS! EVEN AS MR. FANTASTIC FIGHTS THE IMPOSSIBLE FIGHT, WE TURN OUR ATTENTION ELSEWHERE--
--TO THE DISTANT SUB-STRATOSPHERE, WHERE THE ENDLESS VOID BEGINS--
--WHERE A LONE, ALMOST LEGENDARY FIGURE SITS, OBSERVING THE MADNESS BENEATH HIM---
THE FIGURE OF-- THE SILVER SURFER!
SO MANY TIMES HAVE I VOWED TO IGNORE THEIR ENDLESS BATTLES AND TRIBULATIONS! AND YET--
THOUGH THEY HAVE SHUNNED ME-- THOUGH THEY HAVE HOUNDED ME--
AM I NOT WISER THAN THEY?
AND MUST NOT THE WISE-- AND THE STRONG-- BE MERCIFUL, TOO!
I MUST NOT LET MY GRIEVANCES TURN MY HEART AS COLD, AND AS BITTER AS THEIRS!
I HAVE WITNESSED YOUR PLIGHT!
YOU CANNOT PREVAIL, FOR YOU ARE BUT MORTAL!
BUT MINE IS-- THE POWER COSMIC!*
THE SILVER SURFER!
* --AS SHOWN IN ISSUES #49, #50, AND A KABOODLE OF OTHERS! IF YOU MISSED 'EM, DON'T WORRY --WORRYING IS OUR JOB! --SYMPATHETIC STAN.
HE--HE CLAIMS HE'S THE ANGEL GABRIEL! HE'S COME TO HERALD THE END OF THE HUMAN RACE!
PERHAPS SUCH A FATE HAS BEEN LONG OVERDUE!
NO! YOU CAN'T MEAN THAT!

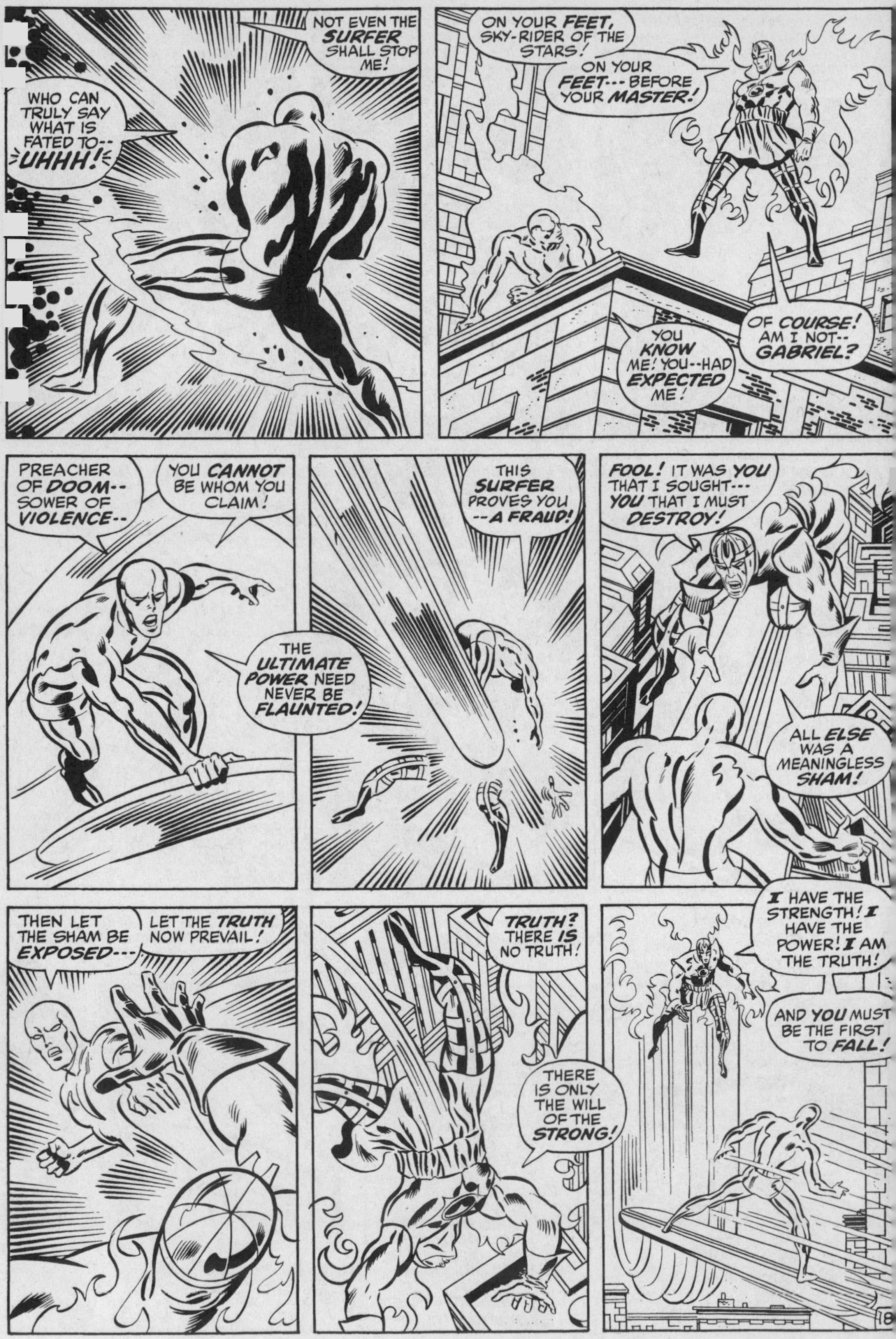
NOT EVEN THE SURFER SHALL STOP ME!
WHO CAN TRULY SAY WHAT IS FATED TO-- UHHH!
ON YOUR FEET, SKY-RIDER OF THE STARS!
ON YOUR FEET--- BEFORE YOUR MASTER!
YOU KNOW ME! YOU--HAD EXPECTED ME!
OF COURSE! AM I NOT-- GABRIEL?
PREACHER OF DOOM-- SOWER OF VIOLENCE--
YOU CANNOT BE WHOM YOU CLAIM!
THE ULTIMATE POWER NEED NEVER BE FLAUNTED!
THIS SURFER PROVES YOU --A FRAUD!
FOOL! IT WAS YOU THAT I SOUGHT--- YOU THAT I MUST DESTROY!
ALL ELSE WAS A MEANINGLESS SHAM!
THEN LET THE SHAM BE EXPOSED---
LET THE TRUTH NOW PREVAIL!
TRUTH? THERE IS NO TRUTH!
THERE IS ONLY THE WILL OF THE STRONG!
I HAVE THE STRENGTH! I HAVE THE POWER! I AM THE TRUTH!
AND YOU MUST BE THE FIRST TO FALL!
18

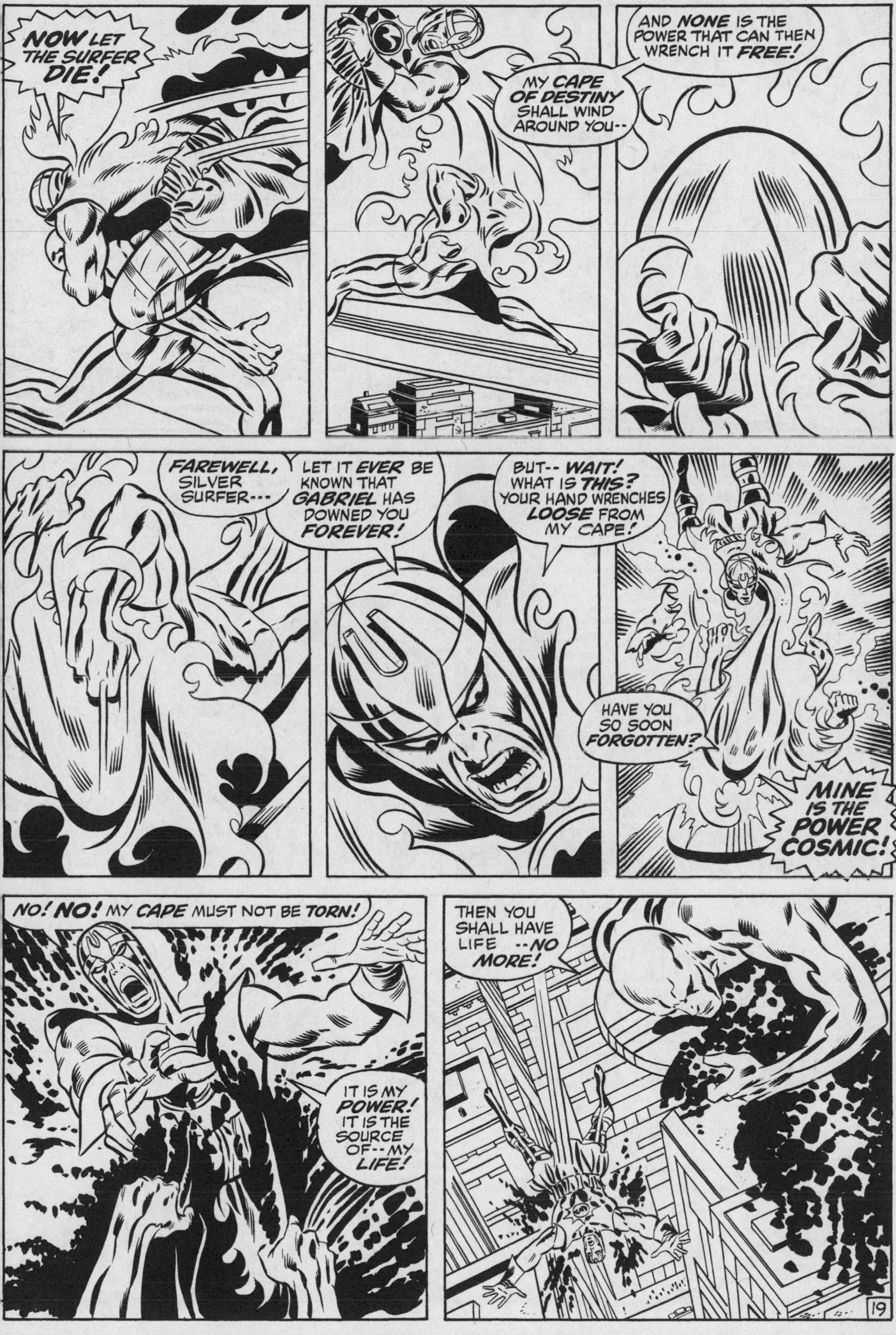

NOW LET THE SURFER DIE!
MY CAPE OF DESTINY SHALL WIND AROUND YOU--
AND NONE IS THE POWER THAT CAN THEN WRENCH IT FREE!
FAREWELL, SILVER SURFER---
LET IT EVER BE KNOWN THAT GABRIEL HAS DOWNED YOU FOREVER!
BUT-- WAIT! WHAT IS THIS? YOUR HAND WRENCHES LOOSE FROM MY CAPE!
HAVE YOU SO SOON FORGOTTEN?
MINE IS THE POWER COSMIC!
NO! NO! MY CAPE MUST NOT BE TORN!
IT IS MY POWER! IT IS THE SOURCE OF-- MY LIFE!
THEN YOU SHALL HAVE LIFE --NO MORE!
19

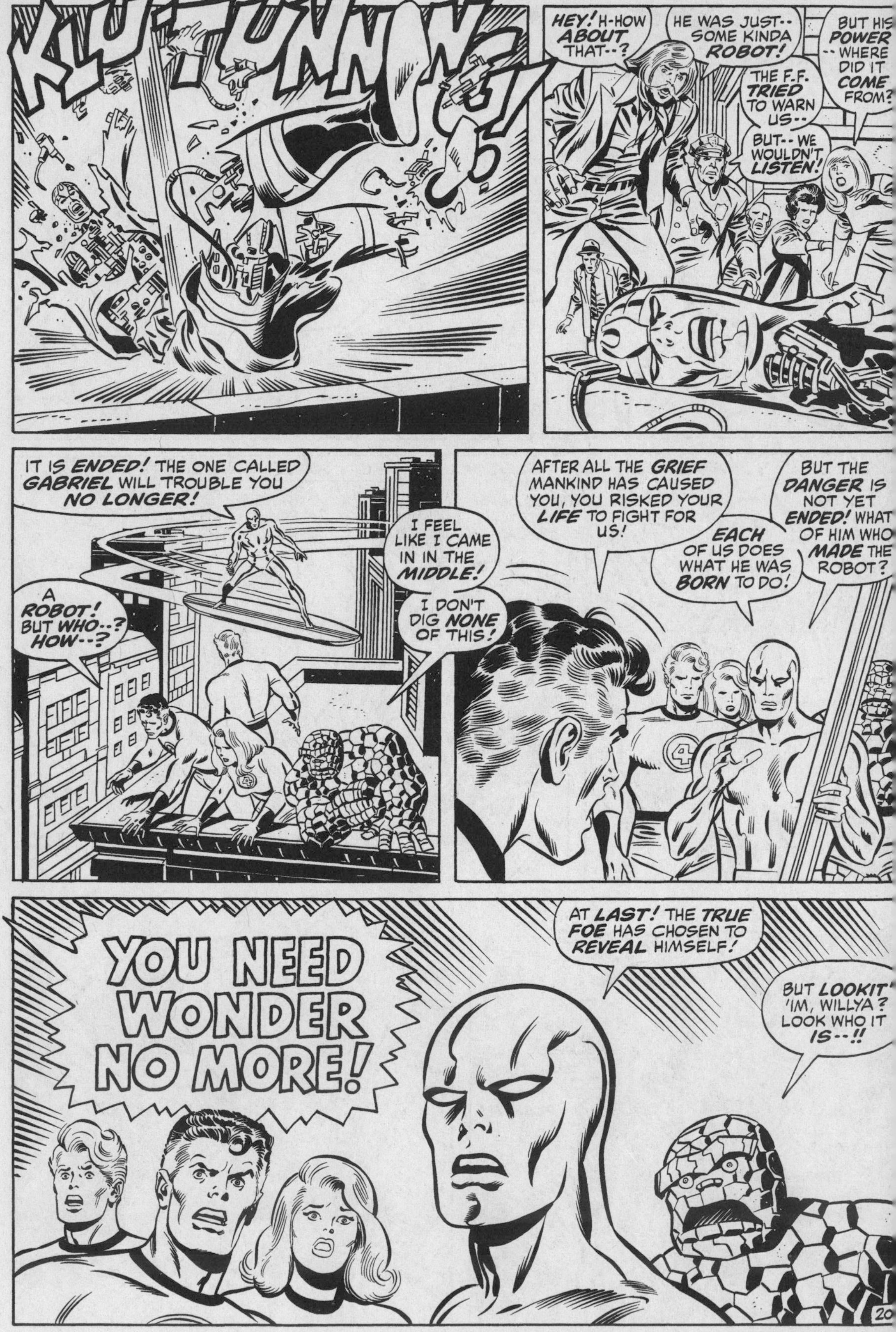
KLU-TUNNNNG!
HEY! H-HOW ABOUT THAT--?
HE WAS JUST-- SOME KINDA ROBOT!
THE F.F. TRIED TO WARN US--
BUT-- WE WOULDN'T LISTEN!
BUT HIS POWER--WHERE DID IT COME FROM?
IT IS ENDED! THE ONE CALLED GABRIEL WILL TROUBLE YOU NO LONGER!
A ROBOT! BUT WHO--? HOW--?
I FEEL LIKE I CAME IN IN THE MIDDLE!
I DON'T DIG NONE OF THIS!
AFTER ALL THE GRIEF MANKIND HAS CAUSED YOU, YOU RISKED YOUR LIFE TO FIGHT FOR US!
EACH OF US DOES WHAT HE WAS BORN TO DO!
BUT THE DANGER IS NOT YET ENDED! WHAT OF HIM WHO MADE THE ROBOT?
YOU NEED WONDER NO MORE!
AT LAST! THE TRUE FOE HAS CHOSEN TO REVEAL HIMSELF!
BUT LOOKIT 'IM, WILLYA? LOOK WHO IT IS--!!
20

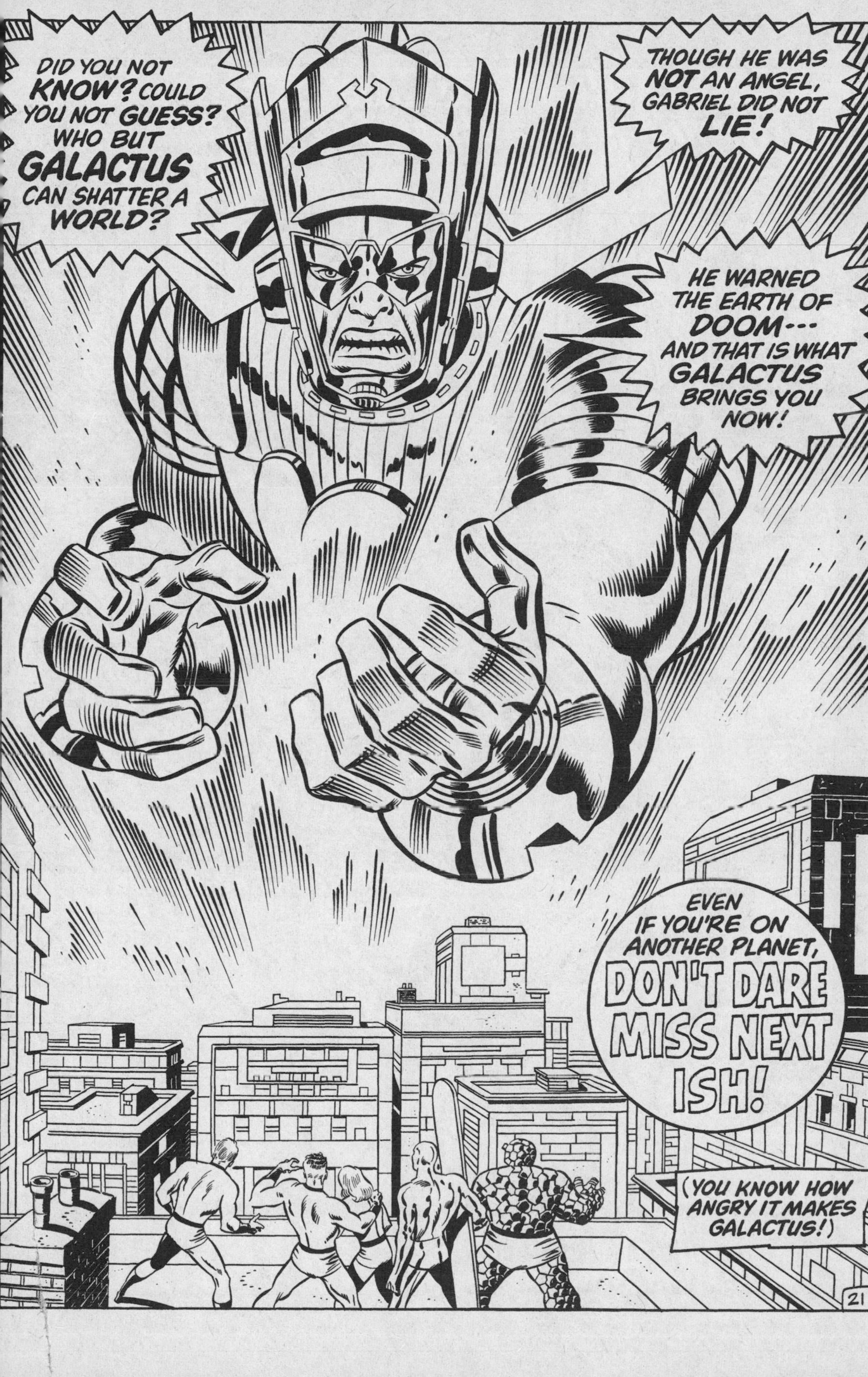
DID YOU NOT KNOW? COULD YOU NOT GUESS? WHO BUT GALACTUS CAN SHATTER A WORLD?
THOUGH HE WAS NOT AN ANGEL, GABRIEL DID NOT LIE!
HE WARNED THE EARTH OF DOOM--- AND THAT IS WHAT GALACTUS BRINGS YOU NOW!
EVEN IF YOU'RE ON ANOTHER PLANET, DON'T DARE MISS NEXT ISH!
(YOU KNOW HOW ANGRY IT MAKES GALACTUS!)
21

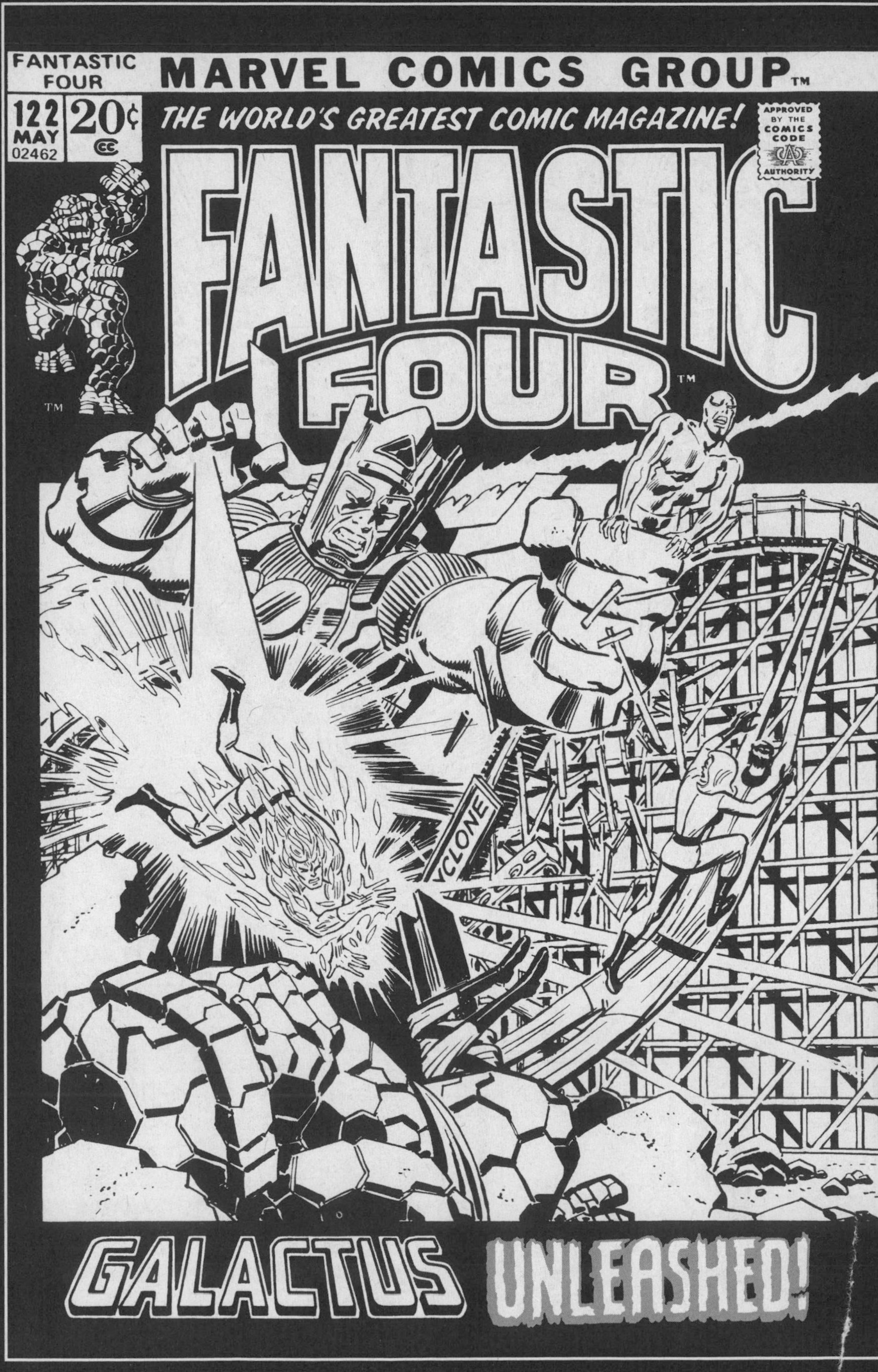
FANTASTIC FOUR
MARVEL COMICS GROUP™
122 MAY 02462
20¢ CC
THE WORLD'S GREATEST COMIC MAGAZINE!
APPROVED BY THE COMICS CODE CA AUTHORITY
FANTASTIC FOUR™
™
CYCLONE
GALACTUS UNLEASHED!

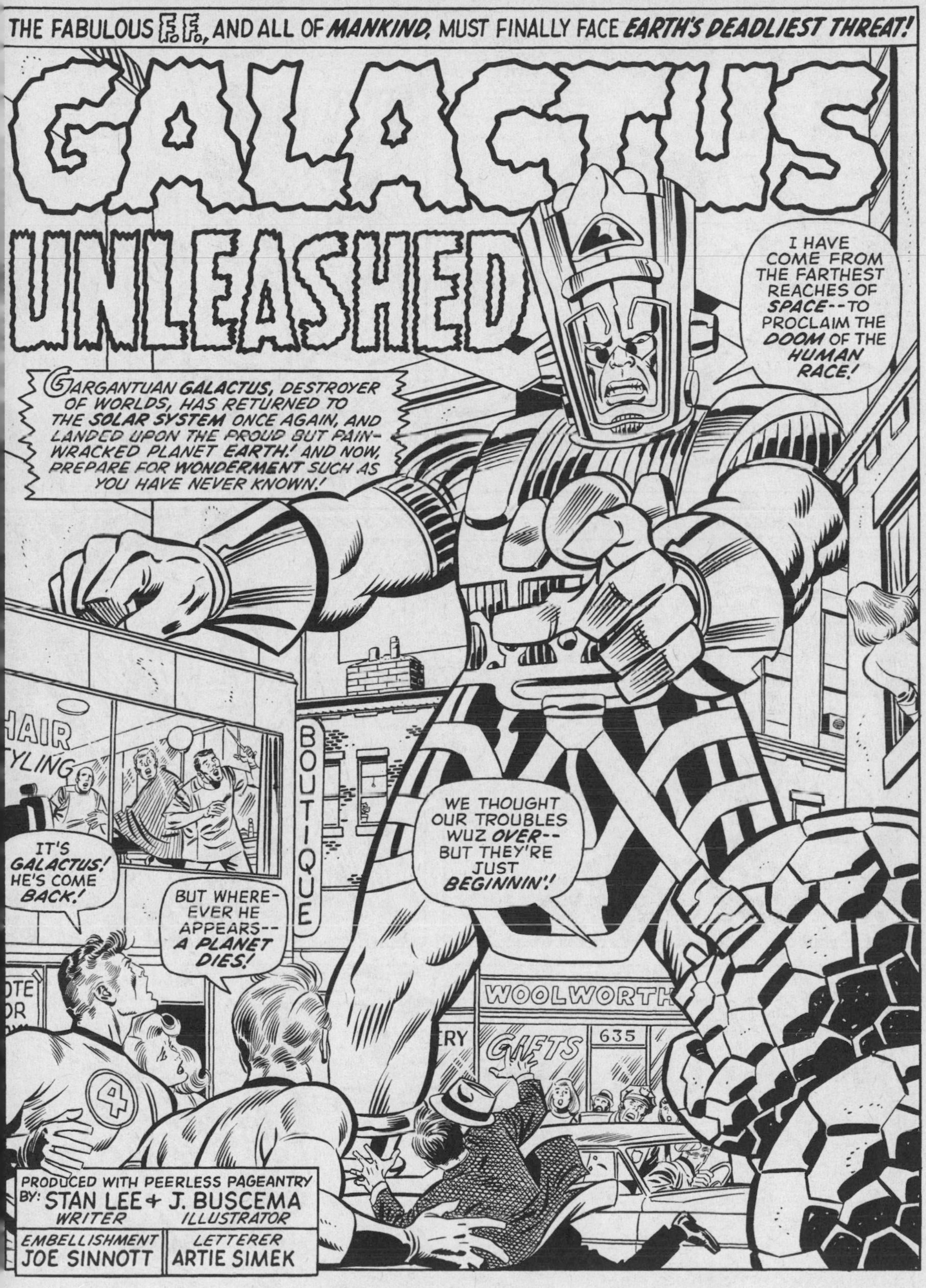
THE FABULOUS F.F., AND ALL OF MANKIND, MUST FINALLY FACE EARTH'S DEADLIEST THREAT!
GALACTUS UNLEASHED
GARGANTUAN GALACTUS, DESTROYER OF WORLDS, HAS RETURNED TO THE SOLAR SYSTEM ONCE AGAIN, AND LANDED UPON THE PROUD BUT PAIN-WRACKED PLANET EARTH! AND NOW, PREPARE FOR WONDERMENT SUCH AS YOU HAVE NEVER KNOWN!
I HAVE COME FROM THE FARTHEST REACHES OF SPACE--TO PROCLAIM THE DOOM OF THE HUMAN RACE!
HAIR STYLING
BOUTIQUE
IT'S GALACTUS! HE'S COME BACK!
BUT WHEREEVER HE APPEARS-- A PLANET DIES!
WE THOUGHT OUR TROUBLES WUZ OVER-- BUT THEY'RE JUST BEGINNIN'!
WOOLWORTH
GIFTS
635
PRODUCED WITH PEERLESS PAGEANTRY BY: STAN LEE + J. BUSCEMA
WRITER ILLUSTRATOR
EMBELLISHMENT JOE SINNOTT
LETTERER ARTIE SIMEK

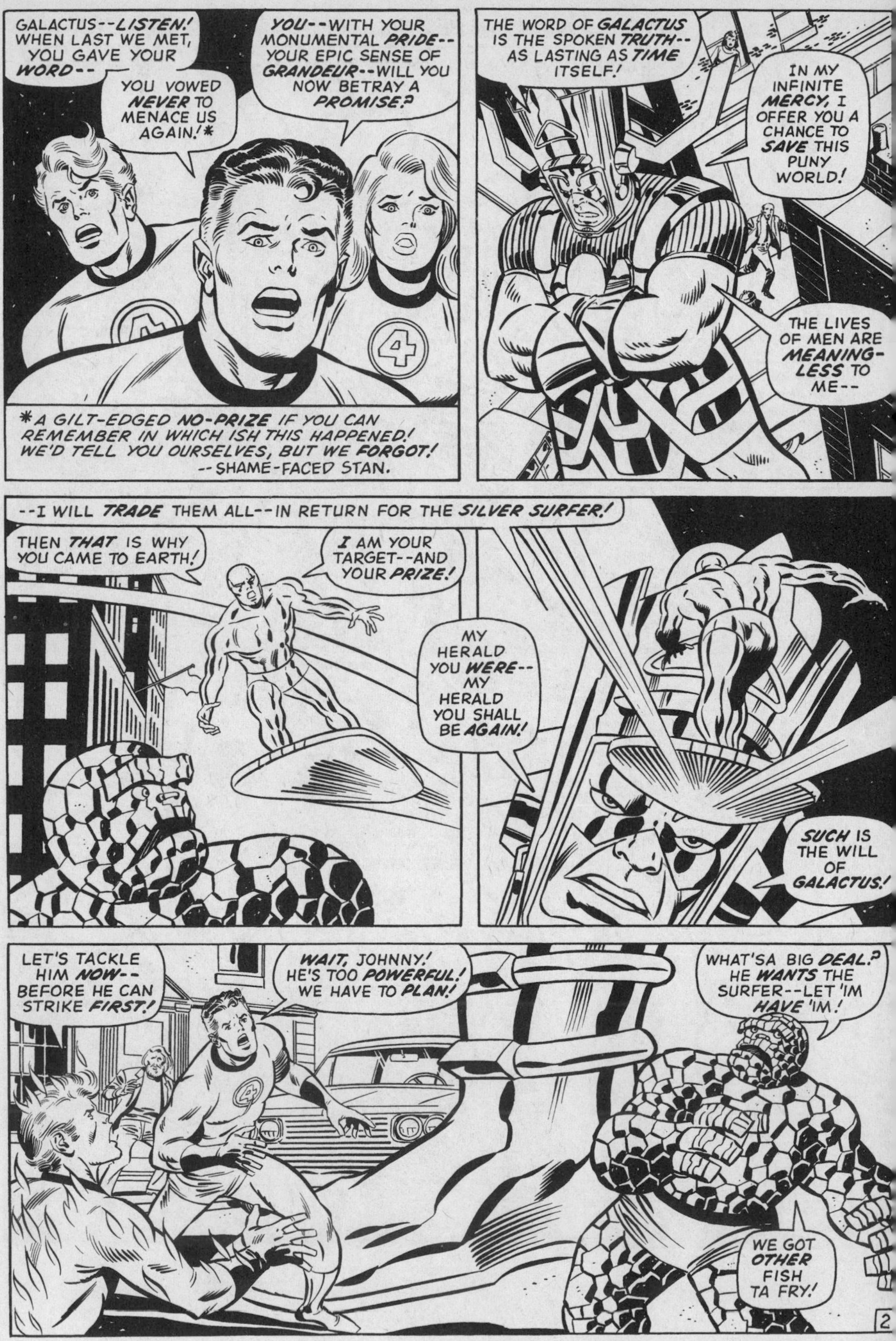
GALACTUS--LISTEN! WHEN LAST WE MET, YOU GAVE YOUR WORD--
YOU VOWED NEVER TO MENACE US AGAIN!*
YOU--WITH YOUR MONUMENTAL PRIDE--YOUR EPIC SENSE OF GRANDEUR--WILL YOU NOW BETRAY A PROMISE?
*A GILT-EDGED NO-PRIZE IF YOU CAN REMEMBER IN WHICH ISH THIS HAPPENED! WE'D TELL YOU OURSELVES, BUT WE FORGOT! --SHAME-FACED STAN.
THE WORD OF GALACTUS IS THE SPOKEN TRUTH--AS LASTING AS TIME ITSELF!
IN MY INFINITE MERCY, I OFFER YOU A CHANCE TO SAVE THIS PUNY WORLD!
THE LIVES OF MEN ARE MEANINGLESS TO ME--
--I WILL TRADE THEM ALL--IN RETURN FOR THE SILVER SURFER!
THEN THAT IS WHY YOU CAME TO EARTH!
I AM YOUR TARGET--AND YOUR PRIZE!
MY HERALD YOU WERE--MY HERALD YOU SHALL BE AGAIN!
SUCH IS THE WILL OF GALACTUS!
LET'S TACKLE HIM NOW--BEFORE HE CAN STRIKE FIRST!
WAIT, JOHNNY! HE'S TOO POWERFUL! WE HAVE TO PLAN!
WHAT'SA BIG DEAL? HE WANTS THE SURFER--LET 'IM HAVE 'IM!
WE GOT OTHER FISH TA FRY!
2

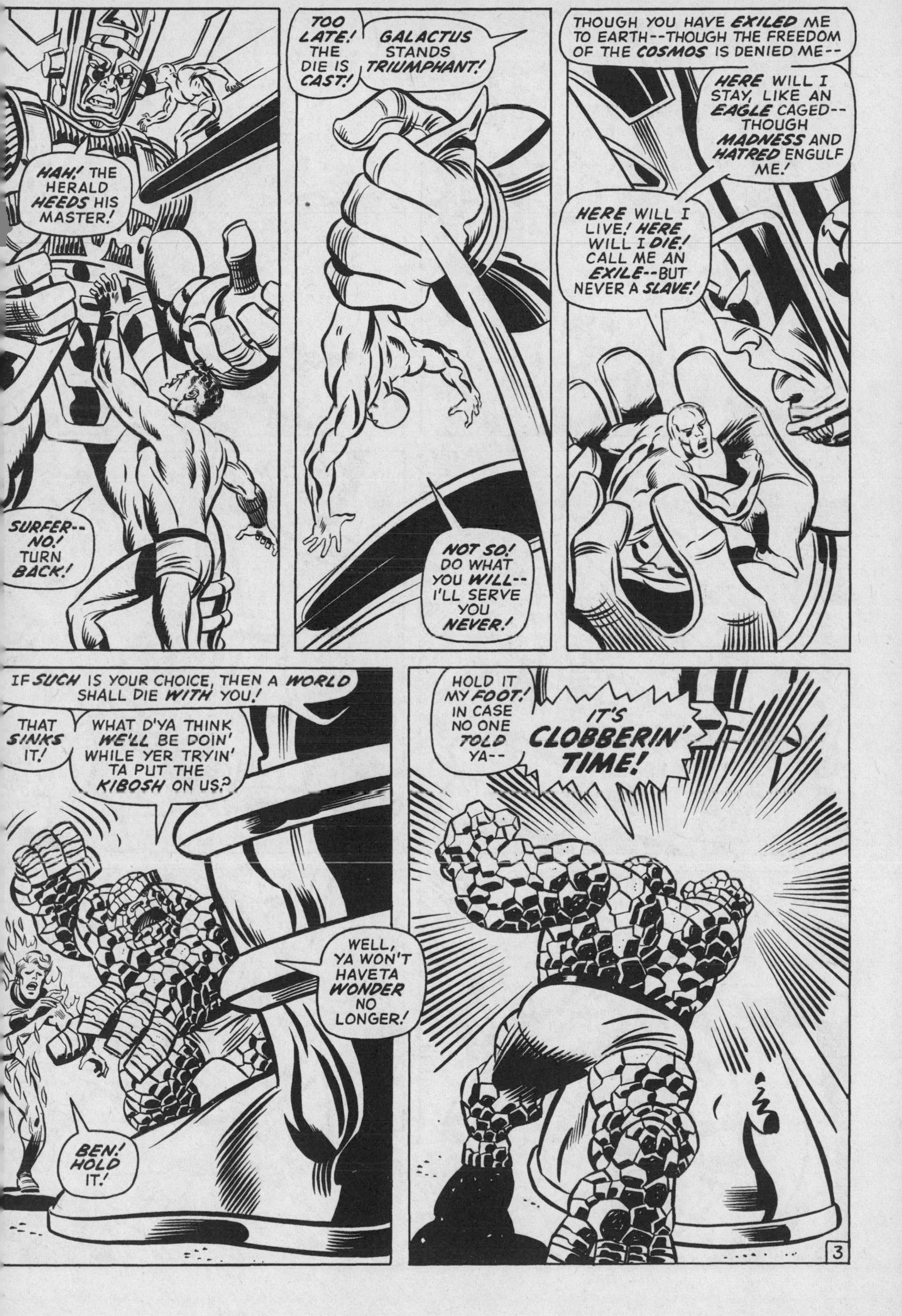
HAH! THE HERALD HEEDS HIS MASTER!
SURFER-- NO! TURN BACK!
TOO LATE! THE DIE IS CAST!
GALACTUS STANDS TRIUMPHANT!
NOT SO! DO WHAT YOU WILL-- I'LL SERVE YOU NEVER!
THOUGH YOU HAVE EXILED ME TO EARTH--THOUGH THE FREEDOM OF THE COSMOS IS DENIED ME--
HERE WILL I STAY, LIKE AN EAGLE CAGED-- THOUGH MADNESS AND HATRED ENGULF ME!
HERE WILL I LIVE! HERE WILL I DIE! CALL ME AN EXILE--BUT NEVER A SLAVE!
IF SUCH IS YOUR CHOICE, THEN A WORLD SHALL DIE WITH YOU!
THAT SINKS IT!
WHAT D'YA THINK WE'LL BE DOIN' WHILE YER TRYIN' TA PUT THE KIBOSH ON US?
WELL, YA WON'T HAVETA WONDER NO LONGER!
BEN! HOLD IT!
HOLD IT MY FOOT! IN CASE NO ONE TOLD YA--
IT'S CLOBBERIN' TIME!
3

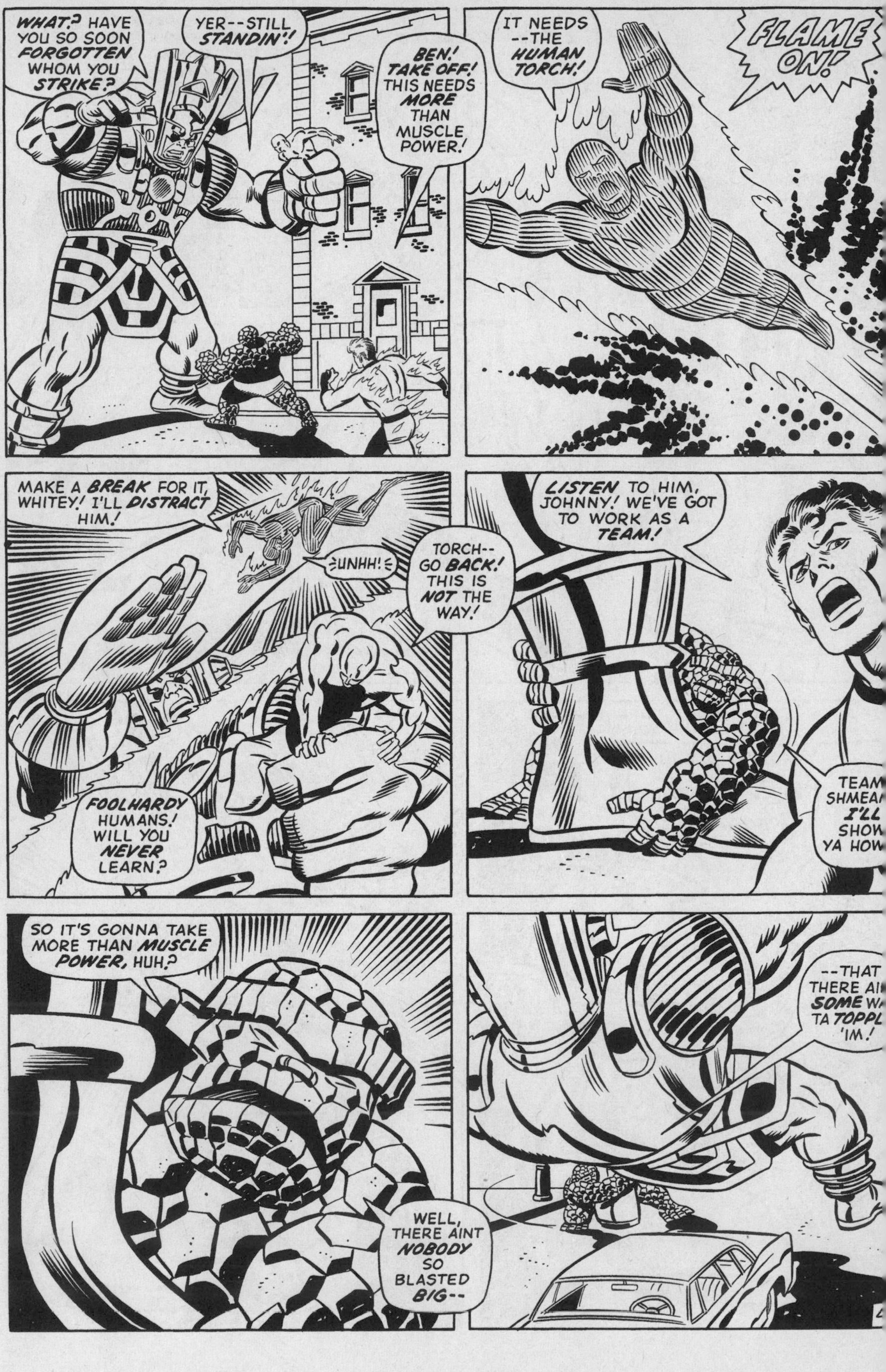
WHAT? HAVE YOU SO SOON FORGOTTEN WHOM YOU STRIKE?
YER--STILL STANDIN'!
BEN! TAKE OFF! THIS NEEDS MORE THAN MUSCLE POWER!
IT NEEDS --THE HUMAN TORCH!
FLAME ON!
MAKE A BREAK FOR IT, WHITEY! I'LL DISTRACT HIM!
UNHH!
TORCH-- GO BACK! THIS IS NOT THE WAY!
FOOLHARDY HUMANS! WILL YOU NEVER LEARN?
LISTEN TO HIM, JOHNNY! WE'VE GOT TO WORK AS A TEAM!
SO IT'S GONNA TAKE MORE THAN MUSCLE POWER, HUH?
WELL, THERE AINT NOBODY SO BLASTED BIG--

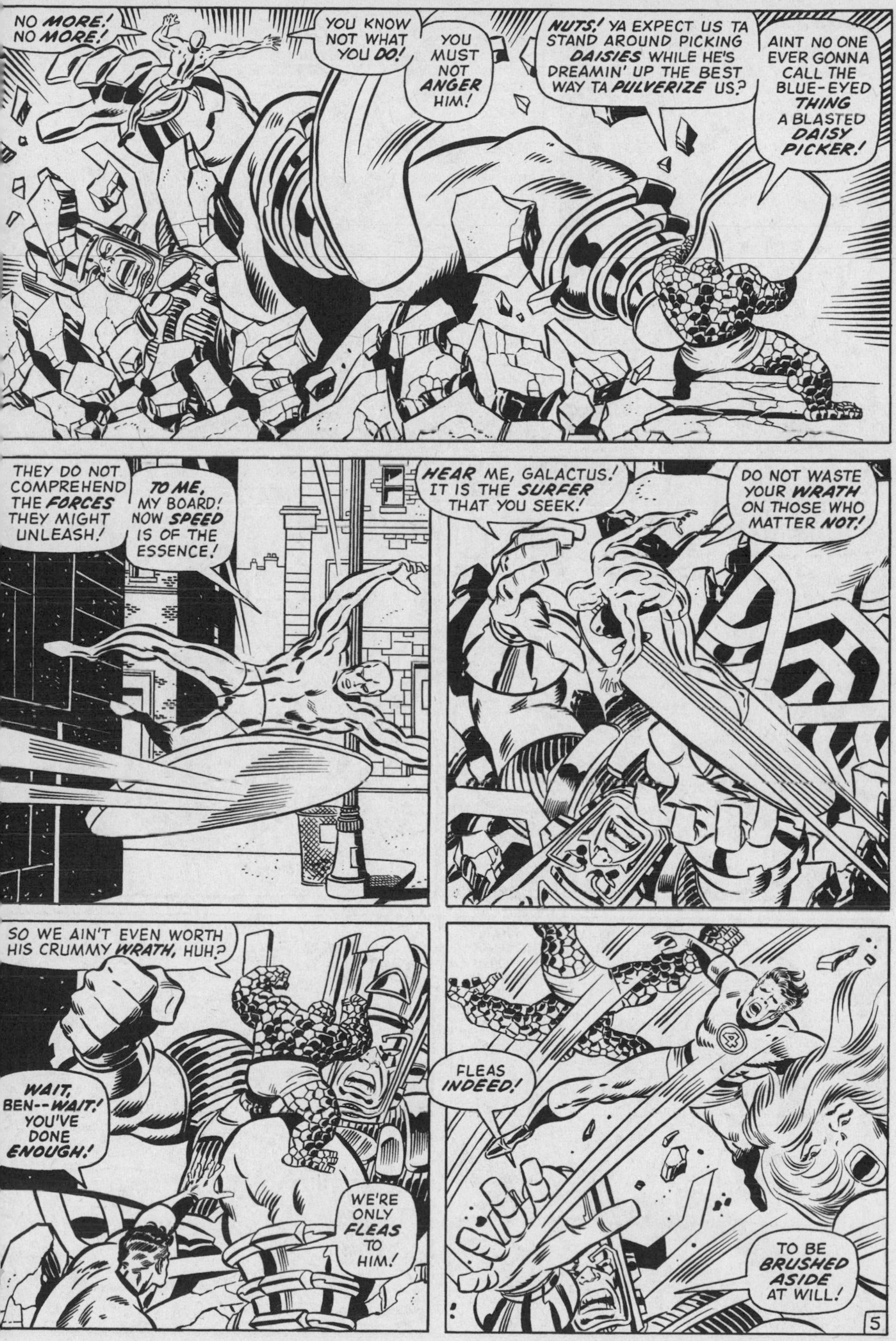
NO MORE! NO MORE!
YOU KNOW NOT WHAT YOU DO!
YOU MUST NOT ANGER HIM!
NUTS! YA EXPECT US TA STAND AROUND PICKING DAISIES WHILE HE'S DREAMIN' UP THE BEST WAY TA PULVERIZE US?
AINT NO ONE EVER GONNA CALL THE BLUE-EYED THING A BLASTED DAISY PICKER!
THEY DO NOT COMPREHEND THE FORCES THEY MIGHT UNLEASH!
TO ME, MY BOARD! NOW SPEED IS OF THE ESSENCE!
HEAR ME, GALACTUS! IT IS THE SURFER THAT YOU SEEK!
DO NOT WASTE YOUR WRATH ON THOSE WHO MATTER NOT!
SO WE AIN'T EVEN WORTH HIS CRUMMY WRATH, HUH?
WAIT, BEN--WAIT! YOU'VE DONE ENOUGH!
WE'RE ONLY FLEAS TO HIM!
FLEAS INDEED!
TO BE BRUSHED ASIDE AT WILL!
5

I TRIED TO WARN THEM--

NEVER MIND THE "I TOLD YOU SO'S"!

WE'VE GOT TO CATCH THEM!

STRETCH, BLAST YA-- WHY DON'TCHA STRETCH?

HE CAN'T, BEN! THE IMPACT KNOCKED HIM OUT!

MY FORCE FIELD! I'LL USE IT TO SAVE REED, EVEN THOUGH IT MEANS I'LL--

NO! JUST RELAX! GO LIMP!

THE SURFER WILL CATCH YOU!

BUT REED--

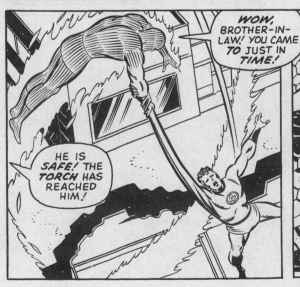

WOW, BROTHER-IN-LAW! YOU CAME TO JUST IN TIME!

HE IS SAFE! THE TORCH HAS REACHED HIM!

SO HOW COME NO ONE WORRIES ABOUT ME?

WHAT AM I? A MACKERAL OR SOMETHIN'?

6

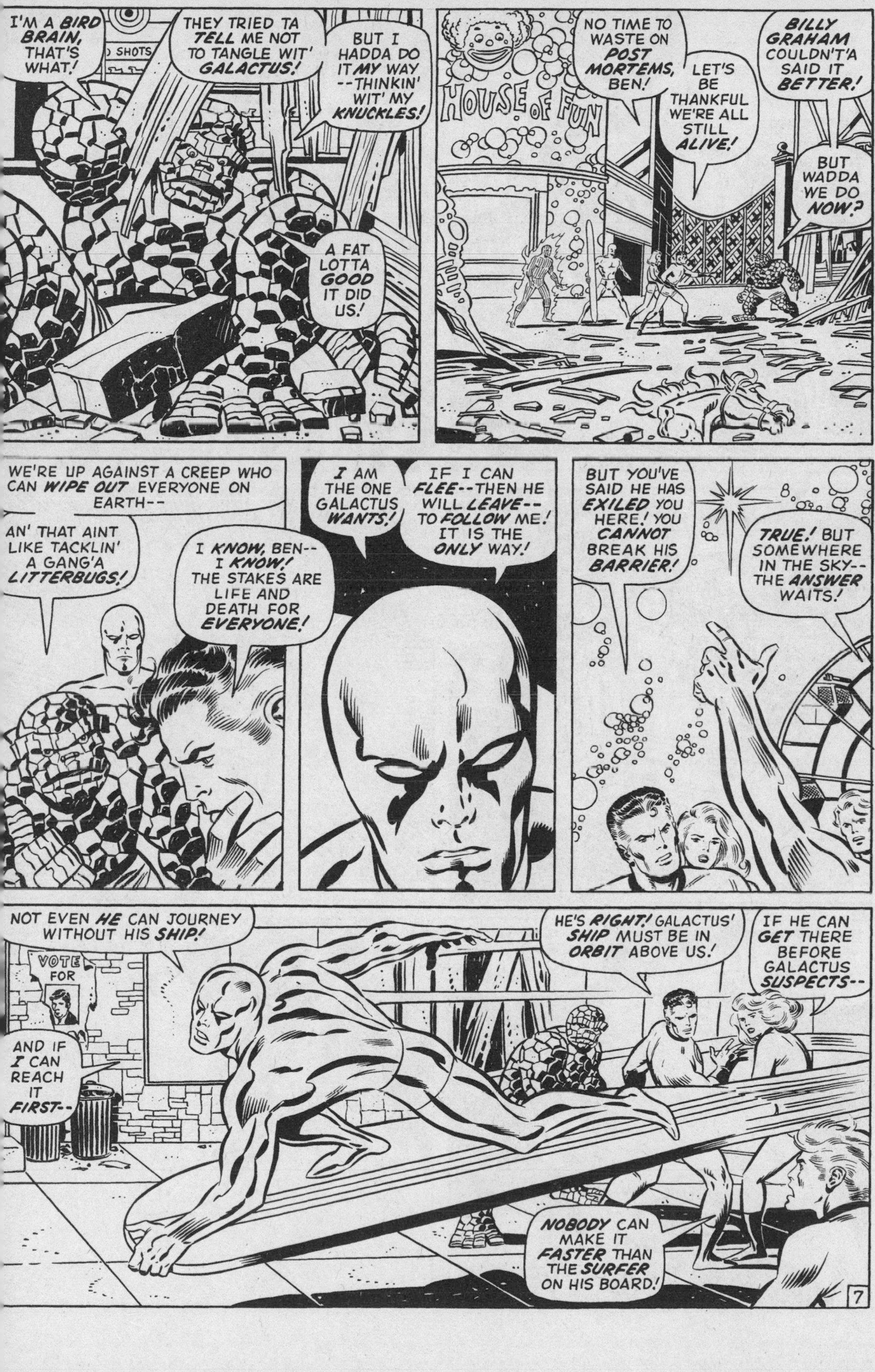
I'M A BIRD BRAIN, THAT'S WHAT!
THEY TRIED TA TELL ME NOT TO TANGLE WIT' GALACTUS!
BUT I HADDA DO IT MY WAY --THINKIN' WIT' MY KNUCKLES!
A FAT LOTTA GOOD IT DID US!
HOUSE OF FUN
NO TIME TO WASTE ON POST MORTEMS, BEN!
LET'S BE THANKFUL WE'RE ALL STILL ALIVE!
BILLY GRAHAM COULDN'T'A SAID IT BETTER!
BUT WADDA WE DO NOW?
WE'RE UP AGAINST A CREEP WHO CAN WIPE OUT EVERYONE ON EARTH--
AN' THAT AINT LIKE TACKLIN' A GANG'A LITTERBUGS!
I KNOW, BEN-- I KNOW! THE STAKES ARE LIFE AND DEATH FOR EVERYONE!
I AM THE ONE GALACTUS WANTS!
IF I CAN FLEE--THEN HE WILL LEAVE-- TO FOLLOW ME! IT IS THE ONLY WAY!
BUT YOU'VE SAID HE HAS EXILED YOU HERE! YOU CANNOT BREAK HIS BARRIER!
TRUE! BUT SOMEWHERE IN THE SKY-- THE ANSWER WAITS!
NOT EVEN HE CAN JOURNEY WITHOUT HIS SHIP!
AND IF I CAN REACH IT FIRST--
VOTE FOR
HE'S RIGHT! GALACTUS' SHIP MUST BE IN ORBIT ABOVE US!
IF HE CAN GET THERE BEFORE GALACTUS SUSPECTS--
NOBODY CAN MAKE IT FASTER THAN THE SURFER ON HIS BOARD!
7

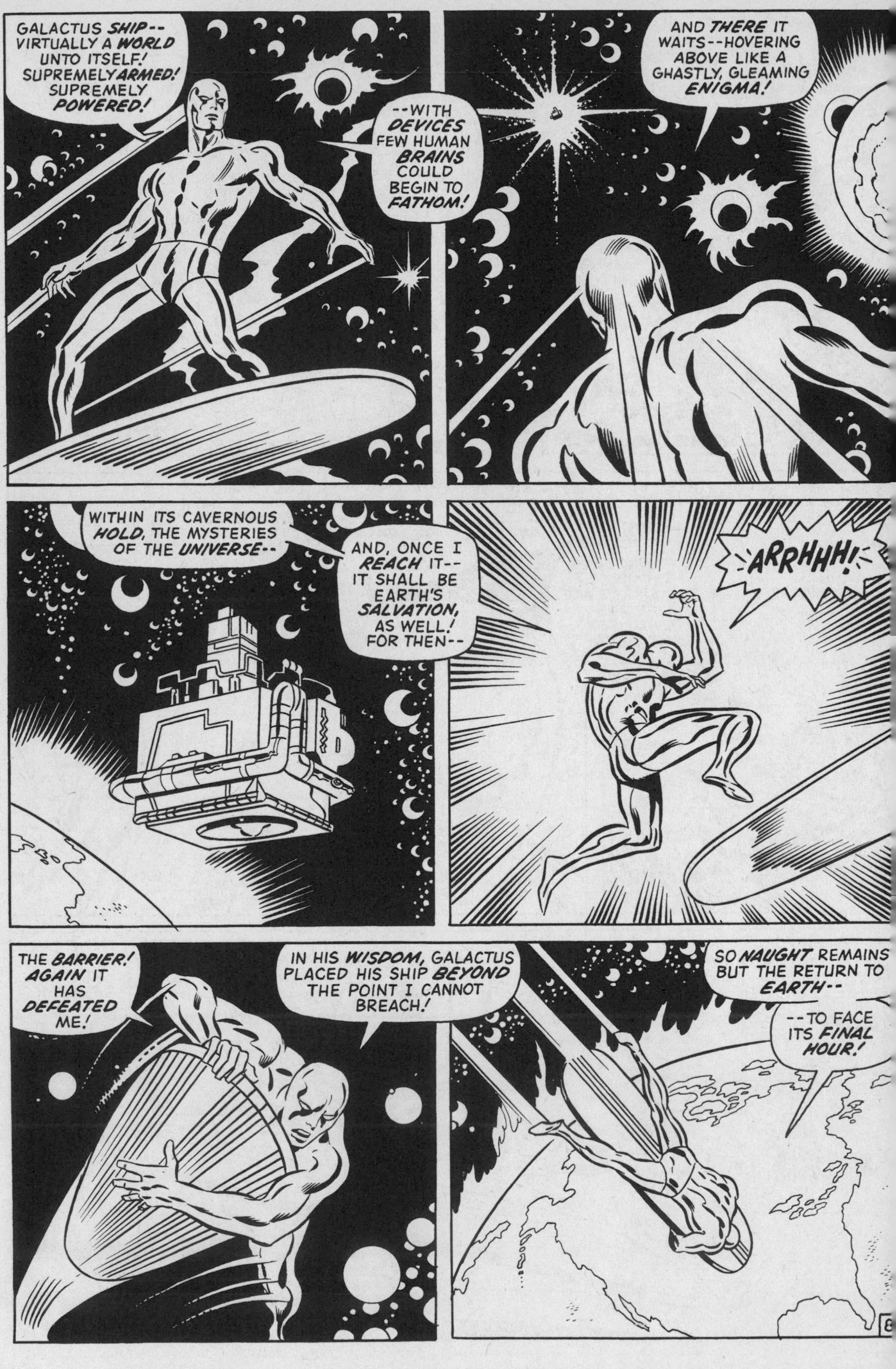

GALACTUS SHIP-- VIRTUALLY A WORLD UNTO ITSELF! SUPREMELY ARMED! SUPREMELY POWERED!
--WITH DEVICES FEW HUMAN BRAINS COULD BEGIN TO FATHOM!
AND THERE IT WAITS--HOVERING ABOVE LIKE A GHASTLY, GLEAMING ENIGMA!
WITHIN ITS CAVERNOUS HOLD, THE MYSTERIES OF THE UNIVERSE--
AND, ONCE I REACH IT-- IT SHALL BE EARTH'S SALVATION, AS WELL! FOR THEN--
ARRHHH!
THE BARRIER! AGAIN IT HAS DEFEATED ME!
IN HIS WISDOM, GALACTUS PLACED HIS SHIP BEYOND THE POINT I CANNOT BREACH!
SO NAUGHT REMAINS BUT THE RETURN TO EARTH--
--TO FACE ITS FINAL HOUR!
8

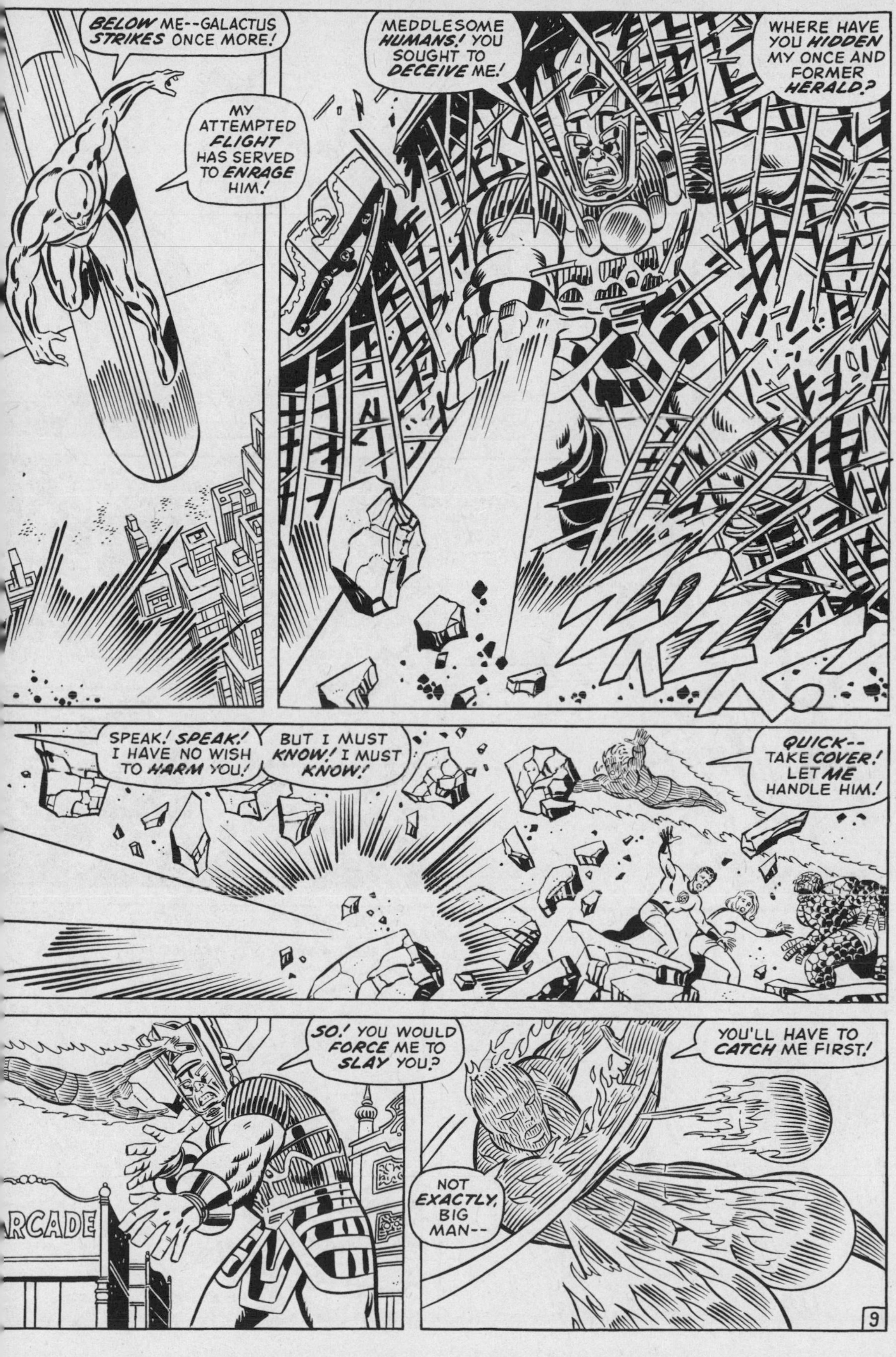
BELOW ME--GALACTUS STRIKES ONCE MORE!
MY ATTEMPTED FLIGHT HAS SERVED TO ENRAGE HIM!
MEDDLESOME HUMANS! YOU SOUGHT TO DECEIVE ME!
WHERE HAVE YOU HIDDEN MY ONCE AND FORMER HERALD?
SPEAK! SPEAK! I HAVE NO WISH TO HARM YOU!
BUT I MUST KNOW! I MUST KNOW!
QUICK-- TAKE COVER! LET ME HANDLE HIM!
SO! YOU WOULD FORCE ME TO SLAY YOU?
RCADE
YOU'LL HAVE TO CATCH ME FIRST!
NOT EXACTLY, BIG MAN--

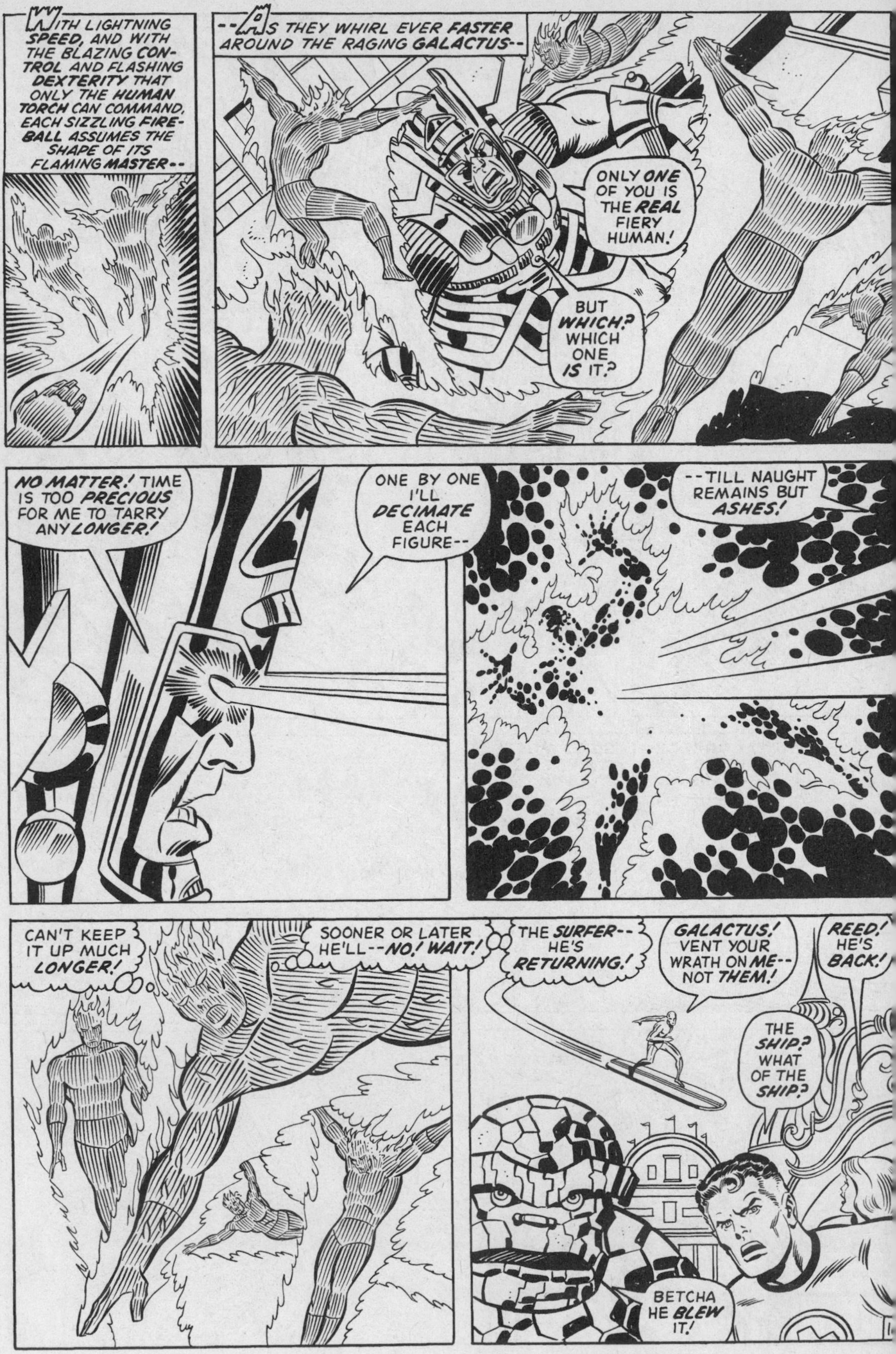
WITH LIGHTNING SPEED, AND WITH THE BLAZING CONTROL AND FLASHING DEXTERITY THAT ONLY THE HUMAN TORCH CAN COMMAND, EACH SIZZLING FIRE-BALL ASSUMES THE SHAPE OF ITS FLAMING MASTER--
--AS THEY WHIRL EVER FASTER AROUND THE RAGING GALACTUS--
ONLY ONE OF YOU IS THE REAL FIERY HUMAN!
BUT WHICH? WHICH ONE IS IT?
NO MATTER! TIME IS TOO PRECIOUS FOR ME TO TARRY ANY LONGER!
ONE BY ONE I'LL DECIMATE EACH FIGURE--
--TILL NAUGHT REMAINS BUT ASHES!
CAN'T KEEP IT UP MUCH LONGER!
SOONER OR LATER HE'LL--NO! WAIT!
THE SURFER--HE'S RETURNING!
GALACTUS! VENT YOUR WRATH ON ME--NOT THEM!
REED! HE'S BACK!
THE SHIP? WHAT OF THE SHIP?
BETCHA HE BLEW IT!

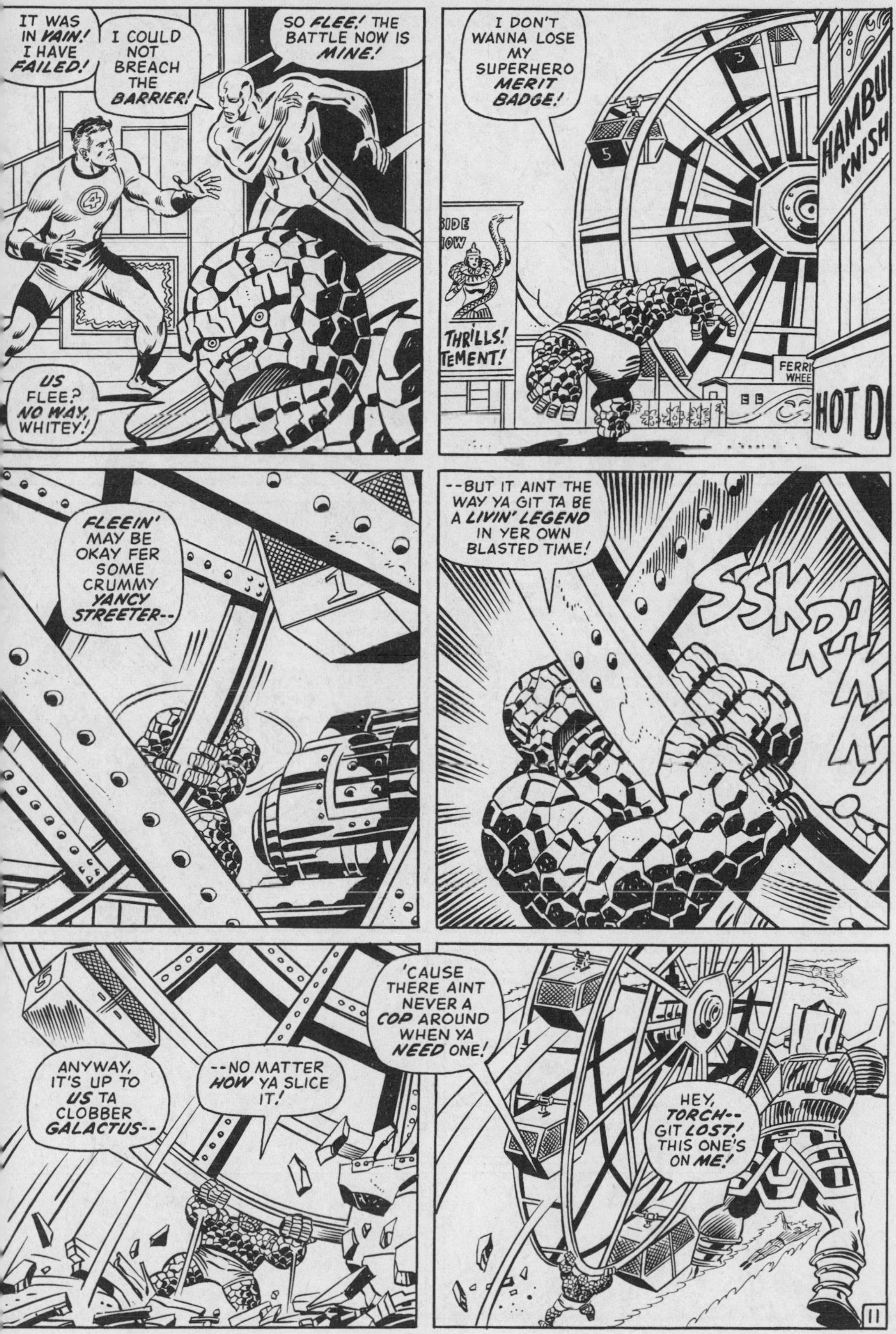
IT WAS IN VAIN! I HAVE FAILED!
I COULD NOT BREACH THE BARRIER!
SO FLEE! THE BATTLE NOW IS MINE!
US FLEE? NO WAY, WHITEY!
I DON'T WANNA LOSE MY SUPERHERO MERIT BADGE!
THRILLS!
TEMENT!
HAMBU
KNISH
FERRI
WHEE
HOT D
FLEEIN' MAY BE OKAY FER SOME CRUMMY YANCY STREETER--
--BUT IT AINT THE WAY YA GIT TA BE A LIVIN' LEGEND IN YER OWN BLASTED TIME!
SSKRAKK
ANYWAY, IT'S UP TO US TA CLOBBER GALACTUS--
--NO MATTER HOW YA SLICE IT!
'CAUSE THERE AINT NEVER A COP AROUND WHEN YA NEED ONE!
HEY, TORCH-- GIT LOST! THIS ONE'S ON ME!
11

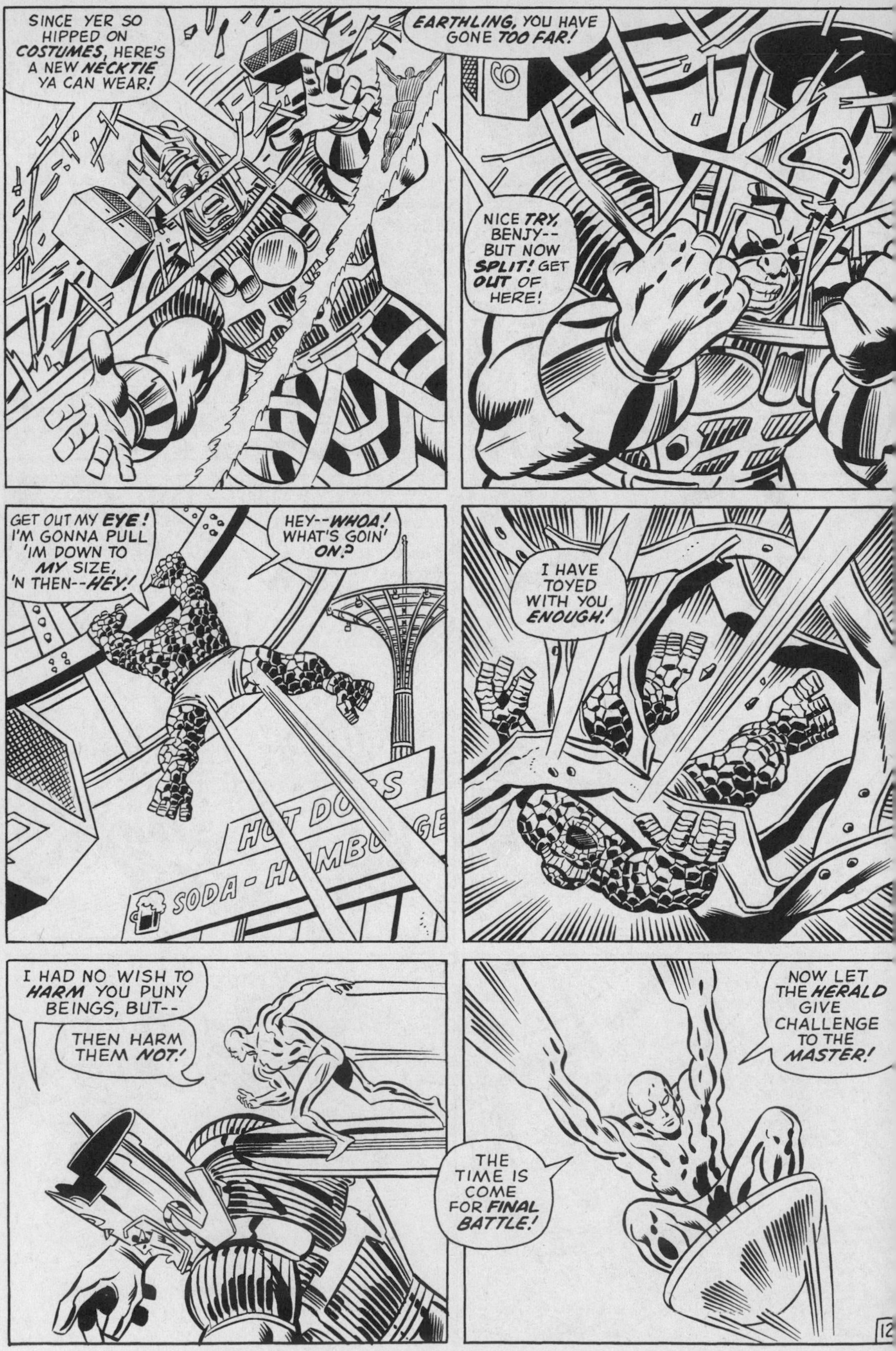

SINCE YER SO HIPPED ON COSTUMES, HERE'S A NEW NECKTIE YA CAN WEAR!
EARTHLING, YOU HAVE GONE TOO FAR!
NICE TRY, BENJY-- BUT NOW SPLIT! GET OUT OF HERE!
GET OUT MY EYE! I'M GONNA PULL 'IM DOWN TO MY SIZE, 'N THEN--HEY!
HEY--WHOA! WHAT'S GOIN' ON?
HOT DOGS
SODA - HAMBURGE
I HAVE TOYED WITH YOU ENOUGH!
I HAD NO WISH TO HARM YOU PUNY BEINGS, BUT--
THEN HARM THEM NOT!
THE TIME IS COME FOR FINAL BATTLE!
NOW LET THE HERALD GIVE CHALLENGE TO THE MASTER!
12

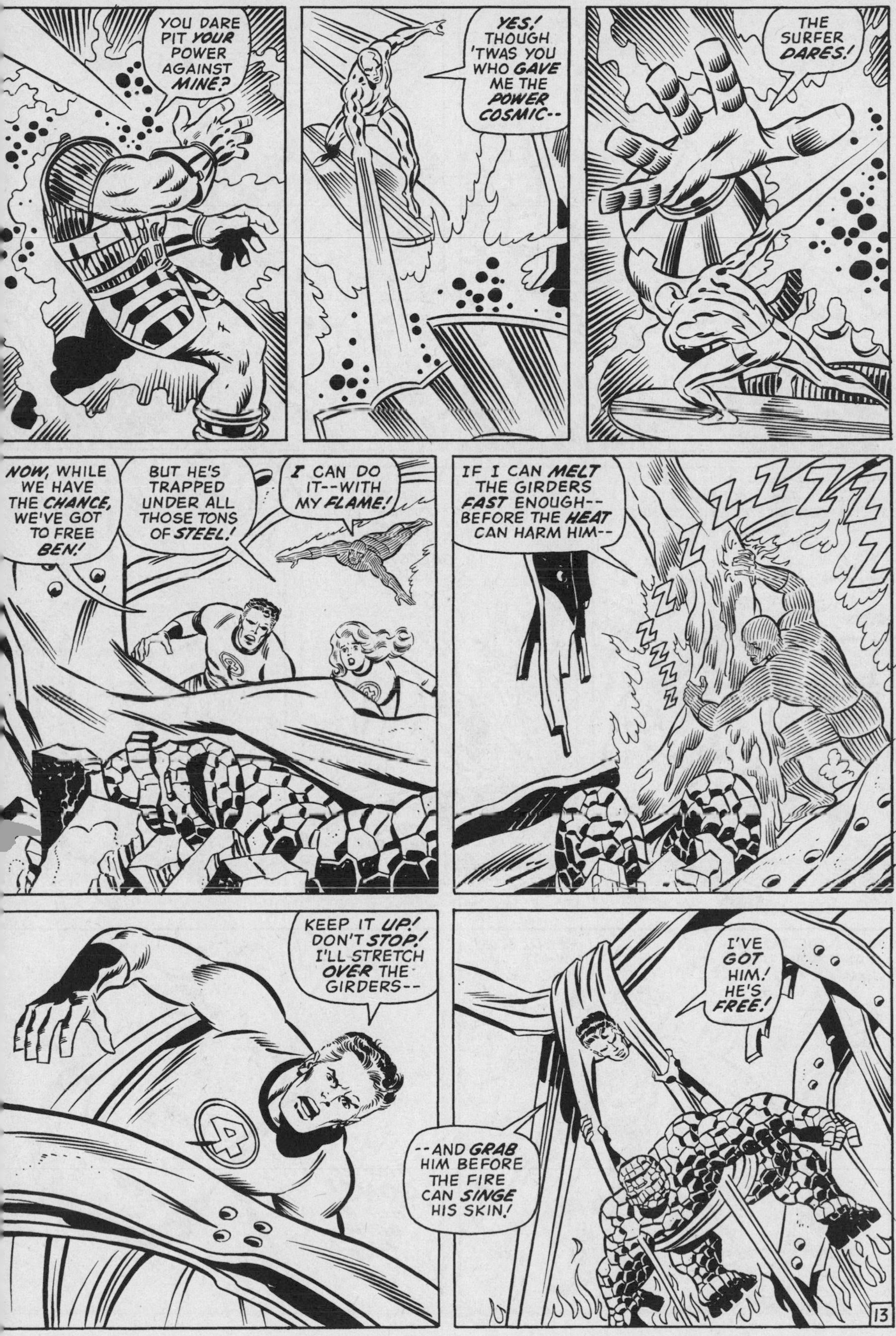
YOU DARE PIT YOUR POWER AGAINST MINE?
YES! THOUGH 'TWAS YOU WHO GAVE ME THE POWER COSMIC--
THE SURFER DARES!
NOW, WHILE WE HAVE THE CHANCE, WE'VE GOT TO FREE BEN!
BUT HE'S TRAPPED UNDER ALL THOSE TONS OF STEEL!
I CAN DO IT--WITH MY FLAME!
IF I CAN MELT THE GIRDERS FAST ENOUGH-- BEFORE THE HEAT CAN HARM HIM--
KEEP IT UP! DON'T STOP! I'LL STRETCH OVER THE GIRDERS--
--AND GRAB HIM BEFORE THE FIRE CAN SINGE HIS SKIN!
I'VE GOT HIM! HE'S FREE!
13

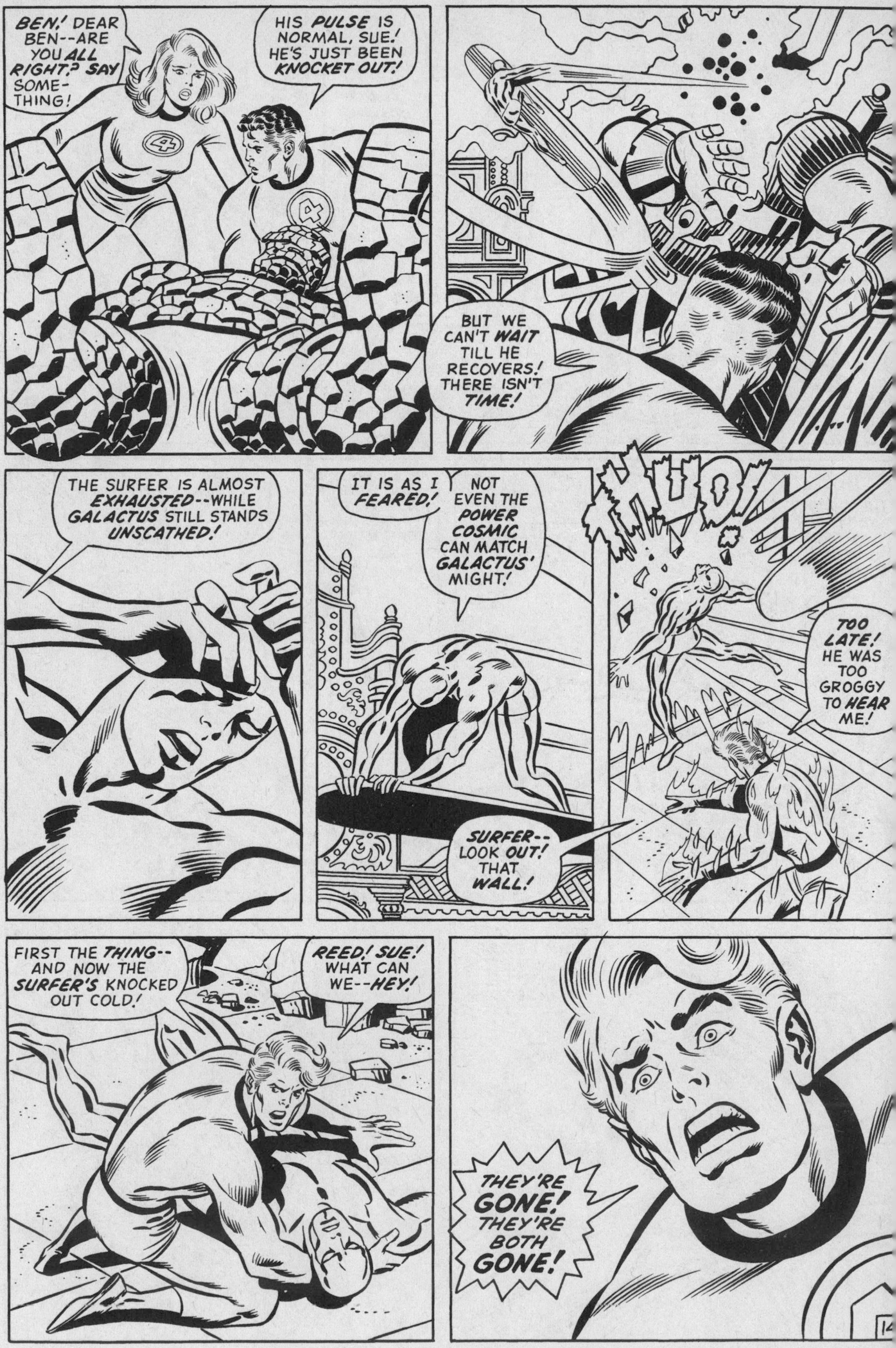
BEN! DEAR BEN--ARE YOU ALL RIGHT? SAY SOME-THING!
HIS PULSE IS NORMAL, SUE! HE'S JUST BEEN KNOCKET OUT!
BUT WE CAN'T WAIT TILL HE RECOVERS! THERE ISN'T TIME!
THE SURFER IS ALMOST EXHAUSTED--WHILE GALACTUS STILL STANDS UNSCATHED!
IT IS AS I FEARED!
NOT EVEN THE POWER COSMIC CAN MATCH GALACTUS' MIGHT!
SURFER--LOOK OUT! THAT WALL!
THUD!
TOO LATE! HE WAS TOO GROGGY TO HEAR ME!
FIRST THE THING--AND NOW THE SURFER'S KNOCKED OUT COLD!
REED! SUE! WHAT CAN WE--HEY!
THEY'RE GONE! THEY'RE BOTH GONE!
14

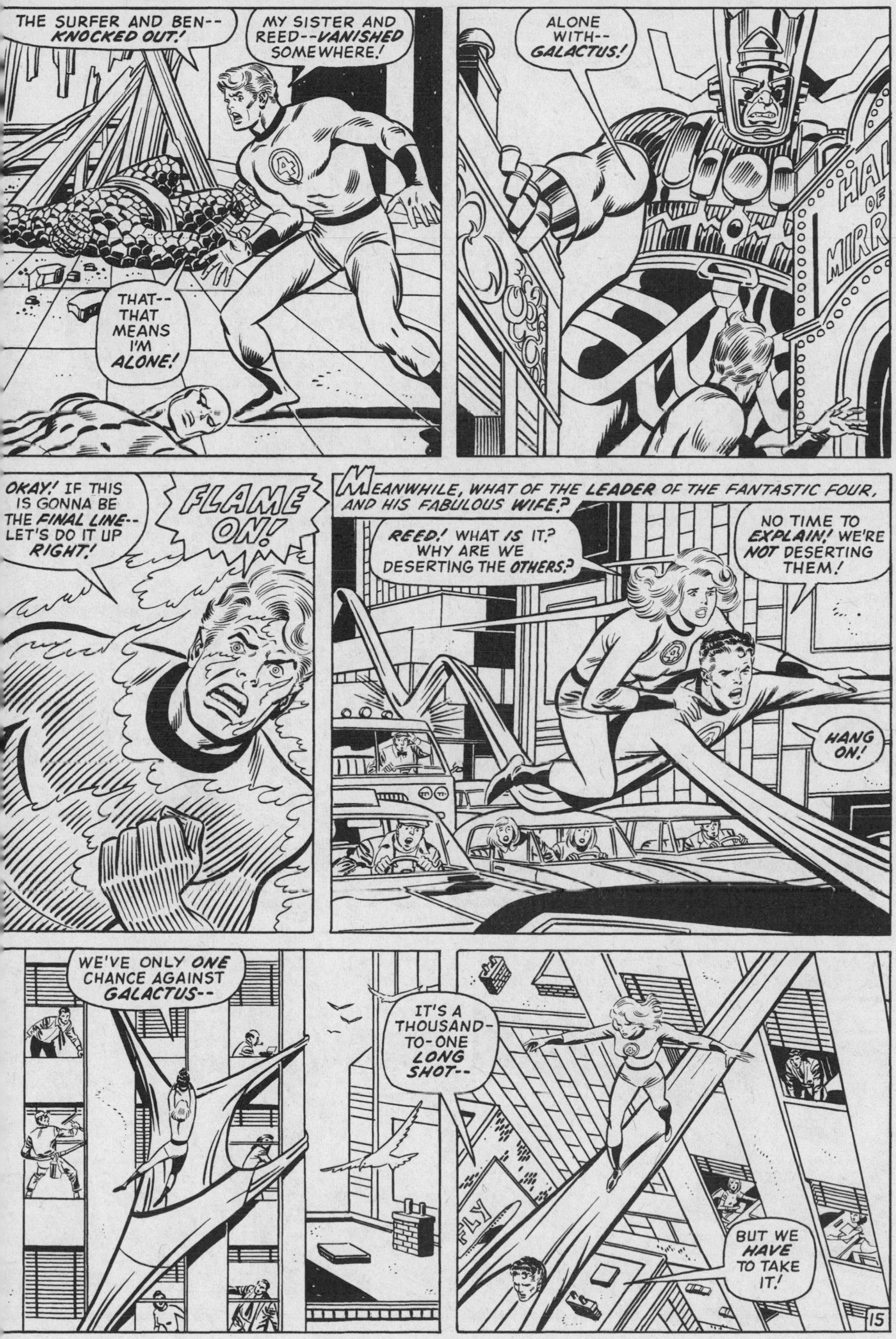
THE SURFER AND BEN-- KNOCKED OUT!
MY SISTER AND REED--VANISHED SOMEWHERE!
THAT--THAT MEANS I'M ALONE!
ALONE WITH--GALACTUS!
HALL OF MIRR
OKAY! IF THIS IS GONNA BE THE FINAL LINE--LET'S DO IT UP RIGHT!
FLAME ON!
MEANWHILE, WHAT OF THE LEADER OF THE FANTASTIC FOUR, AND HIS FABULOUS WIFE?
REED! WHAT IS IT? WHY ARE WE DESERTING THE OTHERS?
NO TIME TO EXPLAIN! WE'RE NOT DESERTING THEM!
HANG ON!
WE'VE ONLY ONE CHANCE AGAINST GALACTUS--
IT'S A THOUSAND-TO-ONE LONG SHOT--
FLY
BUT WE HAVE TO TAKE IT!
15

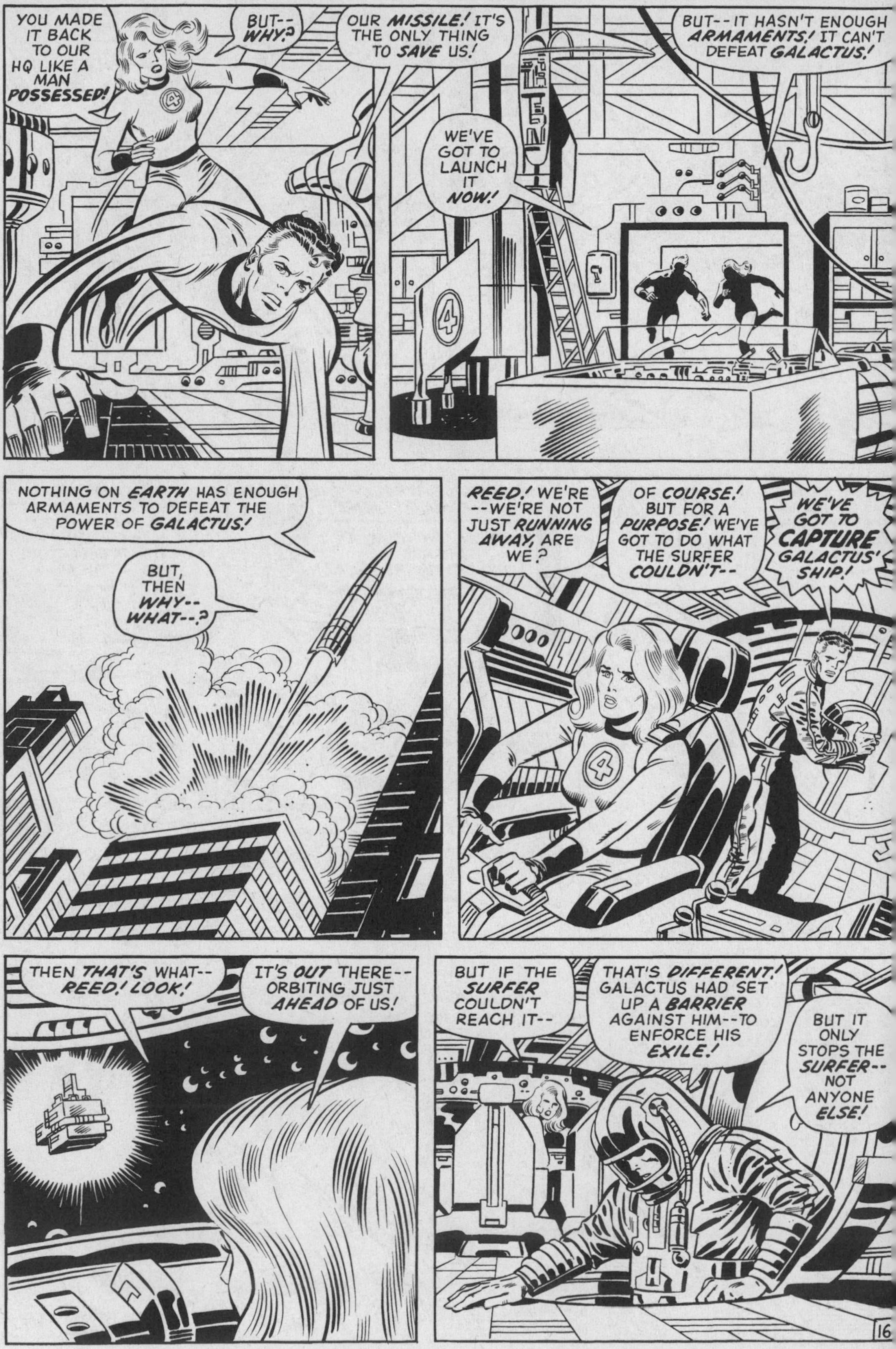
YOU MADE IT BACK TO OUR HQ LIKE A MAN POSSESSED!
BUT--WHY?
OUR MISSILE! IT'S THE ONLY THING TO SAVE US!
WE'VE GOT TO LAUNCH IT NOW!
BUT--IT HASN'T ENOUGH ARMAMENTS! IT CAN'T DEFEAT GALACTUS!
NOTHING ON EARTH HAS ENOUGH ARMAMENTS TO DEFEAT THE POWER OF GALACTUS!
BUT, THEN WHY--WHAT--?
REED! WE'RE--WE'RE NOT JUST RUNNING AWAY, ARE WE?
OF COURSE! BUT FOR A PURPOSE! WE'VE GOT TO DO WHAT THE SURFER COULDN'T--
WE'VE GOT TO CAPTURE GALACTUS' SHIP!
THEN THAT'S WHAT--REED! LOOK!
IT'S OUT THERE--ORBITING JUST AHEAD OF US!
BUT IF THE SURFER COULDN'T REACH IT--
THAT'S DIFFERENT! GALACTUS HAD SET UP A BARRIER AGAINST HIM--TO ENFORCE HIS EXILE!
BUT IT ONLY STOPS THE SURFER--NOT ANYONE ELSE!
16

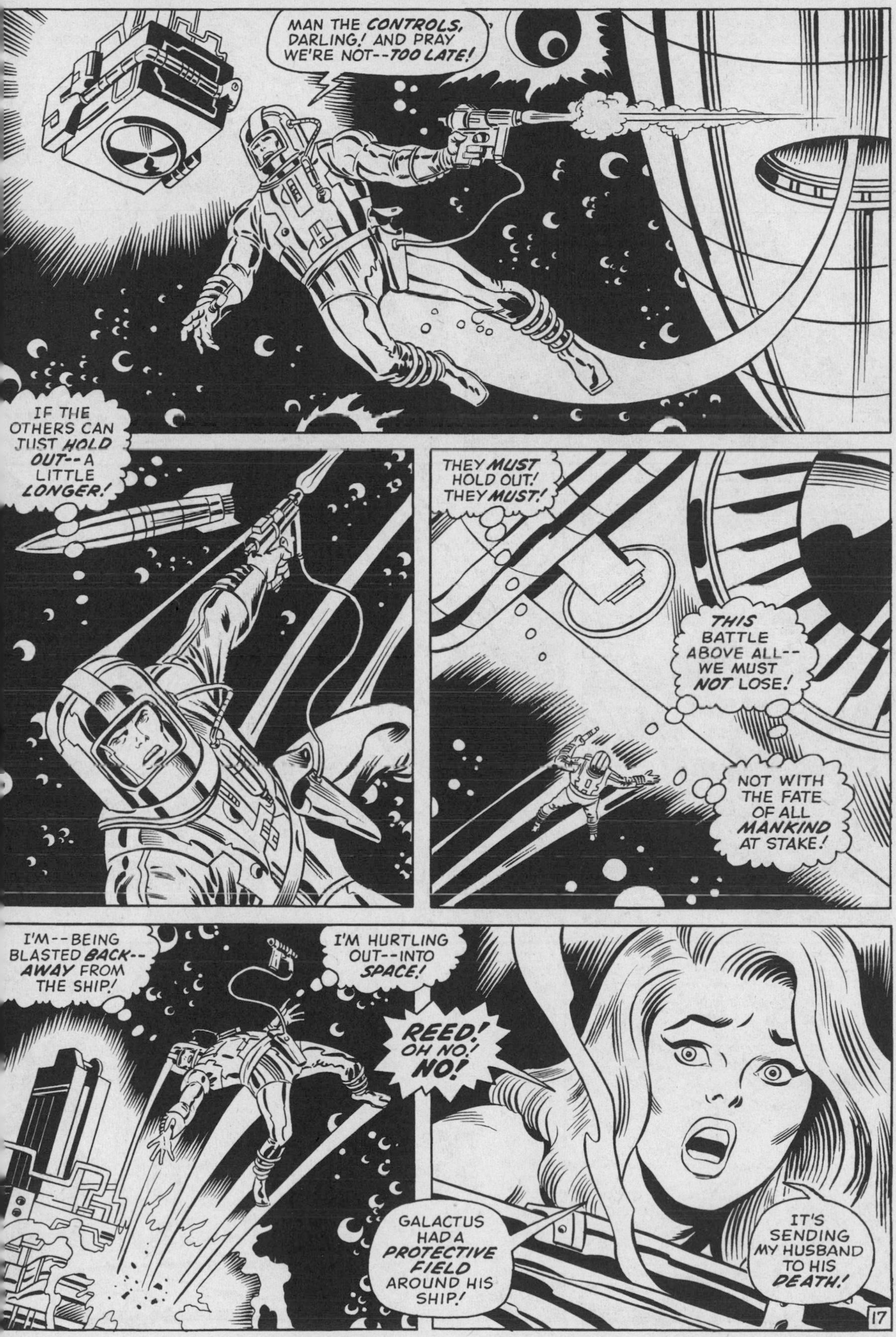
MAN THE CONTROLS, DARLING! AND PRAY WE'RE NOT--TOO LATE!
IF THE OTHERS CAN JUST HOLD OUT--A LITTLE LONGER!
THEY MUST HOLD OUT! THEY MUST!
THIS BATTLE ABOVE ALL--WE MUST NOT LOSE!
NOT WITH THE FATE OF ALL MANKIND AT STAKE!
I'M--BEING BLASTED BACK--AWAY FROM THE SHIP!
I'M HURTLING OUT--INTO SPACE!
REED! OH NO! NO!
GALACTUS HAD A PROTECTIVE FIELD AROUND HIS SHIP!
IT'S SENDING MY HUSBAND TO HIS DEATH!

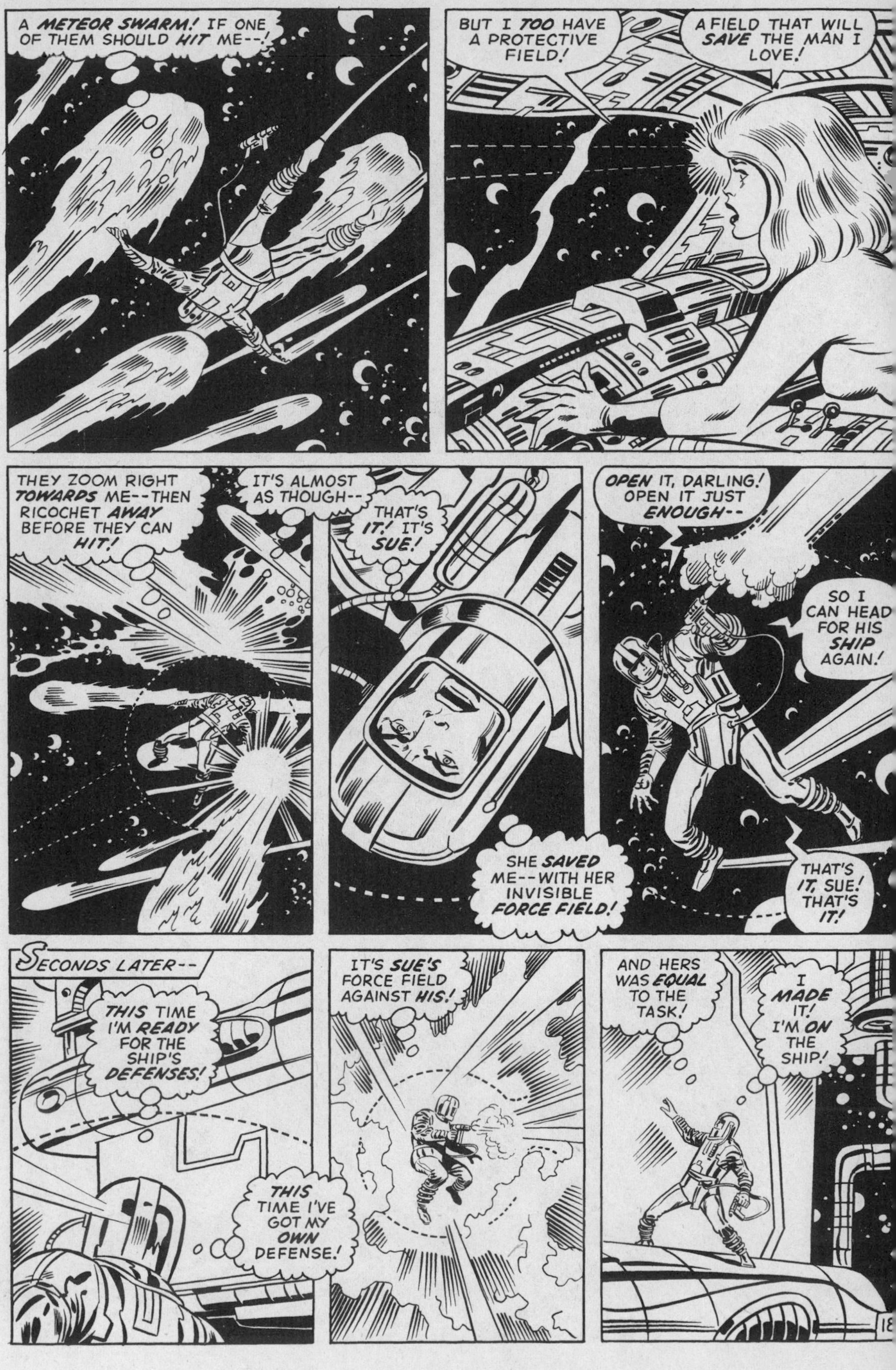
A METEOR SWARM! IF ONE OF THEM SHOULD HIT ME--!
BUT I TOO HAVE A PROTECTIVE FIELD!
A FIELD THAT WILL SAVE THE MAN I LOVE!
THEY ZOOM RIGHT TOWARDS ME--THEN RICOCHET AWAY BEFORE THEY CAN HIT!
IT'S ALMOST AS THOUGH--
THAT'S IT! IT'S SUE!
SHE SAVED ME--WITH HER INVISIBLE FORCE FIELD!
OPEN IT, DARLING! OPEN IT JUST ENOUGH--
SO I CAN HEAD FOR HIS SHIP AGAIN!
THAT'S IT, SUE! THAT'S IT!
SECONDS LATER--
THIS TIME I'M READY FOR THE SHIP'S DEFENSES!
THIS TIME I'VE GOT MY OWN DEFENSE!
IT'S SUE'S FORCE FIELD AGAINST HIS!
AND HERS WAS EQUAL TO THE TASK!
I MADE IT! I'M ON THE SHIP!
18

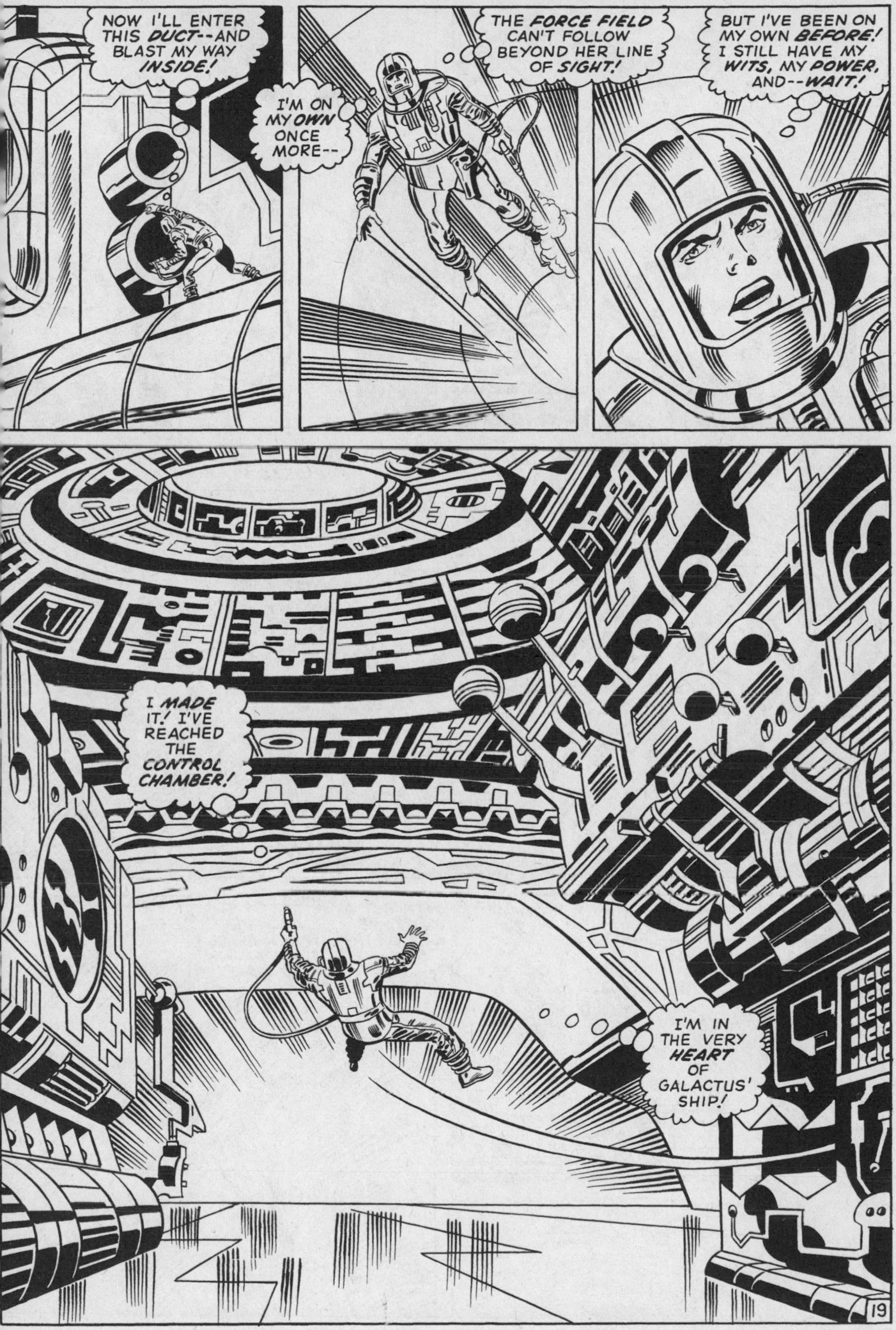
NOW I'LL ENTER THIS DUCT--AND BLAST MY WAY INSIDE!
I'M ON MY OWN ONCE MORE--
THE FORCE FIELD CAN'T FOLLOW BEYOND HER LINE OF SIGHT!
BUT I'VE BEEN ON MY OWN BEFORE! I STILL HAVE MY WITS, MY POWER, AND--WAIT!
I MADE IT! I'VE REACHED THE CONTROL CHAMBER!
I'M IN THE VERY HEART OF GALACTUS' SHIP!
19

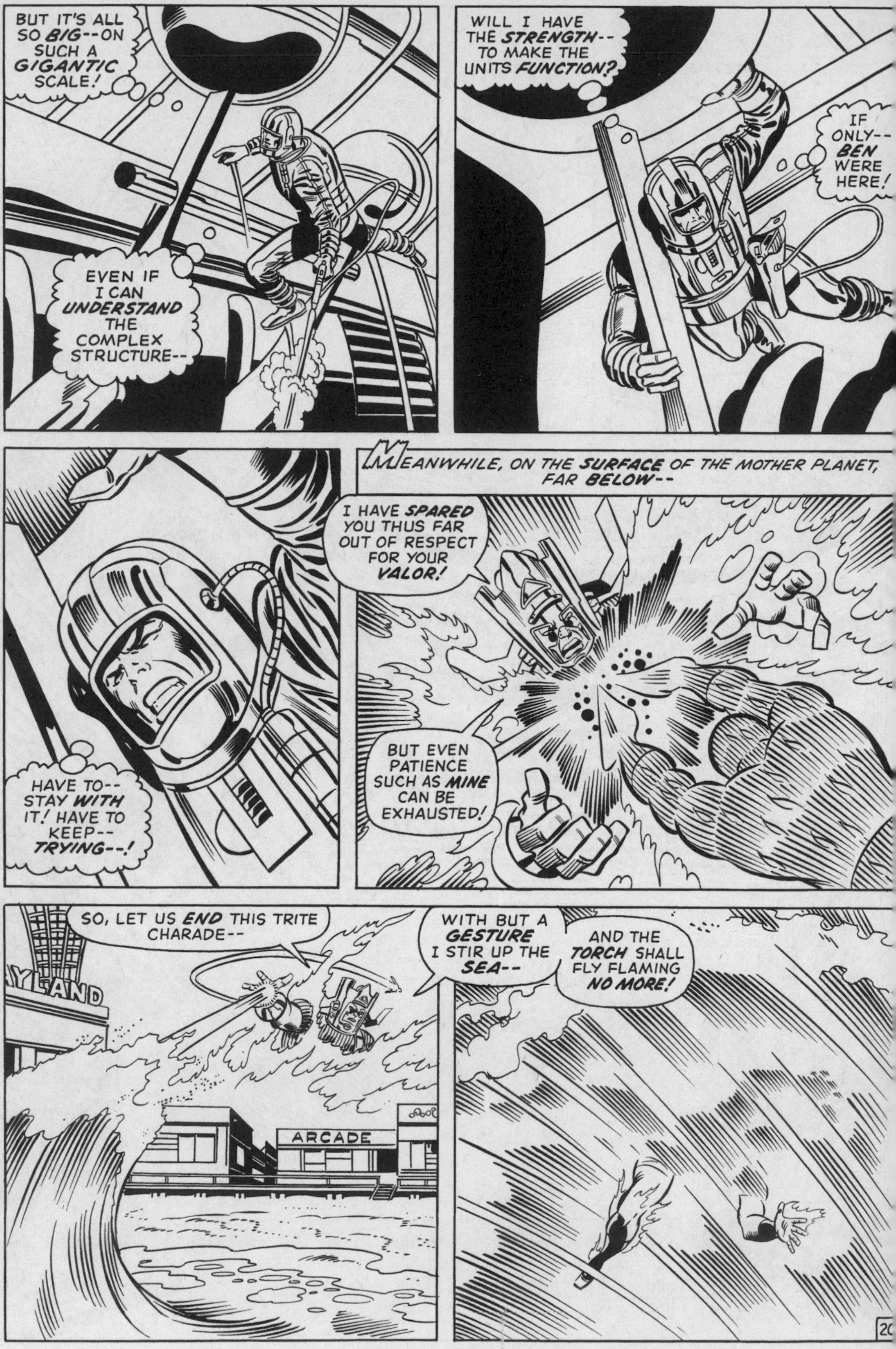

BUT IT'S ALL SO BIG--ON SUCH A GIGANTIC SCALE!
EVEN IF I CAN UNDERSTAND THE COMPLEX STRUCTURE--
WILL I HAVE THE STRENGTH--TO MAKE THE UNITS FUNCTION?
IF ONLY--BEN WERE HERE!
HAVE TO--STAY WITH IT! HAVE TO KEEP--TRYING--!
MEANWHILE, ON THE SURFACE OF THE MOTHER PLANET, FAR BELOW--
I HAVE SPARED YOU THUS FAR OUT OF RESPECT FOR YOUR VALOR!
BUT EVEN PATIENCE SUCH AS MINE CAN BE EXHAUSTED!
SO, LET US END THIS TRITE CHARADE--
WITH BUT A GESTURE I STIR UP THE SEA--
AND THE TORCH SHALL FLY FLAMING NO MORE!
ARCADE
20

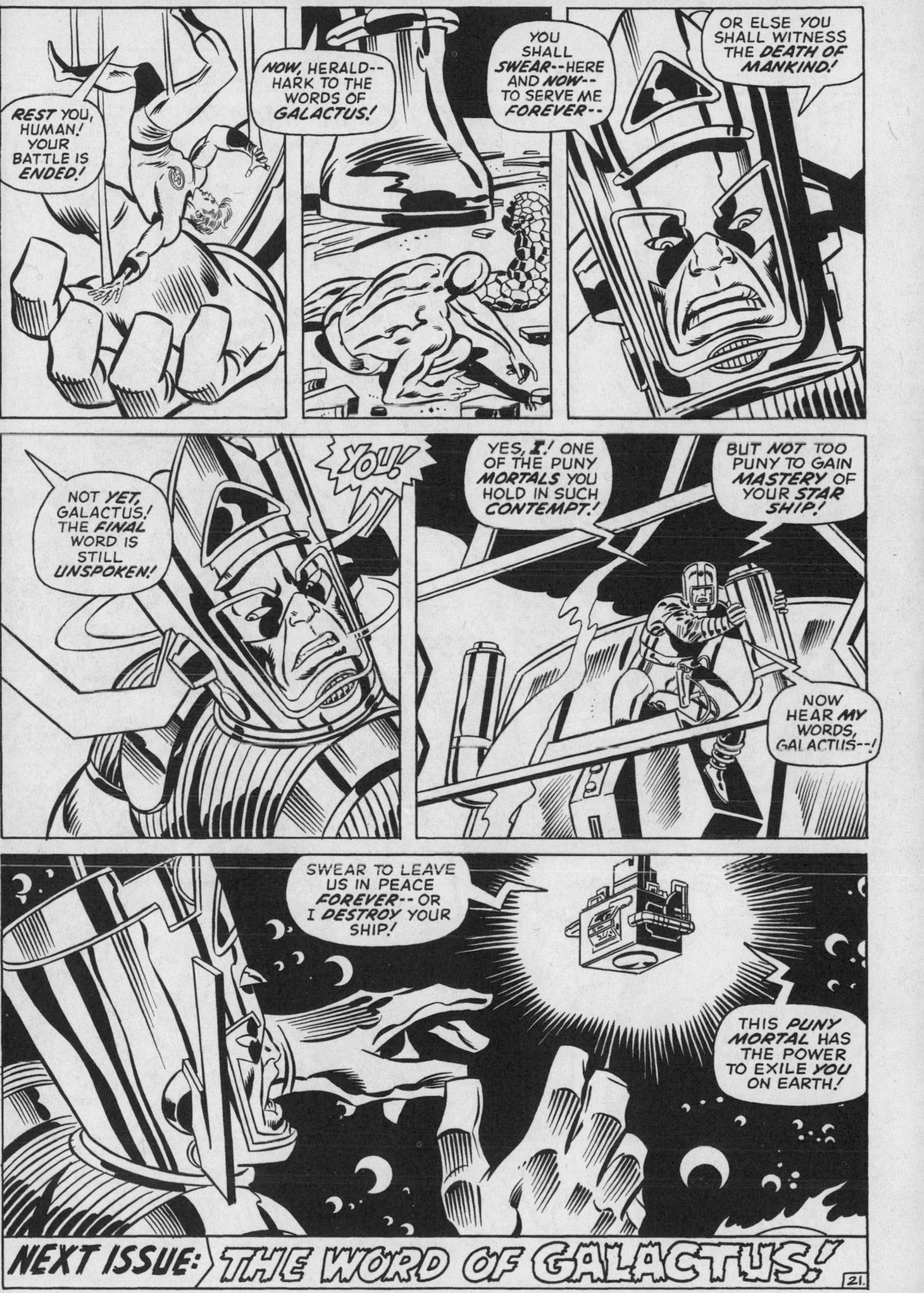
REST YOU, HUMAN! YOUR BATTLE IS ENDED!
NOW, HERALD-- HARK TO THE WORDS OF GALACTUS!
YOU SHALL SWEAR--HERE AND NOW-- TO SERVE ME FOREVER--
OR ELSE YOU SHALL WITNESS THE DEATH OF MANKIND!
NOT YET, GALACTUS! THE FINAL WORD IS STILL UNSPOKEN!
YOU!
YES, I! ONE OF THE PUNY MORTALS YOU HOLD IN SUCH CONTEMPT!
BUT NOT TOO PUNY TO GAIN MASTERY OF YOUR STAR SHIP!
NOW HEAR MY WORDS, GALACTUS--!
SWEAR TO LEAVE US IN PEACE FOREVER-- OR I DESTROY YOUR SHIP!
THIS PUNY MORTAL HAS THE POWER TO EXILE YOU ON EARTH!
NEXT ISSUE: THE WORD OF GALACTUS!
21.

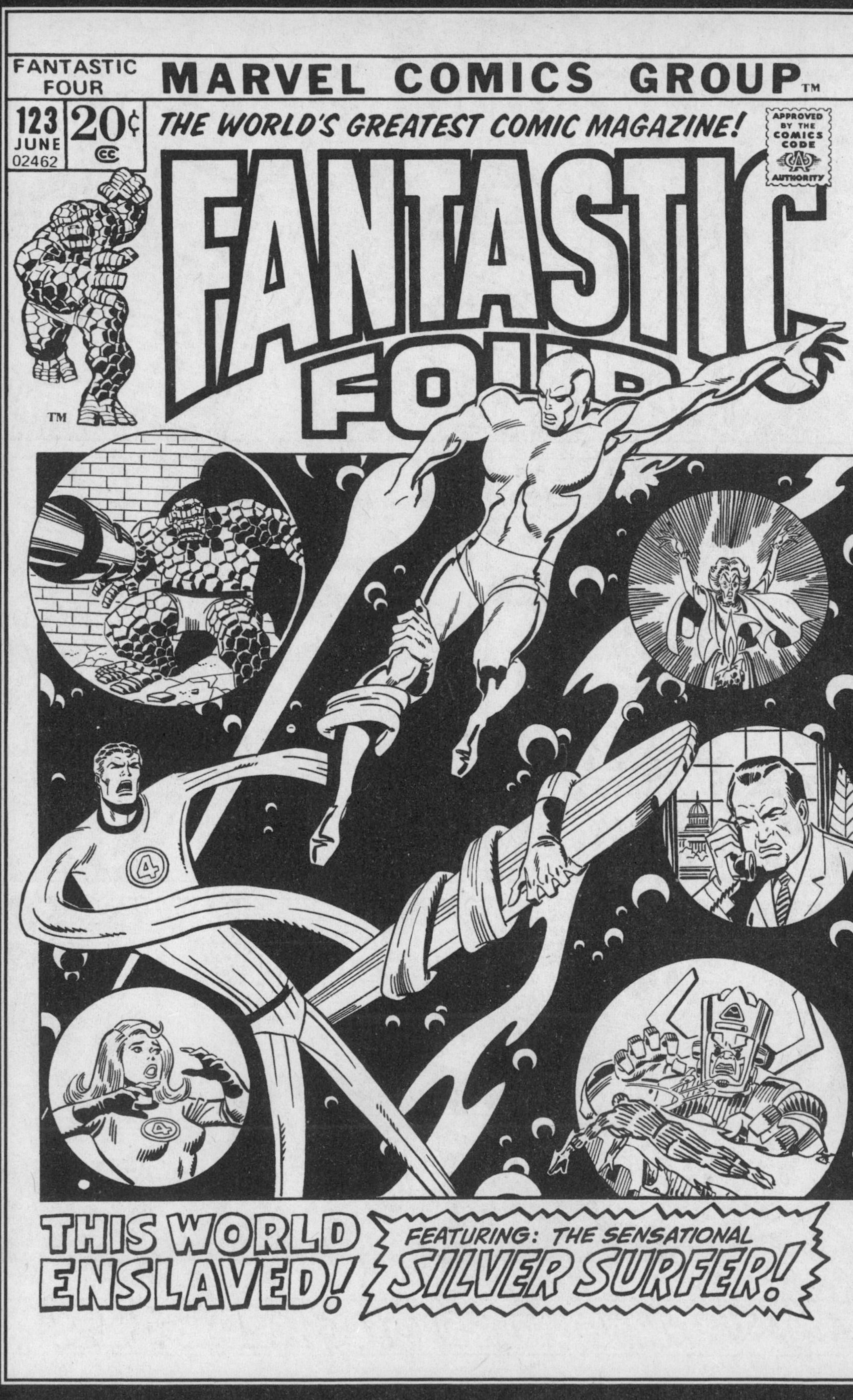
FANTASTIC FOUR
MARVEL COMICS GROUP™
123 JUNE 02462
20¢
THE WORLD'S GREATEST COMIC MAGAZINE!
APPROVED BY THE COMICS CODE AUTHORITY
FANTASTIC FOUR
THIS WORLD ENSLAVED!
FEATURING: THE SENSATIONAL SILVER SURFER!

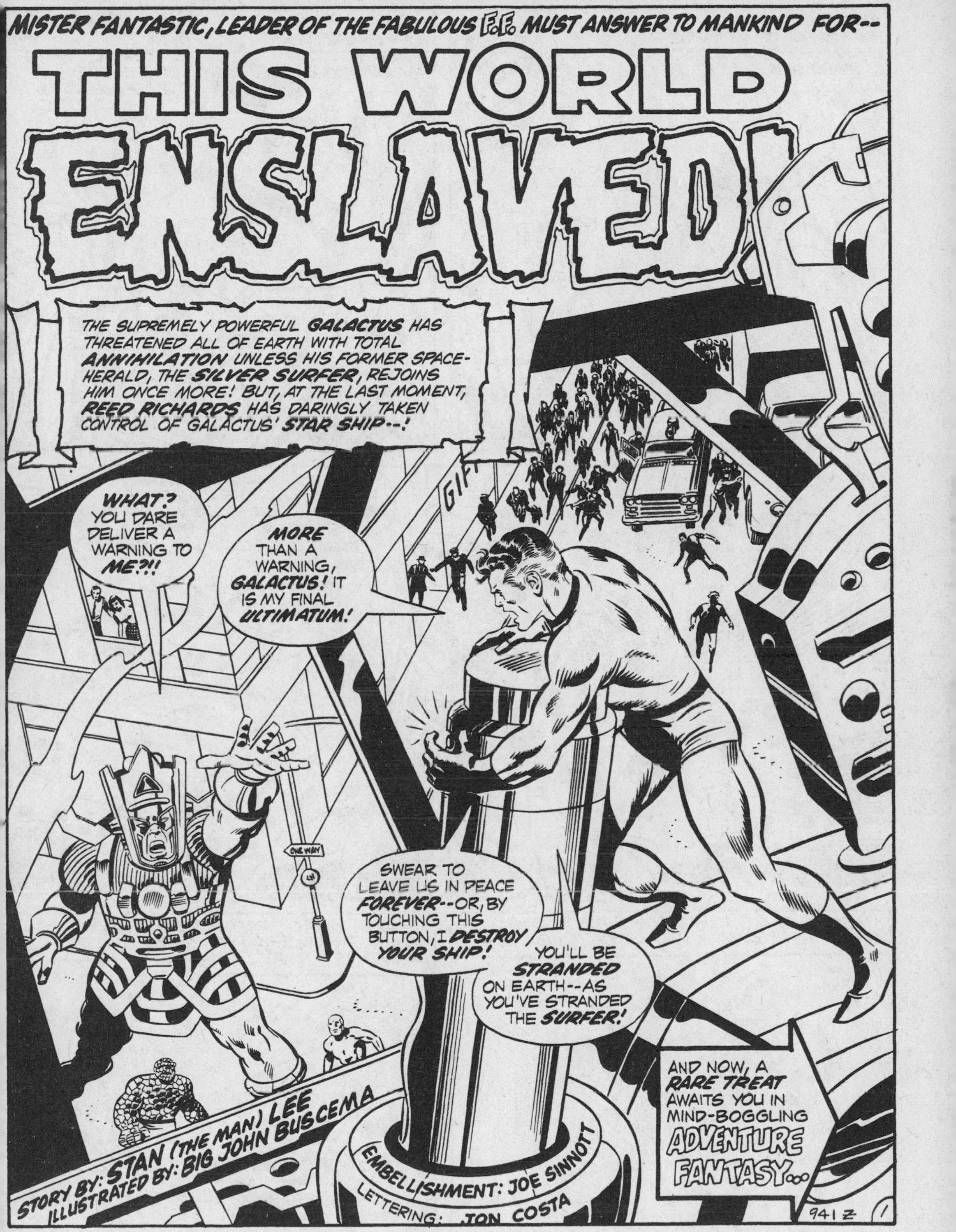
MISTER FANTASTIC, LEADER OF THE FABULOUS F.F. MUST ANSWER TO MANKIND FOR--
THIS WORLD ENSLAVED!
THE SUPREMELY POWERFUL GALACTUS HAS THREATENED ALL OF EARTH WITH TOTAL ANNIHILATION UNLESS HIS FORMER SPACE-HERALD, THE SILVER SURFER, REJOINS HIM ONCE MORE! BUT, AT THE LAST MOMENT, REED RICHARDS HAS DARINGLY TAKEN CONTROL OF GALACTUS' STAR SHIP--!
WHAT? YOU DARE DELIVER A WARNING TO ME?!!
MORE THAN A WARNING, GALACTUS! IT IS MY FINAL ULTIMATUM!
ONE WAY
SWEAR TO LEAVE US IN PEACE FOREVER--OR, BY TOUCHING THIS BUTTON, I DESTROY YOUR SHIP!
YOU'LL BE STRANDED ON EARTH--AS YOU'VE STRANDED THE SURFER!
AND NOW, A RARE TREAT AWAITS YOU IN MIND-BOGGLING ADVENTURE FANTASY...
STORY BY: STAN (THE MAN) LEE
ILLUSTRATED BY: BIG JOHN BUSCEMA
EMBELLISHMENT: JOE SINNOTT
LETTERING: JON COSTA
941 Z
1

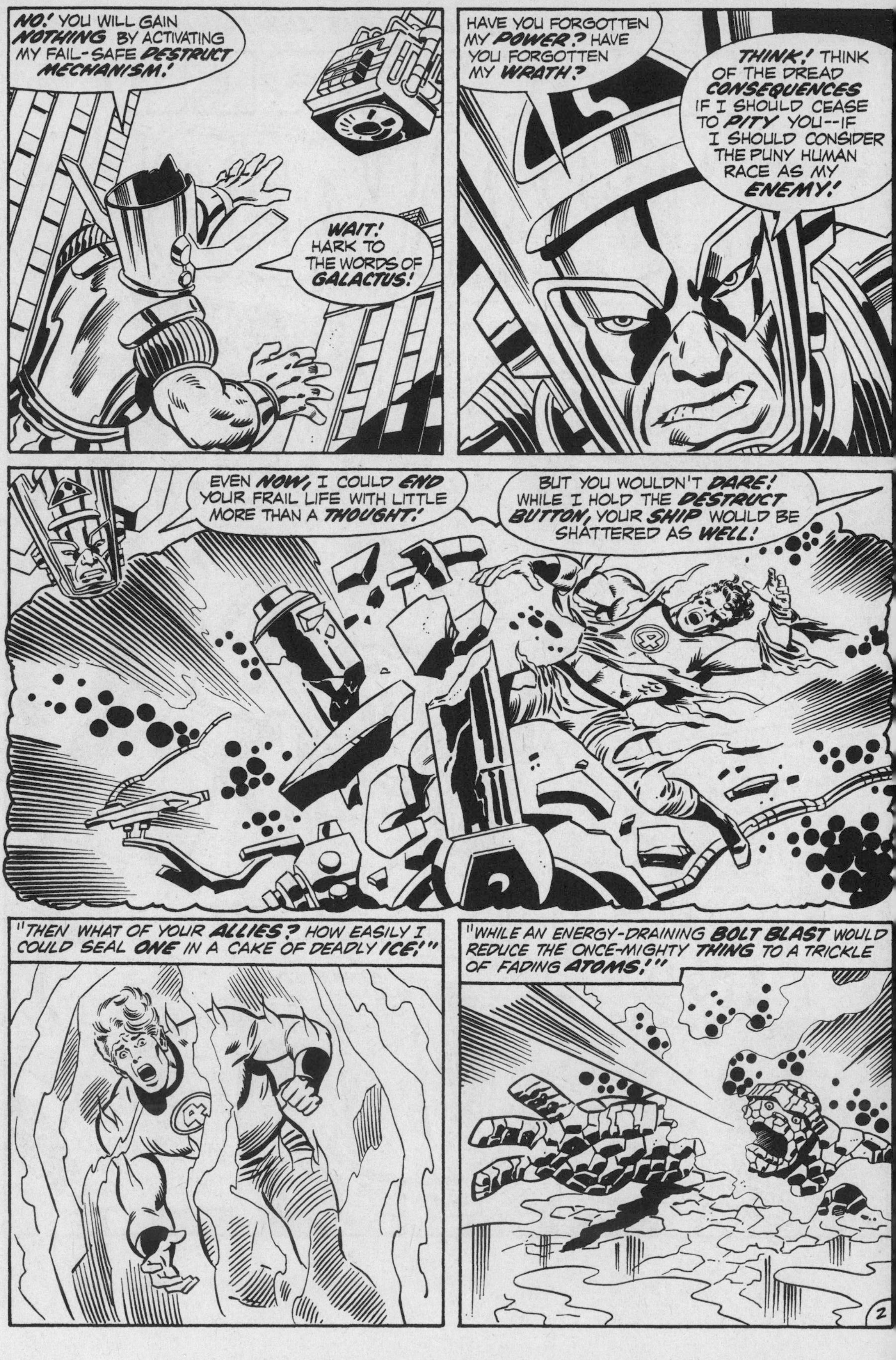
NO! YOU WILL GAIN NOTHING BY ACTIVATING MY FAIL-SAFE DESTRUCT MECHANISM!
WAIT! HARK TO THE WORDS OF GALACTUS!
HAVE YOU FORGOTTEN MY POWER? HAVE YOU FORGOTTEN MY WRATH?
THINK! THINK OF THE DREAD CONSEQUENCES IF I SHOULD CEASE TO PITY YOU--IF I SHOULD CONSIDER THE PUNY HUMAN RACE AS MY ENEMY!
EVEN NOW, I COULD END YOUR FRAIL LIFE WITH LITTLE MORE THAN A THOUGHT!
BUT YOU WOULDN'T DARE! WHILE I HOLD THE DESTRUCT BUTTON, YOUR SHIP WOULD BE SHATTERED AS WELL!
"THEN WHAT OF YOUR ALLIES? HOW EASILY I COULD SEAL ONE IN A CAKE OF DEADLY ICE!"
"WHILE AN ENERGY-DRAINING BOLT BLAST WOULD REDUCE THE ONCE-MIGHTY THING TO A TRICKLE OF FADING ATOMS!"
2

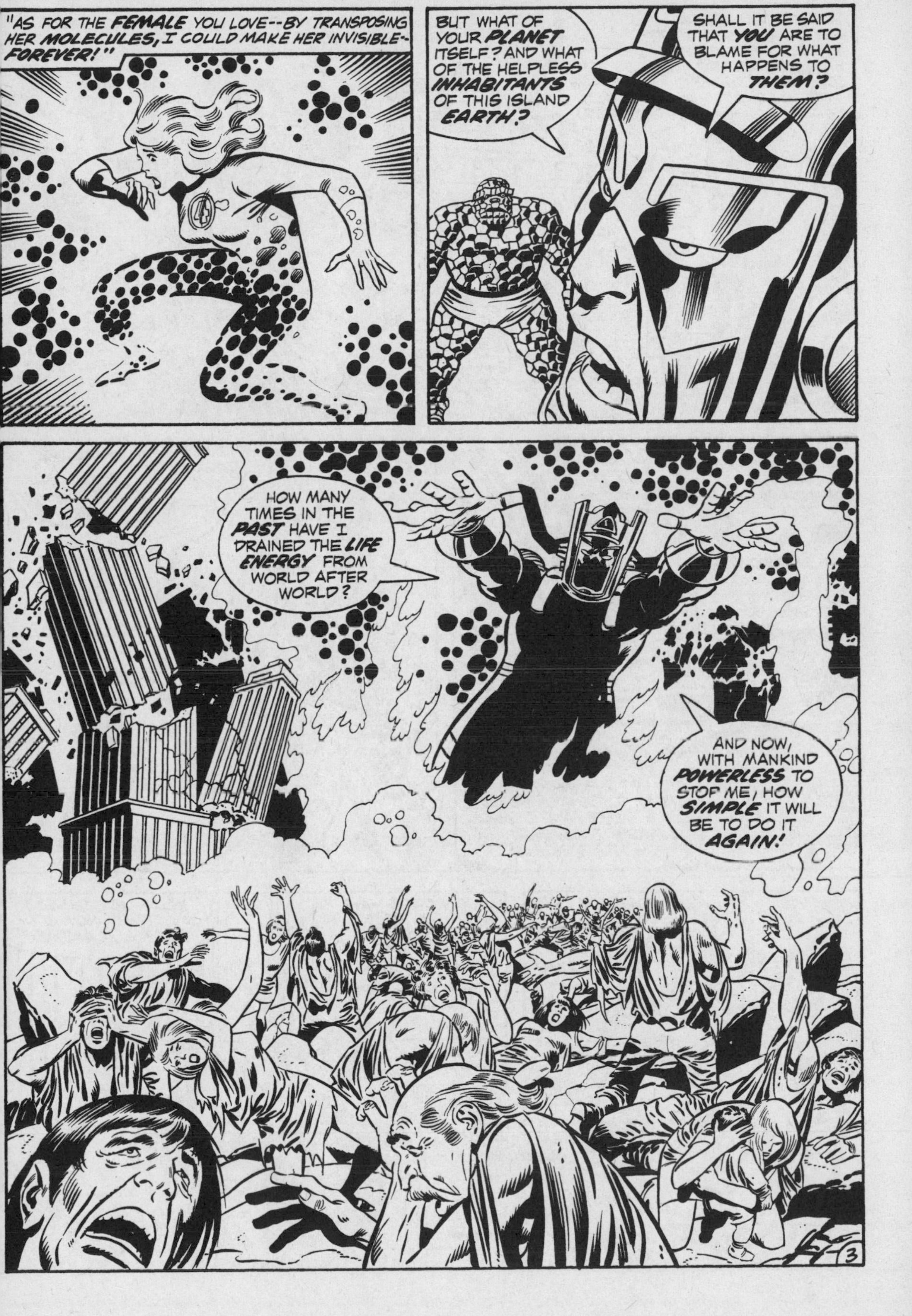
"AS FOR THE **FEMALE** YOU LOVE--BY TRANSPOSING HER **MOLECULES**, I COULD MAKE HER INVISIBLE-**FOREVER!**"
BUT WHAT OF YOUR **PLANET** ITSELF? AND WHAT OF THE HELPLESS **INHABITANTS** OF THIS ISLAND **EARTH?**
SHALL IT BE SAID THAT **YOU** ARE TO BLAME FOR WHAT HAPPENS TO **THEM?**
HOW MANY TIMES IN THE **PAST** HAVE I DRAINED THE **LIFE ENERGY** FROM WORLD AFTER WORLD?
AND NOW, WITH MANKIND **POWERLESS** TO STOP ME, HOW **SIMPLE** IT WILL BE TO DO IT **AGAIN!**
3

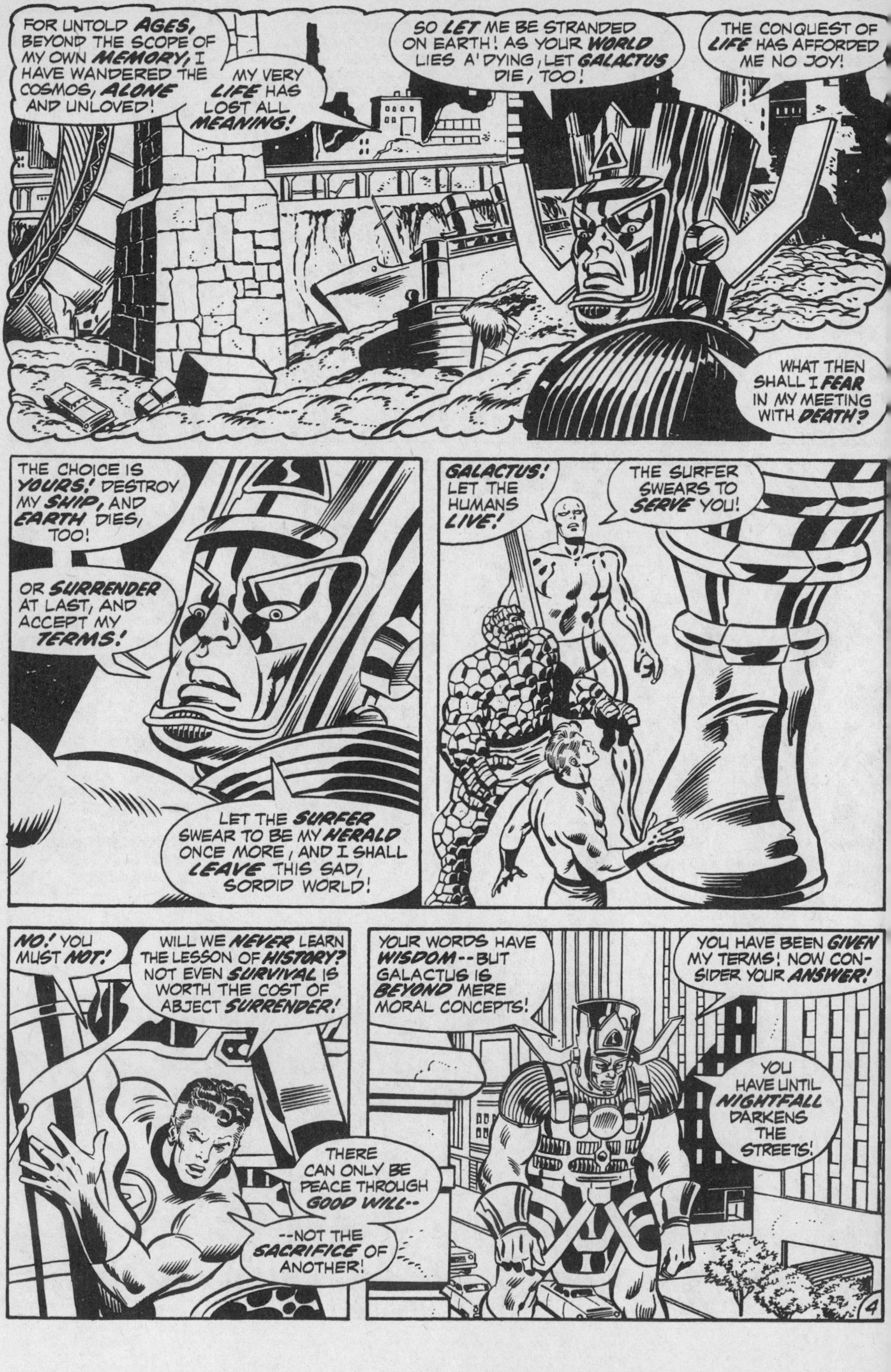
FOR UNTOLD AGES, BEYOND THE SCOPE OF MY OWN MEMORY, I HAVE WANDERED THE COSMOS, ALONE AND UNLOVED!
MY VERY LIFE HAS LOST ALL MEANING!
SO LET ME BE STRANDED ON EARTH! AS YOUR WORLD LIES A'DYING, LET GALACTUS DIE, TOO!
THE CONQUEST OF LIFE HAS AFFORDED ME NO JOY!
WHAT THEN SHALL I FEAR IN MY MEETING WITH DEATH?
THE CHOICE IS YOURS! DESTROY MY SHIP, AND EARTH DIES, TOO!
OR SURRENDER AT LAST, AND ACCEPT MY TERMS!
LET THE SURFER SWEAR TO BE MY HERALD ONCE MORE, AND I SHALL LEAVE THIS SAD, SORDID WORLD!
GALACTUS! LET THE HUMANS LIVE!
THE SURFER SWEARS TO SERVE YOU!
NO! YOU MUST NOT!
WILL WE NEVER LEARN THE LESSON OF HISTORY? NOT EVEN SURVIVAL IS WORTH THE COST OF ABJECT SURRENDER!
THERE CAN ONLY BE PEACE THROUGH GOOD WILL--
--NOT THE SACRIFICE OF ANOTHER!
YOUR WORDS HAVE WISDOM--BUT GALACTUS IS BEYOND MERE MORAL CONCEPTS!
YOU HAVE BEEN GIVEN MY TERMS! NOW CONSIDER YOUR ANSWER!
YOU HAVE UNTIL NIGHTFALL DARKENS THE STREETS!
4

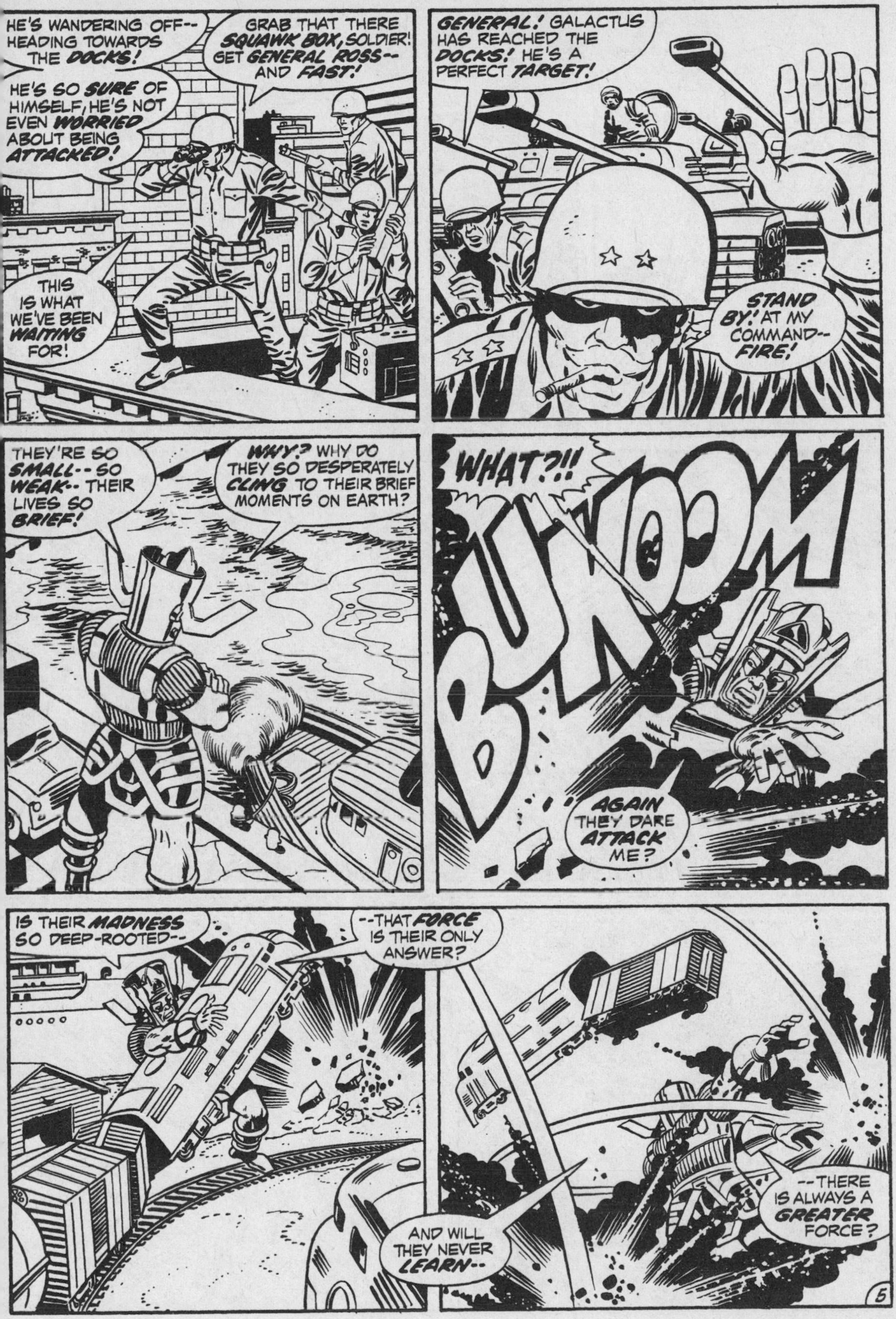
HE'S WANDERING OFF-- HEADING TOWARDS THE DOCKS!
GRAB THAT THERE SQUAWK BOX, SOLDIER! GET GENERAL ROSS-- AND FAST!
HE'S SO SURE OF HIMSELF, HE'S NOT EVEN WORRIED ABOUT BEING ATTACKED!
THIS IS WHAT WE'VE BEEN WAITING FOR!
GENERAL! GALACTUS HAS REACHED THE DOCKS! HE'S A PERFECT TARGET!
STAND BY! AT MY COMMAND-- FIRE!
THEY'RE SO SMALL-- SO WEAK-- THEIR LIVES SO BRIEF!
WHY? WHY DO THEY SO DESPERATELY CLING TO THEIR BRIEF MOMENTS ON EARTH?
WHAT?!!
BUKOOM
AGAIN THEY DARE ATTACK ME?
IS THEIR MADNESS SO DEEP-ROOTED--
--THAT FORCE IS THEIR ONLY ANSWER?
AND WILL THEY NEVER LEARN--
--THERE IS ALWAYS A GREATER FORCE?

I COULD HAVE *CRUSHED* THEM WITH A *GLANCE*-- BUT I SOUGHT TO *REASON!*

THE *FOOLS!* ONLY THE *UNTHINKING* MISTAKE PATIENCE FOR *WEAKNESS!*

L-LOOK! THAT *TRAIN!* IT--IT'S FLYING IN THE *AIR!!*

FLOATING AROUND THE *BUILDINGS*-- LIKE SOMETHING'S *GUIDING* IT!

GALACTUS! IT MUST BE-- *GALACTUS!*

LOOK OUT!

TAKE COVER!

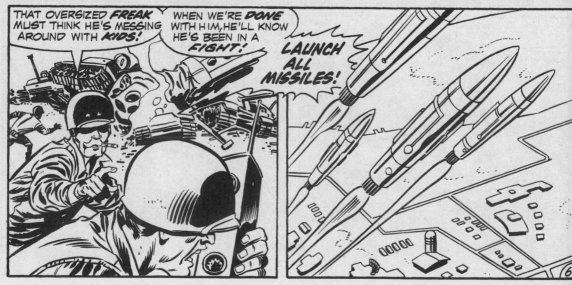

THAT OVERSIZED *FREAK* MUST THINK HE'S MESSING AROUND WITH *KIDS!*

WHEN WE'RE *DONE* WITH HIM, HE'LL KNOW HE'S BEEN IN A *FIGHT!*

LAUNCH ALL MISSILES!

6

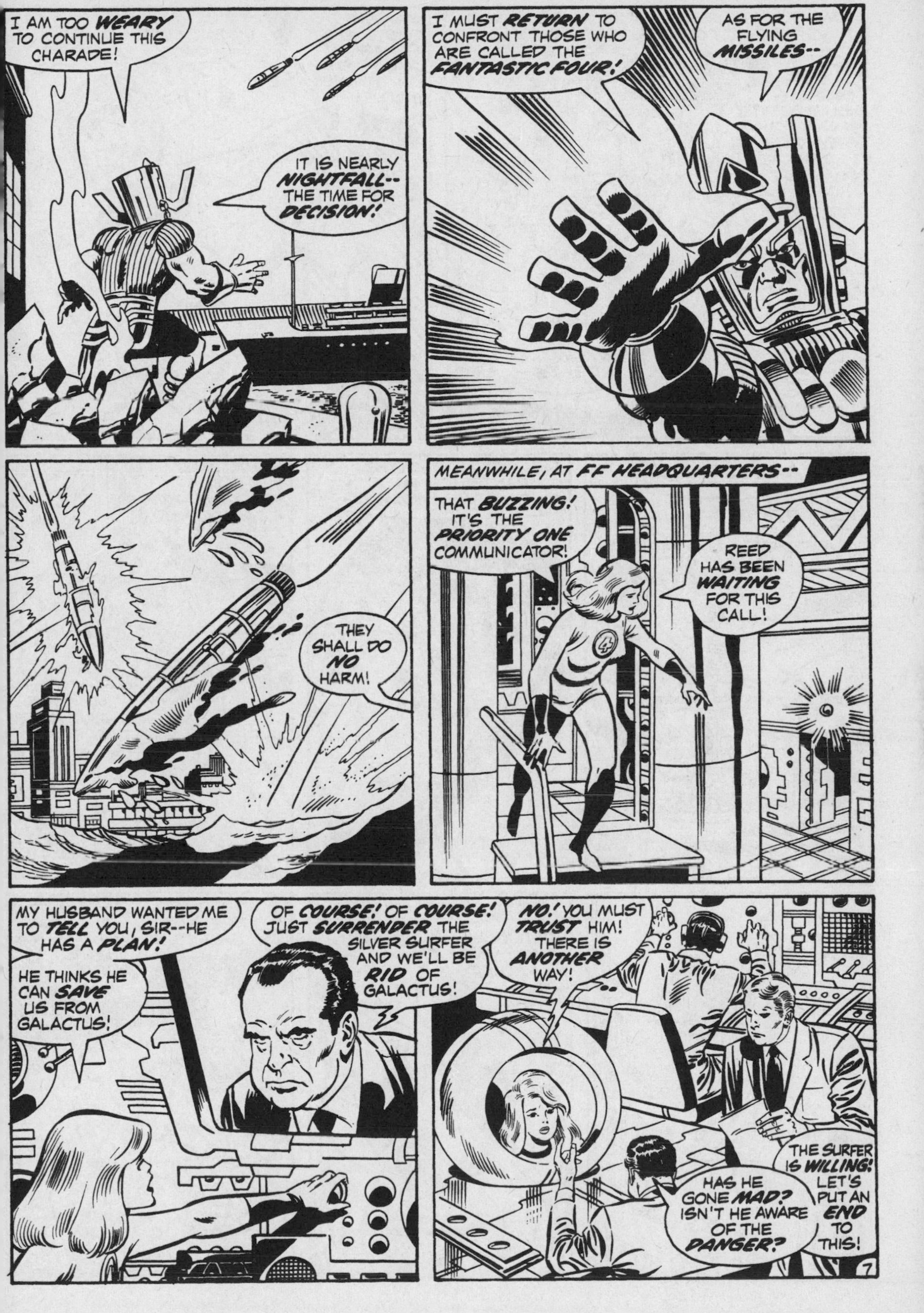
I AM TOO WEARY TO CONTINUE THIS CHARADE!
IT IS NEARLY NIGHTFALL-- THE TIME FOR DECISION!
I MUST RETURN TO CONFRONT THOSE WHO ARE CALLED THE FANTASTIC FOUR!
AS FOR THE FLYING MISSILES--
THEY SHALL DO NO HARM!
MEANWHILE, AT FF HEADQUARTERS--
THAT BUZZING! IT'S THE PRIORITY ONE COMMUNICATOR!
REED HAS BEEN WAITING FOR THIS CALL!
MY HUSBAND WANTED ME TO TELL YOU, SIR--HE HAS A PLAN!
HE THINKS HE CAN SAVE US FROM GALACTUS!
OF COURSE! OF COURSE! JUST SURRENDER THE SILVER SURFER AND WE'LL BE RID OF GALACTUS!
NO! YOU MUST TRUST HIM! THERE IS ANOTHER WAY!
HAS HE GONE MAD? ISN'T HE AWARE OF THE DANGER?
THE SURFER IS WILLING! LET'S PUT AN END TO THIS!
7

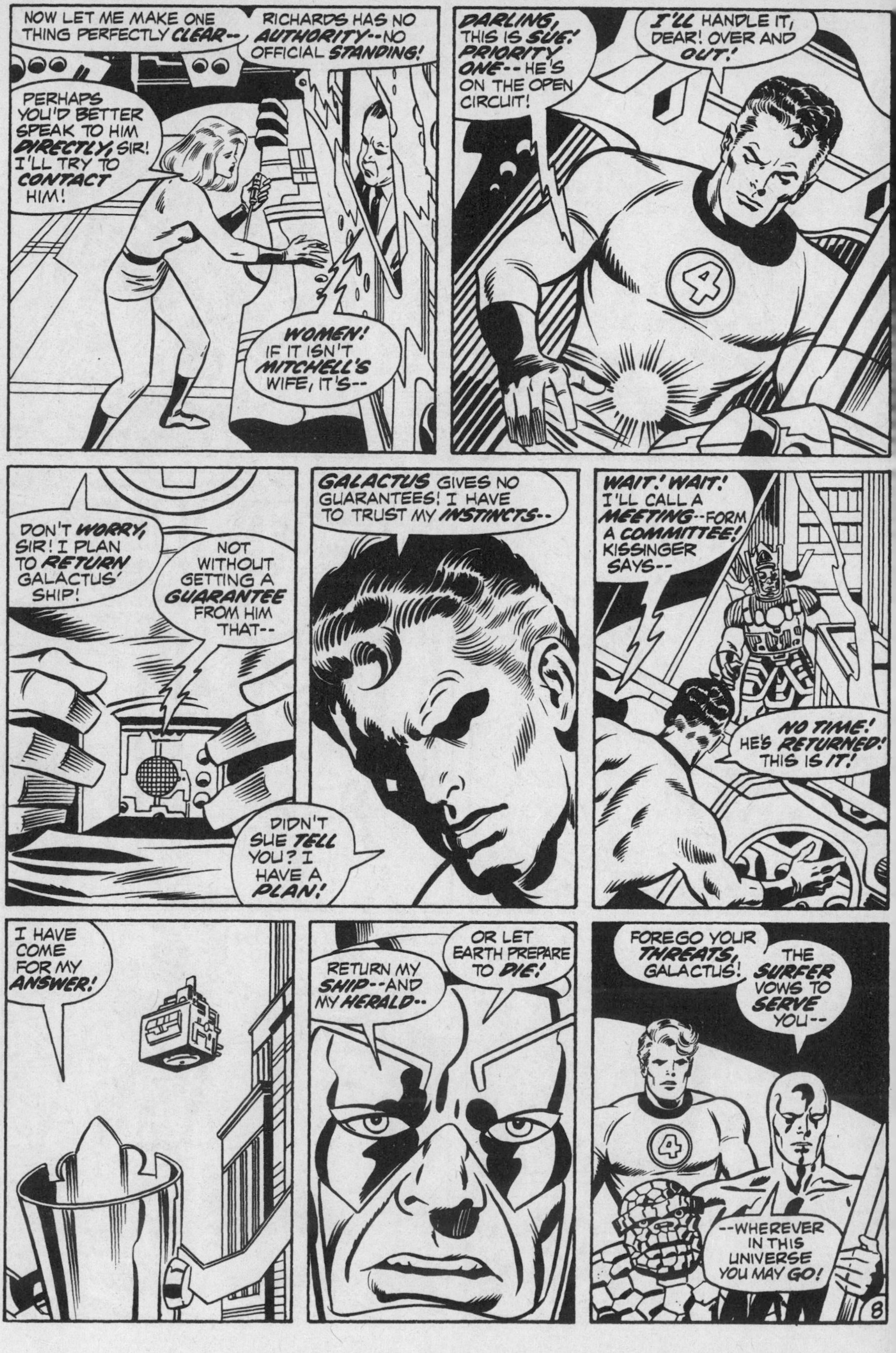
NOW LET ME MAKE ONE THING PERFECTLY CLEAR--
RICHARDS HAS NO AUTHORITY--NO OFFICIAL STANDING!
PERHAPS YOU'D BETTER SPEAK TO HIM DIRECTLY, SIR! I'LL TRY TO CONTACT HIM!
WOMEN! IF IT ISN'T MITCHELL'S WIFE, IT'S--
DARLING, THIS IS SUE! PRIORITY ONE--HE'S ON THE OPEN CIRCUIT!
I'LL HANDLE IT, DEAR! OVER AND OUT!
DON'T WORRY, SIR! I PLAN TO RETURN GALACTUS' SHIP!
NOT WITHOUT GETTING A GUARANTEE FROM HIM THAT--
GALACTUS GIVES NO GUARANTEES! I HAVE TO TRUST MY INSTINCTS--
DIDN'T SUE TELL YOU? I HAVE A PLAN!
WAIT! WAIT! I'LL CALL A MEETING--FORM A COMMITTEE! KISSINGER SAYS--
NO TIME! HE'S RETURNED! THIS IS IT!
I HAVE COME FOR MY ANSWER!
RETURN MY SHIP--AND MY HERALD--
OR LET EARTH PREPARE TO DIE!
FOREGO YOUR THREATS, GALACTUS!
THE SURFER VOWS TO SERVE YOU--
--WHEREVER IN THIS UNIVERSE YOU MAY GO!
8

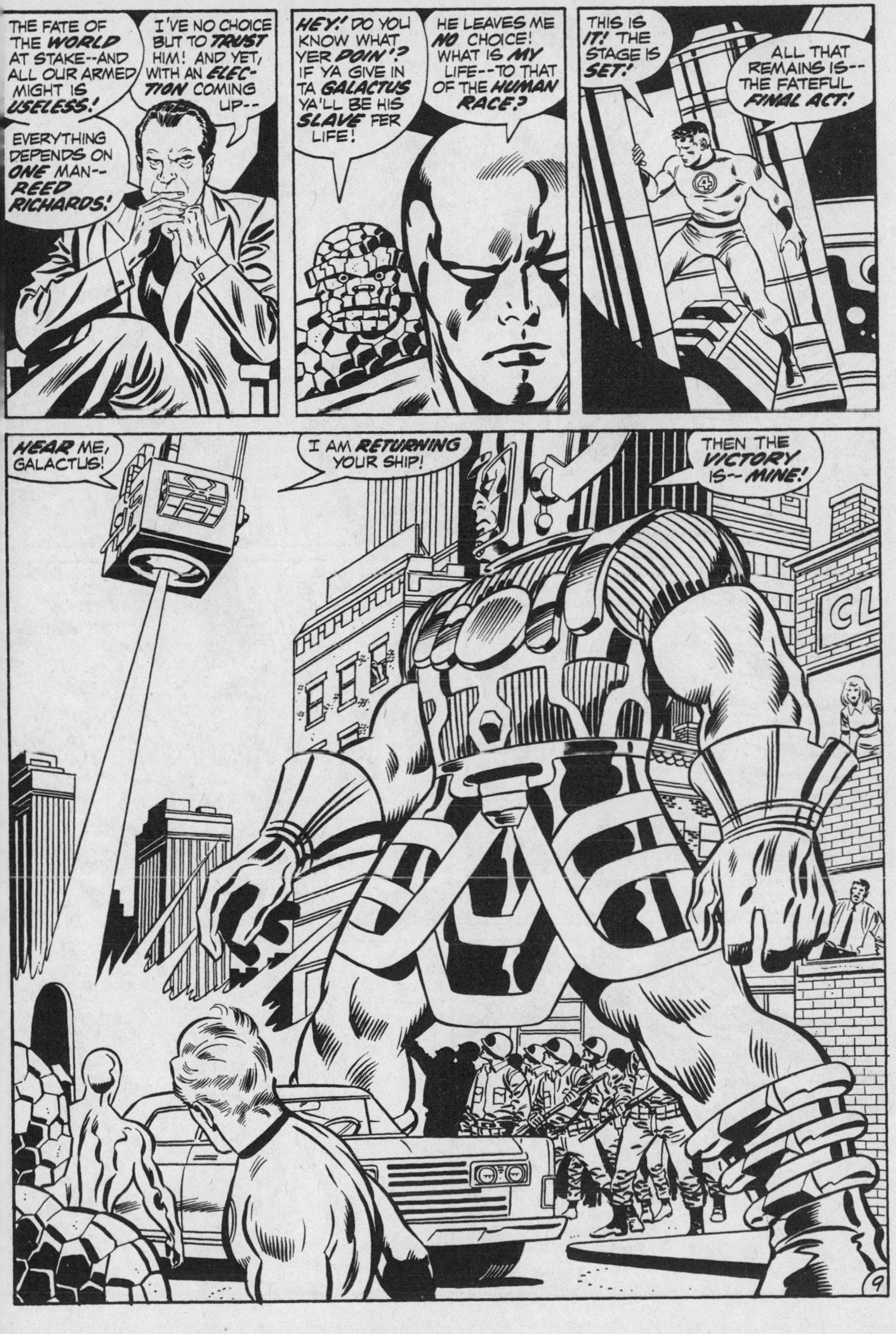
THE FATE OF THE WORLD AT STAKE--AND ALL OUR ARMED MIGHT IS USELESS!
I'VE NO CHOICE BUT TO TRUST HIM! AND YET, WITH AN ELECTION COMING UP--
EVERYTHING DEPENDS ON ONE MAN--REED RICHARDS!
HEY! DO YOU KNOW WHAT YER DOIN'? IF YA GIVE IN TA GALACTUS YA'LL BE HIS SLAVE FER LIFE!
HE LEAVES ME NO CHOICE! WHAT IS MY LIFE--TO THAT OF THE HUMAN RACE?
THIS IS IT! THE STAGE IS SET!
ALL THAT REMAINS IS--THE FATEFUL FINAL ACT!
HEAR ME, GALACTUS!
I AM RETURNING YOUR SHIP!
THEN THE VICTORY IS--MINE!
CL
9

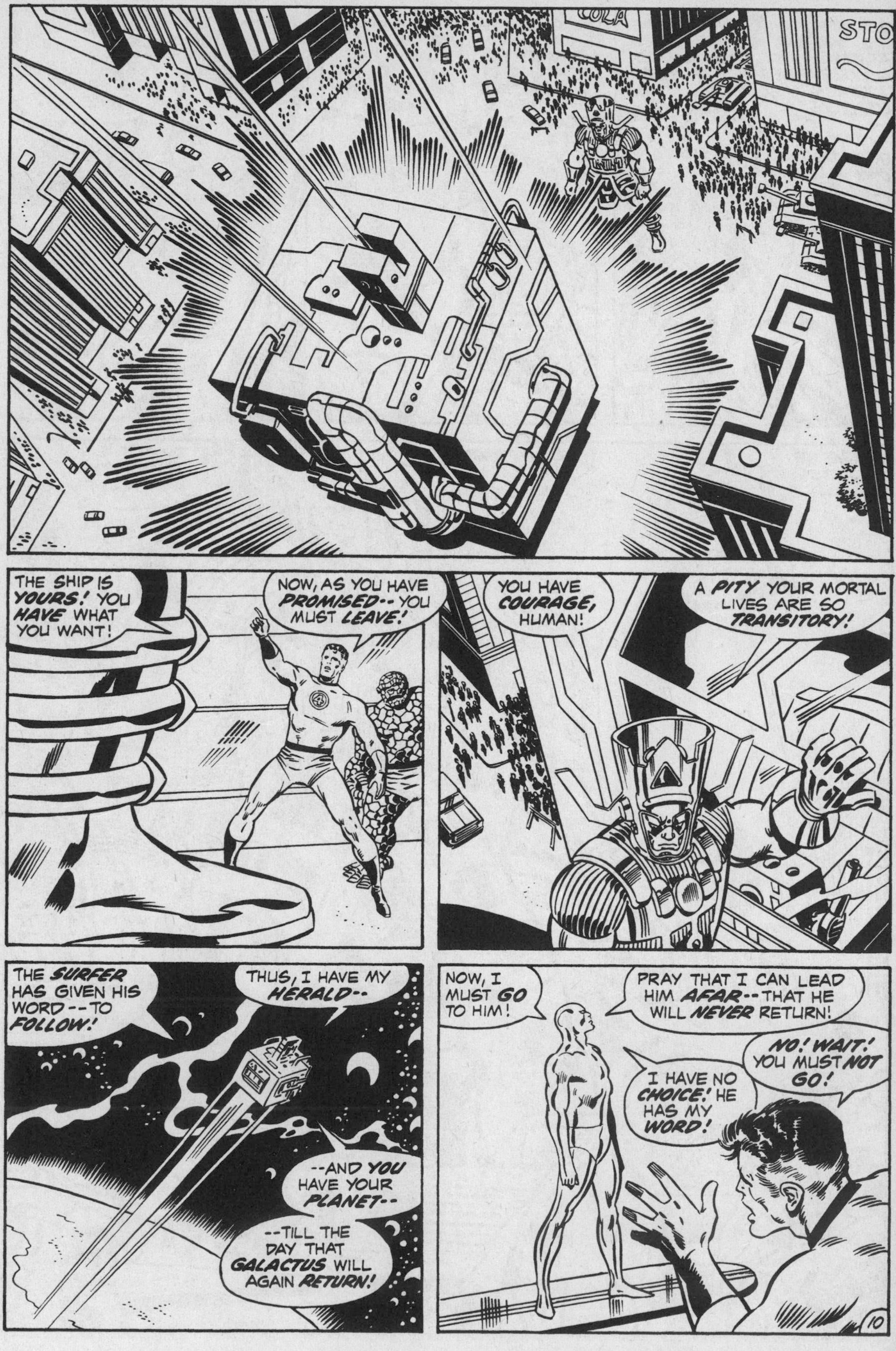
COLA
STO
THE SHIP IS YOURS! YOU HAVE WHAT YOU WANT!
NOW, AS YOU HAVE PROMISED-- YOU MUST LEAVE!
YOU HAVE COURAGE, HUMAN!
A PITY YOUR MORTAL LIVES ARE SO TRANSITORY!
THE SURFER HAS GIVEN HIS WORD -- TO FOLLOW!
THUS, I HAVE MY HERALD--
--AND YOU HAVE YOUR PLANET--
--TILL THE DAY THAT GALACTUS WILL AGAIN RETURN!
NOW, I MUST GO TO HIM!
PRAY THAT I CAN LEAD HIM AFAR--THAT HE WILL NEVER RETURN!
NO! WAIT! YOU MUST NOT GO!
I HAVE NO CHOICE! HE HAS MY WORD!
10

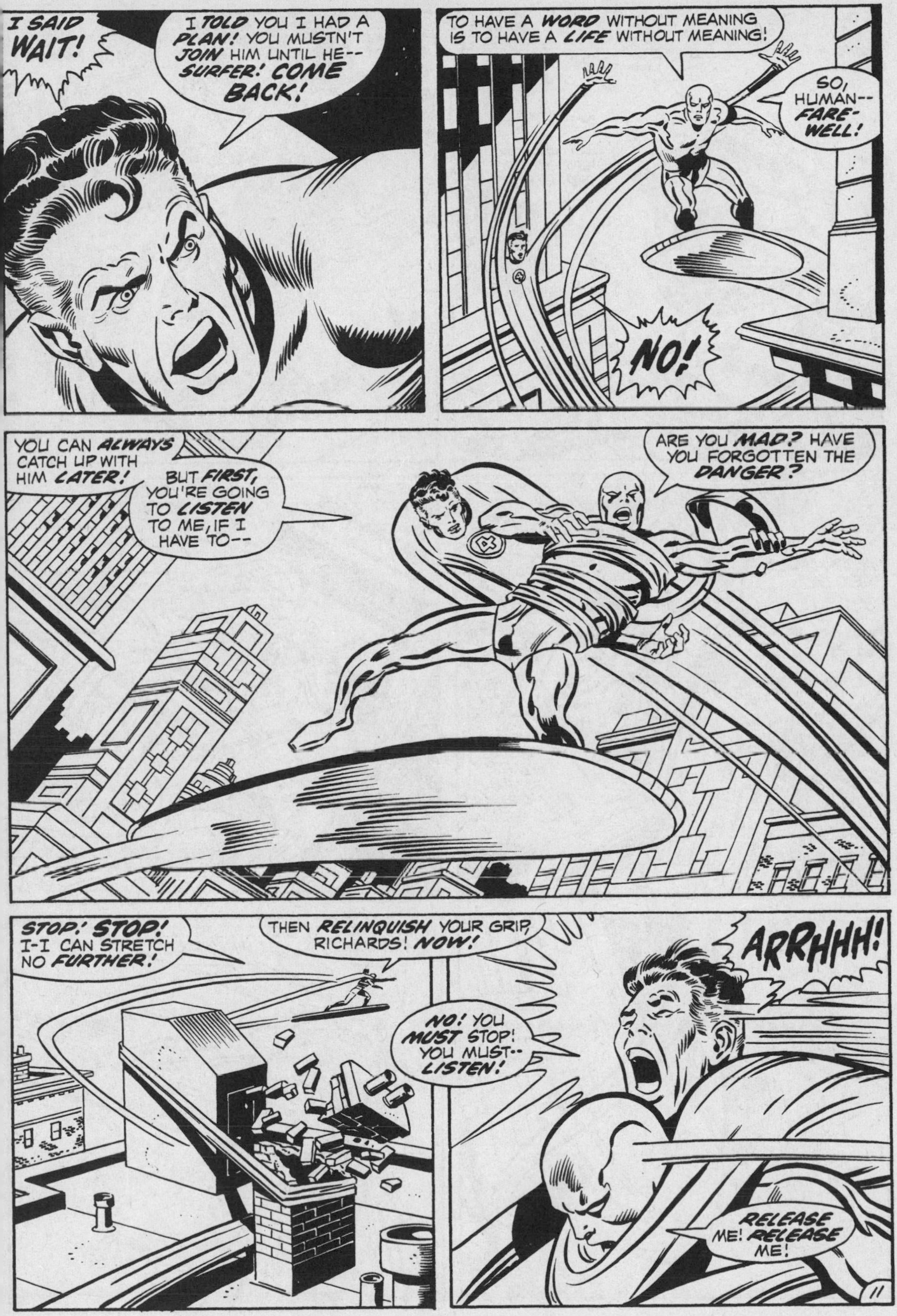
I SAID WAIT!
I TOLD YOU I HAD A PLAN! YOU MUSTN'T JOIN HIM UNTIL HE-- SURFER! COME BACK!
TO HAVE A WORD WITHOUT MEANING IS TO HAVE A LIFE WITHOUT MEANING!
SO, HUMAN-- FARE-WELL!
NO!
YOU CAN ALWAYS CATCH UP WITH HIM LATER!
BUT FIRST, YOU'RE GOING TO LISTEN TO ME, IF I HAVE TO--
ARE YOU MAD? HAVE YOU FORGOTTEN THE DANGER?
STOP! STOP! I-I CAN STRETCH NO FURTHER!
THEN RELINQUISH YOUR GRIP, RICHARDS! NOW!
ARRHHH!
NO! YOU MUST STOP! YOU MUST-- LISTEN!
RELEASE ME! RELEASE ME!
11

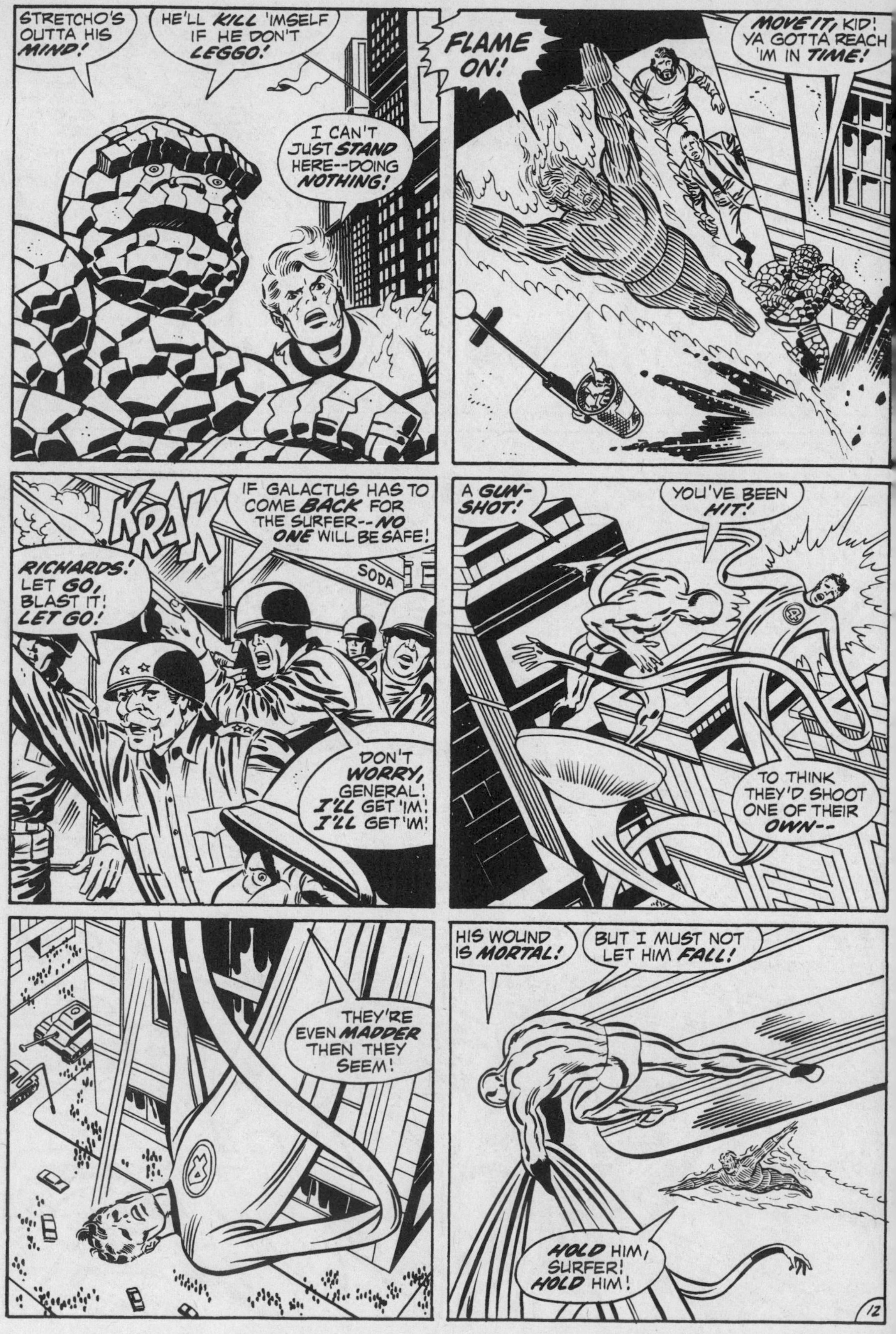
STRETCHO'S OUTTA HIS MIND!
HE'LL KILL 'IMSELF IF HE DON'T LEGGO!
I CAN'T JUST STAND HERE--DOING NOTHING!
FLAME ON!
MOVE IT, KID! YA GOTTA REACH 'IM IN TIME!
KRAK
IF GALACTUS HAS TO COME BACK FOR THE SURFER--NO ONE WILL BE SAFE!
SODA
RICHARDS! LET GO, BLAST IT! LET GO!
DON'T WORRY, GENERAL! I'LL GET 'IM! I'LL GET 'IM!
A GUN-SHOT!
YOU'VE BEEN HIT!
TO THINK THEY'D SHOOT ONE OF THEIR OWN--
THEY'RE EVEN MADDER THEN THEY SEEM!
HIS WOUND IS MORTAL!
BUT I MUST NOT LET HIM FALL!
HOLD HIM, SURFER! HOLD HIM!
12

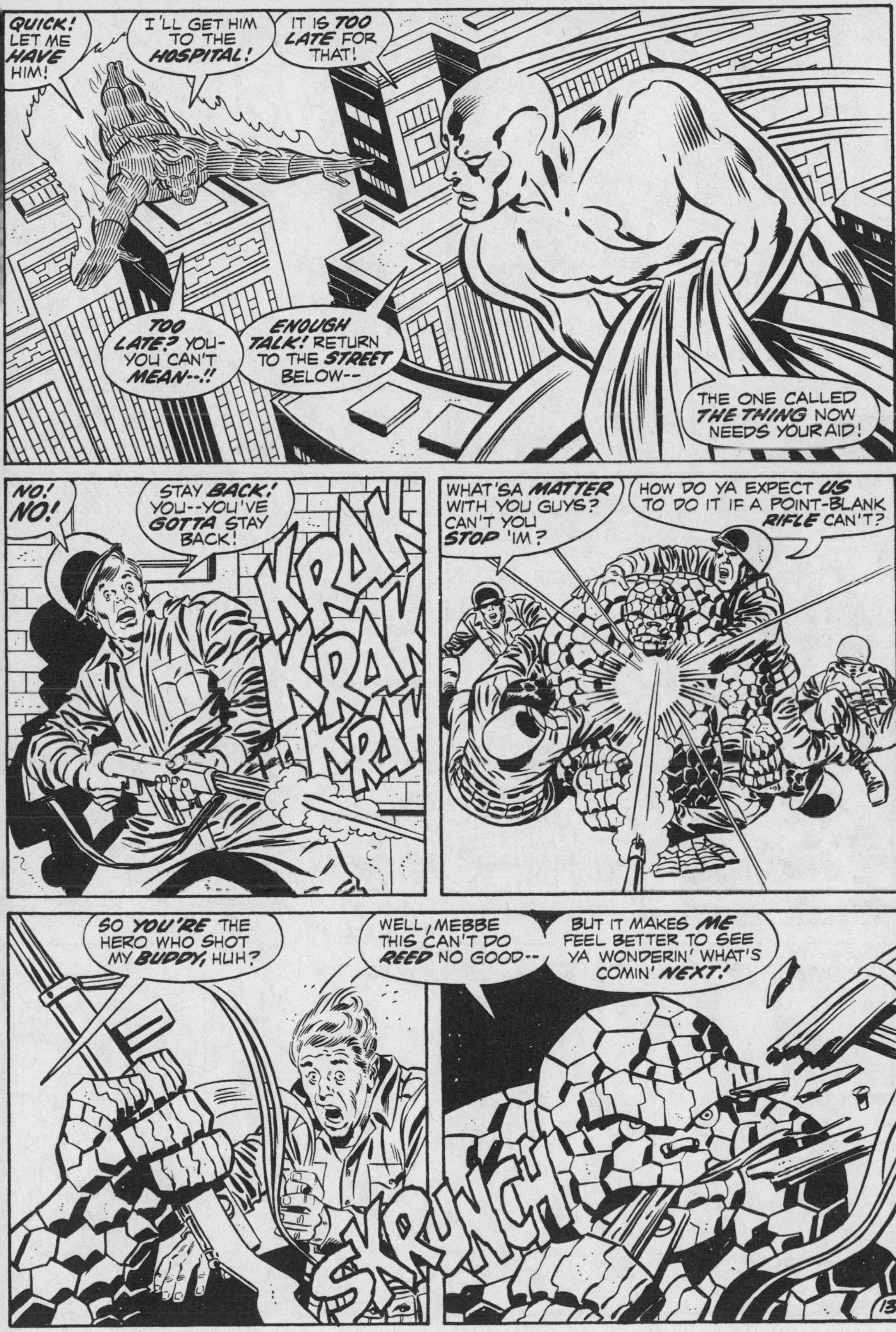
QUICK! LET ME HAVE HIM!
I'LL GET HIM TO THE HOSPITAL!
IT IS TOO LATE FOR THAT!
TOO LATE? YOU-YOU CAN'T MEAN--!!
ENOUGH TALK! RETURN TO THE STREET BELOW--
THE ONE CALLED THE THING NOW NEEDS YOUR AID!
NO! NO!
STAY BACK! YOU--YOU'VE GOTTA STAY BACK!
KRAK KRAK KRAK
WHAT'SA MATTER WITH YOU GUYS? CAN'T YOU STOP 'IM?
HOW DO YA EXPECT US TO DO IT IF A POINT-BLANK RIFLE CAN'T?
SO YOU'RE THE HERO WHO SHOT MY BUDDY, HUH?
WELL, MEBBE THIS CAN'T DO REED NO GOOD--
BUT IT MAKES ME FEEL BETTER TO SEE YA WONDERIN' WHAT'S COMIN' NEXT!
SKRUNCH
13

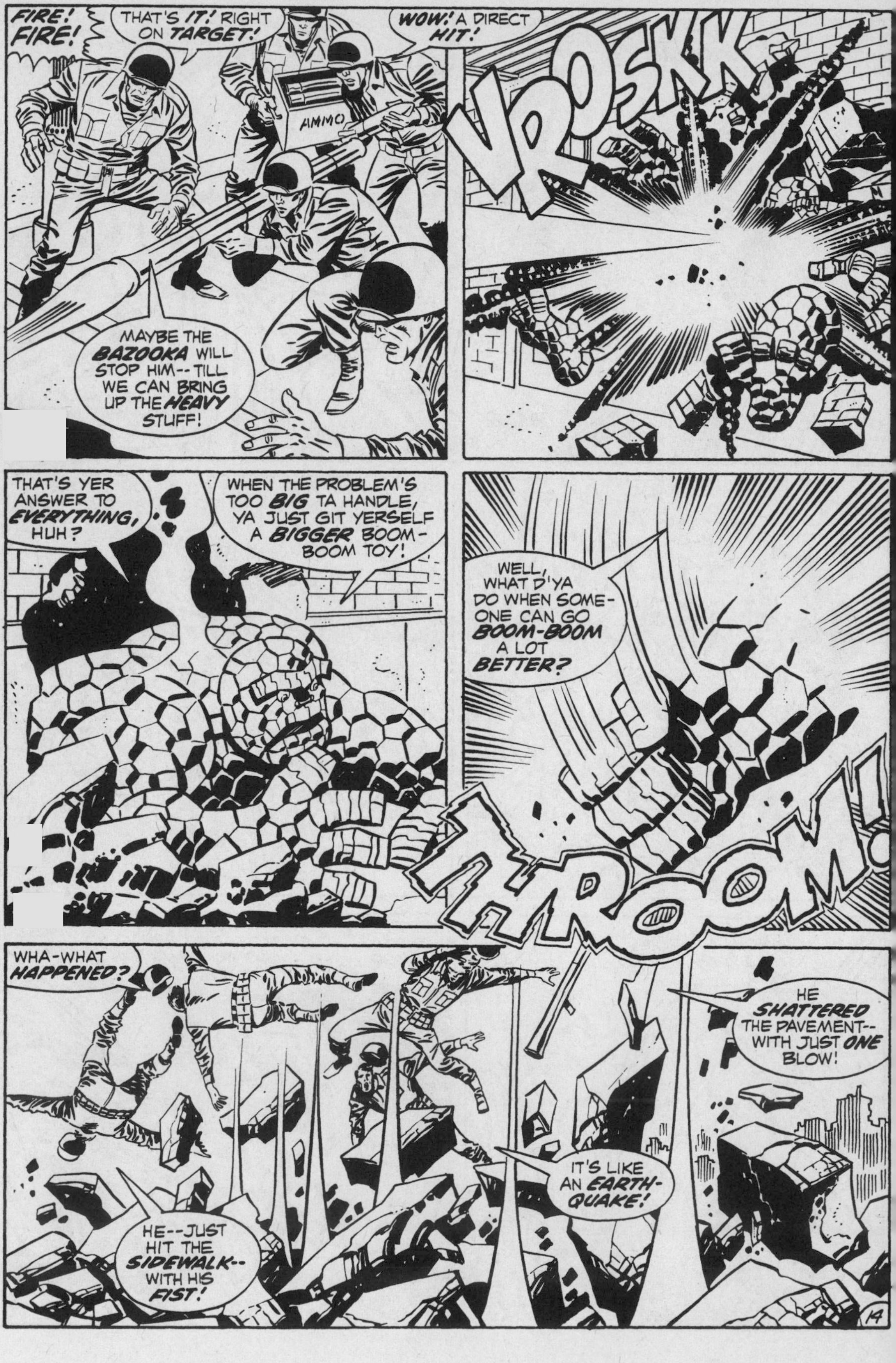
FIRE! FIRE!
THAT'S IT! RIGHT ON TARGET!
AMMO
MAYBE THE BAZOOKA WILL STOP HIM--TILL WE CAN BRING UP THE HEAVY STUFF!
WOW! A DIRECT HIT!
VROSKK
THAT'S YER ANSWER TO EVERYTHING, HUH?
WHEN THE PROBLEM'S TOO BIG TA HANDLE, YA JUST GIT YERSELF A BIGGER BOOM-BOOM TOY!
WELL, WHAT D'YA DO WHEN SOME-ONE CAN GO BOOM-BOOM A LOT BETTER?
THROOM!
WHA-WHAT HAPPENED?
HE SHATTERED THE PAVEMENT--WITH JUST ONE BLOW!
IT'S LIKE AN EARTH-QUAKE!
HE--JUST HIT THE SIDEWALK--WITH HIS FIST!
14

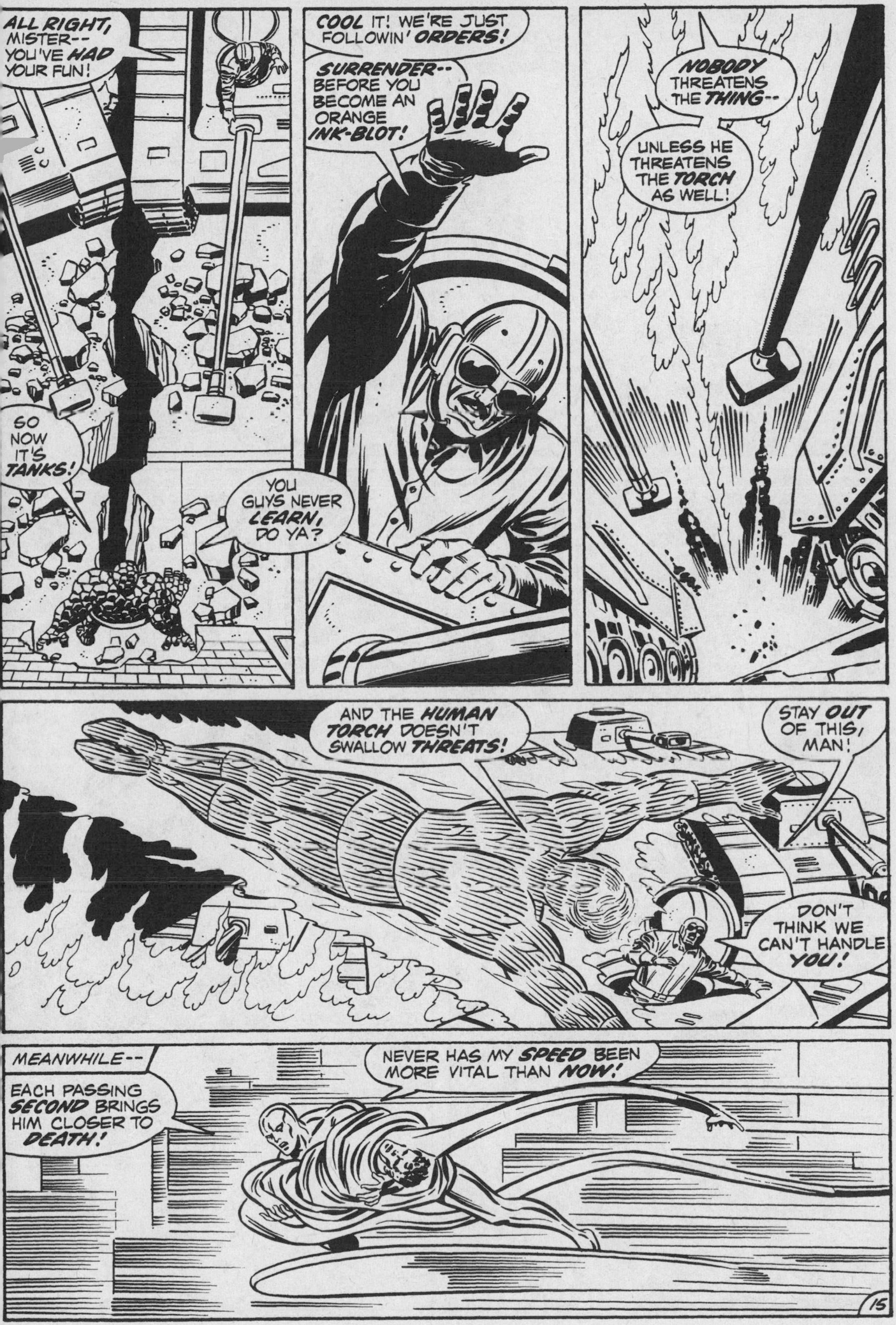
ALL RIGHT, MISTER-- YOU'VE HAD YOUR FUN!
COOL IT! WE'RE JUST FOLLOWIN' ORDERS!
SURRENDER-- BEFORE YOU BECOME AN ORANGE INK-BLOT!
SO NOW IT'S TANKS!
YOU GUYS NEVER LEARN, DO YA?
NOBODY THREATENS THE THING--
UNLESS HE THREATENS THE TORCH AS WELL!
AND THE HUMAN TORCH DOESN'T SWALLOW THREATS!
STAY OUT OF THIS, MAN!
DON'T THINK WE CAN'T HANDLE YOU!
MEANWHILE--
EACH PASSING SECOND BRINGS HIM CLOSER TO DEATH!
NEVER HAS MY SPEED BEEN MORE VITAL THAN NOW!
15

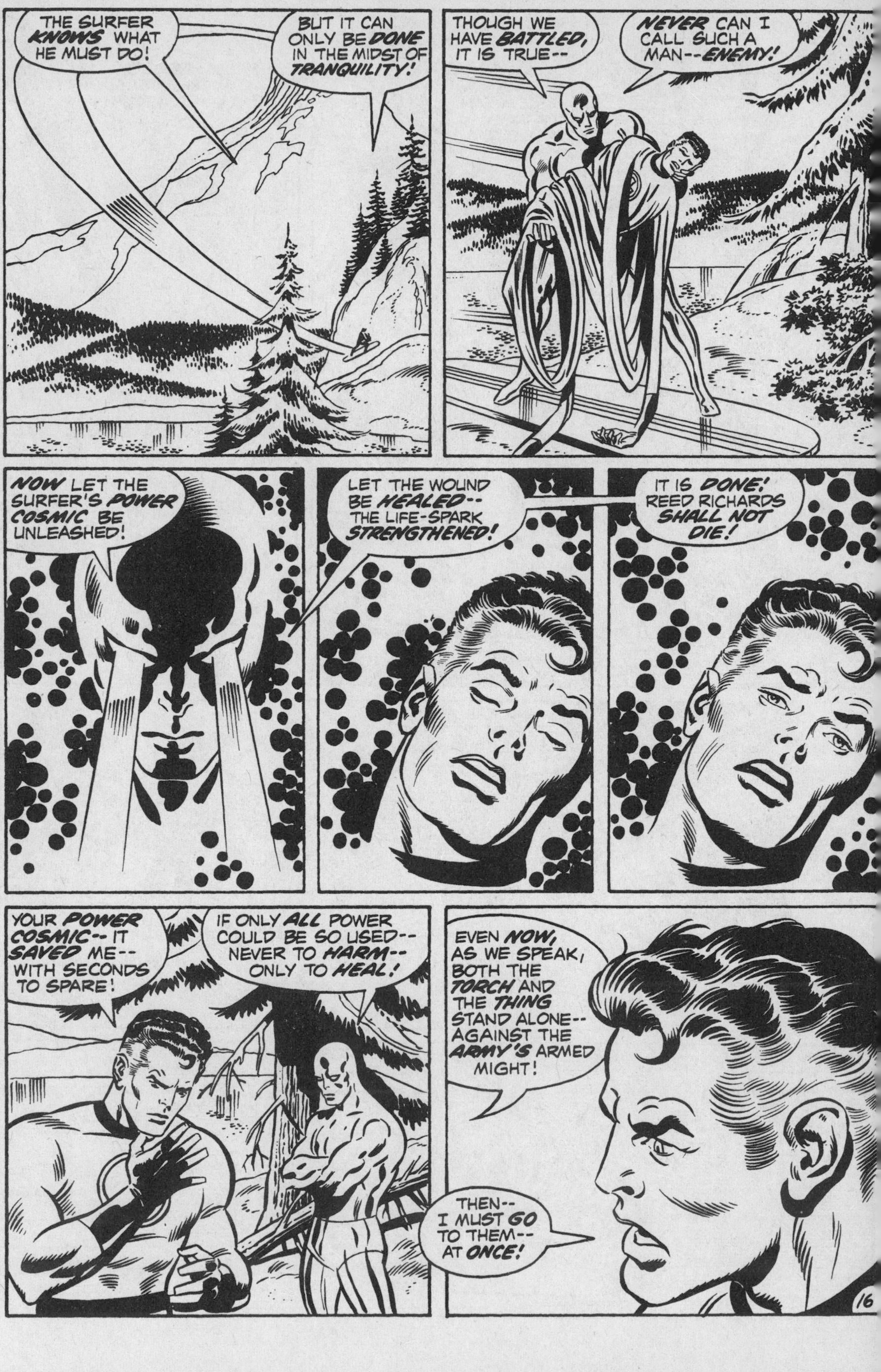

THE SURFER KNOWS WHAT HE MUST DO!
BUT IT CAN ONLY BE DONE IN THE MIDST OF TRANQUILITY!
THOUGH WE HAVE BATTLED, IT IS TRUE--
NEVER CAN I CALL SUCH A MAN--ENEMY!
NOW LET THE SURFER'S POWER COSMIC BE UNLEASHED!
LET THE WOUND BE HEALED-- THE LIFE-SPARK STRENGTHENED!
IT IS DONE! REED RICHARDS SHALL NOT DIE!
YOUR POWER COSMIC-- IT SAVED ME-- WITH SECONDS TO SPARE!
IF ONLY ALL POWER COULD BE SO USED-- NEVER TO HARM-- ONLY TO HEAL!
EVEN NOW, AS WE SPEAK, BOTH THE TORCH AND THE THING STAND ALONE-- AGAINST THE ARMY'S ARMED MIGHT!
THEN-- I MUST GO TO THEM-- AT ONCE!

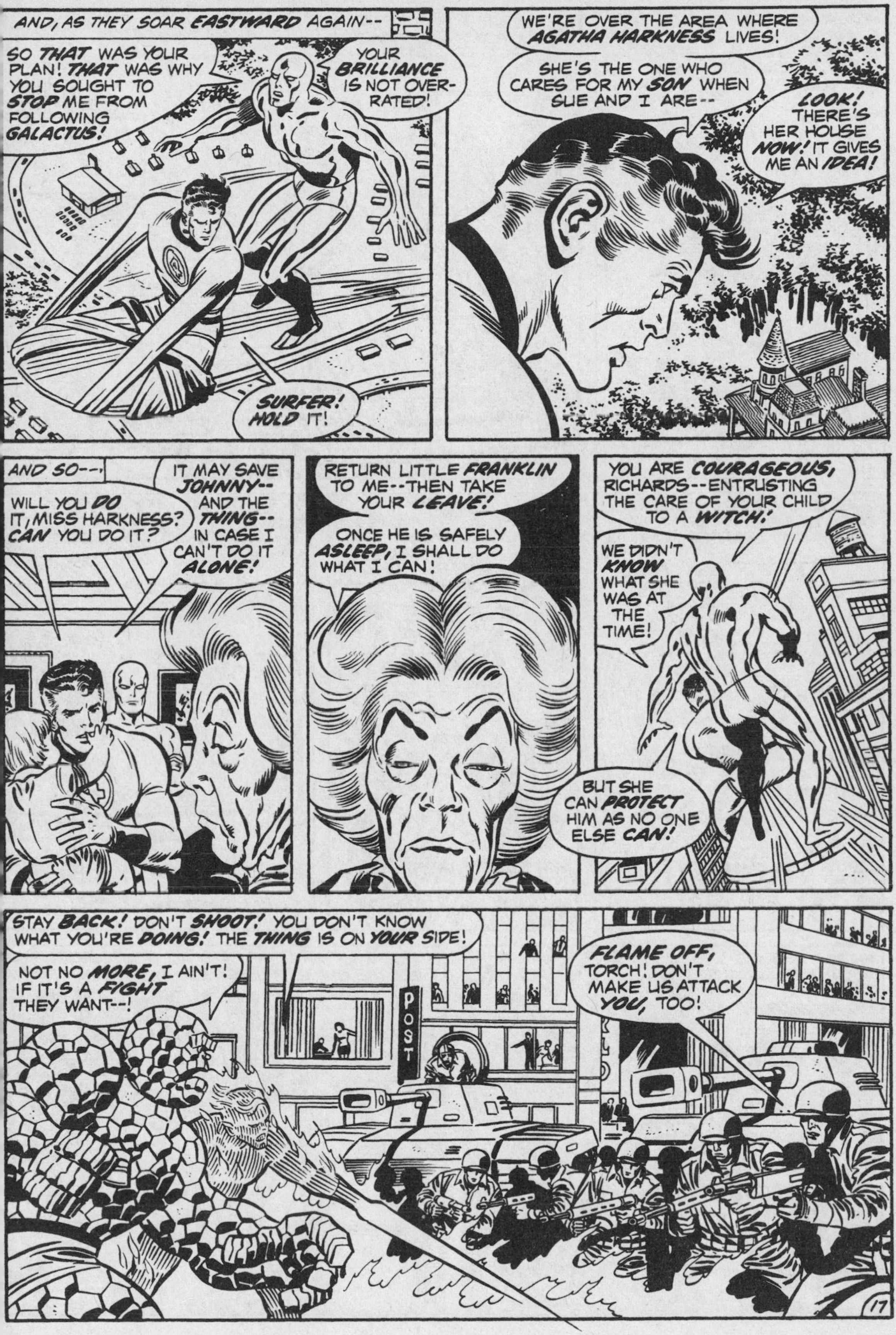
AND, AS THEY SOAR EASTWARD AGAIN--
SO THAT WAS YOUR PLAN! THAT WAS WHY YOU SOUGHT TO STOP ME FROM FOLLOWING GALACTUS!
YOUR BRILLIANCE IS NOT OVER-RATED!
SURFER! HOLD IT!
WE'RE OVER THE AREA WHERE AGATHA HARKNESS LIVES!
SHE'S THE ONE WHO CARES FOR MY SON WHEN SUE AND I ARE--
LOOK! THERE'S HER HOUSE NOW! IT GIVES ME AN IDEA!
AND SO--
WILL YOU DO IT, MISS HARKNESS? CAN YOU DO IT?
IT MAY SAVE JOHNNY-- AND THE THING-- IN CASE I CAN'T DO IT ALONE!
RETURN LITTLE FRANKLIN TO ME--THEN TAKE YOUR LEAVE!
ONCE HE IS SAFELY ASLEEP, I SHALL DO WHAT I CAN!
YOU ARE COURAGEOUS, RICHARDS--ENTRUSTING THE CARE OF YOUR CHILD TO A WITCH!
WE DIDN'T KNOW WHAT SHE WAS AT THE TIME!
BUT SHE CAN PROTECT HIM AS NO ONE ELSE CAN!
STAY BACK! DON'T SHOOT! YOU DON'T KNOW WHAT YOU'RE DOING! THE THING IS ON YOUR SIDE!
NOT NO MORE, I AIN'T! IF IT'S A FIGHT THEY WANT--!
FLAME OFF, TORCH! DON'T MAKE US ATTACK YOU, TOO!
POST
17

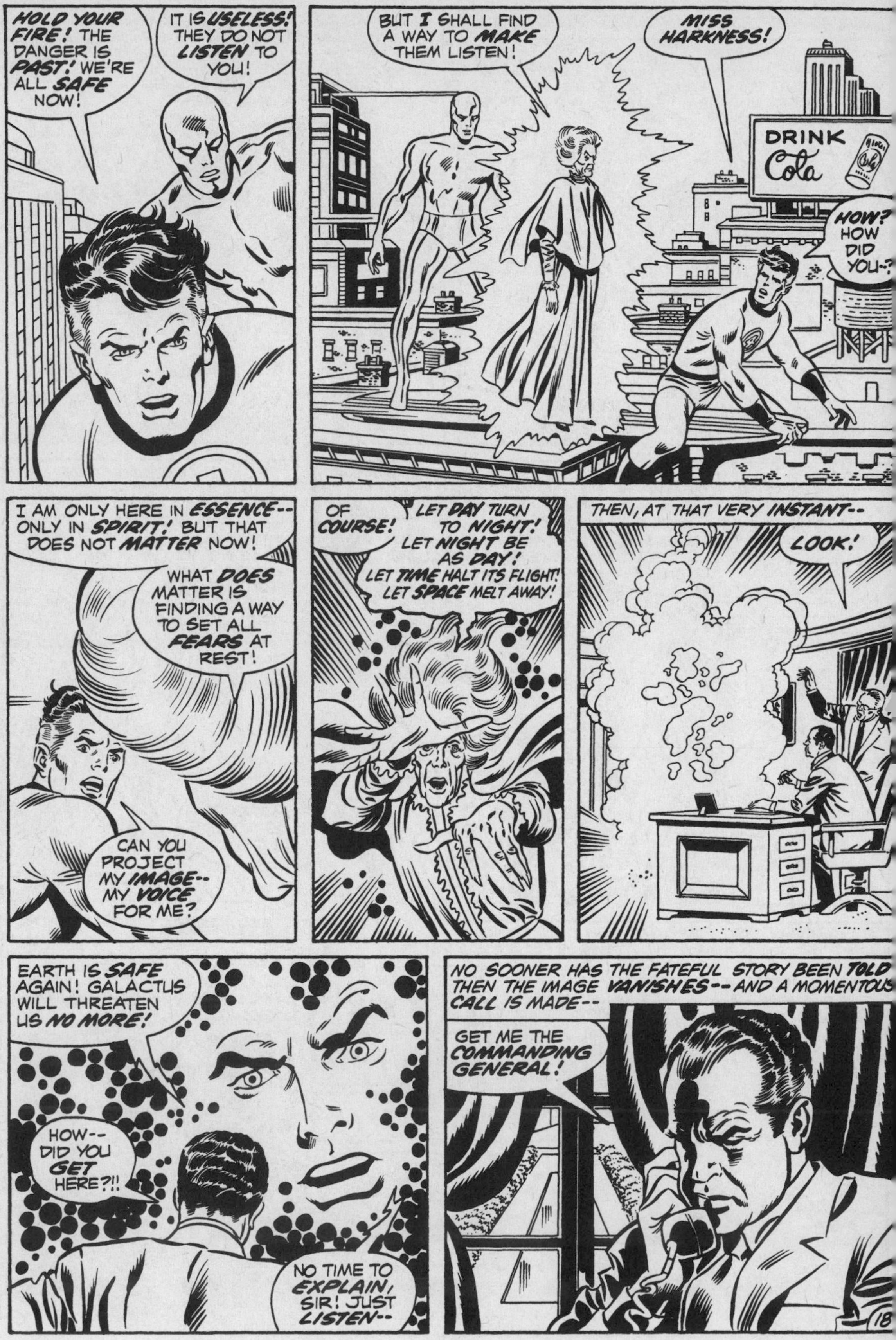
HOLD YOUR FIRE! THE DANGER IS PAST! WE'RE ALL SAFE NOW!
IT IS USELESS! THEY DO NOT LISTEN TO YOU!
BUT I SHALL FIND A WAY TO MAKE THEM LISTEN!
MISS HARKNESS!
DRINK Cola
HOW? HOW DID YOU--?
I AM ONLY HERE IN ESSENCE-- ONLY IN SPIRIT! BUT THAT DOES NOT MATTER NOW!
WHAT DOES MATTER IS FINDING A WAY TO SET ALL FEARS AT REST!
CAN YOU PROJECT MY IMAGE-- MY VOICE FOR ME?
OF COURSE!
LET DAY TURN TO NIGHT! LET NIGHT BE AS DAY! LET TIME HALT ITS FLIGHT! LET SPACE MELT AWAY!
THEN, AT THAT VERY INSTANT--
LOOK!
EARTH IS SAFE AGAIN! GALACTUS WILL THREATEN US NO MORE!
HOW-- DID YOU GET HERE?!!
NO TIME TO EXPLAIN, SIR! JUST LISTEN--
NO SOONER HAS THE FATEFUL STORY BEEN TOLD THEN THE IMAGE VANISHES-- AND A MOMENTOUS CALL IS MADE--
GET ME THE COMMANDING GENERAL!
18

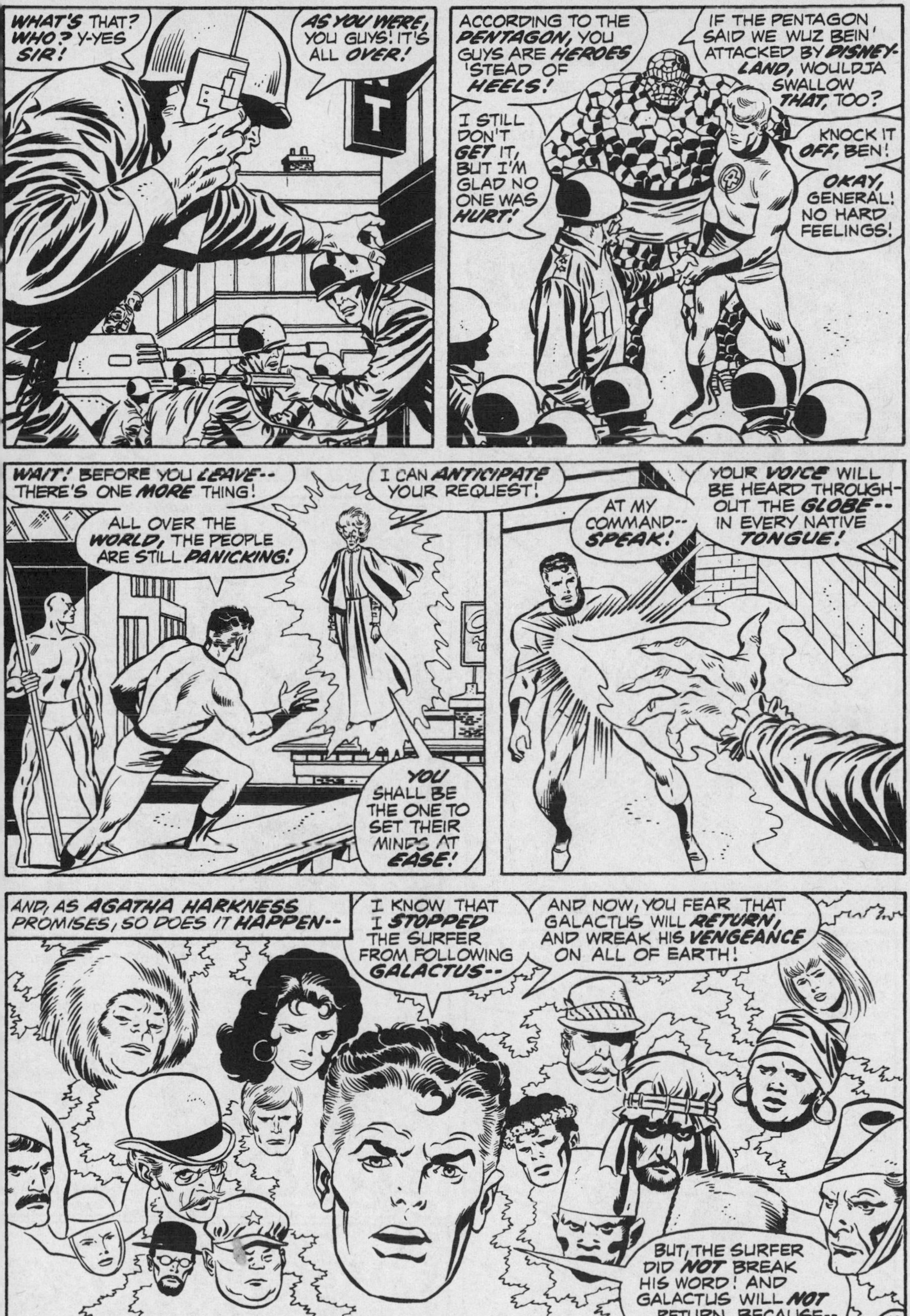
WHAT'S THAT? WHO? Y-YES SIR!
AS YOU WERE, YOU GUYS! IT'S ALL OVER!
ACCORDING TO THE PENTAGON, YOU GUYS ARE HEROES 'STEAD OF HEELS!
IF THE PENTAGON SAID WE WUZ BEIN' ATTACKED BY DISNEY-LAND, WOULDJA SWALLOW THAT, TOO?
I STILL DON'T GET IT, BUT I'M GLAD NO ONE WAS HURT!
KNOCK IT OFF, BEN!
OKAY, GENERAL! NO HARD FEELINGS!
WAIT! BEFORE YOU LEAVE-- THERE'S ONE MORE THING!
ALL OVER THE WORLD, THE PEOPLE ARE STILL PANICKING!
I CAN ANTICIPATE YOUR REQUEST!
YOU SHALL BE THE ONE TO SET THEIR MINDS AT EASE!
AT MY COMMAND-- SPEAK!
YOUR VOICE WILL BE HEARD THROUGH-OUT THE GLOBE-- IN EVERY NATIVE TONGUE!
AND, AS AGATHA HARKNESS PROMISES, SO DOES IT HAPPEN--
I KNOW THAT I STOPPED THE SURFER FROM FOLLOWING GALACTUS--
AND NOW, YOU FEAR THAT GALACTUS WILL RETURN, AND WREAK HIS VENGEANCE ON ALL OF EARTH!
BUT, THE SURFER DID NOT BREAK HIS WORD! AND GALACTUS WILL NOT RETURN, BECAUSE--
19

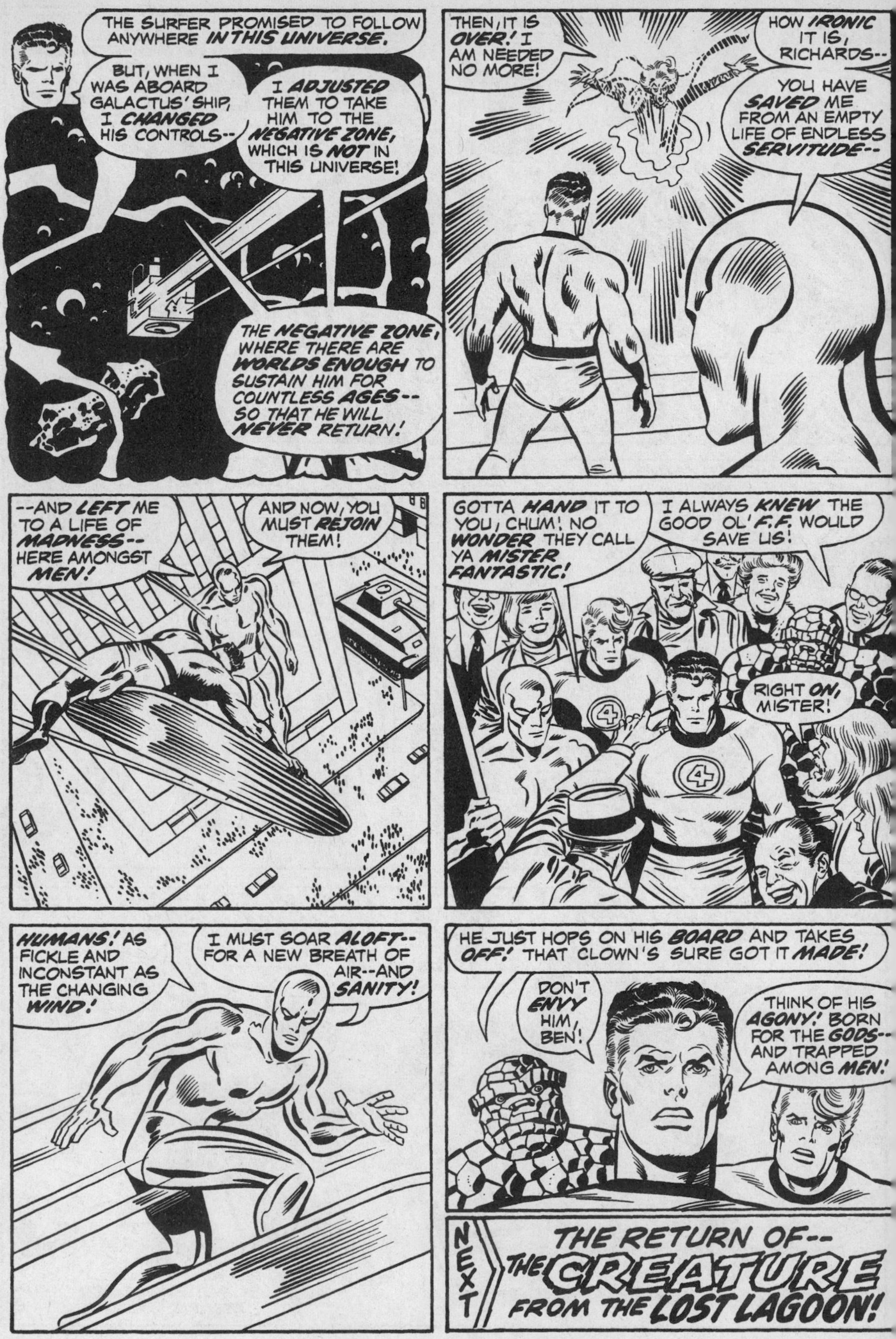
THE SURFER PROMISED TO FOLLOW ANYWHERE IN THIS UNIVERSE.
BUT, WHEN I WAS ABOARD GALACTUS' SHIP, I CHANGED HIS CONTROLS--
I ADJUSTED THEM TO TAKE HIM TO THE NEGATIVE ZONE, WHICH IS NOT IN THIS UNIVERSE!
THE NEGATIVE ZONE, WHERE THERE ARE WORLDS ENOUGH TO SUSTAIN HIM FOR COUNTLESS AGES--SO THAT HE WILL NEVER RETURN!
THEN, IT IS OVER! I AM NEEDED NO MORE!
HOW IRONIC IT IS, RICHARDS--
YOU HAVE SAVED ME FROM AN EMPTY LIFE OF ENDLESS SERVITUDE--
--AND LEFT ME TO A LIFE OF MADNESS--HERE AMONGST MEN!
AND NOW, YOU MUST REJOIN THEM!
GOTTA HAND IT TO YOU, CHUM! NO WONDER THEY CALL YA MISTER FANTASTIC!
I ALWAYS KNEW THE GOOD OL' F.F. WOULD SAVE US!
RIGHT ON, MISTER!
HUMANS! AS FICKLE AND INCONSTANT AS THE CHANGING WIND!
I MUST SOAR ALOFT--FOR A NEW BREATH OF AIR--AND SANITY!
HE JUST HOPS ON HIS BOARD AND TAKES OFF! THAT CLOWN'S SURE GOT IT MADE!
DON'T ENVY HIM, BEN!
THINK OF HIS AGONY! BORN FOR THE GODS--AND TRAPPED AMONG MEN!
NEXT
THE RETURN OF--THE CREATURE FROM THE LOST LAGOON!

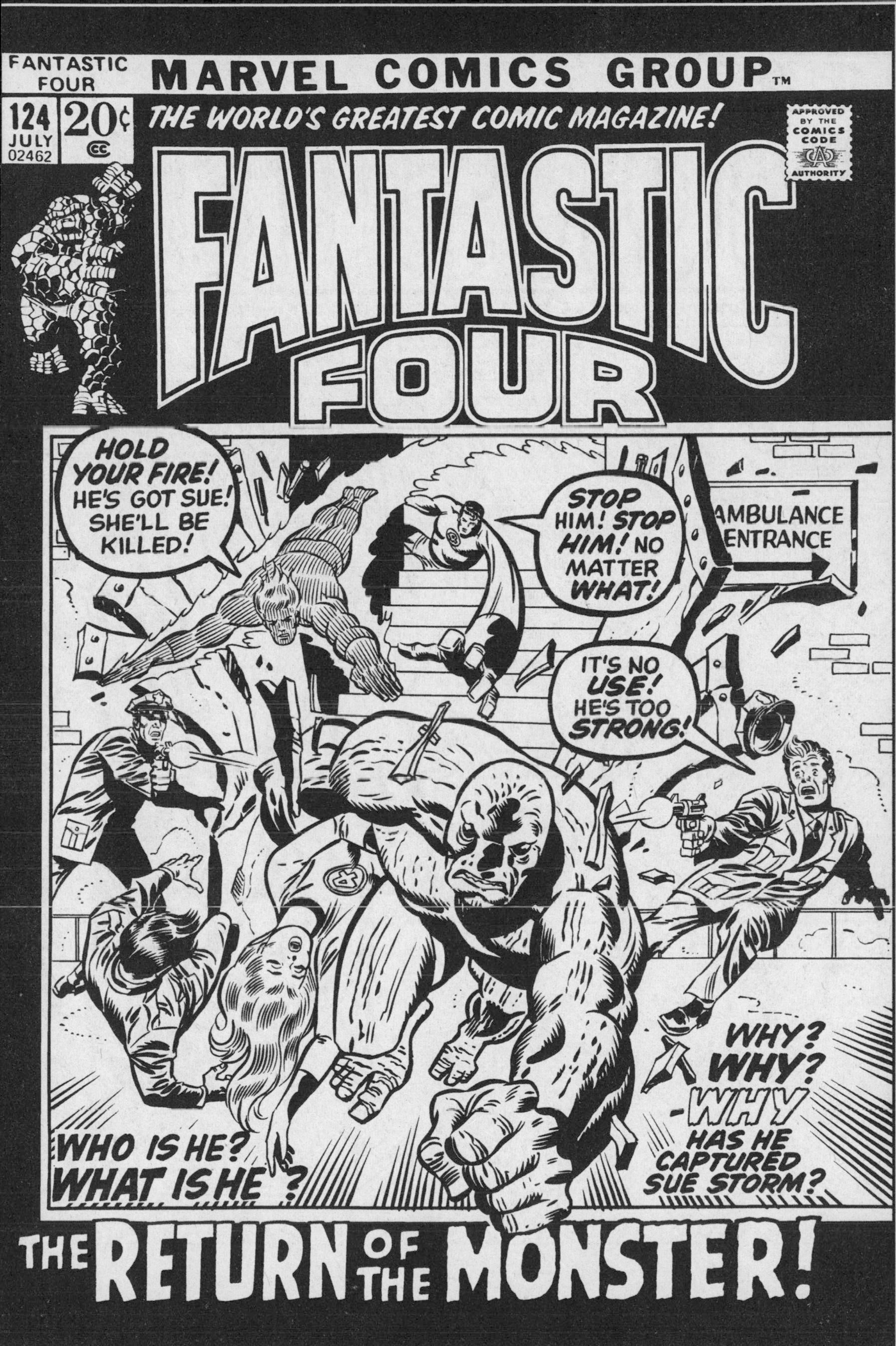
FANTASTIC FOUR
MARVEL COMICS GROUP™
124 JULY 02462
20¢
THE WORLD'S GREATEST COMIC MAGAZINE!
APPROVED BY THE COMICS CODE AUTHORITY
FANTASTIC FOUR
HOLD YOUR FIRE! HE'S GOT SUE! SHE'LL BE KILLED!
STOP HIM! STOP HIM! NO MATTER WHAT!
AMBULANCE ENTRANCE
IT'S NO USE! HE'S TOO STRONG!
WHO IS HE? WHAT IS HE?
WHY? WHY? WHY HAS HE CAPTURED SUE STORM?
THE RETURN OF THE MONSTER!

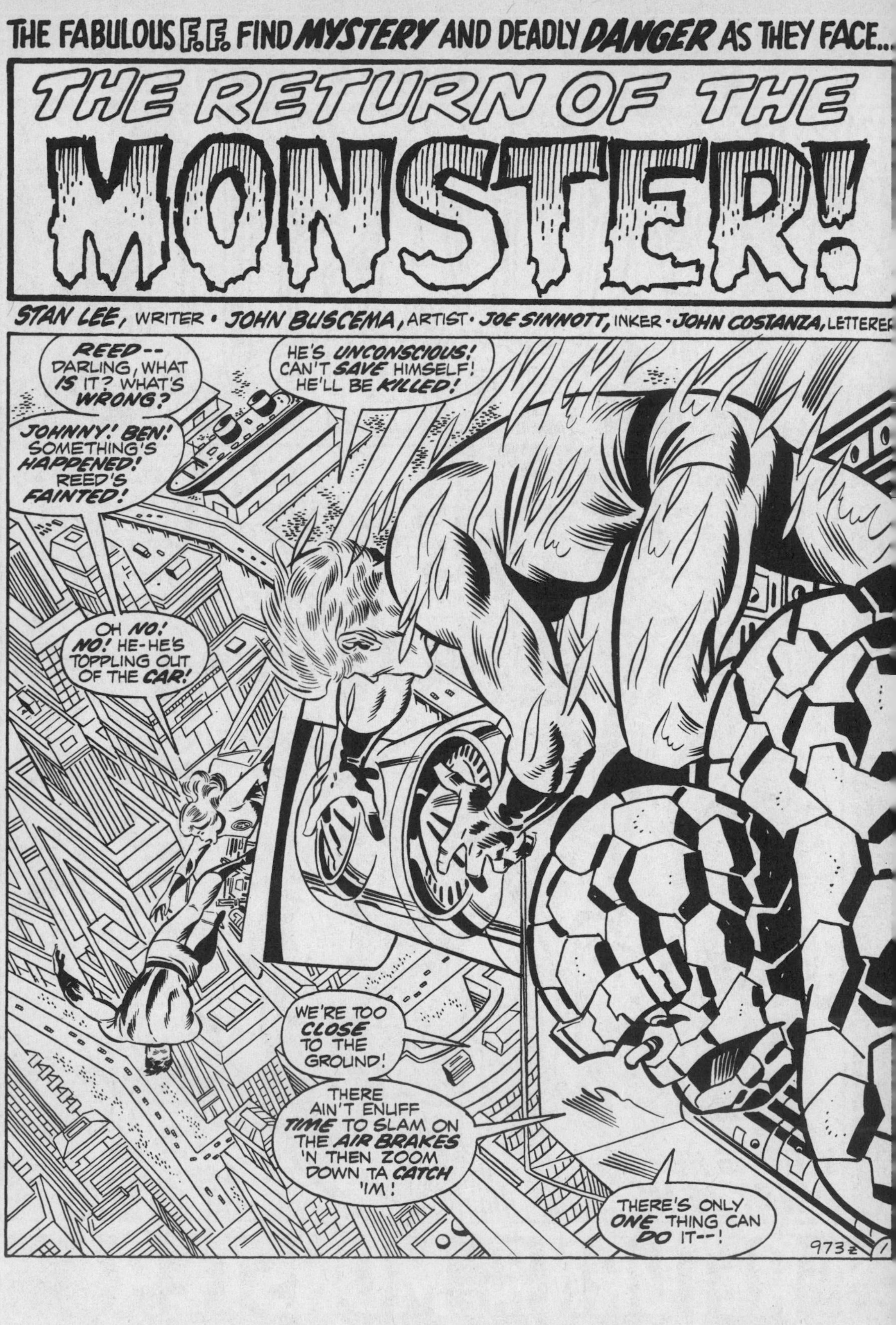
THE FABULOUS F.F. FIND MYSTERY AND DEADLY DANGER AS THEY FACE...
THE RETURN OF THE MONSTER!
STAN LEE, WRITER • JOHN BUSCEMA, ARTIST • JOE SINNOTT, INKER • JOHN COSTANZA, LETTERER
REED-- DARLING, WHAT IS IT? WHAT'S WRONG?
JOHNNY! BEN! SOMETHING'S HAPPENED! REED'S FAINTED!
HE'S UNCONSCIOUS! CAN'T SAVE HIMSELF! HE'LL BE KILLED!
OH NO! NO! HE-HE'S TOPPLING OUT OF THE CAR!
WE'RE TOO CLOSE TO THE GROUND!
THERE AIN'T ENUFF TIME TO SLAM ON THE AIR BRAKES 'N THEN ZOOM DOWN TA CATCH 'IM!
THERE'S ONLY ONE THING CAN DO IT--!

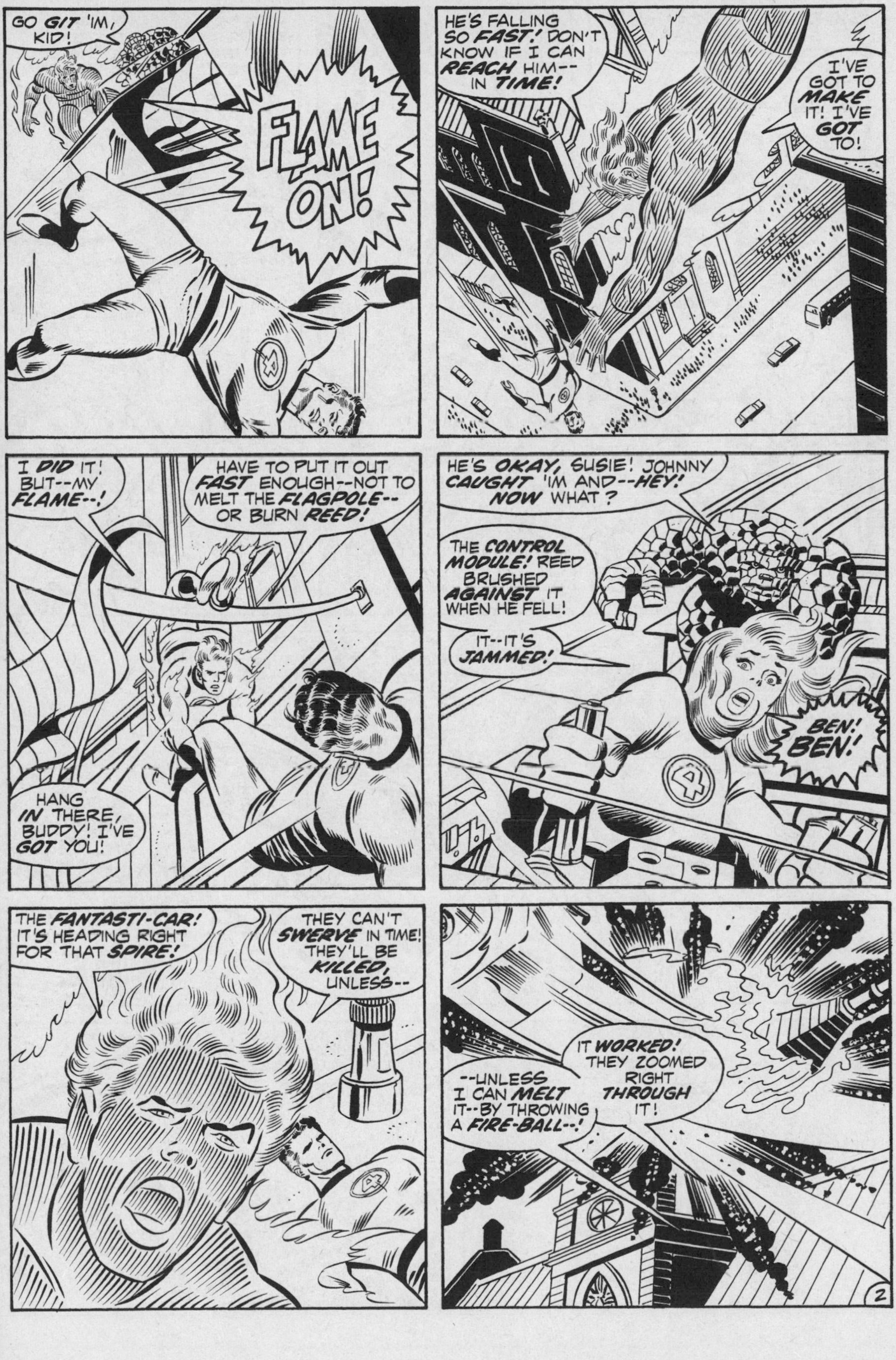
GO GIT 'IM, KID!
FLAME ON!
HE'S FALLING SO FAST! DON'T KNOW IF I CAN REACH HIM-- IN TIME!
I'VE GOT TO MAKE IT! I'VE GOT TO!
I DID IT! BUT--MY FLAME--!
HAVE TO PUT IT OUT FAST ENOUGH--NOT TO MELT THE FLAGPOLE-- OR BURN REED!
HANG IN THERE, BUDDY! I'VE GOT YOU!
HE'S OKAY, SUSIE! JOHNNY CAUGHT 'IM AND--HEY! NOW WHAT?
THE CONTROL MODULE! REED BRUSHED AGAINST IT WHEN HE FELL!
IT--IT'S JAMMED!
BEN! BEN!
THE FANTASTI-CAR! IT'S HEADING RIGHT FOR THAT SPIRE!
THEY CAN'T SWERVE IN TIME! THEY'LL BE KILLED, UNLESS--
--UNLESS I CAN MELT IT--BY THROWING A FIRE-BALL--!
IT WORKED! THEY ZOOMED RIGHT THROUGH IT!
2

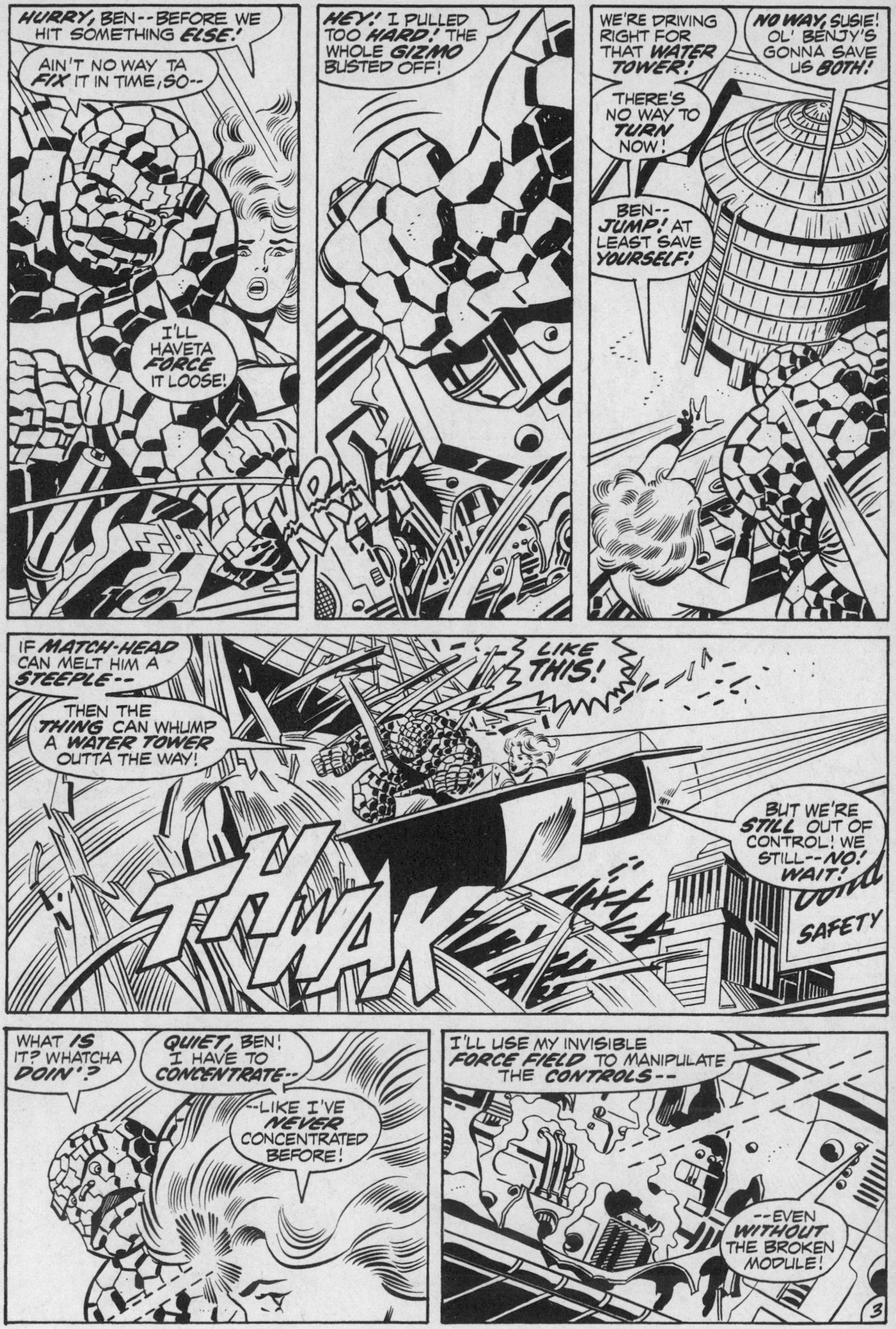
HURRY, BEN--BEFORE WE HIT SOMETHING ELSE!
AIN'T NO WAY TA FIX IT IN TIME, SO--
I'LL HAVETA FORCE IT LOOSE!
HEY! I PULLED TOO HARD! THE WHOLE GIZMO BUSTED OFF!
WE'RE DRIVING RIGHT FOR THAT WATER TOWER!
NO WAY, SUSIE! OL' BENJY'S GONNA SAVE US BOTH!
THERE'S NO WAY TO TURN NOW!
BEN--JUMP! AT LEAST SAVE YOURSELF!
IF MATCH-HEAD CAN MELT HIM A STEEPLE--
THEN THE THING CAN WHUMP A WATER TOWER OUTTA THE WAY!
LIKE THIS!
THWAK
BUT WE'RE STILL OUT OF CONTROL! WE STILL--NO! WAIT!
SAFETY
WHAT IS IT? WHATCHA DOIN'?
QUIET, BEN! I HAVE TO CONCENTRATE--
--LIKE I'VE NEVER CONCENTRATED BEFORE!
I'LL USE MY INVISIBLE FORCE FIELD TO MANIPULATE THE CONTROLS--
--EVEN WITHOUT THE BROKEN MODULE!
3

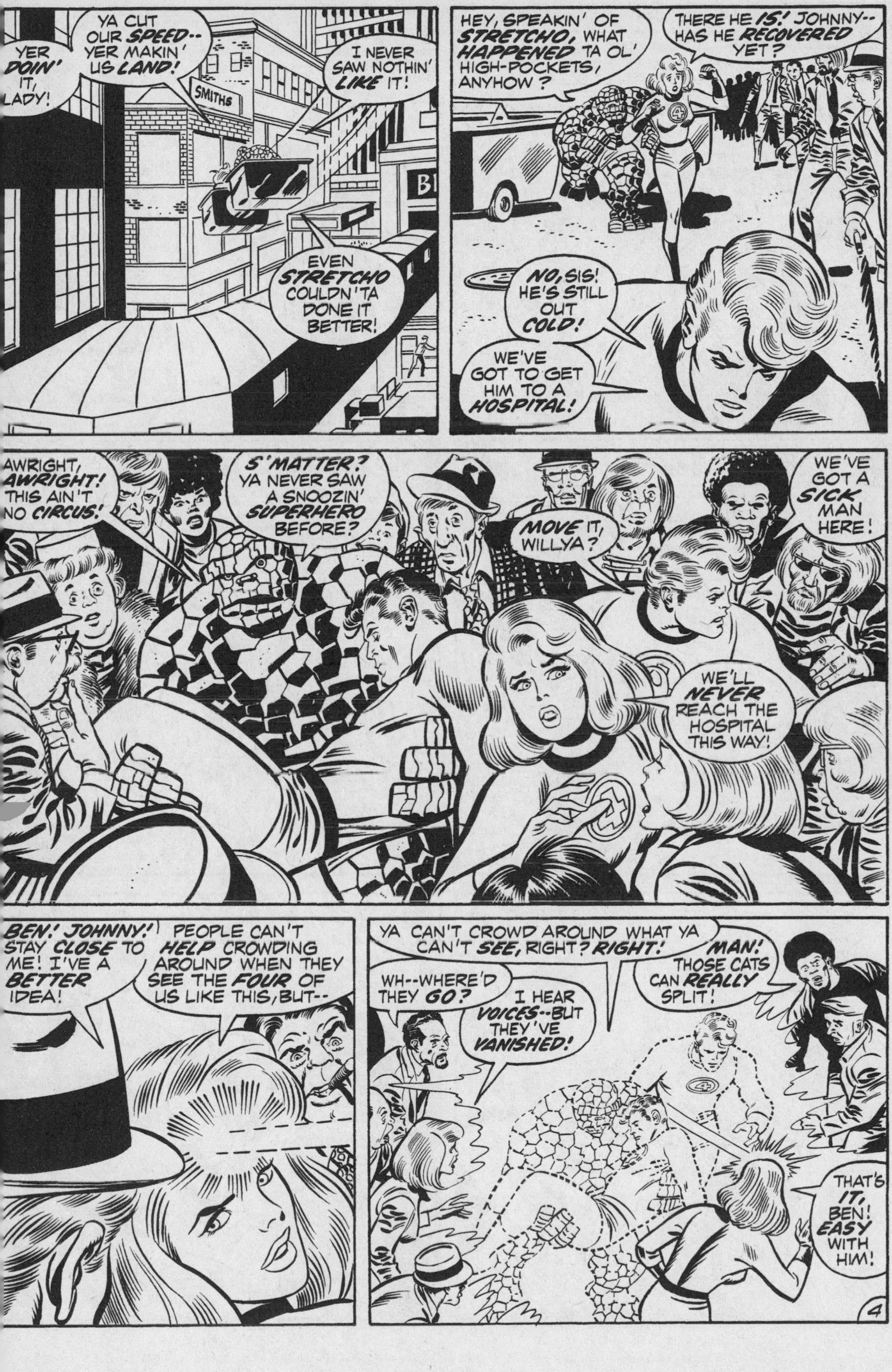

YER DOIN' IT, LADY!
YA CUT OUR SPEED-- YER MAKIN' US LAND!
I NEVER SAW NOTHIN' LIKE IT!
SMITHS
EVEN STRETCHO COULDN'TA DONE IT BETTER!
HEY, SPEAKIN' OF STRETCHO, WHAT HAPPENED TA OL' HIGH-POCKETS, ANYHOW?
THERE HE IS! JOHNNY-- HAS HE RECOVERED YET?
NO, SIS! HE'S STILL OUT COLD!
WE'VE GOT TO GET HIM TO A HOSPITAL!
AWRIGHT, AWRIGHT! THIS AIN'T NO CIRCUS!
S'MATTER? YA NEVER SAW A SNOOZIN' SUPERHERO BEFORE?
MOVE IT, WILLYA?
WE'VE GOT A SICK MAN HERE!
WE'LL NEVER REACH THE HOSPITAL THIS WAY!
BEN! JOHNNY! STAY CLOSE TO ME! I'VE A BETTER IDEA!
PEOPLE CAN'T HELP CROWDING AROUND WHEN THEY SEE THE FOUR OF US LIKE THIS, BUT--
YA CAN'T CROWD AROUND WHAT YA CAN'T SEE, RIGHT? RIGHT!
WH--WHERE'D THEY GO?
I HEAR VOICES--BUT THEY'VE VANISHED!
MAN! THOSE CATS CAN REALLY SPLIT!
THAT'S IT, BEN! EASY WITH HIM!
4

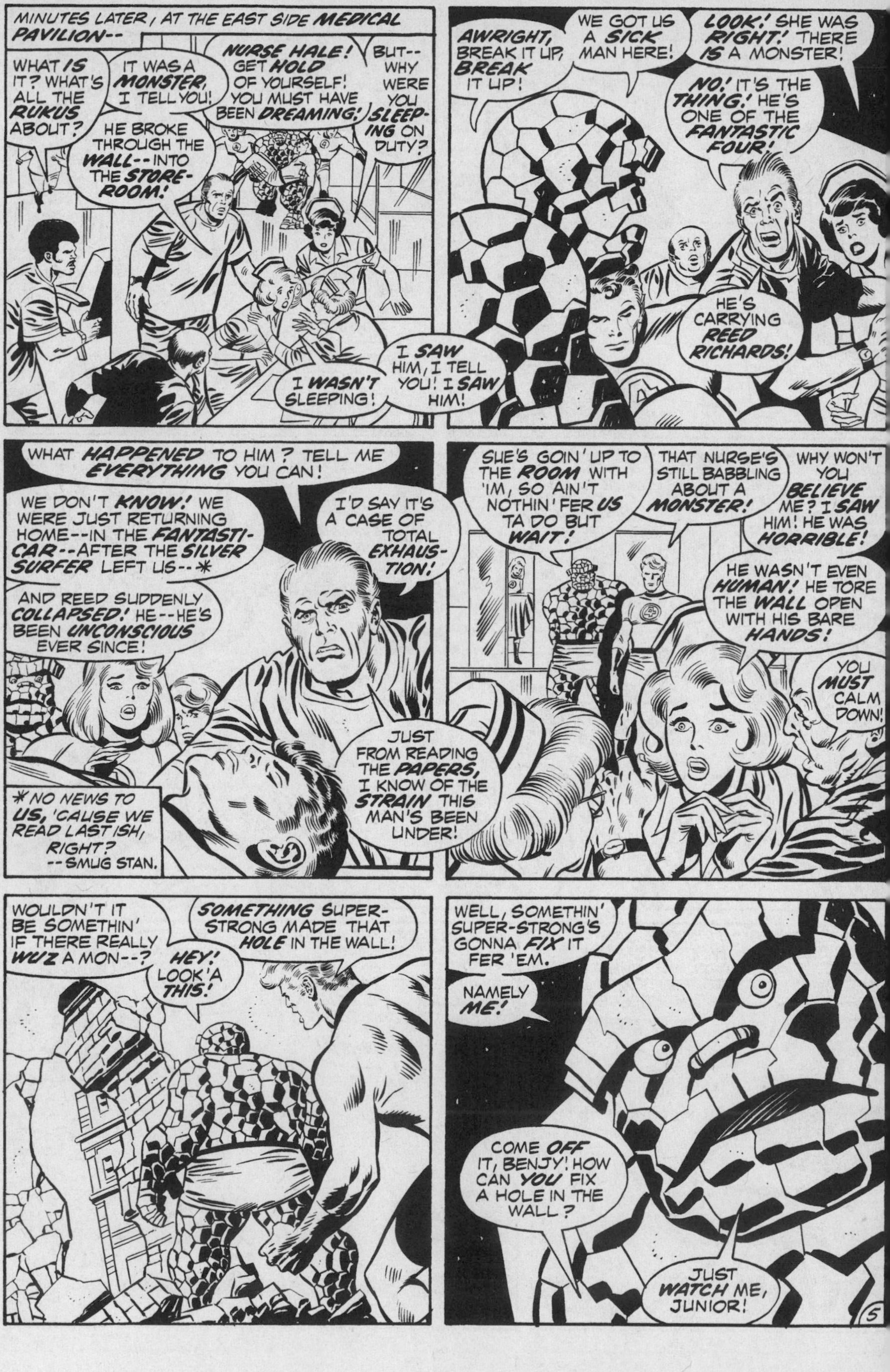
MINUTES LATER, AT THE EAST SIDE MEDICAL PAVILION--
WHAT IS IT? WHAT'S ALL THE RUKUS ABOUT?
IT WAS A MONSTER, I TELL YOU!
HE BROKE THROUGH THE WALL--INTO THE STORE-ROOM!
NURSE HALE! GET HOLD OF YOURSELF! YOU MUST HAVE BEEN DREAMING!
BUT--WHY WERE YOU SLEEPING ON DUTY?
I WASN'T SLEEPING!
I SAW HIM, I TELL YOU! I SAW HIM!
AWRIGHT, BREAK IT UP, BREAK IT UP!
WE GOT US A SICK MAN HERE!
LOOK! SHE WAS RIGHT! THERE IS A MONSTER!
NO! IT'S THE THING! HE'S ONE OF THE FANTASTIC FOUR!
HE'S CARRYING REED RICHARDS!
WHAT HAPPENED TO HIM? TELL ME EVERYTHING YOU CAN!
WE DON'T KNOW! WE WERE JUST RETURNING HOME--IN THE FANTASTI-CAR--AFTER THE SILVER SURFER LEFT US--*
AND REED SUDDENLY COLLAPSED! HE--HE'S BEEN UNCONSCIOUS EVER SINCE!
I'D SAY IT'S A CASE OF TOTAL EXHAUS-TION!
JUST FROM READING THE PAPERS, I KNOW OF THE STRAIN THIS MAN'S BEEN UNDER!
*NO NEWS TO US, 'CAUSE WE READ LAST ISH, RIGHT? --SMUG STAN.
SUE'S GOIN' UP TO THE ROOM WITH 'IM, SO AIN'T NOTHIN' FER US TA DO BUT WAIT!
THAT NURSE'S STILL BABBLING ABOUT A MONSTER!
WHY WON'T YOU BELIEVE ME? I SAW HIM! HE WAS HORRIBLE!
HE WASN'T EVEN HUMAN! HE TORE THE WALL OPEN WITH HIS BARE HANDS!
YOU MUST CALM DOWN!
WOULDN'T IT BE SOMETHIN' IF THERE REALLY WUZ A MON--?
SOMETHING SUPER-STRONG MADE THAT HOLE IN THE WALL!
HEY! LOOK 'A THIS!
WELL, SOMETHIN' SUPER-STRONG'S GONNA FIX IT FER 'EM.
NAMELY ME!
COME OFF IT, BENJY! HOW CAN YOU FIX A HOLE IN THE WALL?
JUST WATCH ME, JUNIOR!
5

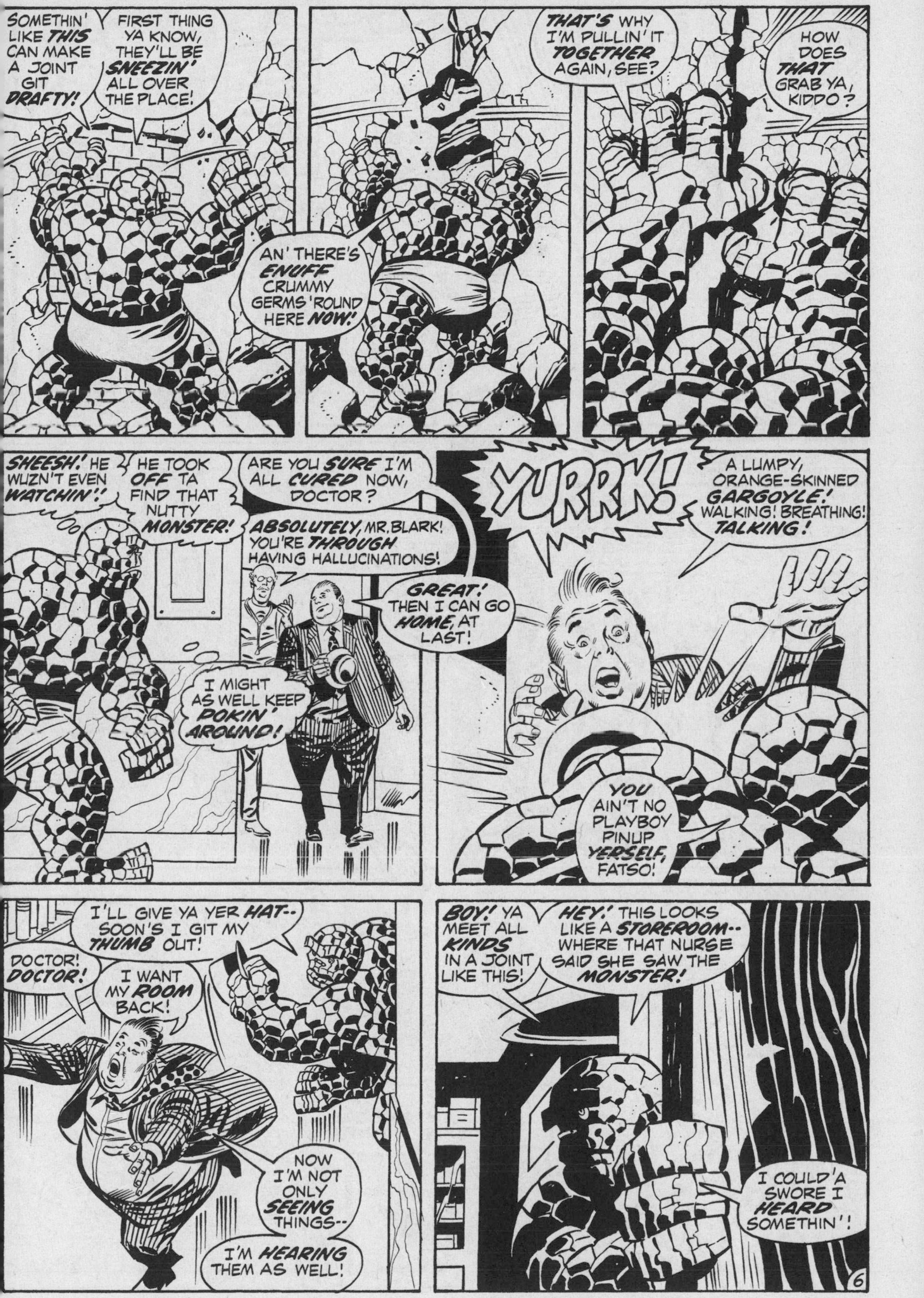
SOMETHIN' LIKE THIS CAN MAKE A JOINT GIT DRAFTY!
FIRST THING YA KNOW, THEY'LL BE SNEEZIN' ALL OVER THE PLACE!
AN' THERE'S ENUFF CRUMMY GERMS 'ROUND HERE NOW!
THAT'S WHY I'M PULLIN' IT TOGETHER AGAIN, SEE?
HOW DOES THAT GRAB YA, KIDDO?
SHEESH! HE WUZN'T EVEN WATCHIN'!
HE TOOK OFF TA FIND THAT NUTTY MONSTER!
I MIGHT AS WELL KEEP POKIN' AROUND!
ARE YOU SURE I'M ALL CURED NOW, DOCTOR?
ABSOLUTELY, MR. BLARK! YOU'RE THROUGH HAVING HALLUCINATIONS!
GREAT! THEN I CAN GO HOME, AT LAST!
YURRK!
A LUMPY, ORANGE-SKINNED GARGOYLE! WALKING! BREATHING! TALKING!
YOU AIN'T NO PLAYBOY PINUP YERSELF, FATSO!
I'LL GIVE YA YER HAT-- SOON'S I GIT MY THUMB OUT!
DOCTOR! DOCTOR!
I WANT MY ROOM BACK!
NOW I'M NOT ONLY SEEING THINGS--
I'M HEARING THEM AS WELL!
BOY! YA MEET ALL KINDS IN A JOINT LIKE THIS!
HEY! THIS LOOKS LIKE A STOREROOM-- WHERE THAT NURSE SAID SHE SAW THE MONSTER!
I COULD'A SWORE I HEARD SOMETHIN'!
6

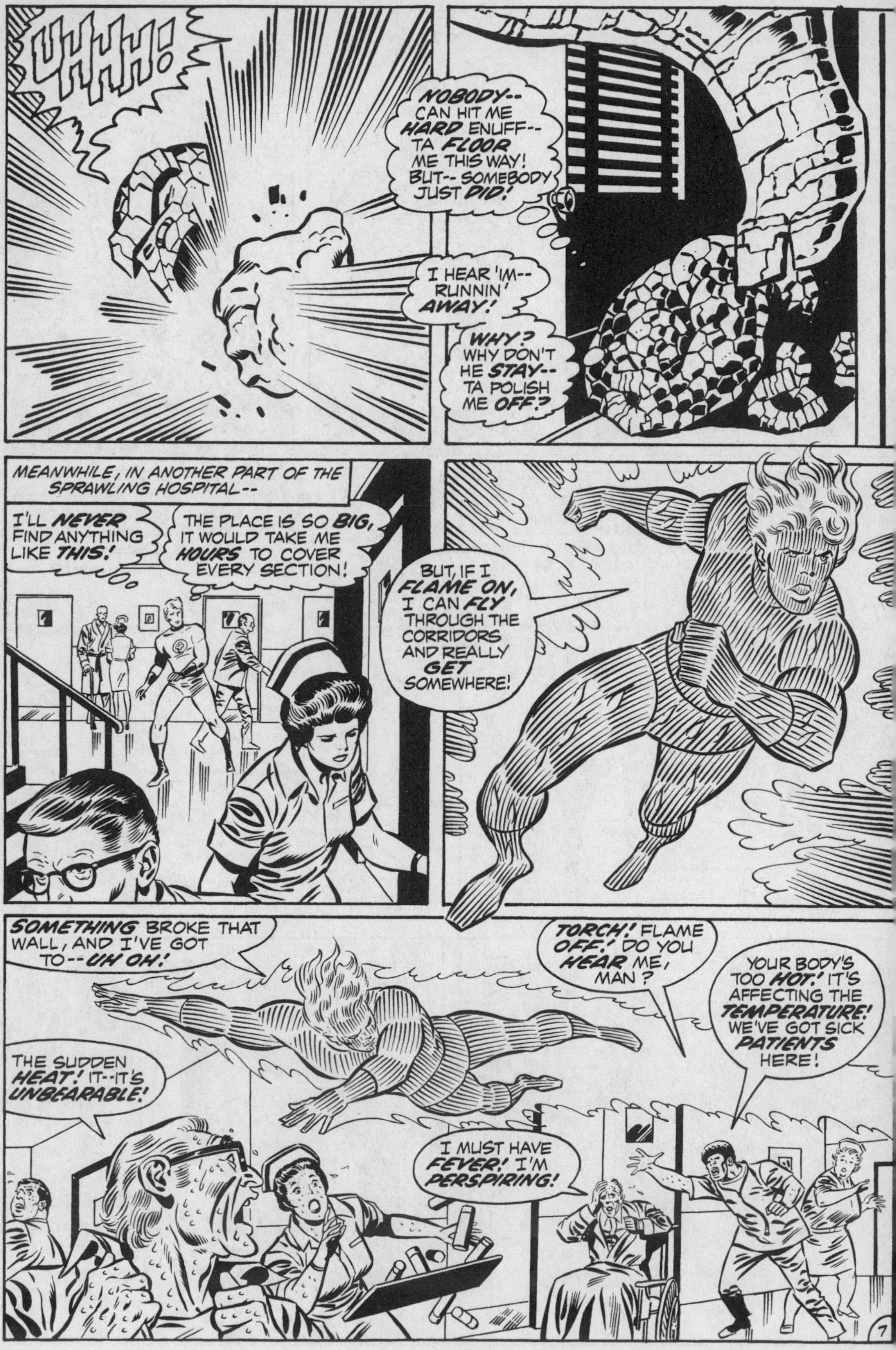
UHHH!
NOBODY-- CAN HIT ME HARD ENUFF-- TA FLOOR ME THIS WAY! BUT-- SOMEBODY JUST DID!
I HEAR 'IM-- RUNNIN' AWAY!
WHY? WHY DON'T HE STAY-- TA POLISH ME OFF?
MEANWHILE, IN ANOTHER PART OF THE SPRAWLING HOSPITAL--
I'LL NEVER FIND ANYTHING LIKE THIS!
THE PLACE IS SO BIG, IT WOULD TAKE ME HOURS TO COVER EVERY SECTION!
BUT, IF I FLAME ON, I CAN FLY THROUGH THE CORRIDORS AND REALLY GET SOMEWHERE!
SOMETHING BROKE THAT WALL, AND I'VE GOT TO-- UH OH!
TORCH! FLAME OFF! DO YOU HEAR ME, MAN?
YOUR BODY'S TOO HOT! IT'S AFFECTING THE TEMPERATURE! WE'VE GOT SICK PATIENTS HERE!
THE SUDDEN HEAT! IT--IT'S UNBEARABLE!
I MUST HAVE FEVER! I'M PERSPIRING!
7

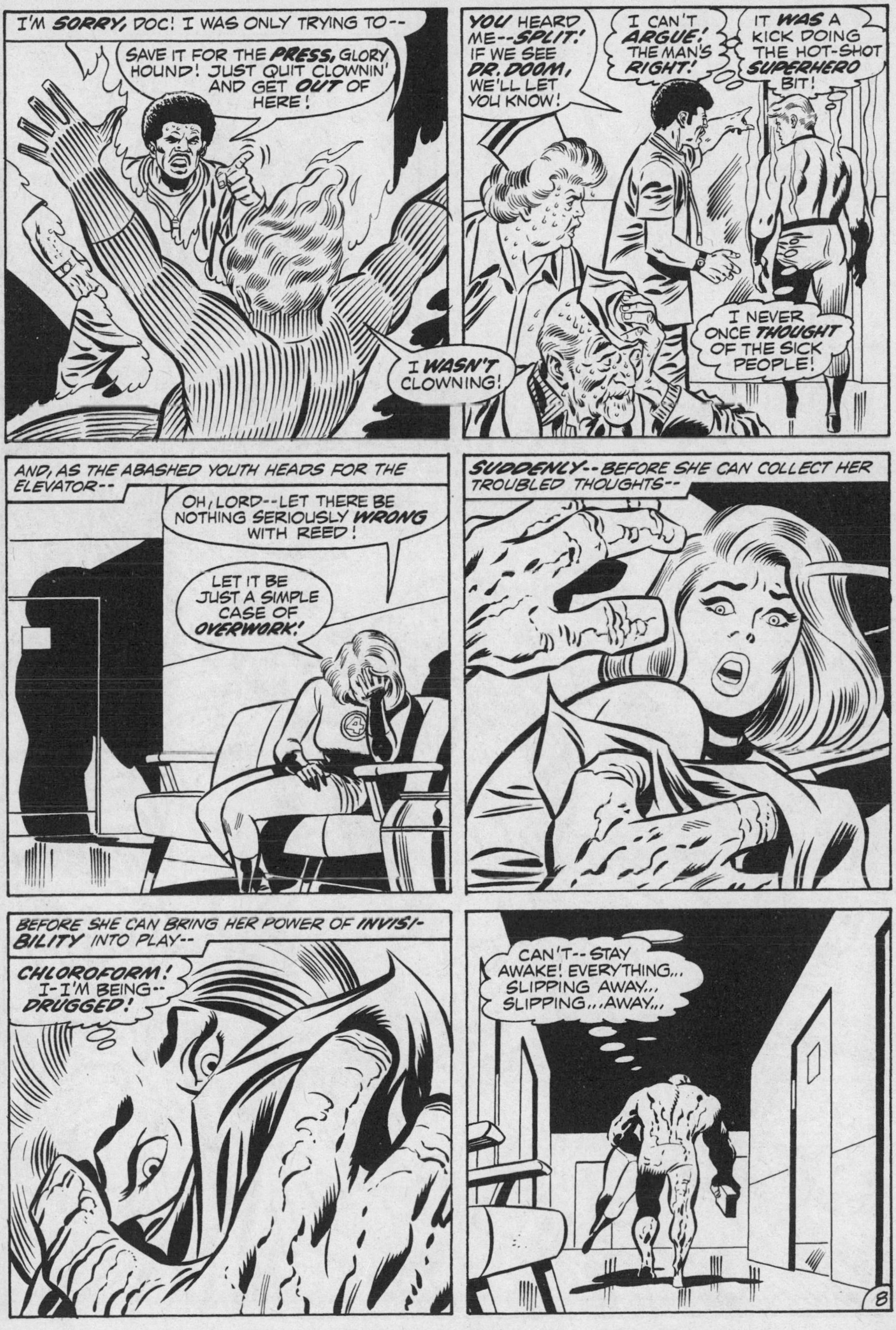

I'M SORRY, DOC! I WAS ONLY TRYING TO--
SAVE IT FOR THE PRESS, GLORY HOUND! JUST QUIT CLOWNIN' AND GET OUT OF HERE!
I WASN'T CLOWNING!
YOU HEARD ME--SPLIT! IF WE SEE DR. DOOM, WE'LL LET YOU KNOW!
I CAN'T ARGUE! THE MAN'S RIGHT!
IT WAS A KICK DOING THE HOT-SHOT SUPERHERO BIT!
I NEVER ONCE THOUGHT OF THE SICK PEOPLE!
AND, AS THE ABASHED YOUTH HEADS FOR THE ELEVATOR--
OH, LORD--LET THERE BE NOTHING SERIOUSLY WRONG WITH REED!
LET IT BE JUST A SIMPLE CASE OF OVERWORK!
SUDDENLY--BEFORE SHE CAN COLLECT HER TROUBLED THOUGHTS--
BEFORE SHE CAN BRING HER POWER OF INVISIBILITY INTO PLAY--
CHLOROFORM! I-I'M BEING--DRUGGED!
CAN'T--STAY AWAKE! EVERYTHING... SLIPPING AWAY... SLIPPING...AWAY...
8

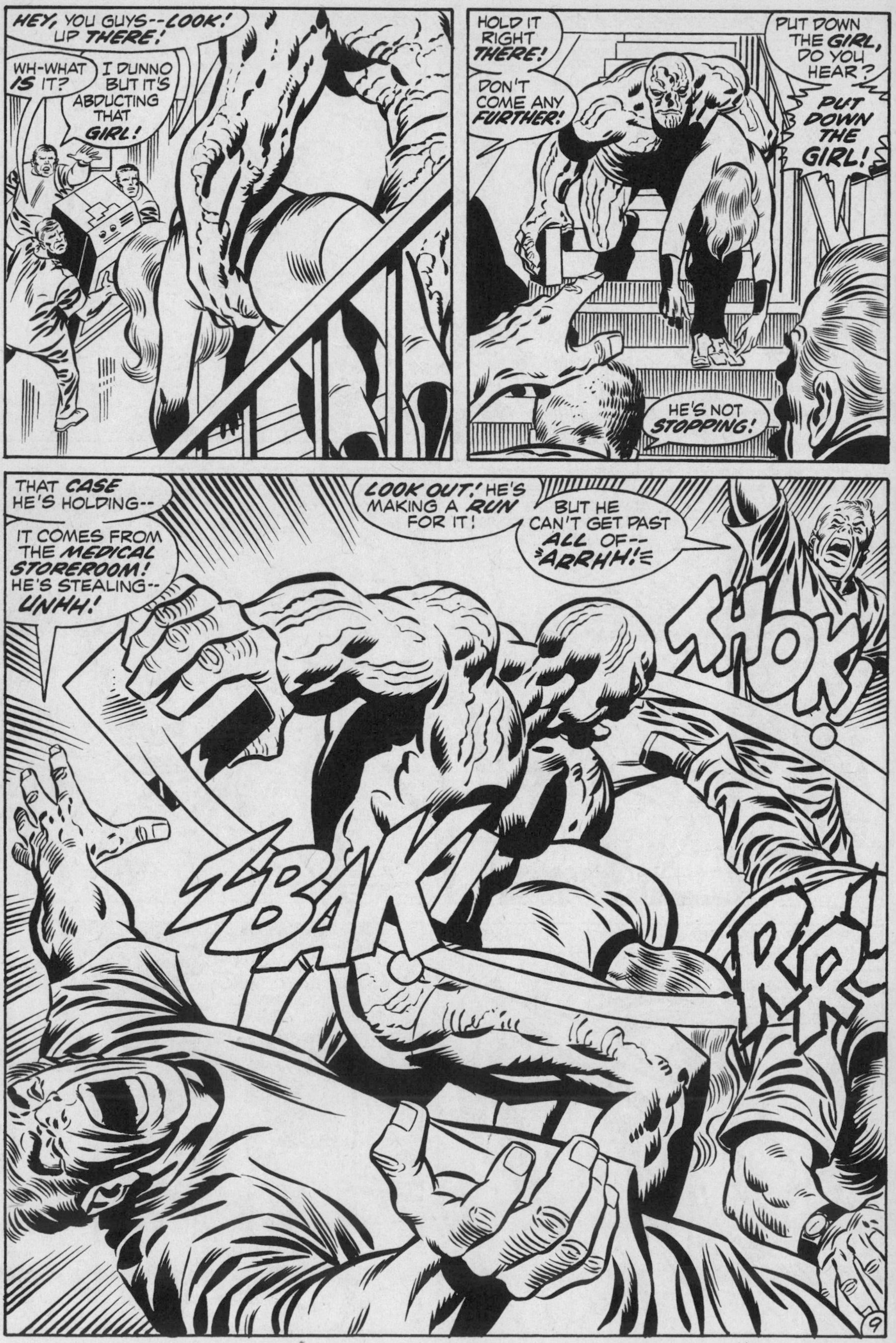
HEY, YOU GUYS--LOOK! UP THERE!
WH-WHAT IS IT?
I DUNNO BUT IT'S ABDUCTING THAT GIRL!
HOLD IT RIGHT THERE!
DON'T COME ANY FURTHER!
PUT DOWN THE GIRL, DO YOU HEAR?
PUT DOWN THE GIRL!
HE'S NOT STOPPING!
THAT CASE HE'S HOLDING--
IT COMES FROM THE MEDICAL STOREROOM! HE'S STEALING-- UNHH!
LOOK OUT! HE'S MAKING A RUN FOR IT!
BUT HE CAN'T GET PAST ALL OF-- ARRHH!
THOK!
ZBAK!
RR
9

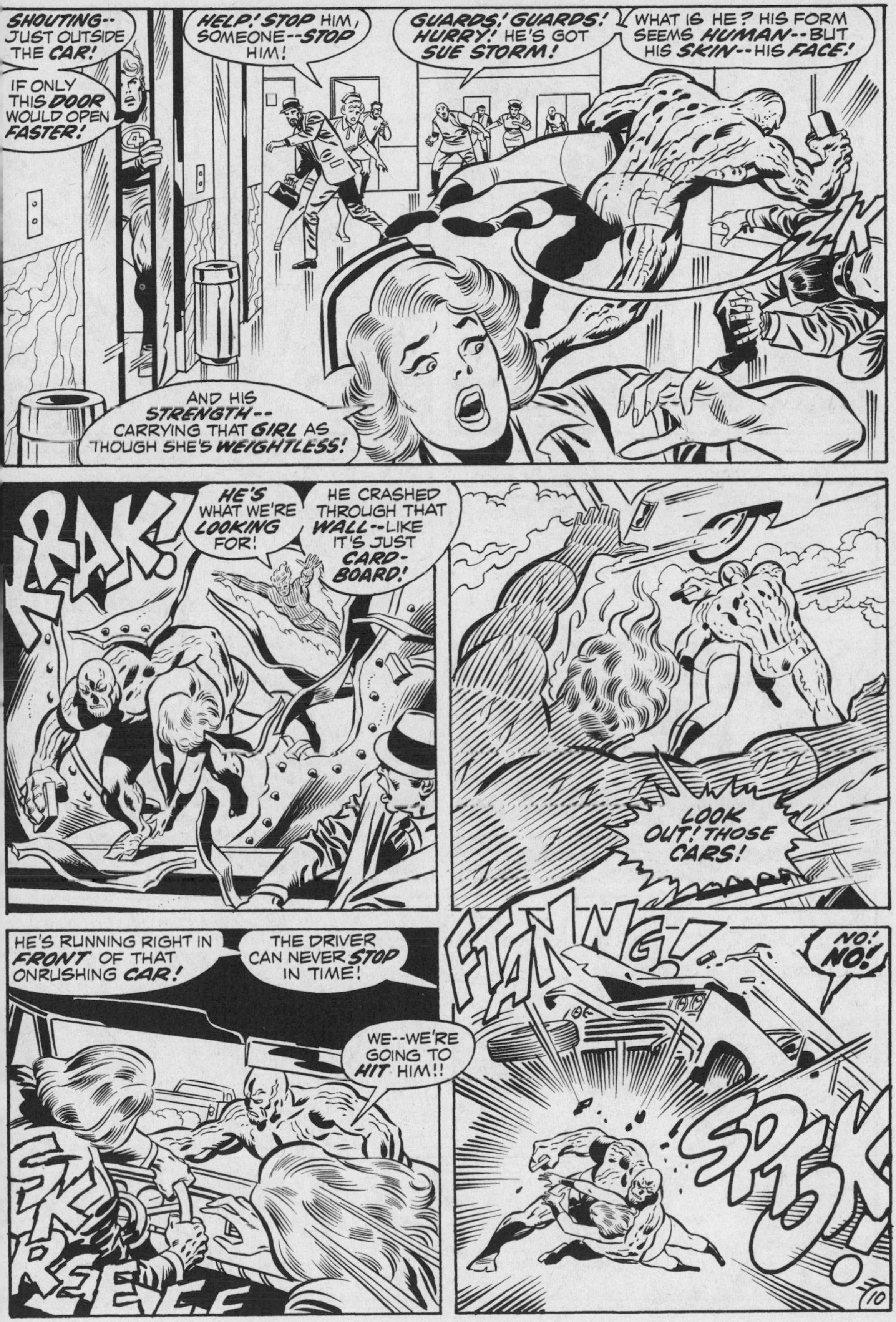

SHOUTING-- JUST OUTSIDE THE CAR!
IF ONLY THIS DOOR WOULD OPEN FASTER!
HELP! STOP HIM, SOMEONE--STOP HIM!
GUARDS! GUARDS! HURRY! HE'S GOT SUE STORM!
WHAT IS HE? HIS FORM SEEMS HUMAN--BUT HIS SKIN--HIS FACE!
AND HIS STRENGTH-- CARRYING THAT GIRL AS THOUGH SHE'S WEIGHTLESS!
HE'S WHAT WE'RE LOOKING FOR!
HE CRASHED THROUGH THAT WALL--LIKE IT'S JUST CARD-BOARD!
LOOK OUT! THOSE CARS!
HE'S RUNNING RIGHT IN FRONT OF THAT ONRUSHING CAR!
THE DRIVER CAN NEVER STOP IN TIME!
WE--WE'RE GOING TO HIT HIM!!
NO! NO!

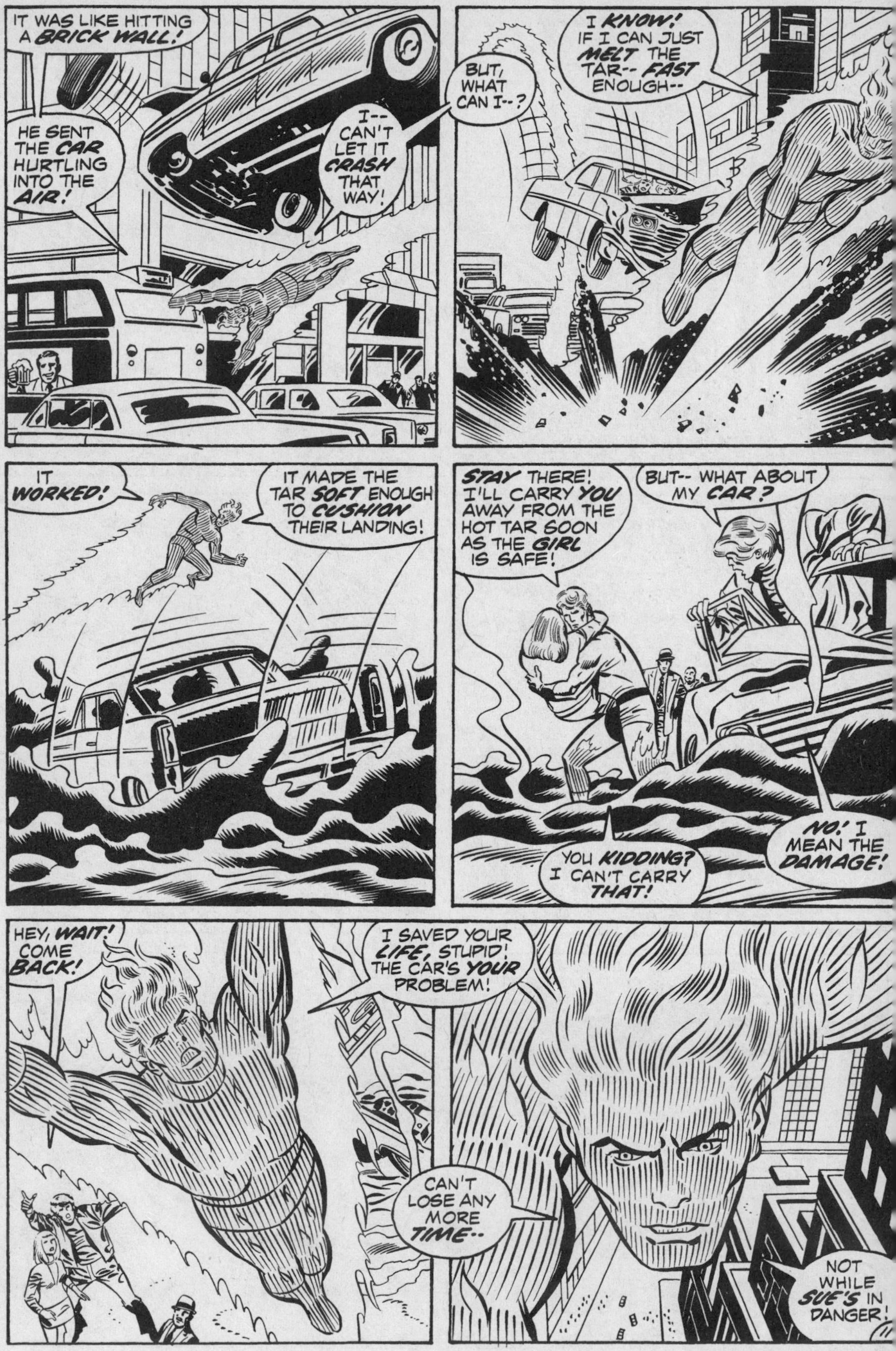
IT WAS LIKE HITTING A BRICK WALL!
HE SENT THE CAR HURTLING INTO THE AIR!
I-- CAN'T LET IT CRASH THAT WAY!
BUT, WHAT CAN I--?
I KNOW! IF I CAN JUST MELT THE TAR-- FAST ENOUGH--
IT WORKED!
IT MADE THE TAR SOFT ENOUGH TO CUSHION THEIR LANDING!
STAY THERE! I'LL CARRY YOU AWAY FROM THE HOT TAR SOON AS THE GIRL IS SAFE!
BUT-- WHAT ABOUT MY CAR?
YOU KIDDING? I CAN'T CARRY THAT!
NO! I MEAN THE DAMAGE!
HEY, WAIT! COME BACK!
I SAVED YOUR LIFE, STUPID! THE CAR'S YOUR PROBLEM!
CAN'T LOSE ANY MORE TIME--
NOT WHILE SUE'S IN DANGER!

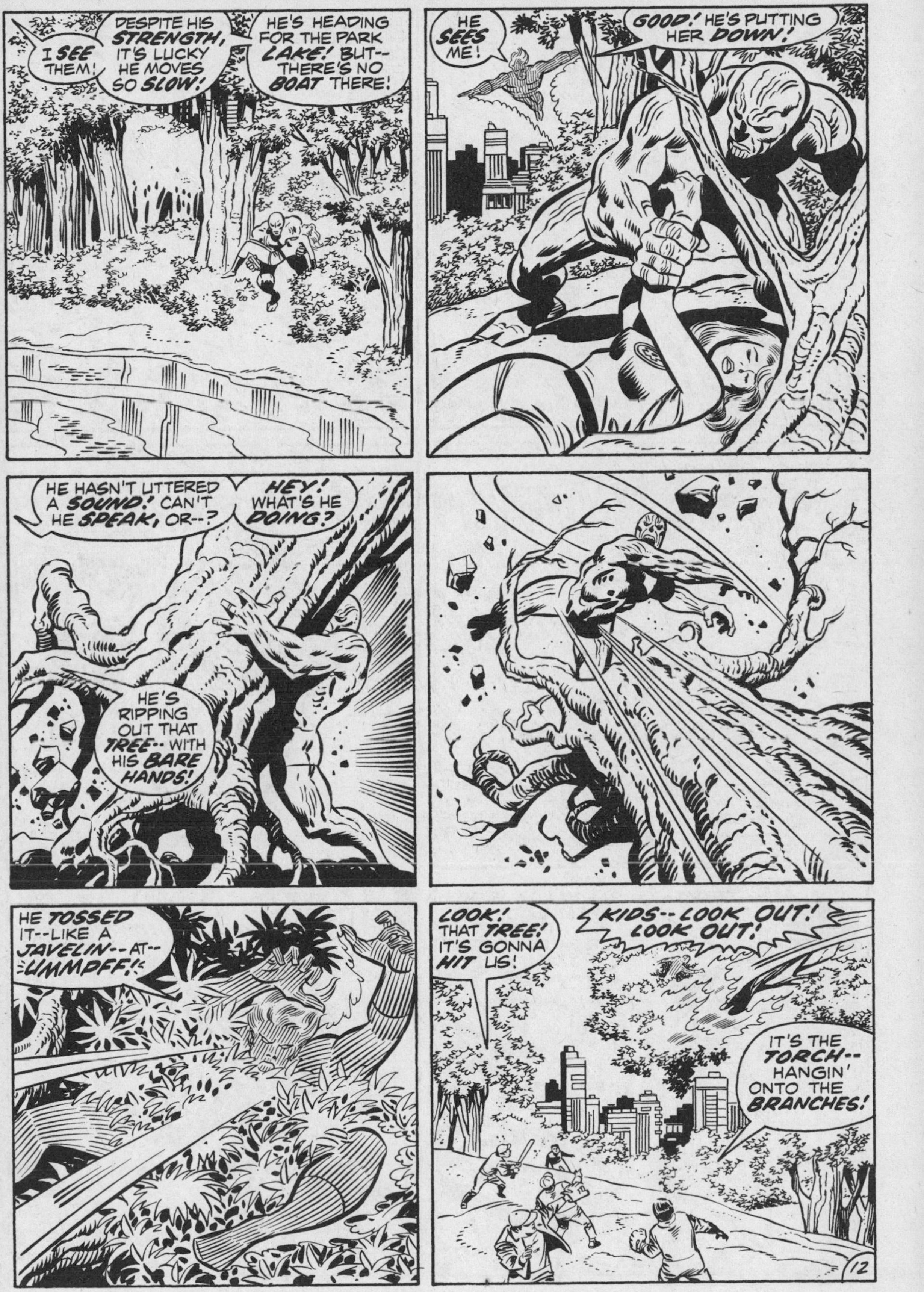
I SEE THEM!
DESPITE HIS STRENGTH, IT'S LUCKY HE MOVES SO SLOW!
HE'S HEADING FOR THE PARK LAKE! BUT-- THERE'S NO BOAT THERE!
HE SEES ME!
GOOD! HE'S PUTTING HER DOWN!
HE HASN'T UTTERED A SOUND! CAN'T HE SPEAK, OR--?
HEY! WHAT'S HE DOING?
HE'S RIPPING OUT THAT TREE-- WITH HIS BARE HANDS!
HE TOSSED IT--LIKE A JAVELIN--AT-- UMMPFF!
LOOK! THAT TREE! IT'S GONNA HIT US!
KIDS-- LOOK OUT! LOOK OUT!
IT'S THE TORCH-- HANGIN' ONTO THE BRANCHES!
12

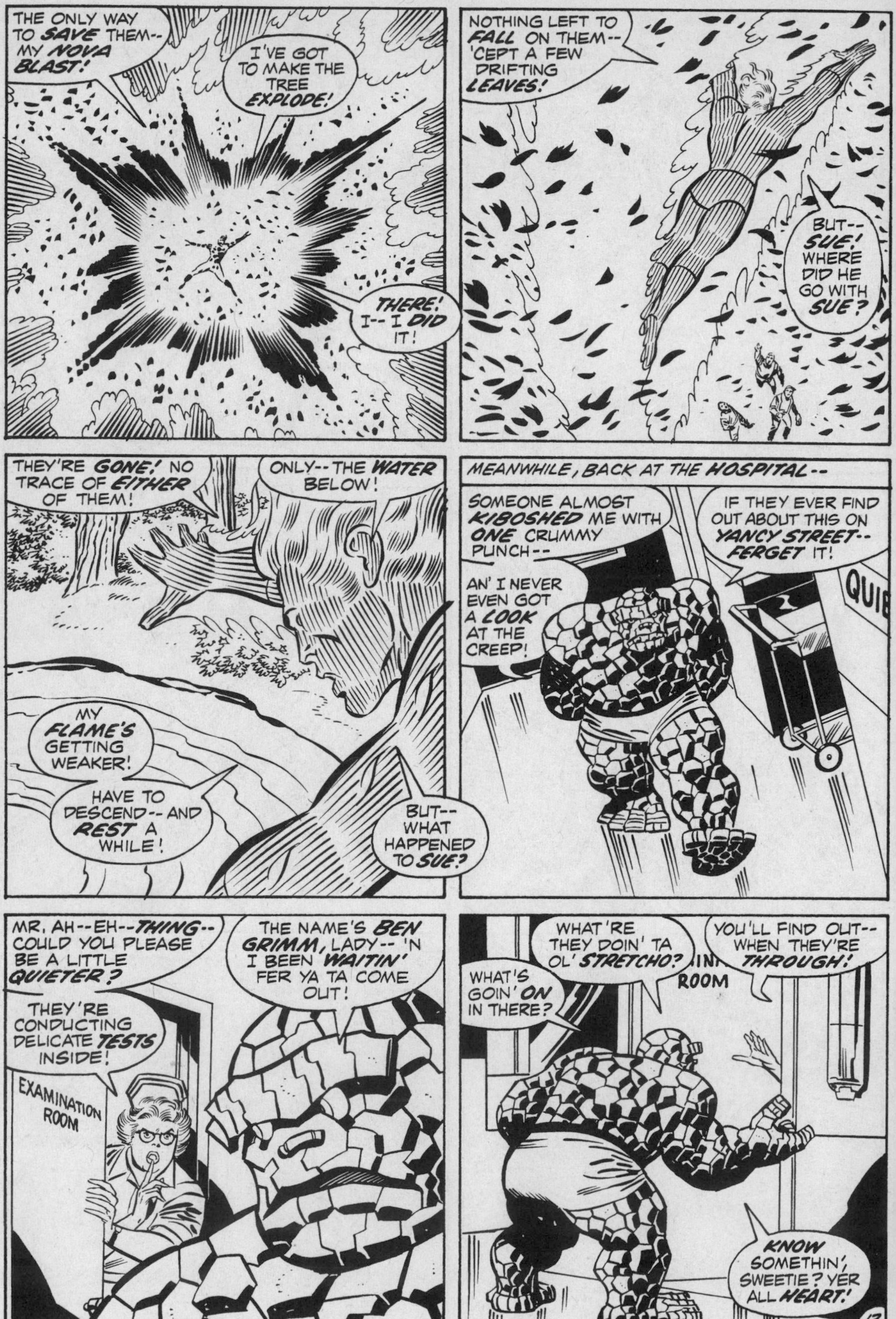
THE ONLY WAY TO SAVE THEM-- MY NOVA BLAST!
I'VE GOT TO MAKE THE TREE EXPLODE!
THERE! I-- I DID IT!
NOTHING LEFT TO FALL ON THEM-- 'CEPT A FEW DRIFTING LEAVES!
BUT-- SUE! WHERE DID HE GO WITH SUE?
THEY'RE GONE! NO TRACE OF EITHER OF THEM!
ONLY-- THE WATER BELOW!
MY FLAME'S GETTING WEAKER!
HAVE TO DESCEND-- AND REST A WHILE!
BUT-- WHAT HAPPENED TO SUE?
MEANWHILE, BACK AT THE HOSPITAL--
SOMEONE ALMOST KIBOSHED ME WITH ONE CRUMMY PUNCH--
AN' I NEVER EVEN GOT A LOOK AT THE CREEP!
IF THEY EVER FIND OUT ABOUT THIS ON YANCY STREET-- FERGET IT!
MR. AH--EH--THING-- COULD YOU PLEASE BE A LITTLE QUIETER?
THEY'RE CONDUCTING DELICATE TESTS INSIDE!
EXAMINATION ROOM
THE NAME'S BEN GRIMM, LADY-- 'N I BEEN WAITIN' FER YA TA COME OUT!
WHAT'S GOIN' ON IN THERE?
WHAT'RE THEY DOIN' TA OL' STRETCHO?
ROOM
YOU'LL FIND OUT-- WHEN THEY'RE THROUGH!
KNOW SOMETHIN', SWEETIE? YER ALL HEART!
13

AND, WITHIN THE PRIVATE *TESTING* COMPLEX--

EVERYTHING CHECKS OUT *PERFECTLY!*

HIS *STRETCHING POWER* IS AS *FANTASTIC* AS EVER!

AND LUCKILY, HIS *BRAIN CELLS* SHOW NO DETERIORATION!

RELEASE HIM, NOW!

ONLY *ONE* TEST REMAINS--

HIS *BONE STRUCTURE* STILL VARIES FROM THE *AVERAGE* MAN--

--BUT IS PERFECTLY *NORMAL*-- FOR *HIM!*

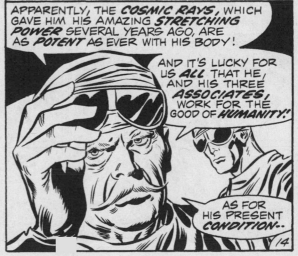

APPARENTLY, THE *COSMIC RAYS,* WHICH GAVE HIM HIS AMAZING *STRETCHING POWER* SEVERAL YEARS AGO, ARE AS *POTENT* AS EVER WITH HIS BODY!

AND IT'S LUCKY FOR US *ALL* THAT HE, AND HIS THREE *ASSOCIATES,* WORK FOR THE GOOD OF *HUMANITY!*

AS FOR HIS PRESENT *CONDITION*--

14

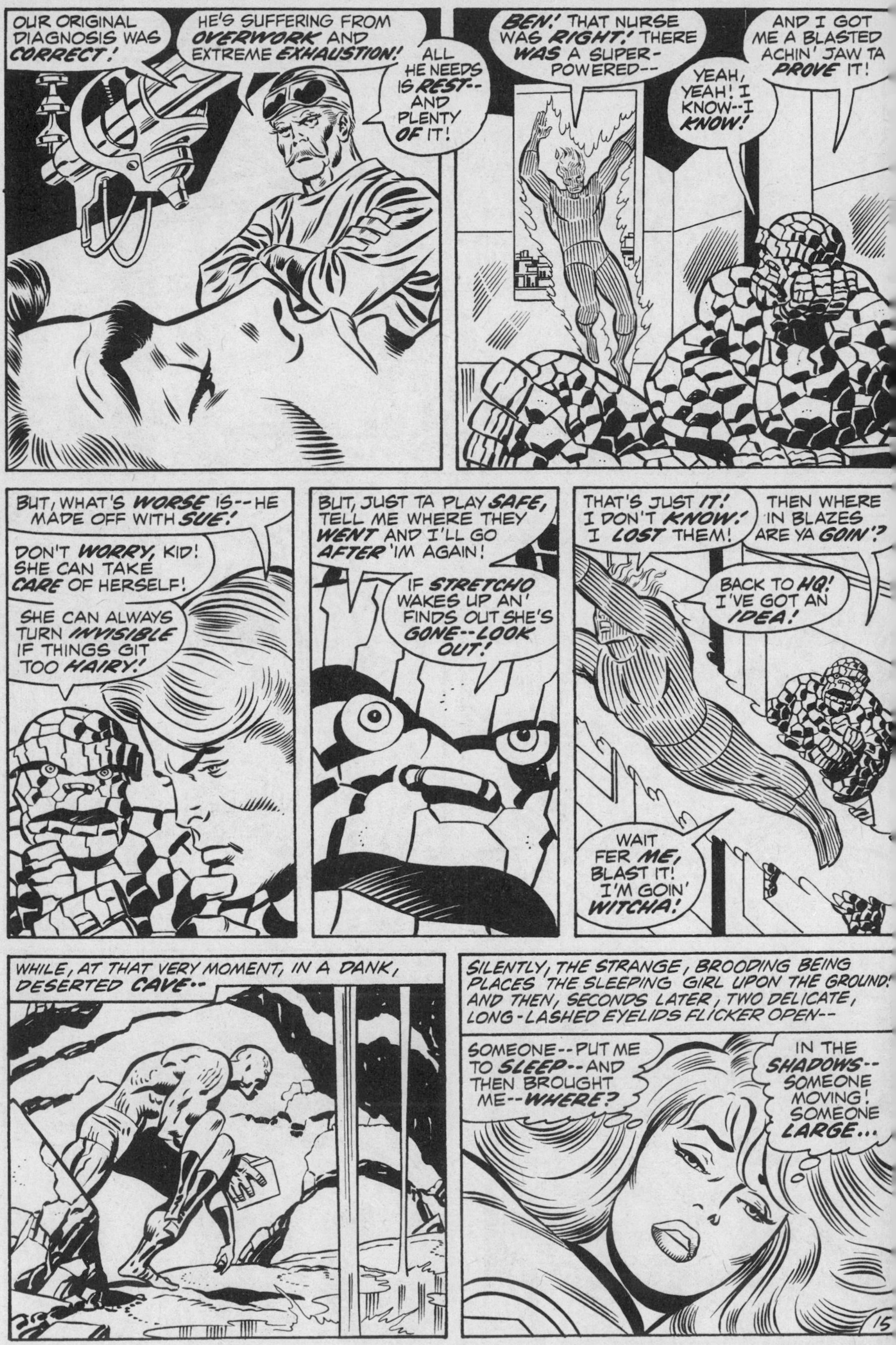

OUR ORIGINAL DIAGNOSIS WAS CORRECT!
HE'S SUFFERING FROM OVERWORK AND EXTREME EXHAUSTION!
ALL HE NEEDS IS REST-- AND PLENTY OF IT!
BEN! THAT NURSE WAS RIGHT! THERE WAS A SUPER-POWERED--
AND I GOT ME A BLASTED ACHIN' JAW TA PROVE IT!
YEAH, YEAH! I KNOW--I KNOW!
BUT, WHAT'S WORSE IS--HE MADE OFF WITH SUE!
DON'T WORRY, KID! SHE CAN TAKE CARE OF HERSELF!
SHE CAN ALWAYS TURN INVISIBLE IF THINGS GIT TOO HAIRY!
BUT, JUST TA PLAY SAFE, TELL ME WHERE THEY WENT AND I'LL GO AFTER 'IM AGAIN!
IF STRETCHO WAKES UP AN' FINDS OUT SHE'S GONE--LOOK OUT!
THAT'S JUST IT! I DON'T KNOW! I LOST THEM!
THEN WHERE IN BLAZES ARE YA GOIN'?
BACK TO HQ! I'VE GOT AN IDEA!
WAIT FER ME, BLAST IT! I'M GOIN' WITCHA!
WHILE, AT THAT VERY MOMENT, IN A DANK, DESERTED CAVE--
SILENTLY, THE STRANGE, BROODING BEING PLACES THE SLEEPING GIRL UPON THE GROUND! AND THEN, SECONDS LATER, TWO DELICATE, LONG-LASHED EYELIDS FLICKER OPEN--
SOMEONE--PUT ME TO SLEEP--AND THEN BROUGHT ME--WHERE?
IN THE SHADOWS--SOMEONE MOVING! SOMEONE LARGE...
15

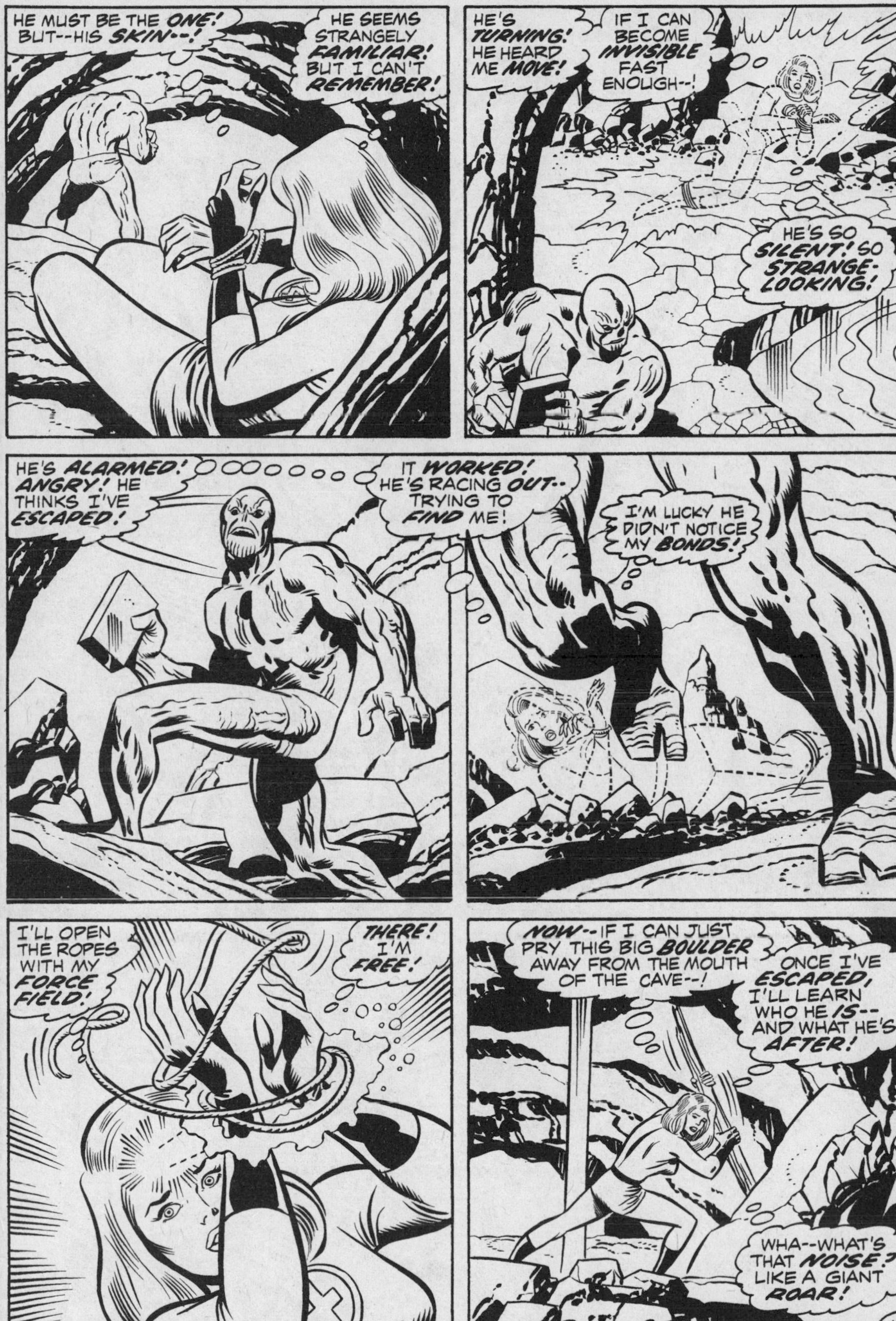
HE MUST BE THE ONE! BUT--HIS SKIN--!
HE SEEMS STRANGELY FAMILIAR! BUT I CAN'T REMEMBER!
HE'S TURNING! HE HEARD ME MOVE!
IF I CAN BECOME INVISIBLE FAST ENOUGH--!
HE'S SO SILENT! SO STRANGE-LOOKING!
HE'S ALARMED! ANGRY! HE THINKS I'VE ESCAPED!
IT WORKED! HE'S RACING OUT.. TRYING TO FIND ME!
I'M LUCKY HE DIDN'T NOTICE MY BONDS!
I'LL OPEN THE ROPES WITH MY FORCE FIELD!
THERE! I'M FREE!
NOW--IF I CAN JUST PRY THIS BIG BOULDER AWAY FROM THE MOUTH OF THE CAVE--!
ONCE I'VE ESCAPED, I'LL LEARN WHO HE IS-- AND WHAT HE'S AFTER!
WHA--WHAT'S THAT NOISE? LIKE A GIANT ROAR!
16

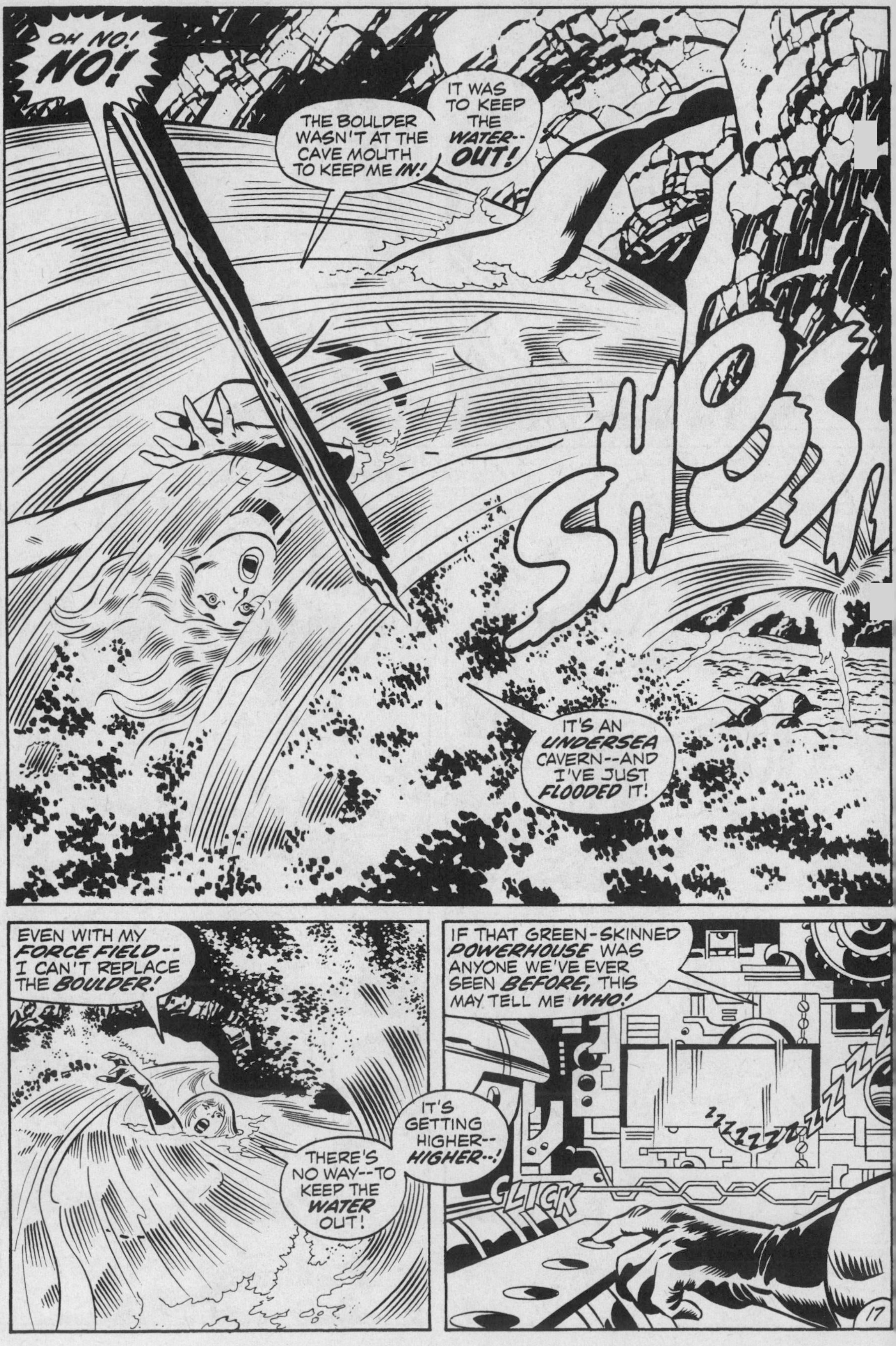
OH NO! NO!
THE BOULDER WASN'T AT THE CAVE MOUTH TO KEEP ME IN!
IT WAS TO KEEP THE WATER--OUT!
SHOOSH
IT'S AN UNDERSEA CAVERN--AND I'VE JUST FLOODED IT!
EVEN WITH MY FORCE FIELD--I CAN'T REPLACE THE BOULDER!
IT'S GETTING HIGHER--HIGHER--!
THERE'S NO WAY--TO KEEP THE WATER OUT!
IF THAT GREEN-SKINNED POWERHOUSE WAS ANYONE WE'VE EVER SEEN BEFORE, THIS MAY TELL ME WHO!
ZZZZZZZZZZZ
CLICK
17

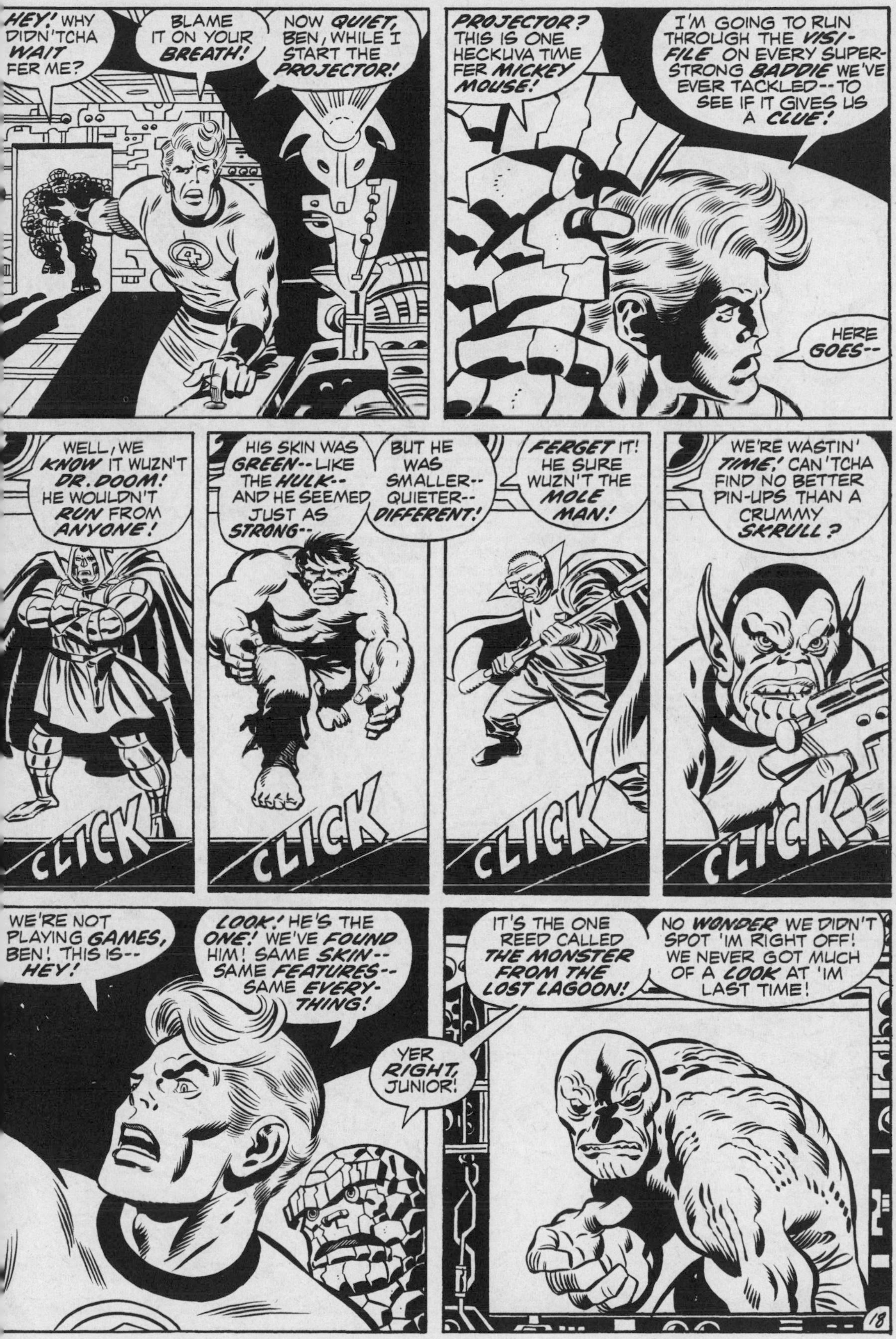
HEY! WHY DIDN'TCHA WAIT FER ME?
BLAME IT ON YOUR BREATH!
NOW QUIET, BEN, WHILE I START THE PROJECTOR!
PROJECTOR? THIS IS ONE HECKUVA TIME FER MICKEY MOUSE!
I'M GOING TO RUN THROUGH THE VISI-FILE ON EVERY SUPER-STRONG BADDIE WE'VE EVER TACKLED--TO SEE IF IT GIVES US A CLUE!
HERE GOES--
WELL, WE KNOW IT WUZN'T DR. DOOM! HE WOULDN'T RUN FROM ANYONE!
CLICK
HIS SKIN WAS GREEN--LIKE THE HULK--AND HE SEEMED JUST AS STRONG--
BUT HE WAS SMALLER--QUIETER--DIFFERENT!
CLICK
FERGET IT! HE SURE WUZN'T THE MOLE MAN!
CLICK
WE'RE WASTIN' TIME! CAN'TCHA FIND NO BETTER PIN-UPS THAN A CRUMMY SKRULL?
CLICK
WE'RE NOT PLAYING GAMES, BEN! THIS IS--HEY!
LOOK! HE'S THE ONE! WE'VE FOUND HIM! SAME SKIN--SAME FEATURES--SAME EVERY-THING!
YER RIGHT, JUNIOR!
IT'S THE ONE REED CALLED THE MONSTER FROM THE LOST LAGOON!
NO WONDER WE DIDN'T SPOT 'IM RIGHT OFF! WE NEVER GOT MUCH OF A LOOK AT 'IM LAST TIME!
18

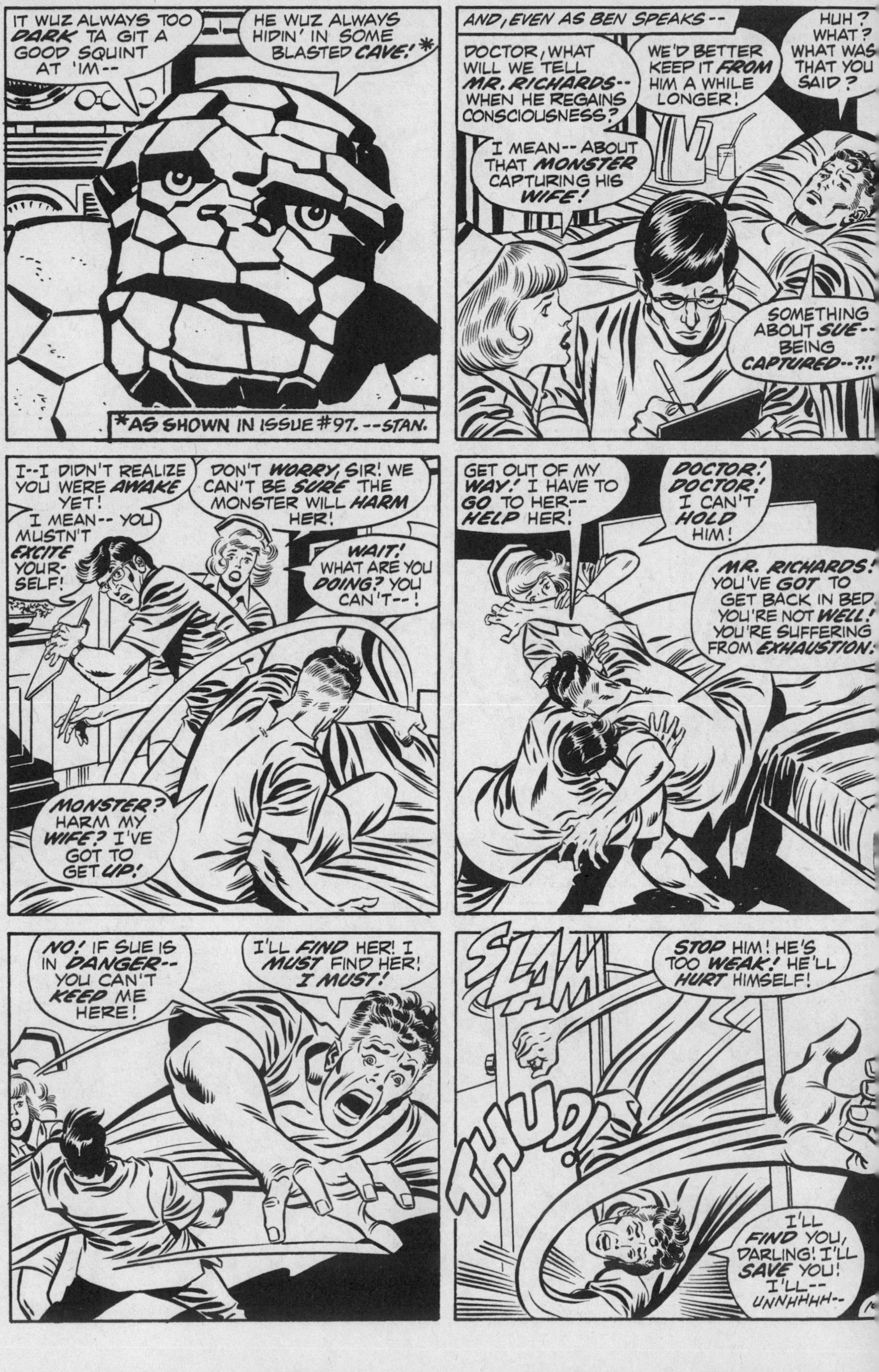
IT WUZ ALWAYS TOO DARK TA GIT A GOOD SQUINT AT 'IM--
HE WUZ ALWAYS HIDIN' IN SOME BLASTED CAVE! *
*AS SHOWN IN ISSUE #97. --STAN.
AND, EVEN AS BEN SPEAKS--
DOCTOR, WHAT WILL WE TELL MR. RICHARDS-- WHEN HE REGAINS CONSCIOUSNESS?
I MEAN-- ABOUT THAT MONSTER CAPTURING HIS WIFE!
WE'D BETTER KEEP IT FROM HIM A WHILE LONGER!
HUH? WHAT? WHAT WAS THAT YOU SAID?
SOMETHING ABOUT SUE-- BEING CAPTURED--?!!
I--I DIDN'T REALIZE YOU WERE AWAKE YET!
I MEAN-- YOU MUSTN'T EXCITE YOURSELF!
DON'T WORRY, SIR! WE CAN'T BE SURE THE MONSTER WILL HARM HER!
WAIT! WHAT ARE YOU DOING? YOU CAN'T--!
MONSTER? HARM MY WIFE? I'VE GOT TO GET UP!
GET OUT OF MY WAY! I HAVE TO GO TO HER-- HELP HER!
DOCTOR! DOCTOR! I CAN'T HOLD HIM!
MR. RICHARDS! YOU'VE GOT TO GET BACK IN BED. YOU'RE NOT WELL! YOU'RE SUFFERING FROM EXHAUSTION!
NO! IF SUE IS IN DANGER-- YOU CAN'T KEEP ME HERE!
I'LL FIND HER! I MUST FIND HER! I MUST!
SLAM
STOP HIM! HE'S TOO WEAK! HE'LL HURT HIMSELF!
THUD!
I'LL FIND YOU, DARLING! I'LL SAVE YOU! I'LL-- UNNHHHH--

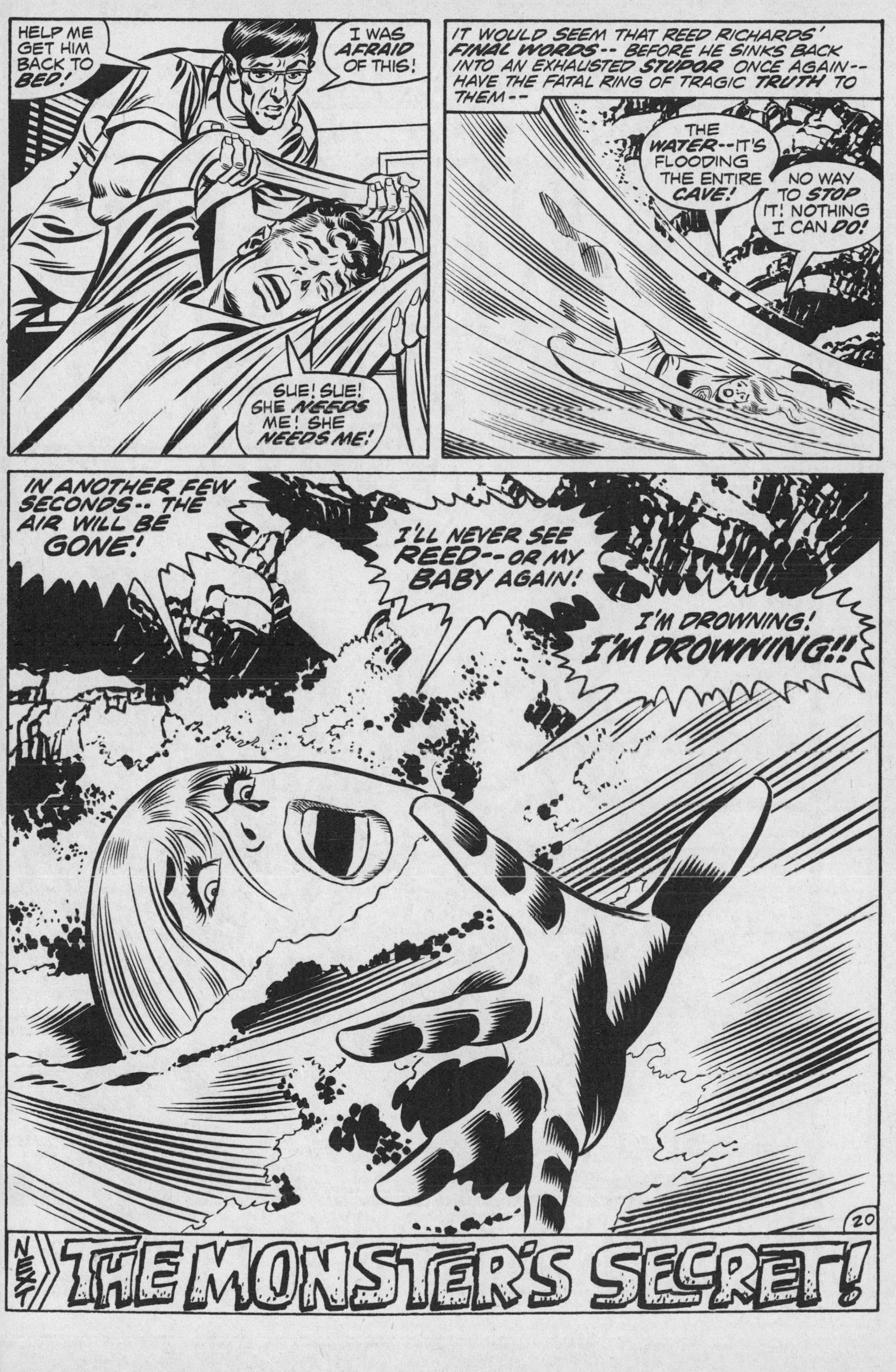

HELP ME GET HIM BACK TO BED!
I WAS AFRAID OF THIS!
SUE! SUE! SHE NEEDS ME! SHE NEEDS ME!
IT WOULD SEEM THAT REED RICHARDS' FINAL WORDS-- BEFORE HE SINKS BACK INTO AN EXHAUSTED STUPOR ONCE AGAIN-- HAVE THE FATAL RING OF TRAGIC TRUTH TO THEM--
THE WATER--IT'S FLOODING THE ENTIRE CAVE!
NO WAY TO STOP IT! NOTHING I CAN DO!
IN ANOTHER FEW SECONDS-- THE AIR WILL BE GONE!
I'LL NEVER SEE REED--OR MY BABY AGAIN!
I'M DROWNING! I'M DROWNING!!
20
NEXT THE MONSTER'S SECRET!

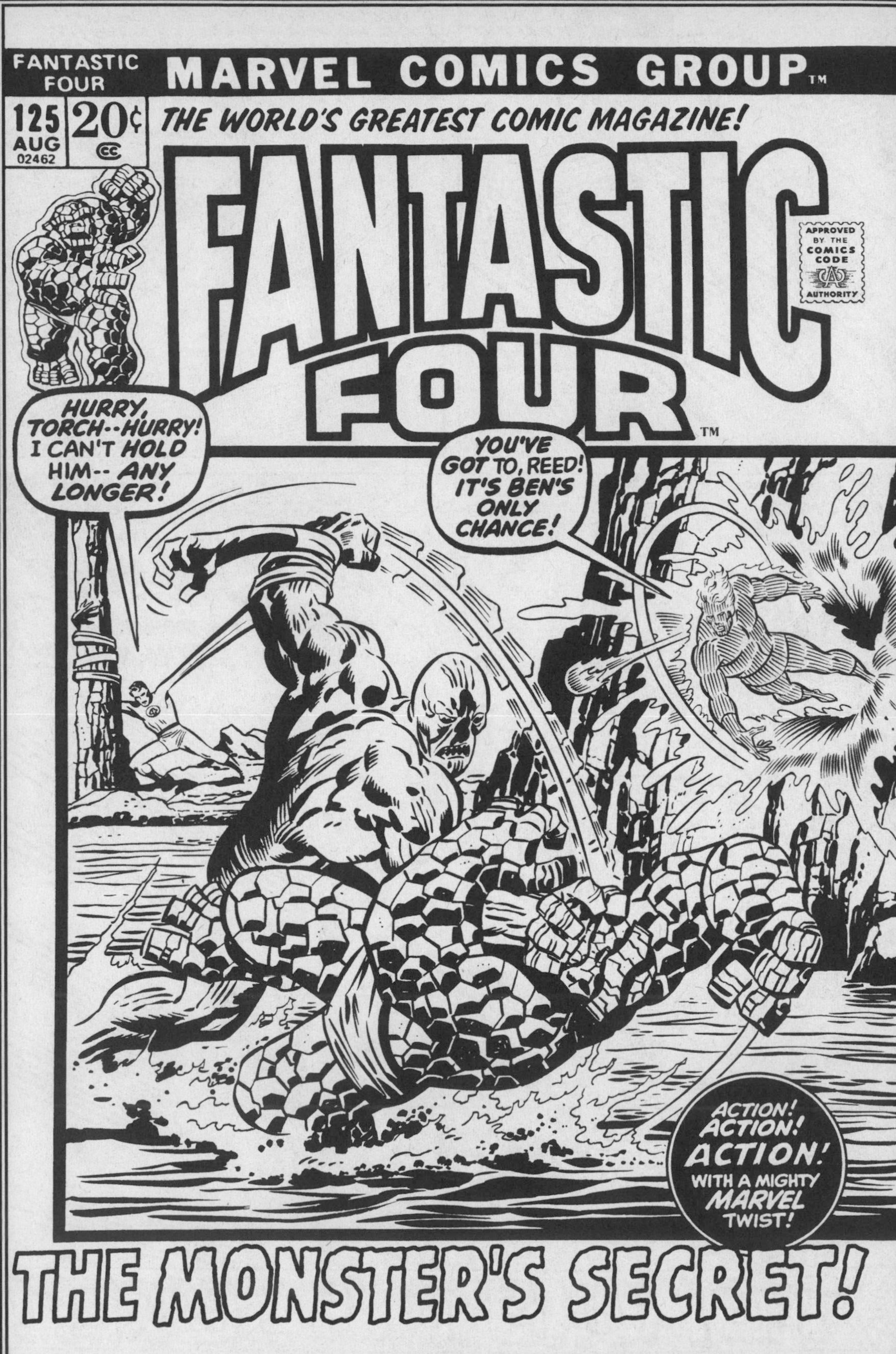

FANTASTIC FOUR
MARVEL COMICS GROUP™
125 AUG 02462
20¢
CC
THE WORLD'S GREATEST COMIC MAGAZINE!
FANTASTIC FOUR™
APPROVED BY THE COMICS CODE AUTHORITY
HURRY, TORCH--HURRY! I CAN'T HOLD HIM-- ANY LONGER!
YOU'VE GOT TO, REED! IT'S BEN'S ONLY CHANCE!
ACTION! ACTION! ACTION! WITH A MIGHTY MARVEL TWIST!
THE MONSTER'S SECRET!

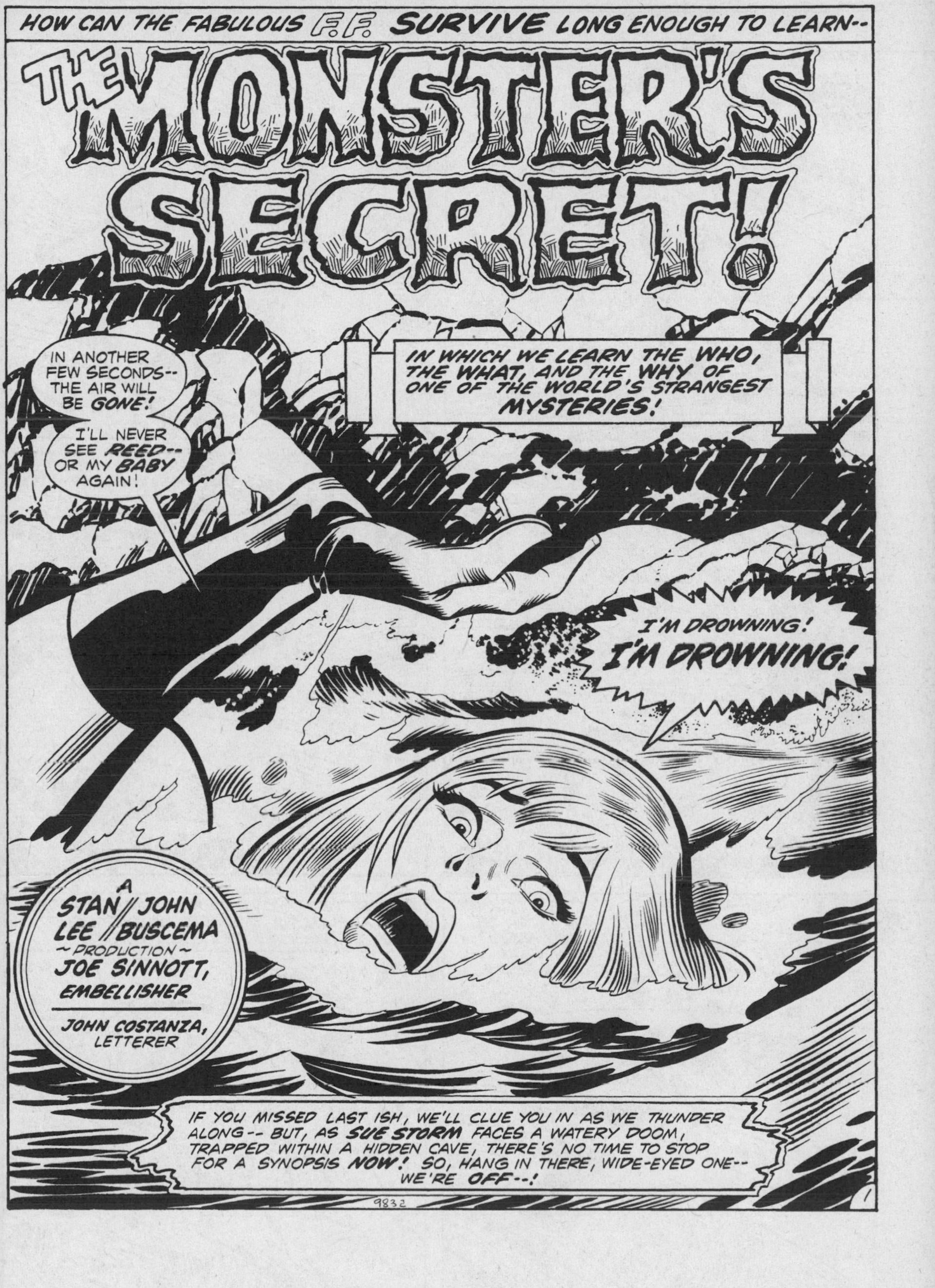
HOW CAN THE FABULOUS F.F. SURVIVE LONG ENOUGH TO LEARN--
THE MONSTER'S SECRET!
IN WHICH WE LEARN THE WHO, THE WHAT, AND THE WHY OF ONE OF THE WORLD'S STRANGEST MYSTERIES!
IN ANOTHER FEW SECONDS-- THE AIR WILL BE GONE!
I'LL NEVER SEE REED-- OR MY BABY AGAIN!
I'M DROWNING! I'M DROWNING!
A STAN LEE // JOHN BUSCEMA ~PRODUCTION~ JOE SINNOTT, EMBELLISHER
JOHN COSTANZA, LETTERER
IF YOU MISSED LAST ISH, WE'LL CLUE YOU IN AS WE THUNDER ALONG-- BUT, AS SUE STORM FACES A WATERY DOOM, TRAPPED WITHIN A HIDDEN CAVE, THERE'S NO TIME TO STOP FOR A SYNOPSIS NOW! SO, HANG IN THERE, WIDE-EYED ONE-- WE'RE OFF--!
1
9832

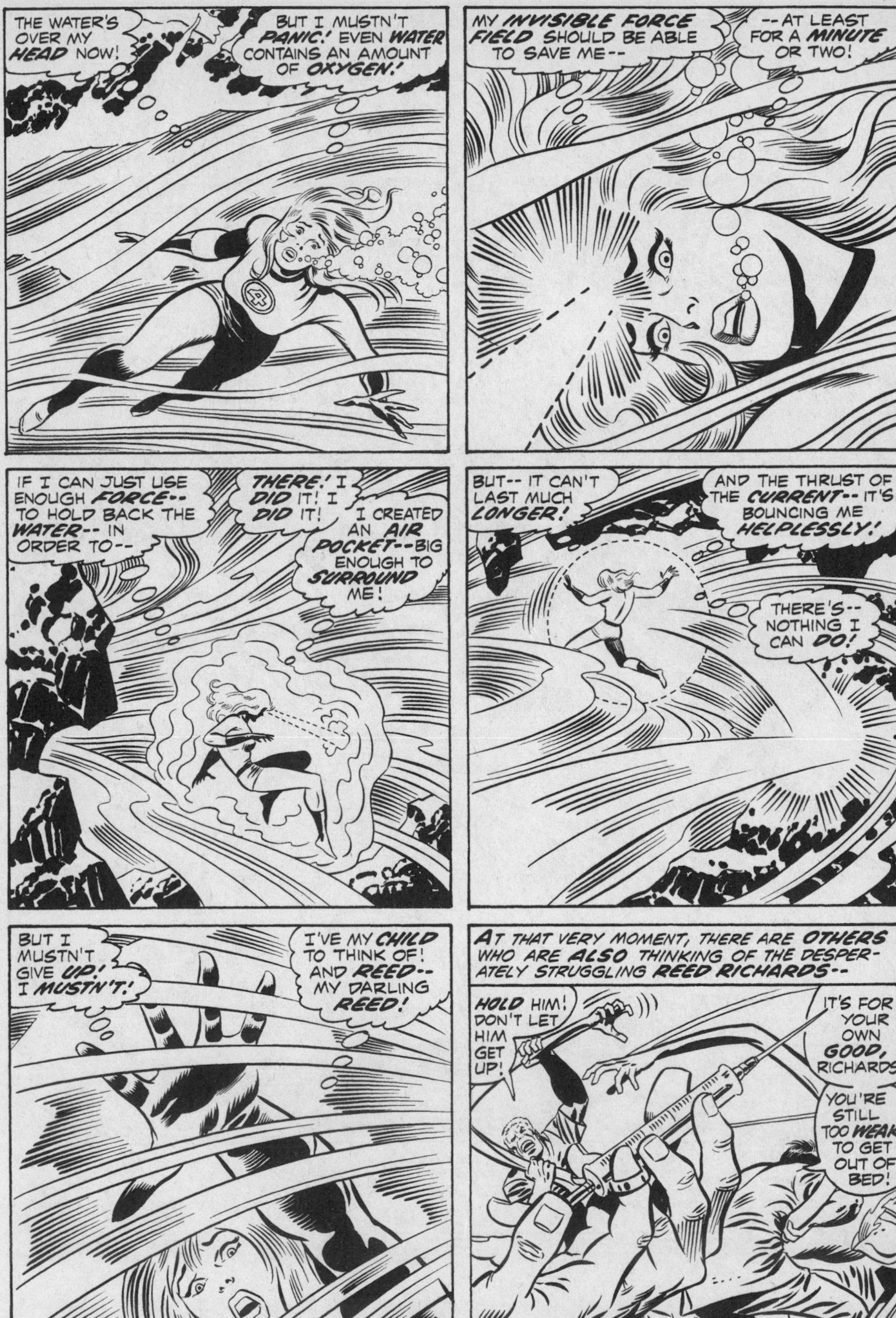

THE WATER'S OVER MY HEAD NOW!
BUT I MUSTN'T PANIC! EVEN WATER CONTAINS AN AMOUNT OF OXYGEN!
MY INVISIBLE FORCE FIELD SHOULD BE ABLE TO SAVE ME--
--AT LEAST FOR A MINUTE OR TWO!
IF I CAN JUST USE ENOUGH FORCE-- TO HOLD BACK THE WATER-- IN ORDER TO--
THERE! I DID IT! I DID IT!
I CREATED AN AIR POCKET--BIG ENOUGH TO SURROUND ME!
BUT-- IT CAN'T LAST MUCH LONGER!
AND THE THRUST OF THE CURRENT-- IT'S BOUNCING ME HELPLESSLY!
THERE'S-- NOTHING I CAN DO!
BUT I MUSTN'T GIVE UP! I MUSTN'T!
I'VE MY CHILD TO THINK OF! AND REED-- MY DARLING REED!
AT THAT VERY MOMENT, THERE ARE OTHERS WHO ARE ALSO THINKING OF THE DESPERATELY STRUGGLING REED RICHARDS--
HOLD HIM! DON'T LET HIM GET UP!
IT'S FOR YOUR OWN GOOD, RICHARDS!
YOU'RE STILL TOO WEAK TO GET OUT OF BED!
2

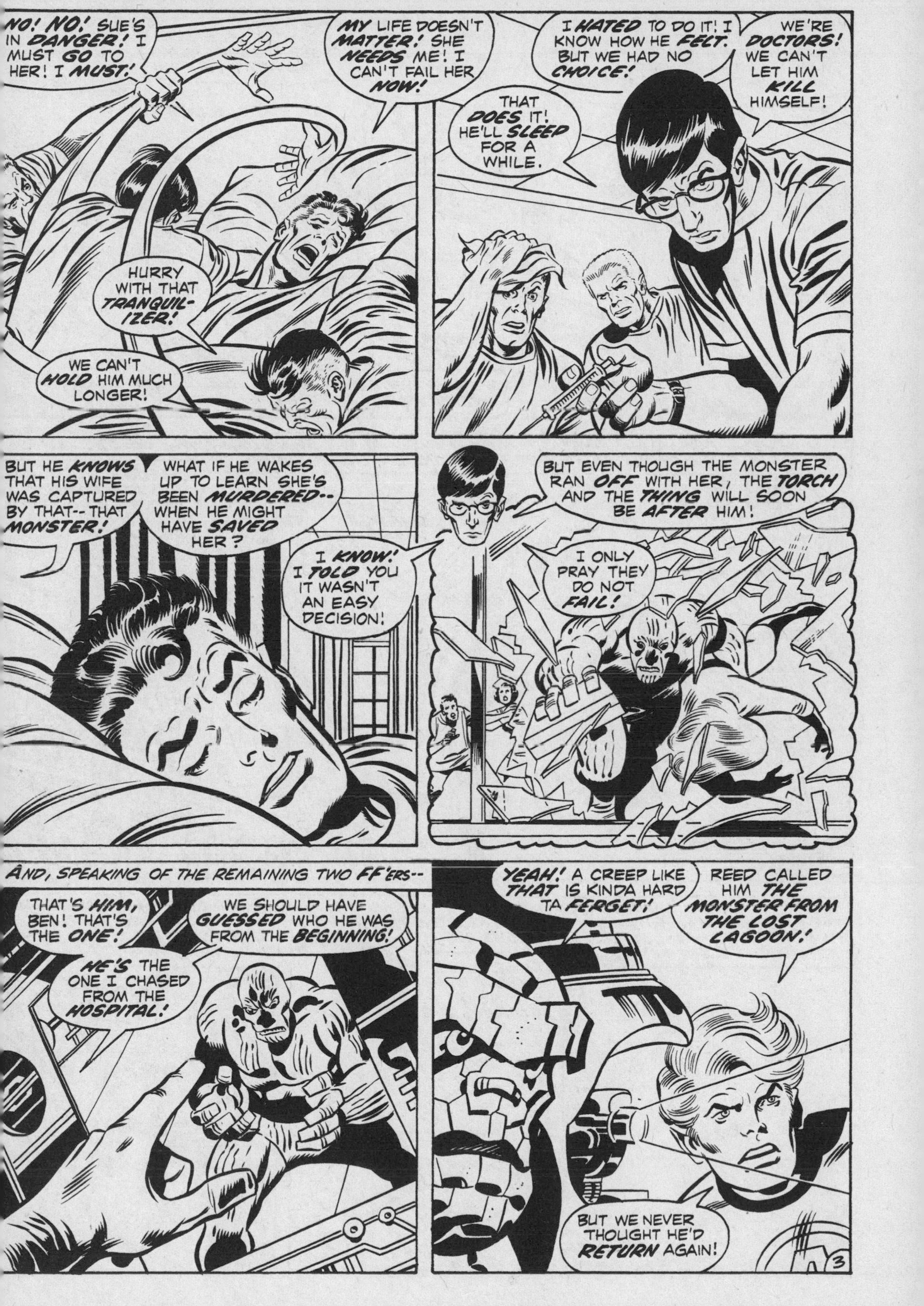
NO! NO! SUE'S IN DANGER! I MUST GO TO HER! I MUST!
MY LIFE DOESN'T MATTER! SHE NEEDS ME! I CAN'T FAIL HER NOW!
HURRY WITH THAT TRANQUIL-IZER!
WE CAN'T HOLD HIM MUCH LONGER!
I HATED TO DO IT! I KNOW HOW HE FELT. BUT WE HAD NO CHOICE!
WE'RE DOCTORS! WE CAN'T LET HIM KILL HIMSELF!
THAT DOES IT! HE'LL SLEEP FOR A WHILE.
BUT HE KNOWS THAT HIS WIFE WAS CAPTURED BY THAT-- THAT MONSTER!
WHAT IF HE WAKES UP TO LEARN SHE'S BEEN MURDERED-- WHEN HE MIGHT HAVE SAVED HER?
I KNOW! I TOLD YOU IT WASN'T AN EASY DECISION!
BUT EVEN THOUGH THE MONSTER RAN OFF WITH HER, THE TORCH AND THE THING WILL SOON BE AFTER HIM!
I ONLY PRAY THEY DO NOT FAIL!
AND, SPEAKING OF THE REMAINING TWO FF'ERS--
THAT'S HIM, BEN! THAT'S THE ONE!
WE SHOULD HAVE GUESSED WHO HE WAS FROM THE BEGINNING!
HE'S THE ONE I CHASED FROM THE HOSPITAL!
YEAH! A CREEP LIKE THAT IS KINDA HARD TA FERGET!
REED CALLED HIM THE MONSTER FROM THE LOST LAGOON!
BUT WE NEVER THOUGHT HE'D RETURN AGAIN!
3

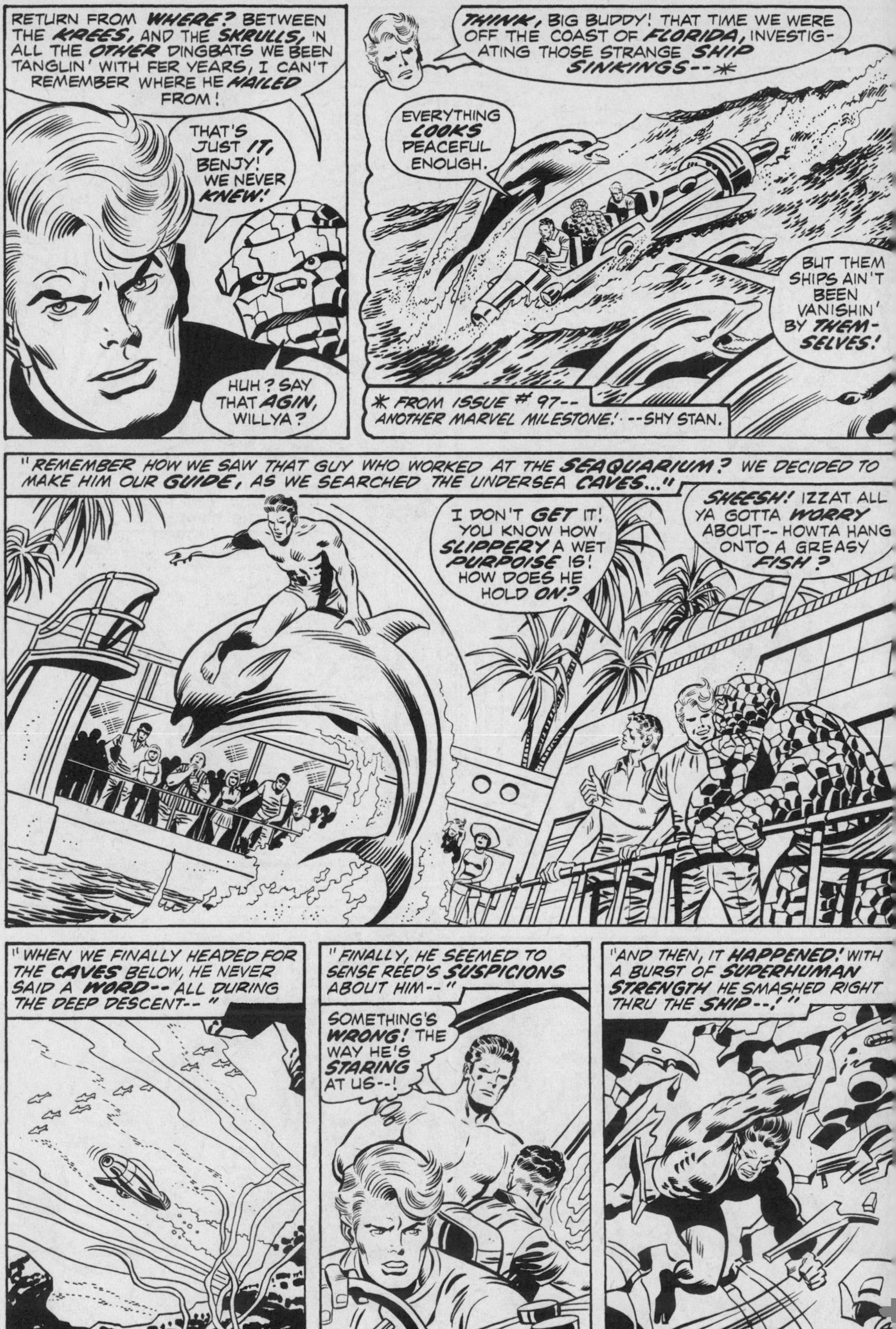
RETURN FROM WHERE? BETWEEN THE KREES, AND THE SKRULLS, 'N ALL THE OTHER DINGBATS WE BEEN TANGLIN' WITH FER YEARS, I CAN'T REMEMBER WHERE HE HAILED FROM!
THAT'S JUST IT, BENJY! WE NEVER KNEW!
HUH? SAY THAT AGIN, WILLYA?
THINK, BIG BUDDY! THAT TIME WE WERE OFF THE COAST OF FLORIDA, INVESTIG-ATING THOSE STRANGE SHIP SINKINGS-- *
EVERYTHING LOOKS PEACEFUL ENOUGH.
BUT THEM SHIPS AIN'T BEEN VANISHIN' BY THEM-SELVES!
* FROM ISSUE # 97-- ANOTHER MARVEL MILESTONE! --SHY STAN.
"REMEMBER HOW WE SAW THAT GUY WHO WORKED AT THE SEAQUARIUM? WE DECIDED TO MAKE HIM OUR GUIDE, AS WE SEARCHED THE UNDERSEA CAVES..."
I DON'T GET IT! YOU KNOW HOW SLIPPERY A WET PURPOISE IS! HOW DOES HE HOLD ON?
SHEESH! IZZAT ALL YA GOTTA WORRY ABOUT-- HOWTA HANG ONTO A GREASY FISH?
"WHEN WE FINALLY HEADED FOR THE CAVES BELOW, HE NEVER SAID A WORD-- ALL DURING THE DEEP DESCENT--"
"FINALLY, HE SEEMED TO SENSE REED'S SUSPICIONS ABOUT HIM--"
SOMETHING'S WRONG! THE WAY HE'S STARING AT US--!
"AND THEN, IT HAPPENED! WITH A BURST OF SUPERHUMAN STRENGTH HE SMASHED RIGHT THRU THE SHIP--!"
4

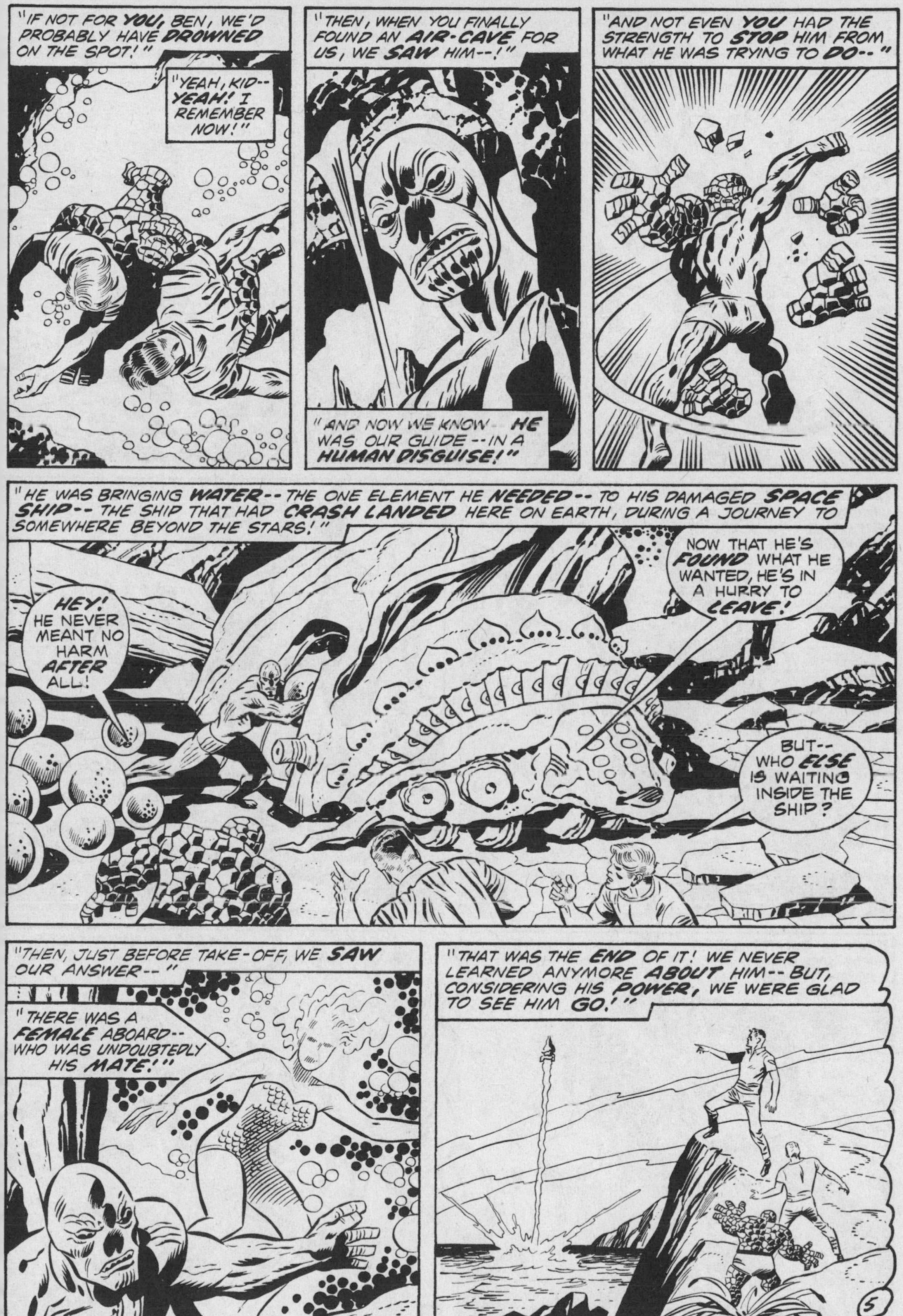
"IF NOT FOR YOU, BEN, WE'D PROBABLY HAVE DROWNED ON THE SPOT!"
"YEAH, KID-- YEAH! I REMEMBER NOW!"
"THEN, WHEN YOU FINALLY FOUND AN AIR-CAVE FOR US, WE SAW HIM--!"
"AND NOW WE KNOW-- HE WAS OUR GUIDE--IN A HUMAN DISGUISE!"
"AND NOT EVEN YOU HAD THE STRENGTH TO STOP HIM FROM WHAT HE WAS TRYING TO DO--"
"HE WAS BRINGING WATER-- THE ONE ELEMENT HE NEEDED-- TO HIS DAMAGED SPACE SHIP-- THE SHIP THAT HAD CRASH LANDED HERE ON EARTH, DURING A JOURNEY TO SOMEWHERE BEYOND THE STARS!"
HEY! HE NEVER MEANT NO HARM AFTER ALL!
NOW THAT HE'S FOUND WHAT HE WANTED, HE'S IN A HURRY TO LEAVE!
BUT-- WHO ELSE IS WAITING INSIDE THE SHIP?
"THEN, JUST BEFORE TAKE-OFF, WE SAW OUR ANSWER--"
"THERE WAS A FEMALE ABOARD-- WHO WAS UNDOUBTEDLY HIS MATE!"
"THAT WAS THE END OF IT! WE NEVER LEARNED ANYMORE ABOUT HIM-- BUT, CONSIDERING HIS POWER, WE WERE GLAD TO SEE HIM GO!"
5

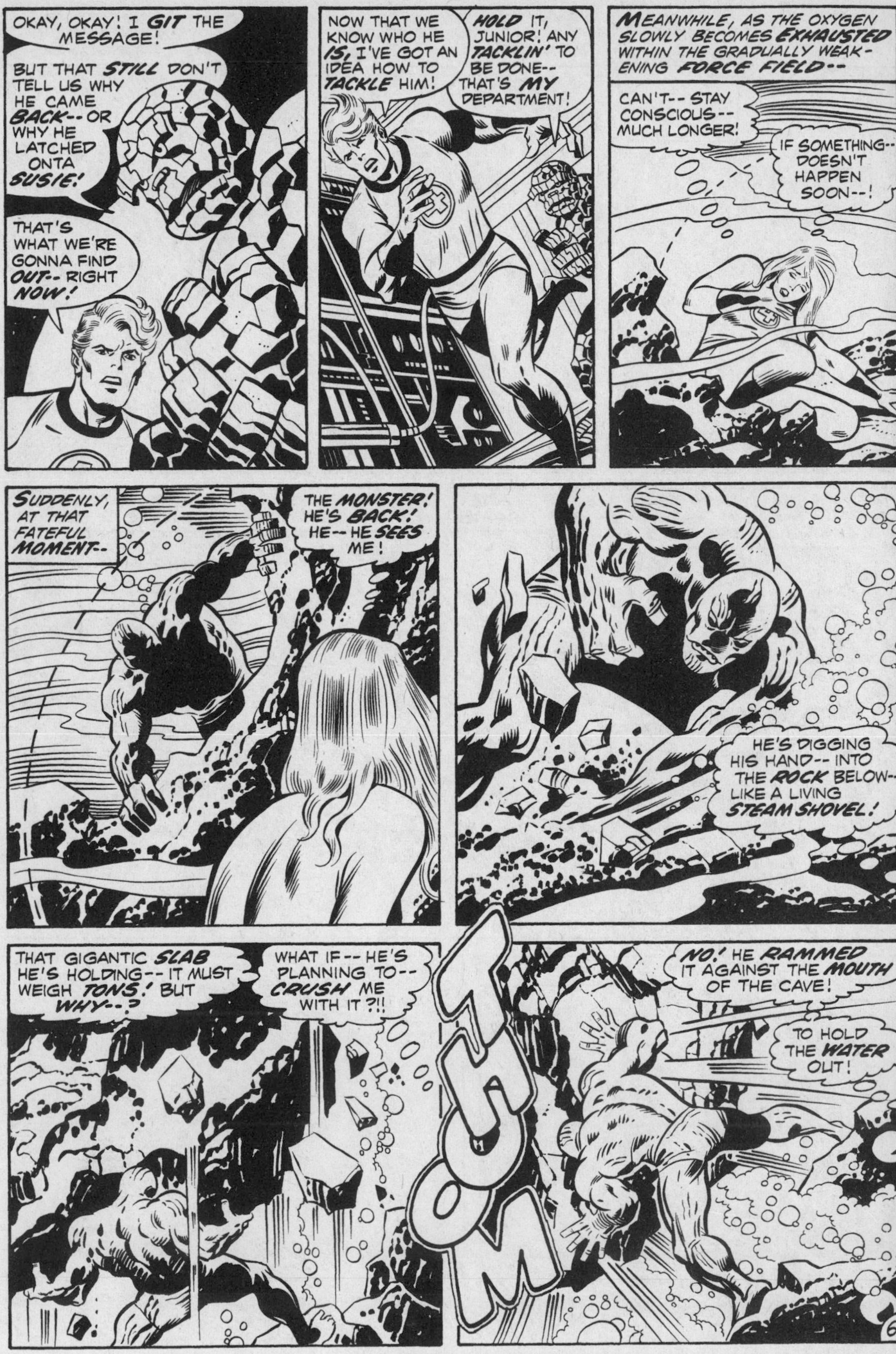
OKAY, OKAY! I GIT THE MESSAGE!
BUT THAT STILL DON'T TELL US WHY HE CAME BACK-- OR WHY HE LATCHED ONTA SUSIE!
THAT'S WHAT WE'RE GONNA FIND OUT-- RIGHT NOW!
NOW THAT WE KNOW WHO HE IS, I'VE GOT AN IDEA HOW TO TACKLE HIM!
HOLD IT, JUNIOR! ANY TACKLIN' TO BE DONE-- THAT'S MY DEPARTMENT!
MEANWHILE, AS THE OXYGEN SLOWLY BECOMES EXHAUSTED WITHIN THE GRADUALLY WEAKENING FORCE FIELD--
CAN'T-- STAY CONSCIOUS-- MUCH LONGER!
IF SOMETHING-- DOESN'T HAPPEN SOON--!
SUDDENLY, AT THAT FATEFUL MOMENT--
THE MONSTER! HE'S BACK! HE-- HE SEES ME!
HE'S DIGGING HIS HAND-- INTO THE ROCK BELOW-- LIKE A LIVING STEAM SHOVEL!
THAT GIGANTIC SLAB HE'S HOLDING-- IT MUST WEIGH TONS! BUT WHY--?
WHAT IF-- HE'S PLANNING TO-- CRUSH ME WITH IT?!!
THOOM
NO! HE RAMMED IT AGAINST THE MOUTH OF THE CAVE!
TO HOLD THE WATER OUT!
6

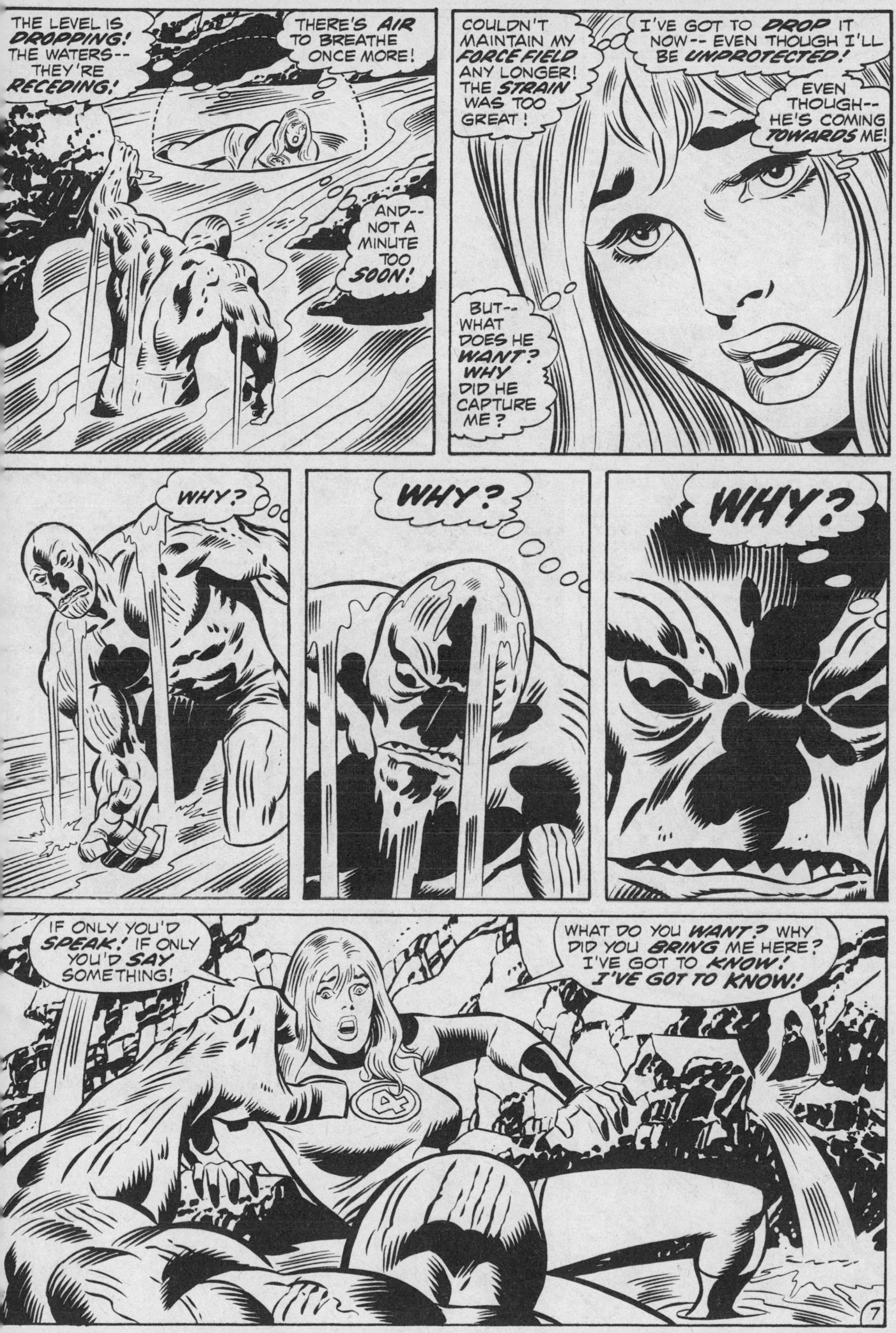
THE LEVEL IS DROPPING! THE WATERS-- THEY'RE RECEDING!
THERE'S AIR TO BREATHE ONCE MORE!
AND-- NOT A MINUTE TOO SOON!
COULDN'T MAINTAIN MY FORCE FIELD ANY LONGER! THE STRAIN WAS TOO GREAT!
I'VE GOT TO DROP IT NOW-- EVEN THOUGH I'LL BE UNPROTECTED!
EVEN THOUGH-- HE'S COMING TOWARDS ME!
BUT-- WHAT DOES HE WANT? WHY DID HE CAPTURE ME?
WHY?
WHY?
WHY?
IF ONLY YOU'D SPEAK! IF ONLY YOU'D SAY SOMETHING!
WHAT DO YOU WANT? WHY DID YOU BRING ME HERE? I'VE GOT TO KNOW! I'VE GOT TO KNOW!
7

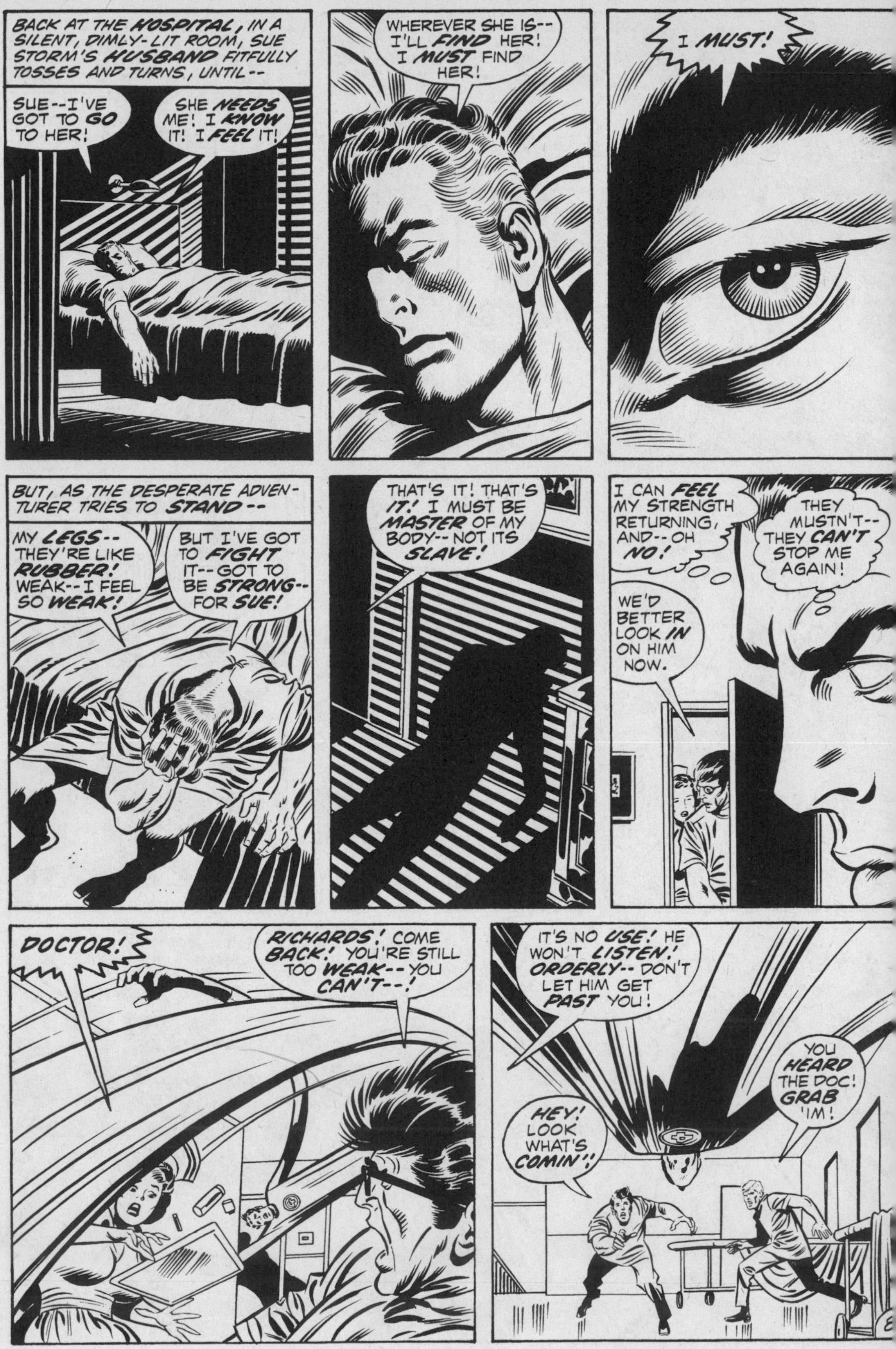

BACK AT THE HOSPITAL, IN A SILENT, DIMLY-LIT ROOM, SUE STORM'S HUSBAND FITFULLY TOSSES AND TURNS, UNTIL--
SUE--I'VE GOT TO GO TO HER!
SHE NEEDS ME! I KNOW IT! I FEEL IT!
WHEREVER SHE IS-- I'LL FIND HER! I MUST FIND HER!
I MUST!
BUT, AS THE DESPERATE ADVENTURER TRIES TO STAND--
MY LEGS-- THEY'RE LIKE RUBBER! WEAK--I FEEL SO WEAK!
BUT I'VE GOT TO FIGHT IT--GOT TO BE STRONG-- FOR SUE!
THAT'S IT! THAT'S IT! I MUST BE MASTER OF MY BODY--NOT ITS SLAVE!
I CAN FEEL MY STRENGTH RETURNING, AND--OH NO!
THEY MUSTN'T-- THEY CAN'T STOP ME AGAIN!
WE'D BETTER LOOK IN ON HIM NOW.
DOCTOR!
RICHARDS! COME BACK! YOU'RE STILL TOO WEAK--YOU CAN'T--!
IT'S NO USE! HE WON'T LISTEN! ORDERLY-- DON'T LET HIM GET PAST YOU!
HEY! LOOK WHAT'S COMIN'!
YOU HEARD THE DOC! GRAB 'IM!

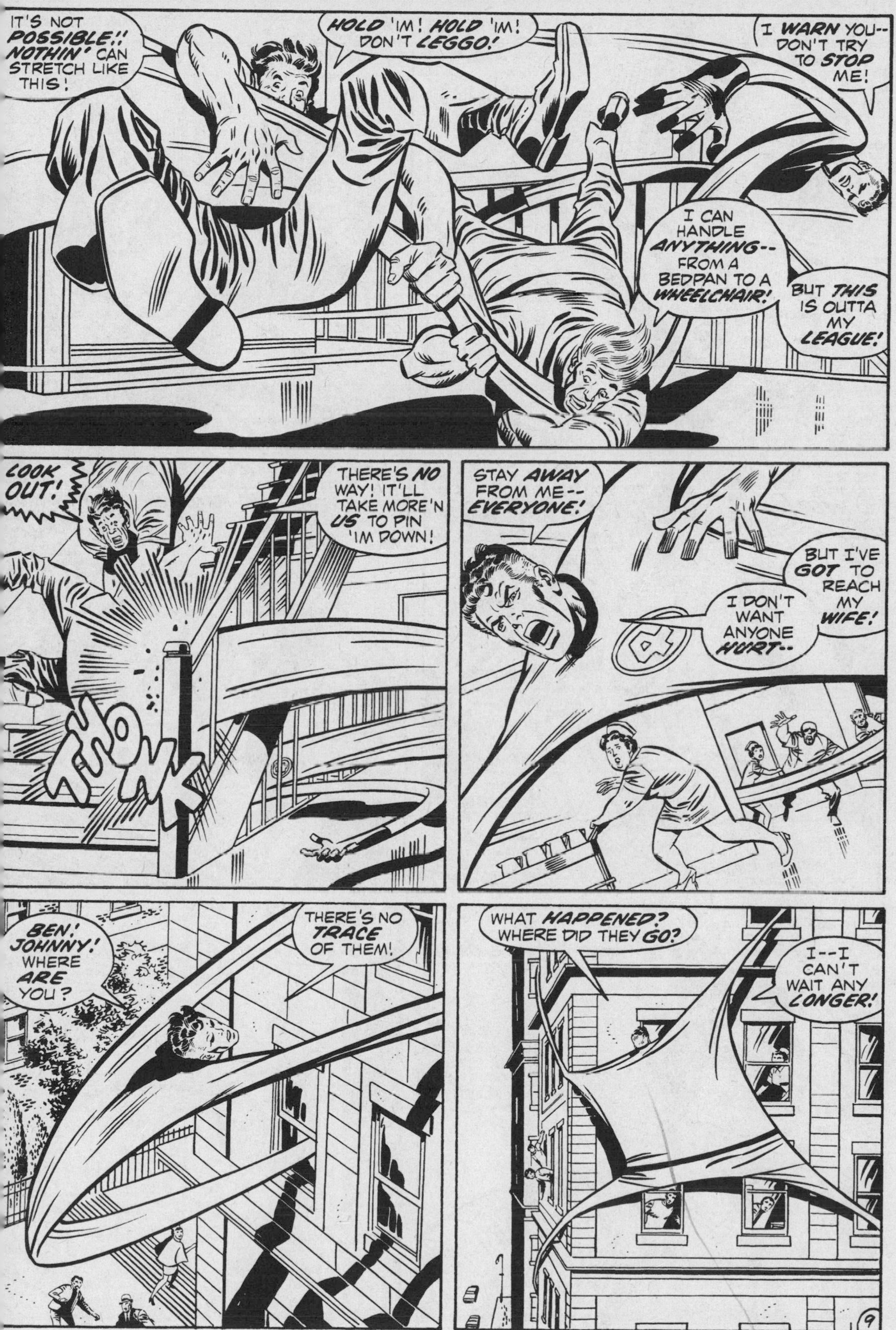

IT'S NOT POSSIBLE!! NOTHIN' CAN STRETCH LIKE THIS!
HOLD 'IM! HOLD 'IM! DON'T LEGGO!
I WARN YOU-- DON'T TRY TO STOP ME!
I CAN HANDLE ANYTHING-- FROM A BEDPAN TO A WHEELCHAIR!
BUT THIS IS OUTTA MY LEAGUE!
LOOK OUT!
THERE'S NO WAY! IT'LL TAKE MORE'N US TO PIN 'IM DOWN!
THONK
STAY AWAY FROM ME-- EVERYONE!
BUT I'VE GOT TO REACH MY WIFE!
I DON'T WANT ANYONE HURT--
BEN! JOHNNY! WHERE ARE YOU?
THERE'S NO TRACE OF THEM!
WHAT HAPPENED? WHERE DID THEY GO?
I--I CAN'T WAIT ANY LONGER!
9

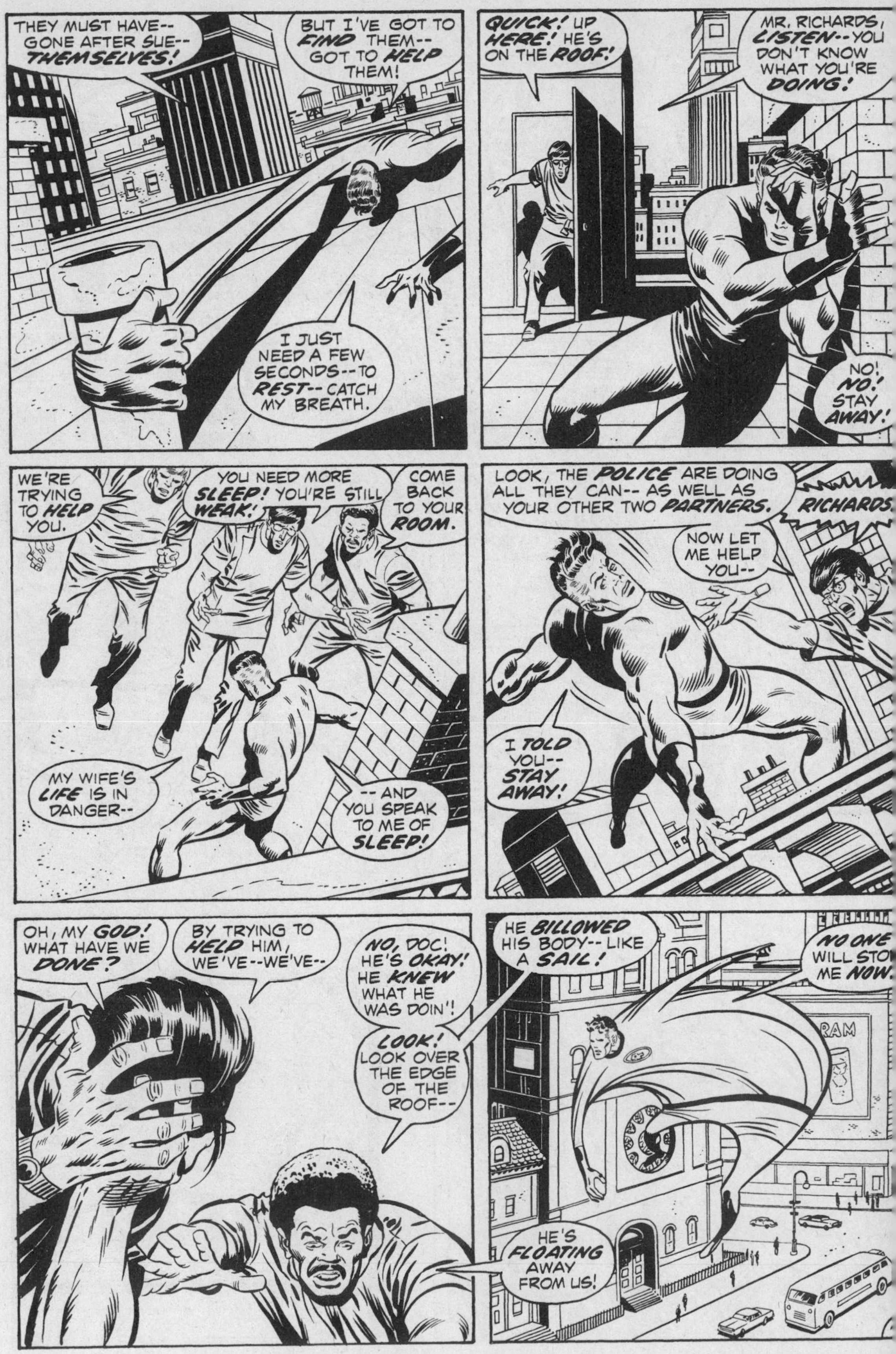
THEY MUST HAVE-- GONE AFTER SUE-- THEMSELVES!
BUT I'VE GOT TO FIND THEM-- GOT TO HELP THEM!
I JUST NEED A FEW SECONDS--TO REST--CATCH MY BREATH.
QUICK! UP HERE! HE'S ON THE ROOF!
MR. RICHARDS, LISTEN--YOU DON'T KNOW WHAT YOU'RE DOING!
NO! NO! STAY AWAY!
WE'RE TRYING TO HELP YOU.
YOU NEED MORE SLEEP! YOU'RE STILL WEAK!
COME BACK TO YOUR ROOM.
MY WIFE'S LIFE IS IN DANGER--
--AND YOU SPEAK TO ME OF SLEEP!
LOOK, THE POLICE ARE DOING ALL THEY CAN-- AS WELL AS YOUR OTHER TWO PARTNERS.
RICHARDS
NOW LET ME HELP YOU--
I TOLD YOU-- STAY AWAY!
OH, MY GOD! WHAT HAVE WE DONE?
BY TRYING TO HELP HIM, WE'VE--WE'VE--
NO, DOC! HE'S OKAY! HE KNEW WHAT HE WAS DOIN'!
LOOK! LOOK OVER THE EDGE OF THE ROOF--
HE'S FLOATING AWAY FROM US!
HE BILLOWED HIS BODY--LIKE A SAIL!
NO ONE WILL STO ME NOW.

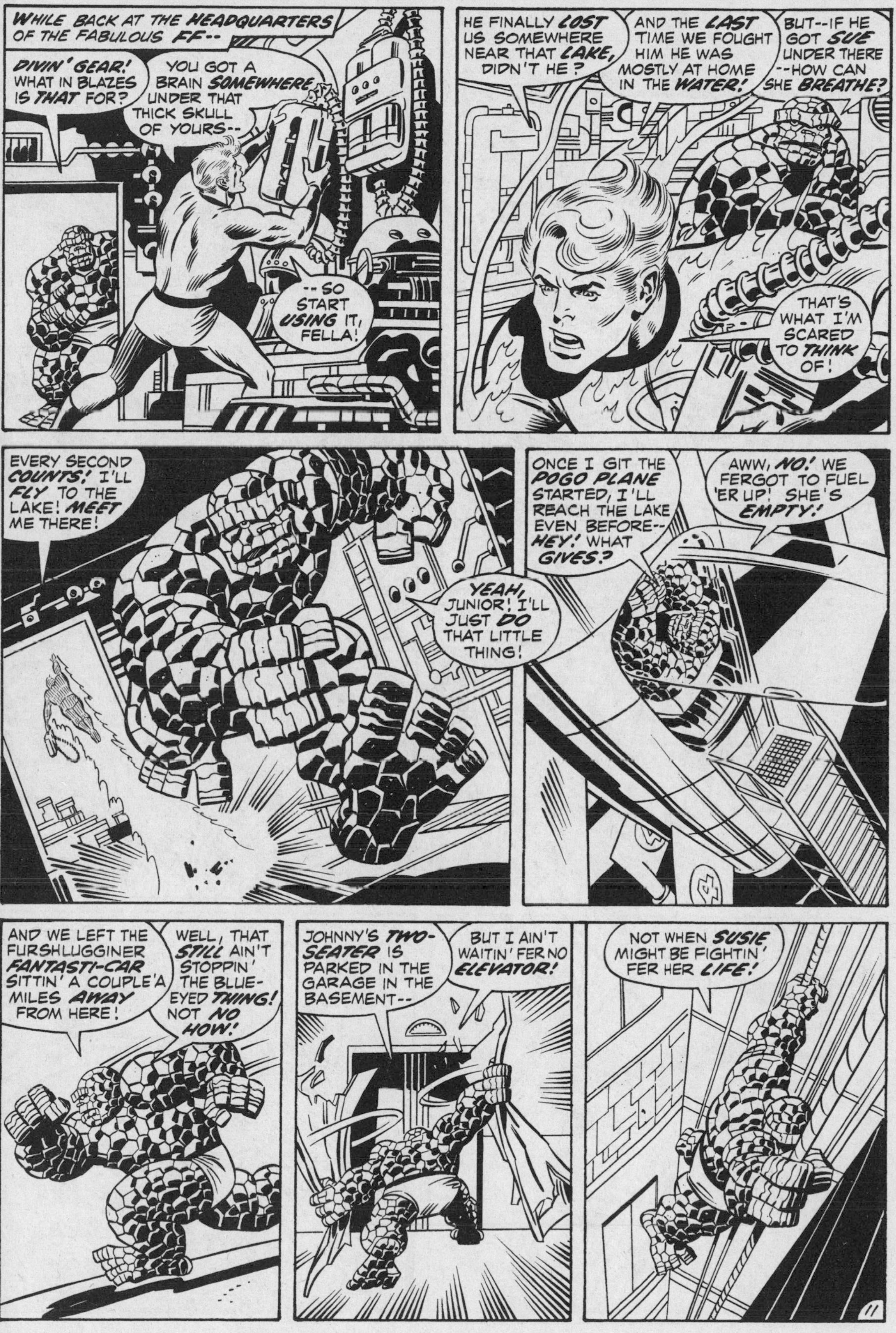

WHILE BACK AT THE HEADQUARTERS OF THE FABULOUS FF--
DIVIN' GEAR! WHAT IN BLAZES IS THAT FOR?
YOU GOT A BRAIN SOMEWHERE UNDER THAT THICK SKULL OF YOURS--
--SO START USING IT, FELLA!
HE FINALLY LOST US SOMEWHERE NEAR THAT LAKE, DIDN'T HE?
AND THE LAST TIME WE FOUGHT HIM HE WAS MOSTLY AT HOME IN THE WATER!
BUT--IF HE GOT SUE UNDER THERE --HOW CAN SHE BREATHE?
THAT'S WHAT I'M SCARED TO THINK OF!
EVERY SECOND COUNTS! I'LL FLY TO THE LAKE! MEET ME THERE!
YEAH, JUNIOR! I'LL JUST DO THAT LITTLE THING!
ONCE I GIT THE POGO PLANE STARTED, I'LL REACH THE LAKE EVEN BEFORE--HEY! WHAT GIVES?
AWW, NO! WE FERGOT TO FUEL 'ER UP! SHE'S EMPTY!
AND WE LEFT THE FURSHLUGGINER FANTASTI-CAR SITTIN' A COUPLE'A MILES AWAY FROM HERE!
WELL, THAT STILL AIN'T STOPPIN' THE BLUE-EYED THING! NOT NO HOW!
JOHNNY'S TWO-SEATER IS PARKED IN THE GARAGE IN THE BASEMENT--
BUT I AIN'T WAITIN' FER NO ELEVATOR!
NOT WHEN SUSIE MIGHT BE FIGHTIN' FER HER LIFE!
11

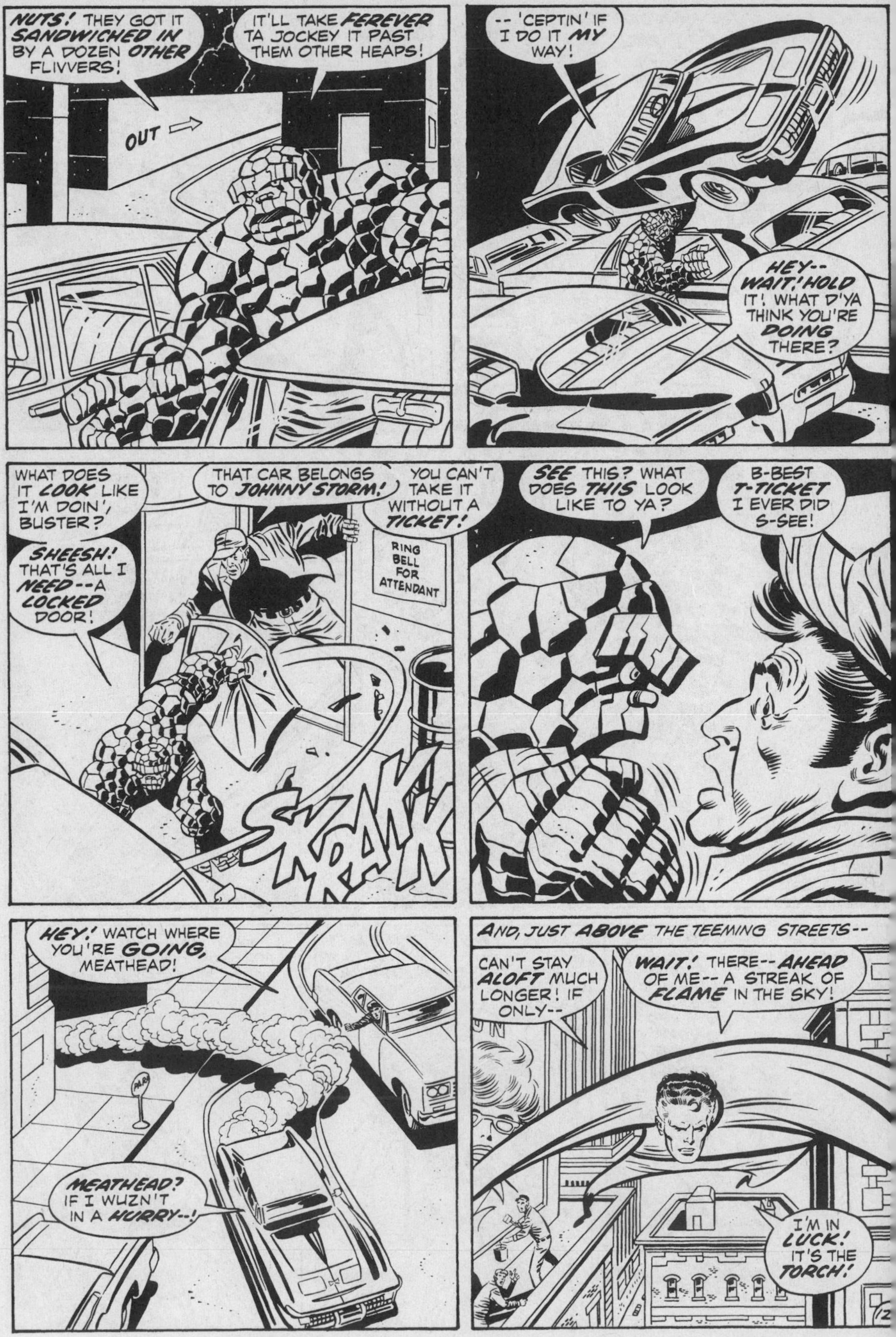
NUTS! THEY GOT IT SANDWICHED IN BY A DOZEN OTHER FLIVVERS!
IT'LL TAKE FEREVER TA JOCKEY IT PAST THEM OTHER HEAPS!
OUT
-- 'CEPTIN' IF I DO IT MY WAY!
HEY-- WAIT! HOLD IT! WHAT D'YA THINK YOU'RE DOING THERE?
WHAT DOES IT LOOK LIKE I'M DOIN', BUSTER?
THAT CAR BELONGS TO JOHNNY STORM!
YOU CAN'T TAKE IT WITHOUT A TICKET!
RING BELL FOR ATTENDANT
SHEESH! THAT'S ALL I NEED--A LOCKED DOOR!
SKRAK
SEE THIS? WHAT DOES THIS LOOK LIKE TO YA?
B-BEST T-TICKET I EVER DID S-SEE!
HEY! WATCH WHERE YOU'RE GOING, MEATHEAD!
MEATHEAD? IF I WUZN'T IN A HURRY--!
AND, JUST ABOVE THE TEEMING STREETS--
CAN'T STAY ALOFT MUCH LONGER! IF ONLY--
WAIT! THERE--AHEAD OF ME-- A STREAK OF FLAME IN THE SKY!
I'M IN LUCK! IT'S THE TORCH!

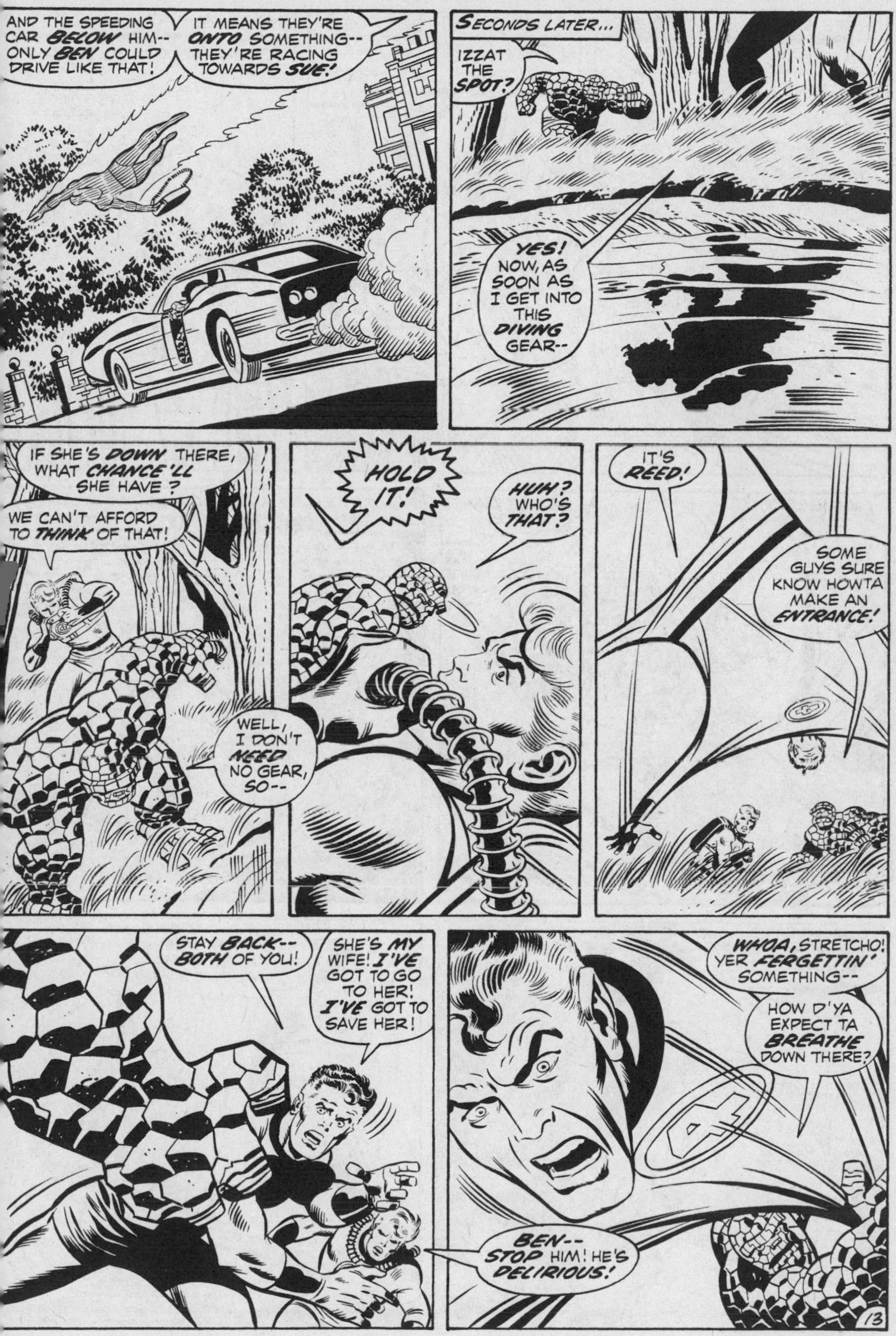
AND THE SPEEDING CAR BELOW HIM-- ONLY BEN COULD DRIVE LIKE THAT!
IT MEANS THEY'RE ONTO SOMETHING-- THEY'RE RACING TOWARDS SUE!
SECONDS LATER...
IZZAT THE SPOT?
YES! NOW, AS SOON AS I GET INTO THIS DIVING GEAR--
IF SHE'S DOWN THERE, WHAT CHANCE'LL SHE HAVE?
WE CAN'T AFFORD TO THINK OF THAT!
WELL, I DON'T NEED NO GEAR, SO--
HOLD IT!
HUH? WHO'S THAT?
IT'S REED!
SOME GUYS SURE KNOW HOWTA MAKE AN ENTRANCE!
STAY BACK-- BOTH OF YOU!
SHE'S MY WIFE! I'VE GOT TO GO TO HER! I'VE GOT TO SAVE HER!
WHOA, STRETCHO! YER FERGETTIN' SOMETHING--
HOW D'YA EXPECT TA BREATHE DOWN THERE?
BEN-- STOP HIM! HE'S DELIRIOUS!
13

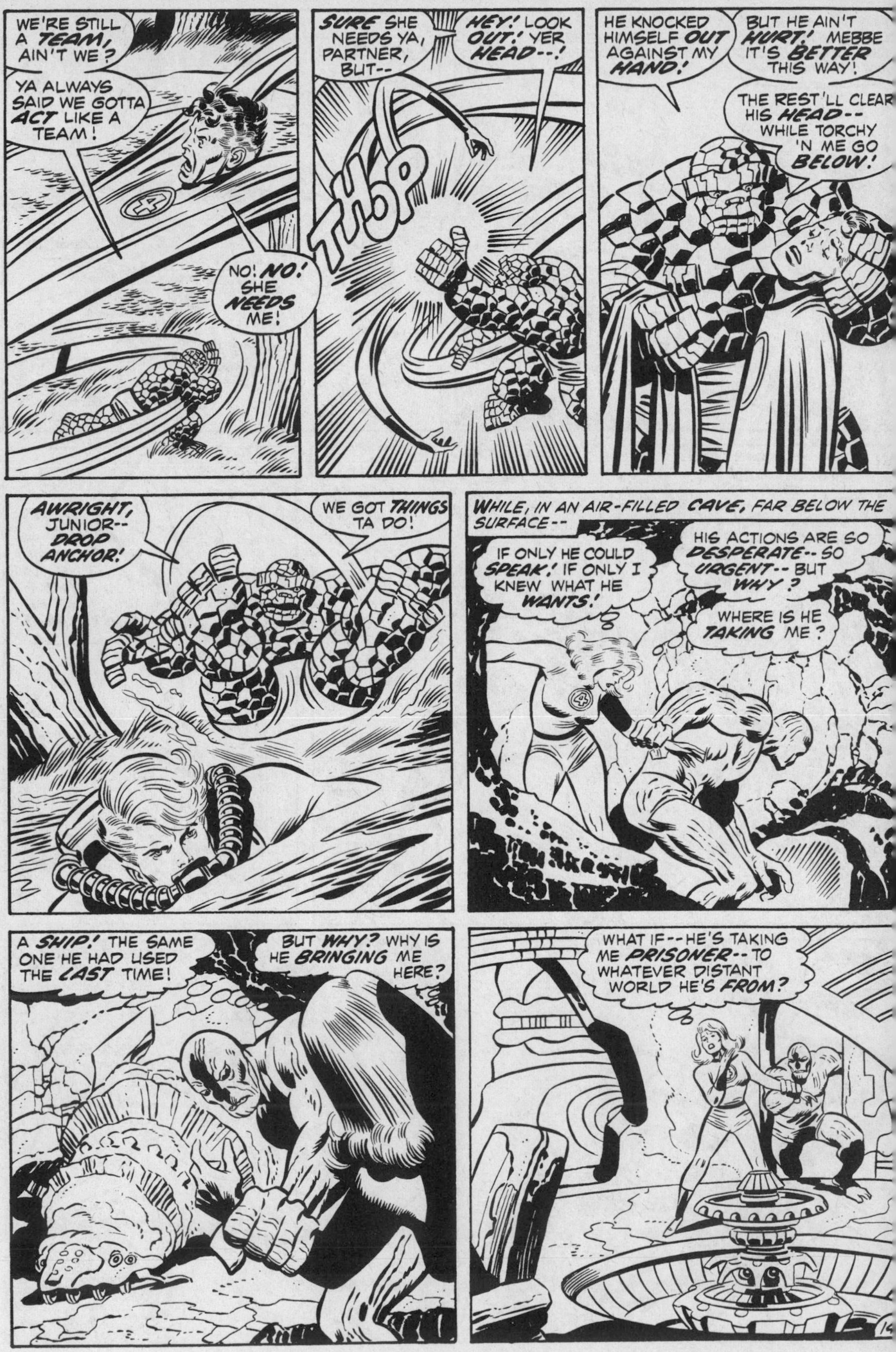
WE'RE STILL A TEAM, AIN'T WE?
YA ALWAYS SAID WE GOTTA ACT LIKE A TEAM!
NO! NO! SHE NEEDS ME!
SURE SHE NEEDS YA, PARTNER, BUT--
HEY! LOOK OUT! YER HEAD--!
THOP
HE KNOCKED HIMSELF OUT AGAINST MY HAND!
BUT HE AIN'T HURT! MEBBE IT'S BETTER THIS WAY!
THE REST'LL CLEAR HIS HEAD-- WHILE TORCHY 'N ME GO BELOW!
AWRIGHT, JUNIOR-- DROP ANCHOR!
WE GOT THINGS TA DO!
WHILE, IN AN AIR-FILLED CAVE, FAR BELOW THE SURFACE--
IF ONLY HE COULD SPEAK! IF ONLY I KNEW WHAT HE WANTS!
HIS ACTIONS ARE SO DESPERATE-- SO URGENT-- BUT WHY?
WHERE IS HE TAKING ME?
A SHIP! THE SAME ONE HE HAD USED THE LAST TIME!
BUT WHY? WHY IS HE BRINGING ME HERE?
WHAT IF--HE'S TAKING ME PRISONER-- TO WHATEVER DISTANT WORLD HE'S FROM?

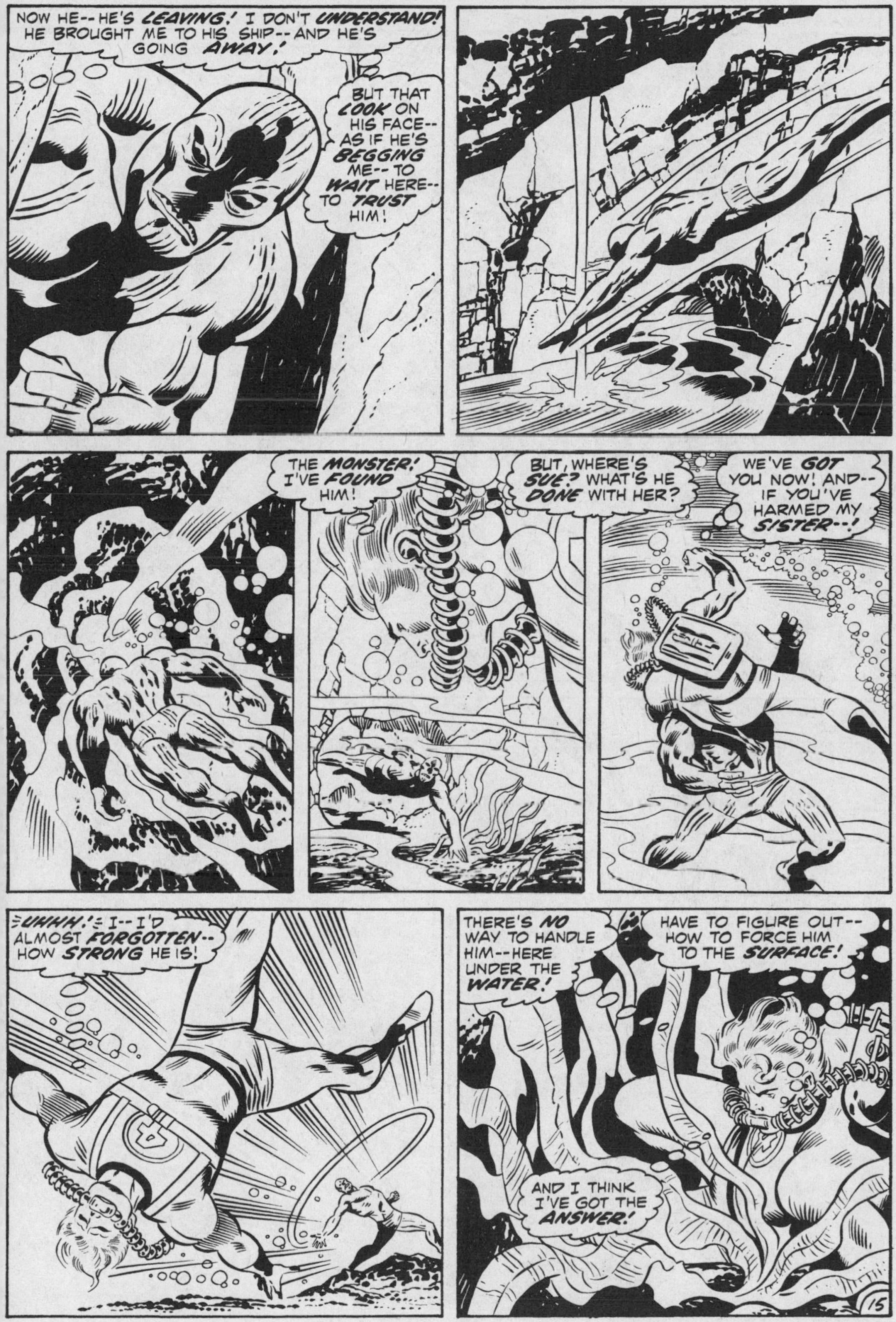

NOW HE-- HE'S LEAVING! I DON'T UNDERSTAND! HE BROUGHT ME TO HIS SHIP-- AND HE'S GOING AWAY!
BUT THAT LOOK ON HIS FACE-- AS IF HE'S BEGGING ME-- TO WAIT HERE-- TO TRUST HIM!
THE MONSTER! I'VE FOUND HIM!
BUT, WHERE'S SUE? WHAT'S HE DONE WITH HER?
WE'VE GOT YOU NOW! AND-- IF YOU'VE HARMED MY SISTER--!
UHHH! I-- I'D ALMOST FORGOTTEN-- HOW STRONG HE IS!
THERE'S NO WAY TO HANDLE HIM--HERE UNDER THE WATER!
HAVE TO FIGURE OUT-- HOW TO FORCE HIM TO THE SURFACE!
AND I THINK I'VE GOT THE ANSWER!
15

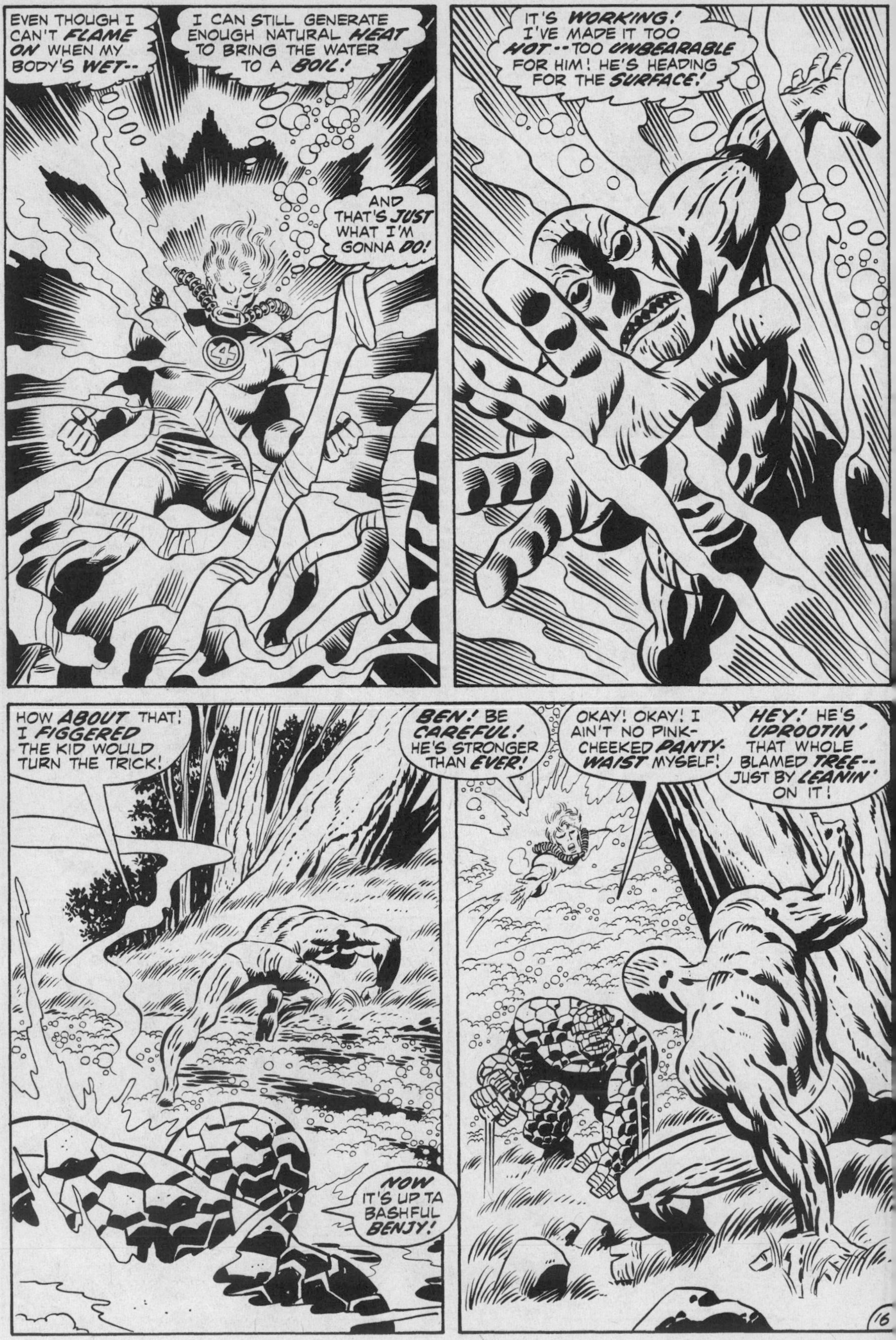

EVEN THOUGH I CAN'T FLAME ON WHEN MY BODY'S WET--
I CAN STILL GENERATE ENOUGH NATURAL HEAT TO BRING THE WATER TO A BOIL!
AND THAT'S JUST WHAT I'M GONNA DO!
IT'S WORKING! I'VE MADE IT TOO HOT--TOO UNBEARABLE FOR HIM! HE'S HEADING FOR THE SURFACE!
HOW ABOUT THAT! I FIGGERED THE KID WOULD TURN THE TRICK!
NOW IT'S UP TA BASHFUL BENJY!
BEN! BE CAREFUL! HE'S STRONGER THAN EVER!
OKAY! OKAY! I AIN'T NO PINK-CHEEKED PANTY-WAIST MYSELF!
HEY! HE'S UPROOTIN' THAT WHOLE BLAMED TREE--JUST BY LEANIN' ON IT!
16

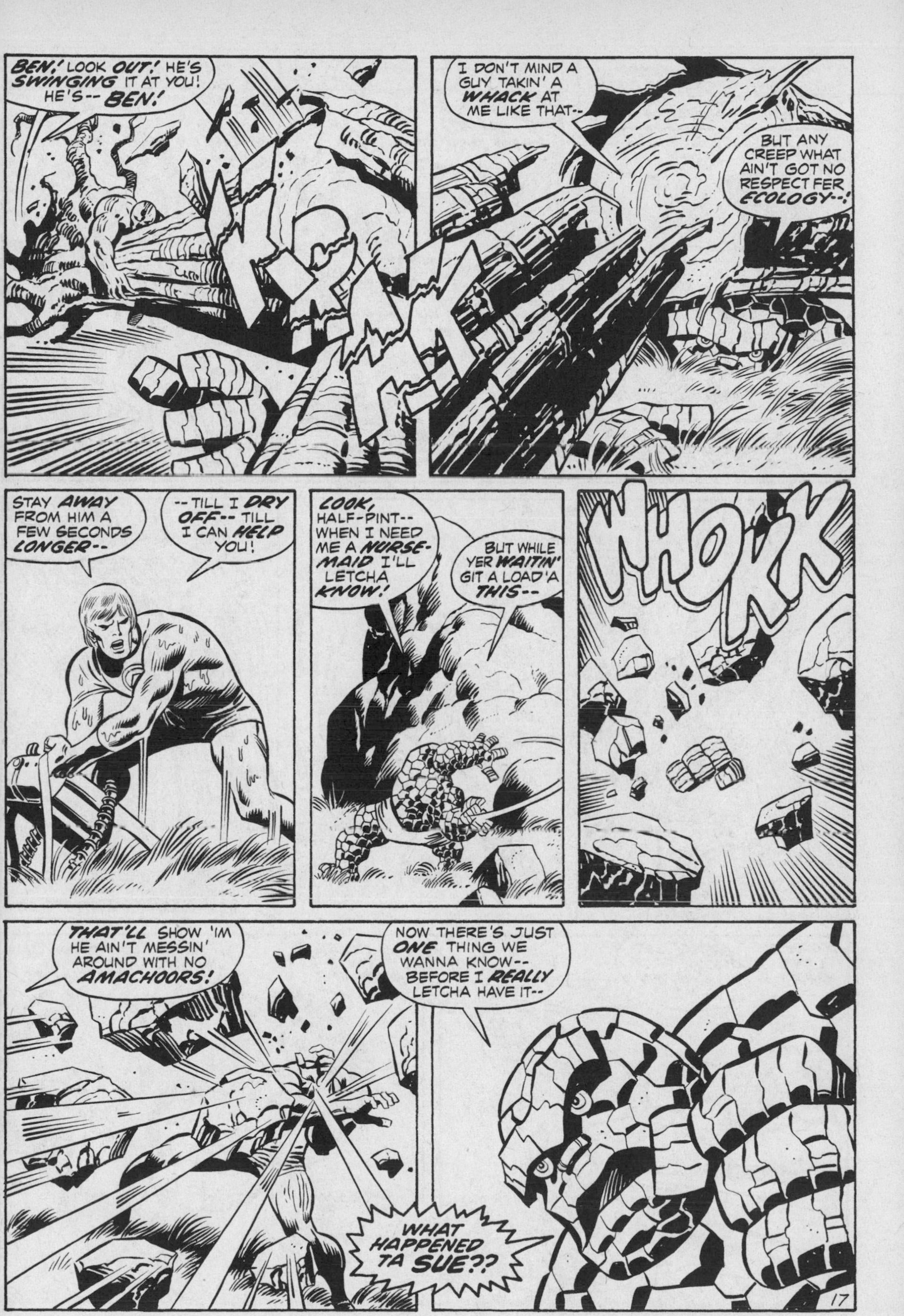
BEN! LOOK OUT! HE'S SWINGING IT AT YOU! HE'S-- BEN!
KRAKK
I DON'T MIND A GUY TAKIN' A WHACK AT ME LIKE THAT--
BUT ANY CREEP WHAT AIN'T GOT NO RESPECT FER ECOLOGY--!
STAY AWAY FROM HIM A FEW SECONDS LONGER--
--TILL I DRY OFF-- TILL I CAN HELP YOU!
LOOK, HALF-PINT-- WHEN I NEED ME A NURSE-MAID I'LL LETCHA KNOW!
BUT WHILE YER WAITIN' GIT A LOAD'A THIS--
WHOKK
THAT'LL SHOW 'IM HE AIN'T MESSIN' AROUND WITH NO AMACHOORS!
NOW THERE'S JUST ONE THING WE WANNA KNOW-- BEFORE I REALLY LETCHA HAVE IT--
WHAT HAPPENED TA SUE??

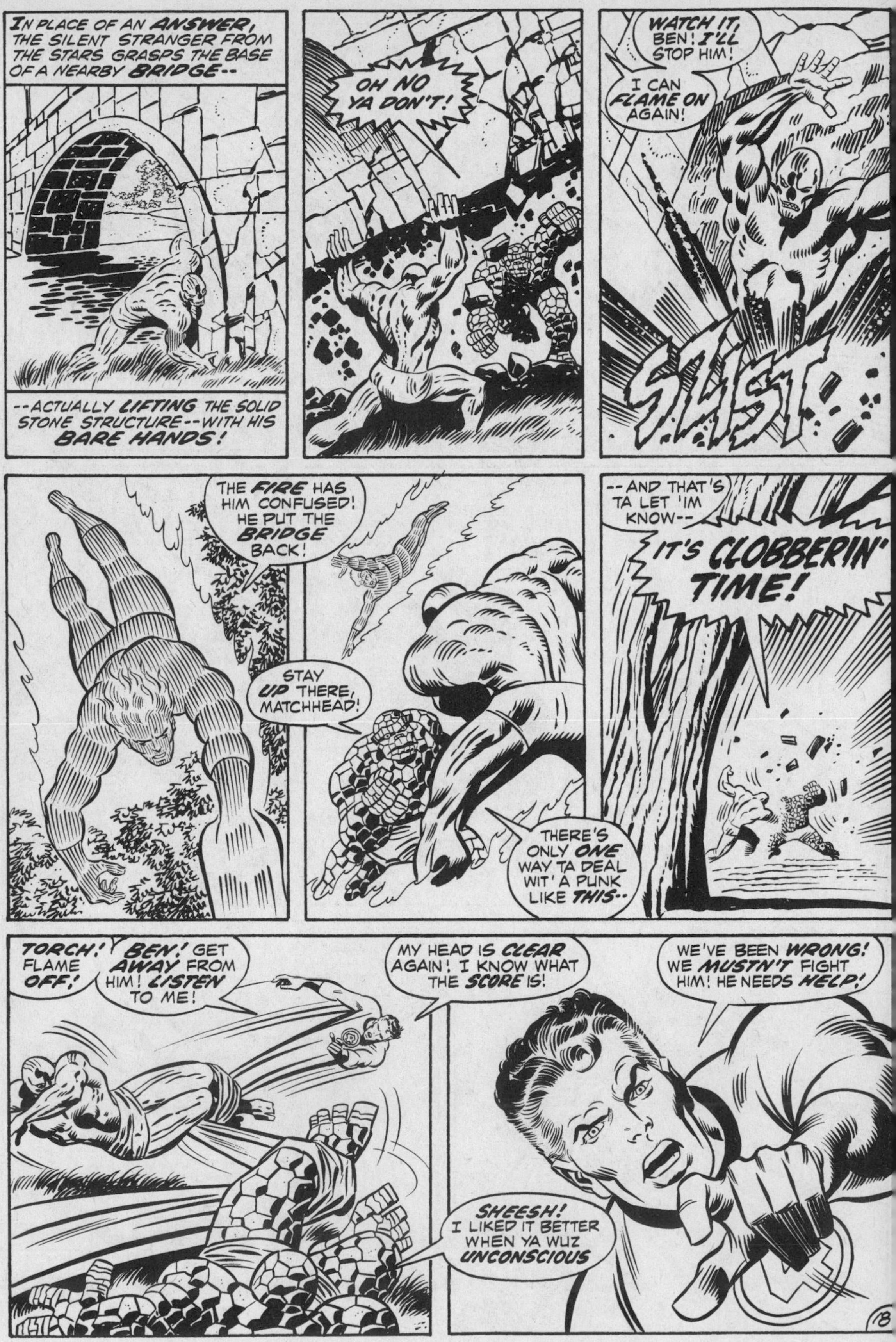
IN PLACE OF AN ANSWER, THE SILENT STRANGER FROM THE STARS GRASPS THE BASE OF A NEARBY BRIDGE--
--ACTUALLY LIFTING THE SOLID STONE STRUCTURE--WITH HIS BARE HANDS!
OH NO YA DON'T!
WATCH IT, BEN! I'LL STOP HIM!
I CAN FLAME ON AGAIN!
SSSST
THE FIRE HAS HIM CONFUSED! HE PUT THE BRIDGE BACK!
STAY UP THERE, MATCHHEAD!
THERE'S ONLY ONE WAY TA DEAL WIT' A PUNK LIKE THIS--
--AND THAT'S TA LET 'IM KNOW--
IT'S CLOBBERIN' TIME!
TORCH! FLAME OFF!
BEN! GET AWAY FROM HIM! LISTEN TO ME!
MY HEAD IS CLEAR AGAIN! I KNOW WHAT THE SCORE IS!
WE'VE BEEN WRONG! WE MUSTN'T FIGHT HIM! HE NEEDS HELP!
SHEESH! I LIKED IT BETTER WHEN YA WUZ UNCONSCIOUS
18

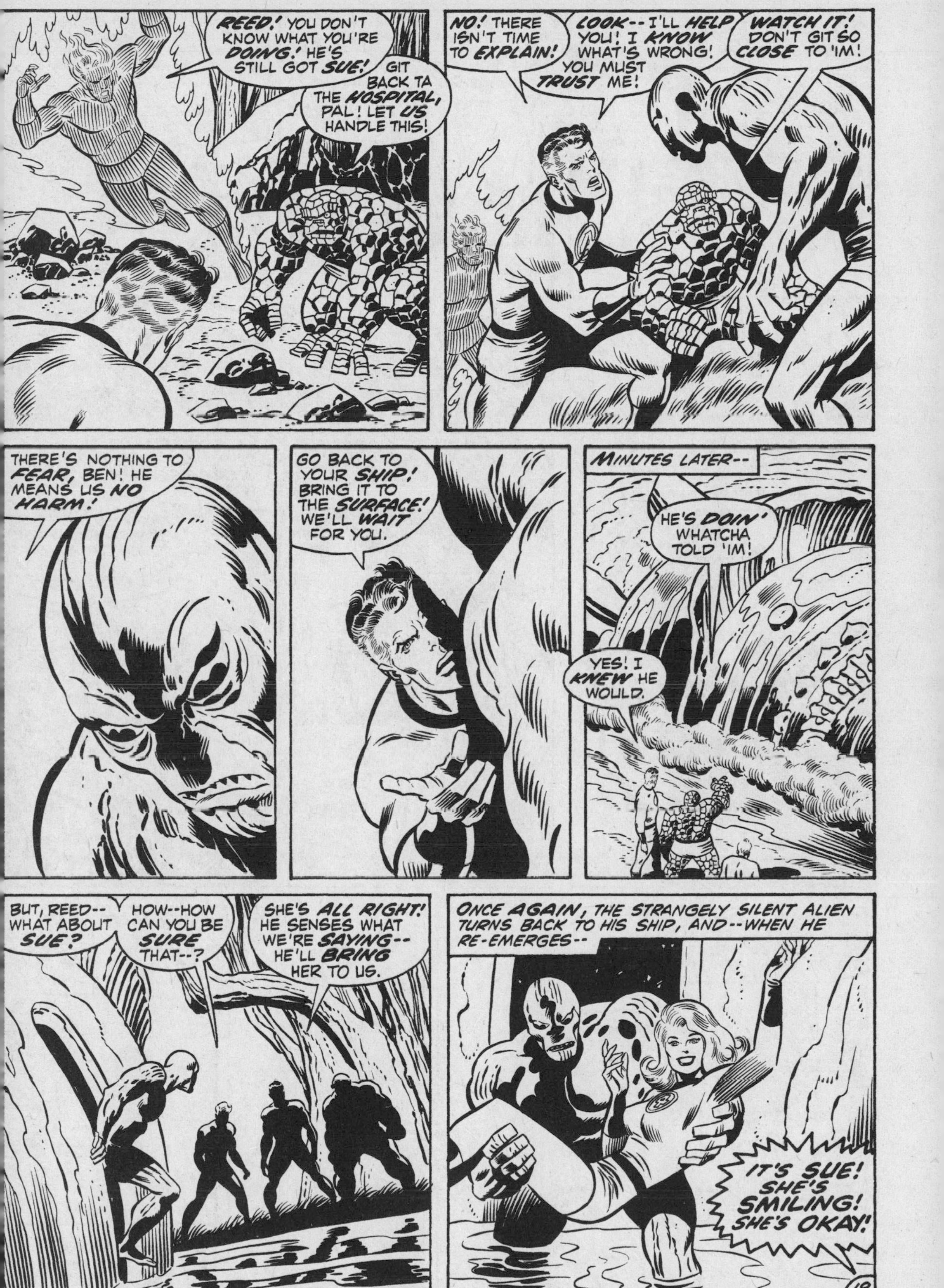
REED! YOU DON'T KNOW WHAT YOU'RE DOING! HE'S STILL GOT SUE!
GIT BACK TA THE HOSPITAL, PAL! LET US HANDLE THIS!
NO! THERE ISN'T TIME TO EXPLAIN!
LOOK--I'LL HELP YOU! I KNOW WHAT'S WRONG! YOU MUST TRUST ME!
WATCH IT! DON'T GIT SO CLOSE TO 'IM!
THERE'S NOTHING TO FEAR, BEN! HE MEANS US NO HARM!
GO BACK TO YOUR SHIP! BRING IT TO THE SURFACE! WE'LL WAIT FOR YOU.
MINUTES LATER--
HE'S DOIN' WHATCHA TOLD 'IM!
YES! I KNEW HE WOULD.
BUT, REED--WHAT ABOUT SUE?
HOW--HOW CAN YOU BE SURE THAT--?
SHE'S ALL RIGHT! HE SENSES WHAT WE'RE SAYING--HE'LL BRING HER TO US.
ONCE AGAIN, THE STRANGELY SILENT ALIEN TURNS BACK TO HIS SHIP, AND--WHEN HE RE-EMERGES--
IT'S SUE! SHE'S SMILING! SHE'S OKAY!
19

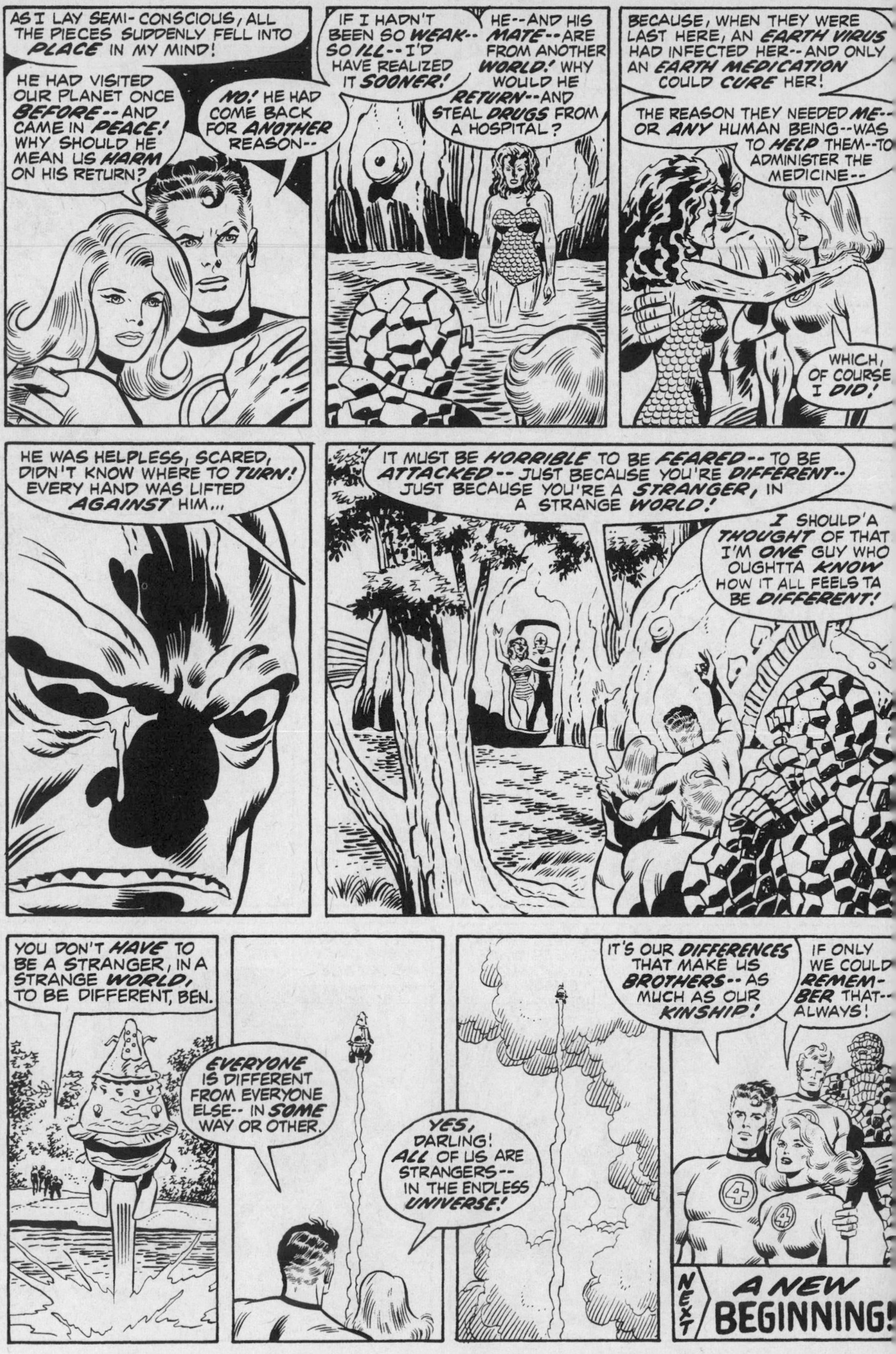
AS I LAY SEMI-CONSCIOUS, ALL THE PIECES SUDDENLY FELL INTO PLACE IN MY MIND!
HE HAD VISITED OUR PLANET ONCE BEFORE--AND CAME IN PEACE! WHY SHOULD HE MEAN US HARM ON HIS RETURN?
NO! HE HAD COME BACK FOR ANOTHER REASON--
IF I HADN'T BEEN SO WEAK-- SO ILL--I'D HAVE REALIZED IT SOONER!
HE--AND HIS MATE--ARE FROM ANOTHER WORLD! WHY WOULD HE RETURN--AND STEAL DRUGS FROM A HOSPITAL?
BECAUSE, WHEN THEY WERE LAST HERE, AN EARTH VIRUS HAD INFECTED HER--AND ONLY AN EARTH MEDICATION COULD CURE HER!
THE REASON THEY NEEDED ME--OR ANY HUMAN BEING--WAS TO HELP THEM--TO ADMINISTER THE MEDICINE--
WHICH, OF COURSE I DID!
HE WAS HELPLESS, SCARED, DIDN'T KNOW WHERE TO TURN! EVERY HAND WAS LIFTED AGAINST HIM...
IT MUST BE HORRIBLE TO BE FEARED--TO BE ATTACKED--JUST BECAUSE YOU'RE DIFFERENT--JUST BECAUSE YOU'RE A STRANGER, IN A STRANGE WORLD!
I SHOULD'A THOUGHT OF THAT. I'M ONE GUY WHO OUGHTTA KNOW HOW IT ALL FEELS TA BE DIFFERENT!
YOU DON'T HAVE TO BE A STRANGER, IN A STRANGE WORLD, TO BE DIFFERENT, BEN.
EVERYONE IS DIFFERENT FROM EVERYONE ELSE--IN SOME WAY OR OTHER.
YES, DARLING! ALL OF US ARE STRANGERS--IN THE ENDLESS UNIVERSE!
IT'S OUR DIFFERENCES THAT MAKE US BROTHERS--AS MUCH AS OUR KINSHIP!
IF ONLY WE COULD REMEMBER THAT--ALWAYS!
NEXT
A NEW BEGINNING!

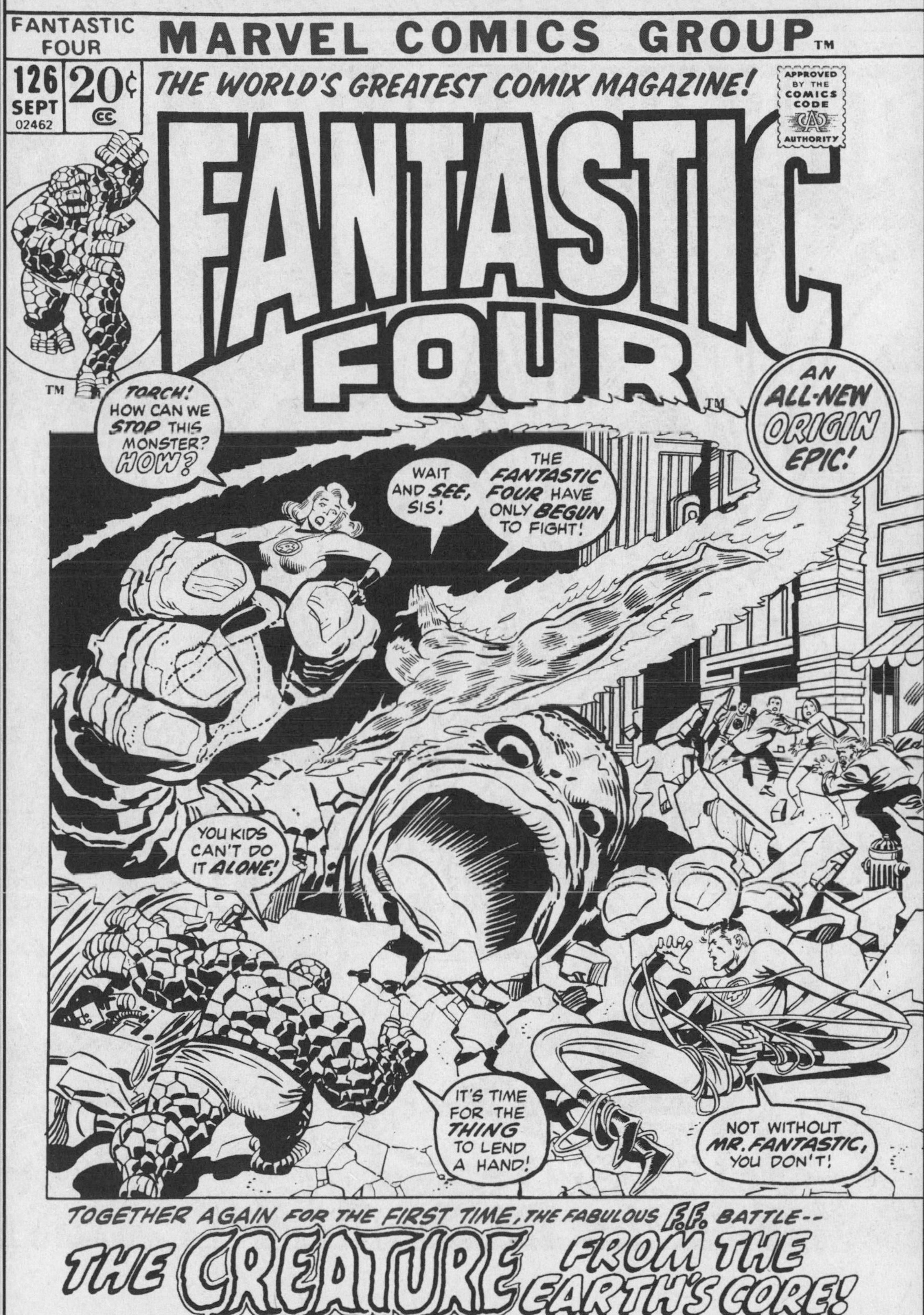
FANTASTIC FOUR
MARVEL COMICS GROUP
126 SEPT 02462
20¢
THE WORLD'S GREATEST COMIX MAGAZINE!
APPROVED BY THE COMICS CODE AUTHORITY
FANTASTIC FOUR
AN ALL-NEW ORIGIN EPIC!
TORCH! HOW CAN WE STOP THIS MONSTER? HOW?
WAIT AND SEE, SIS!
THE FANTASTIC FOUR HAVE ONLY BEGUN TO FIGHT!
YOU KIDS CAN'T DO IT ALONE!
IT'S TIME FOR THE THING TO LEND A HAND!
NOT WITHOUT MR. FANTASTIC, YOU DON'T!
TOGETHER AGAIN FOR THE FIRST TIME, THE FABULOUS F.F. BATTLE--
THE CREATURE FROM THE EARTH'S CORE!

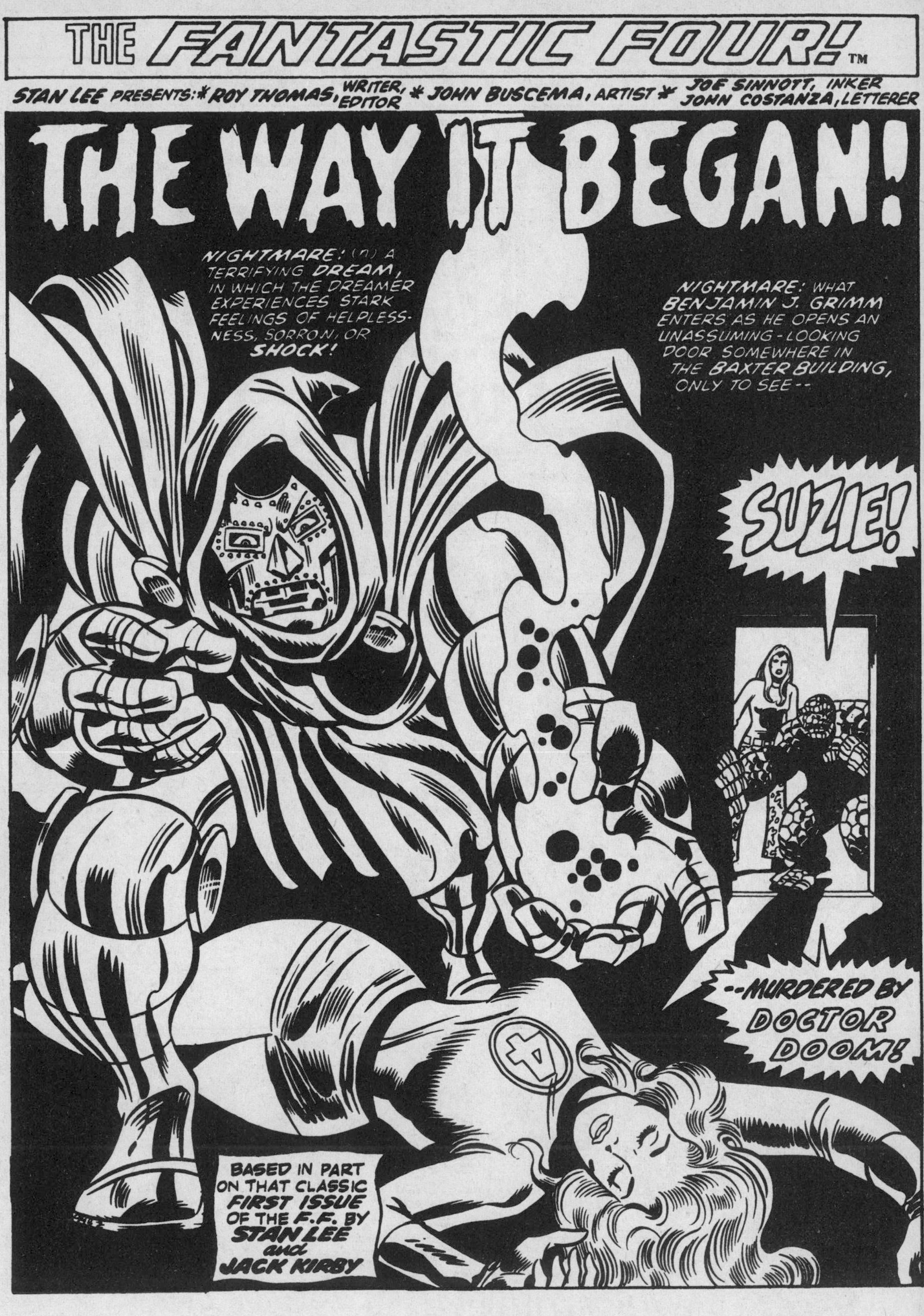
THE FANTASTIC FOUR!™
STAN LEE PRESENTS: * ROY THOMAS, WRITER, EDITOR * JOHN BUSCEMA, ARTIST * JOE SINNOTT, INKER JOHN COSTANZA, LETTERER
THE WAY IT BEGAN!
NIGHTMARE: (n) A TERRIFYING DREAM, IN WHICH THE DREAMER EXPERIENCES STARK FEELINGS OF HELPLESSNESS, SORROW, OR SHOCK!
NIGHTMARE: WHAT BENJAMIN J. GRIMM ENTERS AS HE OPENS AN UNASSUMING-LOOKING DOOR SOMEWHERE IN THE BAXTER BUILDING, ONLY TO SEE--
SUZIE!
--MURDERED BY DOCTOR DOOM!
BASED IN PART ON THAT CLASSIC FIRST ISSUE OF THE F.F. BY STAN LEE and JACK KIRBY

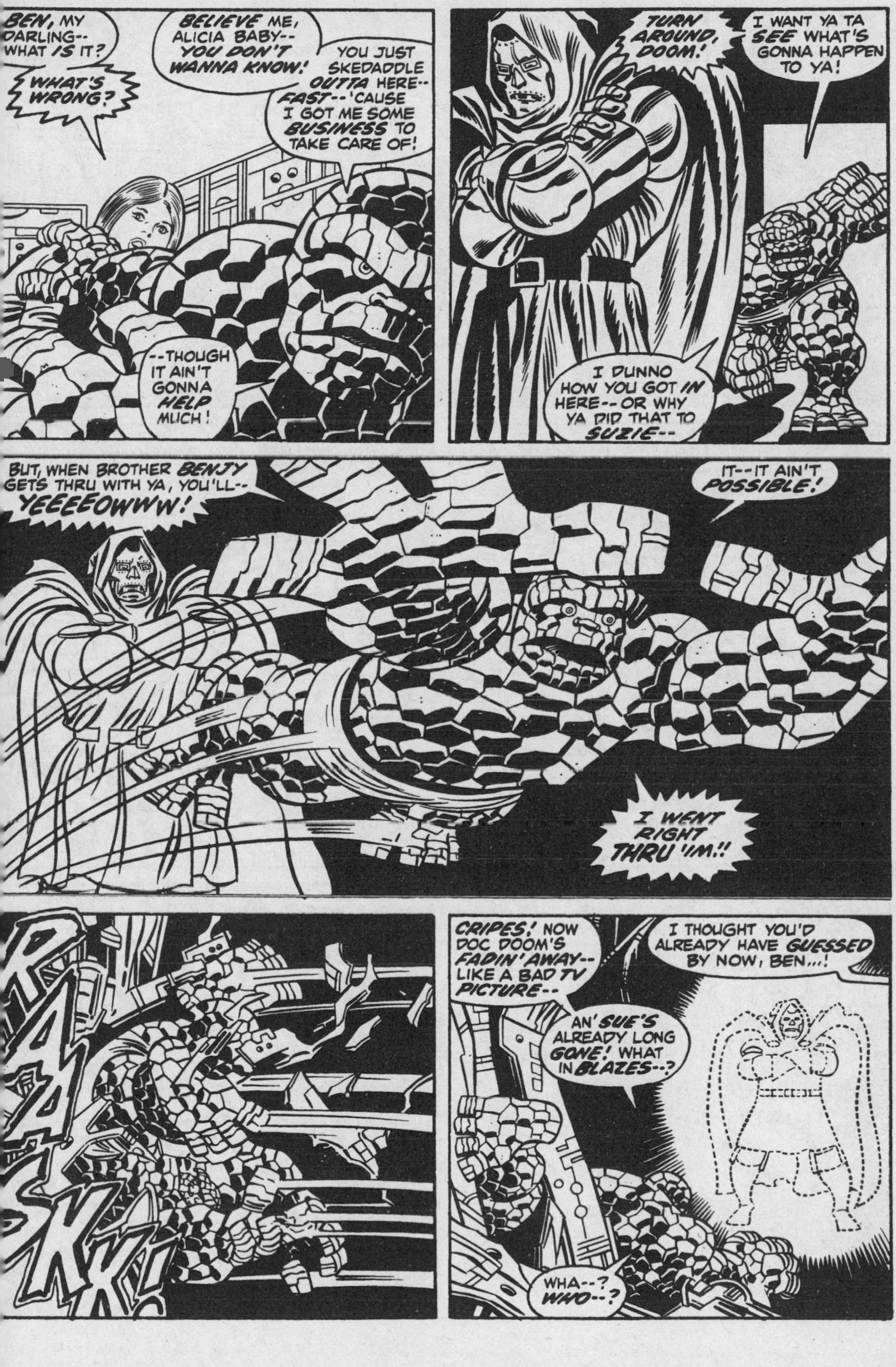
BEN, MY DARLING-- WHAT IS IT?
WHAT'S WRONG?
BELIEVE ME, ALICIA BABY-- YOU DON'T WANNA KNOW!
YOU JUST SKEDADDLE OUTTA HERE-- FAST--'CAUSE I GOT ME SOME BUSINESS TO TAKE CARE OF!
--THOUGH IT AIN'T GONNA HELP MUCH!
TURN AROUND, DOOM!
I WANT YA TA SEE WHAT'S GONNA HAPPEN TO YA!
I DUNNO HOW YOU GOT IN HERE--OR WHY YA DID THAT TO SUZIE--
BUT, WHEN BROTHER BENJY GETS THRU WITH YA, YOU'LL-- YEEEEOWWW!
IT--IT AIN'T POSSIBLE!
I WENT RIGHT THRU 'IM!!
CRIPES! NOW DOC DOOM'S FADIN' AWAY-- LIKE A BAD TV PICTURE--
AN' SUE'S ALREADY LONG GONE! WHAT IN BLAZES--?
I THOUGHT YOU'D ALREADY HAVE GUESSED BY NOW, BEN...!
WHA--? WHO--?

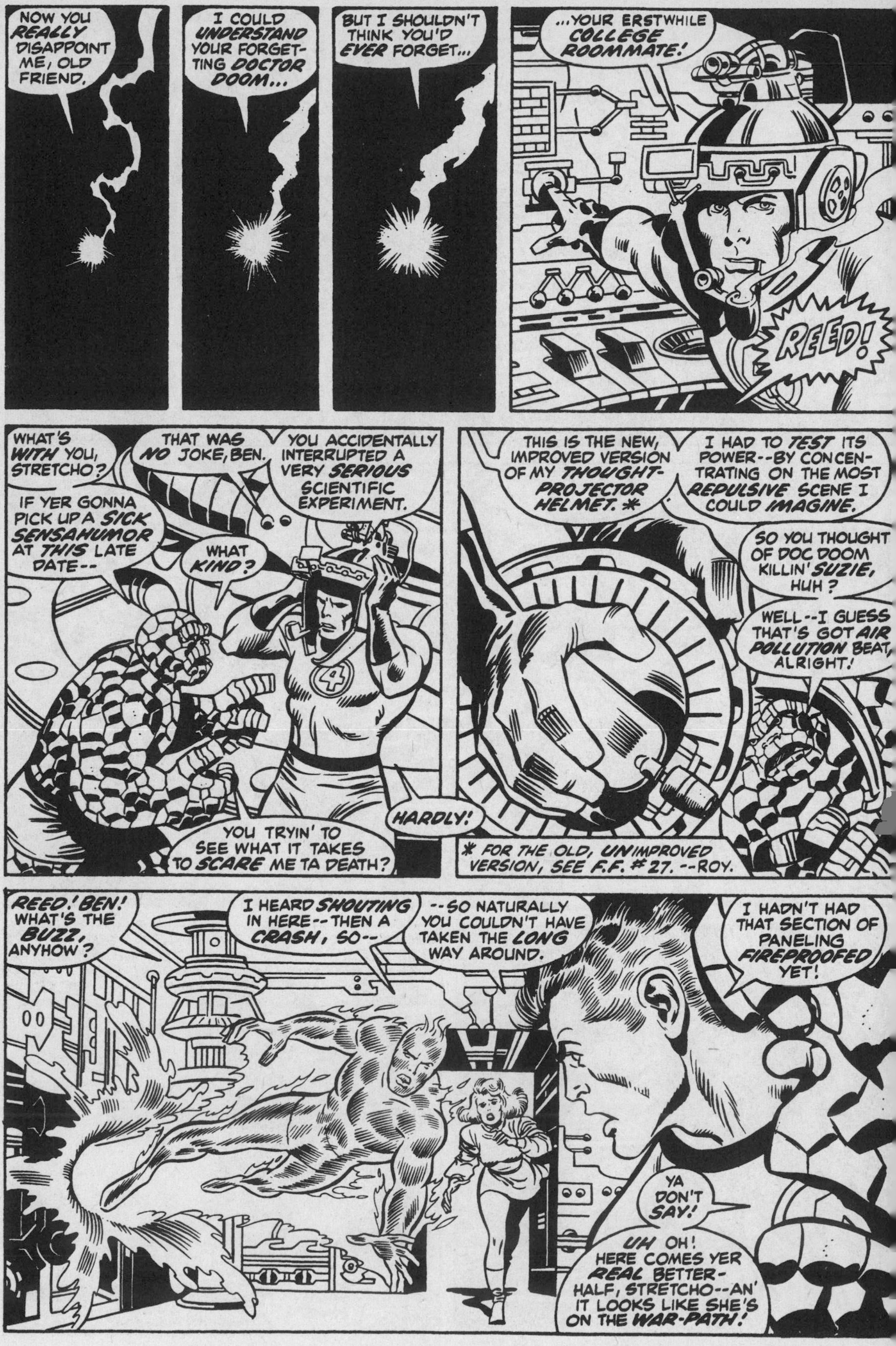
NOW YOU REALLY DISAPPOINT ME, OLD FRIEND.
I COULD UNDERSTAND YOUR FORGETTING DOCTOR DOOM...
BUT I SHOULDN'T THINK YOU'D EVER FORGET...
...YOUR ERSTWHILE COLLEGE ROOMMATE!
REED!
WHAT'S WITH YOU, STRETCHO?
IF YER GONNA PICK UP A SICK SENSAHUMOR AT THIS LATE DATE--
THAT WAS NO JOKE, BEN.
YOU ACCIDENTALLY INTERRUPTED A VERY SERIOUS SCIENTIFIC EXPERIMENT.
WHAT KIND?
YOU TRYIN' TO SEE WHAT IT TAKES TO SCARE ME TA DEATH?
HARDLY!
THIS IS THE NEW, IMPROVED VERSION OF MY THOUGHT-PROJECTOR HELMET. *
I HAD TO TEST ITS POWER--BY CONCENTRATING ON THE MOST REPULSIVE SCENE I COULD IMAGINE.
SO YOU THOUGHT OF DOC DOOM KILLIN' SUZIE, HUH?
WELL--I GUESS THAT'S GOT AIR POLLUTION BEAT, ALRIGHT!
* FOR THE OLD, UNIMPROVED VERSION, SEE F.F. #27. --ROY.
REED! BEN! WHAT'S THE BUZZ, ANYHOW?
I HEARD SHOUTING IN HERE--THEN A CRASH, SO--
--SO NATURALLY YOU COULDN'T HAVE TAKEN THE LONG WAY AROUND.
I HADN'T HAD THAT SECTION OF PANELING FIREPROOFED YET!
YA DON'T SAY!
UH OH! HERE COMES YER REAL BETTER-HALF, STRETCHO--AN' IT LOOKS LIKE SHE'S ON THE WAR-PATH!

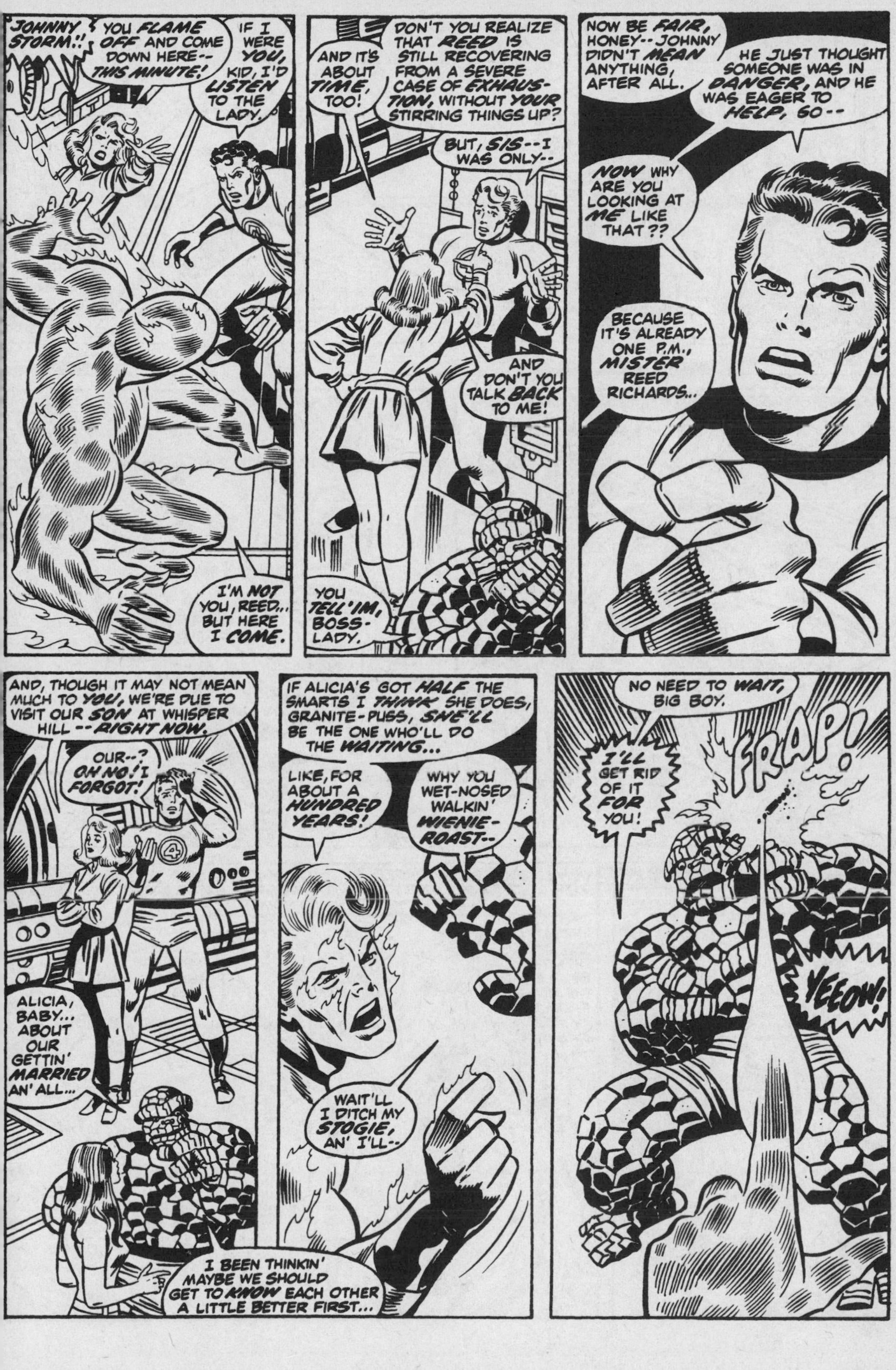

JOHNNY STORM!!
YOU FLAME OFF AND COME DOWN HERE-- THIS MINUTE!
IF I WERE YOU, KID, I'D LISTEN TO THE LADY.
I'M NOT YOU, REED... BUT HERE I COME.
AND IT'S ABOUT TIME, TOO!
DON'T YOU REALIZE THAT REED IS STILL RECOVERING FROM A SEVERE CASE OF EXHAUSTION, WITHOUT YOUR STIRRING THINGS UP?
BUT, SIS--I WAS ONLY--
AND DON'T YOU TALK BACK TO ME!
YOU TELL 'IM, BOSS-LADY.
NOW BE FAIR, HONEY--JOHNNY DIDN'T MEAN ANYTHING, AFTER ALL.
HE JUST THOUGHT SOMEONE WAS IN DANGER, AND HE WAS EAGER TO HELP, SO--
NOW WHY ARE YOU LOOKING AT ME LIKE THAT??
BECAUSE IT'S ALREADY ONE P.M., MISTER REED RICHARDS...
AND, THOUGH IT MAY NOT MEAN MUCH TO YOU, WE'RE DUE TO VISIT OUR SON AT WHISPER HILL --RIGHT NOW.
OUR--? OH NO! I FORGOT!
ALICIA, BABY... ABOUT OUR GETTIN' MARRIED AN' ALL...
I BEEN THINKIN' MAYBE WE SHOULD GET TO KNOW EACH OTHER A LITTLE BETTER FIRST...
IF ALICIA'S GOT HALF THE SMARTS I THINK SHE DOES, GRANITE-PUSS, SHE'LL BE THE ONE WHO'LL DO THE WAITING...
LIKE, FOR ABOUT A HUNDRED YEARS!
WHY YOU WET-NOSED WALKIN' WIENIE-ROAST--
WAIT'LL I DITCH MY STOGIE, AN' I'LL--
NO NEED TO WAIT, BIG BOY.
I'LL GET RID OF IT FOR YOU!
FRAP!
YEEOW!

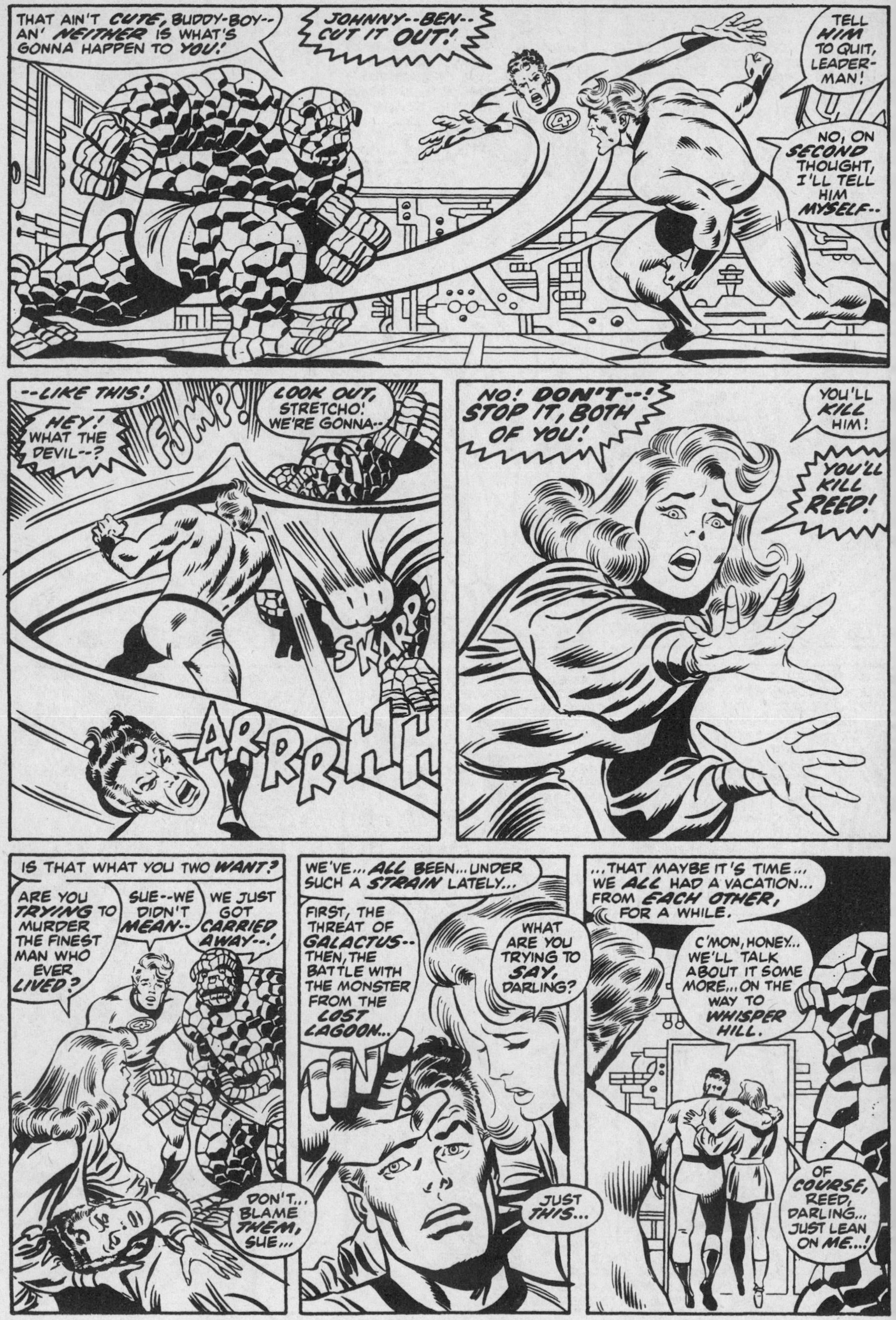
THAT AIN'T CUTE, BUDDY-BOY--AN' NEITHER IS WHAT'S GONNA HAPPEN TO YOU!
JOHNNY--BEN--CUT IT OUT!
TELL HIM TO QUIT, LEADER-MAN!
NO, ON SECOND THOUGHT, I'LL TELL HIM MYSELF--
--LIKE THIS!
HEY! WHAT THE DEVIL--?
FUMP!
LOOK OUT, STRETCHO! WE'RE GONNA--
SKARP!
ARRRHHH
NO! DON'T--! STOP IT, BOTH OF YOU!
YOU'LL KILL HIM!
YOU'LL KILL REED!
IS THAT WHAT YOU TWO WANT?
ARE YOU TRYING TO MURDER THE FINEST MAN WHO EVER LIVED?
SUE--WE DIDN'T MEAN--
WE JUST GOT CARRIED AWAY--!
DON'T... BLAME THEM, SUE...
WE'VE... ALL BEEN... UNDER SUCH A STRAIN LATELY...
FIRST, THE THREAT OF GALACTUS--THEN, THE BATTLE WITH THE MONSTER FROM THE LOST LAGOON...
WHAT ARE YOU TRYING TO SAY, DARLING?
JUST THIS...
...THAT MAYBE IT'S TIME... WE ALL HAD A VACATION... FROM EACH OTHER, FOR A WHILE.
C'MON, HONEY... WE'LL TALK ABOUT IT SOME MORE... ON THE WAY TO WHISPER HILL.
OF COURSE, REED, DARLING... JUST LEAN ON ME...!

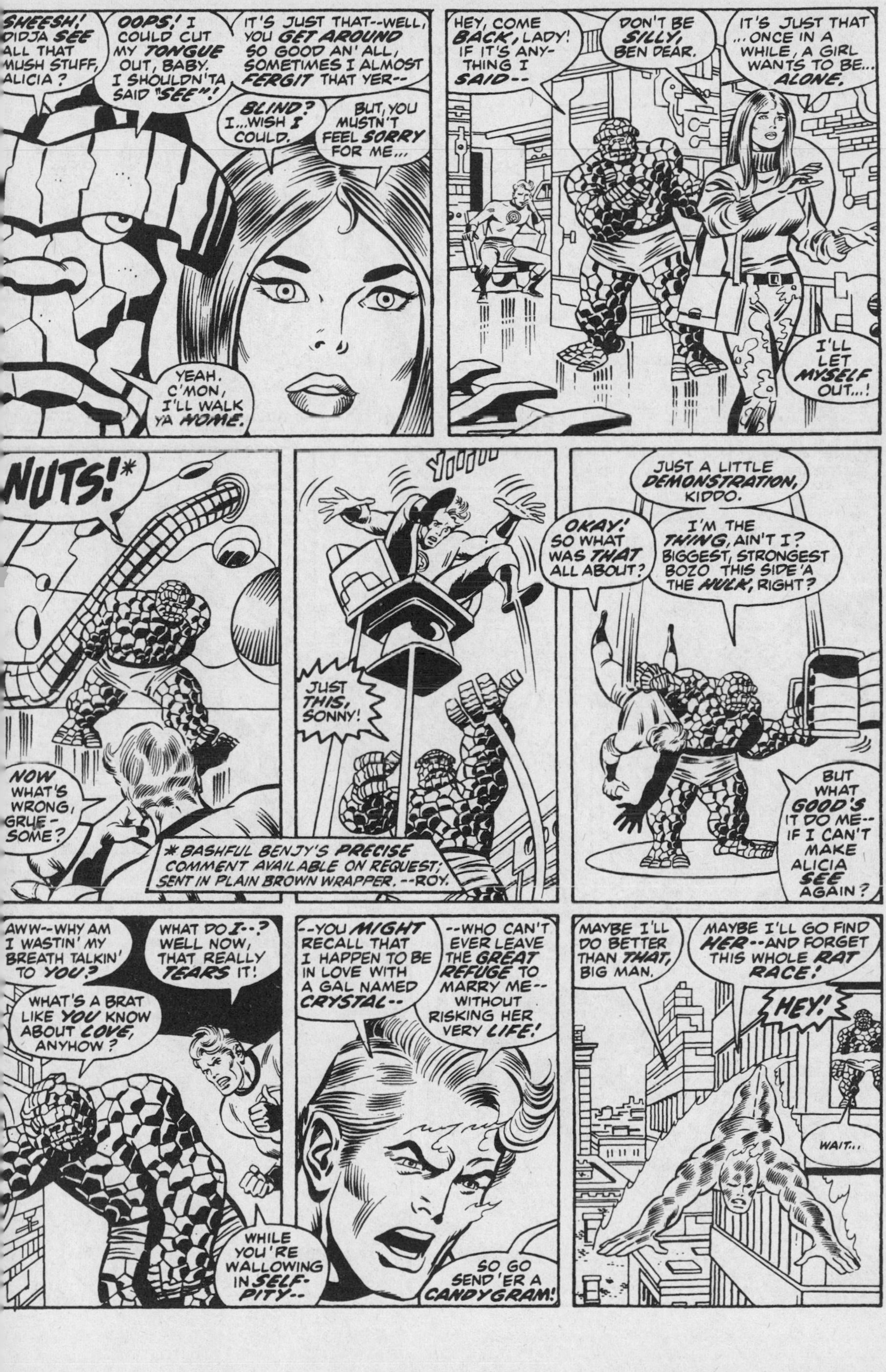
SHEESH! DIDJA SEE ALL THAT MUSH STUFF, ALICIA?
OOPS! I COULD CUT MY TONGUE OUT, BABY. I SHOULDN'TA SAID "SEE"!
IT'S JUST THAT--WELL, YOU GET AROUND SO GOOD AN' ALL, SOMETIMES I ALMOST FERGIT THAT YER--
BLIND? I...WISH I COULD.
BUT, YOU MUSTN'T FEEL SORRY FOR ME...
YEAH. C'MON, I'LL WALK YA HOME.
HEY, COME BACK, LADY! IF IT'S ANY-THING I SAID--
DON'T BE SILLY, BEN DEAR.
IT'S JUST THAT ...ONCE IN A WHILE, A GIRL WANTS TO BE... ALONE.
I'LL LET MYSELF OUT...!
NUTS!*
NOW WHAT'S WRONG, GRUE-SOME?
* BASHFUL BENJY'S PRECISE COMMENT AVAILABLE ON REQUEST; SENT IN PLAIN BROWN WRAPPER. --ROY.
JUST THIS, SONNY!
JUST A LITTLE DEMONSTRATION, KIDDO.
OKAY! SO WHAT WAS THAT ALL ABOUT?
I'M THE THING, AIN'T I? BIGGEST, STRONGEST BOZO THIS SIDE 'A THE HULK, RIGHT?
BUT WHAT GOOD'S IT DO ME-- IF I CAN'T MAKE ALICIA SEE AGAIN?
AWW--WHY AM I WASTIN' MY BREATH TALKIN' TO YOU?
WHAT DO I--? WELL NOW, THAT REALLY TEARS IT!
WHAT'S A BRAT LIKE YOU KNOW ABOUT LOVE, ANYHOW?
--YOU MIGHT RECALL THAT I HAPPEN TO BE IN LOVE WITH A GAL NAMED CRYSTAL--
--WHO CAN'T EVER LEAVE THE GREAT REFUGE TO MARRY ME-- WITHOUT RISKING HER VERY LIFE!
WHILE YOU'RE WALLOWING IN SELF-PITY--
SO GO SEND 'ER A CANDYGRAM!
MAYBE I'LL DO BETTER THAN THAT, BIG MAN.
MAYBE I'LL GO FIND HER--AND FORGET THIS WHOLE RAT RACE!
HEY!
WAIT...

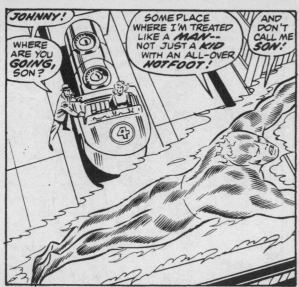

JOHNNY! WHERE ARE YOU *GOING,* SON?

SOME PLACE WHERE I'M TREATED LIKE A *MAN*--NOT JUST A *KID* WITH AN ALL-OVER *HOTFOOT!*

AND DON'T CALL ME *SON!*

SUE...THIS MAY SEEM A BIT *SUPERFLUOUS,* IN LIGHT OF THAT LITTLE SCENE...BUT I'M *WORRIED* ABOUT YOUR BROTHER.

EVER SINCE *CRYSTAL* HAD TO RETURN TO THE *HIDDEN LAND,* HE HASN'T BEEN *HIMSELF.*

BUT--WHAT IF HE *HAS,* REED? WHAT IF THAT BLAZING, *HOSTILE* MAN--IS THE *REAL* JOHNNY STORM?

THEN *PRAY,* HONEY--FOR US, AND FOR THE *WORLD!*

SOME SWINGIN' SUPERHERO *I* AM!

THE CLOSEST THING I GOT TO A *FRIEND* IN THE *WORLD* OUTSIDE 'A REED...

...AN I GOTTA SHOOT OFF MY MOUTH AN' SEND 'IM *PACKIN'!*

STILL, LONG AS I'M *ALONE* AN' ALL...

MAYBE I NEED ME A LITTLE *DISTRACTION...*

LIKE THIS *THOUGHT-PROJECTOR* GIZMO OF REED'S!

HEY, WADDAYA *KNOW!* IT *FITS!*

REED MUST BE MORE *SWELL-HEADED* THAN I *THOUGHT.*

LESSEE NOW...OL' BIG-WORDS DOUSED THE *LIGHTS* FIRST...

THEN, JUST TO TEST IT OUT, HE THOUGHT 'A THE MOST *REPULSIVE* THING HE *COULD.*

GUESS I MIGHT AS WELL DO THE *SAME.*

ONLY CATCH IS, THE MOST REVOLTIN' THING I CAN THINK OF--

--IS *ME!*

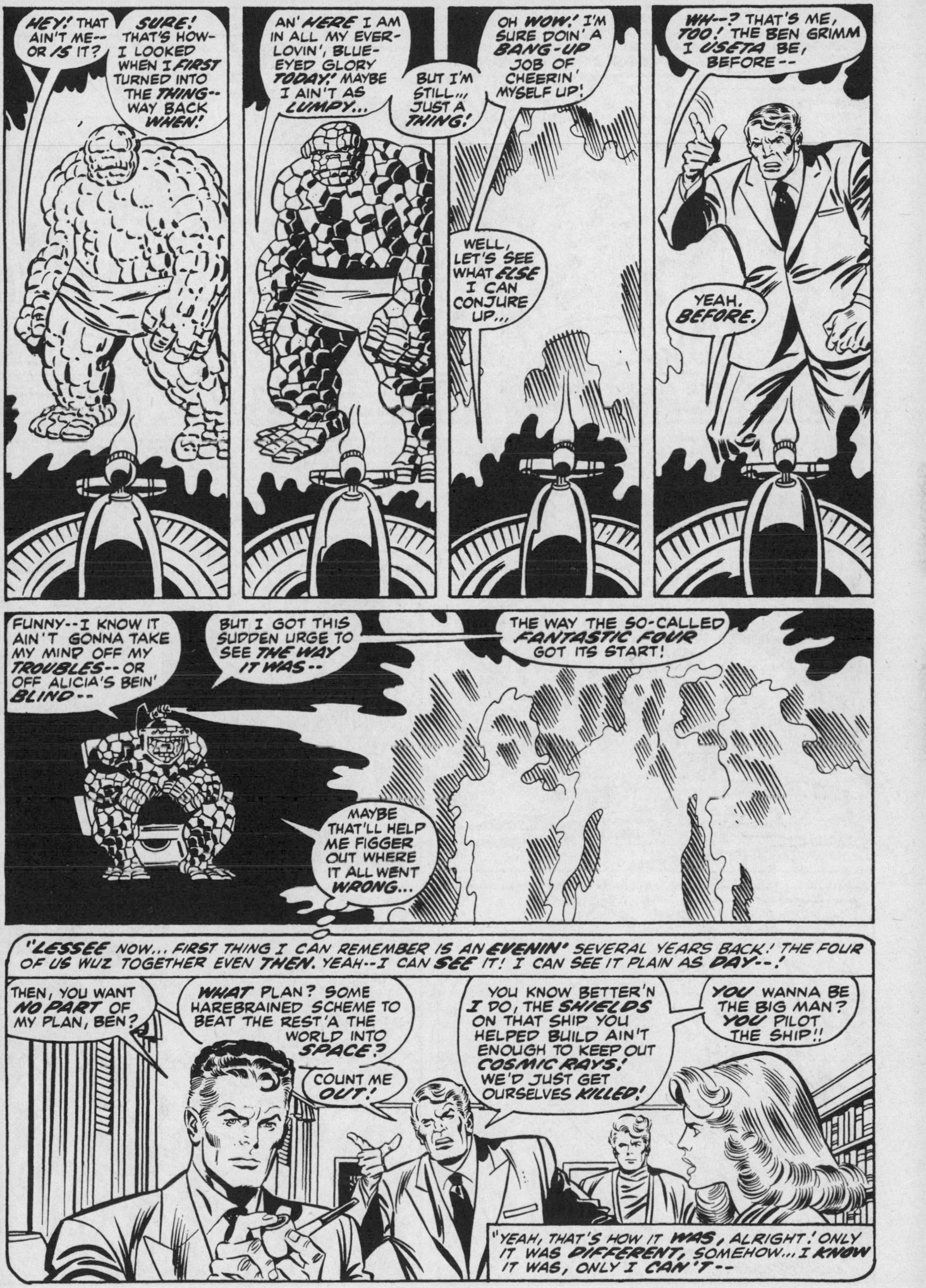
HEY! THAT AIN'T ME-- OR IS IT?
SURE! THAT'S HOW-- I LOOKED WHEN I FIRST TURNED INTO THE THING-- WAY BACK WHEN!
AN' HERE I AM IN ALL MY EVER-LOVIN', BLUE-EYED GLORY TODAY! MAYBE I AIN'T AS LUMPY...
BUT I'M STILL... JUST A THING!
OH WOW! I'M SURE DOIN' A BANG-UP JOB OF CHEERIN' MYSELF UP!
WELL, LET'S SEE WHAT ELSE I CAN CONJURE UP...
WH--? THAT'S ME, TOO! THE BEN GRIMM I USETA BE, BEFORE--
YEAH. BEFORE.
FUNNY--I KNOW IT AIN'T GONNA TAKE MY MIND OFF MY TROUBLES-- OR OFF ALICIA'S BEIN' BLIND--
BUT I GOT THIS SUDDEN URGE TO SEE THE WAY IT WAS--
THE WAY THE SO-CALLED FANTASTIC FOUR GOT ITS START!
MAYBE THAT'LL HELP ME FIGGER OUT WHERE IT ALL WENT WRONG...
"LESSEE NOW... FIRST THING I CAN REMEMBER IS AN EVENIN' SEVERAL YEARS BACK! THE FOUR OF US WUZ TOGETHER EVEN THEN. YEAH--I CAN SEE IT! I CAN SEE IT PLAIN AS DAY--!
THEN, YOU WANT NO PART OF MY PLAN, BEN?
WHAT PLAN? SOME HAREBRAINED SCHEME TO BEAT THE REST'A THE WORLD INTO SPACE?
COUNT ME OUT!
YOU KNOW BETTER'N I DO, THE SHIELDS ON THAT SHIP YOU HELPED BUILD AIN'T ENOUGH TO KEEP OUT COSMIC RAYS! WE'D JUST GET OURSELVES KILLED!
YOU WANNA BE THE BIG MAN? YOU PILOT THE SHIP!!
"YEAH, THAT'S HOW IT WAS, ALRIGHT! ONLY IT WAS DIFFERENT, SOMEHOW... I KNOW IT WAS, ONLY I CAN'T--

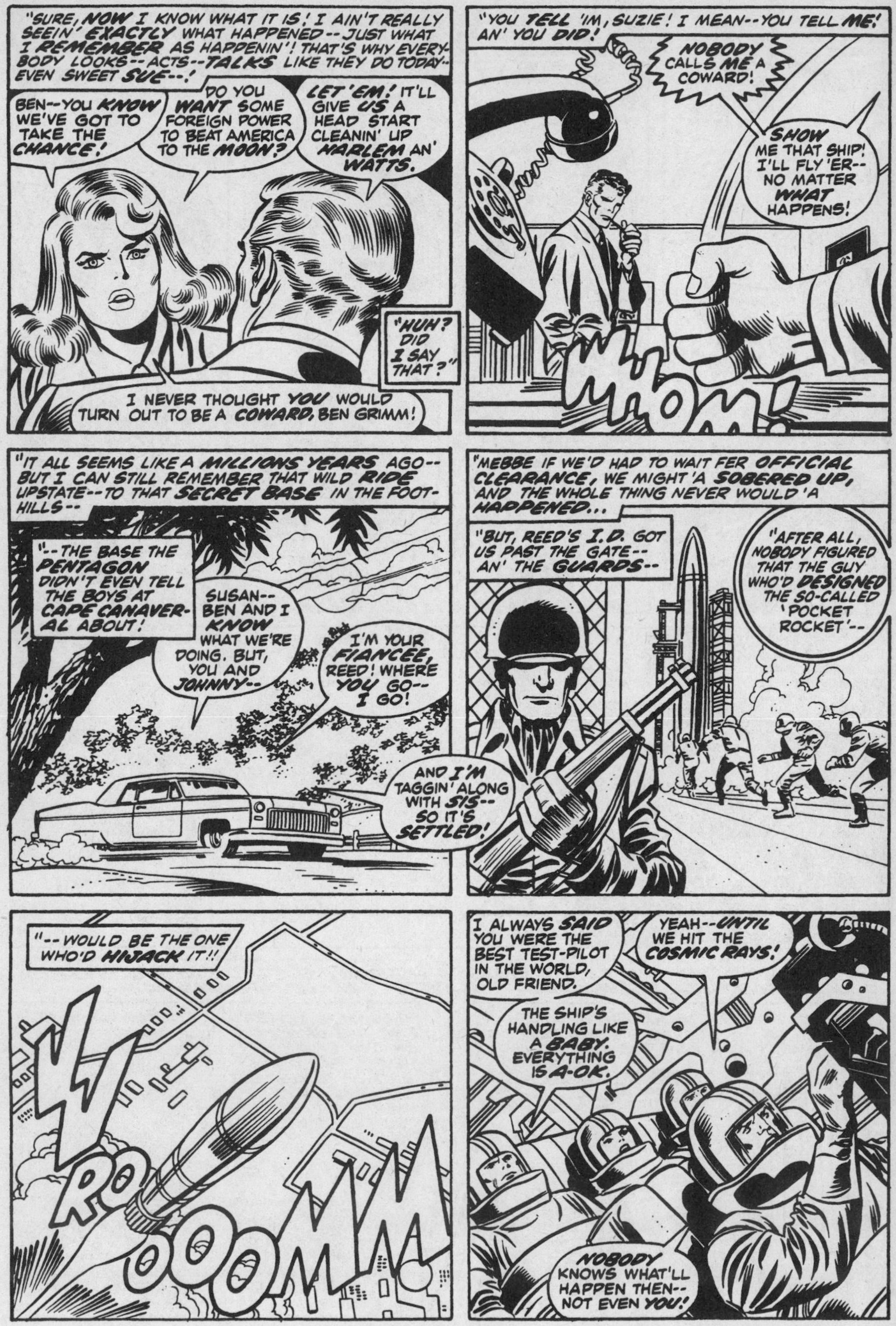
"SURE, NOW I KNOW WHAT IT IS! I AIN'T REALLY SEEIN' EXACTLY WHAT HAPPENED--JUST WHAT I REMEMBER AS HAPPENIN'! THAT'S WHY EVERY-BODY LOOKS--ACTS--TALKS LIKE THEY DO TODAY-EVEN SWEET SUE--!
BEN--YOU KNOW WE'VE GOT TO TAKE THE CHANCE!
DO YOU WANT SOME FOREIGN POWER TO BEAT AMERICA TO THE MOON?
LET 'EM! IT'LL GIVE US A HEAD START CLEANIN' UP HARLEM AN' WATTS.
"HUH? DID I SAY THAT?"
I NEVER THOUGHT YOU WOULD TURN OUT TO BE A COWARD, BEN GRIMM!
"YOU TELL 'IM, SUZIE! I MEAN--YOU TELL ME! AN' YOU DID!
NOBODY CALLS ME A COWARD!
SHOW ME THAT SHIP! I'LL FLY 'ER--NO MATTER WHAT HAPPENS!
WHOM!
"IT ALL SEEMS LIKE A MILLIONS YEARS AGO--BUT I CAN STILL REMEMBER THAT WILD RIDE UPSTATE--TO THAT SECRET BASE IN THE FOOT-HILLS--
"--THE BASE THE PENTAGON DIDN'T EVEN TELL THE BOYS AT CAPE CANAVERAL ABOUT!
SUSAN--BEN AND I KNOW WHAT WE'RE DOING. BUT, YOU AND JOHNNY--
I'M YOUR FIANCEE, REED! WHERE YOU GO--I GO!
AND I'M TAGGIN' ALONG WITH SIS--SO IT'S SETTLED!
"MEBBE IF WE'D HAD TO WAIT FER OFFICIAL CLEARANCE, WE MIGHT 'A SOBERED UP, AND THE WHOLE THING NEVER WOULD 'A HAPPENED...
"BUT, REED'S I.D. GOT US PAST THE GATE--AN' THE GUARDS--
"AFTER ALL, NOBODY FIGURED THAT THE GUY WHO'D DESIGNED THE SO-CALLED 'POCKET ROCKET'--
"--WOULD BE THE ONE WHO'D HIJACK IT!!
VROOOOMM
I ALWAYS SAID YOU WERE THE BEST TEST-PILOT IN THE WORLD, OLD FRIEND.
YEAH--UNTIL WE HIT THE COSMIC RAYS!
THE SHIP'S HANDLING LIKE A BABY. EVERYTHING IS A-OK.
NOBODY KNOWS WHAT'LL HAPPEN THEN--NOT EVEN YOU!

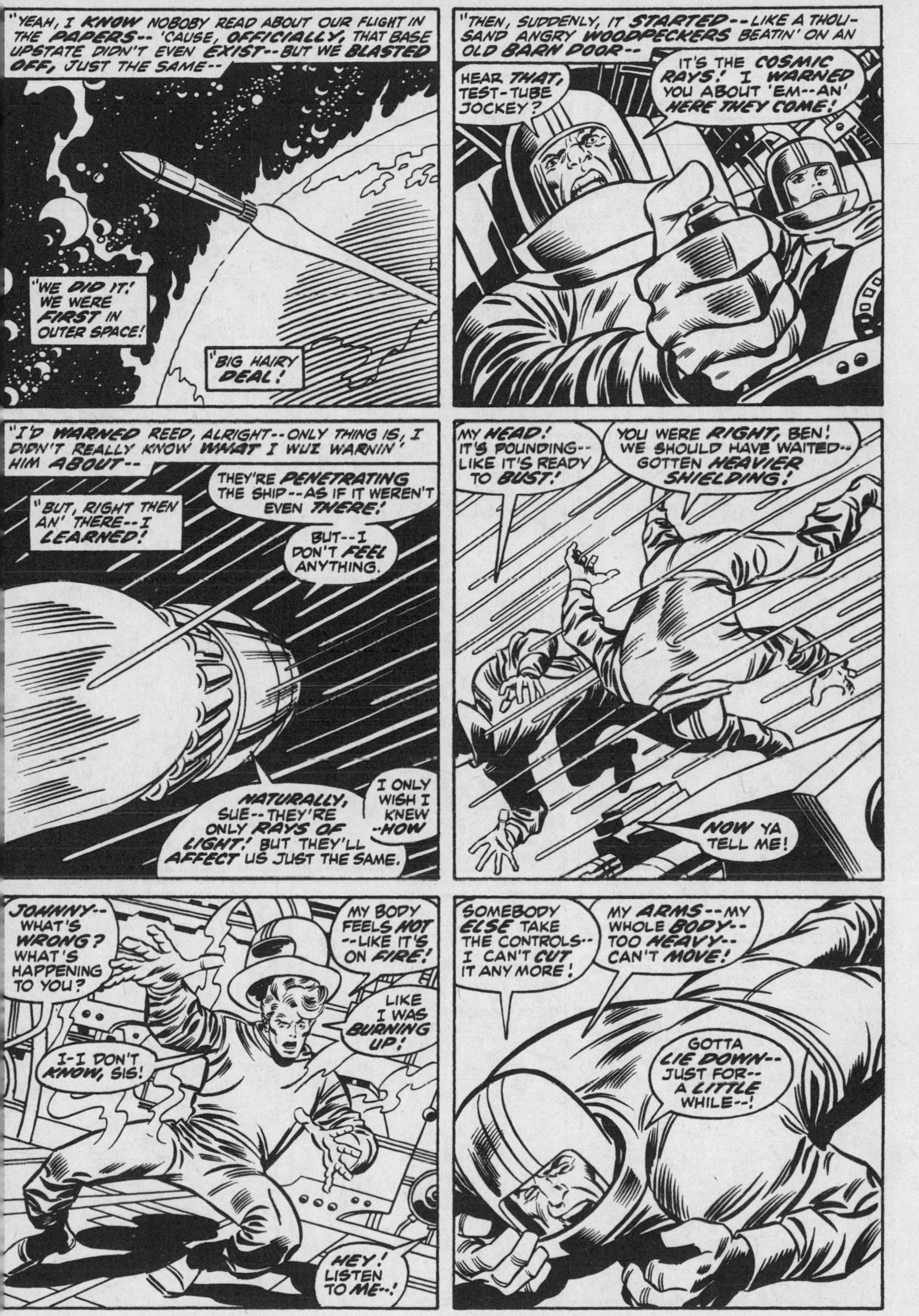
"YEAH, I KNOW NOBOBY READ ABOUT OUR FLIGHT IN THE PAPERS-- 'CAUSE, OFFICIALLY, THAT BASE UPSTATE DIDN'T EVEN EXIST--BUT WE BLASTED OFF, JUST THE SAME--
"WE DID IT! WE WERE FIRST IN OUTER SPACE!
"BIG HAIRY DEAL!
"THEN, SUDDENLY, IT STARTED--LIKE A THOUSAND ANGRY WOODPECKERS BEATIN' ON AN OLD BARN DOOR--
HEAR THAT, TEST-TUBE JOCKEY?
IT'S THE COSMIC RAYS! I WARNED YOU ABOUT 'EM--AN' HERE THEY COME!
"I'D WARNED REED, ALRIGHT--ONLY THING IS, I DIDN'T REALLY KNOW WHAT I WUZ WARNIN' HIM ABOUT--
"BUT, RIGHT THEN AN' THERE--I LEARNED!
THEY'RE PENETRATING THE SHIP--AS IF IT WEREN'T EVEN THERE!
BUT--I DON'T FEEL ANYTHING.
NATURALLY, SUE--THEY'RE ONLY RAYS OF LIGHT! BUT THEY'LL AFFECT US JUST THE SAME.
I ONLY WISH I KNEW --HOW
MY HEAD! IT'S POUNDING--LIKE IT'S READY TO BUST!
YOU WERE RIGHT, BEN! WE SHOULD HAVE WAITED--GOTTEN HEAVIER SHIELDING!
NOW YA TELL ME!
JOHNNY--WHAT'S WRONG? WHAT'S HAPPENING TO YOU?
MY BODY FEELS HOT--LIKE IT'S ON FIRE!
LIKE I WAS BURNING UP!
I-I DON'T KNOW, SIS!
HEY! LISTEN TO ME--!
SOMEBODY ELSE TAKE THE CONTROLS--I CAN'T CUT IT ANY MORE!
MY ARMS--MY WHOLE BODY--TOO HEAVY--CAN'T MOVE!
GOTTA LIE DOWN--JUST FOR--A LITTLE WHILE--!

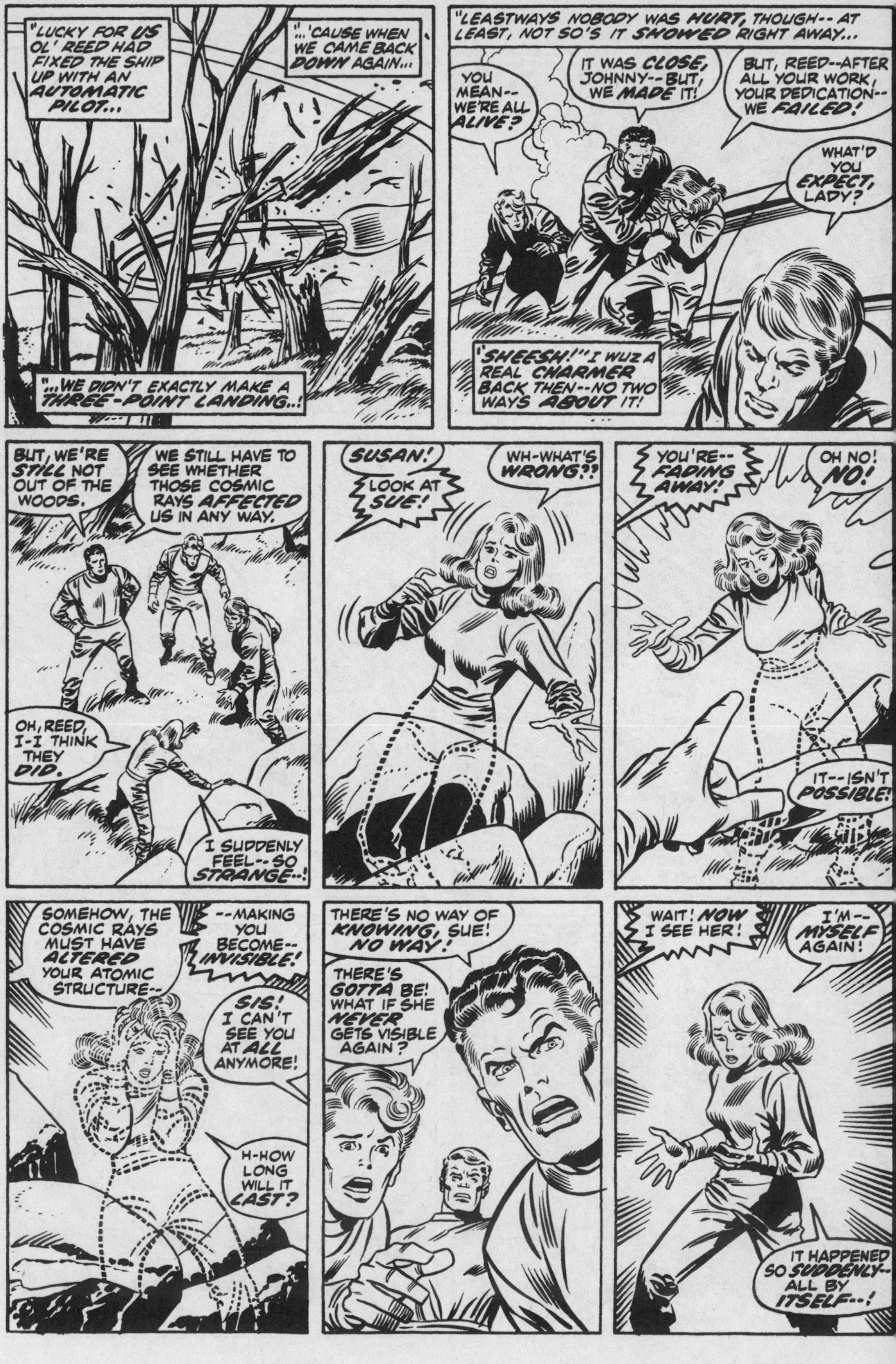
"LUCKY FOR US OL' REED HAD FIXED THE SHIP UP WITH AN AUTOMATIC PILOT...
"...'CAUSE WHEN WE CAME BACK DOWN AGAIN...
"...WE DIDN'T EXACTLY MAKE A THREE-POINT LANDING...!
"LEASTWAYS NOBODY WAS HURT, THOUGH-- AT LEAST, NOT SO'S IT SHOWED RIGHT AWAY...
YOU MEAN-- WE'RE ALL ALIVE?
IT WAS CLOSE, JOHNNY-- BUT, WE MADE IT!
BUT, REED--AFTER ALL YOUR WORK, YOUR DEDICATION-- WE FAILED!
WHAT'D YOU EXPECT, LADY?
"SHEESH!" I WUZ A REAL CHARMER BACK THEN--NO TWO WAYS ABOUT IT!
BUT, WE'RE STILL NOT OUT OF THE WOODS.
WE STILL HAVE TO SEE WHETHER THOSE COSMIC RAYS AFFECTED US IN ANY WAY.
OH, REED, I-I THINK THEY DID.
I SUDDENLY FEEL--SO STRANGE--!
SUSAN!
LOOK AT SUE!
WH-WHAT'S WRONG??
YOU'RE-- FADING AWAY!
OH NO! NO!
IT--ISN'T POSSIBLE!
SOMEHOW, THE COSMIC RAYS MUST HAVE ALTERED YOUR ATOMIC STRUCTURE--
--MAKING YOU BECOME-- INVISIBLE!
SIS! I CAN'T SEE YOU AT ALL ANYMORE!
H-HOW LONG WILL IT LAST?
THERE'S NO WAY OF KNOWING, SUE! NO WAY!
THERE'S GOTTA BE! WHAT IF SHE NEVER GETS VISIBLE AGAIN?
WAIT! NOW I SEE HER!
I'M-- MYSELF AGAIN!
IT HAPPENED SO SUDDENLY-- ALL BY ITSELF--!

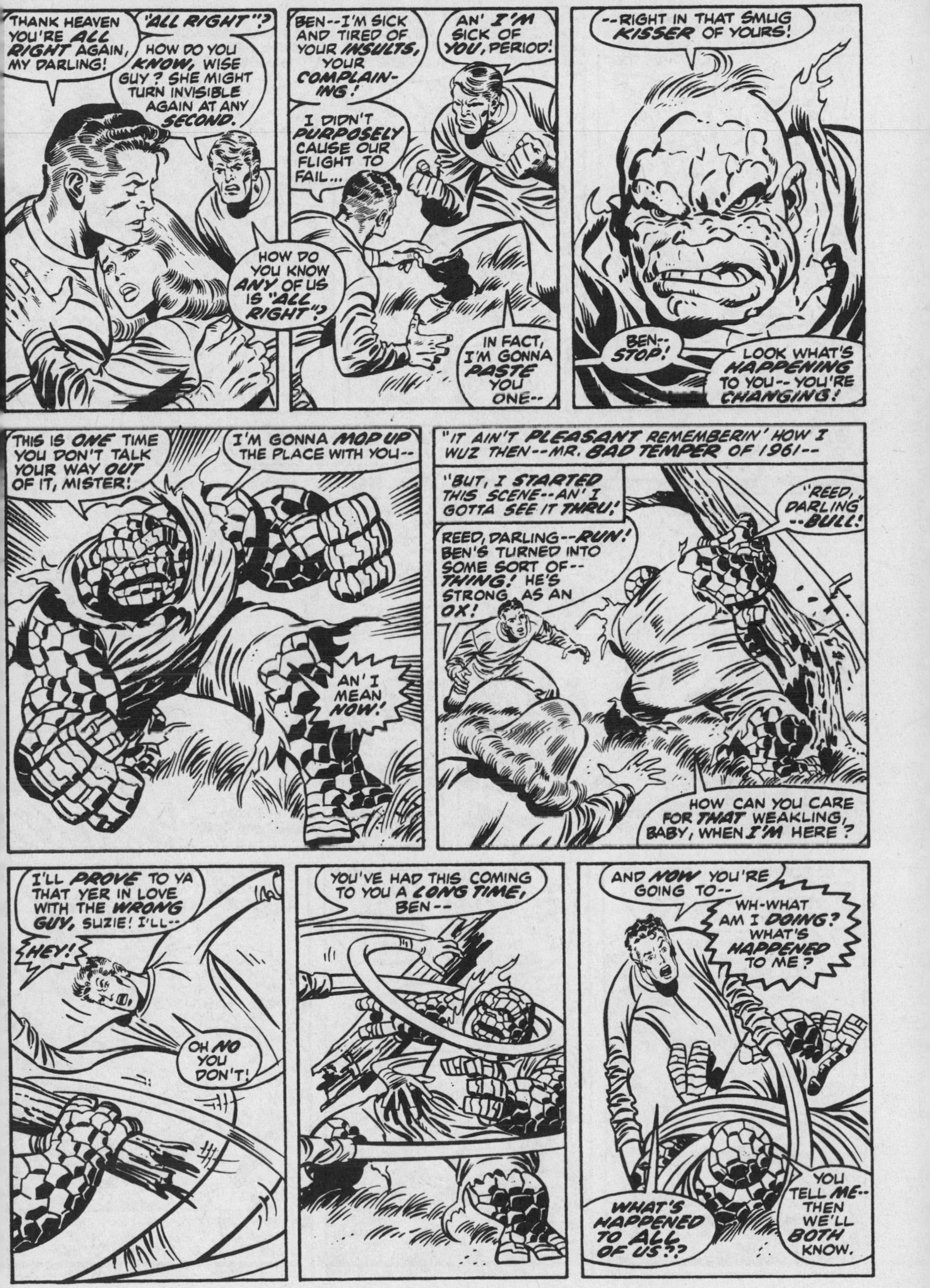
THANK HEAVEN YOU'RE ALL RIGHT AGAIN, MY DARLING!
"ALL RIGHT"? HOW DO YOU KNOW, WISE GUY? SHE MIGHT TURN INVISIBLE AGAIN AT ANY SECOND.
HOW DO YOU KNOW ANY OF US IS "ALL RIGHT"?
BEN--I'M SICK AND TIRED OF YOUR INSULTS, YOUR COMPLAINING!
AN' I'M SICK OF YOU, PERIOD!
I DIDN'T PURPOSELY CAUSE OUR FLIGHT TO FAIL...
IN FACT, I'M GONNA PASTE YOU ONE--
--RIGHT IN THAT SMUG KISSER OF YOURS!
BEN-- STOP!
LOOK WHAT'S HAPPENING TO YOU-- YOU'RE CHANGING!
THIS IS ONE TIME YOU DON'T TALK YOUR WAY OUT OF IT, MISTER!
I'M GONNA MOP UP THE PLACE WITH YOU--
AN' I MEAN NOW!
"IT AIN'T PLEASANT REMEMBERIN' HOW I WUZ THEN--MR. BAD TEMPER OF 1961--
"BUT, I STARTED THIS SCENE--AN' I GOTTA SEE IT THRU!
REED, DARLING--RUN! BEN'S TURNED INTO SOME SORT OF--THING! HE'S STRONG AS AN OX!
"REED, DARLING" --BULL!
HOW CAN YOU CARE FOR THAT WEAKLING, BABY, WHEN I'M HERE?
I'LL PROVE TO YA THAT YER IN LOVE WITH THE WRONG GUY, SUZIE! I'LL--
HEY!
OH NO YOU DON'T!
YOU'VE HAD THIS COMING TO YOU A LONG TIME, BEN--
AND NOW YOU'RE GOING TO--
WH-WHAT AM I DOING? WHAT'S HAPPENED TO ME?
WHAT'S HAPPENED TO ALL OF US??
YOU TELL ME-- THEN WE'LL BOTH KNOW.

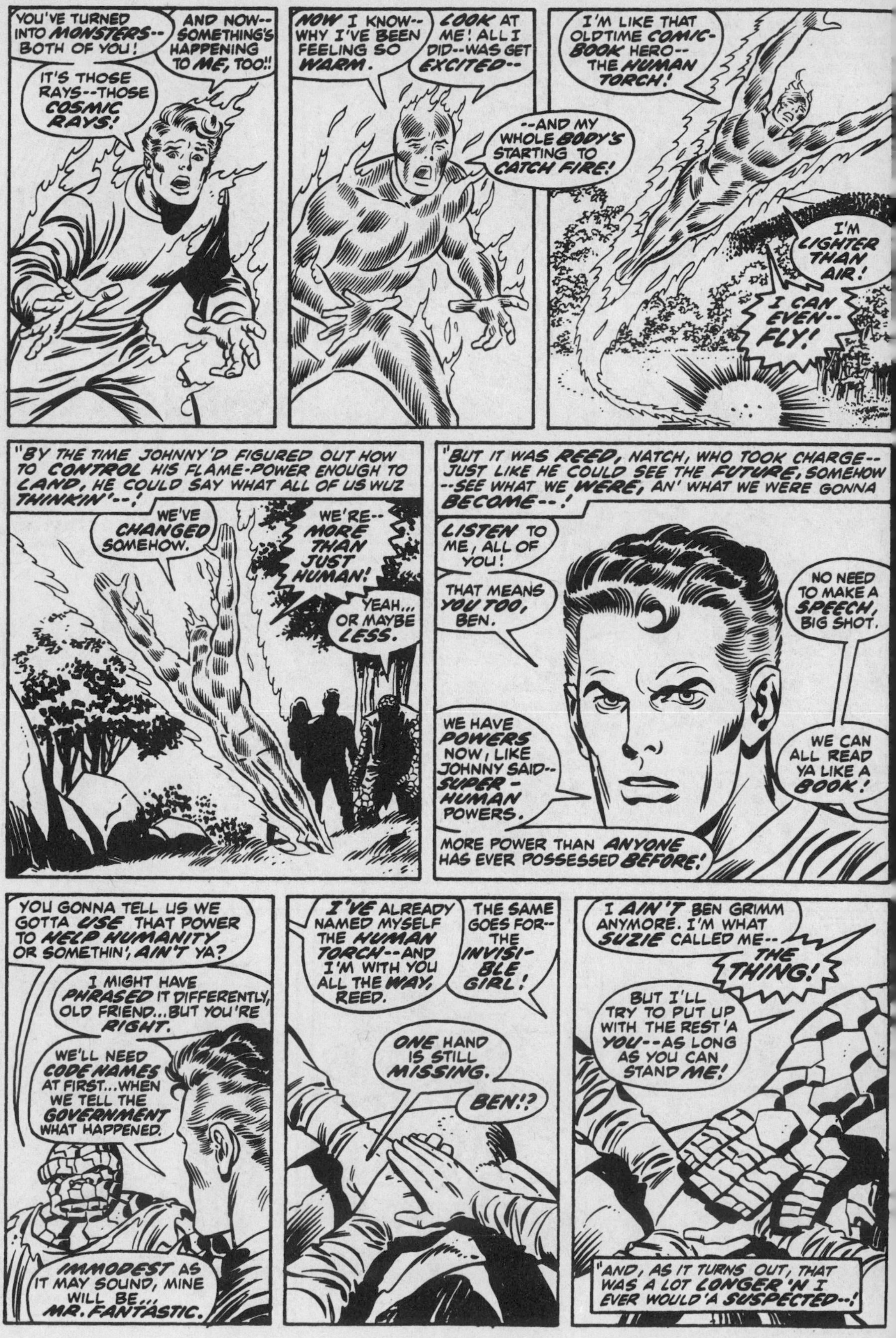

YOU'VE TURNED INTO MONSTERS-- BOTH OF YOU!
AND NOW-- SOMETHING'S HAPPENING TO ME, TOO!!
IT'S THOSE RAYS--THOSE COSMIC RAYS!
NOW I KNOW-- WHY I'VE BEEN FEELING SO WARM.
LOOK AT ME! ALL I DID--WAS GET EXCITED--
--AND MY WHOLE BODY'S STARTING TO CATCH FIRE!
I'M LIKE THAT OLDTIME COMIC-BOOK HERO-- THE HUMAN TORCH!
I'M LIGHTER THAN AIR!
I CAN EVEN-- FLY!
"BY THE TIME JOHNNY'D FIGURED OUT HOW TO CONTROL HIS FLAME-POWER ENOUGH TO LAND, HE COULD SAY WHAT ALL OF US WUZ THINKIN'--!
WE'VE CHANGED SOMEHOW.
WE'RE-- MORE THAN JUST HUMAN!
YEAH... OR MAYBE LESS.
"BUT IT WAS REED, NATCH, WHO TOOK CHARGE-- JUST LIKE HE COULD SEE THE FUTURE, SOMEHOW --SEE WHAT WE WERE, AN' WHAT WE WERE GONNA BECOME--!
LISTEN TO ME, ALL OF YOU!
THAT MEANS YOU TOO, BEN.
NO NEED TO MAKE A SPEECH, BIG SHOT.
WE HAVE POWERS NOW, LIKE JOHNNY SAID-- SUPER-HUMAN POWERS.
WE CAN ALL READ YA LIKE A BOOK!
MORE POWER THAN ANYONE HAS EVER POSSESSED BEFORE!
YOU GONNA TELL US WE GOTTA USE THAT POWER TO HELP HUMANITY OR SOMETHIN', AIN'T YA?
I MIGHT HAVE PHRASED IT DIFFERENTLY, OLD FRIEND...BUT YOU'RE RIGHT.
WE'LL NEED CODE NAMES AT FIRST...WHEN WE TELL THE GOVERNMENT WHAT HAPPENED.
IMMODEST AS IT MAY SOUND, MINE WILL BE... MR. FANTASTIC.
I'VE ALREADY NAMED MYSELF THE HUMAN TORCH--AND I'M WITH YOU ALL THE WAY, REED.
THE SAME GOES FOR-- THE INVISI-BLE GIRL!
ONE HAND IS STILL MISSING.
BEN!?
I AIN'T BEN GRIMM ANYMORE. I'M WHAT SUZIE CALLED ME-- THE THING!
BUT I'LL TRY TO PUT UP WITH THE REST 'A YOU--AS LONG AS YOU CAN STAND ME!
"AND, AS IT TURNS OUT, THAT WAS A LOT LONGER 'N I EVER WOULD 'A SUSPECTED--!

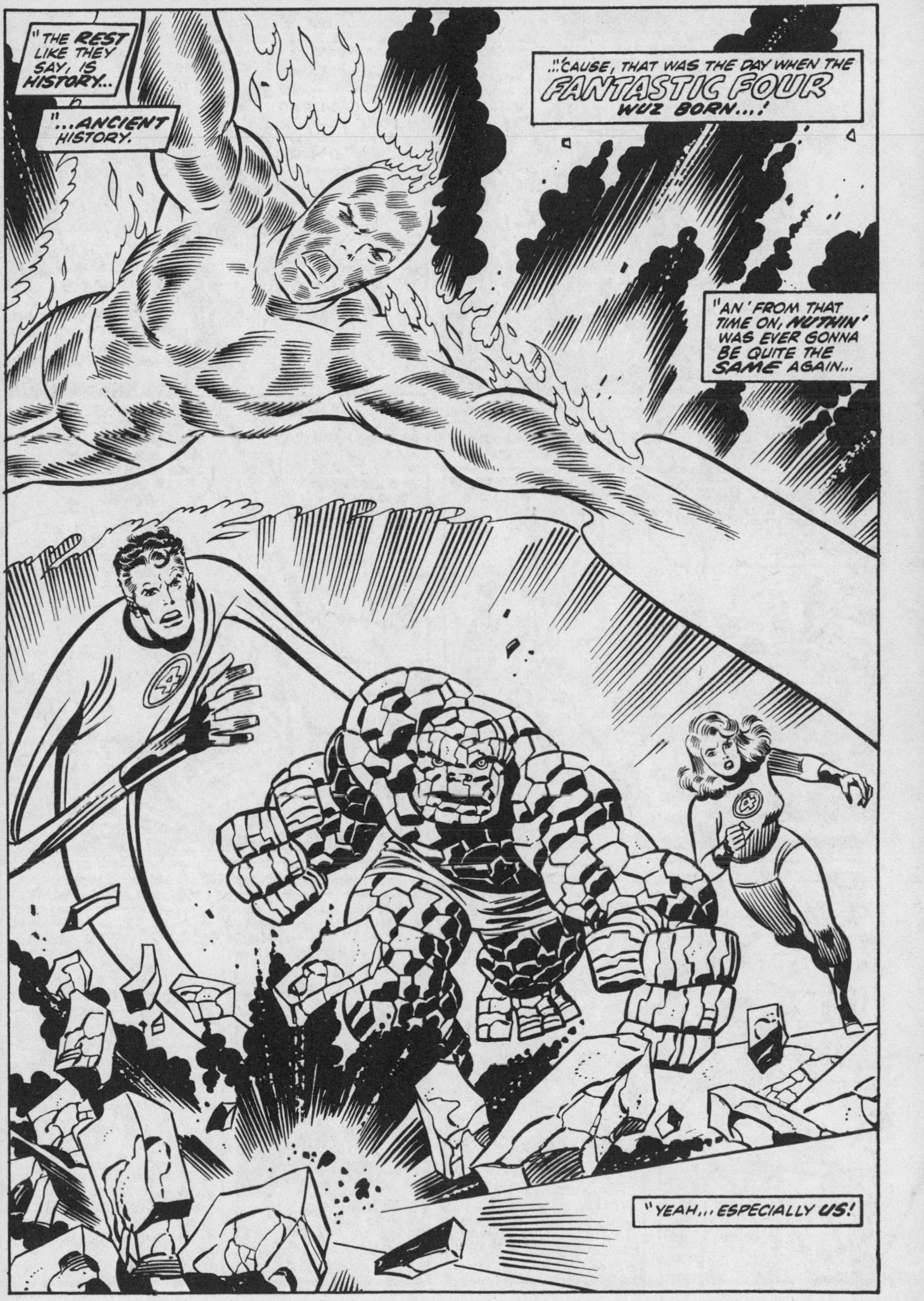
"THE REST LIKE THEY SAY, IS HISTORY...
"...ANCIENT HISTORY.
..."CAUSE, THAT WAS THE DAY WHEN THE FANTASTIC FOUR WUZ BORN...!
"AN' FROM THAT TIME ON, NUTHIN' WAS EVER GONNA BE QUITE THE SAME AGAIN...
"YEAH... ESPECIALLY US!

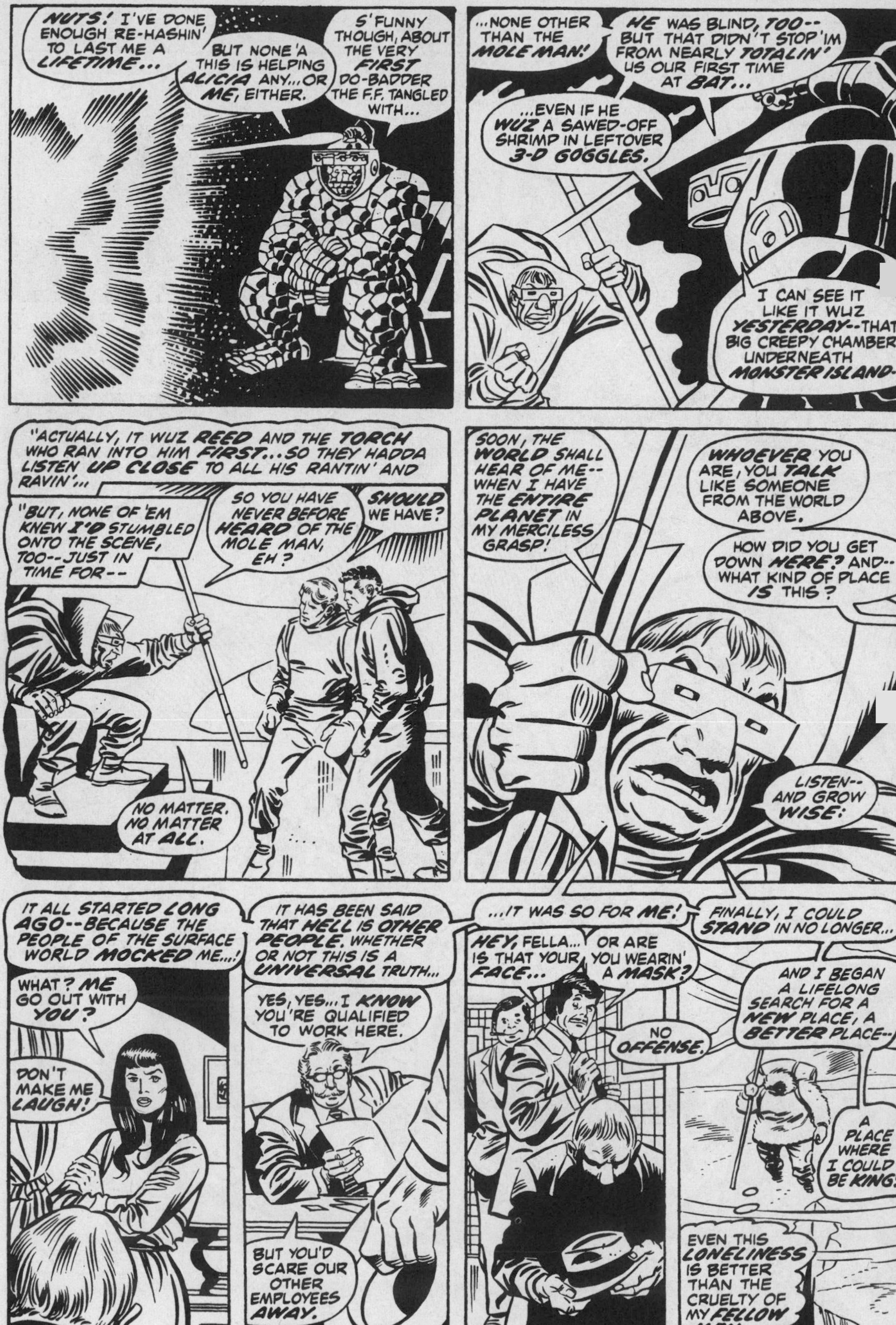
NUTS! I'VE DONE ENOUGH RE-HASHIN' TO LAST ME A LIFETIME...
BUT NONE 'A THIS IS HELPING ALICIA ANY... OR ME, EITHER.
S'FUNNY THOUGH, ABOUT THE VERY FIRST DO-BADDER THE F.F. TANGLED WITH...
...NONE OTHER THAN THE MOLE MAN!
HE WAS BLIND, TOO-- BUT THAT DIDN'T STOP 'IM FROM NEARLY TOTALIN' US OUR FIRST TIME AT BAT...
...EVEN IF HE WUZ A SAWED-OFF SHRIMP IN LEFTOVER 3-D GOGGLES.
I CAN SEE IT LIKE IT WUZ YESTERDAY--THAT BIG CREEPY CHAMBER UNDERNEATH MONSTER ISLAND--
"ACTUALLY, IT WUZ REED AND THE TORCH WHO RAN INTO HIM FIRST...SO THEY HADDA LISTEN UP CLOSE TO ALL HIS RANTIN' AND RAVIN'...
"BUT, NONE OF 'EM KNEW I'D STUMBLED ONTO THE SCENE, TOO--JUST IN TIME FOR--
SO YOU HAVE NEVER BEFORE HEARD OF THE MOLE MAN, EH?
SHOULD WE HAVE?
NO MATTER. NO MATTER AT ALL.
SOON, THE WORLD SHALL HEAR OF ME-- WHEN I HAVE THE ENTIRE PLANET IN MY MERCILESS GRASP!
WHOEVER YOU ARE, YOU TALK LIKE SOMEONE FROM THE WORLD ABOVE.
HOW DID YOU GET DOWN HERE? AND-- WHAT KIND OF PLACE IS THIS?
LISTEN-- AND GROW WISE:
IT ALL STARTED LONG AGO--BECAUSE THE PEOPLE OF THE SURFACE WORLD MOCKED ME...!
WHAT? ME GO OUT WITH YOU?
DON'T MAKE ME LAUGH!
IT HAS BEEN SAID THAT HELL IS OTHER PEOPLE. WHETHER OR NOT THIS IS A UNIVERSAL TRUTH...
YES, YES...I KNOW YOU'RE QUALIFIED TO WORK HERE.
BUT YOU'D SCARE OUR OTHER EMPLOYEES AWAY.
...IT WAS SO FOR ME!
HEY, FELLA... IS THAT YOUR FACE...
OR ARE YOU WEARIN' A MASK?
NO OFFENSE.
FINALLY, I COULD STAND IN NO LONGER...
AND I BEGAN A LIFELONG SEARCH FOR A NEW PLACE, A BETTER PLACE--
A PLACE WHERE I COULD BE KING!
EVEN THIS LONELINESS IS BETTER THAN THE CRUELTY OF MY FELLOW MEN.

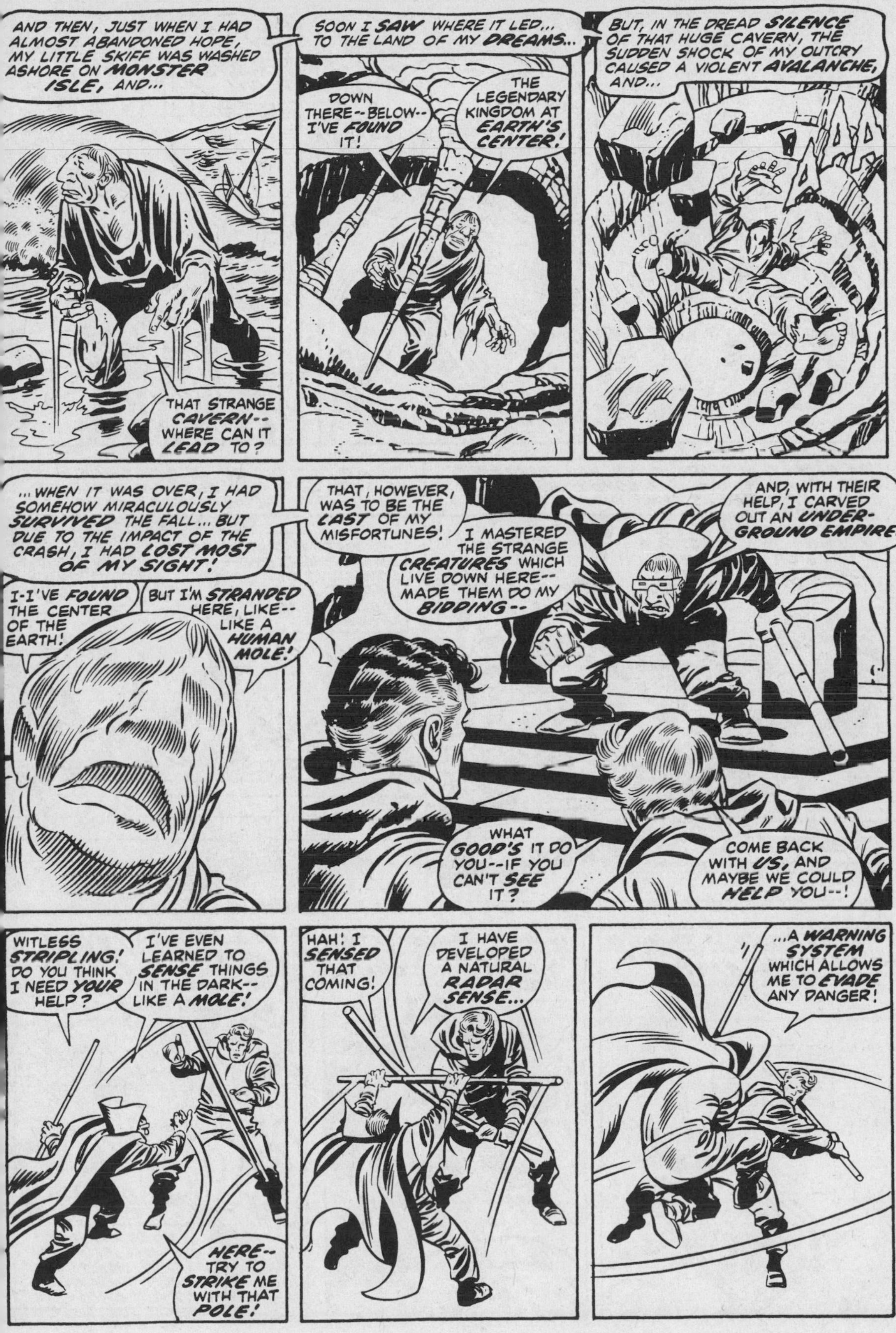
AND THEN, JUST WHEN I HAD ALMOST ABANDONED HOPE, MY LITTLE SKIFF WAS WASHED ASHORE ON MONSTER ISLE, AND...
THAT STRANGE CAVERN-- WHERE CAN IT LEAD TO?
SOON I SAW WHERE IT LED... TO THE LAND OF MY DREAMS...
DOWN THERE--BELOW-- I'VE FOUND IT!
THE LEGENDARY KINGDOM AT EARTH'S CENTER!
BUT, IN THE DREAD SILENCE OF THAT HUGE CAVERN, THE SUDDEN SHOCK OF MY OUTCRY CAUSED A VIOLENT AVALANCHE, AND...
...WHEN IT WAS OVER, I HAD SOMEHOW MIRACULOUSLY SURVIVED THE FALL... BUT DUE TO THE IMPACT OF THE CRASH, I HAD LOST MOST OF MY SIGHT!
I-I'VE FOUND THE CENTER OF THE EARTH!
BUT I'M STRANDED HERE, LIKE-- LIKE A HUMAN MOLE!
THAT, HOWEVER, WAS TO BE THE LAST OF MY MISFORTUNES!
I MASTERED THE STRANGE CREATURES WHICH LIVE DOWN HERE-- MADE THEM DO MY BIDDING--
AND, WITH THEIR HELP, I CARVED OUT AN UNDER-GROUND EMPIRE!
WHAT GOOD'S IT DO YOU--IF YOU CAN'T SEE IT?
COME BACK WITH US, AND MAYBE WE COULD HELP YOU--!
WITLESS STRIPLING! DO YOU THINK I NEED YOUR HELP?
I'VE EVEN LEARNED TO SENSE THINGS IN THE DARK-- LIKE A MOLE!
HERE-- TRY TO STRIKE ME WITH THAT POLE!
HAH! I SENSED THAT COMING!
I HAVE DEVELOPED A NATURAL RADAR SENSE...
...A WARNING SYSTEM WHICH ALLOWS ME TO EVADE ANY DANGER!

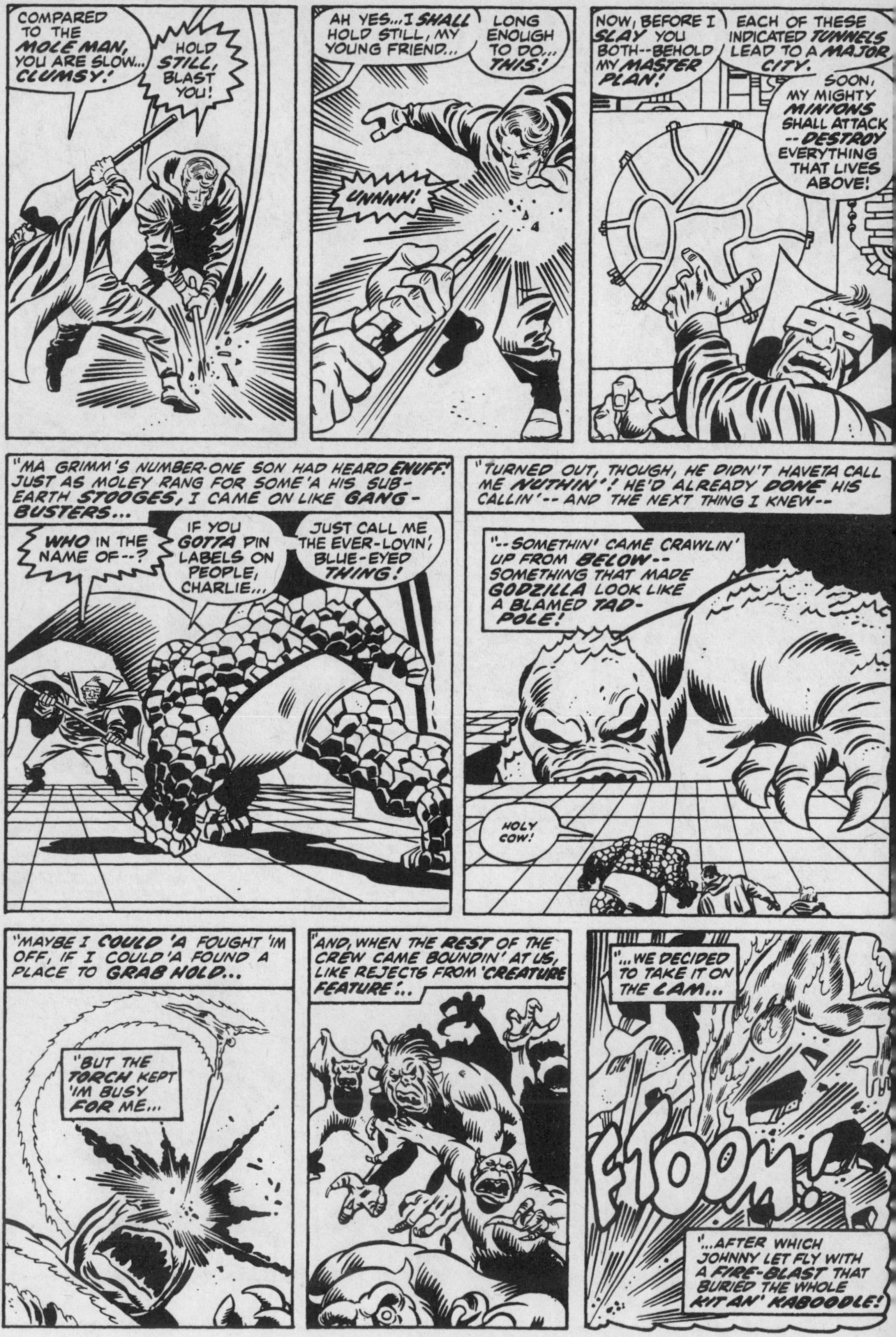
COMPARED TO THE MOLE MAN, YOU ARE SLOW... CLUMSY!
HOLD STILL, BLAST YOU!
AH YES...I SHALL HOLD STILL, MY YOUNG FRIEND...
LONG ENOUGH TO DO... THIS!
UNNNH!
NOW, BEFORE I SLAY YOU BOTH--BEHOLD MY MASTER PLAN!
EACH OF THESE INDICATED TUNNELS LEAD TO A MAJOR CITY.
SOON, MY MIGHTY MINIONS SHALL ATTACK --DESTROY EVERYTHING THAT LIVES ABOVE!
"MA GRIMM'S NUMBER-ONE SON HAD HEARD ENUFF! JUST AS MOLEY RANG FOR SOME 'A HIS SUB-EARTH STOOGES, I CAME ON LIKE GANG-BUSTERS...
WHO IN THE NAME OF--?
IF YOU GOTTA PIN LABELS ON PEOPLE, CHARLIE...
JUST CALL ME THE EVER-LOVIN', BLUE-EYED THING!
"TURNED OUT, THOUGH, HE DIDN'T HAVETA CALL ME NUTHIN'! HE'D ALREADY DONE HIS CALLIN'-- AND THE NEXT THING I KNEW--
"--SOMETHIN' CAME CRAWLIN' UP FROM BELOW-- SOMETHING THAT MADE GODZILLA LOOK LIKE A BLAMED TAD-POLE!
HOLY COW!
"MAYBE I COULD 'A FOUGHT 'IM OFF, IF I COULD'A FOUND A PLACE TO GRAB HOLD...
"BUT THE TORCH KEPT 'IM BUSY FOR ME...
"AND, WHEN THE REST OF THE CREW CAME BOUNDIN' AT US, LIKE REJECTS FROM 'CREATURE FEATURE'...
"...WE DECIDED TO TAKE IT ON THE LAM...
FTOOM!
"...AFTER WHICH JOHNNY LET FLY WITH A FIRE-BLAST THAT BURIED THE WHOLE KIT AN' KABOODLE!

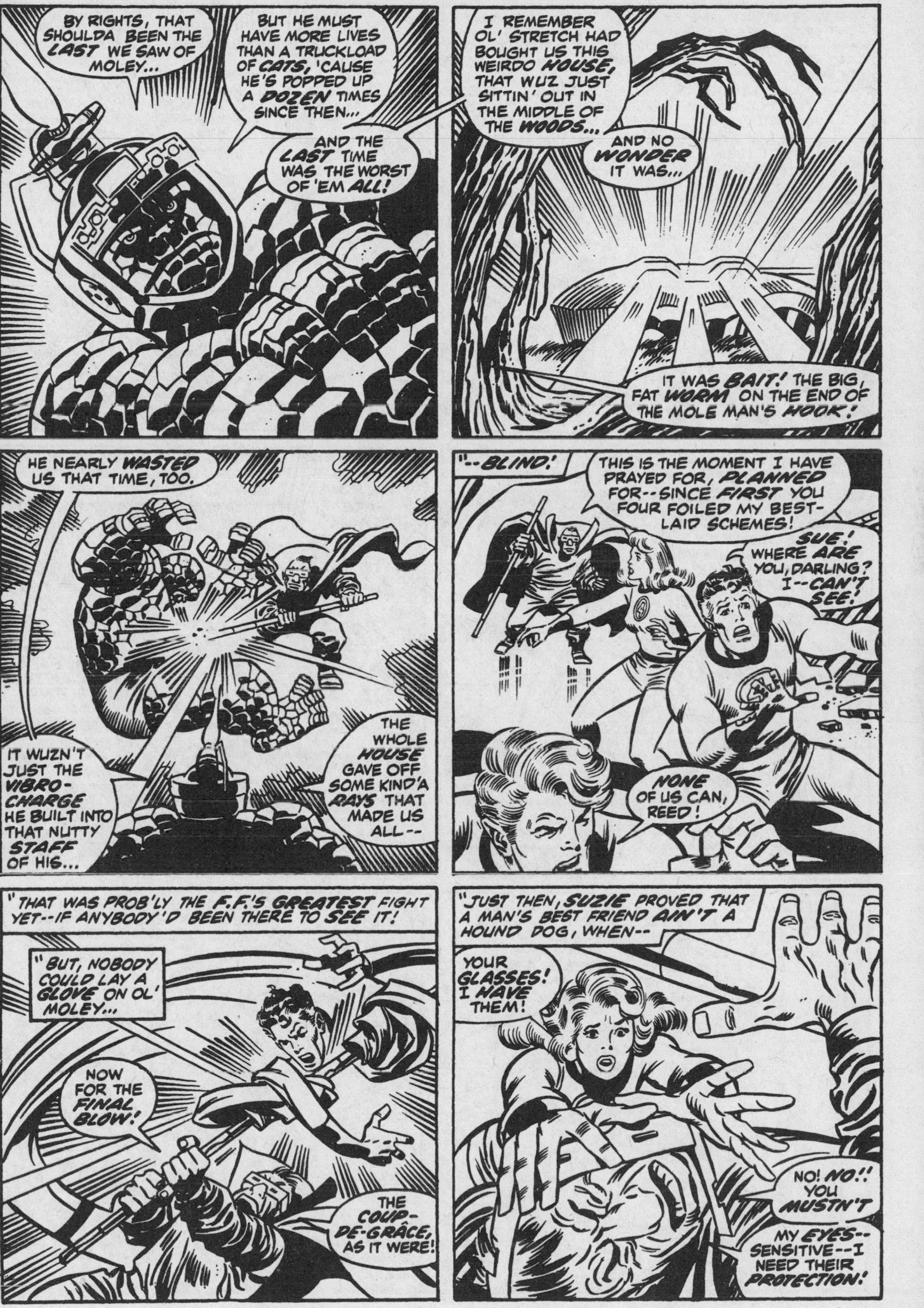
BY RIGHTS, THAT SHOULDA BEEN THE LAST WE SAW OF MOLEY...
BUT HE MUST HAVE MORE LIVES THAN A TRUCKLOAD OF CATS, 'CAUSE HE'S POPPED UP A DOZEN TIMES SINCE THEN...
AND THE LAST TIME WAS THE WORST OF 'EM ALL!
I REMEMBER OL' STRETCH HAD BOUGHT US THIS WEIRDO HOUSE, THAT WUZ JUST SITTIN' OUT IN THE MIDDLE OF THE WOODS...
AND NO WONDER IT WAS...
IT WAS BAIT! THE BIG, FAT WORM ON THE END OF THE MOLE MAN'S HOOK!
HE NEARLY WASTED US THAT TIME, TOO.
IT WUZN'T JUST THE VIBRO-CHARGE HE BUILT INTO THAT NUTTY STAFF OF HIS...
THE WHOLE HOUSE GAVE OFF SOME KIND'A RAYS THAT MADE US ALL--
"--BLIND!
THIS IS THE MOMENT I HAVE PRAYED FOR, PLANNED FOR--SINCE FIRST YOU FOUR FOILED MY BEST-LAID SCHEMES!
SUE! WHERE ARE YOU, DARLING? I--CAN'T SEE!
NONE OF US CAN, REED!
"THAT WAS PROB'LY THE F.F.'S GREATEST FIGHT YET--IF ANYBODY'D BEEN THERE TO SEE IT!
"BUT, NOBODY COULD LAY A GLOVE ON OL' MOLEY...
NOW FOR THE FINAL BLOW!
THE COUP-DE-GRÂCE, AS IT WERE!
"JUST THEN, SUZIE PROVED THAT A MAN'S BEST FRIEND AIN'T A HOUND DOG, WHEN--
YOUR GLASSES! I HAVE THEM!
NO! NO!! YOU MUSTN'T
MY EYES--SENSITIVE--I NEED THEIR PROTECTION!

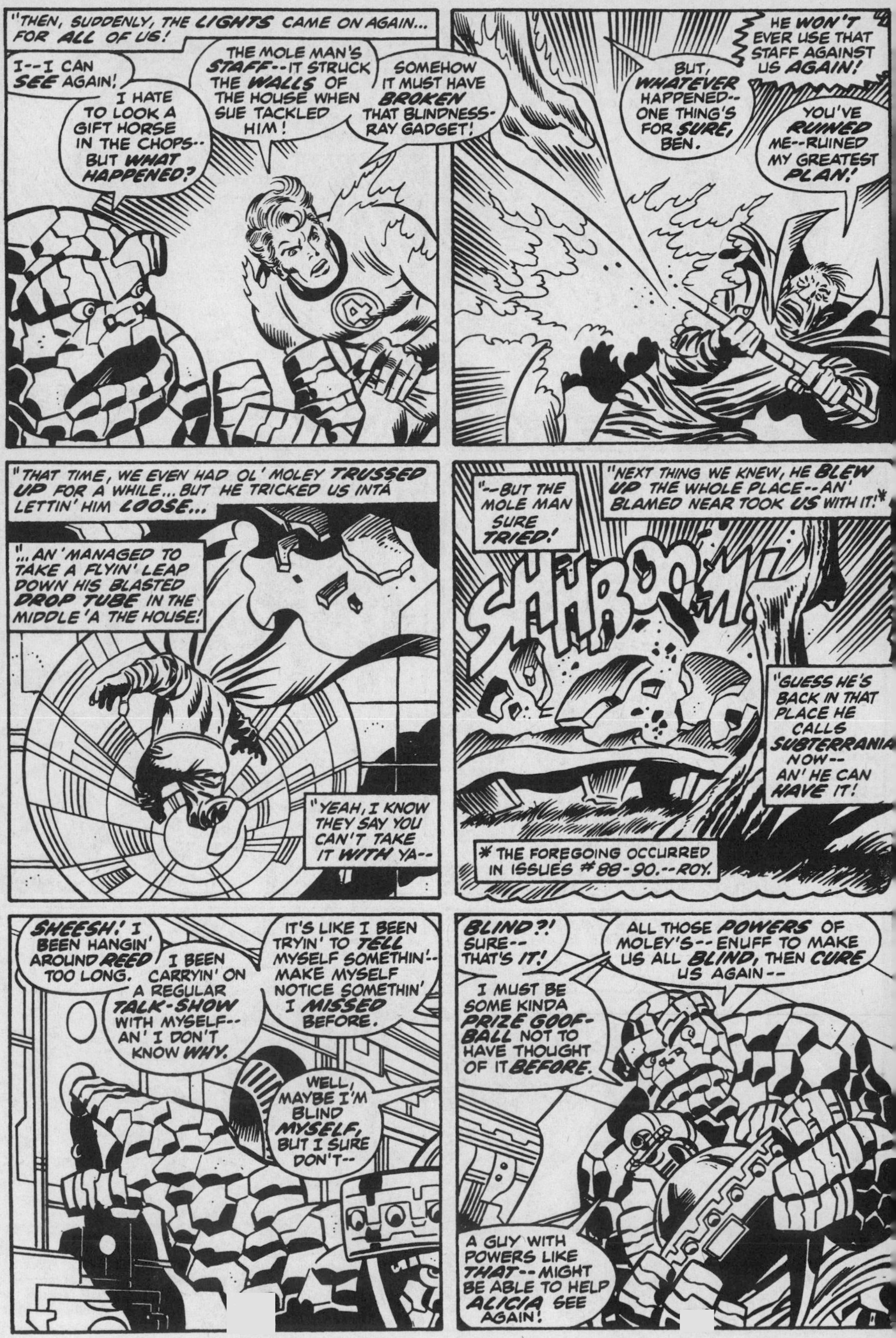

"THEN, SUDDENLY, THE LIGHTS CAME ON AGAIN... FOR ALL OF US!
I--I CAN SEE AGAIN!
I HATE TO LOOK A GIFT HORSE IN THE CHOPS-- BUT WHAT HAPPENED?
THE MOLE MAN'S STAFF--IT STRUCK THE WALLS OF THE HOUSE WHEN SUE TACKLED HIM!
SOMEHOW IT MUST HAVE BROKEN THAT BLINDNESS-RAY GADGET!
BUT, WHATEVER HAPPENED--ONE THING'S FOR SURE, BEN.
HE WON'T EVER USE THAT STAFF AGAINST US AGAIN!
YOU'VE RUINED ME--RUINED MY GREATEST PLAN!
"THAT TIME, WE EVEN HAD OL' MOLEY TRUSSED UP FOR A WHILE... BUT HE TRICKED US INTA LETTIN' HIM LOOSE...
"...AN' MANAGED TO TAKE A FLYIN' LEAP DOWN HIS BLASTED DROP TUBE IN THE MIDDLE 'A THE HOUSE!
"YEAH, I KNOW THEY SAY YOU CAN'T TAKE IT WITH YA--
"--BUT THE MOLE MAN SURE TRIED!
"NEXT THING WE KNEW, HE BLEW UP THE WHOLE PLACE--AN' BLAMED NEAR TOOK US WITH IT!"*
SHHROOM!
"GUESS HE'S BACK IN THAT PLACE HE CALLS SUBTERRANIA NOW--AN' HE CAN HAVE IT!
* THE FOREGOING OCCURRED IN ISSUES #88-90.--ROY.
SHEESH! I BEEN HANGIN' AROUND REED TOO LONG.
I BEEN CARRYIN' ON A REGULAR TALK-SHOW WITH MYSELF--AN' I DON'T KNOW WHY.
IT'S LIKE I BEEN TRYIN' TO TELL MYSELF SOMETHIN'--MAKE MYSELF NOTICE SOMETHIN' I MISSED BEFORE.
WELL, MAYBE I'M BLIND MYSELF, BUT I SURE DON'T--
BLIND?! SURE--THAT'S IT!
ALL THOSE POWERS OF MOLEY'S--ENUFF TO MAKE US ALL BLIND, THEN CURE US AGAIN--
I MUST BE SOME KINDA PRIZE GOOF-BALL NOT TO HAVE THOUGHT OF IT BEFORE.
A GUY WITH POWERS LIKE THAT--MIGHT BE ABLE TO HELP ALICIA SEE AGAIN!

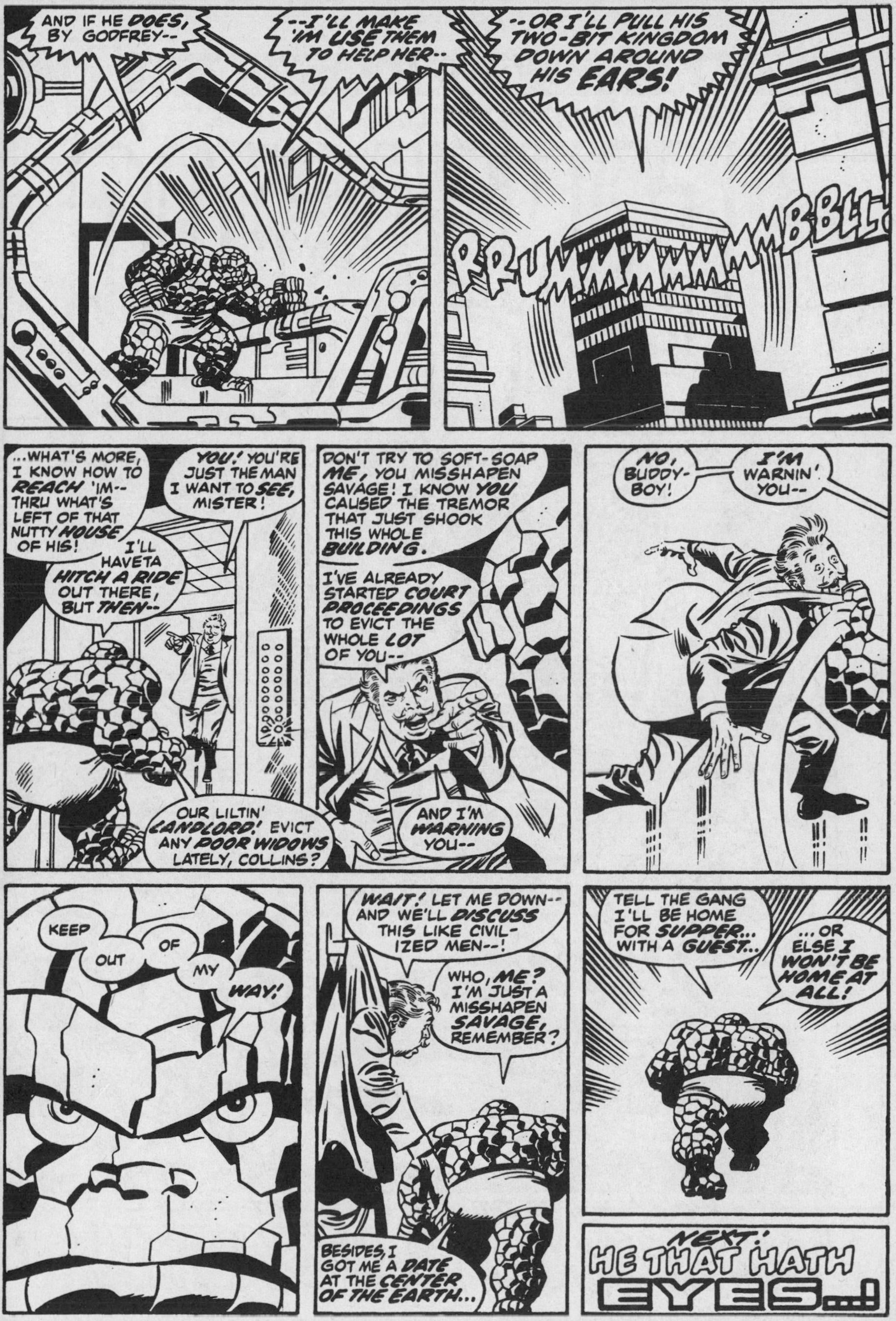
AND IF HE DOES, BY GODFREY--
--I'LL MAKE 'IM USE THEM TO HELP HER--
--OR I'LL PULL HIS TWO-BIT KINGDOM DOWN AROUND HIS EARS!
RRUMMMMMMMMBBLL!
...WHAT'S MORE, I KNOW HOW TO REACH 'IM--THRU WHAT'S LEFT OF THAT NUTTY HOUSE OF HIS!
I'LL HAVETA HITCH A RIDE OUT THERE, BUT THEN--
YOU! YOU'RE JUST THE MAN I WANT TO SEE, MISTER!
OUR LILTIN' LANDLORD! EVICT ANY POOR WIDOWS LATELY, COLLINS?
DON'T TRY TO SOFT-SOAP ME, YOU MISSHAPEN SAVAGE! I KNOW YOU CAUSED THE TREMOR THAT JUST SHOOK THIS WHOLE BUILDING.
I'VE ALREADY STARTED COURT PROCEEDINGS TO EVICT THE WHOLE LOT OF YOU--
AND I'M WARNING YOU--
NO, BUDDY-BOY!
I'M WARNIN' YOU--
KEEP OUT OF MY WAY!
WAIT! LET ME DOWN--AND WE'LL DISCUSS THIS LIKE CIVILIZED MEN--!
WHO, ME? I'M JUST A MISSHAPEN SAVAGE, REMEMBER?
BESIDES, I GOT ME A DATE AT THE CENTER OF THE EARTH...
TELL THE GANG I'LL BE HOME FOR SUPPER... WITH A GUEST...
...OR ELSE I WON'T BE HOME AT ALL!
NEXT: HE THAT HATH EYES...!

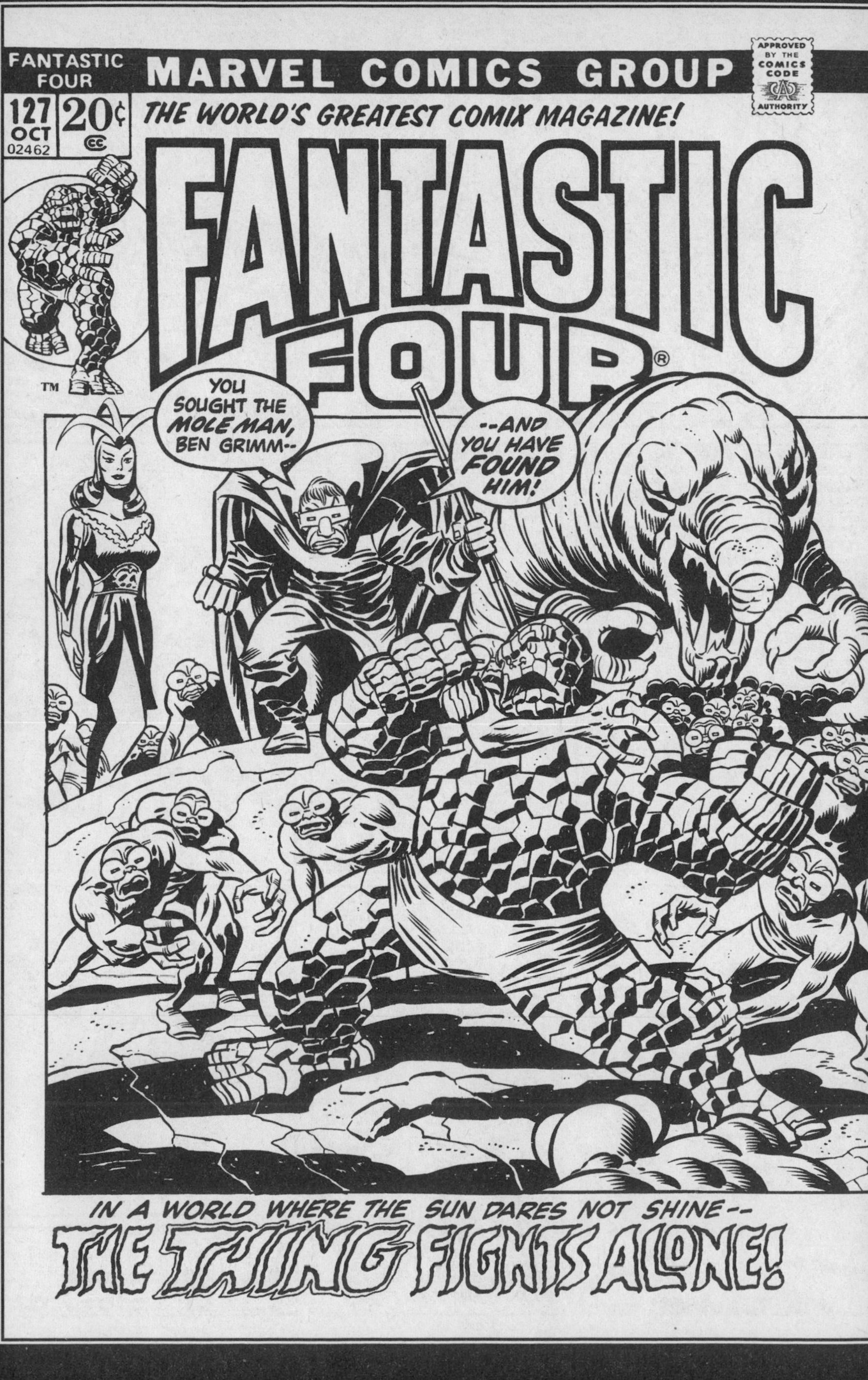
FANTASTIC FOUR
MARVEL COMICS GROUP
APPROVED BY THE COMICS CODE AUTHORITY
127 OCT 02462
20¢
THE WORLD'S GREATEST COMIX MAGAZINE!
FANTASTIC FOUR
YOU SOUGHT THE MOLE MAN, BEN GRIMM--
--AND YOU HAVE FOUND HIM!
IN A WORLD WHERE THE SUN DARES NOT SHINE--
THE THING FIGHTS ALONE!

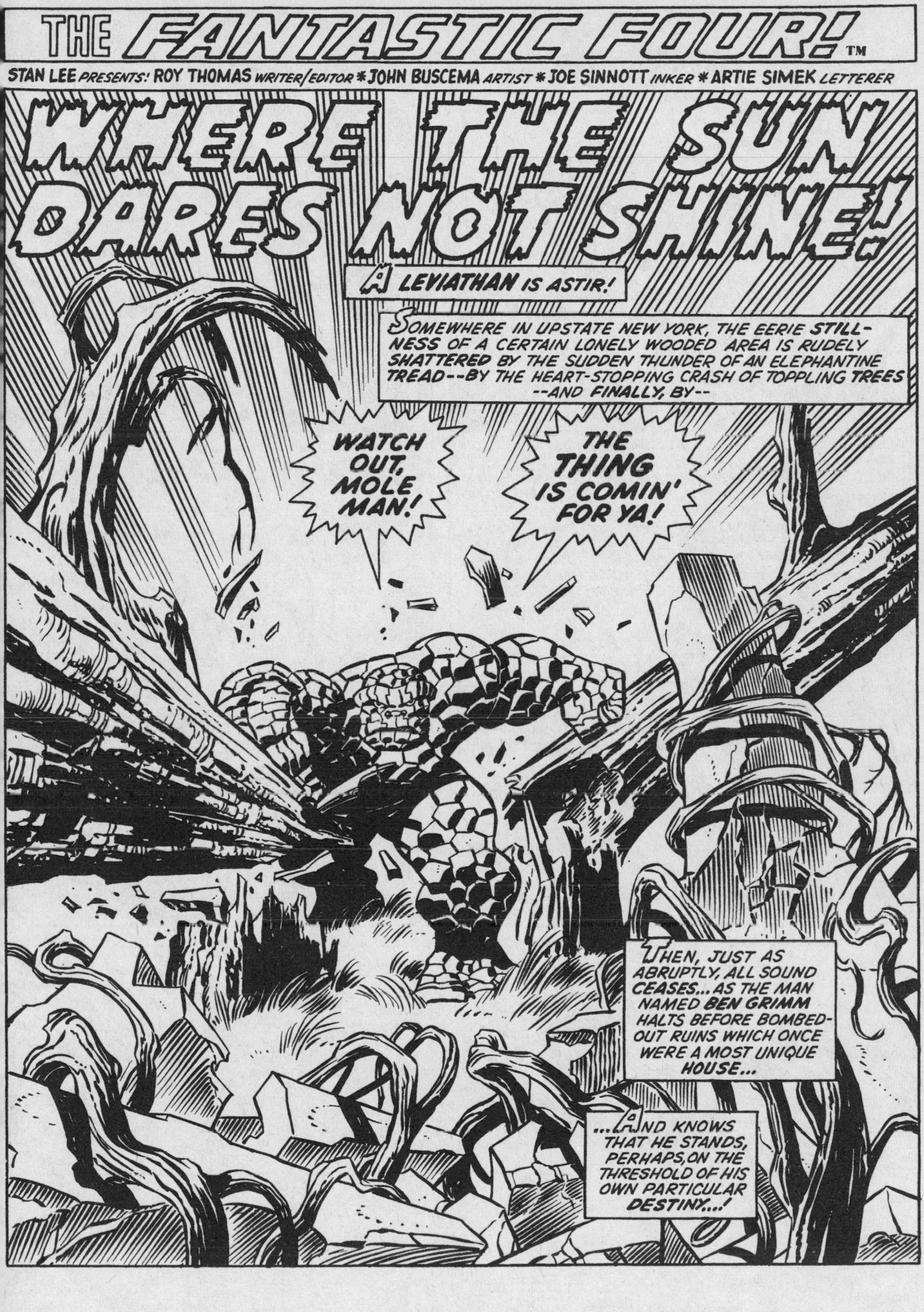
THE FANTASTIC FOUR! ™
STAN LEE PRESENTS: ROY THOMAS WRITER/EDITOR * JOHN BUSCEMA ARTIST * JOE SINNOTT INKER * ARTIE SIMEK LETTERER
WHERE THE SUN DARES NOT SHINE!
A LEVIATHAN IS ASTIR!
SOMEWHERE IN UPSTATE NEW YORK, THE EERIE STILLNESS OF A CERTAIN LONELY WOODED AREA IS RUDELY SHATTERED BY THE SUDDEN THUNDER OF AN ELEPHANTINE TREAD--BY THE HEART-STOPPING CRASH OF TOPPLING TREES --AND FINALLY, BY--
WATCH OUT, MOLE MAN!
THE THING IS COMIN' FOR YA!
THEN, JUST AS ABRUPTLY, ALL SOUND CEASES... AS THE MAN NAMED BEN GRIMM HALTS BEFORE BOMBED-OUT RUINS WHICH ONCE WERE A MOST UNIQUE HOUSE...
...AND KNOWS THAT HE STANDS, PERHAPS, ON THE THRESHOLD OF HIS OWN PARTICULAR DESTINY...!

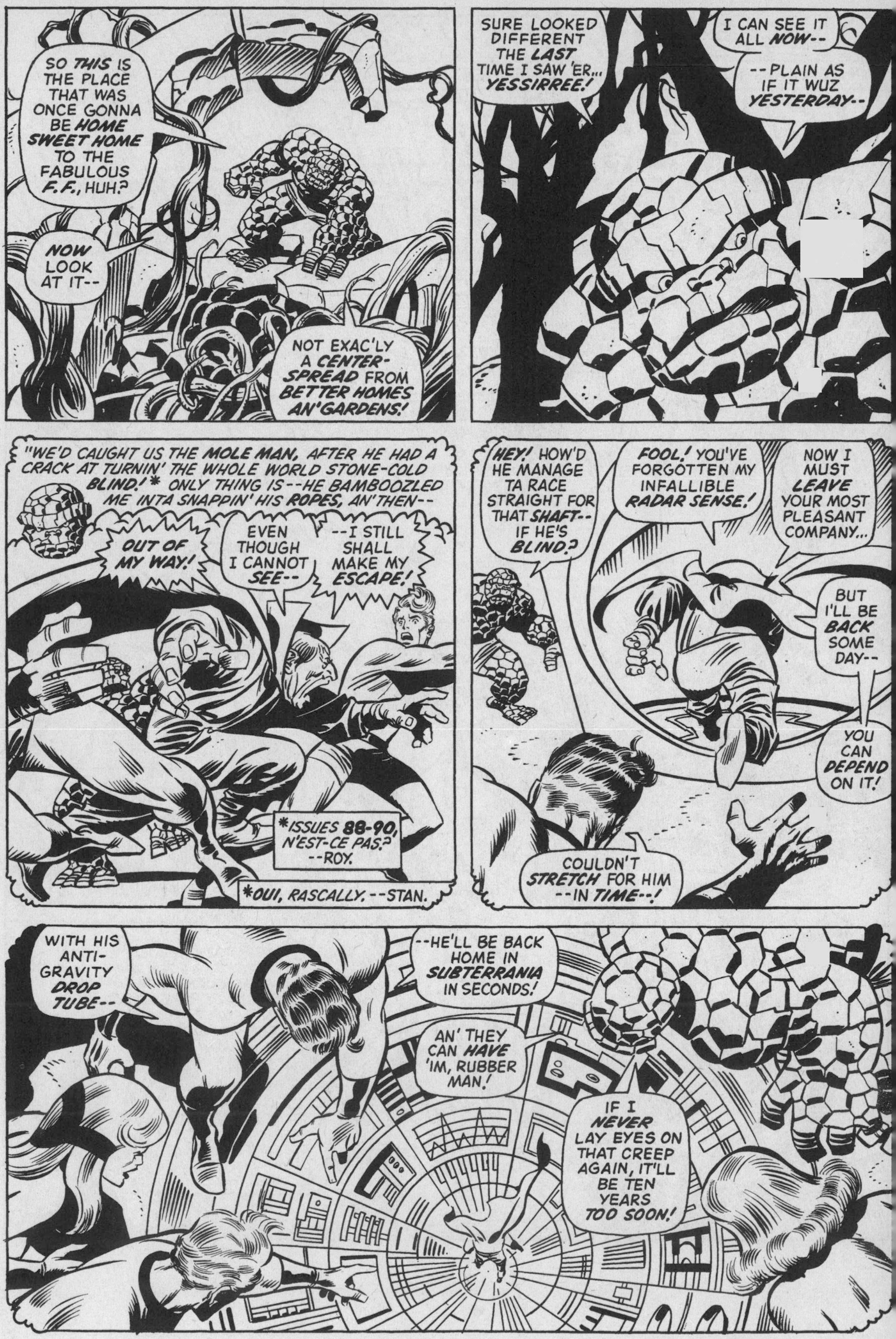

SO THIS IS THE PLACE THAT WAS ONCE GONNA BE HOME SWEET HOME TO THE FABULOUS F.F., HUH?
NOW LOOK AT IT--
NOT EXAC'LY A CENTER-SPREAD FROM BETTER HOMES AN' GARDENS!
SURE LOOKED DIFFERENT THE LAST TIME I SAW 'ER... YESSIRREE!
I CAN SEE IT ALL NOW--
--PLAIN AS IF IT WUZ YESTERDAY--
"WE'D CAUGHT US THE MOLE MAN, AFTER HE HAD A CRACK AT TURNIN' THE WHOLE WORLD STONE-COLD BLIND!* ONLY THING IS--HE BAMBOOZLED ME INTA SNAPPIN' HIS ROPES, AN' THEN--
OUT OF MY WAY!
EVEN THOUGH I CANNOT SEE--
--I STILL SHALL MAKE MY ESCAPE!
*ISSUES 88-90, N'EST-CE PAS? --ROY.
*OUI, RASCALLY. --STAN.
HEY! HOW'D HE MANAGE TA RACE STRAIGHT FOR THAT SHAFT--IF HE'S BLIND?
FOOL! YOU'VE FORGOTTEN MY INFALLIBLE RADAR SENSE!
NOW I MUST LEAVE YOUR MOST PLEASANT COMPANY...
BUT I'LL BE BACK SOME DAY--
YOU CAN DEPEND ON IT!
COULDN'T STRETCH FOR HIM --IN TIME--!
WITH HIS ANTI-GRAVITY DROP TUBE--
--HE'LL BE BACK HOME IN SUBTERRANIA IN SECONDS!
AN' THEY CAN HAVE 'IM, RUBBER MAN!
IF I NEVER LAY EYES ON THAT CREEP AGAIN, IT'LL BE TEN YEARS TOO SOON!

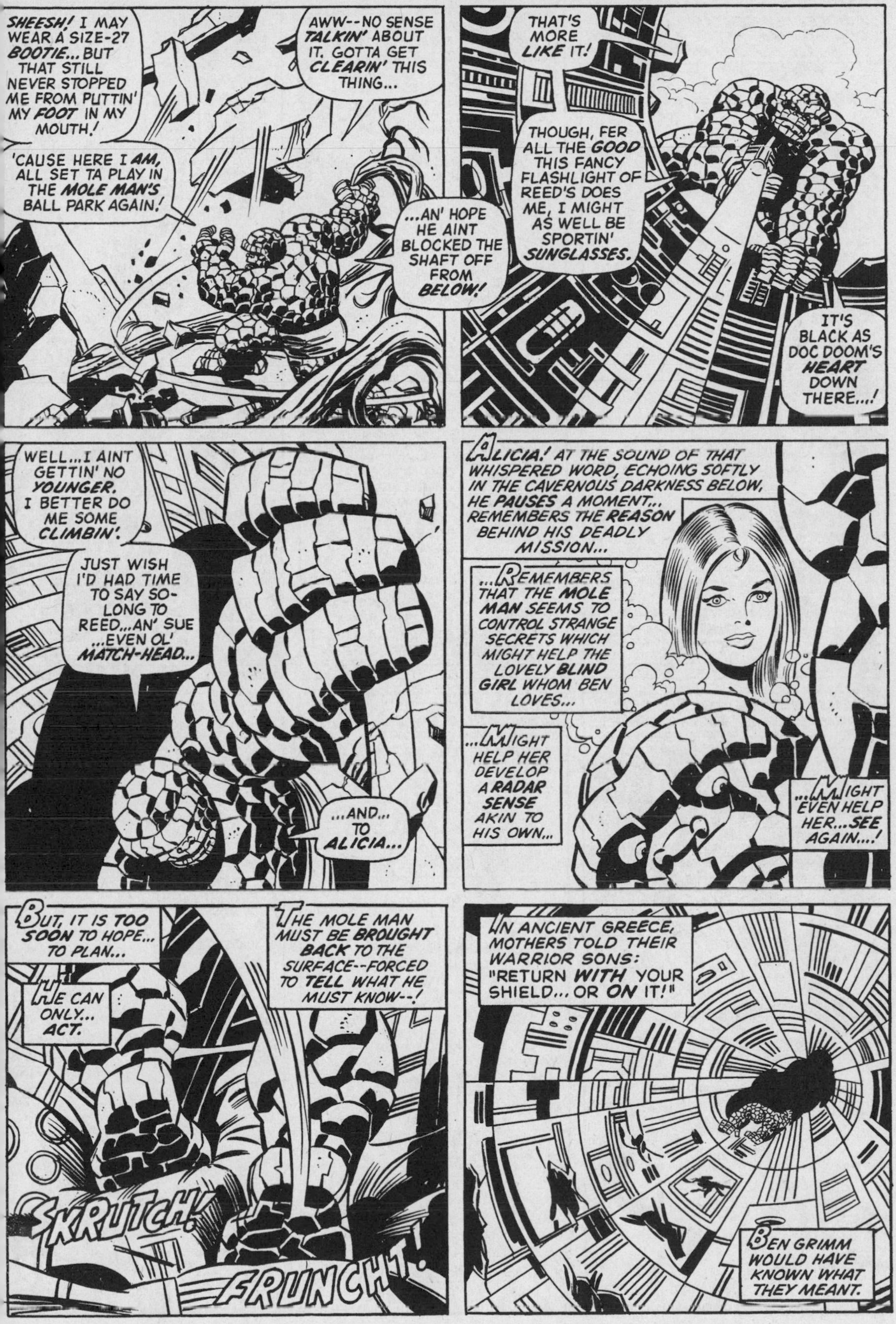
SHEESH! I MAY WEAR A SIZE-27 BOOTIE... BUT THAT STILL NEVER STOPPED ME FROM PUTTIN' MY FOOT IN MY MOUTH!
AWW--NO SENSE TALKIN' ABOUT IT. GOTTA GET CLEARIN' THIS THING...
'CAUSE HERE I AM, ALL SET TA PLAY IN THE MOLE MAN'S BALL PARK AGAIN!
...AN' HOPE HE AINT BLOCKED THE SHAFT OFF FROM BELOW!
THAT'S MORE LIKE IT!
THOUGH, FER ALL THE GOOD THIS FANCY FLASHLIGHT OF REED'S DOES ME, I MIGHT AS WELL BE SPORTIN' SUNGLASSES.
IT'S BLACK AS DOC DOOM'S HEART DOWN THERE...!
WELL...I AINT GETTIN' NO YOUNGER. I BETTER DO ME SOME CLIMBIN'.
JUST WISH I'D HAD TIME TO SAY SO-LONG TO REED...AN' SUE ...EVEN OL' MATCH-HEAD...
...AND... TO ALICIA...
ALICIA! AT THE SOUND OF THAT WHISPERED WORD, ECHOING SOFTLY IN THE CAVERNOUS DARKNESS BELOW, HE PAUSES A MOMENT... REMEMBERS THE REASON BEHIND HIS DEADLY MISSION...
...REMEMBERS THAT THE MOLE MAN SEEMS TO CONTROL STRANGE SECRETS WHICH MIGHT HELP THE LOVELY BLIND GIRL WHOM BEN LOVES...
...MIGHT HELP HER DEVELOP A RADAR SENSE AKIN TO HIS OWN...
...MIGHT EVEN HELP HER...SEE AGAIN...!
BUT, IT IS TOO SOON TO HOPE... TO PLAN...
HE CAN ONLY... ACT.
THE MOLE MAN MUST BE BROUGHT BACK TO THE SURFACE--FORCED TO TELL WHAT HE MUST KNOW--!
SKRUTCH!
FRUNCHT!
IN ANCIENT GREECE, MOTHERS TOLD THEIR WARRIOR SONS: "RETURN WITH YOUR SHIELD... OR ON IT!"
BEN GRIMM WOULD HAVE KNOWN WHAT THEY MEANT.

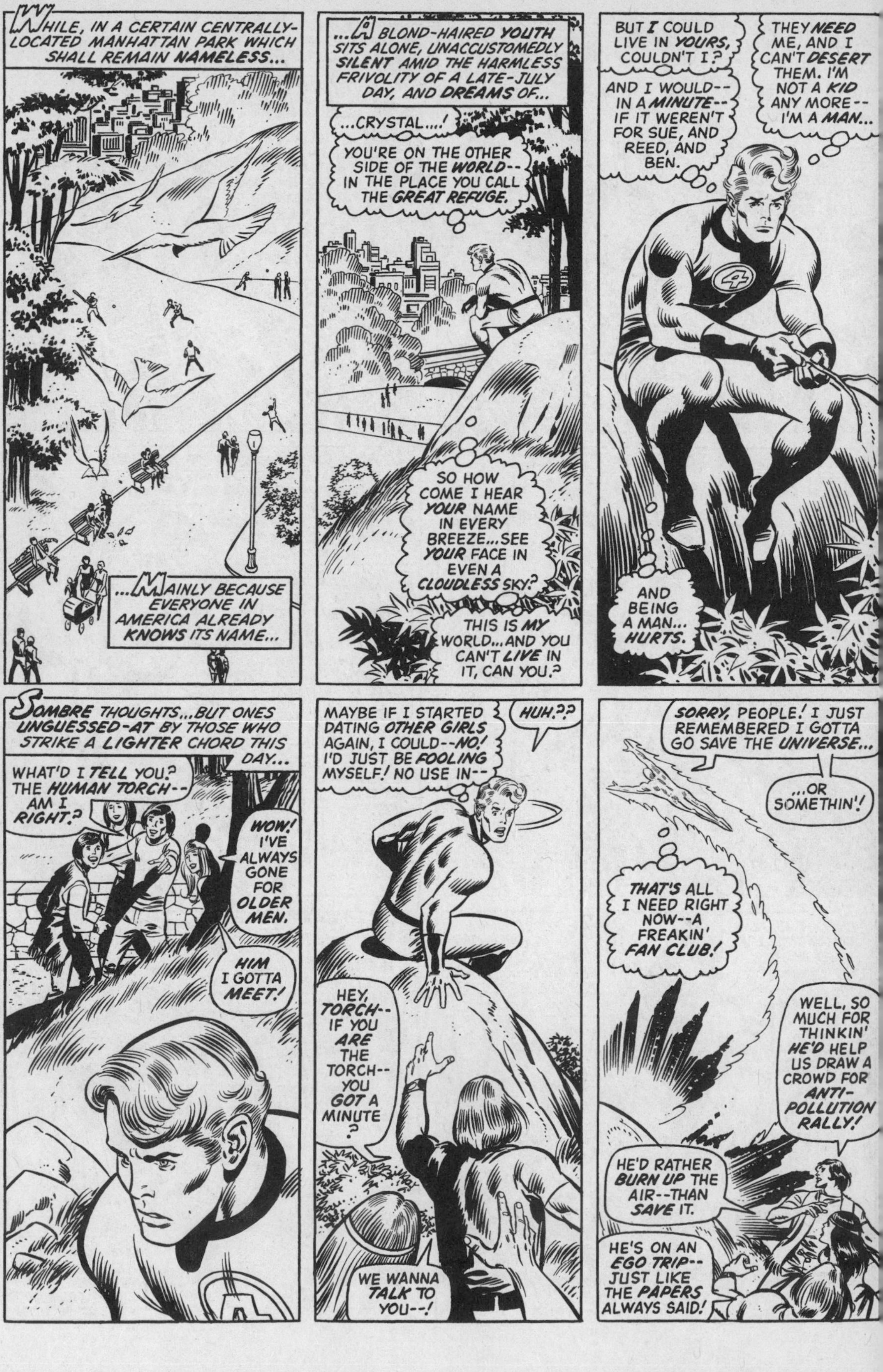
WHILE, IN A CERTAIN CENTRALLY-LOCATED MANHATTAN PARK WHICH SHALL REMAIN NAMELESS...
...MAINLY BECAUSE EVERYONE IN AMERICA ALREADY KNOWS ITS NAME...
...A BLOND-HAIRED YOUTH SITS ALONE, UNACCUSTOMEDLY SILENT AMID THE HARMLESS FRIVOLITY OF A LATE-JULY DAY, AND DREAMS OF...
...CRYSTAL...!
YOU'RE ON THE OTHER SIDE OF THE WORLD--IN THE PLACE YOU CALL THE GREAT REFUGE.
SO HOW COME I HEAR YOUR NAME IN EVERY BREEZE...SEE YOUR FACE IN EVEN A CLOUDLESS SKY?
THIS IS MY WORLD...AND YOU CAN'T LIVE IN IT, CAN YOU.?
BUT I COULD LIVE IN YOURS, COULDN'T I?
AND I WOULD--IN A MINUTE--IF IT WEREN'T FOR SUE, AND REED, AND BEN.
THEY NEED ME, AND I CAN'T DESERT THEM. I'M NOT A KID ANY MORE--I'M A MAN...
AND BEING A MAN... HURTS.
SOMBRE THOUGHTS...BUT ONES UNGUESSED-AT BY THOSE WHO STRIKE A LIGHTER CHORD THIS DAY...
WHAT'D I TELL YOU? THE HUMAN TORCH--AM I RIGHT?
WOW! I'VE ALWAYS GONE FOR OLDER MEN.
HIM I GOTTA MEET!
MAYBE IF I STARTED DATING OTHER GIRLS AGAIN, I COULD--NO! I'D JUST BE FOOLING MYSELF! NO USE IN--
HUH.??
HEY, TORCH--IF YOU ARE THE TORCH--YOU GOT A MINUTE?
WE WANNA TALK TO YOU--!
SORRY, PEOPLE! I JUST REMEMBERED I GOTTA GO SAVE THE UNIVERSE...
...OR SOMETHIN'!
THAT'S ALL I NEED RIGHT NOW--A FREAKIN' FAN CLUB!
WELL, SO MUCH FOR THINKIN' HE'D HELP US DRAW A CROWD FOR ANTI-POLLUTION RALLY!
HE'D RATHER BURN UP THE AIR--THAN SAVE IT.
HE'S ON AN EGO TRIP--JUST LIKE THE PAPERS ALWAYS SAID!

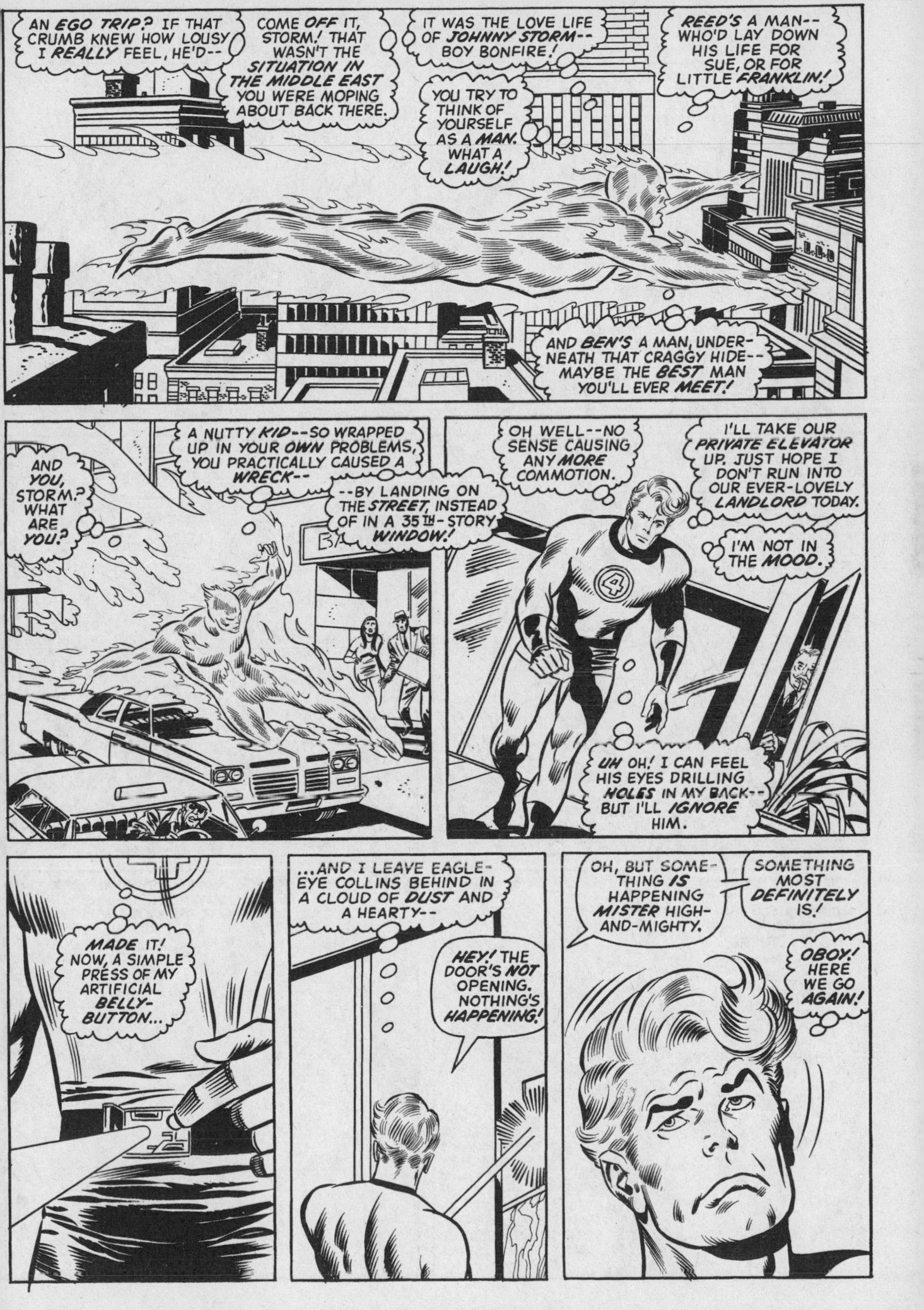
AN EGO TRIP? IF THAT CRUMB KNEW HOW LOUSY I REALLY FEEL, HE'D--
COME OFF IT, STORM! THAT WASN'T THE SITUATION IN THE MIDDLE EAST YOU WERE MOPING ABOUT BACK THERE.
IT WAS THE LOVE LIFE OF JOHNNY STORM-- BOY BONFIRE!
YOU TRY TO THINK OF YOURSELF AS A MAN. WHAT A LAUGH!
REED'S A MAN-- WHO'D LAY DOWN HIS LIFE FOR SUE, OR FOR LITTLE FRANKLIN!
AND BEN'S A MAN, UNDERNEATH THAT CRAGGY HIDE-- MAYBE THE BEST MAN YOU'LL EVER MEET!
AND YOU, STORM? WHAT ARE YOU?
A NUTTY KID--SO WRAPPED UP IN YOUR OWN PROBLEMS, YOU PRACTICALLY CAUSED A WRECK--
--BY LANDING ON THE STREET, INSTEAD OF IN A 35TH-STORY WINDOW!
OH WELL--NO SENSE CAUSING ANY MORE COMMOTION.
I'LL TAKE OUR PRIVATE ELEVATOR UP. JUST HOPE I DON'T RUN INTO OUR EVER-LOVELY LANDLORD TODAY.
I'M NOT IN THE MOOD.
UH OH! I CAN FEEL HIS EYES DRILLING HOLES IN MY BACK-- BUT I'LL IGNORE HIM.
MADE IT! NOW, A SIMPLE PRESS OF MY ARTIFICIAL BELLY-BUTTON...
...AND I LEAVE EAGLE-EYE COLLINS BEHIND IN A CLOUD OF DUST AND A HEARTY--
HEY! THE DOOR'S NOT OPENING. NOTHING'S HAPPENING!
OH, BUT SOMETHING IS HAPPENING MISTER HIGH-AND-MIGHTY.
SOMETHING MOST DEFINITELY IS!
OBOY! HERE WE GO AGAIN!

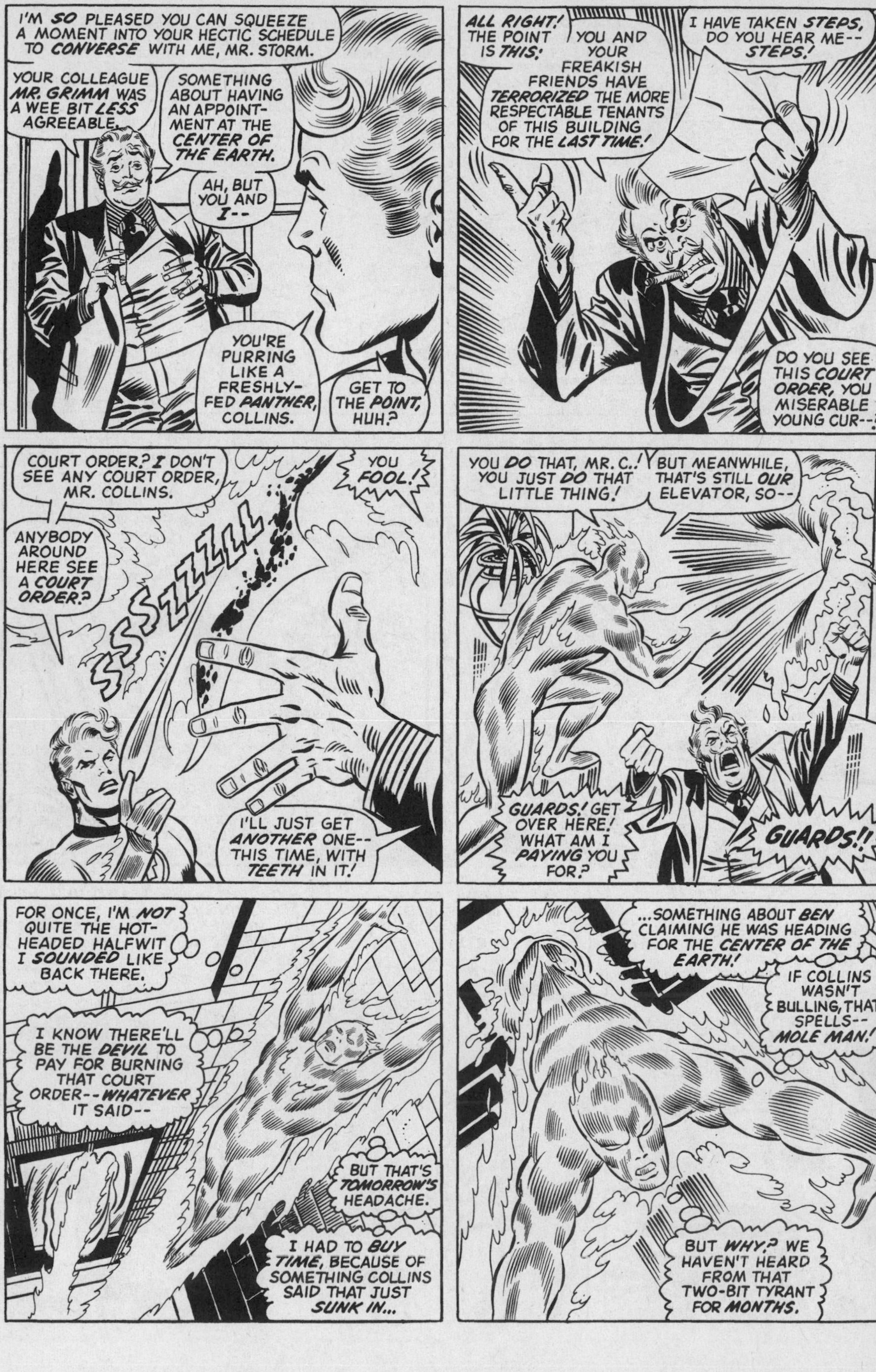
I'M SO PLEASED YOU CAN SQUEEZE A MOMENT INTO YOUR HECTIC SCHEDULE TO CONVERSE WITH ME, MR. STORM.
YOUR COLLEAGUE MR. GRIMM WAS A WEE BIT LESS AGREEABLE.
SOMETHING ABOUT HAVING AN APPOINTMENT AT THE CENTER OF THE EARTH.
AH, BUT YOU AND I--
YOU'RE PURRING LIKE A FRESHLY-FED PANTHER, COLLINS.
GET TO THE POINT, HUH?
ALL RIGHT! THE POINT IS THIS:
YOU AND YOUR FREAKISH FRIENDS HAVE TERRORIZED THE MORE RESPECTABLE TENANTS OF THIS BUILDING FOR THE LAST TIME!
I HAVE TAKEN STEPS, DO YOU HEAR ME-- STEPS!
DO YOU SEE THIS COURT ORDER, YOU MISERABLE YOUNG CUR--?
COURT ORDER? I DON'T SEE ANY COURT ORDER, MR. COLLINS.
ANYBODY AROUND HERE SEE A COURT ORDER?
SSSZZZZLLL
YOU FOOL!
I'LL JUST GET ANOTHER ONE-- THIS TIME, WITH TEETH IN IT!
YOU DO THAT, MR. C.! YOU JUST DO THAT LITTLE THING!
BUT MEANWHILE, THAT'S STILL OUR ELEVATOR, SO--
GUARDS! GET OVER HERE! WHAT AM I PAYING YOU FOR?
GUARDS!!
FOR ONCE, I'M NOT QUITE THE HOT-HEADED HALFWIT I SOUNDED LIKE BACK THERE.
I KNOW THERE'LL BE THE DEVIL TO PAY FOR BURNING THAT COURT ORDER--WHATEVER IT SAID--
BUT THAT'S TOMORROW'S HEADACHE.
I HAD TO BUY TIME, BECAUSE OF SOMETHING COLLINS SAID THAT JUST SUNK IN...
...SOMETHING ABOUT BEN CLAIMING HE WAS HEADING FOR THE CENTER OF THE EARTH!
IF COLLINS WASN'T BULLING, THAT SPELLS-- MOLE MAN!
BUT WHY? WE HAVEN'T HEARD FROM THAT TWO-BIT TYRANT FOR MONTHS.

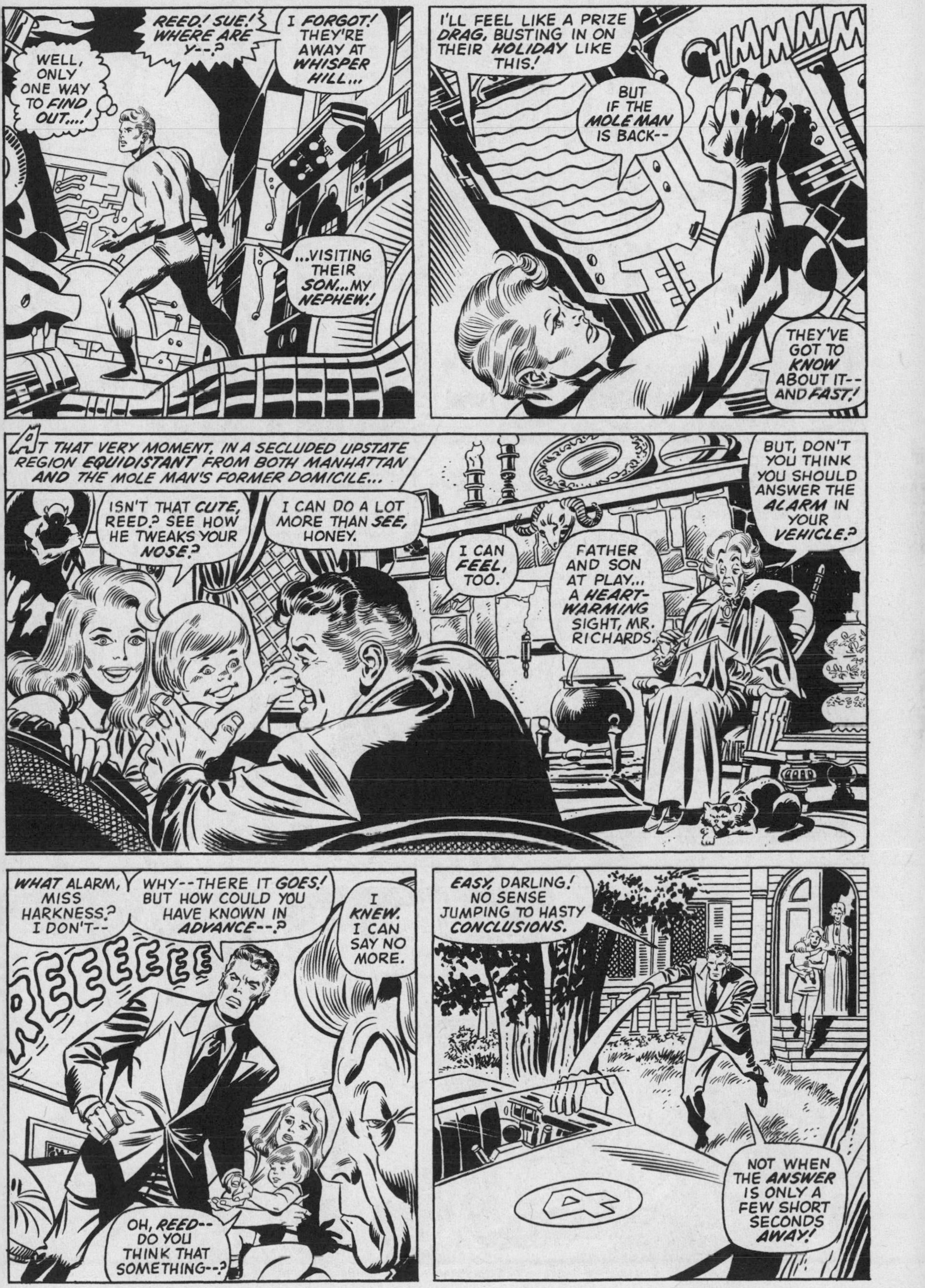
WELL, ONLY ONE WAY TO FIND OUT....!
REED! SUE! WHERE ARE Y--?
I FORGOT! THEY'RE AWAY AT WHISPER HILL...
...VISITING THEIR SON...MY NEPHEW!
I'LL FEEL LIKE A PRIZE DRAG, BUSTING IN ON THEIR HOLIDAY LIKE THIS!
HMMMM
BUT IF THE MOLE MAN IS BACK--
THEY'VE GOT TO KNOW ABOUT IT--AND FAST!
AT THAT VERY MOMENT, IN A SECLUDED UPSTATE REGION EQUIDISTANT FROM BOTH MANHATTAN AND THE MOLE MAN'S FORMER DOMICILE...
ISN'T THAT CUTE, REED? SEE HOW HE TWEAKS YOUR NOSE?
I CAN DO A LOT MORE THAN SEE, HONEY.
I CAN FEEL, TOO.
FATHER AND SON AT PLAY... A HEART-WARMING SIGHT, MR. RICHARDS.
BUT, DON'T YOU THINK YOU SHOULD ANSWER THE ALARM IN YOUR VEHICLE?
WHAT ALARM, MISS HARKNESS? I DON'T--
WHY--THERE IT GOES! BUT HOW COULD YOU HAVE KNOWN IN ADVANCE--?
I KNEW. I CAN SAY NO MORE.
REEEEEE
OH, REED--DO YOU THINK THAT SOMETHING--?
EASY, DARLING! NO SENSE JUMPING TO HASTY CONCLUSIONS.
NOT WHEN THE ANSWER IS ONLY A FEW SHORT SECONDS AWAY!

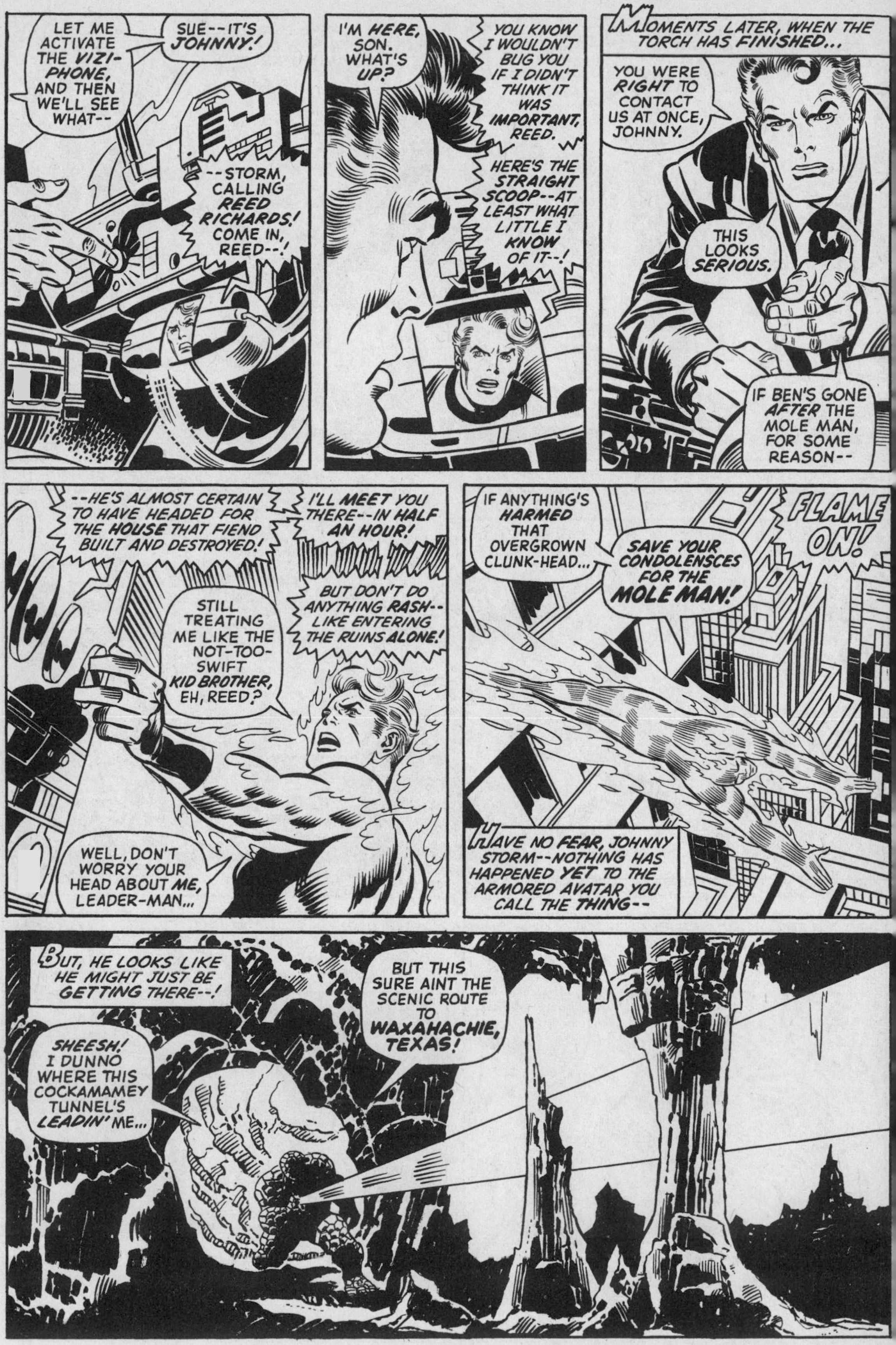
LET ME ACTIVATE THE VIZI-PHONE, AND THEN WE'LL SEE WHAT--
SUE--IT'S JOHNNY!
--STORM, CALLING REED RICHARDS! COME IN, REED--!
I'M HERE, SON. WHAT'S UP?
YOU KNOW I WOULDN'T BUG YOU IF I DIDN'T THINK IT WAS IMPORTANT, REED.
HERE'S THE STRAIGHT SCOOP--AT LEAST WHAT LITTLE I KNOW OF IT--!
MOMENTS LATER, WHEN THE TORCH HAS FINISHED...
YOU WERE RIGHT TO CONTACT US AT ONCE, JOHNNY.
THIS LOOKS SERIOUS.
IF BEN'S GONE AFTER THE MOLE MAN, FOR SOME REASON--
--HE'S ALMOST CERTAIN TO HAVE HEADED FOR THE HOUSE THAT FIEND BUILT AND DESTROYED!
I'LL MEET YOU THERE--IN HALF AN HOUR!
BUT DON'T DO ANYTHING RASH--LIKE ENTERING THE RUINS ALONE!
STILL TREATING ME LIKE THE NOT-TOO-SWIFT KID BROTHER, EH, REED?
WELL, DON'T WORRY YOUR HEAD ABOUT ME, LEADER-MAN...
IF ANYTHING'S HARMED THAT OVERGROWN CLUNK-HEAD...
SAVE YOUR CONDOLENSCES FOR THE MOLE MAN!
FLAME ON!
HAVE NO FEAR, JOHNNY STORM--NOTHING HAS HAPPENED YET TO THE ARMORED AVATAR YOU CALL THE THING--
BUT, HE LOOKS LIKE HE MIGHT JUST BE GETTING THERE--!
SHEESH! I DUNNO WHERE THIS COCKAMAMEY TUNNEL'S LEADIN' ME...
BUT THIS SURE AINT THE SCENIC ROUTE TO WAXAHACHIE, TEXAS!

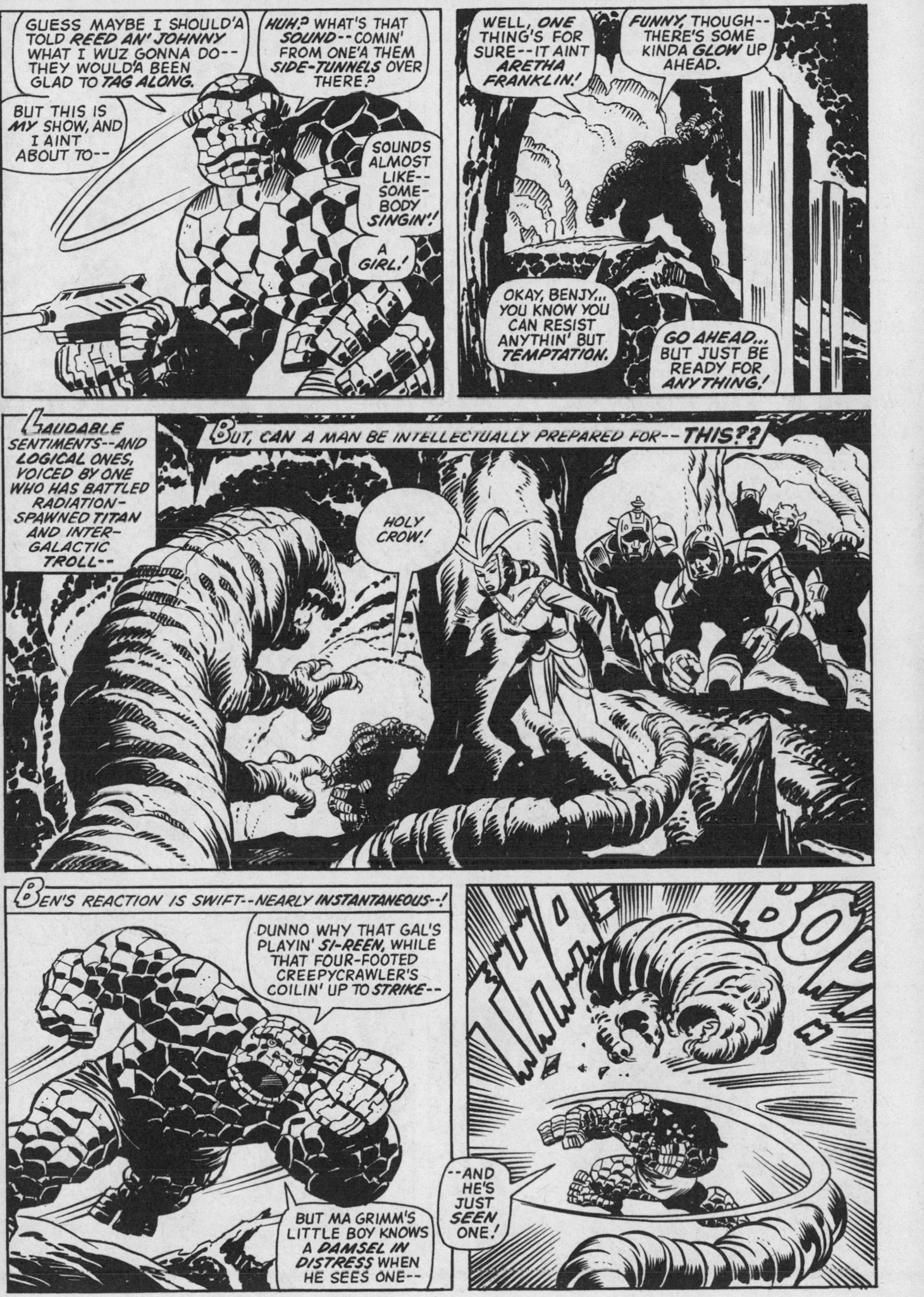
GUESS MAYBE I SHOULD'A TOLD REED AN' JOHNNY WHAT I WUZ GONNA DO-- THEY WOULD'A BEEN GLAD TO TAG ALONG.
BUT THIS IS MY SHOW, AND I AINT ABOUT TO--
HUH? WHAT'S THAT SOUND--COMIN' FROM ONE'A THEM SIDE-TUNNELS OVER THERE?
SOUNDS ALMOST LIKE--SOME-BODY SINGIN'!
A GIRL!
WELL, ONE THING'S FOR SURE--IT AINT ARETHA FRANKLIN!
FUNNY, THOUGH--THERE'S SOME KINDA GLOW UP AHEAD.
OKAY, BENJY... YOU KNOW YOU CAN RESIST ANYTHIN' BUT TEMPTATION.
GO AHEAD... BUT JUST BE READY FOR ANYTHING!
LAUDABLE SENTIMENTS--AND LOGICAL ONES, VOICED BY ONE WHO HAS BATTLED RADIATION-SPAWNED TITAN AND INTER-GALACTIC TROLL--
BUT, CAN A MAN BE INTELLECTUALLY PREPARED FOR--THIS??
HOLY CROW!
BEN'S REACTION IS SWIFT--NEARLY INSTANTANEOUS--!
DUNNO WHY THAT GAL'S PLAYIN' SI-REEN, WHILE THAT FOUR-FOOTED CREEPYCRAWLER'S COILIN' UP TO STRIKE--
BUT MA GRIMM'S LITTLE BOY KNOWS A DAMSEL IN DISTRESS WHEN HE SEES ONE--
THA-BOOM!
--AND HE'S JUST SEEN ONE!

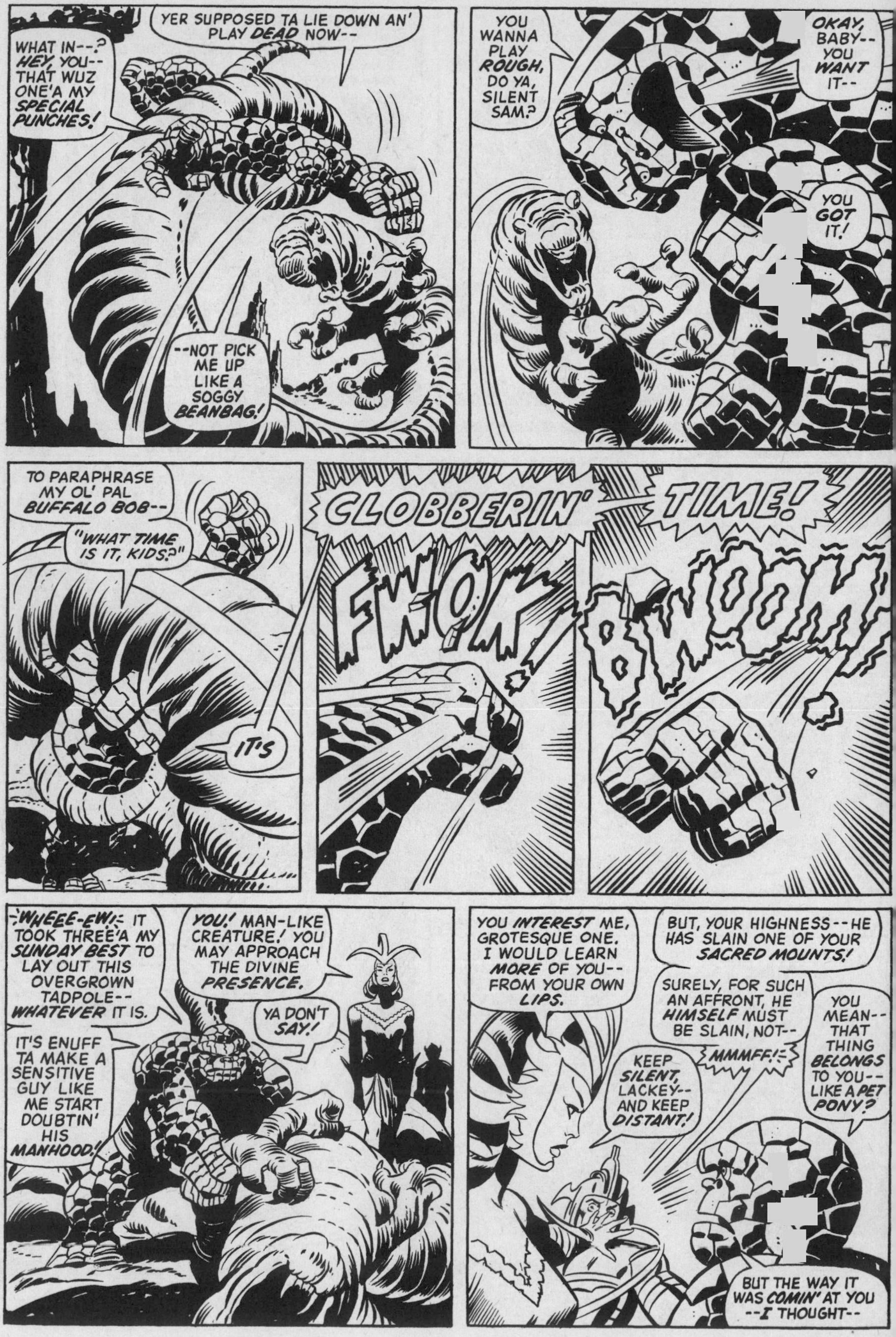

WHAT IN--? HEY, YOU-- THAT WUZ ONE'A MY SPECIAL PUNCHES!
YER SUPPOSED TA LIE DOWN AN' PLAY DEAD NOW--
--NOT PICK ME UP LIKE A SOGGY BEANBAG!
YOU WANNA PLAY ROUGH, DO YA, SILENT SAM?
OKAY, BABY-- YOU WANT IT--
YOU GOT IT!
TO PARAPHRASE MY OL' PAL BUFFALO BOB--
"WHAT TIME IS IT, KIDS?"
IT'S
CLOBBERIN'
TIME!
FWOK
BWOOM
WHEEE-EW! IT TOOK THREE'A MY SUNDAY BEST TO LAY OUT THIS OVERGROWN TADPOLE-- WHATEVER IT IS.
IT'S ENUFF TA MAKE A SENSITIVE GUY LIKE ME START DOUBTIN' HIS MANHOOD!
YOU! MAN-LIKE CREATURE! YOU MAY APPROACH THE DIVINE PRESENCE.
YA DON'T SAY!
YOU INTEREST ME, GROTESQUE ONE. I WOULD LEARN MORE OF YOU-- FROM YOUR OWN LIPS.
BUT, YOUR HIGHNESS--HE HAS SLAIN ONE OF YOUR SACRED MOUNTS!
SURELY, FOR SUCH AN AFFRONT, HE HIMSELF MUST BE SLAIN, NOT--
MMMFF!
KEEP SILENT, LACKEY-- AND KEEP DISTANT!
YOU MEAN--THAT THING BELONGS TO YOU--LIKE A PET PONY?
BUT THE WAY IT WAS COMIN' AT YOU --I THOUGHT--

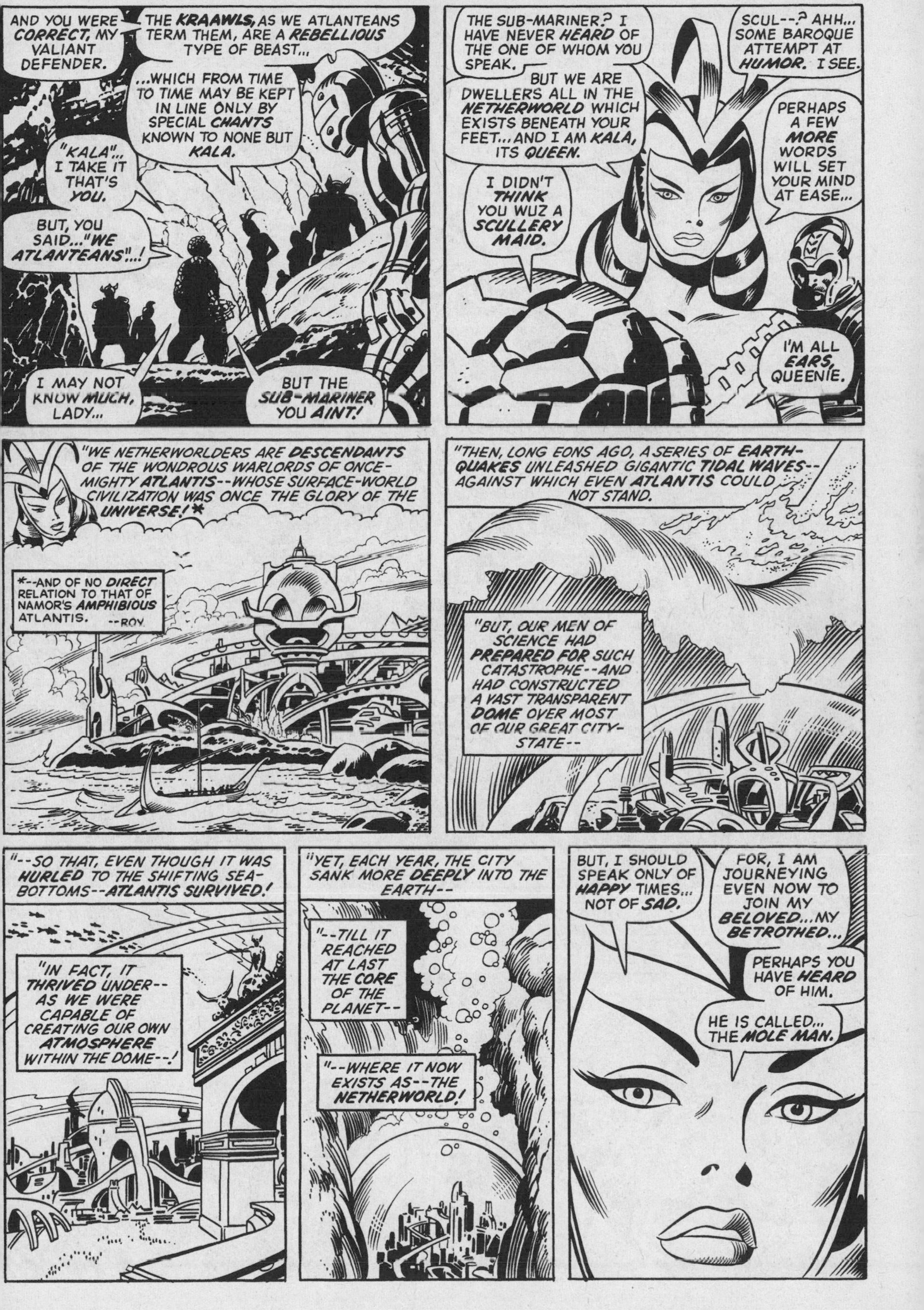
AND YOU WERE CORRECT, MY VALIANT DEFENDER.
THE KRAAWLS, AS WE ATLANTEANS TERM THEM, ARE A REBELLIOUS TYPE OF BEAST...
...WHICH FROM TIME TO TIME MAY BE KEPT IN LINE ONLY BY SPECIAL CHANTS KNOWN TO NONE BUT KALA.
"KALA"... I TAKE IT THAT'S YOU.
BUT, YOU SAID..."WE ATLANTEANS"...!
I MAY NOT KNOW MUCH, LADY...
BUT THE SUB-MARINER YOU AINT!
THE SUB-MARINER? I HAVE NEVER HEARD OF THE ONE OF WHOM YOU SPEAK.
BUT WE ARE DWELLERS ALL IN THE NETHERWORLD WHICH EXISTS BENEATH YOUR FEET... AND I AM KALA, ITS QUEEN.
I DIDN'T THINK YOU WUZ A SCULLERY MAID.
SCUL--? AHH... SOME BAROQUE ATTEMPT AT HUMOR, I SEE.
PERHAPS A FEW MORE WORDS WILL SET YOUR MIND AT EASE...
I'M ALL EARS, QUEENIE.
"WE NETHERWORLDERS ARE DESCENDANTS OF THE WONDROUS WARLORDS OF ONCE-MIGHTY ATLANTIS--WHOSE SURFACE-WORLD CIVILIZATION WAS ONCE THE GLORY OF THE UNIVERSE!*
*--AND OF NO DIRECT RELATION TO THAT OF NAMOR'S AMPHIBIOUS ATLANTIS. --ROY.
"THEN, LONG EONS AGO, A SERIES OF EARTH-QUAKES UNLEASHED GIGANTIC TIDAL WAVES--AGAINST WHICH EVEN ATLANTIS COULD NOT STAND.
"BUT, OUR MEN OF SCIENCE HAD PREPARED FOR SUCH CATASTROPHE--AND HAD CONSTRUCTED A VAST TRANSPARENT DOME OVER MOST OF OUR GREAT CITY-STATE--
"--SO THAT, EVEN THOUGH IT WAS HURLED TO THE SHIFTING SEA-BOTTOMS--ATLANTIS SURVIVED!
"IN FACT, IT THRIVED UNDER--AS WE WERE CAPABLE OF CREATING OUR OWN ATMOSPHERE WITHIN THE DOME--!
"YET, EACH YEAR, THE CITY SANK MORE DEEPLY INTO THE EARTH--
"--TILL IT REACHED AT LAST THE CORE OF THE PLANET--
"--WHERE IT NOW EXISTS AS--THE NETHERWORLD!
BUT, I SHOULD SPEAK ONLY OF HAPPY TIMES... NOT OF SAD.
FOR, I AM JOURNEYING EVEN NOW TO JOIN MY BELOVED... MY BETROTHED...
PERHAPS YOU HAVE HEARD OF HIM.
HE IS CALLED... THE MOLE MAN.

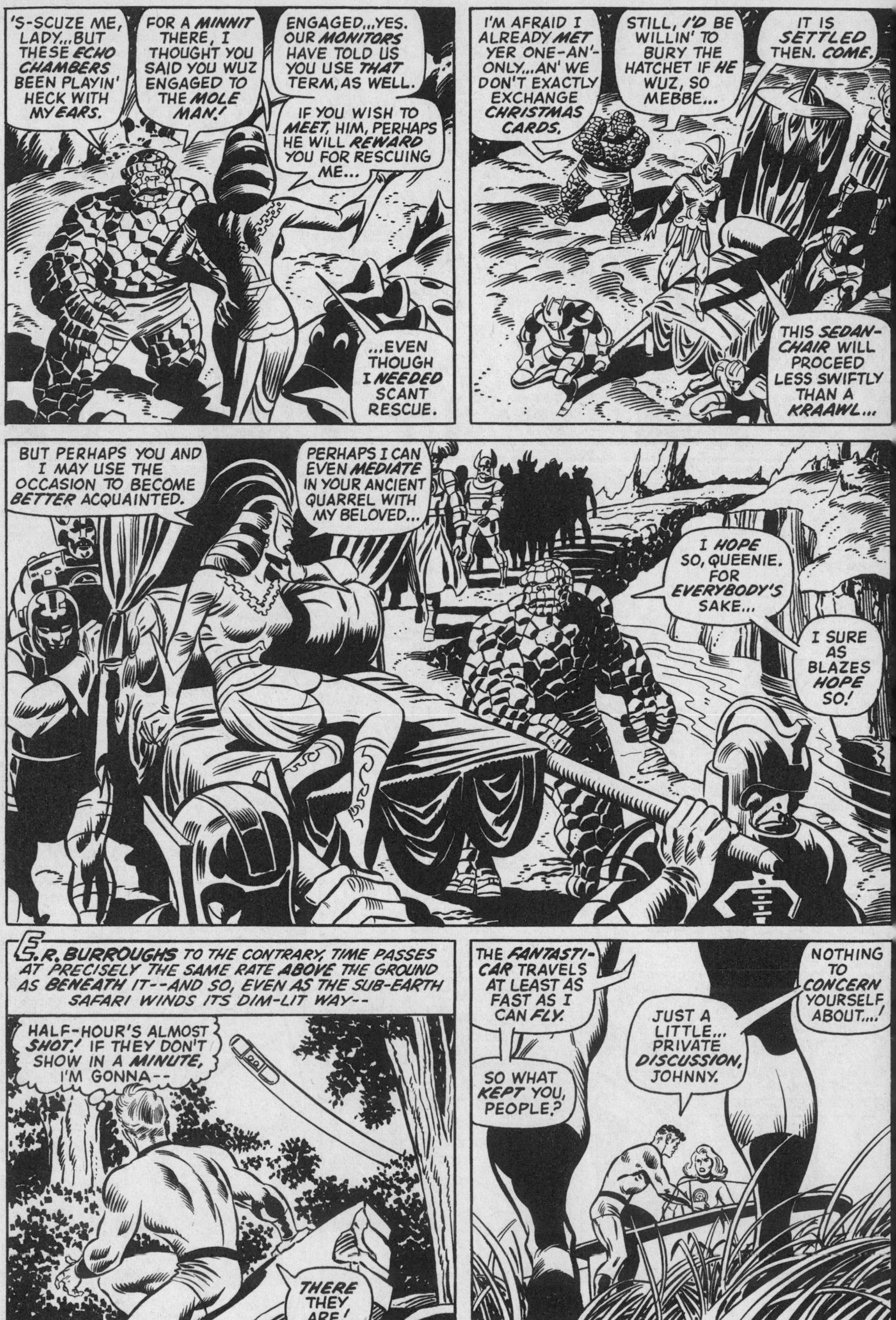
'S-SCUZE ME, LADY... BUT THESE ECHO CHAMBERS BEEN PLAYIN' HECK WITH MY EARS.
FOR A MINNIT THERE, I THOUGHT YOU SAID YOU WUZ ENGAGED TO THE MOLE MAN!
ENGAGED... YES. OUR MONITORS HAVE TOLD US YOU USE THAT TERM, AS WELL.
IF YOU WISH TO MEET, HIM, PERHAPS HE WILL REWARD YOU FOR RESCUING ME...
...EVEN THOUGH I NEEDED SCANT RESCUE.
I'M AFRAID I ALREADY MET YER ONE-AN'-ONLY... AN' WE DON'T EXACTLY EXCHANGE CHRISTMAS CARDS.
STILL, I'D BE WILLIN' TO BURY THE HATCHET IF HE WUZ, SO MEBBE...
IT IS SETTLED THEN. COME.
THIS SEDAN-CHAIR WILL PROCEED LESS SWIFTLY THAN A KRAAWL...
BUT PERHAPS YOU AND I MAY USE THE OCCASION TO BECOME BETTER ACQUAINTED.
PERHAPS I CAN EVEN MEDIATE IN YOUR ANCIENT QUARREL WITH MY BELOVED...
I HOPE SO, QUEENIE. FOR EVERYBODY'S SAKE...
I SURE AS BLAZES HOPE SO!
E.R. BURROUGHS TO THE CONTRARY, TIME PASSES AT PRECISELY THE SAME RATE ABOVE THE GROUND AS BENEATH IT--AND SO, EVEN AS THE SUB-EARTH SAFARI WINDS ITS DIM-LIT WAY--
HALF-HOUR'S ALMOST SHOT! IF THEY DON'T SHOW IN A MINUTE, I'M GONNA--
THERE THEY ARE!
THE FANTASTI-CAR TRAVELS AT LEAST AS FAST AS I CAN FLY.
SO WHAT KEPT YOU, PEOPLE?
NOTHING TO CONCERN YOURSELF ABOUT...!
JUST A LITTLE... PRIVATE DISCUSSION, JOHNNY.

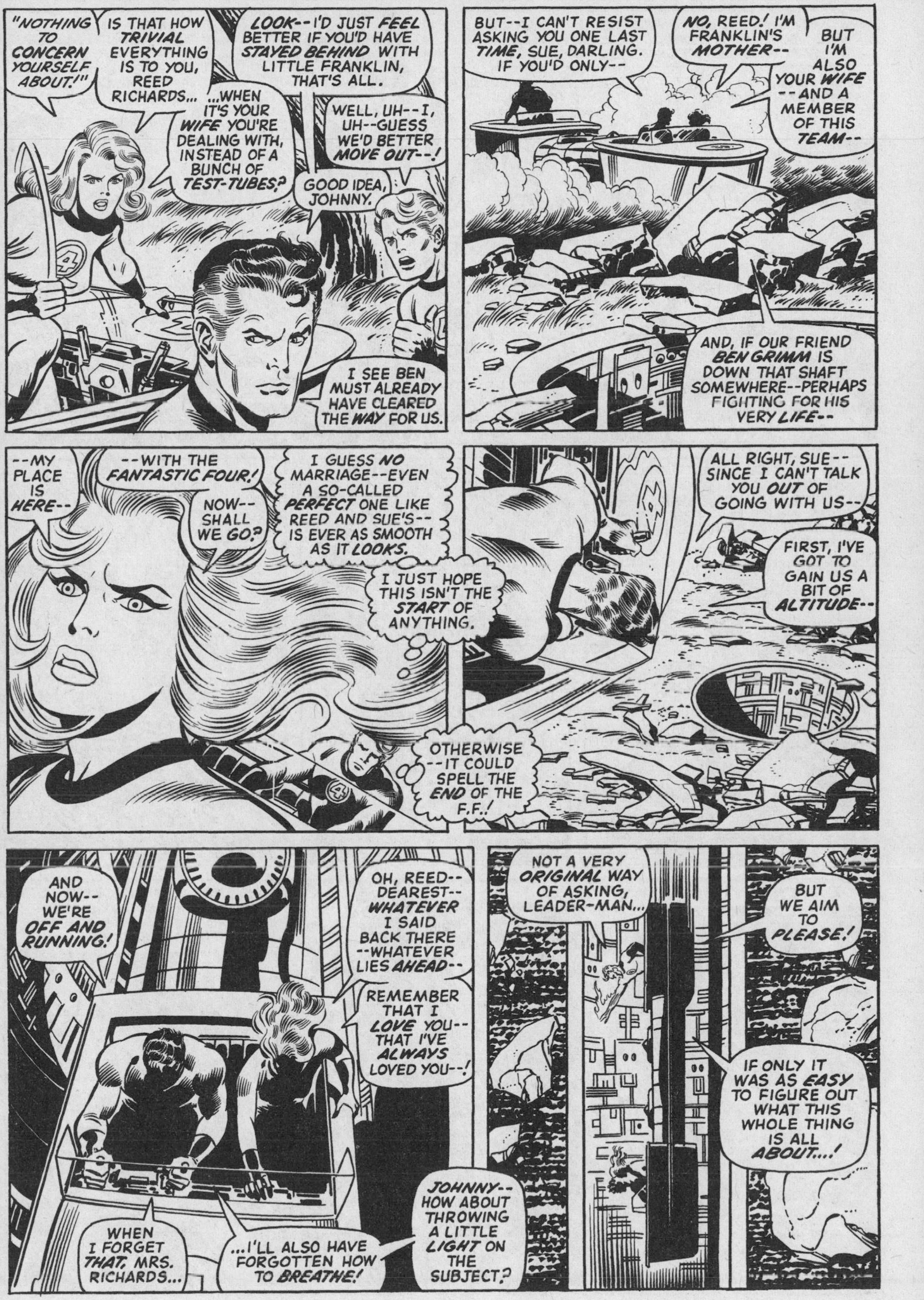
"NOTHING TO CONCERN YOURSELF ABOUT!"
IS THAT HOW TRIVIAL EVERYTHING IS TO YOU, REED RICHARDS...
...WHEN IT'S YOUR WIFE YOU'RE DEALING WITH, INSTEAD OF A BUNCH OF TEST-TUBES?
LOOK--I'D JUST FEEL BETTER IF YOU'D HAVE STAYED BEHIND WITH LITTLE FRANKLIN, THAT'S ALL.
WELL, UH--I, UH--GUESS WE'D BETTER MOVE OUT--!
GOOD IDEA, JOHNNY.
I SEE BEN MUST ALREADY HAVE CLEARED THE WAY FOR US.
BUT--I CAN'T RESIST ASKING YOU ONE LAST TIME, SUE, DARLING. IF YOU'D ONLY--
NO, REED! I'M FRANKLIN'S MOTHER--
BUT I'M ALSO YOUR WIFE --AND A MEMBER OF THIS TEAM--
AND, IF OUR FRIEND BEN GRIMM IS DOWN THAT SHAFT SOMEWHERE--PERHAPS FIGHTING FOR HIS VERY LIFE--
--MY PLACE IS HERE--
--WITH THE FANTASTIC FOUR!
NOW--SHALL WE GO?
I GUESS NO MARRIAGE--EVEN A SO-CALLED PERFECT ONE LIKE REED AND SUE'S--IS EVER AS SMOOTH AS IT LOOKS.
I JUST HOPE THIS ISN'T THE START OF ANYTHING.
OTHERWISE--IT COULD SPELL THE END OF THE F.F.!
ALL RIGHT, SUE--SINCE I CAN'T TALK YOU OUT OF GOING WITH US--
FIRST, I'VE GOT TO GAIN US A BIT OF ALTITUDE--
AND NOW--WE'RE OFF AND RUNNING!
OH, REED--DEAREST--WHATEVER I SAID BACK THERE--WHATEVER LIES AHEAD--
REMEMBER THAT I LOVE YOU--THAT I'VE ALWAYS LOVED YOU--!
WHEN I FORGET THAT, MRS. RICHARDS...
...I'LL ALSO HAVE FORGOTTEN HOW TO BREATHE!
JOHNNY--HOW ABOUT THROWING A LITTLE LIGHT ON THE SUBJECT?
NOT A VERY ORIGINAL WAY OF ASKING, LEADER-MAN...
BUT WE AIM TO PLEASE!
IF ONLY IT WAS AS EASY TO FIGURE OUT WHAT THIS WHOLE THING IS ALL ABOUT...!

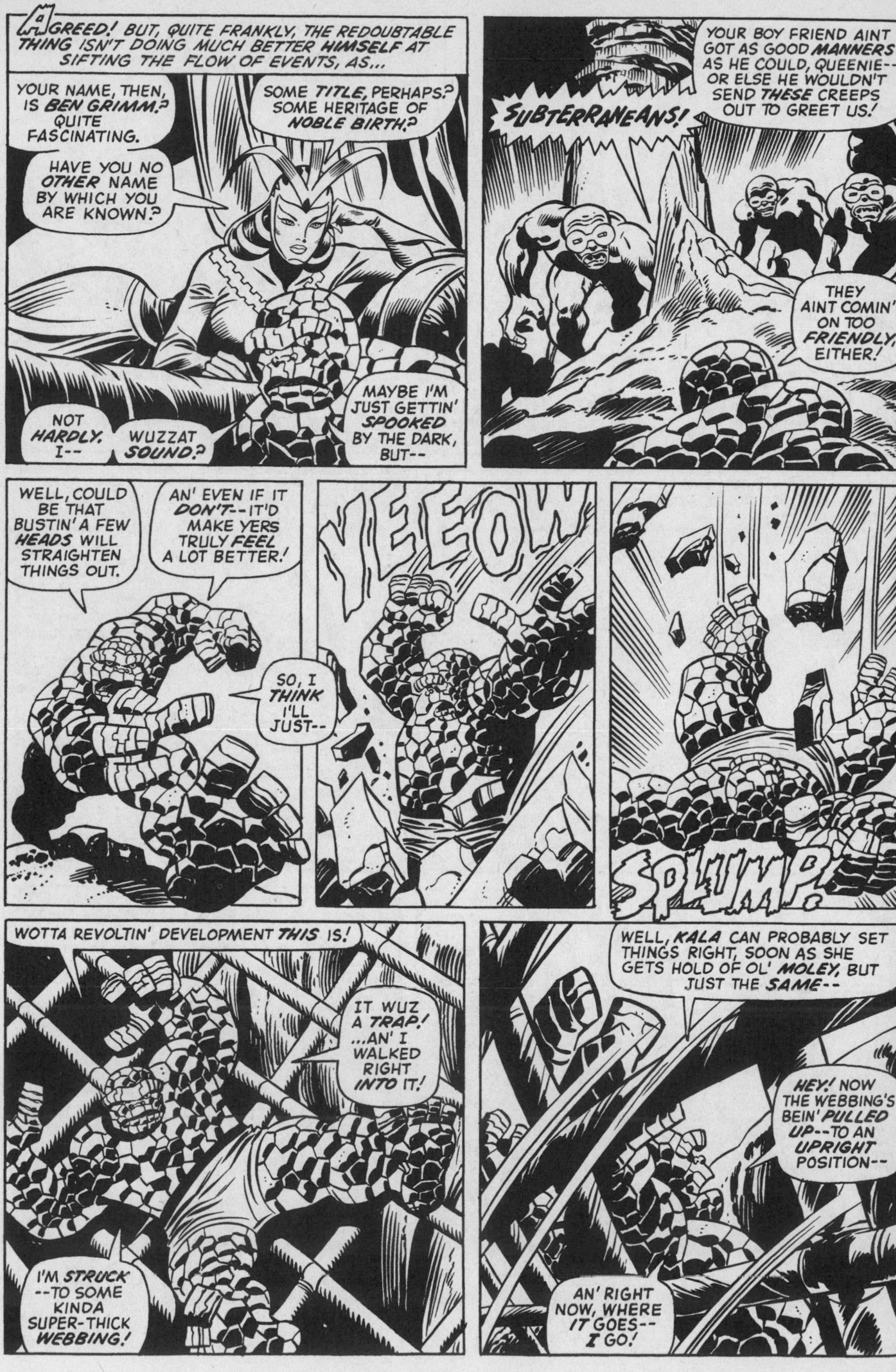
AGREED! BUT, QUITE FRANKLY, THE REDOUBTABLE THING ISN'T DOING MUCH BETTER HIMSELF AT SIFTING THE FLOW OF EVENTS, AS...
YOUR NAME, THEN, IS BEN GRIMM? QUITE FASCINATING.
SOME TITLE, PERHAPS? SOME HERITAGE OF NOBLE BIRTH?
HAVE YOU NO OTHER NAME BY WHICH YOU ARE KNOWN?
NOT HARDLY. I--
WUZZAT SOUND?
MAYBE I'M JUST GETTIN' SPOOKED BY THE DARK, BUT--
SUBTERRANEANS!
YOUR BOY FRIEND AINT GOT AS GOOD MANNERS AS HE COULD, QUEENIE--OR ELSE HE WOULDN'T SEND THESE CREEPS OUT TO GREET US!
THEY AINT COMIN' ON TOO FRIENDLY, EITHER!
WELL, COULD BE THAT BUSTIN' A FEW HEADS WILL STRAIGHTEN THINGS OUT.
AN' EVEN IF IT DON'T--IT'D MAKE YERS TRULY FEEL A LOT BETTER!
SO, I THINK I'LL JUST--
YEEOW
SPLUMP!
WOTTA REVOLTIN' DEVELOPMENT THIS IS!
IT WUZ A TRAP! ...AN' I WALKED RIGHT INTO IT!
I'M STRUCK--TO SOME KINDA SUPER-THICK WEBBING!
WELL, KALA CAN PROBABLY SET THINGS RIGHT, SOON AS SHE GETS HOLD OF OL' MOLEY, BUT JUST THE SAME--
HEY! NOW THE WEBBING'S BEIN' PULLED UP--TO AN UPRIGHT POSITION--
AN' RIGHT NOW, WHERE IT GOES--I GO!

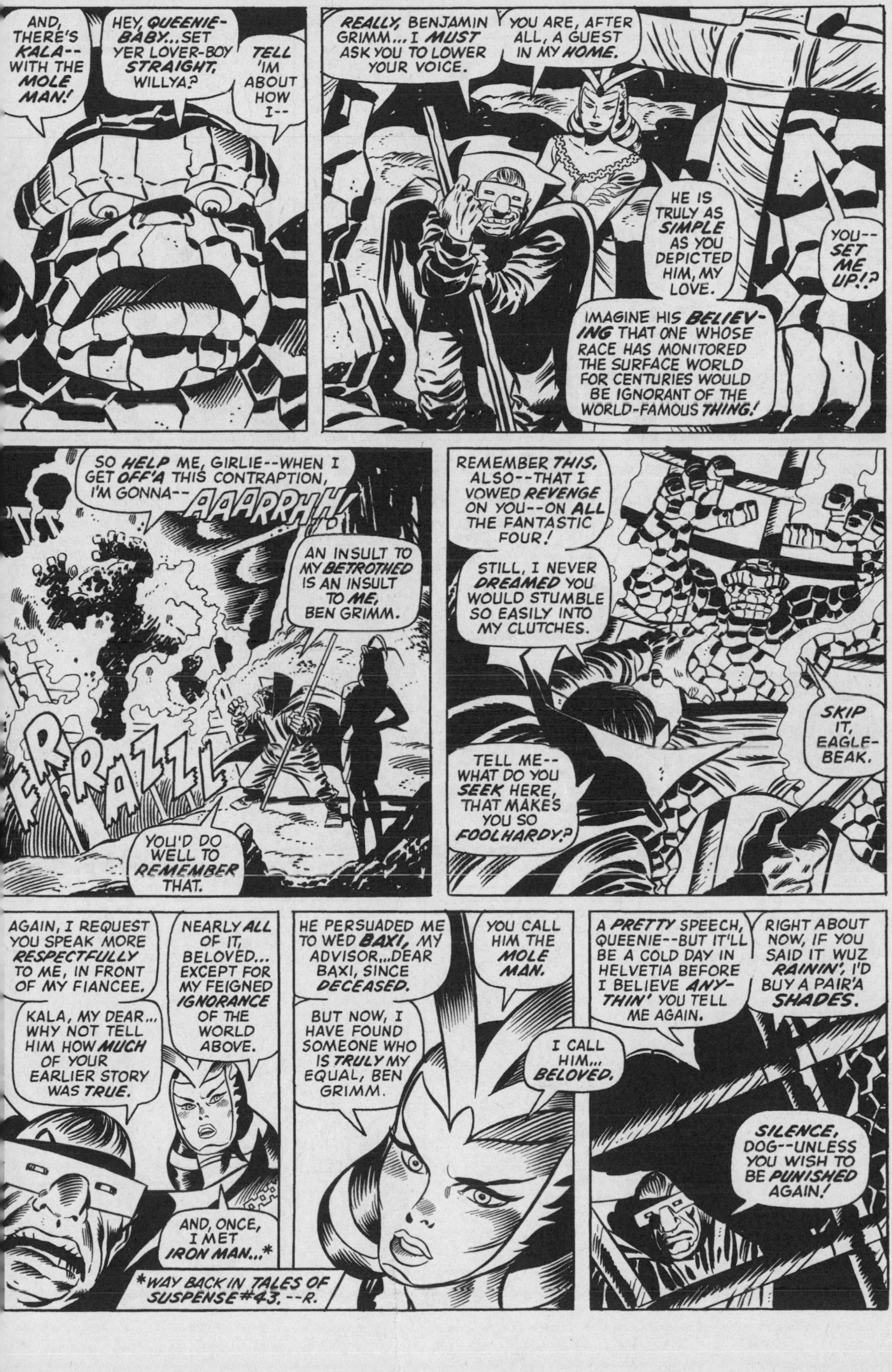
AND, THERE'S KALA-- WITH THE MOLE MAN!
HEY, QUEENIE-BABY...SET YER LOVER-BOY STRAIGHT, WILLYA?
TELL 'IM ABOUT HOW I--
REALLY, BENJAMIN GRIMM... I MUST ASK YOU TO LOWER YOUR VOICE.
YOU ARE, AFTER ALL, A GUEST IN MY HOME.
HE IS TRULY AS SIMPLE AS YOU DEPICTED HIM, MY LOVE.
YOU-- SET ME UP!?
IMAGINE HIS BELIEVING THAT ONE WHOSE RACE HAS MONITORED THE SURFACE WORLD FOR CENTURIES WOULD BE IGNORANT OF THE WORLD-FAMOUS THING!
SO HELP ME, GIRLIE--WHEN I GET OFF'A THIS CONTRAPTION, I'M GONNA-- AAARRHH!
AN INSULT TO MY BETROTHED IS AN INSULT TO ME, BEN GRIMM.
FRAZZL
YOU'D DO WELL TO REMEMBER THAT.
REMEMBER THIS, ALSO--THAT I VOWED REVENGE ON YOU--ON ALL THE FANTASTIC FOUR!
STILL, I NEVER DREAMED YOU WOULD STUMBLE SO EASILY INTO MY CLUTCHES.
SKIP IT, EAGLE-BEAK.
TELL ME-- WHAT DO YOU SEEK HERE, THAT MAKES YOU SO FOOLHARDY?
AGAIN, I REQUEST YOU SPEAK MORE RESPECTFULLY TO ME, IN FRONT OF MY FIANCEE.
KALA, MY DEAR... WHY NOT TELL HIM HOW MUCH OF YOUR EARLIER STORY WAS TRUE.
NEARLY ALL OF IT, BELOVED... EXCEPT FOR MY FEIGNED IGNORANCE OF THE WORLD ABOVE.
AND, ONCE, I MET IRON MAN...*
*WAY BACK IN TALES OF SUSPENSE #43. --R.
HE PERSUADED ME TO WED BAXI, MY ADVISOR...DEAR BAXI, SINCE DECEASED.
YOU CALL HIM THE MOLE MAN.
BUT NOW, I HAVE FOUND SOMEONE WHO IS TRULY MY EQUAL, BEN GRIMM.
I CALL HIM... BELOVED.
A PRETTY SPEECH, QUEENIE--BUT IT'LL BE A COLD DAY IN HELVETIA BEFORE I BELIEVE ANY-THIN' YOU TELL ME AGAIN.
RIGHT ABOUT NOW, IF YOU SAID IT WUZ RAININ', I'D BUY A PAIR'A SHADES.
SILENCE, DOG--UNLESS YOU WISH TO BE PUNISHED AGAIN!

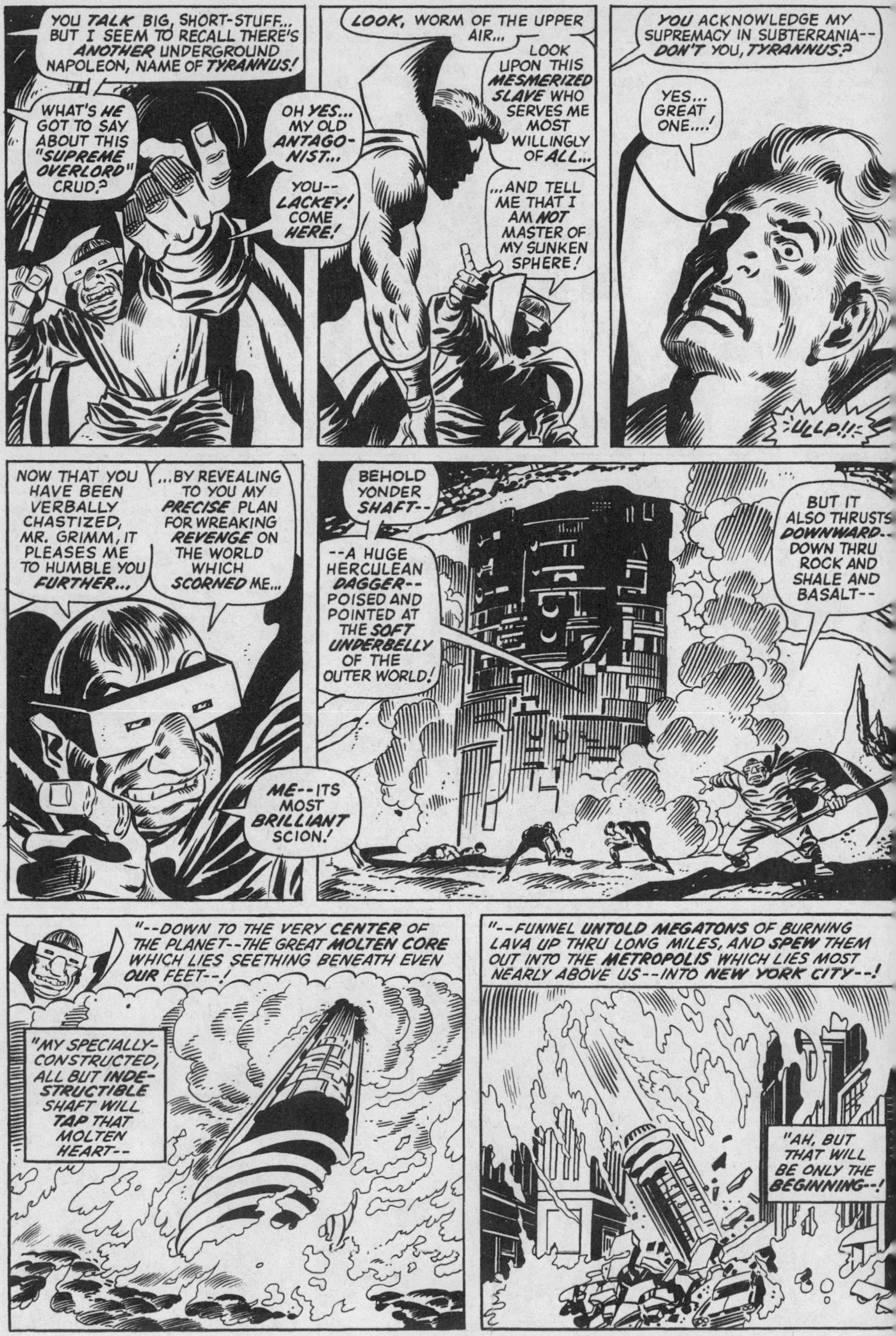
YOU TALK BIG, SHORT-STUFF... BUT I SEEM TO RECALL THERE'S ANOTHER UNDERGROUND NAPOLEON, NAME OF TYRANNUS!
WHAT'S HE GOT TO SAY ABOUT THIS "SUPREME OVERLORD" CRUD?
OH YES... MY OLD ANTAGONIST...
YOU--LACKEY! COME HERE!
LOOK, WORM OF THE UPPER AIR...
LOOK UPON THIS MESMERIZED SLAVE WHO SERVES ME MOST WILLINGLY OF ALL...
...AND TELL ME THAT I AM NOT MASTER OF MY SUNKEN SPHERE!
YOU ACKNOWLEDGE MY SUPREMACY IN SUBTERRANIA--DON'T YOU, TYRANNUS?
YES... GREAT ONE....!
ULLP!!
NOW THAT YOU HAVE BEEN VERBALLY CHASTIZED, MR. GRIMM, IT PLEASES ME TO HUMBLE YOU FURTHER...
...BY REVEALING TO YOU MY PRECISE PLAN FOR WREAKING REVENGE ON THE WORLD WHICH SCORNED ME...
ME--ITS MOST BRILLIANT SCION!
BEHOLD YONDER SHAFT--
--A HUGE HERCULEAN DAGGER--POISED AND POINTED AT THE SOFT UNDERBELLY OF THE OUTER WORLD!
BUT IT ALSO THRUSTS DOWNWARD--DOWN THRU ROCK AND SHALE AND BASALT--
"--DOWN TO THE VERY CENTER OF THE PLANET--THE GREAT MOLTEN CORE WHICH LIES SEETHING BENEATH EVEN OUR FEET--!
"MY SPECIALLY-CONSTRUCTED, ALL BUT INDESTRUCTIBLE SHAFT WILL TAP THAT MOLTEN HEART--
"--FUNNEL UNTOLD MEGATONS OF BURNING LAVA UP THRU LONG MILES, AND SPEW THEM OUT INTO THE METROPOLIS WHICH LIES MOST NEARLY ABOVE US--INTO NEW YORK CITY--!
"AH, BUT THAT WILL BE ONLY THE BEGINNING--!

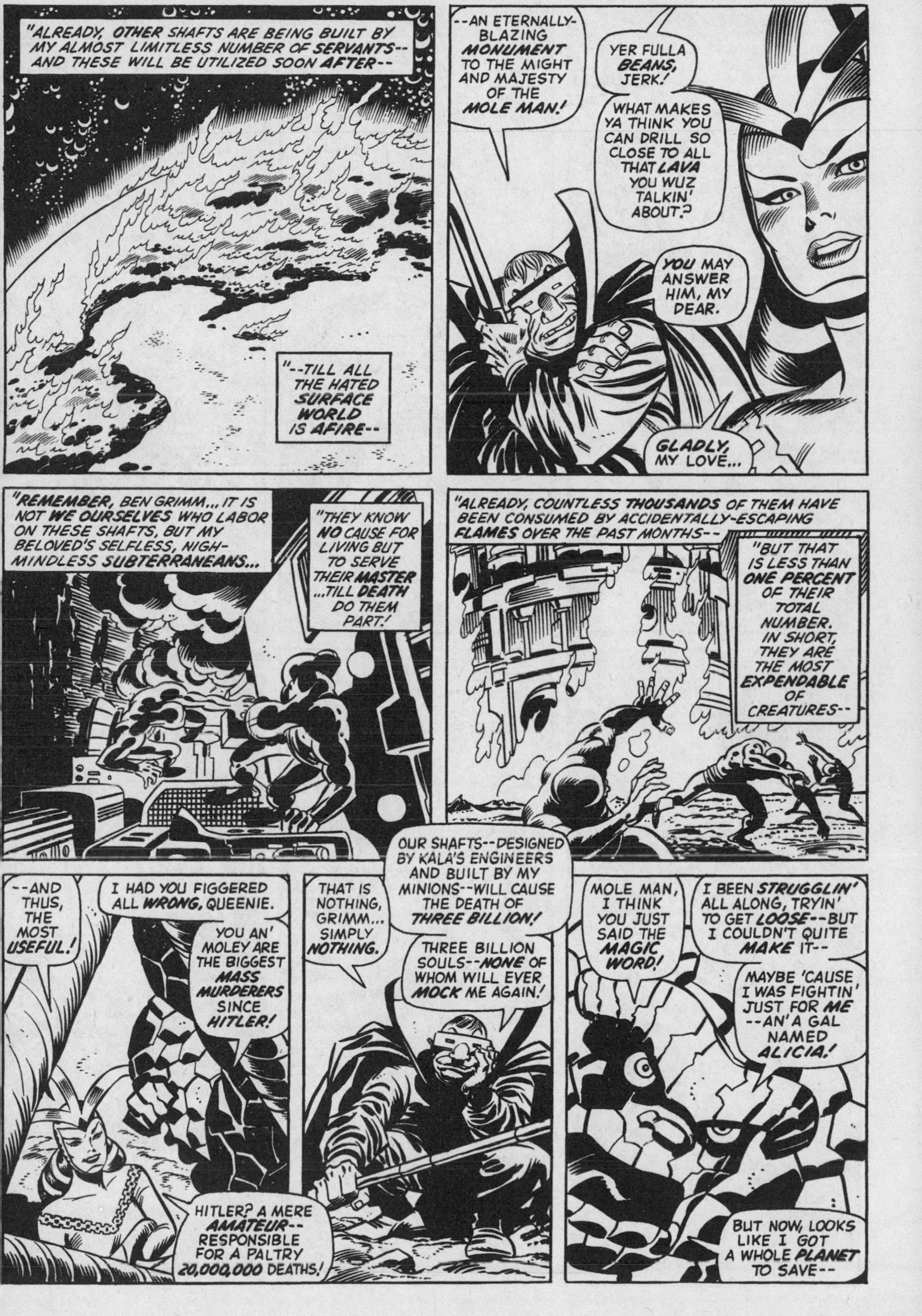
"ALREADY, OTHER SHAFTS ARE BEING BUILT BY MY ALMOST LIMITLESS NUMBER OF SERVANTS-- AND THESE WILL BE UTILIZED SOON AFTER--
"--TILL ALL THE HATED SURFACE WORLD IS AFIRE--
--AN ETERNALLY-BLAZING MONUMENT TO THE MIGHT AND MAJESTY OF THE MOLE MAN!
YER FULLA BEANS, JERK!
WHAT MAKES YA THINK YOU CAN DRILL SO CLOSE TO ALL THAT LAVA YOU WUZ TALKIN' ABOUT?
YOU MAY ANSWER HIM, MY DEAR.
GLADLY, MY LOVE...
"REMEMBER, BEN GRIMM... IT IS NOT WE OURSELVES WHO LABOR ON THESE SHAFTS, BUT MY BELOVED'S SELFLESS, NIGH-MINDLESS SUBTERRANEANS...
"THEY KNOW NO CAUSE FOR LIVING BUT TO SERVE THEIR MASTER ...TILL DEATH DO THEM PART!
"ALREADY, COUNTLESS THOUSANDS OF THEM HAVE BEEN CONSUMED BY ACCIDENTALLY-ESCAPING FLAMES OVER THE PAST MONTHS--
"BUT THAT IS LESS THAN ONE PERCENT OF THEIR TOTAL NUMBER. IN SHORT, THEY ARE THE MOST EXPENDABLE OF CREATURES--
--AND THUS, THE MOST USEFUL!
I HAD YOU FIGGERED ALL WRONG, QUEENIE.
YOU AN' MOLEY ARE THE BIGGEST MASS MURDERERS SINCE HITLER!
HITLER? A MERE AMATEUR-- RESPONSIBLE FOR A PALTRY 20,000,000 DEATHS!
THAT IS NOTHING, GRIMM... SIMPLY NOTHING.
OUR SHAFTS--DESIGNED BY KALA'S ENGINEERS AND BUILT BY MY MINIONS--WILL CAUSE THE DEATH OF THREE BILLION!
THREE BILLION SOULS--NONE OF WHOM WILL EVER MOCK ME AGAIN!
MOLE MAN, I THINK YOU JUST SAID THE MAGIC WORD!
I BEEN STRUGGLIN' ALL ALONG, TRYIN' TO GET LOOSE--BUT I COULDN'T QUITE MAKE IT--
MAYBE 'CAUSE I WAS FIGHTIN' JUST FOR ME --AN' A GAL NAMED ALICIA!
BUT NOW, LOOKS LIKE I GOT A WHOLE PLANET TO SAVE--

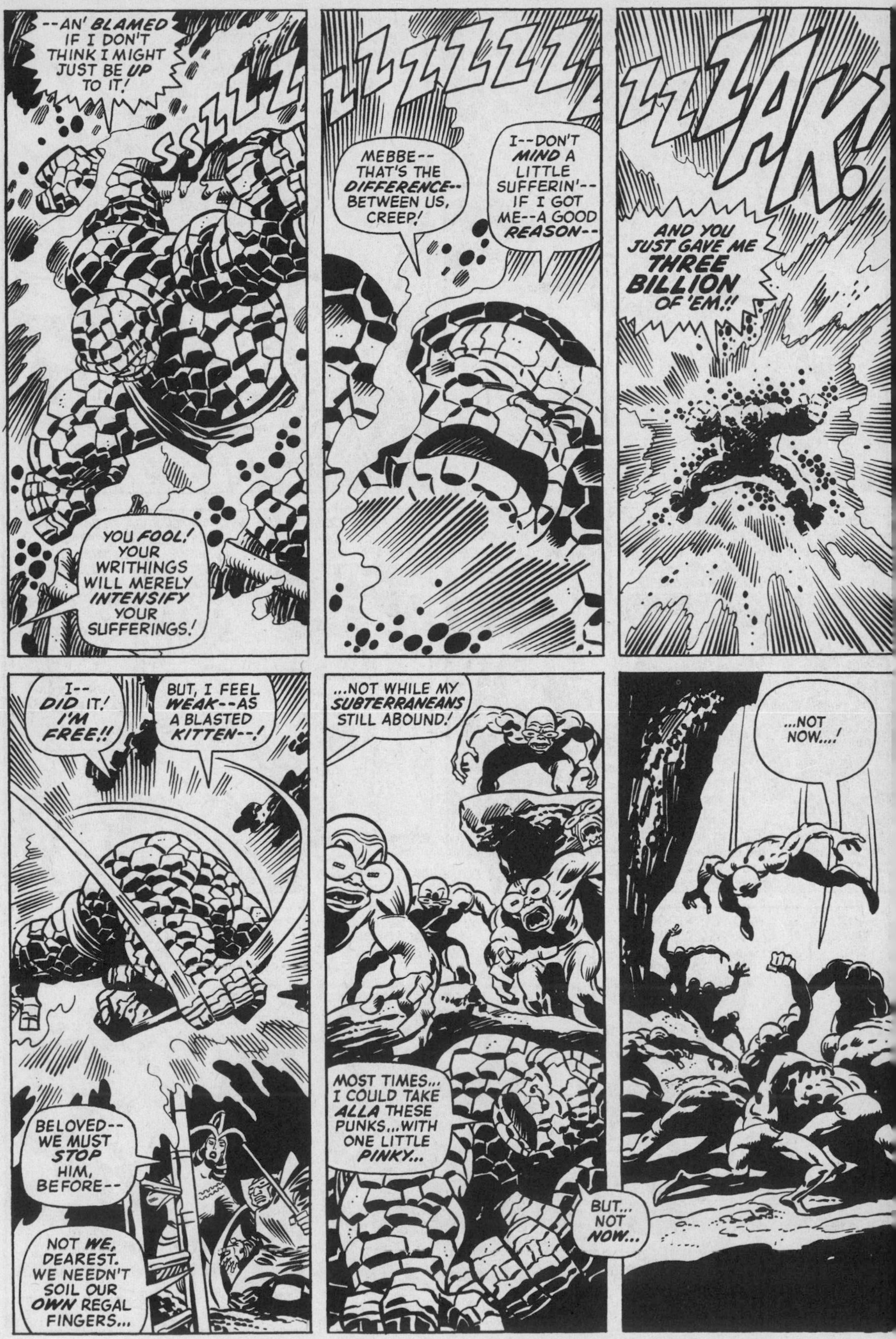
--AN' BLAMED IF I DON'T THINK I MIGHT JUST BE UP TO IT!
SSZZZZZ
YOU FOOL! YOUR WRITHINGS WILL MERELY INTENSIFY YOUR SUFFERINGS!
ZZZZZZZZ
MEBBE-- THAT'S THE DIFFERENCE-- BETWEEN US, CREEP!
I--DON'T MIND A LITTLE SUFFERIN'-- IF I GOT ME--A GOOD REASON--
ZZZZAK!
AND YOU JUST GAVE ME THREE BILLION OF 'EM!!
I-- DID IT! I'M FREE!!
BUT, I FEEL WEAK--AS A BLASTED KITTEN--!
BELOVED-- WE MUST STOP HIM, BEFORE--
NOT WE, DEAREST. WE NEEDN'T SOIL OUR OWN REGAL FINGERS...
...NOT WHILE MY SUBTERRANEANS STILL ABOUND!
MOST TIMES... I COULD TAKE ALLA THESE PUNKS...WITH ONE LITTLE PINKY...
BUT... NOT NOW...
...NOT NOW...!

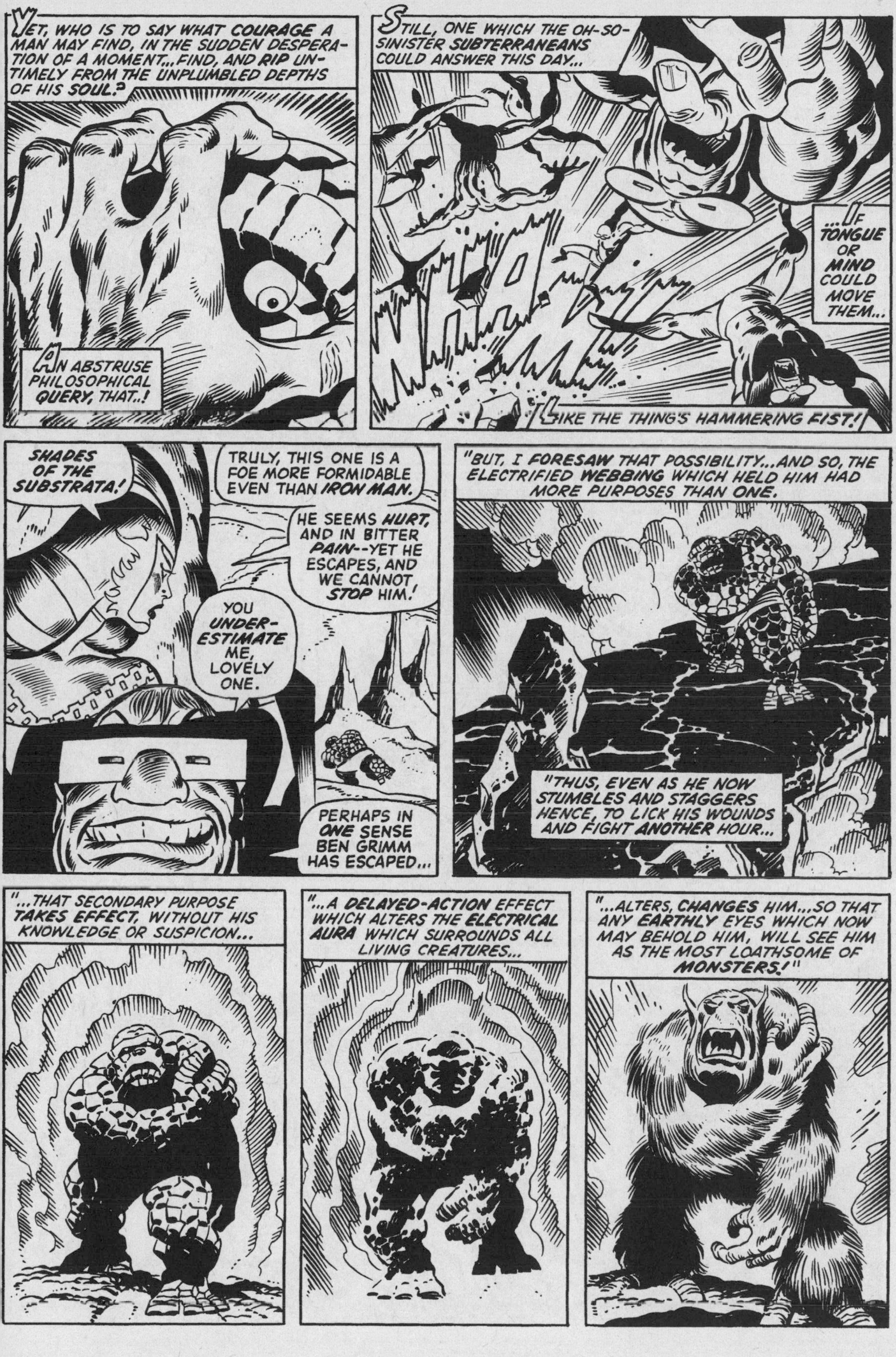
YET, WHO IS TO SAY WHAT COURAGE A MAN MAY FIND, IN THE SUDDEN DESPERATION OF A MOMENT...FIND, AND RIP UNTIMELY FROM THE UNPLUMBLED DEPTHS OF HIS SOUL?
AN ABSTRUSE PHILOSOPHICAL QUERY, THAT..!
STILL, ONE WHICH THE OH-SO-SINISTER SUBTERRANEANS COULD ANSWER THIS DAY...
...IF TONGUE OR MIND COULD MOVE THEM...
...LIKE THE THING'S HAMMERING FIST!
SHADES OF THE SUBSTRATA!
TRULY, THIS ONE IS A FOE MORE FORMIDABLE EVEN THAN IRON MAN.
HE SEEMS HURT, AND IN BITTER PAIN--YET HE ESCAPES, AND WE CANNOT STOP HIM!
YOU UNDER-ESTIMATE ME, LOVELY ONE.
PERHAPS IN ONE SENSE BEN GRIMM HAS ESCAPED...
"BUT, I FORESAW THAT POSSIBILITY...AND SO, THE ELECTRIFIED WEBBING WHICH HELD HIM HAD MORE PURPOSES THAN ONE.
"THUS, EVEN AS HE NOW STUMBLES AND STAGGERS HENCE, TO LICK HIS WOUNDS AND FIGHT ANOTHER HOUR...
"...THAT SECONDARY PURPOSE TAKES EFFECT, WITHOUT HIS KNOWLEDGE OR SUSPICION...
"...A DELAYED-ACTION EFFECT WHICH ALTERS THE ELECTRICAL AURA WHICH SURROUNDS ALL LIVING CREATURES...
"...ALTERS, CHANGES HIM...SO THAT ANY EARTHLY EYES WHICH NOW MAY BEHOLD HIM, WILL SEE HIM AS THE MOST LOATHSOME OF MONSTERS!"

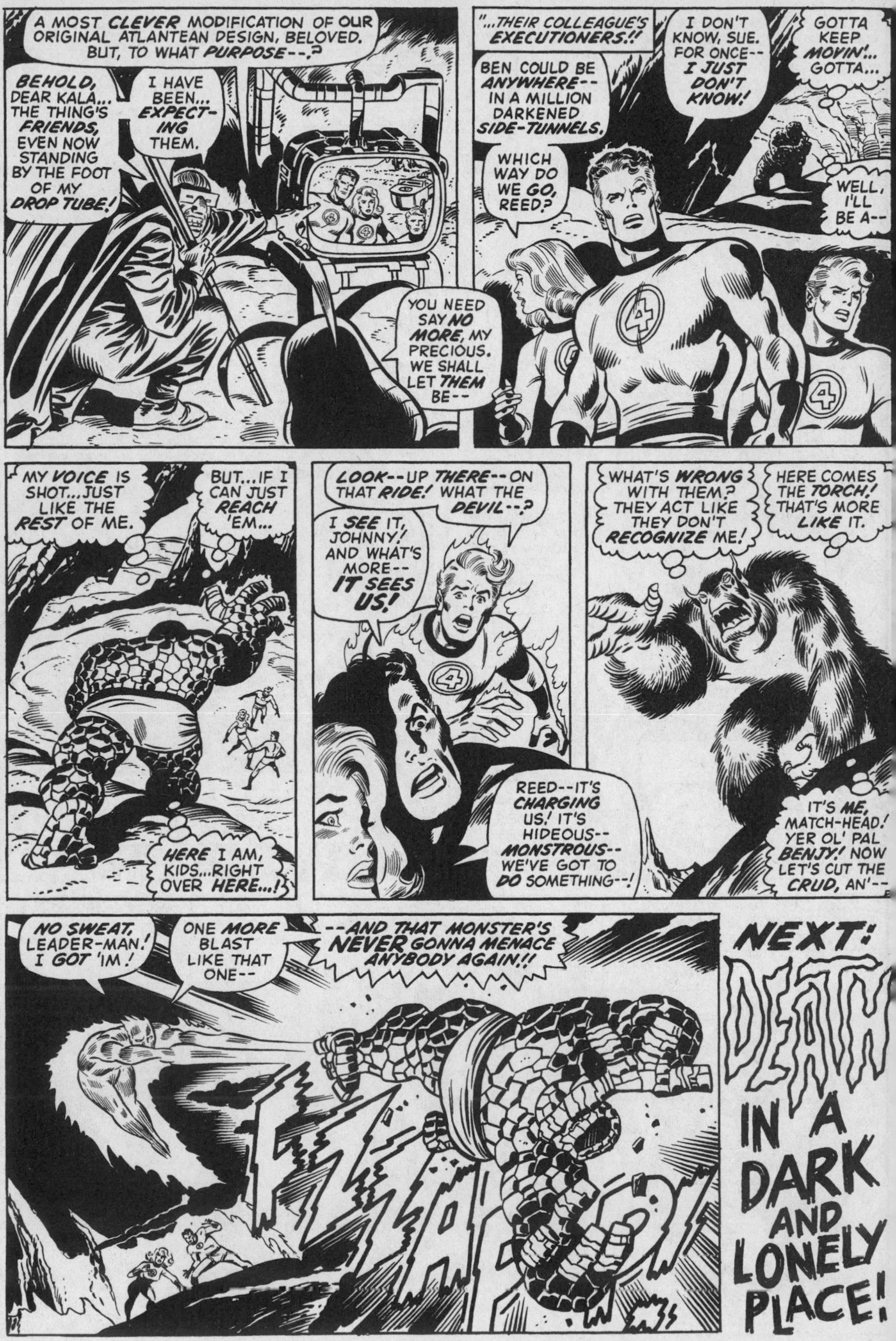
A MOST CLEVER MODIFICATION OF OUR ORIGINAL ATLANTEAN DESIGN, BELOVED. BUT, TO WHAT PURPOSE--?
BEHOLD, DEAR KALA... THE THING'S FRIENDS, EVEN NOW STANDING BY THE FOOT OF MY DROP TUBE!
I HAVE BEEN... EXPECTING THEM.
YOU NEED SAY NO MORE, MY PRECIOUS. WE SHALL LET THEM BE--
"...THEIR COLLEAGUE'S EXECUTIONERS!!
BEN COULD BE ANYWHERE-- IN A MILLION DARKENED SIDE-TUNNELS.
WHICH WAY DO WE GO, REED?
I DON'T KNOW, SUE. FOR ONCE-- I JUST DON'T KNOW!
GOTTA KEEP MOVIN'!... GOTTA...
WELL, I'LL BE A--
MY VOICE IS SHOT... JUST LIKE THE REST OF ME.
BUT... IF I CAN JUST REACH 'EM...
HERE I AM, KIDS... RIGHT OVER HERE...!
LOOK-- UP THERE-- ON THAT RIDE! WHAT THE DEVIL--?
I SEE IT, JOHNNY! AND WHAT'S MORE-- IT SEES US!
REED--IT'S CHARGING US! IT'S HIDEOUS-- MONSTROUS-- WE'VE GOT TO DO SOMETHING--!
WHAT'S WRONG WITH THEM? THEY ACT LIKE THEY DON'T RECOGNIZE ME!
HERE COMES THE TORCH! THAT'S MORE LIKE IT.
IT'S ME, MATCH-HEAD! YER OL' PAL BENJY! NOW LET'S CUT THE CRUD, AN'--
NO SWEAT, LEADER-MAN! I GOT 'IM!
ONE MORE BLAST LIKE THAT ONE--
--AND THAT MONSTER'S NEVER GONNA MENACE ANYBODY AGAIN!!
NEXT:
DEATH IN A DARK AND LONELY PLACE!

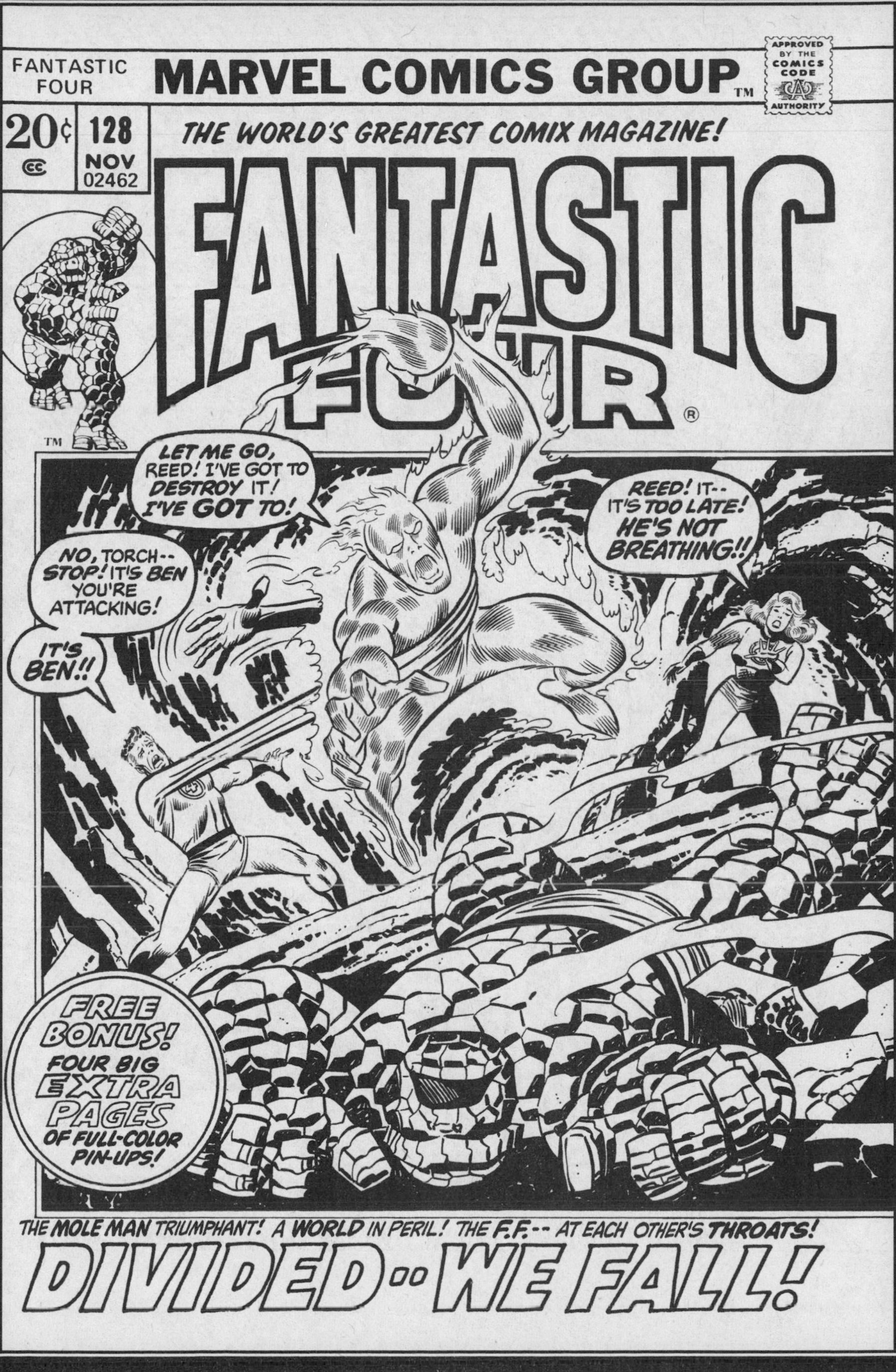
FANTASTIC FOUR
MARVEL COMICS GROUP
APPROVED BY THE COMICS CODE AUTHORITY
20¢
128
NOV
02462
THE WORLD'S GREATEST COMIX MAGAZINE!
FANTASTIC FOUR
LET ME GO, REED! I'VE GOT TO DESTROY IT! I'VE GOT TO!
NO, TORCH-- STOP! IT'S BEN YOU'RE ATTACKING!
IT'S BEN!!
REED! IT-- IT'S TOO LATE! HE'S NOT BREATHING!!
FREE BONUS! FOUR BIG EXTRA PAGES OF FULL-COLOR PIN-UPS!
THE MOLE MAN TRIUMPHANT! A WORLD IN PERIL! THE F.F.-- AT EACH OTHER'S THROATS!
DIVIDED--WE FALL!

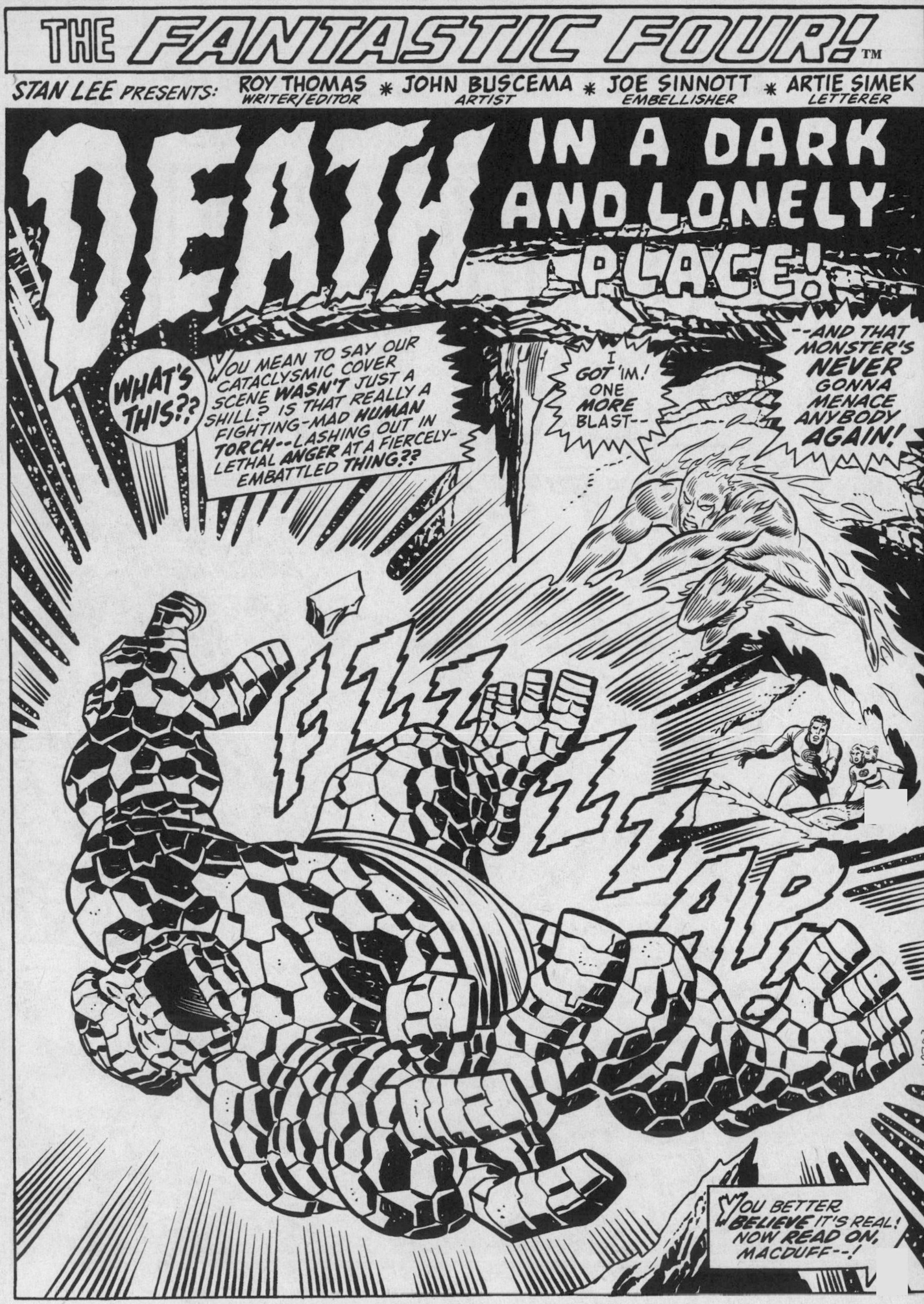
THE FANTASTIC FOUR! ™
STAN LEE PRESENTS: ROY THOMAS WRITER/EDITOR * JOHN BUSCEMA ARTIST * JOE SINNOTT EMBELLISHER * ARTIE SIMEK LETTERER
DEATH IN A DARK AND LONELY PLACE!
WHAT'S THIS??
YOU MEAN TO SAY OUR CATACLYSMIC COVER SCENE WASN'T JUST A SHILL? IS THAT REALLY A FIGHTING-MAD HUMAN TORCH--LASHING OUT IN LETHAL ANGER AT A FIERCELY-EMBATTLED THING??
I GOT 'IM! ONE MORE BLAST--
--AND THAT MONSTER'S NEVER GONNA MENACE ANYBODY AGAIN!
FZZZZ ZAP!
YOU BETTER BELIEVE IT'S REAL! NOW READ ON, MACDUFF--!

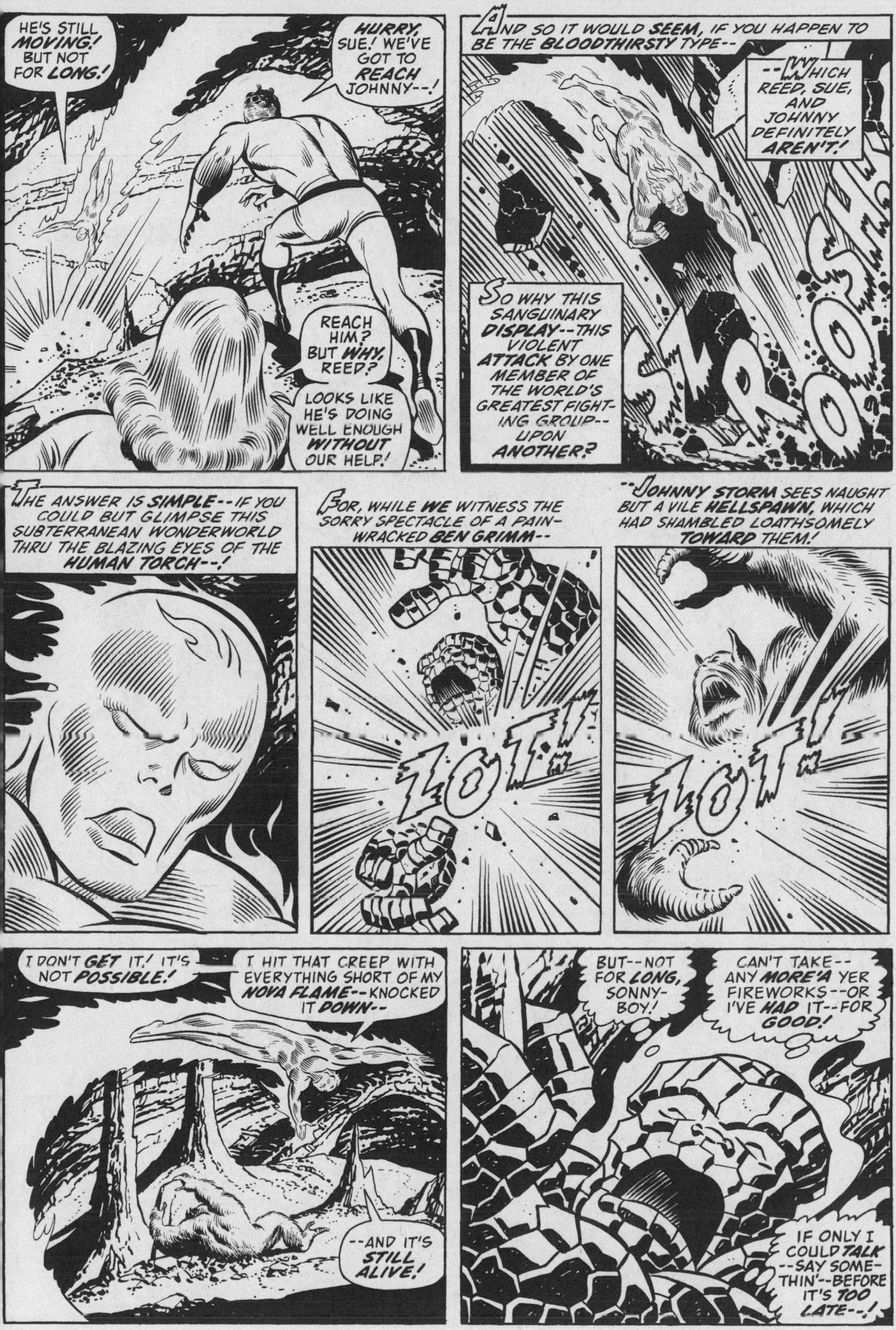
HE'S STILL MOVING! BUT NOT FOR LONG!
HURRY, SUE! WE'VE GOT TO REACH JOHNNY--!
REACH HIM? BUT WHY, REED?
LOOKS LIKE HE'S DOING WELL ENOUGH WITHOUT OUR HELP!
AND SO IT WOULD SEEM, IF YOU HAPPEN TO BE THE BLOODTHIRSTY TYPE--
--WHICH REED, SUE, AND JOHNNY DEFINITELY AREN'T!
SO WHY THIS SANGUINARY DISPLAY--THIS VIOLENT ATTACK BY ONE MEMBER OF THE WORLD'S GREATEST FIGHTING GROUP--UPON ANOTHER?
SZROOSH
THE ANSWER IS SIMPLE--IF YOU COULD BUT GLIMPSE THIS SUBTERRANEAN WONDERWORLD THRU THE BLAZING EYES OF THE HUMAN TORCH--!
FOR, WHILE WE WITNESS THE SORRY SPECTACLE OF A PAIN-WRACKED BEN GRIMM--
ZOT!
--JOHNNY STORM SEES NAUGHT BUT A VILE HELLSPAWN, WHICH HAD SHAMBLED LOATHSOMELY TOWARD THEM!
ZOT!
I DON'T GET IT! IT'S NOT POSSIBLE!
I HIT THAT CREEP WITH EVERYTHING SHORT OF MY NOVA FLAME--KNOCKED IT DOWN--
--AND IT'S STILL ALIVE!
BUT--NOT FOR LONG, SONNY-BOY!
CAN'T TAKE--ANY MORE'A YER FIREWORKS--OR I'VE HAD IT--FOR GOOD!
IF ONLY I COULD TALK--SAY SOMETHIN'--BEFORE IT'S TOO LATE--!

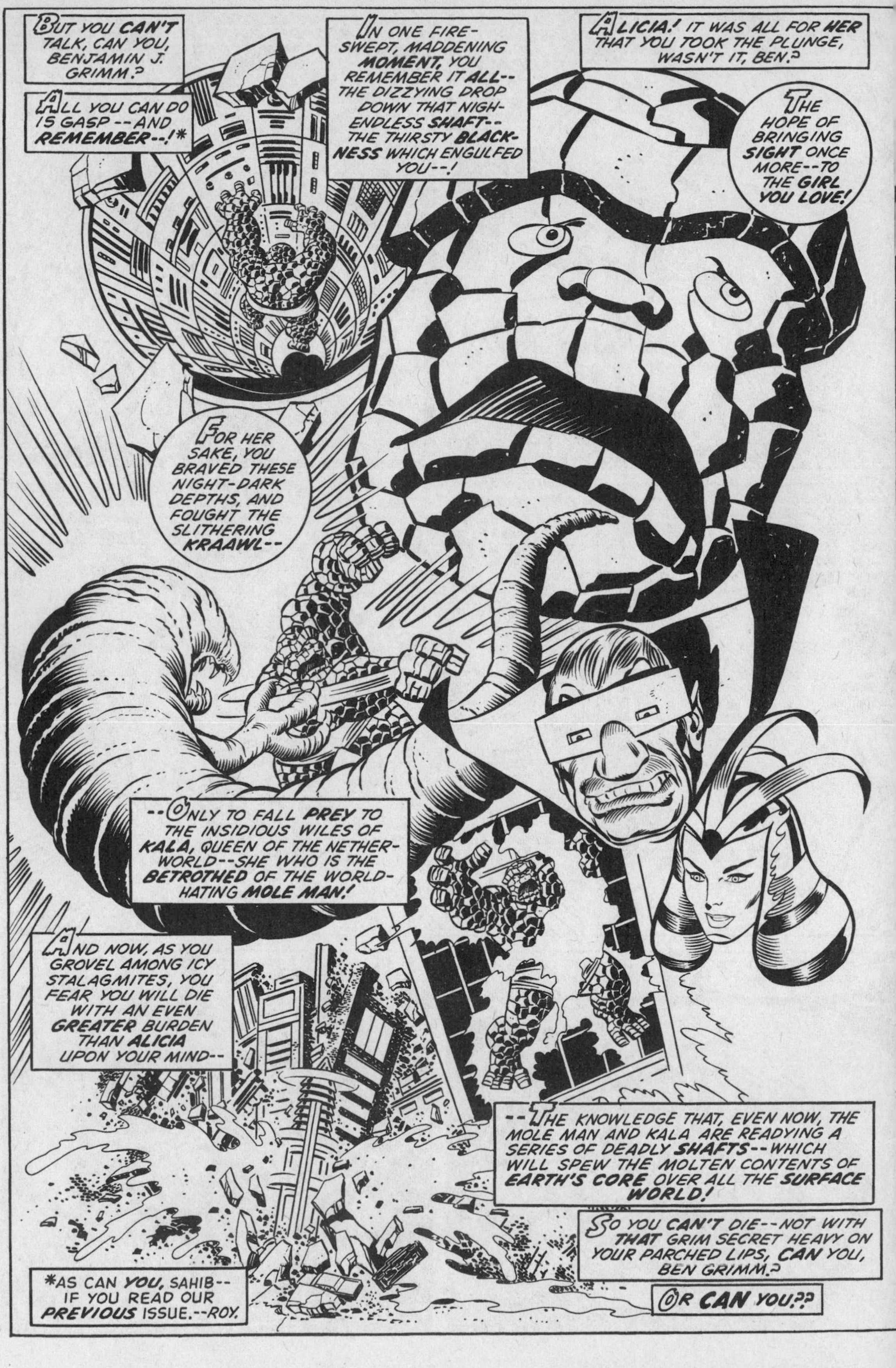
BUT YOU CAN'T TALK, CAN YOU, BENJAMIN J. GRIMM?
ALL YOU CAN DO IS GASP --AND REMEMBER--!*
IN ONE FIRE-SWEPT, MADDENING MOMENT, YOU REMEMBER IT ALL-- THE DIZZYING DROP DOWN THAT NIGH-ENDLESS SHAFT-- THE THIRSTY BLACKNESS WHICH ENGULFED YOU--!
ALICIA! IT WAS ALL FOR HER THAT YOU TOOK THE PLUNGE, WASN'T IT, BEN?
THE HOPE OF BRINGING SIGHT ONCE MORE--TO THE GIRL YOU LOVE!
FOR HER SAKE, YOU BRAVED THESE NIGHT-DARK DEPTHS, AND FOUGHT THE SLITHERING KRAAWL--
--ONLY TO FALL PREY TO THE INSIDIOUS WILES OF KALA, QUEEN OF THE NETHER-WORLD--SHE WHO IS THE BETROTHED OF THE WORLD-HATING MOLE MAN!
AND NOW, AS YOU GROVEL AMONG ICY STALAGMITES, YOU FEAR YOU WILL DIE WITH AN EVEN GREATER BURDEN THAN ALICIA UPON YOUR MIND--
--THE KNOWLEDGE THAT, EVEN NOW, THE MOLE MAN AND KALA ARE READYING A SERIES OF DEADLY SHAFTS--WHICH WILL SPEW THE MOLTEN CONTENTS OF EARTH'S CORE OVER ALL THE SURFACE WORLD!
SO YOU CAN'T DIE--NOT WITH THAT GRIM SECRET HEAVY ON YOUR PARCHED LIPS, CAN YOU, BEN GRIMM?
OR CAN YOU??
*AS CAN YOU, SAHIB-- IF YOU READ OUR PREVIOUS ISSUE.--ROY.

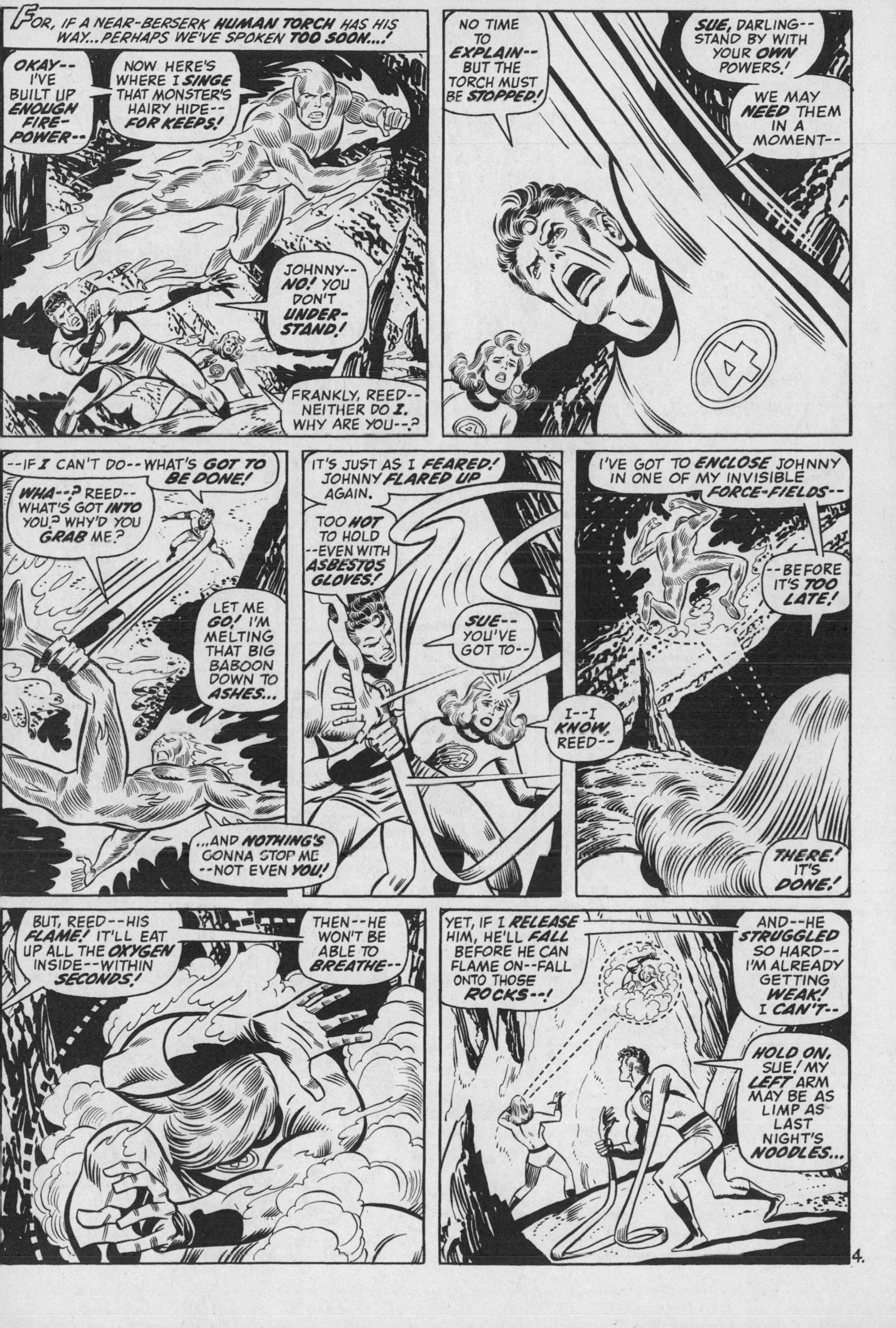
FOR, IF A NEAR-BERSERK HUMAN TORCH HAS HIS WAY... PERHAPS WE'VE SPOKEN TOO SOON...!
OKAY-- I'VE BUILT UP ENOUGH FIRE-POWER--
NOW HERE'S WHERE I SINGE THAT MONSTER'S HAIRY HIDE-- FOR KEEPS!
JOHNNY-- NO! YOU DON'T UNDER-STAND!
FRANKLY, REED-- NEITHER DO I. WHY ARE YOU--?
NO TIME TO EXPLAIN-- BUT THE TORCH MUST BE STOPPED!
SUE, DARLING-- STAND BY WITH YOUR OWN POWERS!
WE MAY NEED THEM IN A MOMENT--
--IF I CAN'T DO-- WHAT'S GOT TO BE DONE!
WHA--? REED-- WHAT'S GOT INTO YOU? WHY'D YOU GRAB ME?
LET ME GO! I'M MELTING THAT BIG BABOON DOWN TO ASHES...
...AND NOTHING'S GONNA STOP ME --NOT EVEN YOU!
IT'S JUST AS I FEARED! JOHNNY FLARED UP AGAIN.
TOO HOT TO HOLD --EVEN WITH ASBESTOS GLOVES!
SUE-- YOU'VE GOT TO--
I--I KNOW, REED--
I'VE GOT TO ENCLOSE JOHNNY IN ONE OF MY INVISIBLE FORCE-FIELDS--
--BEFORE IT'S TOO LATE!
THERE! IT'S DONE!
BUT, REED--HIS FLAME! IT'LL EAT UP ALL THE OXYGEN INSIDE--WITHIN SECONDS!
THEN--HE WON'T BE ABLE TO BREATHE--
YET, IF I RELEASE HIM, HE'LL FALL BEFORE HE CAN FLAME ON--FALL ONTO THOSE ROCKS--!
AND--HE STRUGGLED SO HARD-- I'M ALREADY GETTING WEAK! I CAN'T--
HOLD ON, SUE! MY LEFT ARM MAY BE AS LIMP AS LAST NIGHT'S NOODLES...

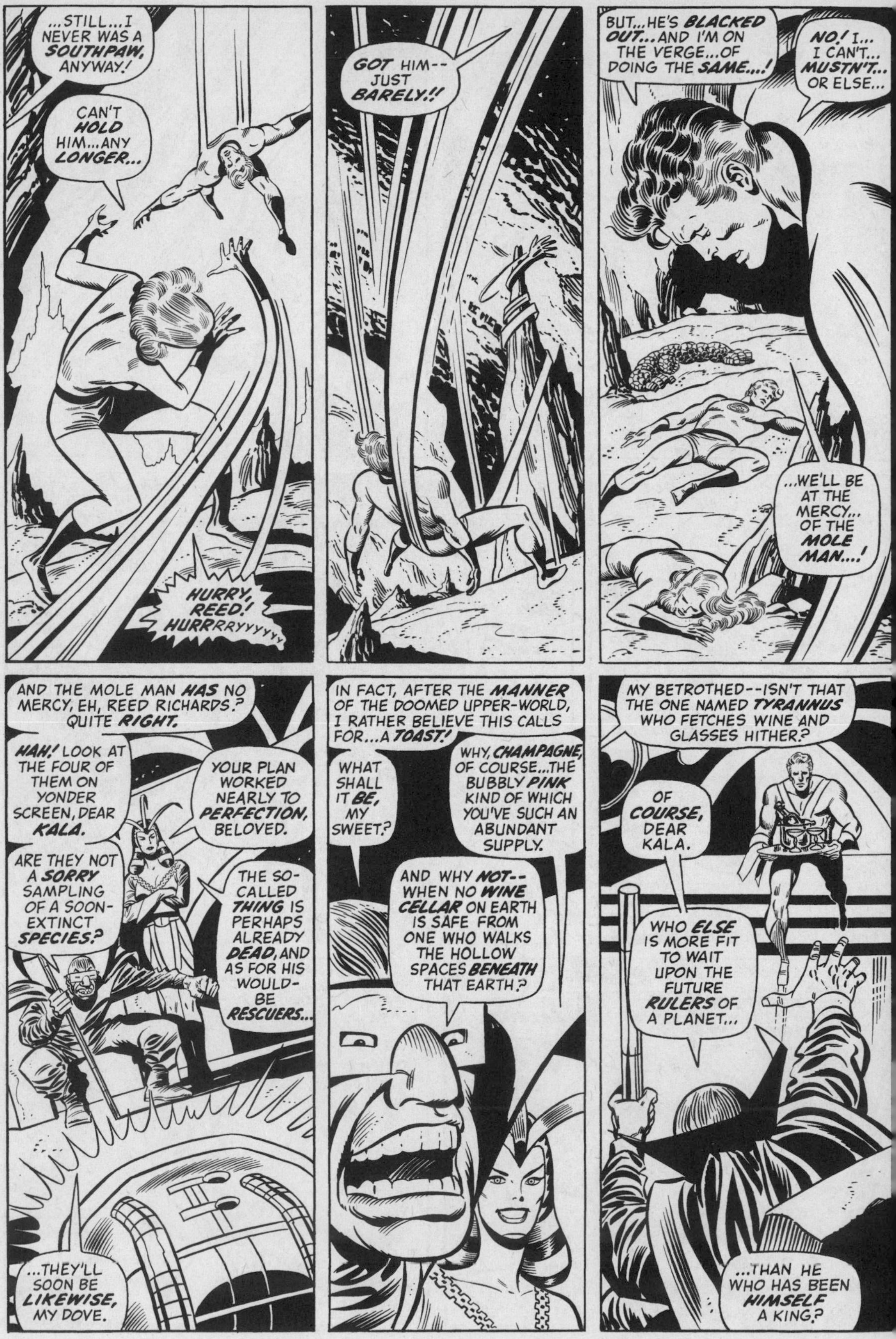
...STILL...I NEVER WAS A SOUTHPAW, ANYWAY!
CAN'T HOLD HIM...ANY LONGER...
HURRY, REED! HURRRRYYYYYY
GOT HIM--JUST BARELY!!
BUT...HE'S BLACKED OUT...AND I'M ON THE VERGE...OF DOING THE SAME...!
NO! I... I CAN'T... MUSTN'T... OR ELSE...
...WE'LL BE AT THE MERCY... OF THE MOLE MAN...!
AND THE MOLE MAN HAS NO MERCY, EH, REED RICHARDS? QUITE RIGHT.
HAH! LOOK AT THE FOUR OF THEM ON YONDER SCREEN, DEAR KALA.
YOUR PLAN WORKED NEARLY TO PERFECTION, BELOVED.
ARE THEY NOT A SORRY SAMPLING OF A SOON-EXTINCT SPECIES?
THE SO-CALLED THING IS PERHAPS ALREADY DEAD, AND AS FOR HIS WOULD-BE RESCUERS...
...THEY'LL SOON BE LIKEWISE, MY DOVE.
IN FACT, AFTER THE MANNER OF THE DOOMED UPPER-WORLD, I RATHER BELIEVE THIS CALLS FOR...A TOAST!
WHAT SHALL IT BE, MY SWEET?
WHY, CHAMPAGNE, OF COURSE...THE BUBBLY PINK KIND OF WHICH YOU'VE SUCH AN ABUNDANT SUPPLY.
AND WHY NOT--WHEN NO WINE CELLAR ON EARTH IS SAFE FROM ONE WHO WALKS THE HOLLOW SPACES BENEATH THAT EARTH?
MY BETROTHED--ISN'T THAT THE ONE NAMED TYRANNUS WHO FETCHES WINE AND GLASSES HITHER?
OF COURSE, DEAR KALA.
WHO ELSE IS MORE FIT TO WAIT UPON THE FUTURE RULERS OF A PLANET...
...THAN HE WHO HAS BEEN HIMSELF A KING?

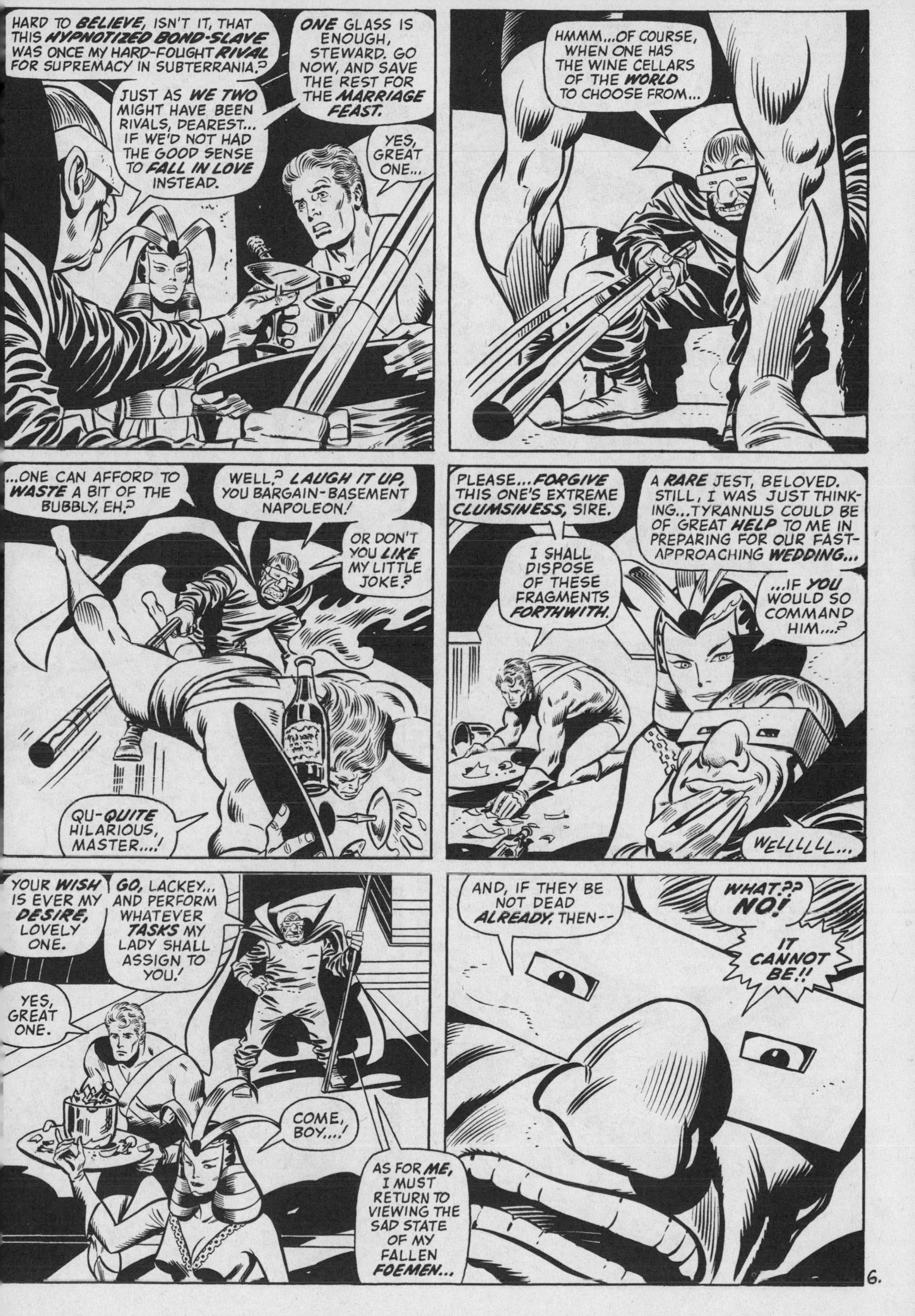
HARD TO BELIEVE, ISN'T IT, THAT THIS HYPNOTIZED BOND-SLAVE WAS ONCE MY HARD-FOUGHT RIVAL FOR SUPREMACY IN SUBTERRANIA?
JUST AS WE TWO MIGHT HAVE BEEN RIVALS, DEAREST... IF WE'D NOT HAD THE GOOD SENSE TO FALL IN LOVE INSTEAD.
ONE GLASS IS ENOUGH, STEWARD. GO NOW, AND SAVE THE REST FOR THE MARRIAGE FEAST.
YES, GREAT ONE...
HMMM...OF COURSE, WHEN ONE HAS THE WINE CELLARS OF THE WORLD TO CHOOSE FROM...
...ONE CAN AFFORD TO WASTE A BIT OF THE BUBBLY, EH?
WELL? LAUGH IT UP, YOU BARGAIN-BASEMENT NAPOLEON!
OR DON'T YOU LIKE MY LITTLE JOKE?
QU-QUITE HILARIOUS, MASTER...!
PLEASE...FORGIVE THIS ONE'S EXTREME CLUMSINESS, SIRE.
I SHALL DISPOSE OF THESE FRAGMENTS FORTHWITH.
A RARE JEST, BELOVED. STILL, I WAS JUST THINKING...TYRANNUS COULD BE OF GREAT HELP TO ME IN PREPARING FOR OUR FAST-APPROACHING WEDDING...
...IF YOU WOULD SO COMMAND HIM...?
WELLLLLLL...
YOUR WISH IS EVER MY DESIRE, LOVELY ONE.
GO, LACKEY... AND PERFORM WHATEVER TASKS MY LADY SHALL ASSIGN TO YOU!
YES, GREAT ONE.
COME, BOY...!
AS FOR ME, I MUST RETURN TO VIEWING THE SAD STATE OF MY FALLEN FOEMEN...
AND, IF THEY BE NOT DEAD ALREADY, THEN--
WHAT?? NO!
IT CANNOT BE!!

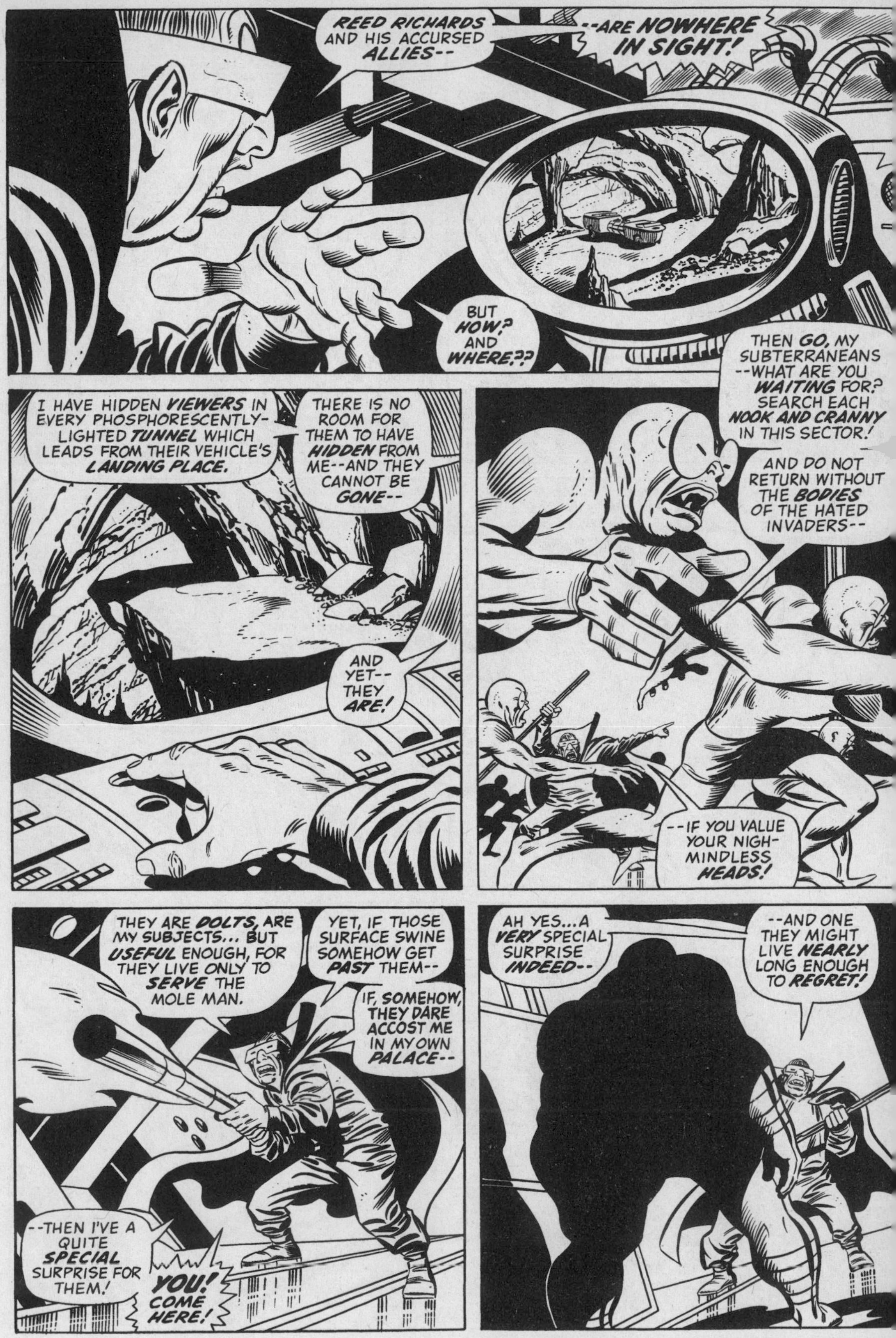

REED RICHARDS AND HIS ACCURSED ALLIES--
--ARE NOWHERE IN SIGHT!
BUT HOW? AND WHERE??
I HAVE HIDDEN VIEWERS IN EVERY PHOSPHORESCENTLY-LIGHTED TUNNEL WHICH LEADS FROM THEIR VEHICLE'S LANDING PLACE.
THERE IS NO ROOM FOR THEM TO HAVE HIDDEN FROM ME--AND THEY CANNOT BE GONE--
AND YET--THEY ARE!
THEN GO, MY SUBTERRANEANS --WHAT ARE YOU WAITING FOR? SEARCH EACH NOOK AND CRANNY IN THIS SECTOR!
AND DO NOT RETURN WITHOUT THE BODIES OF THE HATED INVADERS--
--IF YOU VALUE YOUR NIGH-MINDLESS HEADS!
THEY ARE DOLTS, ARE MY SUBJECTS... BUT USEFUL ENOUGH, FOR THEY LIVE ONLY TO SERVE THE MOLE MAN.
YET, IF THOSE SURFACE SWINE SOMEHOW GET PAST THEM--
IF, SOMEHOW, THEY DARE ACCOST ME IN MY OWN PALACE--
--THEN I'VE A QUITE SPECIAL SURPRISE FOR THEM!
YOU! COME HERE!
AH YES...A VERY SPECIAL SURPRISE INDEED--
--AND ONE THEY MIGHT LIVE NEARLY LONG ENOUGH TO REGRET!

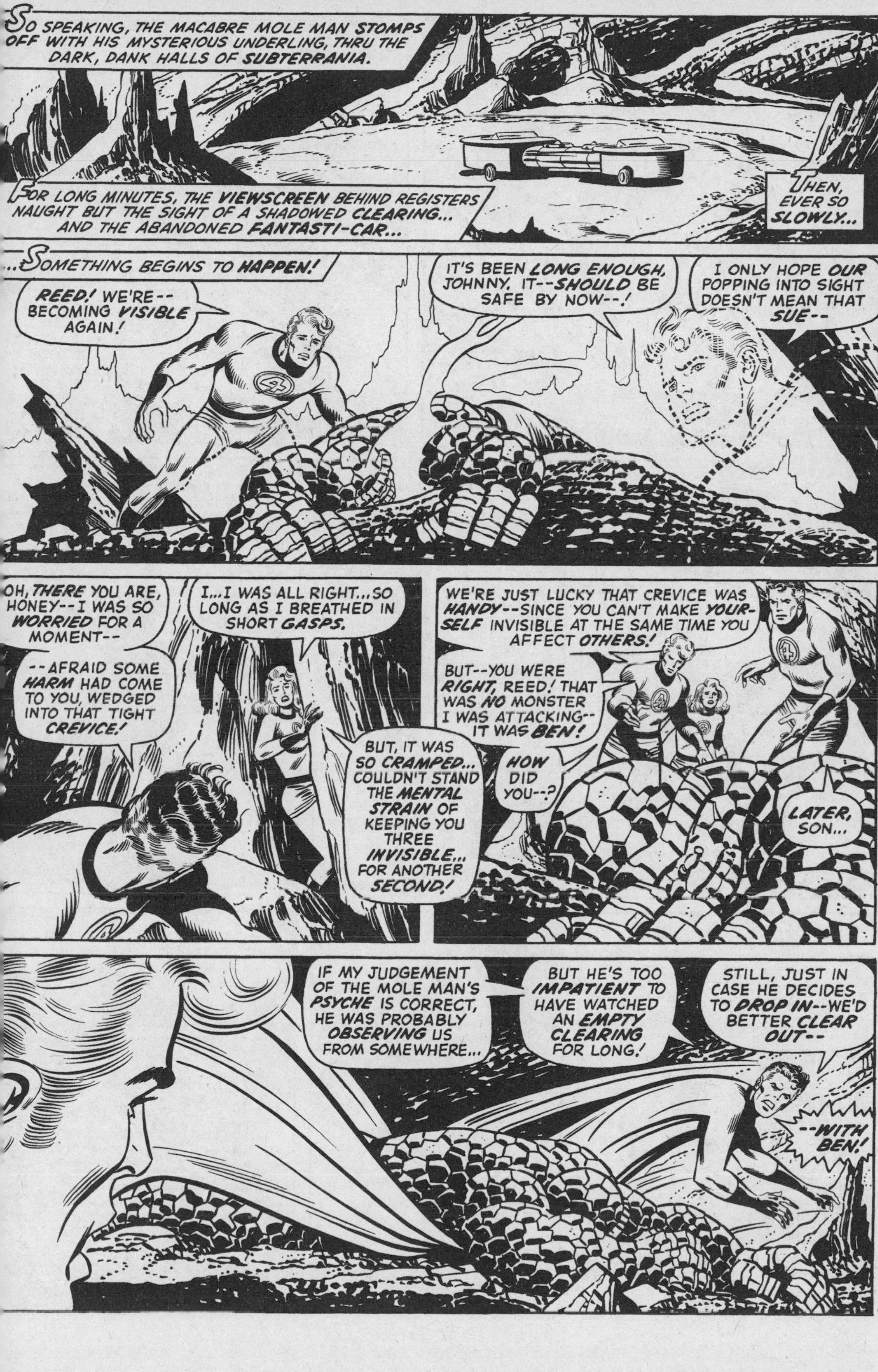

SO SPEAKING, THE MACABRE MOLE MAN STOMPS OFF WITH HIS MYSTERIOUS UNDERLING, THRU THE DARK, DANK HALLS OF SUBTERRANIA.
FOR LONG MINUTES, THE VIEWSCREEN BEHIND REGISTERS NAUGHT BUT THE SIGHT OF A SHADOWED CLEARING... AND THE ABANDONED FANTASTI-CAR...
THEN, EVER SO SLOWLY...
...SOMETHING BEGINS TO HAPPEN!
REED! WE'RE--BECOMING VISIBLE AGAIN!
IT'S BEEN LONG ENOUGH, JOHNNY. IT--SHOULD BE SAFE BY NOW--!
I ONLY HOPE OUR POPPING INTO SIGHT DOESN'T MEAN THAT SUE--
OH, THERE YOU ARE, HONEY--I WAS SO WORRIED FOR A MOMENT--
--AFRAID SOME HARM HAD COME TO YOU, WEDGED INTO THAT TIGHT CREVICE!
I...I WAS ALL RIGHT...SO LONG AS I BREATHED IN SHORT GASPS.
BUT, IT WAS SO CRAMPED... COULDN'T STAND THE MENTAL STRAIN OF KEEPING YOU THREE INVISIBLE... FOR ANOTHER SECOND!
WE'RE JUST LUCKY THAT CREVICE WAS HANDY--SINCE YOU CAN'T MAKE YOURSELF INVISIBLE AT THE SAME TIME YOU AFFECT OTHERS!
BUT--YOU WERE RIGHT, REED! THAT WAS NO MONSTER I WAS ATTACKING--IT WAS BEN!
HOW DID YOU--?
LATER, SON...
IF MY JUDGEMENT OF THE MOLE MAN'S PSYCHE IS CORRECT, HE WAS PROBABLY OBSERVING US FROM SOMEWHERE...
BUT HE'S TOO IMPATIENT TO HAVE WATCHED AN EMPTY CLEARING FOR LONG!
STILL, JUST IN CASE HE DECIDES TO DROP IN--WE'D BETTER CLEAR OUT--
--WITH BEN!

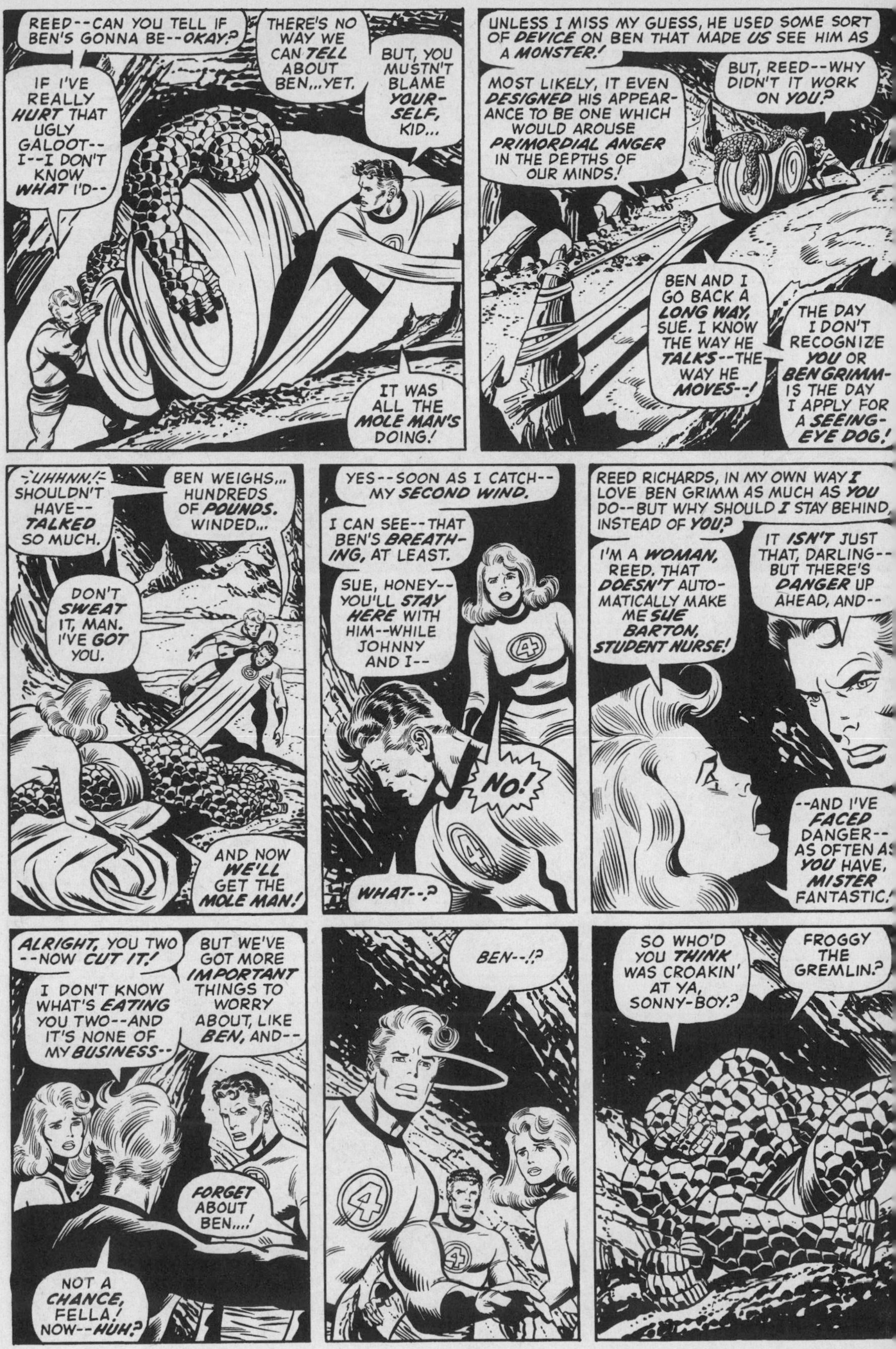

REED--CAN YOU TELL IF BEN'S GONNA BE--OKAY?
IF I'VE REALLY HURT THAT UGLY GALOOT--I--I DON'T KNOW WHAT I'D--
THERE'S NO WAY WE CAN TELL ABOUT BEN...YET.
BUT, YOU MUSTN'T BLAME YOURSELF, KID...
IT WAS ALL THE MOLE MAN'S DOING!
UNLESS I MISS MY GUESS, HE USED SOME SORT OF DEVICE ON BEN THAT MADE US SEE HIM AS A MONSTER!
MOST LIKELY, IT EVEN DESIGNED HIS APPEARANCE TO BE ONE WHICH WOULD AROUSE PRIMORDIAL ANGER IN THE DEPTHS OF OUR MINDS!
BUT, REED--WHY DIDN'T IT WORK ON YOU?
BEN AND I GO BACK A LONG WAY, SUE. I KNOW THE WAY HE TALKS--THE WAY HE MOVES--!
THE DAY I DON'T RECOGNIZE YOU OR BEN GRIMM IS THE DAY I APPLY FOR A SEEING-EYE DOG!
-UHHNN!- SHOULDN'T HAVE--TALKED SO MUCH.
BEN WEIGHS... HUNDREDS OF POUNDS. WINDED...
DON'T SWEAT IT, MAN. I'VE GOT YOU.
AND NOW WE'LL GET THE MOLE MAN!
YES--SOON AS I CATCH--MY SECOND WIND.
I CAN SEE--THAT BEN'S BREATHING, AT LEAST.
SUE, HONEY--YOU'LL STAY HERE WITH HIM--WHILE JOHNNY AND I--
NO!
WHAT--?
REED RICHARDS, IN MY OWN WAY I LOVE BEN GRIMM AS MUCH AS YOU DO--BUT WHY SHOULD I STAY BEHIND INSTEAD OF YOU?
I'M A WOMAN, REED. THAT DOESN'T AUTOMATICALLY MAKE ME SUE BARTON, STUDENT NURSE!
IT ISN'T JUST THAT, DARLING--BUT THERE'S DANGER UP AHEAD, AND--
--AND I'VE FACED DANGER--AS OFTEN AS YOU HAVE, MISTER FANTASTIC!
ALRIGHT, YOU TWO--NOW CUT IT!
I DON'T KNOW WHAT'S EATING YOU TWO--AND IT'S NONE OF MY BUSINESS--
BUT WE'VE GOT MORE IMPORTANT THINGS TO WORRY ABOUT, LIKE BEN, AND--
FORGET ABOUT BEN...!
NOT A CHANCE, FELLA! NOW--HUH?
BEN--!?
SO WHO'D YOU THINK WAS CROAKIN' AT YA, SONNY-BOY?
FROGGY THE GREMLIN?

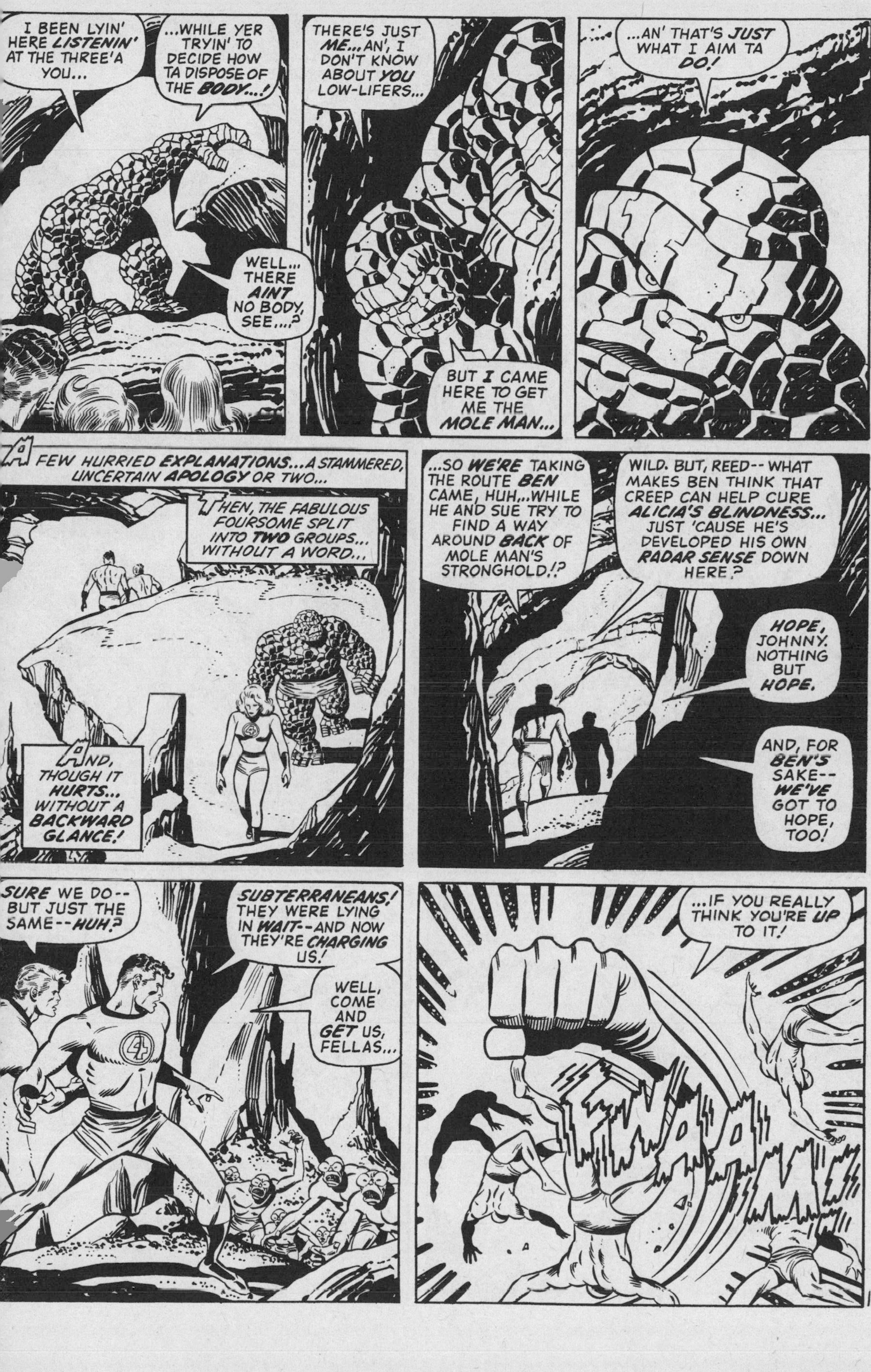
I BEEN LYIN' HERE LISTENIN' AT THE THREE'A YOU...
...WHILE YER TRYIN' TO DECIDE HOW TA DISPOSE OF THE BODY...!
WELL... THERE AINT NO BODY, SEE....?
THERE'S JUST ME... AN', I DON'T KNOW ABOUT YOU LOW-LIFERS...
BUT I CAME HERE TO GET ME THE MOLE MAN...
...AN' THAT'S JUST WHAT I AIM TA DO!
A FEW HURRIED EXPLANATIONS...A STAMMERED, UNCERTAIN APOLOGY OR TWO...
THEN, THE FABULOUS FOURSOME SPLIT INTO TWO GROUPS... WITHOUT A WORD...
AND, THOUGH IT HURTS... WITHOUT A BACKWARD GLANCE!
...SO WE'RE TAKING THE ROUTE BEN CAME, HUH...WHILE HE AND SUE TRY TO FIND A WAY AROUND BACK OF MOLE MAN'S STRONGHOLD!?
WILD. BUT, REED-- WHAT MAKES BEN THINK THAT CREEP CAN HELP CURE ALICIA'S BLINDNESS... JUST 'CAUSE HE'S DEVELOPED HIS OWN RADAR SENSE DOWN HERE?
HOPE, JOHNNY. NOTHING BUT HOPE.
AND, FOR BEN'S SAKE-- WE'VE GOT TO HOPE, TOO!
SURE WE DO-- BUT JUST THE SAME--HUH?
SUBTERRANEANS! THEY WERE LYING IN WAIT--AND NOW THEY'RE CHARGING US!
WELL, COME AND GET US, FELLAS...
...IF YOU REALLY THINK YOU'RE UP TO IT!
FWAAAM

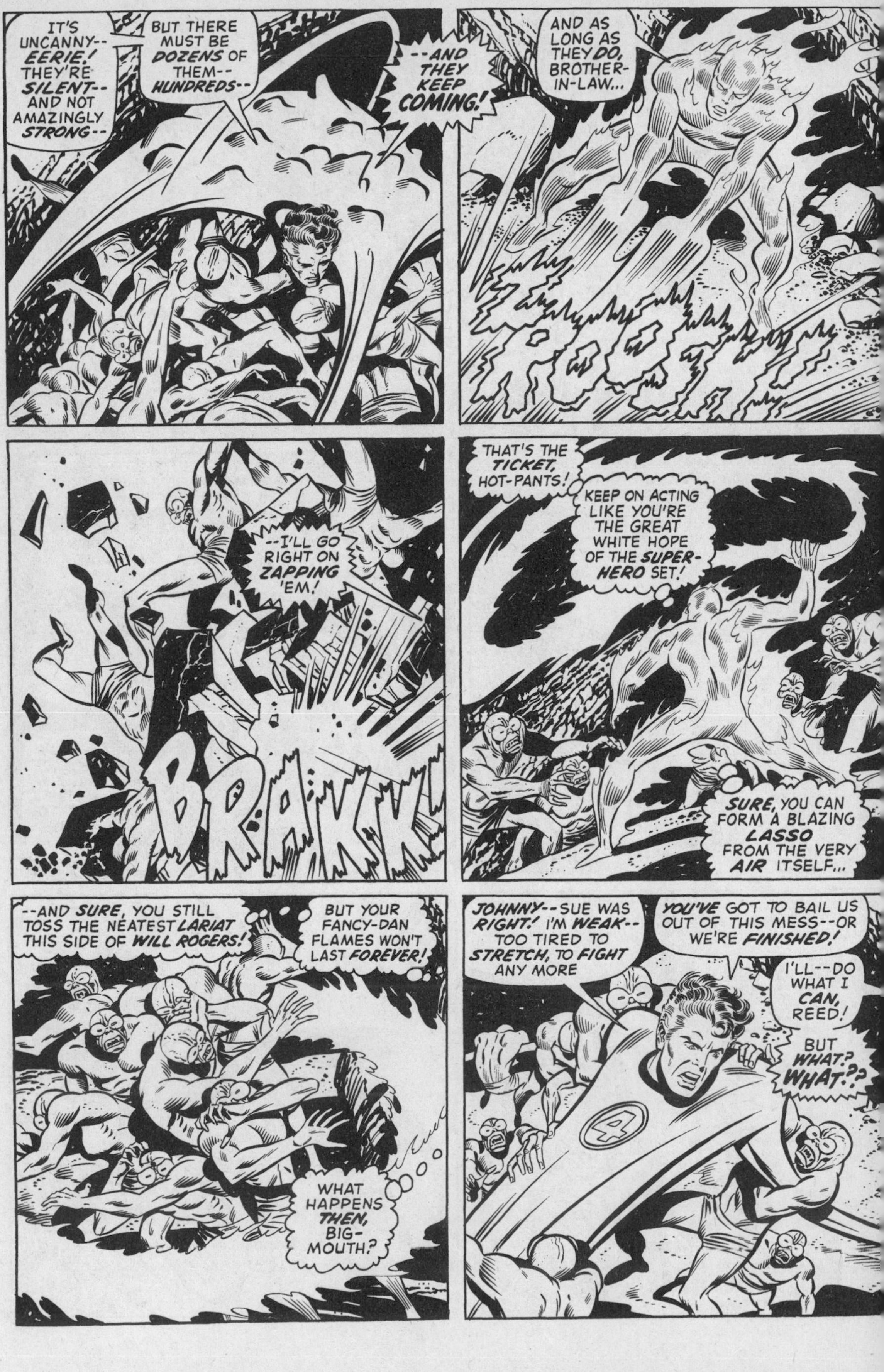

IT'S UNCANNY-- EERIE! THEY'RE SILENT-- AND NOT AMAZINGLY STRONG--
BUT THERE MUST BE DOZENS OF THEM-- HUNDREDS--
--AND THEY KEEP COMING!
AND AS LONG AS THEY DO, BROTHER-IN-LAW...
--I'LL GO RIGHT ON ZAPPING 'EM!
BRAKK!
THAT'S THE TICKET, HOT-PANTS!
KEEP ON ACTING LIKE YOU'RE THE GREAT WHITE HOPE OF THE SUPER-HERO SET!
SURE, YOU CAN FORM A BLAZING LASSO FROM THE VERY AIR ITSELF...
--AND SURE, YOU STILL TOSS THE NEATEST LARIAT THIS SIDE OF WILL ROGERS!
BUT YOUR FANCY-DAN FLAMES WON'T LAST FOREVER!
WHAT HAPPENS THEN, BIG-MOUTH?
JOHNNY--SUE WAS RIGHT! I'M WEAK-- TOO TIRED TO STRETCH, TO FIGHT ANY MORE
YOU'VE GOT TO BAIL US OUT OF THIS MESS--OR WE'RE FINISHED!
I'LL--DO WHAT I CAN, REED!
BUT WHAT? WHAT??

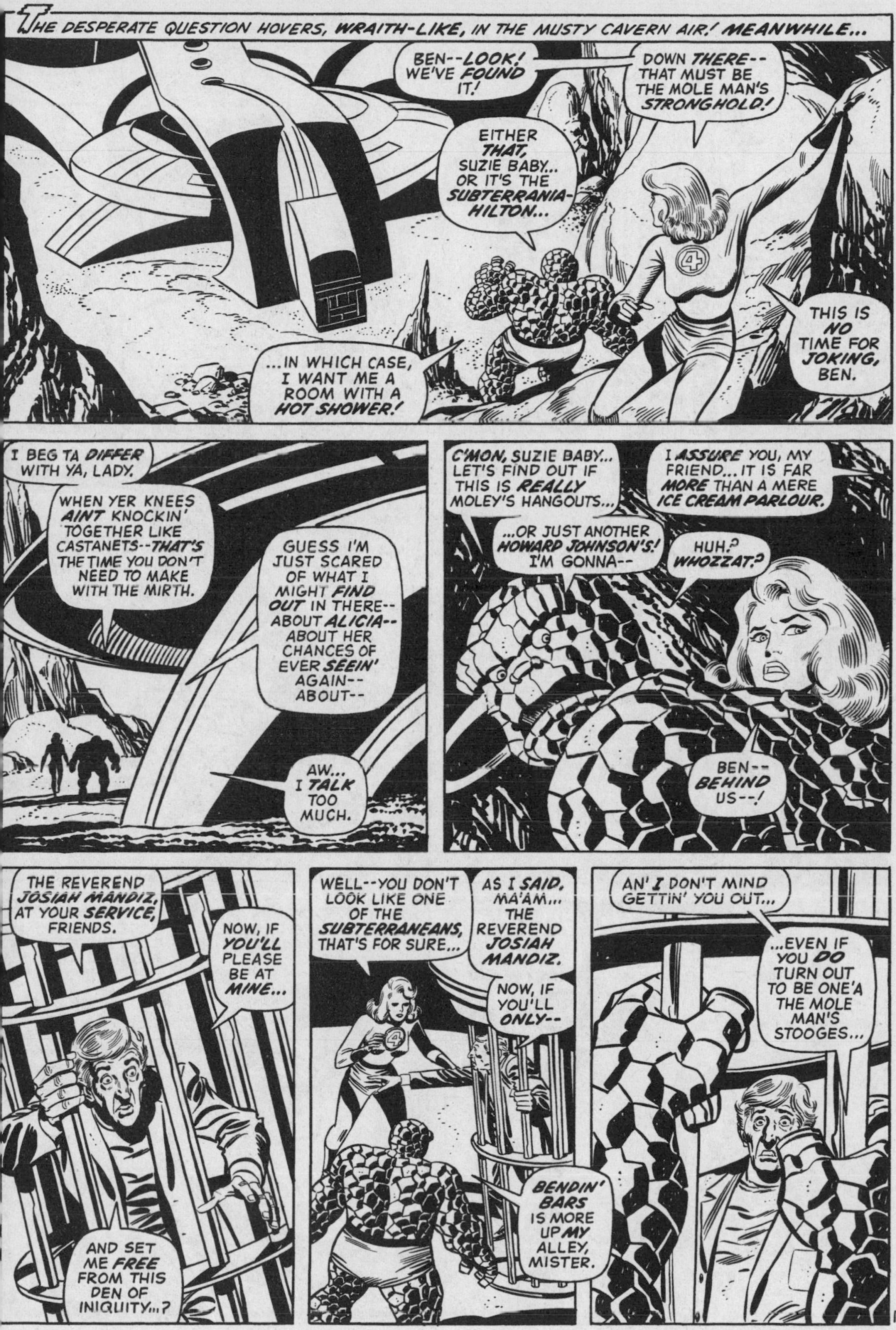
THE DESPERATE QUESTION HOVERS, WRAITH-LIKE, IN THE MUSTY CAVERN AIR! MEANWHILE...
BEN--LOOK! WE'VE FOUND IT!
DOWN THERE-- THAT MUST BE THE MOLE MAN'S STRONGHOLD!
EITHER THAT, SUZIE BABY... OR IT'S THE SUBTERRANIA-HILTON...
...IN WHICH CASE, I WANT ME A ROOM WITH A HOT SHOWER!
THIS IS NO TIME FOR JOKING, BEN.
I BEG TA DIFFER WITH YA, LADY.
WHEN YER KNEES AINT KNOCKIN' TOGETHER LIKE CASTANETS--THAT'S THE TIME YOU DON'T NEED TO MAKE WITH THE MIRTH.
GUESS I'M JUST SCARED OF WHAT I MIGHT FIND OUT IN THERE-- ABOUT ALICIA-- ABOUT HER CHANCES OF EVER SEEIN' AGAIN-- ABOUT--
AW... I TALK TOO MUCH.
C'MON, SUZIE BABY... LET'S FIND OUT IF THIS IS REALLY MOLEY'S HANGOUTS...
...OR JUST ANOTHER HOWARD JOHNSON'S! I'M GONNA--
I ASSURE YOU, MY FRIEND... IT IS FAR MORE THAN A MERE ICE CREAM PARLOUR.
HUH? WHOZZAT?
BEN-- BEHIND US--!
THE REVEREND JOSIAH MANDIZ, AT YOUR SERVICE, FRIENDS.
NOW, IF YOU'LL PLEASE BE AT MINE...
AND SET ME FREE FROM THIS DEN OF INIQUITY...?
WELL--YOU DON'T LOOK LIKE ONE OF THE SUBTERRANEANS, THAT'S FOR SURE...
AS I SAID, MA'AM... THE REVEREND JOSIAH MANDIZ.
NOW, IF YOU'LL ONLY--
BENDIN' BARS IS MORE UP MY ALLEY, MISTER.
AN' I DON'T MIND GETTIN' YOU OUT...
...EVEN IF YOU DO TURN OUT TO BE ONE'A THE MOLE MAN'S STOOGES...

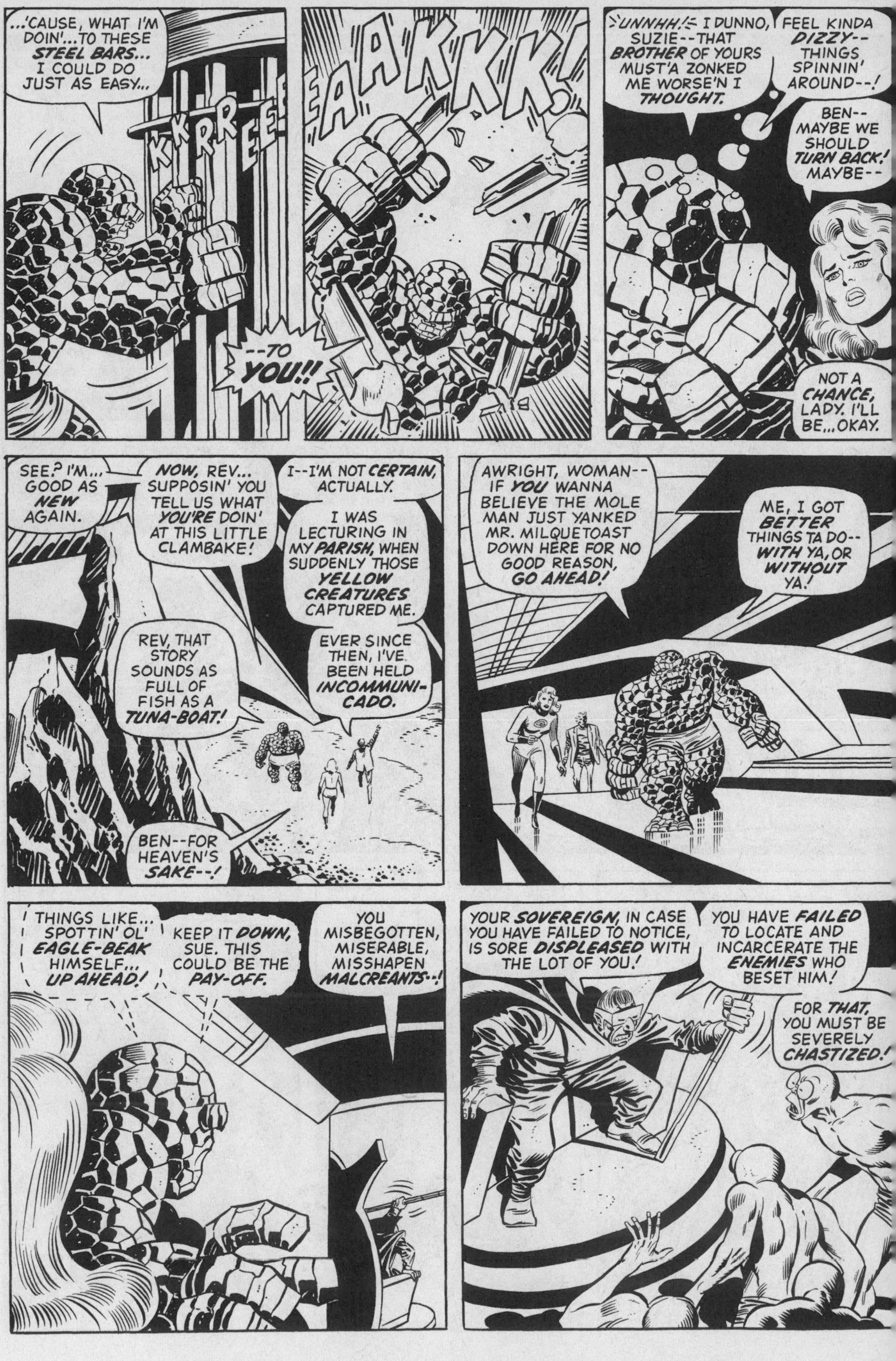
...'CAUSE, WHAT I'M DOIN'...TO THESE STEEL BARS... I COULD DO JUST AS EASY...
KKRREEEEAAKKKK!
--TO YOU!!
UNNHH!-- I DUNNO, SUZIE--THAT BROTHER OF YOURS MUST'A ZONKED ME WORSE'N I THOUGHT.
FEEL KINDA DIZZY-- THINGS SPINNIN' AROUND--!
BEN-- MAYBE WE SHOULD TURN BACK! MAYBE--
NOT A CHANCE, LADY. I'LL BE...OKAY.
SEE? I'M... GOOD AS NEW AGAIN.
NOW, REV... SUPPOSIN' YOU TELL US WHAT YOU'RE DOIN' AT THIS LITTLE CLAMBAKE!
I--I'M NOT CERTAIN, ACTUALLY.
I WAS LECTURING IN MY PARISH, WHEN SUDDENLY THOSE YELLOW CREATURES CAPTURED ME.
EVER SINCE THEN, I'VE BEEN HELD INCOMMUNICADO.
REV, THAT STORY SOUNDS AS FULL OF FISH AS A TUNA-BOAT!
BEN--FOR HEAVEN'S SAKE--!
AWRIGHT, WOMAN-- IF YOU WANNA BELIEVE THE MOLE MAN JUST YANKED MR. MILQUETOAST DOWN HERE FOR NO GOOD REASON, GO AHEAD!
ME, I GOT BETTER THINGS TA DO-- WITH YA, OR WITHOUT YA!
THINGS LIKE... SPOTTIN' OL' EAGLE-BEAK HIMSELF... UP AHEAD!
KEEP IT DOWN, SUE. THIS COULD BE THE PAY-OFF.
YOU MISBEGOTTEN, MISERABLE, MISSHAPEN MALCREANTS--!
YOUR SOVEREIGN, IN CASE YOU HAVE FAILED TO NOTICE, IS SORE DISPLEASED WITH THE LOT OF YOU!
YOU HAVE FAILED TO LOCATE AND INCARCERATE THE ENEMIES WHO BESET HIM!
FOR THAT, YOU MUST BE SEVERELY CHASTIZED!

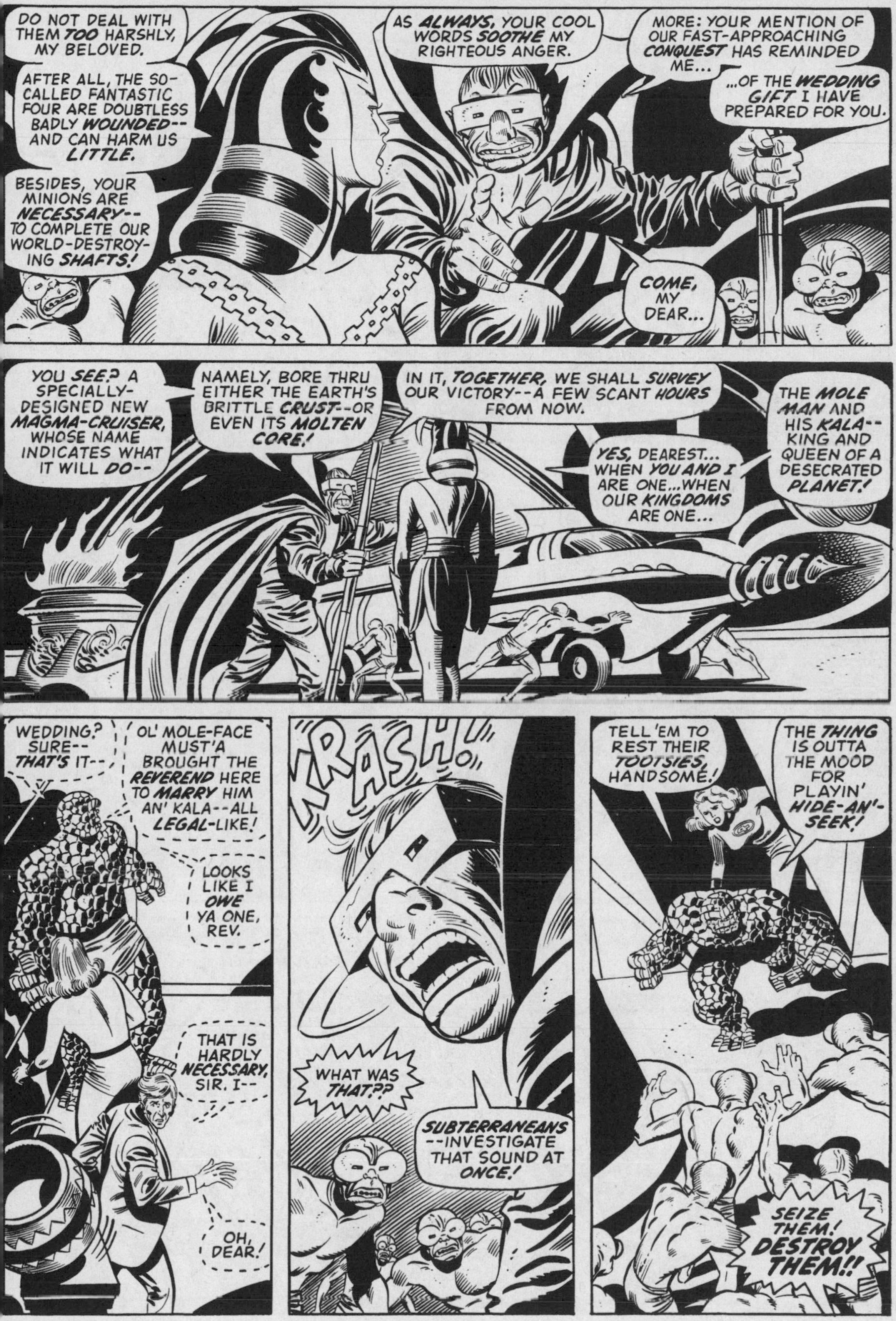

DO NOT DEAL WITH THEM TOO HARSHLY, MY BELOVED.
AFTER ALL, THE SO-CALLED FANTASTIC FOUR ARE DOUBTLESS BADLY WOUNDED-- AND CAN HARM US LITTLE.
BESIDES, YOUR MINIONS ARE NECESSARY-- TO COMPLETE OUR WORLD-DESTROYING SHAFTS!
AS ALWAYS, YOUR COOL WORDS SOOTHE MY RIGHTEOUS ANGER.
MORE: YOUR MENTION OF OUR FAST-APPROACHING CONQUEST HAS REMINDED ME...
...OF THE WEDDING GIFT I HAVE PREPARED FOR YOU.
COME, MY DEAR...
YOU SEE? A SPECIALLY-DESIGNED NEW MAGMA-CRUISER, WHOSE NAME INDICATES WHAT IT WILL DO--
NAMELY, BORE THRU EITHER THE EARTH'S BRITTLE CRUST--OR EVEN ITS MOLTEN CORE!
IN IT, TOGETHER, WE SHALL SURVEY OUR VICTORY--A FEW SCANT HOURS FROM NOW.
YES, DEAREST... WHEN YOU AND I ARE ONE...WHEN OUR KINGDOMS ARE ONE...
THE MOLE MAN AND HIS KALA-- KING AND QUEEN OF A DESECRATED PLANET!
WEDDING? SURE-- THAT'S IT--
OL' MOLE-FACE MUST'A BROUGHT THE REVEREND HERE TO MARRY HIM AN' KALA--ALL LEGAL-LIKE!
LOOKS LIKE I OWE YA ONE, REV.
THAT IS HARDLY NECESSARY, SIR. I--
OH, DEAR!
KRASH!
WHAT WAS THAT??
SUBTERRANEANS --INVESTIGATE THAT SOUND AT ONCE!
TELL 'EM TO REST THEIR TOOTSIES, HANDSOME!
THE THING IS OUTTA THE MOOD FOR PLAYIN' HIDE-AN'-SEEK!
SEIZE THEM! DESTROY THEM!!

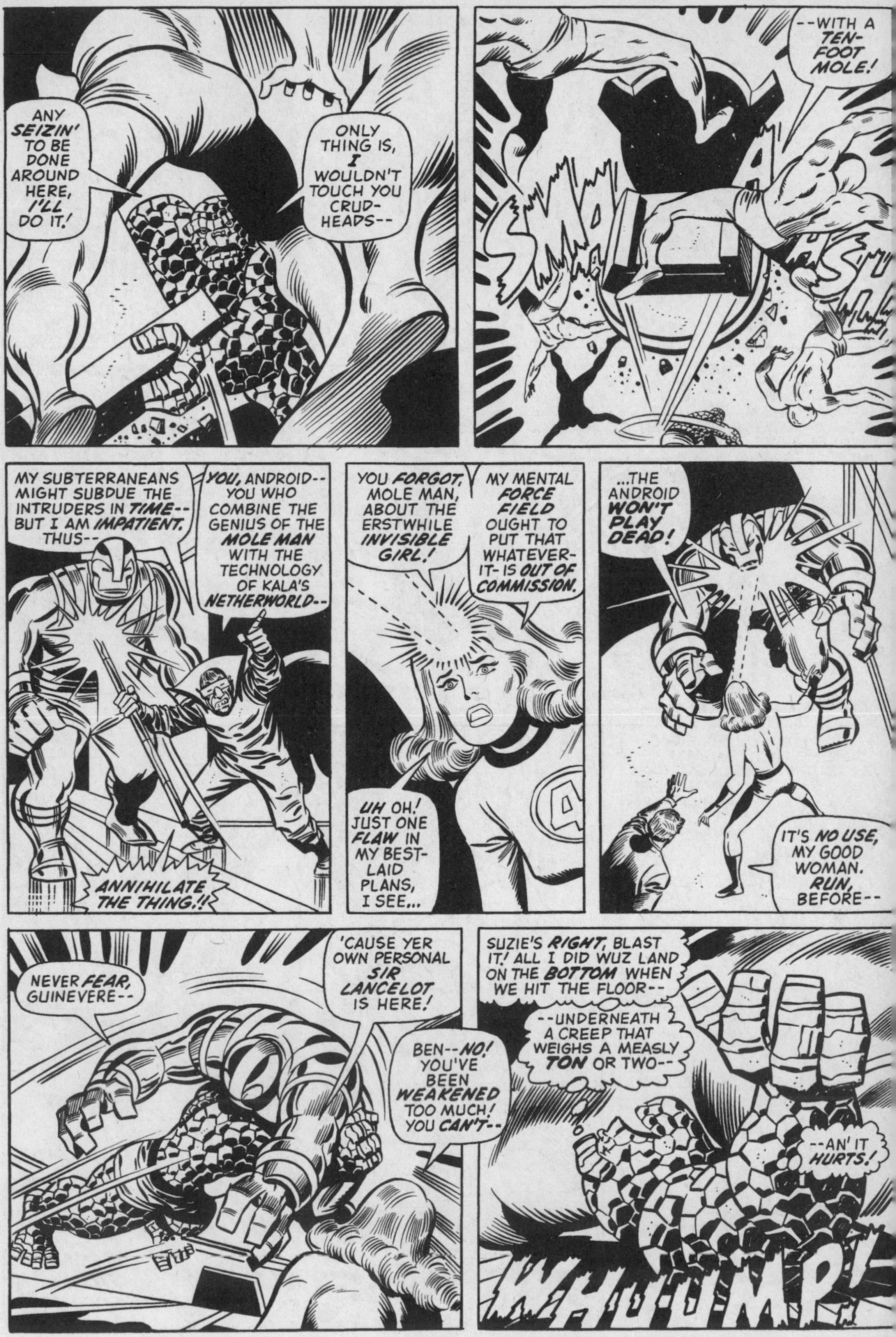

ANY SEIZIN' TO BE DONE AROUND HERE, I'LL DO IT!
ONLY THING IS, I WOULDN'T TOUCH YOU CRUD-HEADS--
--WITH A TEN-FOOT MOLE!
MY SUBTERRANEANS MIGHT SUBDUE THE INTRUDERS IN TIME-- BUT I AM IMPATIENT. THUS--
YOU, ANDROID-- YOU WHO COMBINE THE GENIUS OF THE MOLE MAN WITH THE TECHNOLOGY OF KALA'S NETHERWORLD--
ANNIHILATE THE THING!!
YOU FORGOT, MOLE MAN, ABOUT THE ERSTWHILE INVISIBLE GIRL!
MY MENTAL FORCE FIELD OUGHT TO PUT THAT WHATEVER-IT-IS OUT OF COMMISSION.
UH OH! JUST ONE FLAW IN MY BEST-LAID PLANS, I SEE...
...THE ANDROID WON'T PLAY DEAD!
IT'S NO USE, MY GOOD WOMAN. RUN, BEFORE--
NEVER FEAR, GUINEVERE--
'CAUSE YER OWN PERSONAL SIR LANCELOT IS HERE!
BEN--NO! YOU'VE BEEN WEAKENED TOO MUCH! YOU CAN'T--
SUZIE'S RIGHT, BLAST IT! ALL I DID WUZ LAND ON THE BOTTOM WHEN WE HIT THE FLOOR--
--UNDERNEATH A CREEP THAT WEIGHS A MEASLY TON OR TWO--
--AN' IT HURTS!
WHUUMP!

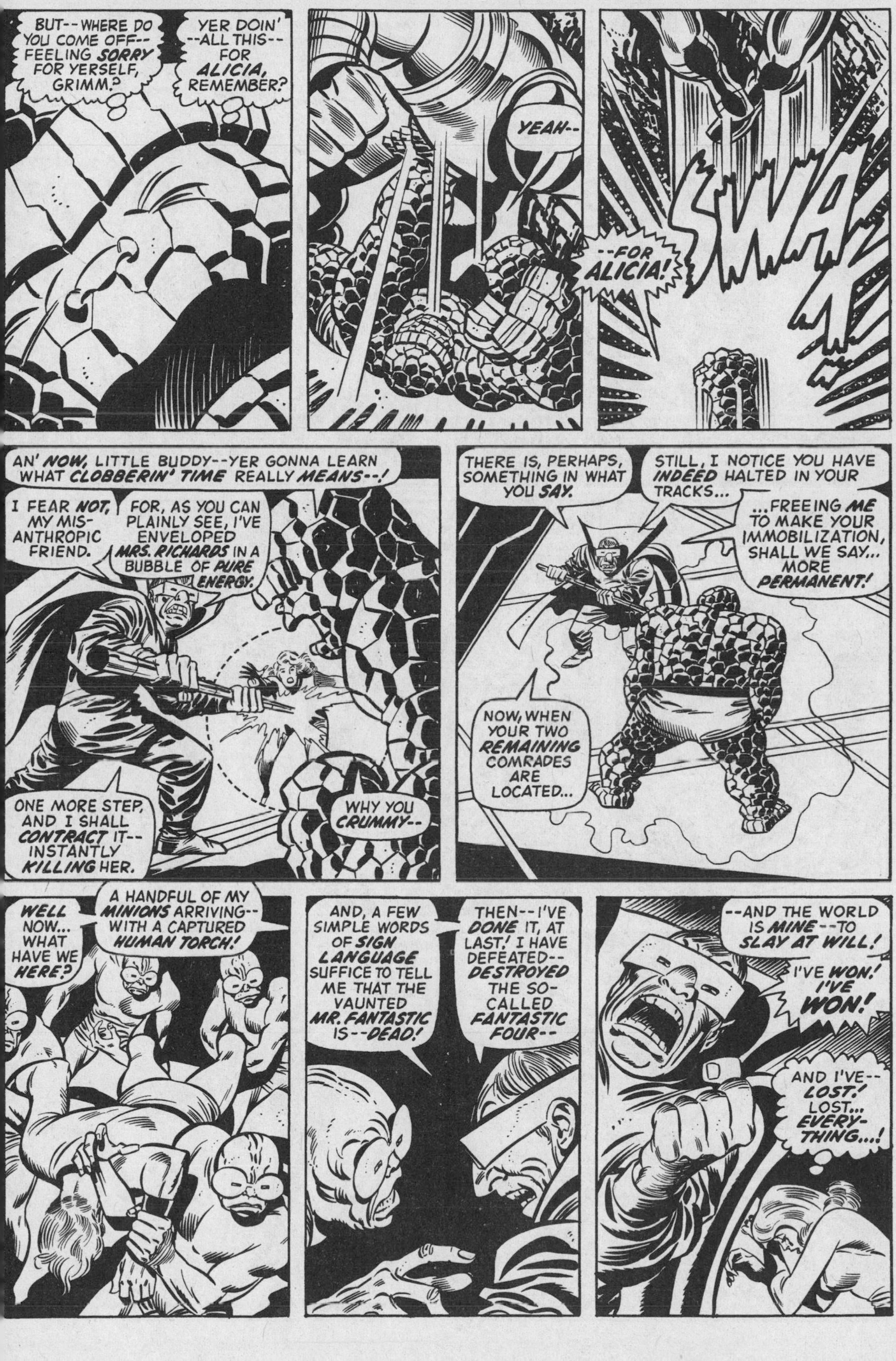

BUT--WHERE DO YOU COME OFF--FEELING SORRY FOR YERSELF, GRIMM?
YER DOIN' --ALL THIS-- FOR ALICIA, REMEMBER?
YEAH--
--FOR ALICIA!
SWA
AN' NOW, LITTLE BUDDY--YER GONNA LEARN WHAT CLOBBERIN' TIME REALLY MEANS--!
I FEAR NOT, MY MIS-ANTHROPIC FRIEND.
FOR, AS YOU CAN PLAINLY SEE, I'VE ENVELOPED MRS. RICHARDS IN A BUBBLE OF PURE ENERGY.
ONE MORE STEP, AND I SHALL CONTRACT IT--INSTANTLY KILLING HER.
WHY YOU CRUMMY--
THERE IS, PERHAPS, SOMETHING IN WHAT YOU SAY.
STILL, I NOTICE YOU HAVE INDEED HALTED IN YOUR TRACKS...
...FREEING ME TO MAKE YOUR IMMOBILIZATION, SHALL WE SAY... MORE PERMANENT!
NOW, WHEN YOUR TWO REMAINING COMRADES ARE LOCATED...
WELL NOW... WHAT HAVE WE HERE?
A HANDFUL OF MY MINIONS ARRIVING--WITH A CAPTURED HUMAN TORCH!
AND, A FEW SIMPLE WORDS OF SIGN LANGUAGE SUFFICE TO TELL ME THAT THE VAUNTED MR. FANTASTIC IS--DEAD!
THEN--I'VE DONE IT, AT LAST! I HAVE DEFEATED--DESTROYED THE SO-CALLED FANTASTIC FOUR--
--AND THE WORLD IS MINE--TO SLAY AT WILL!
I'VE WON! I'VE WON!
AND I'VE--LOST! LOST... EVERY-THING...!

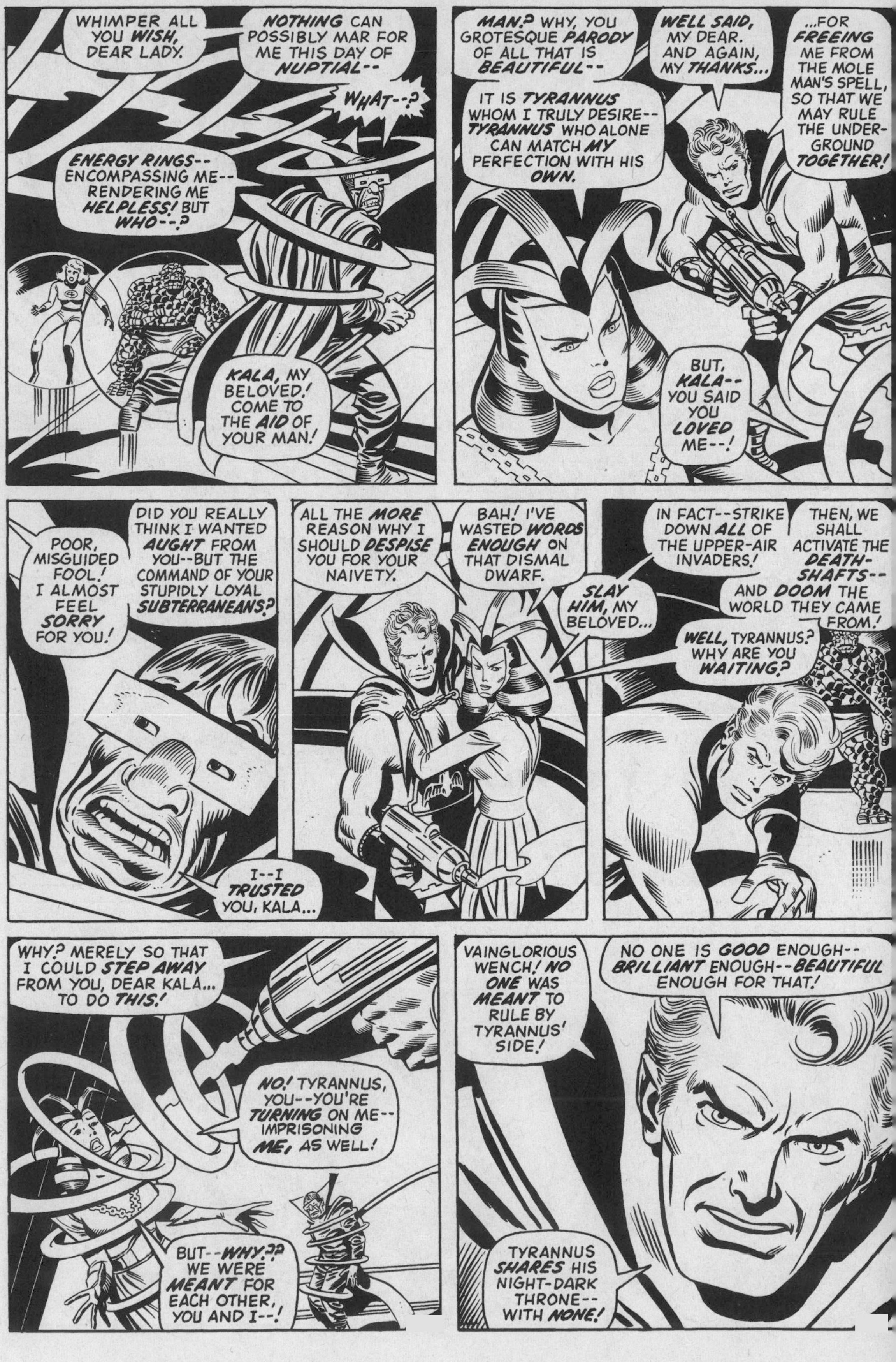
WHIMPER ALL YOU WISH, DEAR LADY.
NOTHING CAN POSSIBLY MAR FOR ME THIS DAY OF NUPTIAL--
WHAT--?
ENERGY RINGS--ENCOMPASSING ME--RENDERING ME HELPLESS! BUT WHO--?
KALA, MY BELOVED! COME TO THE AID OF YOUR MAN!
MAN? WHY, YOU GROTESQUE PARODY OF ALL THAT IS BEAUTIFUL--
IT IS TYRANNUS WHOM I TRULY DESIRE--TYRANNUS WHO ALONE CAN MATCH MY PERFECTION WITH HIS OWN.
WELL SAID, MY DEAR. AND AGAIN, MY THANKS...
...FOR FREEING ME FROM THE MOLE MAN'S SPELL, SO THAT WE MAY RULE THE UNDER-GROUND TOGETHER!
BUT, KALA--YOU SAID YOU LOVED ME--!
POOR, MISGUIDED FOOL! I ALMOST FEEL SORRY FOR YOU!
DID YOU REALLY THINK I WANTED AUGHT FROM YOU--BUT THE COMMAND OF YOUR STUPIDLY LOYAL SUBTERRANEANS?
I--I TRUSTED YOU, KALA...
ALL THE MORE REASON WHY I SHOULD DESPISE YOU FOR YOUR NAIVETY.
BAH! I'VE WASTED WORDS ENOUGH ON THAT DISMAL DWARF.
SLAY HIM, MY BELOVED...
IN FACT--STRIKE DOWN ALL OF THE UPPER-AIR INVADERS!
THEN, WE SHALL ACTIVATE THE DEATH-SHAFTS--
AND DOOM THE WORLD THEY CAME FROM!
WELL, TYRANNUS? WHY ARE YOU WAITING?
WHY? MERELY SO THAT I COULD STEP AWAY FROM YOU, DEAR KALA... TO DO THIS!
NO! TYRANNUS, YOU--YOU'RE TURNING ON ME--IMPRISONING ME, AS WELL!
BUT--WHY?? WE WERE MEANT FOR EACH OTHER, YOU AND I--!
VAINGLORIOUS WENCH! NO ONE WAS MEANT TO RULE BY TYRANNUS' SIDE!
NO ONE IS GOOD ENOUGH--BRILLIANT ENOUGH--BEAUTIFUL ENOUGH FOR THAT!
TYRANNUS SHARES HIS NIGHT-DARK THRONE--WITH NONE!

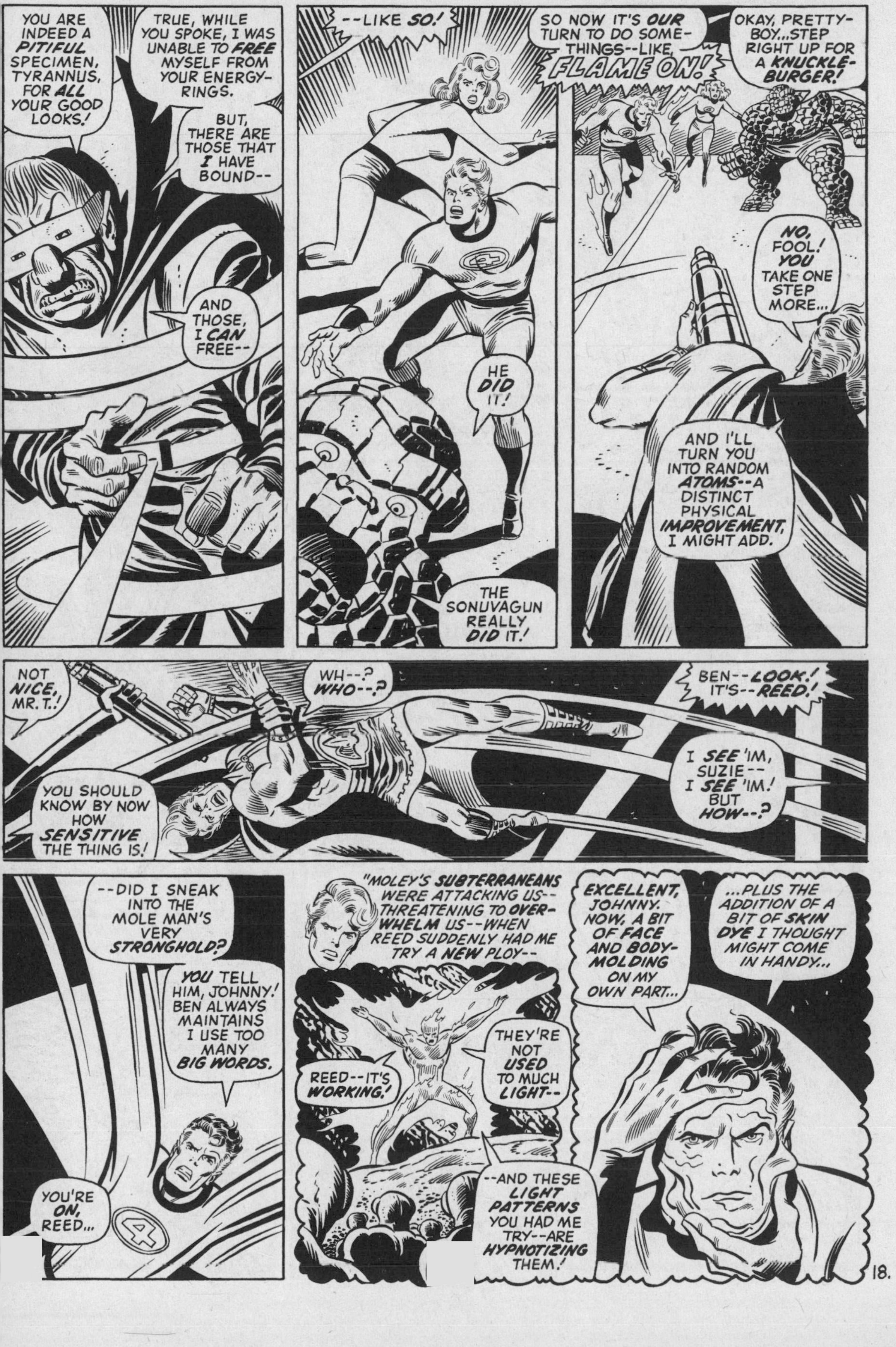
YOU ARE INDEED A PITIFUL SPECIMEN, TYRANNUS, FOR ALL YOUR GOOD LOOKS!
TRUE, WHILE YOU SPOKE, I WAS UNABLE TO FREE MYSELF FROM YOUR ENERGY-RINGS.
BUT, THERE ARE THOSE THAT I HAVE BOUND--
AND THOSE, I CAN FREE--
--LIKE SO!
HE DID IT!
THE SONUVAGUN REALLY DID IT!
SO NOW IT'S OUR TURN TO DO SOME-THINGS--LIKE,
FLAME ON!
OKAY, PRETTY-BOY...STEP RIGHT UP FOR A KNUCKLE-BURGER!
NO, FOOL! YOU TAKE ONE STEP MORE...
AND I'LL TURN YOU INTO RANDOM ATOMS--A DISTINCT PHYSICAL IMPROVEMENT, I MIGHT ADD.
NOT NICE, MR. T.!
YOU SHOULD KNOW BY NOW HOW SENSITIVE THE THING IS!
WH--? WHO--?
BEN--LOOK! IT'S--REED!
I SEE 'IM, SUZIE-- I SEE 'IM! BUT HOW--?
--DID I SNEAK INTO THE MOLE MAN'S VERY STRONGHOLD?
YOU TELL HIM, JOHNNY! BEN ALWAYS MAINTAINS I USE TOO MANY BIG WORDS.
YOU'RE ON, REED...
"MOLEY'S SUBTERRANEANS WERE ATTACKING US--THREATENING TO OVER-WHELM US--WHEN REED SUDDENLY HAD ME TRY A NEW PLOY--
REED--IT'S WORKING!
THEY'RE NOT USED TO MUCH LIGHT--
--AND THESE LIGHT PATTERNS YOU HAD ME TRY--ARE HYPNOTIZING THEM!
EXCELLENT, JOHNNY. NOW, A BIT OF FACE AND BODY-MOLDING ON MY OWN PART...
...PLUS THE ADDITION OF A BIT OF SKIN DYE I THOUGHT MIGHT COME IN HANDY...
4

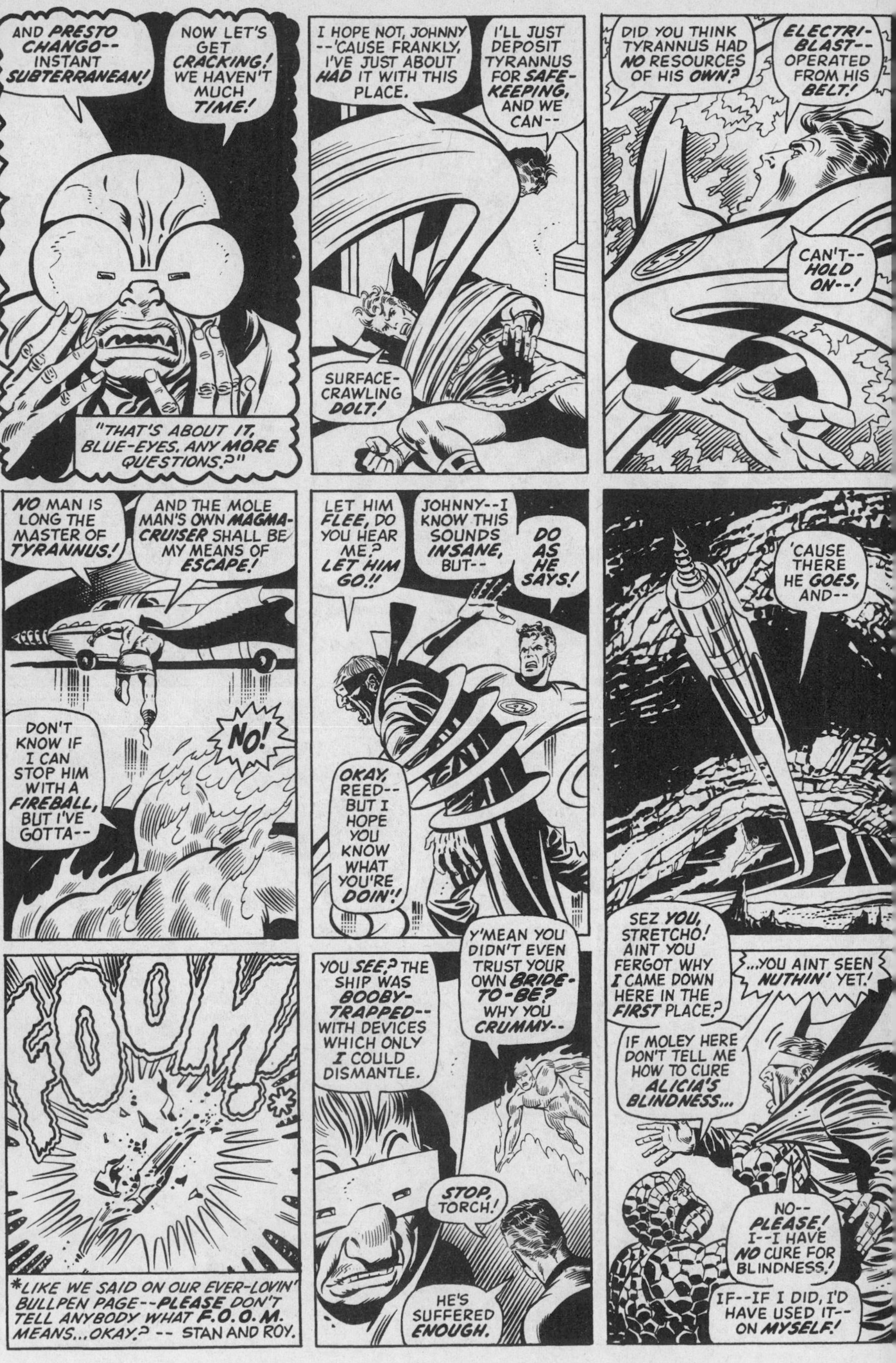

AND PRESTO CHANGO-- INSTANT SUBTERRANEAN!
NOW LET'S GET CRACKING! WE HAVEN'T MUCH TIME!
"THAT'S ABOUT IT, BLUE-EYES. ANY MORE QUESTIONS?"
I HOPE NOT, JOHNNY --'CAUSE FRANKLY, I'VE JUST ABOUT HAD IT WITH THIS PLACE.
I'LL JUST DEPOSIT TYRANNUS FOR SAFE-KEEPING, AND WE CAN--
SURFACE-CRAWLING DOLT!
DID YOU THINK TYRANNUS HAD NO RESOURCES OF HIS OWN?
ELECTRI-BLAST-- OPERATED FROM HIS BELT!
CAN'T-- HOLD ON--!
NO MAN IS LONG THE MASTER OF TYRANNUS!
AND THE MOLE MAN'S OWN MAGMA-CRUISER SHALL BE MY MEANS OF ESCAPE!
DON'T KNOW IF I CAN STOP HIM WITH A FIREBALL, BUT I'VE GOTTA--
NO!
LET HIM FLEE, DO YOU HEAR ME? LET HIM GO!!
JOHNNY--I KNOW THIS SOUNDS INSANE, BUT--
DO AS HE SAYS!
OKAY, REED-- BUT I HOPE YOU KNOW WHAT YOU'RE DOIN'!
'CAUSE THERE HE GOES, AND--
FOOM!
*LIKE WE SAID ON OUR EVER-LOVIN' BULLPEN PAGE--PLEASE DON'T TELL ANYBODY WHAT F.O.O.M. MEANS...OKAY? -- STAN AND ROY.
YOU SEE? THE SHIP WAS BOOBY-TRAPPED-- WITH DEVICES WHICH ONLY I COULD DISMANTLE.
Y'MEAN YOU DIDN'T EVEN TRUST YOUR OWN BRIDE-TO-BE? WHY YOU CRUMMY--
STOP, TORCH!
HE'S SUFFERED ENOUGH.
SEZ YOU, STRETCHO! AINT YOU FERGOT WHY I CAME DOWN HERE IN THE FIRST PLACE?
...YOU AINT SEEN NUTHIN' YET.
IF MOLEY HERE DON'T TELL ME HOW TO CURE ALICIA'S BLINDNESS...
NO-- PLEASE! I--I HAVE NO CURE FOR BLINDNESS!
IF--IF I DID, I'D HAVE USED IT-- ON MYSELF!

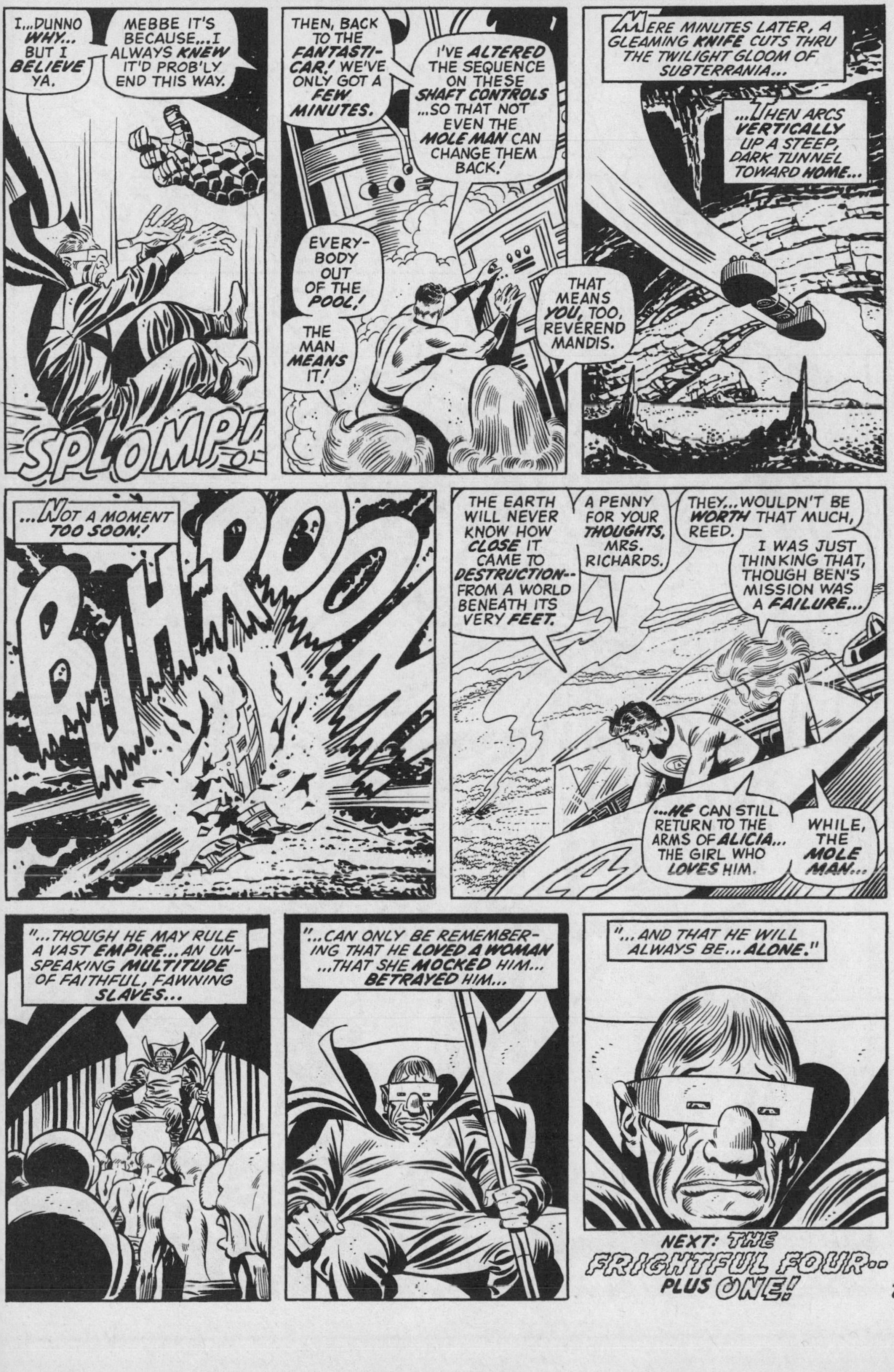
I...DUNNO WHY... BUT I BELIEVE YA.
MEBBE IT'S BECAUSE...I ALWAYS KNEW IT'D PROB'LY END THIS WAY.
SPLOMP!
THEN, BACK TO THE FANTASTI-CAR! WE'VE ONLY GOT A FEW MINUTES.
I'VE ALTERED THE SEQUENCE ON THESE SHAFT CONTROLS ...SO THAT NOT EVEN THE MOLE MAN CAN CHANGE THEM BACK!
EVERY-BODY OUT OF THE POOL!
THE MAN MEANS IT!
THAT MEANS YOU, TOO, REVEREND MANDIS.
MERE MINUTES LATER, A GLEAMING KNIFE CUTS THRU THE TWILIGHT GLOOM OF SUBTERRANIA...
...THEN ARCS VERTICALLY UP A STEEP, DARK TUNNEL TOWARD HOME...
...NOT A MOMENT TOO SOON!
B-H-ROOM
THE EARTH WILL NEVER KNOW HOW CLOSE IT CAME TO DESTRUCTION--FROM A WORLD BENEATH ITS VERY FEET.
A PENNY FOR YOUR THOUGHTS, MRS. RICHARDS.
THEY...WOULDN'T BE WORTH THAT MUCH, REED.
I WAS JUST THINKING THAT, THOUGH BEN'S MISSION WAS A FAILURE...
...HE CAN STILL RETURN TO THE ARMS OF ALICIA... THE GIRL WHO LOVES HIM.
WHILE, THE MOLE MAN...
"...THOUGH HE MAY RULE A VAST EMPIRE...AN UN-SPEAKING MULTITUDE OF FAITHFUL, FAWNING SLAVES...
"...CAN ONLY BE REMEMBER-ING THAT HE LOVED A WOMAN ...THAT SHE MOCKED HIM... BETRAYED HIM...
"...AND THAT HE WILL ALWAYS BE... ALONE."
NEXT: THE FRIGHTFUL FOUR.. PLUS ONE!

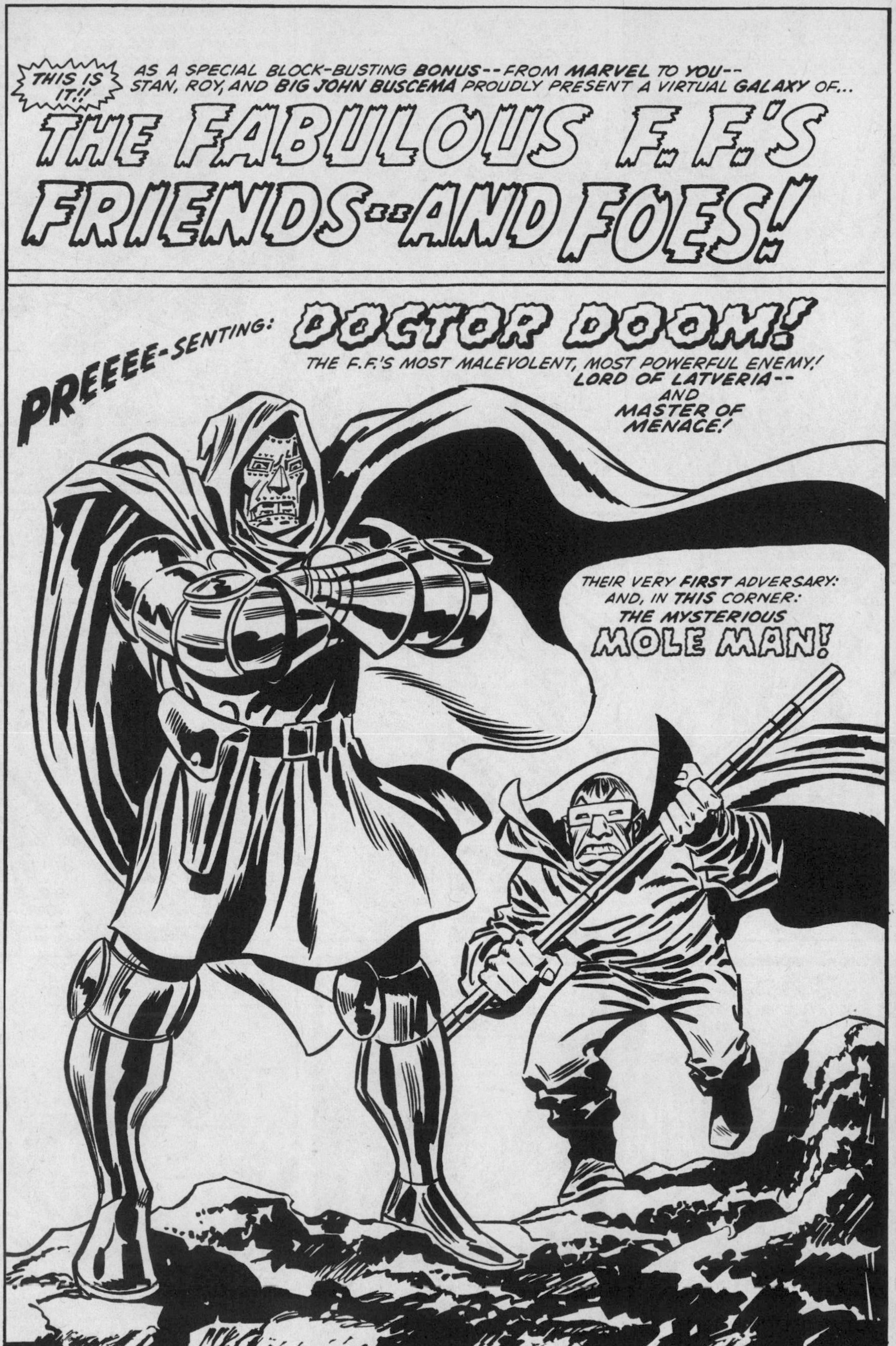
THIS IS IT!!
AS A SPECIAL BLOCK-BUSTING BONUS--FROM MARVEL TO YOU--
STAN, ROY, AND BIG JOHN BUSCEMA PROUDLY PRESENT A VIRTUAL GALAXY OF...
THE FABULOUS F.F.'S FRIENDS--AND FOES!
PREEEEE-SENTING: DOCTOR DOOM!
THE F.F.'S MOST MALEVOLENT, MOST POWERFUL ENEMY! LORD OF LATVERIA-- AND MASTER OF MENACE!
THEIR VERY FIRST ADVERSARY: AND, IN THIS CORNER: THE MYSTERIOUS MOLE MAN!

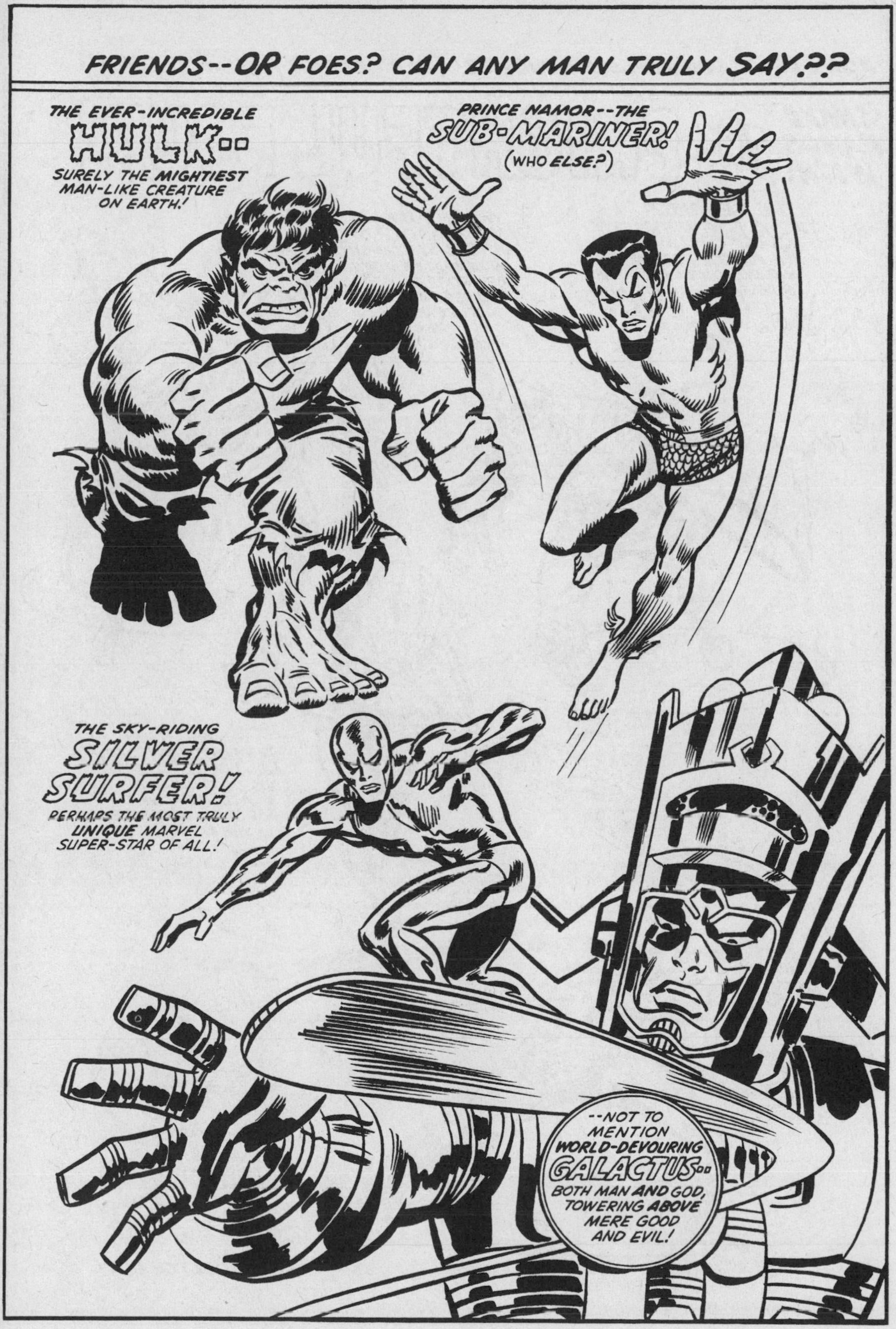
FRIENDS--OR FOES? CAN ANY MAN TRULY SAY??
THE EVER-INCREDIBLE HULK.. SURELY THE MIGHTIEST MAN-LIKE CREATURE ON EARTH!
PRINCE NAMOR--THE SUB-MARINER! (WHO ELSE?)
THE SKY-RIDING SILVER SURFER! PERHAPS THE MOST TRULY UNIQUE MARVEL SUPER-STAR OF ALL!
--NOT TO MENTION WORLD-DEVOURING GALACTUS.. BOTH MAN AND GOD, TOWERING ABOVE MERE GOOD AND EVIL!

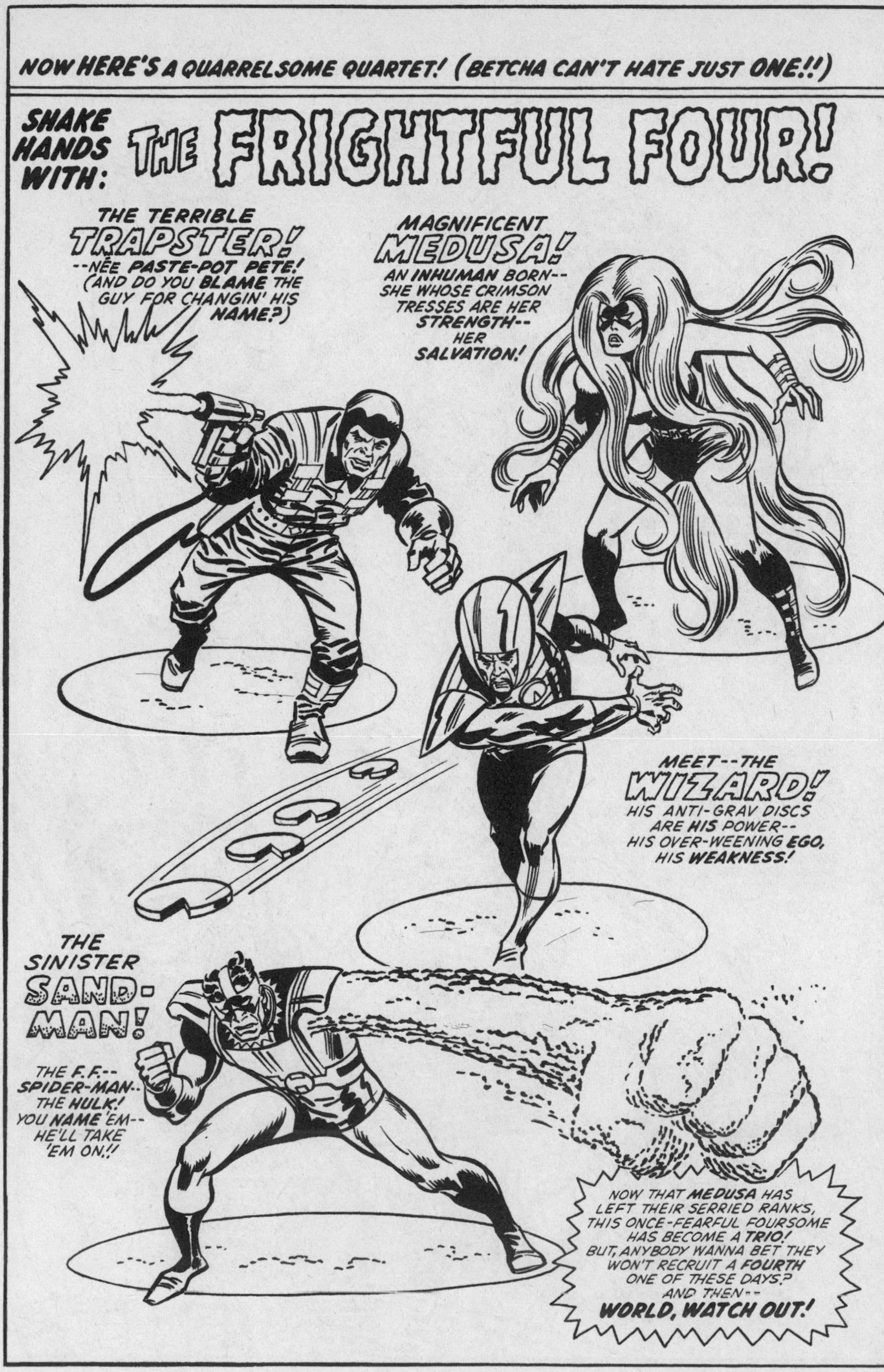
NOW HERE'S A QUARRELSOME QUARTET! (BETCHA CAN'T HATE JUST ONE!!)
SHAKE HANDS WITH: THE FRIGHTFUL FOUR!
THE TERRIBLE TRAPSTER! --NÉE PASTE-POT PETE! (AND DO YOU BLAME THE GUY FOR CHANGIN' HIS NAME?)
MAGNIFICENT MEDUSA! AN INHUMAN BORN-- SHE WHOSE CRIMSON TRESSES ARE HER STRENGTH-- HER SALVATION!
MEET--THE WIZARD! HIS ANTI-GRAV DISCS ARE HIS POWER-- HIS OVER-WEENING EGO, HIS WEAKNESS!
THE SINISTER SAND-MAN!
THE F.F.-- SPIDER-MAN-- THE HULK! YOU NAME 'EM-- HE'LL TAKE 'EM ON!!
NOW THAT MEDUSA HAS LEFT THEIR SERRIED RANKS, THIS ONCE-FEARFUL FOURSOME HAS BECOME A TRIO! BUT, ANYBODY WANNA BET THEY WON'T RECRUIT A FOURTH ONE OF THESE DAYS? AND THEN-- WORLD, WATCH OUT!

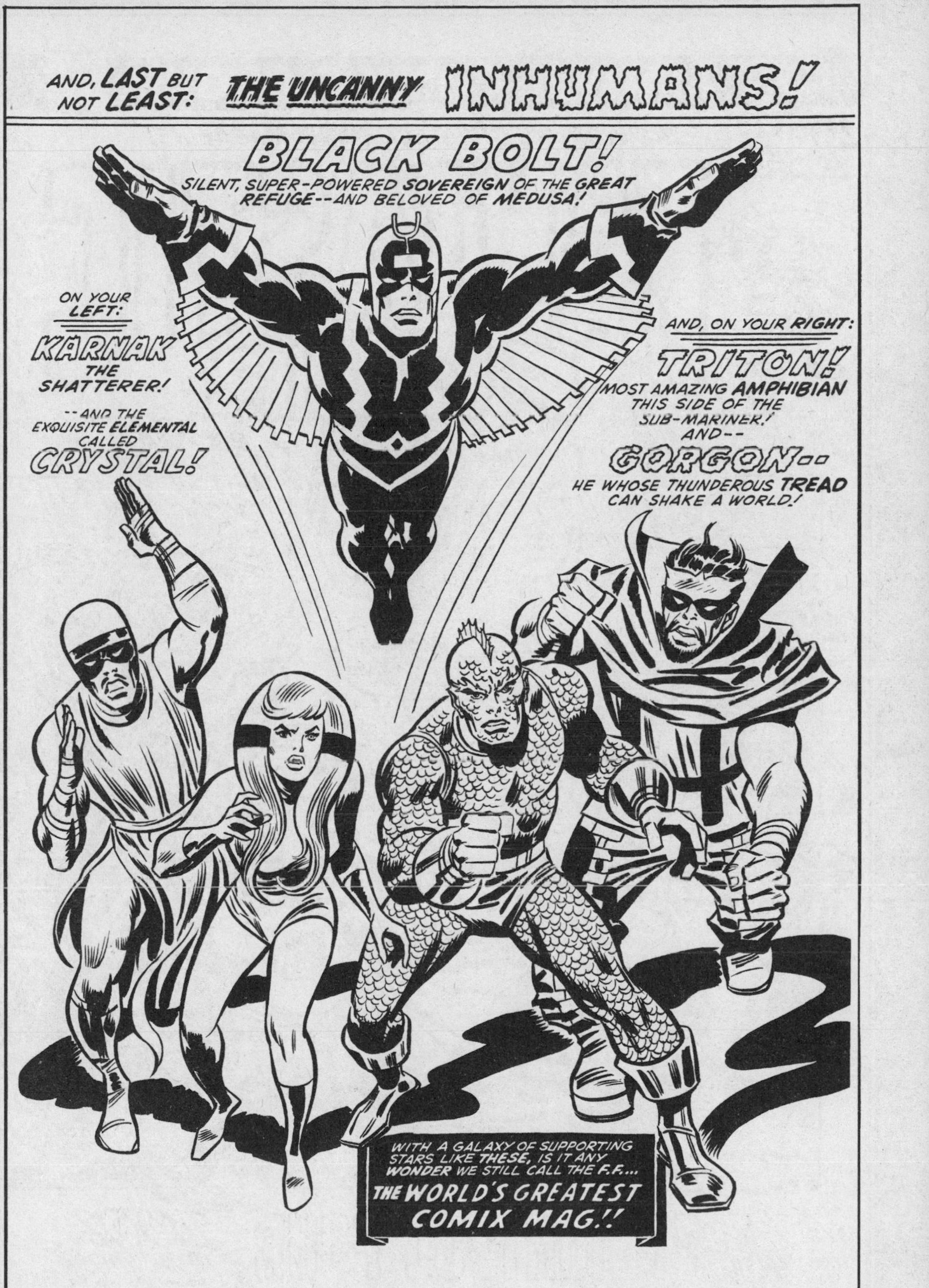
AND, LAST BUT NOT LEAST: THE UNCANNY INHUMANS!
BLACK BOLT!
SILENT, SUPER-POWERED SOVEREIGN OF THE GREAT REFUGE--AND BELOVED OF MEDUSA!
ON YOUR LEFT: KARNAK THE SHATTERER!
--AND THE EXQUISITE ELEMENTAL CALLED CRYSTAL!
AND, ON YOUR RIGHT: TRITON! MOST AMAZING AMPHIBIAN THIS SIDE OF THE SUB-MARINER! AND--
GORGON-- HE WHOSE THUNDEROUS TREAD CAN SHAKE A WORLD!
WITH A GALAXY OF SUPPORTING STARS LIKE THESE, IS IT ANY WONDER WE STILL CALL THE F.F... THE WORLD'S GREATEST COMIX MAG!!

FANTASTIC FOUR
MARVEL COMICS GROUP
APPROVED BY THE COMICS CODE AUTHORITY
20¢
129 DEC 02462
THE WORLD'S GREATEST COMIX MAGAZINE!
FANTASTIC FOUR
EXTRA!! THE HUMAN TORCH QUITS THE F.F.!
STAND AWAY! MEDUSA CLAIMS BEN GRIMM!
NO! HE BELONGS TO THUNDRA--
--OR TO NO ONE!!
ALL THIS, AND THE FRIGHTFUL FOUR, T.O.O! 'NUFF SAID!

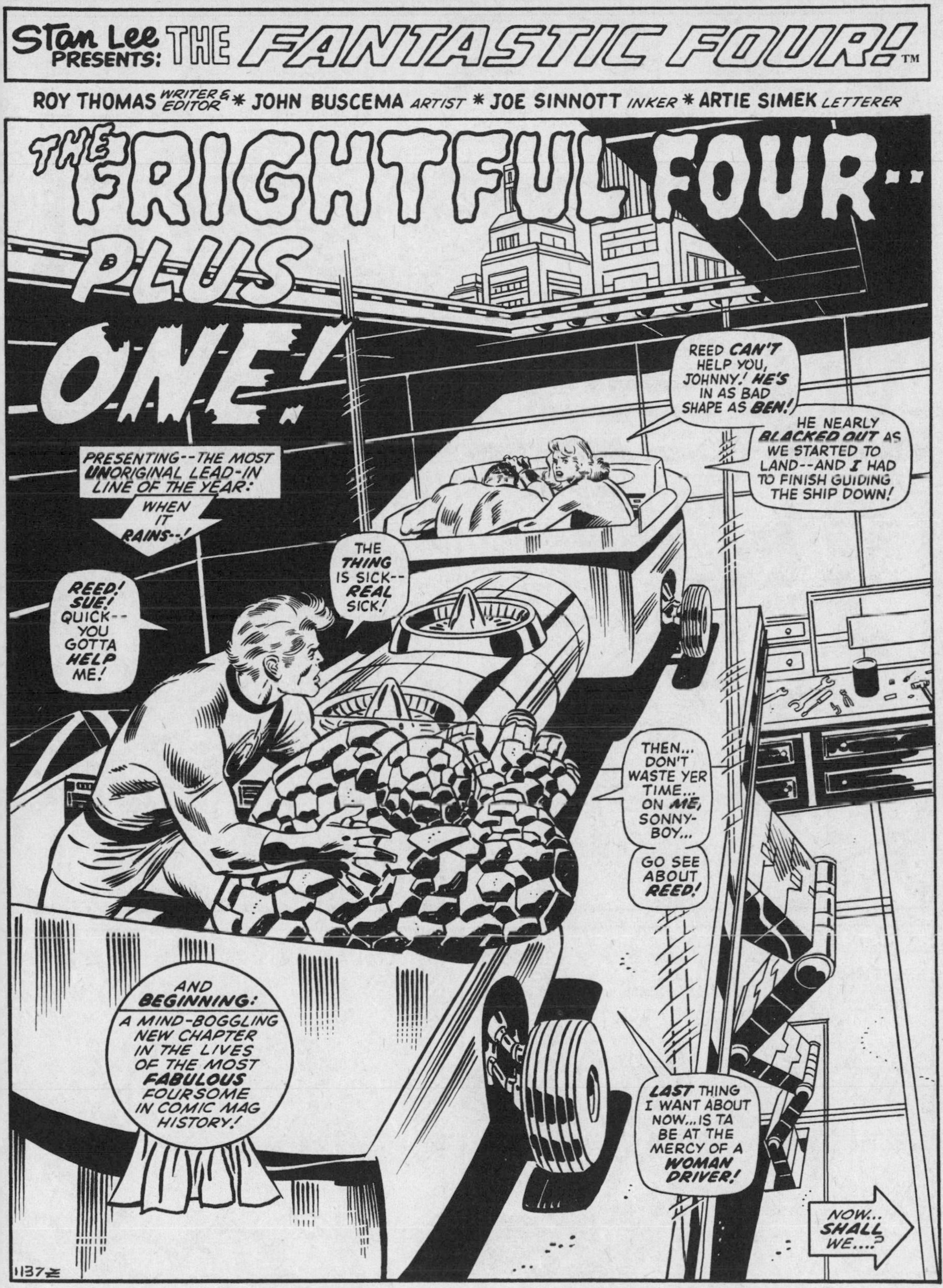
Stan Lee PRESENTS: THE FANTASTIC FOUR! ™
ROY THOMAS WRITER & EDITOR * JOHN BUSCEMA ARTIST * JOE SINNOTT INKER * ARTIE SIMEK LETTERER
THE FRIGHTFUL FOUR-- PLUS ONE!
PRESENTING--THE MOST UNORIGINAL LEAD-IN LINE OF THE YEAR:
WHEN IT RAINS--!
REED CAN'T HELP YOU, JOHNNY! HE'S IN AS BAD SHAPE AS BEN!
HE NEARLY BLACKED OUT AS WE STARTED TO LAND--AND I HAD TO FINISH GUIDING THE SHIP DOWN!
THE THING IS SICK-- REAL SICK!
REED! SUE! QUICK-- YOU GOTTA HELP ME!
THEN... DON'T WASTE YER TIME... ON ME, SONNY-BOY...
GO SEE ABOUT REED!
AND BEGINNING: A MIND-BOGGLING NEW CHAPTER IN THE LIVES OF THE MOST FABULOUS FOURSOME IN COMIC MAG HISTORY!
LAST THING I WANT ABOUT NOW...IS TA BE AT THE MERCY OF A WOMAN DRIVER!
NOW... SHALL WE...?
1137

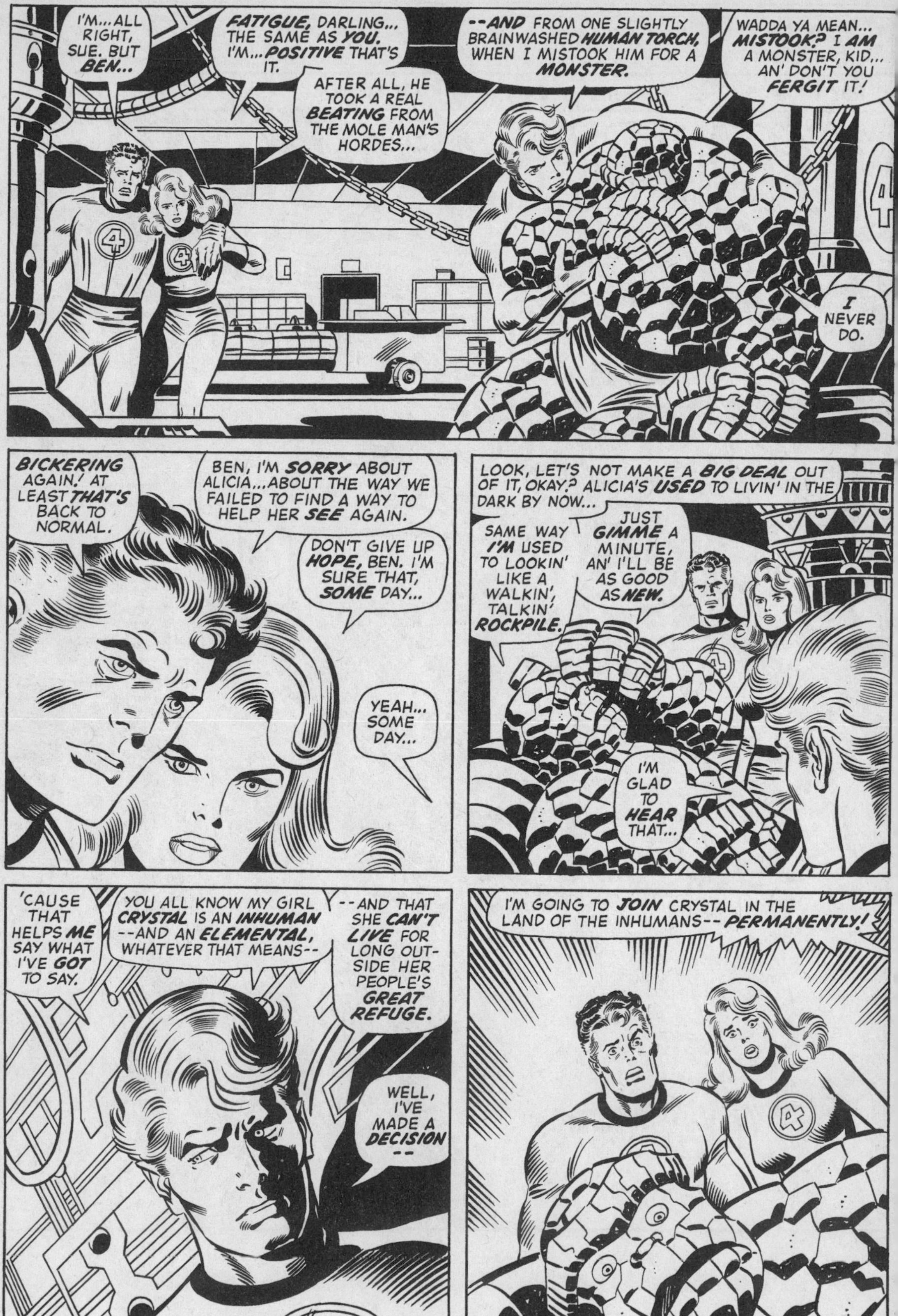

I'M...ALL RIGHT, SUE. BUT BEN...
FATIGUE, DARLING... THE SAME AS YOU. I'M...POSITIVE THAT'S IT.
AFTER ALL, HE TOOK A REAL BEATING FROM THE MOLE MAN'S HORDES...
--AND FROM ONE SLIGHTLY BRAINWASHED HUMAN TORCH, WHEN I MISTOOK HIM FOR A MONSTER.
WADDA YA MEAN... MISTOOK? I AM A MONSTER, KID... AN' DON'T YOU FERGIT IT!
I NEVER DO.
BICKERING AGAIN! AT LEAST THAT'S BACK TO NORMAL.
BEN, I'M SORRY ABOUT ALICIA...ABOUT THE WAY WE FAILED TO FIND A WAY TO HELP HER SEE AGAIN.
DON'T GIVE UP HOPE, BEN. I'M SURE THAT, SOME DAY...
YEAH... SOME DAY...
LOOK, LET'S NOT MAKE A BIG DEAL OUT OF IT, OKAY? ALICIA'S USED TO LIVIN' IN THE DARK BY NOW...
SAME WAY I'M USED TO LOOKIN' LIKE A WALKIN', TALKIN' ROCKPILE.
JUST GIMME A MINUTE, AN' I'LL BE AS GOOD AS NEW.
I'M GLAD TO HEAR THAT...
'CAUSE THAT HELPS ME SAY WHAT I'VE GOT TO SAY.
YOU ALL KNOW MY GIRL CRYSTAL IS AN INHUMAN --AND AN ELEMENTAL, WHATEVER THAT MEANS--
--AND THAT SHE CAN'T LIVE FOR LONG OUTSIDE HER PEOPLE'S GREAT REFUGE.
WELL, I'VE MADE A DECISION--
I'M GOING TO JOIN CRYSTAL IN THE LAND OF THE INHUMANS--PERMANENTLY!

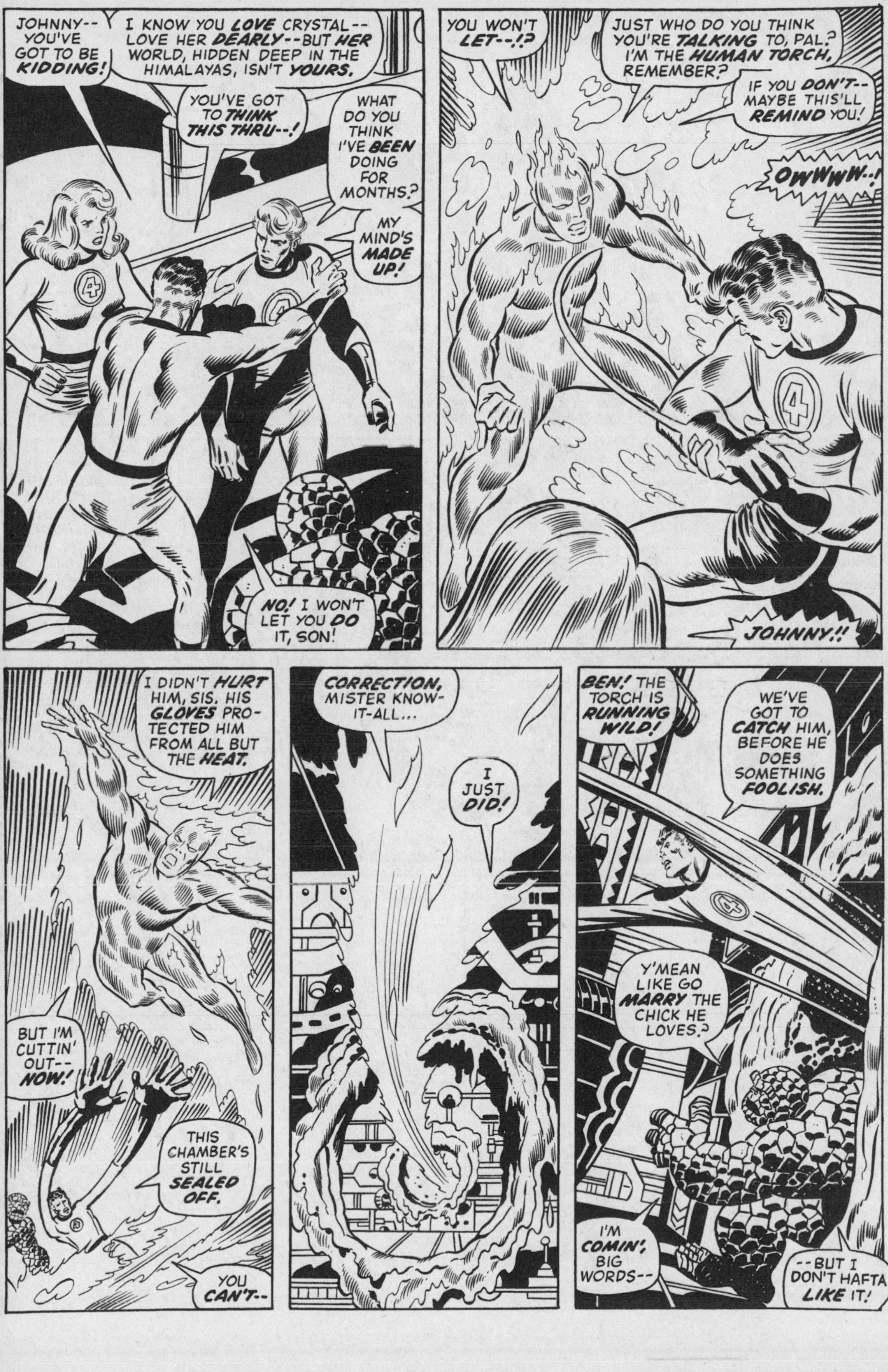
JOHNNY-- YOU'VE GOT TO BE KIDDING!
I KNOW YOU LOVE CRYSTAL-- LOVE HER DEARLY--BUT HER WORLD, HIDDEN DEEP IN THE HIMALAYAS, ISN'T YOURS.
YOU'VE GOT TO THINK THIS THRU--!
WHAT DO YOU THINK I'VE BEEN DOING FOR MONTHS?
MY MIND'S MADE UP!
NO! I WON'T LET YOU DO IT, SON!
YOU WON'T LET--!?
JUST WHO DO YOU THINK YOU'RE TALKING TO, PAL? I'M THE HUMAN TORCH, REMEMBER?
IF YOU DON'T-- MAYBE THIS'LL REMIND YOU!
OWWWW..!
JOHNNY!!
I DIDN'T HURT HIM, SIS. HIS GLOVES PROTECTED HIM FROM ALL BUT THE HEAT.
BUT I'M CUTTIN' OUT-- NOW!
THIS CHAMBER'S STILL SEALED OFF.
YOU CAN'T--
CORRECTION, MISTER KNOW-IT-ALL...
I JUST DID!
BEN! THE TORCH IS RUNNING WILD!
WE'VE GOT TO CATCH HIM, BEFORE HE DOES SOMETHING FOOLISH.
Y'MEAN LIKE GO MARRY THE CHICK HE LOVES?
I'M COMIN', BIG WORDS--
--BUT I DON'T HAFTA LIKE IT!

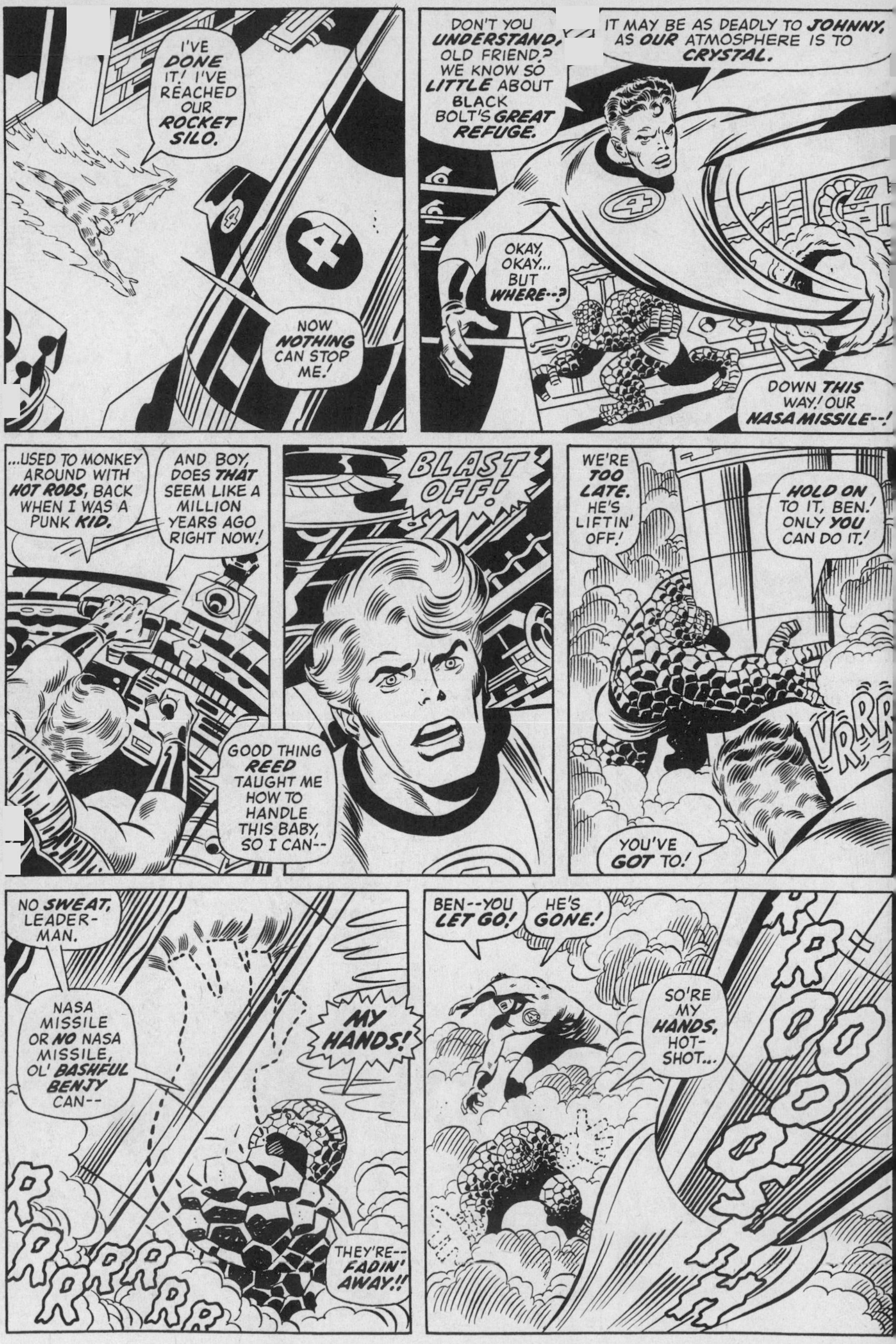

I'VE DONE IT! I'VE REACHED OUR ROCKET SILO.
NOW NOTHING CAN STOP ME!
DON'T YOU UNDERSTAND, OLD FRIEND? WE KNOW SO LITTLE ABOUT BLACK BOLT'S GREAT REFUGE.
IT MAY BE AS DEADLY TO JOHNNY, AS OUR ATMOSPHERE IS TO CRYSTAL.
OKAY, OKAY... BUT WHERE--?
DOWN THIS WAY! OUR NASA MISSILE--!
...USED TO MONKEY AROUND WITH HOT RODS, BACK WHEN I WAS A PUNK KID.
AND BOY, DOES THAT SEEM LIKE A MILLION YEARS AGO RIGHT NOW!
BLAST OFF!
GOOD THING REED TAUGHT ME HOW TO HANDLE THIS BABY, SO I CAN--
WE'RE TOO LATE. HE'S LIFTIN' OFF!
HOLD ON TO IT, BEN! ONLY YOU CAN DO IT!
VRRR
YOU'VE GOT TO!
NO SWEAT, LEADER-MAN.
NASA MISSILE OR NO NASA MISSILE, OL' BASHFUL BENJY CAN--
MY HANDS!
THEY'RE--FADIN' AWAY!!
RRRRRRRR
BEN--YOU LET GO!
HE'S GONE!
SO'RE MY HANDS, HOT-SHOT...
RROOOOOSH

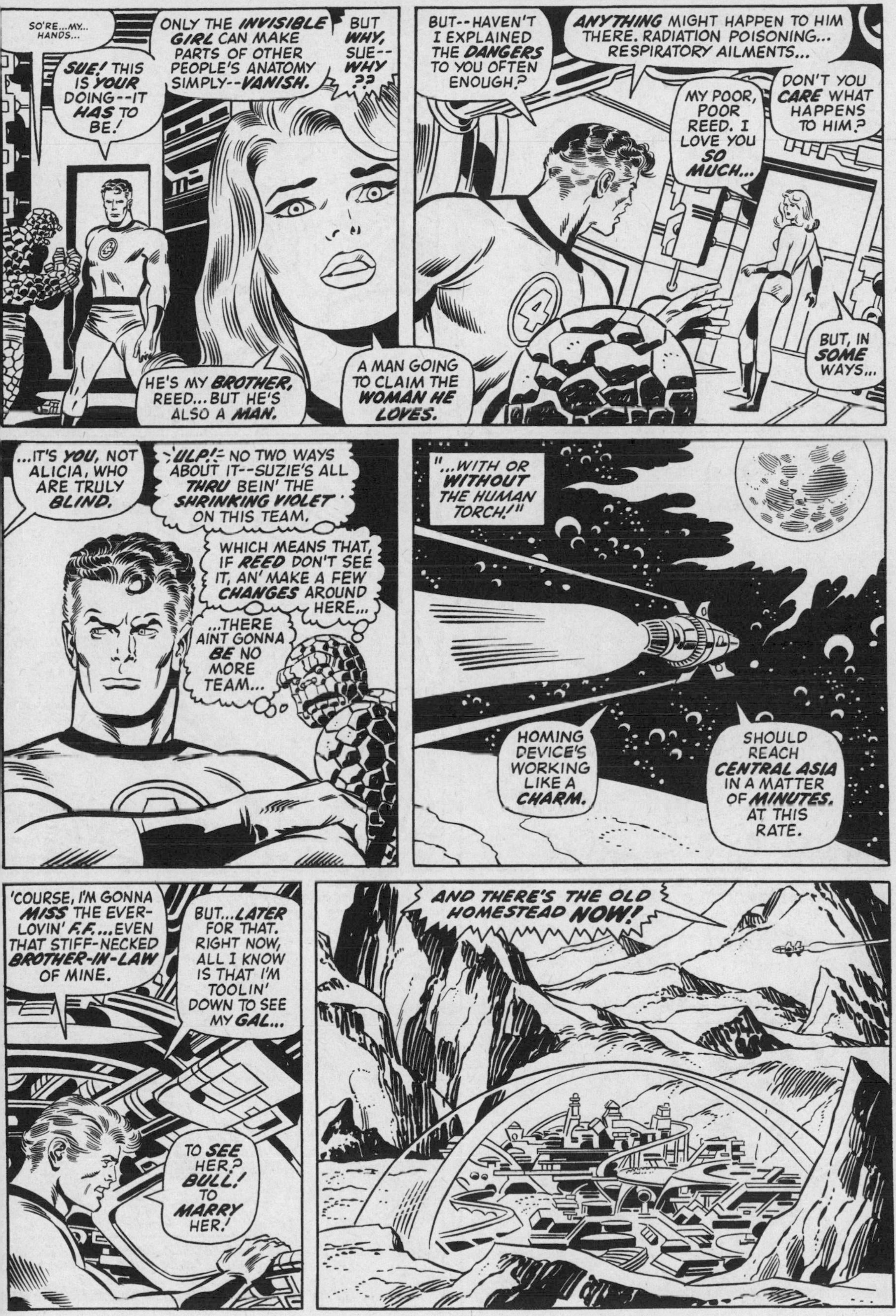
SO'RE...MY... HANDS...
SUE! THIS IS YOUR DOING--IT HAS TO BE!
ONLY THE INVISIBLE GIRL CAN MAKE PARTS OF OTHER PEOPLE'S ANATOMY SIMPLY--VANISH.
BUT WHY, SUE--WHY ??
HE'S MY BROTHER, REED...BUT HE'S ALSO A MAN.
A MAN GOING TO CLAIM THE WOMAN HE LOVES.
BUT--HAVEN'T I EXPLAINED THE DANGERS TO YOU OFTEN ENOUGH?
ANYTHING MIGHT HAPPEN TO HIM THERE. RADIATION POISONING... RESPIRATORY AILMENTS...
MY POOR, POOR REED. I LOVE YOU SO MUCH...
DON'T YOU CARE WHAT HAPPENS TO HIM?
BUT, IN SOME WAYS...
...IT'S YOU, NOT ALICIA, WHO ARE TRULY BLIND.
ULP! NO TWO WAYS ABOUT IT--SUZIE'S ALL THRU BEIN' THE SHRINKING VIOLET ON THIS TEAM.
WHICH MEANS THAT, IF REED DON'T SEE IT, AN' MAKE A FEW CHANGES AROUND HERE...
...THERE AINT GONNA BE NO MORE TEAM...
"...WITH OR WITHOUT THE HUMAN TORCH!"
HOMING DEVICE'S WORKING LIKE A CHARM.
SHOULD REACH CENTRAL ASIA IN A MATTER OF MINUTES. AT THIS RATE.
'COURSE, I'M GONNA MISS THE EVER-LOVIN' F.F. ...EVEN THAT STIFF-NECKED BROTHER-IN-LAW OF MINE.
BUT...LATER FOR THAT. RIGHT NOW, ALL I KNOW IS THAT I'M TOOLIN' DOWN TO SEE MY GAL...
TO SEE HER? BULL! TO MARRY HER!
AND THERE'S THE OLD HOMESTEAD NOW!

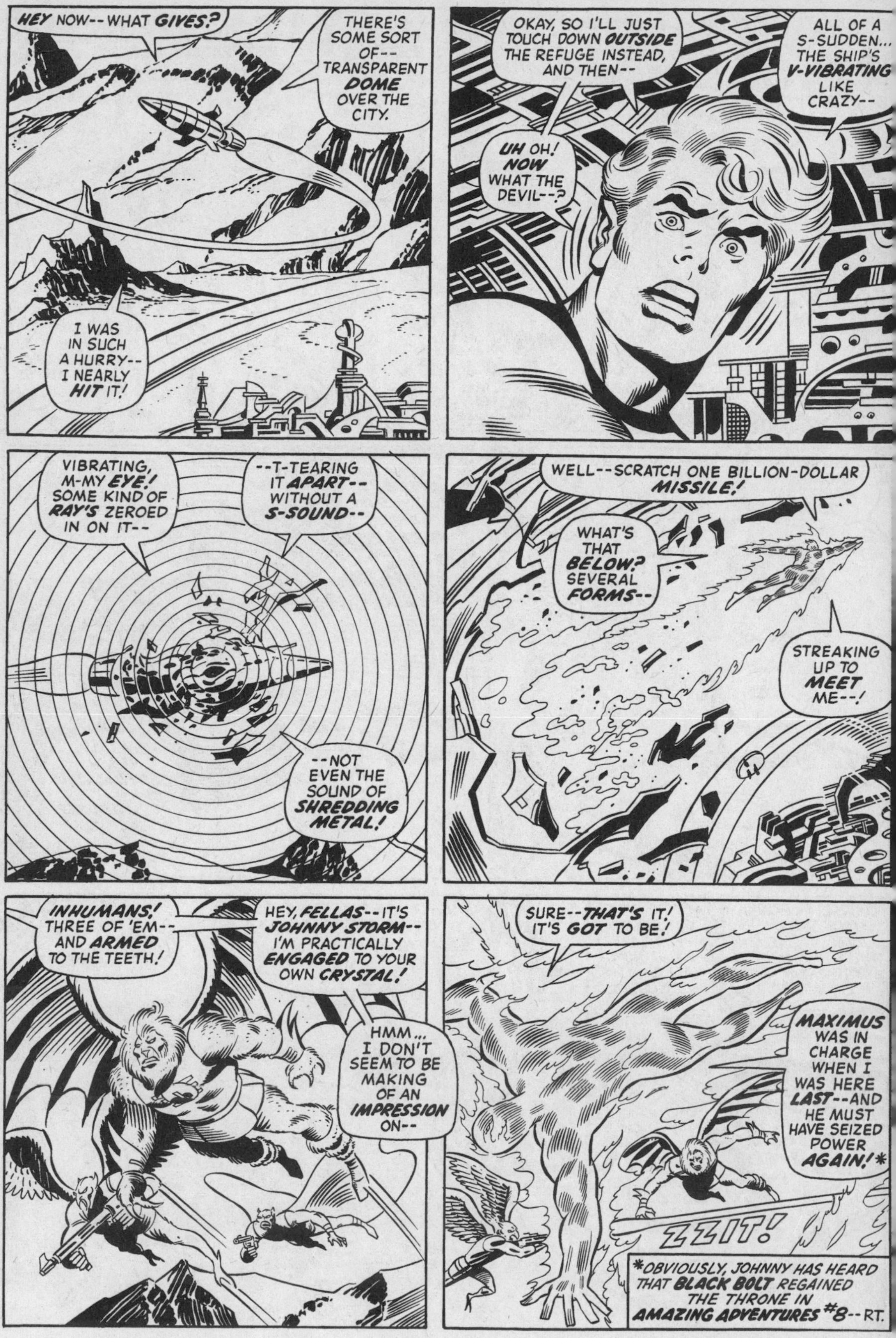
HEY NOW--WHAT GIVES?
THERE'S SOME SORT OF--TRANSPARENT DOME OVER THE CITY.
I WAS IN SUCH A HURRY--I NEARLY HIT IT!
OKAY, SO I'LL JUST TOUCH DOWN OUTSIDE THE REFUGE INSTEAD, AND THEN--
ALL OF A S-SUDDEN... THE SHIP'S V-VIBRATING LIKE CRAZY--
UH OH! NOW WHAT THE DEVIL--?
VIBRATING, M-MY EYE! SOME KIND OF RAY'S ZEROED IN ON IT--
--T-TEARING IT APART--WITHOUT A S-SOUND--
--NOT EVEN THE SOUND OF SHREDDING METAL!
WELL--SCRATCH ONE BILLION-DOLLAR MISSILE!
WHAT'S THAT BELOW? SEVERAL FORMS--
STREAKING UP TO MEET ME--!
INHUMANS! THREE OF 'EM--AND ARMED TO THE TEETH!
HEY, FELLAS--IT'S JOHNNY STORM--I'M PRACTICALLY ENGAGED TO YOUR OWN CRYSTAL!
HMM... I DON'T SEEM TO BE MAKING OF AN IMPRESSION ON--
SURE--THAT'S IT! IT'S GOT TO BE!
MAXIMUS WAS IN CHARGE WHEN I WAS HERE LAST--AND HE MUST HAVE SEIZED POWER AGAIN!*
ZZIT!
*OBVIOUSLY, JOHNNY HAS HEARD THAT BLACK BOLT REGAINED THE THRONE IN AMAZING ADVENTURES #8--RT.

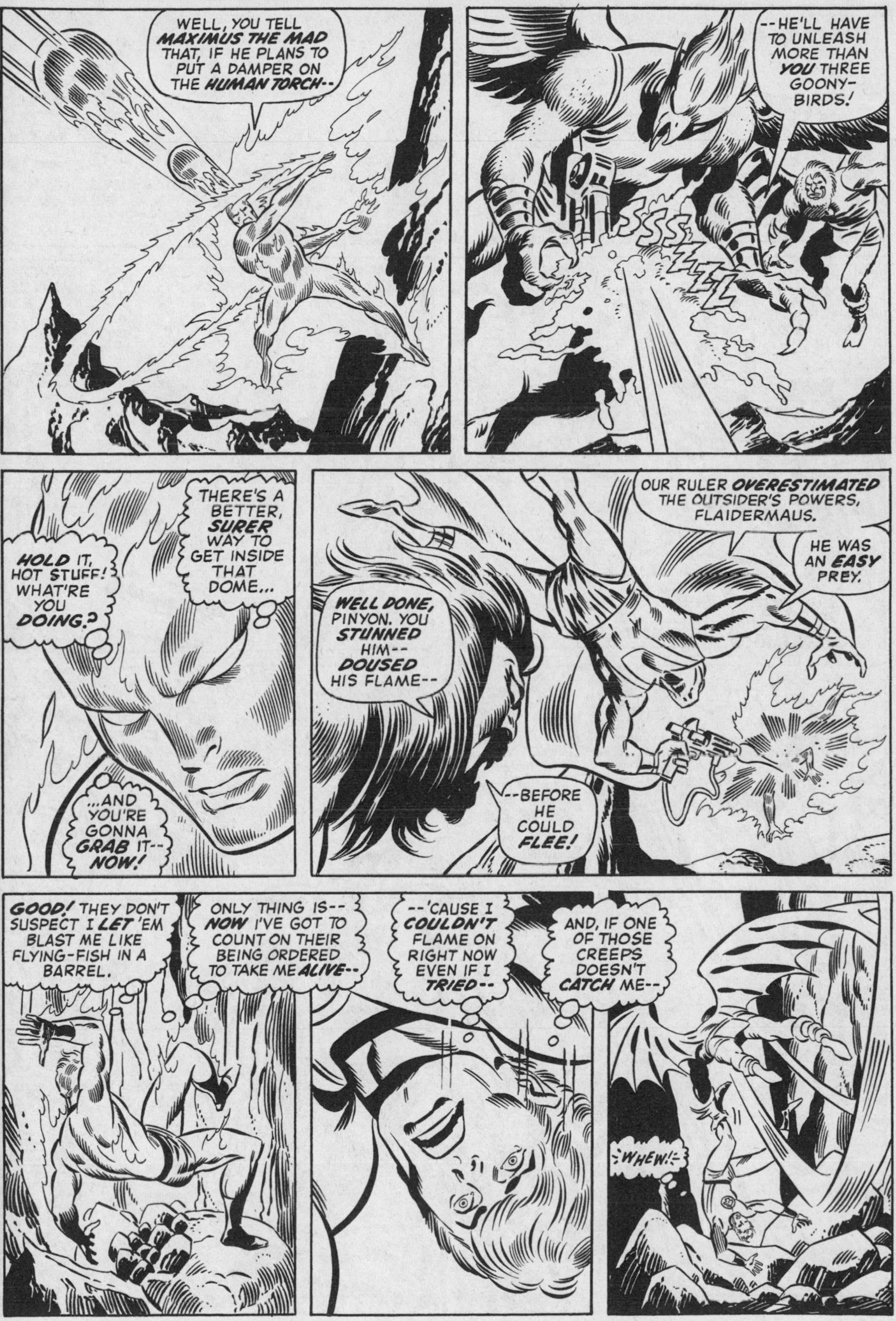
WELL, YOU TELL MAXIMUS THE MAD THAT, IF HE PLANS TO PUT A DAMPER ON THE HUMAN TORCH--
--HE'LL HAVE TO UNLEASH MORE THAN YOU THREE GOONY-BIRDS!
SSSSZZZ
HOLD IT, HOT STUFF! WHAT'RE YOU DOING?
THERE'S A BETTER, SURER WAY TO GET INSIDE THAT DOME...
...AND YOU'RE GONNA GRAB IT--NOW!
OUR RULER OVERESTIMATED THE OUTSIDER'S POWERS, FLAIDERMAUS.
HE WAS AN EASY PREY.
WELL DONE, PINYON. YOU STUNNED HIM--DOUSED HIS FLAME--
--BEFORE HE COULD FLEE!
GOOD! THEY DON'T SUSPECT I LET 'EM BLAST ME LIKE FLYING-FISH IN A BARREL.
ONLY THING IS--NOW I'VE GOT TO COUNT ON THEIR BEING ORDERED TO TAKE ME ALIVE--
--'CAUSE I COULDN'T FLAME ON RIGHT NOW EVEN IF I TRIED--
AND, IF ONE OF THOSE CREEPS DOESN'T CATCH ME--
WHEW!

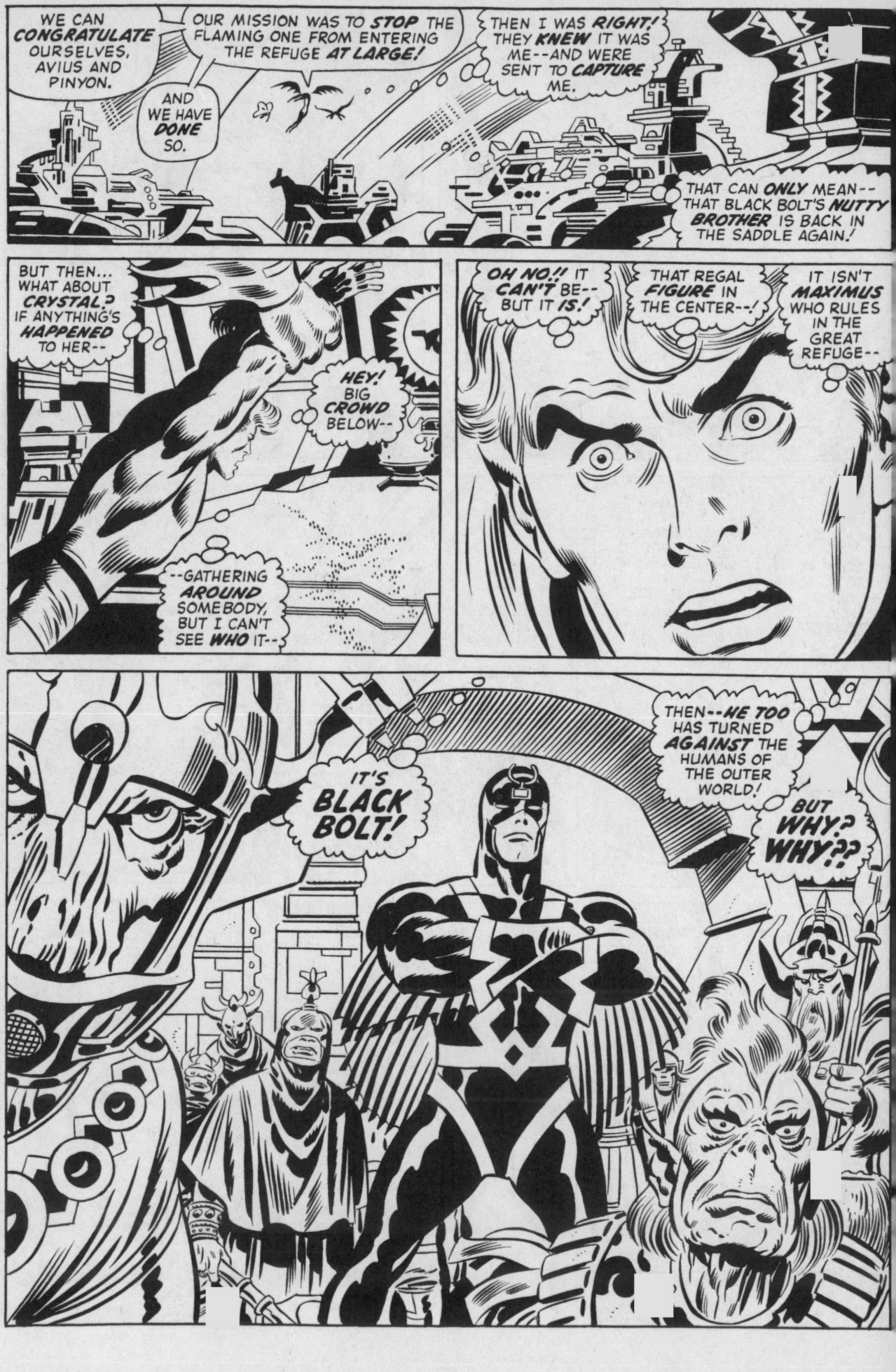
WE CAN CONGRATULATE OURSELVES, AVIUS AND PINYON.
OUR MISSION WAS TO STOP THE FLAMING ONE FROM ENTERING THE REFUGE AT LARGE!
AND WE HAVE DONE SO.
THEN I WAS RIGHT! THEY KNEW IT WAS ME--AND WERE SENT TO CAPTURE ME.
THAT CAN ONLY MEAN--THAT BLACK BOLT'S NUTTY BROTHER IS BACK IN THE SADDLE AGAIN.!
BUT THEN... WHAT ABOUT CRYSTAL? IF ANYTHING'S HAPPENED TO HER--
HEY! BIG CROWD BELOW--
--GATHERING AROUND SOMEBODY, BUT I CAN'T SEE WHO IT--
OH NO!! IT CAN'T BE--BUT IT IS!
THAT REGAL FIGURE IN THE CENTER--!
IT ISN'T MAXIMUS WHO RULES IN THE GREAT REFUGE--
IT'S BLACK BOLT!
THEN--HE TOO HAS TURNED AGAINST THE HUMANS OF THE OUTER WORLD!
BUT WHY? WHY??

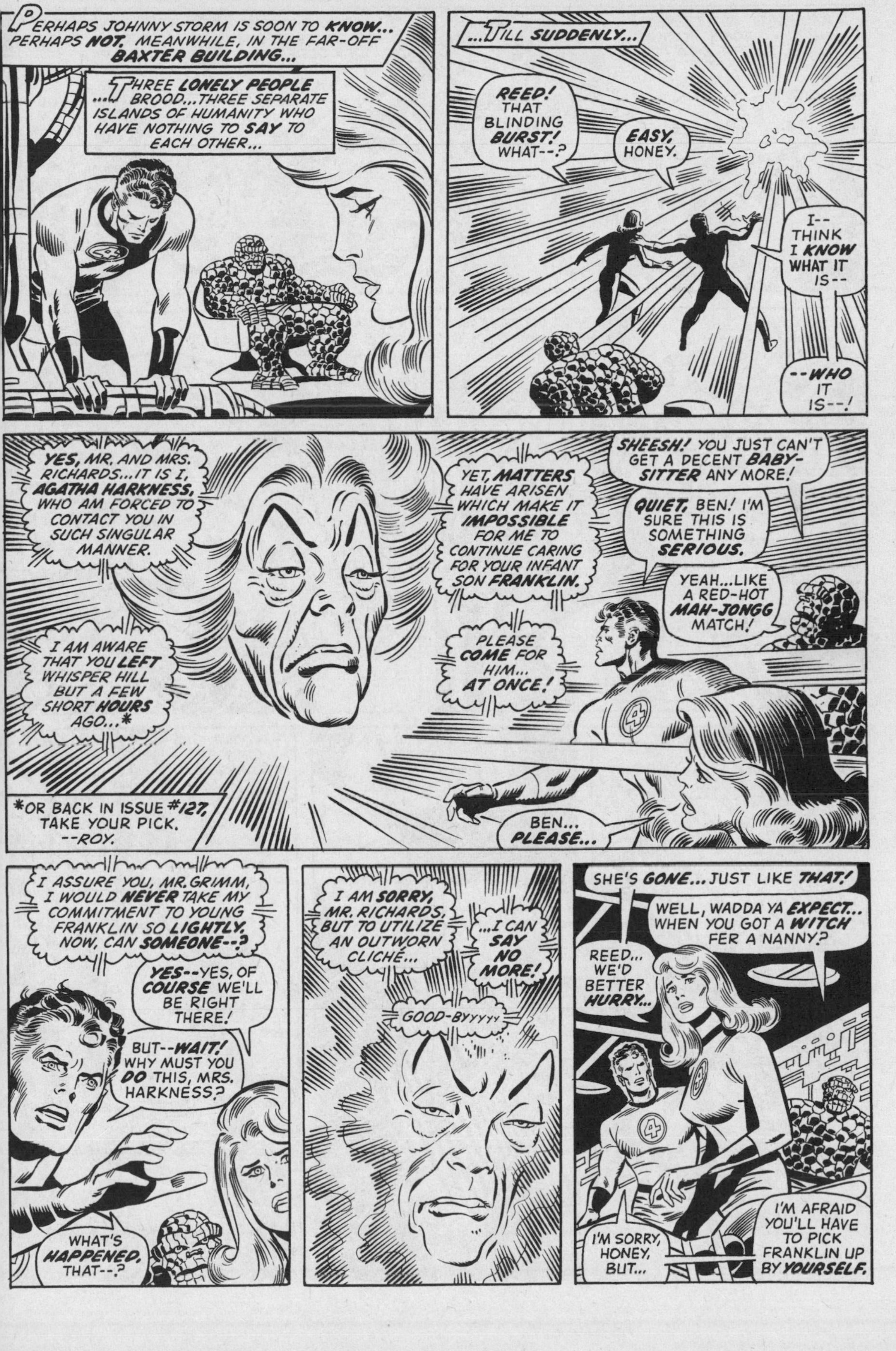
PERHAPS JOHNNY STORM IS SOON TO KNOW... PERHAPS NOT. MEANWHILE, IN THE FAR-OFF BAXTER BUILDING...
...THREE LONELY PEOPLE BROOD...THREE SEPARATE ISLANDS OF HUMANITY WHO HAVE NOTHING TO SAY TO EACH OTHER...
...TILL SUDDENLY...
REED! THAT BLINDING BURST! WHAT--?
EASY, HONEY.
I--THINK I KNOW WHAT IT IS--
--WHO IT IS--!
YES, MR. AND MRS. RICHARDS...IT IS I, AGATHA HARKNESS, WHO AM FORCED TO CONTACT YOU IN SUCH SINGULAR MANNER.
YET, MATTERS HAVE ARISEN WHICH MAKE IT IMPOSSIBLE FOR ME TO CONTINUE CARING FOR YOUR INFANT SON FRANKLIN.
SHEESH! YOU JUST CAN'T GET A DECENT BABY-SITTER ANY MORE!
QUIET, BEN! I'M SURE THIS IS SOMETHING SERIOUS.
YEAH...LIKE A RED-HOT MAH-JONGG MATCH!
I AM AWARE THAT YOU LEFT WHISPER HILL BUT A FEW SHORT HOURS AGO...*
PLEASE COME FOR HIM... AT ONCE!
*OR BACK IN ISSUE #127, TAKE YOUR PICK. --ROY.
BEN... PLEASE...
I ASSURE YOU, MR. GRIMM, I WOULD NEVER TAKE MY COMMITMENT TO YOUNG FRANKLIN SO LIGHTLY. NOW, CAN SOMEONE--?
YES--YES, OF COURSE WE'LL BE RIGHT THERE!
BUT--WAIT! WHY MUST YOU DO THIS, MRS. HARKNESS?
WHAT'S HAPPENED, THAT--?
I AM SORRY, MR. RICHARDS, BUT TO UTILIZE AN OUTWORN CLICHÉ...
...I CAN SAY NO MORE!
GOOD-BYYYYY
SHE'S GONE...JUST LIKE THAT!
WELL, WADDA YA EXPECT... WHEN YOU GOT A WITCH FER A NANNY?
REED... WE'D BETTER HURRY...
I'M SORRY, HONEY, BUT...
I'M AFRAID YOU'LL HAVE TO PICK FRANKLIN UP BY YOURSELF.

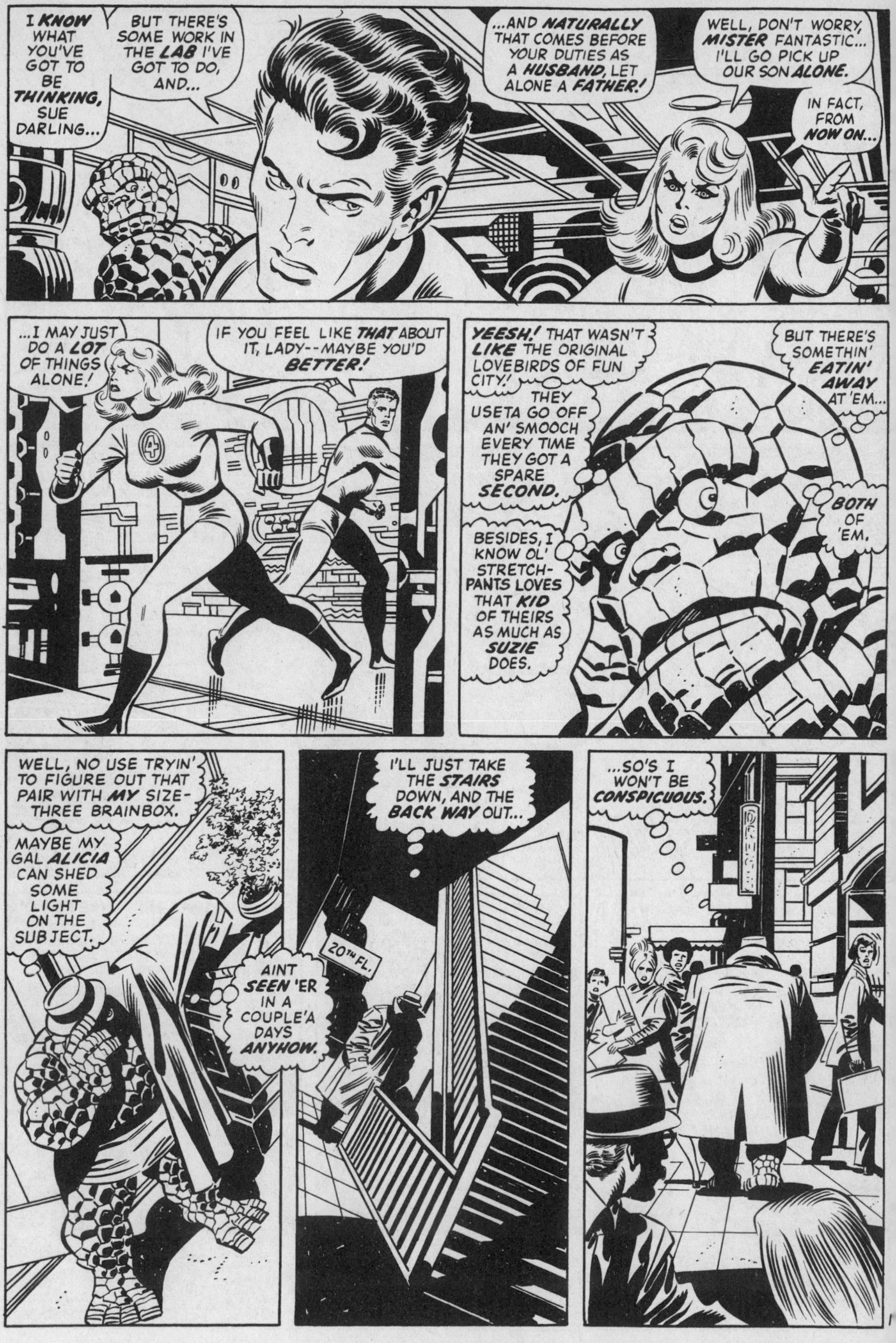
I KNOW WHAT YOU'VE GOT TO BE THINKING, SUE DARLING...
BUT THERE'S SOME WORK IN THE LAB I'VE GOT TO DO, AND...
...AND NATURALLY THAT COMES BEFORE YOUR DUTIES AS A HUSBAND, LET ALONE A FATHER!
WELL, DON'T WORRY, MISTER FANTASTIC... I'LL GO PICK UP OUR SON ALONE.
IN FACT, FROM NOW ON...
...I MAY JUST DO A LOT OF THINGS ALONE!
IF YOU FEEL LIKE THAT ABOUT IT, LADY--MAYBE YOU'D BETTER!
YEESH! THAT WASN'T LIKE THE ORIGINAL LOVEBIRDS OF FUN CITY!
THEY USETA GO OFF AN' SMOOCH EVERY TIME THEY GOT A SPARE SECOND.
BESIDES, I KNOW OL' STRETCH-PANTS LOVES THAT KID OF THEIRS AS MUCH AS SUZIE DOES.
BUT THERE'S SOMETHIN' EATIN' AWAY AT 'EM...
BOTH OF 'EM.
WELL, NO USE TRYIN' TO FIGURE OUT THAT PAIR WITH MY SIZE-THREE BRAINBOX.
MAYBE MY GAL ALICIA CAN SHED SOME LIGHT ON THE SUBJECT.
AINT SEEN 'ER IN A COUPLE'A DAYS ANYHOW.
I'LL JUST TAKE THE STAIRS DOWN, AND THE BACK WAY OUT...
20TH FL.
...SO'S I WON'T BE CONSPICUOUS.

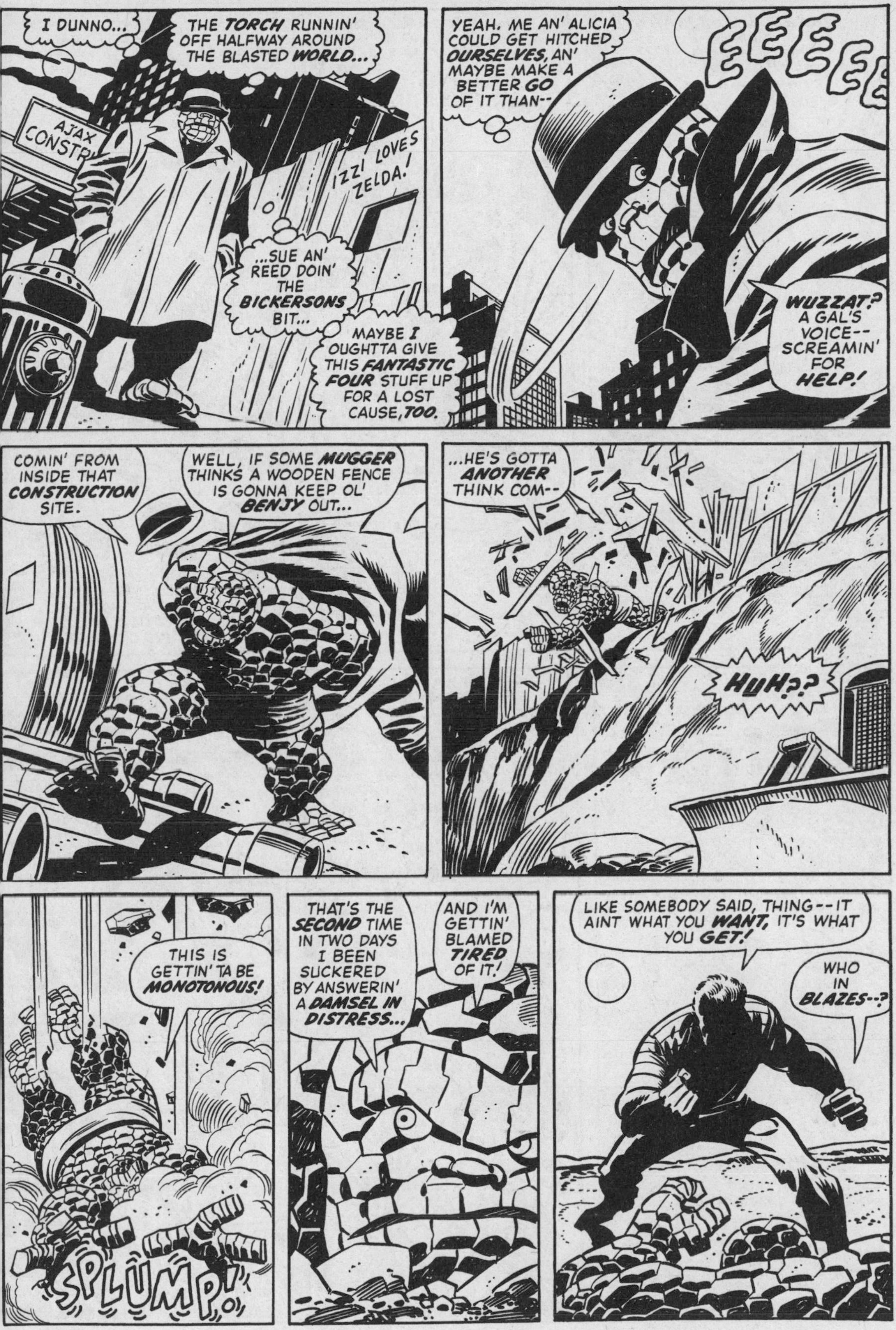
I DUNNO...
THE TORCH RUNNIN' OFF HALFWAY AROUND THE BLASTED WORLD...
AJAX CONSTR
IZZI LOVES ZELDA!
...SUE AN' REED DOIN' THE BICKERSONS BIT...
MAYBE I OUGHTTA GIVE THIS FANTASTIC FOUR STUFF UP FOR A LOST CAUSE, TOO.
YEAH. ME AN' ALICIA COULD GET HITCHED OURSELVES, AN' MAYBE MAKE A BETTER GO OF IT THAN--
EEEEE
WUZZAT? A GAL'S VOICE--SCREAMIN' FOR HELP!
COMIN' FROM INSIDE THAT CONSTRUCTION SITE.
WELL, IF SOME MUGGER THINKS A WOODEN FENCE IS GONNA KEEP OL' BENJY OUT...
...HE'S GOTTA ANOTHER THINK COM--
HUH??
THIS IS GETTIN' TA BE MONOTONOUS!
SPLUMP!
THAT'S THE SECOND TIME IN TWO DAYS I BEEN SUCKERED BY ANSWERIN' A DAMSEL IN DISTRESS...
AND I'M GETTIN' BLAMED TIRED OF IT!
LIKE SOMEBODY SAID, THING--IT AINT WHAT YOU WANT, IT'S WHAT YOU GET!
WHO IN BLAZES--?

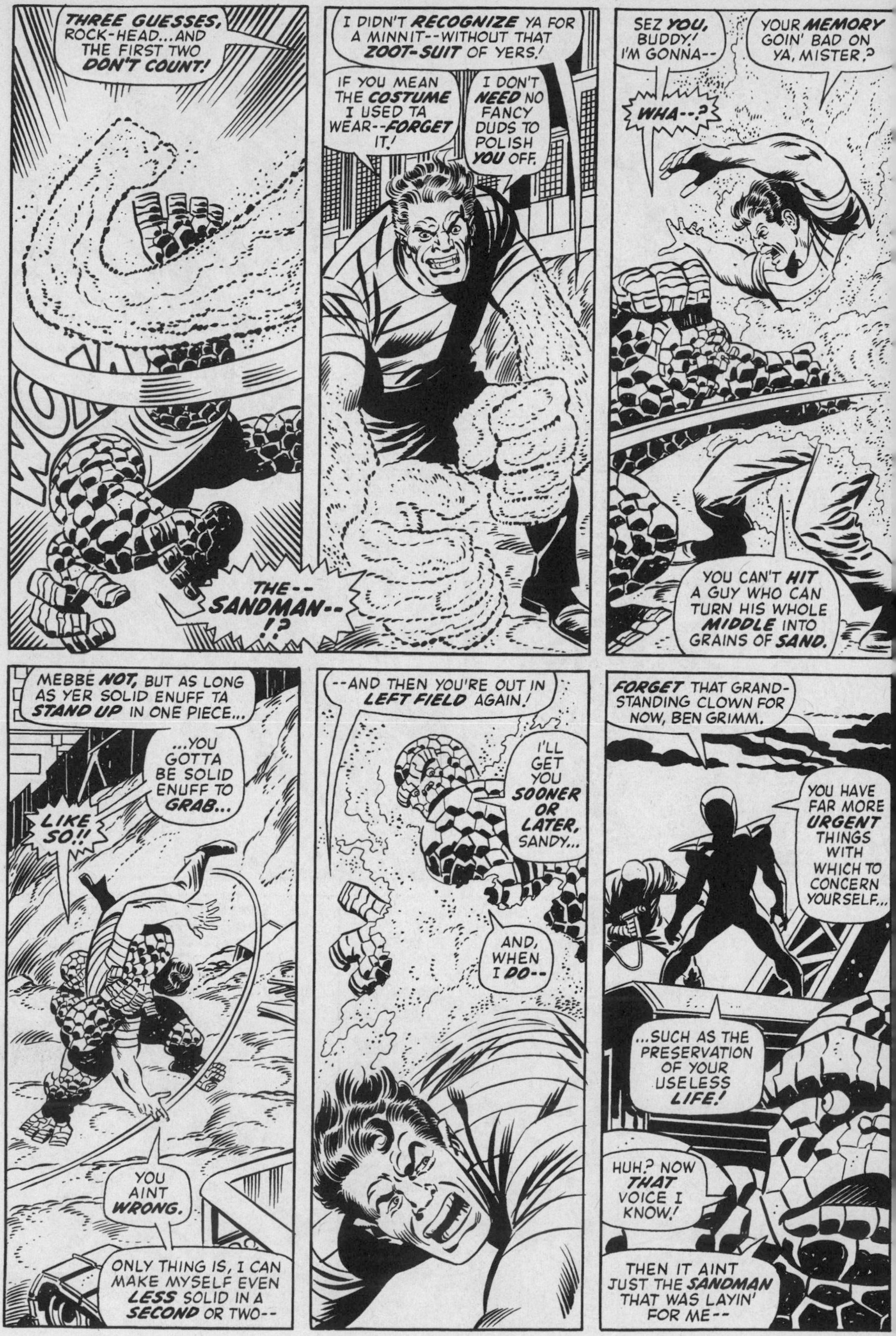
THREE GUESSES, ROCK-HEAD...AND THE FIRST TWO DON'T COUNT!
THE--SANDMAN--!?
I DIDN'T RECOGNIZE YA FOR A MINNIT--WITHOUT THAT ZOOT-SUIT OF YERS!
IF YOU MEAN THE COSTUME I USED TA WEAR--FORGET IT!
I DON'T NEED NO FANCY DUDS TO POLISH YOU OFF.
SEZ YOU, BUDDY! I'M GONNA--
WHA--?
YOUR MEMORY GOIN' BAD ON YA, MISTER?
YOU CAN'T HIT A GUY WHO CAN TURN HIS WHOLE MIDDLE INTO GRAINS OF SAND.
MEBBE NOT, BUT AS LONG AS YER SOLID ENUFF TA STAND UP IN ONE PIECE...
...YOU GOTTA BE SOLID ENUFF TO GRAB...
LIKE SO!!
YOU AINT WRONG.
ONLY THING IS, I CAN MAKE MYSELF EVEN LESS SOLID IN A SECOND OR TWO--
--AND THEN YOU'RE OUT IN LEFT FIELD AGAIN!
I'LL GET YOU SOONER OR LATER, SANDY...
AND, WHEN I DO--
FORGET THAT GRAND-STANDING CLOWN FOR NOW, BEN GRIMM.
YOU HAVE FAR MORE URGENT THINGS WITH WHICH TO CONCERN YOURSELF...
...SUCH AS THE PRESERVATION OF YOUR USELESS LIFE!
HUH? NOW THAT VOICE I KNOW!
THEN IT AINT JUST THE SANDMAN THAT WAS LAYIN' FOR ME--

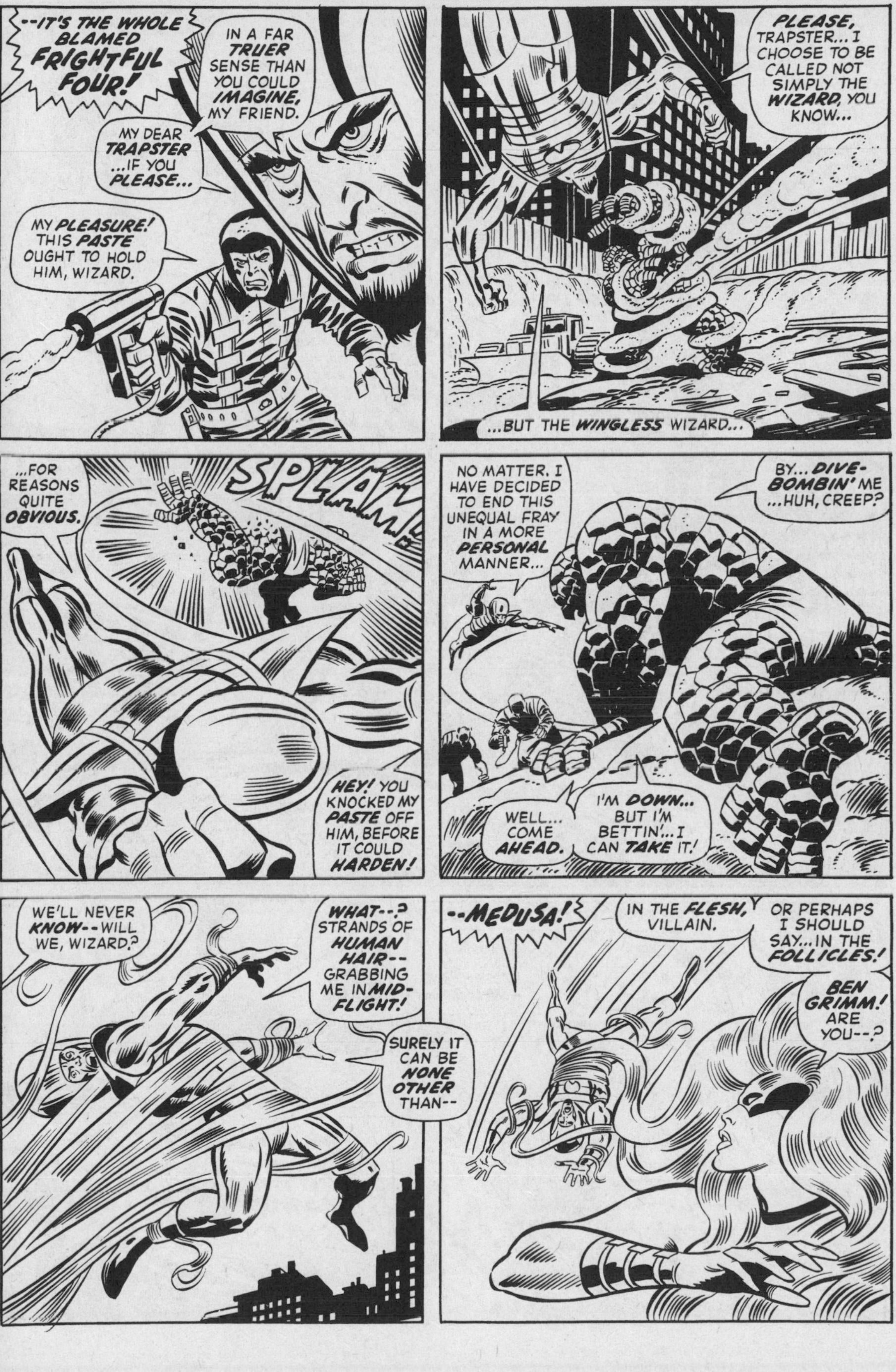

--IT'S THE WHOLE BLAMED FRIGHTFUL FOUR!
IN A FAR TRUER SENSE THAN YOU COULD IMAGINE, MY FRIEND.
MY DEAR TRAPSTER ...IF YOU PLEASE...
MY PLEASURE! THIS PASTE OUGHT TO HOLD HIM, WIZARD.
PLEASE, TRAPSTER... I CHOOSE TO BE CALLED NOT SIMPLY THE WIZARD, YOU KNOW...
...BUT THE WINGLESS WIZARD...
...FOR REASONS QUITE OBVIOUS.
SPLAM
HEY! YOU KNOCKED MY PASTE OFF HIM, BEFORE IT COULD HARDEN!
NO MATTER. I HAVE DECIDED TO END THIS UNEQUAL FRAY IN A MORE PERSONAL MANNER...
BY... DIVE-BOMBIN' ME ...HUH, CREEP?
WELL... COME AHEAD.
I'M DOWN... BUT I'M BETTIN'... I CAN TAKE IT!
WE'LL NEVER KNOW--WILL WE, WIZARD?
WHAT--? STRANDS OF HUMAN HAIR--GRABBING ME IN MID-FLIGHT!
SURELY IT CAN BE NONE OTHER THAN--
--MEDUSA!
IN THE FLESH, VILLAIN.
OR PERHAPS I SHOULD SAY...IN THE FOLLICLES!
BEN GRIMM! ARE YOU--?

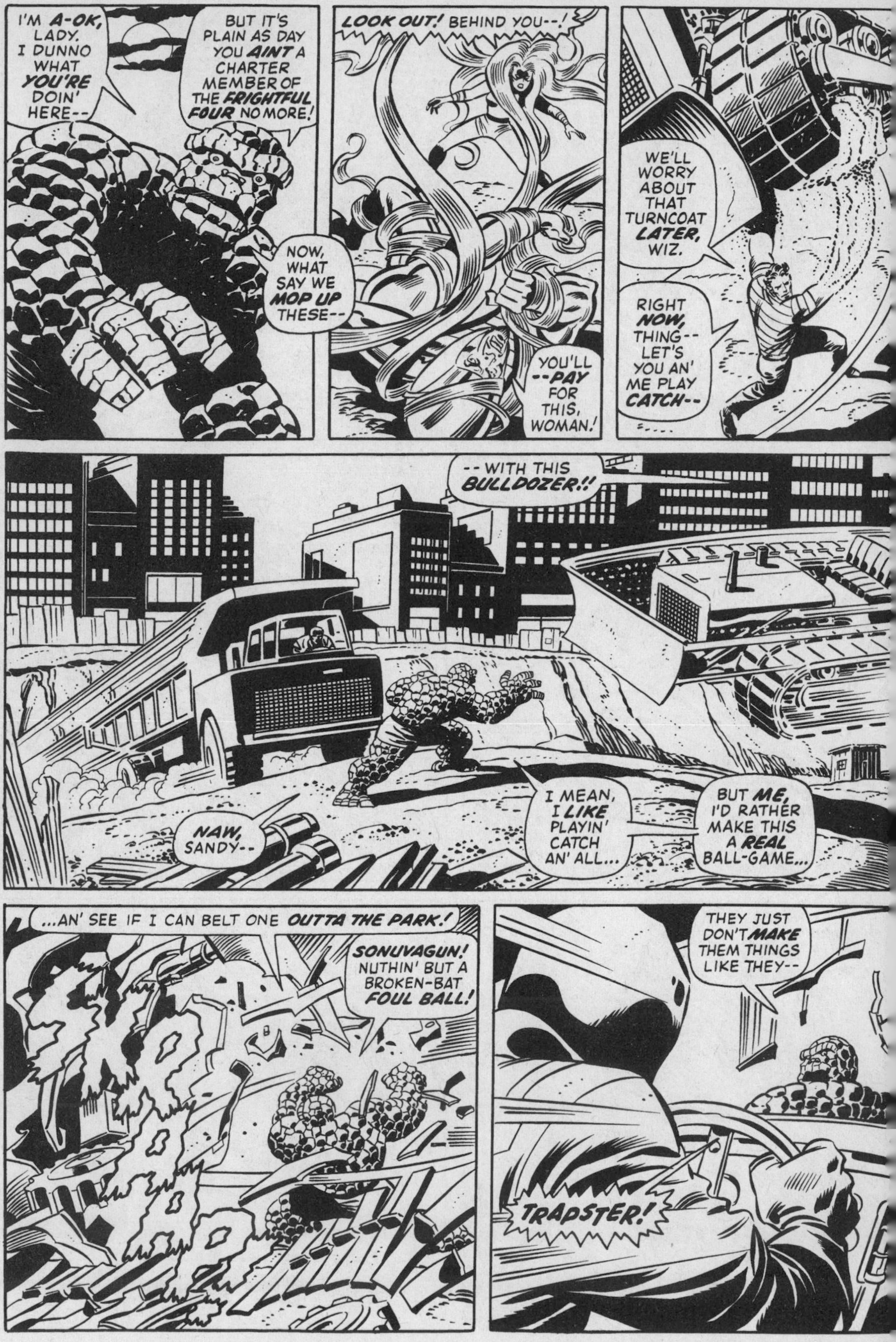

I'M A-OK, LADY. I DUNNO WHAT YOU'RE DOIN' HERE--
BUT IT'S PLAIN AS DAY YOU AINT A CHARTER MEMBER OF THE FRIGHTFUL FOUR NO MORE!
NOW, WHAT SAY WE MOP UP THESE--
LOOK OUT! BEHIND YOU--!
YOU'LL --PAY FOR THIS, WOMAN!
WE'LL WORRY ABOUT THAT TURNCOAT LATER, WIZ.
RIGHT NOW, THING-- LET'S YOU AN' ME PLAY CATCH--
--WITH THIS BULLDOZER!!
NAW, SANDY--
I MEAN, I LIKE PLAYIN' CATCH AN' ALL...
BUT ME, I'D RATHER MAKE THIS A REAL BALL-GAME...
...AN' SEE IF I CAN BELT ONE OUTTA THE PARK!
SONUVAGUN! NUTHIN' BUT A BROKEN-BAT FOUL BALL!
THEY JUST DON'T MAKE THEM THINGS LIKE THEY--
TRAPSTER!

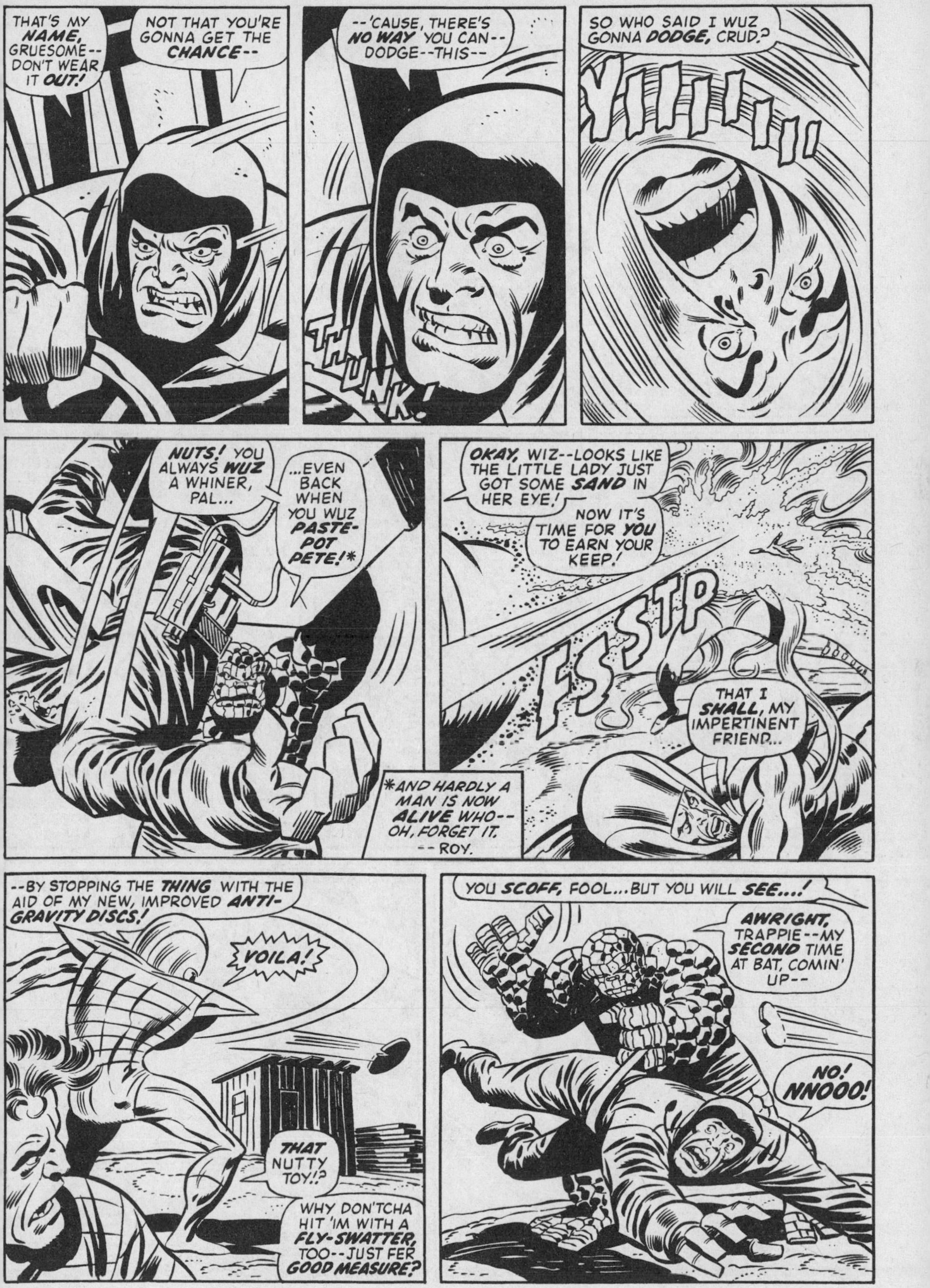
THAT'S MY NAME, GRUESOME-- DON'T WEAR IT OUT!
NOT THAT YOU'RE GONNA GET THE CHANCE--
--'CAUSE, THERE'S NO WAY YOU CAN-- DODGE--THIS--
THUNK!
SO WHO SAID I WUZ GONNA DODGE, CRUD?
YIIIIIIII
NUTS! YOU ALWAYS WUZ A WHINER, PAL...
...EVEN BACK WHEN YOU WUZ PASTE-POT PETE!*
*AND HARDLY A MAN IS NOW ALIVE WHO-- OH, FORGET IT. --ROY.
OKAY, WIZ--LOOKS LIKE THE LITTLE LADY JUST GOT SOME SAND IN HER EYE!
NOW IT'S TIME FOR YOU TO EARN YOUR KEEP!
FSSSTP
THAT I SHALL, MY IMPERTINENT FRIEND...
--BY STOPPING THE THING WITH THE AID OF MY NEW, IMPROVED ANTI-GRAVITY DISCS!
VOILA!
THAT NUTTY TOY!?
WHY DON'TCHA HIT 'IM WITH A FLY-SWATTER, TOO--JUST FER GOOD MEASURE?
YOU SCOFF, FOOL...BUT YOU WILL SEE...!
AWRIGHT, TRAPPIE--MY SECOND TIME AT BAT, COMIN' UP--
NO! NNOOO!

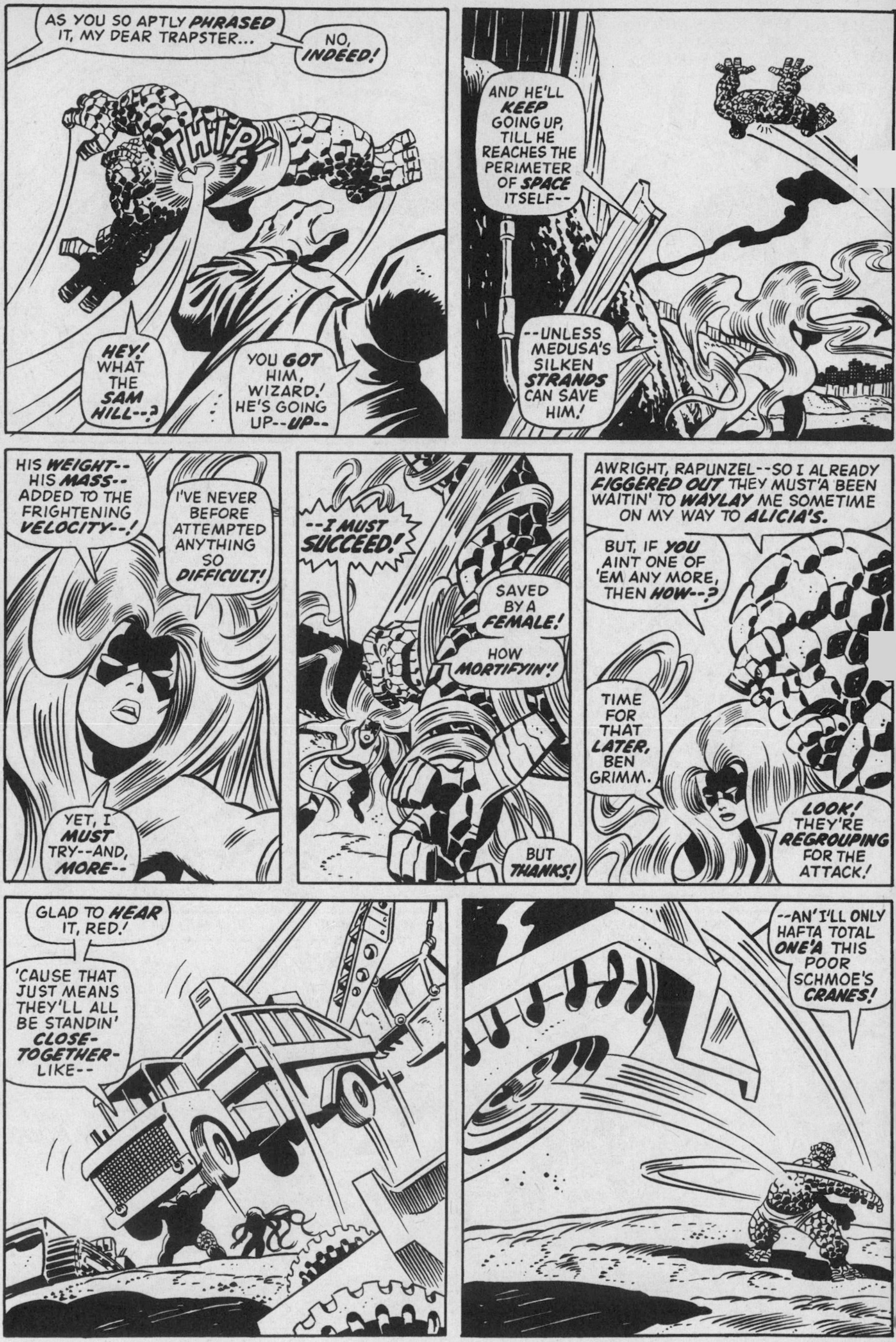

AS YOU SO APTLY PHRASED IT, MY DEAR TRAPSTER...
NO, INDEED!
THIP!
HEY! WHAT THE SAM HILL--?
YOU GOT HIM, WIZARD! HE'S GOING UP--UP--
AND HE'LL KEEP GOING UP, TILL HE REACHES THE PERIMETER OF SPACE ITSELF--
--UNLESS MEDUSA'S SILKEN STRANDS CAN SAVE HIM!
HIS WEIGHT--HIS MASS--ADDED TO THE FRIGHTENING VELOCITY--!
I'VE NEVER BEFORE ATTEMPTED ANYTHING SO DIFFICULT!
YET, I MUST TRY--AND, MORE--
--I MUST SUCCEED!
SAVED BY A FEMALE!
HOW MORTIFYIN'!
BUT THANKS!
AWRIGHT, RAPUNZEL--SO I ALREADY FIGGERED OUT THEY MUST'A BEEN WAITIN' TO WAYLAY ME SOMETIME ON MY WAY TO ALICIA'S.
BUT, IF YOU AINT ONE OF 'EM ANY MORE, THEN HOW--?
TIME FOR THAT LATER, BEN GRIMM.
LOOK! THEY'RE REGROUPING FOR THE ATTACK!
GLAD TO HEAR IT, RED!
'CAUSE THAT JUST MEANS THEY'LL ALL BE STANDIN' CLOSE-TOGETHER-LIKE--
--AN' I'LL ONLY HAFTA TOTAL ONE'A THIS POOR SCHMOE'S CRANES!

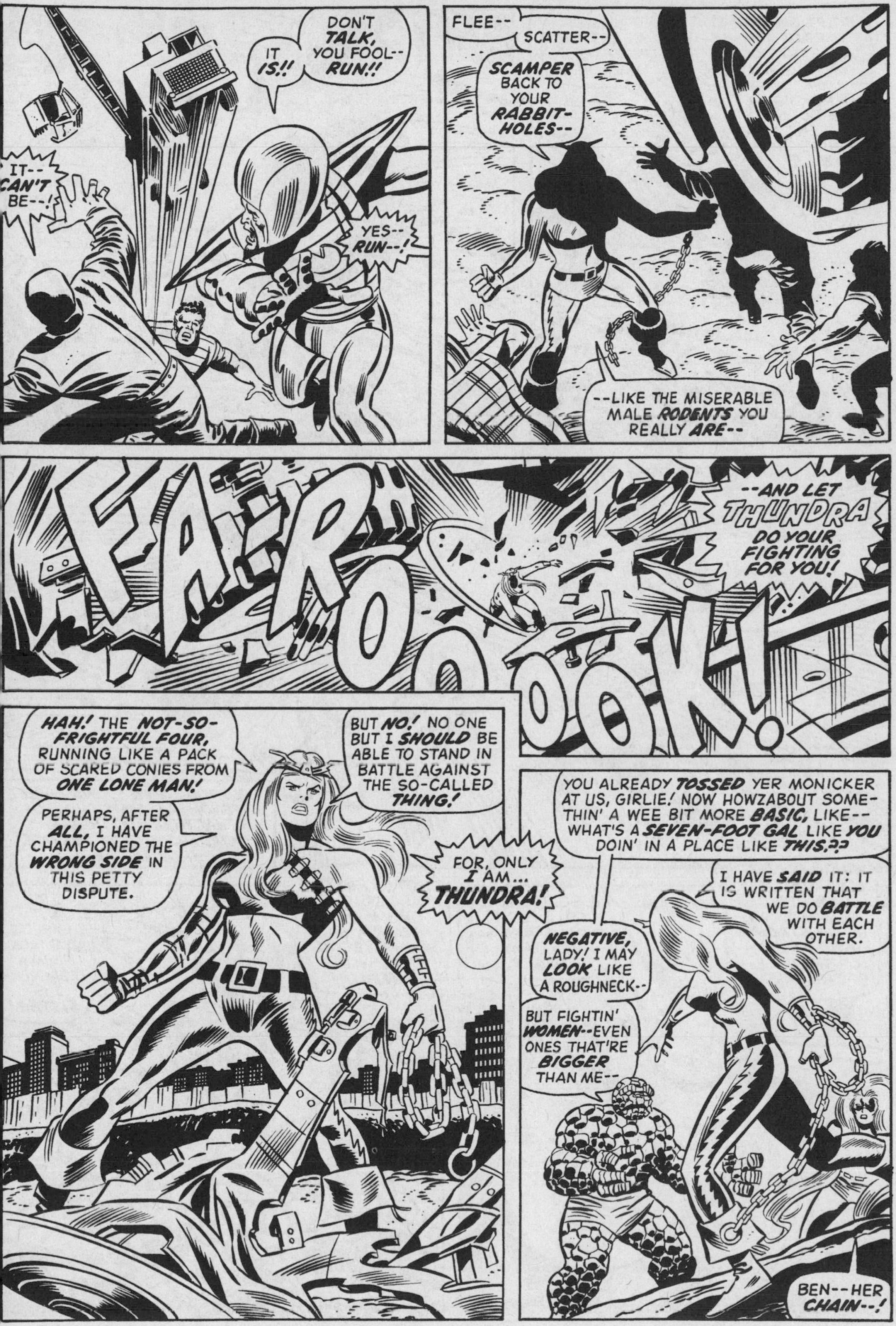

DON'T TALK, YOU FOOL-- RUN!!
IT IS!!
IT-- CAN'T BE--!
YES-- RUN--!
FLEE--
SCATTER--
SCAMPER BACK TO YOUR RABBIT-HOLES--
--LIKE THE MISERABLE MALE RODENTS YOU REALLY ARE--
FA-ROOOOOK!
--AND LET THUNDRA DO YOUR FIGHTING FOR YOU!
HAH! THE NOT-SO-FRIGHTFUL FOUR, RUNNING LIKE A PACK OF SCARED CONIES FROM ONE LONE MAN!
PERHAPS, AFTER ALL, I HAVE CHAMPIONED THE WRONG SIDE IN THIS PETTY DISPUTE.
BUT NO! NO ONE BUT I SHOULD BE ABLE TO STAND IN BATTLE AGAINST THE SO-CALLED THING!
FOR, ONLY I AM... THUNDRA!
YOU ALREADY TOSSED YER MONICKER AT US, GIRLIE! NOW HOWZABOUT SOME-THIN' A WEE BIT MORE BASIC, LIKE-- WHAT'S A SEVEN-FOOT GAL LIKE YOU DOIN' IN A PLACE LIKE THIS?!?
I HAVE SAID IT: IT IS WRITTEN THAT WE DO BATTLE WITH EACH OTHER.
NEGATIVE, LADY! I MAY LOOK LIKE A ROUGHNECK--
BUT FIGHTIN' WOMEN--EVEN ONES THAT'RE BIGGER THAN ME--
BEN--HER CHAIN--!

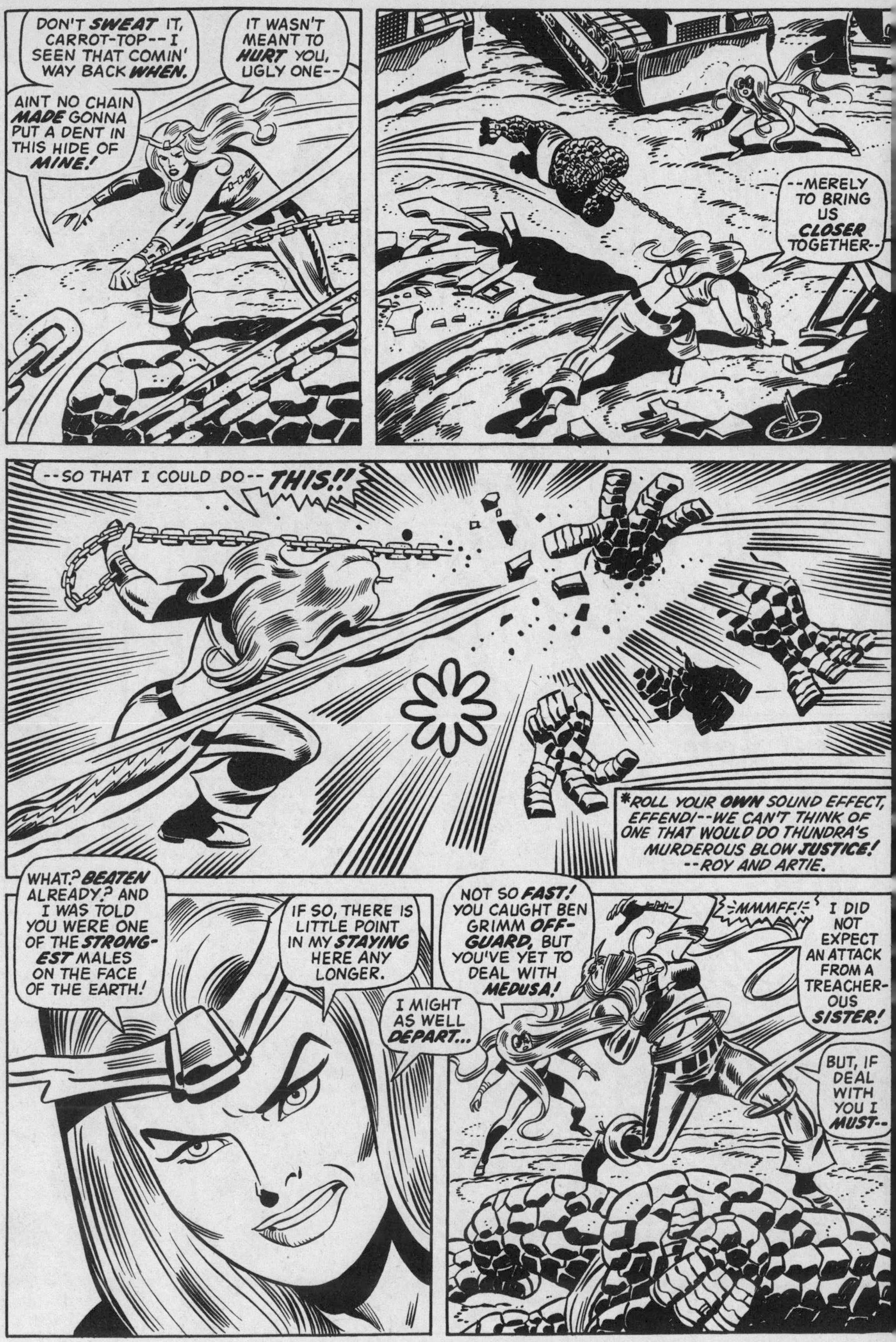
DON'T SWEAT IT, CARROT-TOP-- I SEEN THAT COMIN' WAY BACK WHEN.
AINT NO CHAIN MADE GONNA PUT A DENT IN THIS HIDE OF MINE!
IT WASN'T MEANT TO HURT YOU, UGLY ONE--
--MERELY TO BRING US CLOSER TOGETHER--
--SO THAT I COULD DO-- THIS!!
*ROLL YOUR OWN SOUND EFFECT, EFFENDI--WE CAN'T THINK OF ONE THAT WOULD DO THUNDRA'S MURDEROUS BLOW JUSTICE! --ROY AND ARTIE.
WHAT? BEATEN ALREADY? AND I WAS TOLD YOU WERE ONE OF THE STRONGEST MALES ON THE FACE OF THE EARTH!
IF SO, THERE IS LITTLE POINT IN MY STAYING HERE ANY LONGER.
I MIGHT AS WELL DEPART...
NOT SO FAST! YOU CAUGHT BEN GRIMM OFF-GUARD, BUT YOU'VE YET TO DEAL WITH MEDUSA!
MMMFF!
I DID NOT EXPECT AN ATTACK FROM A TREACHEROUS SISTER!
BUT, IF DEAL WITH YOU I MUST--

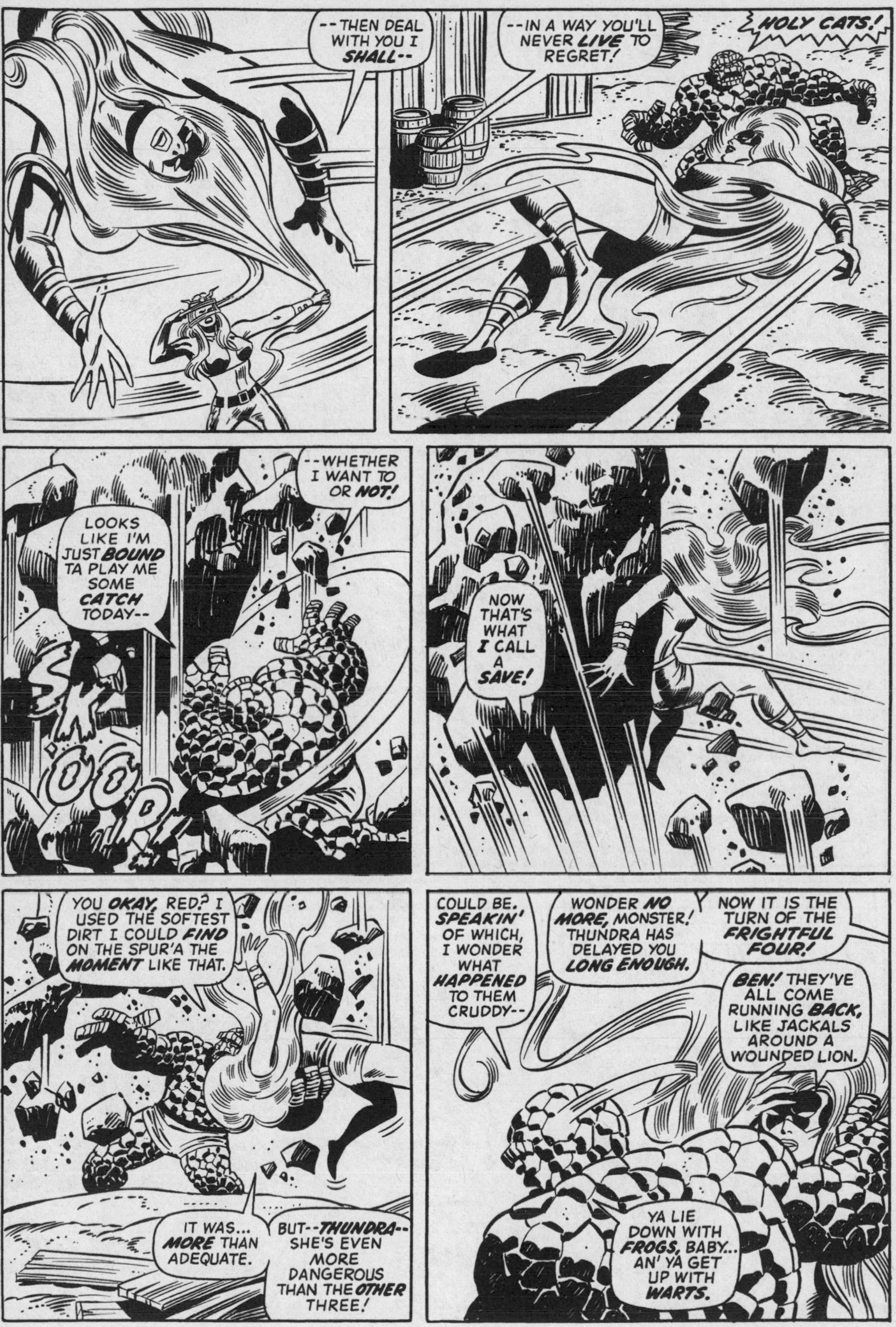
--THEN DEAL WITH YOU I SHALL--
--IN A WAY YOU'LL NEVER LIVE TO REGRET!
HOLY CATS!
LOOKS LIKE I'M JUST BOUND TA PLAY ME SOME CATCH TODAY--
--WHETHER I WANT TO OR NOT!
SKOOOP!
NOW THAT'S WHAT I CALL A SAVE!
YOU OKAY, RED? I USED THE SOFTEST DIRT I COULD FIND ON THE SPUR'A THE MOMENT LIKE THAT.
IT WAS... MORE THAN ADEQUATE.
BUT--THUNDRA--SHE'S EVEN MORE DANGEROUS THAN THE OTHER THREE!
COULD BE. SPEAKIN' OF WHICH, I WONDER WHAT HAPPENED TO THEM CRUDDY--
WONDER NO MORE, MONSTER! THUNDRA HAS DELAYED YOU LONG ENOUGH.
NOW IT IS THE TURN OF THE FRIGHTFUL FOUR!
BEN! THEY'VE ALL COME RUNNING BACK, LIKE JACKALS AROUND A WOUNDED LION.
YA LIE DOWN WITH FROGS, BABY... AN' YA GET UP WITH WARTS.

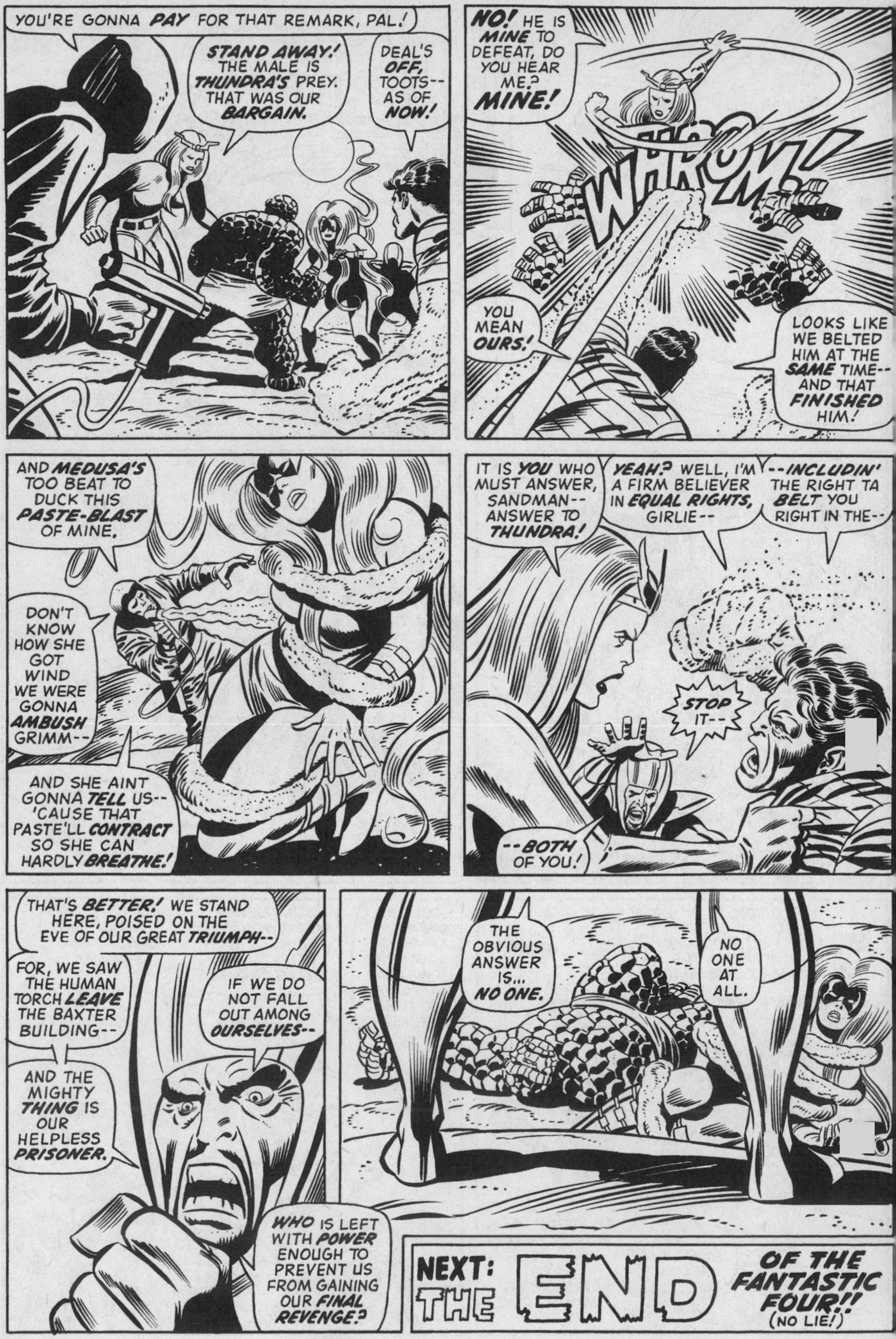

YOU'RE GONNA PAY FOR THAT REMARK, PAL!
STAND AWAY! THE MALE IS THUNDRA'S PREY. THAT WAS OUR BARGAIN.
DEAL'S OFF, TOOTS-- AS OF NOW!
NO! HE IS MINE TO DEFEAT, DO YOU HEAR ME? MINE!
WHROM!
YOU MEAN OURS!
LOOKS LIKE WE BELTED HIM AT THE SAME TIME-- AND THAT FINISHED HIM!
AND MEDUSA'S TOO BEAT TO DUCK THIS PASTE-BLAST OF MINE.
DON'T KNOW HOW SHE GOT WIND WE WERE GONNA AMBUSH GRIMM--
AND SHE AINT GONNA TELL US-- 'CAUSE THAT PASTE'LL CONTRACT SO SHE CAN HARDLY BREATHE!
IT IS YOU WHO MUST ANSWER, SANDMAN-- ANSWER TO THUNDRA!
YEAH? WELL, I'M A FIRM BELIEVER IN EQUAL RIGHTS, GIRLIE--
--INCLUDIN' THE RIGHT TA BELT YOU RIGHT IN THE--
STOP IT--
--BOTH OF YOU!
THAT'S BETTER! WE STAND HERE, POISED ON THE EVE OF OUR GREAT TRIUMPH--
FOR, WE SAW THE HUMAN TORCH LEAVE THE BAXTER BUILDING--
IF WE DO NOT FALL OUT AMONG OURSELVES--
AND THE MIGHTY THING IS OUR HELPLESS PRISONER.
WHO IS LEFT WITH POWER ENOUGH TO PREVENT US FROM GAINING OUR FINAL REVENGE?
THE OBVIOUS ANSWER IS... NO ONE.
NO ONE AT ALL.
NEXT: THE END OF THE FANTASTIC FOUR!! (NO LIE!)

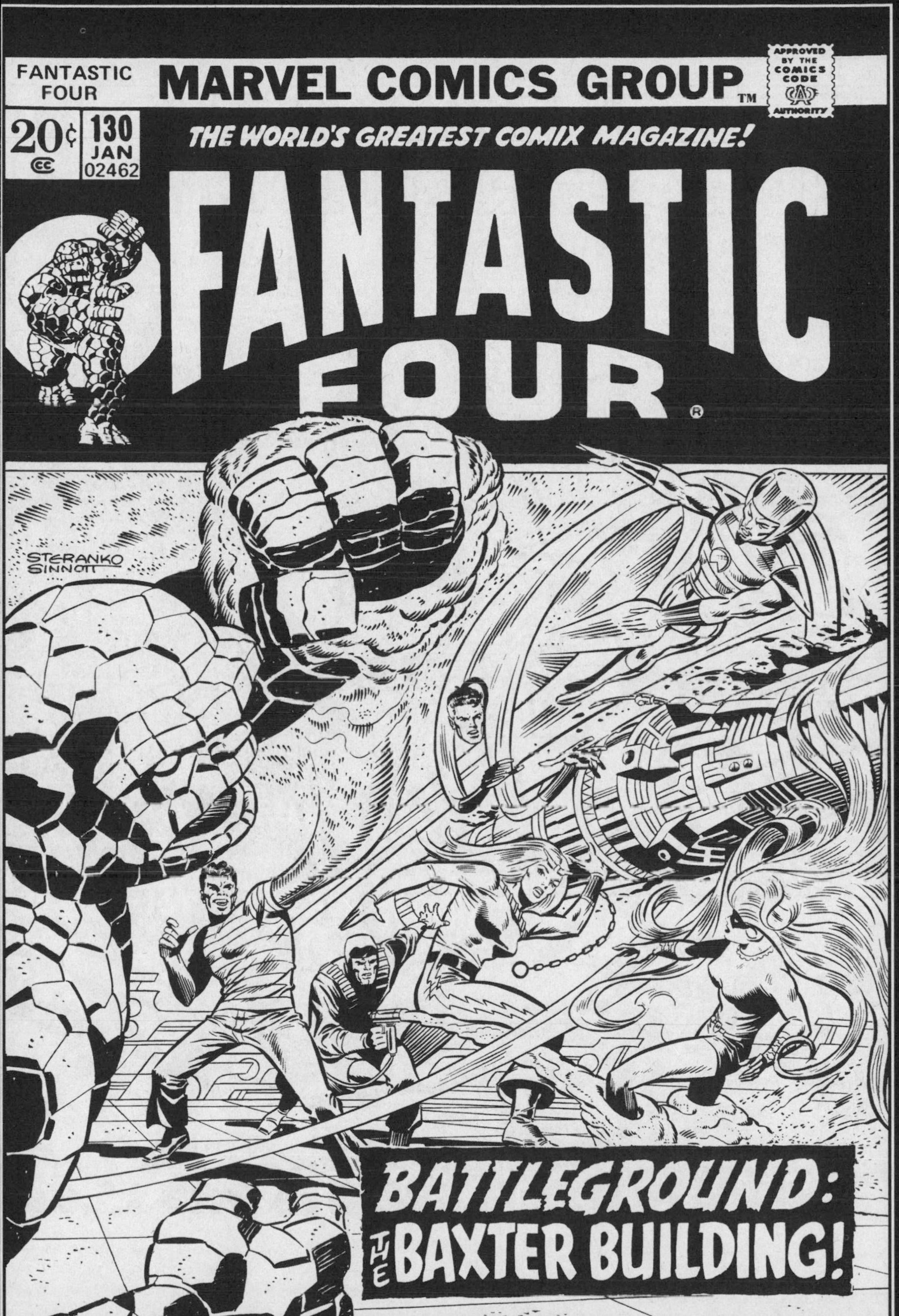
FANTASTIC FOUR
MARVEL COMICS GROUP™
APPROVED BY THE COMICS CODE AUTHORITY
20¢ CC
130 JAN 02462
THE WORLD'S GREATEST COMIX MAGAZINE!
FANTASTIC FOUR®
STERANKO SINNOTT
BATTLEGROUND: THE BAXTER BUILDING!

Stan Lee PRESENTS: THE FANTASTIC FOUR!™

ROY THOMAS WRITER/EDITOR and JOHN BUSCEMA ARTIST * JOE SINNOTT INKER * ARTIE SIMEK, LETTERER PETRA GOLDBERG, COLORIST

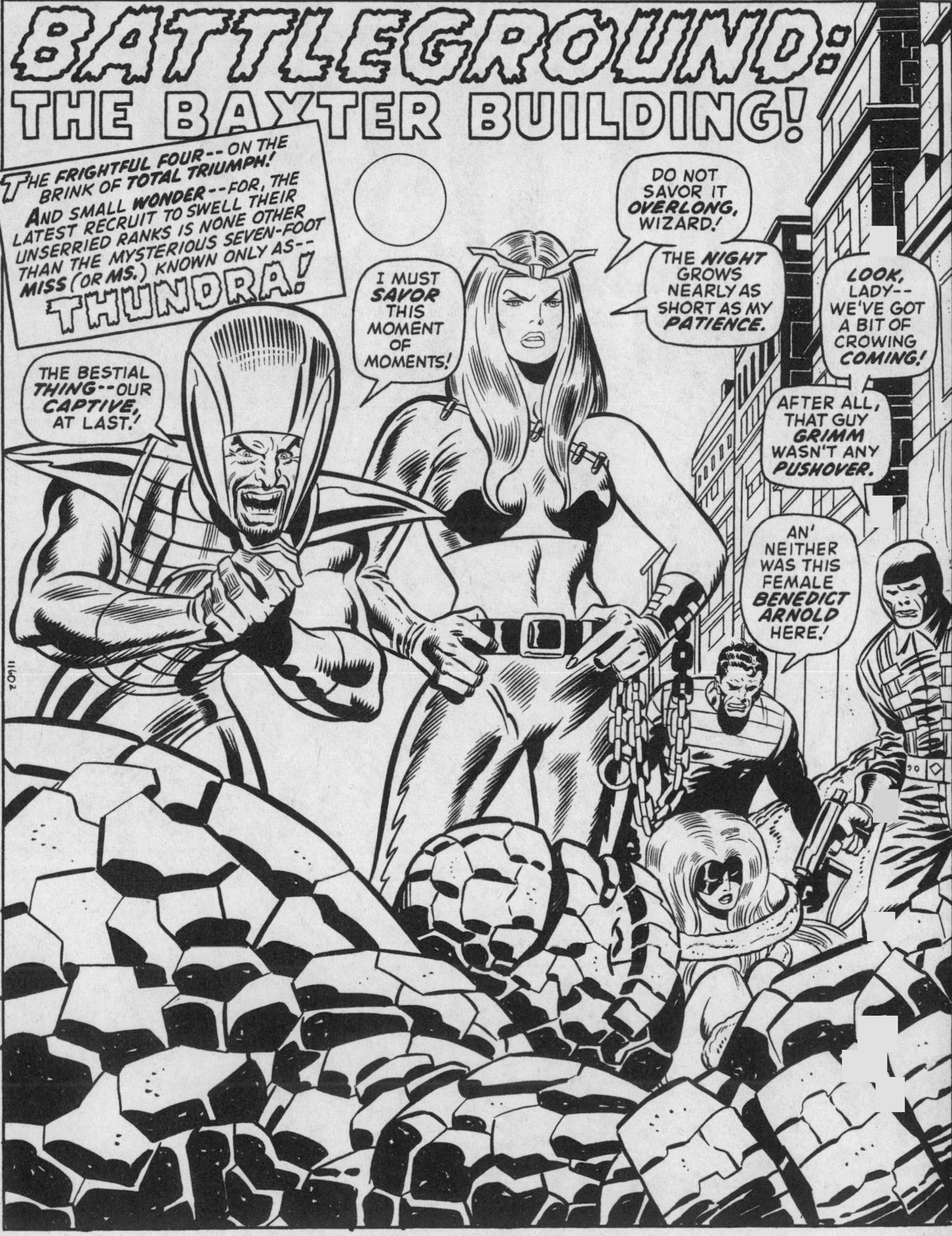
BATTLEGROUND: THE BAXTER BUILDING!
THE FRIGHTFUL FOUR--ON THE BRINK OF TOTAL TRIUMPH! AND SMALL WONDER--FOR, THE LATEST RECRUIT TO SWELL THEIR UNSERRIED RANKS IS NONE OTHER THAN THE MYSTERIOUS SEVEN-FOOT MISS (OR MS.) KNOWN ONLY AS-- THUNDRA!
THE BESTIAL THING--OUR CAPTIVE, AT LAST!
I MUST SAVOR THIS MOMENT OF MOMENTS!
DO NOT SAVOR IT OVERLONG, WIZARD!
THE NIGHT GROWS NEARLY AS SHORT AS MY PATIENCE.
LOOK, LADY-- WE'VE GOT A BIT OF CROWING COMING!
AFTER ALL, THAT GUY GRIMM WASN'T ANY PUSHOVER.
AN' NEITHER WAS THIS FEMALE BENEDICT ARNOLD HERE!

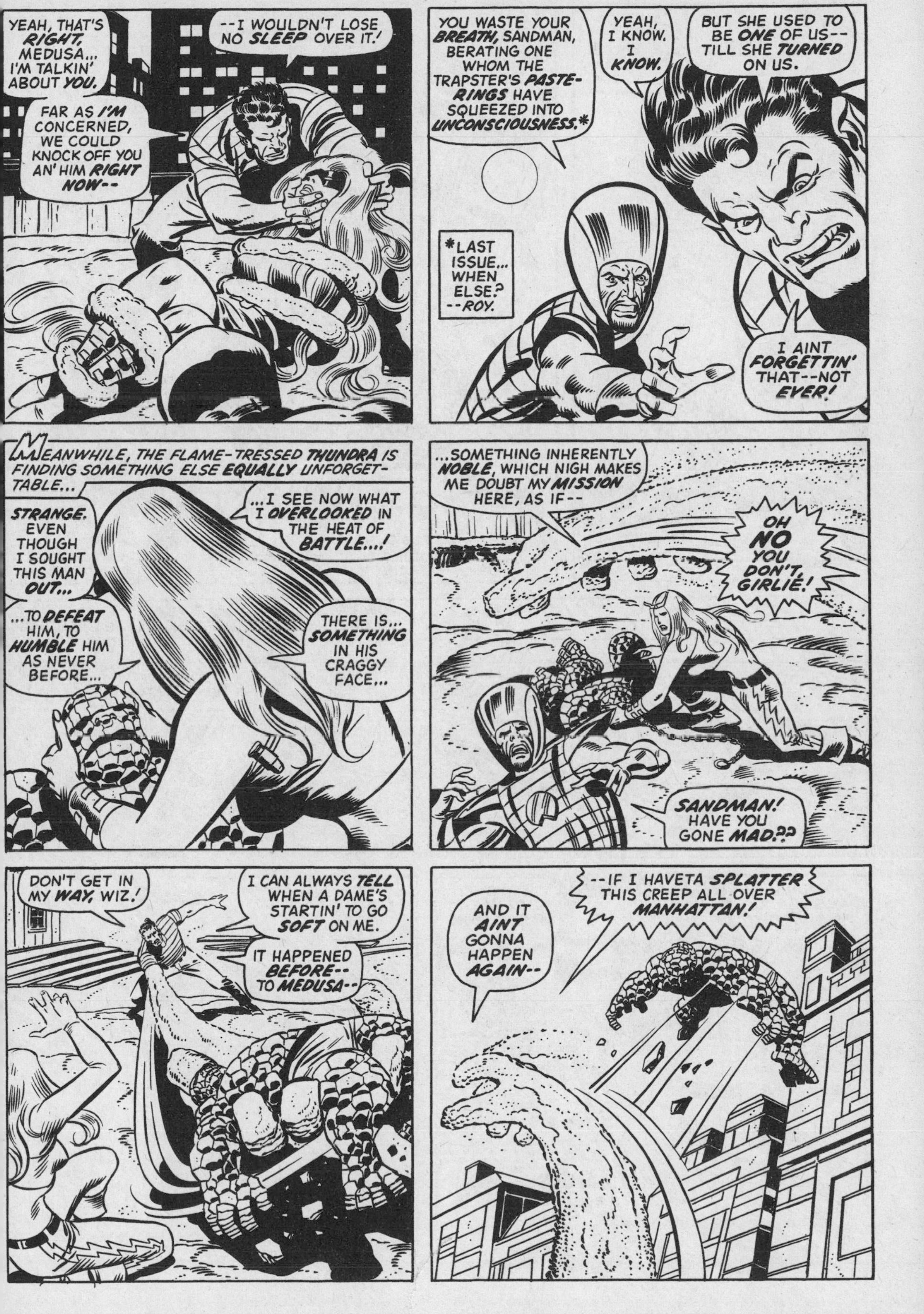
YEAH, THAT'S RIGHT, MEDUSA... I'M TALKIN' ABOUT YOU.
--I WOULDN'T LOSE NO SLEEP OVER IT!
FAR AS I'M CONCERNED, WE COULD KNOCK OFF YOU AN' HIM RIGHT NOW--
YOU WASTE YOUR BREATH, SANDMAN, BERATING ONE WHOM THE TRAPSTER'S PASTE-RINGS HAVE SQUEEZED INTO UNCONSCIOUSNESS.*
YEAH, I KNOW. I KNOW.
BUT SHE USED TO BE ONE OF US--TILL SHE TURNED ON US.
*LAST ISSUE... WHEN ELSE? --ROY.
I AINT FORGETTIN' THAT--NOT EVER!
MEANWHILE, THE FLAME-TRESSED THUNDRA IS FINDING SOMETHING ELSE EQUALLY UNFORGET-TABLE...
STRANGE. EVEN THOUGH I SOUGHT THIS MAN OUT...
...I SEE NOW WHAT I OVERLOOKED IN THE HEAT OF BATTLE...!
...TO DEFEAT HIM, TO HUMBLE HIM AS NEVER BEFORE...
THERE IS... SOMETHING IN HIS CRAGGY FACE...
...SOMETHING INHERENTLY NOBLE, WHICH NIGH MAKES ME DOUBT MY MISSION HERE, AS IF--
OH NO YOU DON'T, GIRLIE!
SANDMAN! HAVE YOU GONE MAD??
DON'T GET IN MY WAY, WIZ.!
I CAN ALWAYS TELL WHEN A DAME'S STARTIN' TO GO SOFT ON ME.
IT HAPPENED BEFORE--TO MEDUSA--
AND IT AINT GONNA HAPPEN AGAIN--
--IF I HAVETA SPLATTER THIS CREEP ALL OVER MANHATTAN!

NO!

I CAME TO HUMBLE-- AYE, EVEN TO HUMILIATE--

BUT **NOT** TO **MURDER!!**

HOLY COW! SHE'S NOT ONLY **STRONG** AS A FREIGHT TRAIN--

--SHE'S **FAST** AS ONE, TO **BOOT!**

AHHH... THE LITTLE ONE IS **UNHARMED.**

BUT THE **TWIN BLOWS** THAT FELLED HIM WILL KEEP HIM UNCONSCIOUS FOR **HOURS.**

AND **NOW**--

NOW **WHAT,** WOMAN?

HEYYYYYYYY

NOW **THIS,** WORM!

IF YOU COME NEAR ENOUGH TO THIS MAN TO SO MUCH AS **BREATHE** UPON HIM--

--YOU'LL ANSWER TO **THUNDRA!!**

I'LL ANSWER TO YA **RIGHT NOW,** LADY--

--WITH A **FIST** RIGHT IN THE--

I THINK WE'VE HAD THIS CONVERSATION **BEFORE,** SANDMAN!

WE'LL **NOT** HAVE IT **AGAIN!**

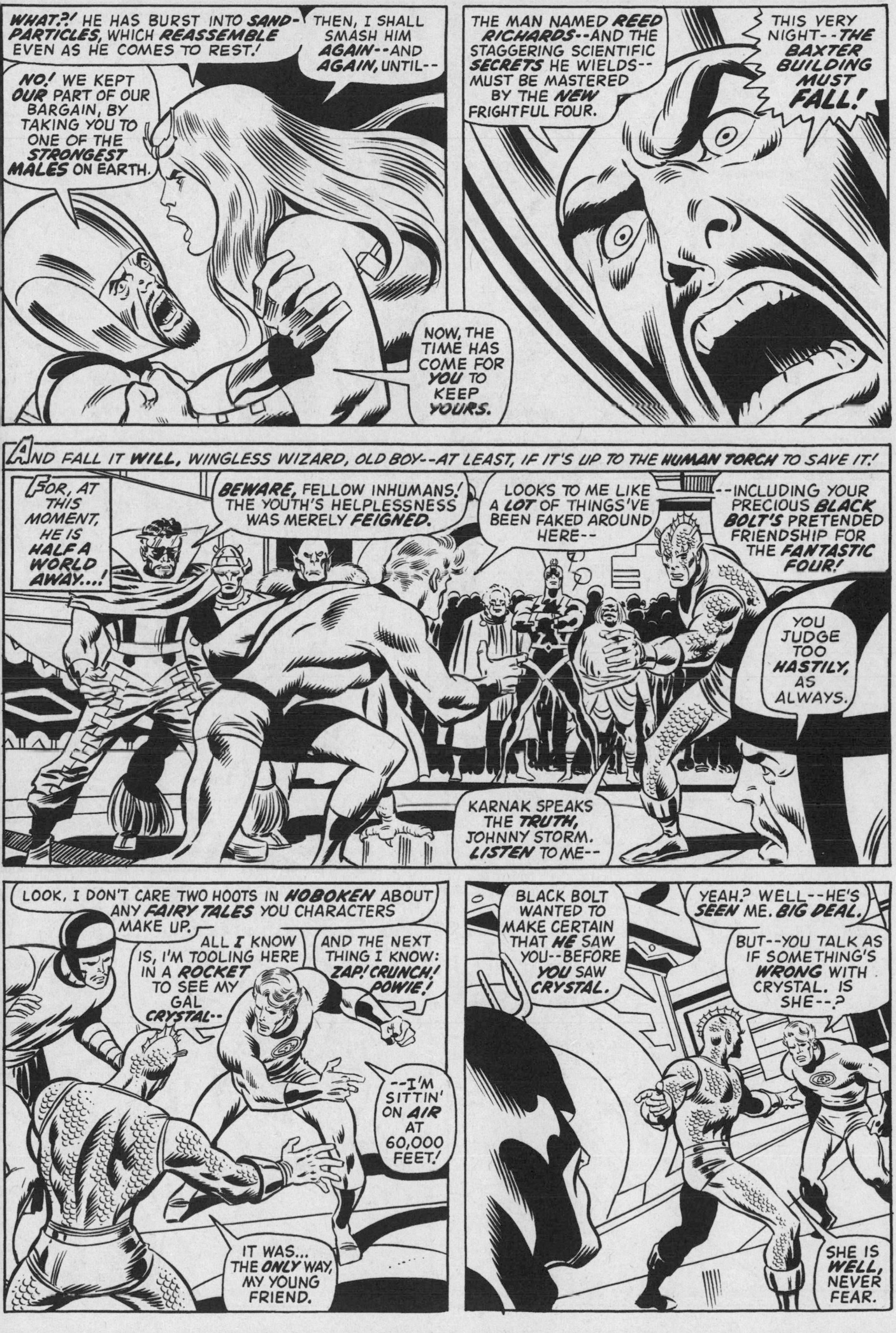

WHAT?!! HE HAS BURST INTO SAND-PARTICLES, WHICH REASSEMBLE EVEN AS HE COMES TO REST!
THEN, I SHALL SMASH HIM AGAIN--AND AGAIN, UNTIL--
NO! WE KEPT OUR PART OF OUR BARGAIN, BY TAKING YOU TO ONE OF THE STRONGEST MALES ON EARTH.
NOW, THE TIME HAS COME FOR YOU TO KEEP YOURS.
THE MAN NAMED REED RICHARDS--AND THE STAGGERING SCIENTIFIC SECRETS HE WIELDS--MUST BE MASTERED BY THE NEW FRIGHTFUL FOUR.
THIS VERY NIGHT--THE BAXTER BUILDING MUST FALL!
AND FALL IT WILL, WINGLESS WIZARD, OLD BOY--AT LEAST, IF IT'S UP TO THE HUMAN TORCH TO SAVE IT!
FOR, AT THIS MOMENT, HE IS HALF A WORLD AWAY...!
BEWARE, FELLOW INHUMANS! THE YOUTH'S HELPLESSNESS WAS MERELY FEIGNED.
LOOKS TO ME LIKE A LOT OF THINGS'VE BEEN FAKED AROUND HERE--
--INCLUDING YOUR PRECIOUS BLACK BOLT'S PRETENDED FRIENDSHIP FOR THE FANTASTIC FOUR!
YOU JUDGE TOO HASTILY, AS ALWAYS.
KARNAK SPEAKS THE TRUTH, JOHNNY STORM. LISTEN TO ME--
LOOK, I DON'T CARE TWO HOOTS IN HOBOKEN ABOUT ANY FAIRY TALES YOU CHARACTERS MAKE UP.
ALL I KNOW IS, I'M TOOLING HERE IN A ROCKET TO SEE MY GAL CRYSTAL--
AND THE NEXT THING I KNOW: ZAP! CRUNCH! POWIE!
--I'M SITTIN' ON AIR AT 60,000 FEET!
IT WAS... THE ONLY WAY, MY YOUNG FRIEND.
BLACK BOLT WANTED TO MAKE CERTAIN THAT HE SAW YOU--BEFORE YOU SAW CRYSTAL.
YEAH? WELL--HE'S SEEN ME. BIG DEAL.
BUT--YOU TALK AS IF SOMETHING'S WRONG WITH CRYSTAL. IS SHE--?
SHE IS WELL, NEVER FEAR.

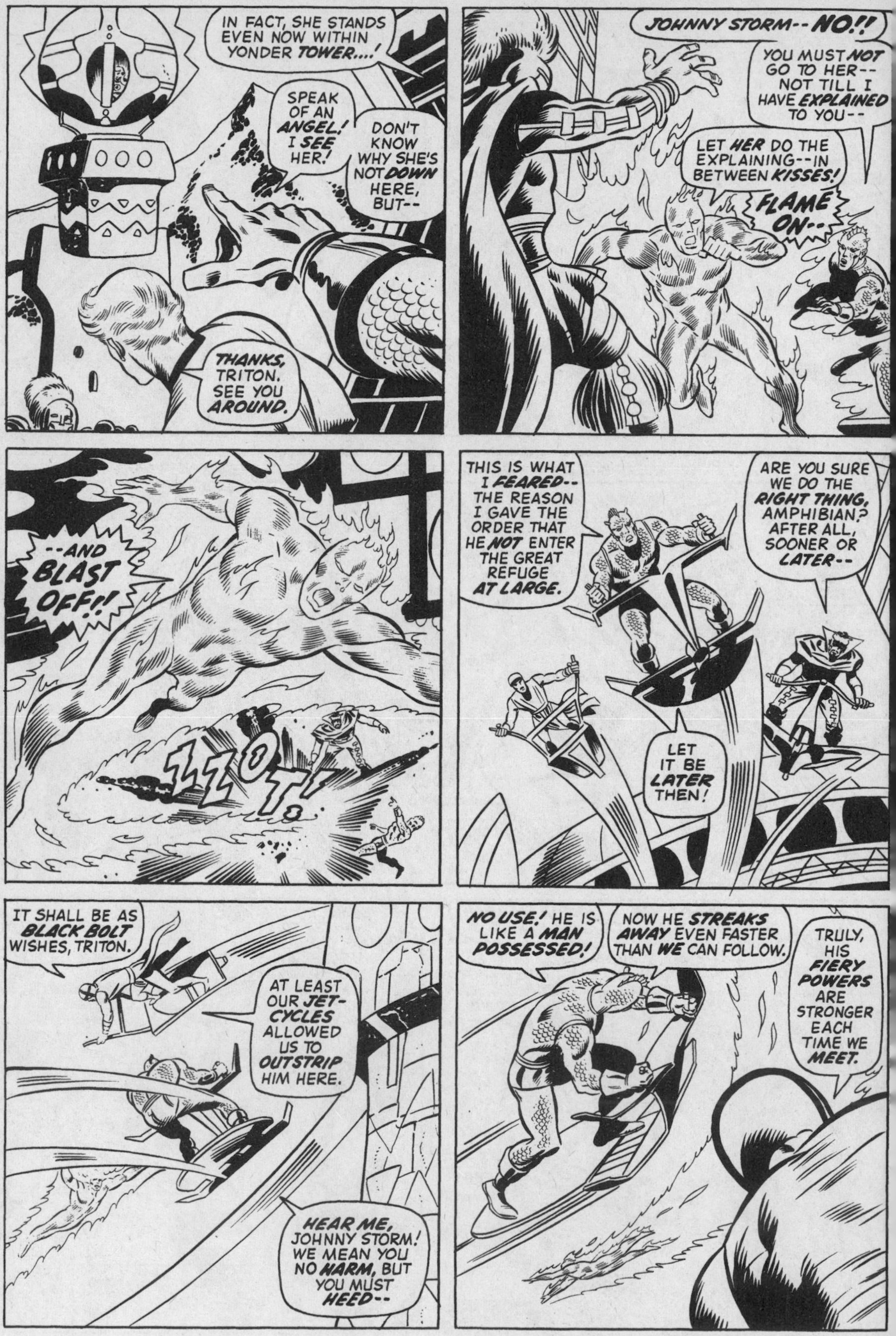
IN FACT, SHE STANDS EVEN NOW WITHIN YONDER TOWER....!
SPEAK OF AN ANGEL! I SEE HER!
DON'T KNOW WHY SHE'S NOT DOWN HERE, BUT--
THANKS, TRITON. SEE YOU AROUND.
JOHNNY STORM--NO!!
YOU MUST NOT GO TO HER--NOT TILL I HAVE EXPLAINED TO YOU--
LET HER DO THE EXPLAINING--IN BETWEEN KISSES!
FLAME ON--
--AND BLAST OFF!!
ZZOT!
THIS IS WHAT I FEARED--THE REASON I GAVE THE ORDER THAT HE NOT ENTER THE GREAT REFUGE AT LARGE.
ARE YOU SURE WE DO THE RIGHT THING, AMPHIBIAN? AFTER ALL, SOONER OR LATER--
LET IT BE LATER THEN!
IT SHALL BE AS BLACK BOLT WISHES, TRITON.
AT LEAST OUR JET-CYCLES ALLOWED US TO OUTSTRIP HIM HERE.
HEAR ME, JOHNNY STORM! WE MEAN YOU NO HARM, BUT YOU MUST HEED--
NO USE! HE IS LIKE A MAN POSSESSED!
NOW HE STREAKS AWAY EVEN FASTER THAN WE CAN FOLLOW.
TRULY, HIS FIERY POWERS ARE STRONGER EACH TIME WE MEET.

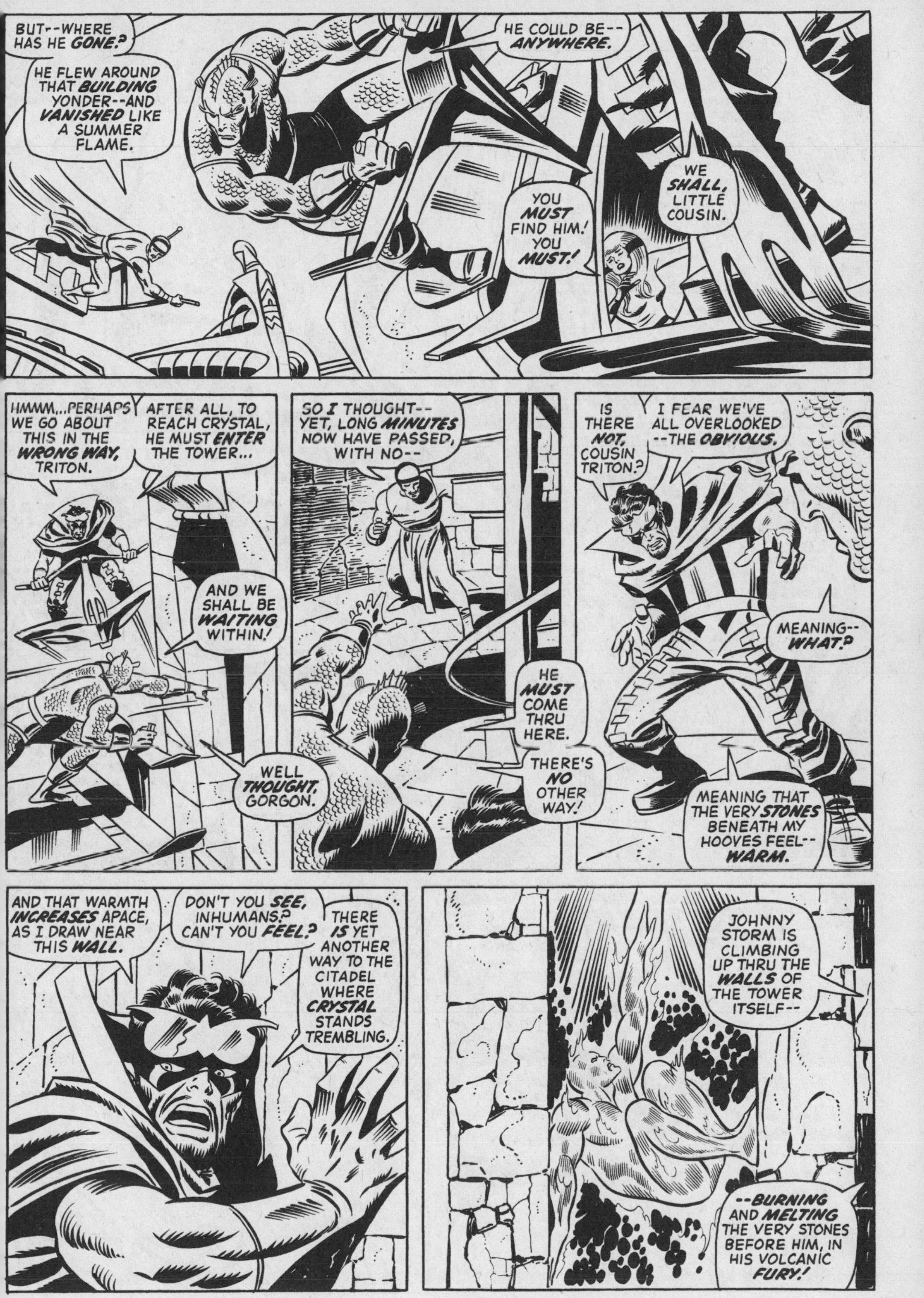

BUT--WHERE HAS HE GONE?
HE FLEW AROUND THAT BUILDING YONDER--AND VANISHED LIKE A SUMMER FLAME.
HE COULD BE--ANYWHERE.
YOU MUST FIND HIM! YOU MUST!
WE SHALL, LITTLE COUSIN.
HMMM...PERHAPS WE GO ABOUT THIS IN THE WRONG WAY, TRITON.
AFTER ALL, TO REACH CRYSTAL, HE MUST ENTER THE TOWER...
AND WE SHALL BE WAITING WITHIN!
WELL THOUGHT, GORGON.
SO I THOUGHT--YET, LONG MINUTES NOW HAVE PASSED, WITH NO--
HE MUST COME THRU HERE.
THERE'S NO OTHER WAY!
IS THERE NOT, COUSIN TRITON?
I FEAR WE'VE ALL OVERLOOKED--THE OBVIOUS.
MEANING--WHAT?
MEANING THAT THE VERY STONES BENEATH MY HOOVES FEEL--WARM.
AND THAT WARMTH INCREASES APACE, AS I DRAW NEAR THIS WALL.
DON'T YOU SEE, INHUMANS? CAN'T YOU FEEL?
THERE IS YET ANOTHER WAY TO THE CITADEL WHERE CRYSTAL STANDS TREMBLING.
JOHNNY STORM IS CLIMBING UP THRU THE WALLS OF THE TOWER ITSELF--
--BURNING AND MELTING THE VERY STONES BEFORE HIM, IN HIS VOLCANIC FURY!

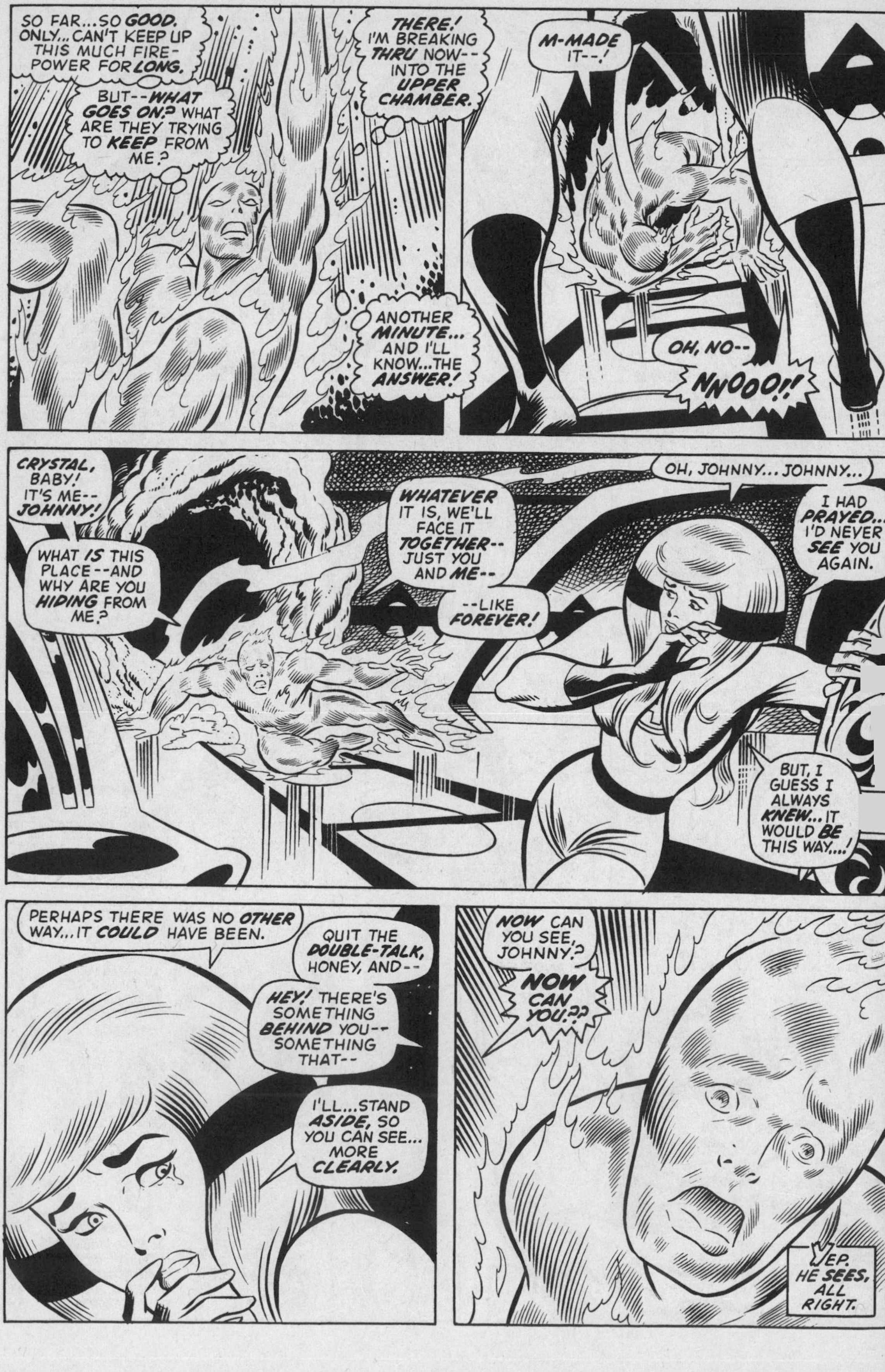
SO FAR...SO GOOD. ONLY...CAN'T KEEP UP THIS MUCH FIRE-POWER FOR LONG.
BUT--WHAT GOES ON? WHAT ARE THEY TRYING TO KEEP FROM ME?
THERE! I'M BREAKING THRU NOW--INTO THE UPPER CHAMBER.
ANOTHER MINUTE... AND I'LL KNOW...THE ANSWER!
M-MADE IT--!
OH, NO--
NNOOO!!
CRYSTAL, BABY! IT'S ME--JOHNNY!
WHAT IS THIS PLACE--AND WHY ARE YOU HIDING FROM ME?
WHATEVER IT IS, WE'LL FACE IT TOGETHER--JUST YOU AND ME--
--LIKE FOREVER!
OH, JOHNNY... JOHNNY...
I HAD PRAYED... I'D NEVER SEE YOU AGAIN.
BUT, I GUESS I ALWAYS KNEW...IT WOULD BE THIS WAY...!
PERHAPS THERE WAS NO OTHER WAY...IT COULD HAVE BEEN.
QUIT THE DOUBLE-TALK, HONEY, AND--
HEY! THERE'S SOMETHING BEHIND YOU--SOMETHING THAT--
I'LL...STAND ASIDE, SO YOU CAN SEE... MORE CLEARLY.
NOW CAN YOU SEE, JOHNNY?
NOW CAN YOU??
YEP. HE SEES, ALL RIGHT.

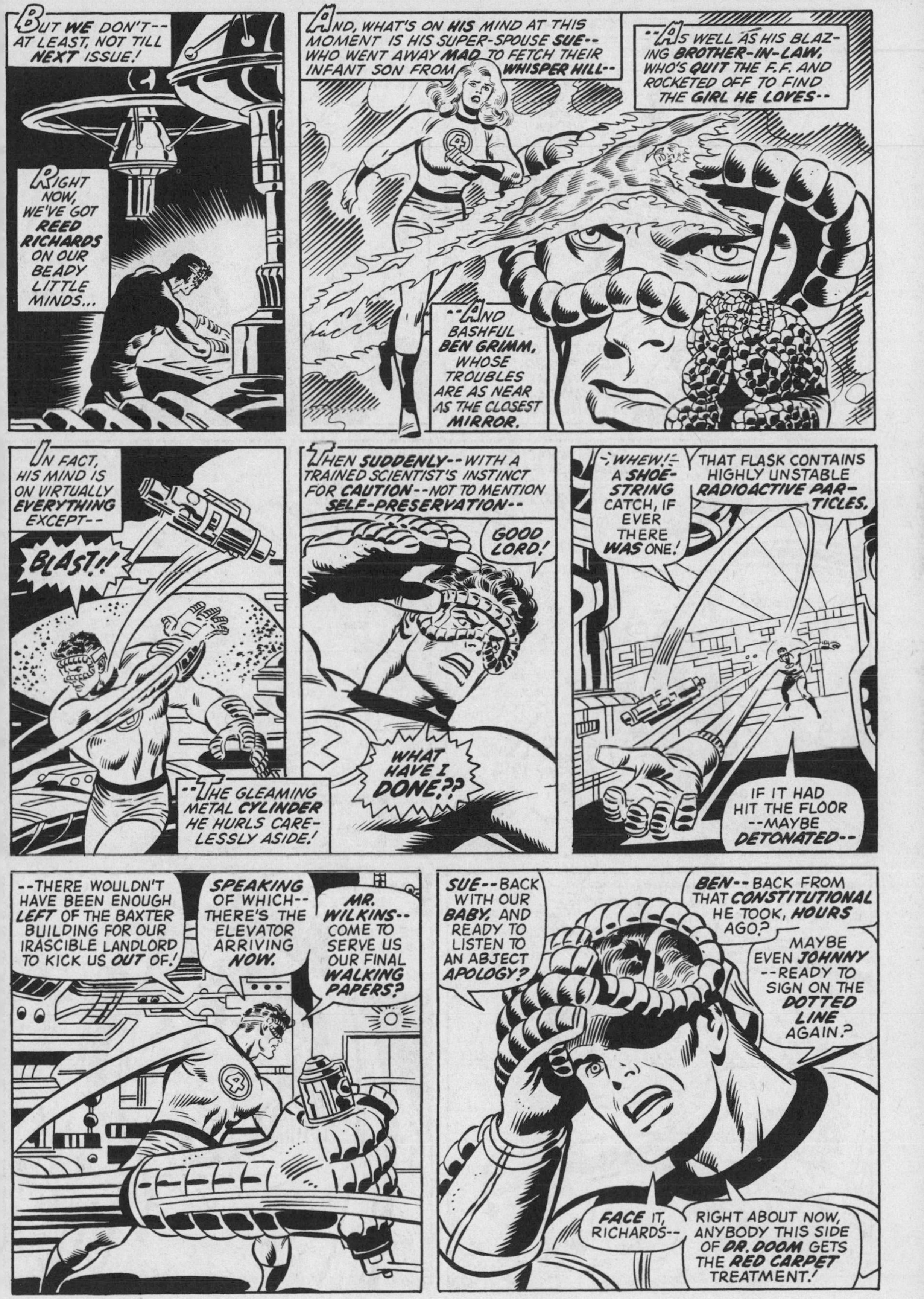
BUT WE DON'T-- AT LEAST, NOT TILL NEXT ISSUE!
RIGHT NOW, WE'VE GOT REED RICHARDS ON OUR BEADY LITTLE MINDS...
AND, WHAT'S ON HIS MIND AT THIS MOMENT IS HIS SUPER-SPOUSE SUE-- WHO WENT AWAY MAD TO FETCH THEIR INFANT SON FROM WHISPER HILL--
--AS WELL AS HIS BLAZING BROTHER-IN-LAW, WHO'S QUIT THE F.F. AND ROCKETED OFF TO FIND THE GIRL HE LOVES--
--AND BASHFUL BEN GRIMM, WHOSE TROUBLES ARE AS NEAR AS THE CLOSEST MIRROR.
IN FACT, HIS MIND IS ON VIRTUALLY EVERYTHING EXCEPT--
BLAST!!
--THE GLEAMING METAL CYLINDER HE HURLS CARELESSLY ASIDE!
THEN SUDDENLY--WITH A TRAINED SCIENTIST'S INSTINCT FOR CAUTION--NOT TO MENTION SELF-PRESERVATION--
GOOD LORD!
WHAT HAVE I DONE??
WHEW! A SHOESTRING CATCH, IF EVER THERE WAS ONE!
THAT FLASK CONTAINS HIGHLY UNSTABLE RADIOACTIVE PARTICLES.
IF IT HAD HIT THE FLOOR --MAYBE DETONATED--
--THERE WOULDN'T HAVE BEEN ENOUGH LEFT OF THE BAXTER BUILDING FOR OUR IRASCIBLE LANDLORD TO KICK US OUT OF!
SPEAKING OF WHICH-- THERE'S THE ELEVATOR ARRIVING NOW.
MR. WILKINS-- COME TO SERVE US OUR FINAL WALKING PAPERS?
SUE--BACK WITH OUR BABY, AND READY TO LISTEN TO AN ABJECT APOLOGY?
BEN--BACK FROM THAT CONSTITUTIONAL HE TOOK, HOURS AGO?
MAYBE EVEN JOHNNY --READY TO SIGN ON THE DOTTED LINE AGAIN?
FACE IT, RICHARDS--
RIGHT ABOUT NOW, ANYBODY THIS SIDE OF DR. DOOM GETS THE RED CARPET TREATMENT!

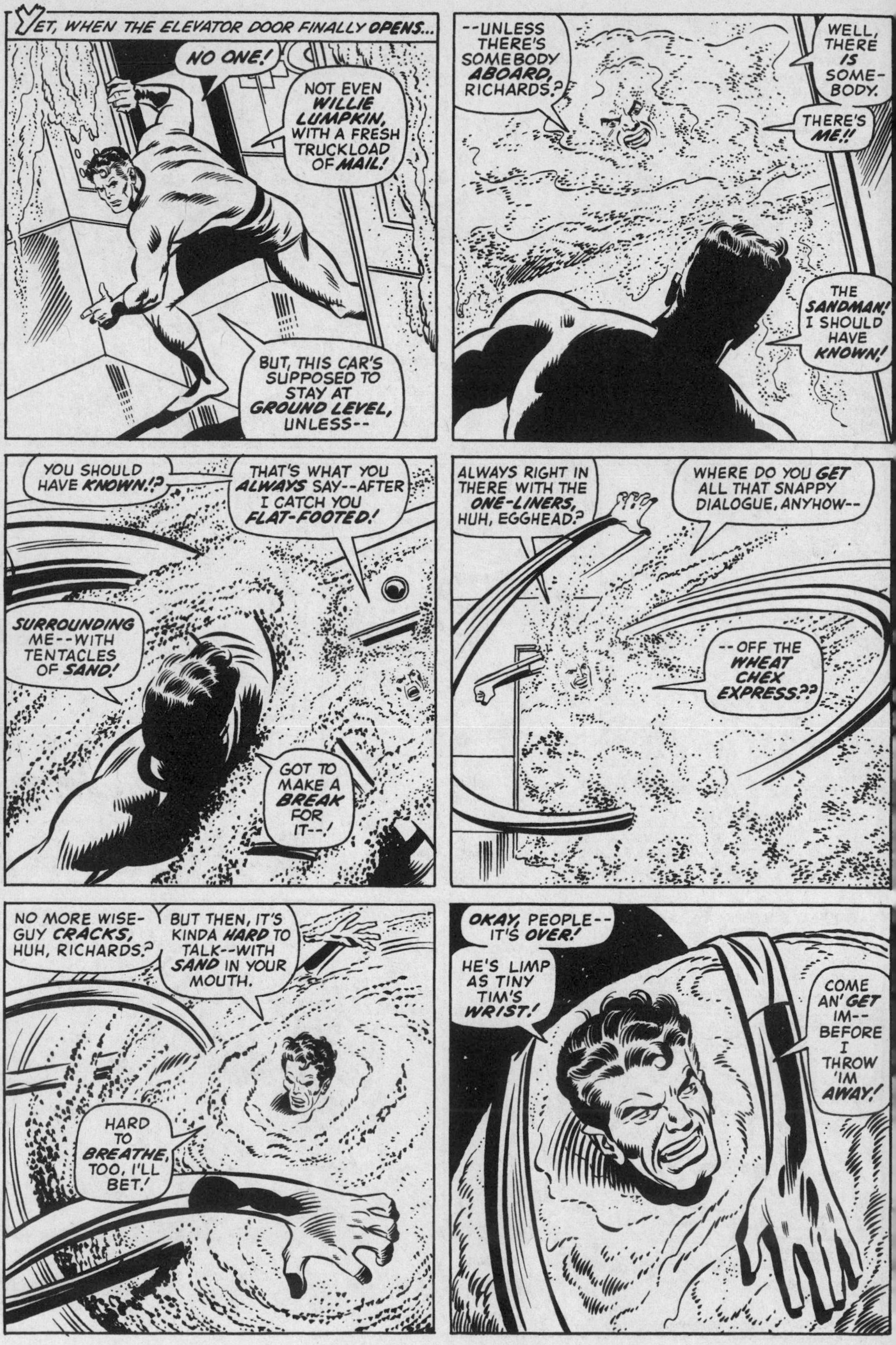
YET, WHEN THE ELEVATOR DOOR FINALLY OPENS...
NO ONE!
NOT EVEN WILLIE LUMPKIN, WITH A FRESH TRUCKLOAD OF MAIL!
BUT, THIS CAR'S SUPPOSED TO STAY AT GROUND LEVEL, UNLESS--
--UNLESS THERE'S SOMEBODY ABOARD, RICHARDS?
WELL, THERE IS SOME-BODY.
THERE'S ME!!
THE SANDMAN! I SHOULD HAVE KNOWN!
YOU SHOULD HAVE KNOWN!?
THAT'S WHAT YOU ALWAYS SAY--AFTER I CATCH YOU FLAT-FOOTED!
SURROUNDING ME--WITH TENTACLES OF SAND!
GOT TO MAKE A BREAK FOR IT--!
ALWAYS RIGHT IN THERE WITH THE ONE-LINERS, HUH, EGGHEAD?
WHERE DO YOU GET ALL THAT SNAPPY DIALOGUE, ANYHOW--
--OFF THE WHEAT CHEX EXPRESS??
NO MORE WISE-GUY CRACKS, HUH, RICHARDS?
BUT THEN, IT'S KINDA HARD TO TALK--WITH SAND IN YOUR MOUTH.
HARD TO BREATHE, TOO, I'LL BET!
OKAY, PEOPLE--IT'S OVER!
HE'S LIMP AS TINY TIM'S WRIST!
COME AN' GET IM--BEFORE I THROW 'IM AWAY!

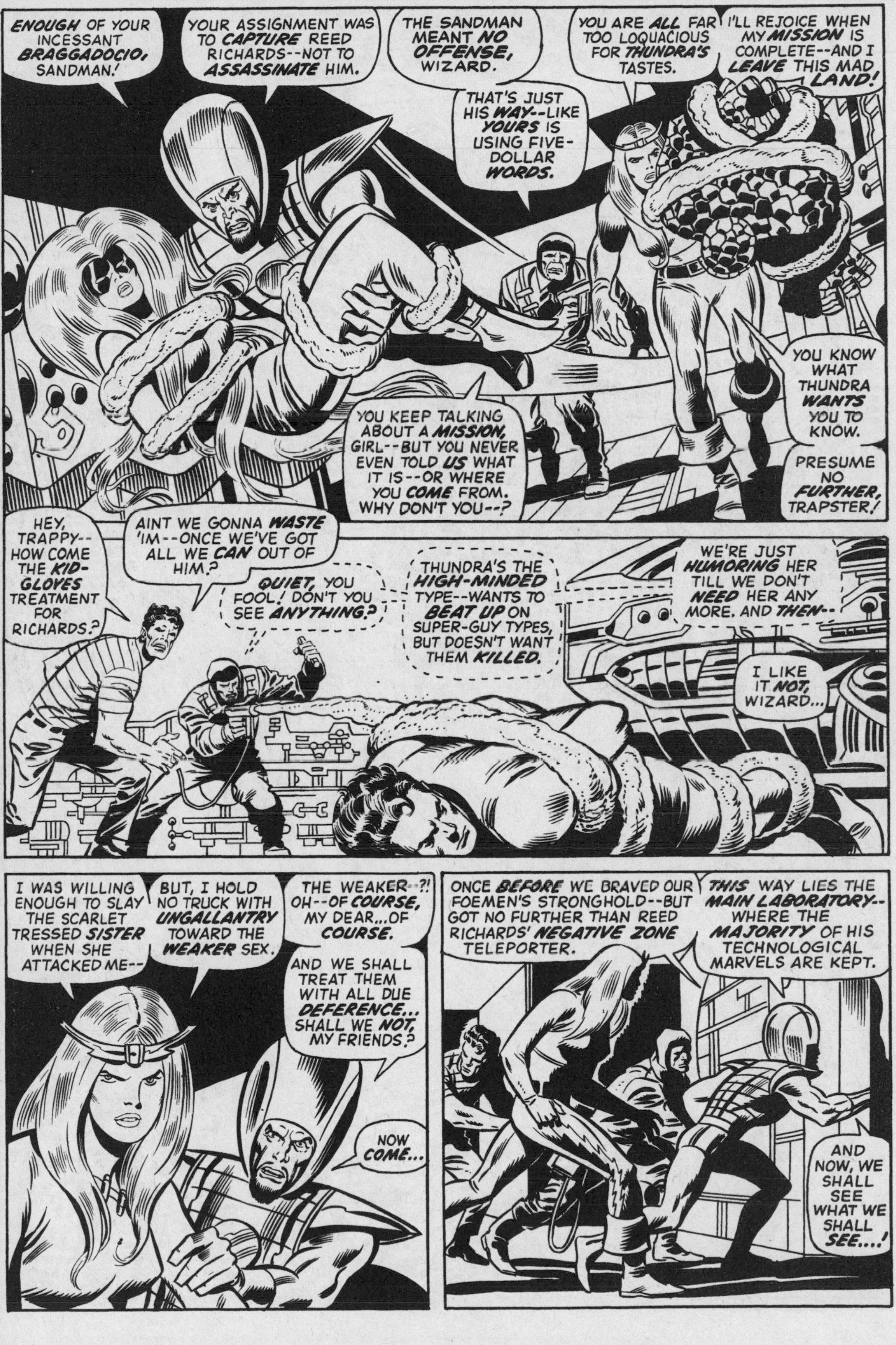

ENOUGH OF YOUR INCESSANT BRAGGADOCIO, SANDMAN!
YOUR ASSIGNMENT WAS TO CAPTURE REED RICHARDS--NOT TO ASSASSINATE HIM.
THE SANDMAN MEANT NO OFFENSE, WIZARD.
THAT'S JUST HIS WAY--LIKE YOURS IS USING FIVE-DOLLAR WORDS.
YOU ARE ALL FAR TOO LOQUACIOUS FOR THUNDRA'S TASTES.
I'LL REJOICE WHEN MY MISSION IS COMPLETE--AND I LEAVE THIS MAD LAND!
YOU KEEP TALKING ABOUT A MISSION, GIRL--BUT YOU NEVER EVEN TOLD US WHAT IT IS--OR WHERE YOU COME FROM. WHY DON'T YOU--?
YOU KNOW WHAT THUNDRA WANTS YOU TO KNOW.
PRESUME NO FURTHER, TRAPSTER!
HEY, TRAPPY--HOW COME THE KID-GLOVES TREATMENT FOR RICHARDS?
AINT WE GONNA WASTE 'IM--ONCE WE'VE GOT ALL WE CAN OUT OF HIM?
QUIET, YOU FOOL! DON'T YOU SEE ANYTHING?
THUNDRA'S THE HIGH-MINDED TYPE--WANTS TO BEAT UP ON SUPER-GUY TYPES, BUT DOESN'T WANT THEM KILLED.
WE'RE JUST HUMORING HER TILL WE DON'T NEED HER ANY MORE. AND THEN--
I LIKE IT NOT, WIZARD...
I WAS WILLING ENOUGH TO SLAY THE SCARLET TRESSED SISTER WHEN SHE ATTACKED ME--
BUT, I HOLD NO TRUCK WITH UNGALLANTRY TOWARD THE WEAKER SEX.
THE WEAKER--?! OH--OF COURSE, MY DEAR...OF COURSE.
AND WE SHALL TREAT THEM WITH ALL DUE DEFERENCE... SHALL WE NOT, MY FRIENDS?
NOW COME...
ONCE BEFORE WE BRAVED OUR FOEMEN'S STRONGHOLD--BUT GOT NO FURTHER THAN REED RICHARDS' NEGATIVE ZONE TELEPORTER.
THIS WAY LIES THE MAIN LABORATORY--WHERE THE MAJORITY OF HIS TECHNOLOGICAL MARVELS ARE KEPT.
AND NOW, WE SHALL SEE WHAT WE SHALL SEE....!

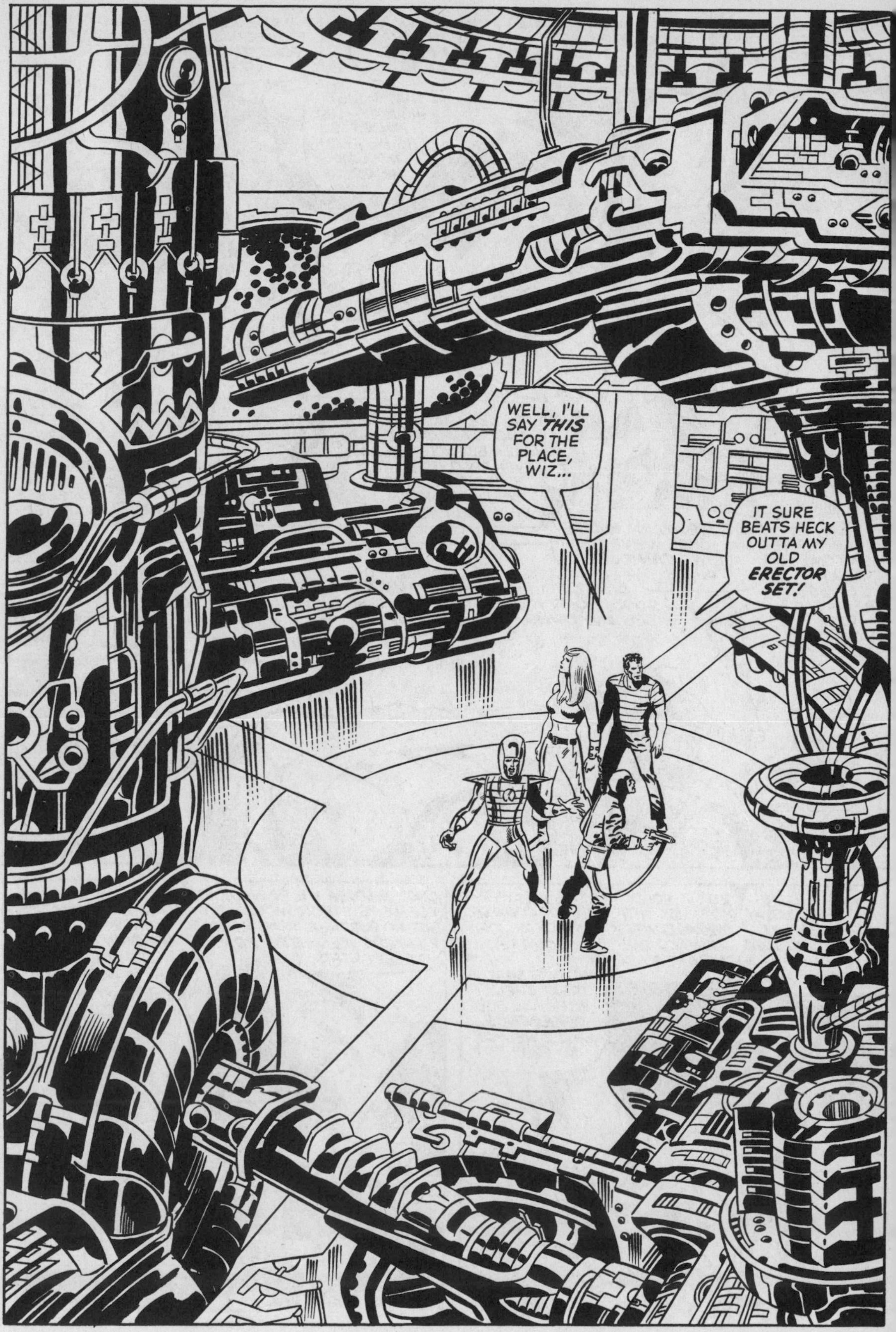
WELL, I'LL SAY THIS FOR THE PLACE, WIZ...
IT SURE BEATS HECK OUTTA MY OLD ERECTOR SET!

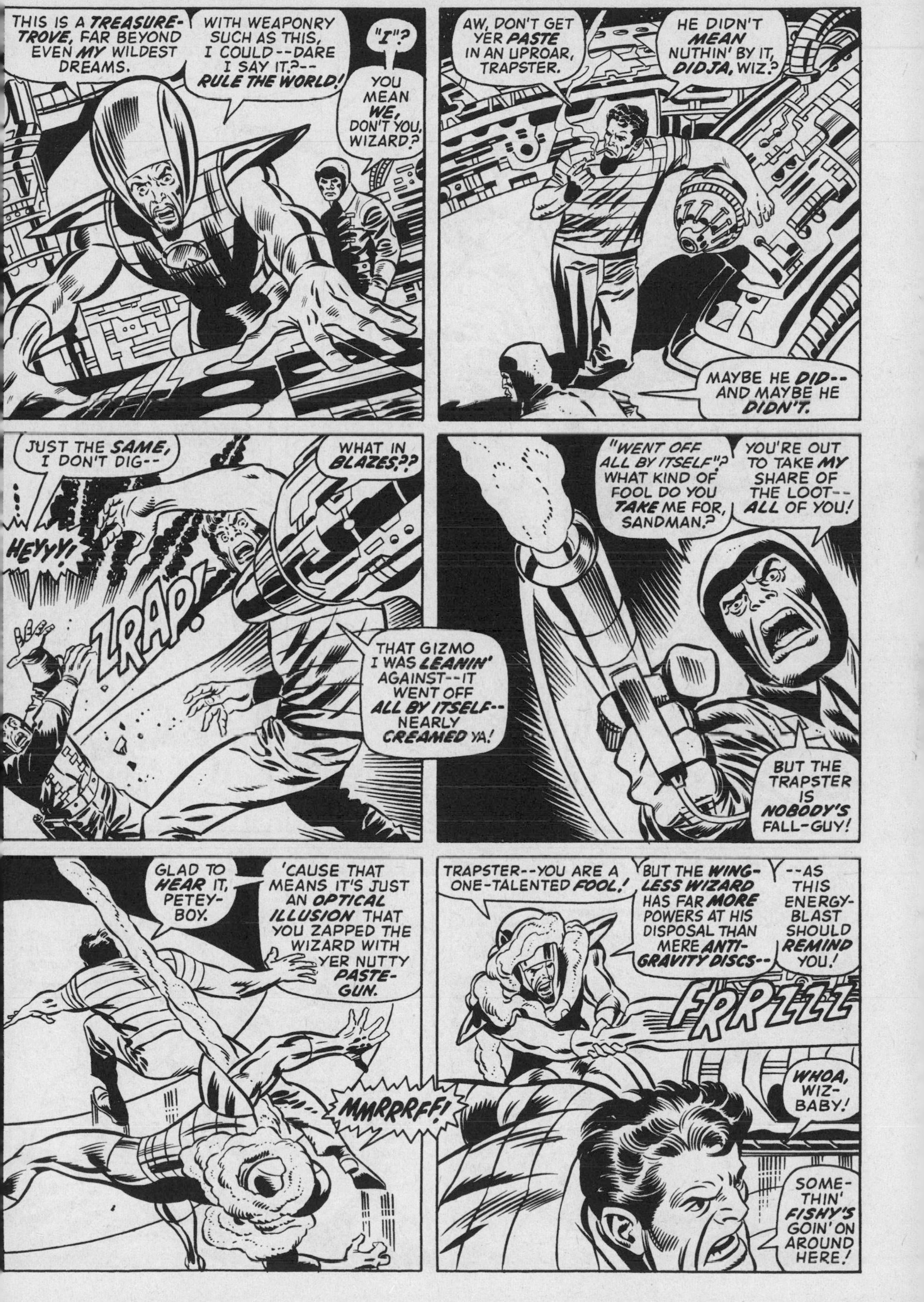
THIS IS A TREASURE-TROVE, FAR BEYOND EVEN MY WILDEST DREAMS.
WITH WEAPONRY SUCH AS THIS, I COULD--DARE I SAY IT?--RULE THE WORLD!
"I"?
YOU MEAN WE, DON'T YOU, WIZARD?
AW, DON'T GET YER PASTE IN AN UPROAR, TRAPSTER.
HE DIDN'T MEAN NUTHIN' BY IT, DIDJA, WIZ?
MAYBE HE DID--AND MAYBE HE DIDN'T.
JUST THE SAME, I DON'T DIG--
HEYYY!
ZRAP!
WHAT IN BLAZES??
THAT GIZMO I WAS LEANIN' AGAINST--IT WENT OFF ALL BY ITSELF--NEARLY CREAMED YA!
"WENT OFF ALL BY ITSELF"? WHAT KIND OF FOOL DO YOU TAKE ME FOR, SANDMAN?
YOU'RE OUT TO TAKE MY SHARE OF THE LOOT--ALL OF YOU!
BUT THE TRAPSTER IS NOBODY'S FALL-GUY!
GLAD TO HEAR IT, PETEY-BOY.
'CAUSE THAT MEANS IT'S JUST AN OPTICAL ILLUSION THAT YOU ZAPPED THE WIZARD WITH YER NUTTY PASTE-GUN.
MMRRRFF!
TRAPSTER--YOU ARE A ONE-TALENTED FOOL!
BUT THE WING-LESS WIZARD HAS FAR MORE POWERS AT HIS DISPOSAL THAN MERE ANTI-GRAVITY DISCS--
--AS THIS ENERGY-BLAST SHOULD REMIND YOU!
FRRZZZ
WHOA, WIZ-BABY!
SOME-THIN' FISHY'S GOIN' ON AROUND HERE!

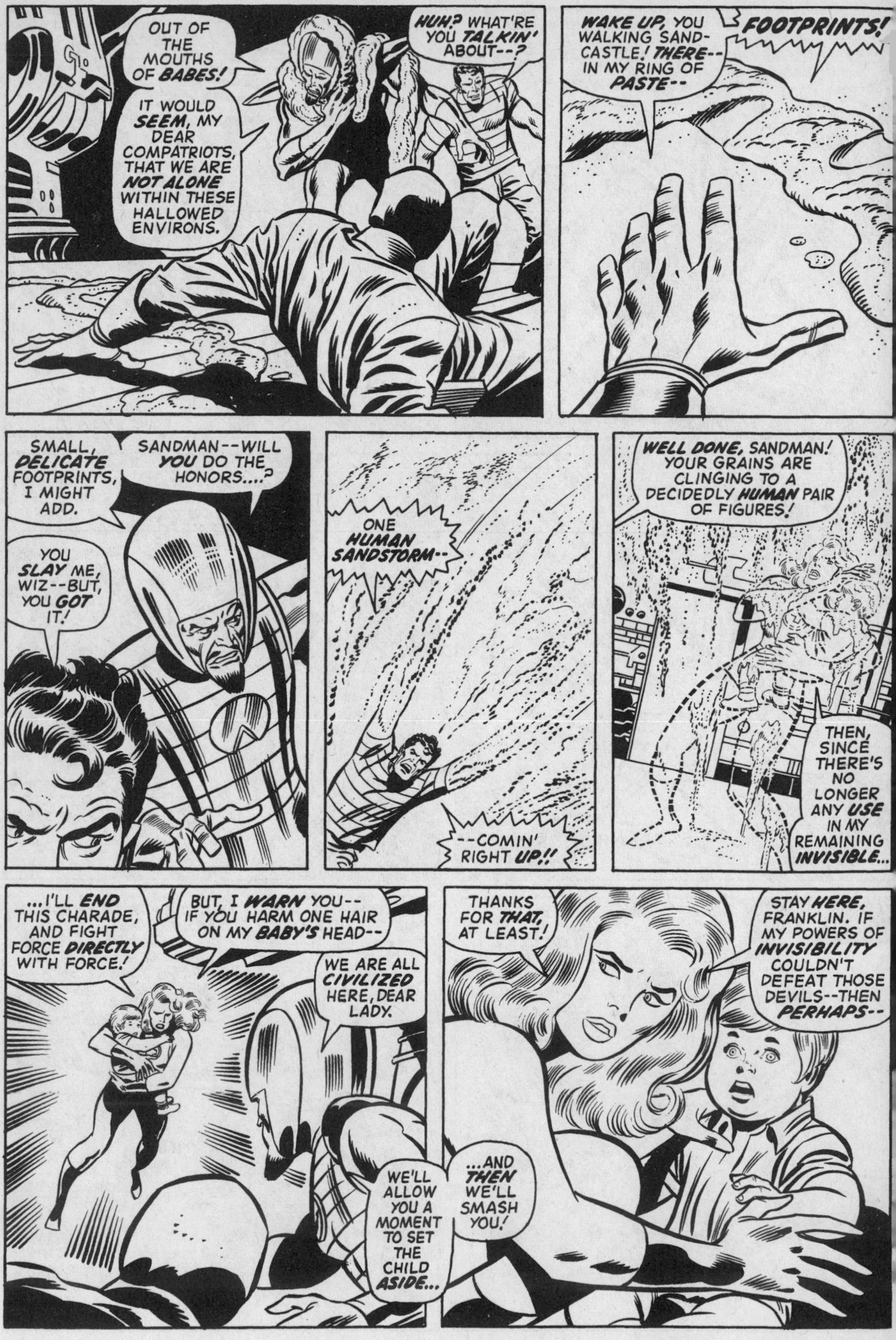

OUT OF THE MOUTHS OF BABES!
IT WOULD SEEM, MY DEAR COMPATRIOTS, THAT WE ARE NOT ALONE WITHIN THESE HALLOWED ENVIRONS.
HUH? WHAT'RE YOU TALKIN' ABOUT--?
WAKE UP, YOU WALKING SAND-CASTLE! THERE--IN MY RING OF PASTE--
FOOTPRINTS!
SMALL, DELICATE FOOTPRINTS, I MIGHT ADD.
SANDMAN--WILL YOU DO THE HONORS...?
YOU SLAY ME, WIZ--BUT, YOU GOT IT!
ONE HUMAN SANDSTORM--
--COMIN' RIGHT UP!!
WELL DONE, SANDMAN! YOUR GRAINS ARE CLINGING TO A DECIDEDLY HUMAN PAIR OF FIGURES!
THEN, SINCE THERE'S NO LONGER ANY USE IN MY REMAINING INVISIBLE...
...I'LL END THIS CHARADE, AND FIGHT FORCE DIRECTLY WITH FORCE!
BUT, I WARN YOU--IF YOU HARM ONE HAIR ON MY BABY'S HEAD--
WE ARE ALL CIVILIZED HERE, DEAR LADY.
WE'LL ALLOW YOU A MOMENT TO SET THE CHILD ASIDE...
...AND THEN WE'LL SMASH YOU!
THANKS FOR THAT, AT LEAST!
STAY HERE, FRANKLIN. IF MY POWERS OF INVISIBILITY COULDN'T DEFEAT THOSE DEVILS--THEN PERHAPS--

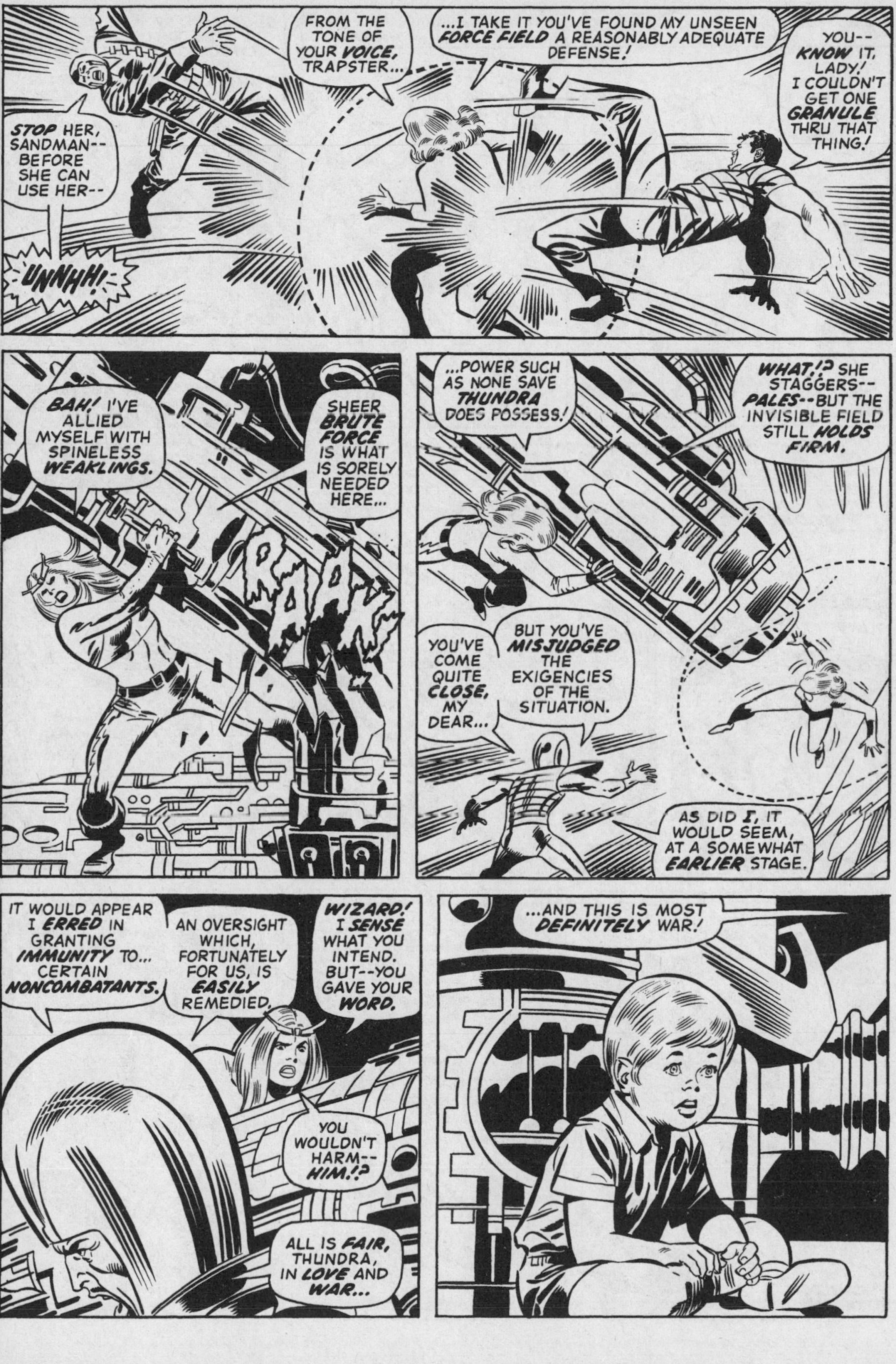
STOP HER, SANDMAN-- BEFORE SHE CAN USE HER--
UNNHH!
FROM THE TONE OF YOUR VOICE, TRAPSTER...
...I TAKE IT YOU'VE FOUND MY UNSEEN FORCE FIELD A REASONABLY ADEQUATE DEFENSE!
YOU-- KNOW IT, LADY! I COULDN'T GET ONE GRANULE THRU THAT THING!
BAH! I'VE ALLIED MYSELF WITH SPINELESS WEAKLINGS.
SHEER BRUTE FORCE IS WHAT IS SORELY NEEDED HERE...
RAAA
...POWER SUCH AS NONE SAVE THUNDRA DOES POSSESS!
WHAT!? SHE STAGGERS-- PALES--BUT THE INVISIBLE FIELD STILL HOLDS FIRM.
YOU'VE COME QUITE CLOSE, MY DEAR...
BUT YOU'VE MISJUDGED THE EXIGENCIES OF THE SITUATION.
AS DID I, IT WOULD SEEM, AT A SOMEWHAT EARLIER STAGE.
IT WOULD APPEAR I ERRED IN GRANTING IMMUNITY TO... CERTAIN NONCOMBATANTS.
AN OVERSIGHT WHICH, FORTUNATELY FOR US, IS EASILY REMEDIED.
WIZARD! I SENSE WHAT YOU INTEND. BUT--YOU GAVE YOUR WORD.
YOU WOULDN'T HARM-- HIM!?
ALL IS FAIR, THUNDRA, IN LOVE AND WAR...
...AND THIS IS MOST DEFINITELY WAR!

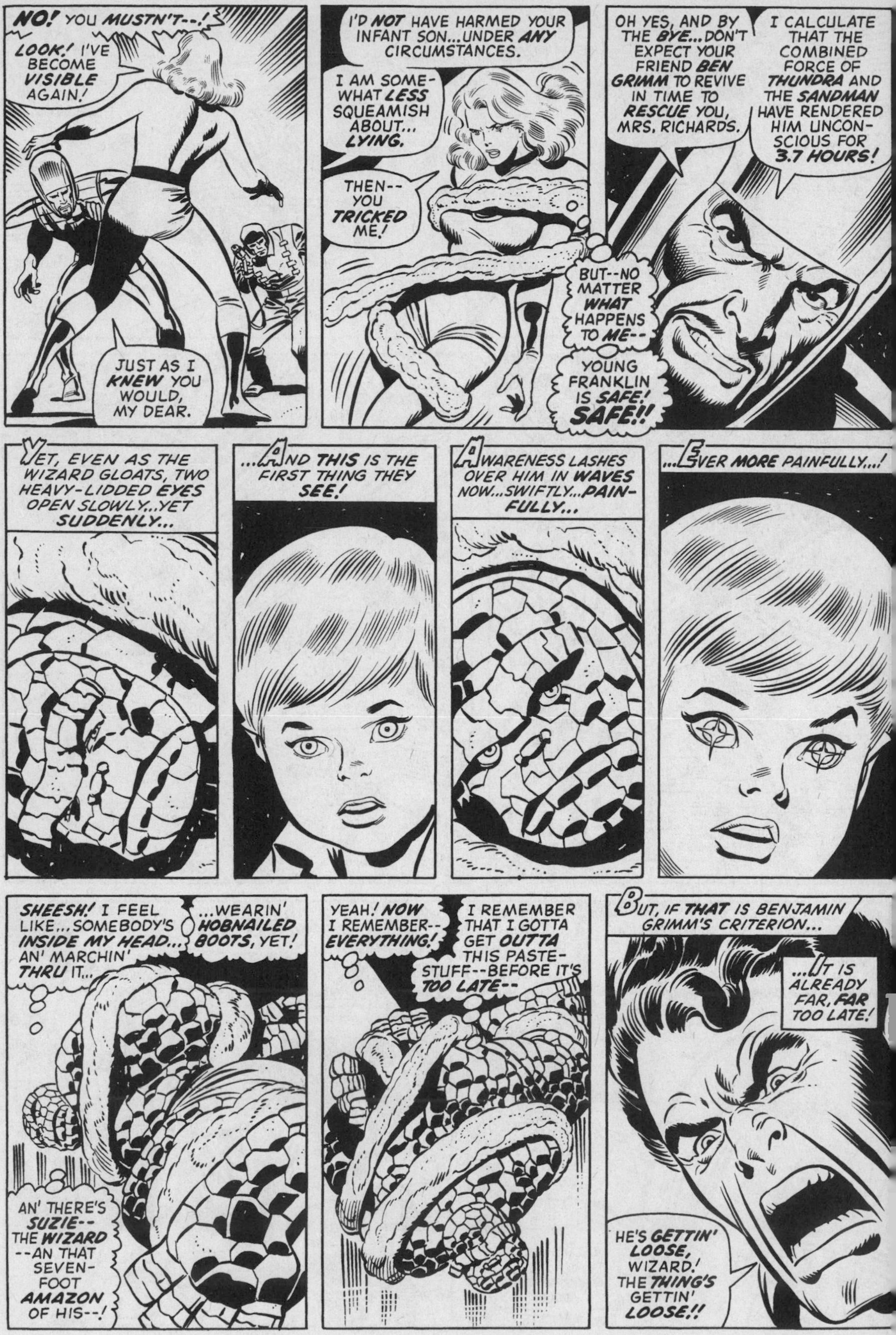
NO! YOU MUSTN'T--!
LOOK! I'VE BECOME VISIBLE AGAIN!
JUST AS I KNEW YOU WOULD, MY DEAR.
I'D NOT HAVE HARMED YOUR INFANT SON...UNDER ANY CIRCUMSTANCES.
I AM SOMEWHAT LESS SQUEAMISH ABOUT... LYING.
THEN--YOU TRICKED ME!
OH YES, AND BY THE BYE...DON'T EXPECT YOUR FRIEND BEN GRIMM TO REVIVE IN TIME TO RESCUE YOU, MRS. RICHARDS.
I CALCULATE THAT THE COMBINED FORCE OF THUNDRA AND THE SANDMAN HAVE RENDERED HIM UNCONSCIOUS FOR 3.7 HOURS!
BUT--NO MATTER WHAT HAPPENS TO ME--
YOUNG FRANKLIN IS SAFE! SAFE!!
YET, EVEN AS THE WIZARD GLOATS, TWO HEAVY-LIDDED EYES OPEN SLOWLY...YET SUDDENLY...
...AND THIS IS THE FIRST THING THEY SEE!
AWARENESS LASHES OVER HIM IN WAVES NOW...SWIFTLY...PAINFULLY...
...EVER MORE PAINFULLY...!
SHEESH! I FEEL LIKE...SOMEBODY'S INSIDE MY HEAD... AN' MARCHIN' THRU IT...
...WEARIN' HOBNAILED BOOTS, YET!
AN' THERE'S SUZIE--THE WIZARD--AN THAT SEVEN-FOOT AMAZON OF HIS--!
YEAH! NOW I REMEMBER--EVERYTHING!
I REMEMBER THAT I GOTTA GET OUTTA THIS PASTE-STUFF--BEFORE IT'S TOO LATE--
BUT, IF THAT IS BENJAMIN GRIMM'S CRITERION...
...IT IS ALREADY FAR, FAR TOO LATE!
HE'S GETTIN' LOOSE, WIZARD! THE THING'S GETTIN' LOOSE!!

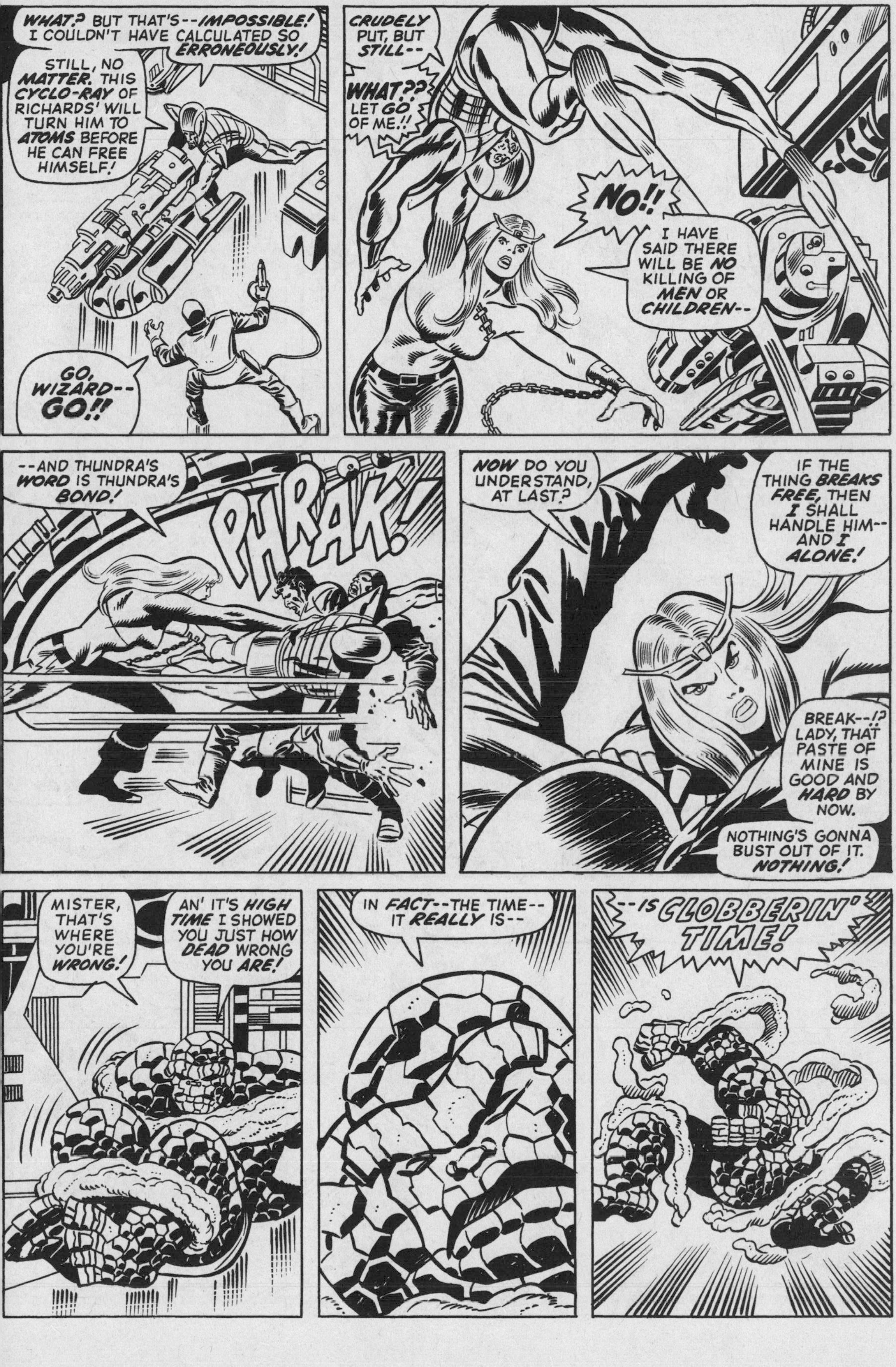
WHAT? BUT THAT'S--IMPOSSIBLE! I COULDN'T HAVE CALCULATED SO ERRONEOUSLY!
STILL, NO MATTER. THIS CYCLO-RAY OF RICHARDS' WILL TURN HIM TO ATOMS BEFORE HE CAN FREE HIMSELF!
GO, WIZARD--GO!!
CRUDELY PUT, BUT STILL--
WHAT?? LET GO OF ME!!
NO!!
I HAVE SAID THERE WILL BE NO KILLING OF MEN OR CHILDREN--
--AND THUNDRA'S WORD IS THUNDRA'S BOND!
PHRAK!
NOW DO YOU UNDERSTAND, AT LAST?
IF THE THING BREAKS FREE, THEN I SHALL HANDLE HIM--AND I ALONE!
BREAK--!? LADY, THAT PASTE OF MINE IS GOOD AND HARD BY NOW.
NOTHING'S GONNA BUST OUT OF IT. NOTHING!
MISTER, THAT'S WHERE YOU'RE WRONG!
AN' IT'S HIGH TIME I SHOWED YOU JUST HOW DEAD WRONG YOU ARE!
IN FACT--THE TIME--IT REALLY IS--
--IS CLOBBERIN' TIME!

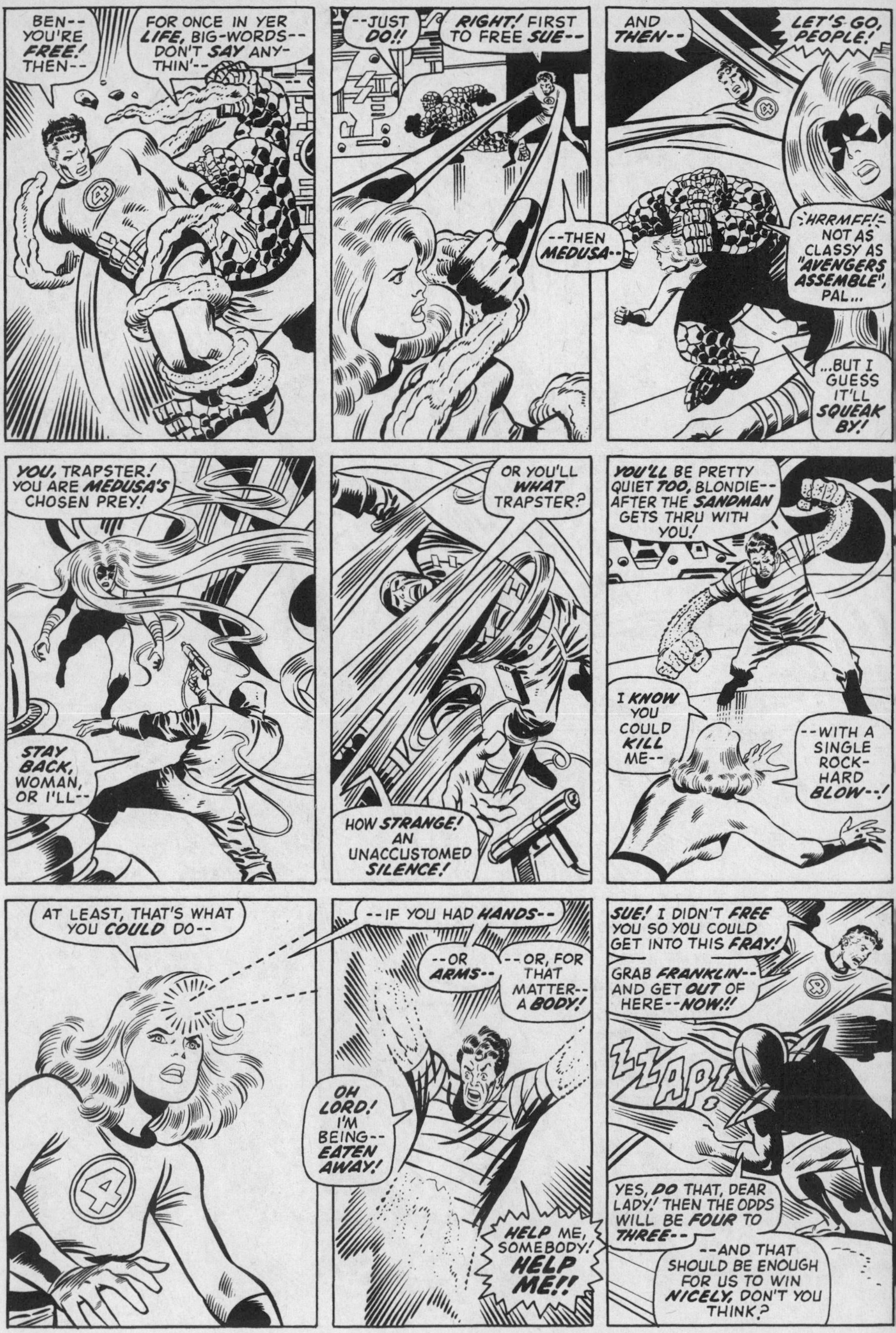
BEN--
YOU'RE
FREE!
THEN--
FOR ONCE IN YER
LIFE, BIG-WORDS--
DON'T SAY ANY-
THIN'--
--JUST
DO!!
RIGHT! FIRST
TO FREE SUE--
--THEN
MEDUSA--
AND
THEN--
LET'S GO,
PEOPLE!
HRRMFF! NOT AS
CLASSY AS
"AVENGERS
ASSEMBLE",
PAL...
...BUT I
GUESS
IT'LL
SQUEAK
BY!
YOU, TRAPSTER!
YOU ARE MEDUSA'S
CHOSEN PREY!
STAY
BACK,
WOMAN,
OR I'LL--
OR YOU'LL
WHAT
TRAPSTER?
HOW STRANGE!
AN
UNACCUSTOMED
SILENCE!
YOU'LL BE PRETTY
QUIET TOO, BLONDIE--
AFTER THE SANDMAN
GETS THRU WITH
YOU!
I KNOW
YOU
COULD
KILL
ME--
--WITH A
SINGLE
ROCK-
HARD
BLOW--!
AT LEAST, THAT'S WHAT
YOU COULD DO--
--IF YOU HAD HANDS--
--OR
ARMS--
--OR, FOR
THAT
MATTER--
A BODY!
OH
LORD!
I'M
BEING--
EATEN
AWAY!
HELP ME,
SOMEBODY!
HELP
ME!!
SUE! I DIDN'T FREE
YOU SO YOU COULD
GET INTO THIS FRAY!
GRAB FRANKLIN--
AND GET OUT OF
HERE--NOW!!
ZZAP!
YES, DO THAT, DEAR
LADY! THEN THE ODDS
WILL BE FOUR TO
THREE--
--AND THAT
SHOULD BE ENOUGH
FOR US TO WIN
NICELY, DON'T YOU
THINK?

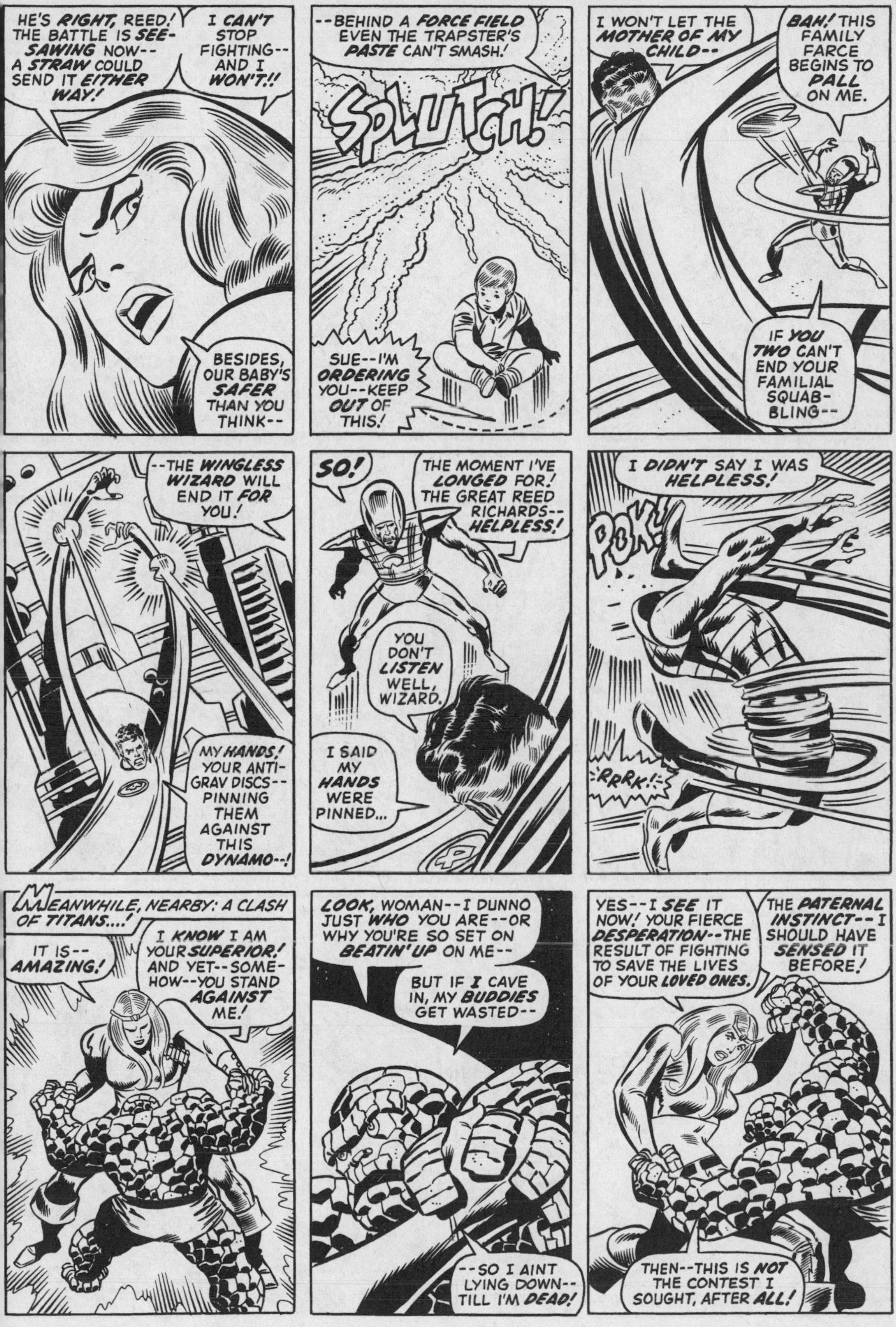
HE'S RIGHT, REED! THE BATTLE IS SEE-SAWING NOW-- A STRAW COULD SEND IT EITHER WAY!
I CAN'T STOP FIGHTING-- AND I WON'T!!
BESIDES, OUR BABY'S SAFER THAN YOU THINK--
--BEHIND A FORCE FIELD EVEN THE TRAPSTER'S PASTE CAN'T SMASH!
SPLUTCH!
SUE--I'M ORDERING YOU--KEEP OUT OF THIS!
I WON'T LET THE MOTHER OF MY CHILD--
BAH! THIS FAMILY FARCE BEGINS TO PALL ON ME.
IF YOU TWO CAN'T END YOUR FAMILIAL SQUAB-BLING--
--THE WINGLESS WIZARD WILL END IT FOR YOU!
MY HANDS! YOUR ANTI-GRAV DISCS--PINNING THEM AGAINST THIS DYNAMO--!
SO!
THE MOMENT I'VE LONGED FOR! THE GREAT REED RICHARDS-- HELPLESS!
YOU DON'T LISTEN WELL, WIZARD.
I SAID MY HANDS WERE PINNED...
I DIDN'T SAY I WAS HELPLESS!
POK!
RRRK!
MEANWHILE, NEARBY: A CLASH OF TITANS...!
IT IS-- AMAZING!
I KNOW I AM YOUR SUPERIOR! AND YET--SOME-HOW--YOU STAND AGAINST ME!
LOOK, WOMAN--I DUNNO JUST WHO YOU ARE--OR WHY YOU'RE SO SET ON BEATIN' UP ON ME--
BUT IF I CAVE IN, MY BUDDIES GET WASTED--
--SO I AINT LYING DOWN-- TILL I'M DEAD!
YES--I SEE IT NOW! YOUR FIERCE DESPERATION--THE RESULT OF FIGHTING TO SAVE THE LIVES OF YOUR LOVED ONES.
THE PATERNAL INSTINCT--I SHOULD HAVE SENSED IT BEFORE!
THEN--THIS IS NOT THE CONTEST I SOUGHT, AFTER ALL!

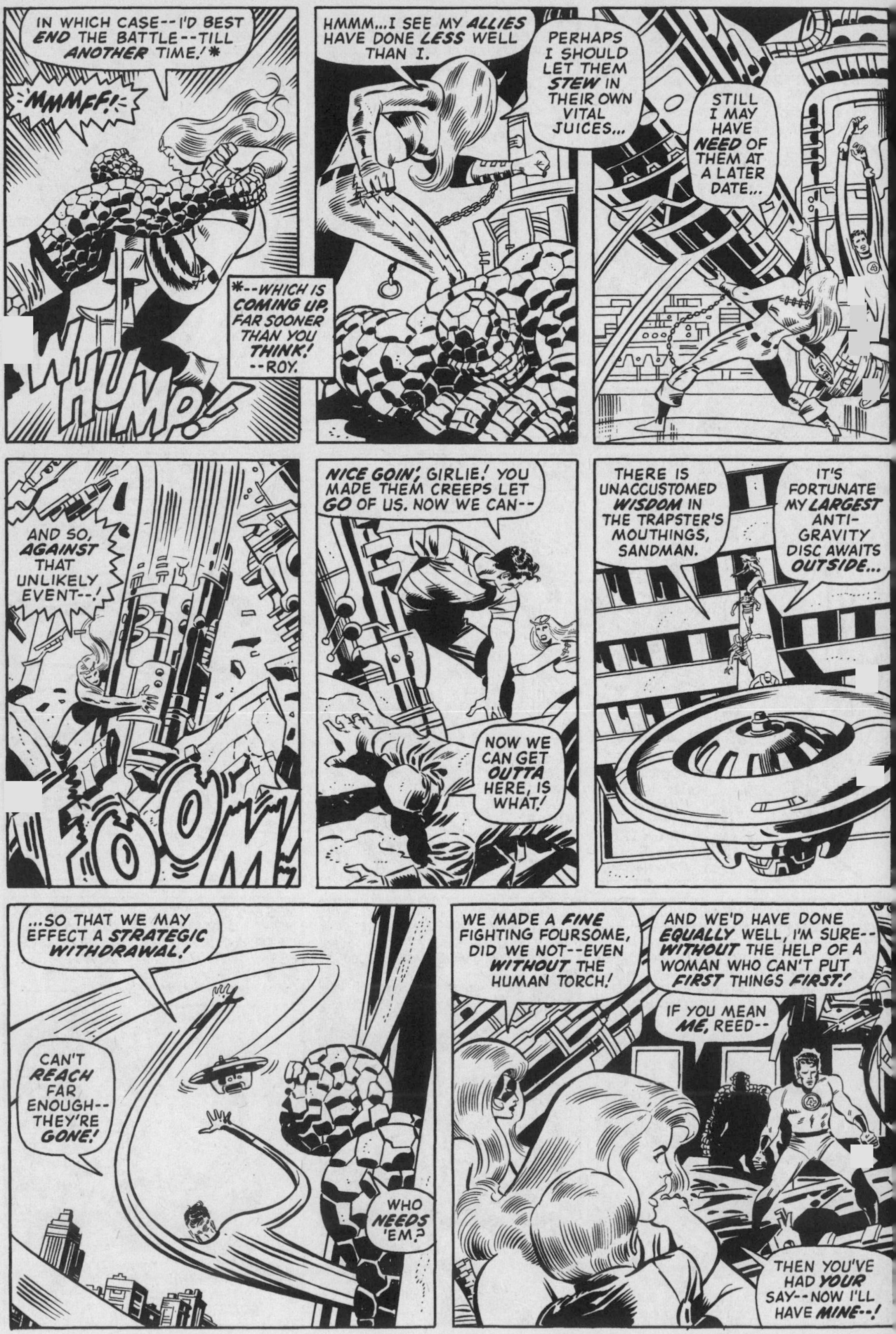
IN WHICH CASE--I'D BEST END THE BATTLE--TILL ANOTHER TIME!*
MMMFF!
*--WHICH IS COMING UP, FAR SOONER THAN YOU THINK! --ROY.
WHUMP!
HMMM...I SEE MY ALLIES HAVE DONE LESS WELL THAN I.
PERHAPS I SHOULD LET THEM STEW IN THEIR OWN VITAL JUICES...
STILL I MAY HAVE NEED OF THEM AT A LATER DATE...
AND SO, AGAINST THAT UNLIKELY EVENT--!
NICE GOIN', GIRLIE! YOU MADE THEM CREEPS LET GO OF US. NOW WE CAN--
NOW WE CAN GET OUTTA HERE, IS WHAT!
THERE IS UNACCUSTOMED WISDOM IN THE TRAPSTER'S MOUTHINGS, SANDMAN.
IT'S FORTUNATE MY LARGEST ANTI-GRAVITY DISC AWAITS OUTSIDE...
...SO THAT WE MAY EFFECT A STRATEGIC WITHDRAWAL!
CAN'T REACH FAR ENOUGH--THEY'RE GONE!
WHO NEEDS 'EM?
WE MADE A FINE FIGHTING FOURSOME, DID WE NOT--EVEN WITHOUT THE HUMAN TORCH!
AND WE'D HAVE DONE EQUALLY WELL, I'M SURE--WITHOUT THE HELP OF A WOMAN WHO CAN'T PUT FIRST THINGS FIRST!
IF YOU MEAN ME, REED--
THEN YOU'VE HAD YOUR SAY--NOW I'LL HAVE MINE--!

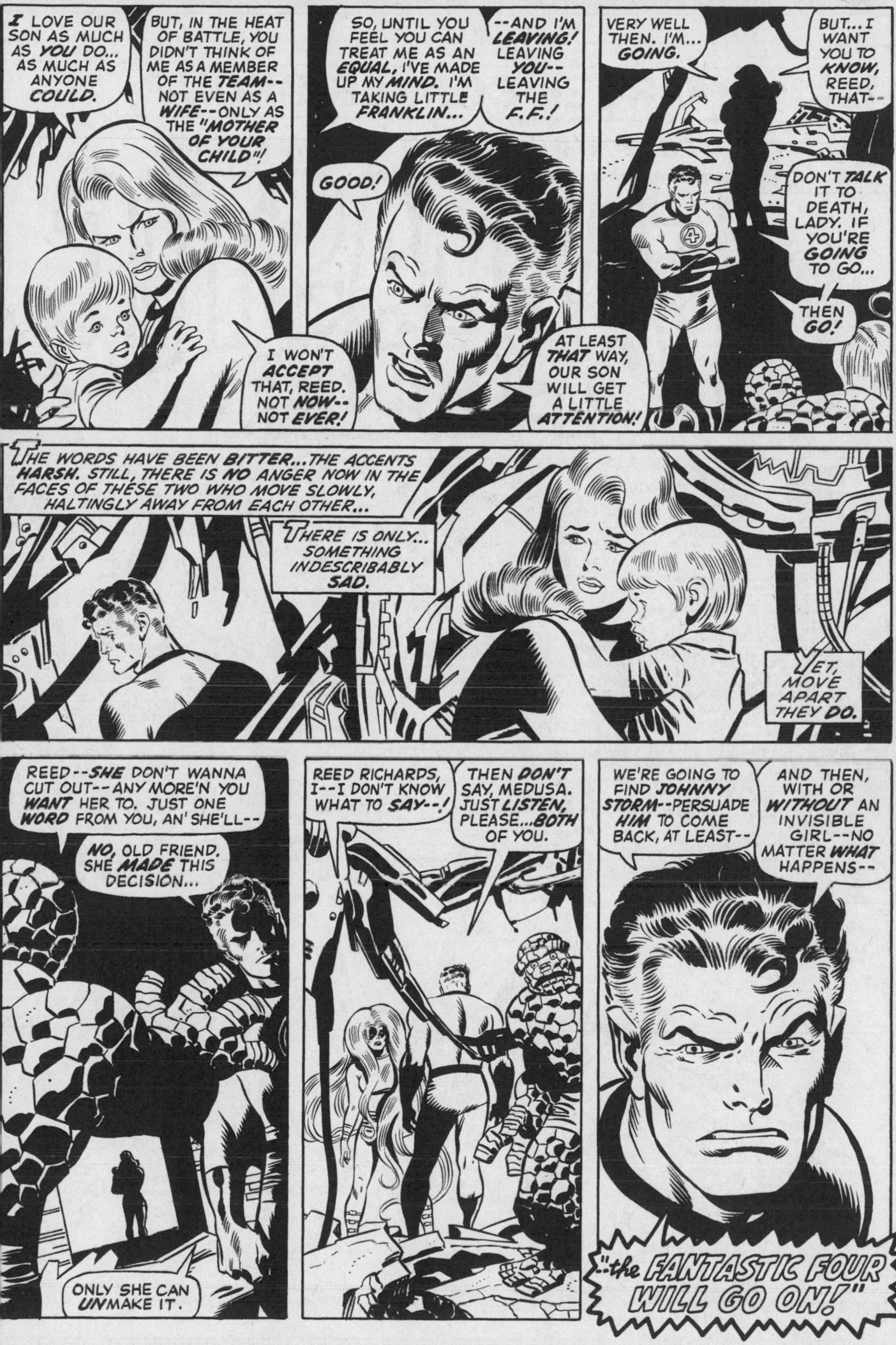

I LOVE OUR SON AS MUCH AS YOU DO... AS MUCH AS ANYONE COULD.
BUT, IN THE HEAT OF BATTLE, YOU DIDN'T THINK OF ME AS A MEMBER OF THE TEAM-- NOT EVEN AS A WIFE--ONLY AS THE "MOTHER OF YOUR CHILD"!
I WON'T ACCEPT THAT, REED. NOT NOW-- NOT EVER!
SO, UNTIL YOU FEEL YOU CAN TREAT ME AS AN EQUAL, I'VE MADE UP MY MIND. I'M TAKING LITTLE FRANKLIN...
--AND I'M LEAVING! LEAVING YOU-- LEAVING THE F.F.!
GOOD!
AT LEAST THAT WAY, OUR SON WILL GET A LITTLE ATTENTION!
VERY WELL THEN. I'M... GOING.
BUT... I WANT YOU TO KNOW, REED, THAT--
DON'T TALK IT TO DEATH, LADY. IF YOU'RE GOING TO GO...
THEN GO!
THE WORDS HAVE BEEN BITTER... THE ACCENTS HARSH. STILL, THERE IS NO ANGER NOW IN THE FACES OF THESE TWO WHO MOVE SLOWLY, HALTINGLY AWAY FROM EACH OTHER...
THERE IS ONLY... SOMETHING INDESCRIBABLY SAD.
YET, MOVE APART THEY DO.
REED--SHE DON'T WANNA CUT OUT--ANY MORE'N YOU WANT HER TO. JUST ONE WORD FROM YOU, AN' SHE'LL--
NO, OLD FRIEND. SHE MADE THIS DECISION...
ONLY SHE CAN UNMAKE IT.
REED RICHARDS, I--I DON'T KNOW WHAT TO SAY--!
THEN DON'T SAY, MEDUSA. JUST LISTEN, PLEASE... BOTH OF YOU.
WE'RE GOING TO FIND JOHNNY STORM--PERSUADE HIM TO COME BACK, AT LEAST--
AND THEN, WITH OR WITHOUT AN INVISIBLE GIRL--NO MATTER WHAT HAPPENS--
"...the FANTASTIC FOUR WILL GO ON!"

FANTASTIC FOUR
MARVEL COMICS GROUP
APPROVED BY THE COMICS CODE AUTHORITY
20¢ CC
131 FEB 02462
THE WORLD'S GREATEST COMIC MAGAZINE!
FANTASTIC FOUR
THE HUMAN TORCH GOES WILD-- IN THE LAND OF THE UNCANNY INHUMANS!
FEATURING-- THE MUTANT CALLED QUICKSILVER! PLUS--THE MOST SHOCKING SURPRISE OF ALL!
STERANKO SINNOTT

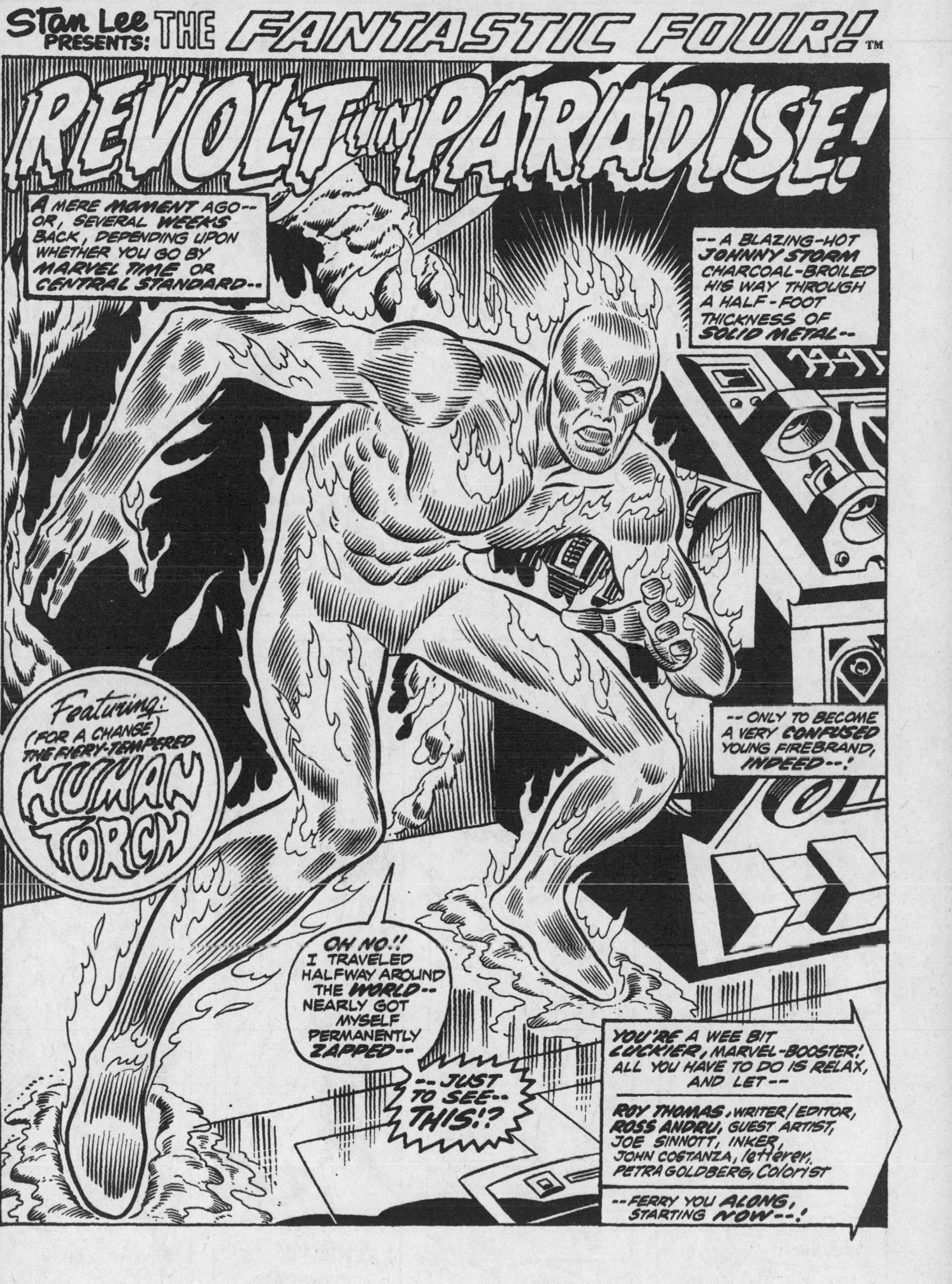

STAN LEE PRESENTS: THE FANTASTIC FOUR!™
REVOLT IN PARADISE!
A MERE MOMENT AGO-- OR, SEVERAL WEEKS BACK, DEPENDING UPON WHETHER YOU GO BY MARVEL TIME OR CENTRAL STANDARD--
--A BLAZING-HOT JOHNNY STORM CHARCOAL-BROILED HIS WAY THROUGH A HALF-FOOT THICKNESS OF SOLID METAL--
--ONLY TO BECOME A VERY CONFUSED YOUNG FIREBRAND, INDEED--!
Featuring: (FOR A CHANGE) THE FIERY-TEMPERED HUMAN TORCH
OH NO!! I TRAVELED HALFWAY AROUND THE WORLD-- NEARLY GOT MYSELF PERMANENTLY ZAPPED--
--JUST TO SEE-- THIS!?
YOU'RE A WEE BIT LUCKIER, MARVEL-BOOSTER! ALL YOU HAVE TO DO IS RELAX, AND LET--
ROY THOMAS, WRITER/EDITOR, ROSS ANDRU, GUEST ARTIST, JOE SINNOTT, INKER, JOHN COSTANZA, letterer, PETRA GOLDBERG, Colorist
--FERRY YOU ALONG, STARTING NOW--!

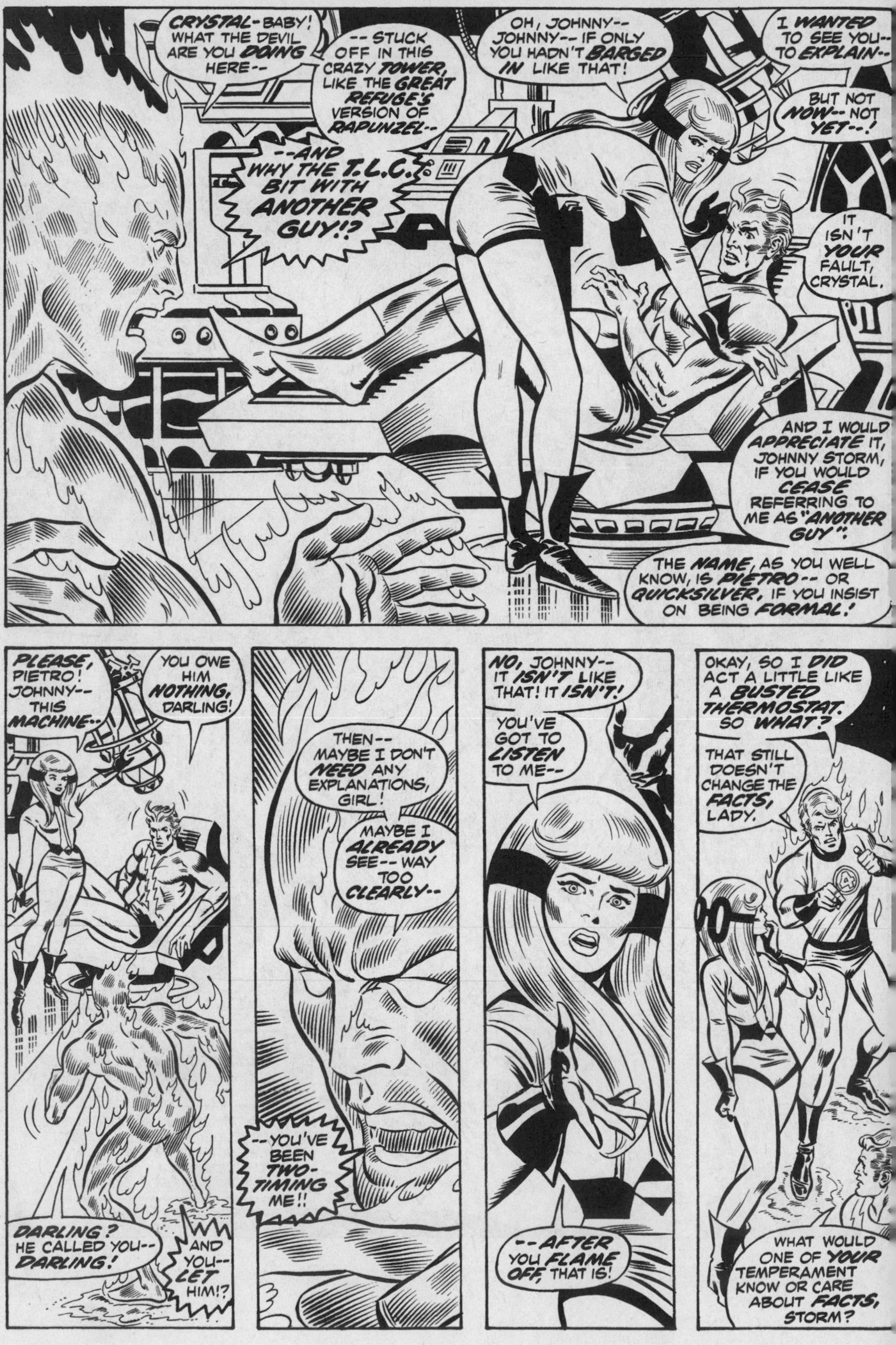
CRYSTAL-BABY! WHAT THE DEVIL ARE YOU DOING HERE--
--STUCK OFF IN THIS CRAZY TOWER, LIKE THE GREAT REFUGE'S VERSION OF RAPUNZEL--
--AND WHY THE T.L.C. BIT WITH ANOTHER GUY!?
OH, JOHNNY-- JOHNNY-- IF ONLY YOU HADN'T BARGED IN LIKE THAT!
I WANTED TO SEE YOU-- TO EXPLAIN--
BUT NOT NOW-- NOT YET--!
IT ISN'T YOUR FAULT, CRYSTAL.
AND I WOULD APPRECIATE IT, JOHNNY STORM, IF YOU WOULD CEASE REFERRING TO ME AS "ANOTHER GUY".
THE NAME, AS YOU WELL KNOW, IS PIETRO-- OR QUICKSILVER, IF YOU INSIST ON BEING FORMAL!
PLEASE, PIETRO! JOHNNY-- THIS MACHINE--
YOU OWE HIM NOTHING, DARLING!
DARLING? HE CALLED YOU-- DARLING!
AND YOU-- LET HIM!?
THEN-- MAYBE I DON'T NEED ANY EXPLANATIONS, GIRL!
MAYBE I ALREADY SEE-- WAY TOO CLEARLY--
--YOU'VE BEEN TWO-TIMING ME!!
NO, JOHNNY-- IT ISN'T LIKE THAT! IT ISN'T!
YOU'VE GOT TO LISTEN TO ME--
--AFTER YOU FLAME OFF, THAT IS!
OKAY, SO I DID ACT A LITTLE LIKE A BUSTED THERMOSTAT. SO WHAT?
THAT STILL DOESN'T CHANGE THE FACTS, LADY.
WHAT WOULD ONE OF YOUR TEMPERAMENT KNOW OR CARE ABOUT FACTS, STORM?

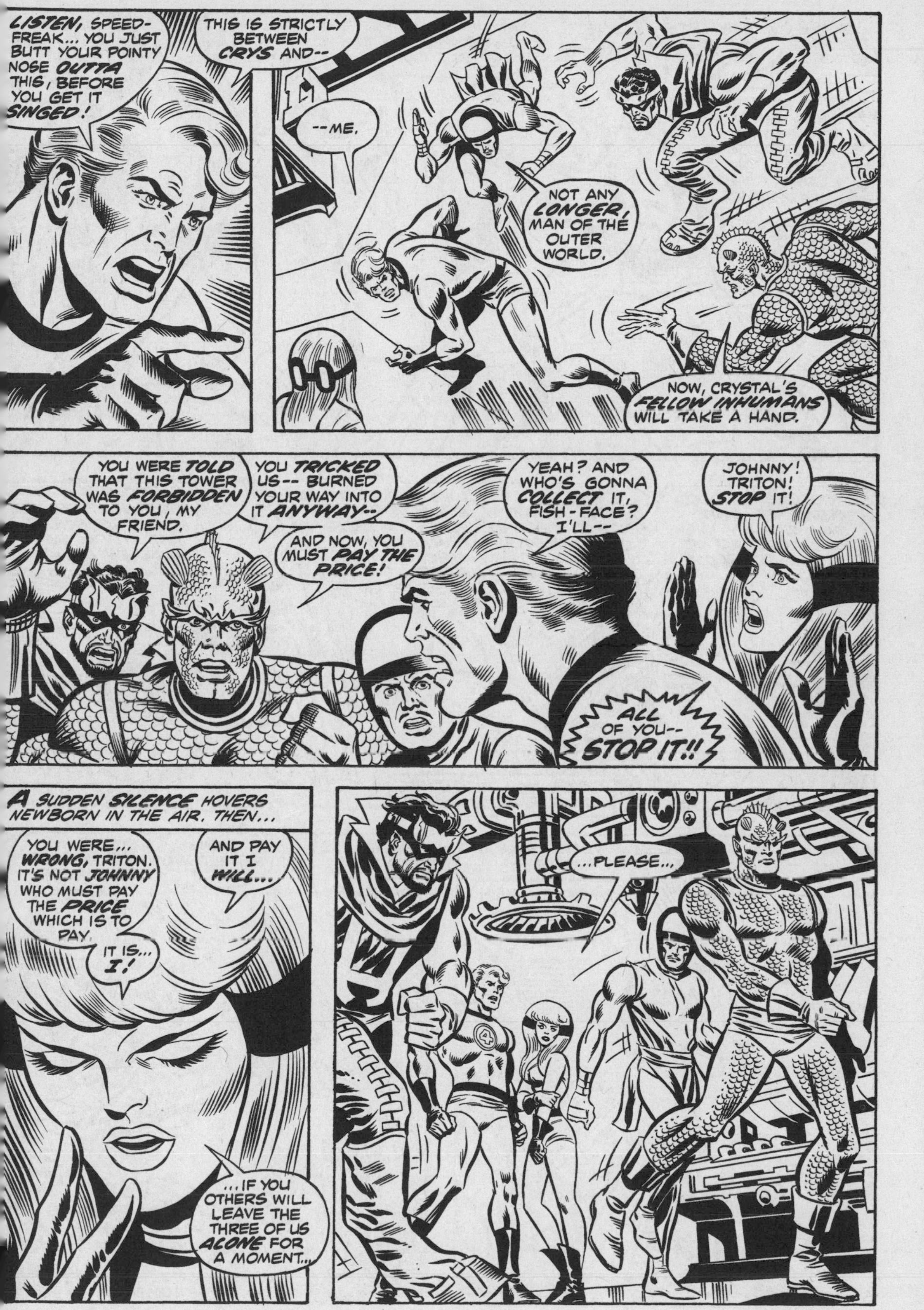

LISTEN, SPEED-FREAK... YOU JUST BUTT YOUR POINTY NOSE OUTTA THIS, BEFORE YOU GET IT SINGED!
THIS IS STRICTLY BETWEEN CRYS AND--
--ME.
NOT ANY LONGER, MAN OF THE OUTER WORLD.
NOW, CRYSTAL'S FELLOW INHUMANS WILL TAKE A HAND.
YOU WERE TOLD THAT THIS TOWER WAS FORBIDDEN TO YOU, MY FRIEND.
YOU TRICKED US-- BURNED YOUR WAY INTO IT ANYWAY--
AND NOW, YOU MUST PAY THE PRICE!
YEAH? AND WHO'S GONNA COLLECT IT, FISH-FACE? I'LL--
JOHNNY! TRITON! STOP IT!
ALL OF YOU-- STOP IT!!
A SUDDEN SILENCE HOVERS NEWBORN IN THE AIR. THEN...
YOU WERE... WRONG, TRITON. IT'S NOT JOHNNY WHO MUST PAY THE PRICE WHICH IS TO PAY.
IT IS... I!
AND PAY IT I WILL...
...PLEASE...
...IF YOU OTHERS WILL LEAVE THE THREE OF US ALONE FOR A MOMENT...

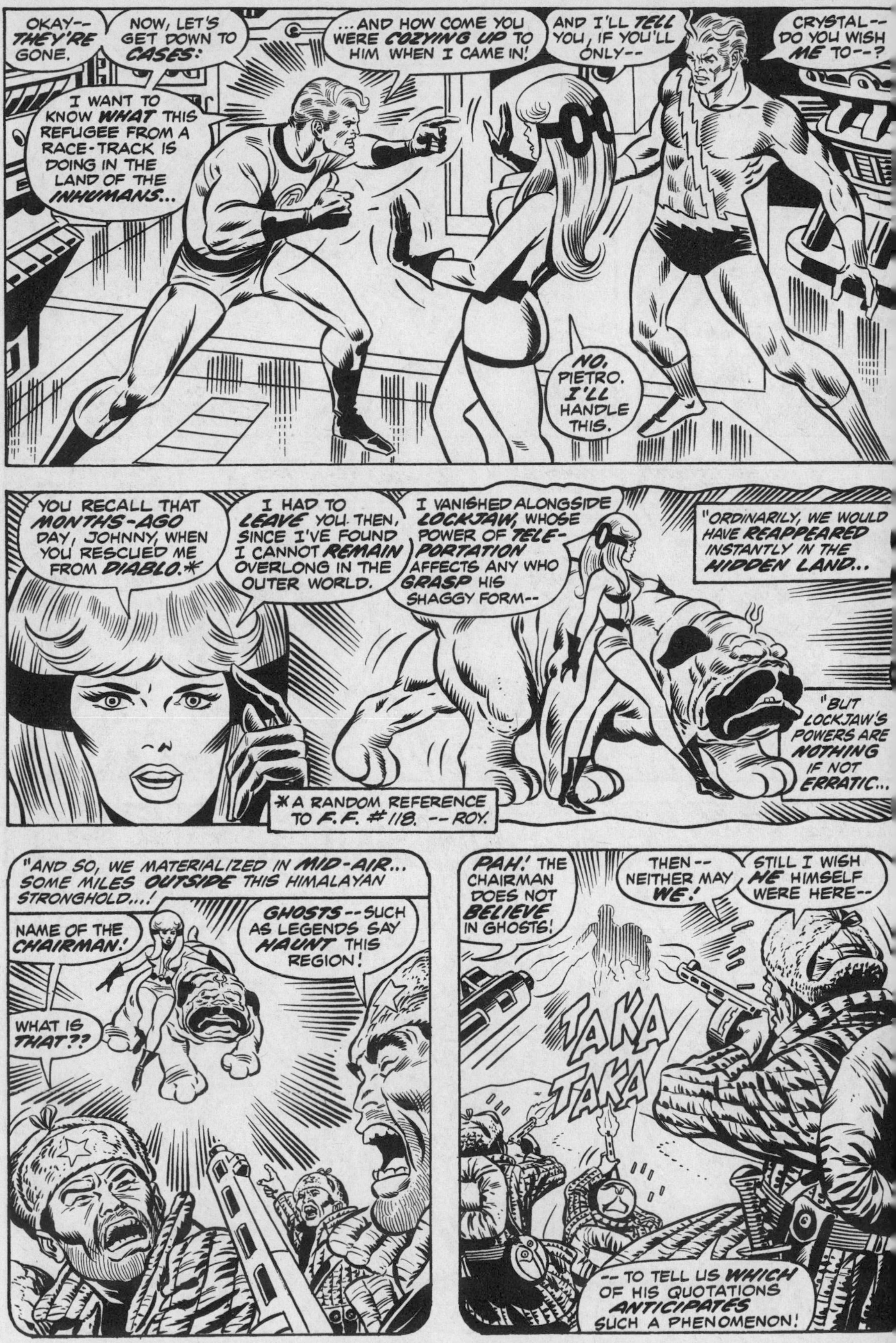
OKAY-- THEY'RE GONE.
NOW, LET'S GET DOWN TO CASES:
I WANT TO KNOW WHAT THIS REFUGEE FROM A RACE-TRACK IS DOING IN THE LAND OF THE INHUMANS...
...AND HOW COME YOU WERE COZYING UP TO HIM WHEN I CAME IN!
AND I'LL TELL YOU, IF YOU'LL ONLY--
CRYSTAL-- DO YOU WISH ME TO--?
NO, PIETRO. I'LL HANDLE THIS.
YOU RECALL THAT MONTHS-AGO DAY, JOHNNY, WHEN YOU RESCUED ME FROM DIABLO.*
I HAD TO LEAVE YOU THEN, SINCE I'VE FOUND I CANNOT REMAIN OVERLONG IN THE OUTER WORLD.
I VANISHED ALONGSIDE LOCKJAW, WHOSE POWER OF TELE-PORTATION AFFECTS ANY WHO GRASP HIS SHAGGY FORM--
"ORDINARILY, WE WOULD HAVE REAPPEARED INSTANTLY IN THE HIDDEN LAND...
"BUT LOCKJAW'S POWERS ARE NOTHING IF NOT ERRATIC...
*A RANDOM REFERENCE TO F.F. #118. --ROY.
"AND SO, WE MATERIALIZED IN MID-AIR... SOME MILES OUTSIDE THIS HIMALAYAN STRONGHOLD...!
NAME OF THE CHAIRMAN!
GHOSTS--SUCH AS LEGENDS SAY HAUNT THIS REGION!
WHAT IS THAT??
PAH! THE CHAIRMAN DOES NOT BELIEVE IN GHOSTS!
THEN-- NEITHER MAY WE!
STILL I WISH HE HIMSELF WERE HERE--
TAKA TAKA
--TO TELL US WHICH OF HIS QUOTATIONS ANTICIPATES SUCH A PHENOMENON!

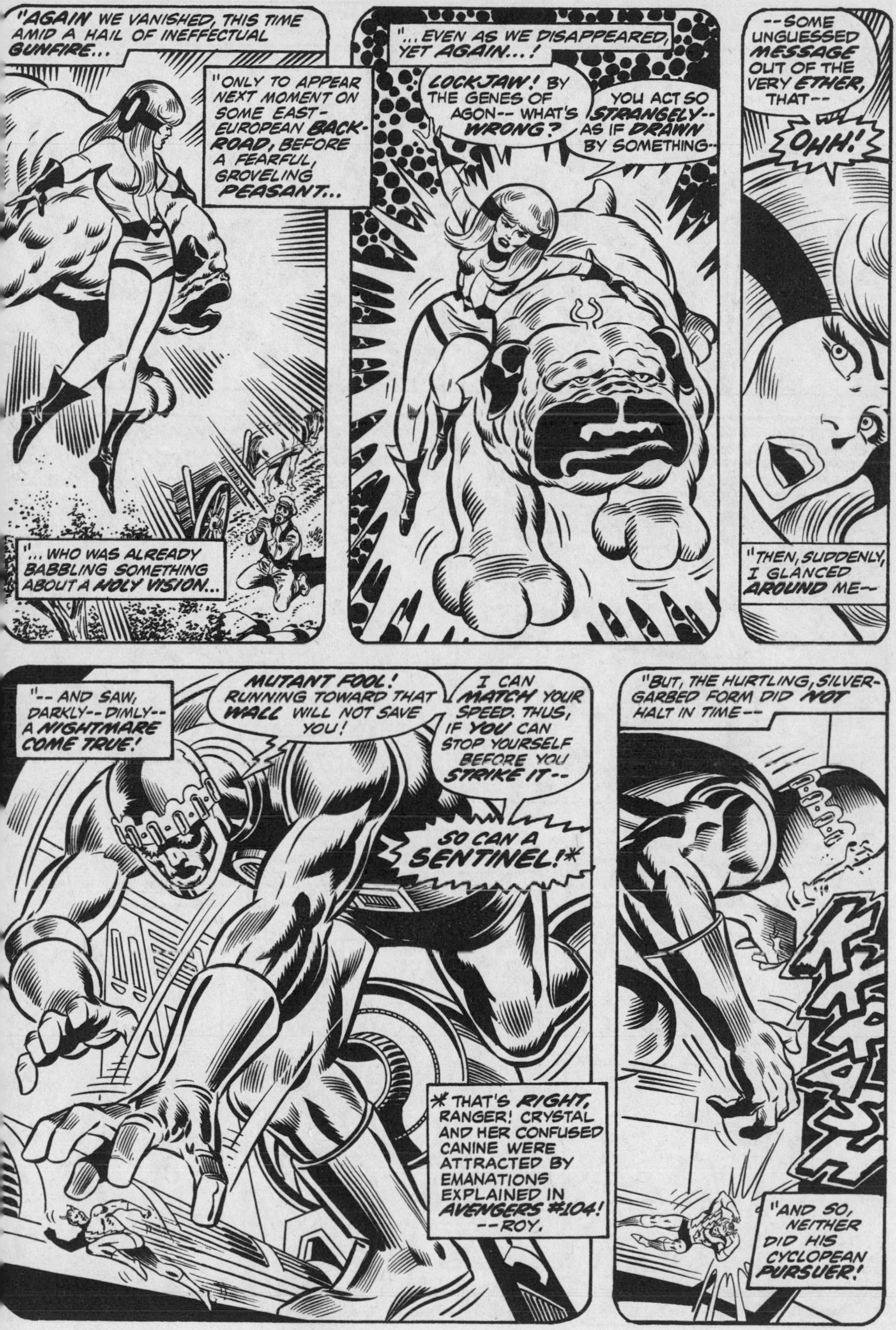
"AGAIN WE VANISHED, THIS TIME AMID A HAIL OF INEFFECTUAL GUNFIRE...
"ONLY TO APPEAR NEXT MOMENT ON SOME EAST-EUROPEAN BACK-ROAD, BEFORE A FEARFUL, GROVELING PEASANT...
"...WHO WAS ALREADY BABBLING SOMETHING ABOUT A HOLY VISION...
"...EVEN AS WE DISAPPEARED, YET AGAIN...!
LOCKJAW! BY THE GENES OF AGON-- WHAT'S WRONG?
YOU ACT SO STRANGELY-- AS IF DRAWN BY SOMETHING--
--SOME UNGUESSED MESSAGE OUT OF THE VERY ETHER, THAT--
OHH!
"THEN, SUDDENLY, I GLANCED AROUND ME--
"-- AND SAW, DARKLY-- DIMLY-- A NIGHTMARE COME TRUE!
MUTANT FOOL! RUNNING TOWARD THAT WALL WILL NOT SAVE YOU!
I CAN MATCH YOUR SPEED. THUS, IF YOU CAN STOP YOURSELF BEFORE YOU STRIKE IT --
SO CAN A SENTINEL!*
*THAT'S RIGHT, RANGER! CRYSTAL AND HER CONFUSED CANINE WERE ATTRACTED BY EMANATIONS EXPLAINED IN AVENGERS #104! --ROY.
"BUT, THE HURTLING, SILVER-GARBED FORM DID NOT HALT IN TIME--
"AND SO, NEITHER DID HIS CYCLOPEAN PURSUER!

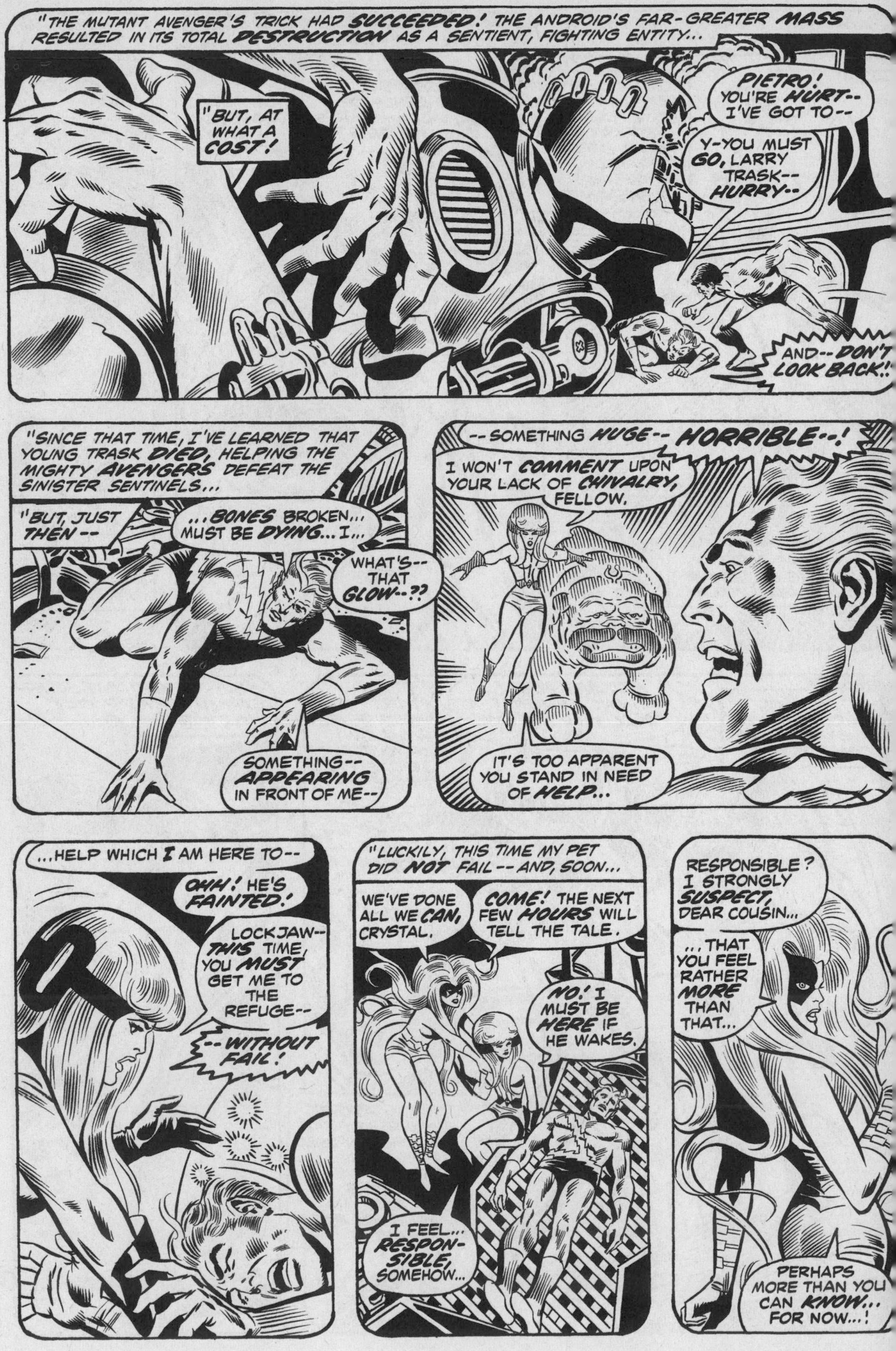
"THE MUTANT AVENGER'S TRICK HAD SUCCEEDED! THE ANDROID'S FAR-GREATER MASS RESULTED IN ITS TOTAL DESTRUCTION AS A SENTIENT, FIGHTING ENTITY...
"BUT, AT WHAT A COST!
PIETRO! YOU'RE HURT-- I'VE GOT TO--
Y-YOU MUST GO, LARRY TRASK-- HURRY--
AND-- DON'T LOOK BACK!
"SINCE THAT TIME, I'VE LEARNED THAT YOUNG TRASK DIED, HELPING THE MIGHTY AVENGERS DEFEAT THE SINISTER SENTINELS...
"BUT, JUST THEN--
...BONES BROKEN... MUST BE DYING... I...
WHAT'S-- THAT GLOW--??
SOMETHING-- APPEARING IN FRONT OF ME--
--SOMETHING HUGE-- HORRIBLE--!
I WON'T COMMENT UPON YOUR LACK OF CHIVALRY, FELLOW.
IT'S TOO APPARENT YOU STAND IN NEED OF HELP...
...HELP WHICH I AM HERE TO--
OHH! HE'S FAINTED!
LOCKJAW-- THIS TIME, YOU MUST GET ME TO THE REFUGE--
--WITHOUT FAIL!
"LUCKILY, THIS TIME MY PET DID NOT FAIL-- AND, SOON...
WE'VE DONE ALL WE CAN, CRYSTAL.
COME! THE NEXT FEW HOURS WILL TELL THE TALE.
NO! I MUST BE HERE IF HE WAKES.
I FEEL... RESPONSIBLE, SOMEHOW...
RESPONSIBLE? I STRONGLY SUSPECT, DEAR COUSIN...
...THAT YOU FEEL RATHER MORE THAN THAT...
PERHAPS MORE THAN YOU CAN KNOW... FOR NOW...!

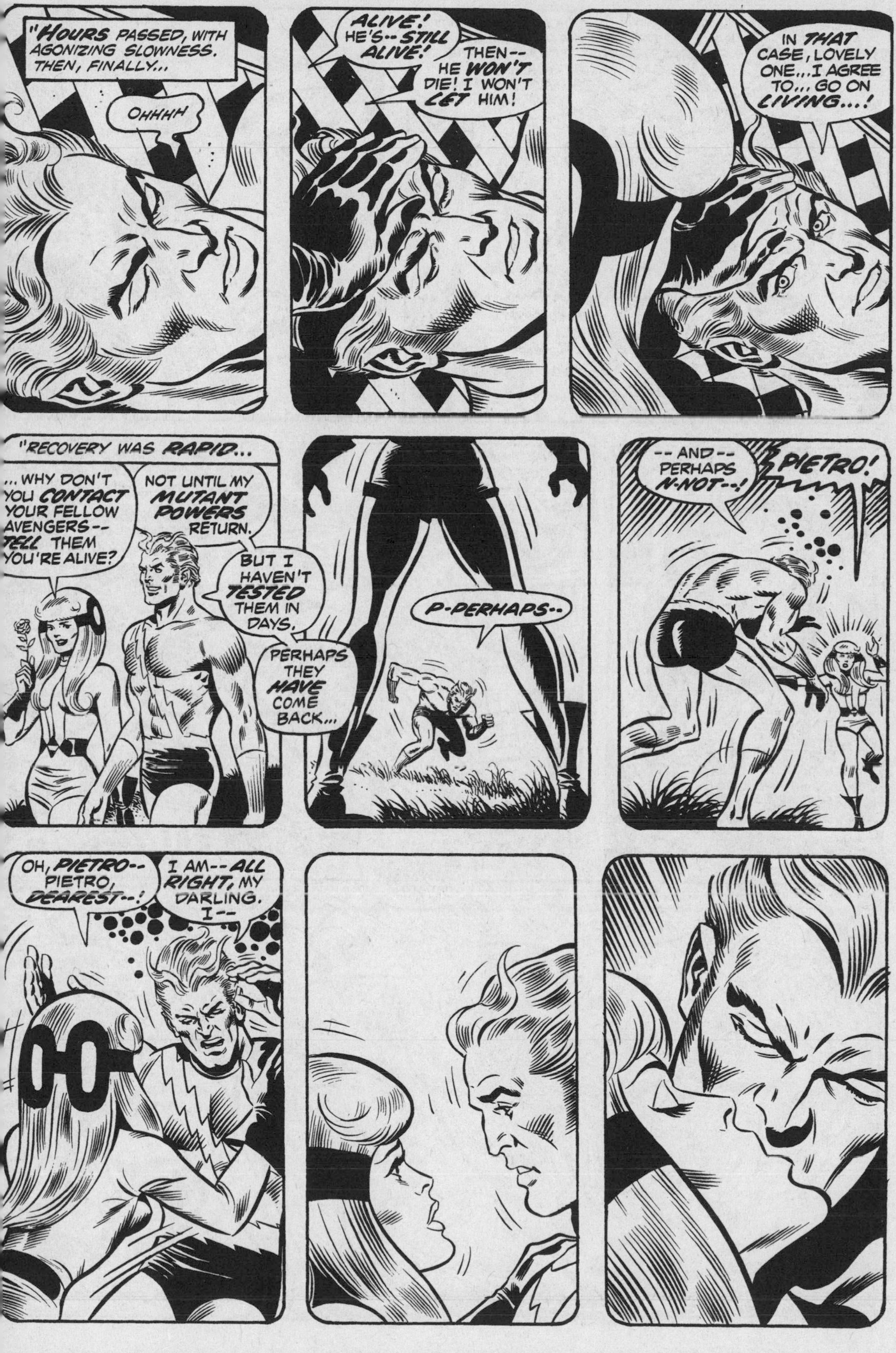
"HOURS PASSED, WITH AGONIZING SLOWNESS. THEN, FINALLY...
OHHHH
ALIVE! HE'S--STILL ALIVE!
THEN--HE WON'T DIE! I WON'T LET HIM!
IN THAT CASE, LOVELY ONE...I AGREE TO...GO ON LIVING...!
"RECOVERY WAS RAPID...
...WHY DON'T YOU CONTACT YOUR FELLOW AVENGERS--TELL THEM YOU'RE ALIVE?
NOT UNTIL MY MUTANT POWERS RETURN.
BUT I HAVEN'T TESTED THEM IN DAYS.
PERHAPS THEY HAVE COME BACK...
P-PERHAPS--
--AND--PERHAPS N-NOT--!
PIETRO!
OH, PIETRO--PIETRO, DEAREST--!
I AM--ALL RIGHT, MY DARLING. I--

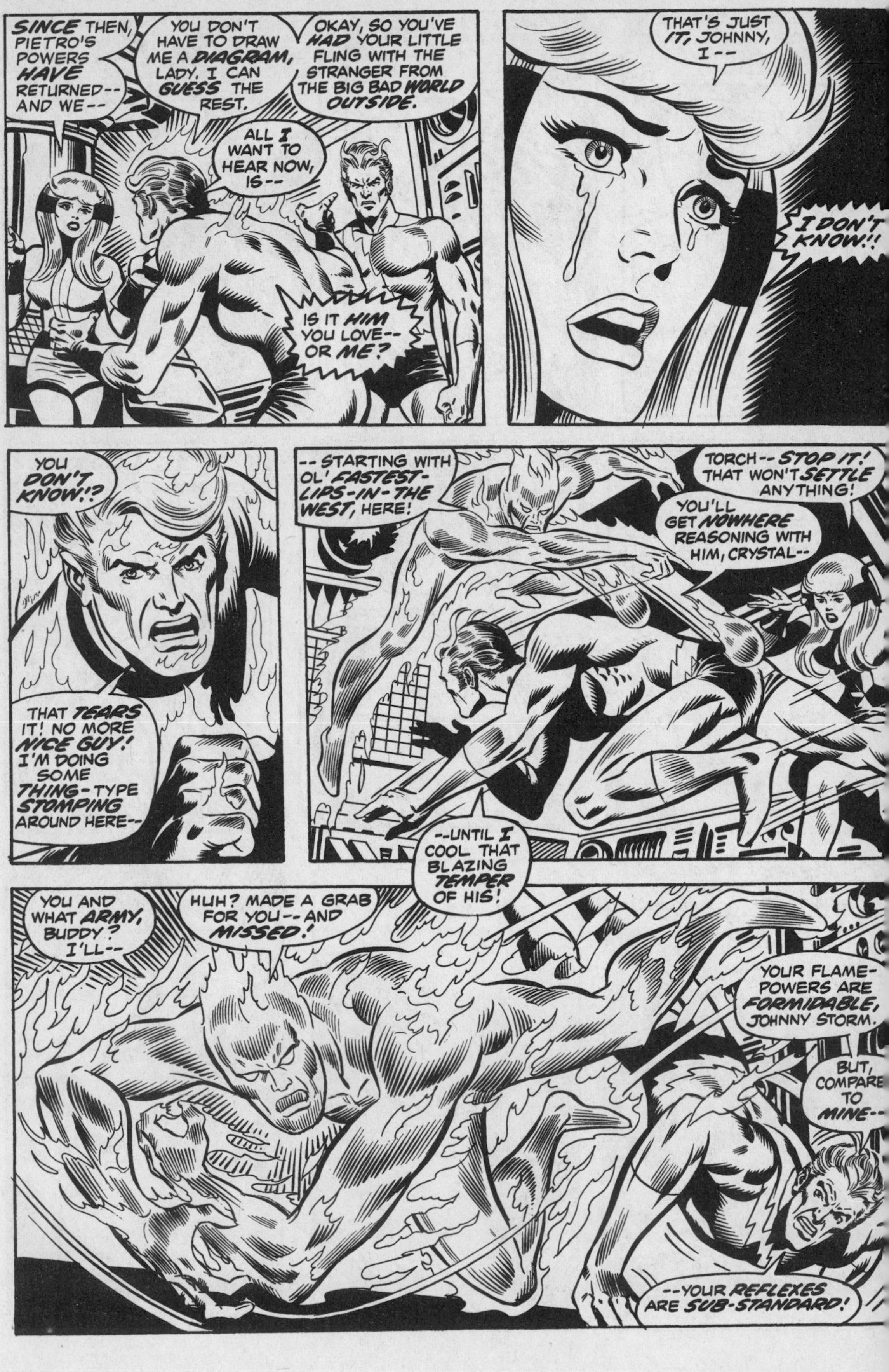
SINCE THEN, PIETRO'S POWERS HAVE RETURNED-- AND WE--
YOU DON'T HAVE TO DRAW ME A DIAGRAM, LADY. I CAN GUESS THE REST.
OKAY, SO YOU'VE HAD YOUR LITTLE FLING WITH THE STRANGER FROM THE BIG BAD WORLD OUTSIDE.
ALL I WANT TO HEAR NOW, IS--
IS IT HIM YOU LOVE-- OR ME?
THAT'S JUST IT, JOHNNY, I--
I DON'T KNOW!!
YOU DON'T KNOW!?
THAT TEARS IT! NO MORE NICE GUY! I'M DOING SOME THING-TYPE STOMPING AROUND HERE--
-- STARTING WITH OL' FASTEST-LIPS-IN-THE WEST, HERE!
TORCH-- STOP IT! THAT WON'T SETTLE ANYTHING!
YOU'LL GET NOWHERE REASONING WITH HIM, CRYSTAL--
--UNTIL I COOL THAT BLAZING TEMPER OF HIS!
YOU AND WHAT ARMY, BUDDY? I'LL--
HUH? MADE A GRAB FOR YOU-- AND MISSED!
YOUR FLAME-POWERS ARE FORMIDABLE, JOHNNY STORM.
BUT, COMPARE TO MINE--
--YOUR REFLEXES ARE SUB-STANDARD!

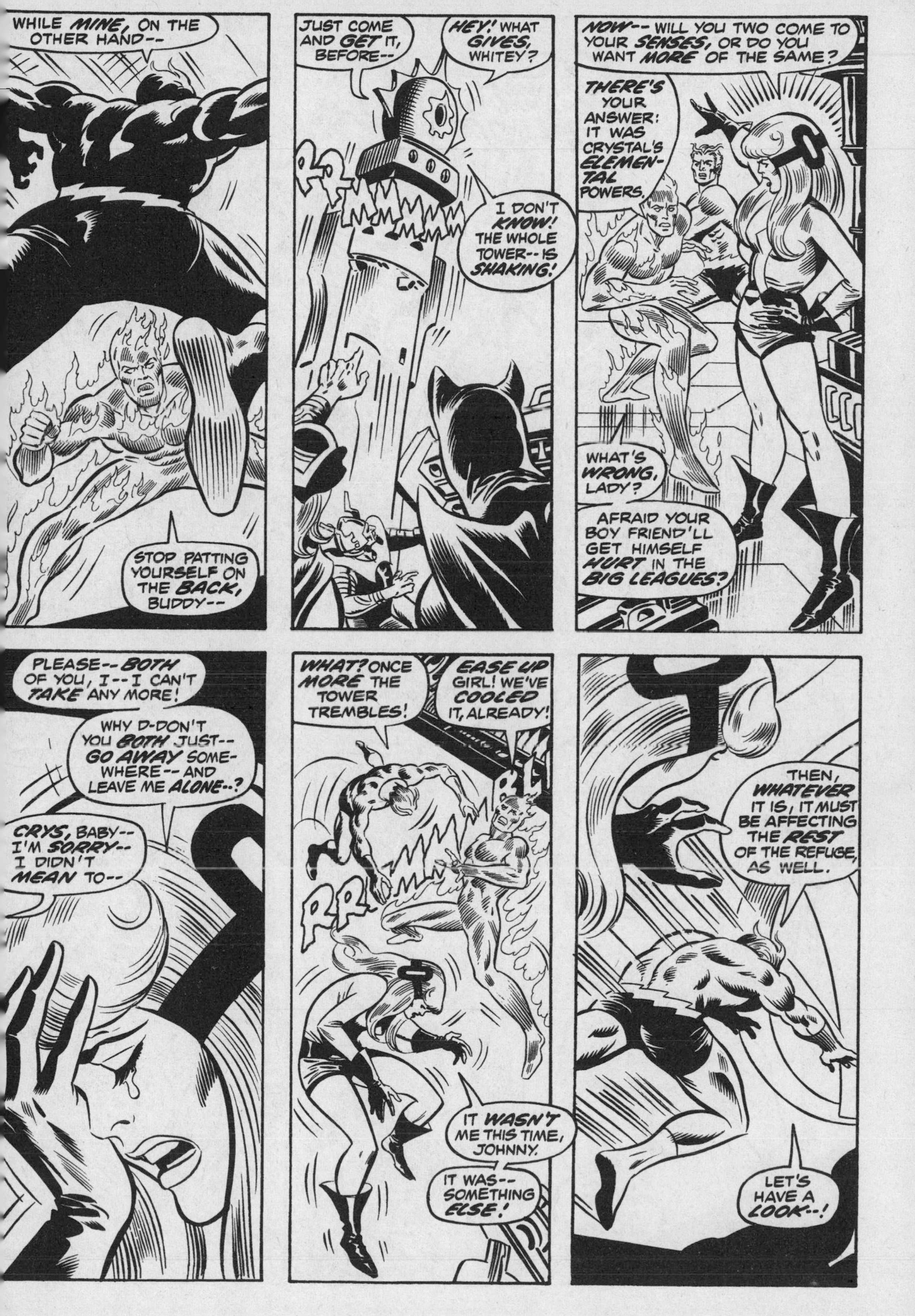
WHILE MINE, ON THE OTHER HAND--
STOP PATTING YOURSELF ON THE BACK, BUDDY--
JUST COME AND GET IT, BEFORE--
HEY! WHAT GIVES, WHITEY?
RR
I DON'T KNOW! THE WHOLE TOWER--IS SHAKING!
NOW-- WILL YOU TWO COME TO YOUR SENSES, OR DO YOU WANT MORE OF THE SAME?
THERE'S YOUR ANSWER: IT WAS CRYSTAL'S ELEMENTAL POWERS.
WHAT'S WRONG, LADY?
AFRAID YOUR BOY FRIEND'LL GET HIMSELF HURT IN THE BIG LEAGUES?
PLEASE-- BOTH OF YOU, I-- I CAN'T TAKE ANY MORE!
WHY D-DON'T YOU BOTH JUST-- GO AWAY SOMEWHERE-- AND LEAVE ME ALONE--?
CRYS, BABY-- I'M SORRY-- I DIDN'T MEAN TO--
WHAT? ONCE MORE THE TOWER TREMBLES!
EASE UP GIRL! WE'VE COOLED IT, ALREADY!
RR
IT WASN'T ME THIS TIME, JOHNNY.
IT WAS-- SOMETHING ELSE!
THEN, WHATEVER IT IS, IT MUST BE AFFECTING THE REST OF THE REFUGE, AS WELL.
LET'S HAVE A LOOK--!

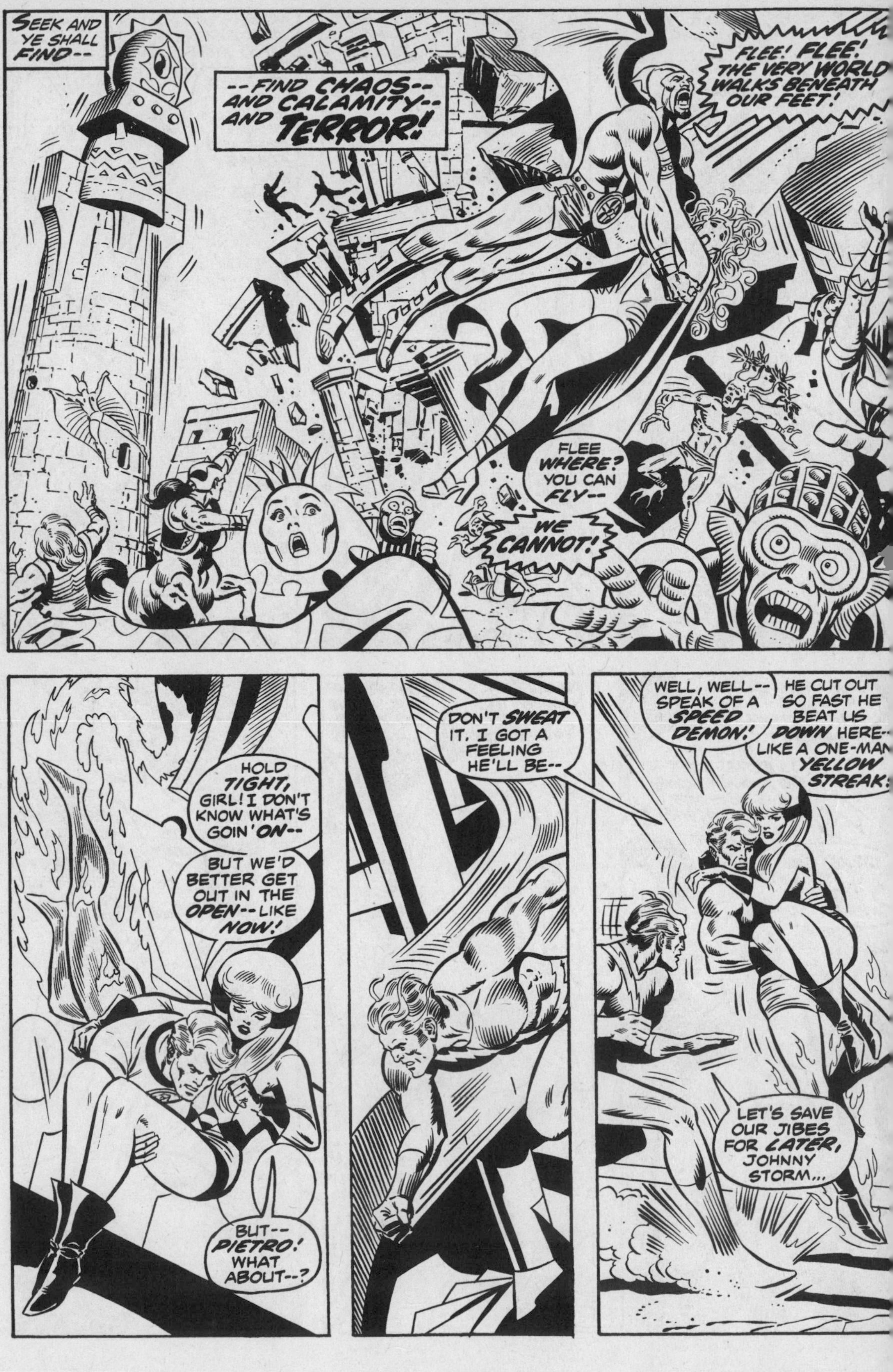
SEEK AND YE SHALL FIND--
--FIND CHAOS-- AND CALAMITY-- AND TERROR!
FLEE! FLEE! THE VERY WORLD WALKS BENEATH OUR FEET!
FLEE WHERE? YOU CAN FLY--
WE CANNOT!
HOLD TIGHT, GIRL! I DON'T KNOW WHAT'S GOIN' ON--
BUT WE'D BETTER GET OUT IN THE OPEN--LIKE NOW!
BUT-- PIETRO! WHAT ABOUT--?
DON'T SWEAT IT. I GOT A FEELING HE'LL BE--
WELL, WELL-- SPEAK OF A SPEED DEMON!
HE CUT OUT SO FAST HE BEAT US DOWN HERE-- LIKE A ONE-MAN YELLOW STREAK!
LET'S SAVE OUR JIBES FOR LATER, JOHNNY STORM...

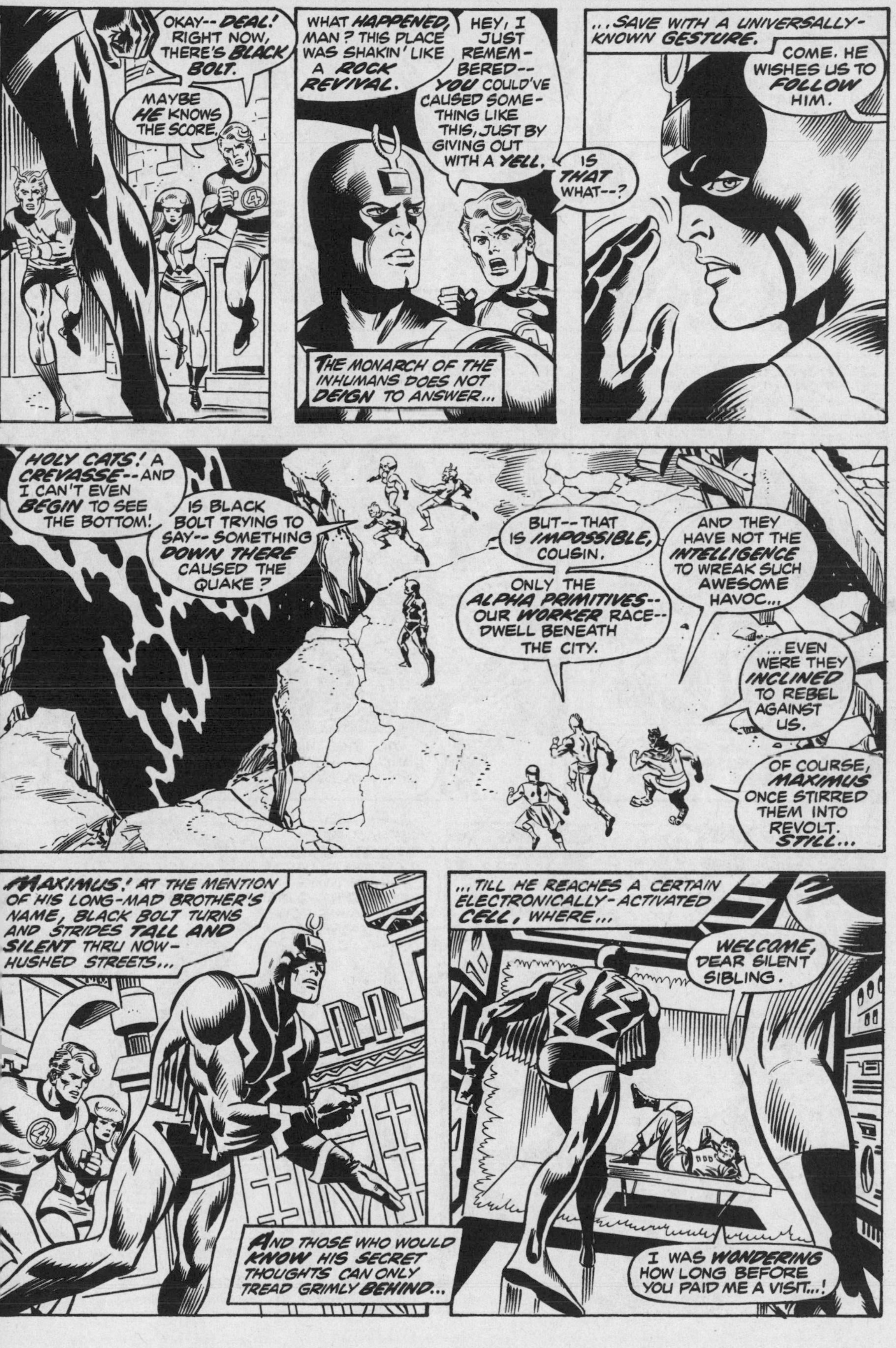
OKAY--DEAL! RIGHT NOW, THERE'S BLACK BOLT.
MAYBE HE KNOWS THE SCORE.
WHAT HAPPENED, MAN? THIS PLACE WAS SHAKIN' LIKE A ROCK REVIVAL.
HEY, I JUST REMEMBERED-- YOU COULD'VE CAUSED SOMETHING LIKE THIS, JUST BY GIVING OUT WITH A YELL.
IS THAT WHAT--?
THE MONARCH OF THE INHUMANS DOES NOT DEIGN TO ANSWER...
...SAVE WITH A UNIVERSALLY-KNOWN GESTURE.
COME. HE WISHES US TO FOLLOW HIM.
HOLY CATS! A CREVASSE--AND I CAN'T EVEN BEGIN TO SEE THE BOTTOM!
IS BLACK BOLT TRYING TO SAY-- SOMETHING DOWN THERE CAUSED THE QUAKE?
BUT--THAT IS IMPOSSIBLE, COUSIN.
ONLY THE ALPHA PRIMITIVES-- OUR WORKER RACE-- DWELL BENEATH THE CITY.
AND THEY HAVE NOT THE INTELLIGENCE TO WREAK SUCH AWESOME HAVOC...
...EVEN WERE THEY INCLINED TO REBEL AGAINST US.
OF COURSE, MAXIMUS ONCE STIRRED THEM INTO REVOLT. STILL...
MAXIMUS! AT THE MENTION OF HIS LONG-MAD BROTHER'S NAME, BLACK BOLT TURNS AND STRIDES TALL AND SILENT THRU NOW-HUSHED STREETS...
AND THOSE WHO WOULD KNOW HIS SECRET THOUGHTS CAN ONLY TREAD GRIMLY BEHIND...
...TILL HE REACHES A CERTAIN ELECTRONICALLY-ACTIVATED CELL, WHERE...
WELCOME, DEAR SILENT SIBLING.
I WAS WONDERING HOW LONG BEFORE YOU PAID ME A VISIT...!

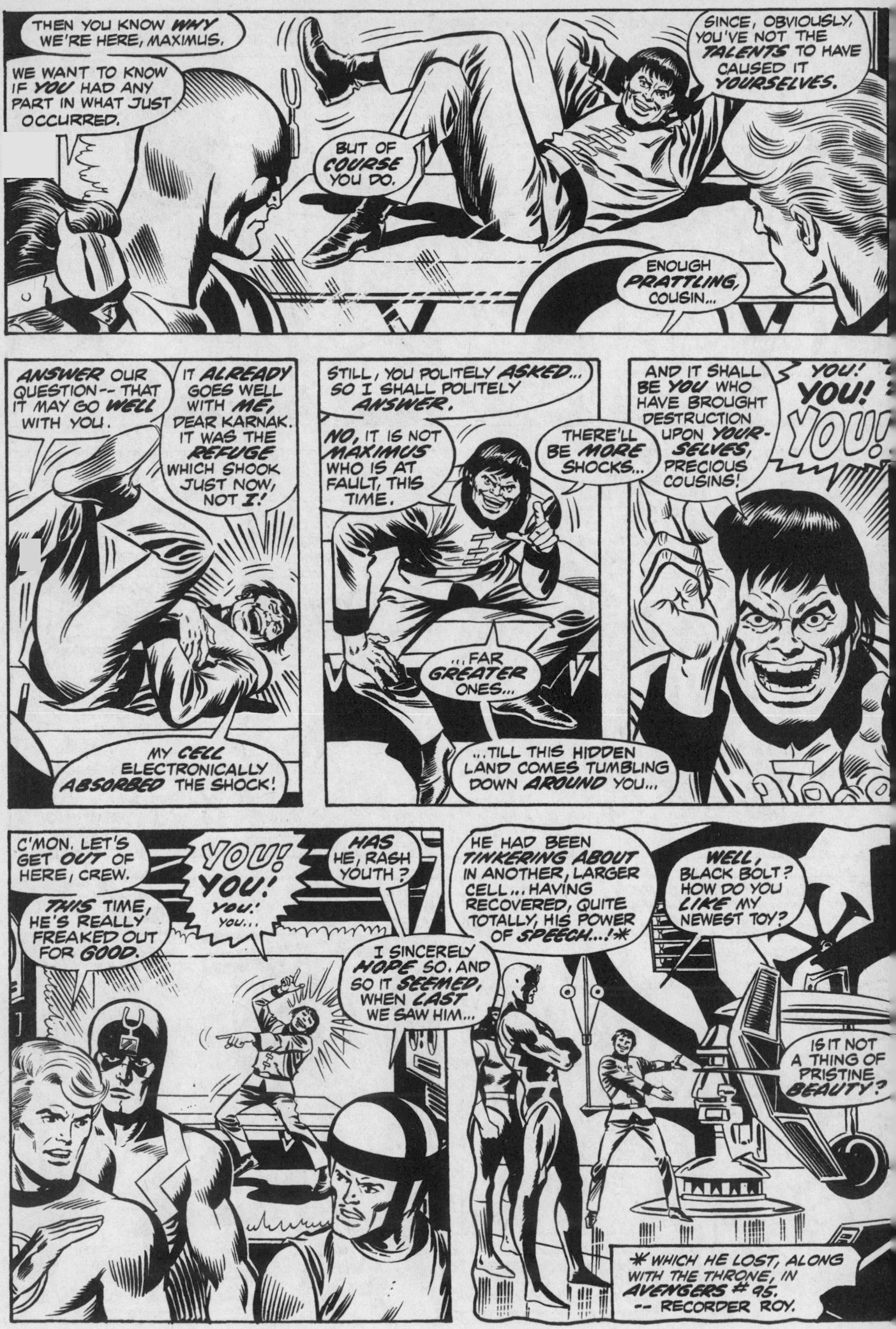
THEN YOU KNOW WHY WE'RE HERE, MAXIMUS.
WE WANT TO KNOW IF YOU HAD ANY PART IN WHAT JUST OCCURRED.
BUT OF COURSE YOU DO.
SINCE, OBVIOUSLY, YOU'VE NOT THE TALENTS TO HAVE CAUSED IT YOURSELVES.
ENOUGH PRATTLING, COUSIN...
ANSWER OUR QUESTION-- THAT IT MAY GO WELL WITH YOU.
IT ALREADY GOES WELL WITH ME, DEAR KARNAK. IT WAS THE REFUGE WHICH SHOOK JUST NOW, NOT I!
MY CELL ELECTRONICALLY ABSORBED THE SHOCK!
STILL, YOU POLITELY ASKED... SO I SHALL POLITELY ANSWER.
NO, IT IS NOT MAXIMUS WHO IS AT FAULT, THIS TIME.
THERE'LL BE MORE SHOCKS...
...FAR GREATER ONES...
...TILL THIS HIDDEN LAND COMES TUMBLING DOWN AROUND YOU...
AND IT SHALL BE YOU WHO HAVE BROUGHT DESTRUCTION UPON YOURSELVES, PRECIOUS COUSINS!
YOU! YOU! YOU!
C'MON. LET'S GET OUT OF HERE, CREW.
THIS TIME, HE'S REALLY FREAKED OUT FOR GOOD.
YOU! YOU! YOU! YOU...
HAS HE, RASH YOUTH?
I SINCERELY HOPE SO. AND SO IT SEEMED, WHEN LAST WE SAW HIM...
HE HAD BEEN TINKERING ABOUT IN ANOTHER, LARGER CELL... HAVING RECOVERED, QUITE TOTALLY, HIS POWER OF SPEECH...!*
WELL, BLACK BOLT? HOW DO YOU LIKE MY NEWEST TOY?
IS IT NOT A THING OF PRISTINE BEAUTY?
* WHICH HE LOST, ALONG WITH THE THRONE, IN AVENGERS #95. -- RECORDER ROY.

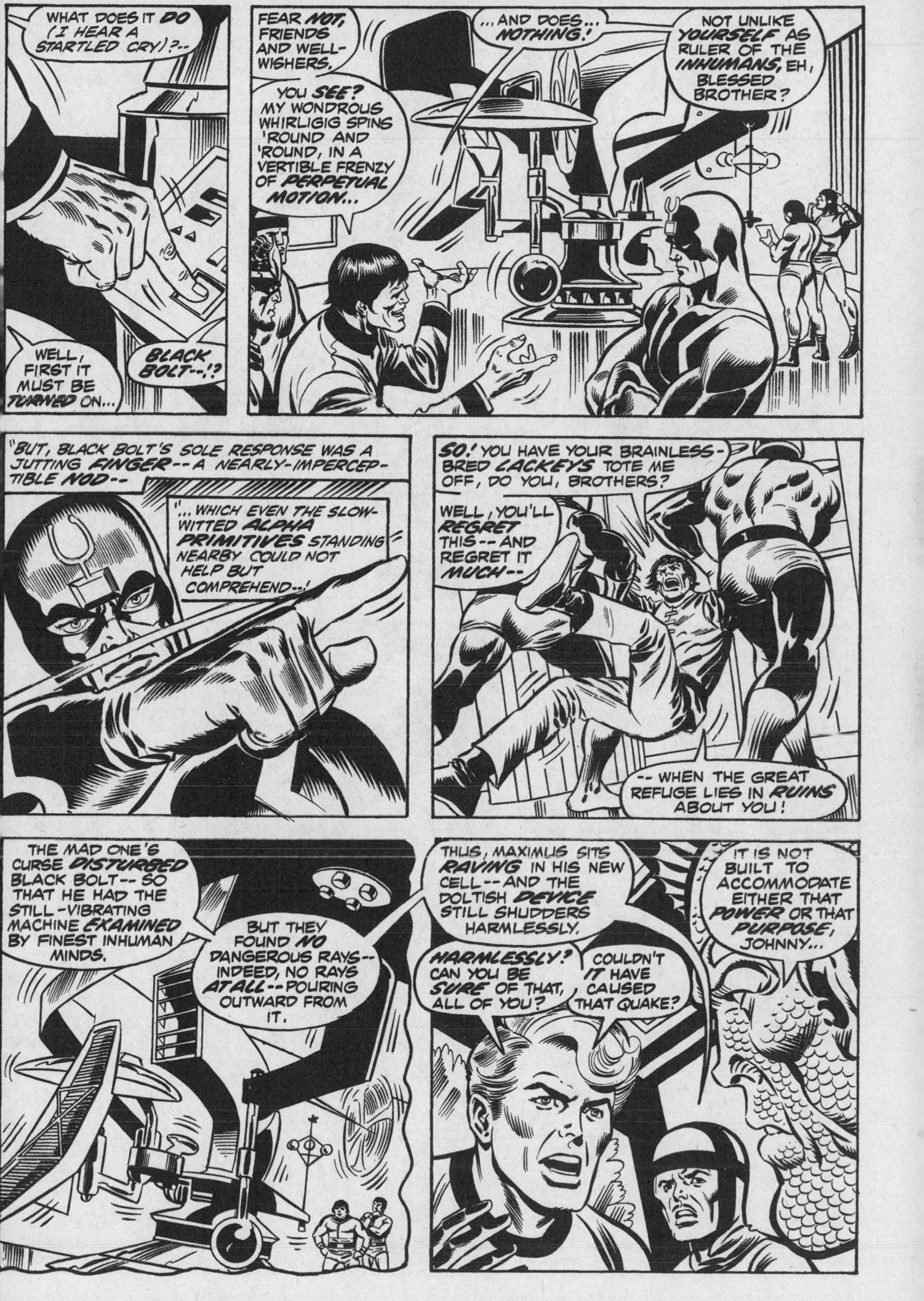
WHAT DOES IT DO (I HEAR A STARTLED CRY)?--
WELL, FIRST IT MUST BE TURNED ON...
BLACK BOLT--!?
FEAR NOT, FRIENDS AND WELL-WISHERS.
YOU SEE? MY WONDROUS WHIRLIGIG SPINS 'ROUND AND 'ROUND, IN A VERTIBLE FRENZY OF PERPETUAL MOTION...
...AND DOES... NOTHING!
NOT UNLIKE YOURSELF AS RULER OF THE INHUMANS, EH, BLESSED BROTHER?
"BUT, BLACK BOLT'S SOLE RESPONSE WAS A JUTTING FINGER-- A NEARLY-IMPERCEPTIBLE NOD--
"...WHICH EVEN THE SLOW-WITTED ALPHA PRIMITIVES STANDING NEARBY COULD NOT HELP BUT COMPREHEND...!
SO! YOU HAVE YOUR BRAINLESS-BRED LACKEYS TOTE ME OFF, DO YOU, BROTHERS?
WELL, YOU'LL REGRET THIS-- AND REGRET IT MUCH--
--WHEN THE GREAT REFUGE LIES IN RUINS ABOUT YOU!
THE MAD ONE'S CURSE DISTURBED BLACK BOLT-- SO THAT HE HAD THE STILL-VIBRATING MACHINE EXAMINED BY FINEST INHUMAN MINDS.
BUT THEY FOUND NO DANGEROUS RAYS-- INDEED, NO RAYS AT ALL-- POURING OUTWARD FROM IT.
THUS, MAXIMUS SITS RAVING IN HIS NEW CELL-- AND THE DOLTISH DEVICE STILL SHUDDERS HARMLESSLY.
HARMLESSLY? CAN YOU BE SURE OF THAT, ALL OF YOU?
COULDN'T IT HAVE CAUSED THAT QUAKE?
IT IS NOT BUILT TO ACCOMMODATE EITHER THAT POWER OR THAT PURPOSE, JOHNNY...

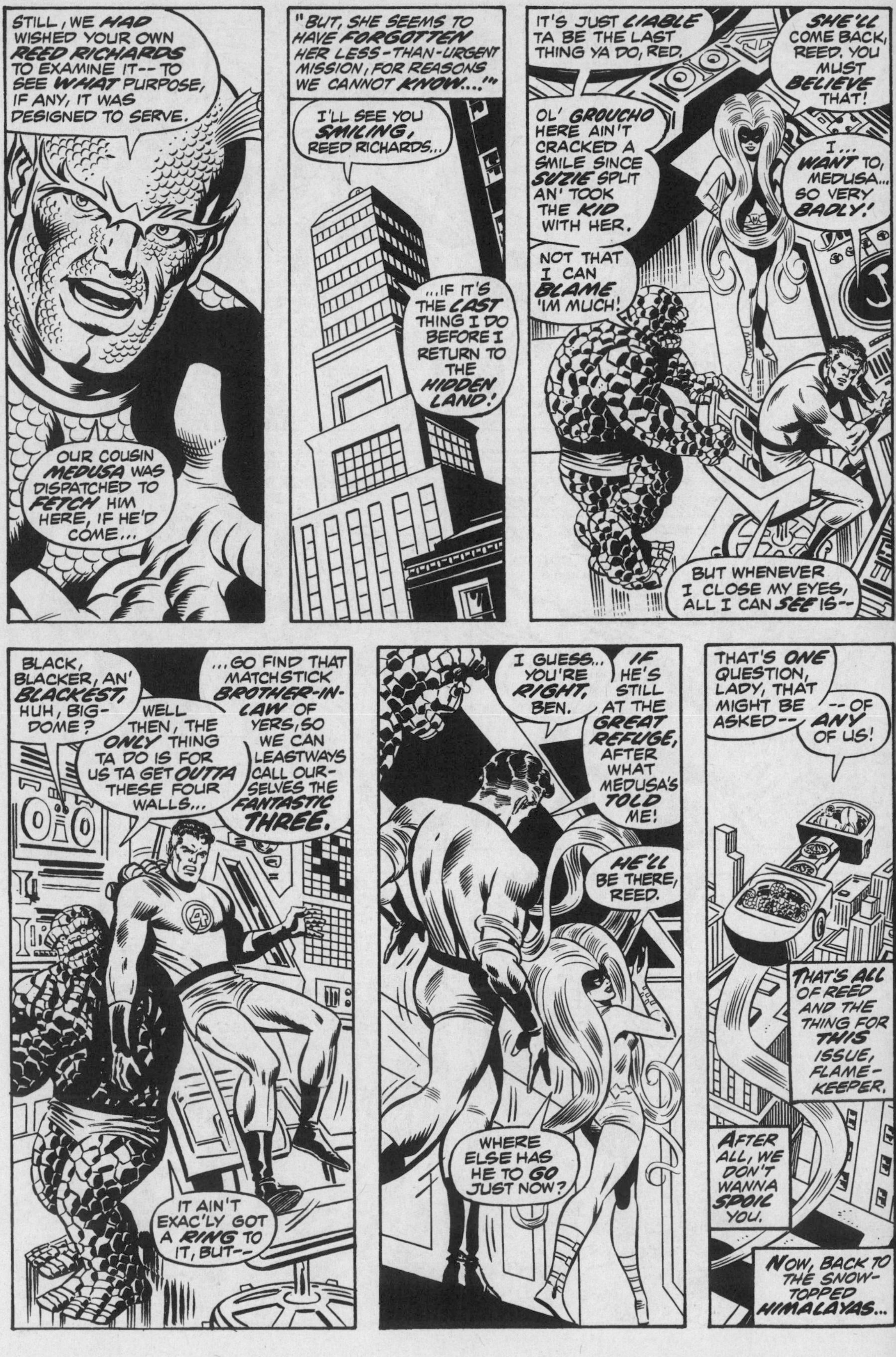
STILL, WE HAD WISHED YOUR OWN REED RICHARDS TO EXAMINE IT-- TO SEE WHAT PURPOSE, IF ANY, IT WAS DESIGNED TO SERVE.
OUR COUSIN MEDUSA WAS DISPATCHED TO FETCH HIM HERE, IF HE'D COME...
"BUT, SHE SEEMS TO HAVE FORGOTTEN HER LESS-THAN-URGENT MISSION, FOR REASONS WE CANNOT KNOW...!"
I'LL SEE YOU SMILING, REED RICHARDS...
...IF IT'S THE LAST THING I DO BEFORE I RETURN TO THE HIDDEN LAND!
IT'S JUST LIABLE TA BE THE LAST THING YA DO, RED.
OL' GROUCHO HERE AIN'T CRACKED A SMILE SINCE SUZIE SPLIT AN' TOOK THE KID WITH HER.
NOT THAT I CAN BLAME 'IM MUCH!
SHE'LL COME BACK, REED. YOU MUST BELIEVE THAT!
I... WANT TO, MEDUSA... SO VERY BADLY!
BUT WHENEVER I CLOSE MY EYES, ALL I CAN SEE IS--
BLACK, BLACKER, AN' BLACKEST, HUH, BIG-DOME?
WELL THEN, THE ONLY THING TA DO IS FOR US TA GET OUTTA THESE FOUR WALLS...
...GO FIND THAT MATCHSTICK BROTHER-IN-LAW OF YERS, SO WE CAN LEASTWAYS CALL OURSELVES THE FANTASTIC THREE.
IT AIN'T EXAC'LY GOT A RING TO IT, BUT--
I GUESS... YOU'RE RIGHT, BEN.
IF HE'S STILL AT THE GREAT REFUGE, AFTER WHAT MEDUSA'S TOLD ME!
HE'LL BE THERE, REED.
WHERE ELSE HAS HE TO GO JUST NOW?
THAT'S ONE QUESTION, LADY, THAT MIGHT BE ASKED--
-- OF ANY OF US!
THAT'S ALL OF REED AND THE THING FOR THIS ISSUE, FLAME-KEEPER.
AFTER ALL, WE DON'T WANNA SPOIL YOU.
NOW, BACK TO THE SNOW-TOPPED HIMALAYAS...

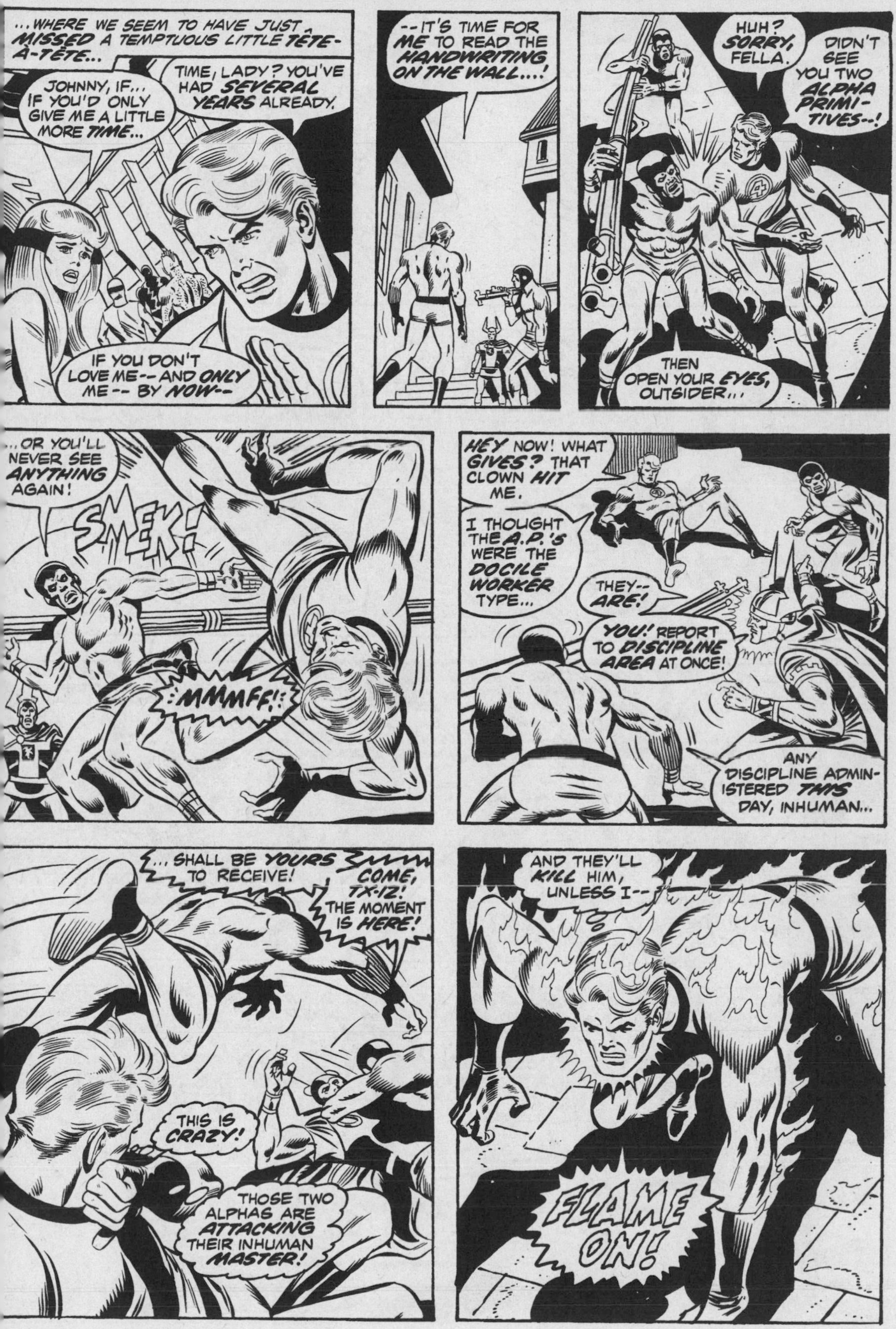

...WHERE WE SEEM TO HAVE JUST MISSED A TEMPTUOUS LITTLE TÊTE-À-TÊTE...
JOHNNY, IF... IF YOU'D ONLY GIVE ME A LITTLE MORE TIME...
TIME, LADY? YOU'VE HAD SEVERAL YEARS ALREADY.
IF YOU DON'T LOVE ME--AND ONLY ME-- BY NOW--
--IT'S TIME FOR ME TO READ THE HANDWRITING ON THE WALL...!
HUH? SORRY, FELLA.
DIDN'T SEE YOU TWO ALPHA PRIMITIVES--!
THEN OPEN YOUR EYES, OUTSIDER...
...OR YOU'LL NEVER SEE ANYTHING AGAIN!
SMEK!
MMMFF!
HEY NOW! WHAT GIVES? THAT CLOWN HIT ME.
I THOUGHT THE A.P.'S WERE THE DOCILE WORKER TYPE...
THEY--ARE!
YOU! REPORT TO DISCIPLINE AREA AT ONCE!
ANY DISCIPLINE ADMINISTERED THIS DAY, INHUMAN...
...SHALL BE YOURS TO RECEIVE!
COME, TX-12! THE MOMENT IS HERE!
THIS IS CRAZY!
THOSE TWO ALPHAS ARE ATTACKING THEIR INHUMAN MASTER!
AND THEY'LL KILL HIM, UNLESS I--
FLAME ON!

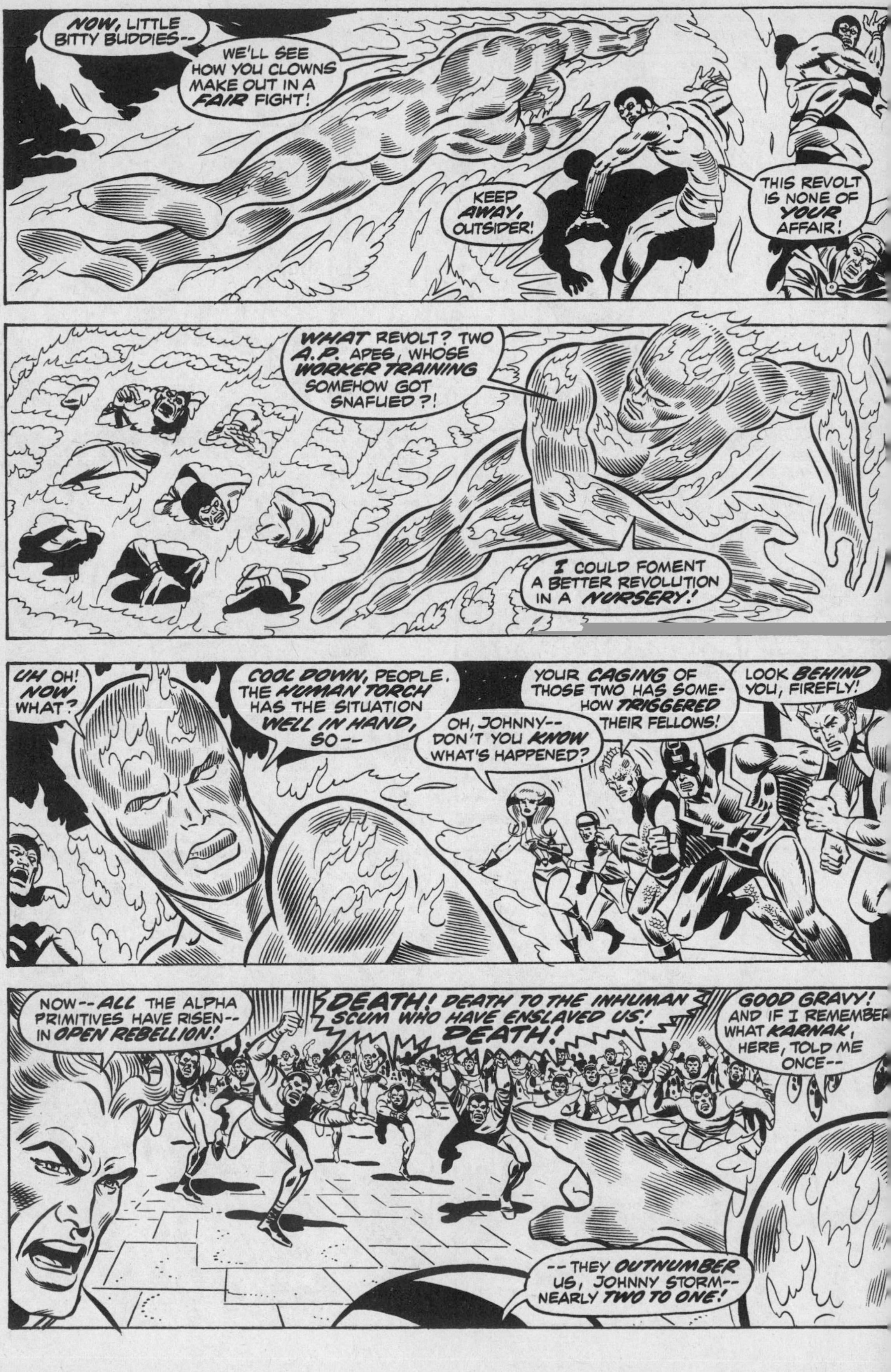
NOW, LITTLE BITTY BUDDIES--
WE'LL SEE HOW YOU CLOWNS MAKE OUT IN A FAIR FIGHT!
KEEP AWAY, OUTSIDER!
THIS REVOLT IS NONE OF YOUR AFFAIR!
WHAT REVOLT? TWO A.P. APES, WHOSE WORKER TRAINING SOMEHOW GOT SNAFUED?!
I COULD FOMENT A BETTER REVOLUTION IN A NURSERY!
UH OH! NOW WHAT?
COOL DOWN, PEOPLE. THE HUMAN TORCH HAS THE SITUATION WELL IN HAND, SO--
OH, JOHNNY-- DON'T YOU KNOW WHAT'S HAPPENED?
YOUR CAGING OF THOSE TWO HAS SOMEHOW TRIGGERED THEIR FELLOWS!
LOOK BEHIND YOU, FIREFLY!
NOW--ALL THE ALPHA PRIMITIVES HAVE RISEN--IN OPEN REBELLION!
DEATH! DEATH TO THE INHUMAN SCUM WHO HAVE ENSLAVED US! DEATH!
GOOD GRAVY! AND IF I REMEMBER WHAT KARNAK, HERE, TOLD ME ONCE--
--THEY OUTNUMBER US, JOHNNY STORM-- NEARLY TWO TO ONE!

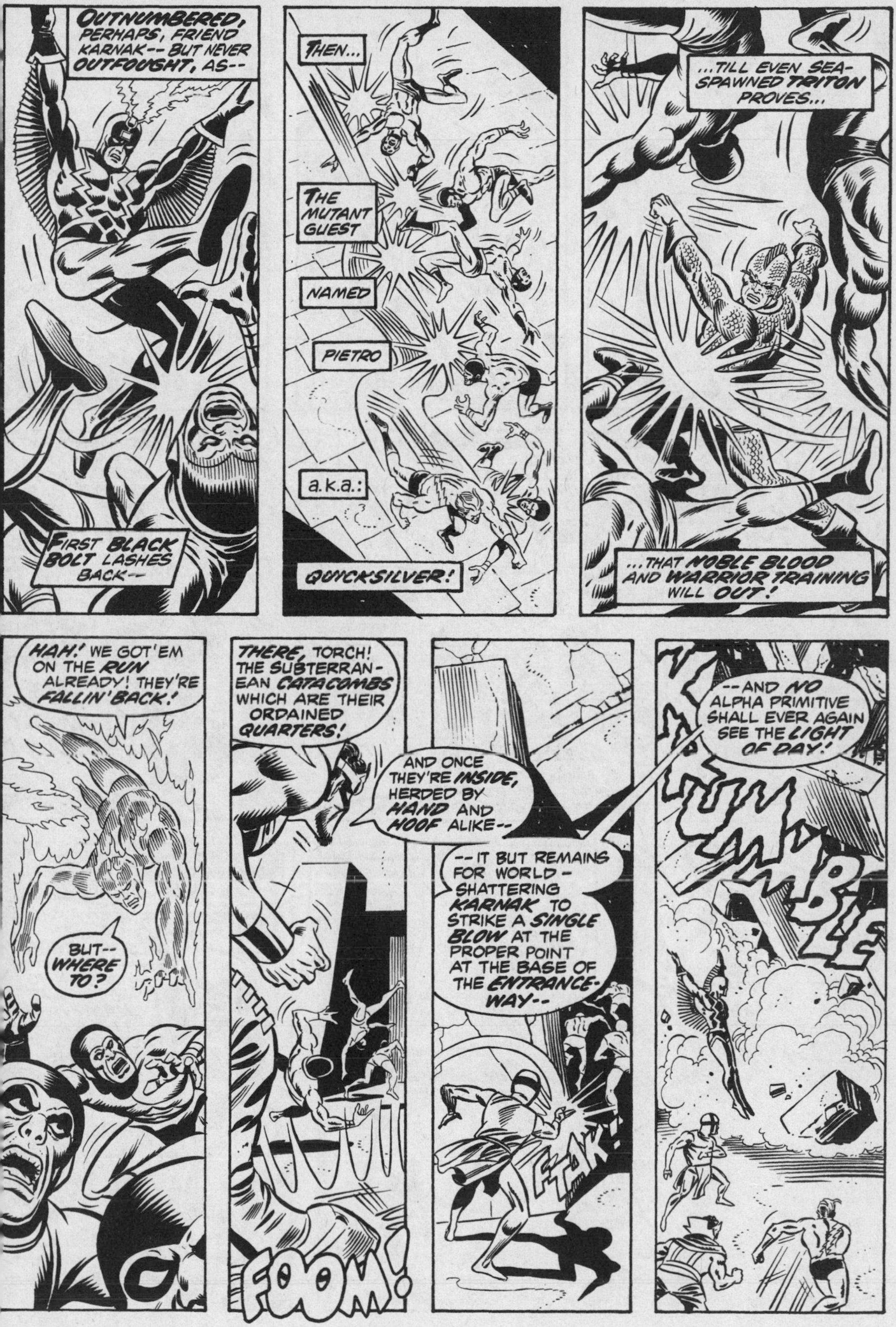

OUTNUMBERED, PERHAPS, FRIEND KARNAK-- BUT NEVER OUTFOUGHT, AS--
FIRST BLACK BOLT LASHES BACK--
THEN...
THE MUTANT GUEST
NAMED
PIETRO
a.k.a.:
QUICKSILVER!
...TILL EVEN SEA-SPAWNED TRITON PROVES...
...THAT NOBLE BLOOD AND WARRIOR TRAINING WILL OUT!
HAH! WE GOT'EM ON THE RUN ALREADY! THEY'RE FALLIN' BACK!
BUT-- WHERE TO?
THERE, TORCH! THE SUBTERRANEAN CATACOMBS WHICH ARE THEIR ORDAINED QUARTERS!
FOOM!
AND ONCE THEY'RE INSIDE, HERDED BY HAND AND HOOF ALIKE--
--IT BUT REMAINS FOR WORLD-SHATTERING KARNAK TO STRIKE A SINGLE BLOW AT THE PROPER POINT AT THE BASE OF THE ENTRANCE-WAY--
--AND NO ALPHA PRIMITIVE SHALL EVER AGAIN SEE THE LIGHT OF DAY!
RUMBLE

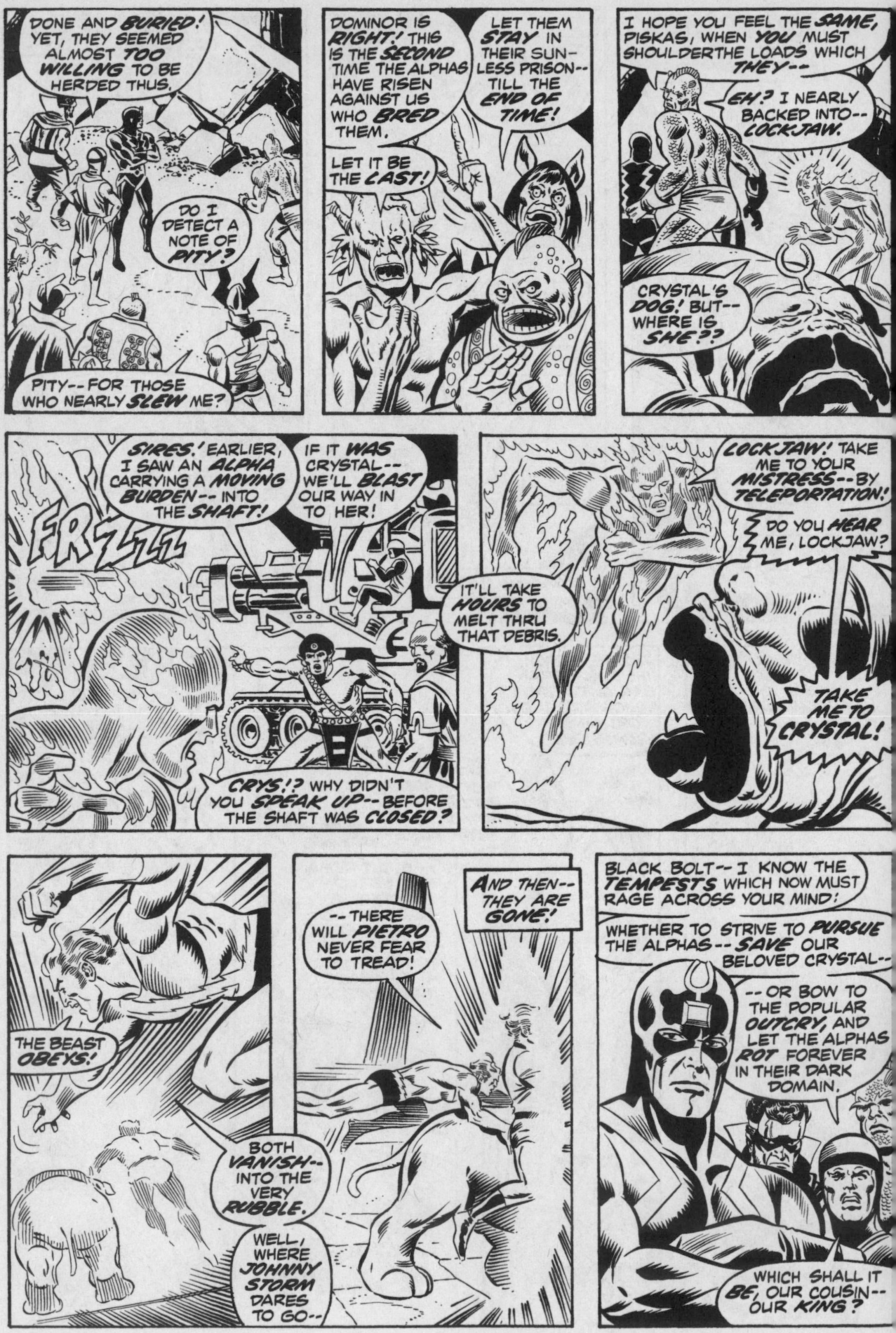

DONE AND BURIED! YET, THEY SEEMED ALMOST TOO WILLING TO BE HERDED THUS.
DO I DETECT A NOTE OF PITY?
PITY--FOR THOSE WHO NEARLY SLEW ME?
DOMINOR IS RIGHT! THIS IS THE SECOND TIME THE ALPHAS HAVE RISEN AGAINST US WHO BRED THEM.
LET THEM STAY IN THEIR SUN-LESS PRISON--TILL THE END OF TIME!
LET IT BE THE LAST!
I HOPE YOU FEEL THE SAME, PISKAS, WHEN YOU MUST SHOULDERTHE LOADS WHICH THEY--
EH? I NEARLY BACKED INTO--LOCKJAW.
CRYSTAL'S DOG! BUT--WHERE IS SHE??
SIRES! EARLIER, I SAW AN ALPHA CARRYING A MOVING BURDEN--INTO THE SHAFT!
IF IT WAS CRYSTAL--WE'LL BLAST OUR WAY IN TO HER!
FRZZZ
IT'LL TAKE HOURS TO MELT THRU THAT DEBRIS.
CRYS!? WHY DIDN'T YOU SPEAK UP--BEFORE THE SHAFT WAS CLOSED?
LOCKJAW! TAKE ME TO YOUR MISTRESS--BY TELEPORTATION!
DO YOU HEAR ME, LOCKJAW?
TAKE ME TO CRYSTAL!
THE BEAST OBEYS!
BOTH VANISH--INTO THE VERY RUBBLE.
WELL, WHERE JOHNNY STORM DARES TO GO--
--THERE WILL PIETRO NEVER FEAR TO TREAD!
AND THEN--THEY ARE GONE!
BLACK BOLT--I KNOW THE TEMPESTS WHICH NOW MUST RAGE ACROSS YOUR MIND:
WHETHER TO STRIVE TO PURSUE THE ALPHAS--SAVE OUR BELOVED CRYSTAL--
--OR BOW TO THE POPULAR OUTCRY, AND LET THE ALPHAS ROT FOREVER IN THEIR DARK DOMAIN.
WHICH SHALL IT BE, OUR COUSIN--OUR KING?

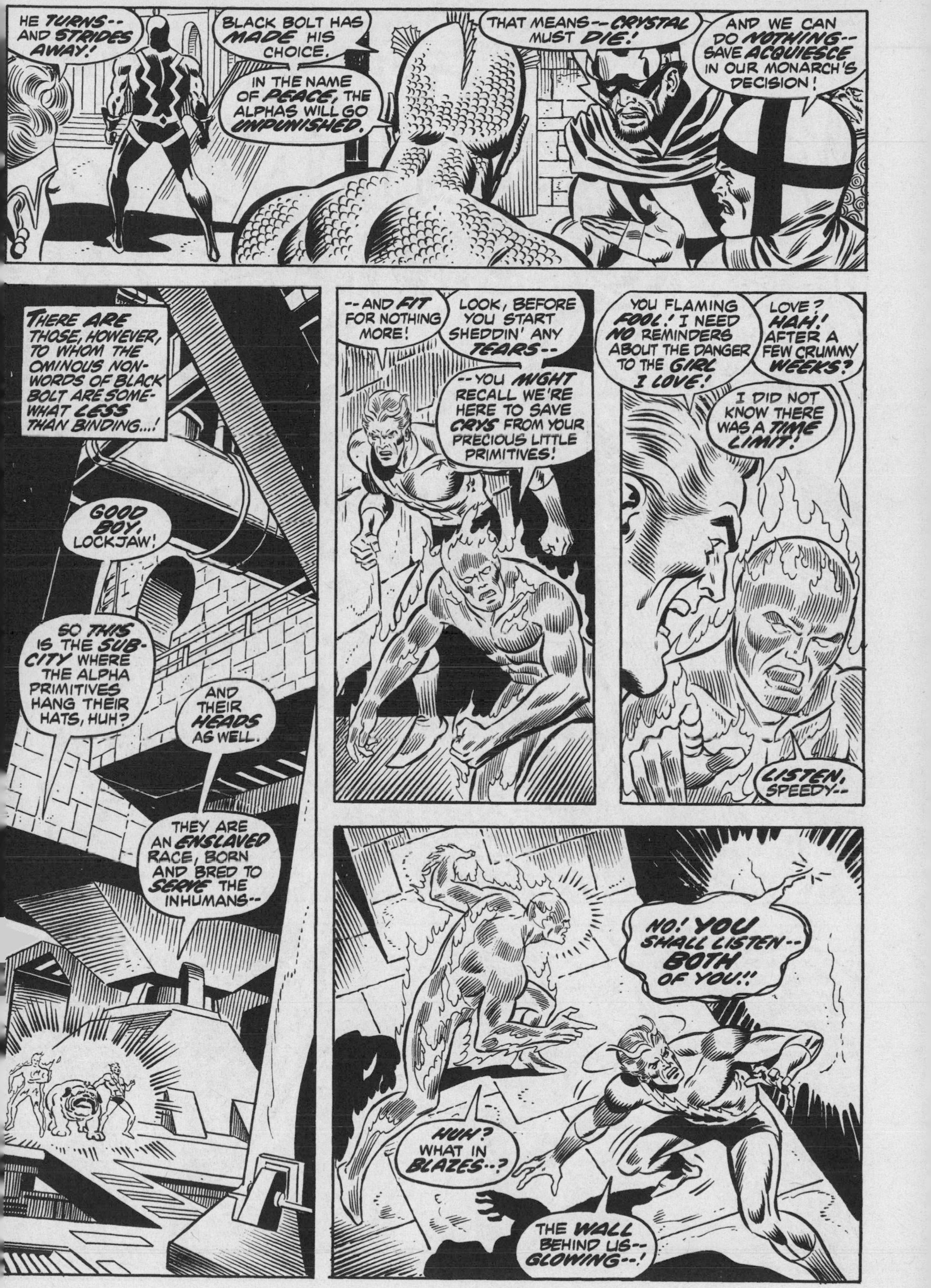

HE TURNS-- AND STRIDES AWAY!
BLACK BOLT HAS MADE HIS CHOICE.
IN THE NAME OF PEACE, THE ALPHAS WILL GO UNPUNISHED.
THAT MEANS--CRYSTAL MUST DIE!
AND WE CAN DO NOTHING-- SAVE ACQUIESCE IN OUR MONARCH'S DECISION!
THERE ARE THOSE, HOWEVER, TO WHOM THE OMINOUS NON-WORDS OF BLACK BOLT ARE SOME-WHAT LESS THAN BINDING...!
GOOD BOY, LOCKJAW!
SO THIS IS THE SUB-CITY WHERE THE ALPHA PRIMITIVES HANG THEIR HATS, HUH?
AND THEIR HEADS AS WELL.
THEY ARE AN ENSLAVED RACE, BORN AND BRED TO SERVE THE INHUMANS--
--AND FIT FOR NOTHING MORE!
LOOK, BEFORE YOU START SHEDDIN' ANY TEARS--
--YOU MIGHT RECALL WE'RE HERE TO SAVE CRYS FROM YOUR PRECIOUS LITTLE PRIMITIVES!
YOU FLAMING FOOL! I NEED NO REMINDERS ABOUT THE DANGER TO THE GIRL I LOVE!
LOVE? HAH! AFTER A FEW CRUMMY WEEKS?
I DID NOT KNOW THERE WAS A TIME LIMIT!
LISTEN, SPEEDY--
NO! YOU SHALL LISTEN-- BOTH OF YOU!!
HUH? WHAT IN BLAZES--?
THE WALL BEHIND US-- GLOWING--!

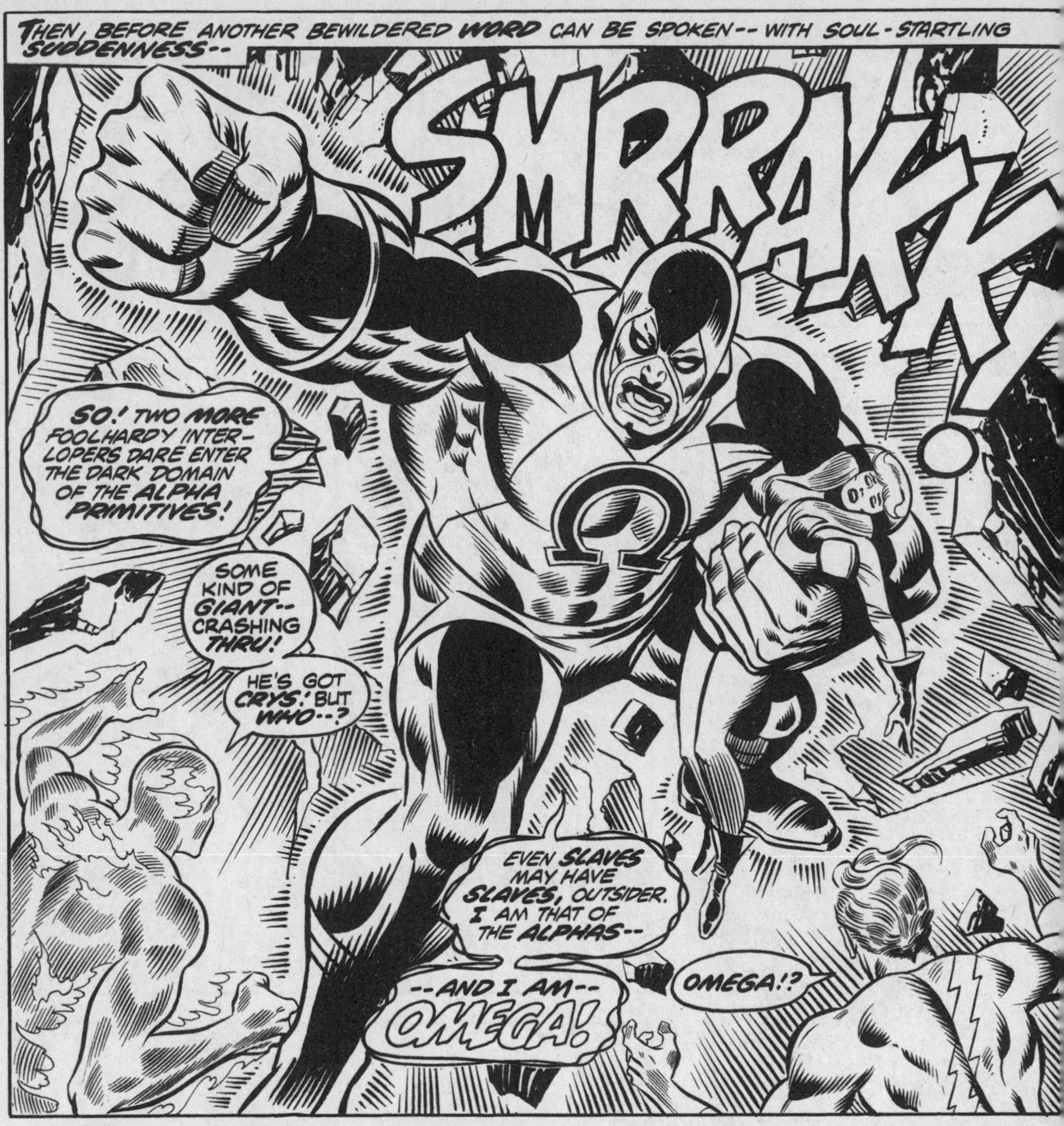
THEN, BEFORE ANOTHER BEWILDERED WORD CAN BE SPOKEN-- WITH SOUL-STARTLING SUDDENNESS--
SMRRAKK!
SO! TWO MORE FOOLHARDY INTERLOPERS DARE ENTER THE DARK DOMAIN OF THE ALPHA PRIMITIVES!
SOME KIND OF GIANT--CRASHING THRU!
HE'S GOT CRYS! BUT WHO--?
EVEN SLAVES MAY HAVE SLAVES, OUTSIDER. I AM THAT OF THE ALPHAS--
--AND I AM-- OMEGA!
OMEGA!?

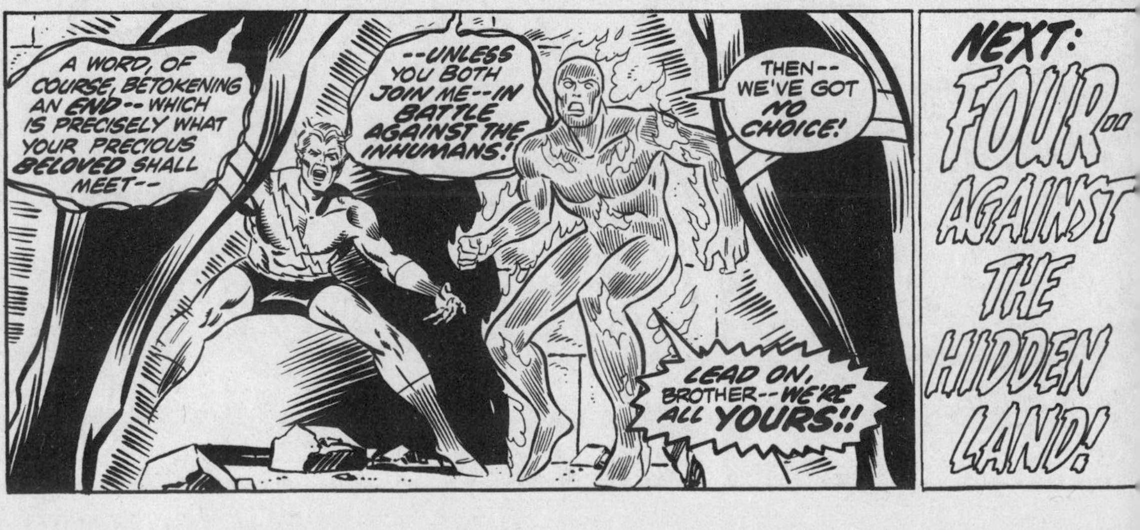
A WORD, OF COURSE, BETOKENING AN END-- WHICH IS PRECISELY WHAT YOUR PRECIOUS BELOVED SHALL MEET--
--UNLESS YOU BOTH JOIN ME--IN BATTLE AGAINST THE INHUMANS!
THEN--WE'VE GOT NO CHOICE!
LEAD ON, BROTHER--WE'RE ALL YOURS!!
NEXT: FOUR-- AGAINST THE HIDDEN LAND!

FANTASTIC FOUR
MARVEL COMICS GROUP
APPROVED BY THE COMICS CODE AUTHORITY
20¢ 132 MAR 02462
THE WORLD'S GREATEST COMIC MAGAZINE!
FANTASTIC FOUR
FIGHT ME! RESIST ME! YOU'LL BUT MAKE ME STRONGER-- EVER STRONGER!
--UNTIL AT LAST DESTROY YOU!!
OMEGA! THE ULTIMATE ASSASSIN!

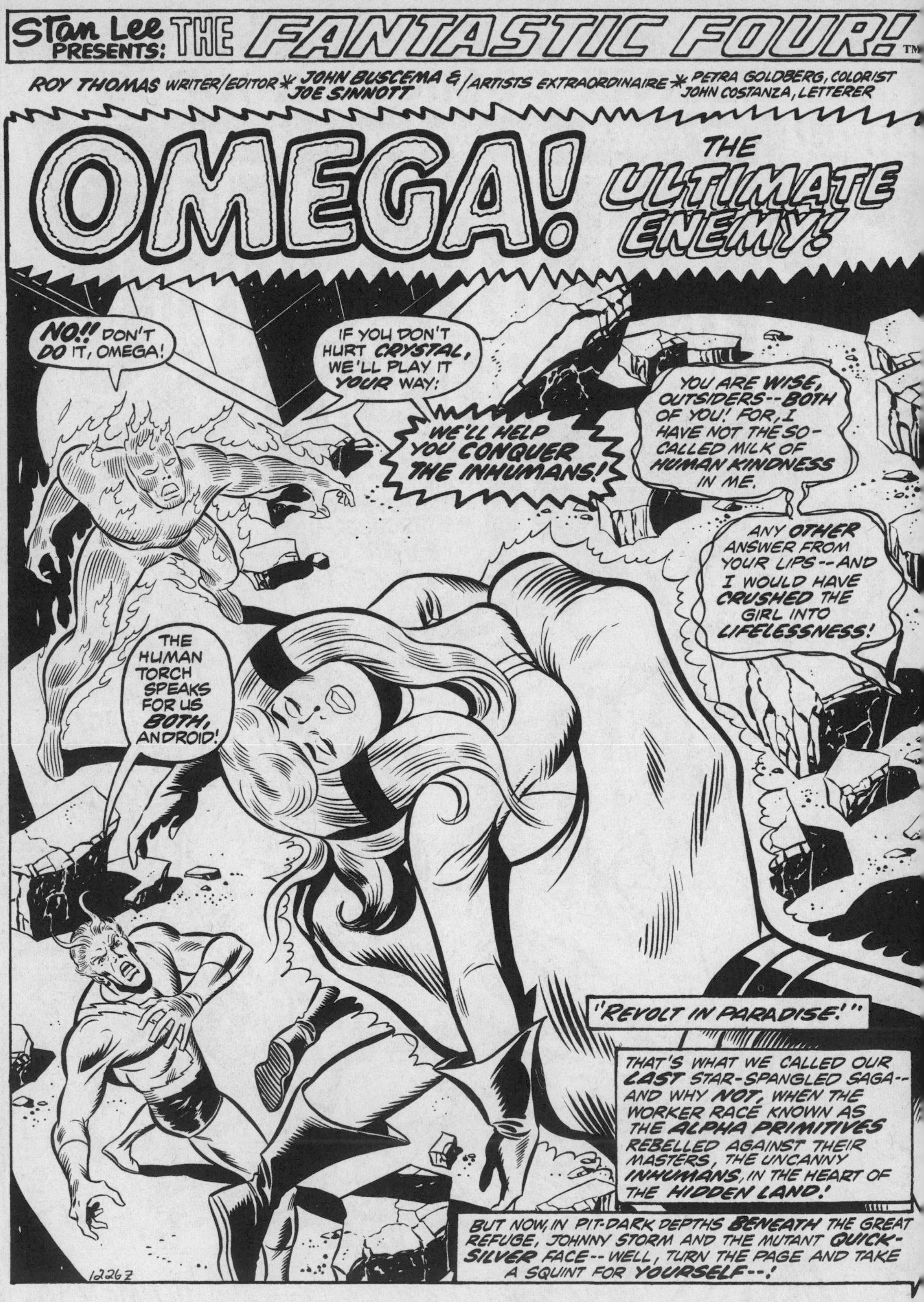
STAN LEE PRESENTS: THE FANTASTIC FOUR!™
ROY THOMAS WRITER/EDITOR ✱ JOHN BUSCEMA & JOE SINNOTT / ARTISTS EXTRAORDINAIRE ✱ PETRA GOLDBERG, COLORIST JOHN COSTANZA, LETTERER
OMEGA! THE ULTIMATE ENEMY!
NO!! DON'T DO IT, OMEGA!
IF YOU DON'T HURT CRYSTAL, WE'LL PLAY IT YOUR WAY:
WE'LL HELP YOU CONQUER THE INHUMANS!
YOU ARE WISE, OUTSIDERS--BOTH OF YOU! FOR, I HAVE NOT THE SO-CALLED MILK OF HUMAN KINDNESS IN ME.
ANY OTHER ANSWER FROM YOUR LIPS--AND I WOULD HAVE CRUSHED THE GIRL INTO LIFELESSNESS!
THE HUMAN TORCH SPEAKS FOR US BOTH, ANDROID!
"REVOLT IN PARADISE!"
THAT'S WHAT WE CALLED OUR LAST STAR-SPANGLED SAGA--AND WHY NOT, WHEN THE WORKER RACE KNOWN AS THE ALPHA PRIMITIVES REBELLED AGAINST THEIR MASTERS, THE UNCANNY INHUMANS, IN THE HEART OF THE HIDDEN LAND!
BUT NOW, IN PIT-DARK DEPTHS BENEATH THE GREAT REFUGE, JOHNNY STORM AND THE MUTANT QUICK-SILVER FACE--WELL, TURN THE PAGE AND TAKE A SQUINT FOR YOURSELF--!
12267

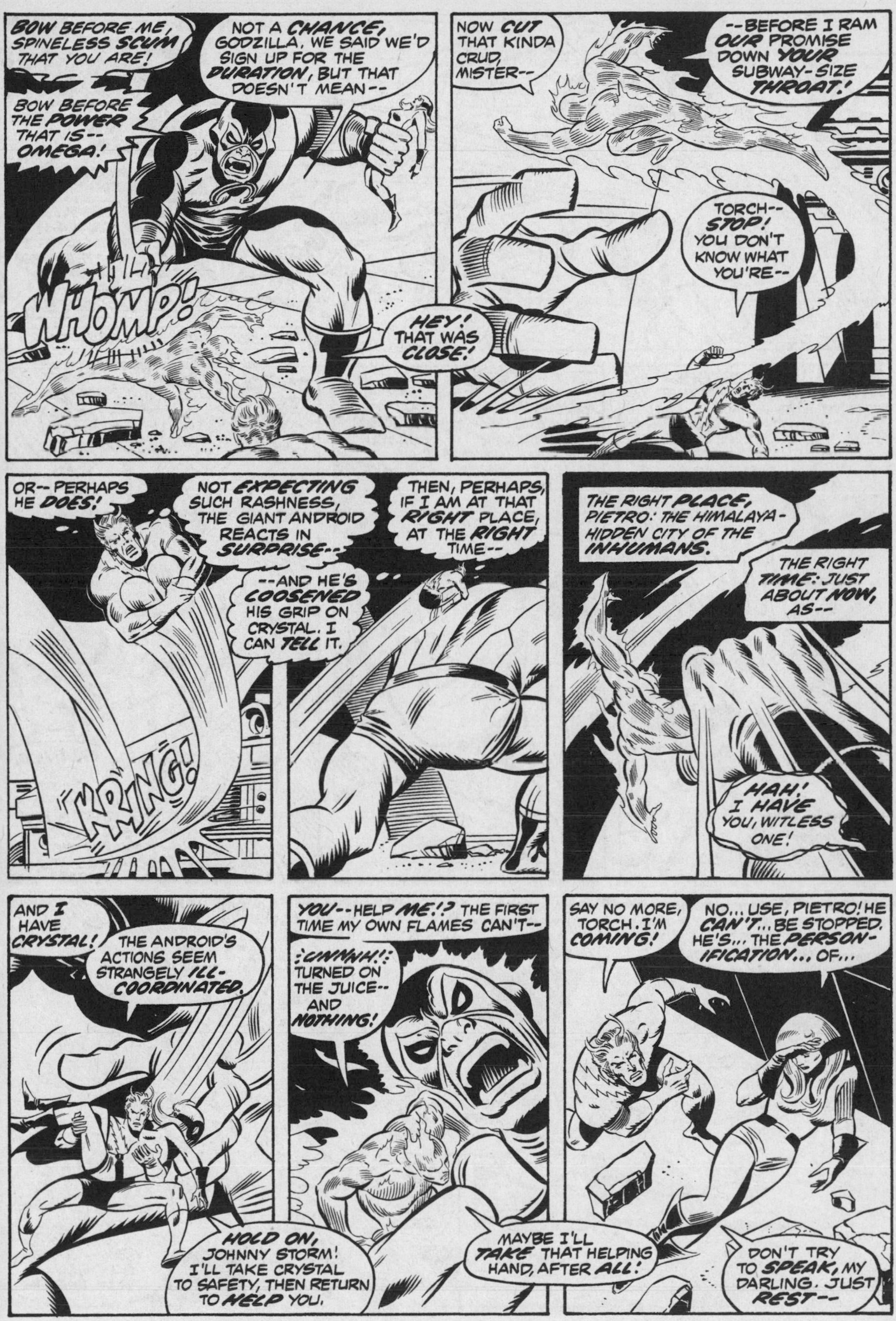
BOW BEFORE ME, SPINELESS SCUM THAT YOU ARE!
BOW BEFORE THE POWER THAT IS-- OMEGA!
NOT A CHANCE, GODZILLA, WE SAID WE'D SIGN UP FOR THE DURATION, BUT THAT DOESN'T MEAN--
WHOMP!
HEY! THAT WAS CLOSE!
NOW CUT THAT KINDA CRUD, MISTER--
--BEFORE I RAM OUR PROMISE DOWN YOUR SUBWAY-SIZE THROAT!
TORCH-- STOP! YOU DON'T KNOW WHAT YOU'RE--
OR-- PERHAPS HE DOES!
NOT EXPECTING SUCH RASHNESS, THE GIANT ANDROID REACTS IN SURPRISE--
KRANG!
THEN, PERHAPS, IF I AM AT THAT RIGHT PLACE, AT THE RIGHT TIME--
--AND HE'S LOOSENED HIS GRIP ON CRYSTAL. I CAN TELL IT.
THE RIGHT PLACE, PIETRO: THE HIMALAYA-HIDDEN CITY OF THE INHUMANS.
THE RIGHT TIME: JUST ABOUT NOW, AS--
HAH! I HAVE YOU, WITLESS ONE!
AND I HAVE CRYSTAL!
THE ANDROID'S ACTIONS SEEM STRANGELY ILL-COORDINATED.
HOLD ON, JOHNNY STORM! I'LL TAKE CRYSTAL TO SAFETY, THEN RETURN TO HELP YOU.
YOU--HELP ME!? THE FIRST TIME MY OWN FLAMES CAN'T--
:UNNNH!: TURNED ON THE JUICE-- AND NOTHING!
MAYBE I'LL TAKE THAT HELPING HAND, AFTER ALL!
SAY NO MORE, TORCH. I'M COMING!
NO... USE, PIETRO! HE CAN'T... BE STOPPED. HE'S... THE PERSON-IFICATION... OF...
DON'T TRY TO SPEAK, MY DARLING. JUST REST--

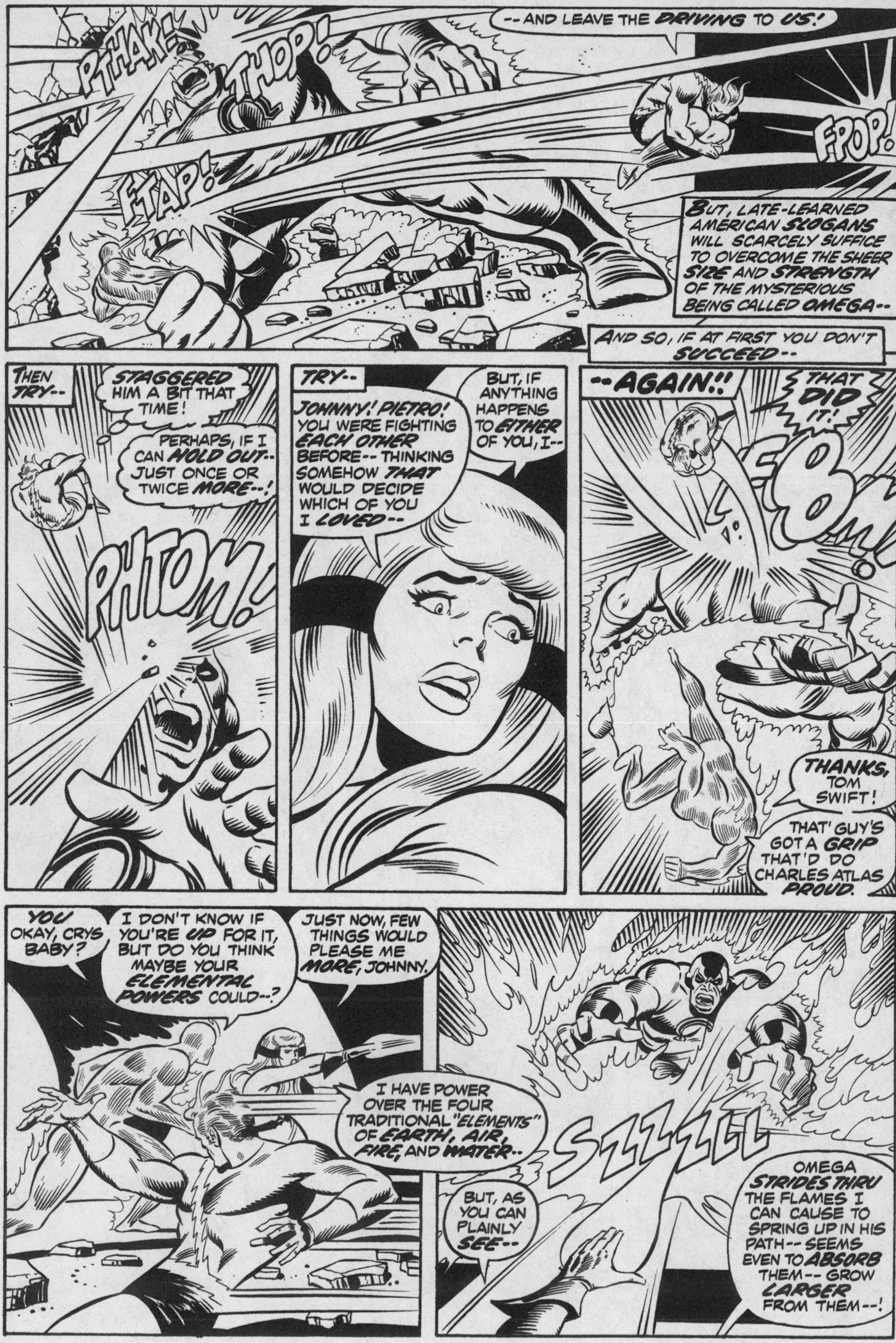
PTHAK!
THOP!
-- AND LEAVE THE DRIVING TO US!
FPOP!
FTAP!
BUT, LATE-LEARNED AMERICAN SLOGANS WILL SCARCELY SUFFICE TO OVERCOME THE SHEER SIZE AND STRENGTH OF THE MYSTERIOUS BEING CALLED OMEGA--
AND SO, IF AT FIRST YOU DON'T SUCCEED--
THEN TRY--
STAGGERED HIM A BIT THAT TIME!
PERHAPS, IF I CAN HOLD OUT-- JUST ONCE OR TWICE MORE--!
PHTOM!
TRY--
JOHNNY! PIETRO! YOU WERE FIGHTING EACH OTHER BEFORE-- THINKING SOMEHOW THAT WOULD DECIDE WHICH OF YOU I LOVED--
BUT, IF ANYTHING HAPPENS TO EITHER OF YOU, I--
--AGAIN!!
THAT DID IT!
THANKS, TOM SWIFT!
THAT' GUY'S GOT A GRIP THAT'D DO CHARLES ATLAS PROUD.
YOU OKAY, CRYS BABY?
I DON'T KNOW IF YOU'RE UP FOR IT, BUT DO YOU THINK MAYBE YOUR ELEMENTAL POWERS COULD--?
JUST NOW, FEW THINGS WOULD PLEASE ME MORE, JOHNNY.
I HAVE POWER OVER THE FOUR TRADITIONAL "ELEMENTS" OF EARTH, AIR, FIRE, AND WATER..
SZZZZZL
BUT, AS YOU CAN PLAINLY SEE--
OMEGA STRIDES THRU THE FLAMES I CAN CAUSE TO SPRING UP IN HIS PATH-- SEEMS EVEN TO ABSORB THEM-- GROW LARGER FROM THEM--!

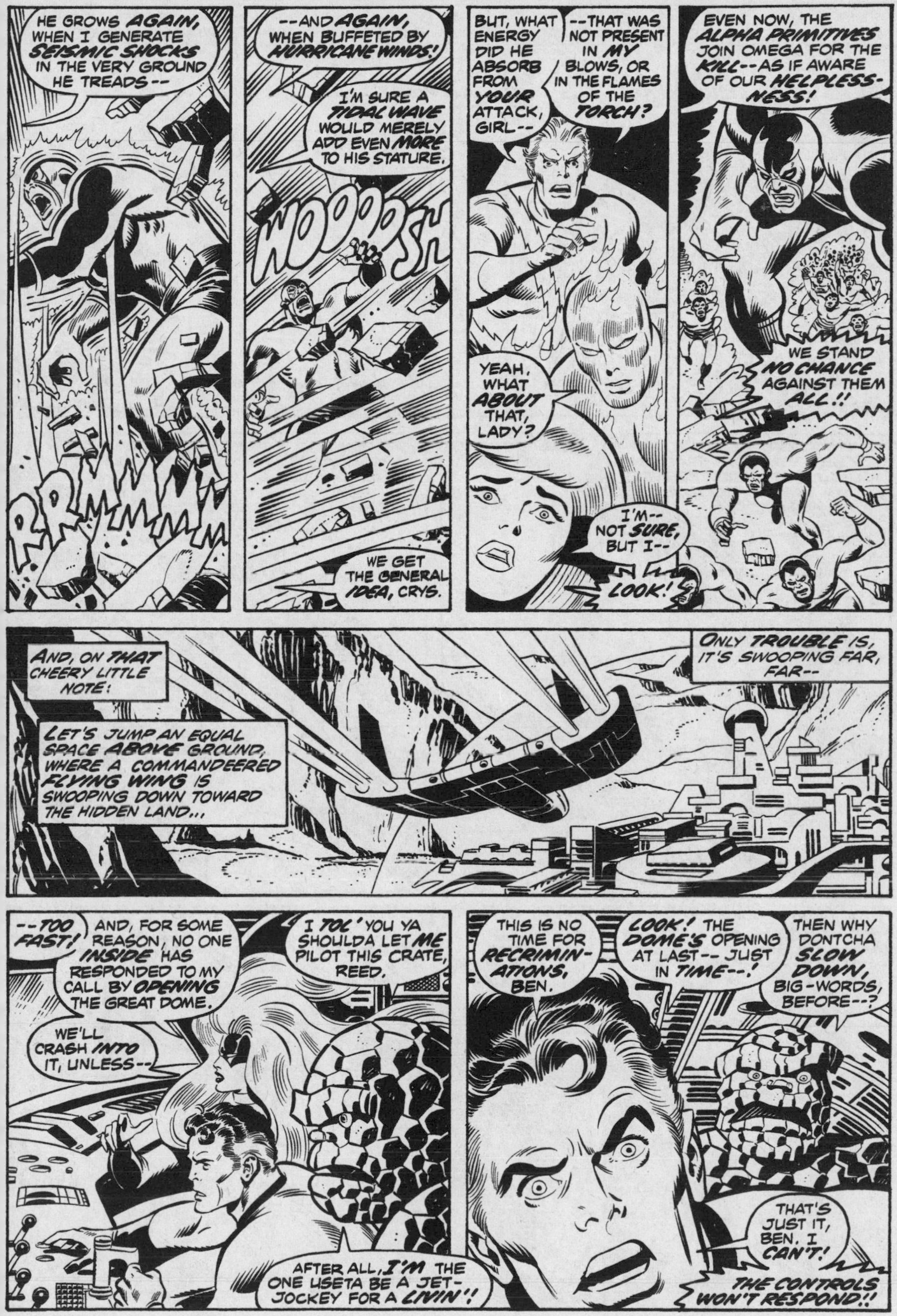

HE GROWS AGAIN, WHEN I GENERATE SEISMIC SHOCKS IN THE VERY GROUND HE TREADS--
RRMMMMM
--AND AGAIN, WHEN BUFFETED BY HURRICANE WINDS!
I'M SURE A TIDAL WAVE WOULD MERELY ADD EVEN MORE TO HIS STATURE.
WOOOOSH
WE GET THE GENERAL IDEA, CRYS.
BUT, WHAT ENERGY DID HE ABSORB FROM YOUR ATTACK, GIRL--
--THAT WAS NOT PRESENT IN MY BLOWS, OR IN THE FLAMES OF THE TORCH?
YEAH, WHAT ABOUT THAT, LADY?
I'M--NOT SURE, BUT I--
LOOK!
EVEN NOW, THE ALPHA PRIMITIVES JOIN OMEGA FOR THE KILL--AS IF AWARE OF OUR HELPLESSNESS!
WE STAND NO CHANCE AGAINST THEM ALL!!
AND, ON THAT CHEERY LITTLE NOTE:
LET'S JUMP AN EQUAL SPACE ABOVE GROUND, WHERE A COMMANDEERED FLYING WING IS SWOOPING DOWN TOWARD THE HIDDEN LAND...
ONLY TROUBLE IS, IT'S SWOOPING FAR, FAR--
--TOO FAST!
AND, FOR SOME REASON, NO ONE INSIDE HAS RESPONDED TO MY CALL BY OPENING THE GREAT DOME.
WE'LL CRASH INTO IT, UNLESS--
I TOL' YOU YA SHOULDA LET ME PILOT THIS CRATE, REED.
AFTER ALL, I'M THE ONE USETA BE A JET-JOCKEY FOR A LIVIN'!!
THIS IS NO TIME FOR RECRIMINATIONS, BEN.
LOOK! THE DOME'S OPENING AT LAST-- JUST IN TIME--!
THEN WHY DONTCHA SLOW DOWN, BIG-WORDS, BEFORE--?
THAT'S JUST IT, BEN. I CAN'T!
THE CONTROLS WON'T RESPOND!!

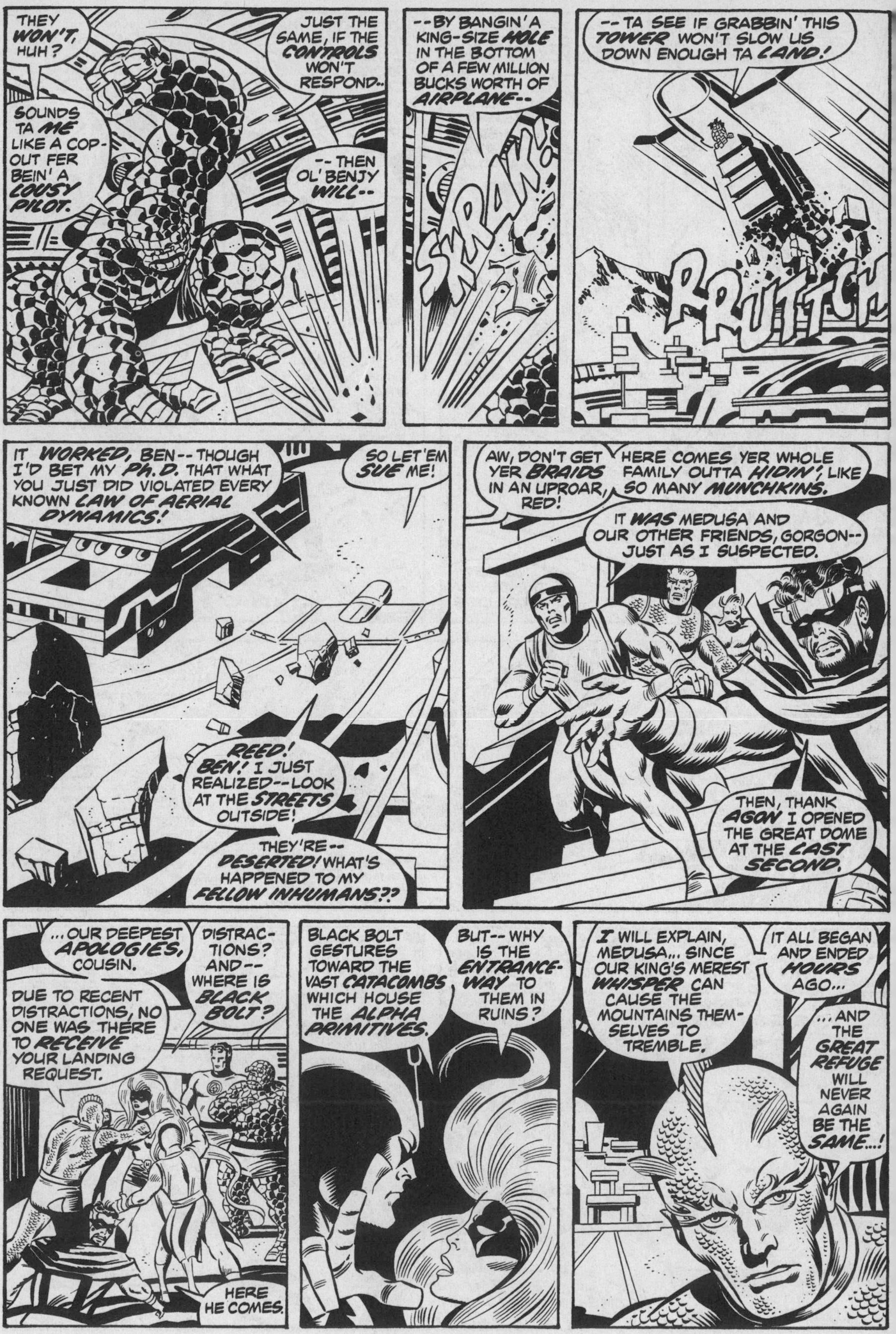
THEY WON'T, HUH?
JUST THE SAME, IF THE CONTROLS WON'T RESPOND..
SOUNDS TA ME LIKE A COP-OUT FER BEIN' A LOUSY PILOT.
--THEN OL' BENJY WILL--
--BY BANGIN' A KING-SIZE HOLE IN THE BOTTOM OF A FEW MILLION BUCKS WORTH OF AIRPLANE--
SKRAK!
--TA SEE IF GRABBIN' THIS TOWER WON'T SLOW US DOWN ENOUGH TA LAND!
RRUTTCH
IT WORKED, BEN--THOUGH I'D BET MY Ph.D. THAT WHAT YOU JUST DID VIOLATED EVERY KNOWN LAW OF AERIAL DYNAMICS!
SO LET'EM SUE ME!
REED! BEN! I JUST REALIZED--LOOK AT THE STREETS OUTSIDE!
THEY'RE--DESERTED! WHAT'S HAPPENED TO MY FELLOW INHUMANS??
AW, DON'T GET YER BRAIDS IN AN UPROAR, RED!
HERE COMES YER WHOLE FAMILY OUTTA HIDIN', LIKE SO MANY MUNCHKINS.
IT WAS MEDUSA AND OUR OTHER FRIENDS, GORGON--JUST AS I SUSPECTED.
THEN, THANK AGON I OPENED THE GREAT DOME AT THE LAST SECOND.
...OUR DEEPEST APOLOGIES, COUSIN.
DUE TO RECENT DISTRACTIONS, NO ONE WAS THERE TO RECEIVE YOUR LANDING REQUEST.
DISTRACTIONS? AND--WHERE IS BLACK BOLT?
HERE HE COMES.
BLACK BOLT GESTURES TOWARD THE VAST CATACOMBS WHICH HOUSE THE ALPHA PRIMITIVES.
BUT--WHY IS THE ENTRANCE-WAY TO THEM IN RUINS?
I WILL EXPLAIN, MEDUSA... SINCE OUR KING'S MEREST WHISPER CAN CAUSE THE MOUNTAINS THEMSELVES TO TREMBLE.
IT ALL BEGAN AND ENDED HOURS AGO...
...AND THE GREAT REFUGE WILL NEVER AGAIN BE THE SAME...!

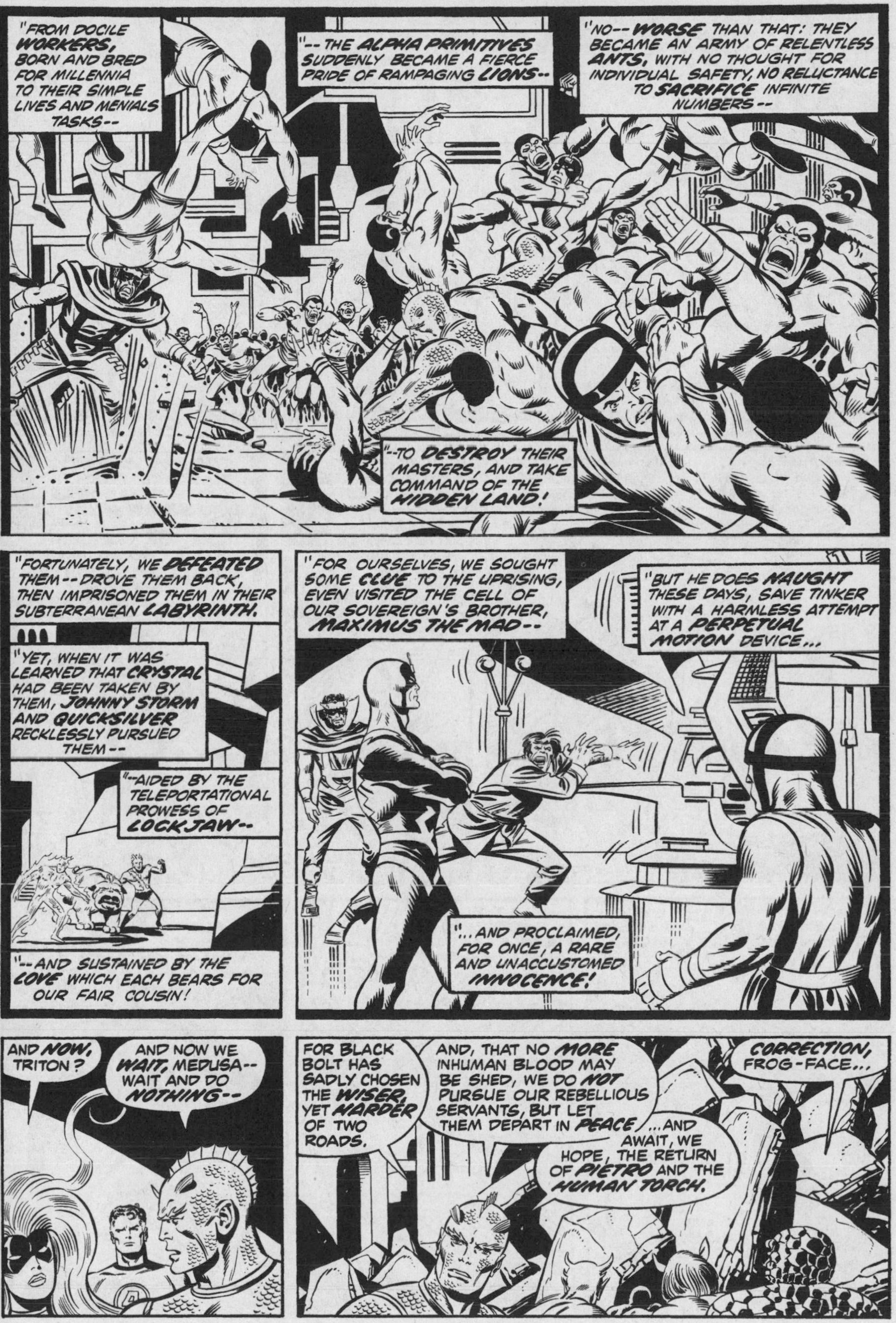
"FROM DOCILE WORKERS, BORN AND BRED FOR MILLENNIA TO THEIR SIMPLE LIVES AND MENIALS TASKS--
"--THE ALPHA PRIMITIVES SUDDENLY BECAME A FIERCE PRIDE OF RAMPAGING LIONS--
"NO--WORSE THAN THAT: THEY BECAME AN ARMY OF RELENTLESS ANTS, WITH NO THOUGHT FOR INDIVIDUAL SAFETY, NO RELUCTANCE TO SACRIFICE INFINITE NUMBERS--
"--TO DESTROY THEIR MASTERS, AND TAKE COMMAND OF THE HIDDEN LAND!
"FORTUNATELY, WE DEFEATED THEM--DROVE THEM BACK, THEN IMPRISONED THEM IN THEIR SUBTERRANEAN LABYRINTH.
"YET, WHEN IT WAS LEARNED THAT CRYSTAL HAD BEEN TAKEN BY THEM, JOHNNY STORM AND QUICKSILVER RECKLESSLY PURSUED THEM--
"--AIDED BY THE TELEPORTATIONAL PROWESS OF LOCKJAW--
"--AND SUSTAINED BY THE LOVE WHICH EACH BEARS FOR OUR FAIR COUSIN!
"FOR OURSELVES, WE SOUGHT SOME CLUE TO THE UPRISING, EVEN VISITED THE CELL OF OUR SOVEREIGN'S BROTHER, MAXIMUS THE MAD--
"BUT HE DOES NAUGHT THESE DAYS, SAVE TINKER WITH A HARMLESS ATTEMPT AT A PERPETUAL MOTION DEVICE...
"...AND PROCLAIMED, FOR ONCE, A RARE AND UNACCUSTOMED INNOCENCE!
AND NOW, TRITON?
AND NOW WE WAIT, MEDUSA--WAIT AND DO NOTHING--
FOR BLACK BOLT HAS SADLY CHOSEN THE WISER, YET HARDER OF TWO ROADS.
AND, THAT NO MORE INHUMAN BLOOD MAY BE SHED, WE DO NOT PURSUE OUR REBELLIOUS SERVANTS, BUT LET THEM DEPART IN PEACE
...AND AWAIT, WE HOPE, THE RETURN OF PIETRO AND THE HUMAN TORCH.
CORRECTION, FROG-FACE...

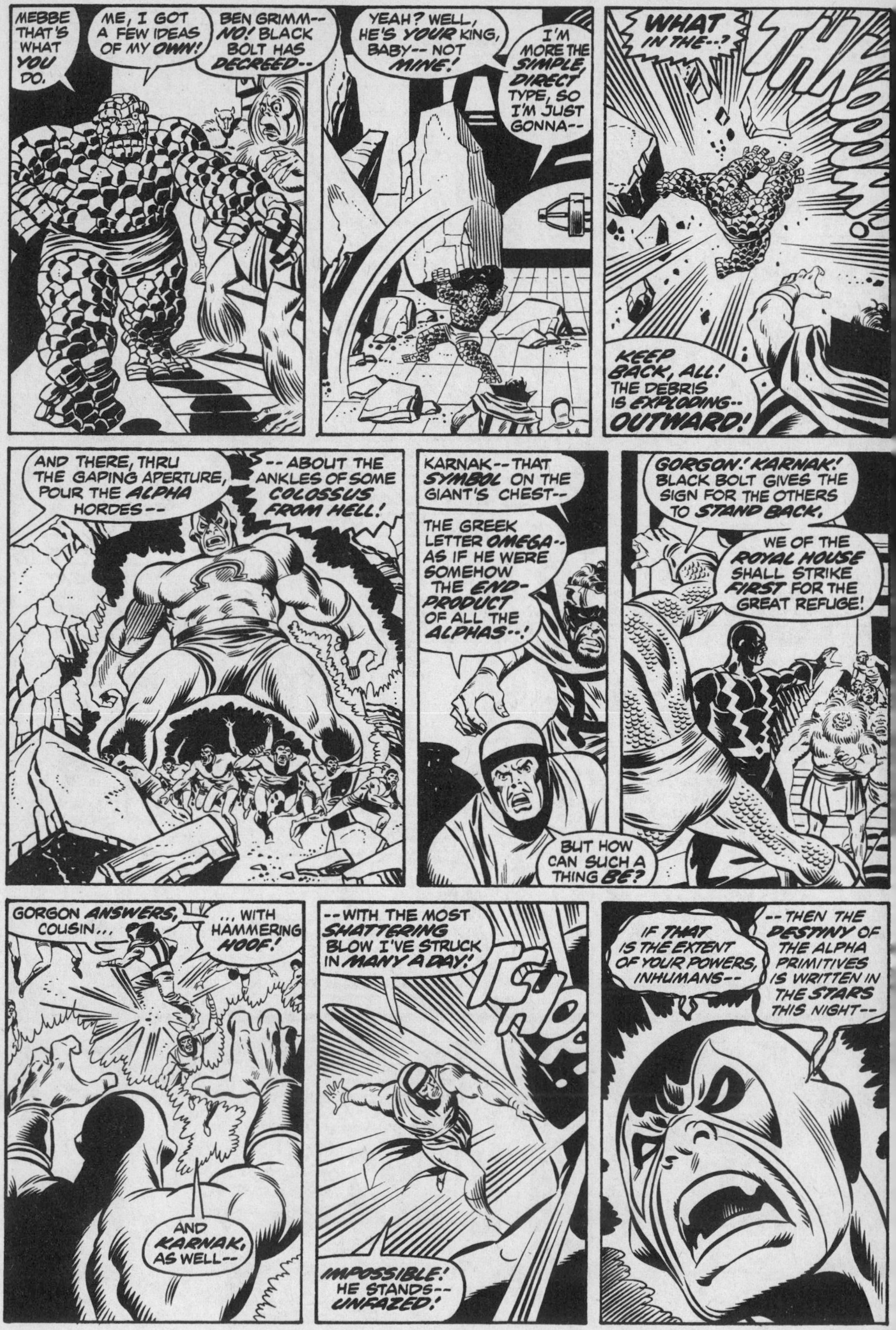
MEBBE THAT'S WHAT YOU DO.
ME, I GOT A FEW IDEAS OF MY OWN!
BEN GRIMM-- NO! BLACK BOLT HAS DECREED--
YEAH? WELL, HE'S YOUR KING, BABY-- NOT MINE!
I'M MORE THE SIMPLE, DIRECT TYPE, SO I'M JUST GONNA--
WHAT IN THE--?
THROOOOM!
KEEP BACK, ALL! THE DEBRIS IS EXPLODING-- OUTWARD!
AND THERE, THRU THE GAPING APERTURE, POUR THE ALPHA HORDES--
-- ABOUT THE ANKLES OF SOME COLOSSUS FROM HELL!
KARNAK--THAT SYMBOL ON THE GIANT'S CHEST--
THE GREEK LETTER OMEGA-- AS IF HE WERE SOMEHOW THE END-PRODUCT OF ALL THE ALPHAS--!
BUT HOW CAN SUCH A THING BE?
GORGON! KARNAK! BLACK BOLT GIVES THE SIGN FOR THE OTHERS TO STAND BACK.
WE OF THE ROYAL HOUSE SHALL STRIKE FIRST FOR THE GREAT REFUGE!
GORGON ANSWERS, COUSIN...
..., WITH HAMMERING HOOF!
AND KARNAK, AS WELL--
--WITH THE MOST SHATTERING BLOW I'VE STRUCK IN MANY A DAY!
TCHOK!
IMPOSSIBLE! HE STANDS-- UNFAZED!
IF THAT IS THE EXTENT OF YOUR POWERS, INHUMANS--
--THEN THE DESTINY OF THE ALPHA PRIMITIVES IS WRITTEN IN THE STARS THIS NIGHT--

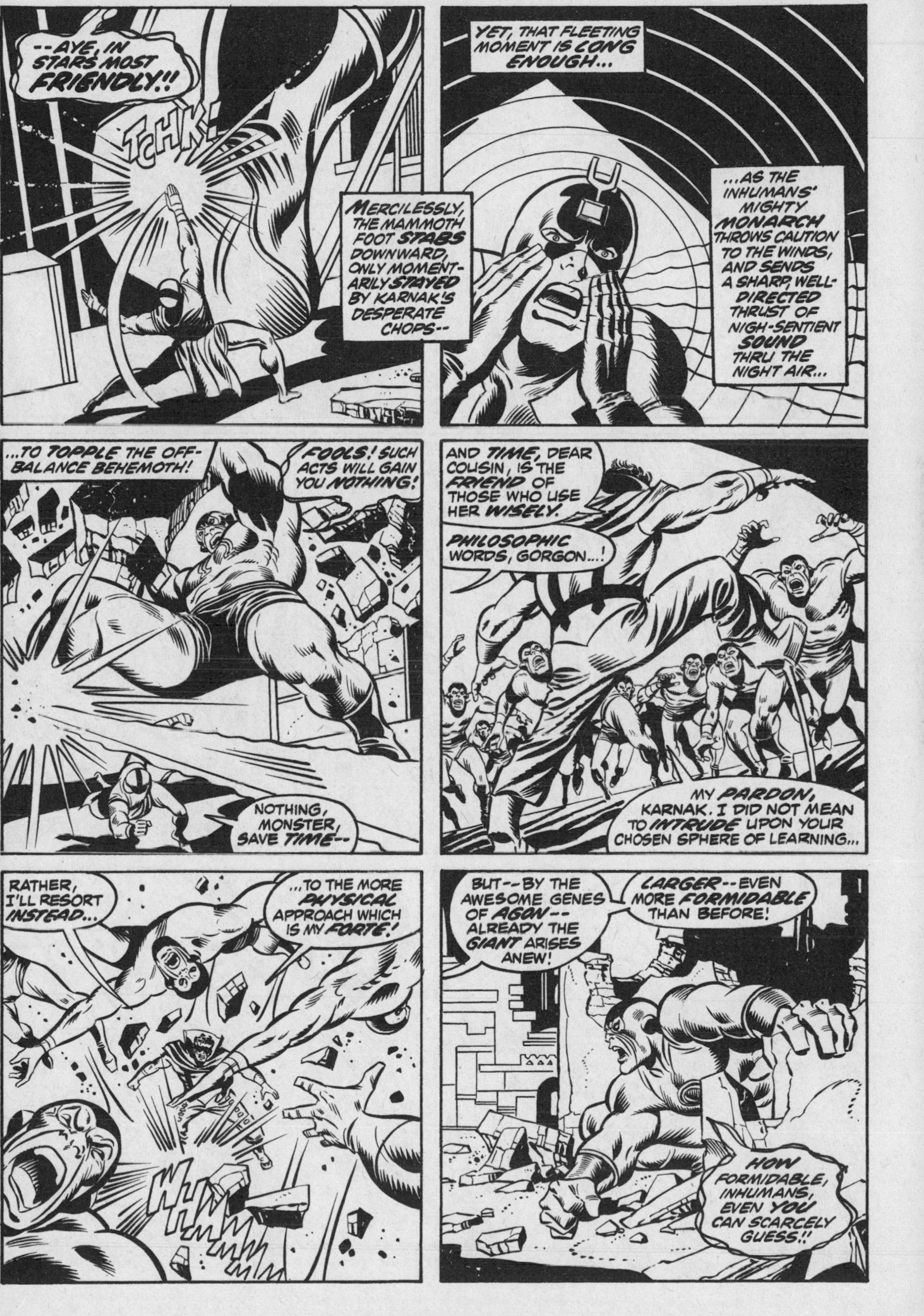
--AYE, IN STARS MOST FRIENDLY!!
TCHK!
MERCILESSLY, THE MAMMOTH FOOT STABS DOWNWARD, ONLY MOMENTARILY STAYED BY KARNAK'S DESPERATE CHOPS--
YET, THAT FLEETING MOMENT IS LONG ENOUGH...
...AS THE INHUMANS' MIGHTY MONARCH THROWS CAUTION TO THE WINDS, AND SENDS A SHARP, WELL-DIRECTED THRUST OF NIGH-SENTIENT SOUND THRU THE NIGHT AIR...
...TO TOPPLE THE OFF-BALANCE BEHEMOTH!
FOOLS! SUCH ACTS WILL GAIN YOU NOTHING!
NOTHING, MONSTER, SAVE TIME--
AND TIME, DEAR COUSIN, IS THE FRIEND OF THOSE WHO USE HER WISELY.
PHILOSOPHIC WORDS, GORGON...!
MY PARDON, KARNAK. I DID NOT MEAN TO INTRUDE UPON YOUR CHOSEN SPHERE OF LEARNING...
RATHER, I'LL RESORT INSTEAD...
...TO THE MORE PHYSICAL APPROACH WHICH IS MY FORTE!
WHMMM
BUT--BY THE AWESOME GENES OF AGON--ALREADY THE GIANT ARISES ANEW!
LARGER--EVEN MORE FORMIDABLE THAN BEFORE!
HOW FORMIDABLE, INHUMANS, EVEN YOU CAN SCARCELY GUESS!!

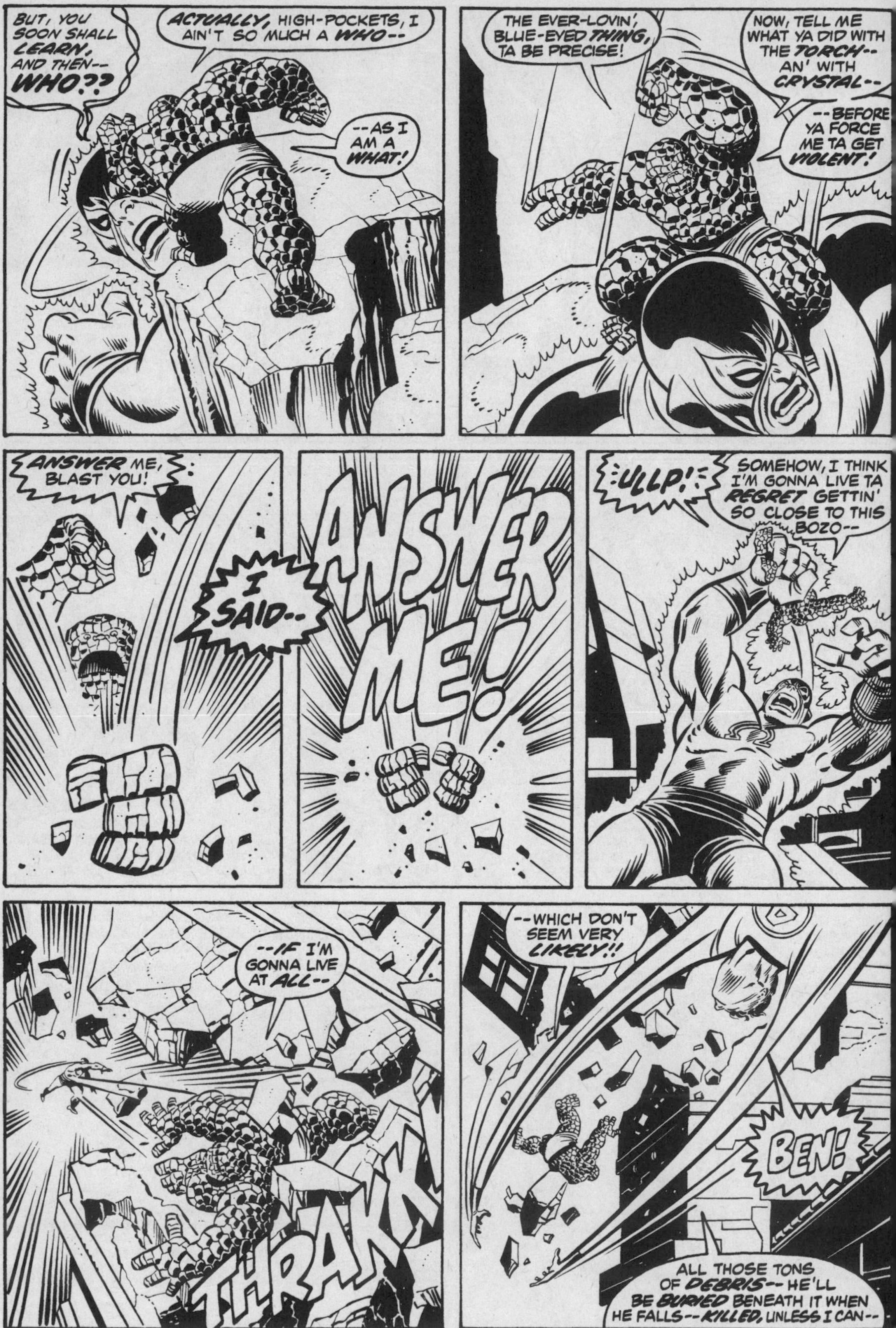
BUT, YOU SOON SHALL LEARN, AND THEN-- WHO??
ACTUALLY, HIGH-POCKETS, I AIN'T SO MUCH A WHO--
--AS I AM A WHAT!
THE EVER-LOVIN', BLUE-EYED THING, TA BE PRECISE!
NOW, TELL ME WHAT YA DID WITH THE TORCH-- AN' WITH CRYSTAL--
--BEFORE YA FORCE ME TA GET VIOLENT!
ANSWER ME, BLAST YOU!
I SAID--
ANSWER ME!
ULLP!
SOMEHOW, I THINK I'M GONNA LIVE TA REGRET GETTIN' SO CLOSE TO THIS BOZO--
--IF I'M GONNA LIVE AT ALL--
THRAKK
--WHICH DON'T SEEM VERY LIKELY!!
BEN!
ALL THOSE TONS OF DEBRIS-- HE'LL BE BURIED BENEATH IT WHEN HE FALLS--KILLED, UNLESS I CAN--

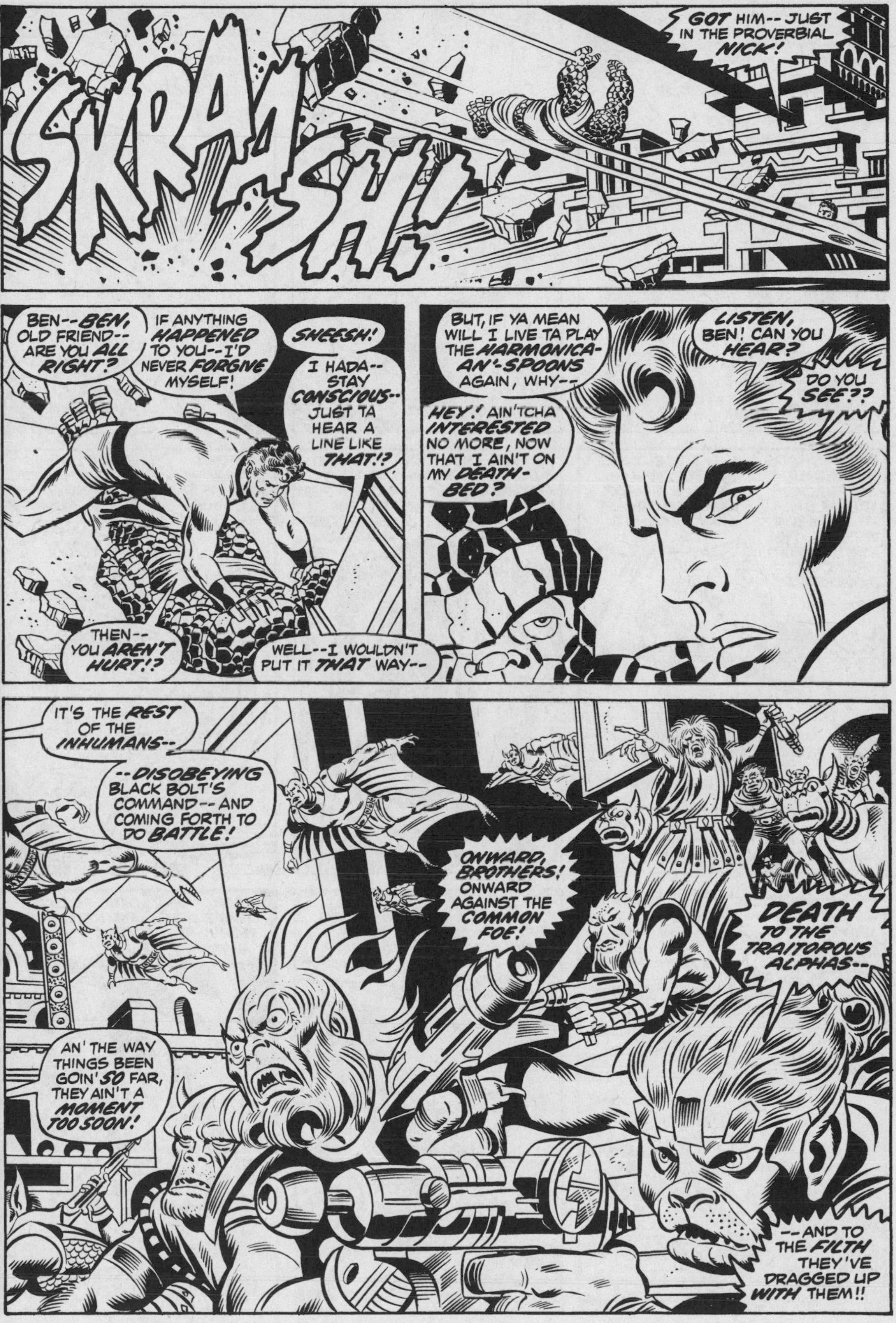
SKRAASH!
GOT HIM-- JUST IN THE PROVERBIAL NICK!
BEN--BEN, OLD FRIEND-- ARE YOU ALL RIGHT?
IF ANYTHING HAPPENED TO YOU--I'D NEVER FORGIVE MYSELF!
SHEESH!
I HADA-- STAY CONSCIOUS-- JUST TA HEAR A LINE LIKE THAT!?
THEN-- YOU AREN'T HURT!?
WELL--I WOULDN'T PUT IT THAT WAY--
BUT, IF YA MEAN WILL I LIVE TA PLAY THE HARMONICA-AN'-SPOONS AGAIN, WHY--
HEY! AIN'TCHA INTERESTED NO MORE, NOW THAT I AIN'T ON MY DEATH-BED?
LISTEN, BEN! CAN YOU HEAR?
DO YOU SEE??
IT'S THE REST OF THE INHUMANS--
--DISOBEYING BLACK BOLT'S COMMAND--AND COMING FORTH TO DO BATTLE!
ONWARD, BROTHERS! ONWARD AGAINST THE COMMON FOE!
DEATH TO THE TRAITOROUS ALPHAS--
AN' THE WAY THINGS BEEN GOIN' SO FAR, THEY AIN'T A MOMENT TOO SOON!
--AND TO THE FILTH THEY'VE DRAGGED UP WITH THEM!!

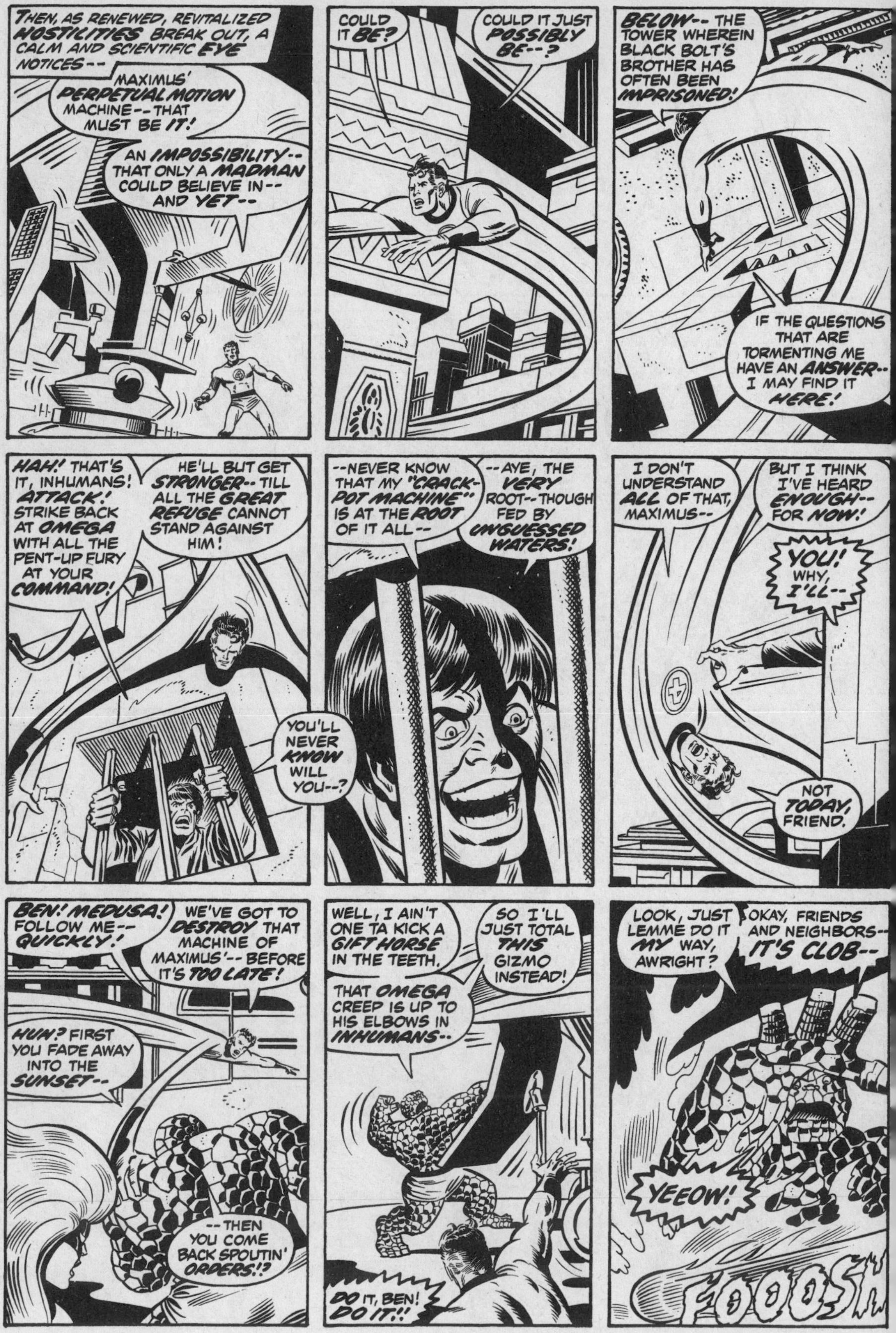
THEN, AS RENEWED, REVITALIZED HOSTILITIES BREAK OUT, A CALM AND SCIENTIFIC EYE NOTICES--
MAXIMUS' PERPETUAL MOTION MACHINE--THAT MUST BE IT!
AN IMPOSSIBILITY--THAT ONLY A MADMAN COULD BELIEVE IN--AND YET--
COULD IT BE?
COULD IT JUST POSSIBLY BE--?
BELOW-- THE TOWER WHEREIN BLACK BOLT'S BROTHER HAS OFTEN BEEN IMPRISONED!
IF THE QUESTIONS THAT ARE TORMENTING ME HAVE AN ANSWER--I MAY FIND IT HERE!
HAH! THAT'S IT, INHUMANS! ATTACK! STRIKE BACK AT OMEGA WITH ALL THE PENT-UP FURY AT YOUR COMMAND!
HE'LL BUT GET STRONGER-- TILL ALL THE GREAT REFUGE CANNOT STAND AGAINST HIM!
YOU'LL NEVER KNOW WILL YOU--?
--NEVER KNOW THAT MY "CRACK-POT MACHINE" IS AT THE ROOT OF IT ALL--
--AYE, THE VERY ROOT--THOUGH FED BY UNGUESSED WATERS!
I DON'T UNDERSTAND ALL OF THAT, MAXIMUS--
BUT I THINK I'VE HEARD ENOUGH--FOR NOW!
YOU! WHY, I'LL--
NOT TODAY, FRIEND.
BEN! MEDUSA! FOLLOW ME--QUICKLY!
WE'VE GOT TO DESTROY THAT MACHINE OF MAXIMUS'--BEFORE IT'S TOO LATE!
HUH? FIRST YOU FADE AWAY INTO THE SUNSET--
--THEN YOU COME BACK SPOUTIN' ORDERS!?
WELL, I AIN'T ONE TA KICK A GIFT HORSE IN THE TEETH.
SO I'LL JUST TOTAL THIS GIZMO INSTEAD!
THAT OMEGA CREEP IS UP TO HIS ELBOWS IN INHUMANS--
DO IT, BEN! DO IT!!
LOOK, JUST LEMME DO IT MY WAY, AWRIGHT?
OKAY, FRIENDS AND NEIGHBORS--IT'S CLOB--
YEEOW!
FOOOSH

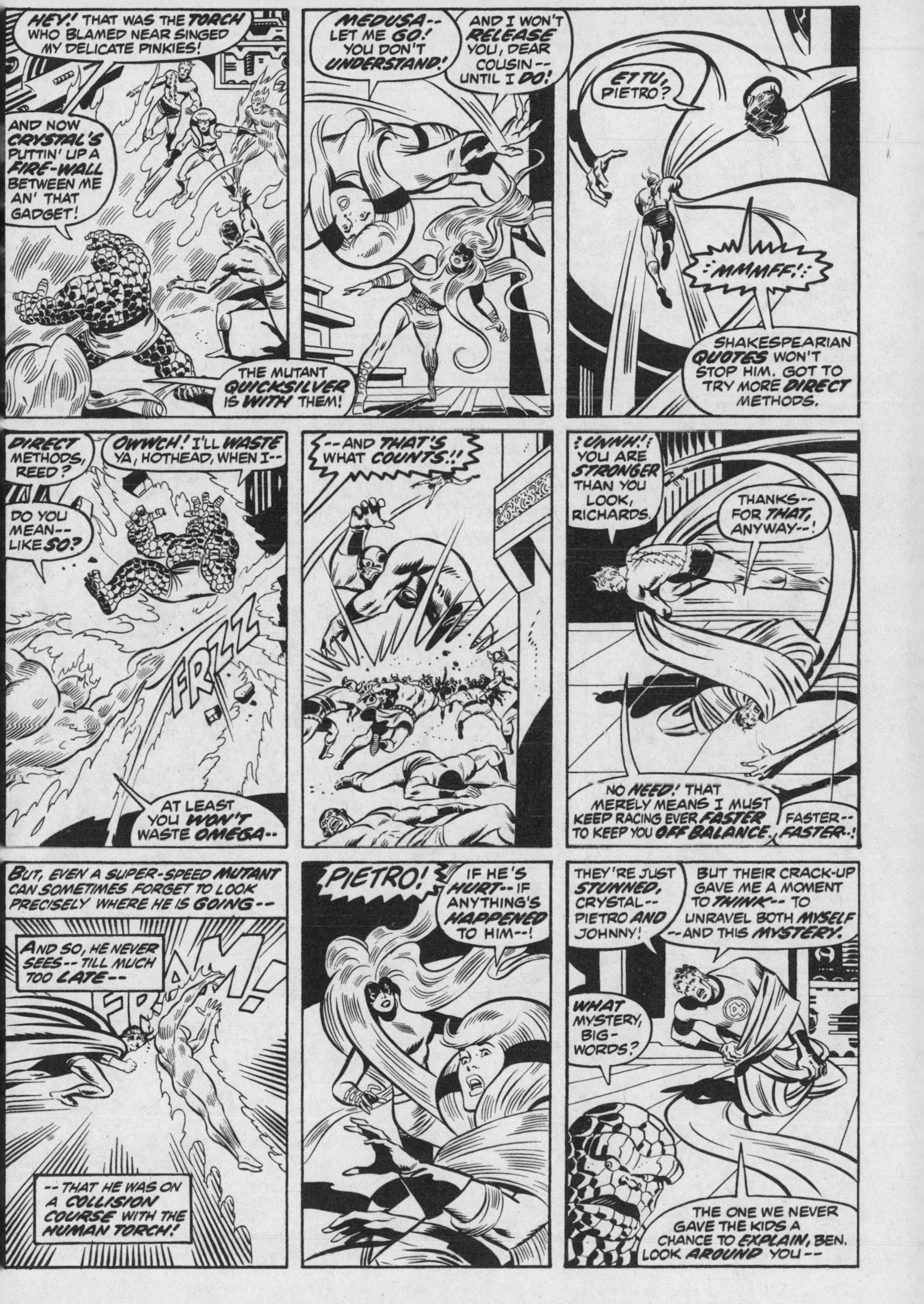
HEY! THAT WAS THE TORCH WHO BLAMED NEAR SINGED MY DELICATE PINKIES!
AND NOW CRYSTAL'S PUTTIN' UP A FIRE-WALL BETWEEN ME AN' THAT GADGET!
THE MUTANT QUICKSILVER IS WITH THEM!
MEDUSA-- LET ME GO! YOU DON'T UNDERSTAND!
AND I WON'T RELEASE YOU, DEAR COUSIN-- UNTIL I DO!
ET TU, PIETRO?
MMMFF!
SHAKESPEARIAN QUOTES WON'T STOP HIM. GOT TO TRY MORE DIRECT METHODS.
DIRECT METHODS, REED?
OWWCH! I'LL WASTE YA, HOTHEAD, WHEN I--
DO YOU MEAN-- LIKE SO?
FRZZZ
AT LEAST YOU WON'T WASTE OMEGA--
--AND THAT'S WHAT COUNTS!!
UNNH! YOU ARE STRONGER THAN YOU LOOK, RICHARDS.
THANKS-- FOR THAT, ANYWAY--!
NO NEED! THAT MERELY MEANS I MUST KEEP RACING EVER FASTER TO KEEP YOU OFF BALANCE.
FASTER-- FASTER--!
BUT, EVEN A SUPER-SPEED MUTANT CAN SOMETIMES FORGET TO LOOK PRECISELY WHERE HE IS GOING--
AND SO, HE NEVER SEES-- TILL MUCH TOO LATE--
FRAM!
--THAT HE WAS ON A COLLISION COURSE WITH THE HUMAN TORCH!
PIETRO!
IF HE'S HURT-- IF ANYTHING'S HAPPENED TO HIM--!
THEY'RE JUST STUNNED, CRYSTAL-- PIETRO AND JOHNNY!
BUT THEIR CRACK-UP GAVE ME A MOMENT TO THINK-- TO UNRAVEL BOTH MYSELF --AND THIS MYSTERY.
WHAT MYSTERY, BIG-WORDS?
THE ONE WE NEVER GAVE THE KIDS A CHANCE TO EXPLAIN, BEN. LOOK AROUND YOU--

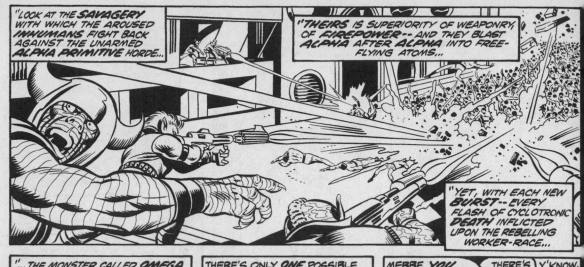

"LOOK AT THE SAVAGERY WITH WHICH THE AROUSED INHUMANS FIGHT BACK AGAINST THE UNARMED ALPHA PRIMITIVE HORDE...

"THEIRS IS SUPERIORITY OF WEAPONRY, OF FIREPOWER -- AND THEY BLAST ALPHA AFTER ALPHA INTO FREE-FLYING ATOMS...

"YET, WITH EACH NEW BURST -- EVERY FLASH OF CYCLOTRONIC DEATH INFLICTED UPON THE REBELLING WORKER-RACE...

"...THE MONSTER CALLED OMEGA GLOWS MORE BRIGHTLY -- AND GROWS EVEN LARGER...

"...TILL IT SEEMS THAT NOTHING CAN STOP HIM!

THERE'S ONLY ONE POSSIBLE ANSWER -- AND I'M A FOOL FOR NOT GUESSING IT BEFORE!

YOU SAID IT, LEADER-MAN... I DIDN'T.

WE COULDN'T TAKE THE TIME TO TELL YOU--

--'CAUSE WE COULDN'T RISK YOUR DESTROYING THAT MACHINE!

YES -- I SEE THAT NOW.

MEBBE YOU SEE IT, STRETCHO-- BUT I'M STILL IN THE DARK. HOWZABOUT--?

THERE'S NO TIME!

Y'KNOW, SOMEHOW I KINDA THOUGHT THAT'S WHAT YOU'D SAY.

JUST WAIT UP, HUH?

BUT, THERE ARE SOME THINGS WHICH A MAN WHOM COSMIC ACCIDENT HAS MADE A HUMAN RUBBER-BAND CAN DO BEST FOR HIMSELF...

AND THIS, IT SEEMS, IS ONE OF THEM.

INHUMANS-- STOP! THIS IS A BATTLE YOU CANNOT-- SHOULD NOT WIN!

LISTEN TO ME-- AND ALL THE BLOOD-LETTING CAN COME TO AN END!

BLACK BOLT GIVES THE SIGN THAT WE SHOULD HEED THIS TRUSTED OUTLANDER.

DONE, THEN! WE'LL GIVE HIM HIS SAY-- IF THE REBELS AND THEIR MONSTER OBEY THE TRUCE, AS WELL!

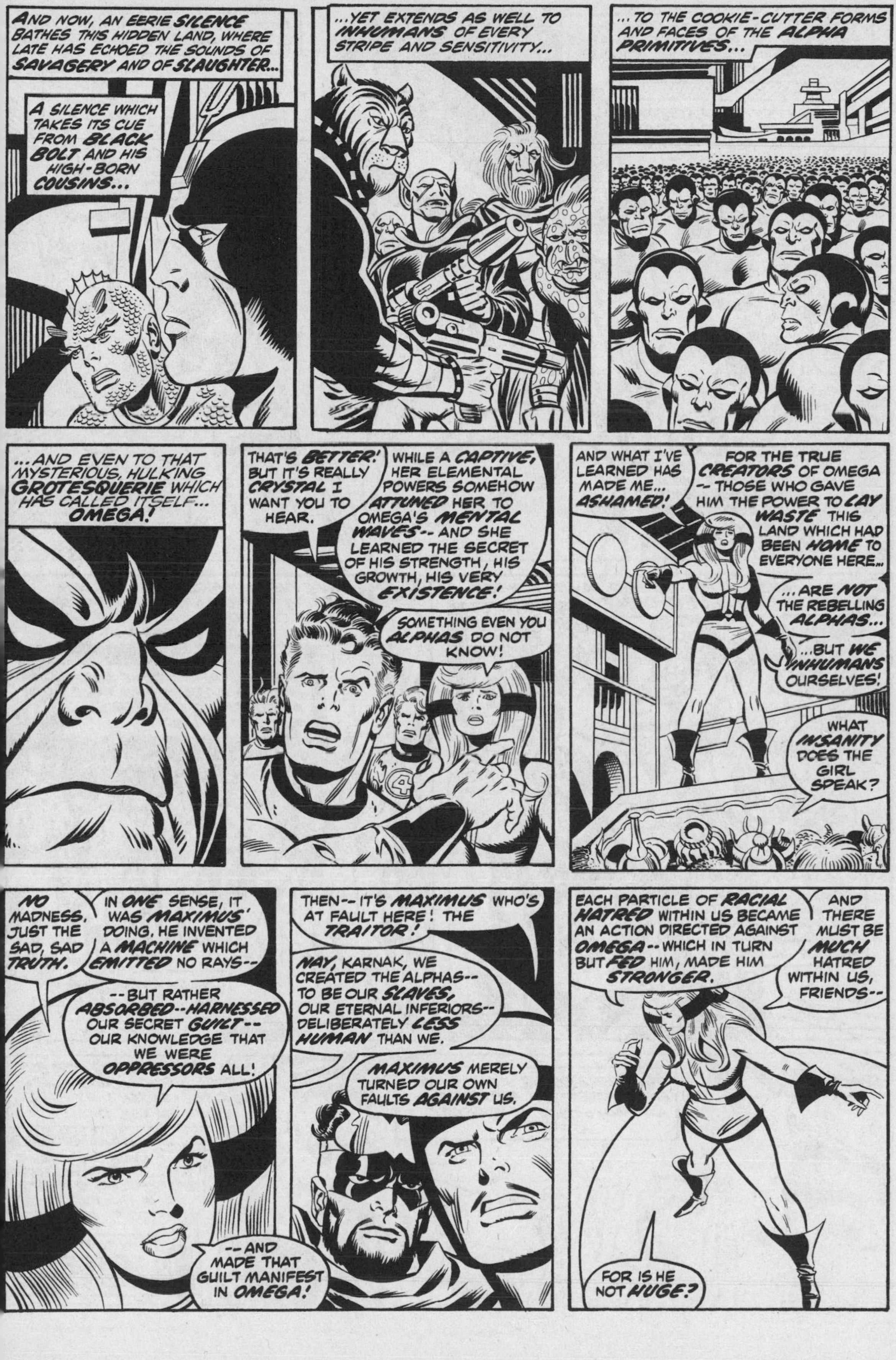
AND NOW, AN EERIE SILENCE BATHES THIS HIDDEN LAND, WHERE LATE HAS ECHOED THE SOUNDS OF SAVAGERY AND OF SLAUGHTER...
A SILENCE WHICH TAKES ITS CUE FROM BLACK BOLT AND HIS HIGH-BORN COUSINS...
...YET EXTENDS AS WELL TO INHUMANS OF EVERY STRIPE AND SENSITIVITY...
...TO THE COOKIE-CUTTER FORMS AND FACES OF THE ALPHA PRIMITIVES...
...AND EVEN TO THAT MYSTERIOUS, HULKING GROTESQUERIE WHICH HAS CALLED ITSELF... OMEGA!
THAT'S BETTER! BUT IT'S REALLY CRYSTAL I WANT YOU TO HEAR.
WHILE A CAPTIVE, HER ELEMENTAL POWERS SOMEHOW ATTUNED HER TO OMEGA'S MENTAL WAVES-- AND SHE LEARNED THE SECRET OF HIS STRENGTH, HIS GROWTH, HIS VERY EXISTENCE!
SOMETHING EVEN YOU ALPHAS DO NOT KNOW!
AND WHAT I'VE LEARNED HAS MADE ME... ASHAMED!
FOR THE TRUE CREATORS OF OMEGA -- THOSE WHO GAVE HIM THE POWER TO LAY WASTE THIS LAND WHICH HAD BEEN HOME TO EVERYONE HERE...
...ARE NOT THE REBELLING ALPHAS...
...BUT WE INHUMANS OURSELVES!
WHAT INSANITY DOES THE GIRL SPEAK?
NO MADNESS. JUST THE SAD, SAD TRUTH.
IN ONE SENSE, IT WAS MAXIMUS' DOING. HE INVENTED A MACHINE WHICH EMITTED NO RAYS--
--BUT RATHER ABSORBED--HARNESSED OUR SECRET GUILT-- --OUR KNOWLEDGE THAT WE WERE OPPRESSORS ALL!
--AND MADE THAT GUILT MANIFEST IN OMEGA!
THEN-- IT'S MAXIMUS WHO'S AT FAULT HERE! THE TRAITOR!
NAY, KARNAK, WE CREATED THE ALPHAS-- TO BE OUR SLAVES, OUR ETERNAL INFERIORS-- DELIBERATELY LESS HUMAN THAN WE.
MAXIMUS MERELY TURNED OUR OWN FAULTS AGAINST US.
EACH PARTICLE OF RACIAL HATRED WITHIN US BECAME AN ACTION DIRECTED AGAINST OMEGA-- WHICH IN TURN BUT FED HIM, MADE HIM STRONGER.
AND THERE MUST BE MUCH HATRED WITHIN US, FRIENDS--
FOR IS HE NOT HUGE?

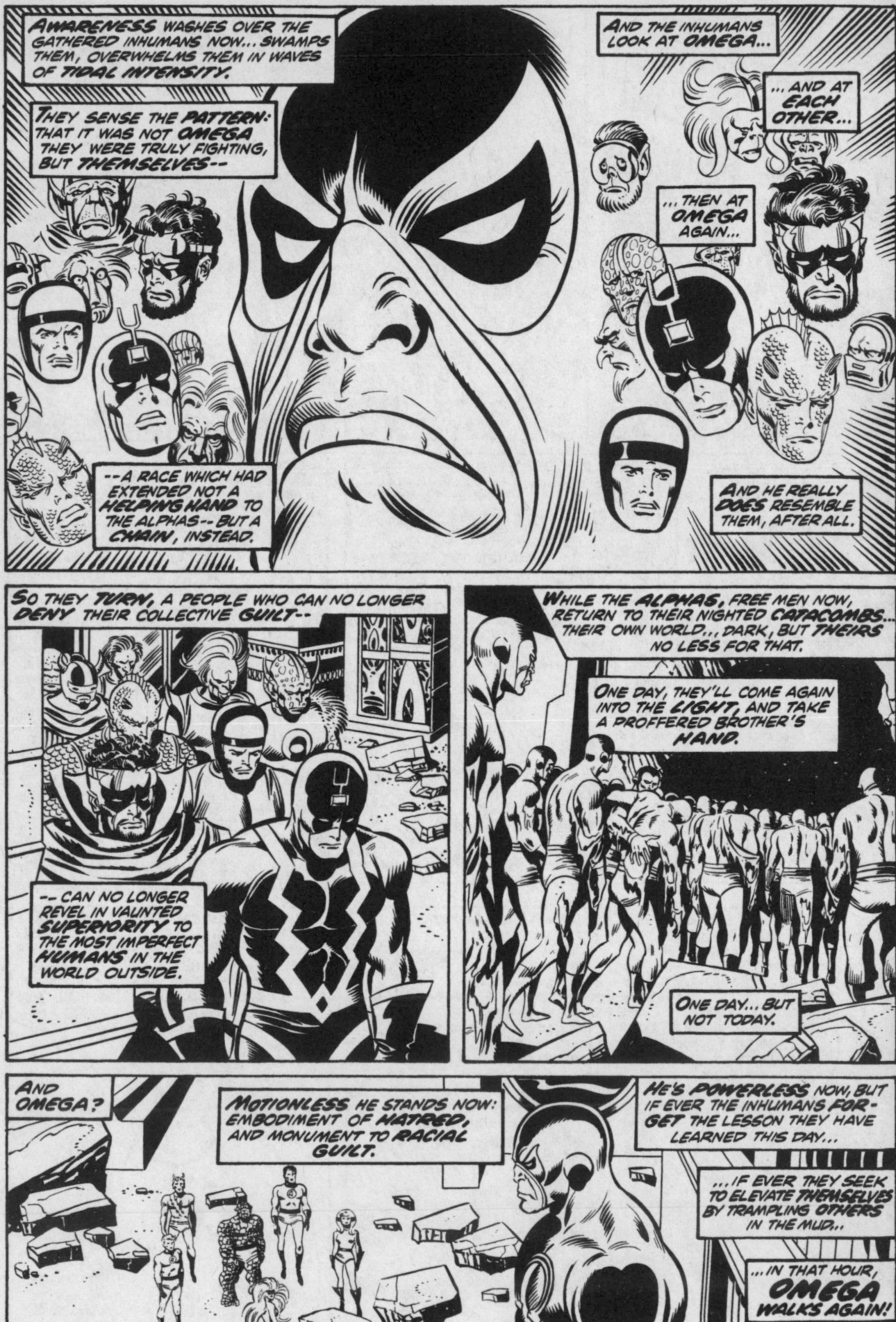
AWARENESS WASHES OVER THE GATHERED INHUMANS NOW... SWAMPS THEM, OVERWHELMS THEM IN WAVES OF TIDAL INTENSITY.
THEY SENSE THE PATTERN: THAT IT WAS NOT OMEGA THEY WERE TRULY FIGHTING, BUT THEMSELVES--
--A RACE WHICH HAD EXTENDED NOT A HELPING HAND TO THE ALPHAS--BUT A CHAIN, INSTEAD.
AND THE INHUMANS LOOK AT OMEGA...
...AND AT EACH OTHER...
...THEN AT OMEGA AGAIN...
AND HE REALLY DOES RESEMBLE THEM, AFTER ALL.
SO THEY TURN, A PEOPLE WHO CAN NO LONGER DENY THEIR COLLECTIVE GUILT--
--CAN NO LONGER REVEL IN VAUNTED SUPERIORITY TO THE MOST IMPERFECT HUMANS IN THE WORLD OUTSIDE.
WHILE THE ALPHAS, FREE MEN NOW, RETURN TO THEIR NIGHTED CATACOMBS... THEIR OWN WORLD... DARK, BUT THEIRS NO LESS FOR THAT.
ONE DAY, THEY'LL COME AGAIN INTO THE LIGHT, AND TAKE A PROFFERED BROTHER'S HAND.
ONE DAY... BUT NOT TODAY.
AND OMEGA?
MOTIONLESS HE STANDS NOW: EMBODIMENT OF HATRED, AND MONUMENT TO RACIAL GUILT.
HE'S POWERLESS NOW, BUT IF EVER THE INHUMANS FOR-GET THE LESSON THEY HAVE LEARNED THIS DAY...
...IF EVER THEY SEEK TO ELEVATE THEMSELVES BY TRAMPLING OTHERS IN THE MUD...
...IN THAT HOUR, OMEGA WALKS AGAIN!

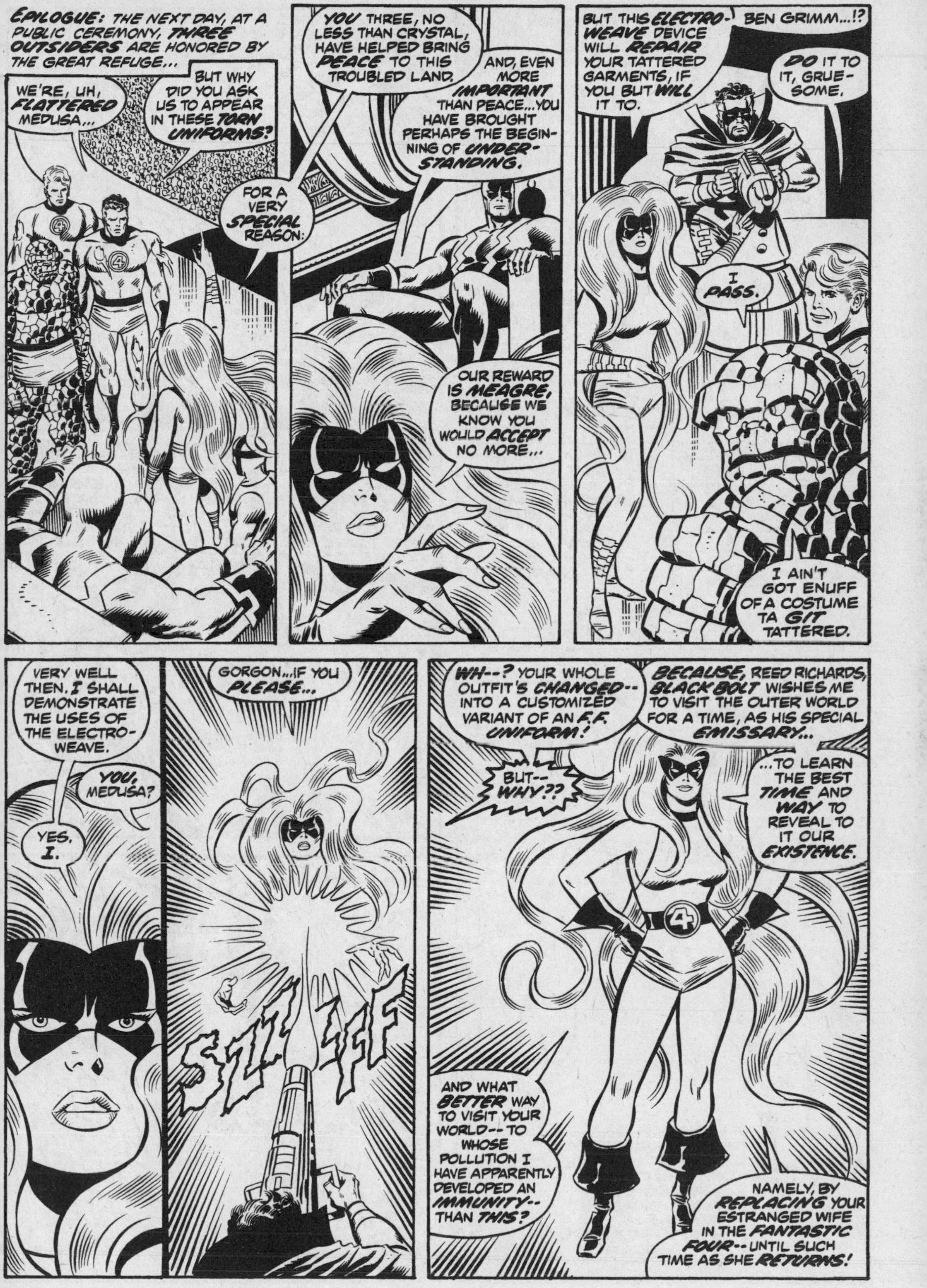
EPILOGUE: THE NEXT DAY, AT A PUBLIC CEREMONY, THREE OUTSIDERS ARE HONORED BY THE GREAT REFUGE...
WE'RE, UH, FLATTERED MEDUSA...
BUT WHY DID YOU ASK US TO APPEAR IN THESE TORN UNIFORMS?
FOR A VERY SPECIAL REASON:
YOU THREE, NO LESS THAN CRYSTAL, HAVE HELPED BRING PEACE TO THIS TROUBLED LAND.
AND, EVEN MORE IMPORTANT THAN PEACE...YOU HAVE BROUGHT PERHAPS THE BEGINNING OF UNDERSTANDING.
OUR REWARD IS MEAGRE, BECAUSE WE KNOW YOU WOULD ACCEPT NO MORE...
BUT THIS ELECTRO-WEAVE DEVICE WILL REPAIR YOUR TATTERED GARMENTS, IF YOU BUT WILL IT TO.
BEN GRIMM...!?
DO IT TO IT, GRUESOME.
I PASS.
I AIN'T GOT ENUFF OF A COSTUME TA GIT TATTERED.
VERY WELL THEN. I SHALL DEMONSTRATE THE USES OF THE ELECTRO-WEAVE.
YOU, MEDUSA?
YES. I.
GORGON...IF YOU PLEASE...
SZZ-FFF
WH--? YOUR WHOLE OUTFIT'S CHANGED--INTO A CUSTOMIZED VARIANT OF AN F.F. UNIFORM!
BUT--WHY??
BECAUSE, REED RICHARDS, BLACK BOLT WISHES ME TO VISIT THE OUTER WORLD FOR A TIME, AS HIS SPECIAL EMISSARY...
...TO LEARN THE BEST TIME AND WAY TO REVEAL TO IT OUR EXISTENCE.
AND WHAT BETTER WAY TO VISIT YOUR WORLD--TO WHOSE POLLUTION I HAVE APPARENTLY DEVELOPED AN IMMUNITY--THAN THIS?
NAMELY, BY REPLACING YOUR ESTRANGED WIFE IN THE FANTASTIC FOUR--UNTIL SUCH TIME AS SHE RETURNS!

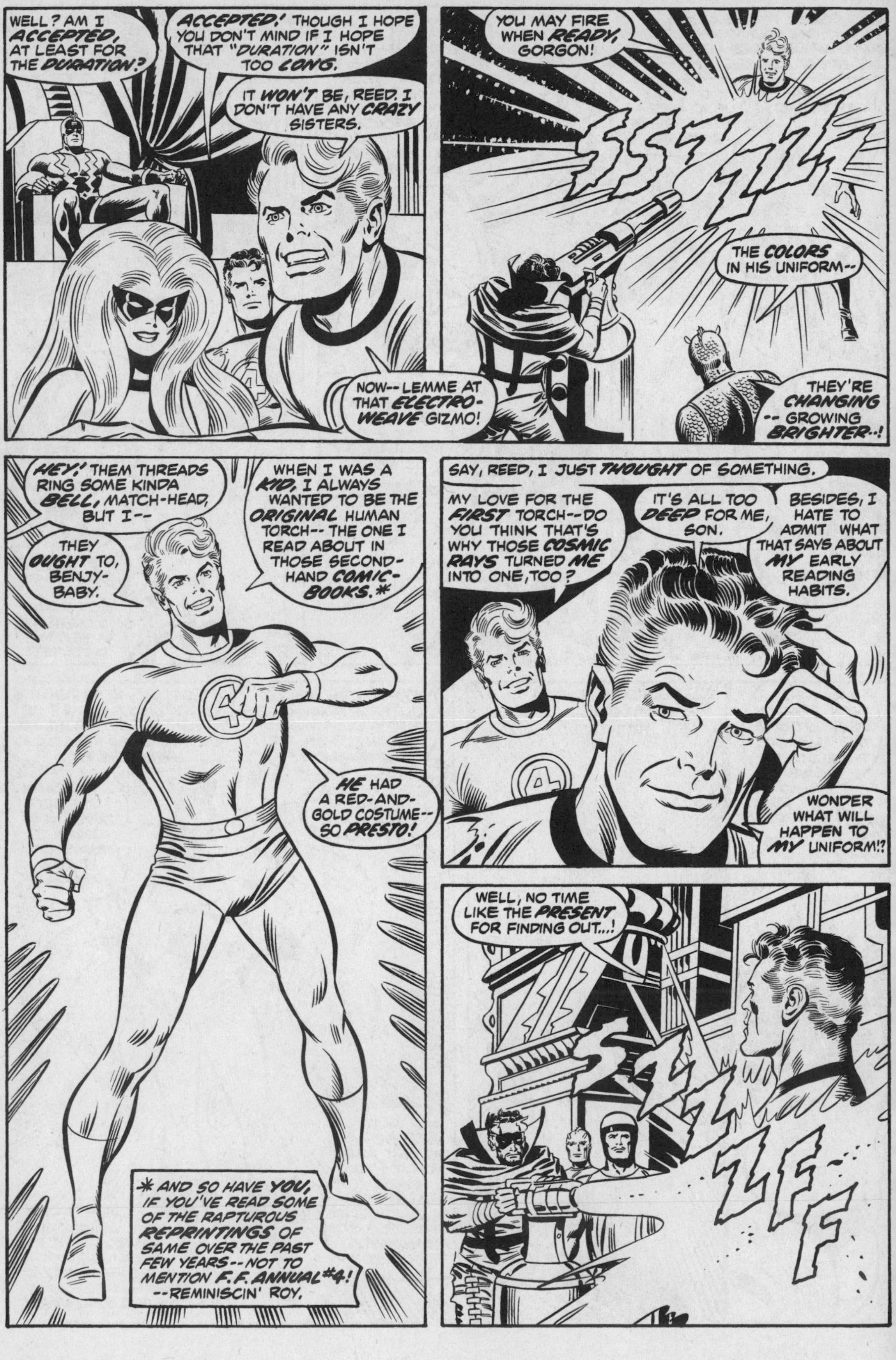
WELL? AM I ACCEPTED, AT LEAST FOR THE DURATION?
ACCEPTED! THOUGH I HOPE YOU DON'T MIND IF I HOPE THAT "DURATION" ISN'T TOO LONG.
IT WON'T BE, REED. I DON'T HAVE ANY CRAZY SISTERS.
NOW--LEMME AT THAT ELECTRO-WEAVE GIZMO!
YOU MAY FIRE WHEN READY, GORGON!
SSSZZZZ
THE COLORS IN HIS UNIFORM--
THEY'RE CHANGING -- GROWING BRIGHTER--!
HEY! THEM THREADS RING SOME KINDA BELL, MATCH-HEAD, BUT I--
THEY OUGHT TO, BENJY-BABY.
WHEN I WAS A KID, I ALWAYS WANTED TO BE THE ORIGINAL HUMAN TORCH-- THE ONE I READ ABOUT IN THOSE SECOND-HAND COMIC-BOOKS.*
HE HAD A RED-AND-GOLD COSTUME--SO PRESTO!
*AND SO HAVE YOU, IF YOU'VE READ SOME OF THE RAPTUROUS REPRINTINGS OF SAME OVER THE PAST FEW YEARS--NOT TO MENTION F.F. ANNUAL #4! --REMINISCIN' ROY.
SAY, REED, I JUST THOUGHT OF SOMETHING.
MY LOVE FOR THE FIRST TORCH--DO YOU THINK THAT'S WHY THOSE COSMIC RAYS TURNED ME INTO ONE, TOO?
IT'S ALL TOO DEEP FOR ME, SON.
BESIDES, I HATE TO ADMIT WHAT THAT SAYS ABOUT MY EARLY READING HABITS.
WONDER WHAT WILL HAPPEN TO MY UNIFORM!?
WELL, NO TIME LIKE THE PRESENT FOR FINDING OUT...!
SZZZZFFF

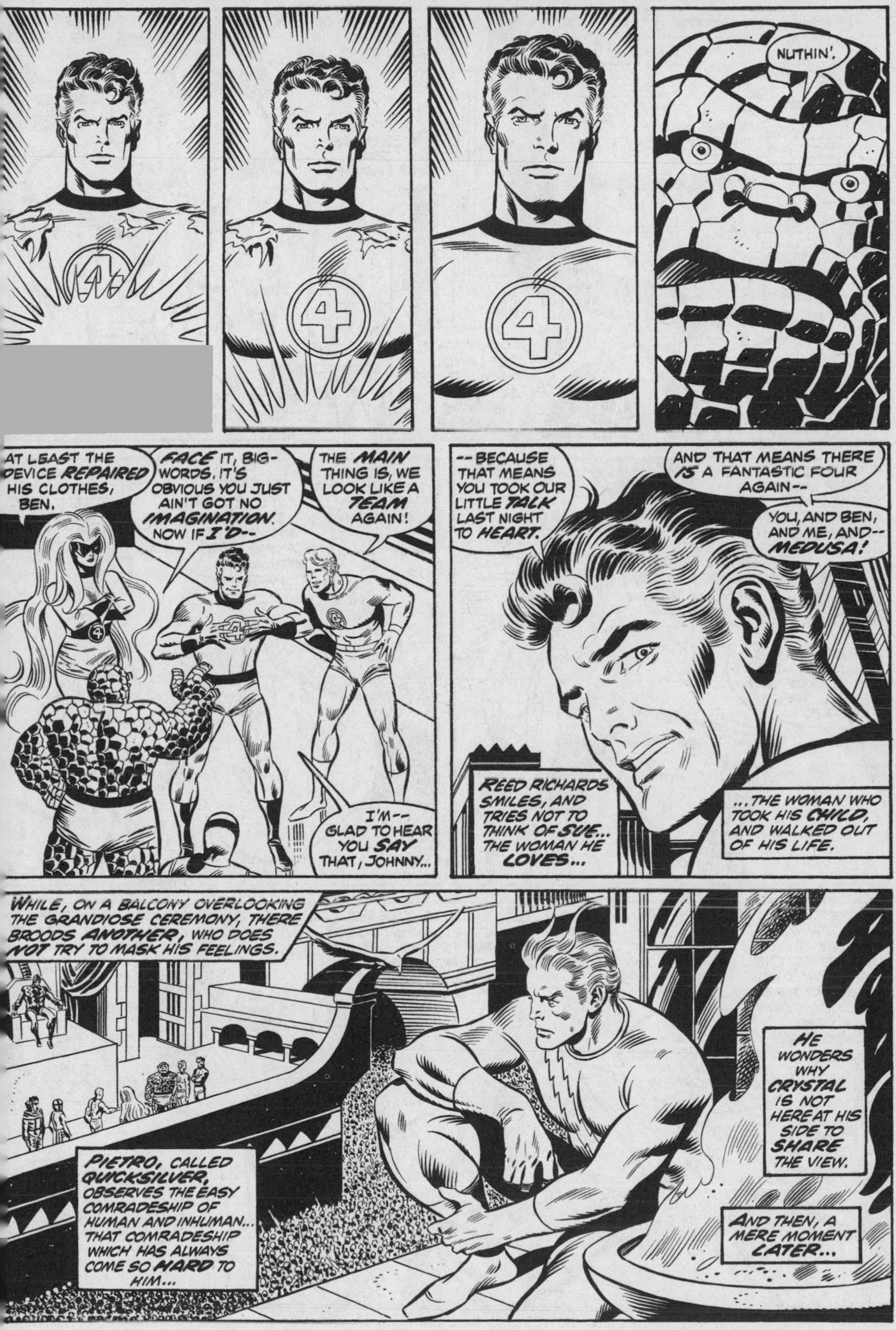
NUTHIN'.
AT LEAST THE DEVICE REPAIRED HIS CLOTHES, BEN.
FACE IT, BIG-WORDS. IT'S OBVIOUS YOU JUST AIN'T GOT NO IMAGINATION. NOW IF I'D--
THE MAIN THING IS, WE LOOK LIKE A TEAM AGAIN!
I'M-- GLAD TO HEAR YOU SAY THAT, JOHNNY...
--BECAUSE THAT MEANS YOU TOOK OUR LITTLE TALK LAST NIGHT TO HEART.
AND THAT MEANS THERE IS A FANTASTIC FOUR AGAIN--
YOU, AND BEN, AND ME, AND-- MEDUSA!
REED RICHARDS SMILES, AND TRIES NOT TO THINK OF SUE... THE WOMAN HE LOVES...
...THE WOMAN WHO TOOK HIS CHILD, AND WALKED OUT OF HIS LIFE.
WHILE, ON A BALCONY OVERLOOKING THE GRANDIOSE CEREMONY, THERE BROODS ANOTHER, WHO DOES NOT TRY TO MASK HIS FEELINGS.
PIETRO, CALLED QUICKSILVER, OBSERVES THE EASY COMRADESHIP OF HUMAN AND INHUMAN... THAT COMRADESHIP WHICH HAS ALWAYS COME SO HARD TO HIM...
HE WONDERS WHY CRYSTAL IS NOT HERE AT HIS SIDE TO SHARE THE VIEW.
AND THEN, A MERE MOMENT LATER...

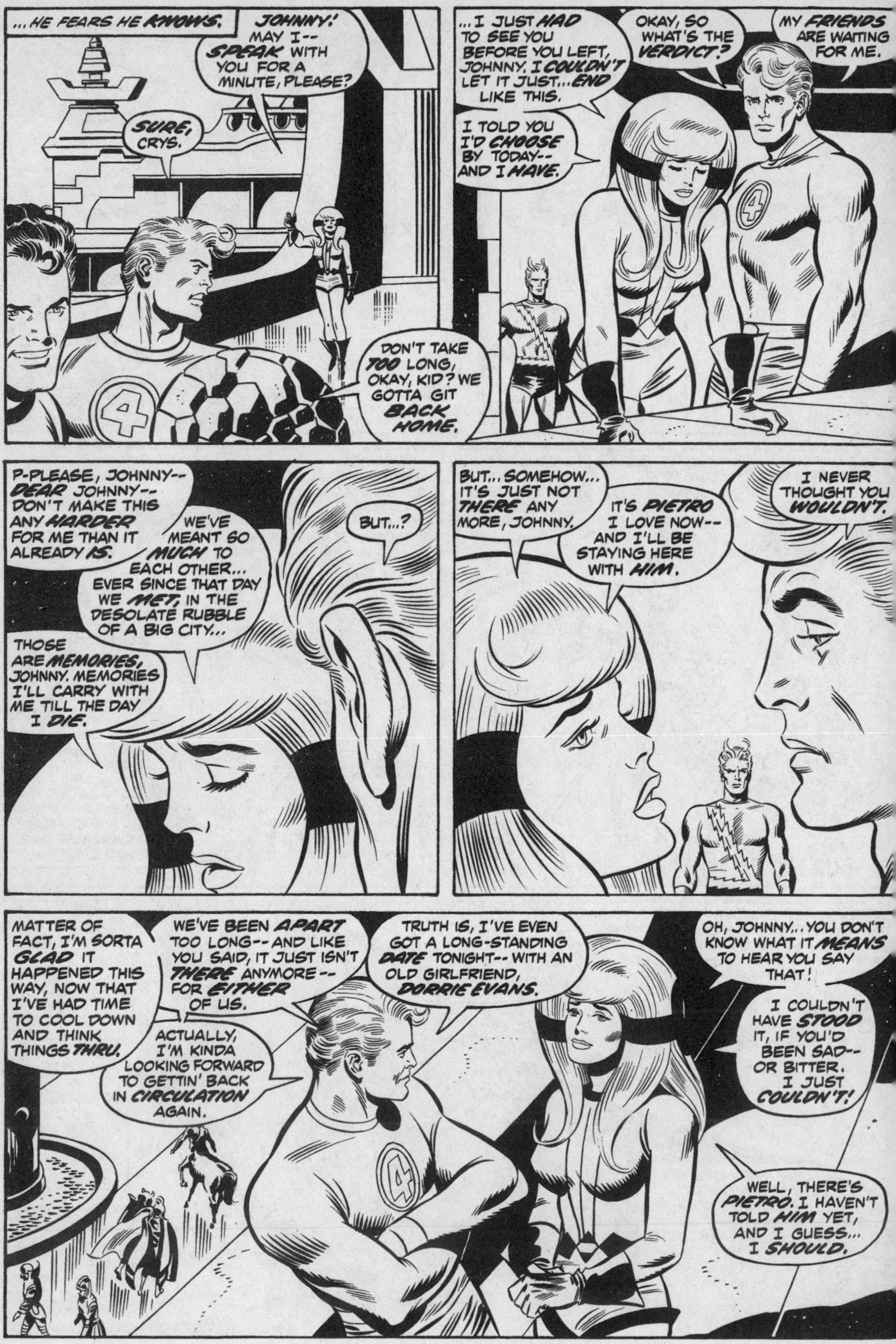

...HE FEARS HE KNOWS.
JOHNNY! MAY I-- SPEAK WITH YOU FOR A MINUTE, PLEASE?
SURE, CRYS.
DON'T TAKE TOO LONG, OKAY, KID? WE GOTTA GIT BACK HOME.
...I JUST HAD TO SEE YOU BEFORE YOU LEFT, JOHNNY. I COULDN'T LET IT JUST...END LIKE THIS.
OKAY, SO WHAT'S THE VERDICT?
MY FRIENDS ARE WAITING FOR ME.
I TOLD YOU I'D CHOOSE BY TODAY-- AND I HAVE.
P-PLEASE, JOHNNY-- DEAR JOHNNY-- DON'T MAKE THIS ANY HARDER FOR ME THAN IT ALREADY IS.
WE'VE MEANT SO MUCH TO EACH OTHER... EVER SINCE THAT DAY WE MET, IN THE DESOLATE RUBBLE OF A BIG CITY...
BUT...?
THOSE ARE MEMORIES, JOHNNY. MEMORIES I'LL CARRY WITH ME TILL THE DAY I DIE.
BUT... SOMEHOW... IT'S JUST NOT THERE ANY MORE, JOHNNY.
IT'S PIETRO I LOVE NOW-- AND I'LL BE STAYING HERE WITH HIM.
I NEVER THOUGHT YOU WOULDN'T.
MATTER OF FACT, I'M SORTA GLAD IT HAPPENED THIS WAY, NOW THAT I'VE HAD TIME TO COOL DOWN AND THINK THINGS THRU.
WE'VE BEEN APART TOO LONG-- AND LIKE YOU SAID, IT JUST ISN'T THERE ANYMORE-- FOR EITHER OF US.
ACTUALLY, I'M KINDA LOOKING FORWARD TO GETTIN' BACK IN CIRCULATION AGAIN.
TRUTH IS, I'VE EVEN GOT A LONG-STANDING DATE TONIGHT-- WITH AN OLD GIRLFRIEND, DORRIE EVANS.
OH, JOHNNY... YOU DON'T KNOW WHAT IT MEANS TO HEAR YOU SAY THAT!
I COULDN'T HAVE STOOD IT, IF YOU'D BEEN SAD-- OR BITTER. I JUST COULDN'T!
WELL, THERE'S PIETRO. I HAVEN'T TOLD HIM YET, AND I GUESS... I SHOULD.

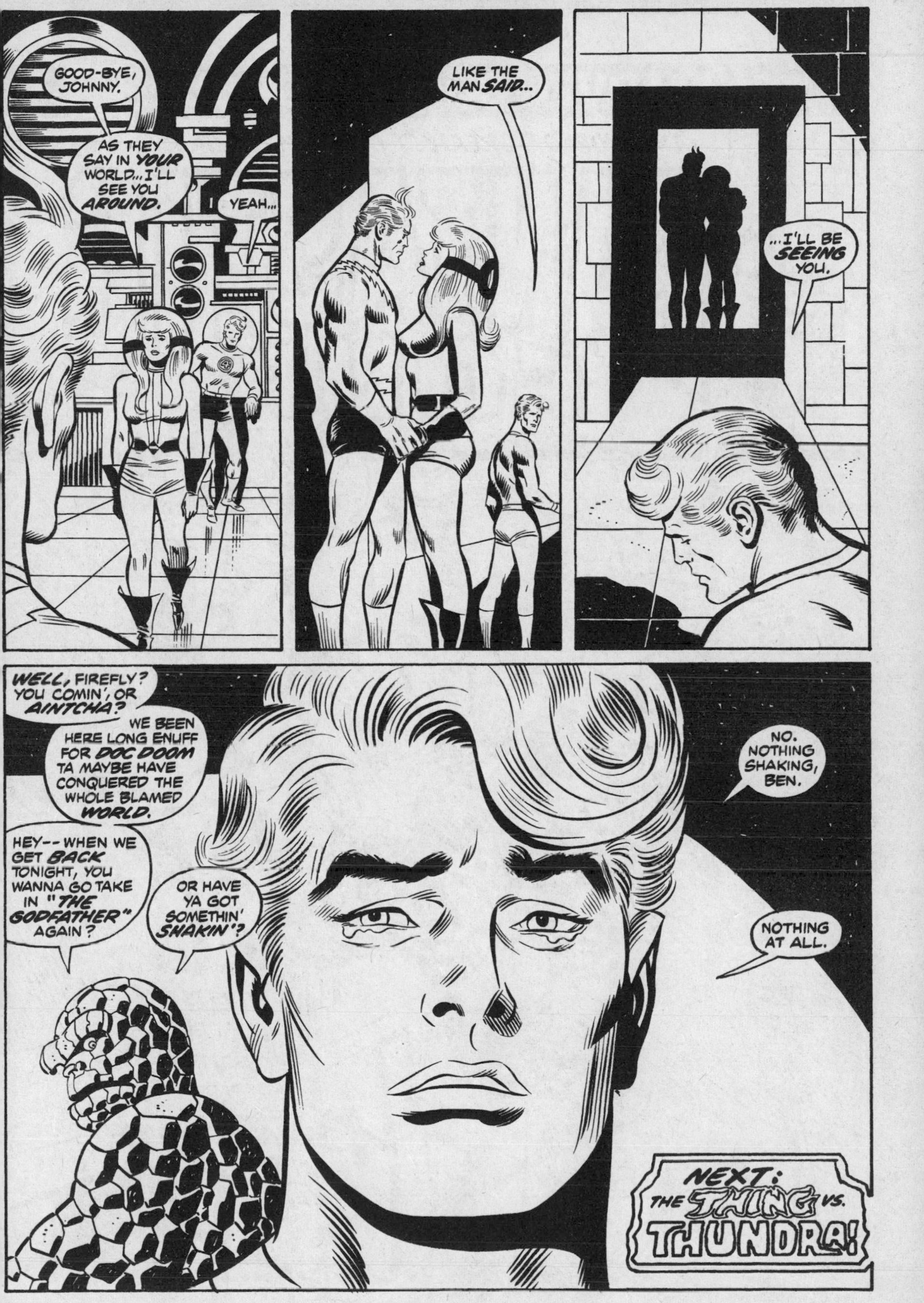
GOOD-BYE, JOHNNY.
AS THEY SAY IN YOUR WORLD... I'LL SEE YOU AROUND.
YEAH...
LIKE THE MAN SAID...
...I'LL BE SEEING YOU.
WELL, FIREFLY? YOU COMIN', OR AINTCHA?
WE BEEN HERE LONG ENUFF FOR DOC DOOM TA MAYBE HAVE CONQUERED THE WHOLE BLAMED WORLD.
HEY--WHEN WE GET BACK TONIGHT, YOU WANNA GO TAKE IN "THE GODFATHER" AGAIN?
OR HAVE YA GOT SOMETHIN' SHAKIN'?
NO. NOTHING SHAKING, BEN.
NOTHING AT ALL.
NEXT: THE THING VS. THUNDRA!

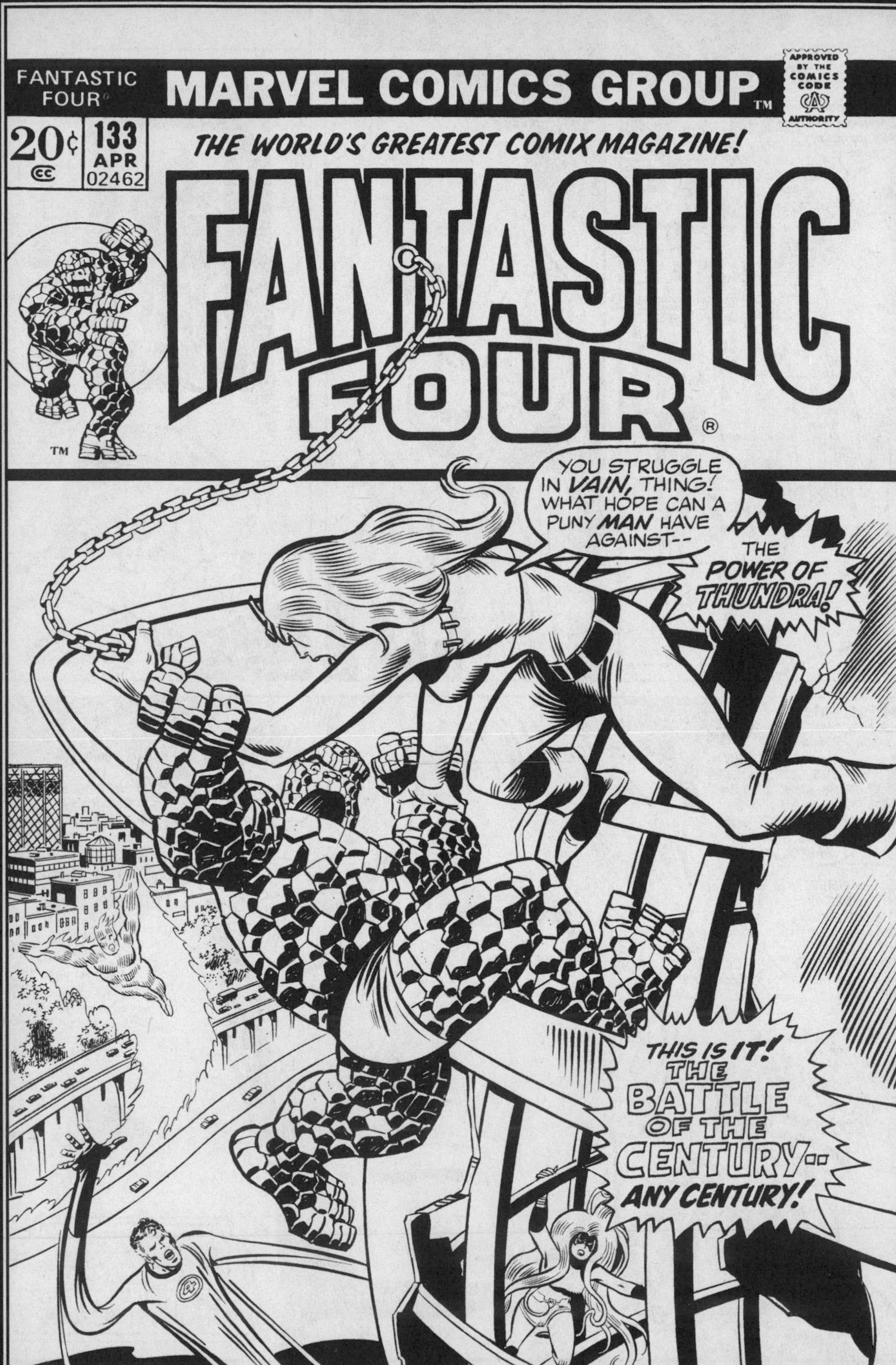

FANTASTIC FOUR
MARVEL COMICS GROUP
APPROVED BY THE COMICS CODE AUTHORITY
20¢
133
APR
02462
THE WORLD'S GREATEST COMIX MAGAZINE!
FANTASTIC FOUR
YOU STRUGGLE IN VAIN, THING! WHAT HOPE CAN A PUNY MAN HAVE AGAINST--
THE POWER OF THUNDRA!
THIS IS IT! THE BATTLE OF THE CENTURY-- ANY CENTURY!

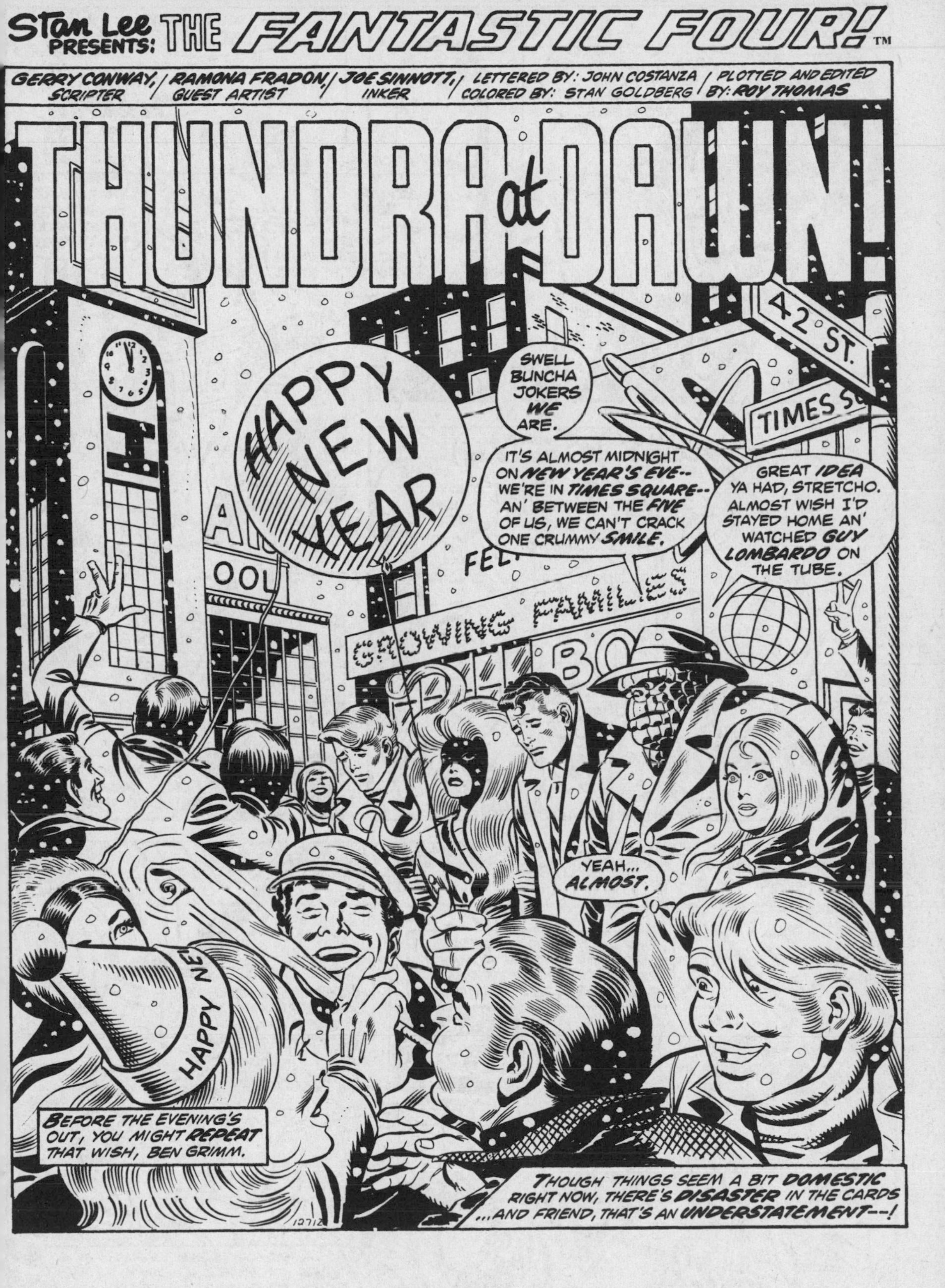

STAN LEE PRESENTS: THE FANTASTIC FOUR!™
GERRY CONWAY, SCRIPTER / RAMONA FRADON, GUEST ARTIST / JOE SINNOTT, INKER / LETTERED BY: JOHN COSTANZA COLORED BY: STAN GOLDBERG / PLOTTED AND EDITED BY: ROY THOMAS
THUNDRA AT DAWN!
42 ST.
TIMES S
HAPPY NEW YEAR
SWELL BUNCHA JOKERS WE ARE.
IT'S ALMOST MIDNIGHT ON NEW YEAR'S EVE-- WE'RE IN TIMES SQUARE-- AN' BETWEEN THE FIVE OF US, WE CAN'T CRACK ONE CRUMMY SMILE.
GREAT IDEA YA HAD, STRETCHO. ALMOST WISH I'D STAYED HOME AN' WATCHED GUY LOMBARDO ON THE TUBE.
GROWING FAMILIES
YEAH... ALMOST.
HAPPY NE
BEFORE THE EVENING'S OUT, YOU MIGHT REPEAT THAT WISH, BEN GRIMM.
THOUGH THINGS SEEM A BIT DOMESTIC RIGHT NOW, THERE'S DISASTER IN THE CARDS ...AND FRIEND, THAT'S AN UNDERSTATEMENT--!

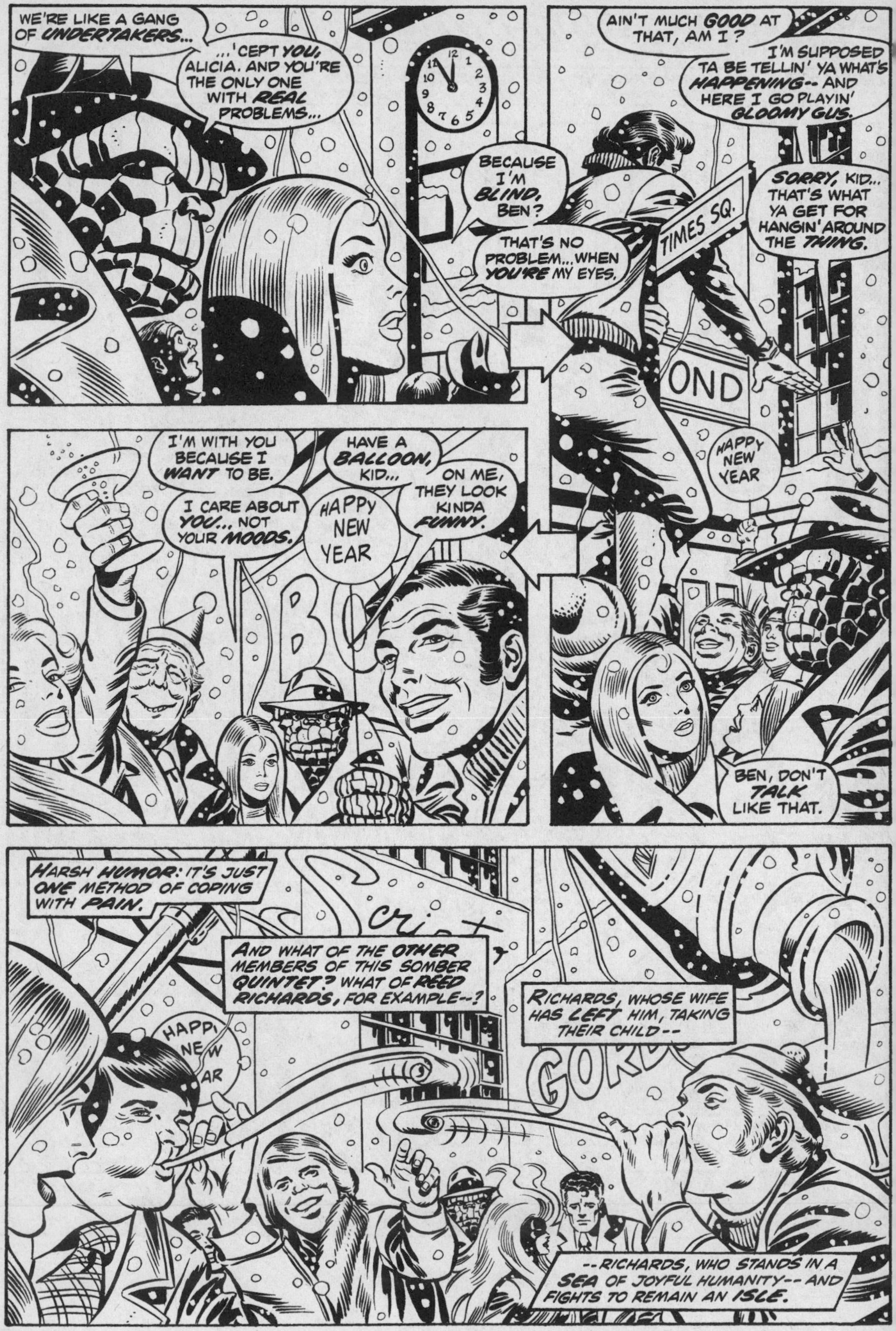

WE'RE LIKE A GANG OF UNDERTAKERS...
...'CEPT YOU, ALICIA. AND YOU'RE THE ONLY ONE WITH REAL PROBLEMS...
BECAUSE I'M BLIND, BEN?
THAT'S NO PROBLEM...WHEN YOU'RE MY EYES.
AIN'T MUCH GOOD AT THAT, AM I?
I'M SUPPOSED TA BE TELLIN' YA WHAT'S HAPPENING-- AND HERE I GO PLAYIN' GLOOMY GUS.
SORRY, KID... THAT'S WHAT YA GET FOR HANGIN' AROUND THE THING.
TIMES SQ.
OND
HAPPY NEW YEAR
I'M WITH YOU BECAUSE I WANT TO BE.
I CARE ABOUT YOU... NOT YOUR MOODS.
HAVE A BALLOON, KID...
ON ME, THEY LOOK KINDA FUNNY.
HAPPY NEW YEAR
BEN, DON'T TALK LIKE THAT.
HARSH HUMOR: IT'S JUST ONE METHOD OF COPING WITH PAIN.
AND WHAT OF THE OTHER MEMBERS OF THIS SOMBER QUINTET? WHAT OF REED RICHARDS, FOR EXAMPLE--?
RICHARDS, WHOSE WIFE HAS LEFT HIM, TAKING THEIR CHILD--
--RICHARDS, WHO STANDS IN A SEA OF JOYFUL HUMANITY-- AND FIGHTS TO REMAIN AN ISLE.

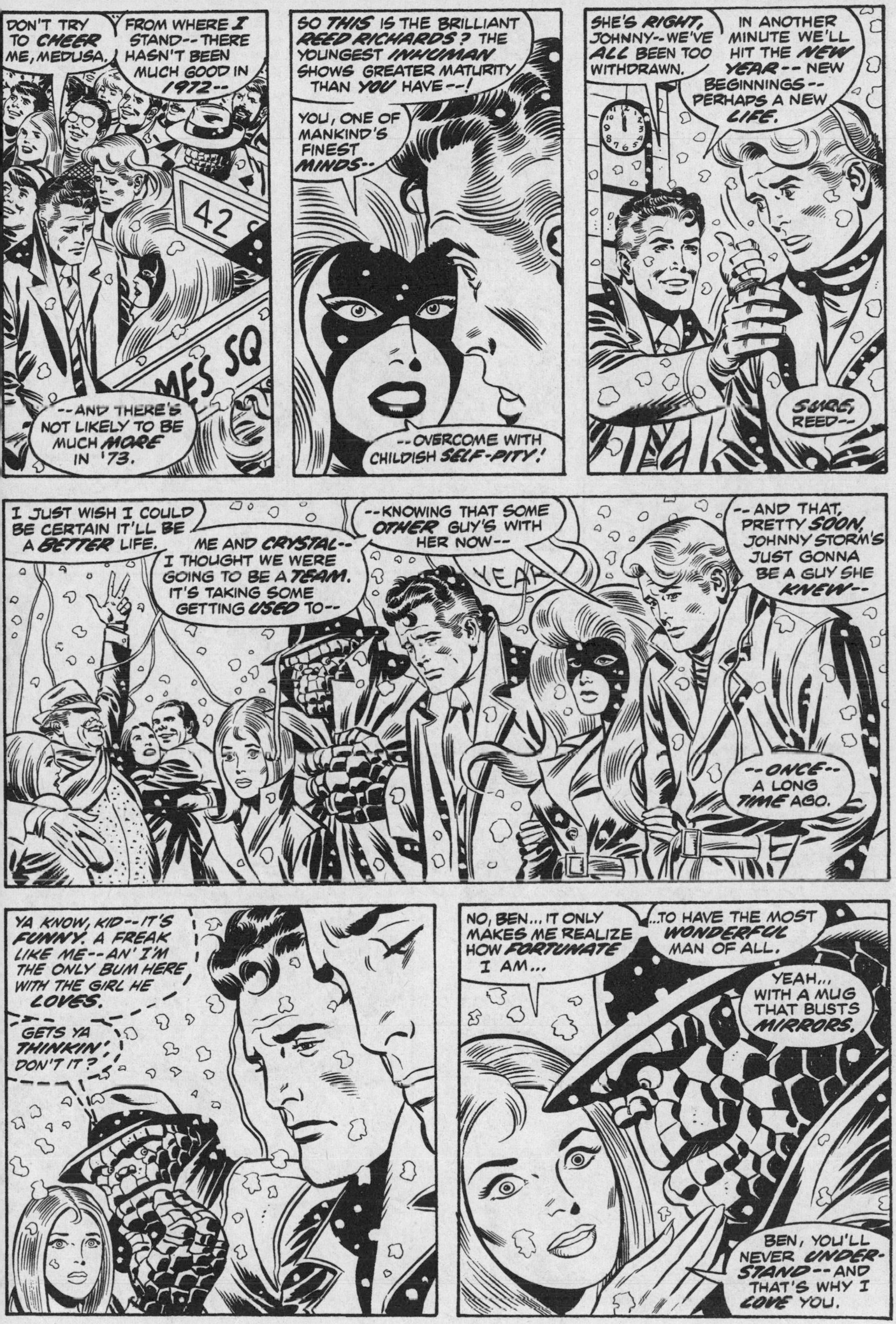
DON'T TRY TO CHEER ME, MEDUSA.
FROM WHERE I STAND--THERE HASN'T BEEN MUCH GOOD IN 1972--
--AND THERE'S NOT LIKELY TO BE MUCH MORE IN '73.
42 S
MES SQ
SO THIS IS THE BRILLIANT REED RICHARDS? THE YOUNGEST INHUMAN SHOWS GREATER MATURITY THAN YOU HAVE--!
YOU, ONE OF MANKIND'S FINEST MINDS--
--OVERCOME WITH CHILDISH SELF-PITY!
SHE'S RIGHT, JOHNNY--WE'VE ALL BEEN TOO WITHDRAWN.
IN ANOTHER MINUTE WE'LL HIT THE NEW YEAR--NEW BEGINNINGS--PERHAPS A NEW LIFE.
SURE, REED--
I JUST WISH I COULD BE CERTAIN IT'LL BE A BETTER LIFE.
ME AND CRYSTAL--I THOUGHT WE WERE GOING TO BE A TEAM. IT'S TAKING SOME GETTING USED TO--
--KNOWING THAT SOME OTHER GUY'S WITH HER NOW--
YEAR
--AND THAT, PRETTY SOON, JOHNNY STORM'S JUST GONNA BE A GUY SHE KNEW--
--ONCE--A LONG TIME AGO.
YA KNOW, KID--IT'S FUNNY. A FREAK LIKE ME--AN' I'M THE ONLY BUM HERE WITH THE GIRL HE LOVES.
GETS YA THINKIN', DON'T IT?
NO, BEN... IT ONLY MAKES ME REALIZE HOW FORTUNATE I AM...
...TO HAVE THE MOST WONDERFUL MAN OF ALL.
YEAH,.. WITH A MUG THAT BUSTS MIRRORS.
BEN, YOU'LL NEVER UNDER-STAND--AND THAT'S WHY I LOVE YOU.

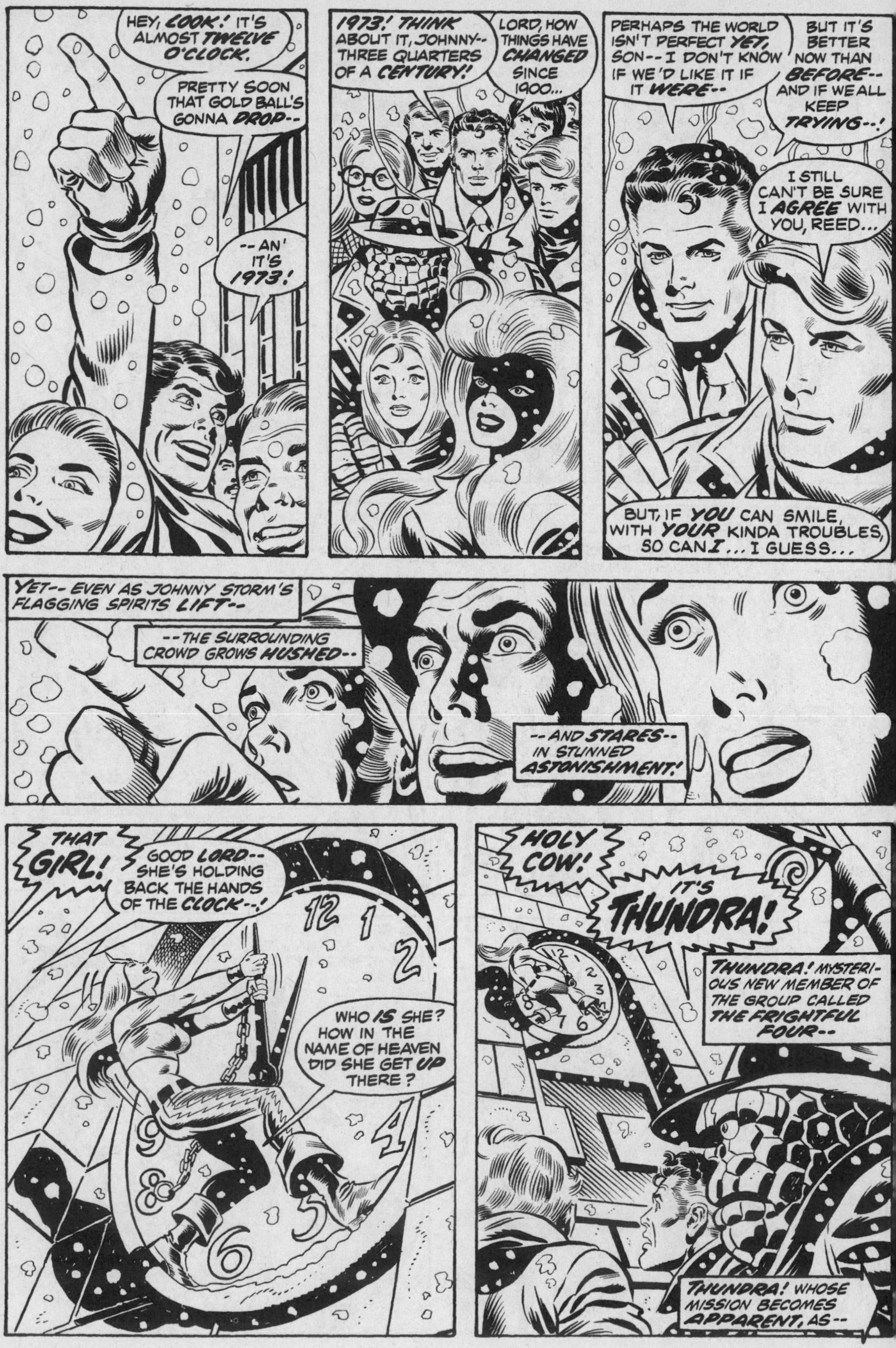
HEY, LOOK! IT'S ALMOST TWELVE O'CLOCK.
PRETTY SOON THAT GOLD BALL'S GONNA DROP--
--AN' IT'S 1973!
1973! THINK ABOUT IT, JOHNNY-- THREE QUARTERS OF A CENTURY!
LORD, HOW THINGS HAVE CHANGED SINCE 1900...
PERHAPS THE WORLD ISN'T PERFECT YET, SON-- I DON'T KNOW IF WE'D LIKE IT IF IT WERE--
BUT IT'S BETTER NOW THAN BEFORE-- AND IF WE ALL KEEP TRYING--!
I STILL CAN'T BE SURE I AGREE WITH YOU, REED...
BUT, IF YOU CAN SMILE, WITH YOUR KINDA TROUBLES, SO CAN I... I GUESS...
YET-- EVEN AS JOHNNY STORM'S FLAGGING SPIRITS LIFT--
--THE SURROUNDING CROWD GROWS HUSHED--
--AND STARES-- IN STUNNED ASTONISHMENT!
THAT GIRL!
GOOD LORD-- SHE'S HOLDING BACK THE HANDS OF THE CLOCK--!
WHO IS SHE? HOW IN THE NAME OF HEAVEN DID SHE GET UP THERE?
HOLY COW!
IT'S THUNDRA!
THUNDRA! MYSTERIOUS NEW MEMBER OF THE GROUP CALLED THE FRIGHTFUL FOUR--
THUNDRA! WHOSE MISSION BECOMES APPARENT, AS--

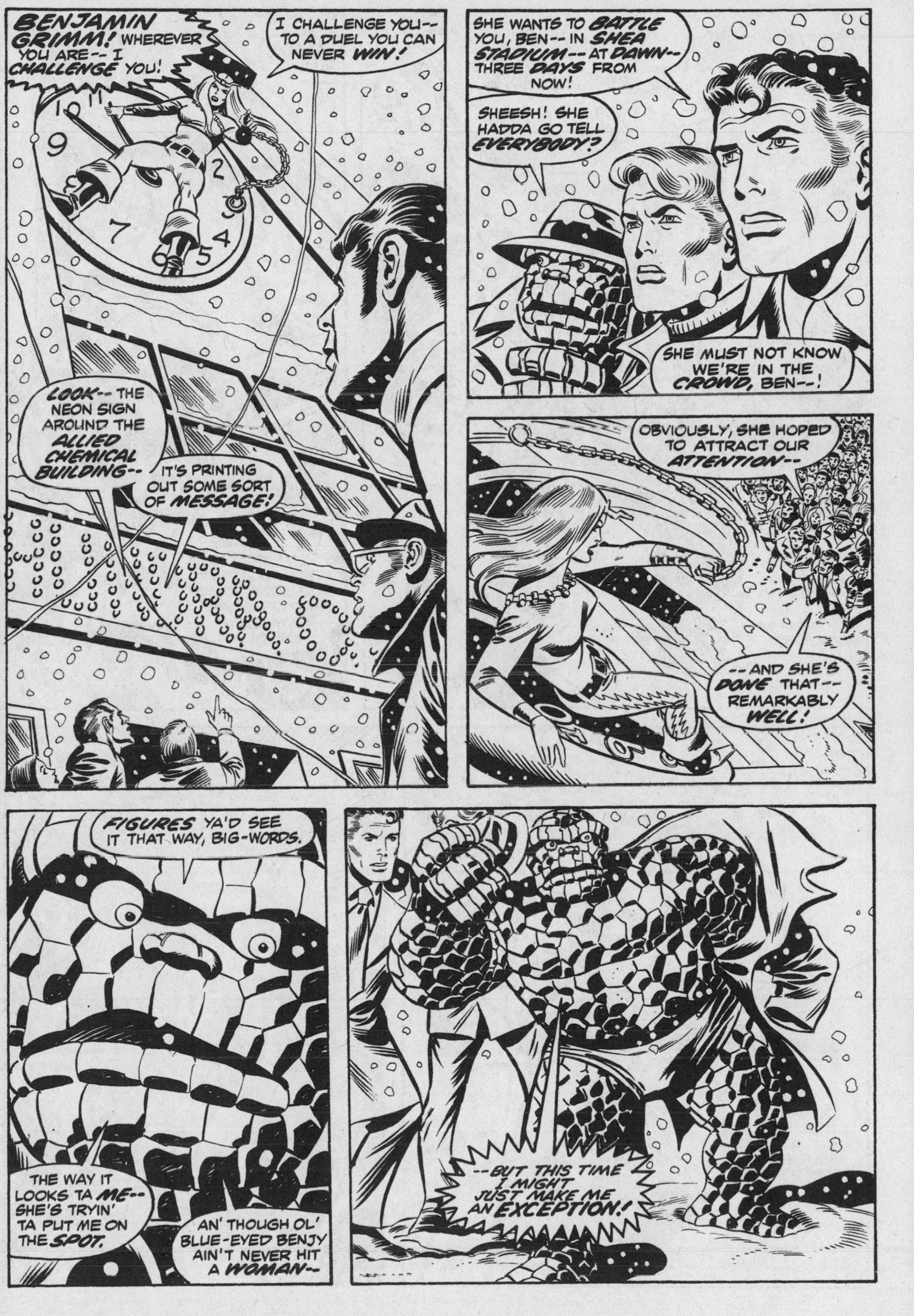

BENJAMIN GRIMM! WHEREVER YOU ARE-- I CHALLENGE YOU!
I CHALLENGE YOU-- TO A DUEL YOU CAN NEVER WIN!
LOOK-- THE NEON SIGN AROUND THE ALLIED CHEMICAL BUILDING--
IT'S PRINTING OUT SOME SORT OF MESSAGE!
SHE WANTS TO BATTLE YOU, BEN-- IN SHEA STADIUM-- AT DAWN-- THREE DAYS FROM NOW!
SHEESH! SHE HADDA GO TELL EVERYBODY?
SHE MUST NOT KNOW WE'RE IN THE CROWD, BEN--!
OBVIOUSLY, SHE HOPED TO ATTRACT OUR ATTENTION--
--AND SHE'S DONE THAT-- REMARKABLY WELL!
FIGURES YA'D SEE IT THAT WAY, BIG-WORDS.
THE WAY IT LOOKS TA ME-- SHE'S TRYIN' TA PUT ME ON THE SPOT.
AN' THOUGH OL' BLUE-EYED BENJY AIN'T NEVER HIT A WOMAN--
--BUT THIS TIME I MIGHT JUST MAKE ME AN EXCEPTION!

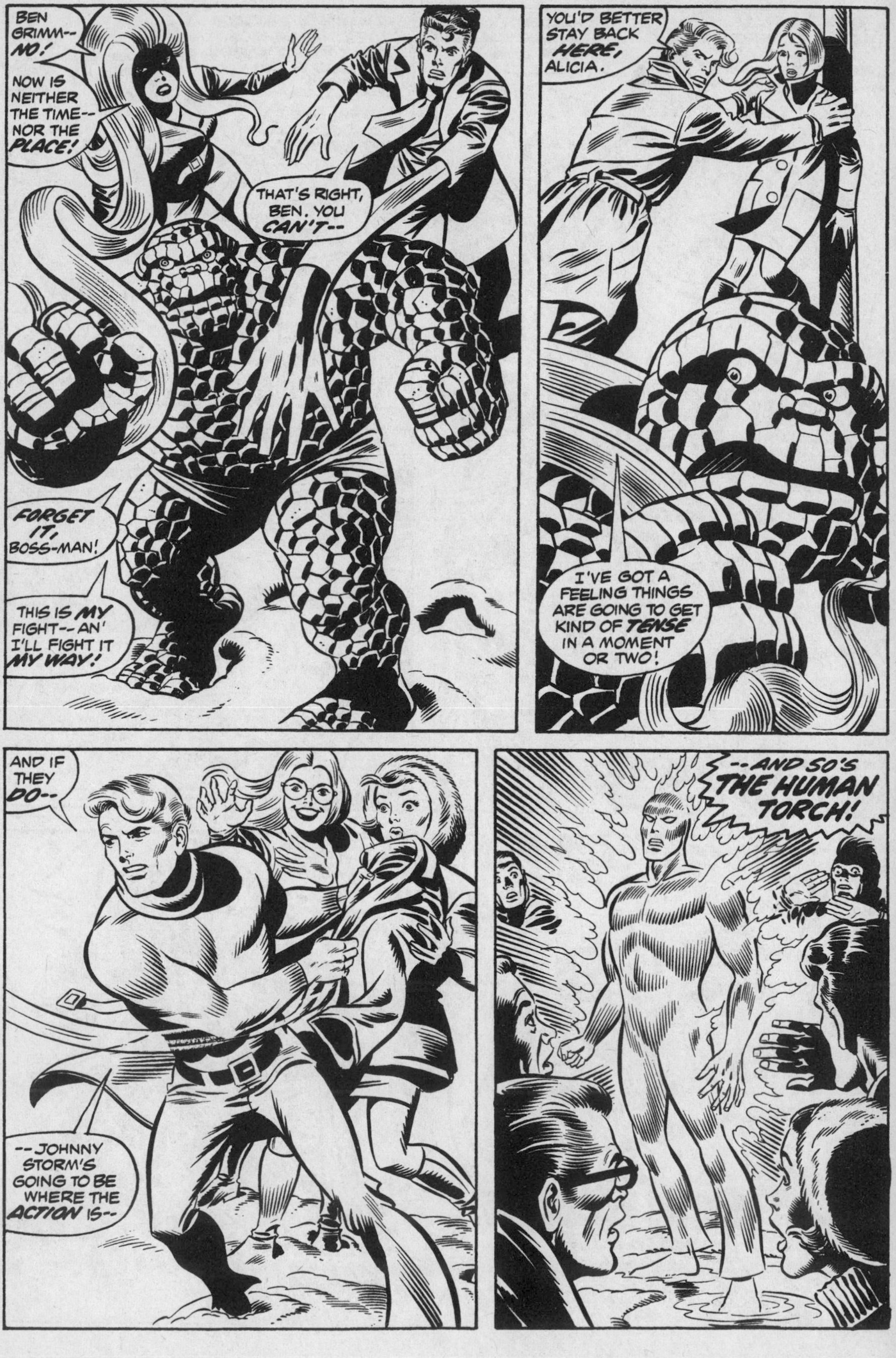

BEN GRIMM-- NO!
NOW IS NEITHER THE TIME-- NOR THE PLACE!
THAT'S RIGHT, BEN. YOU CAN'T--
FORGET IT, BOSS-MAN!
THIS IS MY FIGHT-- AN' I'LL FIGHT IT MY WAY!
YOU'D BETTER STAY BACK HERE, ALICIA.
I'VE GOT A FEELING THINGS ARE GOING TO GET KIND OF TENSE IN A MOMENT OR TWO!
AND IF THEY DO--
--JOHNNY STORM'S GOING TO BE WHERE THE ACTION IS--
--AND SO'S THE HUMAN TORCH!

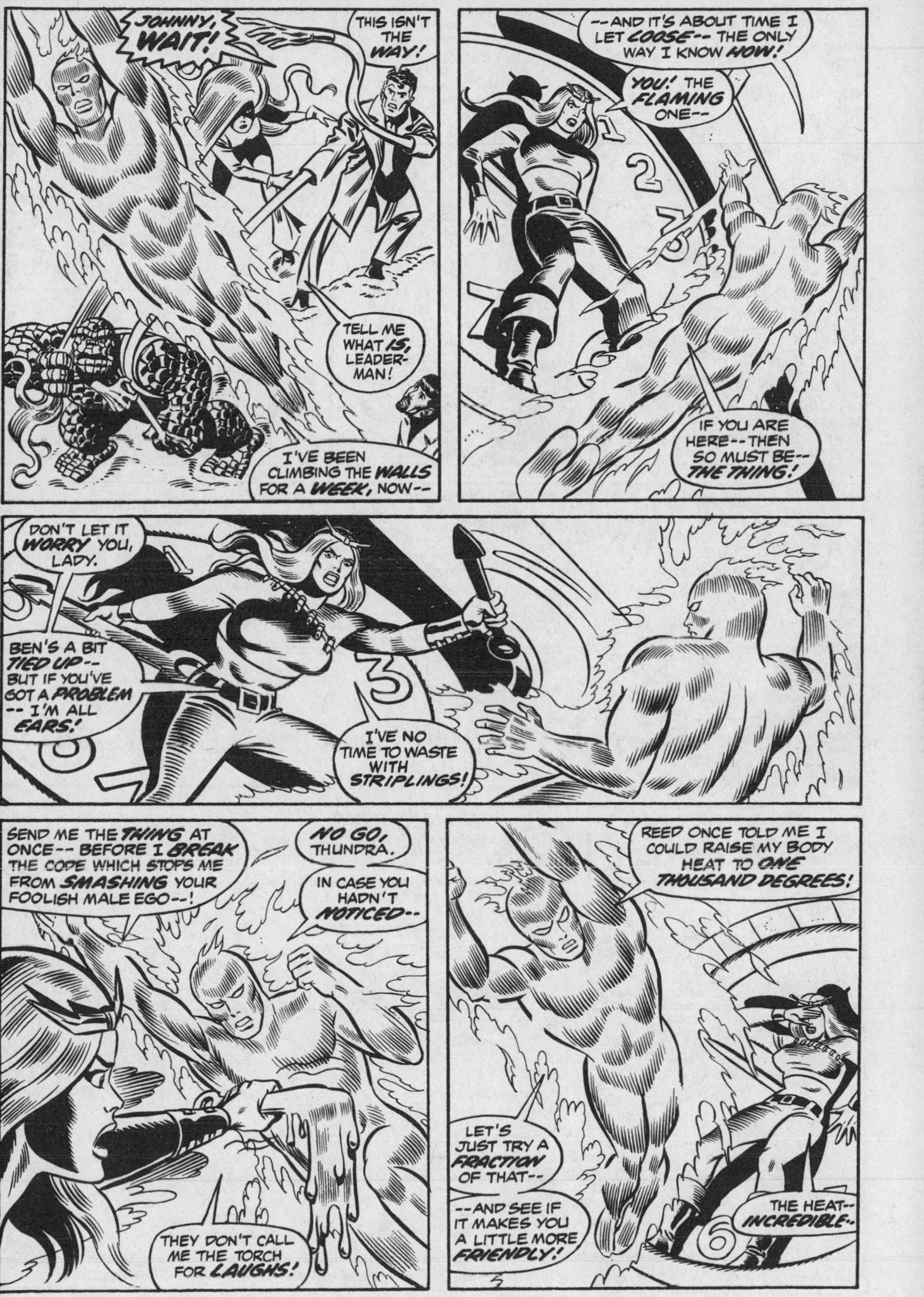
JOHNNY, WAIT!
THIS ISN'T THE WAY!
TELL ME WHAT IS, LEADER-MAN!
I'VE BEEN CLIMBING THE WALLS FOR A WEEK, NOW--
--AND IT'S ABOUT TIME I LET LOOSE-- THE ONLY WAY I KNOW HOW!
YOU! THE FLAMING ONE--
IF YOU ARE HERE--THEN SO MUST BE-- THE THING!
DON'T LET IT WORRY YOU, LADY.
BEN'S A BIT TIED UP-- BUT IF YOU'VE GOT A PROBLEM -- I'M ALL EARS!
I'VE NO TIME TO WASTE WITH STRIPLINGS!
SEND ME THE THING AT ONCE-- BEFORE I BREAK THE CODE WHICH STOPS ME FROM SMASHING YOUR FOOLISH MALE EGO--!
NO GO, THUNDRA.
IN CASE YOU HADN'T NOTICED--
THEY DON'T CALL ME THE TORCH FOR LAUGHS!
REED ONCE TOLD ME I COULD RAISE MY BODY HEAT TO ONE THOUSAND DEGREES!
LET'S JUST TRY A FRACTION OF THAT--
--AND SEE IF IT MAKES YOU A LITTLE MORE FRIENDLY!
THE HEAT-- INCREDIBLE..

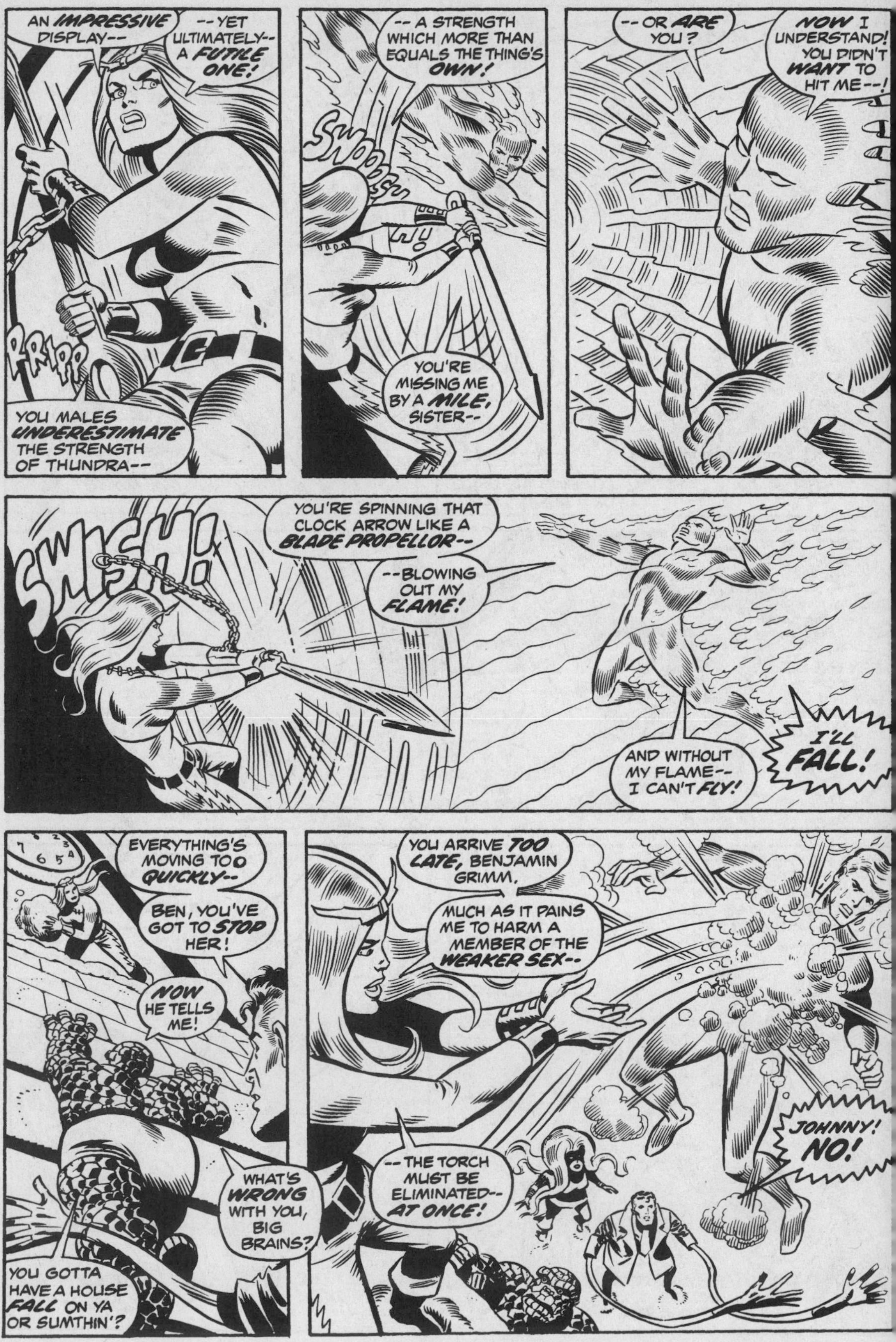

AN IMPRESSIVE DISPLAY--
--YET ULTIMATELY-- A FUTILE ONE!
PRIPP
YOU MALES UNDERESTIMATE THE STRENGTH OF THUNDRA--
-- A STRENGTH WHICH MORE THAN EQUALS THE THING'S OWN!
SWOOSH
YOU'RE MISSING ME BY A MILE, SISTER--
-- OR ARE YOU?
NOW I UNDERSTAND! YOU DIDN'T WANT TO HIT ME--!
SWISH!
YOU'RE SPINNING THAT CLOCK ARROW LIKE A BLADE PROPELLOR--
--BLOWING OUT MY FLAME!
AND WITHOUT MY FLAME-- I CAN'T FLY!
I'LL FALL!
EVERYTHING'S MOVING TOO QUICKLY--
BEN, YOU'VE GOT TO STOP HER!
NOW HE TELLS ME!
WHAT'S WRONG WITH YOU, BIG BRAINS?
YOU GOTTA HAVE A HOUSE FALL ON YA OR SUMTHIN'?
YOU ARRIVE TOO LATE, BENJAMIN GRIMM.
MUCH AS IT PAINS ME TO HARM A MEMBER OF THE WEAKER SEX--
--THE TORCH MUST BE ELIMINATED-- AT ONCE!
JOHNNY! NO!

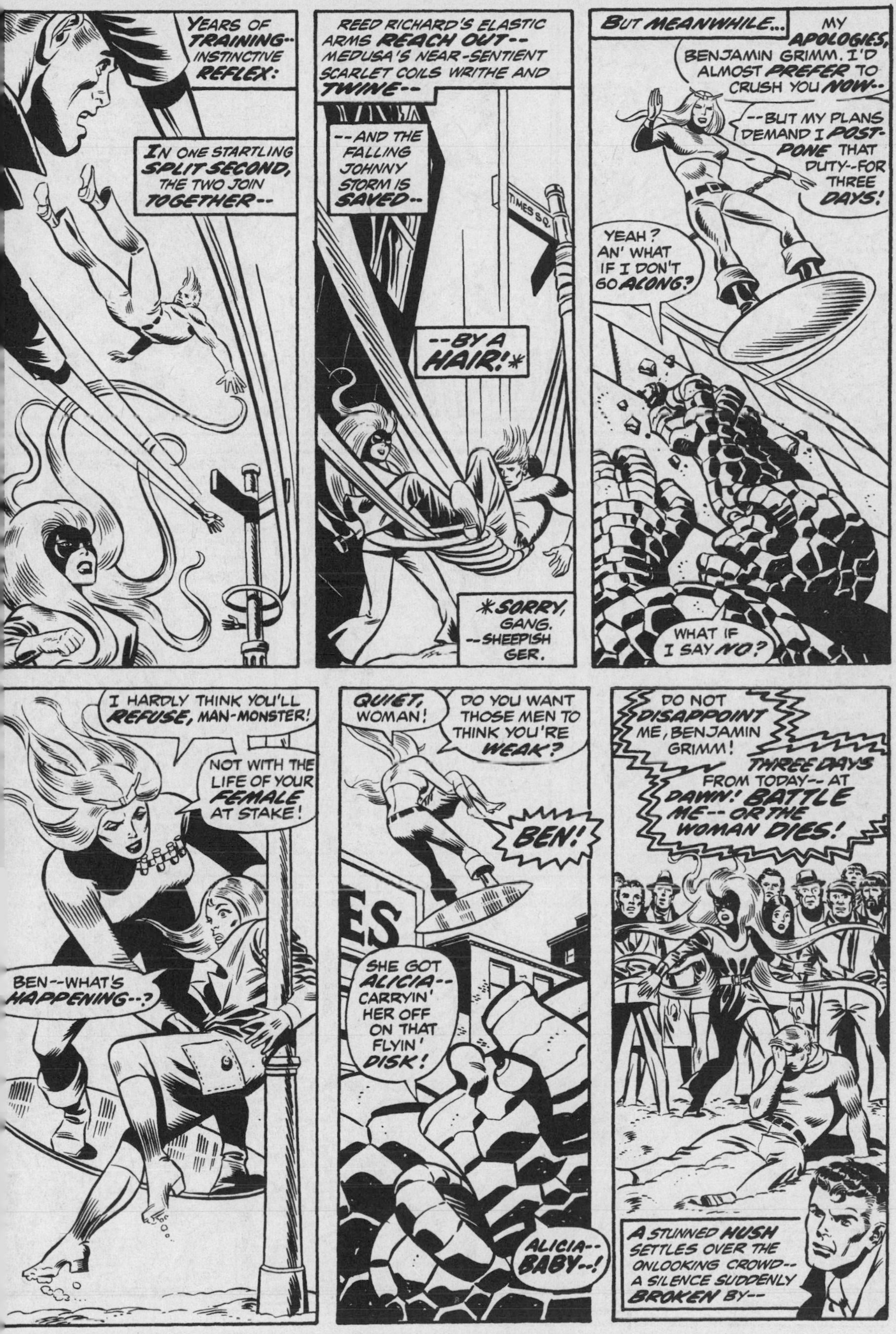

YEARS OF TRAINING-- INSTINCTIVE REFLEX:
IN ONE STARTLING SPLIT SECOND, THE TWO JOIN TOGETHER--
REED RICHARD'S ELASTIC ARMS REACH OUT-- MEDUSA'S NEAR-SENTIENT SCARLET COILS WRITHE AND TWINE--
--AND THE FALLING JOHNNY STORM IS SAVED--
TIMES SQ
--BY A HAIR!*
*SORRY, GANG. --SHEEPISH GER.
BUT MEANWHILE...
MY APOLOGIES, BENJAMIN GRIMM. I'D ALMOST PREFER TO CRUSH YOU NOW--
--BUT MY PLANS DEMAND I POST-PONE THAT DUTY--FOR THREE DAYS!
YEAH? AN' WHAT IF I DON'T GO ALONG?
WHAT IF I SAY NO?
I HARDLY THINK YOU'LL REFUSE, MAN-MONSTER!
NOT WITH THE LIFE OF YOUR FEMALE AT STAKE!
BEN--WHAT'S HAPPENING--?
QUIET, WOMAN!
DO YOU WANT THOSE MEN TO THINK YOU'RE WEAK?
BEN!
ES
SHE GOT ALICIA-- CARRYIN' HER OFF ON THAT FLYIN' DISK!
ALICIA-- BABY--!
DO NOT DISAPPOINT ME, BENJAMIN GRIMM!
THREE DAYS FROM TODAY-- AT DAWN! BATTLE ME-- OR THE WOMAN DIES!
A STUNNED HUSH SETTLES OVER THE ONLOOKING CROWD-- A SILENCE SUDDENLY BROKEN BY--

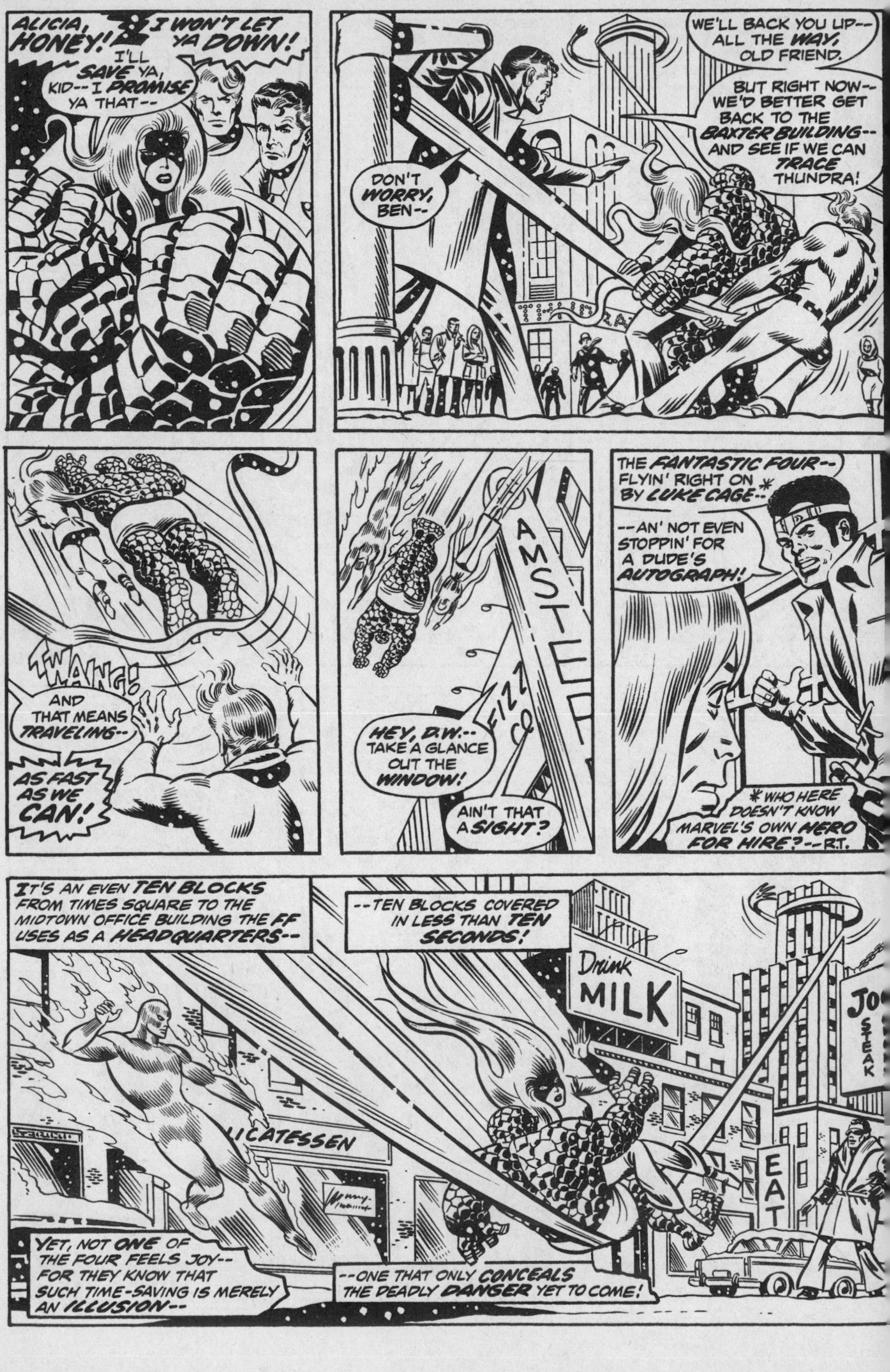
ALICIA, HONEY! I WON'T LET YA DOWN!
I'LL SAVE YA, KID--I PROMISE YA THAT--
WE'LL BACK YOU UP--ALL THE WAY, OLD FRIEND.
BUT RIGHT NOW--WE'D BETTER GET BACK TO THE BAXTER BUILDING--AND SEE IF WE CAN TRACE THUNDRA!
DON'T WORRY, BEN--
TWANG!
AND THAT MEANS TRAVELING--
AS FAST AS WE CAN!
AMSTER
FIZZ CO
HEY, D.W.--TAKE A GLANCE OUT THE WINDOW!
AIN'T THAT A SIGHT?
THE FANTASTIC FOUR--FLYIN' RIGHT ON BY LUKE CAGE--*
--AN' NOT EVEN STOPPIN' FOR A DUDE'S AUTOGRAPH!
*WHO HERE DOESN'T KNOW MARVEL'S OWN HERO FOR HIRE?--R.T.
IT'S AN EVEN TEN BLOCKS FROM TIMES SQUARE TO THE MIDTOWN OFFICE BUILDING THE FF USES AS A HEADQUARTERS--
--TEN BLOCKS COVERED IN LESS THAN TEN SECONDS!
Drink MILK
JO STEAK
LICATESSEN
EAT
YET, NOT ONE OF THE FOUR FEELS JOY--FOR THEY KNOW THAT SUCH TIME-SAVING IS MERELY AN ILLUSION--
--ONE THAT ONLY CONCEALS THE DEADLY DANGER YET TO COME!

...LATE LAST NIGHT, AND SINCE THAT TIME *SPECULATION* ABOUT THURSDAY'S DAWN BATTLE HAS GROWN INCREASINGLY *DRAMATIC*.

ALREADY, THE CITY'S *OFF-TRACK BETTING* CORPORATION HAS ISSUED *ODDS* ON THE FIGHT --

VS THUN 7-5

-- AND MANY OF THE NATION'S LEADING *NEWSPAPERS* HAVE JOINED IN A JOURNAL-ISTIC *RACE* TO GARNER THE WIDEST *OPINION* ON THE SUBJECT!

DAILY LEDGER
BATTLE SET FOR...

MORNING LEDGER
FIGHT OF THE CENTURY

"EVEN SO, MANY OF THE MORE *PUBLIC* SUPER-HEROES -- SUCH AS THE WORLD-FAMOUS *AVENGERS* -- HAVE REFUSED TO COMMENT ON THE UPCOMING CONFLICT --

"-- THOUGH THEY MUST CERTAINLY BE *AWARE* OF IT!"

WELL? WHAT DO YOU *THINK*, THOR?

'TIS *MADNESS* -- NO MORE.

DAILY SUN
THUNDRA vs THING

VERILY, THE WAYS OF MORTALS DO *CONTINUE* TO ASTOUND ME!

...THE THING VERSUS THAT *THUNDRA* CHICK, HM?

MUCH AS I LIKE OLD BENJY*, I HATE TO *ADMIT* IT -- BUT MY MONEY'S ON THE *LADY*!

* BEN AND SPIDEY MET IN TEAM-UP #7. --RT.

HULK DOESN'T *UNDERSTAND*. PICTURES SAY *FIGHT*.

WHY GIRL WANT TO HIT ROCK-THING? MAKE HULK'S *HEAD* HURT.

FIGHT *DUMB*.

DAILY BUGLE
THUNDRA VS TH...

EVERYONE DUMB.

AYE, OPINION RUNS *STRONG ACROSS* THE COUNTRY --

-- BUT CERTAINLY NO STRONGER THAN IT DOES IN AN ABANDONED *WATER TOWER* IN QUEENS --

-- WHERE --

LOSIN' YER *NERVE*, GIRLIE?

HARDLY. I'M MERELY *AMUSED* BY THIS WOMAN'S FAITH IN HER *MALE*.

SHE BELIEVES HE'LL *BEAT* ME.

1000

500

SHE *DOES*, HUH?

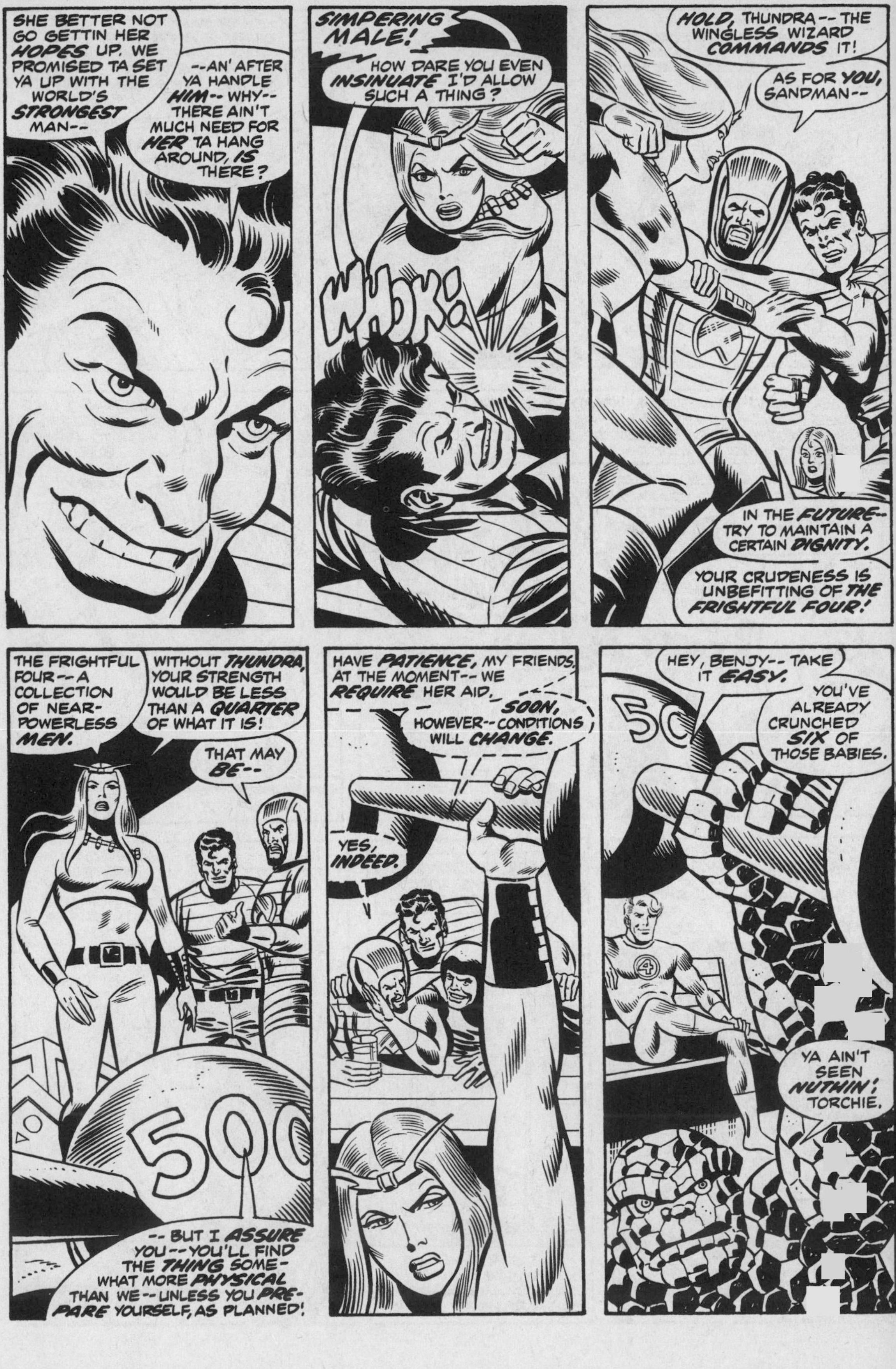
SHE BETTER NOT GO GETTIN HER HOPES UP. WE PROMISED TA SET YA UP WITH THE WORLD'S STRONGEST MAN--
--AN' AFTER YA HANDLE HIM-- WHY-- THERE AIN'T MUCH NEED FOR HER TA HANG AROUND, IS THERE?
SIMPERING MALE!
HOW DARE YOU EVEN INSINUATE I'D ALLOW SUCH A THING?
WHOK!
HOLD, THUNDRA-- THE WINGLESS WIZARD COMMANDS IT!
AS FOR YOU, SANDMAN--
IN THE FUTURE-- TRY TO MAINTAIN A CERTAIN DIGNITY.
YOUR CRUDENESS IS UNBEFITTING OF THE FRIGHTFUL FOUR!
THE FRIGHTFUL FOUR-- A COLLECTION OF NEAR-POWERLESS MEN.
WITHOUT THUNDRA, YOUR STRENGTH WOULD BE LESS THAN A QUARTER OF WHAT IT IS!
THAT MAY BE--
-- BUT I ASSURE YOU--YOU'LL FIND THE THING SOMEWHAT MORE PHYSICAL THAN WE--UNLESS YOU PREPARE YOURSELF, AS PLANNED!
500
HAVE PATIENCE, MY FRIENDS, AT THE MOMENT-- WE REQUIRE HER AID.
SOON, HOWEVER-- CONDITIONS WILL CHANGE.
YES, INDEED.
HEY, BENJY-- TAKE IT EASY.
YOU'VE ALREADY CRUNCHED SIX OF THOSE BABIES.
YA AIN'T SEEN NUTHIN', TORCHIE.

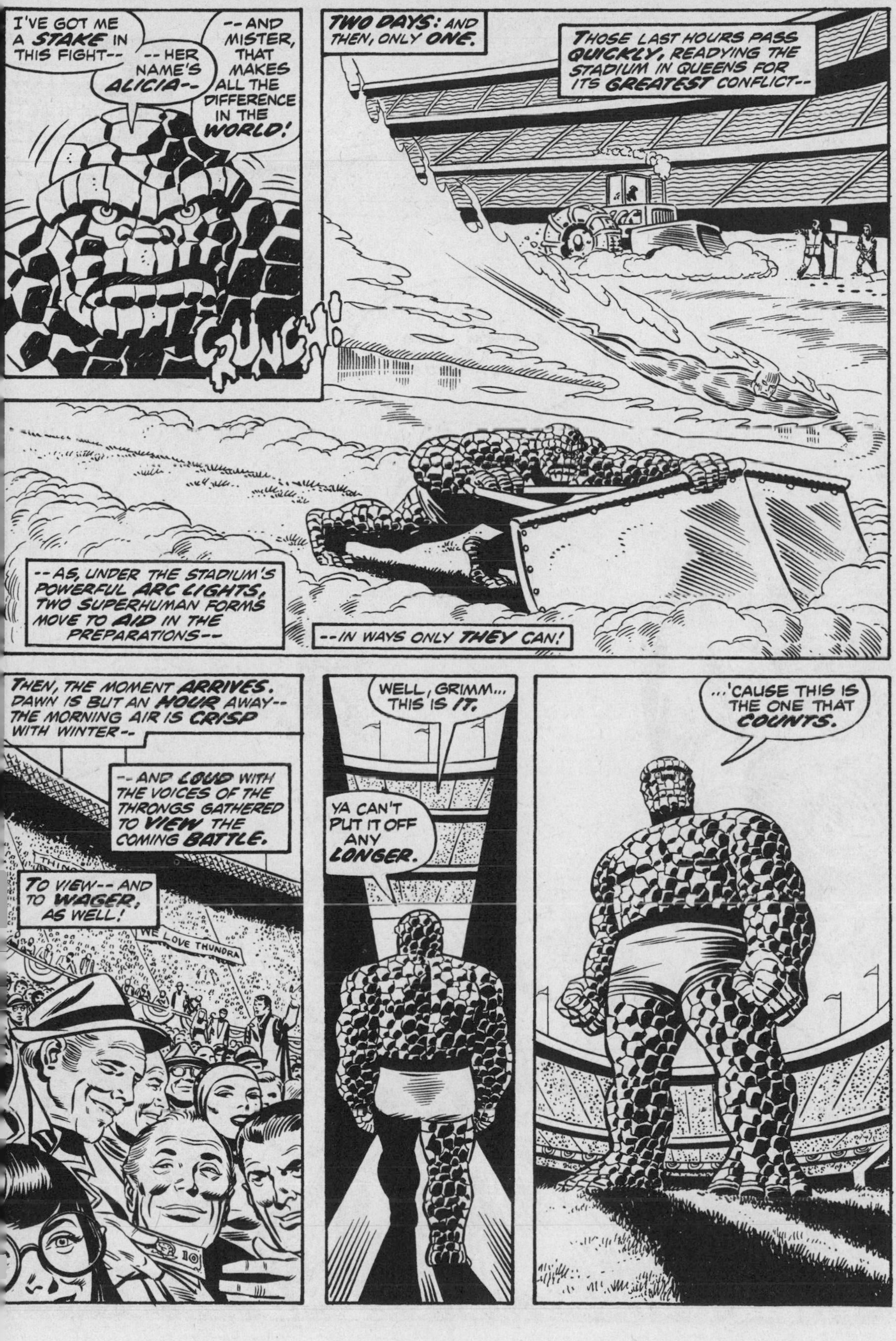
I'VE GOT ME A STAKE IN THIS FIGHT--
--HER NAME'S ALICIA--
--AND MISTER, THAT MAKES ALL THE DIFFERENCE IN THE WORLD!
CRUNCH!
TWO DAYS: AND THEN, ONLY ONE.
THOSE LAST HOURS PASS QUICKLY, READYING THE STADIUM IN QUEENS FOR ITS GREATEST CONFLICT--
--AS, UNDER THE STADIUM'S POWERFUL ARC LIGHTS, TWO SUPERHUMAN FORMS MOVE TO AID IN THE PREPARATIONS--
--IN WAYS ONLY THEY CAN!
THEN, THE MOMENT ARRIVES. DAWN IS BUT AN HOUR AWAY-- THE MORNING AIR IS CRISP WITH WINTER--
--AND LOUD WITH THE VOICES OF THE THRONGS GATHERED TO VIEW THE COMING BATTLE.
TO VIEW-- AND TO WAGER, AS WELL!
WE LOVE THUNDRA
WELL, GRIMM... THIS IS IT.
YA CAN'T PUT IT OFF ANY LONGER.
...'CAUSE THIS IS THE ONE THAT COUNTS.

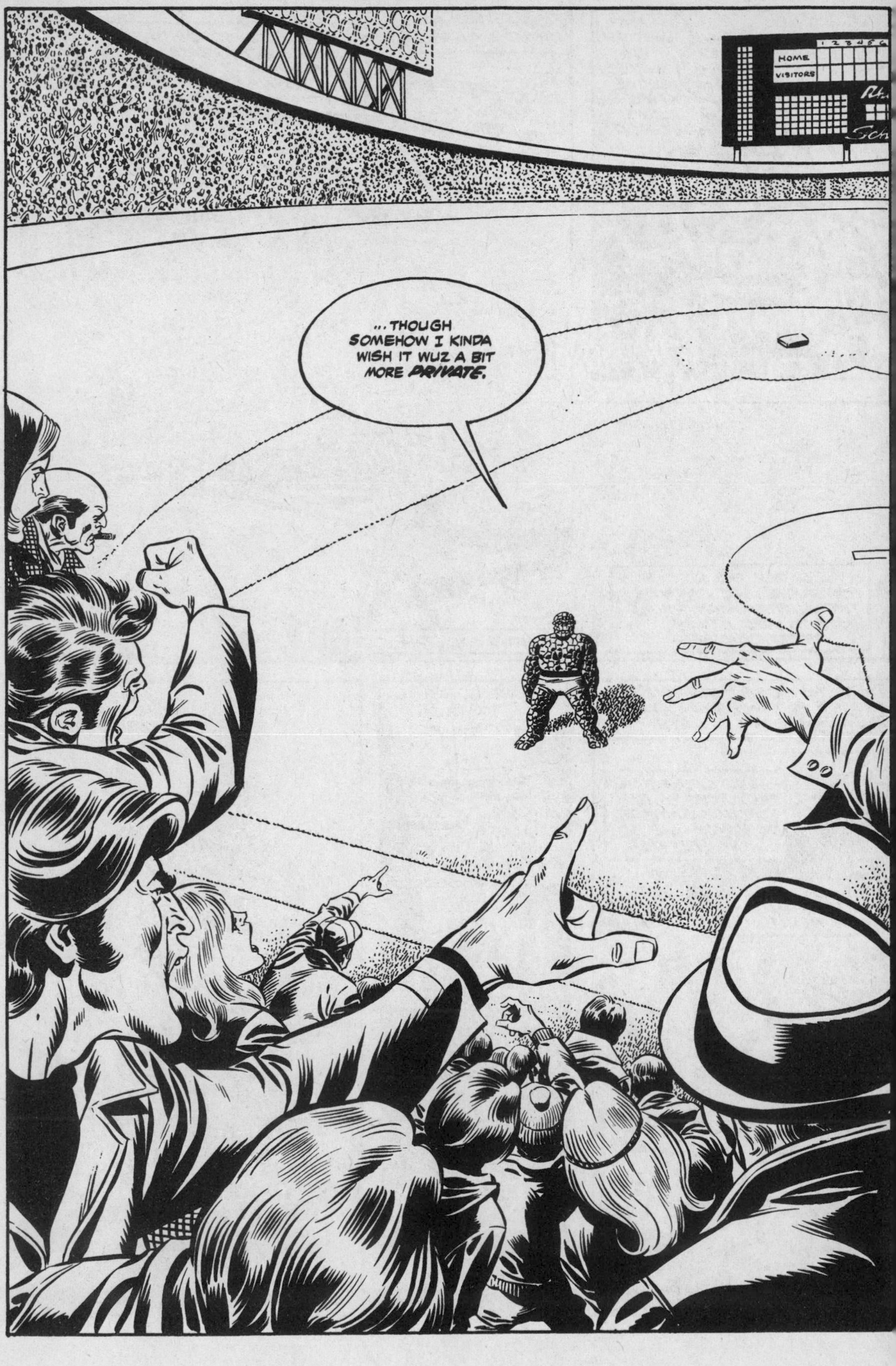
HOME
VISITORS
...THOUGH SOMEHOW I KINDA WISH IT WUZ A BIT MORE PRIVATE.

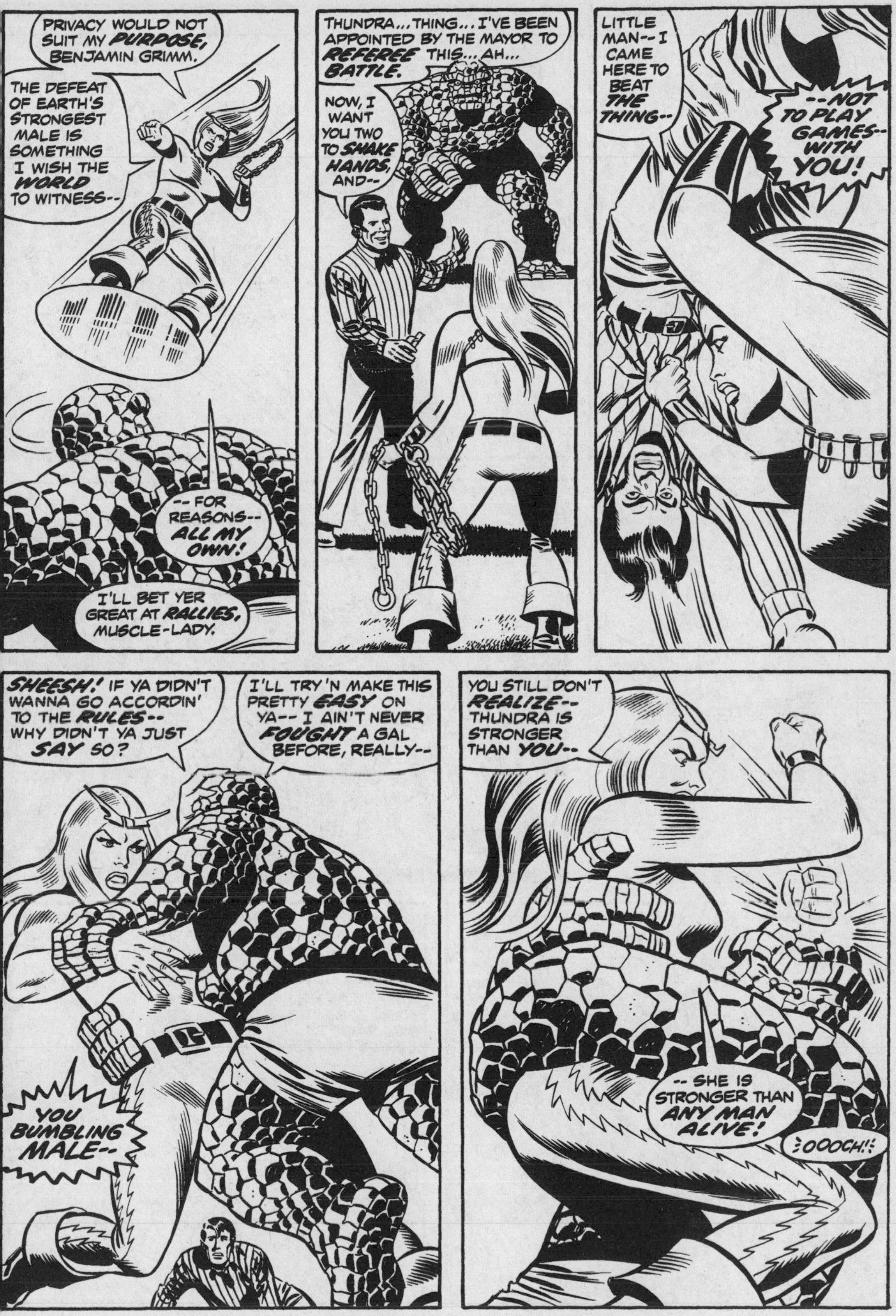
PRIVACY WOULD NOT SUIT MY PURPOSE, BENJAMIN GRIMM.
THE DEFEAT OF EARTH'S STRONGEST MALE IS SOMETHING I WISH THE WORLD TO WITNESS--
--FOR REASONS-- ALL MY OWN!
I'LL BET YER GREAT AT RALLIES, MUSCLE-LADY.
THUNDRA... THING... I'VE BEEN APPOINTED BY THE MAYOR TO REFEREE THIS... AH... BATTLE.
NOW, I WANT YOU TWO TO SHAKE HANDS, AND--
LITTLE MAN-- I CAME HERE TO BEAT THE THING--
--NOT TO PLAY GAMES-- WITH YOU!
SHEESH! IF YA DIDN'T WANNA GO ACCORDIN' TO THE RULES-- WHY DIDN'T YA JUST SAY SO?
I'LL TRY 'N MAKE THIS PRETTY EASY ON YA-- I AIN'T NEVER FOUGHT A GAL BEFORE, REALLY--
YOU BUMBLING MALE--
YOU STILL DON'T REALIZE-- THUNDRA IS STRONGER THAN YOU--
--SHE IS STRONGER THAN ANY MAN ALIVE!
OOOCH!

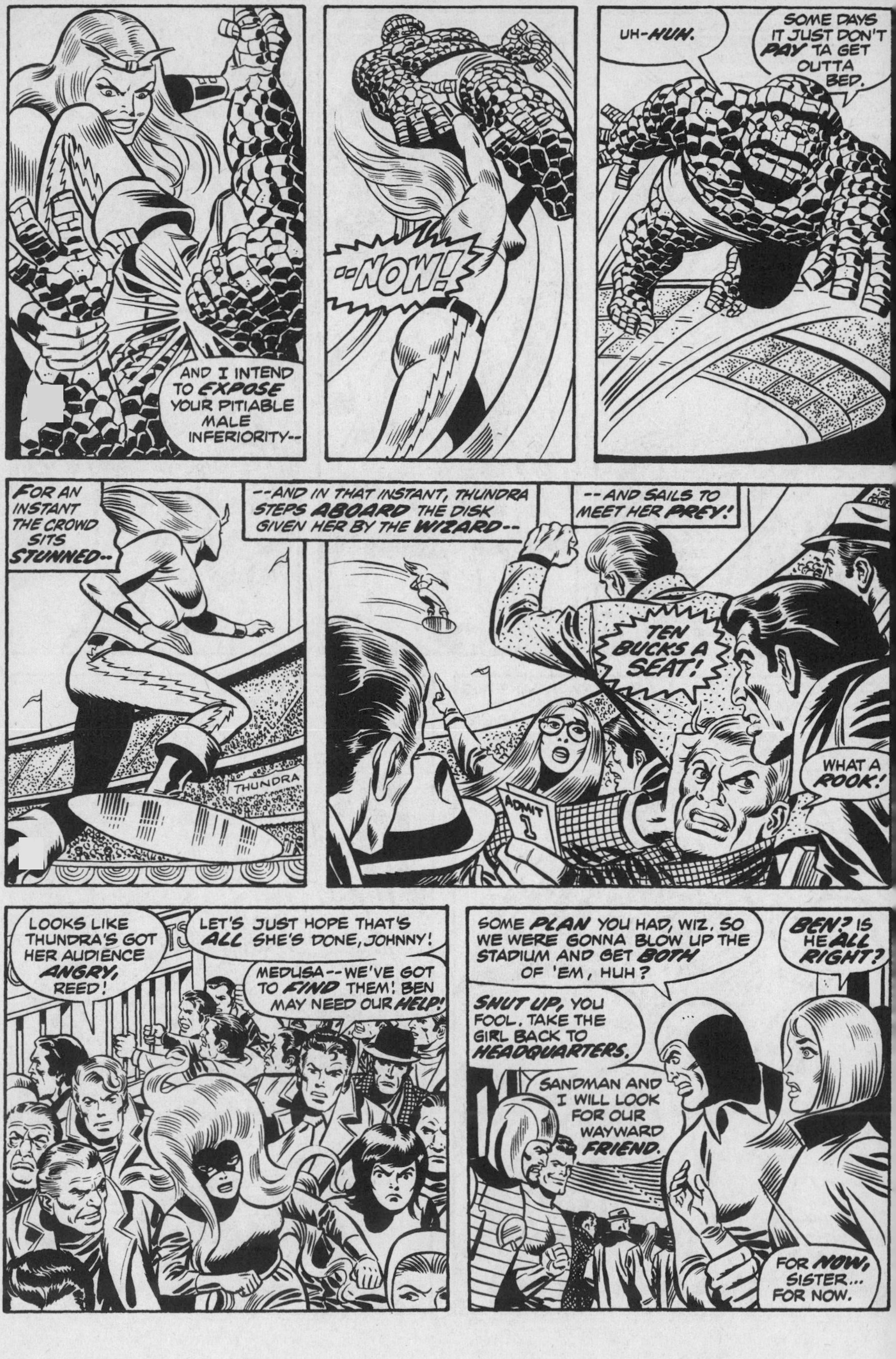

AND I INTEND TO EXPOSE YOUR PITIABLE MALE INFERIORITY--
--NOW!
UH-HUH.
SOME DAYS IT JUST DON'T PAY TA GET OUTTA BED.
FOR AN INSTANT THE CROWD SITS STUNNED--
--AND IN THAT INSTANT, THUNDRA STEPS ABOARD THE DISK GIVEN HER BY THE WIZARD--
--AND SAILS TO MEET HER PREY!
THUNDRA
TEN BUCKS A SEAT!
WHAT A ROOK!
ADMIT 1
LOOKS LIKE THUNDRA'S GOT HER AUDIENCE ANGRY, REED!
LET'S JUST HOPE THAT'S ALL SHE'S DONE, JOHNNY!
MEDUSA--WE'VE GOT TO FIND THEM! BEN MAY NEED OUR HELP!
SOME PLAN YOU HAD, WIZ. SO WE WERE GONNA BLOW UP THE STADIUM AND GET BOTH OF 'EM, HUH?
BEN? IS HE ALL RIGHT?
SHUT UP, YOU FOOL. TAKE THE GIRL BACK TO HEADQUARTERS.
SANDMAN AND I WILL LOOK FOR OUR WAYWARD FRIEND.
FOR NOW, SISTER... FOR NOW.

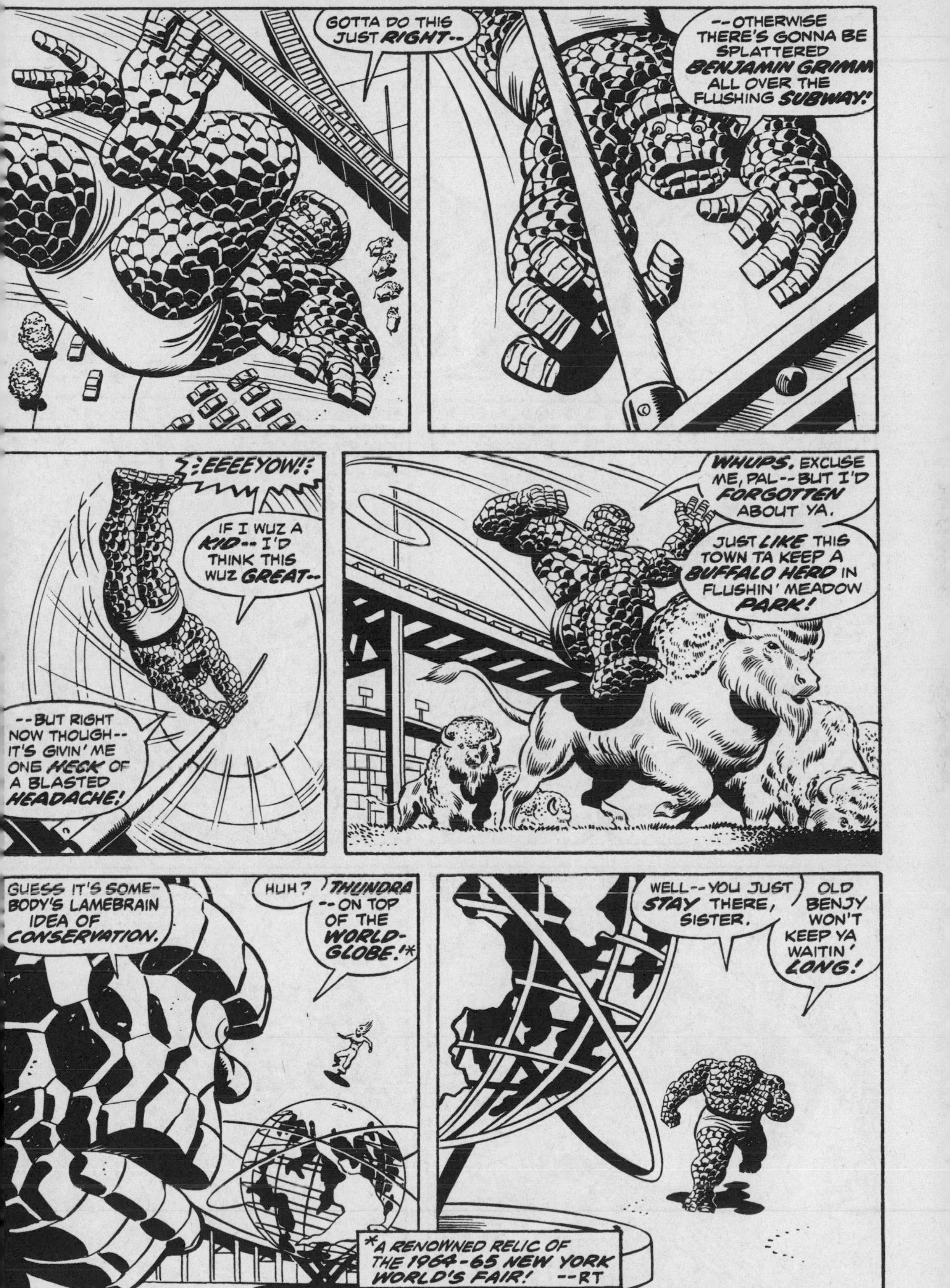
GOTTA DO THIS JUST RIGHT--
--OTHERWISE THERE'S GONNA BE SPLATTERED BENJAMIN GRIMM ALL OVER THE FLUSHING SUBWAY!
EEEEYOW!
IF I WUZ A KID--I'D THINK THIS WUZ GREAT--
--BUT RIGHT NOW THOUGH--IT'S GIVIN' ME ONE HECK OF A BLASTED HEADACHE!
WHUPS. EXCUSE ME, PAL--BUT I'D FORGOTTEN ABOUT YA.
JUST LIKE THIS TOWN TA KEEP A BUFFALO HERD IN FLUSHIN' MEADOW PARK!
GUESS IT'S SOMEBODY'S LAMEBRAIN IDEA OF CONSERVATION.
HUH? THUNDRA--ON TOP OF THE WORLD-GLOBE!*
*A RENOWNED RELIC OF THE 1964-65 NEW YORK WORLD'S FAIR! --RT
WELL--YOU JUST STAY THERE, SISTER.
OLD BENJY WON'T KEEP YA WAITIN' LONG!

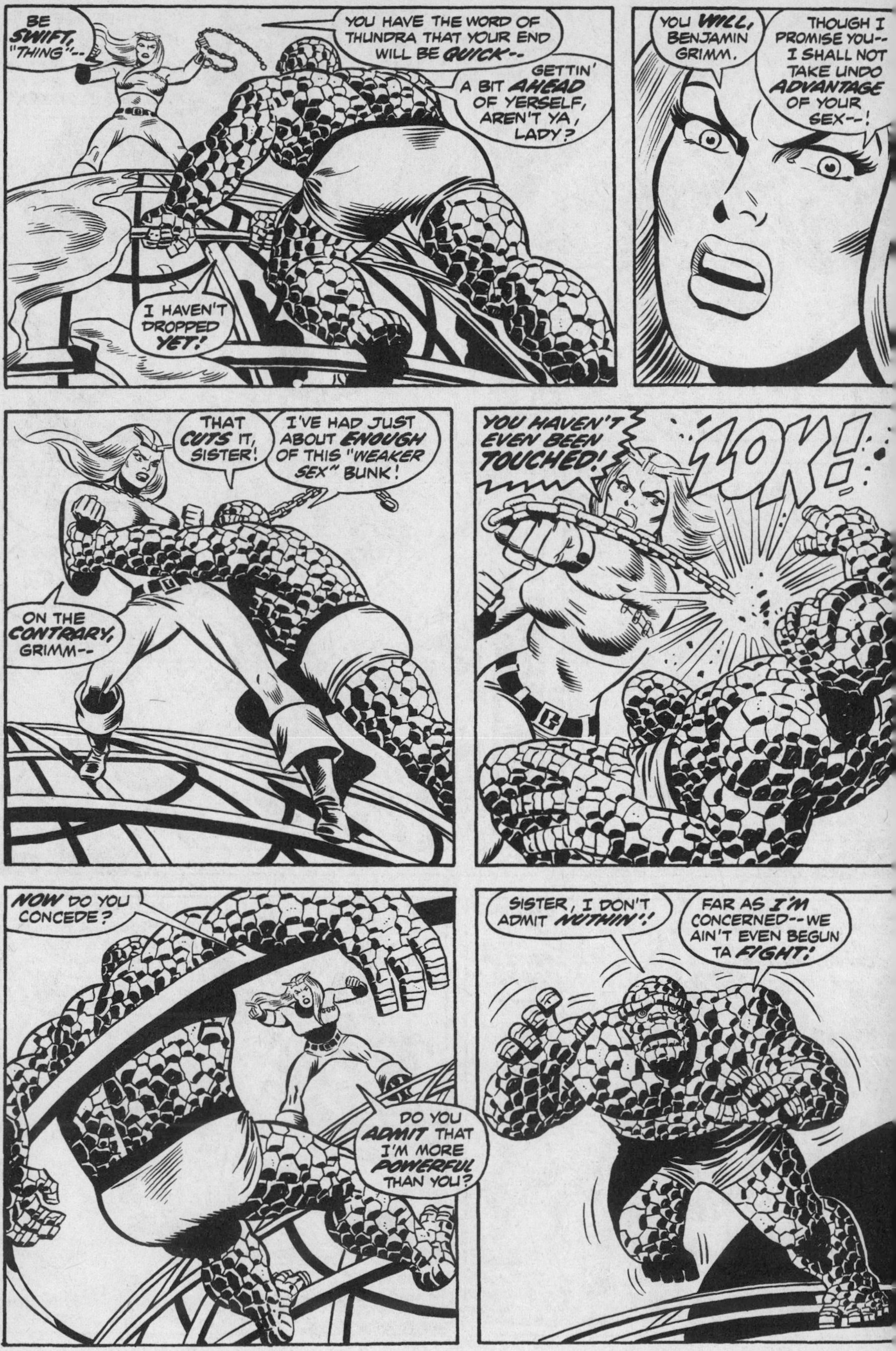
BE SWIFT, "THING"--
YOU HAVE THE WORD OF THUNDRA THAT YOUR END WILL BE QUICK--
GETTIN' A BIT AHEAD OF YERSELF, AREN'T YA, LADY?
I HAVEN'T DROPPED YET!
YOU WILL, BENJAMIN GRIMM.
THOUGH I PROMISE YOU-- I SHALL NOT TAKE UNDO ADVANTAGE OF YOUR SEX--!
THAT CUTS IT, SISTER!
I'VE HAD JUST ABOUT ENOUGH OF THIS "WEAKER SEX" BUNK!
ON THE CONTRARY, GRIMM--
YOU HAVEN'T EVEN BEEN TOUCHED!
ZOK!
NOW DO YOU CONCEDE?
DO YOU ADMIT THAT I'M MORE POWERFUL THAN YOU?
SISTER, I DON'T ADMIT NUTHIN'!
FAR AS I'M CONCERNED--WE AIN'T EVEN BEGUN TA FIGHT!

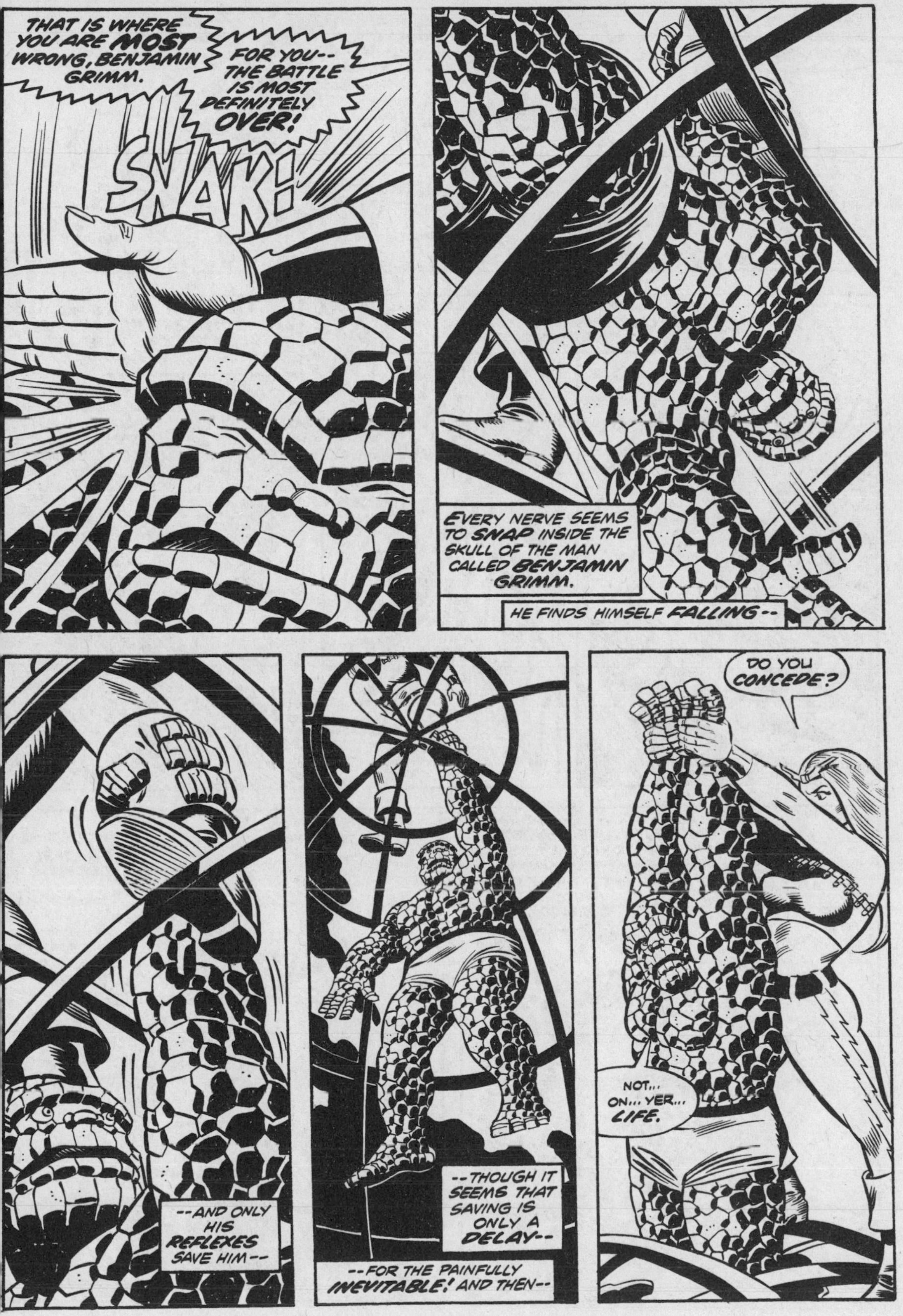
THAT IS WHERE YOU ARE MOST WRONG, BENJAMIN GRIMM.
FOR YOU-- THE BATTLE IS MOST DEFINITELY OVER!
SNAK!
EVERY NERVE SEEMS TO SNAP INSIDE THE SKULL OF THE MAN CALLED BENJAMIN GRIMM.
HE FINDS HIMSELF FALLING--
--AND ONLY HIS REFLEXES SAVE HIM--
--THOUGH IT SEEMS THAT SAVING IS ONLY A DELAY--
--FOR THE PAINFULLY INEVITABLE! AND THEN--
DO YOU CONCEDE?
NOT... ON... YER... LIFE.

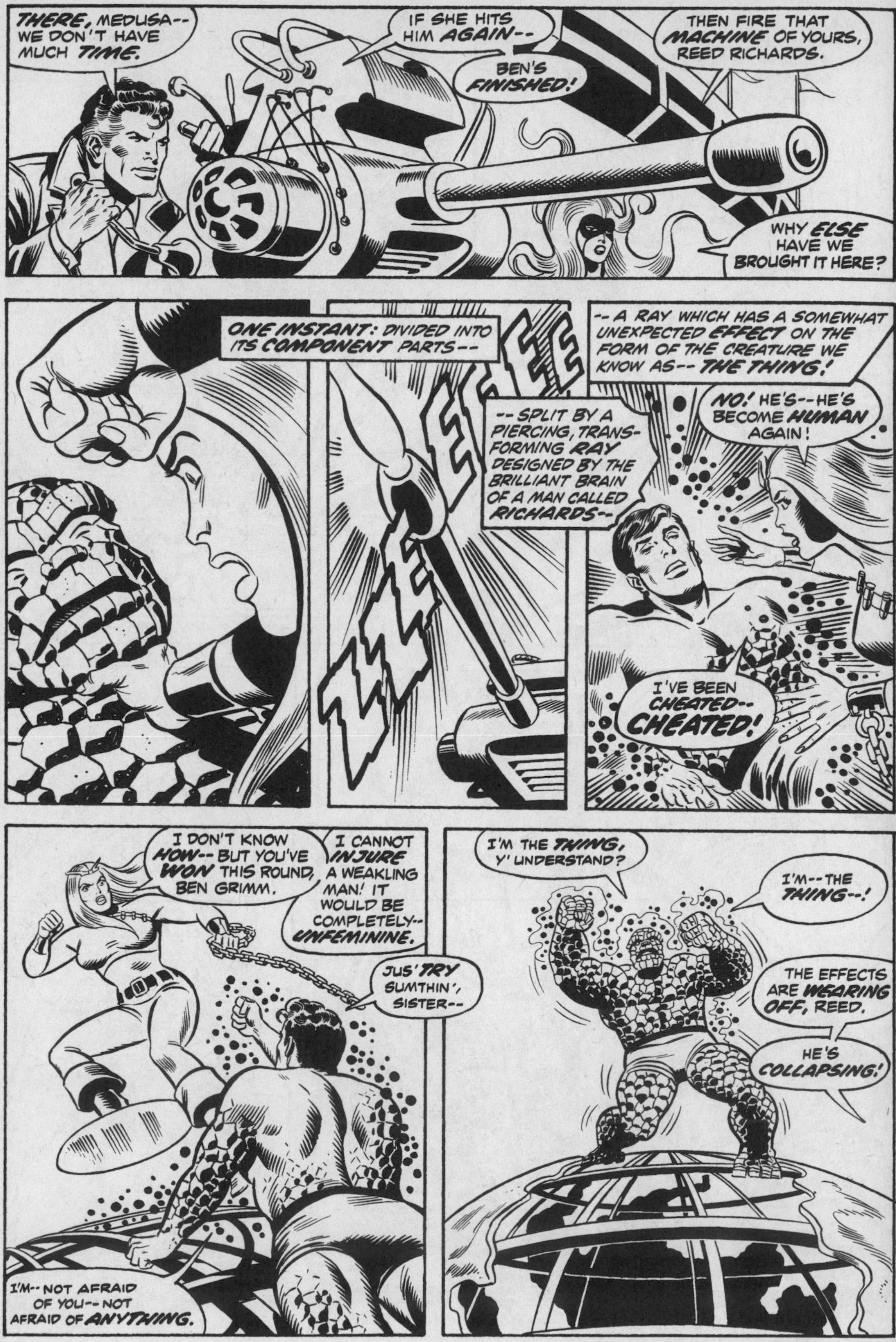

THERE, MEDUSA--WE DON'T HAVE MUCH TIME.
IF SHE HITS HIM AGAIN--
BEN'S FINISHED!
THEN FIRE THAT MACHINE OF YOURS, REED RICHARDS.
WHY ELSE HAVE WE BROUGHT IT HERE?
ONE INSTANT: DIVIDED INTO ITS COMPONENT PARTS--
--SPLIT BY A PIERCING, TRANS-FORMING RAY DESIGNED BY THE BRILLIANT BRAIN OF A MAN CALLED RICHARDS--
ZEEEE
--A RAY WHICH HAS A SOMEWHAT UNEXPECTED EFFECT ON THE FORM OF THE CREATURE WE KNOW AS--THE THING!
NO! HE'S--HE'S BECOME HUMAN AGAIN!
I'VE BEEN CHEATED--CHEATED!
I DON'T KNOW HOW--BUT YOU'VE WON THIS ROUND, BEN GRIMM.
I CANNOT INJURE A WEAKLING MAN! IT WOULD BE COMPLETELY--UNFEMININE.
JUS' TRY SUMTHIN', SISTER--
I'M--NOT AFRAID OF YOU--NOT AFRAID OF ANYTHING.
I'M THE THING, Y' UNDERSTAND?
I'M--THE THING--!
THE EFFECTS ARE WEARING OFF, REED.
HE'S COLLAPSING!

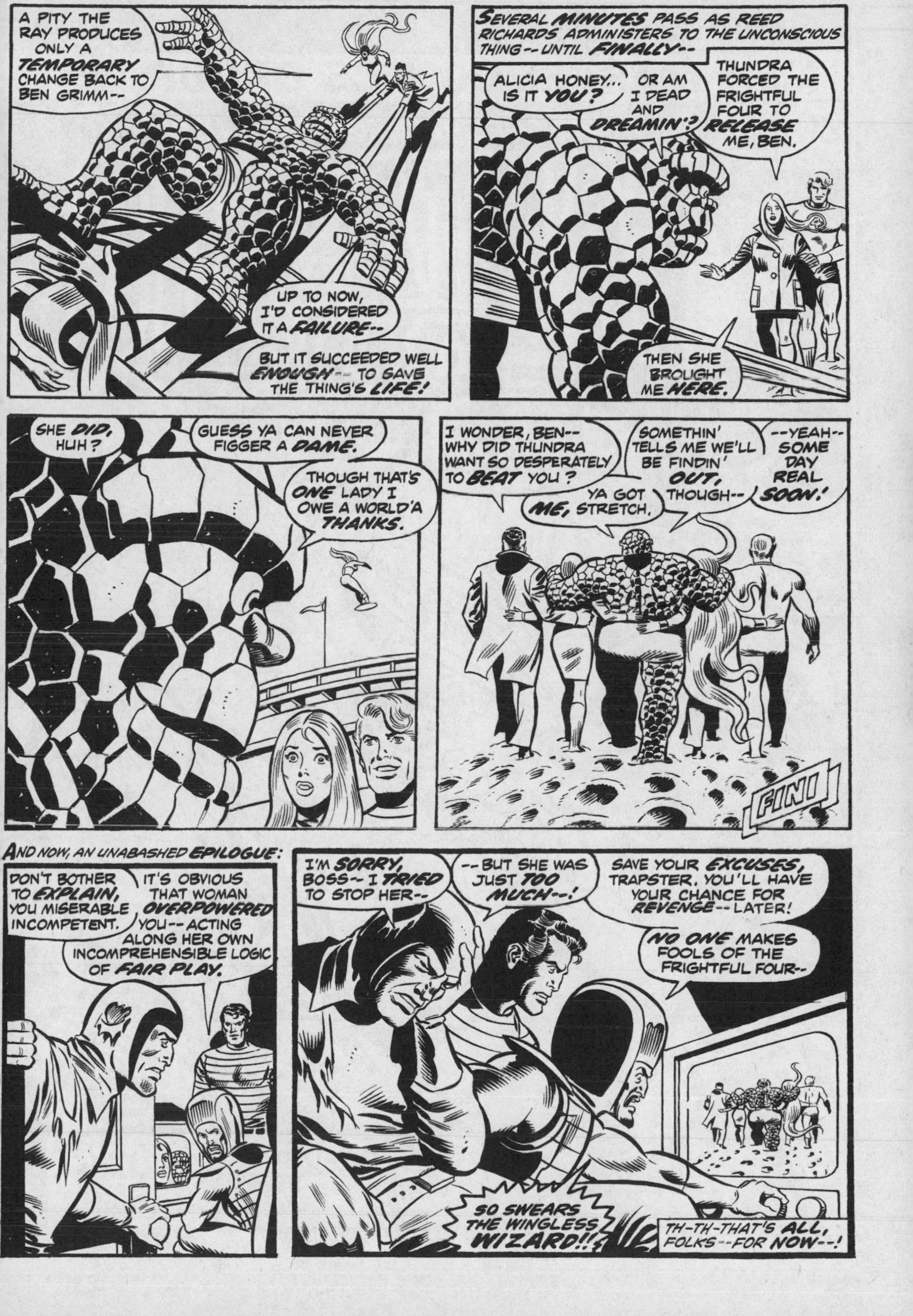
A PITY THE RAY PRODUCES ONLY A TEMPORARY CHANGE BACK TO BEN GRIMM--
UP TO NOW, I'D CONSIDERED IT A FAILURE--
BUT IT SUCCEEDED WELL ENOUGH-- TO SAVE THE THING'S LIFE!
SEVERAL MINUTES PASS AS REED RICHARDS ADMINISTERS TO THE UNCONSCIOUS THING--UNTIL FINALLY--
ALICIA HONEY... IS IT YOU?
OR AM I DEAD AND DREAMIN'?
THUNDRA FORCED THE FRIGHTFUL FOUR TO RELEASE ME, BEN.
THEN SHE BROUGHT ME HERE.
SHE DID, HUH?
GUESS YA CAN NEVER FIGGER A DAME.
THOUGH THAT'S ONE LADY I OWE A WORLD'A THANKS.
I WONDER, BEN-- WHY DID THUNDRA WANT SO DESPERATELY TO BEAT YOU?
YA GOT ME, STRETCH.
SOMETHIN' TELLS ME WE'LL BE FINDIN' OUT, THOUGH--
--YEAH-- SOME DAY REAL SOON!
FINI
AND NOW, AN UNABASHED EPILOGUE:
DON'T BOTHER TO EXPLAIN, YOU MISERABLE INCOMPETENT.
IT'S OBVIOUS THAT WOMAN OVERPOWERED YOU--ACTING ALONG HER OWN INCOMPREHENSIBLE LOGIC OF FAIR PLAY.
I'M SORRY, BOSS-- I TRIED TO STOP HER--
--BUT SHE WAS JUST TOO MUCH--!
SAVE YOUR EXCUSES, TRAPSTER. YOU'LL HAVE YOUR CHANCE FOR REVENGE--LATER!
NO ONE MAKES FOOLS OF THE FRIGHTFUL FOUR--
SO SWEARS THE WINGLESS WIZARD!!
TH-TH-THAT'S ALL, FOLKS--FOR NOW--!

FANTASTIC FOUR
MARVEL COMICS GROUP
APPROVED BY THE COMICS CODE AUTHORITY
20¢ 134 MAY 02462
THE WORLD'S GREATEST COMIC MAGAZINE!
FANTASTIC FOUR
STOP HIM! HE'S GOT MY WIFE-- MY CHILD!
BUT-- IF WE MAKE HIM LET GO OF THEM--
--THEY'LL FALL TO THEIR DEATHS!!
THE DRAGON MAN STALKS THE SKIES!

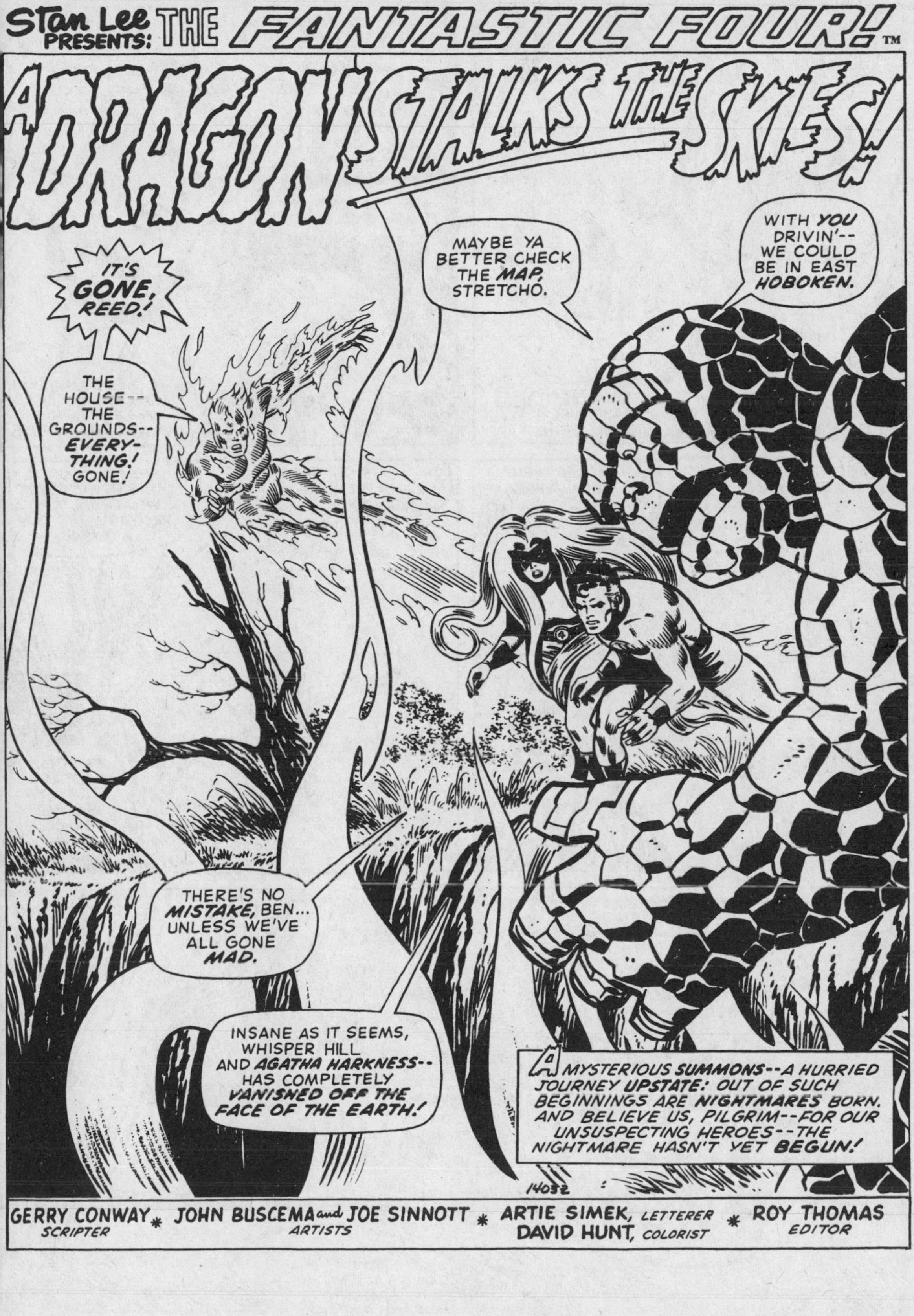

Stan Lee PRESENTS: THE FANTASTIC FOUR!™
A DRAGON STALKS THE SKIES!
IT'S GONE, REED!
THE HOUSE-- THE GROUNDS-- EVERY-THING! GONE!
MAYBE YA BETTER CHECK THE MAP, STRETCHO.
WITH YOU DRIVIN'-- WE COULD BE IN EAST HOBOKEN.
THERE'S NO MISTAKE, BEN... UNLESS WE'VE ALL GONE MAD.
INSANE AS IT SEEMS, WHISPER HILL AND AGATHA HARKNESS-- HAS COMPLETELY VANISHED OFF THE FACE OF THE EARTH!
A MYSTERIOUS SUMMONS--A HURRIED JOURNEY UPSTATE: OUT OF SUCH BEGINNINGS ARE NIGHTMARES BORN. AND BELIEVE US, PILGRIM--FOR OUR UNSUSPECTING HEROES--THE NIGHTMARE HASN'T YET BEGUN!
14032
GERRY CONWAY SCRIPTER * JOHN BUSCEMA and JOE SINNOTT ARTISTS * ARTIE SIMEK, LETTERER DAVID HUNT, COLORIST * ROY THOMAS EDITOR

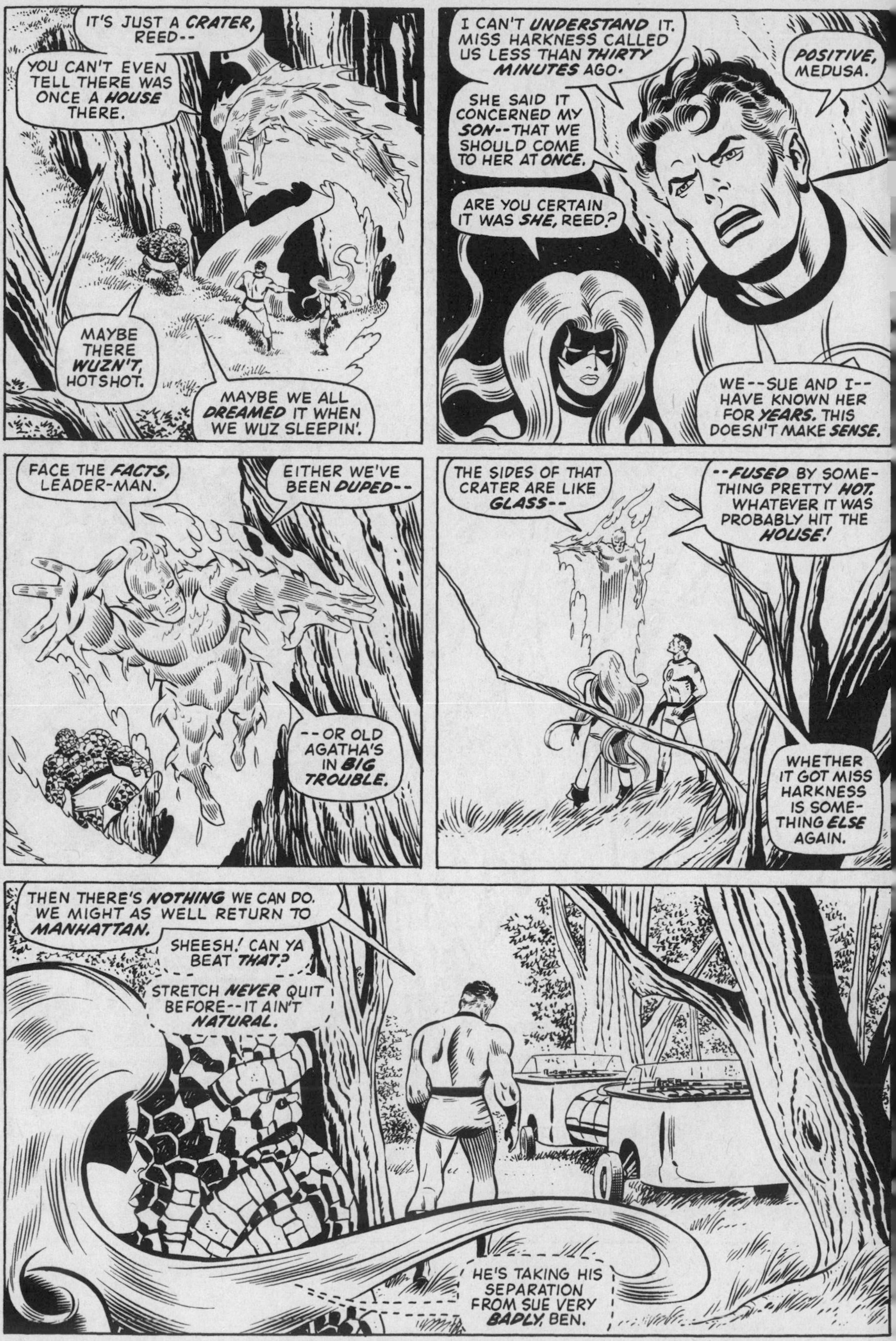
IT'S JUST A CRATER, REED--
YOU CAN'T EVEN TELL THERE WAS ONCE A HOUSE THERE.
MAYBE THERE WUZN'T, HOTSHOT.
MAYBE WE ALL DREAMED IT WHEN WE WUZ SLEEPIN'.
I CAN'T UNDERSTAND IT. MISS HARKNESS CALLED US LESS THAN THIRTY MINUTES AGO.
SHE SAID IT CONCERNED MY SON--THAT WE SHOULD COME TO HER AT ONCE.
ARE YOU CERTAIN IT WAS SHE, REED?
POSITIVE, MEDUSA.
WE--SUE AND I--HAVE KNOWN HER FOR YEARS. THIS DOESN'T MAKE SENSE.
FACE THE FACTS, LEADER-MAN.
EITHER WE'VE BEEN DUPED--
--OR OLD AGATHA'S IN BIG TROUBLE.
THE SIDES OF THAT CRATER ARE LIKE GLASS--
--FUSED BY SOMETHING PRETTY HOT. WHATEVER IT WAS PROBABLY HIT THE HOUSE!
WHETHER IT GOT MISS HARKNESS IS SOMETHING ELSE AGAIN.
THEN THERE'S NOTHING WE CAN DO. WE MIGHT AS WELL RETURN TO MANHATTAN.
SHEESH! CAN YA BEAT THAT?
STRETCH NEVER QUIT BEFORE--IT AIN'T NATURAL.
HE'S TAKING HIS SEPARATION FROM SUE VERY BADLY, BEN.

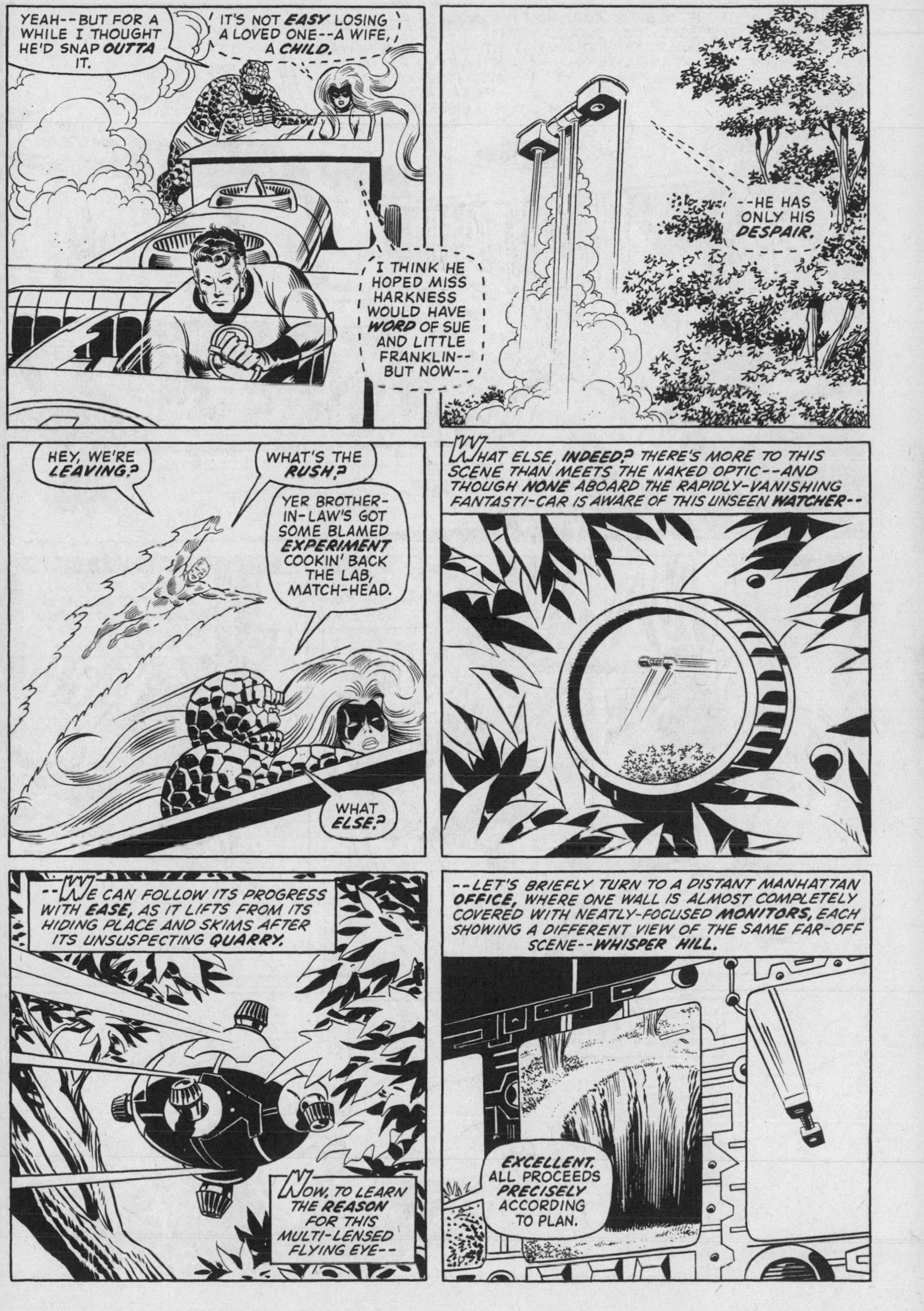
YEAH--BUT FOR A WHILE I THOUGHT HE'D SNAP OUTTA IT.
IT'S NOT EASY LOSING A LOVED ONE--A WIFE, A CHILD.
I THINK HE HOPED MISS HARKNESS WOULD HAVE WORD OF SUE AND LITTLE FRANKLIN--BUT NOW--
--HE HAS ONLY HIS DESPAIR.
HEY, WE'RE LEAVING?
WHAT'S THE RUSH?
YER BROTHER-IN-LAW'S GOT SOME BLAMED EXPERIMENT COOKIN' BACK THE LAB, MATCH-HEAD.
WHAT ELSE?
WHAT ELSE, INDEED? THERE'S MORE TO THIS SCENE THAN MEETS THE NAKED OPTIC--AND THOUGH NONE ABOARD THE RAPIDLY-VANISHING FANTASTI-CAR IS AWARE OF THIS UNSEEN WATCHER--
--WE CAN FOLLOW ITS PROGRESS WITH EASE, AS IT LIFTS FROM ITS HIDING PLACE AND SKIMS AFTER ITS UNSUSPECTING QUARRY.
NOW, TO LEARN THE REASON FOR THIS MULTI-LENSED FLYING EYE--
--LET'S BRIEFLY TURN TO A DISTANT MANHATTAN OFFICE, WHERE ONE WALL IS ALMOST COMPLETELY COVERED WITH NEATLY-FOCUSED MONITORS, EACH SHOWING A DIFFERENT VIEW OF THE SAME FAR-OFF SCENE--WHISPER HILL.
EXCELLENT. ALL PROCEEDS PRECISELY ACCORDING TO PLAN.

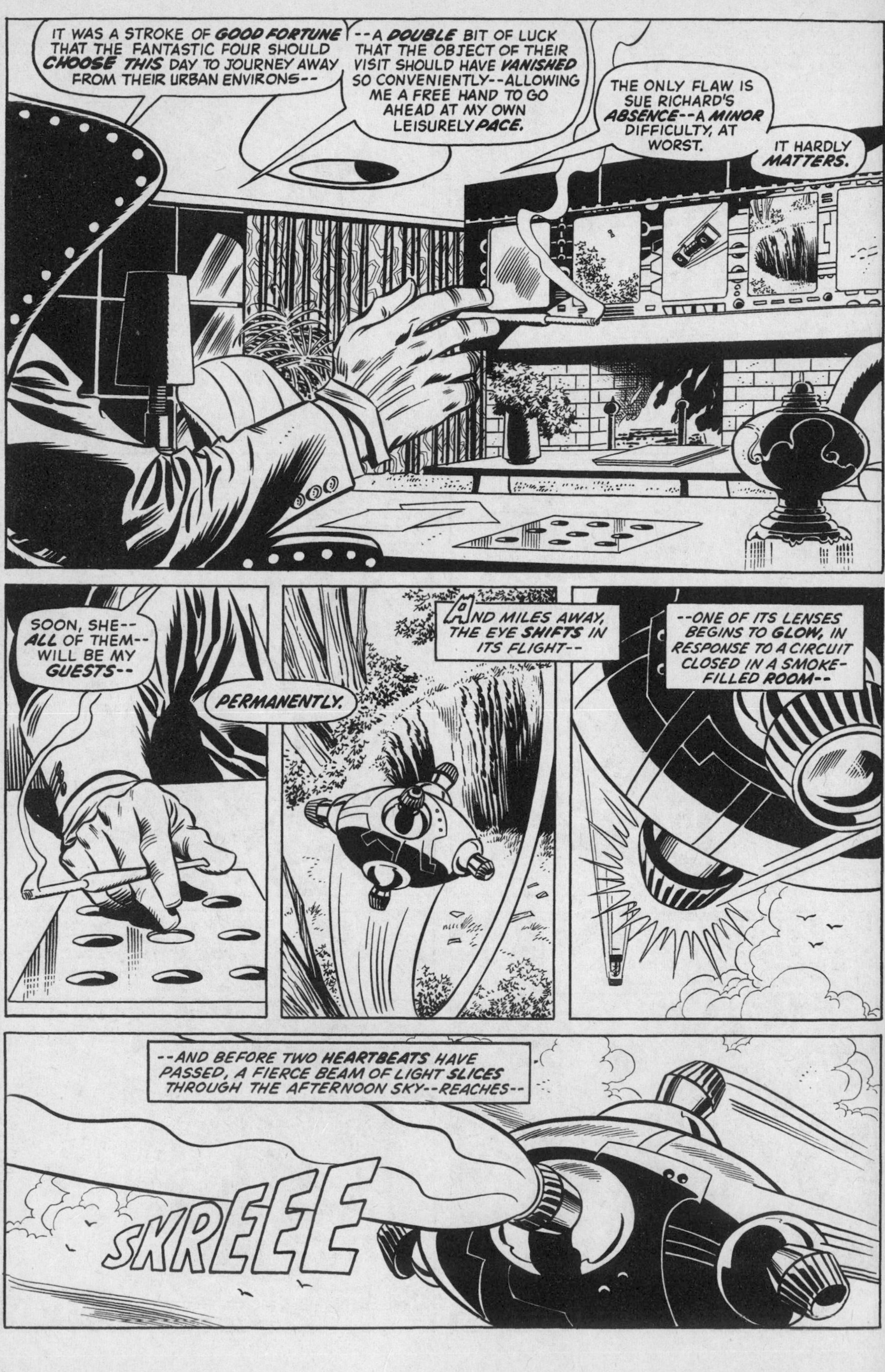
IT WAS A STROKE OF GOOD FORTUNE THAT THE FANTASTIC FOUR SHOULD CHOOSE THIS DAY TO JOURNEY AWAY FROM THEIR URBAN ENVIRONS--
--A DOUBLE BIT OF LUCK THAT THE OBJECT OF THEIR VISIT SHOULD HAVE VANISHED SO CONVENIENTLY--ALLOWING ME A FREE HAND TO GO AHEAD AT MY OWN LEISURELY PACE.
THE ONLY FLAW IS SUE RICHARD'S ABSENCE--A MINOR DIFFICULTY, AT WORST.
IT HARDLY MATTERS.
SOON, SHE--ALL OF THEM--WILL BE MY GUESTS--
PERMANENTLY.
AND MILES AWAY, THE EYE SHIFTS IN ITS FLIGHT--
--ONE OF ITS LENSES BEGINS TO GLOW, IN RESPONSE TO A CIRCUIT CLOSED IN A SMOKE-FILLED ROOM--
--AND BEFORE TWO HEARTBEATS HAVE PASSED, A FIERCE BEAM OF LIGHT SLICES THROUGH THE AFTERNOON SKY--REACHES--
SKREEE

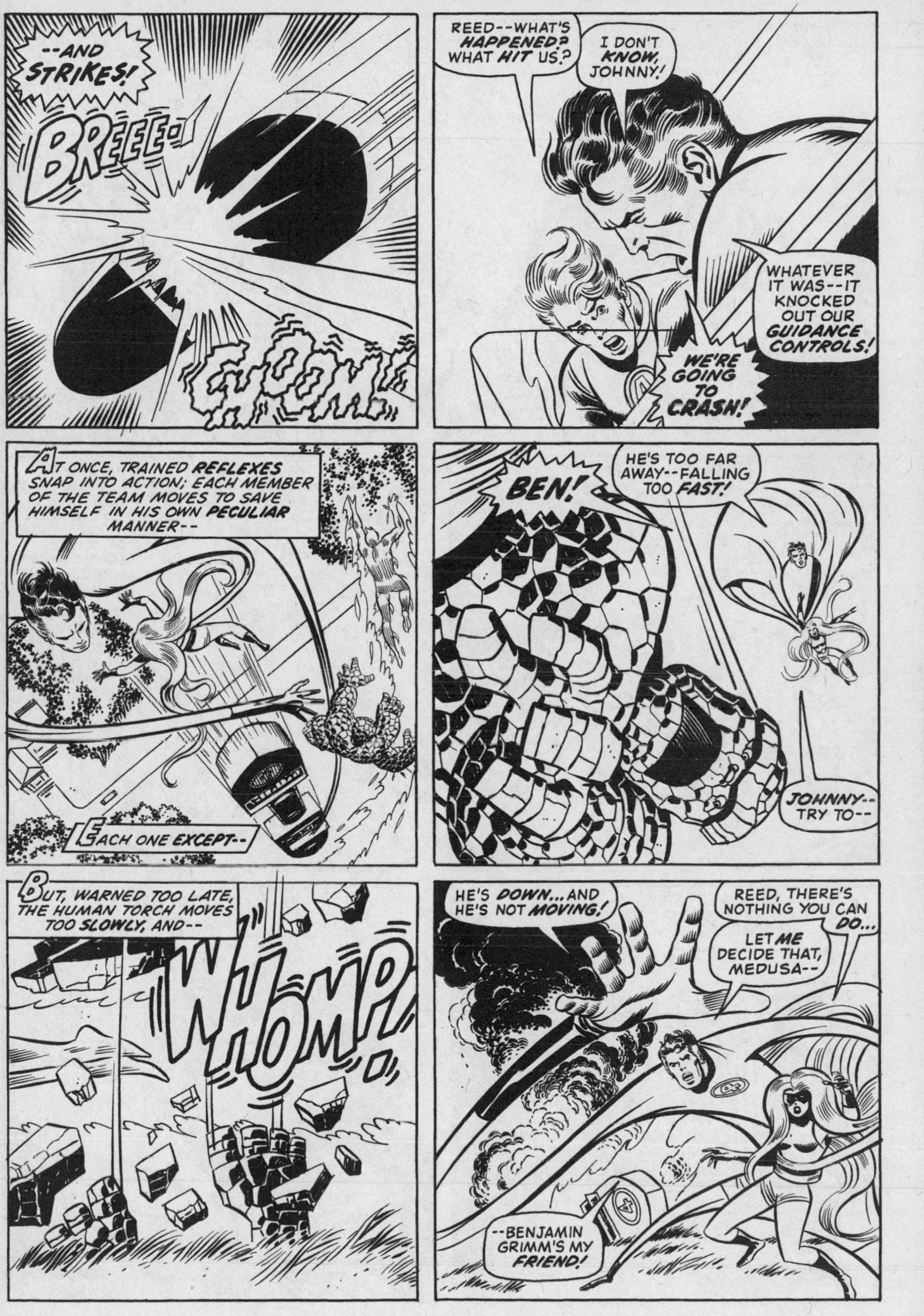
--AND STRIKES!
BREEE--
GROOM!
REED--WHAT'S HAPPENED? WHAT HIT US?
I DON'T KNOW, JOHNNY!
WHATEVER IT WAS--IT KNOCKED OUT OUR GUIDANCE CONTROLS!
WE'RE GOING TO CRASH!
AT ONCE, TRAINED REFLEXES SNAP INTO ACTION; EACH MEMBER OF THE TEAM MOVES TO SAVE HIMSELF IN HIS OWN PECULIAR MANNER--
EACH ONE EXCEPT--
BEN!
HE'S TOO FAR AWAY--FALLING TOO FAST!
JOHNNY-- TRY TO--
BUT, WARNED TOO LATE, THE HUMAN TORCH MOVES TOO SLOWLY, AND--
WHOMP!
HE'S DOWN...AND HE'S NOT MOVING!
REED, THERE'S NOTHING YOU CAN DO...
LET ME DECIDE THAT, MEDUSA--
--BENJAMIN GRIMM'S MY FRIEND!

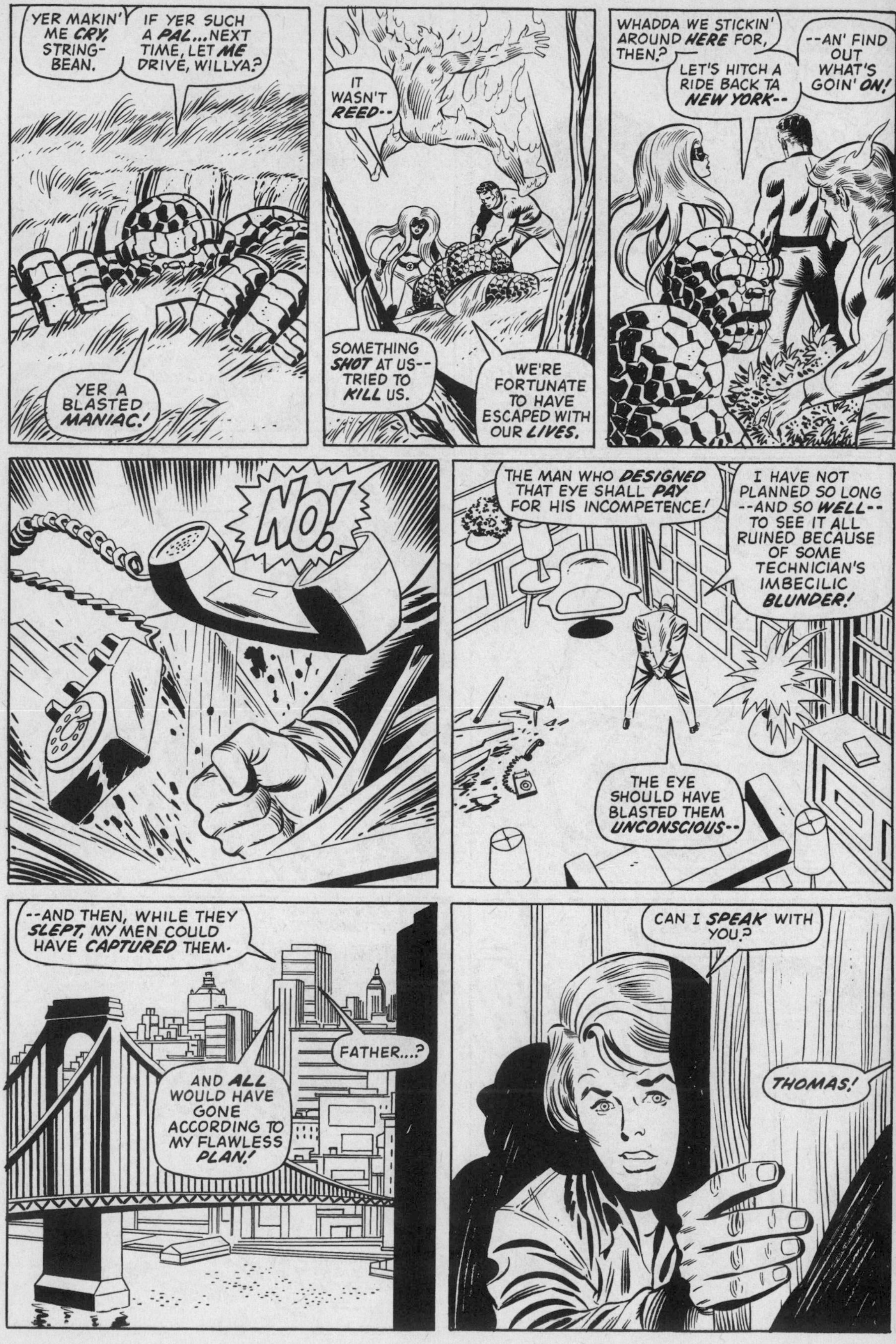
YER MAKIN' ME CRY, STRING-BEAN.
IF YER SUCH A PAL...NEXT TIME, LET ME DRIVE, WILLYA?
YER A BLASTED MANIAC!
IT WASN'T REED--
SOMETHING SHOT AT US--TRIED TO KILL US.
WE'RE FORTUNATE TO HAVE ESCAPED WITH OUR LIVES.
WHADDA WE STICKIN' AROUND HERE FOR, THEN?
LET'S HITCH A RIDE BACK TA NEW YORK--
--AN' FIND OUT WHAT'S GOIN' ON!
NO!
THE MAN WHO DESIGNED THAT EYE SHALL PAY FOR HIS INCOMPETENCE!
I HAVE NOT PLANNED SO LONG --AND SO WELL-- TO SEE IT ALL RUINED BECAUSE OF SOME TECHNICIAN'S IMBECILIC BLUNDER!
THE EYE SHOULD HAVE BLASTED THEM UNCONSCIOUS--
--AND THEN, WHILE THEY SLEPT, MY MEN COULD HAVE CAPTURED THEM.
FATHER...?
AND ALL WOULD HAVE GONE ACCORDING TO MY FLAWLESS PLAN!
CAN I SPEAK WITH YOU?
THOMAS!

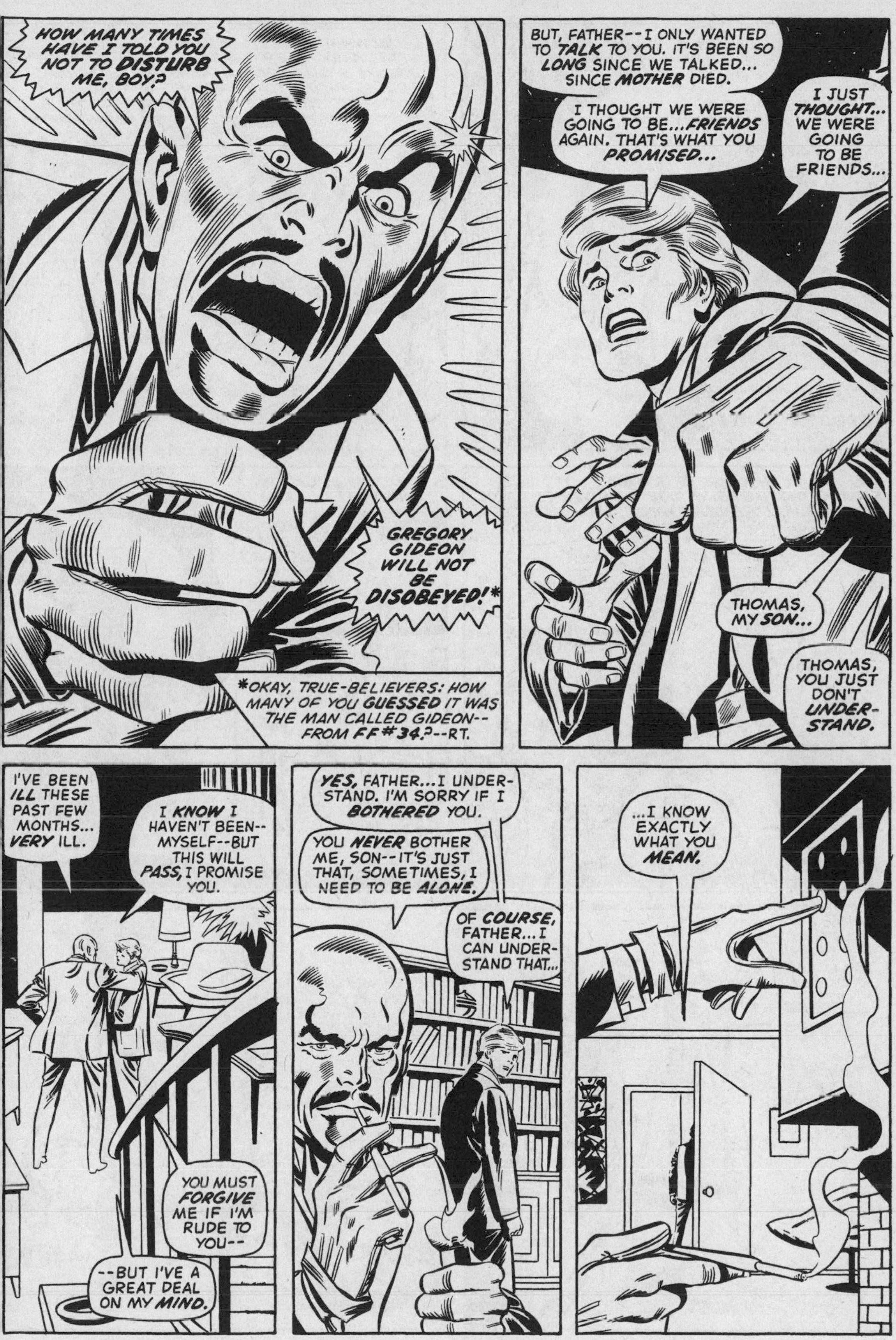
HOW MANY TIMES HAVE I TOLD YOU NOT TO DISTURB ME, BOY?
GREGORY GIDEON WILL NOT BE DISOBEYED!*
*OKAY, TRUE-BELIEVERS: HOW MANY OF YOU GUESSED IT WAS THE MAN CALLED GIDEON--FROM FF #34?--RT.
BUT, FATHER--I ONLY WANTED TO TALK TO YOU. IT'S BEEN SO LONG SINCE WE TALKED... SINCE MOTHER DIED.
I THOUGHT WE WERE GOING TO BE...FRIENDS AGAIN. THAT'S WHAT YOU PROMISED...
I JUST THOUGHT... WE WERE GOING TO BE FRIENDS...
THOMAS, MY SON...
THOMAS, YOU JUST DON'T UNDER-STAND.
I'VE BEEN ILL THESE PAST FEW MONTHS... VERY ILL.
I KNOW I HAVEN'T BEEN--MYSELF--BUT THIS WILL PASS, I PROMISE YOU.
YOU MUST FORGIVE ME IF I'M RUDE TO YOU--
--BUT I'VE A GREAT DEAL ON MY MIND.
YES, FATHER...I UNDER-STAND. I'M SORRY IF I BOTHERED YOU.
YOU NEVER BOTHER ME, SON--IT'S JUST THAT, SOMETIMES, I NEED TO BE ALONE.
OF COURSE, FATHER...I CAN UNDER-STAND THAT...
...I KNOW EXACTLY WHAT YOU MEAN.

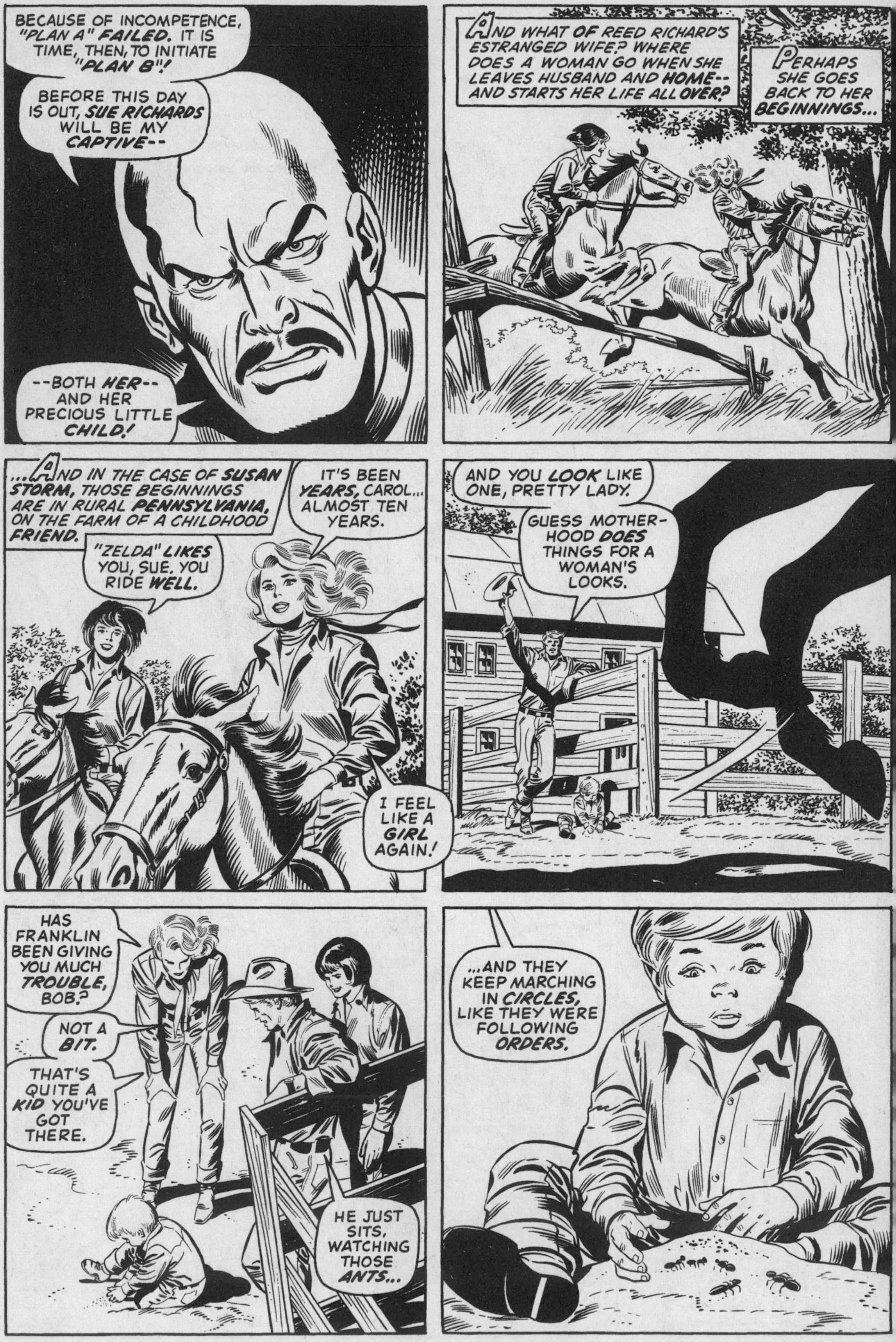
BECAUSE OF INCOMPETENCE, "PLAN A" FAILED. IT IS TIME, THEN, TO INITIATE "PLAN B"!
BEFORE THIS DAY IS OUT, SUE RICHARDS WILL BE MY CAPTIVE--
--BOTH HER-- AND HER PRECIOUS LITTLE CHILD!
AND WHAT OF REED RICHARD'S ESTRANGED WIFE? WHERE DOES A WOMAN GO WHEN SHE LEAVES HUSBAND AND HOME-- AND STARTS HER LIFE ALL OVER?
PERHAPS SHE GOES BACK TO HER BEGINNINGS...
...AND IN THE CASE OF SUSAN STORM, THOSE BEGINNINGS ARE IN RURAL PENNSYLVANIA, ON THE FARM OF A CHILDHOOD FRIEND.
"ZELDA" LIKES YOU, SUE. YOU RIDE WELL.
IT'S BEEN YEARS, CAROL... ALMOST TEN YEARS.
I FEEL LIKE A GIRL AGAIN!
AND YOU LOOK LIKE ONE, PRETTY LADY.
GUESS MOTHERHOOD DOES THINGS FOR A WOMAN'S LOOKS.
HAS FRANKLIN BEEN GIVING YOU MUCH TROUBLE, BOB?
NOT A BIT.
THAT'S QUITE A KID YOU'VE GOT THERE.
HE JUST SITS, WATCHING THOSE ANTS...
...AND THEY KEEP MARCHING IN CIRCLES, LIKE THEY WERE FOLLOWING ORDERS.

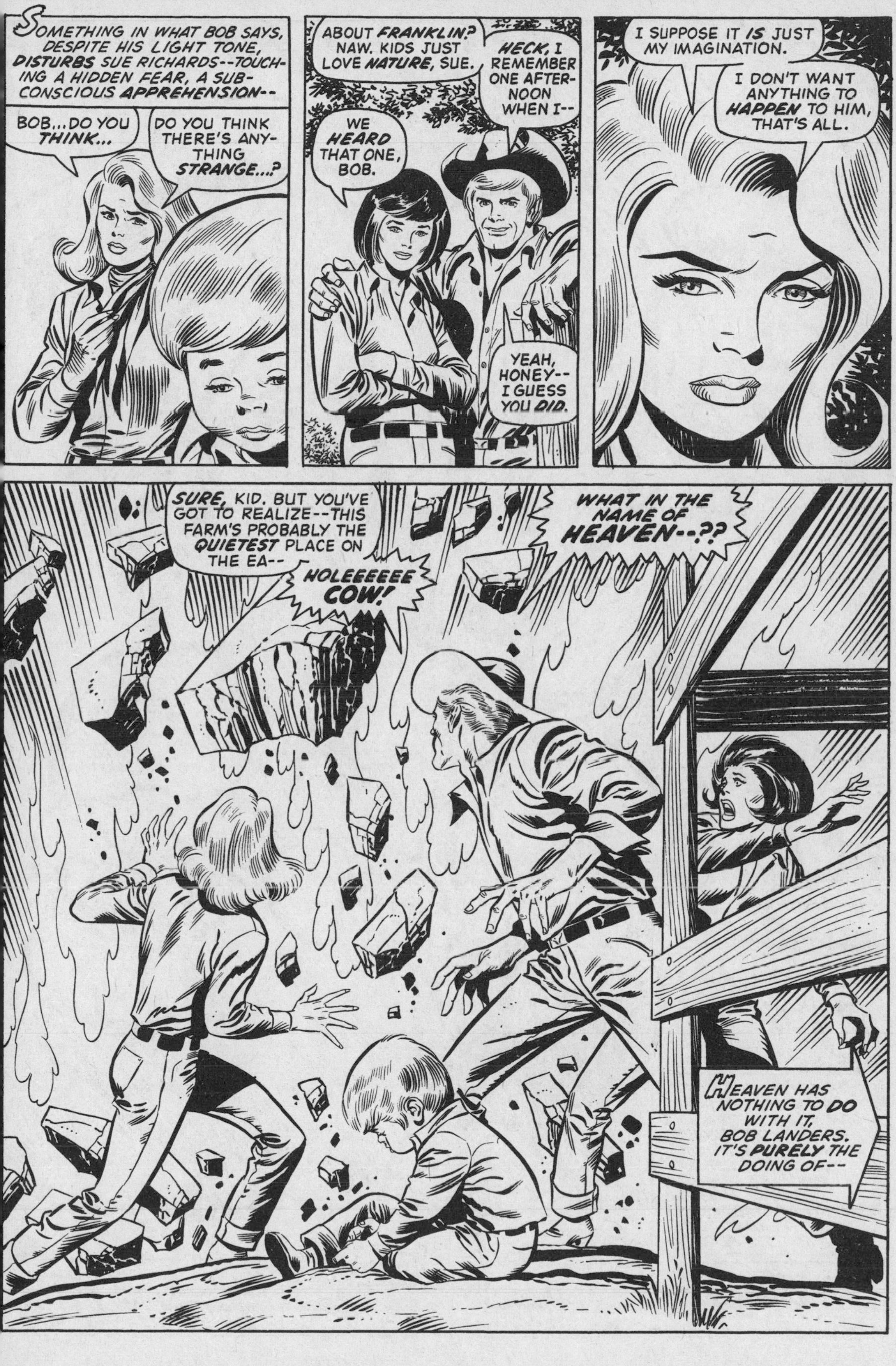

SOMETHING IN WHAT BOB SAYS, DESPITE HIS LIGHT TONE, DISTURBS SUE RICHARDS--TOUCHING A HIDDEN FEAR, A SUB-CONSCIOUS APPREHENSION--
BOB...DO YOU THINK...
DO YOU THINK THERE'S ANYTHING STRANGE...?
ABOUT FRANKLIN? NAW. KIDS JUST LOVE NATURE, SUE.
HECK, I REMEMBER ONE AFTER-NOON WHEN I--
WE HEARD THAT ONE, BOB.
YEAH, HONEY--I GUESS YOU DID.
I SUPPOSE IT IS JUST MY IMAGINATION.
I DON'T WANT ANYTHING TO HAPPEN TO HIM, THAT'S ALL.
SURE, KID. BUT YOU'VE GOT TO REALIZE--THIS FARM'S PROBABLY THE QUIETEST PLACE ON THE EA--
HOLEEEEEE COW!
WHAT IN THE NAME OF HEAVEN--??
HEAVEN HAS NOTHING TO DO WITH IT, BOB LANDERS. IT'S PURELY THE DOING OF--

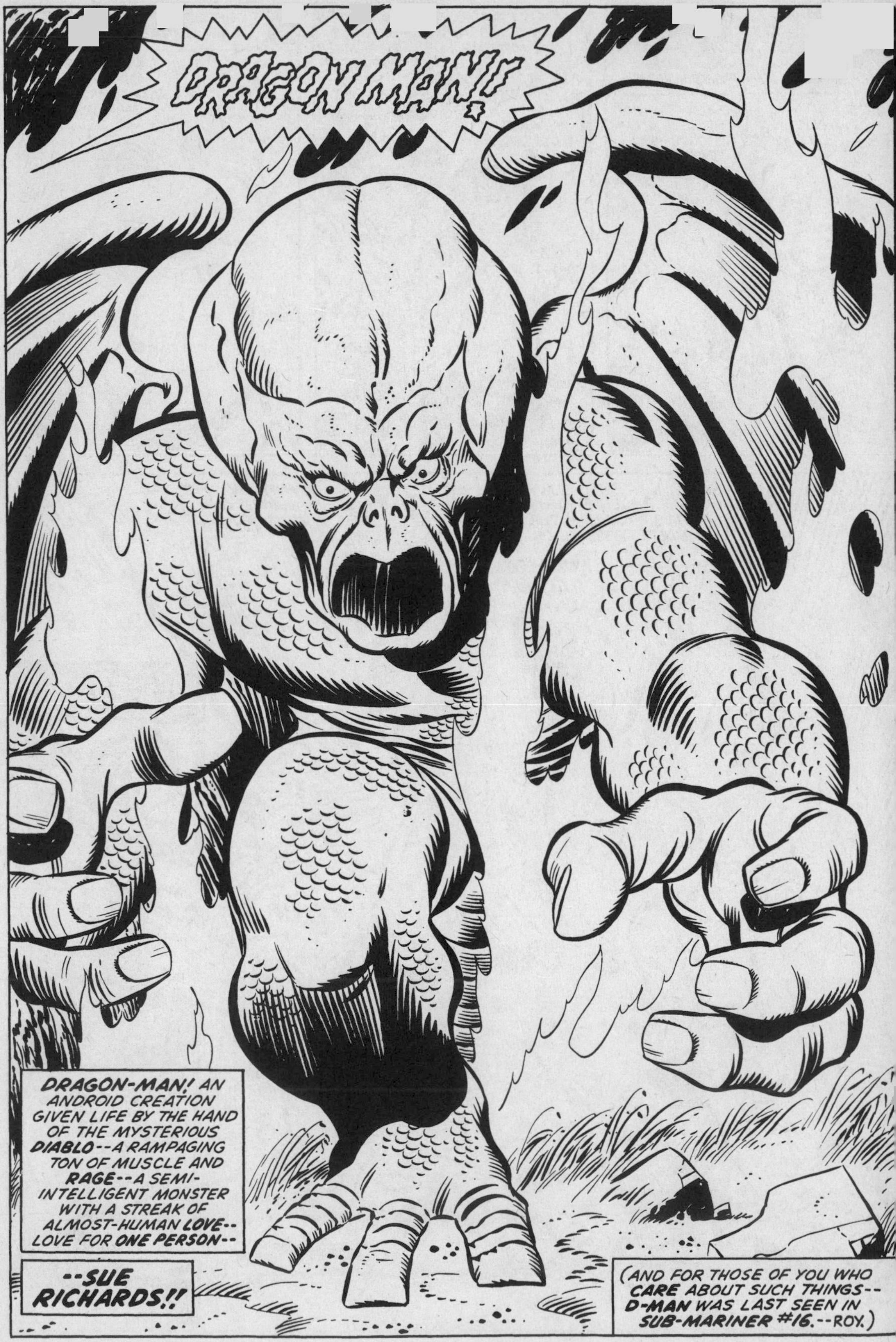
DRAGON MAN!
DRAGON-MAN! AN ANDROID CREATION GIVEN LIFE BY THE HAND OF THE MYSTERIOUS DIABLO--A RAMPAGING TON OF MUSCLE AND RAGE--A SEMI-INTELLIGENT MONSTER WITH A STREAK OF ALMOST-HUMAN LOVE--LOVE FOR ONE PERSON--
--SUE RICHARDS!!
(AND FOR THOSE OF YOU WHO CARE ABOUT SUCH THINGS--D-MAN WAS LAST SEEN IN SUB-MARINER #16.--ROY.)

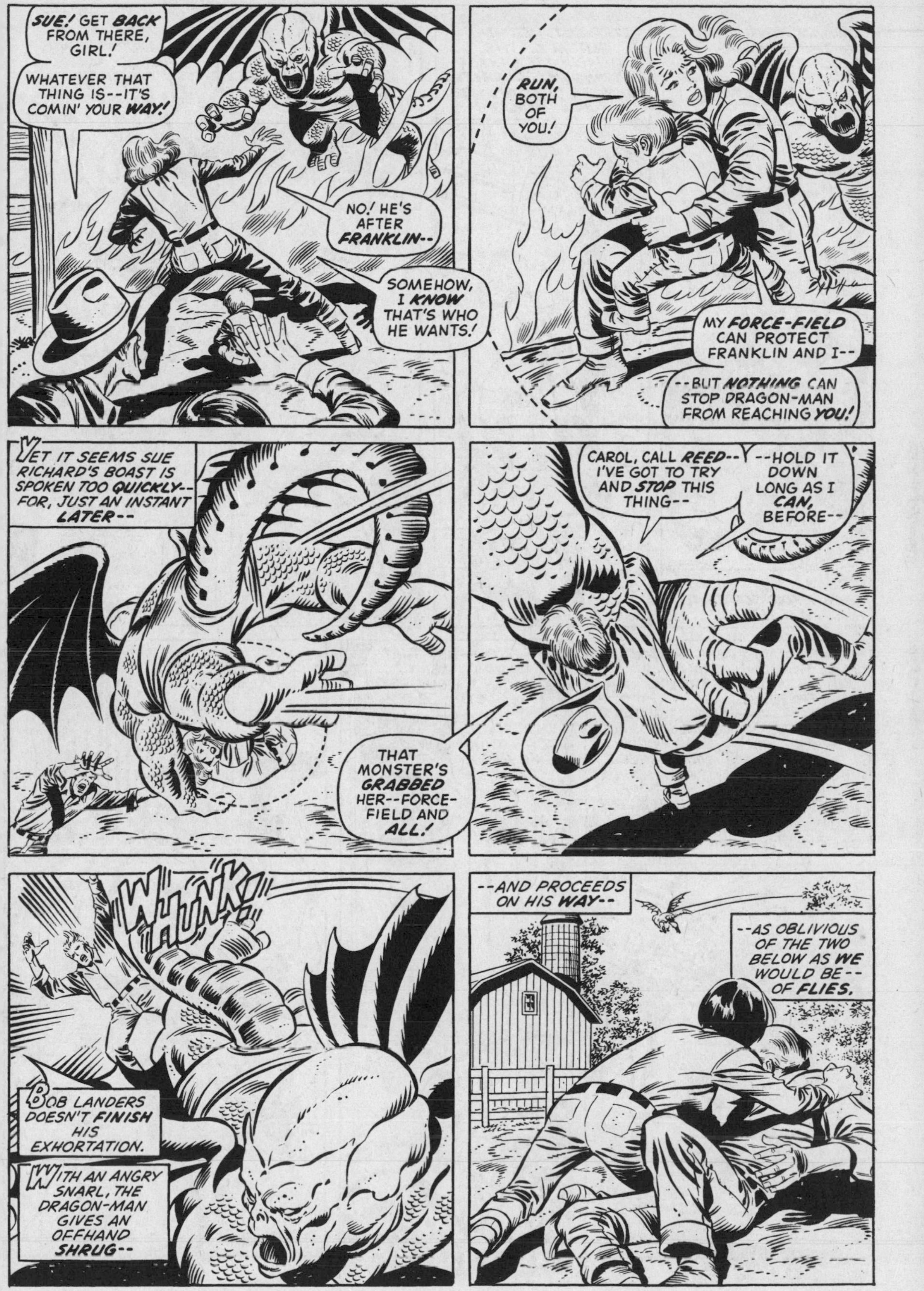
SUE! GET BACK FROM THERE, GIRL!
WHATEVER THAT THING IS--IT'S COMIN' YOUR WAY!
NO! HE'S AFTER FRANKLIN--
SOMEHOW, I KNOW THAT'S WHO HE WANTS!
RUN, BOTH OF YOU!
MY FORCE-FIELD CAN PROTECT FRANKLIN AND I--
--BUT NOTHING CAN STOP DRAGON-MAN FROM REACHING YOU!
YET IT SEEMS SUE RICHARD'S BOAST IS SPOKEN TOO QUICKLY--FOR, JUST AN INSTANT LATER--
THAT MONSTER'S GRABBED HER--FORCE-FIELD AND ALL!
CAROL, CALL REED--I'VE GOT TO TRY AND STOP THIS THING--
--HOLD IT DOWN LONG AS I CAN, BEFORE--
WHUNK!
BOB LANDERS DOESN'T FINISH HIS EXHORTATION.
WITH AN ANGRY SNARL, THE DRAGON-MAN GIVES AN OFFHAND SHRUG--
--AND PROCEEDS ON HIS WAY--
--AS OBLIVIOUS OF THE TWO BELOW AS WE WOULD BE--OF FLIES.

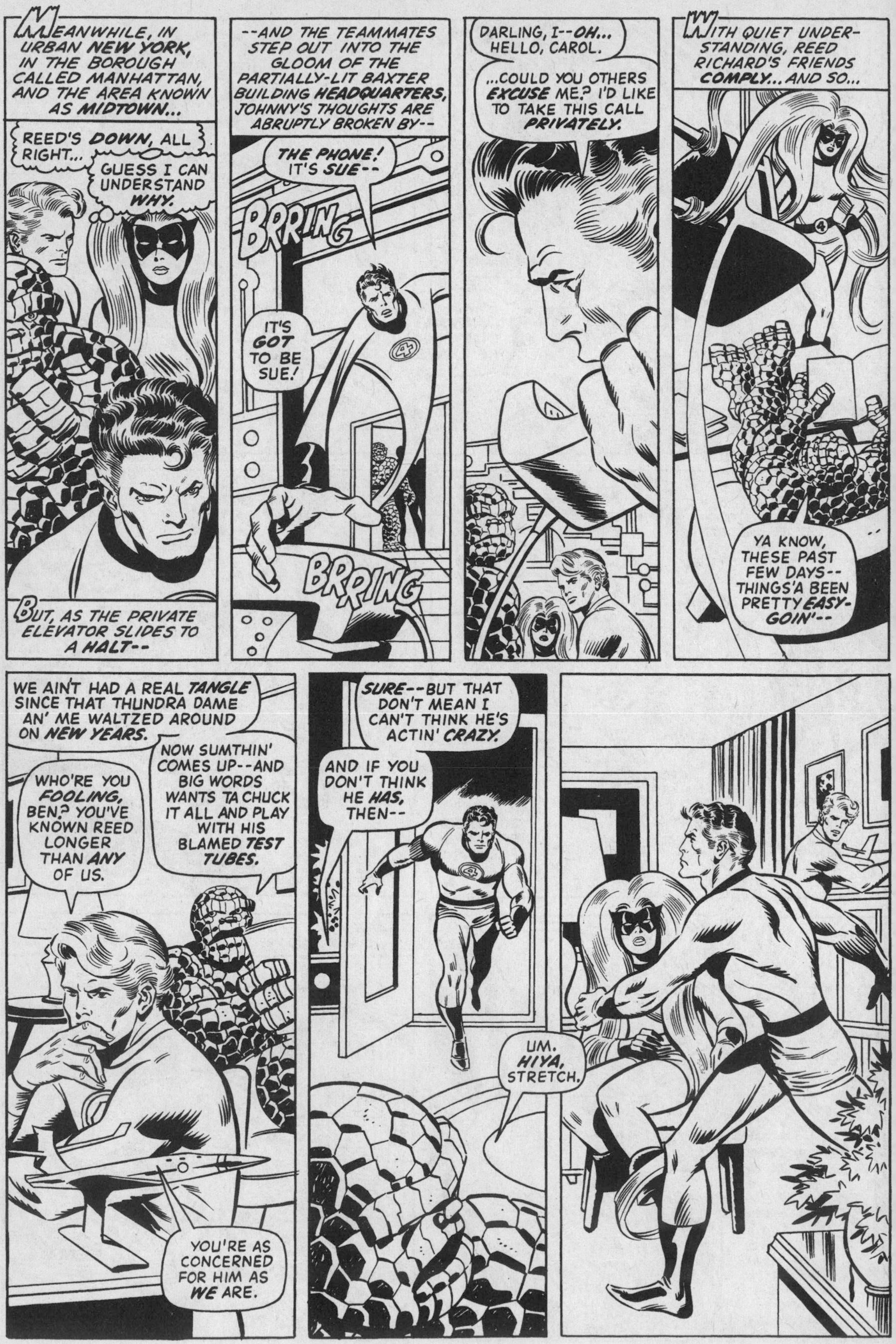
MEANWHILE, IN URBAN NEW YORK, IN THE BOROUGH CALLED MANHATTAN, AND THE AREA KNOWN AS MIDTOWN...
REED'S DOWN, ALL RIGHT...
GUESS I CAN UNDERSTAND WHY.
BUT, AS THE PRIVATE ELEVATOR SLIDES TO A HALT--
--AND THE TEAMMATES STEP OUT INTO THE GLOOM OF THE PARTIALLY-LIT BAXTER BUILDING HEADQUARTERS, JOHNNY'S THOUGHTS ARE ABRUPTLY BROKEN BY--
THE PHONE! IT'S SUE--
BRRING
IT'S GOT TO BE SUE!
BRRING
DARLING, I--OH... HELLO, CAROL.
...COULD YOU OTHERS EXCUSE ME? I'D LIKE TO TAKE THIS CALL PRIVATELY.
WITH QUIET UNDERSTANDING, REED RICHARD'S FRIENDS COMPLY... AND SO...
YA KNOW, THESE PAST FEW DAYS-- THINGS'A BEEN PRETTY EASY-GOIN'--
WE AIN'T HAD A REAL TANGLE SINCE THAT THUNDRA DAME AN' ME WALTZED AROUND ON NEW YEARS.
NOW SUMTHIN' COMES UP--AND BIG WORDS WANTS TA CHUCK IT ALL AND PLAY WITH HIS BLAMED TEST TUBES.
WHO'RE YOU FOOLING, BEN? YOU'VE KNOWN REED LONGER THAN ANY OF US.
YOU'RE AS CONCERNED FOR HIM AS WE ARE.
SURE--BUT THAT DON'T MEAN I CAN'T THINK HE'S ACTIN' CRAZY.
AND IF YOU DON'T THINK HE HAS, THEN--
UM. HIYA, STRETCH.

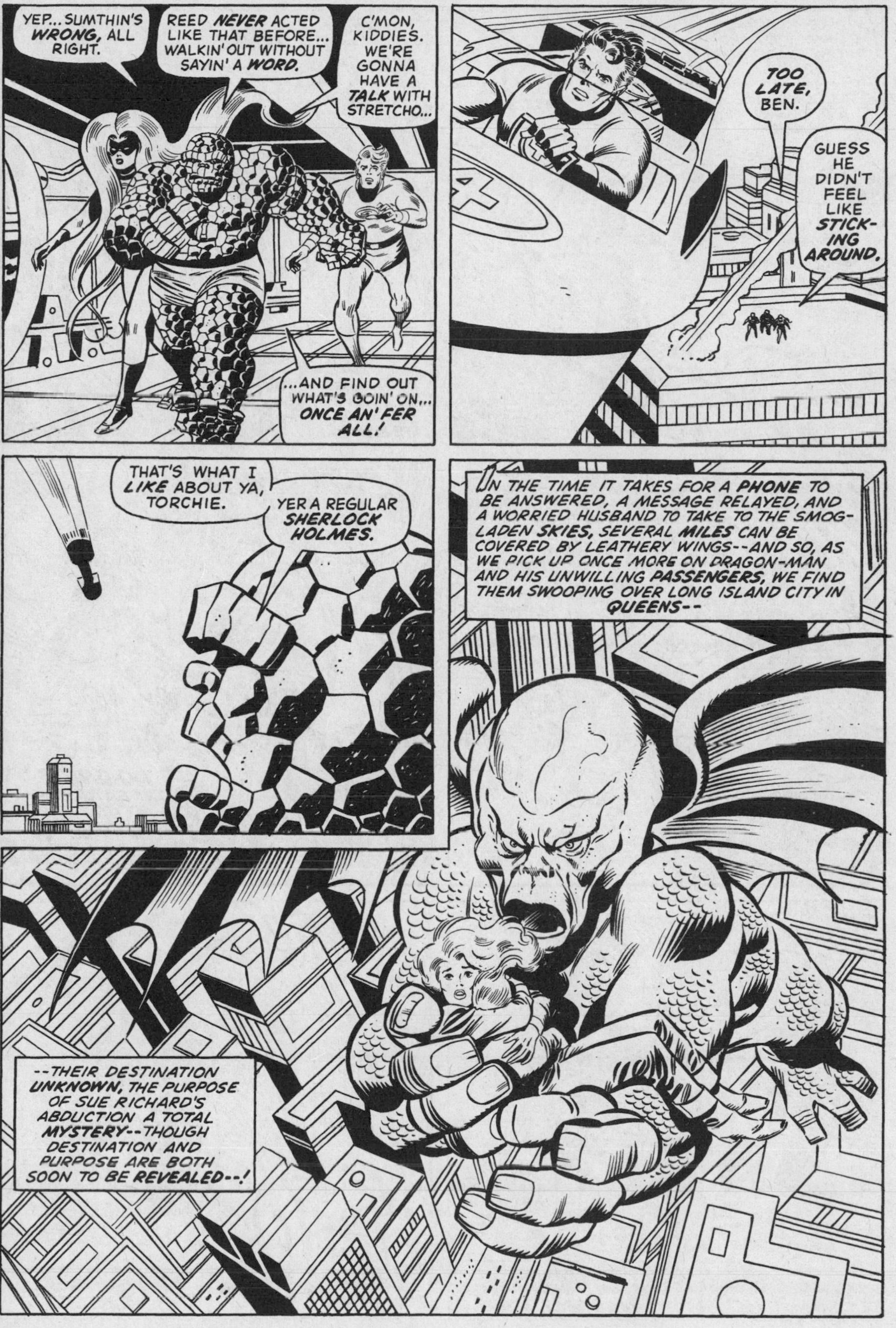

YEP... SUMTHIN'S WRONG, ALL RIGHT.
REED NEVER ACTED LIKE THAT BEFORE... WALKIN' OUT WITHOUT SAYIN' A WORD.
C'MON, KIDDIES. WE'RE GONNA HAVE A TALK WITH STRETCHO...
...AND FIND OUT WHAT'S GOIN' ON... ONCE AN' FER ALL!
TOO LATE, BEN.
GUESS HE DIDN'T FEEL LIKE STICKING AROUND.
THAT'S WHAT I LIKE ABOUT YA, TORCHIE.
YER A REGULAR SHERLOCK HOLMES.
IN THE TIME IT TAKES FOR A PHONE TO BE ANSWERED, A MESSAGE RELAYED, AND A WORRIED HUSBAND TO TAKE TO THE SMOG-LADEN SKIES, SEVERAL MILES CAN BE COVERED BY LEATHERY WINGS--AND SO, AS WE PICK UP ONCE MORE ON DRAGON-MAN AND HIS UNWILLING PASSENGERS, WE FIND THEM SWOOPING OVER LONG ISLAND CITY IN QUEENS--
--THEIR DESTINATION UNKNOWN, THE PURPOSE OF SUE RICHARD'S ABDUCTION A TOTAL MYSTERY--THOUGH DESTINATION AND PURPOSE ARE BOTH SOON TO BE REVEALED--!

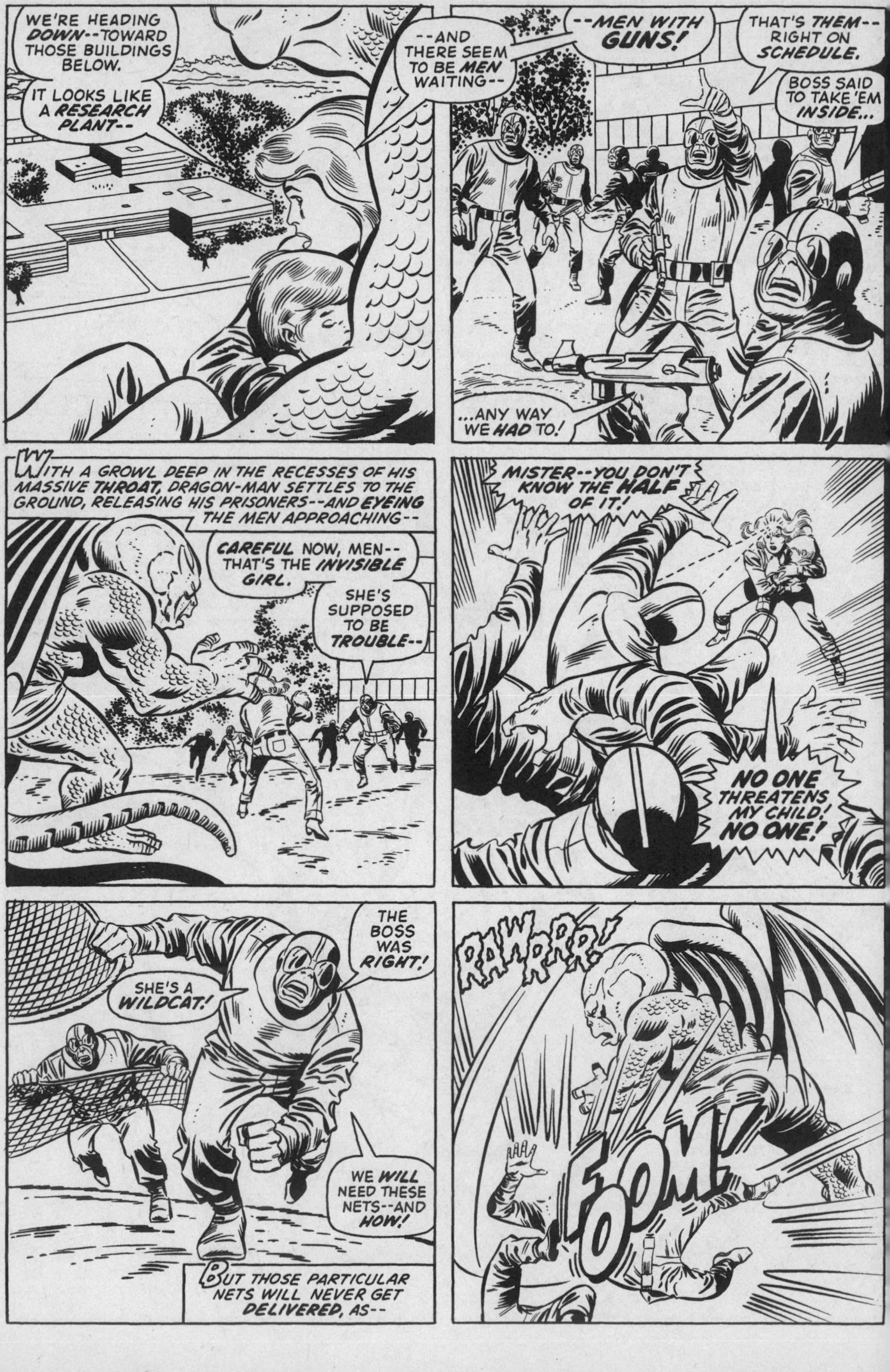
WE'RE HEADING DOWN--TOWARD THOSE BUILDINGS BELOW.
IT LOOKS LIKE A RESEARCH PLANT--
--AND THERE SEEM TO BE MEN WAITING--
--MEN WITH GUNS!
THAT'S THEM--RIGHT ON SCHEDULE.
BOSS SAID TO TAKE 'EM INSIDE...
...ANY WAY WE HAD TO!
WITH A GROWL DEEP IN THE RECESSES OF HIS MASSIVE THROAT, DRAGON-MAN SETTLES TO THE GROUND, RELEASING HIS PRISONERS--AND EYEING THE MEN APPROACHING--
CAREFUL NOW, MEN--THAT'S THE INVISIBLE GIRL.
SHE'S SUPPOSED TO BE TROUBLE--
MISTER--YOU DON'T KNOW THE HALF OF IT!
NO ONE THREATENS MY CHILD! NO ONE!
SHE'S A WILDCAT!
THE BOSS WAS RIGHT!
WE WILL NEED THESE NETS--AND HOW!
BUT THOSE PARTICULAR NETS WILL NEVER GET DELIVERED, AS--
RAWRRR!
FOOM!

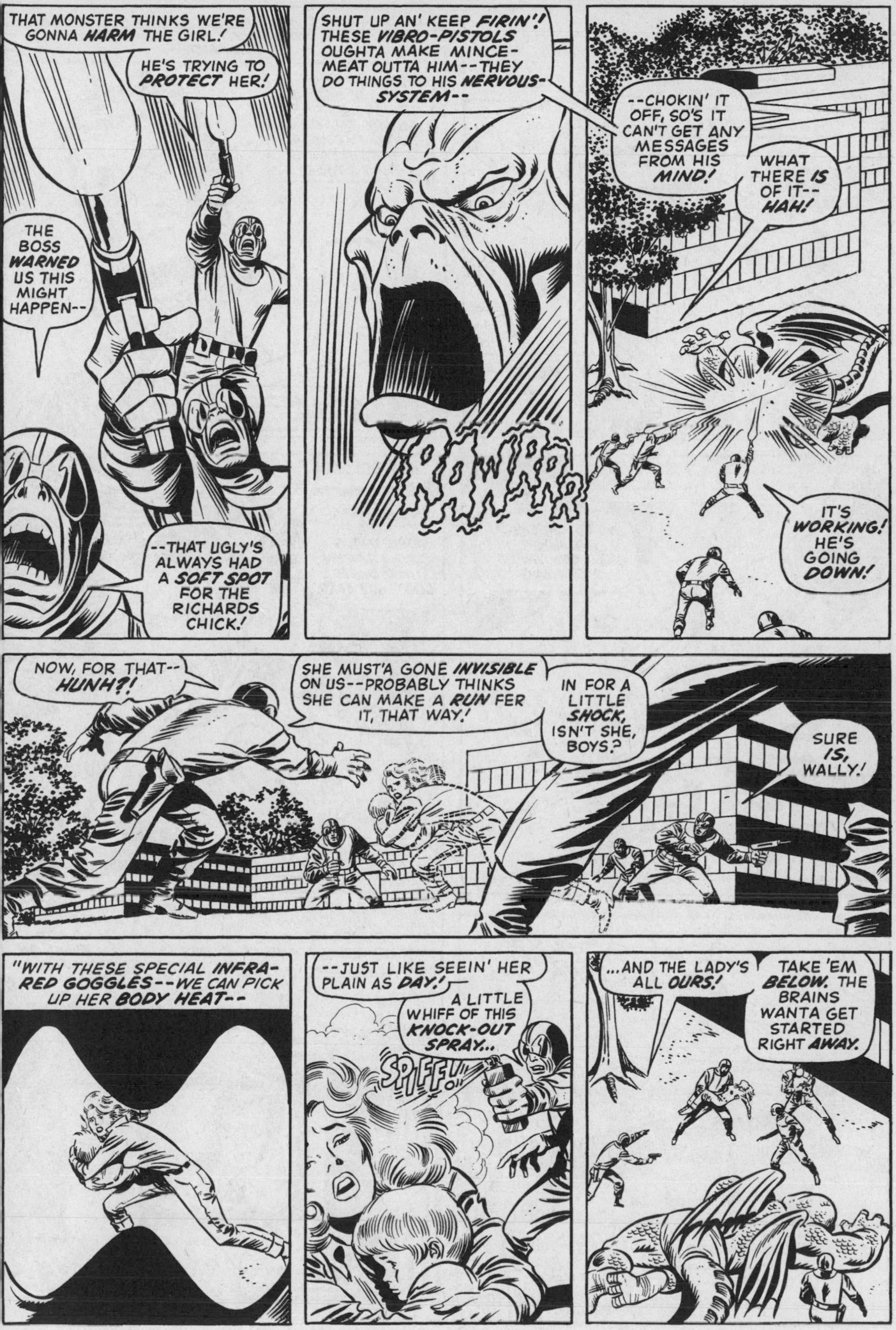
THAT MONSTER THINKS WE'RE GONNA HARM THE GIRL!
HE'S TRYING TO PROTECT HER!
THE BOSS WARNED US THIS MIGHT HAPPEN--
--THAT UGLY'S ALWAYS HAD A SOFT SPOT FOR THE RICHARDS CHICK!
SHUT UP AN' KEEP FIRIN'! THESE VIBRO-PISTOLS OUGHTA MAKE MINCE-MEAT OUTTA HIM--THEY DO THINGS TO HIS NERVOUS-SYSTEM--
RAWRR
--CHOKIN' IT OFF, SO'S IT CAN'T GET ANY MESSAGES FROM HIS MIND!
WHAT THERE IS OF IT--HAH!
IT'S WORKING! HE'S GOING DOWN!
NOW, FOR THAT--HUNH?!
SHE MUST'A GONE INVISIBLE ON US--PROBABLY THINKS SHE CAN MAKE A RUN FER IT, THAT WAY!
IN FOR A LITTLE SHOCK, ISN'T SHE, BOYS?
SURE IS, WALLY!
"WITH THESE SPECIAL INFRA-RED GOGGLES--WE CAN PICK UP HER BODY HEAT--
--JUST LIKE SEEIN' HER PLAIN AS DAY!
A LITTLE WHIFF OF THIS KNOCK-OUT SPRAY...
SPIFFF!
...AND THE LADY'S ALL OURS!
TAKE 'EM BELOW. THE BRAINS WANTA GET STARTED RIGHT AWAY.

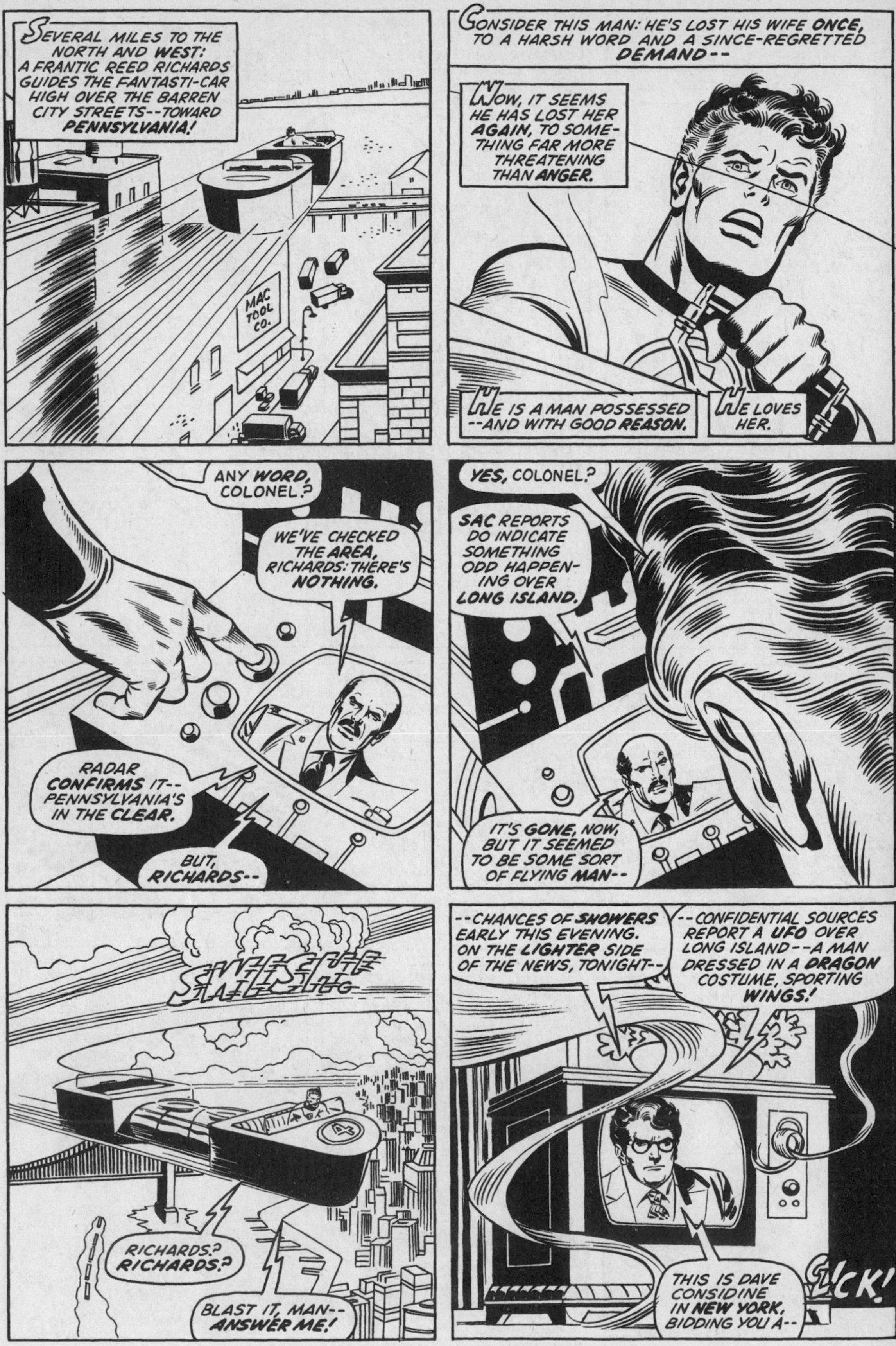
SEVERAL MILES TO THE NORTH AND WEST: A FRANTIC REED RICHARDS GUIDES THE FANTASTI-CAR HIGH OVER THE BARREN CITY STREETS--TOWARD PENNSYLVANIA!
MAC TOOL CO.
CONSIDER THIS MAN: HE'S LOST HIS WIFE ONCE, TO A HARSH WORD AND A SINCE-REGRETTED DEMAND--
NOW, IT SEEMS HE HAS LOST HER AGAIN, TO SOMETHING FAR MORE THREATENING THAN ANGER.
HE IS A MAN POSSESSED --AND WITH GOOD REASON.
HE LOVES HER.
ANY WORD, COLONEL?
WE'VE CHECKED THE AREA, RICHARDS: THERE'S NOTHING.
RADAR CONFIRMS IT-- PENNSYLVANIA'S IN THE CLEAR.
BUT, RICHARDS--
YES, COLONEL?
SAC REPORTS DO INDICATE SOMETHING ODD HAPPENING OVER LONG ISLAND.
IT'S GONE, NOW, BUT IT SEEMED TO BE SOME SORT OF FLYING MAN--
RICHARDS? RICHARDS?
BLAST IT, MAN-- ANSWER ME!
--CHANCES OF SHOWERS EARLY THIS EVENING. ON THE LIGHTER SIDE OF THE NEWS, TONIGHT--
--CONFIDENTIAL SOURCES REPORT A UFO OVER LONG ISLAND--A MAN DRESSED IN A DRAGON COSTUME, SPORTING WINGS!
THIS IS DAVE CONSIDINE IN NEW YORK, BIDDING YOU A--
CLICK!

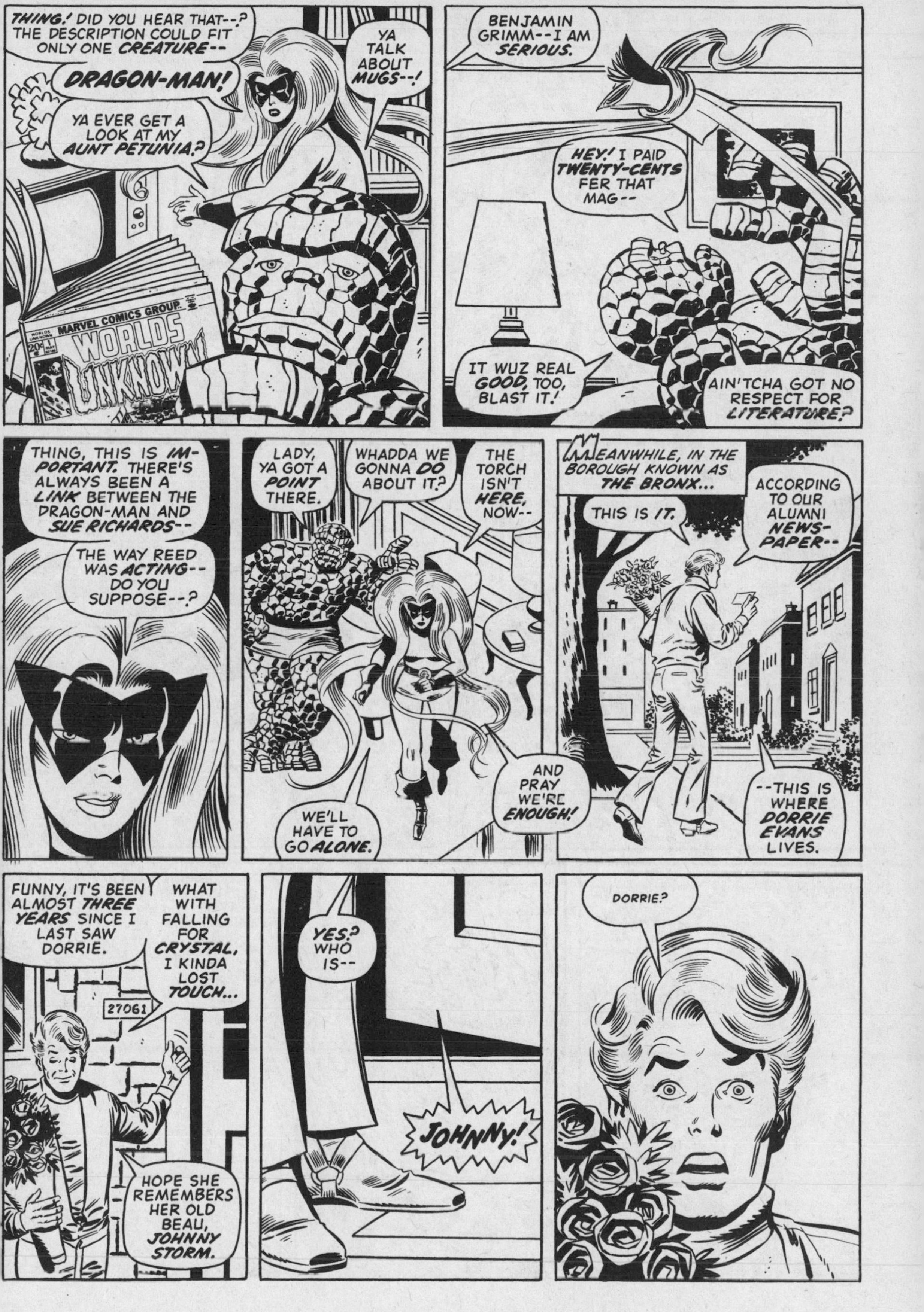

THING! DID YOU HEAR THAT--? THE DESCRIPTION COULD FIT ONLY ONE CREATURE--
DRAGON-MAN!
YA EVER GET A LOOK AT MY AUNT PETUNIA?
YA TALK ABOUT MUGS--!
MARVEL COMICS GROUP
WORLDS UNKNOWN
BENJAMIN GRIMM--I AM SERIOUS.
HEY! I PAID TWENTY-CENTS FER THAT MAG--
IT WUZ REAL GOOD, TOO, BLAST IT!
AIN'TCHA GOT NO RESPECT FOR LITERATURE?
THING, THIS IS IMPORTANT. THERE'S ALWAYS BEEN A LINK BETWEEN THE DRAGON-MAN AND SUE RICHARDS--
THE WAY REED WAS ACTING--DO YOU SUPPOSE--?
LADY, YA GOT A POINT THERE.
WHADDA WE GONNA DO ABOUT IT?
THE TORCH ISN'T HERE, NOW--
WE'LL HAVE TO GO ALONE.
AND PRAY WE'RE ENOUGH!
MEANWHILE, IN THE BOROUGH KNOWN AS THE BRONX...
THIS IS IT.
ACCORDING TO OUR ALUMNI NEWSPAPER--
--THIS IS WHERE DORRIE EVANS LIVES.
FUNNY, IT'S BEEN ALMOST THREE YEARS SINCE I LAST SAW DORRIE.
WHAT WITH FALLING FOR CRYSTAL, I KINDA LOST TOUCH...
27061
HOPE SHE REMEMBERS HER OLD BEAU, JOHNNY STORM.
YES? WHO IS--
JOHNNY!
DORRIE?

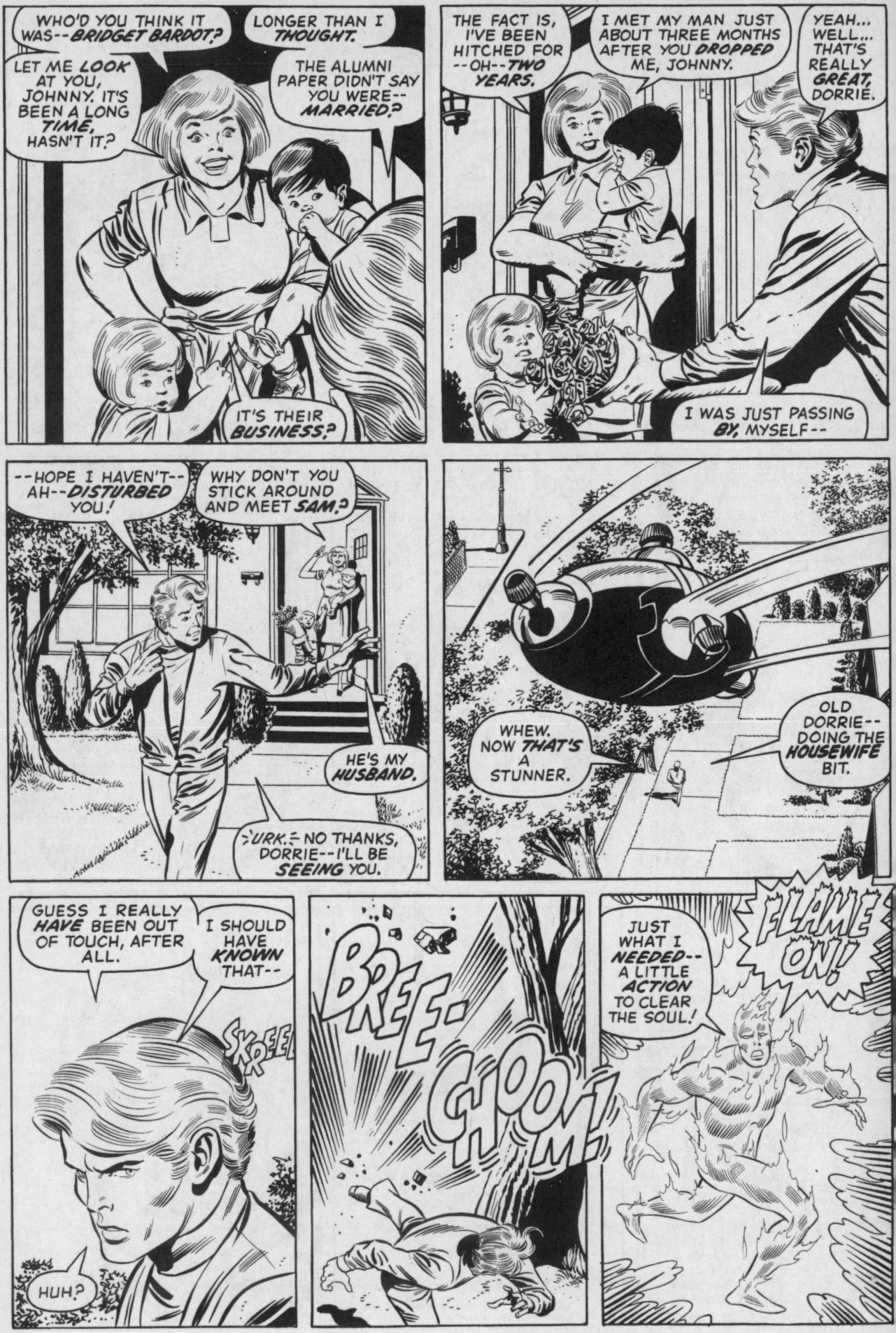
WHO'D YOU THINK IT WAS--BRIDGET BARDOT?
LET ME LOOK AT YOU, JOHNNY. IT'S BEEN A LONG TIME, HASN'T IT?
LONGER THAN I THOUGHT.
THE ALUMNI PAPER DIDN'T SAY YOU WERE--MARRIED?
IT'S THEIR BUSINESS?
THE FACT IS, I'VE BEEN HITCHED FOR --OH--TWO YEARS.
I MET MY MAN JUST ABOUT THREE MONTHS AFTER YOU DROPPED ME, JOHNNY.
YEAH... WELL... THAT'S REALLY GREAT, DORRIE.
I WAS JUST PASSING BY, MYSELF--
--HOPE I HAVEN'T--AH--DISTURBED YOU!
WHY DON'T YOU STICK AROUND AND MEET SAM?
HE'S MY HUSBAND.
URK.--NO THANKS, DORRIE--I'LL BE SEEING YOU.
WHEW. NOW THAT'S A STUNNER.
OLD DORRIE--DOING THE HOUSEWIFE BIT.
GUESS I REALLY HAVE BEEN OUT OF TOUCH, AFTER ALL.
I SHOULD HAVE KNOWN THAT--
SKREEE
HUH?
BREE-CHOOM!
JUST WHAT I NEEDED--A LITTLE ACTION TO CLEAR THE SOUL!
FLAME ON!

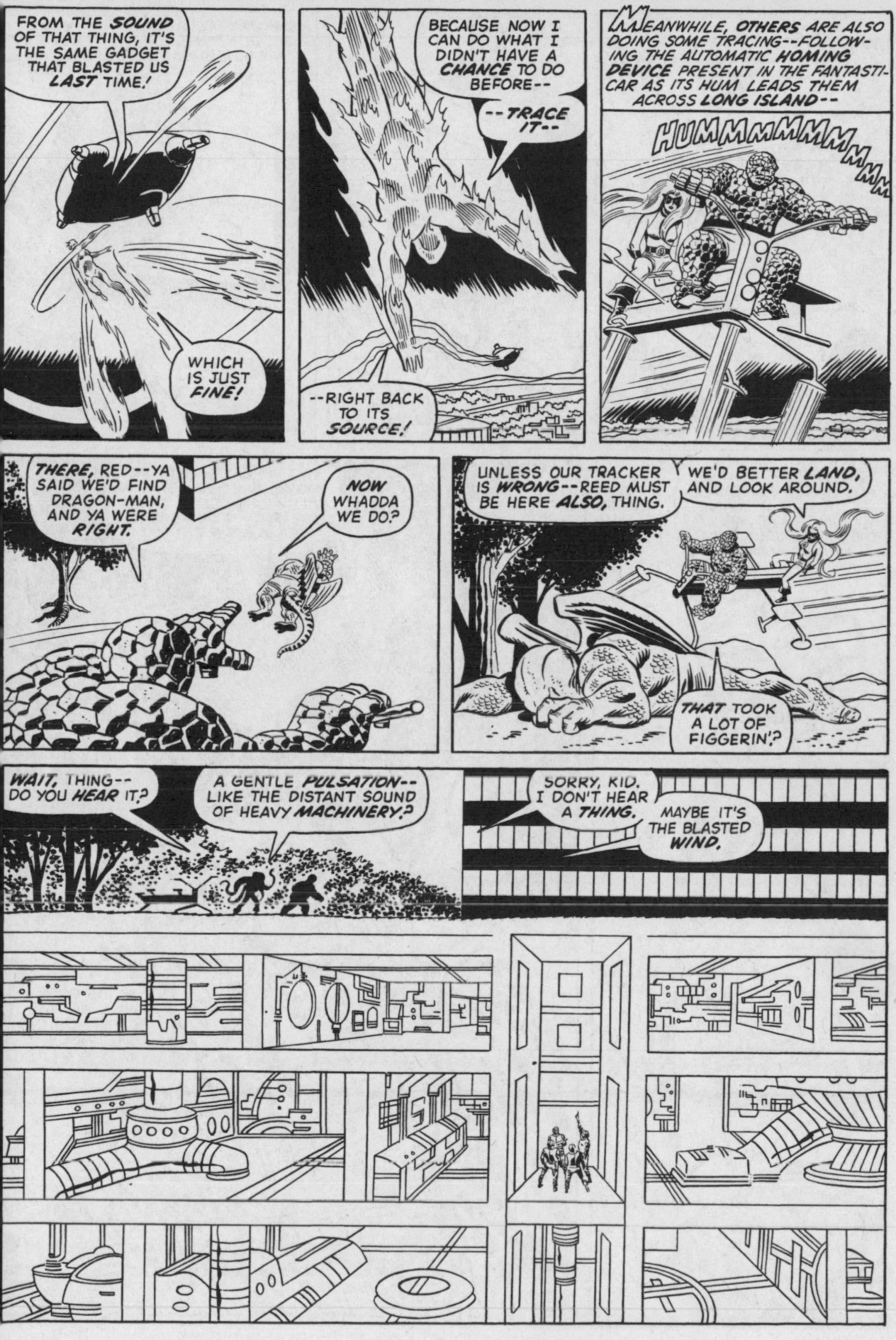
FROM THE SOUND OF THAT THING, IT'S THE SAME GADGET THAT BLASTED US LAST TIME!
WHICH IS JUST FINE!
BECAUSE NOW I CAN DO WHAT I DIDN'T HAVE A CHANCE TO DO BEFORE--
--TRACE IT--
--RIGHT BACK TO ITS SOURCE!
MEANWHILE, OTHERS ARE ALSO DOING SOME TRACING--FOLLOWING THE AUTOMATIC HOMING DEVICE PRESENT IN THE FANTASTI-CAR AS ITS HUM LEADS THEM ACROSS LONG ISLAND--
HUMMMMMMMMMMM
THERE, RED--YA SAID WE'D FIND DRAGON-MAN, AND YA WERE RIGHT.
NOW WHADDA WE DO?
UNLESS OUR TRACKER IS WRONG--REED MUST BE HERE ALSO, THING.
WE'D BETTER LAND, AND LOOK AROUND.
THAT TOOK A LOT OF FIGGERIN'?
WAIT, THING--DO YOU HEAR IT?
A GENTLE PULSATION--LIKE THE DISTANT SOUND OF HEAVY MACHINERY?
SORRY, KID. I DON'T HEAR A THING.
MAYBE IT'S THE BLASTED WIND.

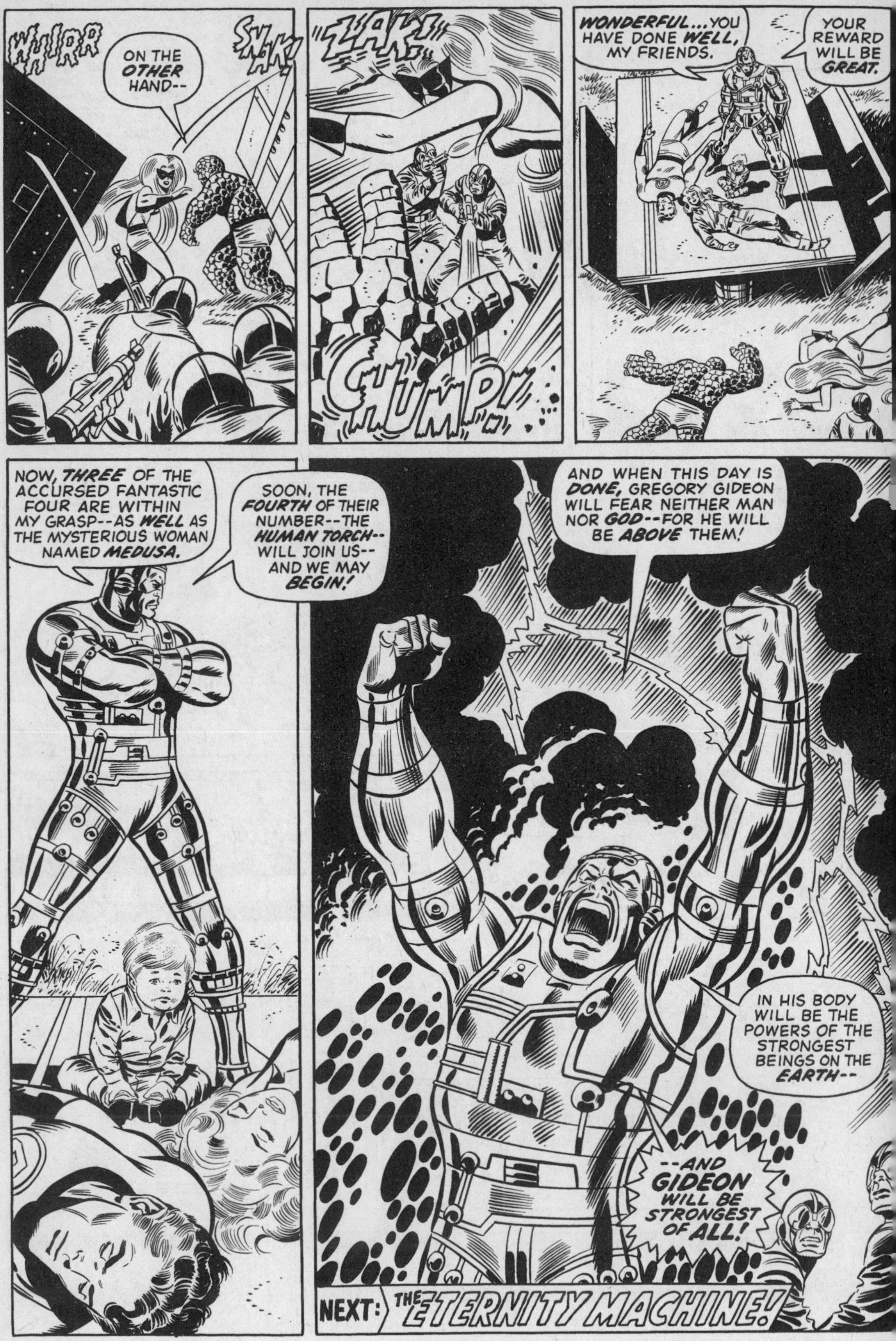
WHIRR
ON THE OTHER HAND--
SNAK
ZZAK!
CHUMP!
WONDERFUL...YOU HAVE DONE WELL, MY FRIENDS.
YOUR REWARD WILL BE GREAT.
NOW, THREE OF THE ACCURSED FANTASTIC FOUR ARE WITHIN MY GRASP--AS WELL AS THE MYSTERIOUS WOMAN NAMED MEDUSA.
SOON, THE FOURTH OF THEIR NUMBER--THE HUMAN TORCH--WILL JOIN US--AND WE MAY BEGIN!
AND WHEN THIS DAY IS DONE, GREGORY GIDEON WILL FEAR NEITHER MAN NOR GOD--FOR HE WILL BE ABOVE THEM!
IN HIS BODY WILL BE THE POWERS OF THE STRONGEST BEINGS ON THE EARTH--
--AND GIDEON WILL BE STRONGEST OF ALL!
NEXT: THE ETERNITY MACHINE!

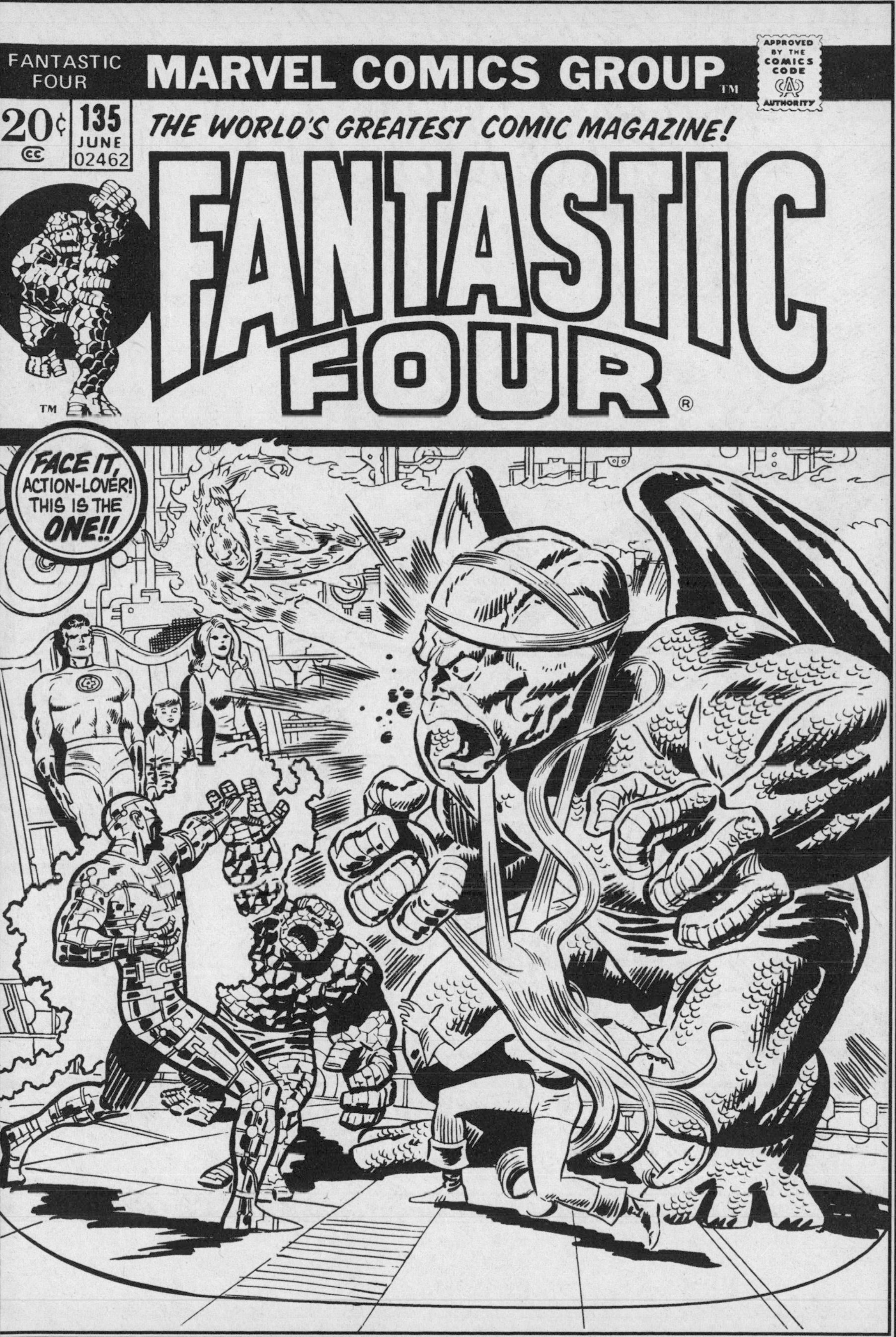

FANTASTIC FOUR
MARVEL COMICS GROUP
TM
APPROVED BY THE COMICS CODE AUTHORITY
20¢
135
JUNE
02462
THE WORLD'S GREATEST COMIC MAGAZINE!
FANTASTIC FOUR
TM
®
FACE IT, ACTION-LOVER! THIS IS THE ONE!!

Stan Lee PRESENTS: THE FANTASTIC FOUR!™
THE ETERNITY MACHINE
HOLY COW! IT'S DRAGON-MAN!
I FOLLOW THIS CRAZY FLYING EYE ACROSS HALF OF LONG ISLAND, THINKING I'M GOING TO FIND THE JOKERS WHO TRIED TO BLAST US*--
--AND INSTEAD OF SOME GADGET-FILLED ARSENAL-- I FIND HIM!
*LAST ISSUE--ROY.
GERRY CONWAY, WRITER * JOHN BUSCEMA & JOE SINNOTT, ARTISTS * LETTERED BY: ARTIE SIMEK COLORED BY: P. GOLDBERG * ROY THOMAS, EDITOR

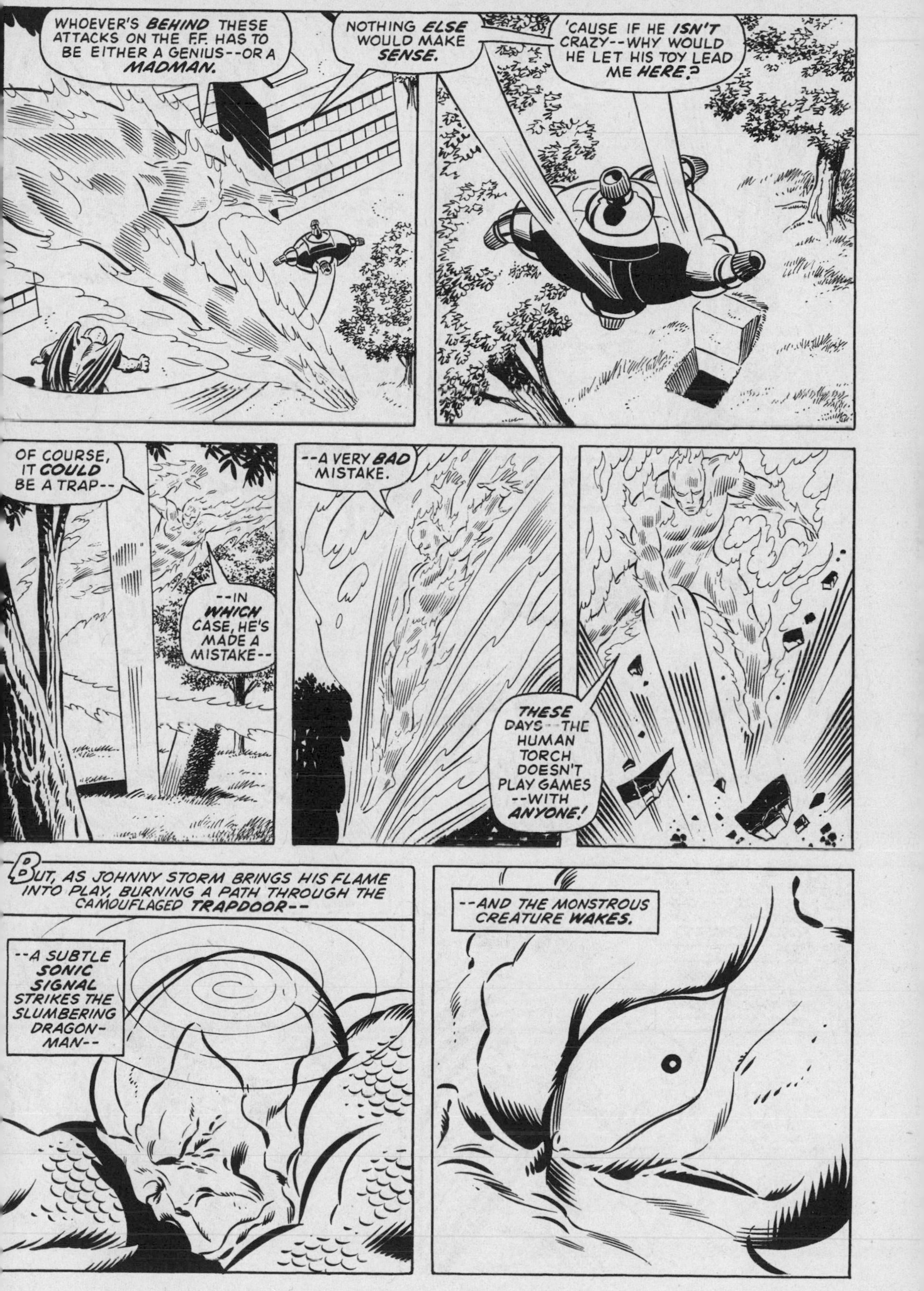
WHOEVER'S BEHIND THESE ATTACKS ON THE F.F. HAS TO BE EITHER A GENIUS--OR A MADMAN.
NOTHING ELSE WOULD MAKE SENSE.
'CAUSE IF HE ISN'T CRAZY--WHY WOULD HE LET HIS TOY LEAD ME HERE?
OF COURSE, IT COULD BE A TRAP--
--IN WHICH CASE, HE'S MADE A MISTAKE--
--A VERY BAD MISTAKE.
THESE DAYS--THE HUMAN TORCH DOESN'T PLAY GAMES--WITH ANYONE!
BUT, AS JOHNNY STORM BRINGS HIS FLAME INTO PLAY, BURNING A PATH THROUGH THE CAMOUFLAGED TRAPDOOR--
--A SUBTLE SONIC SIGNAL STRIKES THE SLUMBERING DRAGON-MAN--
--AND THE MONSTROUS CREATURE WAKES.

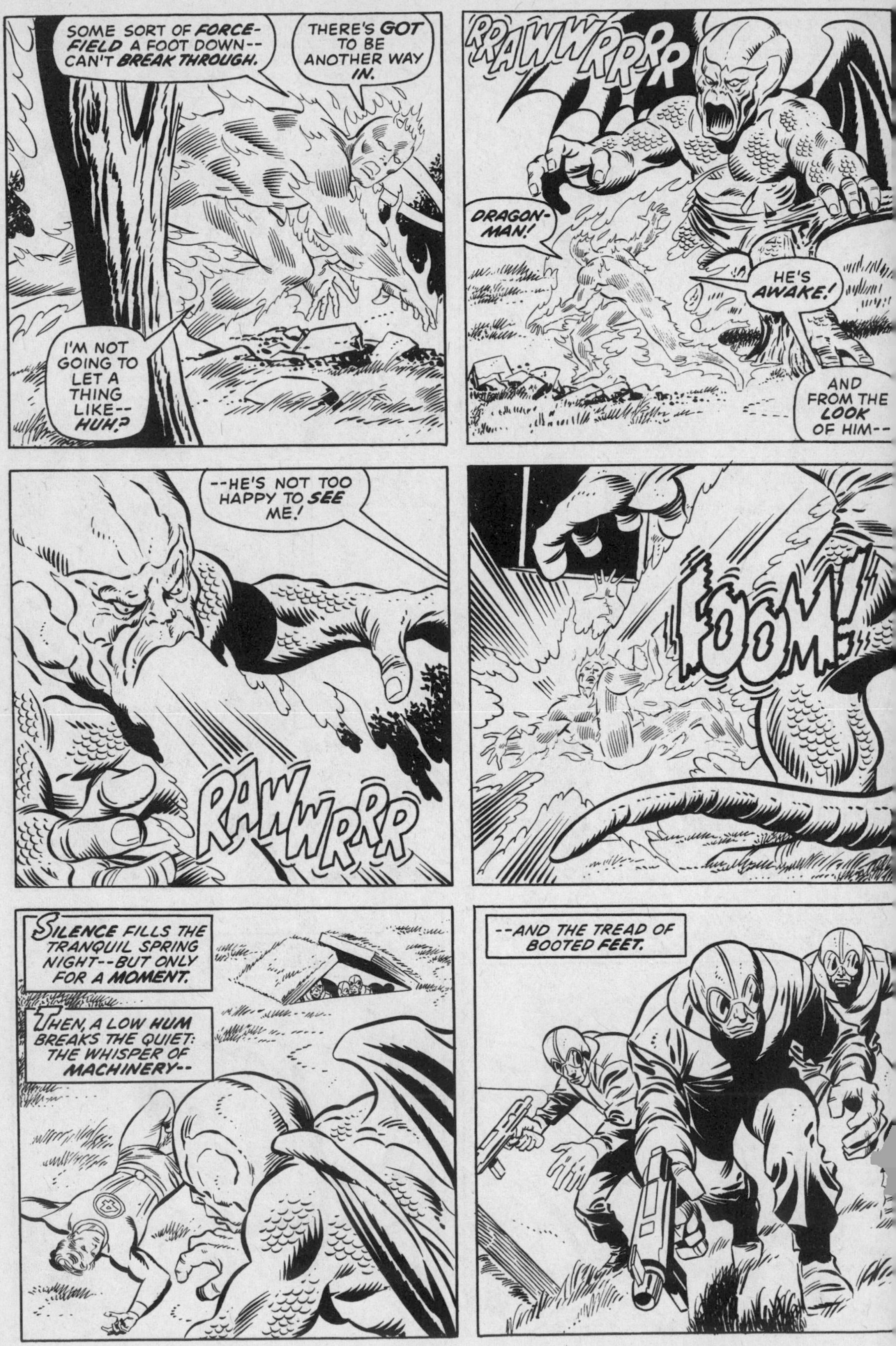
SOME SORT OF FORCE-FIELD A FOOT DOWN-- CAN'T BREAK THROUGH.
THERE'S GOT TO BE ANOTHER WAY IN.
I'M NOT GOING TO LET A THING LIKE-- HUH?
RRAWWRRRR
DRAGON-MAN!
HE'S AWAKE!
AND FROM THE LOOK OF HIM--
--HE'S NOT TOO HAPPY TO SEE ME!
RAWWRRR
FOOM!
SILENCE FILLS THE TRANQUIL SPRING NIGHT--BUT ONLY FOR A MOMENT.
THEN, A LOW HUM BREAKS THE QUIET: THE WHISPER OF MACHINERY--
--AND THE TREAD OF BOOTED FEET.

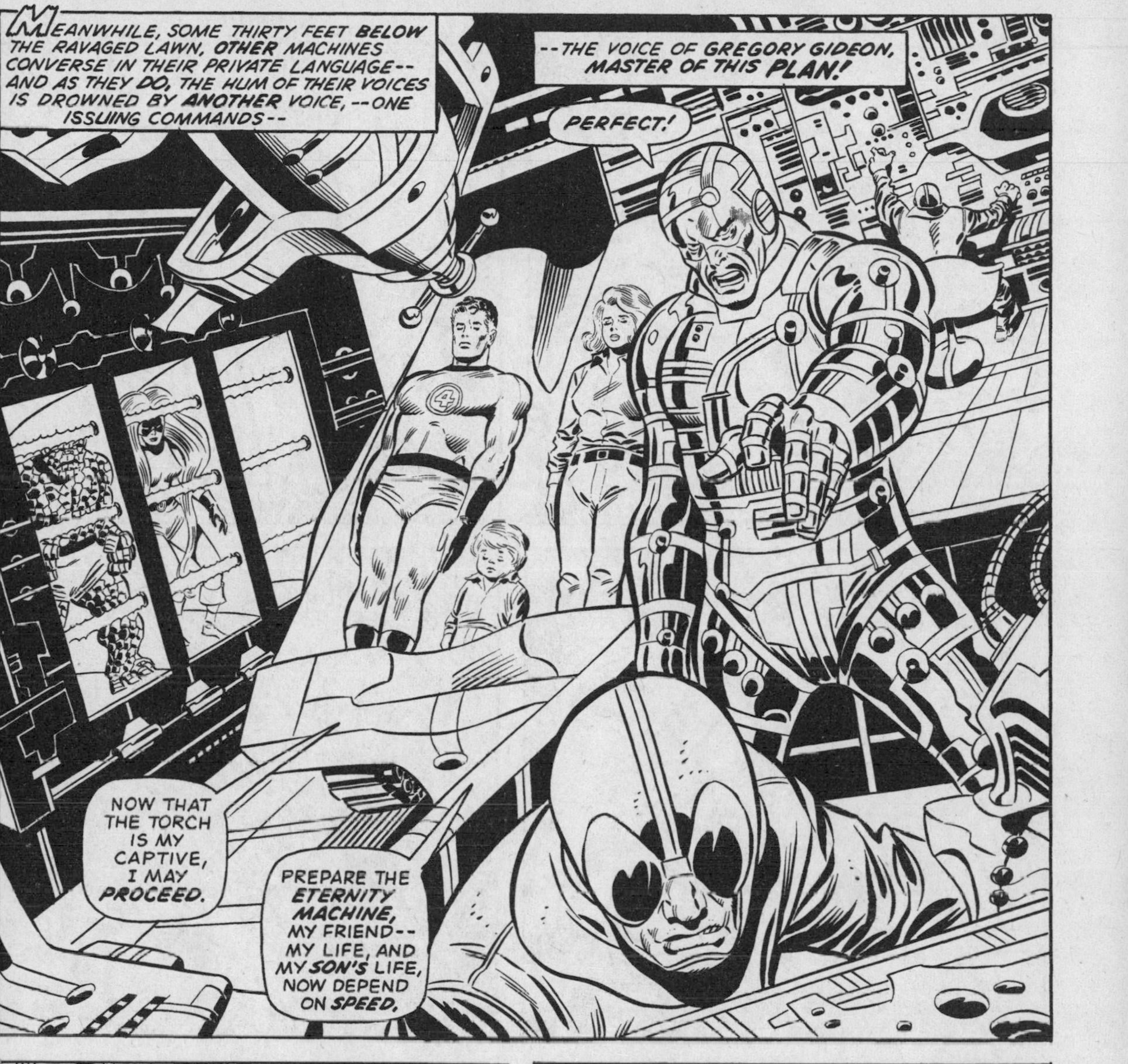
MEANWHILE, SOME THIRTY FEET BELOW THE RAVAGED LAWN, OTHER MACHINES CONVERSE IN THEIR PRIVATE LANGUAGE-- AND AS THEY DO, THE HUM OF THEIR VOICES IS DROWNED BY ANOTHER VOICE, --ONE ISSUING COMMANDS--
--THE VOICE OF GREGORY GIDEON, MASTER OF THIS PLAN!
PERFECT!
NOW THAT THE TORCH IS MY CAPTIVE, I MAY PROCEED.
PREPARE THE ETERNITY MACHINE, MY FRIEND-- MY LIFE, AND MY SON'S LIFE, NOW DEPEND ON SPEED.

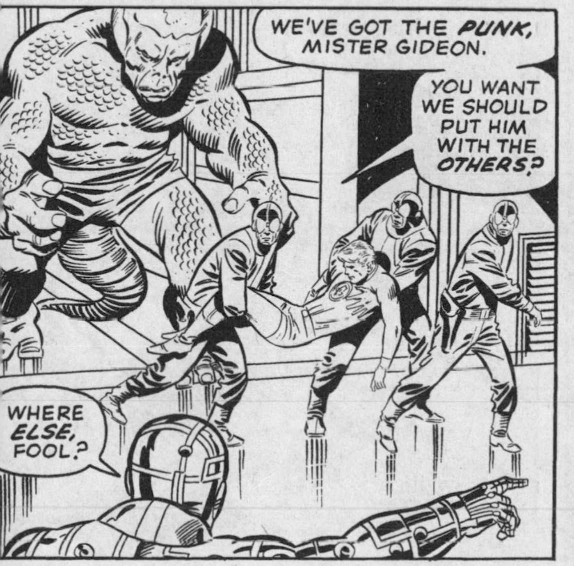
WE'VE GOT THE PUNK, MISTER GIDEON.
YOU WANT WE SHOULD PUT HIM WITH THE OTHERS?
WHERE ELSE, FOOL?

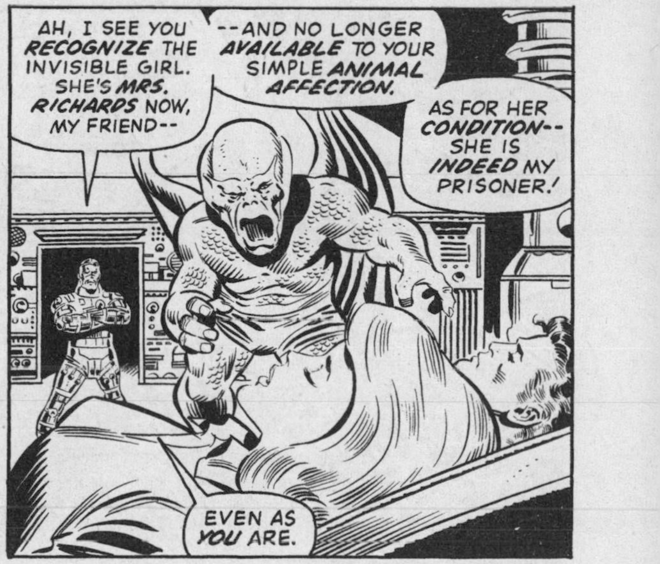
AH, I SEE YOU RECOGNIZE THE INVISIBLE GIRL. SHE'S MRS. RICHARDS NOW, MY FRIEND--
--AND NO LONGER AVAILABLE TO YOUR SIMPLE ANIMAL AFFECTION.
AS FOR HER CONDITION-- SHE IS INDEED MY PRISONER!
EVEN AS YOU ARE.

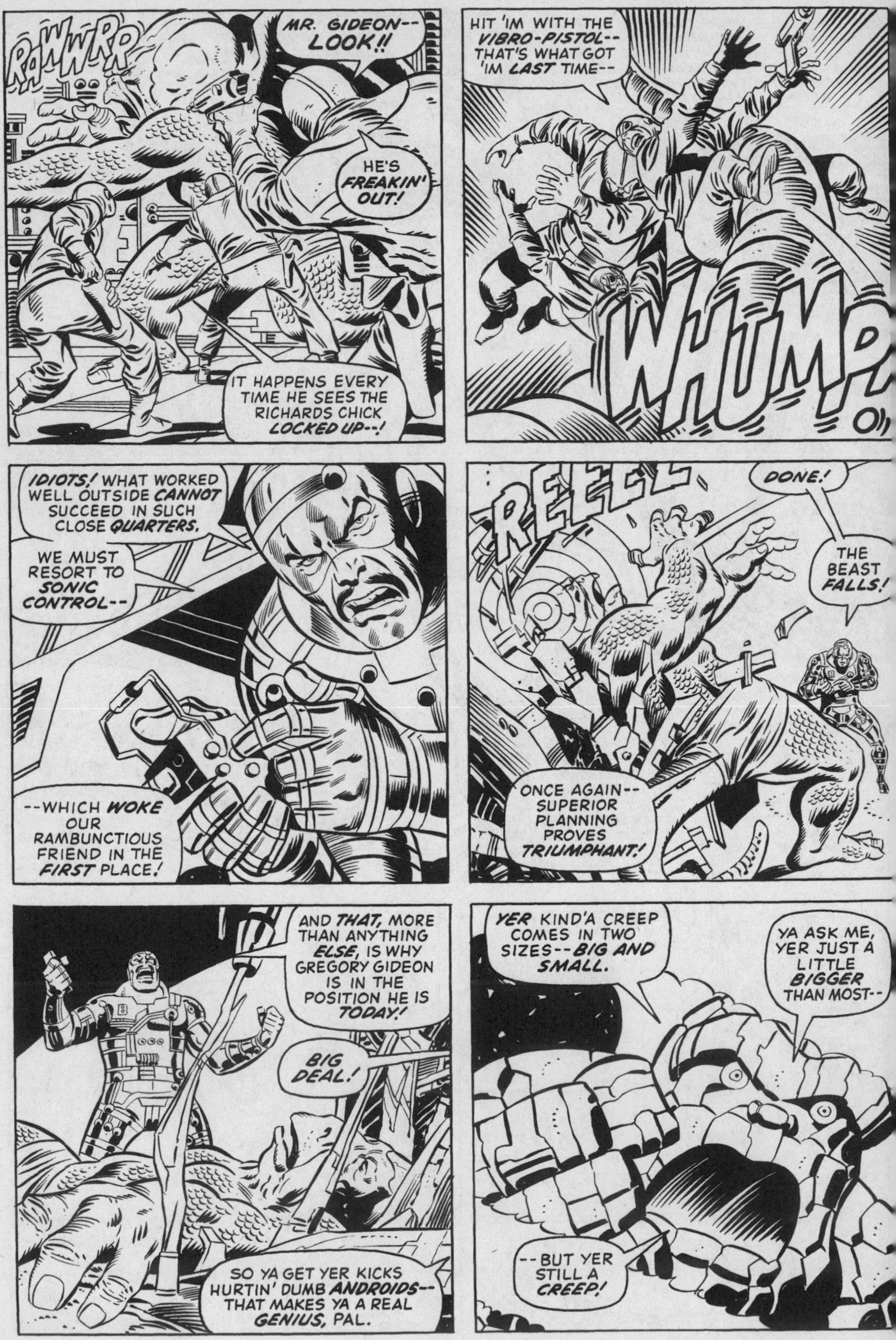
RAWWRR
MR. GIDEON-- LOOK!!
HE'S FREAKIN' OUT!
IT HAPPENS EVERY TIME HE SEES THE RICHARDS CHICK LOCKED UP--!
HIT 'IM WITH THE VIBRO-PISTOL-- THAT'S WHAT GOT 'IM LAST TIME--
WHUMP!
IDIOTS! WHAT WORKED WELL OUTSIDE CANNOT SUCCEED IN SUCH CLOSE QUARTERS.
WE MUST RESORT TO SONIC CONTROL--
--WHICH WOKE OUR RAMBUNCTIOUS FRIEND IN THE FIRST PLACE!
REEEL
DONE!
THE BEAST FALLS!
ONCE AGAIN-- SUPERIOR PLANNING PROVES TRIUMPHANT!
AND THAT, MORE THAN ANYTHING ELSE, IS WHY GREGORY GIDEON IS IN THE POSITION HE IS TODAY!
BIG DEAL!
SO YA GET YER KICKS HURTIN' DUMB ANDROIDS-- THAT MAKES YA A REAL GENIUS, PAL.
YER KIND'A CREEP COMES IN TWO SIZES--BIG AND SMALL.
YA ASK ME, YER JUST A LITTLE BIGGER THAN MOST--
--BUT YER STILL A CREEP!

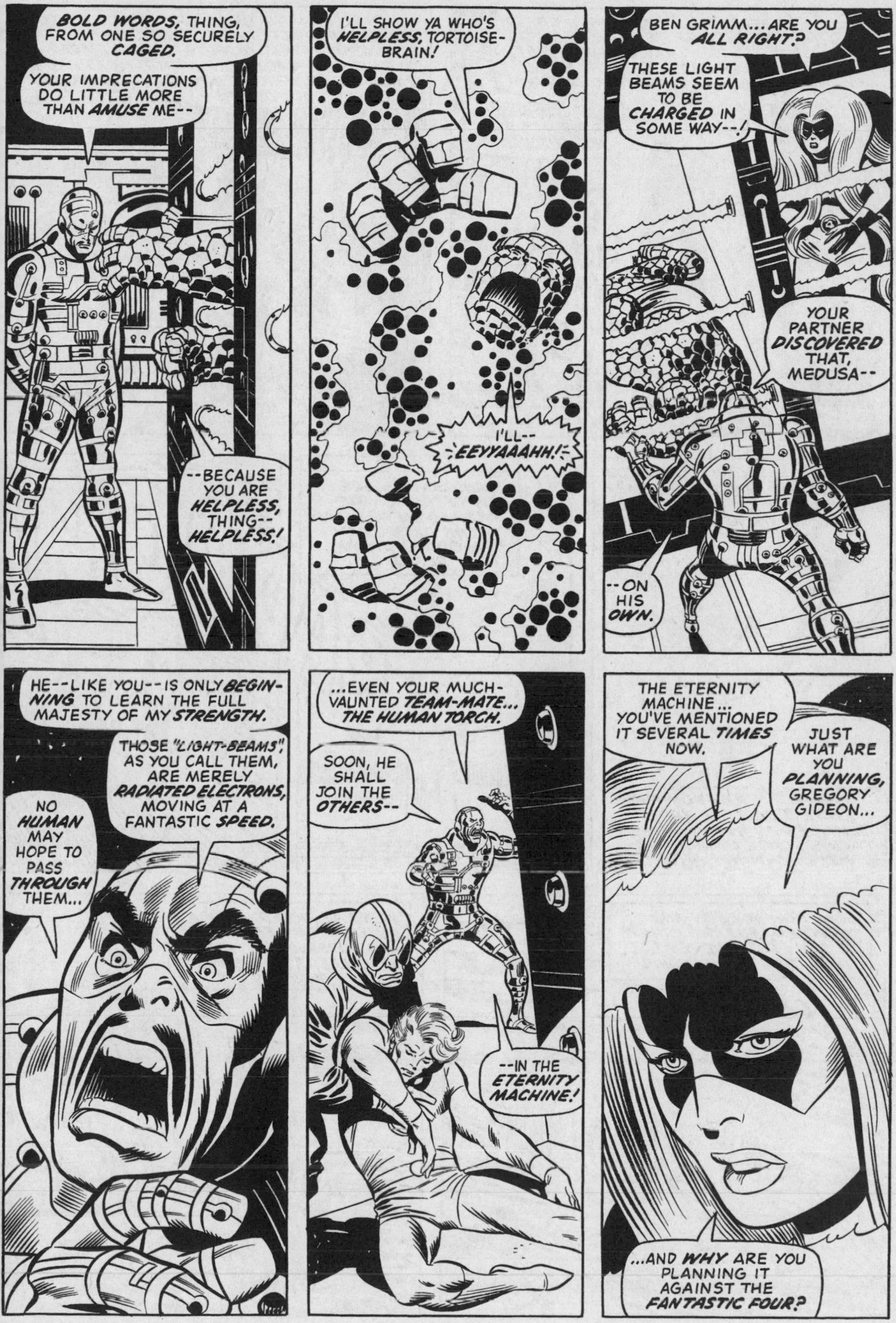
BOLD WORDS, THING, FROM ONE SO SECURELY CAGED.
YOUR IMPRECATIONS DO LITTLE MORE THAN AMUSE ME--
--BECAUSE YOU ARE HELPLESS, THING-- HELPLESS!
I'LL SHOW YA WHO'S HELPLESS, TORTOISE-BRAIN!
I'LL-- EEYYAAAHH!
BEN GRIMM... ARE YOU ALL RIGHT?
THESE LIGHT BEAMS SEEM TO BE CHARGED IN SOME WAY--!
YOUR PARTNER DISCOVERED THAT, MEDUSA--
--ON HIS OWN.
HE--LIKE YOU--IS ONLY BEGINNING TO LEARN THE FULL MAJESTY OF MY STRENGTH.
THOSE "LIGHT-BEAMS", AS YOU CALL THEM, ARE MERELY RADIATED ELECTRONS, MOVING AT A FANTASTIC SPEED.
NO HUMAN MAY HOPE TO PASS THROUGH THEM...
...EVEN YOUR MUCH-VAUNTED TEAM-MATE... THE HUMAN TORCH.
SOON, HE SHALL JOIN THE OTHERS--
--IN THE ETERNITY MACHINE!
THE ETERNITY MACHINE... YOU'VE MENTIONED IT SEVERAL TIMES NOW.
JUST WHAT ARE YOU PLANNING, GREGORY GIDEON...
...AND WHY ARE YOU PLANNING IT AGAINST THE FANTASTIC FOUR?

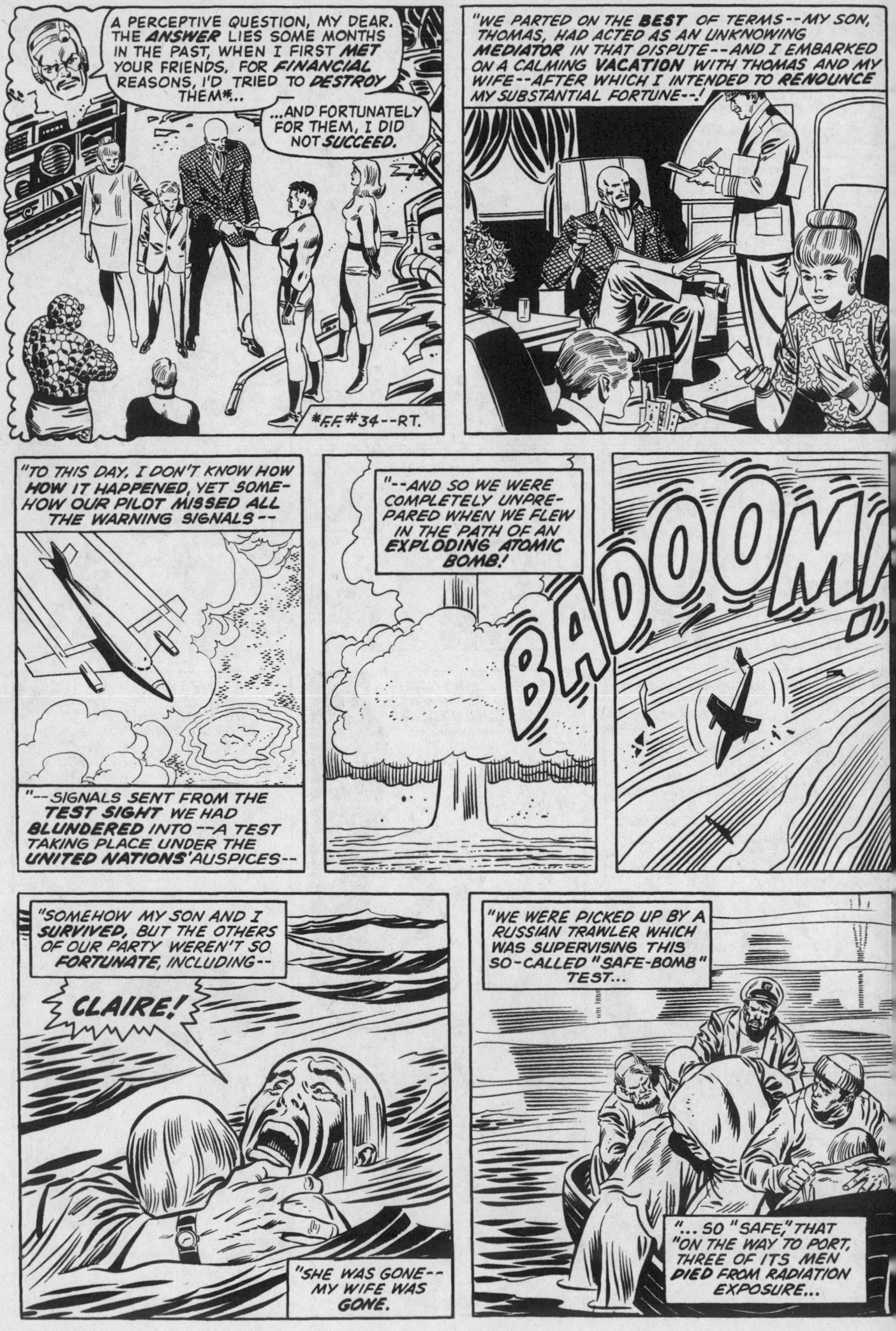
A PERCEPTIVE QUESTION, MY DEAR. THE ANSWER LIES SOME MONTHS IN THE PAST, WHEN I FIRST MET YOUR FRIENDS. FOR FINANCIAL REASONS, I'D TRIED TO DESTROY THEM*...
...AND FORTUNATELY FOR THEM, I DID NOT SUCCEED.
*F.F. #34--RT.
"WE PARTED ON THE BEST OF TERMS--MY SON, THOMAS, HAD ACTED AS AN UNKNOWING MEDIATOR IN THAT DISPUTE--AND I EMBARKED ON A CALMING VACATION WITH THOMAS AND MY WIFE--AFTER WHICH I INTENDED TO RENOUNCE MY SUBSTANTIAL FORTUNE--!
"TO THIS DAY, I DON'T KNOW HOW HOW IT HAPPENED, YET SOMEHOW OUR PILOT MISSED ALL THE WARNING SIGNALS--
"--SIGNALS SENT FROM THE TEST SIGHT WE HAD BLUNDERED INTO--A TEST TAKING PLACE UNDER THE UNITED NATIONS' AUSPICES--
"--AND SO WE WERE COMPLETELY UNPREPARED WHEN WE FLEW IN THE PATH OF AN EXPLODING ATOMIC BOMB!
BADOOM
"SOMEHOW MY SON AND I SURVIVED, BUT THE OTHERS OF OUR PARTY WEREN'T SO FORTUNATE, INCLUDING--
CLAIRE!
"SHE WAS GONE--MY WIFE WAS GONE.
"WE WERE PICKED UP BY A RUSSIAN TRAWLER WHICH WAS SUPERVISING THIS SO-CALLED "SAFE-BOMB" TEST...
"... SO "SAFE," THAT "ON THE WAY TO PORT, THREE OF ITS MEN DIED FROM RADIATION EXPOSURE...

"...AND FOR A TIME, IT SEEMED *WE* WOULD BE AS *UNLUCKY*, UNTIL..."

--REPORTS ARE ALL *NEGATIVE*, MR. GIDEON.

HOWEVER, RADIATION DECAY *HAS* SET IN...

DON'T TRY TO *SPARE* ME, DOCTOR.

I DIDN'T BECOME A BILLIONAIRE BY IGNORING *REALITY.*

HERE IT *IS*, THEN, MR. GIDEON: YOU AND YOUR *SON* HAVE APPROXIMATELY *TWO YEARS*--YOUR *SON* A LITTLE *LONGER*, BECAUSE OF HIS AGE.

THERE'S NOTHING YOU CAN *DO*.?

NOTHING. I'M *SORRY*, SIR.

DON'T BE. JUST *GET OUT.*

"DURING THE FOLLOWING SIX MONTHS, I CONTINUED TO GROW *WEAKER*-- BUT EVEN AS MY STRENGTH WANED, I *STUDIED*--"

"--FILLING MYSELF WITH KNOWLEDGE, LEARNING ALL I *COULD* ABOUT THE DISEASE WHICH AFFECTED ME."

"I TRIED A *THOUSAND* CURES...BUT *NONE* MET WITH SUCCESS."

"MY VERY *ATOMIC* STRUCTURE WAS COLLAPSING--AND I WAS *HELPLESS.*"

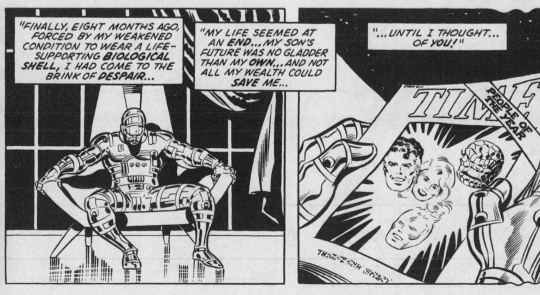

"FINALLY, EIGHT MONTHS AGO, FORCED BY MY WEAKENED CONDITION TO WEAR A LIFE-SUPPORTING *BIOLOGICAL* SHELL, I HAD COME TO THE BRINK OF *DESPAIR*..."

"MY LIFE SEEMED AT AN *END*...MY SON'S FUTURE WAS NO GLADDER THAN MY *OWN*...AND NOT ALL MY WEALTH COULD *SAVE* ME..."

"...UNTIL I THOUGHT... OF *YOU!*"

TIME
PEOPLE OF THE YEAR

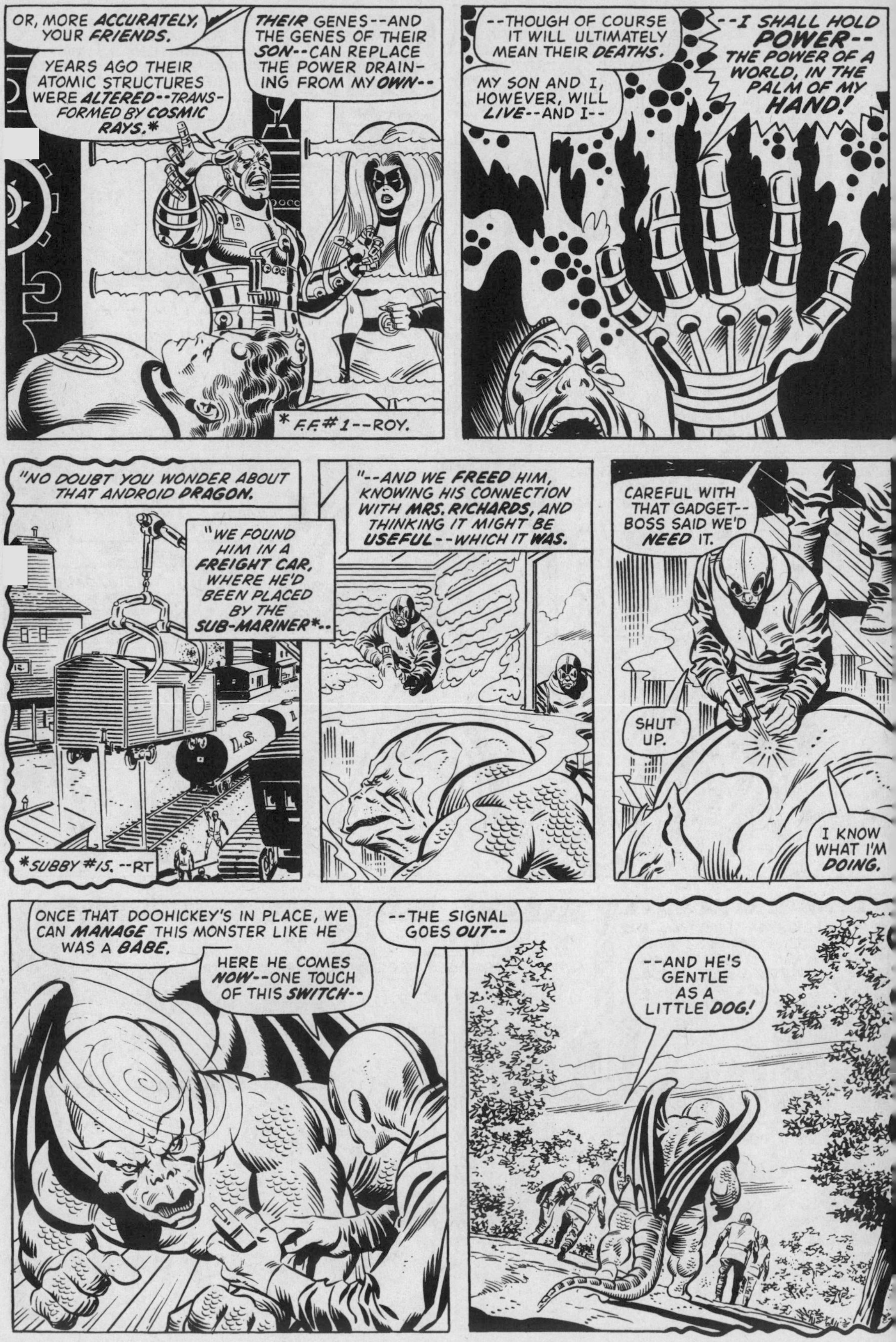
OR, MORE ACCURATELY, YOUR FRIENDS.
YEARS AGO THEIR ATOMIC STRUCTURES WERE ALTERED--TRANSFORMED BY COSMIC RAYS.*
THEIR GENES--AND THE GENES OF THEIR SON--CAN REPLACE THE POWER DRAINING FROM MY OWN--
*F.F. #1--ROY.
--THOUGH OF COURSE IT WILL ULTIMATELY MEAN THEIR DEATHS.
MY SON AND I, HOWEVER, WILL LIVE--AND I--
--I SHALL HOLD POWER-- THE POWER OF A WORLD, IN THE PALM OF MY HAND!
"NO DOUBT YOU WONDER ABOUT THAT ANDROID DRAGON.
"WE FOUND HIM IN A FREIGHT CAR, WHERE HE'D BEEN PLACED BY THE SUB-MARINER*..
*SUBBY #15. --RT
"--AND WE FREED HIM, KNOWING HIS CONNECTION WITH MRS. RICHARDS, AND THINKING IT MIGHT BE USEFUL--WHICH IT WAS.
CAREFUL WITH THAT GADGET-- BOSS SAID WE'D NEED IT.
SHUT UP.
I KNOW WHAT I'M DOING.
ONCE THAT DOOHICKEY'S IN PLACE, WE CAN MANAGE THIS MONSTER LIKE HE WAS A BABE.
HERE HE COMES NOW--ONE TOUCH OF THIS SWITCH--
--THE SIGNAL GOES OUT--
--AND HE'S GENTLE AS A LITTLE DOG!

AND *THAT*, MY DEAR MEDUSA--IS HOW THINGS *ARE*.

NEITHER YOU NOR YOUR FRIENDS WILL EVER AGAIN LEAVE THIS *CHAMBER*.

IT IS THE *ONLY WAY* --THAT MY SON AND I MIGHT *SURVIVE!*

IF YOU THINK *THAT*, GREGORY GIDEON--

--YOU ARE A *GREATER* FOOL THAN I *IMAGINED!*

*B*UT, BEFORE WE LET OUR-SELVES BE DRAWN INTO STILL *ANOTHER* ANGRY EXCHANGE, LET'S SWITCH *SCENES*--FOR AN INTERLUDE IN MANHATTAN, AT THE *BAXTER BUILDING!*

WILL YOU *LOOK* AT THAT GUY?

MAYBE IT'S TIME I TOOK TO THE *GYM* AGAIN....!

*A*ND FOR THOSE OF YOU WHO ARE *UNFAMILIAR* WITH THE *FANTASTIC FOUR* (ALL SIX OF YOU HIDING IN BOISE, IDAHO), THE BAXTER BUILDING'S WHERE THEY KEEP THEIR *HEADQUARTERS*--

--AND THE MAN IN THE *GRAY SUIT* IS THEIR *POSTMAN*-- *WILLIE LUMPKIN.*

HAVEN'T BEEN *DELIVERIN'* THE MAIL TO THE F.F. ALL THESE YEARS WITHOUT LEARNIN' WHAT SORT OF FOLK COME *CALLING.*

BIG FELLA'S IN FOR A *SHOCK*, THOUGH--

NOBODY GETS IN 'LESS REED RICHARDS *LETS* THEM--OR THEY GOT THE GADGET TO WORK THAT *PRIVATE ELEVATOR.*

AND *NOBODY* HAS THAT GA--

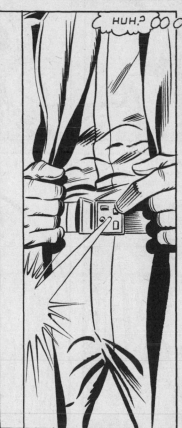

HUH?

CAN YOU BEAT *THAT?*

THOUGHT I KNEW *EVERYTHING* 'BOUT THOSE CRAZY SUPER-FOLKS...

I GUESS EVEN *WILLIE LUMPKIN* CAN BE *WRONG*-- ONCE OR *TWICE!*

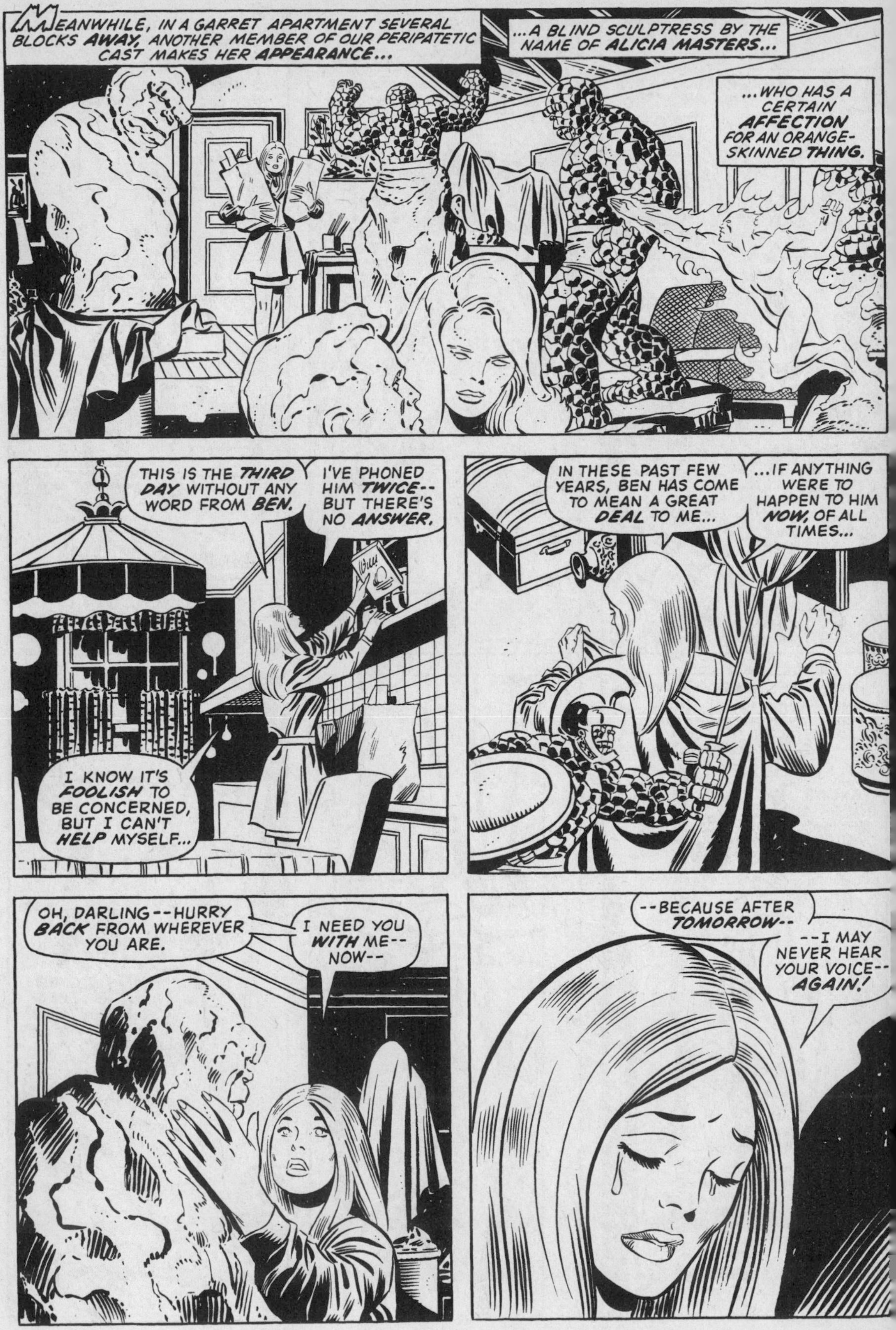
MEANWHILE, IN A GARRET APARTMENT SEVERAL BLOCKS AWAY, ANOTHER MEMBER OF OUR PERIPATETIC CAST MAKES HER APPEARANCE...
...A BLIND SCULPTRESS BY THE NAME OF ALICIA MASTERS...
...WHO HAS A CERTAIN AFFECTION FOR AN ORANGE-SKINNED THING.
THIS IS THE THIRD DAY WITHOUT ANY WORD FROM BEN.
I'VE PHONED HIM TWICE-- BUT THERE'S NO ANSWER.
I KNOW IT'S FOOLISH TO BE CONCERNED, BUT I CAN'T HELP MYSELF...
IN THESE PAST FEW YEARS, BEN HAS COME TO MEAN A GREAT DEAL TO ME...
...IF ANYTHING WERE TO HAPPEN TO HIM NOW, OF ALL TIMES...
OH, DARLING--HURRY BACK FROM WHEREVER YOU ARE.
I NEED YOU WITH ME-- NOW--
--BECAUSE AFTER TOMORROW--
--I MAY NEVER HEAR YOUR VOICE-- AGAIN!

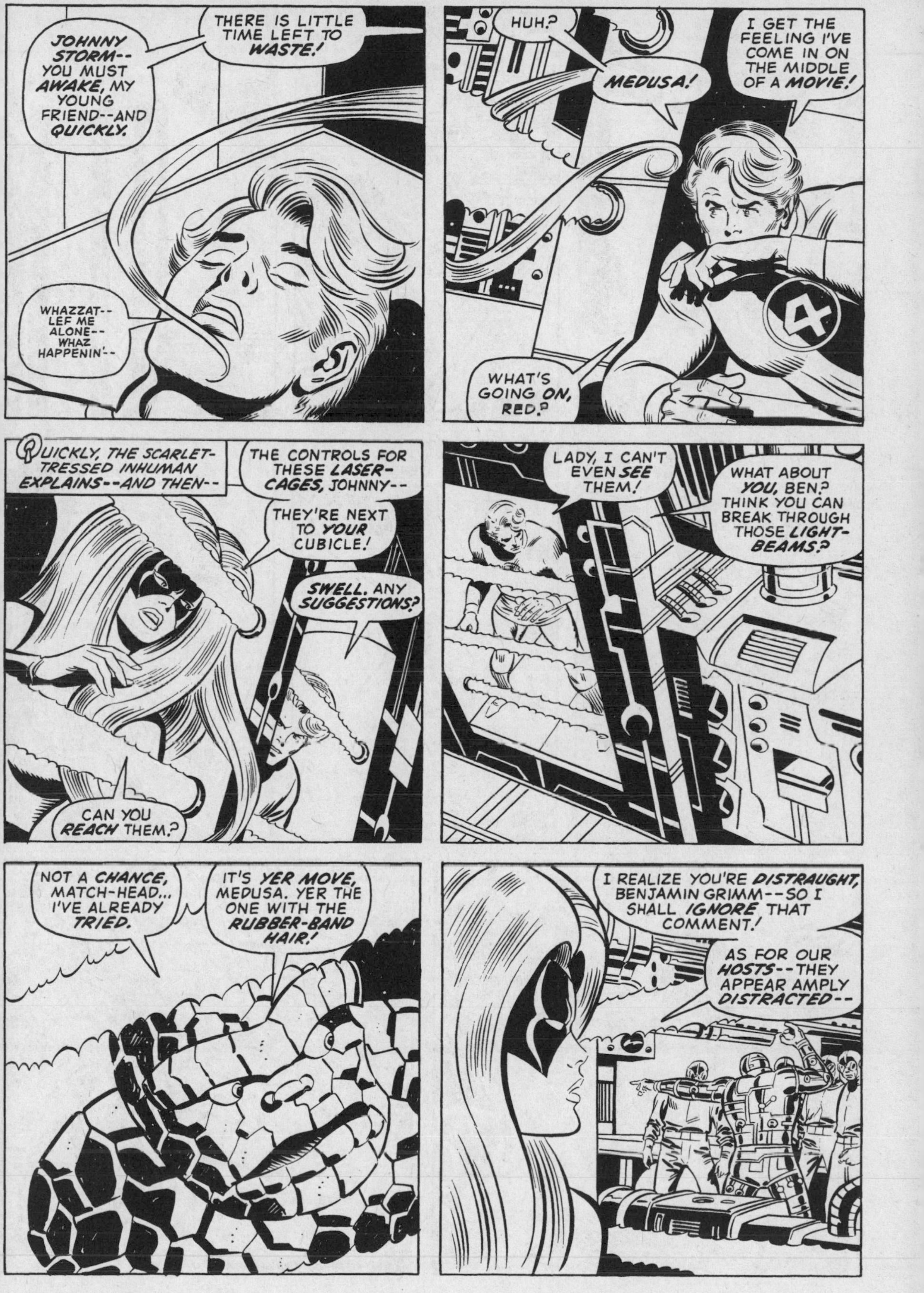

JOHNNY STORM--YOU MUST AWAKE, MY YOUNG FRIEND--AND QUICKLY.
THERE IS LITTLE TIME LEFT TO WASTE!
WHAZZAT--LEF ME ALONE--WHAZ HAPPENIN'--
HUH?
MEDUSA!
I GET THE FEELING I'VE COME IN ON THE MIDDLE OF A MOVIE!
WHAT'S GOING ON, RED?
QUICKLY, THE SCARLET-TRESSED INHUMAN EXPLAINS--AND THEN--
THE CONTROLS FOR THESE LASER-CAGES, JOHNNY--
THEY'RE NEXT TO YOUR CUBICLE!
SWELL. ANY SUGGESTIONS?
CAN YOU REACH THEM?
LADY, I CAN'T EVEN SEE THEM!
WHAT ABOUT YOU, BEN? THINK YOU CAN BREAK THROUGH THOSE LIGHT-BEAMS?
NOT A CHANCE, MATCH-HEAD... I'VE ALREADY TRIED.
IT'S YER MOVE, MEDUSA. YER THE ONE WITH THE RUBBER-BAND HAIR!
I REALIZE YOU'RE DISTRAUGHT, BENJAMIN GRIMM--SO I SHALL IGNORE THAT COMMENT!
AS FOR OUR HOSTS--THEY APPEAR AMPLY DISTRACTED--

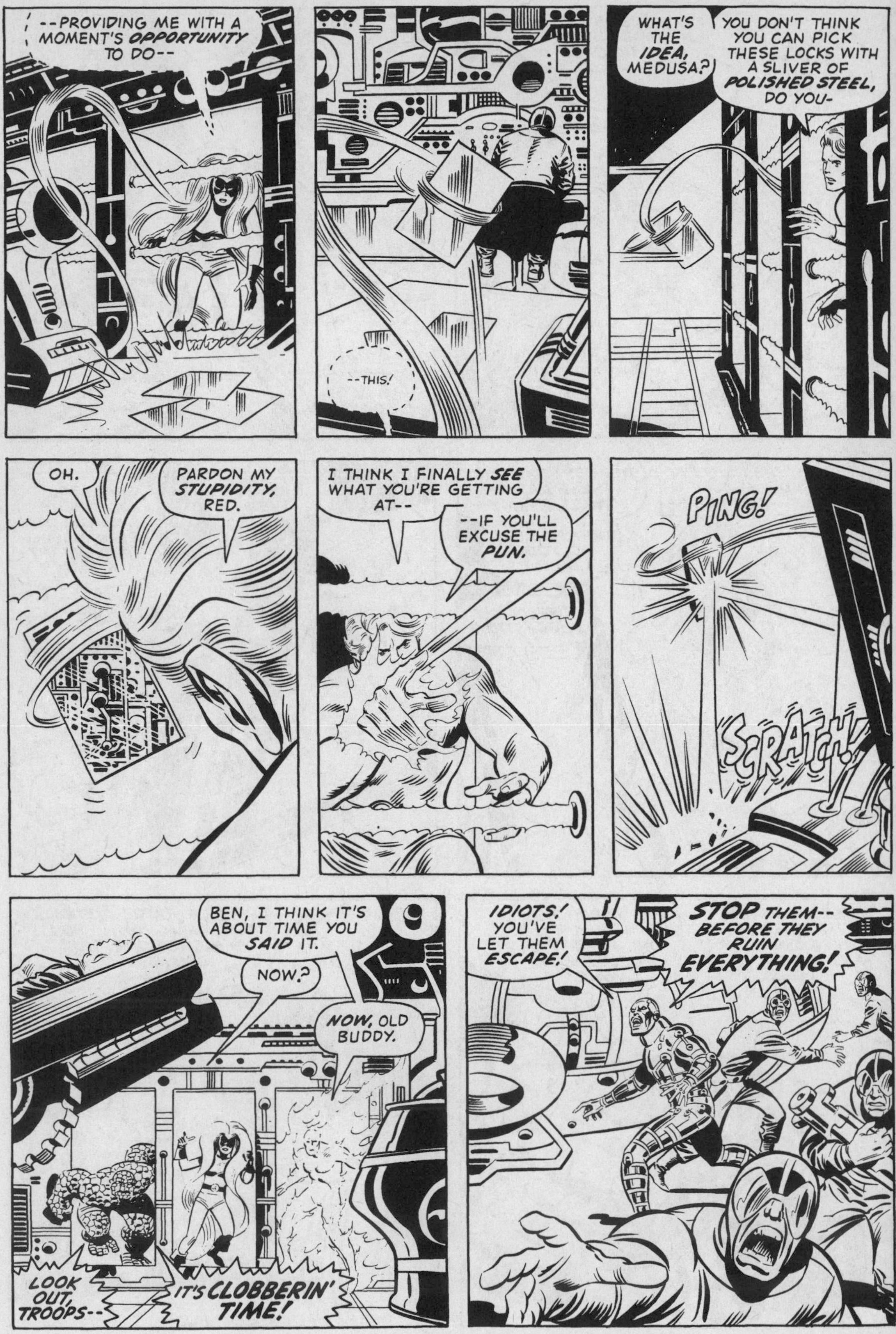
--PROVIDING ME WITH A MOMENT'S OPPORTUNITY TO DO--
--THIS!
WHAT'S THE IDEA, MEDUSA?
YOU DON'T THINK YOU CAN PICK THESE LOCKS WITH A SLIVER OF POLISHED STEEL, DO YOU-
OH.
PARDON MY STUPIDITY, RED.
I THINK I FINALLY SEE WHAT YOU'RE GETTING AT--
--IF YOU'LL EXCUSE THE PUN.
PING!
SCRATCH!
BEN, I THINK IT'S ABOUT TIME YOU SAID IT.
NOW?
NOW, OLD BUDDY.
LOOK OUT, TROOPS--
IT'S CLOBBERIN' TIME!
IDIOTS! YOU'VE LET THEM ESCAPE!
STOP THEM-- BEFORE THEY RUIN EVERYTHING!

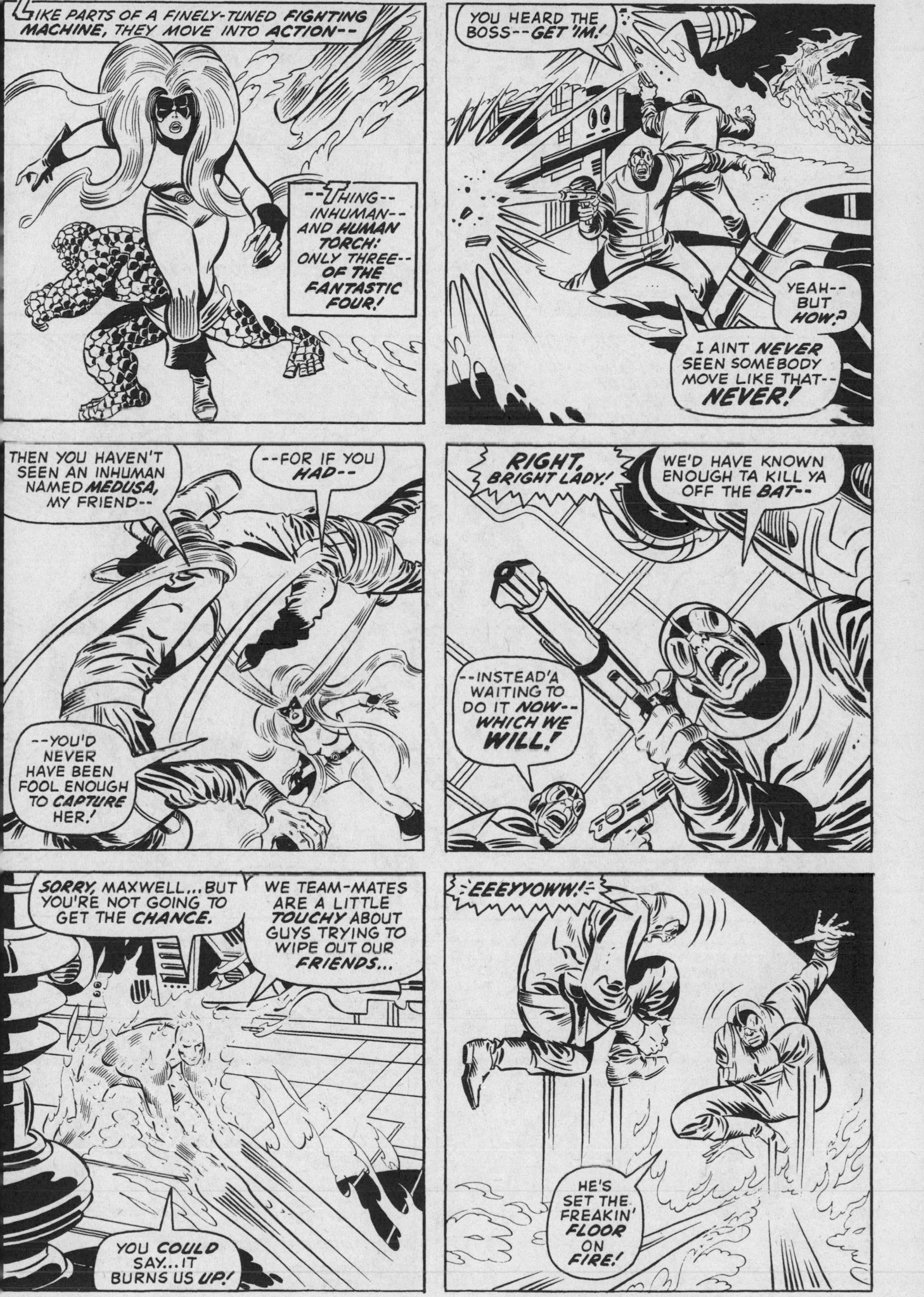
LIKE PARTS OF A FINELY-TUNED FIGHTING MACHINE, THEY MOVE INTO ACTION--
--THING--INHUMAN--AND HUMAN TORCH: ONLY THREE--OF THE FANTASTIC FOUR!
YOU HEARD THE BOSS--GET 'IM!
YEAH--BUT HOW?
I AINT NEVER SEEN SOMEBODY MOVE LIKE THAT--NEVER!
THEN YOU HAVEN'T SEEN AN INHUMAN NAMED MEDUSA, MY FRIEND--
--FOR IF YOU HAD--
--YOU'D NEVER HAVE BEEN FOOL ENOUGH TO CAPTURE HER!
RIGHT, BRIGHT LADY!
WE'D HAVE KNOWN ENOUGH TA KILL YA OFF THE BAT--
--INSTEAD'A WAITING TO DO IT NOW--WHICH WE WILL!
SORRY, MAXWELL... BUT YOU'RE NOT GOING TO GET THE CHANCE.
WE TEAM-MATES ARE A LITTLE TOUCHY ABOUT GUYS TRYING TO WIPE OUT OUR FRIENDS...
YOU COULD SAY... IT BURNS US UP!
EEEYYOWW!
HE'S SET THE FREAKIN' FLOOR ON FIRE!

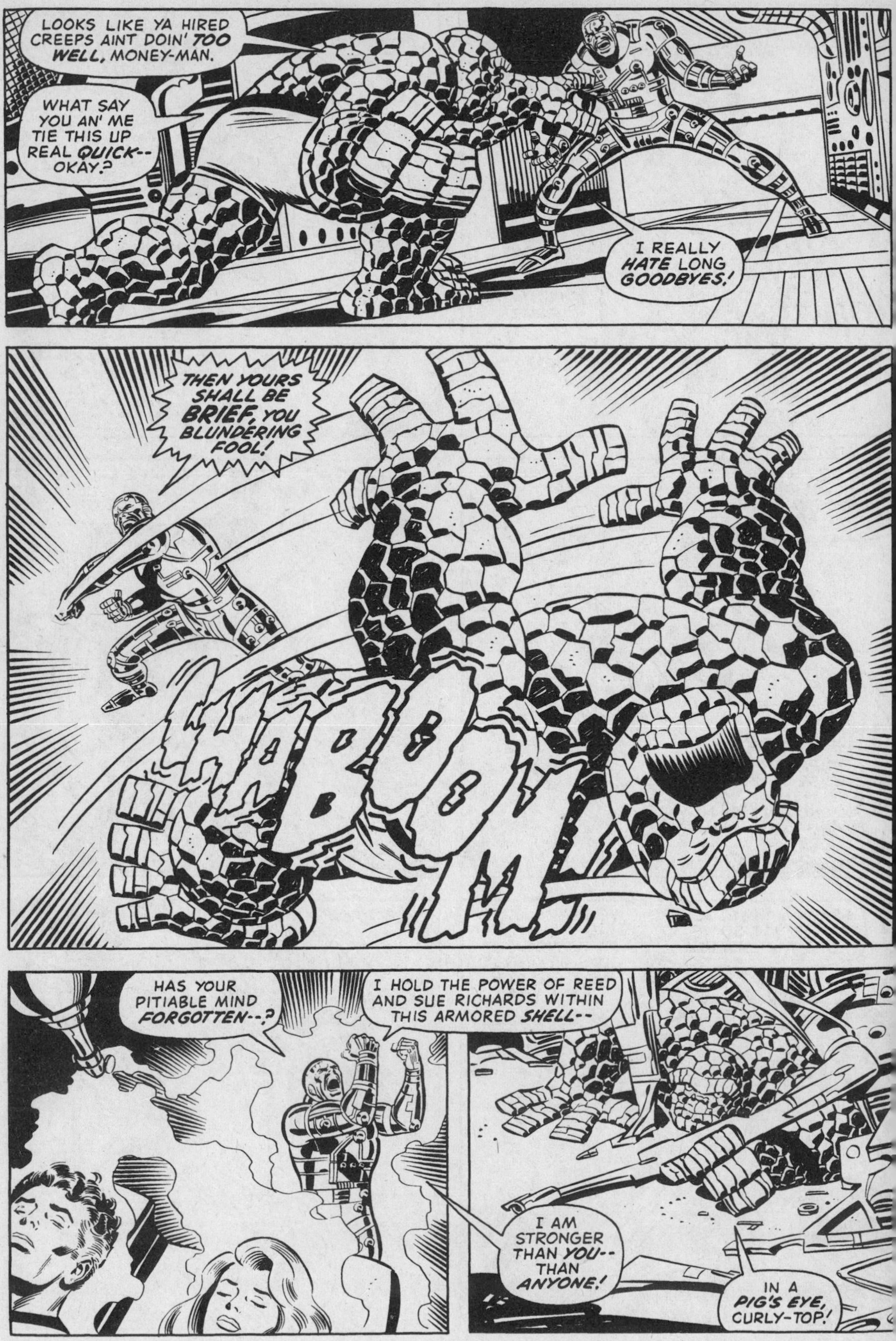

LOOKS LIKE YA HIRED CREEPS AINT DOIN' TOO WELL, MONEY-MAN.
WHAT SAY YOU AN' ME TIE THIS UP REAL QUICK--OKAY?
I REALLY HATE LONG GOODBYES!
THEN YOURS SHALL BE BRIEF, YOU BLUNDERING FOOL!
KABOOM
HAS YOUR PITIABLE MIND FORGOTTEN--?
I HOLD THE POWER OF REED AND SUE RICHARDS WITHIN THIS ARMORED SHELL--
I AM STRONGER THAN YOU--THAN ANYONE!
IN A PIG'S EYE, CURLY-TOP!

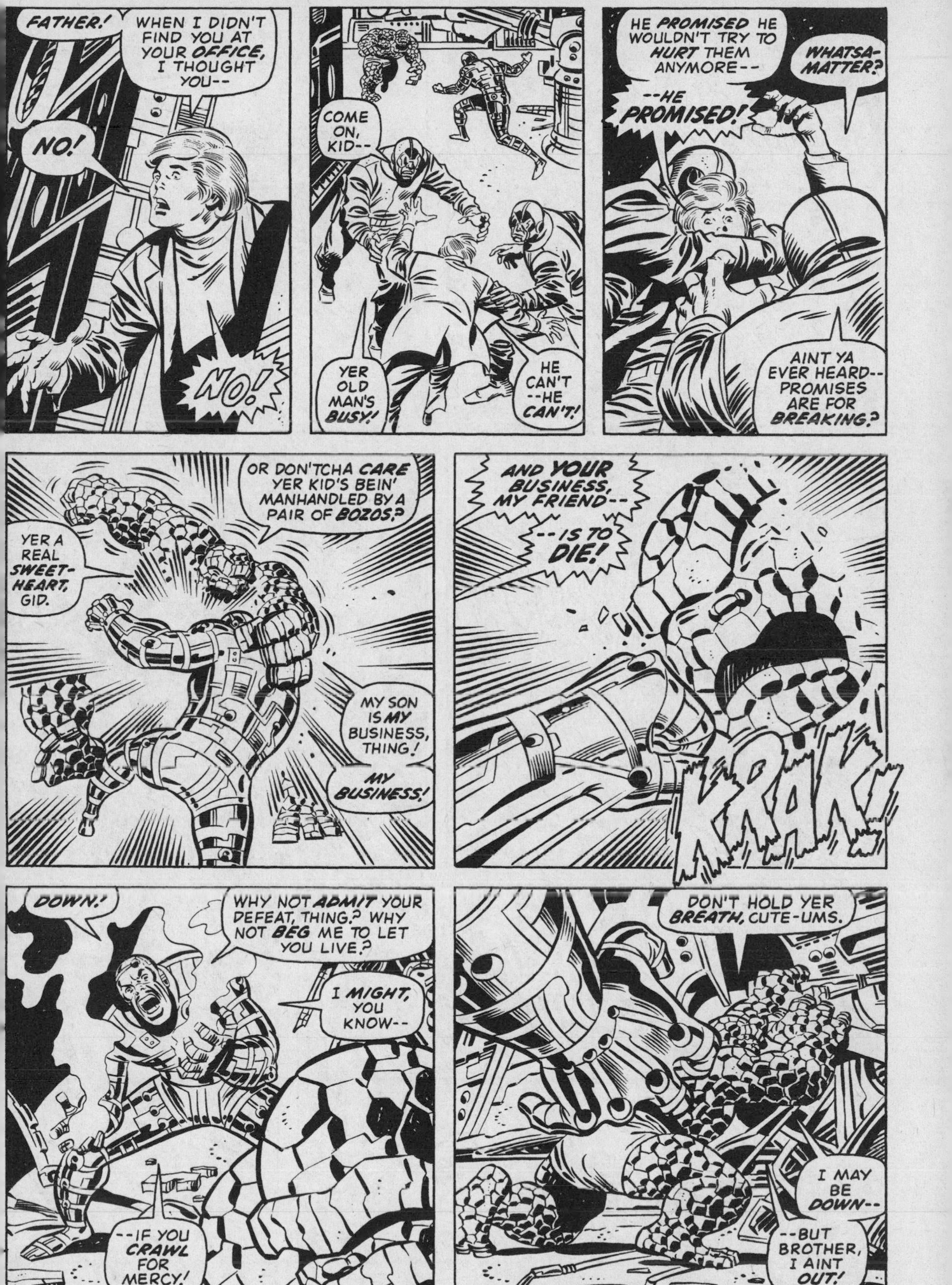
FATHER!
WHEN I DIDN'T FIND YOU AT YOUR OFFICE, I THOUGHT YOU--
NO!
NO!
COME ON, KID--
YER OLD MAN'S BUSY!
HE CAN'T --HE CAN'T!
HE PROMISED HE WOULDN'T TRY TO HURT THEM ANYMORE--
--HE PROMISED!
WHATSA-MATTER?
AINT YA EVER HEARD--PROMISES ARE FOR BREAKING?
OR DON'TCHA CARE YER KID'S BEIN' MANHANDLED BY A PAIR OF BOZOS?
YER A REAL SWEET-HEART, GID.
MY SON IS MY BUSINESS, THING!
MY BUSINESS!
AND YOUR BUSINESS, MY FRIEND--
--IS TO DIE!
KRAK!
DOWN!
WHY NOT ADMIT YOUR DEFEAT, THING? WHY NOT BEG ME TO LET YOU LIVE?
I MIGHT, YOU KNOW--
--IF YOU CRAWL FOR MERCY!
DON'T HOLD YER BREATH, CUTE-UMS.
I MAY BE DOWN--
--BUT BROTHER, I AINT OUT!

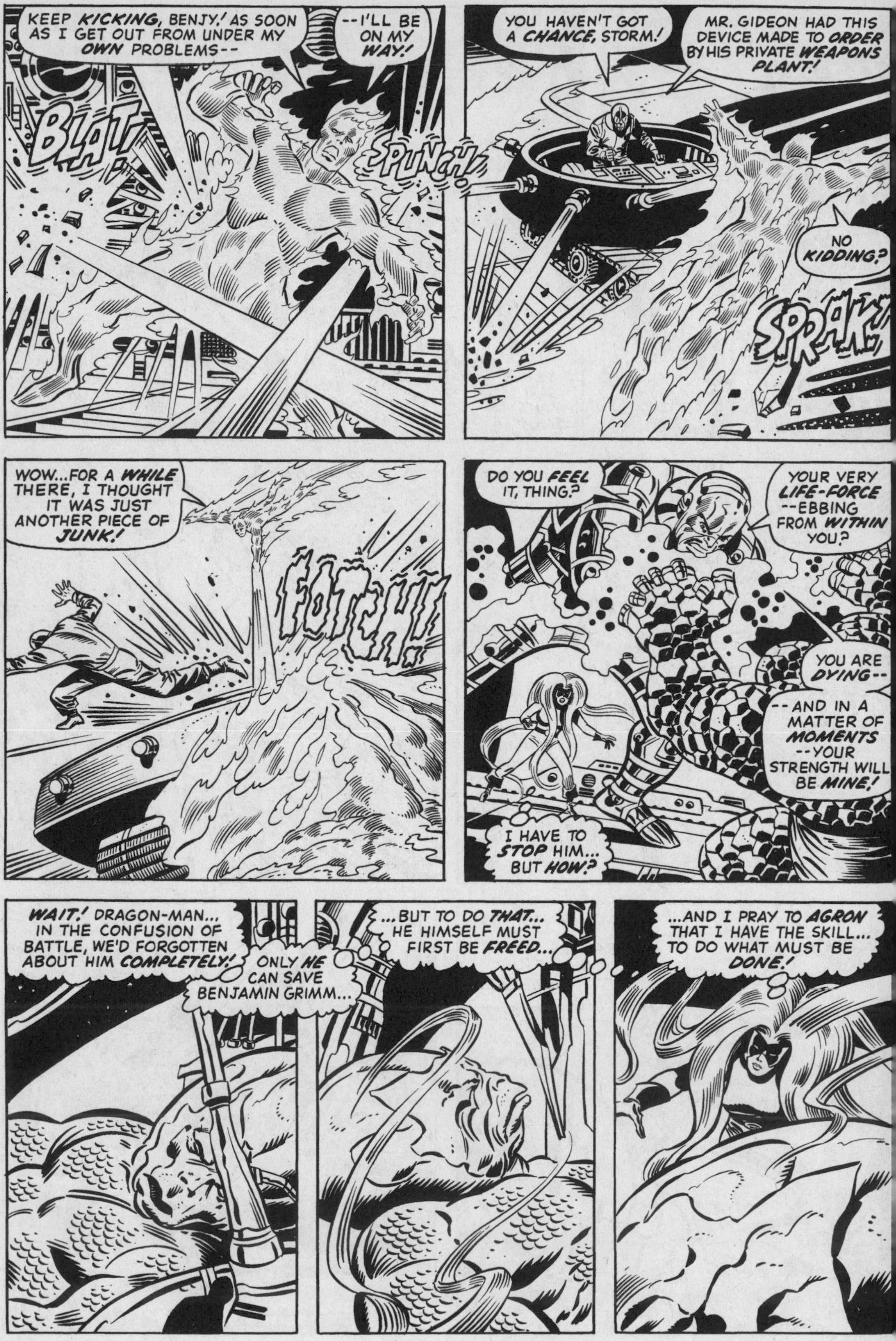
KEEP KICKING, BENJY! AS SOON AS I GET OUT FROM UNDER MY OWN PROBLEMS--
--I'LL BE ON MY WAY!
BLAT
SPUNCH
YOU HAVEN'T GOT A CHANCE, STORM!
MR. GIDEON HAD THIS DEVICE MADE TO ORDER BY HIS PRIVATE WEAPONS PLANT!
NO KIDDING?
WOW...FOR A WHILE THERE, I THOUGHT IT WAS JUST ANOTHER PIECE OF JUNK!
DO YOU FEEL IT, THING?
YOUR VERY LIFE-FORCE --EBBING FROM WITHIN YOU?
YOU ARE DYING--
--AND IN A MATTER OF MOMENTS --YOUR STRENGTH WILL BE MINE!
I HAVE TO STOP HIM... BUT HOW?
WAIT! DRAGON-MAN... IN THE CONFUSION OF BATTLE, WE'D FORGOTTEN ABOUT HIM COMPLETELY!
ONLY HE CAN SAVE BENJAMIN GRIMM...
...BUT TO DO THAT... HE HIMSELF MUST FIRST BE FREED...
...AND I PRAY TO AGRON THAT I HAVE THE SKILL... TO DO WHAT MUST BE DONE!

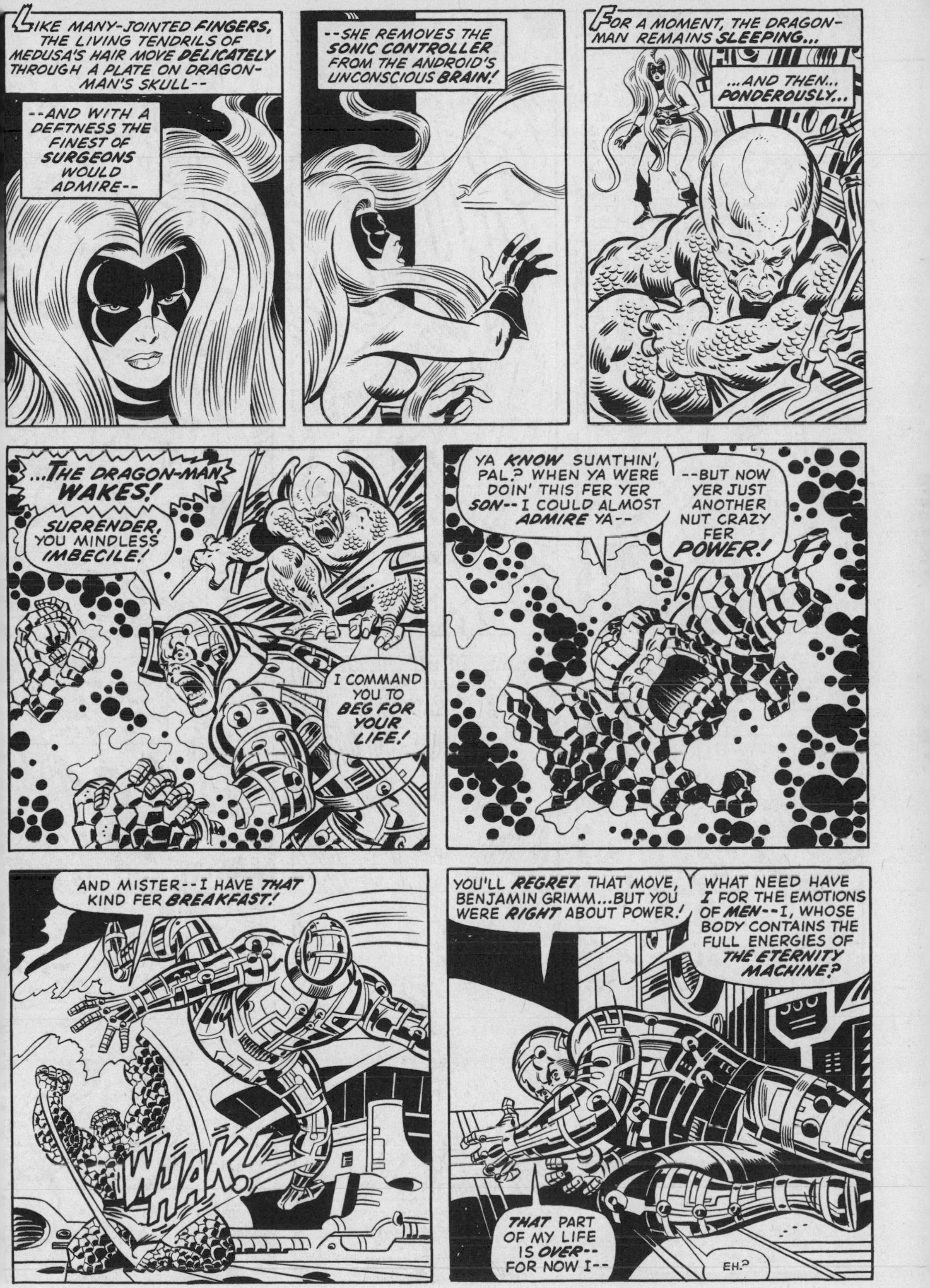
LIKE MANY-JOINTED FINGERS, THE LIVING TENDRILS OF MEDUSA'S HAIR MOVE DELICATELY THROUGH A PLATE ON DRAGON-MAN'S SKULL--
--AND WITH A DEFTNESS THE FINEST OF SURGEONS WOULD ADMIRE--
--SHE REMOVES THE SONIC CONTROLLER FROM THE ANDROID'S UNCONSCIOUS BRAIN!
FOR A MOMENT, THE DRAGON-MAN REMAINS SLEEPING...
...AND THEN... PONDEROUSLY...
...THE DRAGON-MAN WAKES!
SURRENDER, YOU MINDLESS IMBECILE!
I COMMAND YOU TO BEG FOR YOUR LIFE!
YA KNOW SUMTHIN', PAL? WHEN YA WERE DOIN' THIS FER YER SON--I COULD ALMOST ADMIRE YA--
--BUT NOW YER JUST ANOTHER NUT CRAZY FER POWER!
AND MISTER--I HAVE THAT KIND FER BREAKFAST!
WHAK!
YOU'LL REGRET THAT MOVE, BENJAMIN GRIMM...BUT YOU WERE RIGHT ABOUT POWER!
WHAT NEED HAVE I FOR THE EMOTIONS OF MEN--I, WHOSE BODY CONTAINS THE FULL ENERGIES OF THE ETERNITY MACHINE?
THAT PART OF MY LIFE IS OVER--FOR NOW I--
EH?

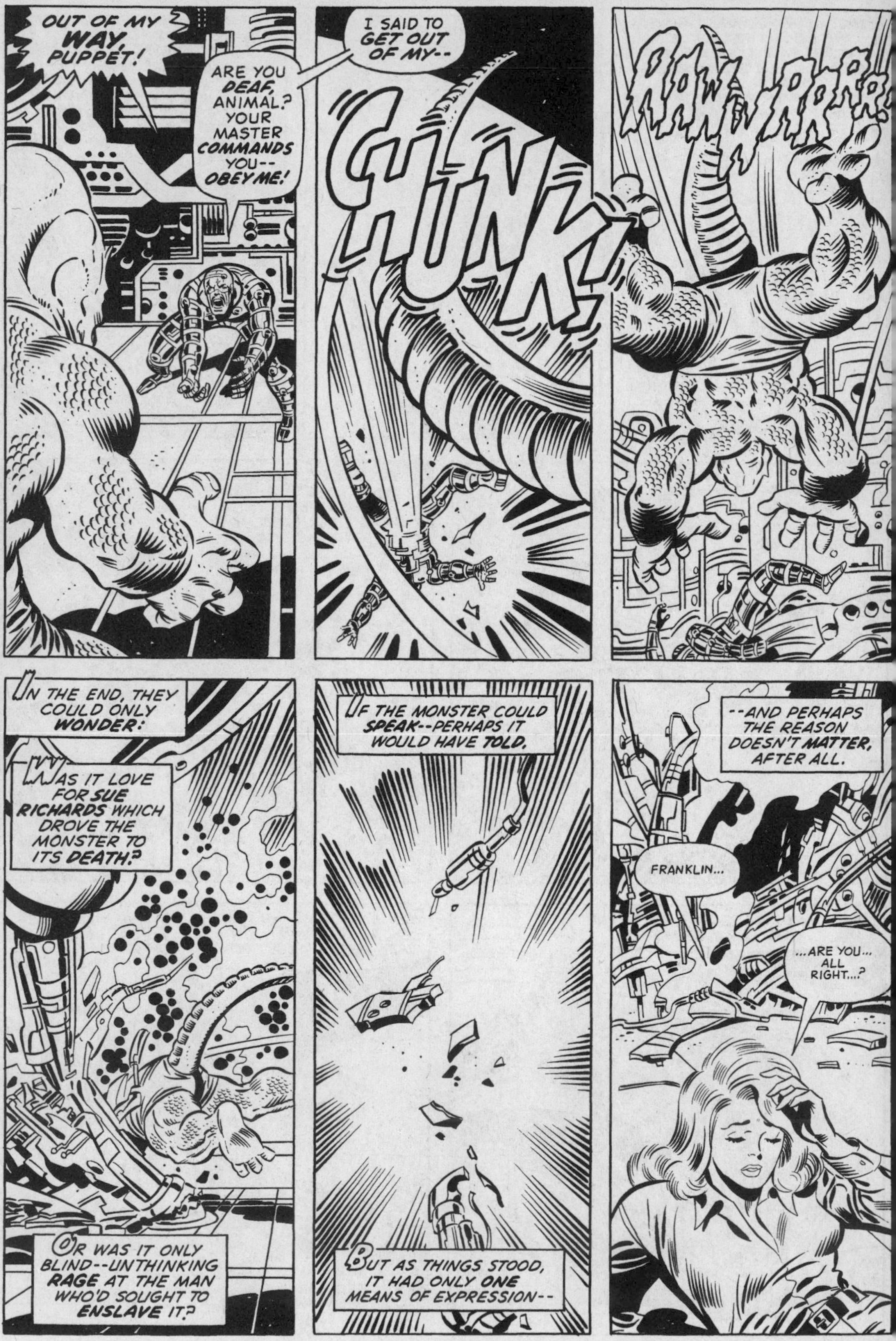
OUT OF MY WAY, PUPPET!
ARE YOU DEAF, ANIMAL? YOUR MASTER COMMANDS YOU-- OBEY ME!
I SAID TO GET OUT OF MY--
CHUNK!
RAWRRRR!
IN THE END, THEY COULD ONLY WONDER:
WAS IT LOVE FOR SUE RICHARDS WHICH DROVE THE MONSTER TO ITS DEATH?
OR WAS IT ONLY BLIND--UNTHINKING RAGE AT THE MAN WHO'D SOUGHT TO ENSLAVE IT?
IF THE MONSTER COULD SPEAK--PERHAPS IT WOULD HAVE TOLD.
BUT AS THINGS STOOD, IT HAD ONLY ONE MEANS OF EXPRESSION--
--AND PERHAPS THE REASON DOESN'T MATTER, AFTER ALL.
FRANKLIN...
...ARE YOU... ALL RIGHT...?

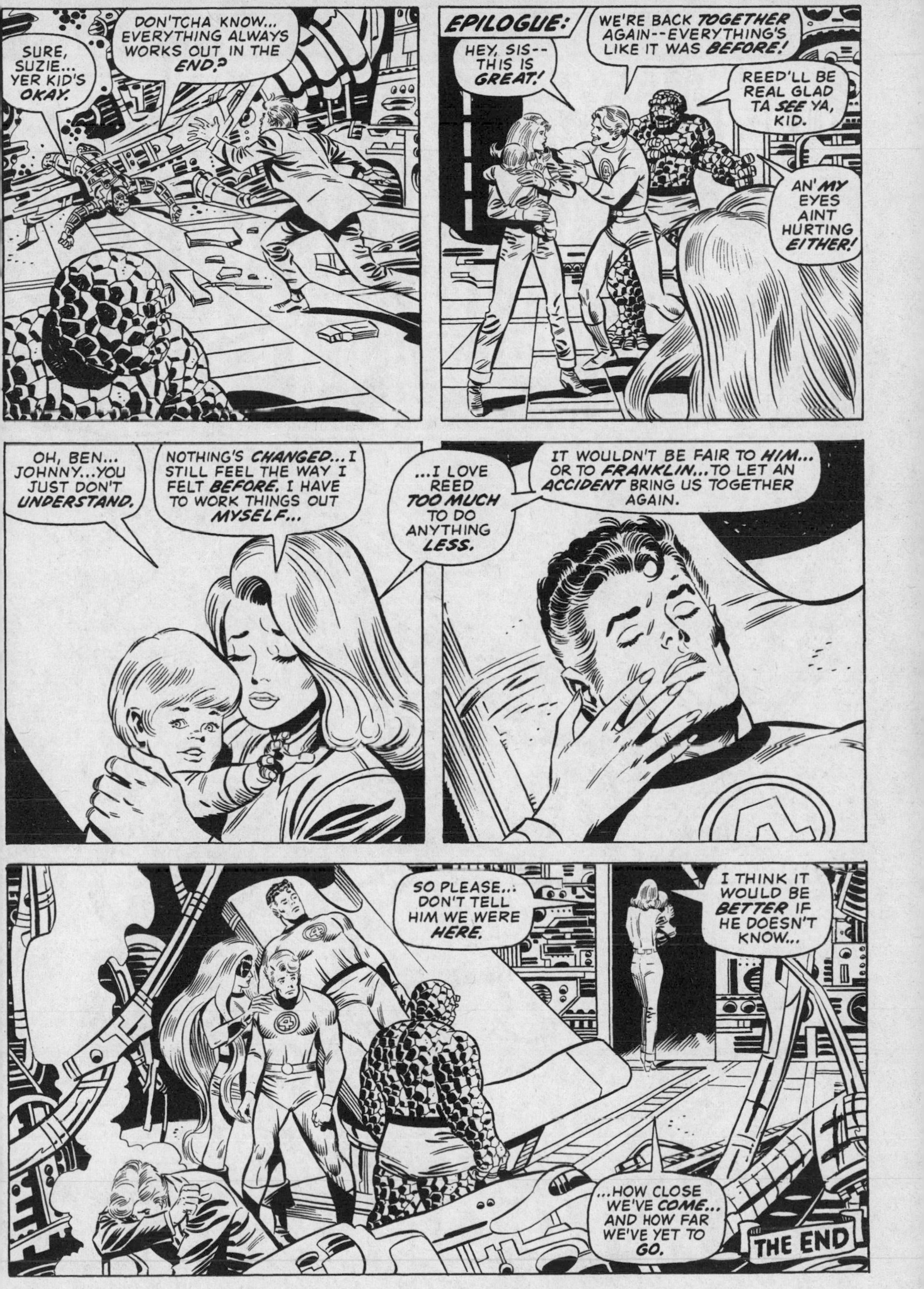
SURE, SUZIE... YER KID'S OKAY.
DON'TCHA KNOW... EVERYTHING ALWAYS WORKS OUT IN THE END?
EPILOGUE:
HEY, SIS-- THIS IS GREAT!
WE'RE BACK TOGETHER AGAIN--EVERYTHING'S LIKE IT WAS BEFORE!
REED'LL BE REAL GLAD TA SEE YA, KID.
AN' MY EYES AINT HURTING EITHER!
OH, BEN... JOHNNY...YOU JUST DON'T UNDERSTAND.
NOTHING'S CHANGED...I STILL FEEL THE WAY I FELT BEFORE. I HAVE TO WORK THINGS OUT MYSELF...
...I LOVE REED TOO MUCH TO DO ANYTHING LESS.
IT WOULDN'T BE FAIR TO HIM... OR TO FRANKLIN...TO LET AN ACCIDENT BRING US TOGETHER AGAIN.
SO PLEASE... DON'T TELL HIM WE WERE HERE.
I THINK IT WOULD BE BETTER IF HE DOESN'T KNOW...
...HOW CLOSE WE'VE COME... AND HOW FAR WE'VE YET TO GO.
THE END

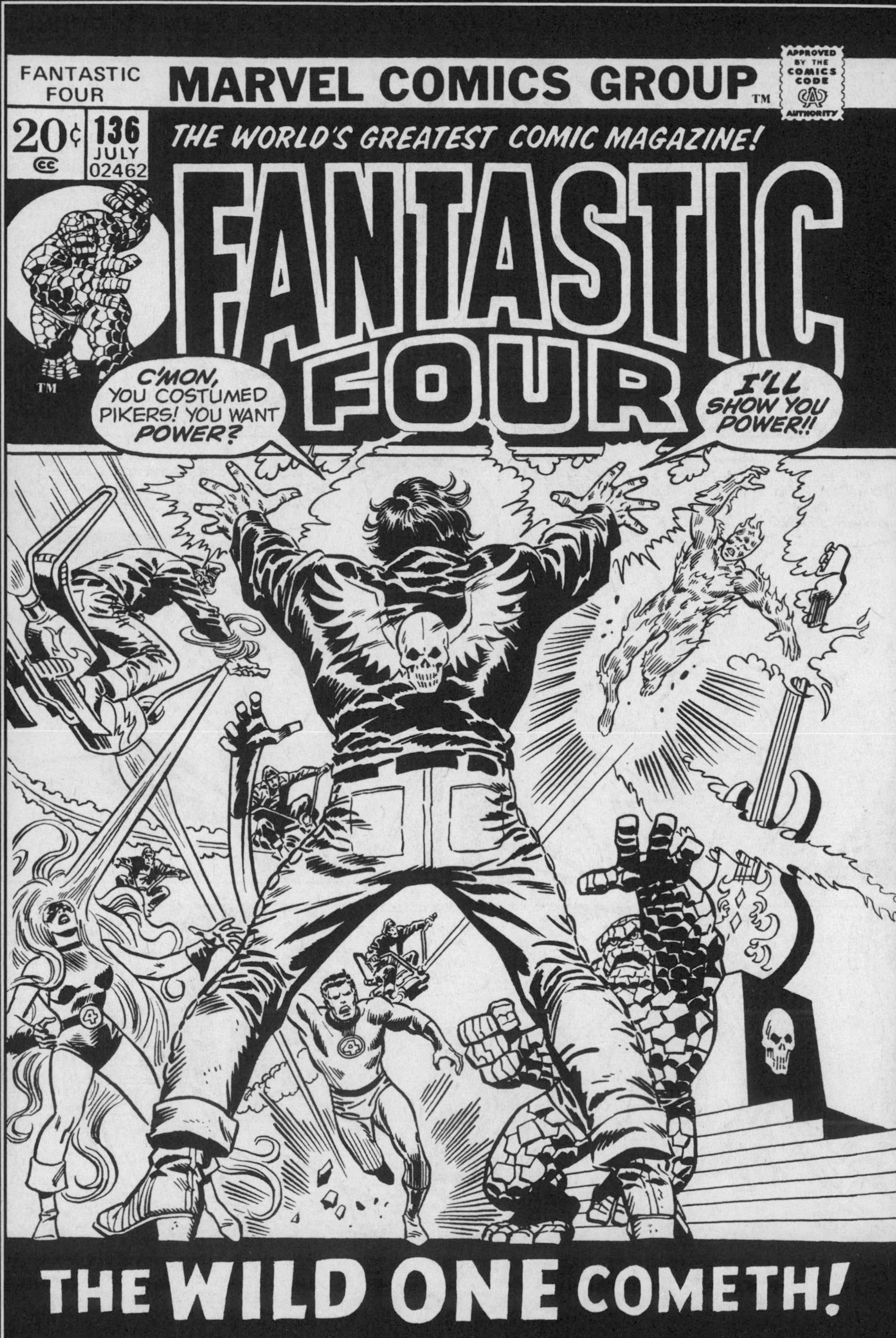
FANTASTIC FOUR
MARVEL COMICS GROUP
APPROVED BY THE COMICS CODE AUTHORITY
20¢
136
JULY
02462
THE WORLD'S GREATEST COMIC MAGAZINE!
FANTASTIC FOUR
C'MON, YOU COSTUMED PIKERS! YOU WANT POWER?
I'LL SHOW YOU POWER!!
THE WILD ONE COMETH!

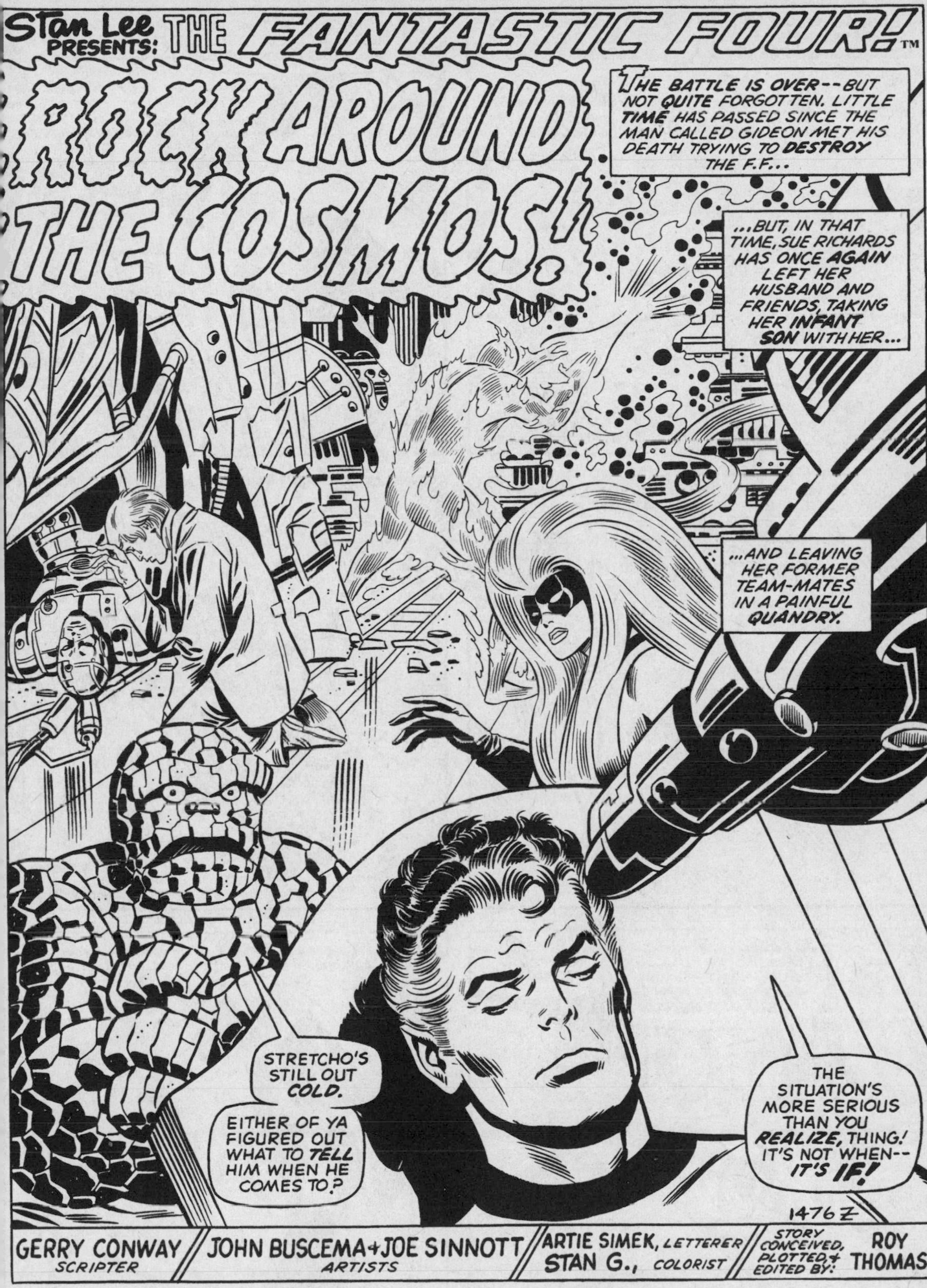
Stan Lee PRESENTS: THE FANTASTIC FOUR! ™
ROCK AROUND THE COSMOS!
THE BATTLE IS OVER--BUT NOT QUITE FORGOTTEN. LITTLE TIME HAS PASSED SINCE THE MAN CALLED GIDEON MET HIS DEATH TRYING TO DESTROY THE F.F...
...BUT, IN THAT TIME, SUE RICHARDS HAS ONCE AGAIN LEFT HER HUSBAND AND FRIENDS, TAKING HER INFANT SON WITH HER...
...AND LEAVING HER FORMER TEAM-MATES IN A PAINFUL QUANDRY.
STRETCHO'S STILL OUT COLD.
EITHER OF YA FIGURED OUT WHAT TO TELL HIM WHEN HE COMES TO?
THE SITUATION'S MORE SERIOUS THAN YOU REALIZE, THING! IT'S NOT WHEN-- IT'S IF!
1476Z
GERRY CONWAY SCRIPTER
JOHN BUSCEMA + JOE SINNOTT ARTISTS
ARTIE SIMEK, LETTERER
STAN G., COLORIST
STORY CONCEIVED, PLOTTED + EDITED BY: ROY THOMAS

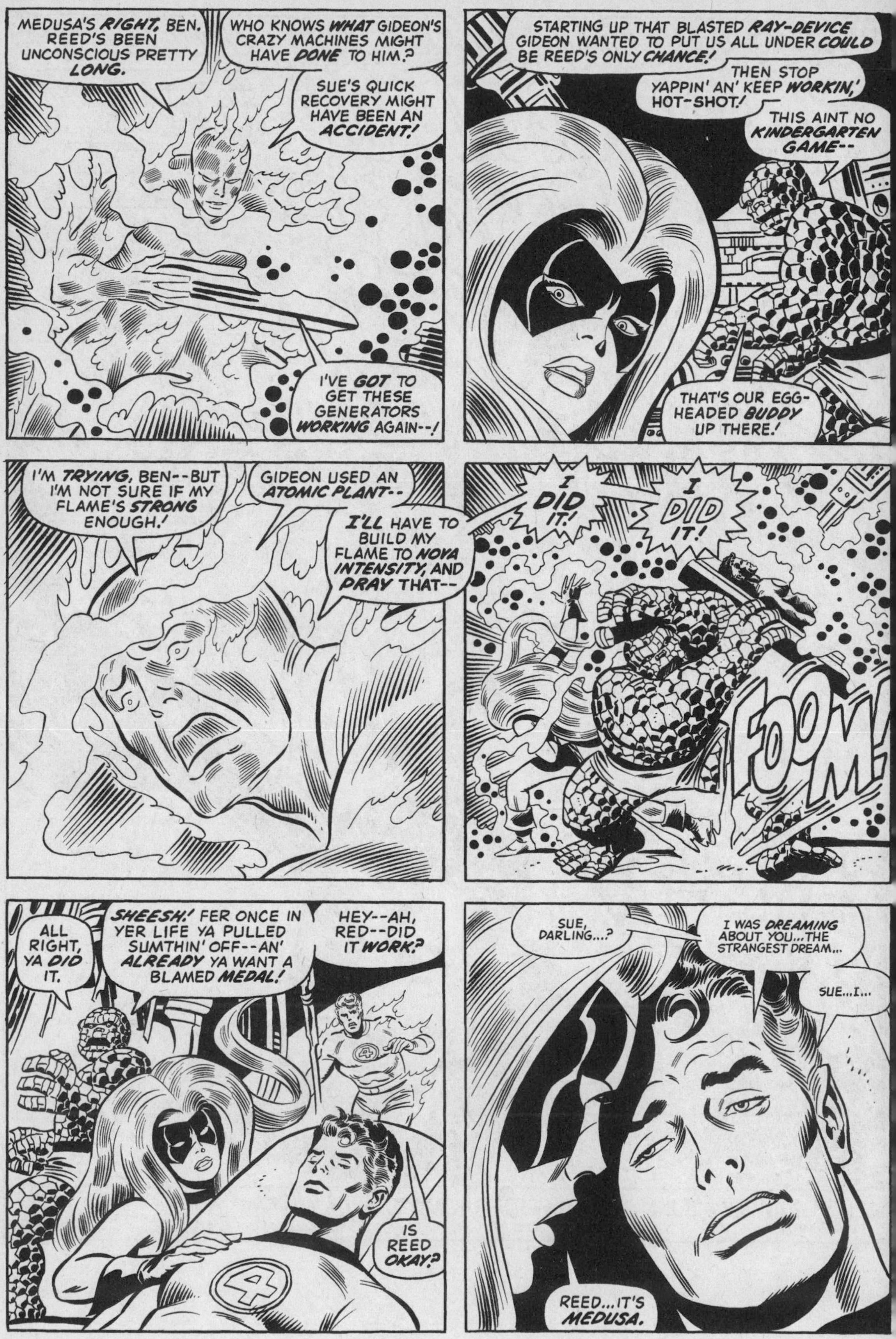
MEDUSA'S RIGHT, BEN. REED'S BEEN UNCONSCIOUS PRETTY LONG.
WHO KNOWS WHAT GIDEON'S CRAZY MACHINES MIGHT HAVE DONE TO HIM?
SUE'S QUICK RECOVERY MIGHT HAVE BEEN AN ACCIDENT!
I'VE GOT TO GET THESE GENERATORS WORKING AGAIN--!
STARTING UP THAT BLASTED RAY-DEVICE GIDEON WANTED TO PUT US ALL UNDER COULD BE REED'S ONLY CHANCE!
THEN STOP YAPPIN' AN' KEEP WORKIN,' HOT-SHOT!
THIS AINT NO KINDERGARTEN GAME--
THAT'S OUR EGG-HEADED BUDDY UP THERE!
I'M TRYING, BEN--BUT I'M NOT SURE IF MY FLAME'S STRONG ENOUGH!
GIDEON USED AN ATOMIC PLANT--
I'LL HAVE TO BUILD MY FLAME TO NOVA INTENSITY, AND PRAY THAT--
I DID IT!
I DID IT!
FOOM!
ALL RIGHT, YA DID IT.
SHEESH! FER ONCE IN YER LIFE YA PULLED SUMTHIN' OFF--AN' ALREADY YA WANT A BLAMED MEDAL!
HEY--AH, RED--DID IT WORK?
IS REED OKAY?
SUE, DARLING...?
I WAS DREAMING ABOUT YOU...THE STRANGEST DREAM...
SUE...I...
REED...IT'S MEDUSA.

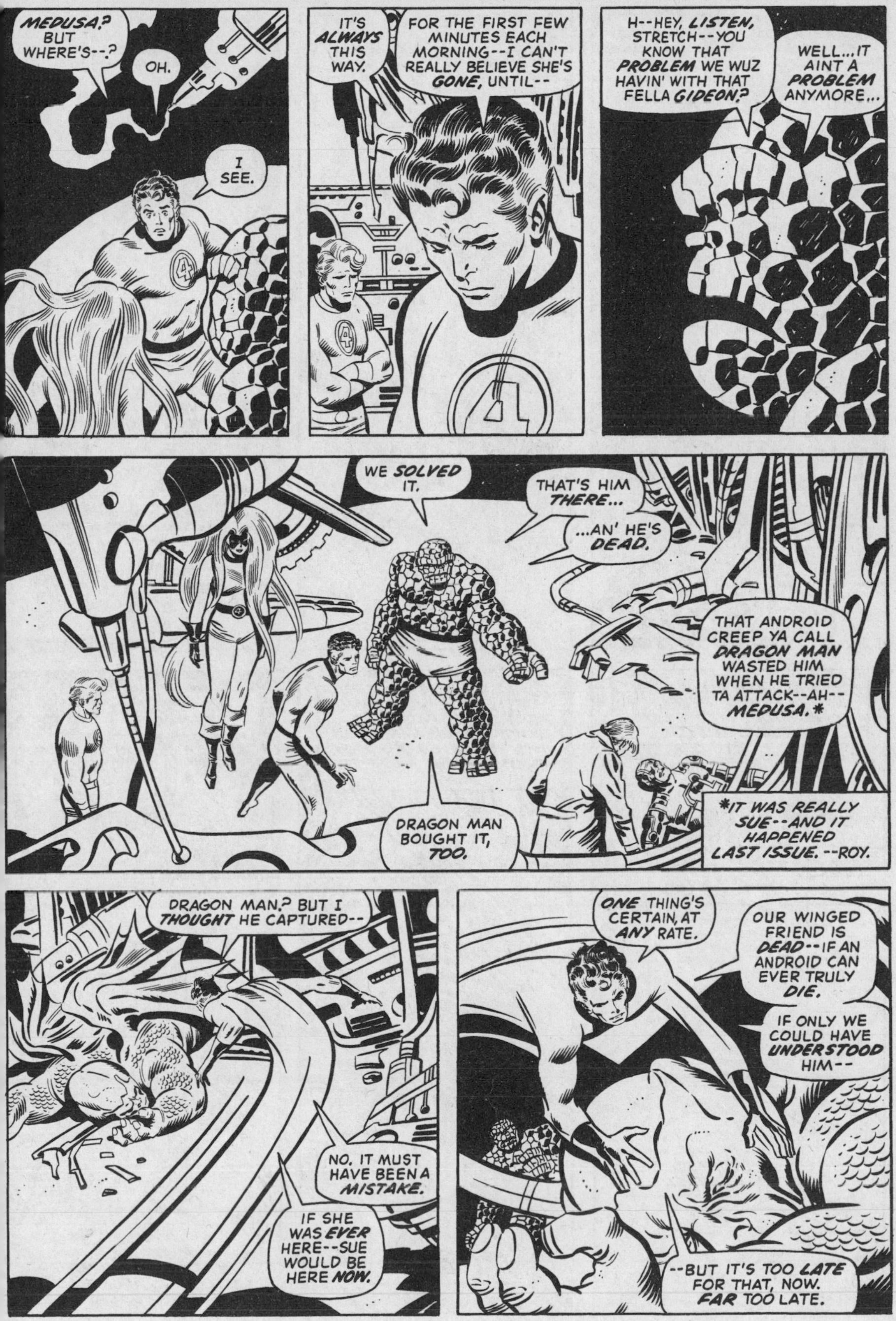
MEDUSA? BUT WHERE'S--?
OH.
I SEE.
IT'S ALWAYS THIS WAY.
FOR THE FIRST FEW MINUTES EACH MORNING--I CAN'T REALLY BELIEVE SHE'S GONE, UNTIL--
H--HEY, LISTEN, STRETCH--YOU KNOW THAT PROBLEM WE WUZ HAVIN' WITH THAT FELLA GIDEON?
WELL...IT AINT A PROBLEM ANYMORE...
WE SOLVED IT.
THAT'S HIM THERE...
...AN' HE'S DEAD.
THAT ANDROID CREEP YA CALL DRAGON MAN WASTED HIM WHEN HE TRIED TA ATTACK--AH--MEDUSA.*
DRAGON MAN BOUGHT IT, TOO.
*IT WAS REALLY SUE--AND IT HAPPENED LAST ISSUE. --ROY.
DRAGON MAN? BUT I THOUGHT HE CAPTURED--
NO, IT MUST HAVE BEEN A MISTAKE.
IF SHE WAS EVER HERE--SUE WOULD BE HERE NOW.
ONE THING'S CERTAIN, AT ANY RATE.
OUR WINGED FRIEND IS DEAD--IF AN ANDROID CAN EVER TRULY DIE.
IF ONLY WE COULD HAVE UNDERSTOOD HIM--
--BUT IT'S TOO LATE FOR THAT, NOW. FAR TOO LATE.

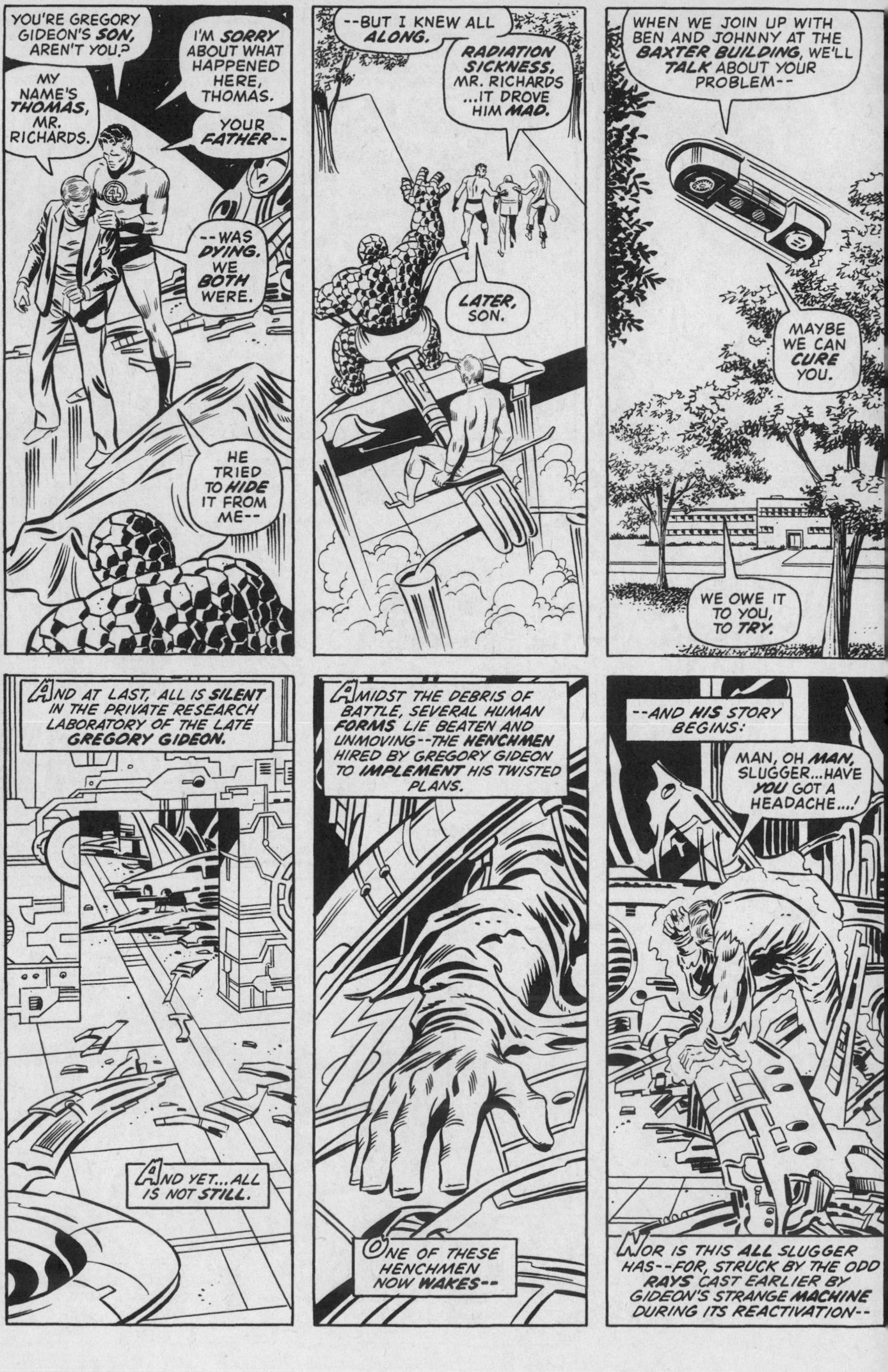

YOU'RE GREGORY GIDEON'S SON, AREN'T YOU?
MY NAME'S THOMAS, MR. RICHARDS.
I'M SORRY ABOUT WHAT HAPPENED HERE, THOMAS.
YOUR FATHER--
--WAS DYING. WE BOTH WERE.
HE TRIED TO HIDE IT FROM ME--
--BUT I KNEW ALL ALONG.
RADIATION SICKNESS, MR. RICHARDS ...IT DROVE HIM MAD.
LATER, SON.
WHEN WE JOIN UP WITH BEN AND JOHNNY AT THE BAXTER BUILDING, WE'LL TALK ABOUT YOUR PROBLEM--
MAYBE WE CAN CURE YOU.
WE OWE IT TO YOU, TO TRY.
AND AT LAST, ALL IS SILENT IN THE PRIVATE RESEARCH LABORATORY OF THE LATE GREGORY GIDEON.
AND YET... ALL IS NOT STILL.
AMIDST THE DEBRIS OF BATTLE, SEVERAL HUMAN FORMS LIE BEATEN AND UNMOVING--THE HENCHMEN HIRED BY GREGORY GIDEON TO IMPLEMENT HIS TWISTED PLANS.
ONE OF THESE HENCHMEN NOW WAKES--
--AND HIS STORY BEGINS:
MAN, OH MAN, SLUGGER... HAVE YOU GOT A HEADACHE....!
NOR IS THIS ALL SLUGGER HAS--FOR, STRUCK BY THE ODD RAYS CAST EARLIER BY GIDEON'S STRANGE MACHINE DURING ITS REACTIVATION--

--HIS BODY IS SUFFUSED WITH AN UNEARTHLY *GLOW*--OF WHICH HE IS BLITHELY *UNAWARE!*

LOOKS LIKE *OUR* SIDE *LOST.*

FACE IT, SLUGGER--YOU BOMBED OUT *AGAIN.*

FROM THE *LOOK* OF THINGS--THIS TURF'S *HOT.*

GOTTA FIGURE AN ANGLE TO GET *OUTTA* HERE--

--BEFORE I'M SPOTTED BY THE *FUZZ.*

THE WAY MY *LUCK'S* BEEN HOLDING, *I'LL* CATCH THE BLAME FOR THIS MESS.

WISH THINGS WERE LIKE THEY WUZ IN THE *FIFTIES*--

"--WHEN ME AN' THE *OTHER* J.D.'s USED TA HANG OUT 'ROUND *POP DANVER'S* JOINT--

"--EYEIN' THE BROADS AND FIGURIN' ON WAYS TO SCORE THE *REAL* PAYOLA. YEAH, *THOSE* WERE THE DAYS--CHUGALUGGIN' BEER AN DIGGIN' OL' *ELVIS.*

"FUNNY HOW IT ALL SORTA *ENDED* IN '58, WHEN I FINALLY PULLED A PASSIN' GRADE AND GRADUATED *HIGH SCHOOL*--!

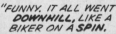

"FUNNY. IT ALL WENT *DOWNHILL,* LIKE A BIKER ON A *SPIN.*

"ALL I COULD GET WERE *ODD JOBS*-- GARAGE MECHANIC, BUM WORK LIKE *THAT*--

"--UNTIL I READ THAT *AD* IN THE CLASSIFIED SECTION OF THE *DAILY BUGLE*--ABOUT SOMEONE NEEDIN' A *BODY-GUARD* WHO DIDN'T CARE ABOUT 'TRADITIONAL LEGALITIES'!

"I KNEW WHAT *THAT* MEANT-- AND I WAS ALL *FOR* IT--

--AN' LOOK WHERE IT'S *GOT* ME.

I'M IN *MORE* HOT WATER THAN I EVER WUZ WITH--

HUH?

SOME SORT'A *GLOW* BEHIND ME--?

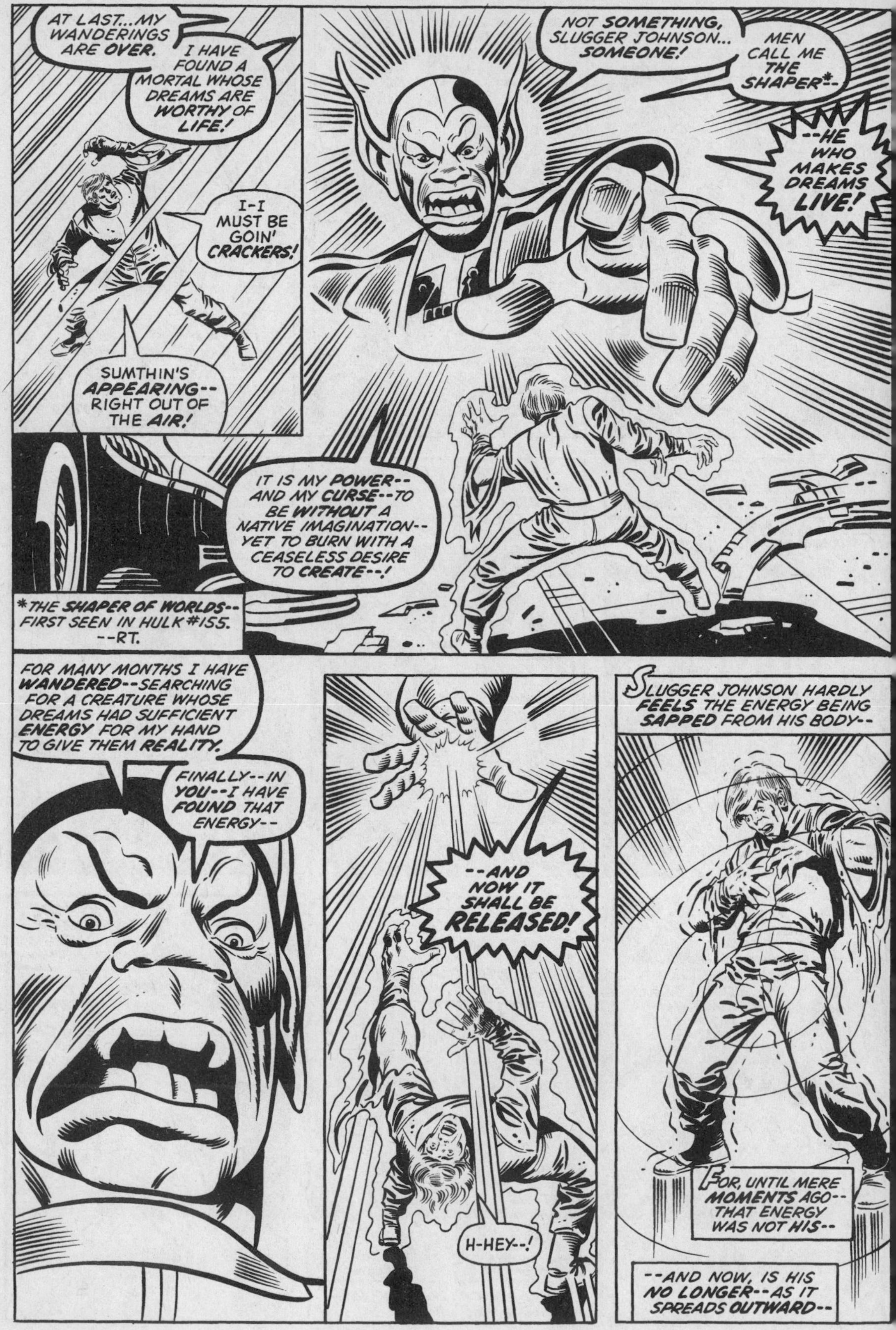
AT LAST... MY WANDERINGS ARE OVER.
I HAVE FOUND A MORTAL WHOSE DREAMS ARE WORTHY OF LIFE!
I-I MUST BE GOIN' CRACKERS!
SUMTHIN'S APPEARING-- RIGHT OUT OF THE AIR!
NOT SOMETHING, SLUGGER JOHNSON... SOMEONE!
MEN CALL ME THE SHAPER*--
--HE WHO MAKES DREAMS LIVE!
IT IS MY POWER-- AND MY CURSE--TO BE WITHOUT A NATIVE IMAGINATION-- YET TO BURN WITH A CEASELESS DESIRE TO CREATE--!
*THE SHAPER OF WORLDS-- FIRST SEEN IN HULK #155. --RT.
FOR MANY MONTHS I HAVE WANDERED--SEARCHING FOR A CREATURE WHOSE DREAMS HAD SUFFICIENT ENERGY FOR MY HAND TO GIVE THEM REALITY.
FINALLY--IN YOU--I HAVE FOUND THAT ENERGY--
--AND NOW IT SHALL BE RELEASED!
H-HEY--!
SLUGGER JOHNSON HARDLY FEELS THE ENERGY BEING SAPPED FROM HIS BODY--
FOR, UNTIL MERE MOMENTS AGO-- THAT ENERGY WAS NOT HIS--
--AND NOW, IS HIS NO LONGER--AS IT SPREADS OUTWARD--

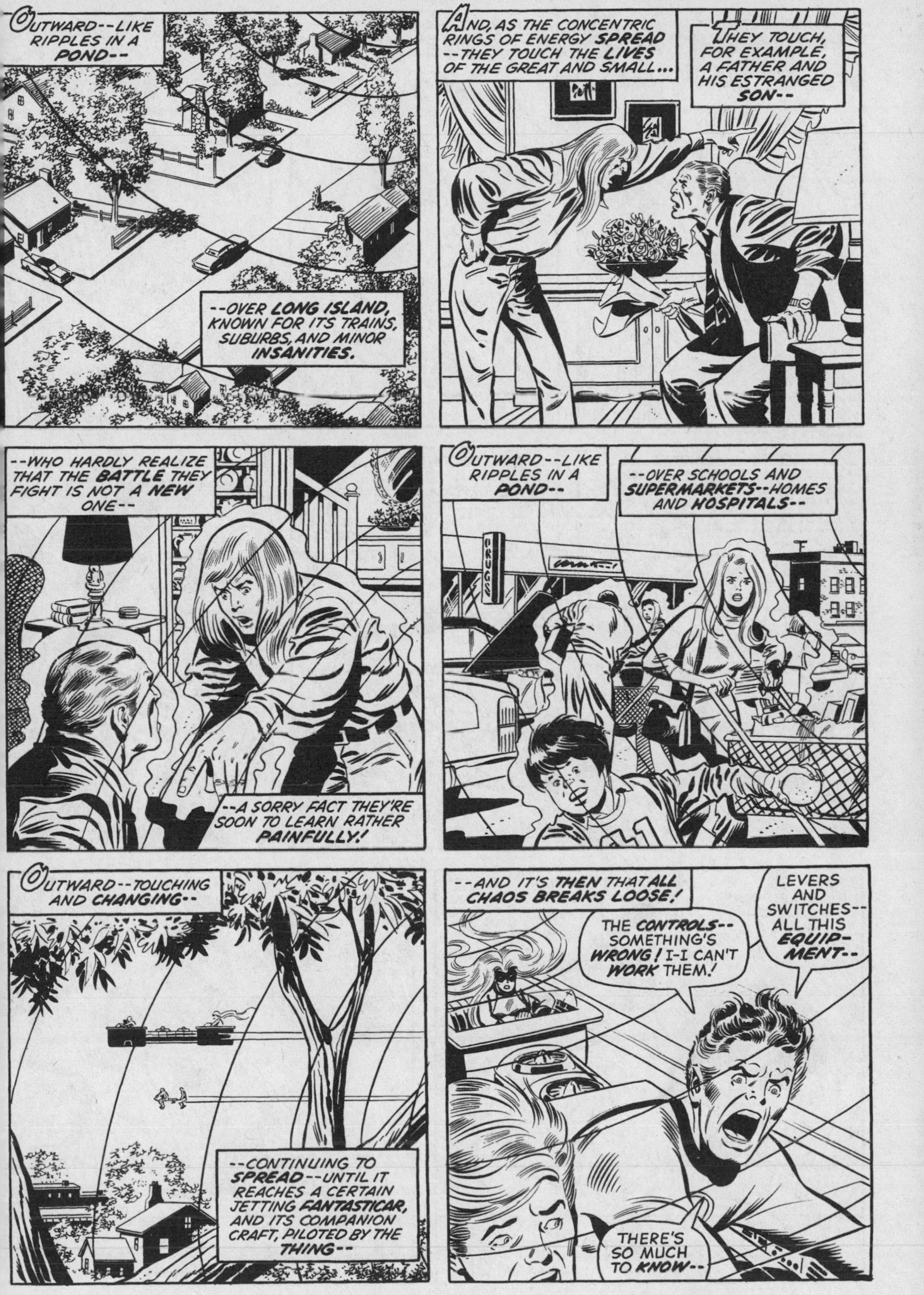
OUTWARD--LIKE RIPPLES IN A POND--
--OVER LONG ISLAND, KNOWN FOR ITS TRAINS, SUBURBS, AND MINOR INSANITIES.
AND, AS THE CONCENTRIC RINGS OF ENERGY SPREAD --THEY TOUCH THE LIVES OF THE GREAT AND SMALL...
THEY TOUCH, FOR EXAMPLE, A FATHER AND HIS ESTRANGED SON--
--WHO HARDLY REALIZE THAT THE BATTLE THEY FIGHT IS NOT A NEW ONE--
--A SORRY FACT THEY'RE SOON TO LEARN RATHER PAINFULLY!
OUTWARD--LIKE RIPPLES IN A POND--
--OVER SCHOOLS AND SUPERMARKETS--HOMES AND HOSPITALS--
DRUGS
OUTWARD--TOUCHING AND CHANGING--
--CONTINUING TO SPREAD--UNTIL IT REACHES A CERTAIN JETTING FANTASTICAR, AND ITS COMPANION CRAFT, PILOTED BY THE THING--
--AND IT'S THEN THAT ALL CHAOS BREAKS LOOSE!
THE CONTROLS-- SOMETHING'S WRONG! I-I CAN'T WORK THEM!
LEVERS AND SWITCHES-- ALL THIS EQUIPMENT--
THERE'S SO MUCH TO KNOW--

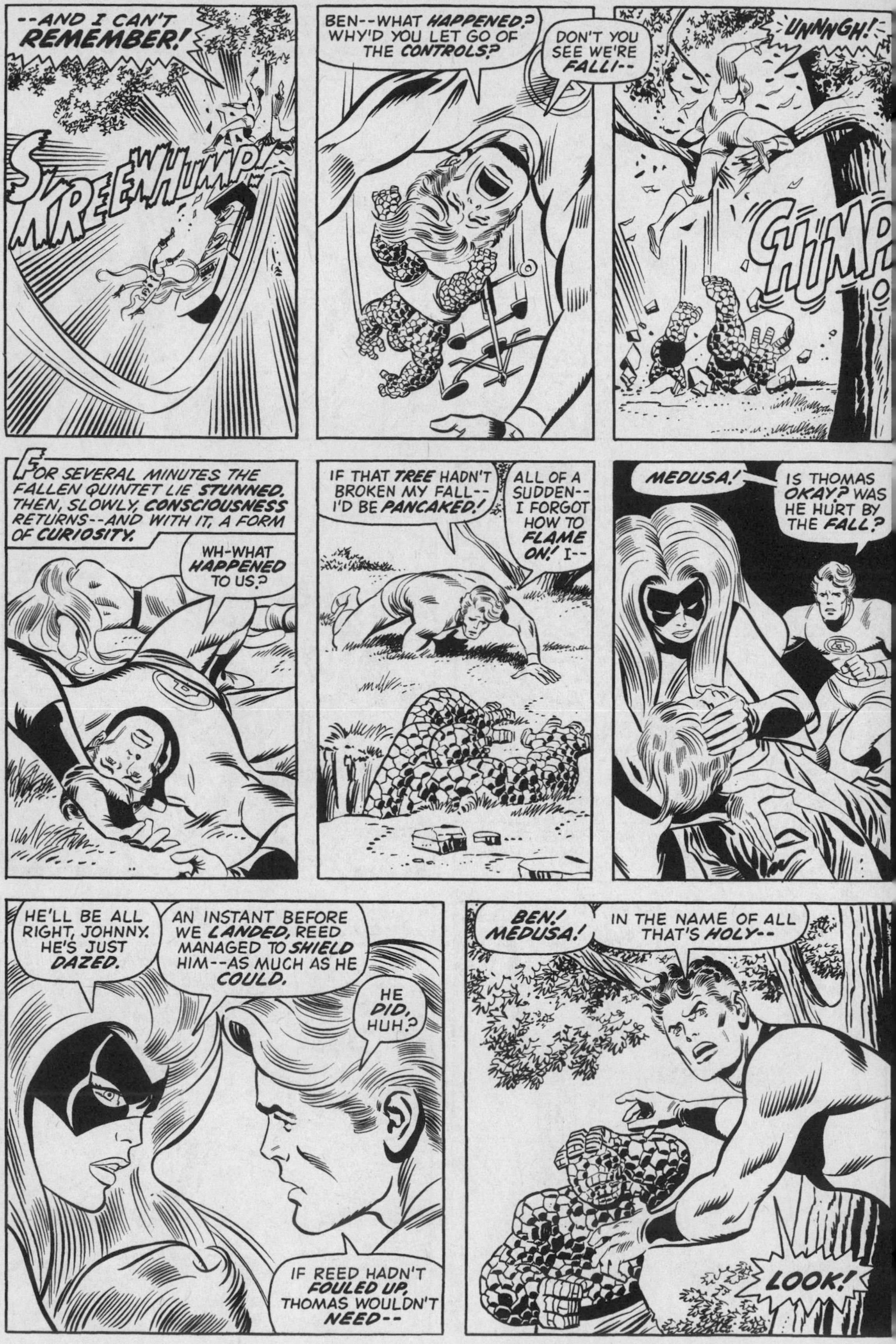
--AND I CAN'T REMEMBER!
SKREEWHUMP!
BEN--WHAT HAPPENED? WHY'D YOU LET GO OF THE CONTROLS?
DON'T YOU SEE WE'RE FALLI--
UNNNGH!
CHUMP
FOR SEVERAL MINUTES THE FALLEN QUINTET LIE STUNNED. THEN, SLOWLY, CONSCIOUSNESS RETURNS--AND WITH IT, A FORM OF CURIOSITY.
WH-WHAT HAPPENED TO US?
IF THAT TREE HADN'T BROKEN MY FALL--I'D BE PANCAKED!
ALL OF A SUDDEN--I FORGOT HOW TO FLAME ON! I--
MEDUSA!
IS THOMAS OKAY? WAS HE HURT BY THE FALL?
HE'LL BE ALL RIGHT, JOHNNY. HE'S JUST DAZED.
AN INSTANT BEFORE WE LANDED, REED MANAGED TO SHIELD HIM--AS MUCH AS HE COULD.
HE DID, HUH?
IF REED HADN'T FOULED UP, THOMAS WOULDN'T NEED--
BEN! MEDUSA!
IN THE NAME OF ALL THAT'S HOLY--
LOOK!

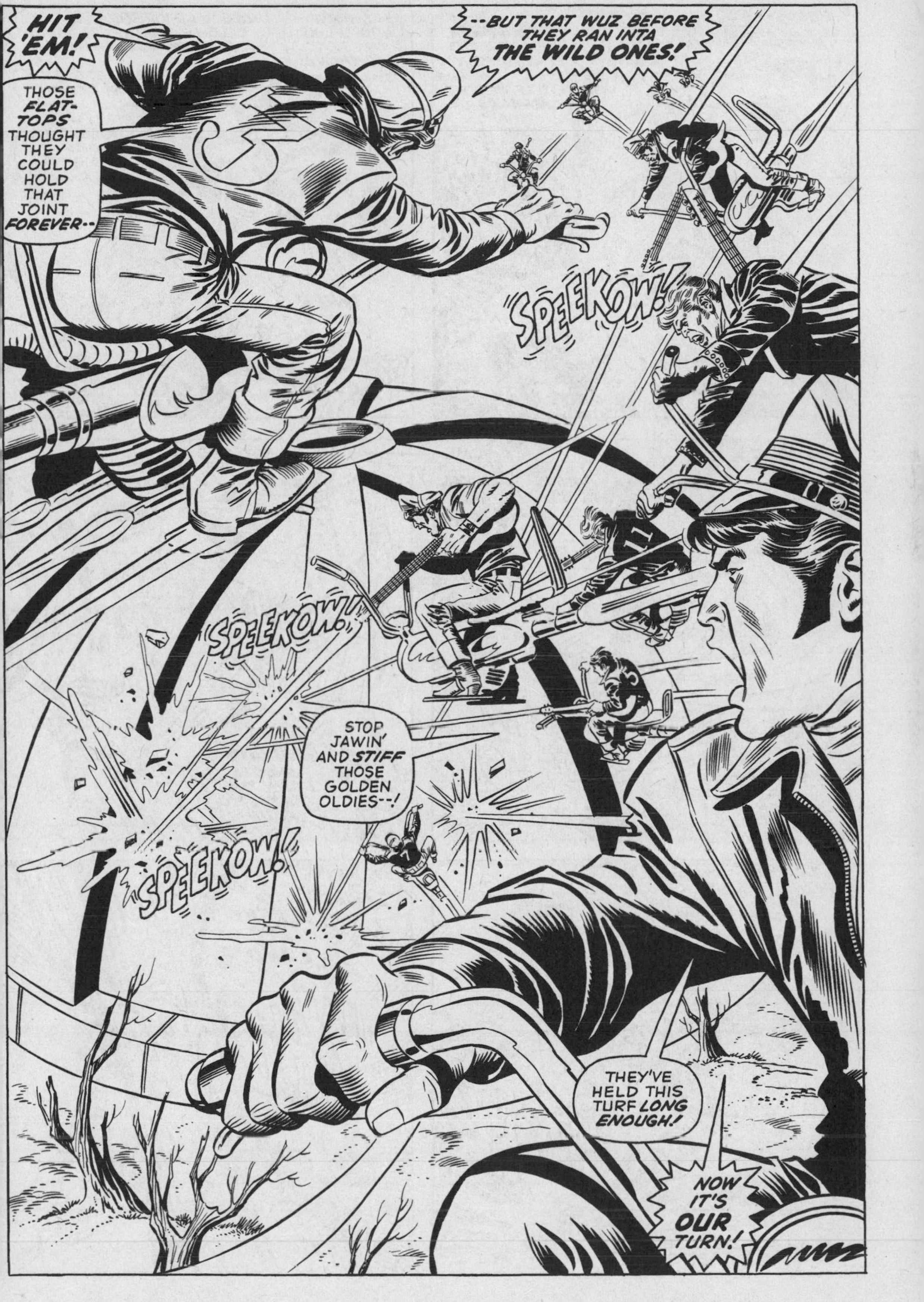

HIT 'EM!
THOSE FLAT-TOPS THOUGHT THEY COULD HOLD THAT JOINT FOREVER--
--BUT THAT WUZ BEFORE THEY RAN INTA THE WILD ONES!
SPEEKOW!
SPEEKOW!
STOP JAWIN' AND STIFF THOSE GOLDEN OLDIES--!
SPEEKOW!
THEY'VE HELD THIS TURF LONG ENOUGH!
NOW IT'S OUR TURN!

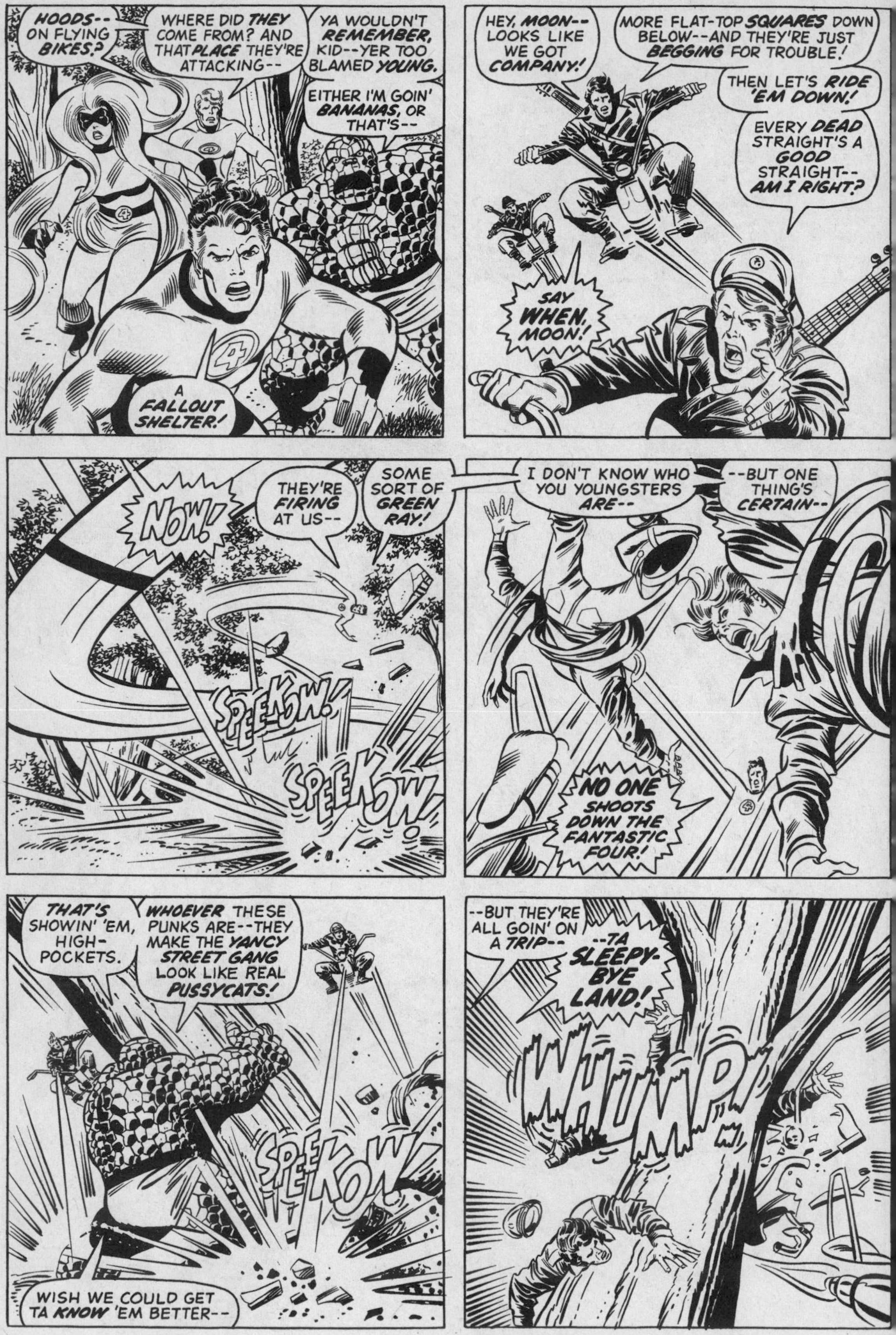
HOODS--ON FLYING BIKES?
WHERE DID THEY COME FROM? AND THAT PLACE THEY'RE ATTACKING--
YA WOULDN'T REMEMBER, KID--YER TOO BLAMED YOUNG.
EITHER I'M GOIN' BANANAS, OR THAT'S--
A FALLOUT SHELTER!
HEY, MOON--LOOKS LIKE WE GOT COMPANY!
MORE FLAT-TOP SQUARES DOWN BELOW--AND THEY'RE JUST BEGGING FOR TROUBLE!
THEN LET'S RIDE 'EM DOWN!
EVERY DEAD STRAIGHT'S A GOOD STRAIGHT--AM I RIGHT?
SAY WHEN, MOON!
NOW!
THEY'RE FIRING AT US--
SOME SORT OF GREEN RAY!
SPEEKOW!
SPEEKOW
I DON'T KNOW WHO YOU YOUNGSTERS ARE--
--BUT ONE THING'S CERTAIN--
NO ONE SHOOTS DOWN THE FANTASTIC FOUR!
THAT'S SHOWIN' 'EM, HIGH-POCKETS.
WHOEVER THESE PUNKS ARE--THEY MAKE THE YANCY STREET GANG LOOK LIKE REAL PUSSYCATS!
SPEEKOW
WISH WE COULD GET TA KNOW 'EM BETTER--
--BUT THEY'RE ALL GOIN' ON A TRIP--
--TA SLEEPY-BYE LAND!
WHUMP!

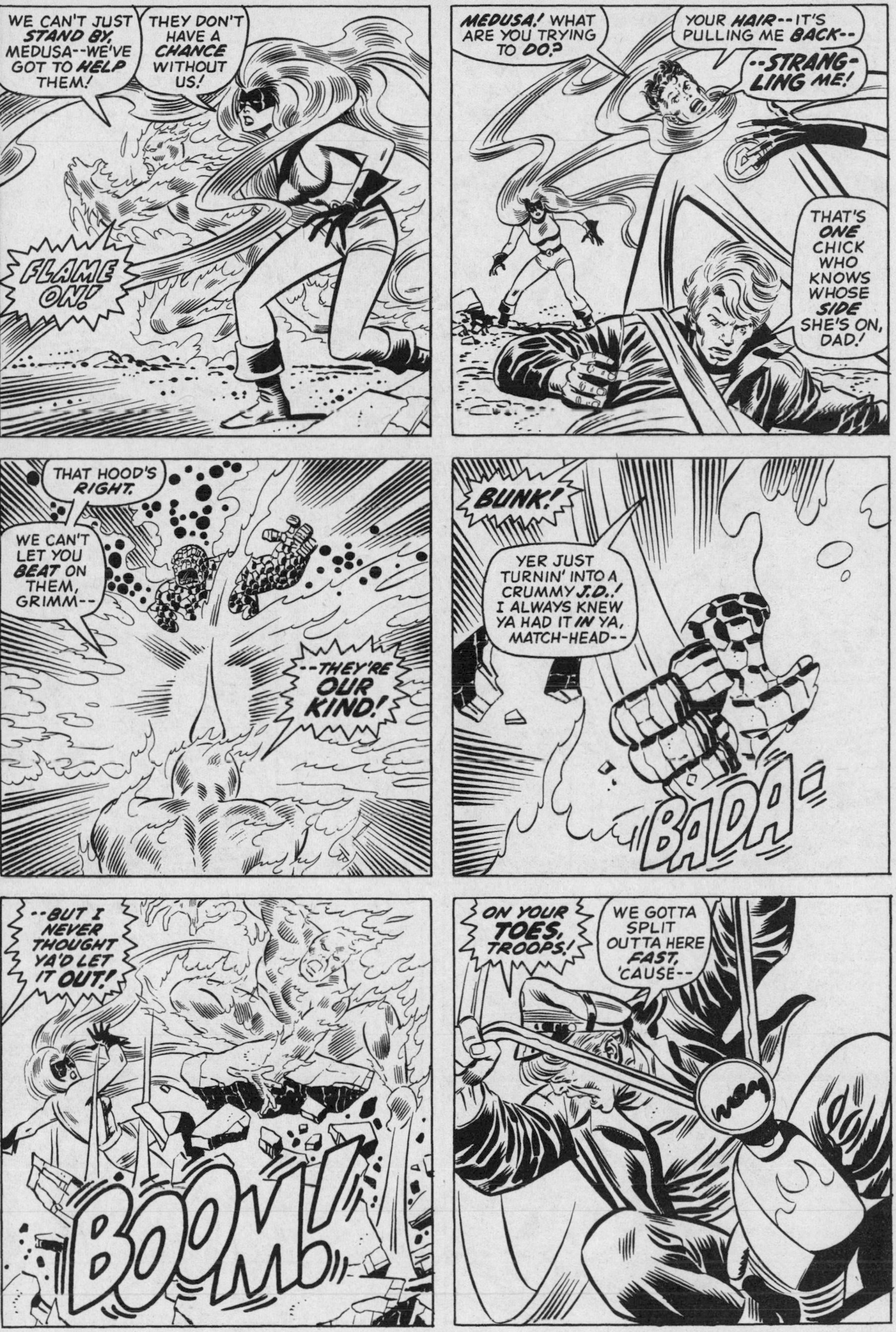
WE CAN'T JUST STAND BY, MEDUSA--WE'VE GOT TO HELP THEM!
THEY DON'T HAVE A CHANCE WITHOUT US!
FLAME ON!
MEDUSA! WHAT ARE YOU TRYING TO DO?
YOUR HAIR--IT'S PULLING ME BACK--
--STRANGLING ME!
THAT'S ONE CHICK WHO KNOWS WHOSE SIDE SHE'S ON, DAD!
THAT HOOD'S RIGHT.
WE CAN'T LET YOU BEAT ON THEM, GRIMM--
--THEY'RE OUR KIND!
BUNK!
YER JUST TURNIN' INTO A CRUMMY J.D.! I ALWAYS KNEW YA HAD IT IN YA, MATCH-HEAD--
BADA-
--BUT I NEVER THOUGHT YA'D LET IT OUT!
BOOMB!
ON YOUR TOES, TROOPS!
WE GOTTA SPLIT OUTTA HERE FAST, 'CAUSE--

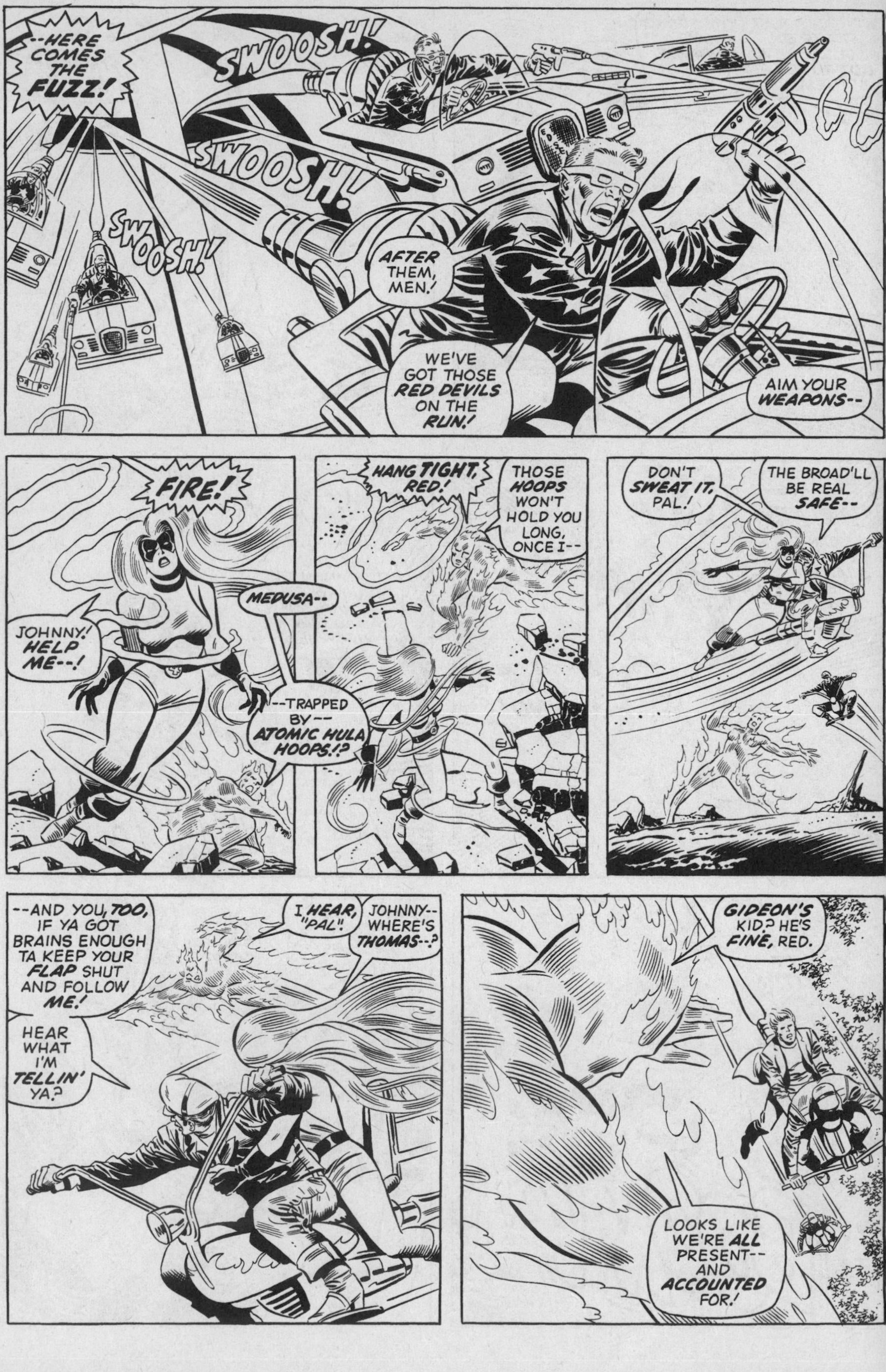
--HERE COMES THE FUZZ!
SWOOSH!
SWOOSH!
SWOOSH!
AFTER THEM, MEN.!
WE'VE GOT THOSE RED DEVILS ON THE RUN!
AIM YOUR WEAPONS--
FIRE!
JOHNNY! HELP ME--!
MEDUSA--
--TRAPPED BY-- ATOMIC HULA HOOPS!?
HANG TIGHT, RED!
THOSE HOOPS WON'T HOLD YOU LONG, ONCE I--
DON'T SWEAT IT, PAL.!
THE BROAD'LL BE REAL SAFE--
--AND YOU, TOO, IF YA GOT BRAINS ENOUGH TA KEEP YOUR FLAP SHUT AND FOLLOW ME.!
HEAR WHAT I'M TELLIN' YA?
I HEAR, "PAL"!
JOHNNY-- WHERE'S THOMAS--?
GIDEON'S KID? HE'S FINE, RED.
LOOKS LIKE WE'RE ALL PRESENT-- AND ACCOUNTED FOR.!

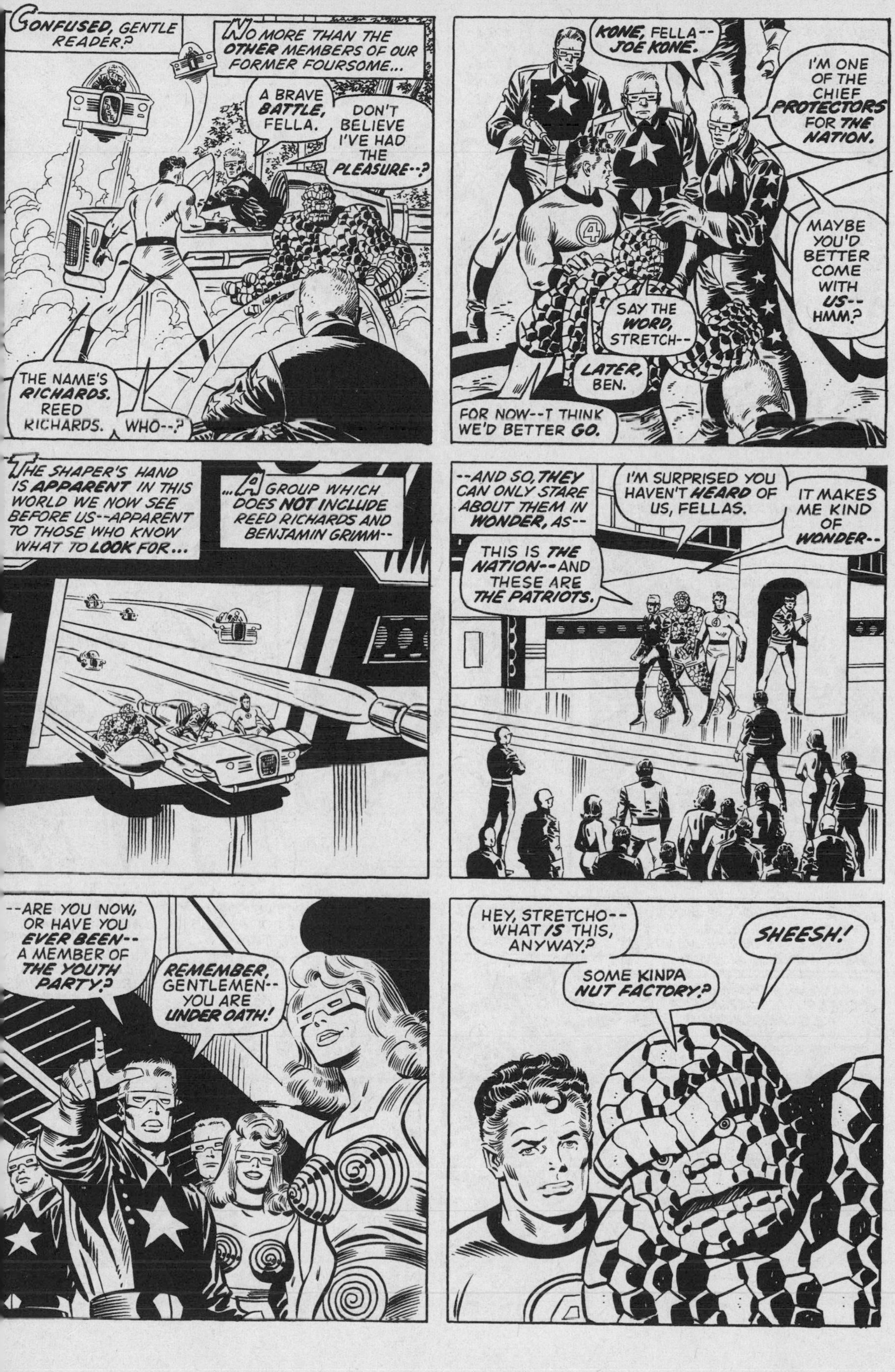

CONFUSED, GENTLE READER?
NO MORE THAN THE OTHER MEMBERS OF OUR FORMER FOURSOME...
A BRAVE BATTLE, FELLA.
DON'T BELIEVE I'VE HAD THE PLEASURE--?
THE NAME'S RICHARDS. REED RICHARDS.
WHO--?
KONE, FELLA-- JOE KONE.
I'M ONE OF THE CHIEF PROTECTORS FOR THE NATION.
MAYBE YOU'D BETTER COME WITH US-- HMM?
SAY THE WORD, STRETCH--
LATER, BEN.
FOR NOW--I THINK WE'D BETTER GO.
THE SHAPER'S HAND IS APPARENT IN THIS WORLD WE NOW SEE BEFORE US--APPARENT TO THOSE WHO KNOW WHAT TO LOOK FOR...
...A GROUP WHICH DOES NOT INCLUDE REED RICHARDS AND BENJAMIN GRIMM--
--AND SO, THEY CAN ONLY STARE ABOUT THEM IN WONDER, AS--
THIS IS THE NATION--AND THESE ARE THE PATRIOTS.
I'M SURPRISED YOU HAVEN'T HEARD OF US, FELLAS.
IT MAKES ME KIND OF WONDER--
--ARE YOU NOW, OR HAVE YOU EVER BEEN-- A MEMBER OF THE YOUTH PARTY?
REMEMBER, GENTLEMEN-- YOU ARE UNDER OATH!
HEY, STRETCHO-- WHAT IS THIS, ANYWAY?
SOME KINDA NUT FACTORY?
SHEESH!

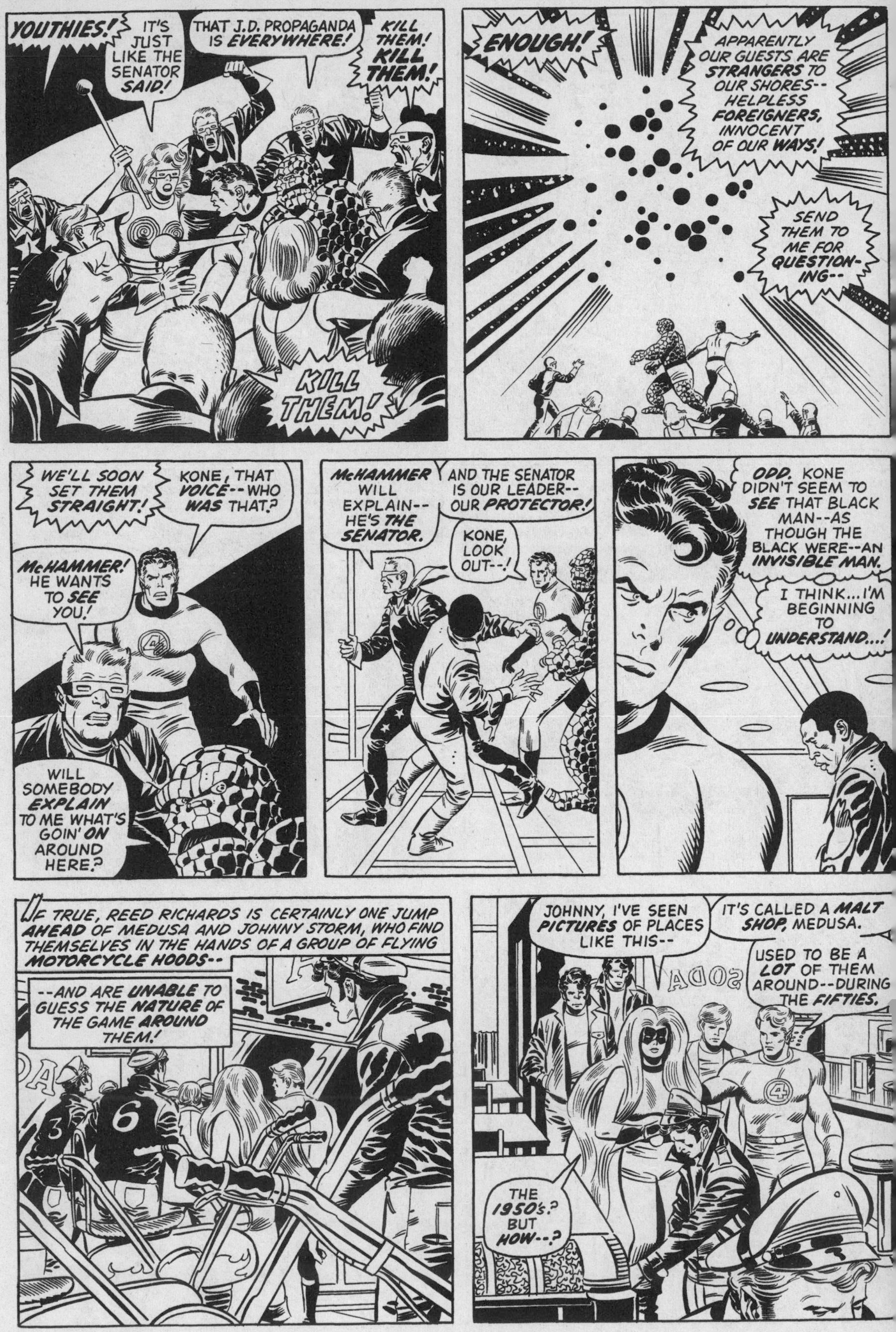
YOUTHIES!
IT'S JUST LIKE THE SENATOR SAID!
THAT J.D. PROPAGANDA IS EVERYWHERE!
KILL THEM! KILL THEM!
KILL THEM!
ENOUGH!
APPARENTLY OUR GUESTS ARE STRANGERS TO OUR SHORES--HELPLESS FOREIGNERS, INNOCENT OF OUR WAYS!
SEND THEM TO ME FOR QUESTIONING--
WE'LL SOON SET THEM STRAIGHT!
KONE, THAT VOICE--WHO WAS THAT?
McHAMMER! HE WANTS TO SEE YOU!
WILL SOMEBODY EXPLAIN TO ME WHAT'S GOIN' ON AROUND HERE?
McHAMMER WILL EXPLAIN--HE'S THE SENATOR.
AND THE SENATOR IS OUR LEADER--OUR PROTECTOR!
KONE, LOOK OUT--!
ODD. KONE DIDN'T SEEM TO SEE THAT BLACK MAN--AS THOUGH THE BLACK WERE--AN INVISIBLE MAN.
I THINK...I'M BEGINNING TO UNDERSTAND...!
IF TRUE, REED RICHARDS IS CERTAINLY ONE JUMP AHEAD OF MEDUSA AND JOHNNY STORM, WHO FIND THEMSELVES IN THE HANDS OF A GROUP OF FLYING MOTORCYCLE HOODS--
--AND ARE UNABLE TO GUESS THE NATURE OF THE GAME AROUND THEM!
JOHNNY, I'VE SEEN PICTURES OF PLACES LIKE THIS--
IT'S CALLED A MALT SHOP, MEDUSA.
USED TO BE A LOT OF THEM AROUND--DURING THE FIFTIES.
THE 1950's? BUT HOW--?

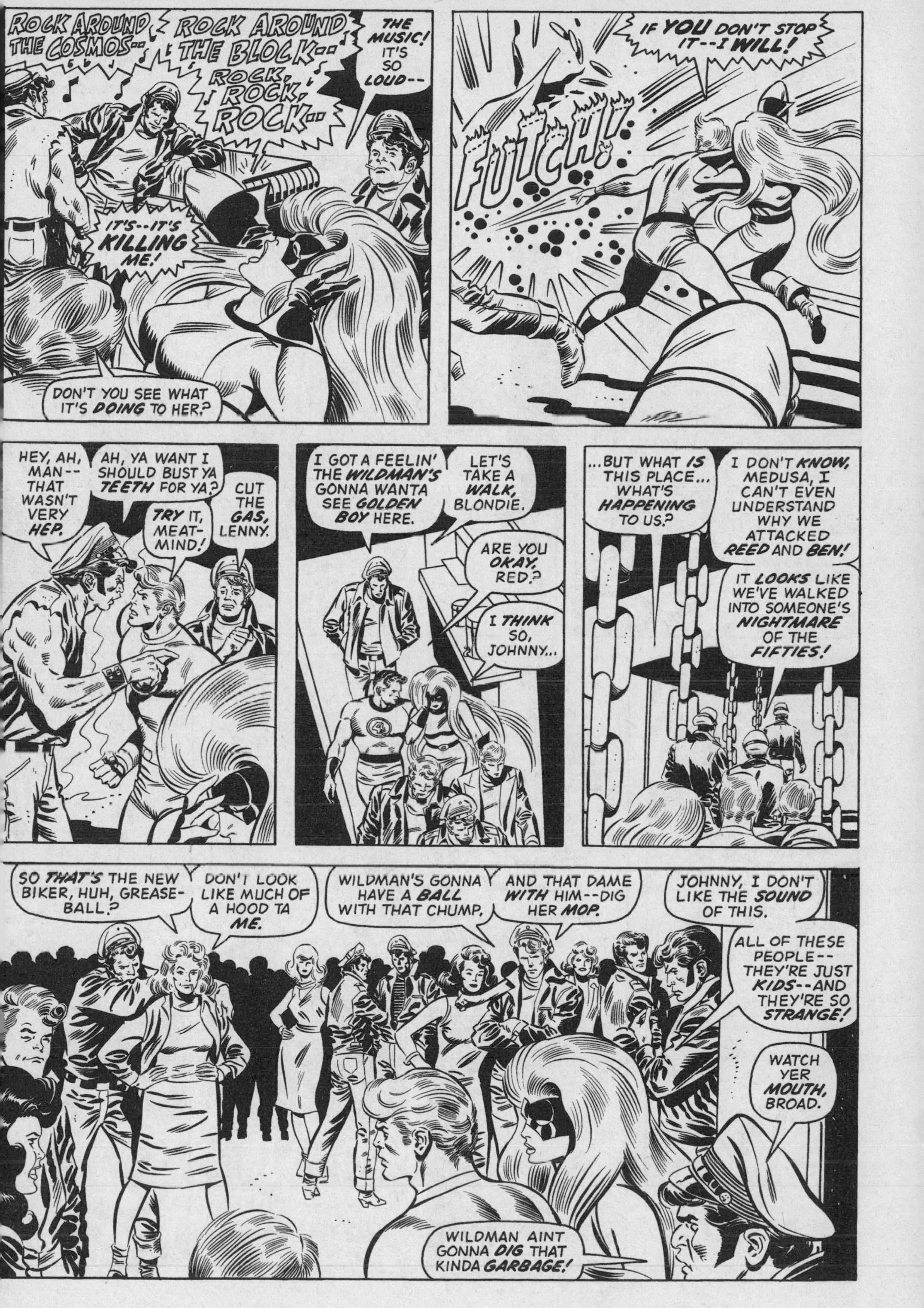
ROCK AROUND THE COSMOS--
ROCK AROUND THE BLOCK-- ROCK, ROCK, ROCK--
THE MUSIC! IT'S SO LOUD--
IT'S--IT'S KILLING ME!
DON'T YOU SEE WHAT IT'S DOING TO HER?
IF YOU DON'T STOP IT--I WILL!
FUTCH!
HEY, AH, MAN--THAT WASN'T VERY HEP.
AH, YA WANT I SHOULD BUST YA TEETH FOR YA?
TRY IT, MEAT-MIND!
CUT THE GAS, LENNY.
I GOT A FEELIN' THE WILDMAN'S GONNA WANTA SEE GOLDEN BOY HERE.
LET'S TAKE A WALK, BLONDIE.
ARE YOU OKAY, RED?
I THINK SO, JOHNNY...
...BUT WHAT IS THIS PLACE... WHAT'S HAPPENING TO US?
I DON'T KNOW, MEDUSA, I CAN'T EVEN UNDERSTAND WHY WE ATTACKED REED AND BEN!
IT LOOKS LIKE WE'VE WALKED INTO SOMEONE'S NIGHTMARE OF THE FIFTIES!
SO THAT'S THE NEW BIKER, HUH, GREASE-BALL?
DON'T LOOK LIKE MUCH OF A HOOD TA ME.
WILDMAN'S GONNA HAVE A BALL WITH THAT CHUMP.
AND THAT DAME WITH HIM--DIG HER MOP.
JOHNNY, I DON'T LIKE THE SOUND OF THIS.
ALL OF THESE PEOPLE--THEY'RE JUST KIDS--AND THEY'RE SO STRANGE!
WATCH YER MOUTH, BROAD.
WILDMAN AINT GONNA DIG THAT KINDA GARBAGE!

I DON'T *GET* IT-- WHO'S THIS *WILDMAN* YOU KEEP TALKING ABOUT?

PAL, HAVE YOU BEEN LIVIN' IN ANOTHER *UNIVERSE?*

HE'S OUR *ELVIS*-- OUR *BRANDO*-- OUR VERY OWN HEAD *DEAN!*

HE'S THE MAN WHO'S GONNA DECIDE WHAT TO *DO* WITH YOU! HE'S--

WILDMAN!

*F*ROM SOMEWHERE COMES THE FAINTEST STRUMMING OF AN ELECTRIC *GUITAR.*

A WHISPER-- AS SOFT AS A REVVING *MOTORCYCLE*--

--AS GENTLE AS THE SCREAM OF A VICTIM IN *PAIN!*

NOW, IF I AINT A LOVE-SICK *HOUND DOG!*

WHAT HAVE WE HERE? SEEMS I'VE SEEN THOSE PRETTY FACES *BEFORE*--

--BUT I JUST CAN'T REMEMBER *WHERE!**

*TAKE A *CLOSE* LOOK-- AND THEN FLIP BACK TO *PAGE 7*, AND TELL US WHAT YOU SEE! --SNEAKY ROY.

THE BOYS TELL ME YOU'RE *NEW*--

--AN' WHILE THAT AINT EXACTLY A *CRIME*--

--IT *IS* KINDA *SUSPICIOUS!*

SOOOO-- MEET YER *INTERRO- GATORS*--

--THE TWO BEST *DISK JOCKEYS* IN THE WHOLE WILD AND WOOLLY *WESTERN* HEMISPHERE.

HIYA HIYA *HIYA*, KIDDIES AND KOOL KATS--

WANNA STUFF A *PHONE BOOTH!?*

JOHNNY...WHAT DOES IT ALL *MEAN?*

I THINK I UNDER- STAND NOW, RED...

I THINK I UNDER- STAND NOW, RED...

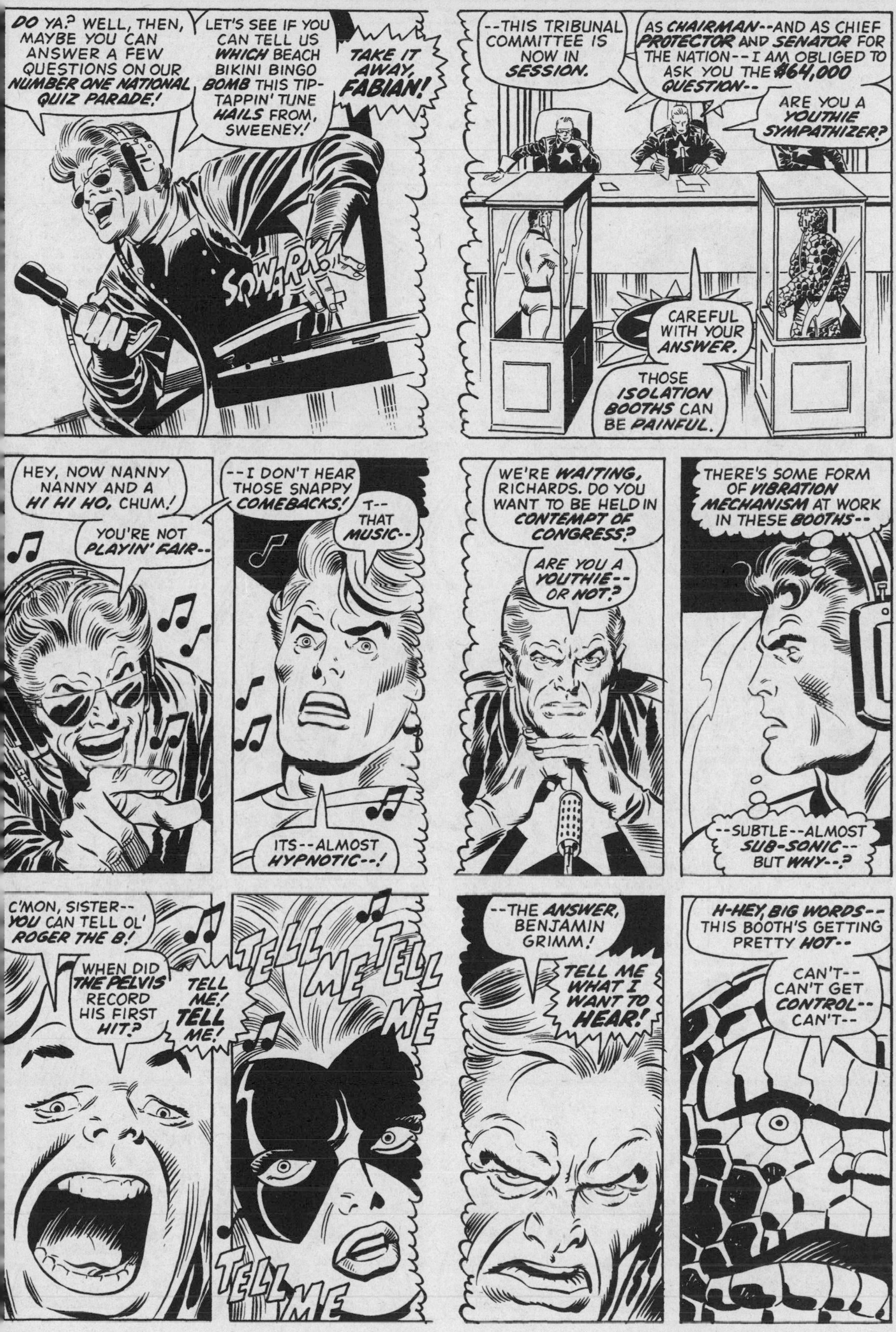
DO YA? WELL, THEN, MAYBE YOU CAN ANSWER A FEW QUESTIONS ON OUR NUMBER ONE NATIONAL QUIZ PARADE!
LET'S SEE IF YOU CAN TELL US WHICH BEACH BIKINI BINGO BOMB THIS TIP-TAPPIN' TUNE HAILS FROM, SWEENEY!
TAKE IT AWAY, FABIAN!
SQWARK!
--THIS TRIBUNAL COMMITTEE IS NOW IN SESSION.
AS CHAIRMAN--AND AS CHIEF PROTECTOR AND SENATOR FOR THE NATION--I AM OBLIGED TO ASK YOU THE $64,000 QUESTION--
ARE YOU A YOUTHIE SYMPATHIZER?
CAREFUL WITH YOUR ANSWER.
THOSE ISOLATION BOOTHS CAN BE PAINFUL.
HEY, NOW NANNY NANNY AND A HI HI HO, CHUM!
YOU'RE NOT PLAYIN' FAIR--
--I DON'T HEAR THOSE SNAPPY COMEBACKS!
T--THAT MUSIC--
ITS--ALMOST HYPNOTIC--!
WE'RE WAITING, RICHARDS. DO YOU WANT TO BE HELD IN CONTEMPT OF CONGRESS?
ARE YOU A YOUTHIE--OR NOT?
THERE'S SOME FORM OF VIBRATION MECHANISM AT WORK IN THESE BOOTHS--
--SUBTLE--ALMOST SUB-SONIC--BUT WHY--?
C'MON, SISTER--YOU CAN TELL OL' ROGER THE B!
WHEN DID THE PELVIS RECORD HIS FIRST HIT?
TELL ME! TELL ME!
TELL ME TELL ME
TELL ME
--THE ANSWER, BENJAMIN GRIMM!
TELL ME WHAT I WANT TO HEAR!
H-HEY, BIG WORDS--THIS BOOTH'S GETTING PRETTY HOT--
CAN'T--CAN'T GET CONTROL--CAN'T--

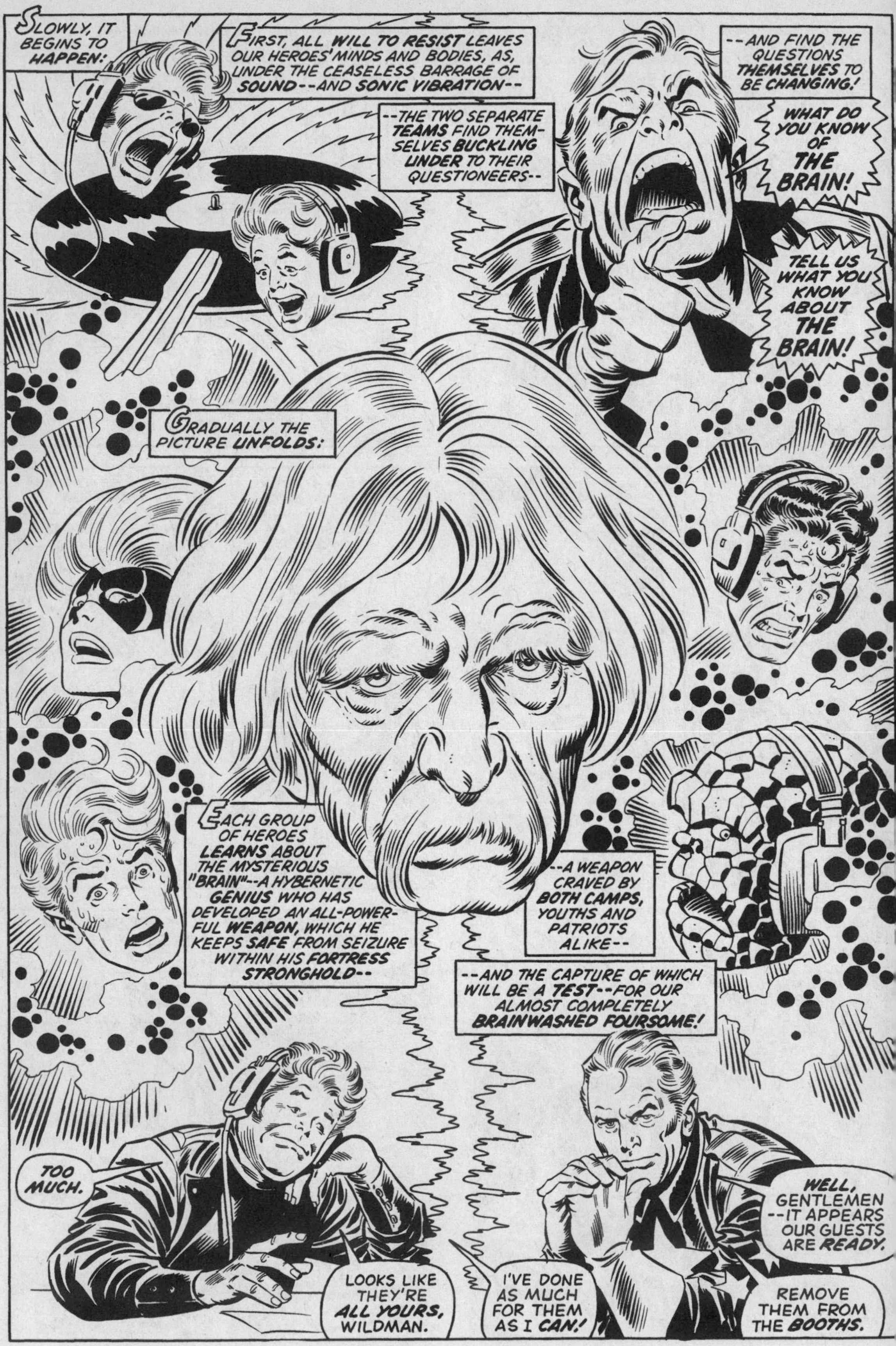
SLOWLY, IT BEGINS TO HAPPEN:
FIRST, ALL WILL TO RESIST LEAVES OUR HEROES' MINDS AND BODIES, AS, UNDER THE CEASELESS BARRAGE OF SOUND--AND SONIC VIBRATION--
--THE TWO SEPARATE TEAMS FIND THEMSELVES BUCKLING UNDER TO THEIR QUESTIONEERS--
--AND FIND THE QUESTIONS THEMSELVES TO BE CHANGING!
WHAT DO YOU KNOW OF THE BRAIN!
TELL US WHAT YOU KNOW ABOUT THE BRAIN!
GRADUALLY THE PICTURE UNFOLDS:
EACH GROUP OF HEROES LEARNS ABOUT THE MYSTERIOUS "BRAIN"--A HYBERNETIC GENIUS WHO HAS DEVELOPED AN ALL-POWERFUL WEAPON, WHICH HE KEEPS SAFE FROM SEIZURE WITHIN HIS FORTRESS STRONGHOLD--
--A WEAPON CRAVED BY BOTH CAMPS, YOUTHS AND PATRIOTS ALIKE--
--AND THE CAPTURE OF WHICH WILL BE A TEST--FOR OUR ALMOST COMPLETELY BRAINWASHED FOURSOME!
TOO MUCH.
LOOKS LIKE THEY'RE ALL YOURS, WILDMAN.
I'VE DONE AS MUCH FOR THEM AS I CAN!
WELL, GENTLEMEN--IT APPEARS OUR GUESTS ARE READY.
REMOVE THEM FROM THE BOOTHS.

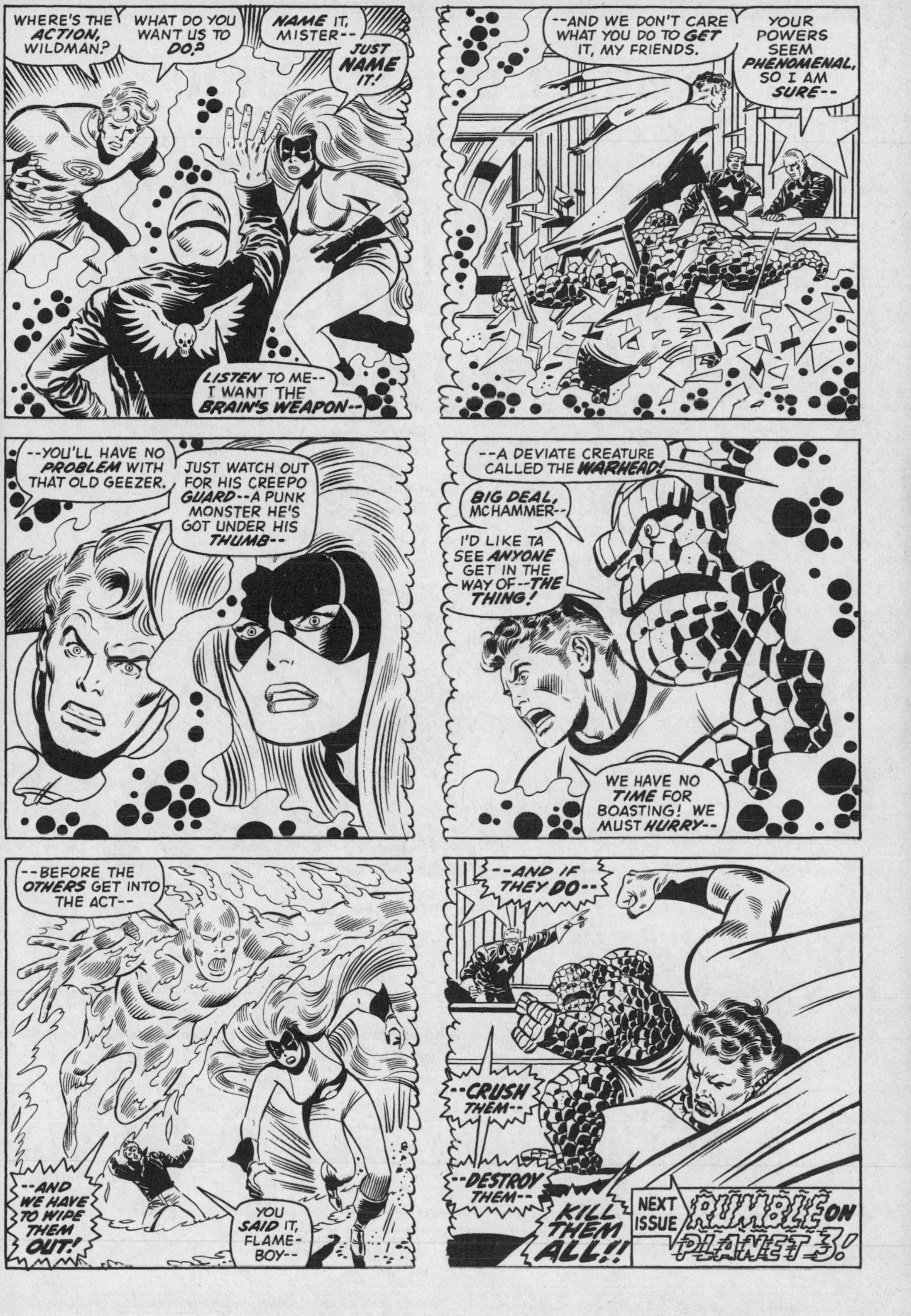

WHERE'S THE ACTION, WILDMAN?
WHAT DO YOU WANT US TO DO?
NAME IT, MISTER--
JUST NAME IT!
LISTEN TO ME-- I WANT THE BRAIN'S WEAPON--
--AND WE DON'T CARE WHAT YOU DO TO GET IT, MY FRIENDS.
YOUR POWERS SEEM PHENOMENAL, SO I AM SURE--
--YOU'LL HAVE NO PROBLEM WITH THAT OLD GEEZER.
JUST WATCH OUT FOR HIS CREEPO GUARD--A PUNK MONSTER HE'S GOT UNDER HIS THUMB--
--A DEVIATE CREATURE CALLED THE WARHEAD!
BIG DEAL, MCHAMMER--
I'D LIKE TA SEE ANYONE GET IN THE WAY OF --THE THING!
WE HAVE NO TIME FOR BOASTING! WE MUST HURRY--
--BEFORE THE OTHERS GET INTO THE ACT--
--AND WE HAVE TO WIPE THEM OUT!
YOU SAID IT, FLAME-BOY--
--AND IF THEY DO--
--CRUSH THEM--
--DESTROY THEM--
KILL THEM ALL!!
NEXT ISSUE
RUMBLE ON PLANET 3!

FANTASTIC FOUR
MARVEL COMICS GROUP
APPROVED BY THE COMICS CODE AUTHORITY
20¢
137 AUG 02462
THE WORLD'S GREATEST COMIC MAGAZINE!
FANTASTIC FOUR
REED! BEN'S DOWN-- AND NOW THAT CREEP'S GOT MEDUSA!
DON'T GIVE UP, TORCH-- NO MATTER WHAT!
IF WE FALL-- THE WORLD IS FINISHED!
WHERE WALKS WAR-HEAD!

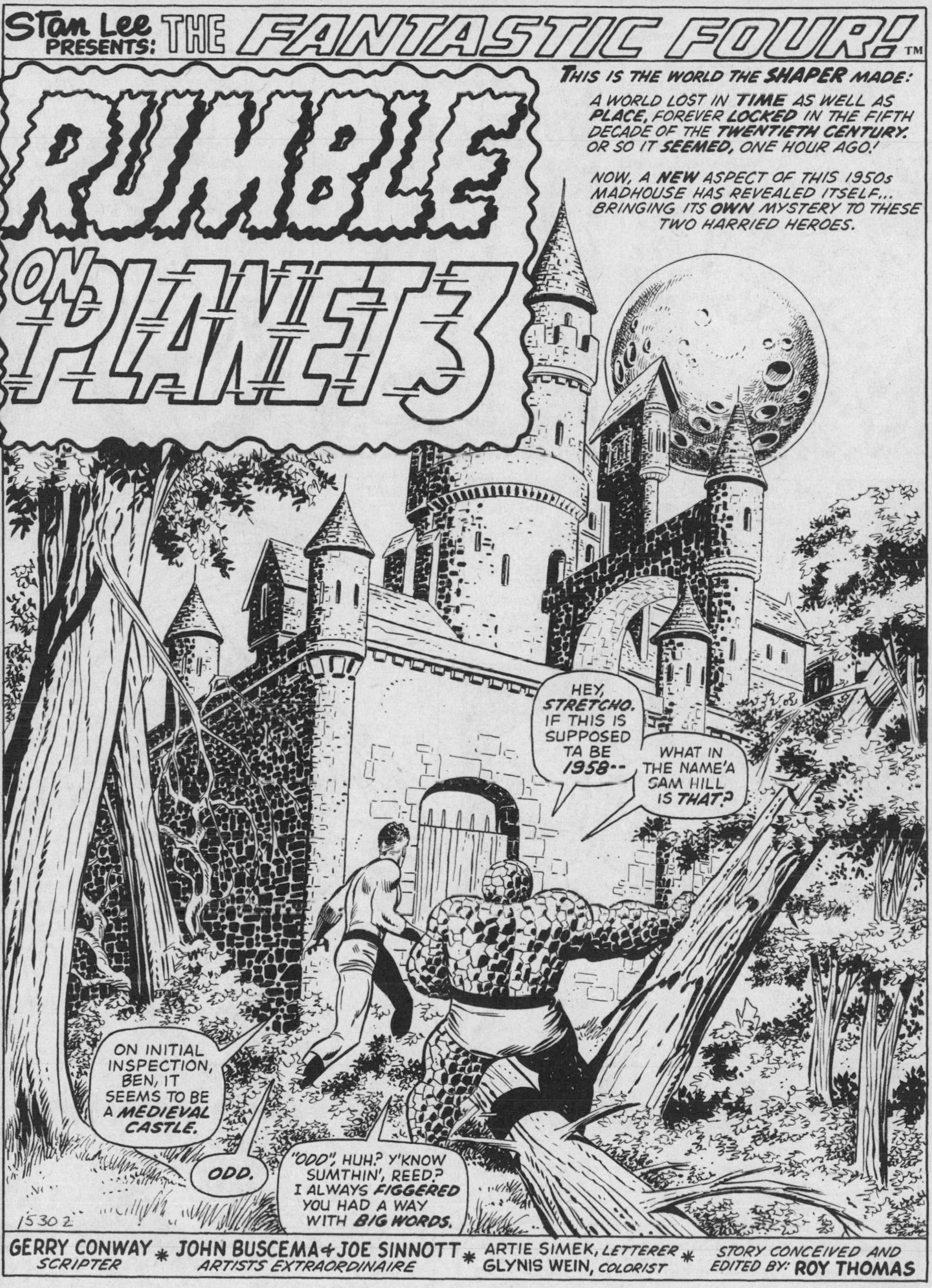

STAN LEE PRESENTS: THE FANTASTIC FOUR!™
RUMBLE ON PLANET 3
THIS IS THE WORLD THE SHAPER MADE:
A WORLD LOST IN TIME AS WELL AS PLACE, FOREVER LOCKED IN THE FIFTH DECADE OF THE TWENTIETH CENTURY. OR SO IT SEEMED, ONE HOUR AGO!
NOW, A NEW ASPECT OF THIS 1950s MADHOUSE HAS REVEALED ITSELF... BRINGING ITS OWN MYSTERY TO THESE TWO HARRIED HEROES.
HEY, STRETCHO. IF THIS IS SUPPOSED TA BE 1958--
WHAT IN THE NAME'A SAM HILL IS THAT?
ON INITIAL INSPECTION, BEN, IT SEEMS TO BE A MEDIEVAL CASTLE.
ODD.
"ODD", HUH? Y'KNOW SUMTHIN', REED? I ALWAYS FIGGERED YOU HAD A WAY WITH BIG WORDS.
15302
GERRY CONWAY SCRIPTER * JOHN BUSCEMA & JOE SINNOTT ARTISTS EXTRAORDINAIRE * ARTIE SIMEK, LETTERER GLYNIS WEIN, COLORIST * STORY CONCEIVED AND EDITED BY: ROY THOMAS

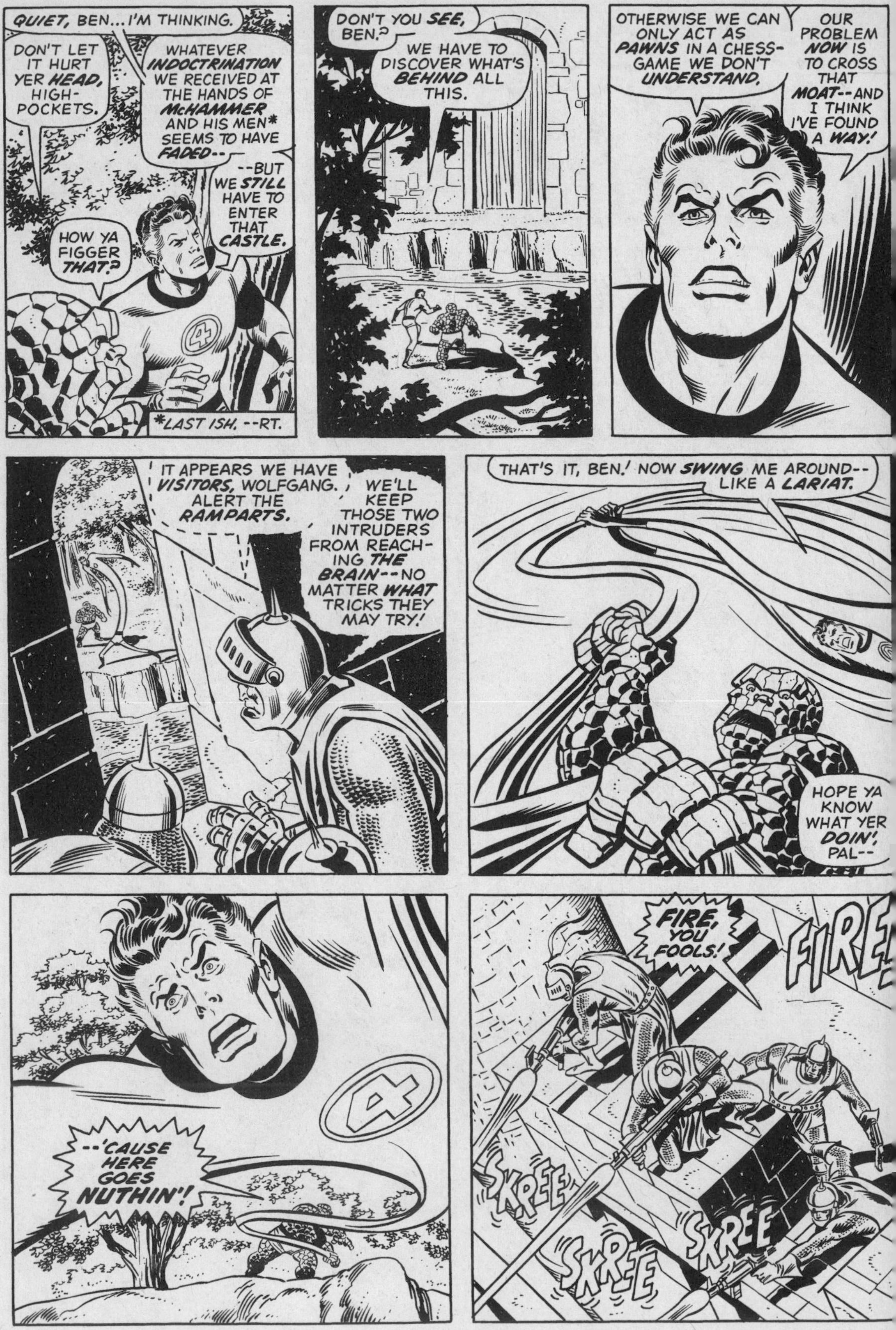

QUIET, BEN... I'M THINKING.
DON'T LET IT HURT YER HEAD, HIGH-POCKETS.
WHATEVER INDOCTRINATION WE RECEIVED AT THE HANDS OF McHAMMER AND HIS MEN* SEEMS TO HAVE FADED--
--BUT WE STILL HAVE TO ENTER THAT CASTLE.
HOW YA FIGGER THAT?
*LAST ISH. --RT.
DON'T YOU SEE, BEN?
WE HAVE TO DISCOVER WHAT'S BEHIND ALL THIS.
OTHERWISE WE CAN ONLY ACT AS PAWNS IN A CHESS-GAME WE DON'T UNDERSTAND.
OUR PROBLEM NOW IS TO CROSS THAT MOAT--AND I THINK I'VE FOUND A WAY!
IT APPEARS WE HAVE VISITORS, WOLFGANG. ALERT THE RAMPARTS.
WE'LL KEEP THOSE TWO INTRUDERS FROM REACHING THE BRAIN--NO MATTER WHAT TRICKS THEY MAY TRY!
THAT'S IT, BEN! NOW SWING ME AROUND--LIKE A LARIAT.
HOPE YA KNOW WHAT YER DOIN'! PAL--
--'CAUSE HERE GOES NUTHIN'!
FIRE, YOU FOOLS!
FIRE
SKREE
SKREE
SKREE

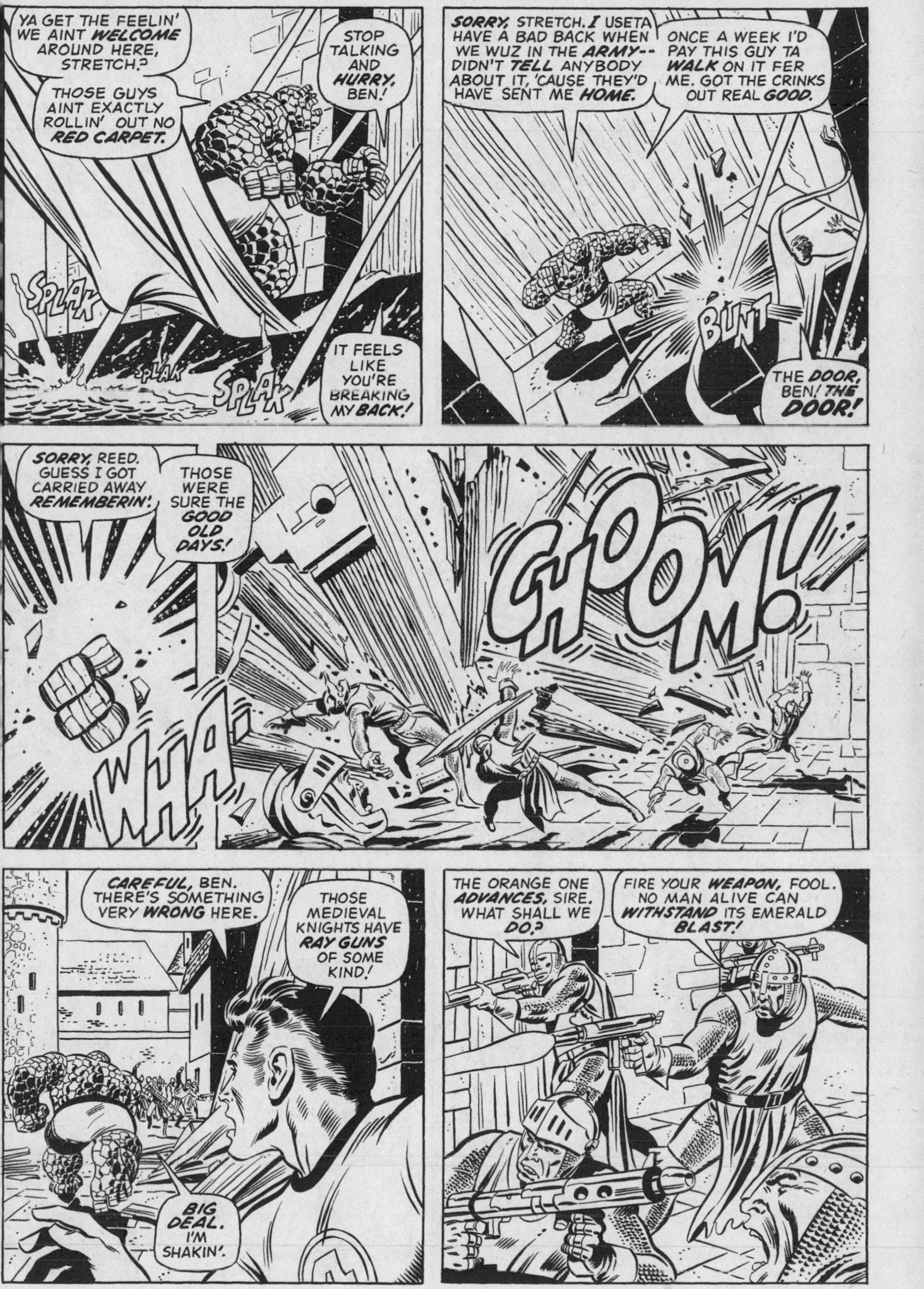
YA GET THE FEELIN' WE AINT WELCOME AROUND HERE, STRETCH?
THOSE GUYS AINT EXACTLY ROLLIN' OUT NO RED CARPET.
STOP TALKING AND HURRY, BEN!
SPLAK
SPLAK
SPLAK
IT FEELS LIKE YOU'RE BREAKING MY BACK!
SORRY, STRETCH. I USETA HAVE A BAD BACK WHEN WE WUZ IN THE ARMY-- DIDN'T TELL ANYBODY ABOUT IT, 'CAUSE THEY'D HAVE SENT ME HOME.
ONCE A WEEK I'D PAY THIS GUY TA WALK ON IT FER ME. GOT THE CRINKS OUT REAL GOOD.
BUNT
THE DOOR, BEN! THE DOOR!
SORRY, REED. GUESS I GOT CARRIED AWAY REMEMBERIN'.
THOSE WERE SURE THE GOOD OLD DAYS!
CHOOM!
WHA
CAREFUL, BEN. THERE'S SOMETHING VERY WRONG HERE.
THOSE MEDIEVAL KNIGHTS HAVE RAY GUNS OF SOME KIND!
BIG DEAL. I'M SHAKIN'.
THE ORANGE ONE ADVANCES, SIRE. WHAT SHALL WE DO?
FIRE YOUR WEAPON, FOOL. NO MAN ALIVE CAN WITHSTAND ITS EMERALD BLAST!

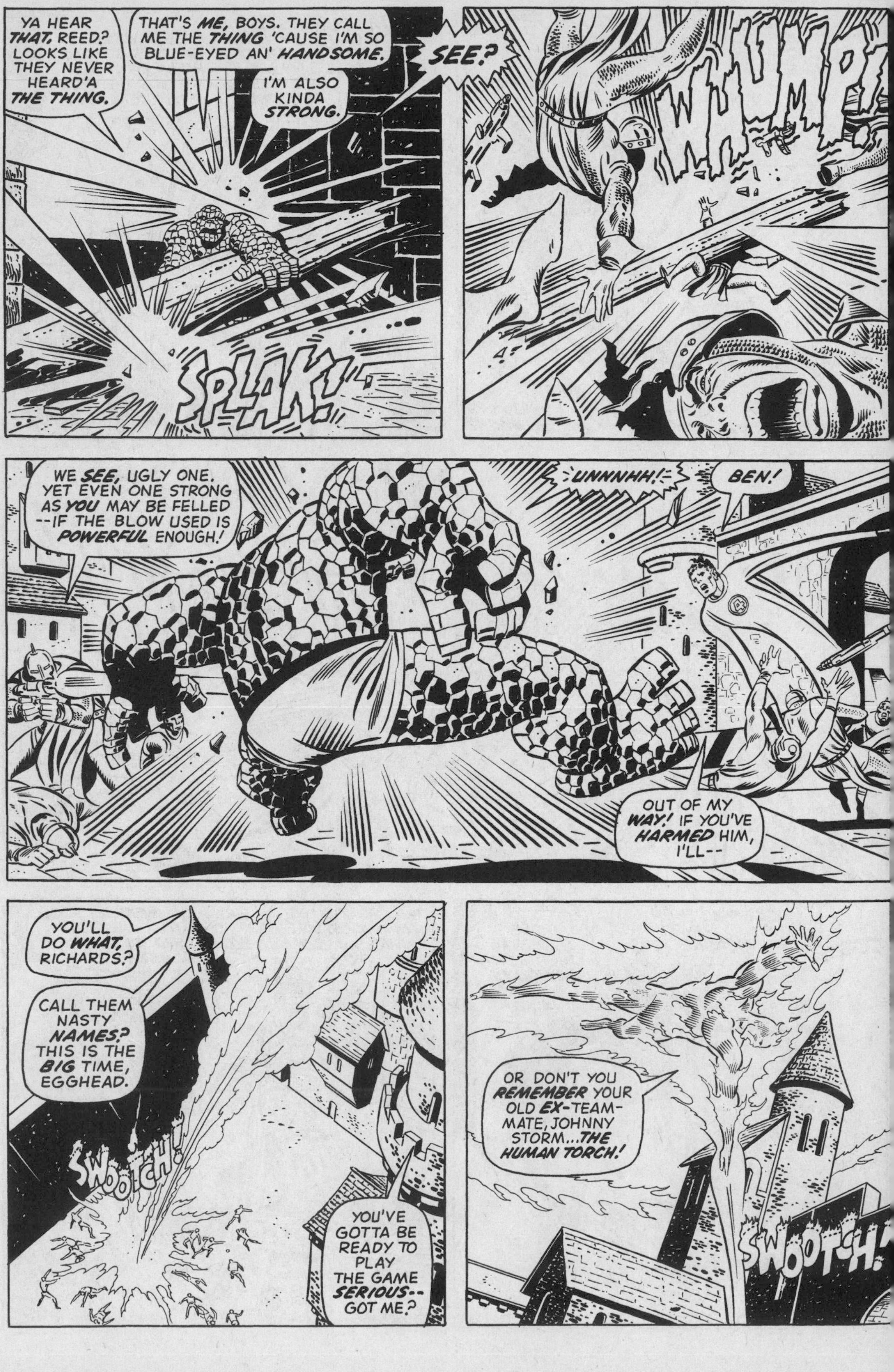

YA HEAR THAT, REED? LOOKS LIKE THEY NEVER HEARD'A THE THING.
THAT'S ME, BOYS. THEY CALL ME THE THING 'CAUSE I'M SO BLUE-EYED AN' HANDSOME.
I'M ALSO KINDA STRONG.
SPLAK!
SEE?
WHUMP!
WE SEE, UGLY ONE. YET EVEN ONE STRONG AS YOU MAY BE FELLED --IF THE BLOW USED IS POWERFUL ENOUGH!
UNNNHH!
BEN!
OUT OF MY WAY! IF YOU'VE HARMED HIM, I'LL--
YOU'LL DO WHAT, RICHARDS?
CALL THEM NASTY NAMES? THIS IS THE BIG TIME, EGGHEAD.
SWOOTCH!
YOU'VE GOTTA BE READY TO PLAY THE GAME SERIOUS-- GOT ME?
OR DON'T YOU REMEMBER YOUR OLD EX-TEAM-MATE, JOHNNY STORM...THE HUMAN TORCH!
SWOOTCH!

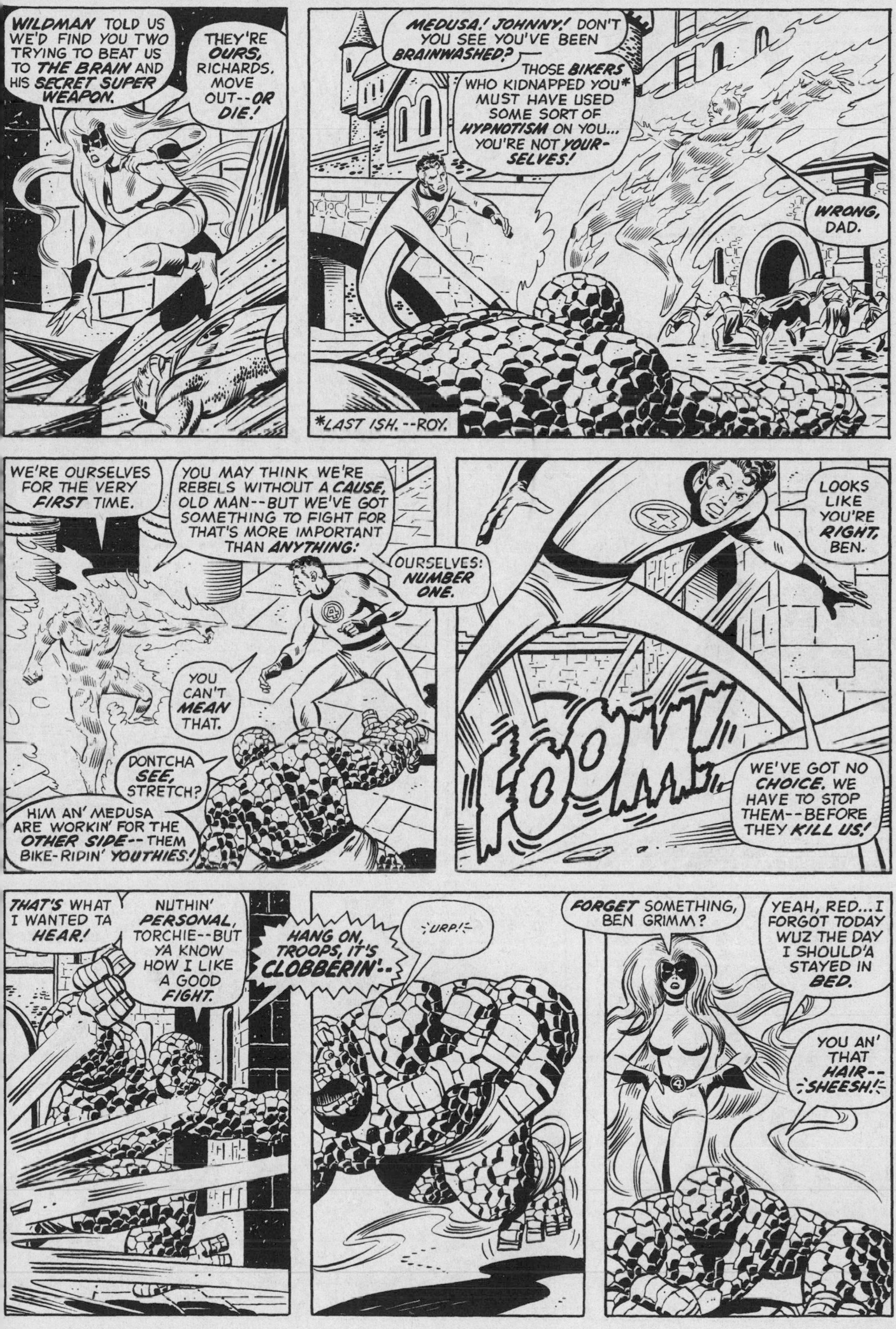

WILDMAN TOLD US WE'D FIND YOU TWO TRYING TO BEAT US TO THE BRAIN AND HIS SECRET SUPER WEAPON.
THEY'RE OURS, RICHARDS. MOVE OUT--OR DIE!
MEDUSA! JOHNNY! DON'T YOU SEE YOU'VE BEEN BRAINWASHED?
THOSE BIKERS WHO KIDNAPPED YOU* MUST HAVE USED SOME SORT OF HYPNOTISM ON YOU... YOU'RE NOT YOURSELVES!
WRONG, DAD.
*LAST ISH. --ROY.
WE'RE OURSELVES FOR THE VERY FIRST TIME.
YOU MAY THINK WE'RE REBELS WITHOUT A CAUSE, OLD MAN--BUT WE'VE GOT SOMETHING TO FIGHT FOR THAT'S MORE IMPORTANT THAN ANYTHING:
OURSELVES: NUMBER ONE.
YOU CAN'T MEAN THAT.
DONTCHA SEE, STRETCH?
HIM AN' MEDUSA ARE WORKIN' FOR THE OTHER SIDE--THEM BIKE-RIDIN' YOUTHIES!
LOOKS LIKE YOU'RE RIGHT, BEN.
FOOM!
WE'VE GOT NO CHOICE. WE HAVE TO STOP THEM--BEFORE THEY KILL US!
THAT'S WHAT I WANTED TA HEAR!
NUTHIN' PERSONAL, TORCHIE--BUT YA KNOW HOW I LIKE A GOOD FIGHT.
HANG ON, TROOPS, IT'S CLOBBERIN'..
URP!
FORGET SOMETHING, BEN GRIMM?
YEAH, RED...I FORGOT TODAY WUZ THE DAY I SHOULD'A STAYED IN BED.
YOU AN' THAT HAIR-- SHEESH!

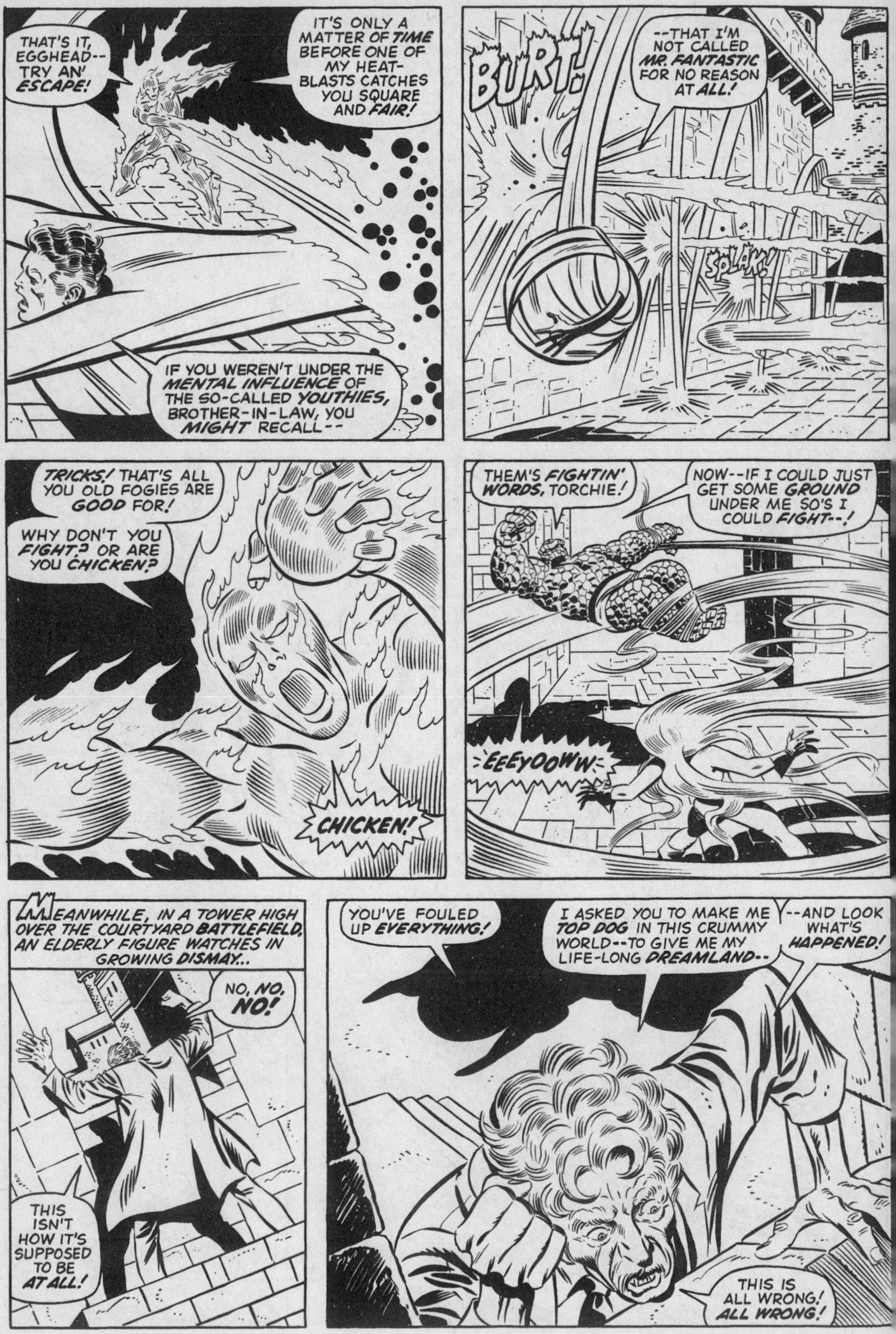
THAT'S IT, EGGHEAD-- TRY AN' ESCAPE!
IT'S ONLY A MATTER OF TIME BEFORE ONE OF MY HEAT-BLASTS CATCHES YOU SQUARE AND FAIR!
IF YOU WEREN'T UNDER THE MENTAL INFLUENCE OF THE SO-CALLED YOUTHIES, BROTHER-IN-LAW, YOU MIGHT RECALL--
BURT!
--THAT I'M NOT CALLED MR. FANTASTIC FOR NO REASON AT ALL!
SPLAK!
TRICKS! THAT'S ALL YOU OLD FOGIES ARE GOOD FOR!
WHY DON'T YOU FIGHT? OR ARE YOU CHICKEN?
CHICKEN!
THEM'S FIGHTIN' WORDS, TORCHIE!
NOW--IF I COULD JUST GET SOME GROUND UNDER ME SO'S I COULD FIGHT--!
EEEYOOWW
MEANWHILE, IN A TOWER HIGH OVER THE COURTYARD BATTLEFIELD, AN ELDERLY FIGURE WATCHES IN GROWING DISMAY...
NO, NO, NO!
THIS ISN'T HOW IT'S SUPPOSED TO BE AT ALL!
YOU'VE FOULED UP EVERYTHING!
I ASKED YOU TO MAKE ME TOP DOG IN THIS CRUMMY WORLD--TO GIVE ME MY LIFE-LONG DREAMLAND--
--AND LOOK WHAT'S HAPPENED!
THIS IS ALL WRONG! ALL WRONG!

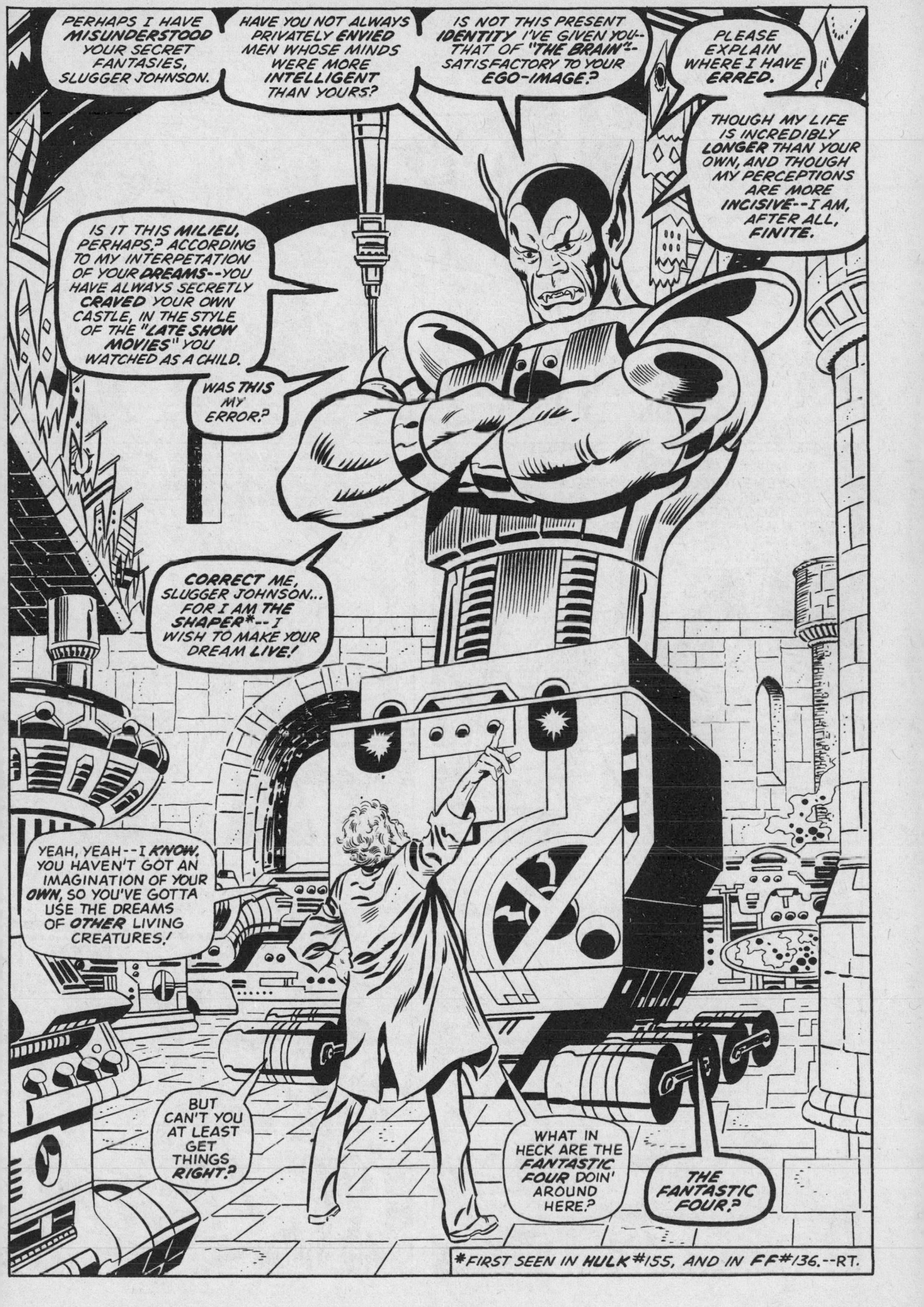

PERHAPS I HAVE MISUNDERSTOOD YOUR SECRET FANTASIES, SLUGGER JOHNSON.
HAVE YOU NOT ALWAYS PRIVATELY ENVIED MEN WHOSE MINDS WERE MORE INTELLIGENT THAN YOURS?
IS NOT THIS PRESENT IDENTITY I'VE GIVEN YOU--THAT OF "THE BRAIN"--SATISFACTORY TO YOUR EGO-IMAGE?
PLEASE EXPLAIN WHERE I HAVE ERRED.
THOUGH MY LIFE IS INCREDIBLY LONGER THAN YOUR OWN, AND THOUGH MY PERCEPTIONS ARE MORE INCISIVE--I AM, AFTER ALL, FINITE.
IS IT THIS MILIEU, PERHAPS? ACCORDING TO MY INTERPETATION OF YOUR DREAMS--YOU HAVE ALWAYS SECRETLY CRAVED YOUR OWN CASTLE, IN THE STYLE OF THE "LATE SHOW MOVIES" YOU WATCHED AS A CHILD.
WAS THIS MY ERROR?
CORRECT ME, SLUGGER JOHNSON... FOR I AM THE SHAPER*--I WISH TO MAKE YOUR DREAM LIVE!
YEAH, YEAH--I KNOW. YOU HAVEN'T GOT AN IMAGINATION OF YOUR OWN, SO YOU'VE GOTTA USE THE DREAMS OF OTHER LIVING CREATURES!
BUT CAN'T YOU AT LEAST GET THINGS RIGHT?
WHAT IN HECK ARE THE FANTASTIC FOUR DOIN' AROUND HERE?
THE FANTASTIC FOUR?
*FIRST SEEN IN HULK #155, AND IN FF #136.--RT.

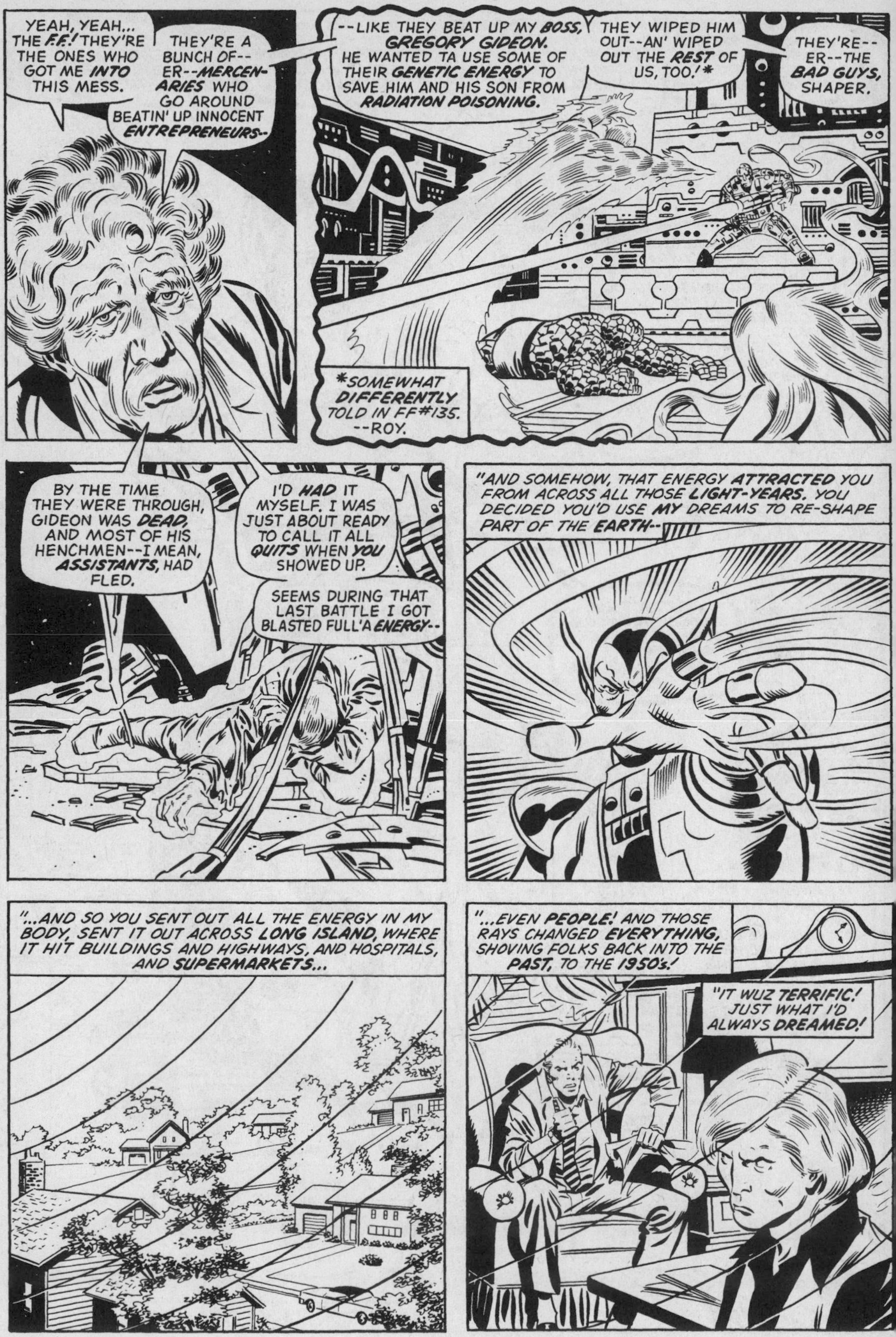
YEAH, YEAH... THE F.F.! THEY'RE THE ONES WHO GOT ME INTO THIS MESS.
THEY'RE A BUNCH OF-- ER--MERCENARIES WHO GO AROUND BEATIN' UP INNOCENT ENTREPRENEURS--
--LIKE THEY BEAT UP MY BOSS, GREGORY GIDEON. HE WANTED TA USE SOME OF THEIR GENETIC ENERGY TO SAVE HIM AND HIS SON FROM RADIATION POISONING.
THEY WIPED HIM OUT--AN' WIPED OUT THE REST OF US, TOO!*
THEY'RE-- ER--THE BAD GUYS, SHAPER.
*SOMEWHAT DIFFERENTLY TOLD IN FF#135. --ROY.
BY THE TIME THEY WERE THROUGH, GIDEON WAS DEAD, AND MOST OF HIS HENCHMEN--I MEAN, ASSISTANTS, HAD FLED.
I'D HAD IT MYSELF. I WAS JUST ABOUT READY TO CALL IT ALL QUITS WHEN YOU SHOWED UP.
SEEMS DURING THAT LAST BATTLE I GOT BLASTED FULL'A ENERGY--
"AND SOMEHOW, THAT ENERGY ATTRACTED YOU FROM ACROSS ALL THOSE LIGHT-YEARS. YOU DECIDED YOU'D USE MY DREAMS TO RE-SHAPE PART OF THE EARTH--
"...AND SO YOU SENT OUT ALL THE ENERGY IN MY BODY, SENT IT OUT ACROSS LONG ISLAND, WHERE IT HIT BUILDINGS AND HIGHWAYS, AND HOSPITALS, AND SUPERMARKETS...
"...EVEN PEOPLE! AND THOSE RAYS CHANGED EVERYTHING, SHOVING FOLKS BACK INTO THE PAST, TO THE 1950's!
"IT WUZ TERRIFIC! JUST WHAT I'D ALWAYS DREAMED!

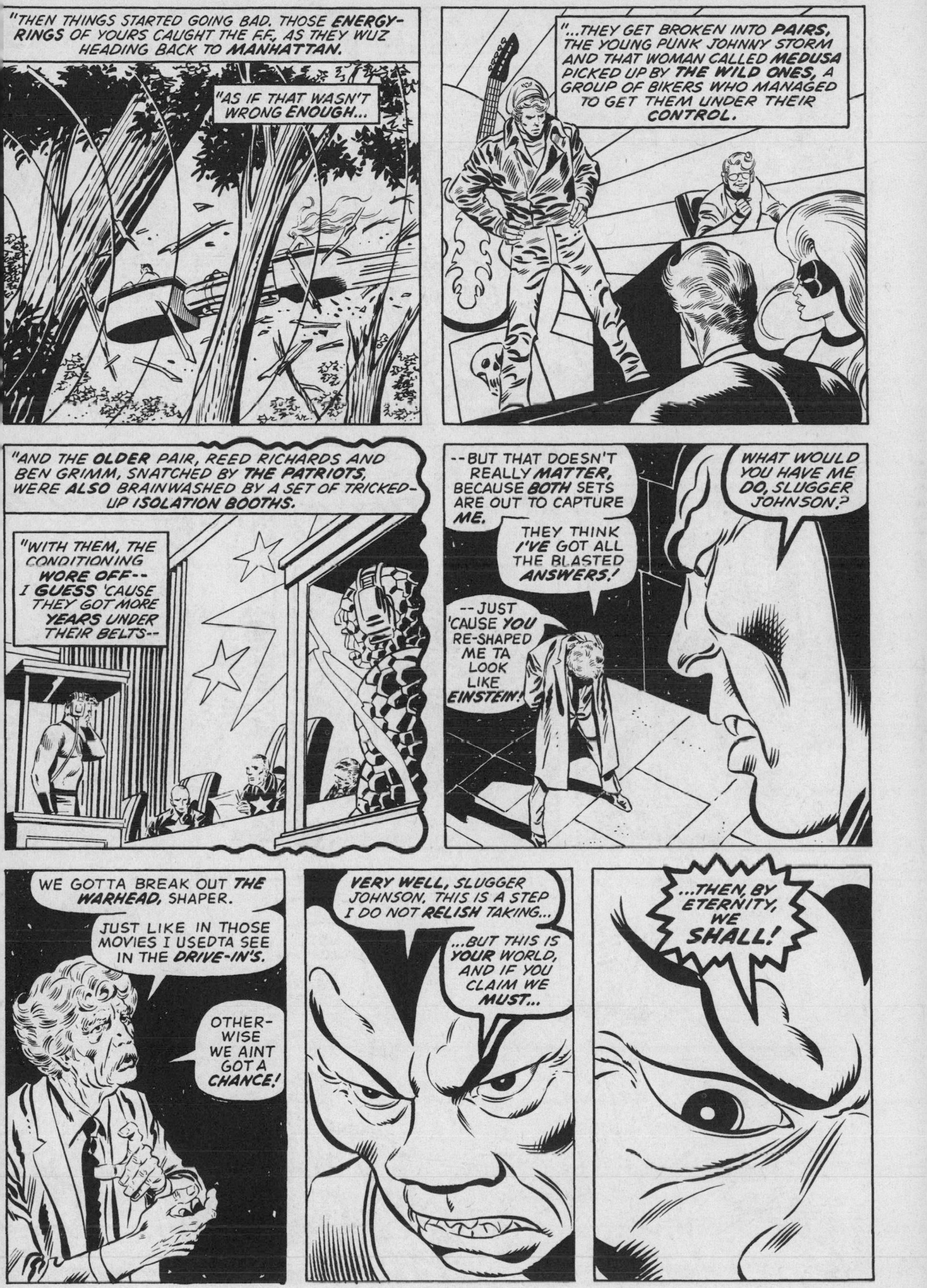
"THEN THINGS STARTED GOING BAD. THOSE ENERGY-RINGS OF YOURS CAUGHT THE F.F., AS THEY WUZ HEADING BACK TO MANHATTAN.
"AS IF THAT WASN'T WRONG ENOUGH...
"...THEY GET BROKEN INTO PAIRS, THE YOUNG PUNK JOHNNY STORM AND THAT WOMAN CALLED MEDUSA PICKED UP BY THE WILD ONES, A GROUP OF BIKERS WHO MANAGED TO GET THEM UNDER THEIR CONTROL.
"AND THE OLDER PAIR, REED RICHARDS AND BEN GRIMM, SNATCHED BY THE PATRIOTS, WERE ALSO BRAINWASHED BY A SET OF TRICKED-UP ISOLATION BOOTHS.
"WITH THEM, THE CONDITIONING WORE OFF-- I GUESS 'CAUSE THEY GOT MORE YEARS UNDER THEIR BELTS--
--BUT THAT DOESN'T REALLY MATTER, BECAUSE BOTH SETS ARE OUT TO CAPTURE ME.
THEY THINK I'VE GOT ALL THE BLASTED ANSWERS!
--JUST 'CAUSE YOU RE-SHAPED ME TA LOOK LIKE EINSTEIN!
WHAT WOULD YOU HAVE ME DO, SLUGGER JOHNSON?
WE GOTTA BREAK OUT THE WARHEAD, SHAPER.
JUST LIKE IN THOSE MOVIES I USEDTA SEE IN THE DRIVE-IN'S.
OTHER-WISE WE AINT GOT A CHANCE!
VERY WELL, SLUGGER JOHNSON. THIS IS A STEP I DO NOT RELISH TAKING...
...BUT THIS IS YOUR WORLD, AND IF YOU CLAIM WE MUST...
...THEN, BY ETERNITY, WE SHALL!

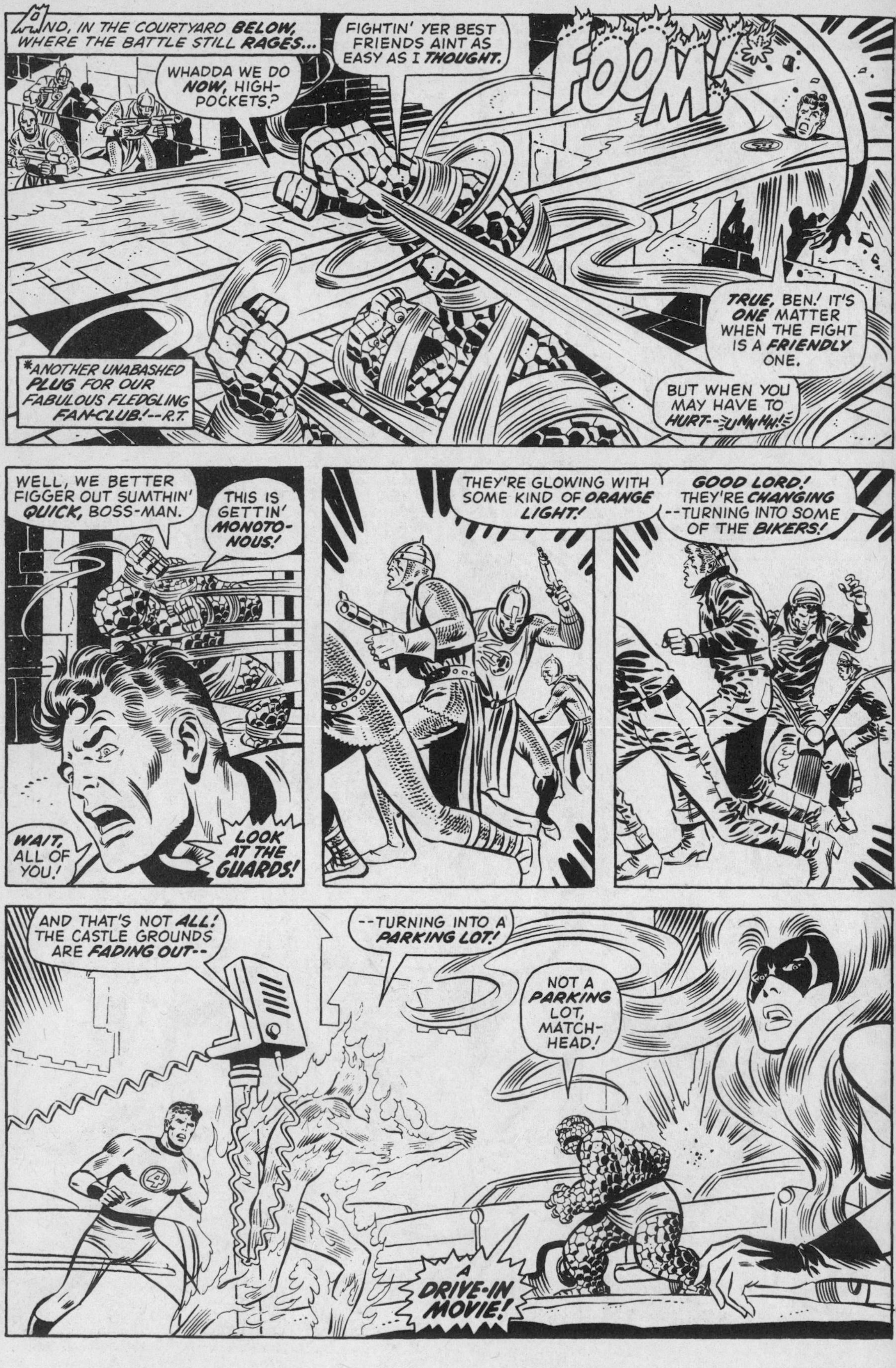
AND, IN THE COURTYARD BELOW, WHERE THE BATTLE STILL RAGES...
WHADDA WE DO NOW, HIGH-POCKETS?
FIGHTIN' YER BEST FRIENDS AINT AS EASY AS I THOUGHT.
FOOM!
TRUE, BEN! IT'S ONE MATTER WHEN THE FIGHT IS A FRIENDLY ONE.
BUT WHEN YOU MAY HAVE TO HURT--UNNHH!
*ANOTHER UNABASHED PLUG FOR OUR FABULOUS FLEDGLING FAN-CLUB!--R.T.
WELL, WE BETTER FIGGER OUT SUMTHIN' QUICK, BOSS-MAN.
THIS IS GETTIN' MONOTONOUS!
WAIT, ALL OF YOU!
LOOK AT THE GUARDS!
THEY'RE GLOWING WITH SOME KIND OF ORANGE LIGHT!
GOOD LORD! THEY'RE CHANGING --TURNING INTO SOME OF THE BIKERS!
AND THAT'S NOT ALL! THE CASTLE GROUNDS ARE FADING OUT--
--TURNING INTO A PARKING LOT!
NOT A PARKING LOT, MATCH-HEAD!
A DRIVE-IN MOVIE!

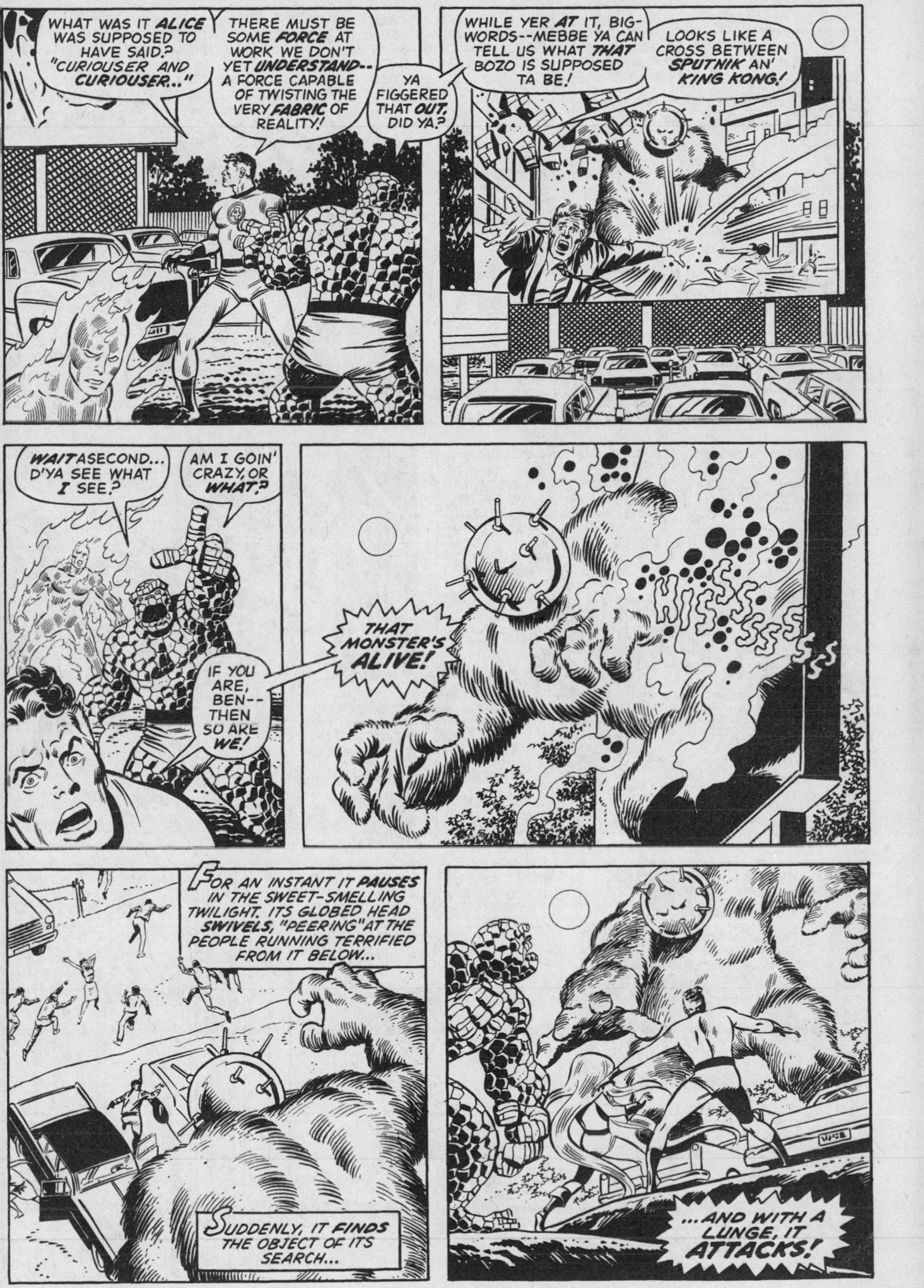
WHAT WAS IT ALICE WAS SUPPOSED TO HAVE SAID? "CURIOUSER AND CURIOUSER..."
THERE MUST BE SOME FORCE AT WORK WE DON'T YET UNDERSTAND-- A FORCE CAPABLE OF TWISTING THE VERY FABRIC OF REALITY!
YA FIGGERED THAT OUT, DID YA?
WHILE YER AT IT, BIG-WORDS--MEBBE YA CAN TELL US WHAT THAT BOZO IS SUPPOSED TA BE!
LOOKS LIKE A CROSS BETWEEN SPUTNIK AN' KING KONG!
WAIT A SECOND... D'YA SEE WHAT I SEE?
AM I GOIN' CRAZY, OR WHAT?
THAT MONSTER'S ALIVE!
IF YOU ARE, BEN-- THEN SO ARE WE!
HISSSSSSS
FOR AN INSTANT IT PAUSES IN THE SWEET-SMELLING TWILIGHT. ITS GLOBED HEAD SWIVELS, "PEERING" AT THE PEOPLE RUNNING TERRIFIED FROM IT BELOW...
SUDDENLY, IT FINDS THE OBJECT OF ITS SEARCH...
...AND WITH A LUNGE, IT ATTACKS!

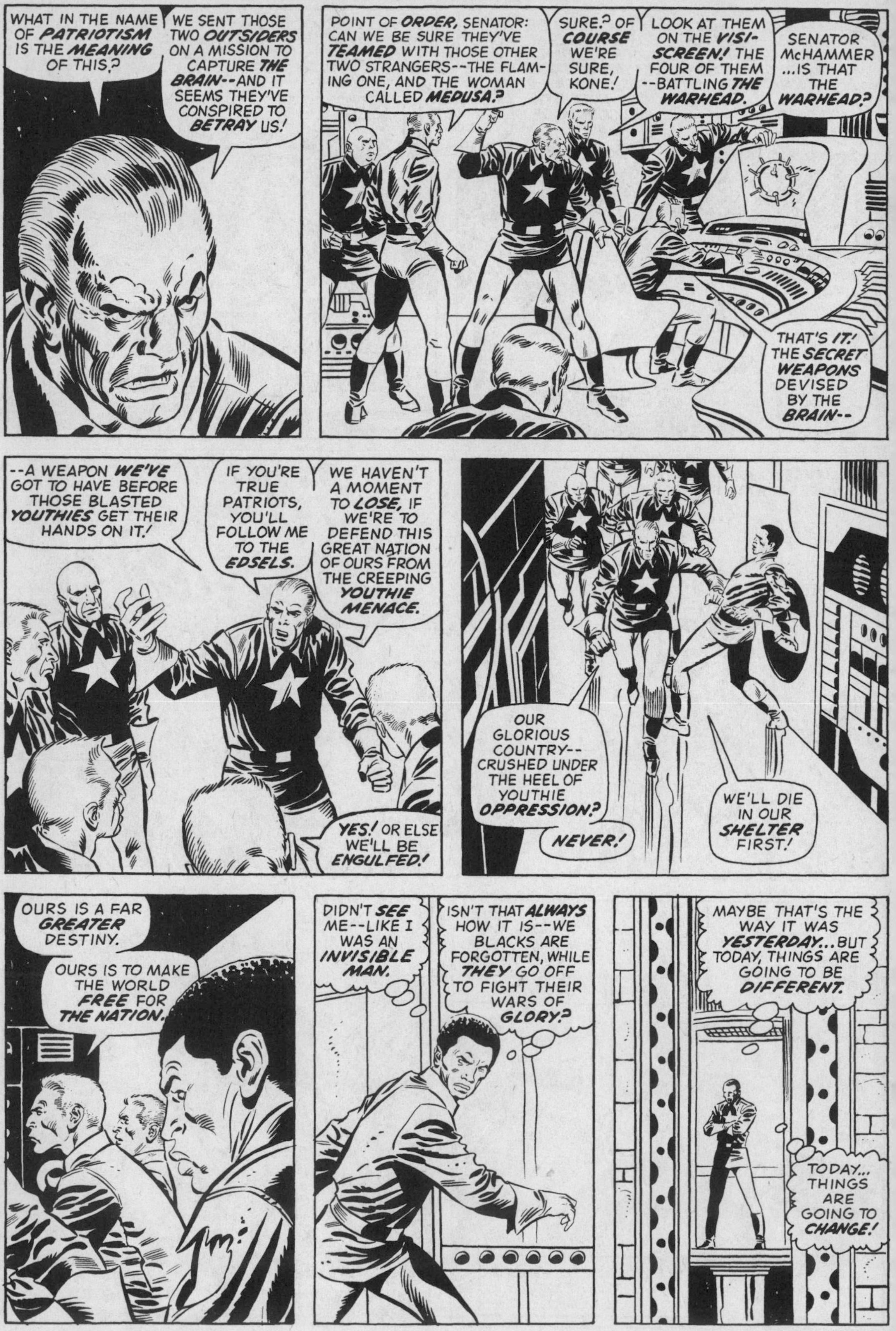
WHAT IN THE NAME OF PATRIOTISM IS THE MEANING OF THIS?
WE SENT THOSE TWO OUTSIDERS ON A MISSION TO CAPTURE THE BRAIN--AND IT SEEMS THEY'VE CONSPIRED TO BETRAY US!
POINT OF ORDER, SENATOR: CAN WE BE SURE THEY'VE TEAMED WITH THOSE OTHER TWO STRANGERS--THE FLAMING ONE, AND THE WOMAN CALLED MEDUSA?
SURE? OF COURSE WE'RE SURE, KONE!
LOOK AT THEM ON THE VISI-SCREEN! THE FOUR OF THEM --BATTLING THE WARHEAD.
SENATOR McHAMMER ...IS THAT THE WARHEAD?
THAT'S IT! THE SECRET WEAPONS DEVISED BY THE BRAIN--
--A WEAPON WE'VE GOT TO HAVE BEFORE THOSE BLASTED YOUTHIES GET THEIR HANDS ON IT!
IF YOU'RE TRUE PATRIOTS, YOU'LL FOLLOW ME TO THE EDSELS.
WE HAVEN'T A MOMENT TO LOSE, IF WE'RE TO DEFEND THIS GREAT NATION OF OURS FROM THE CREEPING YOUTHIE MENACE.
YES! OR ELSE WE'LL BE ENGULFED!
OUR GLORIOUS COUNTRY--CRUSHED UNDER THE HEEL OF YOUTHIE OPPRESSION?
NEVER!
WE'LL DIE IN OUR SHELTER FIRST!
OURS IS A FAR GREATER DESTINY.
OURS IS TO MAKE THE WORLD FREE FOR THE NATION.
DIDN'T SEE ME--LIKE I WAS AN INVISIBLE MAN.
ISN'T THAT ALWAYS HOW IT IS--WE BLACKS ARE FORGOTTEN, WHILE THEY GO OFF TO FIGHT THEIR WARS OF GLORY?
MAYBE THAT'S THE WAY IT WAS YESTERDAY... BUT TODAY, THINGS ARE GOING TO BE DIFFERENT.
TODAY... THINGS ARE GOING TO CHANGE!

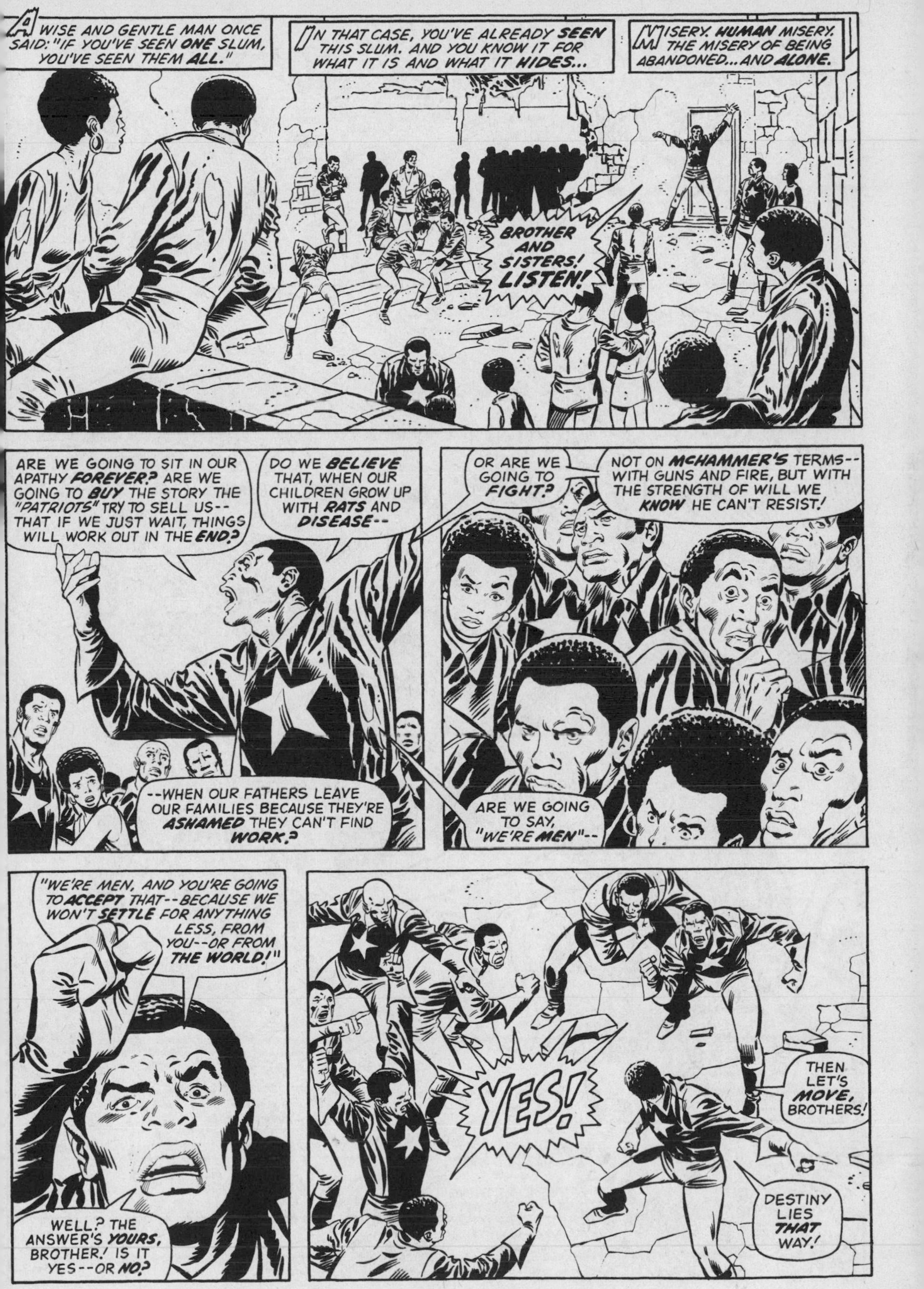
A WISE AND GENTLE MAN ONCE SAID: "IF YOU'VE SEEN ONE SLUM, YOU'VE SEEN THEM ALL."
IN THAT CASE, YOU'VE ALREADY SEEN THIS SLUM. AND YOU KNOW IT FOR WHAT IT IS AND WHAT IT HIDES...
MISERY. HUMAN MISERY. THE MISERY OF BEING ABANDONED...AND ALONE.
BROTHER AND SISTERS! LISTEN!
ARE WE GOING TO SIT IN OUR APATHY FOREVER? ARE WE GOING TO BUY THE STORY THE "PATRIOTS" TRY TO SELL US--THAT IF WE JUST WAIT, THINGS WILL WORK OUT IN THE END?
DO WE BELIEVE THAT, WHEN OUR CHILDREN GROW UP WITH RATS AND DISEASE--
--WHEN OUR FATHERS LEAVE OUR FAMILIES BECAUSE THEY'RE ASHAMED THEY CAN'T FIND WORK?
OR ARE WE GOING TO FIGHT?
NOT ON MCHAMMER'S TERMS--WITH GUNS AND FIRE, BUT WITH THE STRENGTH OF WILL WE KNOW HE CAN'T RESIST!
ARE WE GOING TO SAY, "WE'RE MEN"--
"WE'RE MEN, AND YOU'RE GOING TO ACCEPT THAT--BECAUSE WE WON'T SETTLE FOR ANYTHING LESS, FROM YOU--OR FROM THE WORLD!"
WELL? THE ANSWER'S YOURS, BROTHER! IS IT YES--OR NO?
YES!
THEN LET'S MOVE, BROTHERS!
DESTINY LIES THAT WAY!

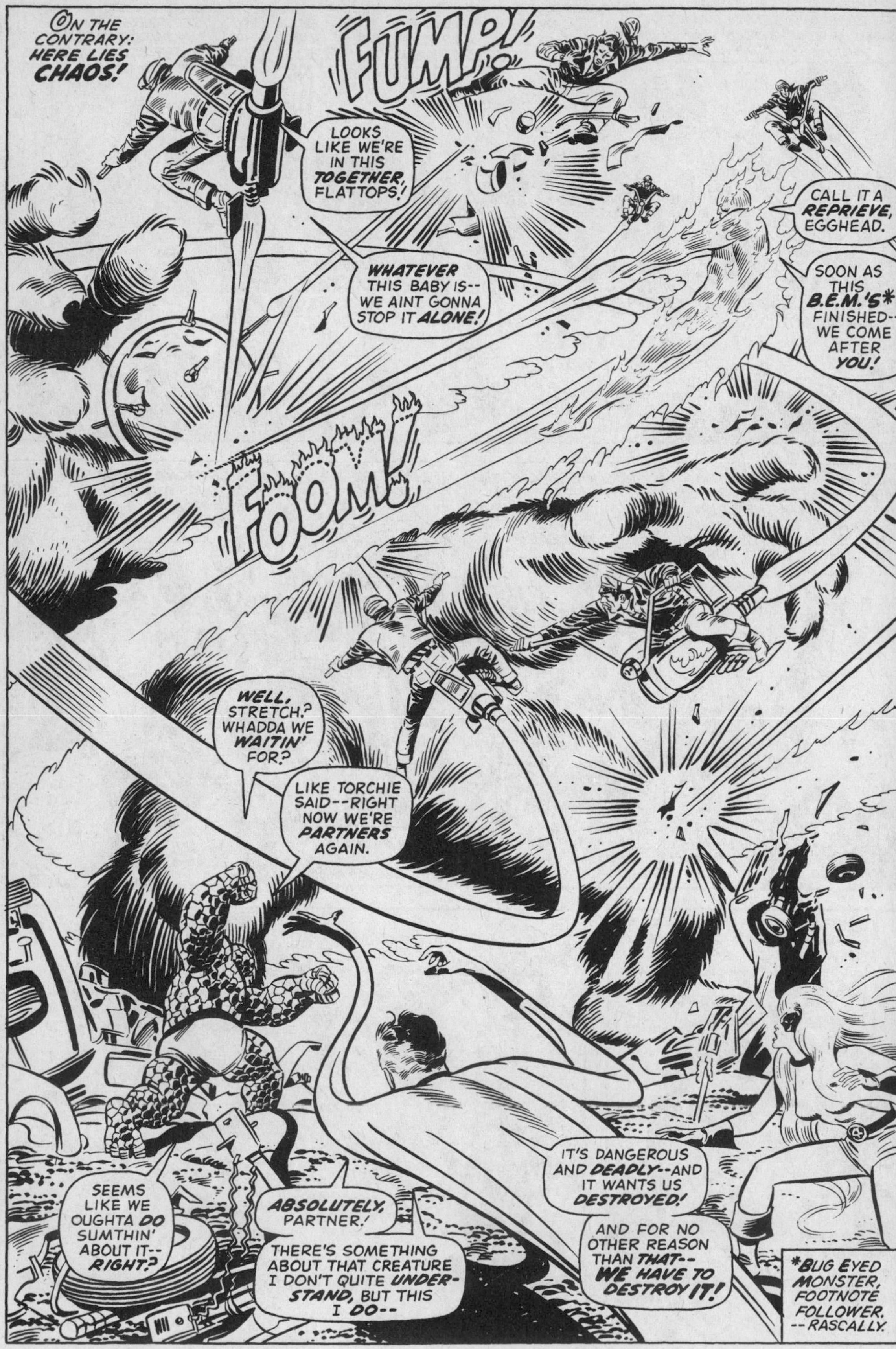
ON THE CONTRARY: HERE LIES CHAOS!
FUMP!
LOOKS LIKE WE'RE IN THIS TOGETHER, FLATTOPS!
WHATEVER THIS BABY IS-- WE AINT GONNA STOP IT ALONE!
CALL IT A REPRIEVE, EGGHEAD.
SOON AS THIS B.E.M.'S* FINISHED-- WE COME AFTER YOU!
FOOM!
WELL, STRETCH? WHADDA WE WAITIN' FOR?
LIKE TORCHIE SAID--RIGHT NOW WE'RE PARTNERS AGAIN.
SEEMS LIKE WE OUGHTA DO SUMTHIN' ABOUT IT--RIGHT?
ABSOLUTELY, PARTNER!
THERE'S SOMETHING ABOUT THAT CREATURE I DON'T QUITE UNDER-STAND, BUT THIS I DO--
IT'S DANGEROUS AND DEADLY--AND IT WANTS US DESTROYED!
AND FOR NO OTHER REASON THAN THAT-- WE HAVE TO DESTROY IT!
*BUG EYED MONSTER, FOOTNOTE FOLLOWER. --RASCALLY.

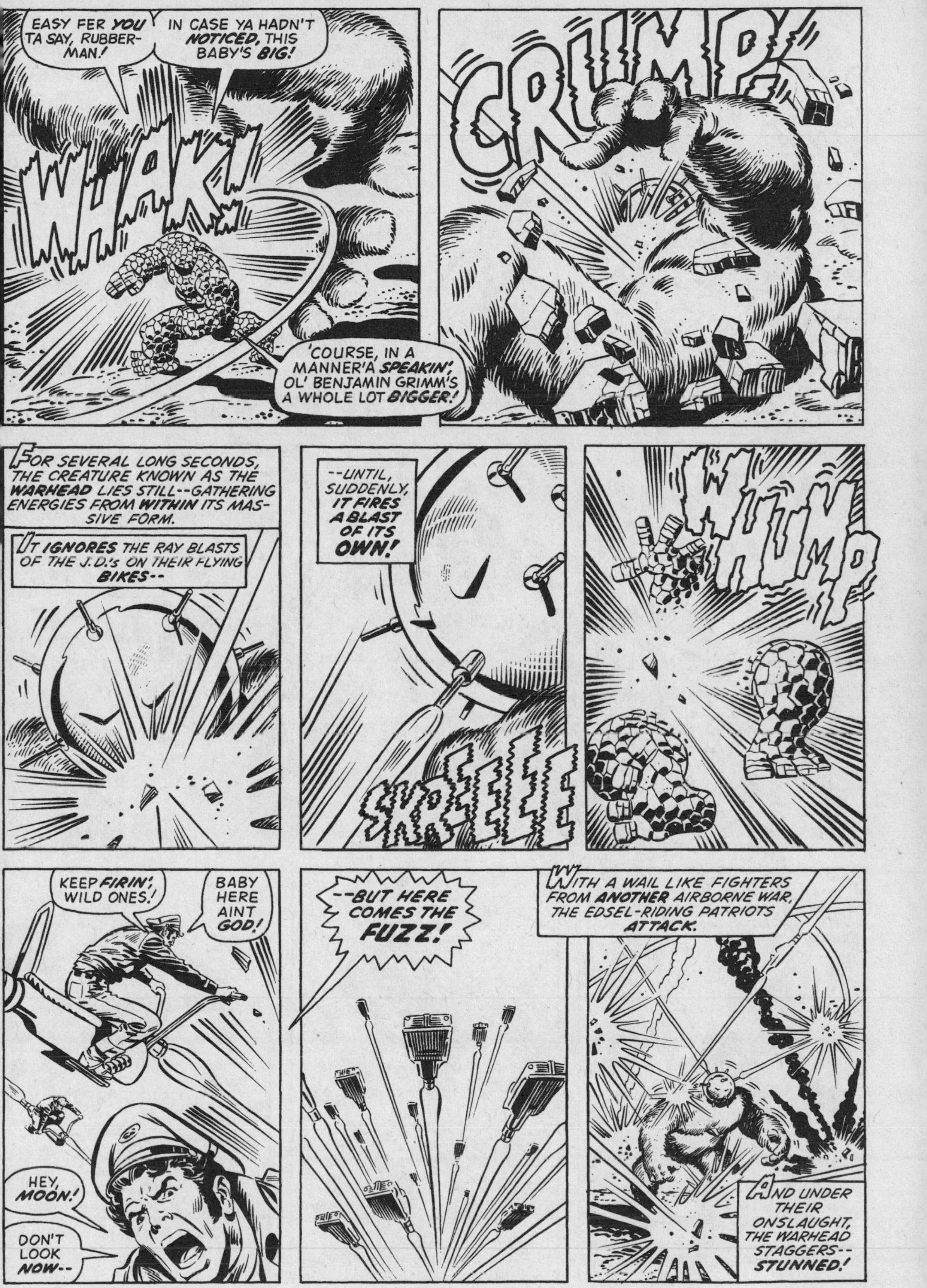
EASY FER YOU TA SAY, RUBBER-MAN!
IN CASE YA HADN'T NOTICED, THIS BABY'S BIG!
WAK!
'COURSE, IN A MANNER'A SPEAKIN', OL' BENJAMIN GRIMM'S A WHOLE LOT BIGGER!
CRUMP!
FOR SEVERAL LONG SECONDS, THE CREATURE KNOWN AS THE WARHEAD LIES STILL--GATHERING ENERGIES FROM WITHIN ITS MASSIVE FORM.
IT IGNORES THE RAY BLASTS OF THE J.D.'s ON THEIR FLYING BIKES--
--UNTIL, SUDDENLY, IT FIRES A BLAST OF ITS OWN!
SKREELE
WHUMP
KEEP FIRIN', WILD ONES!
BABY HERE AINT GOD!
HEY, MOON!
DON'T LOOK NOW--
--BUT HERE COMES THE FUZZ!
WITH A WAIL LIKE FIGHTERS FROM ANOTHER AIRBORNE WAR, THE EDSEL-RIDING PATRIOTS ATTACK.
AND UNDER THEIR ONSLAUGHT, THE WARHEAD STAGGERS--STUNNED!

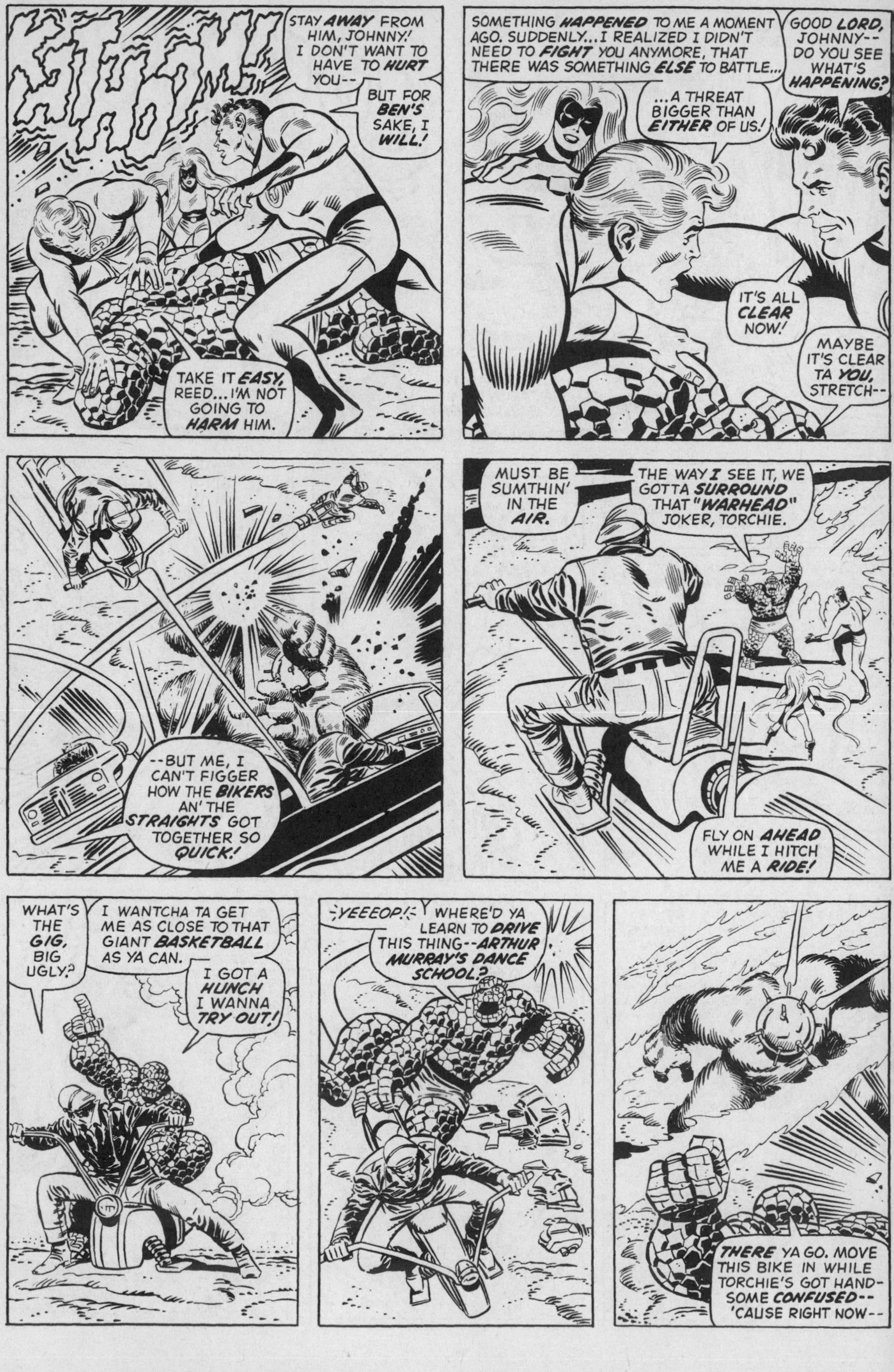
STHOOM!
STAY AWAY FROM HIM, JOHNNY! I DON'T WANT TO HAVE TO HURT YOU--
BUT FOR BEN'S SAKE, I WILL!
TAKE IT EASY, REED... I'M NOT GOING TO HARM HIM.
SOMETHING HAPPENED TO ME A MOMENT AGO. SUDDENLY... I REALIZED I DIDN'T NEED TO FIGHT YOU ANYMORE, THAT THERE WAS SOMETHING ELSE TO BATTLE...
...A THREAT BIGGER THAN EITHER OF US!
GOOD LORD, JOHNNY-- DO YOU SEE WHAT'S HAPPENING?
IT'S ALL CLEAR NOW!
MAYBE IT'S CLEAR TA YOU, STRETCH--
--BUT ME, I CAN'T FIGGER HOW THE BIKERS AN' THE STRAIGHTS GOT TOGETHER SO QUICK!
MUST BE SUMTHIN' IN THE AIR.
THE WAY I SEE IT, WE GOTTA SURROUND THAT "WARHEAD" JOKER, TORCHIE.
FLY ON AHEAD WHILE I HITCH ME A RIDE!
WHAT'S THE GIG, BIG UGLY?
I WANTCHA TA GET ME AS CLOSE TO THAT GIANT BASKETBALL AS YA CAN.
I GOT A HUNCH I WANNA TRY OUT!
-YEEEOP!-
WHERE'D YA LEARN TO DRIVE THIS THING--ARTHUR MURRAY'S DANCE SCHOOL?
THERE YA GO. MOVE THIS BIKE IN WHILE TORCHIE'S GOT HAND-SOME CONFUSED-- 'CAUSE RIGHT NOW--

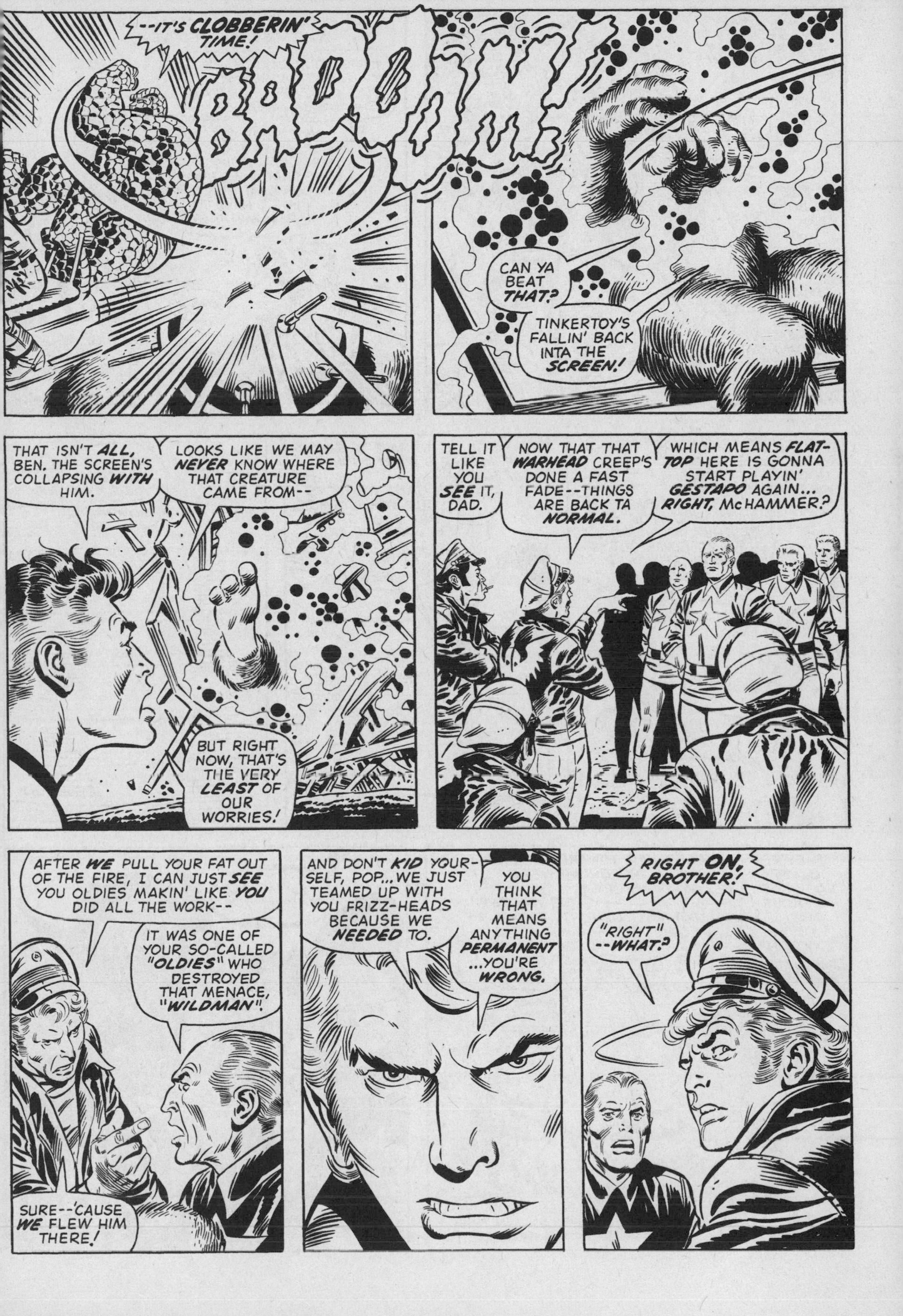
--IT'S CLOBBERIN' TIME!
BADOOM!
CAN YA BEAT THAT?
TINKERTOY'S FALLIN' BACK INTA THE SCREEN!
THAT ISN'T ALL, BEN. THE SCREEN'S COLLAPSING WITH HIM.
LOOKS LIKE WE MAY NEVER KNOW WHERE THAT CREATURE CAME FROM--
BUT RIGHT NOW, THAT'S THE VERY LEAST OF OUR WORRIES!
TELL IT LIKE YOU SEE IT, DAD.
NOW THAT THAT WARHEAD CREEP'S DONE A FAST FADE--THINGS ARE BACK TA NORMAL.
WHICH MEANS FLAT-TOP HERE IS GONNA START PLAYIN' GESTAPO AGAIN... RIGHT, McHAMMER?
AFTER WE PULL YOUR FAT OUT OF THE FIRE, I CAN JUST SEE YOU OLDIES MAKIN' LIKE YOU DID ALL THE WORK--
IT WAS ONE OF YOUR SO-CALLED "OLDIES" WHO DESTROYED THAT MENACE, "WILDMAN".
SURE--'CAUSE WE FLEW HIM THERE!
AND DON'T KID YOURSELF, POP...WE JUST TEAMED UP WITH YOU FRIZZ-HEADS BECAUSE WE NEEDED TO.
YOU THINK THAT MEANS ANYTHING PERMANENT ...YOU'RE WRONG.
RIGHT ON, BROTHER!
"RIGHT" --WHAT?

WE SAID, "RIGHT ON, BROTHER," AND WE MEAN WHAT WE SAY!

THINGS ARE GOING TO BE DIFFERENT FROM NOW ON. YOU KNOW IT.

YOU TELL HIM, MARTY!

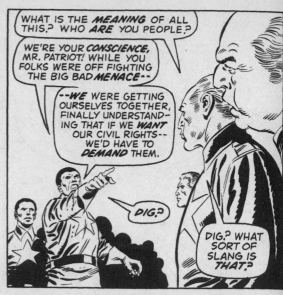

WHAT IS THE MEANING OF ALL THIS? WHO ARE YOU PEOPLE?

WE'RE YOUR CONSCIENCE, MR. PATRIOT! WHILE YOU FOLKS WERE OFF FIGHTING THE BIG BAD MENACE--

--WE WERE GETTING OURSELVES TOGETHER, FINALLY UNDERSTANDING THAT IF WE WANT OUR CIVIL RIGHTS-- WE'D HAVE TO DEMAND THEM.

DIG?

DIG? WHAT SORT OF SLANG IS THAT?

IT'S THE SLANG OF THE SIXTIES, MISTER--AND THAT'S WHERE WE ARE NOW!

NO MORE SAFE AN' COZY 1950's FOR YOU, BROTHER. YOU'RE GONNA HAVE TO COME OUT OF YOUR EISENHOWER COCOON--

YOU'RE GOING TO HAVE TO GROW UP, MISTER SUPERNATIONAL PATRIOT.

I SAID WE WERE YOUR CONSCIENCE... AND BABY, THAT'S WHAT WE ARE... WHAT WE'RE GOING TO BE.

FACE IT, BUSTER... YOU JUST CAN'T GO HOME AGAIN...

THEY'RE GONE! VANISHED... AS THOUGH THEY'D NEVER EXISTED!

STRANGE...BUT TOWARD THE END, IT WAS AS THOUGH WE WERE RELIVING HISTORY.

THE WAY THE NATION JOINED TO BATTLE A COMMON ENEMY--AND THE WARHEAD'S RESEMBLANCE TO THE RUSSIAN SPUTNIK OF THE LATE '50's.. IS IT POSSIBLE--?

IS WHAT POSSIBLE, STRETCH?

COULD WE HAVE BEEN SHOWN THIS FOR A REASON....?

YES AND NO, EARTHLINGS.

THERE IS REASON IN ALL THINGS...

...THOUGH AT TIMES THE REASON IS UNCLEAR.

WHO IN THE NAME OF AGON--?

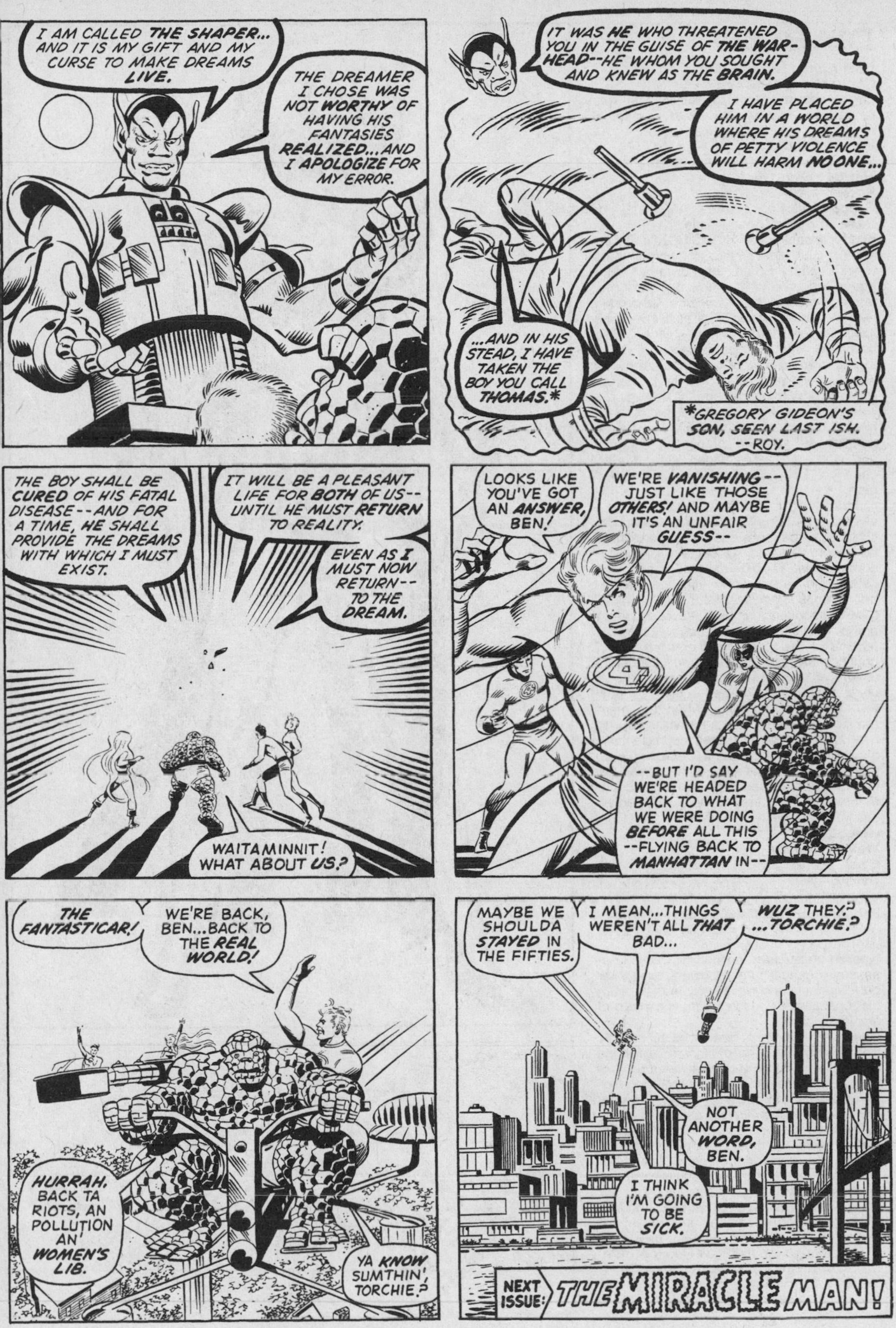
I AM CALLED THE SHAPER... AND IT IS MY GIFT AND MY CURSE TO MAKE DREAMS LIVE.
THE DREAMER I CHOSE WAS NOT WORTHY OF HAVING HIS FANTASIES REALIZED... AND I APOLOGIZE FOR MY ERROR.
IT WAS HE WHO THREATENED YOU IN THE GUISE OF THE WAR-HEAD--HE WHOM YOU SOUGHT AND KNEW AS THE BRAIN.
I HAVE PLACED HIM IN A WORLD WHERE HIS DREAMS OF PETTY VIOLENCE WILL HARM NO ONE...
...AND IN HIS STEAD, I HAVE TAKEN THE BOY YOU CALL THOMAS.*
*GREGORY GIDEON'S SON, SEEN LAST ISH. --ROY.
THE BOY SHALL BE CURED OF HIS FATAL DISEASE--AND FOR A TIME, HE SHALL PROVIDE THE DREAMS WITH WHICH I MUST EXIST.
IT WILL BE A PLEASANT LIFE FOR BOTH OF US--UNTIL HE MUST RETURN TO REALITY.
EVEN AS I MUST NOW RETURN--TO THE DREAM.
WAITAMINNIT! WHAT ABOUT US?
LOOKS LIKE YOU'VE GOT AN ANSWER, BEN!
WE'RE VANISHING--JUST LIKE THOSE OTHERS! AND MAYBE IT'S AN UNFAIR GUESS--
--BUT I'D SAY WE'RE HEADED BACK TO WHAT WE WERE DOING BEFORE ALL THIS--FLYING BACK TO MANHATTAN IN--
THE FANTASTICAR!
WE'RE BACK, BEN... BACK TO THE REAL WORLD!
HURRAH. BACK TA RIOTS, AN POLLUTION AN' WOMEN'S LIB.
YA KNOW SUMTHIN', TORCHIE?
MAYBE WE SHOULDA STAYED IN THE FIFTIES.
I MEAN... THINGS WEREN'T ALL THAT BAD...
WUZ THEY? ...TORCHIE?
NOT ANOTHER WORD, BEN.
I THINK I'M GOING TO BE SICK.
NEXT ISSUE: THE MIRACLE MAN!

DIABLO

Real Name: Esteban Diablo
Occupation: Alchemist
Legal status: Spanish citizen who has moved to Transylvania, with a criminal record in the United States
Identity: Publicly known
Place of birth: Saragossa, Spain
Marital status: Single
Known relatives: None
Group affiliation: None
Base of operations: Mobile
First appearance: FANTASTIC FOUR #30
History: Esteban Diablo was born in early Ninth Century Spain, the son of a nobleman. Curious and inventive by nature, the restless young man became fascinated with the ancient science of alchemy. Using funds borrowed from his inheritance, Diablo began to roam Europe in search of documents and artifacts of ancient alchemy, as well as rare potions and herbs to experiment with. Within a decade, he became the world's greatest living authority on alchemy, having discovered or concocted countless potions with bizarre properties. Haughty and cunning, Diablo began to put his alchemical knowledge to use for personal gain.

Journeying to Transylvania to investigate its legendary secrets, Diablo decided to settle there and set up permanent laboratory facilities. Under suspicious circumstances, Diablo acquired a spacious castle and began work. Although most of his potions had very transitory effects, Diablo discovered an elixir that could retard aging. Drinking it, Diablo began a reign of terror over the surrounding Transylvanians, until one day a mob of villagers caught him unawares and imprisoned him in a massive crypt. Diablo was trapped in the crypt until the Twentieth Century, when he mesmerized the Thing of the Fantastic Four to free him. Not having aged appreciably in his century of confinement, Diablo began to plot his alchemical conquests anew. He has plagued humanity on numerous occasions, and most frequently is opposed by the Fantastic Four.
Height: 6′ 3″
Weight: 190 lbs
Eyes: Brown
Hair: Black
Strength level: Diablo possesses the normal human strength of a man of his age, height, and build who engages in no regular exercise.
Known superhuman powers: Diablo possesses no superhuman powers, except for prolonged life and vitality granted him by an alchemical elixir which he must partake of from time to time.
Weapons: Diablo's powers stem entirely from the huge arsenal of alchemical potions and pellets that he has discovered or concocted. His entire costume is lined with hidden pockets and pouches where he keeps his array of alchemical weapons.

The diversity and extent of the effects of his alchemy at times seem magical in nature. The basis of the ancient science of alchemy was the transmutation of elements (lead into gold being the most sought after effect) by means unknown to modern science. Since all matter is made up of elements, a mastery of alchemy gives one a wide range of materials to work with. Diablo's alchemy enables him to control or influence his own body, the bodies of others, or the environment itself.

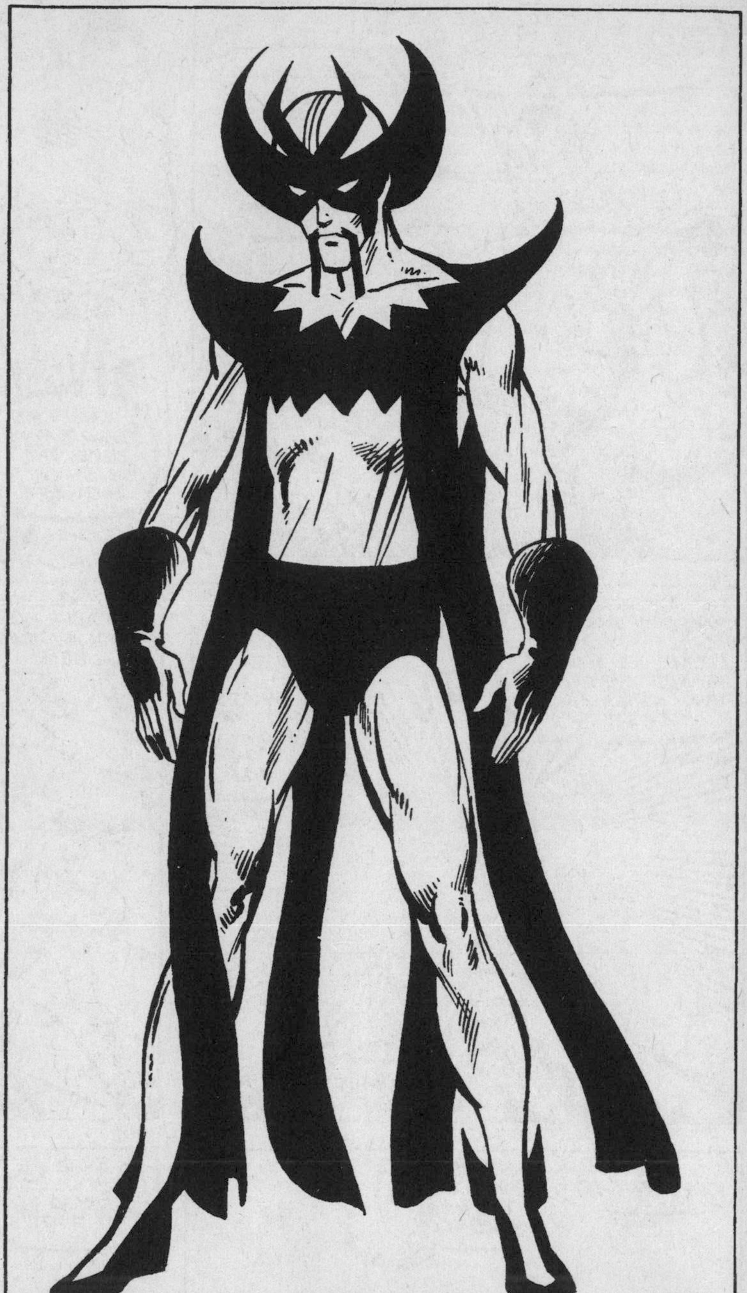

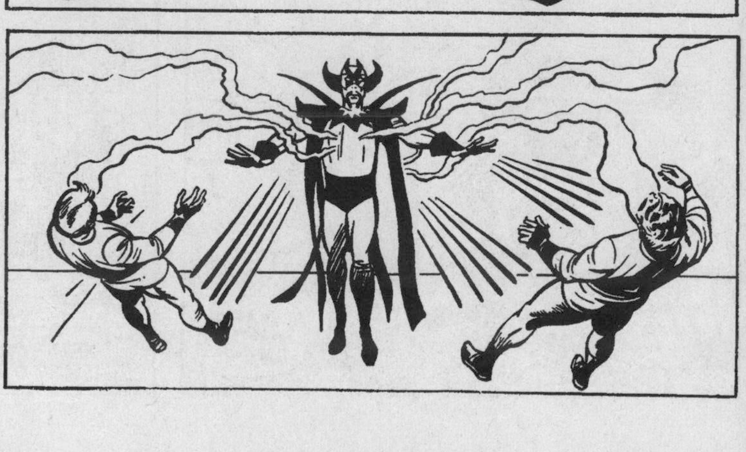

Among the effects of his alchemy upon himself are the capacity to alter his appearance by making the flesh of his face and body pliable, and the capacity to change his human form into "nerveless protoplasm," thus protecting him from certain forms of harm. He can also use on himself any of the alchemical substances designed to give him control over others, if he so desires.

Among the many alchemical mixtures giving him control over others are a nerve-gas pellet, a sleeping potion, a potion permitting a dying person to resist death for a short time (perhaps a variant of his own life-prolonging elixir), a potion that renders a person inert by lowering his or her body temperature rapidly, and a pellet that makes a person susceptible to Diablo's hypnotic commands.

Among the alchemical feats he can perform on non-organic matter are temporary molecular transmutations such as stones into feathers, the generation of explosions equivalent to 50 pounds of TNT, the animation of inanimate matter (see *Dragon Man*), massive conversions of water into ice, and the creation and control of objects or beings composed of the ancient elements of fire, water, earth, and air. The latter feat is accomplished by numerous alchemical substances working jointly.

Although the scope of Diablo's alchemical wizardry is wide, all of the feats are temporary in nature, lasting no more than several hours without repeated administrations. The only exception is the potion he used on Dragon Man, and his longevity elixir, whose length of effectiveness is as yet unknown. (He probably had a supply of it with him during his century of imprisonment.) ■

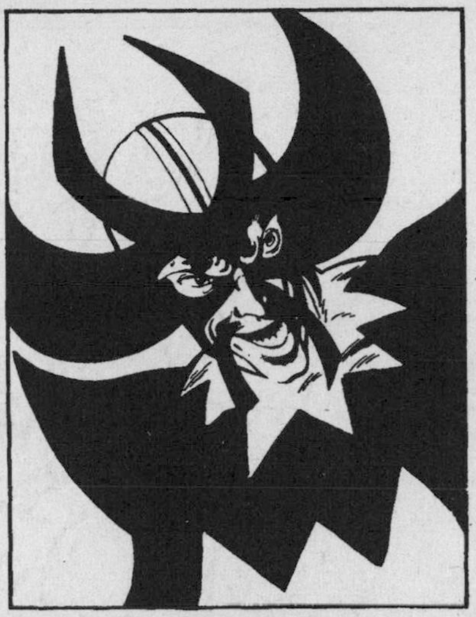

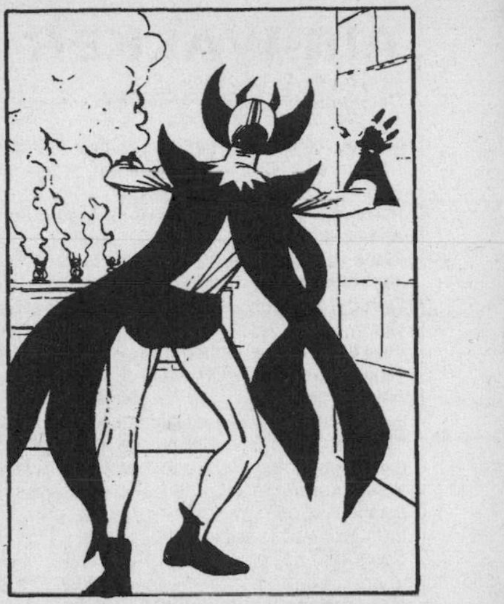

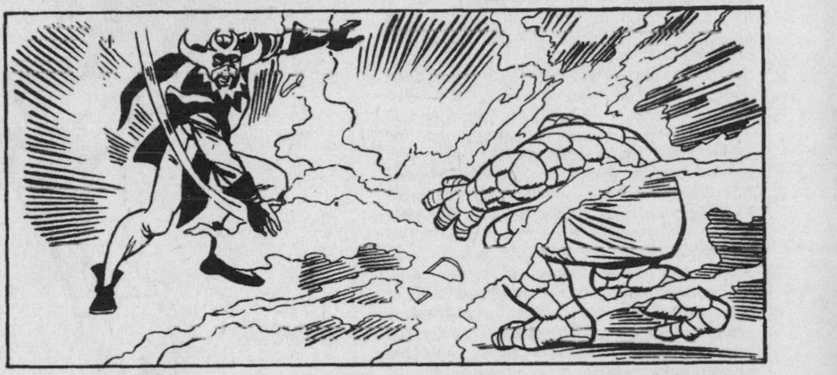

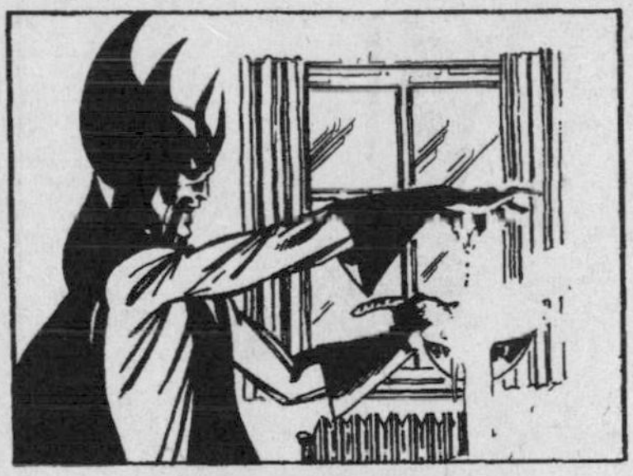

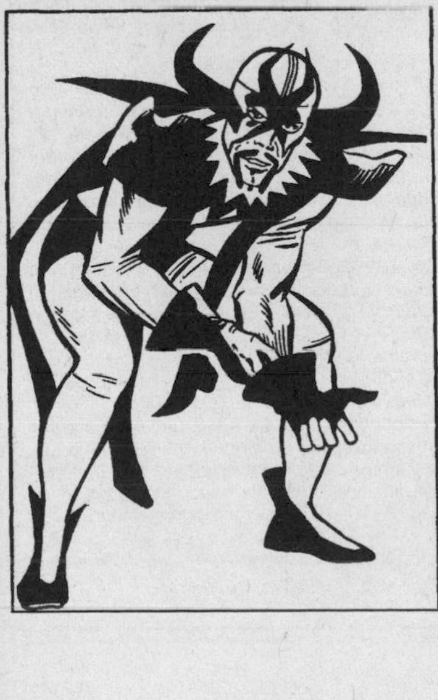

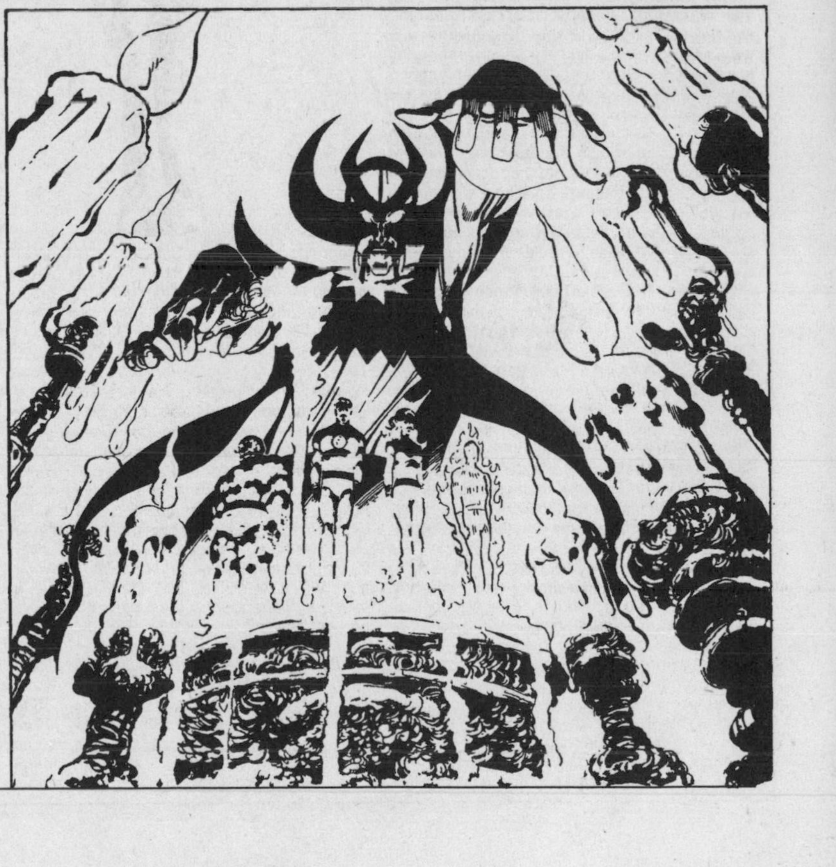

AIR-WALKER

DECEASED

Real Name: Gabriel Lan
Occupation: Former starship captain, herald of Galactus
Identity: Unknown to general populace of Earth
Legal status: Citizen of Xandar
Former aliases: Nova Centurion
Place of birth: Xandar, planet in the Tranta system, Andromeda Galaxy
Place of death: Interstellar space between Sekar and Janstak systems, Milky Way Galaxy
Group affiliation: Former member of the Nova Corps
First appearance: (robot form) FANTASTIC FOUR #123, (real form) THOR #306
Final appearance: THOR #306 (Air-Walker died some time prior to his first appearance on Earth)
History: Gabriel Lan was the captain of the Xandarian explorer-ship *Way-Opener*, whose mission was to seek out and establish peaceful relationships with neighboring alien civilizations. Lan had previously distinguished himself in Xandar's military, the Nova Corps, and welcomed his appointment to an explorer-ship since he was filled with wanderlust and love of open space. Returning from his seven year tour of duty, Lan neared his home solar system when a spherical craft of an unidentified nature approached. A teleport-beam took Lan from the bridge of the *Way-Opener* and brought him aboard the spherical ship into the presence of the world-devourer Galactus. Galactus announced that he was looking for a new herald to replace the defected Silver Surfer, and having scanned Lan's mind, deemed him an appropriate candidate. Hearing Galactus's offer of vast power and unlimited travel, Lan readily accepted and was transformed by a tiny fraction of Galactus's cosmic might into the Air-Walker, second of Galactus's great heralds.

Voluntarily putting all thought of his previous life behind, the Air-Walker served Galactus faithfully for years, seeking out new worlds to suit his master's appetites. He came to befriend Galactus, and would pass long hours listening to Galactus's tales of the wonders and mysteries of the universe. One day after he had found a new world for Galactus to drain and was returning to Galactus's ship to tell him of it, the Air-Walker saw a fleet of warships in battle formation approaching The ships contained members of the Ovoids, a highly advanced civilization, who feared Galactus's presence so close to their star system (see *Alien Races: Ovoids*). The Air-Walker launched an attack on the Ovoid fleet and was struck down by Ovoidian weaponry designed to slay Galactus himself. Because Galactus was weak from hunger, he was unable to retaliate with full force and decided to retreat from that space sector. His power still at a low ebb, Galactus could not afford to give up any of his personal energy to resuscitate the dying spark of life in his faithful herald. However, once he had renewed himself, Galactus transferred the consciousness of the herald who laid down his life for him to a perfect robotic replica. Still, there was something intangible missing from the replica, a vitality, a passion for the mysteries of space that Galactus liked in the original Air-Walker. Therefore, Galactus determined to dispatch the Air-Walker robot to Earth to reenlist his original herald, the Silver Surfer. The Surfer declined Galactus's invitation, however, and in battle with his new messenger, destroyed the Air-Walker robot. Galactus grimly abandoned both the Surfer and the defective Air-Walker robot.

The Air-Walker robot was taken into custody by robots of the Machinesmith (see *Appendix: Machinesmith*) who sought to repair the robot but could not understand its alien circuitry. The Machinesmith did manage to accidentally activate the Air-Walker's self-repair functions, however, and after several months, the Air-Walker regained its artificial consciousness. Seeking a rematch with the Silver Surfer, the Air-Walker instead attracted the attention of the thunder god Thor. Thor damaged the robot in battle, apparently destroying its self-repair circuitry. The Air-Walker's remains were taken into custody by Galactus's third herald, Firelord, a colleague and friend of Gabriel Lan, the original Air-Walker. Firelord buried the robot's remains on an asteroid in the Tranta system near Xandar, with cosmic flame marking his grave.

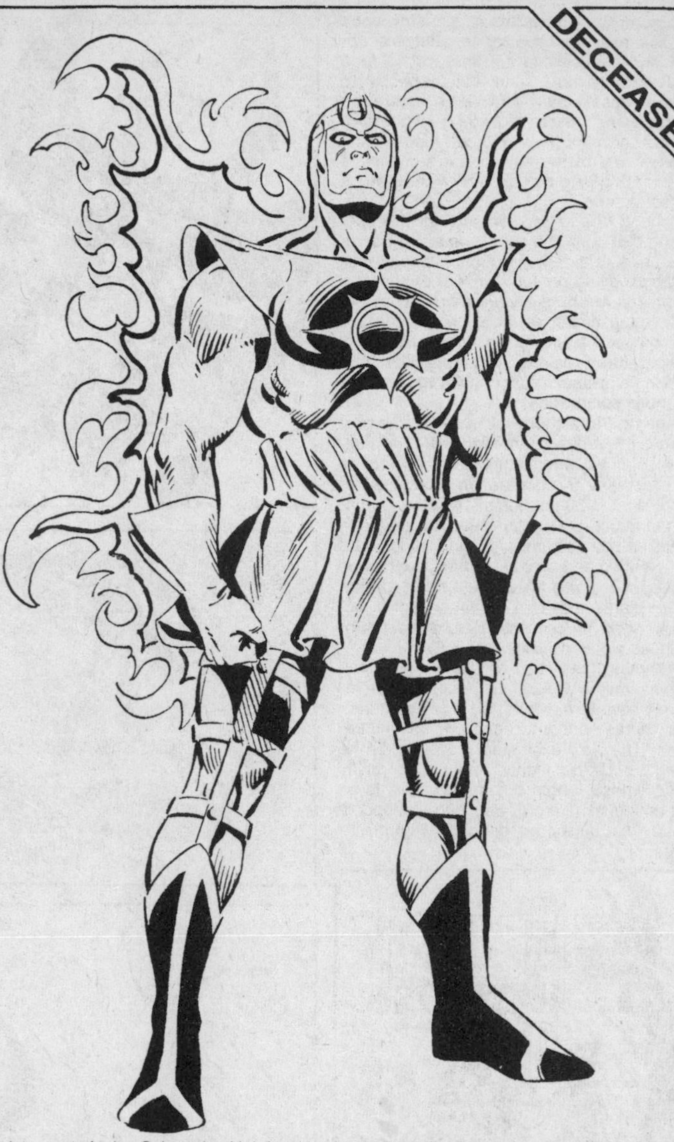

Height: 6' 1" **Weight:** 210 lbs. (Earth gravity)
Eyes: Blue **Hair:** White
Powers: The original Air-Walker possessed the vast cosmic power that Galactus granted to all of his heralds upon their initiation (see *Firelord, Nova, Silver Surfer, Terrax*) His body restructured to be a living battery for cosmic energy, the Air-Walker could utilize cosmic power for a variety of effects: heat, concussive force, magnetism, electricity, etc Unlike most of the other heralds, the Air-Walker utilized his cosmic energy without an accompanying visible manifestation (such as Firelord's "cosmic flame"). The Air-Walker could also use his cosmic energy to rearrange molecules, although he never became adept at it as did the Silver Surfer. The cosmic energy augmented his strength, endurance and durability. At maximum exertion, the Air-Walker could match the strength of the Thing (see *Thing*). He could use his cosmic powers to peak capacity for several Earth-months without resting before fatigue or the need to dream woud begin to impair his functions. His skin was treated to be immune to virtually all the conventional rigors of space. It took a force greater than the cosmic force invested in him by Galactus to kill him. The Air-Walker did not need to eat or breathe since he absorbed life-maintaining cosmic energy through his cells.

The Air-Walker could fly through space at hyper-light velocities. While moving through planetary atmospheres, he would curtail his speed so as not to cause any catastrophic side effects. The Air-Walker did not employ such conveyances as the Silver Surfer's surfboard or Firelord's baton in order to travel: he apparently traveled and navigated by his own power.

The Air-Walker robot replicated all of the original's powers to approximate levels. It was endowed with automatic self-repair circuitry in its chest cavity, capable of functioning as long as .35 of the total system was intact. The robot's power source was in its fiery cloak, apparently some form of cosmic energy receptor.
Paraphenalia: The Air-Walker robot employed a golden trumpet like device to summon Galactus. Apparently the horn emitted some sort of hyper-spatial signal. When the robot first appeared on Earth it was mistaken for the Biblical archangel due to its imposing appearance its "horn," and the coincidence that the Air-Walker's first name was also Gabriel.

OVERMIND

Real Name: Grom
Occupation: Former gladiator
Identity: Unknown to the general public of Earth
Legal status: None
Former aliases: Champion of Champions
Place of birth: Planet Eternus (now non-existent), somewhere in the Andromeda Galaxy
Marital status: Single
Known relatives: None
Group affiliation: Defenders
Base of operations: Mobile
First appearance: FANTASTIC FOUR #111

Origin: Grom was born on the ancient planet Eternus, a member of a highly advanced, belligerent race of humanoid aliens who are now extinct. Eons ago, the Eternians learned to control aging and eliminate natural death. To prevent overpopulation, the Eternian governments sanctioned interstellar warfare and conquest which regularly claimed the lives of multitudes. When enemies could not be found to wage war against, the government held gladiatorial spectacles called The Games. Grom was a naturally skilled gladiator who earned in combat the title Champion of Champions. Soon after Grom's coronation, the Eternians discovered Gigantus, a huge planet on which dwelled an equally advanced but peaceful civilization. Immediately they launched an attack upon the world. Because Gigantus was several hundred times larger than Eternus (about the size of Jupiter), the war became very costly and difficult for the Eternians to sustain. Finally it was decided to simply obliterate the planet. The Eternians showered Gigantus with immensely powerful nuclear warheads and detonated them, destroying the planet. A huge armada of Gigantians, however, who had learned the ways of war after eons of peace, escaped the world's destruction and attacked Eternus in retaliation. Unprepared for so devastating an attack, the Eternian defenses fell. Government leaders realized that their race faced total extinction. Desperately Eternian scientists prepared to transform Grom, the race's most outstanding physical specimen, into the receptacle of the collective consciousness and mental might of Eternus. As the surviving population of Eternus marched into huge "synthesizing chambers" scattered across the planet, their organic brains were converted to pure mental energy and projected into Grom. When the process was complete, and only the scientists who conducted the process were left alive, the capsule containing Grom was launched into space to incubate until the being learned to control the powers of his group mind. Eons passed. Then Grom emerged as the Overmind, a warrior who possessed the collective psionic power of one billion brains and who carried in his memory the subliminal command to subdue the universe.

The Overmind attacked the first inhabited planet he came upon, the Earth, but was defeated by the Fantastic Four with the aid of the enigmatic alien being called the Stranger. The Stranger claimed to be the embodiment of the collective psionic power of all the surviving Gigantians (see *Stranger*). The Stranger's psionic abilities proved to be more powerful than those of the Overmind and he shrunk the Overmind to microscopic stature and exiled him to a mote of dust. Several years later, a demonic creature called Null the Living Darkness located the Overmind and decided to use him as a pawn in his scheme of conquest. However, when he restored the Eternian to his original power and stature, Null accidentally transported the Overmind to an alternate Earth other than the one upon which he had met his defeat. This Earth was the home of the Squadron Supreme. Null and the Overmind battled the Squadron, who sent for reinforcements in the persons of the Defenders. A being composed of the psychic union of six of

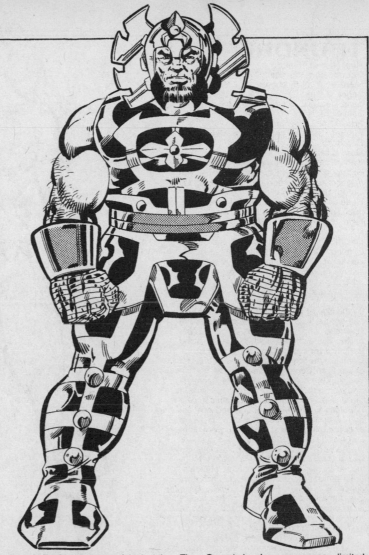

the alternate Earth's most powerful telepaths also aided in the struggle, and were instrumental in neutralizing Null and the Overmind. At the battle's end, the Overmind's Eternian consciousness was driven out of its body and the six telepaths, lacking physical bodies, took refuge inside him. Now possessing a benevolent mind and a small fraction of his former mental might, the Overmind returned with the Defenders to their world. After parting company with the group, he set forth for parts unknown.

Height: 10'   **Weight:** 750 lbs
Eyes: Black   **Hair:** Red
Powers: Overmind possesses superhuman physical attributes derived from his alien nature as well as vast psionic powers. As the ultimate physical specimen of an ancient alien race, Overmind's body is far superior to a human being's, able to lift (press) approximately 10 tons (without the augmentation of his psionic powers). He is also immune to disease and aging and has greater than human endurance and recovery time by a factor of 5.

Overmind possesses the combined psionic powers of six moderately-powerful human psionic/telepaths. He can "read" the thoughts of others and project his own thoughts into others' minds, within an as yet undetermined radius. He can also project illusions of apparently opaque 3-dimensional objects into the minds of those within his field of view, providing it is a single image. It is not known how long he can sustain a given illusion or how many minds he can project illusions into at once.

The Overmind also possesses limited psychokinetic ability, enabling him to levitate objects (whose weights do not exceed that which he can physically lift without psionic augmentation) within approximately 50 feet of him. He can project psychokinetic force over a range of .001 pounds per square inch to 20 pounds per square inch of overpressure (equivalent to an explosion of 10 pounds of TNT at a range of 15 feet). By directing concussive psychokinetic blasts at people or objects, he could kill a human being at a maximum range of 10 feet or eventually severely deform a plate of 1-inch thick steel. The Overmind also appears to have a degree of precognitive ability, the extent of which is yet unknown. It is also not known how long the Overmind can project his psionic energy before fatigue impairs his abilities.

As a group intelligence made up of six once-separate consciousnesses, the Overmind has a gestalt personality greater than the sum of its parts. Through concentration, he can allow one of his six component personalities to temporarily manifest itself as dominant. When doing so, he usually creates an illusion of the physical image of the manifest group member.

By generating as much psionic energy as he can and channeling it back into his physical body, the Overmind can augment his physical strength by a factor of 7 for brief periods of exertion. Hence, he can sometimes lift (press) 70 tons. This channeling takes such concentration that he cannot use any of his other abilities at the same time.

THUNDRA

Real Name: Thundra
Occupation: Warrior
Identity: Publicly known
Legal status: Citizen of the United Sisterhood Republic in an alternate future of the 23rd Century
Former aliases: None
Place of birth: Greater Milago, Midwestern Republic
Marital status: Single
Known relatives: None
Group affiliation: Former member of the Frightful Four, former agent of Roxxon Oil Corporation
Base of operations: United Sisterhood Republic of North America
First appearance: FANTASTIC FOUR #129
Origin: Thundra was born in the Central Birthing Center of Greater Milago (Milwaukee-Chicago), a government-run laboratory where fetuses are brought to term in artificial wombs. Genetically engineered for strength and endurance, Thundra was sent to military school when she was 8 years old. By the age of 18, she had distinguished herself as the finest warrior in the Midwestern Republic and became an officer in the militia. There she led assaults against roving bands of renegades and the armies of the Central American Empire. Toward the end of the 20th Century on the timeline that diverged Thundra's alternate future, chemical and biological warfare broke out, resulting in the sterilization of 95% of the Earth's female population. The fertile 5% seized political power, and began a systematized program of oppression against men, who were seen as having nearly exterminated the species. By the early 23rd Century, natural childbirth was totally supplanted by laboratory birthing, and men were bred only as servants, entertainers, and breeding stock. The major concerns of the United Sisterhood Republic, one of the leading nations of the new world, were exterminating the renegade bands of roving free men and preventing incursions from foreign nations and powers.

In the middle of Thundra's military career, the U.S.R. faced an invasion from an unexpected quarter. Men from a contemporary alternate Earth where, generations previously, renegade men had managed to overthrow their female oppressors, had developed the technology for interdimensional travel, and decided to journey to Thundra's Earth to liberate the men of that world. In a strange attempt to strike back at the men of Machus, as the leading nation of this alternate Earth was called, Thundra stole their dimensional apparatus and journeyed back to the 20th Century. Her goal was to humble the strongest man on Earth, thereby, she believed, preventing the world of Machus from ever coming about. Upon her arrival in the 20th Century, she was befriended by the Wizard of the Frightful Four and became a temporary member of that group. She engaged the Thing of the Fantastic Four in a battle, besting him fairly on at least one occasion. She soon saw that her actions in the past would have little bearing on the future and became an ally of the Fantastic Four.

Mahkizmo, the greatest warrior of Machus, eventually trailed Thundra to the 20th Century and brought her back to her own time to stand trial for her theft of the inter-dimension travel equipment. The Fantastic Four followed Thundra, using their own transportation, however, and helped Thundra battle against the dimensional invaders of Machus. Before leaving the future for their own time, the Fantastic Four destroyed the mind-domination equipment of the Machians and hoped that the two worlds would settle their differences amicably. Thundra returned to the 20th Century with them, believing that her world would be changed unfavorably by the presence of the extradimensional men.

Months later, however, Thundra was contacted by the Nth Command, a subsidiary of the Roxxon Oil Company devoted to extradimensional research. They told her that a divergent future world existed which was never invaded by Machus. She agreed to carry out a mission for them in exchange for being restored to her world. Although she did as agreed, she later learned of the Nth Command's sinister motives and stole one of their Nth Projectors, a dimensional aperture synthesizer. Creating a portal to her own time, she traveled back after bidding a fond farewell to the Thing, the 20th Century male she had most learned to admire.

Height: 7' 2" **Weight:** 450 lbs
Eyes: Green **Hair:** Red

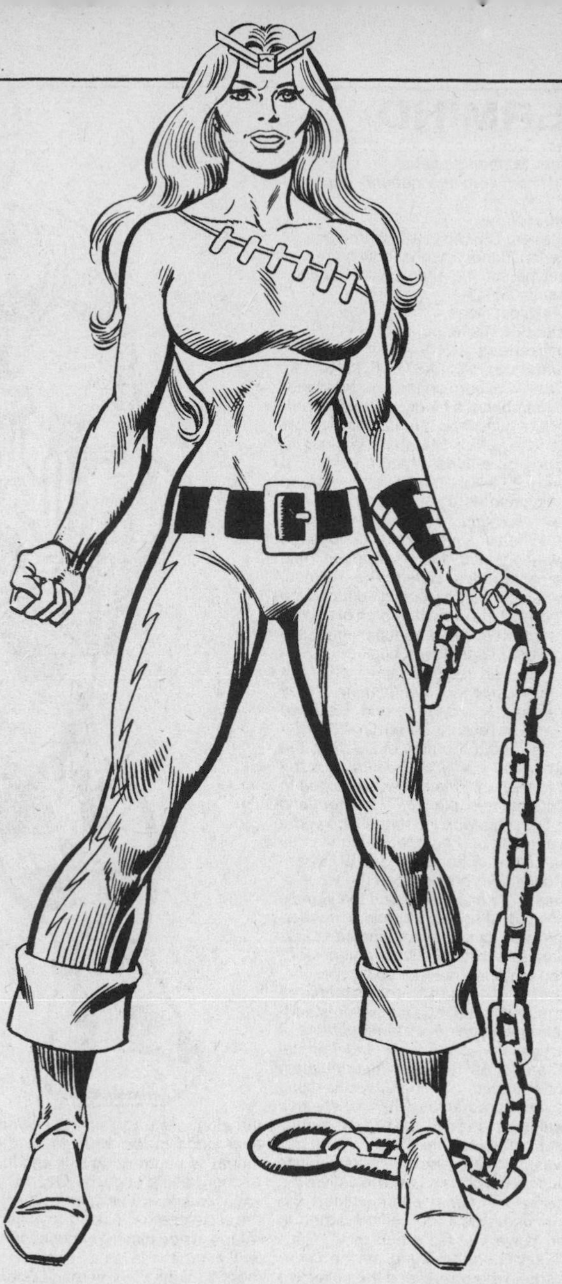

Powers: Thundra possesses superhuman strength, endurance, and resilience. Due to her genetic engineering, her skin, muscle, and bone tissue have been enhanced to the limits of human efficiency. Thundra can lift (press) 60 tons. Her powerful leg muscles enable her to make a standing high jump of about 45 feet. Her physiology is so robust that she can exert herself at peak levels for about 50 minutes before accumulated fatigue-poisons in her bloodstream force her to reduce her activity or rest. Her great skin density gives her a hardness of 7.5 on the Mohs hardness scale, enabling her to resist penetration of small caliber bullets. She can run a maximum of about 32 miles per hour.

Thundra has been extensively trained in boxing and wrestling and the military arts of her century. She is experienced in the use of the broadsword. She is a seasoned combat veteran of many anti-renegade raids. Thundra has had little experience with firearms because of their virtual elimination in her own time.